Far East Pinyin
Chinese-English Dictionary

遠東
拼音漢英辭典

Editor in Chief
Yeh, Teh-Ming

Compiled by
The Far East Book Co.,
Editorial Committee

遠東圖書公司印行
The Far East Book Co., Ltd.

Published by

The Far East Book Co., Ltd.
66-1 Chungking South Road, Section 1 Taipei, Taiwan
http://www.fareast.com.tw

Distributed by
US International Publishing Inc.
39 West 38th Street
New York, New York 10018
U.S.A.

ISBN 957-612-463-8

Table of Contents

序

序

　　《遠東拼音漢英辭典》是為順應現代世界各地人士需要而重新改編的。時代在進步，語文也在社會潮流中不斷地變動，而學習語文的工具書—字典，自然必須因人們應用的語音符號、詞彙不斷地增加而擴充其使用的幅度。

　　鑑於原《遠東漢英辭典》自出版以來廣受中外各界人士熱愛使用，故該書於出版之初即已許諾將視需要隨時修訂，才能延續發揮一本優良辭典的學術使命及功能。

　　這部重新按照「漢語拼音」編排的辭典，共收錄了以通用頻率最高的四千個漢字為基礎，衍生出的漢語詞條、片語、成語等共計四萬餘言。而且全書的詞條均按照「漢語拼音」的規則排序，與一般英文辭典按英文字母排列的方式一樣，便利讀者查閱。

　　本辭典內容順序依次是：漢語拼音、漢字、英譯。注音包括海峽兩地，大陸與台灣的標準音，於不同處特加以說明。若慣用詞彙在兩地用法相異時，則兩者均予列出。

　　如：計程車／出租汽車（taxi）、番茄／西紅柿（tomato）等。

　　為了因應當今社會文化的變遷，本辭典同時增錄了兩地科技與社會方面的流行詞彙。

如：網路／網絡（internet），多媒體／多介質（multimedia）等。

有關英文翻譯，除了保存原版內容之外，也參考最新出版之其他漢英、英英詞典之解釋，充實本辭典的信度。

本辭典檢附「部首索引」、「拼音索引」、「漢字筆畫數索引」，以因應各人在使用本辭典時之查詢習慣。

附錄內容包括「漢語拼音字母系統表」、「國語注音符號與漢語拼音對照表」，及「世界各國及首都一覽表」。

遠東圖書公司編輯部同仁在迎接千禧年新世紀之初，長時間運用大量人力改編此一鉅著，其目的在於貢獻給眾多喜愛傳譯中、英文的讀者們，一部更有用的工具書。敬請各界學者專家不吝指教。

葉德明

Preface

The Far East Pinyin Chinese English Dictionary is aimed to meet the growing needs of Chinese scholars and students all over the world. As society is developing and changing so is the language. The demand for updated language teaching and training materials is ever increasing. As a tool for language learning, the dictionary must keep up with the ever changing world with its new edition and the latest terms for today's high-tech and business environment.

Arranged alphabetically according to Hanyu Pinyin, and based on 4,000 most commonly used characters. This dictionary includes 40,000 entries, phrases and idiomatic expressions.

Each entry is in three parts. The first part is the Pinyin entry, the second is the Chinese characters and the third is an English translation and explanation. Beijing dialect is used as the standard pronunciation. The pronunciation used in Taiwan is also provided if there is any variation.

Different words and expressions as used in Taiwan and PRC are both included such as **chūzūchē** 出租車 and **jìchéngchē** 計程車 for taxi, **xīhóngshì** 西紅柿 and **fānqié** 蕃茄 for tomato.

New words and phrases with a strong focus on the language used on both sides of the straits are added to this edition, such as **wǎngluò** 網絡 (the Mainland term) and **wǎnglù** 網路 (the Taiwan term) for the internet, **duōjièzhì** 多介質 (the Mainland term) and **duōméitǐ** 多媒體 (the Taiwan term) for multimedia.

In addition, the Radical Index, the Stroke Numbers Index and the Pinyin Index are juxtaposed in this edition for different users to take his/her choice.

Appendices include a thorough explanation of the Hanyu Pinyin table and a comparative table of Hanyu Pinyin and Mandarin Phonetic Symbols.　There is also a chart of countries of the world and their capitals.

The Far East editorial staff has made great effort to publish this valuable dictionary. It is a real treasure for Chinese language teaching and learning as well as translation. We will appreciate any comments from scholars and specialists.

Yeh, Teh-Ming

User's Guide

Arrangement of Entries

All the entries are listed in alphabetical order. Characters with identical spelling but different tones are arranged in the ascending order according to the order of their tones (i.e., the 1st, 2nd, 3rd, 4th, and the neutral tone). For entries with identical spelling, including tones, arrangement is by order of their stroke numbers.

Standard for Pronunciation

Separate entries are printed for characters with more than one pronunciation. The pronunciation of Beijing dialect is used as the standard in this dictionary. The pronunciation used in Taiwan is also provided in reference to that in Beijing dialect if there are any differences.

For example, the character "期" is pronounced as **qī** in Beijing but **qí** in Taiwan. Therefore, the users need to look up the entry "**qí** 期" for the full explanation of the character even though the entry "**qī** 期" is provided as well.

qī 期 also **qí**

1. periods; times 2. a designated time; a time limit 3. to expect; to hope; to wait

qí 期

refer to **qī** 期

Phrases are treated in the same way.

dǎjī 打擊 to give a blow to

dǎjí 打擊 refer to **dǎjí** 打擊

"Neutral Tone" and "-r" Suffixation

The "neutral tone" (as in **fúqi** 福氣) and "-r" suffixation (as in **dǎgér** 打嗝兒) are marked in this dictionary; however, they might be lost with some dialect speakers.

Tone Modification

All syllables are marked with their primary tones. The tone of certain characters (i.e., **yī** 一, **qī** 七, **bā** 八, **bù** 不) changes when the following character has a fourth spelling tone. However, in this dictionary, the primary tone is marked with an annotation to explain the phenomenon of the tone modification.

Segmentation

Generally speaking, phrases and idioms are segmented disyllabically, though there are some exceptions.

yǔyán zhōngxīn 語言中心 a language center

hǎohàn bùchī yǎnqíankuī 好漢不吃眼前虧 A wise man knows how to avoid being beaten.

With characters has ambiguous spelling, and with characters beginning with "a", "e", or "o", an apostrophe (') is used to separate syllables.

shēn'ào 深奧 deep; abstruse; profound

shēn'gāo 身高 stature; height

Pinyin Index

In this index the characters are arranged according to the alphabetical order of their Pinyin transcription. Characters with the same pronunciation are arranged by the ascending order of their stroke numbers. The figure to the right of each character is the page number under which the character can be found in the body of the dictionary.

If the dictionary user knows the pronunciation of the character s/he is looking for, s/he can find it in the index according to the alphabetical order of Pinyin. Uning the page number as a guide, s/he can locate in the the dictionary the character and the entries beneath it.

A		哎	1	矮	2	礙(碍)	2	闇	5	熬	5
ā		埃	1	嗳	2	ān		黯	5	áo	
阿	1	唉	1	藹	2	安	3	āng		嗷	5
啊	1	挨	1	靄	2	庵	4	肮	5	獒	5
腌	1	ái		ài		鞍	4	航	5	熬	6
à		呆	1	艾	2	諳	4	áng		遨	6
阿	1	挨	1	隘	2	àn		昂	5	翱	6
a		捱	1	愛	2	岸	4	àng		鏖	6
啊	1	皑	1	嗳	2	按	4	盎	5	鼇(鰲)	6
āi		癌	1	嫒	2	案	4	āo		ǎo	
哀	1	ǎi		曖	2	暗	4	凹	5	拗	6

幻 233	迥 238	諢 242	嘰 246	給 252	夾 258
宦 233	迴 238	**huō**	機 246	擠 252	莢 258
浣 233	蛔 238	豁 242	積 247	濟 252	頰 258
患 233	**huǐ**	**huó**	激 247	**jì**	**jiǎ**
換 234	悔 238	和 242	績 248	伎 252	甲 258
澳 234	賄 238	活 242	擊 248	忌 252	岬 258
喚 234	毀 238	**huǒ**	雞 248	技 253	夏 258
煥 234	誨 239	火 243	譏 249	妓 253	假 258
瘓 234	燬 239	伙 244	饑 249	季 253	賈 259
huāng	**huì**	夥 244	鷄(雞) 249	紀 253	鉀 259
荒 234	卉 239	**huò**	齎 249	計 253	**jià**
慌 234	晦 239	和 244	羇 249	記 254	夾 259
huáng	彗 239	或 244	羈 249	寄 254	架 259
皇 234	喙 239	貨 244	**jí**	寂 254	假 259
凰 235	惠 239	惑 245	及 249	祭 254	嫁 259
惶 235	賄 239	禍 245	吃 249	悸 255	稼 259
黃 235	彙 239	霍 245	吉 249	既 255	駕 259
徨 235	會 239	豁 245	汲 249	際 255	價 260
遑 236	匯 240	獲 245	岌 249	稷 255	**jiān**
潢 236	誨 240	壑 245	即 250	髻 255	尖 260
蝗 236	慧 240	穫 245	急 250	暨 255	奸 260
磺 236	諱 240	**J**	亟 250	劑 255	肩 260
簧 236	蕙 240	**jī**	脊 250	寬 255	戔 260
huǎng	薈 240	几 245	疾 250	覬 255	兼 260
恍 236	燴 240	兀 245	級 250	濟 255	堅 261
晃 236	穢 240	肌 245	唧 251	騎 255	菅 261
幌 236	繪 241	圾 245	寂 251	繫 255	湔 261
謊 236	**hūn**	奇 245	棘 251	繼 255	間 261
huàng	昏 241	迹 245	集 251	鯽 255	煎 261
晃 236	婚 241	飢 245	極 251	霽 255	犍 261
huī	葷 241	唧 246	嫉 251	驥 255	監 261
灰 236	**hún**	姬 246	瘠 251	**jiā**	箋 262
恢 236	混 241	基 246	輯 252	加 256	漸 262
揮 236	渾 241	幾 246	擊 252	夾 256	緘 262
暉 237	魂 241	畸 246	藉 252	佳 256	艱 262
詼 237	餛 242	期 246	籍 252	枷 257	鶼 262
輝 237	**hǔn**	畸 246	**jǐ**	痂 257	殲 262
麾 237	混 242	跡 246	几 252	家 257	**jiǎn**
徽 237	**hùn**	箕 246	己 252	袈 258	柬 262
huí	混 242	緝 246	紀 252	傢 258	剪 262
回 237	溷 242	畿 246	脊 252	嘉 258	減 263
徊 238		稽 246	幾 252	**jiá**	

máo
毛 369 / 矛 370 / 茅 370 / 髦 370 / 錨 370

mǎo
卯 370

mào
冒 370 / 茂 370 / 貿 370 / 帽 370 / 貌 371

me
麼 371

méi
沒 371 / 玫 371 / 枚 371 / 眉 372 / 梅 372 / 莓 372 / 湄 372 / 媒 372 / 楣 372 / 煤 372 / 霉 372 / 黴 372

měi
每 372 / 美 373 / 浼 373 / 鎂 373

mèi
妹 373 / 昧 373 / 寐 374 / 媚 374 / 瑁 374 / 魅 374 / 謎 374

mēn
悶 374 / 燜 374

mén
門 374 / 們 375 / 捫 375 / 悶 375 / 燜 375

men
們 375

mēng
矇 375

méng
萌 375 / 盟 375 / 蒙 375 / 濛 375 / 檬 375 / 朦 375 / 懵 376 / 瞢 376

měng
猛 376 / 蒙 376 / 錳 376 / 懵 376

mèng
孟 376 / 夢 376

mī
咪 376

mí
迷 376 / 麋 377 / 糜 377 / 謎 377 / 彌 377 / 靡 377 / 瀰 377 / 獼 377

mǐ
米 377 / 弭 377 / 靡 377

mì
汨 378 / 泌 378 / 祕 378 / 密 378 / 覓 378 / 蜜 378 / 冪 378 / 謐 378 / 謎 378

mián
眠 378 / 棉 378 / 綿 379

miǎn
免 379 / 勉 379 / 娩 379 / 冕 379 / 湎 379 / 愐 379 / 腼(靦) 379 / 緬 379

miàn
面 380 / 瞑 380 / 麵 380

miáo
苗 381 / 描 381 / 瞄 381

miǎo
眇 381 / 秒 381 / 渺 381 / 淼 381 / 藐 381 / 邈 381

miào
妙 381 / 廟 381

miē
乜 382 / 哶 382

miè
滅 382 / 蔑 382

mín
民 382 / 閩 383

mǐn
皿 383 / 泯 383 / 抿 383 / 敏 383 / 黽 383 / 憫 383 / 閔 383 / 憫 383

míng
名 383 / 明 384 / 冥 385 / 茗 386 / 溟 386 / 銘 386 / 鳴 386

mǐng
皿 386 / 茗 386 / 酩 386 / 瞑 386

mìng
命 386

miù
謬 386

mō
摸 387

mó
摩 387 / 模 387 / 摹 387 / 摩 387 / 膜 387 / 磨 387 / 魔 388

mǒ
抹 388

mò
末 388 / 沒 388 / 沫 388 / 歿 388 / 抹 388 / 陌 388 / 茉 388 / 脈 388 / 麥 388 / 莫 389 / 寞 389 / 漠 389 / 膜 389 / 墨 389 / 默 389 / 磨 389 / 驀 389

móu
牟 389 / 車 389 / 眸 389 / 謀 390

mǒu
某 390

mòu
茂 390

mú
模 390

mǔ
母 390 / 牡 390 / 姆 390 / 拇 391 / 畝 391

mù
木 391 / 目 391 / 沐 392 / 牧 392 / 睦 392 / 募 392 / 墓 392 / 幕 392 / 慕 392 / 暮 392 / 穆 393

N

ná
拿 393

nǎ
哪 393

nà
那 393 / 吶 393 / 納 393 / 娜 393

na
哪 393

nǎi
乃 393 / 奶 393

nài
奈 394 / 耐 394

nán
男 394 / 南 394 / 喃 395 / 難 395

nǎn
赧 396

nàn	逆 399	nín	nù	pá	磅 412
難 396	匿 399	您 402	怒 406	扒 408	膀 412
náng	溺 399	níng	nǚ	爬 408	螃 412
囊 396	暱 399	寧 402	女 406	耙 408	龐 412
nǎng	膩 399	凝 403	nǜ	琶 408	pàng
曩 396	niān	獰 403	衄 406	pà	胖 412
náo	拈 399	嚀 403	nuǎn	怕 408	pāo
撓 396	nián	檸 403	暖 407	帕 408	泡 412
鐃 396	年 400	nǐng	nüè	pāi	抛 412
nǎo	秥 400	擰 403	虐 407	拍 408	páo
惱 396	黏 401	nìng	瘧 407	pái	刨 412
瑙 396	niǎn	佞 403	謔 407	排 409	咆 412
腦 396	捻 401	寧 403	nuó	徘 409	庖 412
nào	撚 401	擰 403	娜 407	牌 409	炮 412
淖 396	輦(碾) 401	濘 403	挪 407	pài	袍 412
鬧 396	攆 401	niū	nuò	派 410	pǎo
nè	niàn	妞 403	娜 407	湃 410	跑 412
那 397	念 401	niú	諾 407	pān	pào
ne	唸 401	牛 403	儒 407	番 410	泡 413
呢 397	niáng	niǔ	糯 407	潘 410	炮 413
něi	娘 401	扭 404	**O**	攀 410	疱 413
哪 397	niàng	忸 404	ō	pán	皰 413
餒 397	釀 401	紐 404	喔 407	胖 410	礮(砲) 413
nèi	niǎo	鈕 404	ó	槃 410	pēi
內 397	鳥 401	niù	哦 407	盤 410	披 413
那 398	裊 402	拗 404	ōu	磐 410	胚 413
nèn	嬈 402	糅 404	嘔 407	蟠 411	péi
嫩 398	niào	謬 404	歐 407	蹣 411	陪 413
néng	尿 402	nóng	毆 407	pàn	培 414
能 398	niē	農 404	謳 407	判 411	裴 414
nèng	捏(揑) 402	儂 405	鷗 407	拚 411	賠 414
濘 398	niè	濃 405	ǒu	叛 411	pèi
ní	涅(湼) 402	膿 405	偶 408	盼 411	沛 414
尼 398	鎳 402	穠 405	嘔 408	畔 411	佩 414
泥 398	闑 402	nòng	慪 408	pāng	珮 414
呢 399	孽 402	弄 405	**P**	乓 411	配 414
霓 399	囓 402	nú	pā	滂 411	轡 414
nǐ	齧 402	奴 405	趴 408	磅 411	pēn
你 399	鑷 402	nǔ		páng	噴 414
擬 399		努 406		彷 411	pén
nì				旁(傍) 411	盆 415
泥 399				徬 412	pēng

鉗	440	僑	444	**qín**		秋	454	全	458	**rāng**	
箝	440	憔	444	芹	448	蚯	454	泉	459	嚷	462
潛	440	橋	444	衾	448	鞦	454	拳	459	**ráng**	
錢	441	樵	445	秦	448	**qiú**		痊	459	攘	462
黔	441	瞧	445	琴	448			詮	459	**rǎng**	
qiǎn		翹	445	禽	448	囚	455	銓	459	壤	462
淺	441	**qiǎo**		勤	448	泅	455	蜷	459	攘	462
遣	441	巧	445	擒	448	酋	455	鬈	460	嚷	462
繾	441	悄	445	**qǐn**		球	455	權	460	**ràng**	
譴	441	雀	445	寢	448	裘	456	**quǎn**		讓	462
qiàn		愀	445	**qìn**		逑	456	犬	460	**ráo**	
欠	441	鵲	445	沁	448	赇	456	綣	460	饒	463
倩	442	**qiào**		**qīng**		糗	456	**quàn**		**rǎo**	
嵌	442	俏	445	青	449	**qū**		券	460	擾	463
慊	442	峭	445	氫	449	曲	456	勸	460	**rào**	
歉	442	殼	446	清	449	沏	456	**quē**		遶	463
塹	442	撬	446	卿	451	屈	456	缺	460	繞	463
qiāng		鞘	446	傾	451	祛	456	闕	461	**rě**	
戕	442	翹	446	蜻	451	區	456	**qué**		若	463
腔	442	竅	446	輕	451	幅	456	瘸	461	惹	463
搶	442	**qiē**		**qíng**		趨	456	**què**		**rè**	
嗆	442	切	446	情	452	麴	457	怯	461	熱	463
槍	442	**qié**		晴	453	驅	457	恪	461	**rén**	
鎗	442	茄	446	傾	453	驪	457	卻	461	人	464
鏘	443	**qiě**		黥	453	**qú**		雀	461	壬	466
qiáng		且	446	**qǐng**		劬	457	殼	461	仁	466
戕	443	**qiè**		頃	453	渠	457	榷	461	任	466
強	443	切	446	請	453	麴	457	確	461	**rěn**	
薔	443	怯	446	慶	453	衢	457	闋	461	忍	466
牆	443	妾	446	親	453	**qǔ**		鵲	461	荏	466
qiǎng		契	446	磬	454	曲	457	**qún**		稔	467
強	443	挈	446	**qióng**		取	457	裙	461	**rèn**	
搶	443	愜	446	穹	454	娶	458	群	461	刃	467
襁	444	慊	446	**qióng**		麟	458	**R**		任	467
qiàng		鍥	446	穹	454	**qù**		**rán**		妊	467
嗆	444	竊	446	穹	454	去	458	然	462	紉	467
qiāo		**qīn**		窮	454	漆	458	髯	462	軔	467
敲	444	侵	447	瓊	458	趣	458	燃	462	飪	467
橇	444	衾	447	**qiū**		闃	458	**rǎn**		認	467
蹺	444	欽	447	丘	454	**quān**		冉	462	**rēng**	
qiáo		嶔	447	邱	454	圈	458	苒	462	扔	467
喬	444	親	447			**quán**		染	462	**réng**	

速	537	唆	541	汰	545	**tǎng**		蹄	553	貼	559
宿	538	娑	541	泰	545	倘	548	題	553	**tiě**	
粟	538	棱	541	態	545	淌	548	**tǐ**		帖	560
訴	538	蓑	541	**tān**		躺	548	體	553	鐵	560
溯(泝)	538	縮	541	坍	545	**tàng**		**tì**		**tīng**	
肅	538	**suó**		探	545	趟	548	剃	554	汀	560
塑	538	索	541	貪	545	燙	548	倜	554	聽	560
縮	538	**suǒ**		灘	545	**tāo**		悌	554	廳	561
suān		所	541	攤	545	叨	549	涕	554	**tíng**	
痠	538	索	542	癱	545	掏	549	屜	554	廷	561
酸	538	嗩	542	**tán**		洮	549	惕	554	亭	561
suàn		瑣	542	覃	546	滔	549	替	554	庭	561
蒜	539	鎖	542	痰	546	韜	549	嚏	554	停	561
算	539	**T**		潭	546	饕	549	**tiān**		婷	562
suī		**tā**		彈	546	**táo**		天	554	**tǐng**	
綏	539	他	542	談	546	桃	549	添	556	町	562
雖	539	它	542	壇	546	逃	549	**tián**		挺	562
suí		她	543	曇	546	淘	550	田	557	艇	562
隋	539	牠	543	檀	546	陶	550	恬	557	鋌	562
遂	539	塌	543	罈	546	萄	550	畋	557	**tìng**	
綏	539	**tǎ**		譚	546	濤	550	甜	557	聽	562
隨	539	塔	543	**tǎn**		**tǎo**		填	557	**tōng**	
雖	540	獺	543	忐	546	討	550	湉	557	恫	562
suǐ		**tà**		坦	546	**tào**		**tiǎn**		通	562
髓	540	拓	543	袒	546	套	550	忝	557	**tóng**	
suì		沓	543	毯	547	**tē**		殄	557	同	563
祟	540	榻	543	**tàn**		忚	550	腆	558	桐	564
碎	540	踏	543	炭	547	**tè**		**tiāo**		銅	564
遂	540	躂	543	探	547	特	550	挑	558	筒	564
歲	540	**tāi**		碳	547	**téng**		**tiáo**		童	565
隧	540	苔	543	歎	547	疼	551	迢	558	僮	565
穗	540	胎	543	**tāng**		膯	551	條	558	瞳	565
燧	541	**tái**		湯	547	藤(籐)	551	調	558	**tǒng**	
sūn		台	543	**táng**		謄	551	齠	559	桶	565
孫	541	苔	543	唐	548	**tī**		**tiǎo**		統	565
sǔn		跆	543	堂	548	剔	552	挑	559	筒	565
筍	541	颱	543	棠	548	梯	552	窕	559	**tòng**	
損	541	臺(台)	543	搪	548	踢	552	**tiào**		痛	565
榫	541	擡(抬)	544	塘	548	**tí**		眺	559	慟	566
sùn		檯(枱)	544	膛	548	堤(隄)	552	跳	559	**tōu**	
遜	541	**tài**		糖	548	提	552	**tiē**		偷	566
suō		太	544	螳	548	啼	553	帖	559	**tóu**	

幟 751	咒 757	蛀 762	錐 768	**zǐ**	祖 778
質 751	宙 758	粥 762	**zhuì**	子 771	組 778
緻 751	紂 758	註 762	綴 768	仔 772	詛 779
摯 751	胄 758	貯 762	墜 768	姊 772	**zuān**
櫛 751	晝 758	著 763	贅 768	梓 772	鑽 779
擲 751	軸 758	箸 763	**zhūn**	紫 772	**zuǎn**
zhōng	皺 758	駐 763	諄 768	滓 772	纂 779
中 752	縐 758	築 763	**zhǔn**	**zì**	鑽 779
忪 753	驟 758	鑄 763	准 768	自 772	**zuàn**
忠 753	**zhū**	**zhuā**	準 768	字 774	鑽 779
盅 754	朱 758	抓 763	**zhuō**	恣 775	**zuǐ**
衷 754	侏 758	**zhuǎ**	拙 769	漬 775	嘴 779
終 754	珠 758	爪 763	卓 769	**zōng**	**zuì**
鍾 754	株 758	**zhuān**	捉 769	宗 775	最 780
鐘 754	硃 758	專 763	桌 769	棕 775	罪 780
zhǒng	蛛 758	甄 764	**zhuó**	綜 775	醉 780
冢 754	誅 759	(磚,塼)	灼 769	縱 775	最 780
腫 754	銖 759	**zhuǎn**	卓 769	蹤(踪) 775	**zūn**
塚 754	豬 759	轉 764	拙 769	**zǒng**	尊 780
種 754	諸 759	囀 765	茁 769	總 775	樽 780
踵 755	竹 759	**zhuàn**	酌 769	**zòng**	遵 780
zhòng	逐 759	傳 765	啄 770	從 776	**zuō**
中 755	軸 759	撰 765	琢 770	綜 776	作 780
仲 755	築 759	篆 765	著(着) 770	粽 776	**zuó**
重 755	燭 759	賺 765	濁 770	縱 776	作 781
眾 756	**zhǔ**	轉 765	擢 770	**zōu**	昨 781
種 756	主 759	饌 766	濯 770	鄒 777	琢 781
zhōu	貯 761	囀 766	鐲 770	**zǒu**	**zuǒ**
舟 756	渚 761	**zhuāng**	**zī**	走 777	左 781
州 756	煮 761	妝(粧) 766	孜 770	**zòu**	佐 781
周 756	麈 761	莊(庄) 766	吱 770	奏 777	**zuò**
洲 757	屬 761	裝 766	咨 770	揍 777	坐 781
週 757	囑 761	椿 766	姿 770	驟 777	作 782
粥 757	矚 761	**zhuàng**	茲 770	**zū**	座 783
賙 757	**zhù**	壯 767	孳 770	租 777	做 783
zhóu	住 761	狀 767	滋 771	**zú**	鑿 784
妯 757	助 761	僮 767	資 771	足 778	
軸 757	佇(竚) 762	撞 767	輜 771	卒 778	
zhǒu	注 762	**zhuī**	錙 771	族 778	
肘 757	柱 762	隹 767	髭 771	**zǔ**	
帚 757	祝 762	追 767	諮 771	阻 778	
zhòu		椎 768	鯔 771		

ā 阿 also **à**

1. an initial particle; a prefix to a name or a term of address 2. a word often used in transliterations

Āfùhàn 阿富汗 Afghanistan

Āgēntíng 阿根廷 Argentina; the Argentine

Ālā 阿拉 (Mohammedan) Allah

Ālābó 阿拉伯 1. Arabia 2. Arab

Ālābó shùzì 阿拉伯數字 Arabic numerals

Ālǐshān 阿里山 Mt. Ali, Taiwan

āmén 阿門 amen

āsīpǐlín 阿斯匹林 aspirin

āyí 阿姨 1. an aunt 2. a stepmother

ā 啊

an exclamatory particle

āyo 啊唷 the sound uttered when suddenly get hurt

ā 醃

refer to **āng** 醃

à 阿

refer to **ā** 阿

a 啊

a phrase-final particle

āi 哀

1. to grieve; to mourn; to lament 2. to pity; to sympathize; to commiserate; compassion 3. sad; sorrowful; lamentable 4. sadness; sorrow; grief

āichóu 哀愁 sad; sorrowful

āidào 哀悼 to mourn over, or lament (someone's death)

āigē 哀歌 a lament; an elegy; a dirge

āiháo 哀號 to wail

āilián 哀憐 to pity; to commiserate

āimíng 哀鳴 to give mournful cries; to wail

āiqiú 哀求 to beg or appeal pathetically

āishāng 哀傷 to feel sorrow or grief

āitàn 哀歎 to lament; to bewail

āitòng 哀痛 to feel the anguish

of sorrow

āiyuè 哀樂 funeral music

āi 哎

an interjection of surprise mixed with regret

āi 埃

1. fine dust 2. Egypt

Āijí 埃及 Egypt

āi 唉

(an interjection of regret or disgust) alas

āishēng tànqì 唉聲歎氣 to moan and groan

āi 挨 also **ái**

1. (to stay) near, next to, close to; to lean to 2. to suffer (from cold, hunger, etc.) 3. to wait; to delay; to put off 4. according to order 5. (now rarely) to rub

āidǎ 挨打 to suffer a beating

āi'è 挨餓 to suffer from hunger or starvation

āijìn 挨近 near to; to be close to

āilěng shòudòng 挨冷受凍 to suffer from cold

āimà 挨罵 to be blamed; to be scolded

āimén āihù 挨門挨戶 to go from door to door

āizhe 挨著 1. next to 2. one by one

āizòu 挨揍 to take a beating

ái 呆

refer to **dāi** 呆

ái 挨

refer to **āi** 挨

ái 捱

1. to suffer; to endure 2. to procrastinate; to put off 3. to rub (shoulders) 4. to draw near; to come close to

ái 皚

pure white; white and clean; brightly white

ái'ái 皚皚 (usually said of snow) white and clean

ái 癌 also **yán**

cancer

áixìbāo 癌細胞 cancer cells

ǎi 矮

1. a short person; a dwarf 2. short; low; low-ranking

ǎidèngzi 矮凳子 a low bench or stool

ǎigèr 矮個兒 a person of short stature

ǎipàng 矮胖 short and fat; stout

ǎixiǎo 矮小 short-statured

ǎi 噯

an interjection

ǎiqì 噯氣 (medicine) belch; eructation

ǎi 藹

1. exuberant; luxuriant; lush 2. gentle; kind; amiable

ǎi 靄

cloudy; haze; mist

ǎi'ǎi 靄靄 1. luxuriant growth 2. numerous 3. cloudy—thick and dusky

ài 艾

1. moxa 2. fine; fair; beautiful; good 3. old 4. to cease; to stop; to discontinue

ài 隘

1. a strategic pass 2. narrow 3. urgent 4. destitute

àikǒu 隘口 a (mountain) pass

ài 愛

1. to love; to like; to be fond of; to be kind to 2. love; affection; kindness; benevolence; likes 3. to be apt to

àibù shìshǒu 愛不釋手 loving something too much to part with it

àidài 愛戴 to love and support

Ài'ěrlán 愛爾蘭 Ireland

àifǔ 愛撫 to caress

àiguó 愛國 patriotic

àiguóxīn 愛國心 patriotism

àihào 愛好 to be interested in, or to love (sport, art, etc.)

àihàozhě 愛好者 a lover (of art, sports, etc.); a fan

àihù 愛護 to give kind protection

to; to take kind care of

àikèsīguāng 愛克司光 X rays; Roentgen rays

àilián 愛憐 to show love or fondness for

àiliàn 愛戀 to be in love with

àilǚ dòngwù 愛侶動物 a pet

àimò néngzhù 愛莫能助 desirous but unable to help

àimù 愛慕 to adore; adoration

àinǚ 愛女 a beloved daughter

àiqiè 愛妾 a beloved concubine

àiqíng 愛情 love

àiren 愛人 1. a sweetheart; a lover 2. to love others 3. a spouse

àishén 愛神 Cupid

Àisījīmórén 愛斯基摩人 the Eskimos

àiwū jíwū 愛屋及烏 to extend love to someone who is close or dear to one's direct object of love

àixī 愛惜 to prize; to cherish; to value

àixí 愛惜 refer to **àixī** 愛惜

àixīn 愛心 compassion; kindness

àixūróng 愛虛榮 vainglorious

àizībìng 愛滋病 AIDS (Acquired Immune Deficiency Syndrome)

àizī bìngdú 愛滋病毒 AIDS virus

ài 噯

an interjection

ài 嬡

the daughter (a complimentary term referring to the daughter of the person one is speaking to)

ài 曖

1. dim; indistinct 2. vague; ambiguous

àimèi 曖昧 1. ambiguous; obscure 2. a secret impropriety

ài 礙(碍)

1. to obstruct; to hinder; to be in the way 2. harmful; detrimental

àishì 礙事 to be in the way

àishǒu àijiǎo 礙手礙腳 to be

very much in the way

àiyǎn 礙眼 to be an eyesore

àiyú qíngmiàn 礙於情面 for fear of hurting somebody's feelings

ān 安
1. peaceful; quiet; calm; tranquil 2. to quiet; to stabilize; to pacify; to console 3. to put; to place; to arrange 4. to be content with 5. how; why 6. safe; secure; stable 7. a Chinese family name

ānbù dāngchē 安步當車 1. to be content to go on foot instead of riding in a vehicle 2. to be content with a simple life

ānbù dāngjū 安步當車 refer to **ānbù dāngchē** 安步當車

ānchā 安插 to plant; to get a position (for a person) in an organization

āndìng 安定 stable; steadfast; to stabilize

āndìng rénxīn 安定人心 to reassure the public

āndùn 安頓 to put in order; to help settle down

ānfēitāmìng 安非他命 amphetamine

ānfèn 安分 to be law-abiding

ānfèn shǒujǐ 安分守己 content or happy to be what one is; law-abiding

ānfǔ 安撫 to pacify

ānhǎo 安好 well; safe and sound

ānjìng 安靜 quiet; tranquil; still; peaceful

ānjū lèyè 安居樂業 to live and work in peace and content

ānkāng 安康 in a state of peace and good health

ānlè 安樂 comfort

ānlèsǐ 安樂死 euthanasia

ānmiányào 安眠藥 hypnotics; soporifics

ānnèi rángwài 安內攘外 to maintain internal security and to expel foreign invasion

ānníng 安寧 peace; repose; tranquility

ānpái 安排 arrangements; to arrange

ānpín lèdào 安貧樂道 happy to lead a simple, virtuous life

ānquán 安全 1. safe; secure 2. safety; security

ānquándài 安全帶 a safety belt (or strap)

ānquándǎo 安全島 a traffic island

ānquán dìyī 安全第一 safety first

ānquángǎn 安全感 a sense of security

ānquánmào 安全帽 a safety helmet

ānquánmén 安全門 a safety exit

ānquán shèshī 安全設施 safety devices (or equipment, installations)

ānrán wúyàng 安然無恙 completely uninjured; safe and sound

ānrú Tàishān 安如泰山 not in the slightest danger

ānshēn 安身 to find settled place for life

ānshēn lìmìng 安身立命 to enjoy peace and stability both physically and spiritually

ānshì 安適 peaceful and comfortable

ānshuì 安睡 to sleep soundly

āntài 安泰 in good health

ānwēi 安危 security and danger

ānwéi 安危 refer to **ānwēi** 安危

ānwèi 安慰 to console; to soothe

ānwěn 安穩 1. smoothly 2. peacefully

ānxí 安息 to rest

ānxí 安息 refer to **ānxí** 安息

ānxiáng 安詳 (said of one's manner) undisturbed; composed

ānxiē 安歇 to rest; to sleep

ānxīn 安心 to have peace of mind; to be relieved

ānyì 安逸 ease and comfort

ānyú 安於 to be content with

ānzàng 安葬 to bury (the dead); to inter

ānzhì 安置 1. to put in a proper place 2. to settle (people in need of employment, refugees, etc.)

ānzhuāng 安裝 to install (a device)

ān 庵
1. a hut; a cottage 2. a nunnery

ānsì 庵寺 1. a nunnery 2. a temple

ān 鞍
a saddle; a saddle-like terrain or thing

ānmǎ 鞍馬 1. a pommel horse; a side horse 2. saddle and horse

ān 諳
skilled in; versed in; familiar with

ānliàn 諳練 skilled in; versed in; familiar with

àn 岸
1. a shore; a bank; a beach; a coast 2. majestic 3. proud

ànrán 岸然 a solemn and dignified look

àn 按
1. to place the hand on; to press, control, etc. with one's hand 2. to examine 3. to stop; to halt; to repress 4. to impeach; to censure 5. according to; in (good order); as 6. to follow (a map, river, etc.) 7. a note; a comment

ànbīng bùdòng 按兵不動 to refuse to send troops; not to take actions at the moment

ànbù jiùbān 按部就班 (to do things) in good order or according to logical order

ànlǐ 按理 according to common practice or simple reasoning; normally

ànlì 按例 according to precedents

ànlíng 按鈴 to ring the bell

ànmó 按摩 1. massage 2. to massage

ànnà 按捺 to restrain, repress or hold back (one's anger, etc.)

ànniǔ 按鈕 1. a push button 2. to push the button

ànqī 按期 according to the dates, periods, etc. agreed upon or specified

ànqí 按期 refer to **ànqī** 按期

ànrì 按日 daily; every day

ànshí 按時 1. according to the time specified or agreed upon 2. on time 3. regularly

ànyuè 按月 monthly; by the month

ànzhào 按照 in accordance with; according to

ànzhù 按住 to repress or restrain

àn 案
1. a narrow, long table 2. according to; on the strength of; following this precedent 3. a legal case; legal records; a legal offense 4. (按) to press

ànfā 案發 a crime or conspiracy coming to the open

ànjiàn 案件 a legal case; a crime

ànqíng 案情 the ins and outs of a crime

ànqíng dàbái 案情大白 The riddle of a puzzling case has been completely unraveled.

àntóu 案頭 on the desk

ànyóu 案由 a brief; a summary

ànzi 案子 a legal case; a project

àn 暗
1. dim; dark; obscure 2. stupid; ignorant 3. secret; clandestine; stealthy 4. hidden

àncáng 暗藏 to hide; to conceal

ànchù 暗處 an obscure corner; a secret place

àndàn 暗淡 1. (said of colors, etc.) faded, dull and not fresh 2. (said of business, etc.) dim

àndìlǐ 暗地裡 secretly; stealthily; clandestinely

àndù Chéncāng 暗渡陳倉 illicit affairs; adultery

ànfáng 暗房 (photography) a darkroom

ànfǎng 暗訪 to investigate in secret

àngōu 暗溝 a sewer

ànhào 暗號 a secret mark, sign, signal or password

ànjì 暗計 1. to calculate or count in one's heart 2. a conspiracy

ànjiàn shāngrén 暗箭傷人 to stab somebody in the back

ànjiāo 暗礁 1. a submerged (or hidden) reef 2. an unseen obstacle

ànliú 暗流 a subterranean flow

ànpán 暗盤 a price or quotation which is kept from public knowledge but made known to selected few

ànqì 暗泣 to weep behind others' backs

ànsè 暗色 dark colors; deep colors

ànshā 暗殺 assassination; to assassinate

ànshì 暗示 1. to hint; to suggest 2. a hint; a suggestion

ànsuàn 暗算 a secret plot; to plot in secret

ànwú tiānrì 暗無天日 1. (said of a place, room, etc.) very dark 2. (said of a nation, locality, etc.) lawlessness

ànxǐ 暗喜 to feel happy secretly

ànxiǎng 暗想 to muse; to ponder

ànxiào 暗笑 to laugh in one's heart

ànyǔ 暗語 a code word

ànyù 暗喻 a metaphor; a concealed analogy

ànzhōng 暗中 1. in secret 2. (to do something) in the dark or without light

ànzhōng mōsuǒ 暗中摸索 to grope in the dark

ànzì 暗自 inwardly; to oneself; secretly

àn 闇

1. to shut the door 2. dark; obscure; obscurity 3. evening; night 4. lunar or solar eclipses 5. stupid and dull

ànrán 闇然 obscure; concealed

àn 黯

1. very dark; pitch-dark 2. miserable; dismal

ànrán shénshāng 黯然神傷 to feel dejected (or depressed)

ànrán shīsè 黯然失色 to appear very dull or poor in comparison; to be outshone; to be eclipsed

ànrán xiāohún 黯然銷魂 deeply affected (as by the sorrow of parting)

āng 腌 also **ā**

unclean; dirty; filthy

āngzāng 腌臢 unclean; dirty; filthy

āng 骯

dirty; filthy; foul

āngzāng 骯髒 dirty

áng 昂

1. to raise 2. lofty and proud; bold and not easily bent; straightforward 3. high 4. expensive; costly

ánguì 昂貴 expensive; costly

ángrán 昂然 proud and bold; haughtily

ángshǒu 昂首 to raise one's head high

ángshǒu kuòbù 昂首闊步 to stride proudly ahead

ángyáng 昂揚 high-spirited

àng 盎

1. a basin; a pot; a bowl 2. abundant; plentiful; rich

àngrán 盎然 abundant; full; exuberant

àngsī 盎斯 an ounce

āo 凹

1. indented; an indention 2. hollow; concave

āotòujìng 凹透鏡 a concave lens

āoxiàn 凹陷 a hollow or depression

áo 熬

1. to cook; to stew 2. to be worn down by worries, cares; discouraged or despondent; dejected

áo 嗷

a cry of hunger

áo'áo dàibǔ 嗷嗷待哺 waiting to be fed with cries of hunger

áo 獒

a large fierce dog; a mastiff

áo 熬

B

1. to extract (oil, etc.) by applying heat 2. to cook; to stew or simmer 3. to endure with perseverance; to suffer with patience (an ordeal, etc.); to sustain

áochūlai 熬出來 to have gone through all sorts of ordeal

áochūtóu 熬出頭 to have gone through all sorts of ordeal

áoyào 熬藥 to decoct medicinal herbs

áoyè 熬夜 to burn the midnight oil

áozhōu 熬粥 to cook congee or gruel by simmering

áo 遨
to travel for pleasure; to ramble

áoyóu 遨遊 to ramble; to travel

áo 翱
1. to soar; to fly 2. to roam; to wander

áoxiáng 翱翔 1. to soar; to fly 2. to roam

áo 鏖
to fight hard

áozhàn 鏖戰 to engage in hard fighting

áo 鰲(鼇)
a huge sea turtle

áotóu 鰲頭 the top successful candidate in a civil service examination under the former system

ǎo 拗
to bend or twist so as to break

ǎo 襖
a coat; a jacket or top garment padded with cotton or lined with fur

ào 拗
1. (also **yào**) hard to pronounce 2. refer to **niù** 拗

àokǒu 拗口 to twist the tongue

ào 奧
1. mysterious; obscure; profound (learning) 2. a secret cabin or corner of a house or palace

Àolínpǐkè Yùndònghuì 奧林匹克運動會 the Olympic Games

àomì 奧祕 deep, profound and mysterious subtle

àomiào 奧妙 1. mysterious; marvelous 2. the secret of doing something

ào 傲
1. proud; haughty; overbearing 2. to disdain; to despise; to look down upon 3. rash and impatient

àomàn 傲慢 haughty and overbearing; impudent

àoqì 傲氣 an air of arrogance; haughtiness

àoshì 傲視 to turn up one's nose at

ào 懊
to regret; to resent; regretful

àohuǐ 懊悔 to regret; remorseful; regretful

àonǎo 懊惱 to feel remorseful and angry

ào 澳
1. deep waters—where seagoing vessels can moor 2. name of various places (see below)

Àodàlìyà 澳大利亞 Australia

Àomén 澳門 Macao

Àozhōu 澳洲 refer to **Àodàlìyà** 澳大利亞

ào 燠
very hot; sweltering

àorè 燠熱 very hot; sweltering

bā 八
eight (Note: When **bā** precedes a 4th-tone sound, it is pronounced as **bá**.)

bābài zhījiāo 八拜之交 sworn brotherhood

bāchéng 八成 nearly; almost; very likely

bāfāng 八方 all directions

bāgēr 八哥兒 a mynah

bāgǔ 八股 corny; lacking in originality

bājiǎo 八角 Japanese star anise

bājiǎoxíng 八角形 an octagon

bā jiǔ bùlí shí 八九不離十 pretty close; very near

bākāi 八開 octavo (books, paper,

etc.)

bāmiàn línglóng 八面玲瓏 to be pleasant all round

bāmiàn wēifēng 八面威風 having an awe-inspiring reputation everywhere

Bāxiān 八仙 the Eight Immortals of Taoism

bāyuè 八月 1. August 2. eight months 3. the eighth month of the lunar calendar

bā 巴
1. name of an ancient state which occupied today's eastern Sichuan 2. a crust formed as a result of heat or dryness 3. to expect; to hope for anxiously 4. used with parts of human body (such as hands, cheeks, chin, etc.) 5. a final particle implying closeness or adhesion 6. to be close to 7. (physics) a bar

bābude 巴不得 can't wait to...; would that

bājie 巴結 1. to curry favor; to toady; to flatter 2. to exert oneself for advancement

Bālèsītǎn 巴勒斯坦 Palestine

Bālí 巴黎 Paris

Bā'námǎ 巴拿馬 Panama

bāshì 巴士 a bus

bāwàng 巴望 to hope for anxiously

Bāxī 巴西 Brazil

bāzhang 巴掌 1. the palm of the hand 2. a slap

bā 叭
a trumpet

bā 扒
1. to claw; to strip 2. to rake 3. to climb; to scale

bāpí 扒皮 to peel off the skin

bā 吧
bānǚ 吧女 a bar girl

bā 芭
1. a fragrant plant 2. a palmetto; a plantain

bājiāo 芭蕉 a plantain

bālè 芭樂 guava

bālěiwǔ 芭蕾舞 ballet

bā 疤
1. a scar 2. a birthmark

bāhén 疤痕 a scar

bā 笆
a bamboo fence

bā 捌
an elaborate form of 八(eight) used in documents or checks to prevent forgery

B

bá 拔
1. to pull out; to uproot 2. to promote (another to a higher position, etc.) 3. to stand out; outstanding; remarkable 4. to attack and take (a city); to capture

bácǎo 拔草 to weed

báchú 拔除 to uproot; to eradicate

bácuì 拔萃 (said of persons) to stand out; outstanding

bádāo xiāngzhù 拔刀相助 to help another (usually a stranger) for the sake of justice

bádé tóuchóu 拔得頭籌 to become the first to do something

báhé 拔河 a tug of war

báqǔ 拔取 to take or capture

báqù yǎnzhōngdīng 拔去眼中釘 (figuratively) to remove a person one hates most

báqún 拔群 (said of persons) to stand out; outstanding

bátuǐ 拔腿 to take to one's heels

báyá 拔牙 to extract a tooth

báyíng 拔營 to strike camp

bázhuó 拔擢 to promote; to raise

bá 跋
1. to travel 2. a postscript 3. to trample

báhù 跋扈 to be rampant in defiance of authority

báshè 跋涉 to trudge; to trek; to wade

bǎ 把
1. a handle; a hold 2. to take 3. to hold 4. to guard; to watch over; to keep under surveillance

B

5. a bundle; a grasp; a handful 6. around; about; approximately; more or less 7. sworn

bǎbǐng 把柄 a hold (on somebody); a handle

bǎchí 把持 to monopolize; to dominate or control

bǎchí bùdìng 把持不定 vacillating; undecided

bǎduò 把舵 1. to steer the rudder 2. a helmsman

bǎfēng 把風 a person posted as a look out, especially, in a robbery or other criminal acts

bǎguān 把關 1. to guard a pass 2. to check on

bǎláo 把牢 strong; dependable

bǎshì 把式 1. movements in Chinese boxing 2. a skilled laborer 3. a skill

bǎshǒu 把守 to guard or defend

bǎshou 把手 1. to hold hands 2. a handle

bǎwán 把玩 to fondle

bǎwò 把握 1. something one holds in hand 2. confident 3. to have a firm grasp of the situation

bǎxì 把戲 1. acrobatic performances as juggling, etc. 2. a trick or scheme 3. a child; a toddler

bǎxiōngdì 把兄弟 sworn brothers

bǎ 靶
1. the target 2. the splashboard of a chariot

bǎchǎng 靶場 a firing range; a shooting range

bǎxīn 靶心 the bull's-eye

bǎzi 靶子 a target

bà 把
a handle

bà 爸
father

bàba 爸爸 father; papa

bà 耙
refer to **pá** 耙

bà 罷
to cease; to stop; to finish; to be

done with

bàchù 罷黜 to remove from office; to fire

bàgōng 罷工 (said of workers) to strike

bàguān 罷官 to remove from office

bàkè 罷課 to boycott classes

bàle 罷了 (as a sentence-final phrase) merely; only; that's all

bàmiǎn 罷免 to recall (officials by the people)

bàshǒu 罷手 to stop; to pause; to give up

bàxiū 罷休 to cease; to stop

bàzhí 罷職 to remove from office

bà 霸
1. to dominate; to rule by might rather than right 2. a feudal lord; a chief or leader; an oppressor 3. something in which one is specially talented or gifted; outstanding

bàdao 霸道 to throw one's weight or to bully around; overbearing; high-handed

bàjù 霸據 to occupy by force

bàqì 霸氣 aggressiveness

bàquán 霸權 the authority of a powerful feudal prince; hegemony

bàwáng 霸王 1. the leader of feudal lords 2. the supreme chief or leader

bàyè 霸業 the achievement, career, etc. of a powerful head of feudal lords

bàzhàn 霸占 to occupy or take by force

Bà 灞
name of a river in Shanxi

Bàqiáo zhéliǔ 灞橋折柳 to part from friends; to bid farewell

bà 壩
1. an embankment; a dike 2. a dam

ba 吧(罷)
a particle used after an imperative sentence

bāi 掰

to pull apart with hands

bāikāi 掰開 to pull apart with hands

bái 白 also bó

1. white; clear; bright; clean; pure; plain 2. empty; blank 3. in vain; for nothing 4. free of charge; gratis 5. the spoken part in an opera, etc. 6. to state; to explain 7. a Chinese family name

báibì wēixiá 白璧微瑕 a small defect

báibì wéixiá 白璧微瑕 refer to **báibì wēixiá** 白璧微瑕

báibù 白布 plain white cloth; calico

báicài 白菜
1. Chinese cabbage 2. white rape

báichī 白癡 an idiot

báicù 白醋 plain vinegar

báidā 白搭 futile; in vain; to no avail

báidài 白帶 (medicine) leucorrhea

báifà cāngcāng 白髮蒼蒼 refer to **báifà cāngcāng** 白髮蒼蒼

báifà cāngcāng 白髮蒼蒼 hoary-headed

báifèi xīnjī 白費心機 to scheme in vain

Báigōng 白宮 the White House, Washington D.C.

báihuà 白話 spoken Chinese; vernacular Chinese

báihuàwén 白話文 writings in vernacular Chinese

báijīn 白金 1. platinum 2. silver

Báijīnhàngōng 白金漢宮 Buckingham Palace, England

báijìng 白淨 perfectly clean; immaculate

báijū guòxì 白駒過隙 the swiftness of the lapse of time

báikāishuǐ 白開水 boiled water

báilándì 白蘭地 brandy

báilǐng jiējí 白領階級 the white-collar class

báilù 白鷺 an egret

báimǎyǐ 白螞蟻 a termite

báimáng 白忙 to busy oneself to no purpose

báimángmáng 白茫茫 showing a vast expanse of whiteness

báimǐ 白米 white polished rice

báimiàn shūshēng 白面書生
1. an inexperienced young scholar 2. a fair-complexioned young scholar

báipǎo yītàng 白跑一趟 to make a futile trip

báipútáojiǔ 白葡萄酒 sherry

báirèhuà 白熱化 (said of a contest, movement, etc.) to reach the climax

báirì 白日 1. daytime; daylight 2. the sun

báirìmèng 白日夢 a daydream; reverie

báisè rénzhǒng 白色人種 the white race

báishǒu 白首 a hoary head—the old age

báishǒu qǐjiā 白手起家 to rise in life by one's own efforts

báisòng 白送 to give away; to give gratis

báitáng 白糖 white sugar; refined sugar

báitiān 白天 daytime

báitóu xiélǎo 白頭偕老 (said of a married couple)to stick to each other to the end of their lives

báixī 白皙 white-skinned

báixiěbìng 白血病 refer to **báixuèbìng** 白血病

báixiěqiú 白血球 refer to **báixuèqiú** 白血球

báixióng 白熊 a polar bear

báixuǎn 白癬 favus; honeycomb ringworm

báixuèbìng 白血病 leukemia

báixuèqiú 白血球 white blood cells; leucocytes

báiyǎn 白眼 1. the whites of the eyes 2. disdain; contempt

báiyī tiānshǐ 白衣天使 angels in white—nurses

báiyǐ 白蟻 a termite

báiyín 白銀 silver

B

báiyòng xīnjī 白用心機 to scheme in vain

báiyún 白雲 white clouds

báizhǒngrén 白種人 the white people; the Caucasians

báizhòu 白晝 broad daylight

báizhuàn 白賺 to earn with little or no effort

bǎi 百 also **bó**
1. hundred 2. many; numerous 3. all

bǎibān 百般 all sorts; every kind

bǎibǎoxiāng 百寶箱 a jewel case; a treasure box

bǎibèi 百倍 one hundred times

bǎibì cóngshēng 百弊叢生 All the ill effects appear.

bǎibù chuānyáng 百步穿楊 (archery) superior marksmanship

bǎichǐ gāntóu, gèngjìn yībù 百尺竿頭，更進一步 to make still further progress

bǎidú bùyàn 百讀不厭 (said of a book) not boring even after repeated reading; very interesting

bǎifā bǎizhòng 百發百中 to hit the target at every shot

bǎifèi dàixìng 百廢待興 All neglected matters are yet to be dealt with.

bǎifēnbǐ 百分比 a percentage

bǎifēnlù 百分率 a percentage

bǎifēn zhībǎi 百分之百 absolutely

bǎigǎn jiāojí 百感交集 Lots of emotions crowd into the heart.

bǎigōng 百工 1. all sorts of officers 2. all sorts of handicraftsmen

bǎihéhuā 百合花 the lily

bǎihuā qífàng 百花齊放 All flowers are in bloom.

bǎihuò gōngsī 百貨公司 a department store

bǎihuò shāngchǎng 百貨商場 an emporium

bǎijiā zhēngmíng 百家爭鳴 All schools of thoughts contend for attention.

bǎijiǎnqún 百襉裙 a pleated skirt

bǎikē quánshū 百科全書 an encyclopedia

bǎikǒng qiānchuāng 百孔千瘡 in a state of ruin or extreme distress

bǎikǒu mòbiàn 百口莫辯 unable to give a convincing explanation for self-defense

bǎiliàn chénggāng 百鍊成鋼 Mastery comes from long training.

bǎimǐ sàipǎo 百米賽跑 the 100-meter dash

bǎinián 百年 1. a hundred years; a century 2. a lifetime

bǎinián dàjì 百年大計 a project of vital and lasting importance

bǎinián hǎohé 百年好合 harmonious union lasting a hundred years (a conventional congratulatory message on a wedding)

bǎinián shùrén 百年樹人 It takes one hundred years to cultivate a man.

bǎirìké 百日咳 whooping cough

bǎishìtōng 百事通 an expert in everything; an all-rounder

bǎishòu zhīwáng 百獸之王 the king of all animals—the lion

bǎisī mòjiě 百思莫解 incomprehensible

bǎitīng bùyàn 百聽不厭 worth hearing a hundred times

bǎiwàn 百萬 a million

bǎiwàn fùwēng 百萬富翁 a millionaire

bǎiwén bùrú yījiàn 百聞不如一見 Seeing is believing.

bǎiwú jìnjì 百無禁忌 There are no taboos or restrictions at all.

bǎiwú yīshī 百無一失 sure to succeed if certain rules are followed

bǎixìng 百姓 1. the common people; the people 2. all existing family names

bǎiyèchuāng 百葉窗 Venetian blinds

bǎiyī bǎishùn 百依百順 to

yield to all the wishes (of a child, etc.)

bǎizhàn bǎishèng 百戰百勝 victorious in every battle

bǎizhé bùnáo 百折不撓 indomitable; unswerving

bǎizhéqún 百褶裙 a pleated skirt

bǎi 伯
refer to **bó** 伯

bǎi 柏 also **bó, bò**
a cypress

bǎishù 柏樹 a cypress

bǎiyóu 柏油 asphalt

bǎi 擺
1. to arrange; to display; to place; to put 2. to wave; to swing; to oscillate; to wag 3. a pendulum 4. to assume; to put on

bǎibu 擺布 1. to manage or handle (a person) 2. to arrange

bǎidòng 擺動 to sway; to swing

bǎidù 擺渡 to ferry

bǎijiàzi 擺架子 to be snobbish; to put on airs

bǎikuò 擺闊 to show off one's wealth

bǎinòng 擺弄 1. to toy with; to play with 2. to make fun of; to trick

bǎipíng 擺平 1. (slang) to make satisfied 2. to put down something securely

bǎisher 擺設兒 to furnish and decorate (a room)

bǎishǒu 擺手 to swing one's arms

bǎituō 擺脫 to free oneself from; to cast off; to shake off (a tailer)

bǎiwūlóng 擺烏龍 to talk irresponsibly

bài 拜
1. to do obeisance; to salute; to pay respects to 2. to appoint (as a government official); an appointment 3. to visit; to pay a visit to; to call on (or at)

bàibài 拜拜
1. to bring hands together and take a bow 2. a worshipping festival in Taiwan

bàibié 拜別 to say good-bye or farewell

bàidǎo shíliúqún xià 拜倒石榴裙下 to fall head over heels for a woman

bàidú 拜讀 (a polite expression) to read with respect

bàifǎng 拜訪 to pay a visit to; to visit

bàifú 拜服 to admire (another's erudition, courage, moral strength, etc.)

bàiguān 拜官 to be appointed to a public office

bàihè 拜賀 to congratulate

bàihòu 拜候 to visit; to call on

bàihuì 拜會 to visit; to call on

bàijiàn 拜見 to visit, or call on (an elder or superior)

bàijīn zhǔyì 拜金主義 mammonism

bàinián 拜年 to call on another and offer New Year's greetings

bàishén 拜神 to worship gods

bàishòu 拜壽 to congratulate one on his birthday

bàituō 拜託 a polite expression in asking another to do something for oneself

bàiwàng 拜望 to visit; to call on

bàixiè 拜謝 to express one's thanks

bàiyè 拜謁 to pay a courtesy call

bài 敗
1. to defeat or be defeated; to fail; to go down 2. to decline; to decay; to wither 3. to spoil or be spoiled; to corrupt or be corrupted

bàiběi 敗北 to suffer defeat; a defeat

bàibǐ 敗筆 1. poor calligraphy 2. a flaw

bàihuài 敗壞 to ruin or be ruined

bàihuài ménméi 敗壞門楣 to disgrace one's family

bàijī 敗績 a defeat

bàijiāzi 敗家子 a wastrel; a prodigal; a spendthrift

bàijiàng 敗將 1. a defeated

enemy general 2. one who is defeated in a contest

bàilèi 敗類 1. to ruin or corrupt one's fellows 2. corrupt people

bàilù 敗露 (said of a crime, plot, etc.) to fail and be exposed

bàisù 敗訴 to lose a lawsuit

bàiwáng 敗亡 to be defeated and overthrown

bàixiěbìng 敗血病 refer to **bàixuěbìng** 敗血病

bàixìng érguī 敗興而歸 to come back disappointed

bàixuěbìng 敗血病 septicemia

bàizhàng 敗仗 a defeat

bàizhèn 敗陣 a defeat

bài 稗

1. barnyard grass 2. small; little 3. novels, legends, etc.

bàiguān yěshǐ 稗官野史 unofficial historical writings

bān 扳

1. to pull 2. to count (on one's fingers)

bāndǎo 扳倒 to pull down

bānjī 扳機 a trigger

bānkāi 扳開 to pull open

bānshou 扳手 1. a spanner; a wrench 2. a lever (on a machine)

bān 般

1. kind; sort; class 2. (搬) to carry; to move 3. (班) to return; to call back

bān 班

1. a grade; a seat or position 2. a class or company; a set; a group 3. a squad (of soldiers) 4. to distribute 5. to return 6. (斑) variegated; of different colors 7. of equal rank, same generation, etc. 8. a shift; duty 9. scheduled runs (of the bus, etc.) 10. a Chinese family name

bānchē 班車 a regular bus

bāncì 班次 1. the flight number of an airliner 2. the designated number of a scheduled train 3. the grade or class (of a student) 4. sequence

bāndǐ 班底 1. ordinary members of a theatrical troupe 2. (in poli-

tics, etc.) hard-core followers

bānjī 班機 an airliner on the scheduled flight

bānjí 班級 1. a grade 2. a class

Bānmén nòngfǔ 班門弄斧 to show off one's talent or skill before an expert

bānshī 班師 to withdraw troops after a victorious campaign

bānzhǎng 班長 1. (military) a squad leader 2. (in school) the leader of a class

bān 斑

1. speckles; spots; mottles 2. mottled; variegated; motley

bānbái 斑白 (said of hair) gray

bānbó 斑駁 motley (in color)

bāndiǎn 斑點 specks; spots; mottles

bānjiū 斑鳩 the ringdove; the cushat

bānlán 斑斕 gorgeous; resplendent

bānmǎ 斑馬 a zebra

bānmǎxiàn 斑馬線 a zebra crossing

bānwén 斑紋 stripes; striped

bān 搬

1. to move; to transport 2. to present

bāndòng 搬動 to move; to shift

bānjiā 搬家 to move from one dwelling to another

bānjiùbīng 搬救兵 to ask for help

bānnòng shìfēi 搬弄是非 to stir up or incite trouble between people

bānqiān 搬遷 to move

bānyí 搬移 to move

bānyùn 搬運 to move; to transport; to carry

bānyùnfèi 搬運費 carriage; freight

bānyùn gōngrén 搬運工人 a porter; a docker

bān 頒

1. to bestow on; to grant; to confer on 2. to proclaim; to make public; to promulgate 3. to dis-

tribute; to send out

bānbù 頌布 to proclaim or promulgate

bānfā 頌發 to bestow; to award or distribute (prizes, etc.)

bānjiǎng 頌獎 to hand out an award or prize

bǎn 版

1. household registers 2. printing plate 3. edition 4. supporting boards used in building walls

bǎnběn 版本 an edition; a version

bǎnhuà 版畫 a print

bǎnmiàn 版面 1. space of a whole page 2. layout of a printed sheet

bǎnquán 版權 copyright

bǎnquán suǒyǒu 版權所有 All rights reserved.

bǎnshuì 版稅 royalties (on books)

bǎntú 版圖 1. population and territory 2. territory; dominion

bǎn 板

1. a board; a plank 2. a plate (of tin, aluminum, etc.) 3. a slab 4. printing blocks 5. rigid; stern; stiff

bǎncār 板擦兒 a wiper or an eraser (for a blackboard, etc.)

bǎndèng 板凳 a wooden stool

bǎnhuà 板畫 a woodcut; a print

bǎnqǐ miànkǒng 板起面孔 to make a long face

bǎnqiú 板球 (sports) cricket

bǎnzheliǎn 板著臉 to make a long face

bǎnzi 板子 1. a flogging board 2. a printing block

bǎn 闆

the boss; the owner

bàn 半

1. half 2. very little 3. in the middle 4. partly; about half

bànbǎi 半百 fifty; half a hundred

bànbèizi 半輩子 a lifetime

bànbì jiāngshān 半壁江山 half of the national territory

bànbiān 半邊 half of something

bànbiān jiātíng 半邊家庭 a single-parent family

bànchǎng 半場 1. a half of a game 2. half-court

bàndá 半打 half a dozen

bàndǎo 半島 a peninsula

bàndǎotǐ 半導體 a semiconductor

bàndiàozi 半吊子 1. a dabbler 2. a rash person

bàngōng bàndú 半工半讀 part work, and part study

bàngōngkāi 半公開 semi-overt

bànguānfāng 半官方 semiofficial

bànjià 半價 half-price; 50 percent discount

bànjié 半截 a half part; half (a section)

bànjīn bāliǎng 半斤八兩 tweedledum and tweedledee

bànjìng 半徑 a radius

bànkōngzhōng 半空中 in midair; in the air

bànlù 半路 halfway; midway

bànlù chūjiā 半路出家 to start midway

bànmài bànsòng 半賣半送 to sell goods at rock-bottom prices

bànpiào 半票 a half-price ticket

bànpíngcù 半瓶醋 a half-educated person

bànqiú 半球 a hemisphere

bànshǎng 半晌 (for) quite some time; a long time

bànshēn bùsuí 半身不遂 hemiplegia—paralysis of half of one's body

bànshēn bùsuì 半身不遂 refer to **bànshēn bùsuí** 半身不遂

bànshēng bùshóu 半生不熟 1. half-cooked; half-raw 2. casual acquaintance

bànshù 半數 half the number; half

bànsǐ bùhuó 半死不活 1. dying 2. listless; lethargic 3. more dead than alive

bàntiān 半天 1. midair; in the air 2. half-day; half a day 3. quite a while

bàntú 半途 halfway; midway

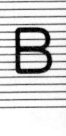

B

bàntú érfèi 半途而廢 to stop (a task) halfway

bàntuī bànjiù 半推半就 to be half willing (at heart) and half unwilling (in appearance)

bànxìn bànyí 半信半疑 half-believing and half-doubting

bànyè 半夜 1. half a night 2. midnight

bànyè sān'gēng 半夜三更 in the depth of night

bànyè sānjīng 半夜三更 refer to bànyè sān'gēng 半夜三更

bànyuán 半圓 a semicircle

bànyuèkān 半月刊 a semi-monthly; a fortnightly

bàn 伴

1. a companion 2. to accompany

bànchàng 伴唱 1. a vocal accompaniment 2. to accompany (a singer)

bànchàngjī 伴唱機 a karaoke

bànláng 伴郎 the best man

bànlǚ 伴侶 a companion; a pal

bànniáng 伴娘 the maid of honor

bànsuí 伴隨 to accompany; to follow

bànwǔ 伴舞 to be a dancing partner

bànzòu 伴奏 to accompany (a soloist)

bàn 扮

to dress up; to disguise; to play

bànguǐliǎn 扮鬼臉 to make faces

bànyǎn 扮演 to play or act (a part or role)

bànzuò 扮作 to dress up as

bàn 拌

to mix

bànyún 拌匀 to mix evenly or properly

bànzuǐ 拌嘴 to wrangle; to quarrel

bàn 絆

1. shackles; fetters 2. to stumble; to trip over; to trip

bàndǎo 絆倒 to trip over; to trip

bànjiǎoshí 絆腳石 a stumbling block

bànzhù 絆住 to be detained, hindered or held back; to be bogged down

bàn 辦

1. to manage; to handle; to transact; to deal with; to attend to 2. to try and punish 3. to purchase

bàn'àn 辦案 to handle a (legal or business) case

bàndào 辦到 to accomplish or manage

bànfǎ 辦法 means; schemes; ways; resources

bàngōng 辦公 to attend to business; to do office work

bàngōngshì 辦公室 an office

bànlǐ 辦理 to handle; to manage

bànshì 辦事 to handle business; to manage an affair

bàntuǒ 辦妥 to complete (procedures); to finish doing something properly

bànxǐshì 辦喜事 to host a party on a joyous occasion (especially a wedding)

bàn 瓣

1. petals 2. sections (as of oranges) 3. a valve; a lamella 4. fragments

bāng 邦

1. a state; a country; a nation 2. a manor given to a nobleman by the emperor in feudal China

bāngguó 邦國 a nation; a country; a state

bāngjiāo 邦交 international relations

bānglián 邦聯 a confederation

bāng 梆

a watchman's rattle made of wood or bamboo

bāngzi 梆子 1. watchman's clapper 2. a general term for local operas performed to the accompaniment of bangzi

bāng 傍

refer to bàng 傍

bāng 幫

1. to help; to assist 2. a gang; a group; a class; a fleet 3. the sides of a shoe or gutter

bāngchèn 幫襯 help; aid; assistance

bāngdàománg 幫倒忙 to cause trouble while trying to help

bānggōng 幫工 an assistant of a skilled worker

bānghuì 幫會 1. secret societies 2. an underworld gang

bāngmáng 幫忙 help; assistance; to help or assist

bāngpài 幫派 a faction

bāngpǔ 幫浦 a pump

bāngqiāng 幫腔 to give verbal support to a person

bāngshou 幫手 a helper; an assistant

bāngxiōng 幫兇 an accomplice in a crime

bāngzhù 幫助 help; assistance; to help or assist

bǎng 綁

to tie; to bind; to fasten

bǎngfěi 綁匪 a kidnaper

bǎngjià 綁架 to kidnap for ransoms

bǎngjǐn 綁緊 to bind or fasten tight

bǎngpiào 綁票 to kidnap for ransoms

bǎng 膀

the upper arms

bǎngbì 膀臂 1. the arms 2. capable aides

bǎng 榜

a publicly posted roll of successful examinees

bǎngshàng wúmíng 榜上無名 to fail in an examination

bǎngshì 榜示 to post for public attention

bǎngshǒu 榜首 the top candidate of an examination

bǎngyàng 榜樣 an example; a model

bàng 蚌

an oyster

bàng 傍 also **bāng**

1. to depend on 2. to draw near; to be close to

bàngwǎn 傍晚 dusk; twilight; nightfall

bàngwǔ 傍午 near noontime; shortly before noon

bàng 棒

1. a club; a stick; a truncheon 2. to hit with a club 3. good; strong; wonderful

bàngbàngtáng 棒棒糖 a lollipop

bànghè 棒喝 1. to bang and bawl in rebuke of a student 2. to arouse a person from his evil ways—as if by using a club

bàngqiú 棒球 baseball

bàng 膀

to make passes at

bàng 磅

1. a pound 2. scales 3. to weigh

bàngchèng 磅秤 scales giving the weight in avoirdupois

bàng 謗

to slander; to libel; to condemn

bàngyán 謗言 a libel; a slander; defamatory remarks

bàng 鎊

pound sterling

bāo 包

1. to wrap 2. to include; to contain 3. to surround 4. to guarantee 5. a parcel; a package; a bundle 6. a Chinese family name

bāobàn 包辦 to undertake completely

bāobì 包庇 to harbor; to shelter

bāocáng 包藏 to contain; to conceal

bāocáng huòxīn 包藏禍心 to harbor evil intentions or malicious intent

bāochǎng 包場 to reserve a whole theater or cinema

bāochāo 包抄 (military) to outflank

bāofàn 包飯 to board

bāofu 包袱 1. a cloth wrapper 2.

a bundle in a cloth wrapper 3. a

bāoguā 包括 refer to **bāokuò** 括

bāoguǎn 包管 to guarantee or assure

bāoguǒ 包裹 1. to wrap up 2. a parcel

bāohán 包含 to contain; to comprise

bāohan 包涵 to forgive or pardon

bāohuǒ 包伙 to board

bāojī 包機 a chartered airplane

bāokuò 包括 to include; to comprise

bāolǎn 包攬 to monopolize

bāoluó wànxiàng 包羅萬象 inclusive of everything

bāopí 包皮 1. a wrapper; a covering 2. the prepuce

bāopiào 包票 a guaranty

bāoróng 包容 to tolerate; to forgive

bāoshāng 包商 a contractor

bāowéi 包圍 to surround; to encircle

bāoxiāng 包廂 a box (in a theater, stadium, etc.)

bāoxīncài 包心菜 a cabbage

bāozā 包紮 to wrap; to bind up

bāozhuāng 包裝 to pack; packing

bāozi 包子 a steamed stuffed bun

bāo 炮(炰)
quick-fry

bāo 苞
1. a variety of rush 2. a bract 3. to wrap 4. profuse; thick 5. seeds with the germ ready to burst; seeds bursting up

bāo 胞
1. the placenta 2. children of the same parents

bāo 剝
to strip

bāokāi 剝開 to strip the covering off

bāo 褒(襃)

1. to praise; to cite; to commend; a citation 2. big; great

bāobiǎn 褒貶 to praise and disparage; criticisms

bāojiǎng 褒獎 to praise and cite; to commend and award

báo 薄
refer to **bó** 薄

bǎo 保

1. to guard; to shelter; to protect 2. to be responsible; to guarantee; to insure 3. to keep; to maintain

bǎo'ān 保安 1. to ensure local security 2. to ensure the workers' safety 3. public security

bǎo'ān rényuán 保安人員 security personnel

bǎobiāo 保鏢 1. a bodyguard; an armed escort 2. to act as a bodyguard

bǎobuzhù 保不住 most likely; may well

bǎochí 保持 to maintain; to keep

bǎocún 保存 1. to safeguard 2. to preserve

bǎocún qīxiàn 保存期限 1. the shelf life of a commodity 2. the period for keeping official papers on file

bǎocún qíxiàn 保存期限 refer to **bǎocún qīxiàn** 保存期限

bǎodān 保單 1. a formal note or document of guaranty 2. an insurance policy

bǎofáng gōngzuò 保防工作 security measures

bǎoguǎn 保管 to safeguard; to safekeep

bǎoguǎnfèi 保管費 storage charges

bǎohù 保護 to protect; to guard; protection

bǎohù guānshuì 保護關稅 a protective tariff

bǎohùrén 保護人 a guardian

bǎohùsè 保護色 protective coloration

bǎohuángdǎng 保皇黨 the royalist

Bǎojiālìyà 保加利亞 Bulgaria

bǎojiàn 保健 health protection; health care

bǎojiàn 保薦 to recommend (somebody for a job, etc.)

bǎojiànxiāng 保健箱 a medical kit

bǎolíngqiú 保齡球 bowling

bǎoliú 保留 to preserve; to reserve

bǎomì 保密 to keep the secret

bǎomǔ 保母 a nurse who looks after small children

bǎoquán 保全 to assure the safety of

bǎoshì 保釋 to release on bail

bǎoshìjīn 保釋金 bail

bǎoshǒu 保守 conservative

bǎoshǒu zhǔyì 保守主義 conservatism

bǎosòng 保送 to send a student to school or college without an entrance examination, usually for his high scholastic qualifications

bǎowèi 保衛 to defend; to guard against

bǎowēn 保溫 1. heat preservation 2. to keep (water, etc.) hot; to preserve heat

bǎowēnbēi 保溫杯 a thermos cup or container

bǎoxiǎn 保險 1. insurance 2. to guarantee

bǎoxiǎnfèi 保險費 insurance premiums

bǎoxiǎngàng 保險槓 a bumper

bǎoxiǎn gōngsī 保險公司 an insurance company

bǎoxiǎnrén 保險人 an insurer; an underwriter

bǎoxiǎnsī 保險絲 a fuse wire

bǎoxiǎntào 保險套 a condom; a sheath

bǎoxiǎnxiāng 保險箱 a safe; a strongbox

bǎoyǎng 保養 1. maintenance 2. to take care (of health) 3. to maintain

bǎoyǎngfèi 保養費 maintenance cost; upkeep

bǎoyǒu 保有 to keep

bǎoyòu 保佑 1. to protect or bless 2. a blessing

bǎoyùyuàn 保育院 an orphanage

bǎozhàng 保障 to safeguard; to protect

bǎozhèng 保證 to guarantee; to assure

bǎozhèngjīn 保證金 guaranty money

bǎozhèngrén 保證人 a guarantor; a guarantee

bǎozhèngshū 保證書 a guaranty; a warrant

bǎozhí 保值 to preserve the value (of currency)

bǎozhòng 保重 Please take good care (of yourself).

bǎo 堡
1. a walled village; a town 2. a petty military station; a fort; a fortress

bǎolěi 堡壘 a fortress; a bastion

bǎo 飽
1. to eat to the full; surfeited 2. satisfied 3. full; plump 4. fully; to the full

bǎohé 飽和 saturation; saturated

bǎojīng fēngshuāng 飽經風霜 to have experienced the hardships of life

bǎojīng shìgù 飽經世故 well-experienced in the ways of the world

bǎomǎn 飽滿 well-stacked (figures, etc.); full; plump

bǎorù sīnáng 飽入私囊 to embezzle public funds

bǎoshí zhōngrì 飽食終日 well-fed all day (without doing anything worthwhile)

bǎoshòu 飽受 to suffer (insult, grievances, etc.) to the fullest extent

bǎoxué zhīshì 飽學之士 a learned scholar; an erudite person

bǎo 褓
swaddling bands; swaddling clothes

bǎo 鴇
1. a bird resembling the wild

B

goose 2. a prostitute 3. a procuress

bǎomǔ 鴇母 a procuress

bǎo 寶
1. treasure 2. precious; valuable 3. respectable; honorable

bǎobǎo 寶寶 baby

bǎobèi 寶貝 1. a cherished thing 2. darling

bǎodāo wèilǎo 寶刀未老 old but still vigorous in mind and body

bǎodǎo 寶島 a treasure island

bǎodiǎn 寶典 a valuable book

bǎoguì 寶貴 valuable; precious

bǎojiàn 寶劍 a treasured sword

bǎokù 寶庫 a treasury; a treasure house

bǎoshān kōnghuí 寶山空回 to gain nothing from a rare opportunity

bǎoshí 寶石 a precious stone; a gem; a jewel

bǎotǎ 寶塔 a pagoda

bǎowù 寶物 a treasure; a treasury

bǎoyù 寶玉 a precious stone

bǎozàng 寶藏 a treasure; a treasury

bǎozuò 寶座 the throne

bào 抱
1. to embrace; to enfold; to hold in the arms 2. to harbor; to cherish; to bosom 3. to adopt 4. ambition

bàobìng 抱病 indisposed; sick or ill

bàobùpíng 抱不平 indignant at injustice

bàocán shǒuquē 抱殘守缺 sticking to old ways

bàodìng juéxīn 抱定決心 determined

bàofù 抱負 aspirations; ambition

bàohàn 抱憾 to deplore; to regret

bàohèn zhōngshēn 抱恨終身 to regret something to the end of one's days

bàojǐn 抱緊 to hold tightly in one's arms

bàoqiàn 抱歉 to feel sorry about; to regret

bàotóu shǔcuàn 抱頭鼠竄 to run helter-skelter

bàotóu tòngkū 抱頭痛哭 to bury one's head in one's arms and cry bitterly

bàoxīn jiùhuǒ 抱薪救火 to add fuel to the fire—to make the situation even worse

bàoyàng 抱恙 indisposed; sick or ill

bàoyuàn 抱怨 to complain; to grumble

bàozhe 抱著 to hold in one's arms; to embrace

bào 豹
a leopard; a panther

bào 報
1. to repay; to recompense; to requite 2. a reward; a retribution 3. to report; to announce 4. a report; a newspaper

bào'àn 報案 to report a case (such as a theft, murder, etc.) to the police

bàobèi 報備 to inform the authorities of what one plans to do

bàobiǎo 報表 forms for reporting statistics, etc.; report forms

bàochóu 報仇 to avenge (a grievance, etc.)

bàochou 報酬 1. pay; a salary 2. remuneration; reward

bàodá 報答 to repay another's kindness

bàodǎo 報導 1. to report (news) 2. a news report

bàodào 報到 to check in; to register

bào'ēn 報恩 repay another's kindness

bàofèi 報費 a newspaper subscription bill

bàofèi 報廢 1. to report (worn-out office equipment, etc.) as unserviceable or useless 2. to scrap

bàofù 復仇 1. to avenge; to revenge 2. to report back (after investigation)

bàogào 報告 1. to report 2. a

report

bàoguān 報關 to declare something at the customs

bàoguānháng 報關行 a customs broker

bàoguǎn 報館 a newspaper office

bàoguó 報國 to devote oneself to the national cause

bàohùkǒu 報戶口 1. to apply for a residence permit 2. to register

bàojiāyīn 報佳音 to carol; caroling

bàojiā 報夾 a newspaper holder or clip

bàojiā 報夾 refer to **bàojiā** 報夾

bàojiè 報界 the press; the news circles

bàojǐng 報警 1. to report an alarm or emergency 2. to report to the police

bàokān 報刊 newspapers and periodicals

bàokǎo 報考 to enter one's name in an examination

bàomíng 報名 to enroll; to enlist

bàoshè 報社 a newspaper office

bàoshí 報時 to give the correct time

bàoshuì 報稅 to report tax returns

bàotān 報攤 a newsstand; a news stall

bàotóng 報童 a newsboy

bàoxǐ 報喜 to announce good news

bàoxiāo 報銷 1. to give a statement on one's expenses 2. to write off

bàoxiào 報效 to work for; to repay another's kindness by working hard for him 2. to give private means for public use

bàoxìn 報信 to report news; to announce

bàoyè 報業 the business of the press

bàoyìng 報應 retribution

bàozǎi 報載 according to newspaper reports

bàozhāng 報章 1. newspapers 2. reply letters

bàozhàng 報帳 to present a bill of expenses (to the employer or the accountant)

bàozhǐ 報紙 1. a newspaper 2. news print

B

bào 暴
1. cruel; savage; fierce; violent 2. (also **pù**) sudden 3. short-tempered

bàobì 暴斃 to meet a sudden death

bàodiē 暴跌 (said of prices) to slump

bàodié 暴跌 refer to **bàodiē** 暴跌

bàodòng 暴動 a riot; a rebellion

bàofā 暴發
1. a violent eruption 2. to break out 3. to become rich or to attain a high position all of a sudden

bàofāhù 暴發戶 an upstart; a parvenu

bàofēng 暴風 a storm; a tempest

bàofēngxuě 暴風雪 a snowstorm; a blizzard

bàofēngyǔ 暴風雨 a storm; a tempest

bàojūn 暴君 a tyrant; a despot

bàolì 暴力 violence; brute force

bàolì 暴戾 despotic and tyrannical

bàoluàn 暴亂 a riot; a rebellion

bàomín 暴民 mobs or mobsters

bàonù 暴怒 furious; to blow one's top

bàotiǎn tiānwù 暴殄天物 a reckless waste of grains, etc.

bàotiào rúléi 暴跳如雷 to be infuriated; to be enraged; furious

bàotóu 暴投 (baseball) a wild pitch

bàoxíng 暴行 violence; atrocities

bàoyǐn bàoshí 暴飲暴食 to eat and drink excessively

bàozào 暴躁 irritable; fretful; irascible

bàozhǎng 暴漲 (said of a water level or a commodity price) to

rise sharply or quickly

bàozhèng 暴政 tyrannical rule

bào 鮑

1. an abalone 2. salted fish 3. a Chinese family name

bàoyú 鮑魚 1. an abalone 2. salted fish

bàoyú zhīsì 鮑魚之肆 a market for salted fish—an objectionable environment

bào 瀑

a pouring rain which comes all of a sudden; a sudden shower

bào 爆

1. to explode; to burst; to crack 2. to quick-boil; to quick-fry

bàofā 爆發 1. to explode; to blow up 2. to break out; to erupt; to flare up

bàoliè 爆裂 to burst; to erupt; to crack

bàomǐhuā 爆米花 popcorn

bàopò 爆破 to demolish by explosives; demolition

bàozhà 爆炸 to explode; to blow up

bàozhàlì 爆炸力 explosive force; the impact of explosion

bàozhú 爆竹 firecrackers

bēi 杯

a cup; a tumbler; a glass; a goblet

bēigé 杯葛 1. a boycott 2. to boycott

bēigōng shéyǐng 杯弓蛇影 extremely suspicious

bēipán lángjí 杯盤狼藉 (literally) Empty glasses and plates are scattered all over—The feast is over.

bēishuǐ chēxīn 杯水車薪 too inadequate and useless

bēizhōngwù 杯中物 wine; alcoholic drinks

bēi 卑

1. low 2. debased; depraved; vile 3. inferior 4. a modest expression referring to oneself

bēibǐ 卑鄙 1. mean 2. low; inferior

bēibǐ shǒuduàn 卑鄙手段 dirty tricks

bēigōng qūxī 卑躬屈膝 obsequious; fawning; servile

bēijiàn 卑賤 low; inferior; mean; humble

bēixià 卑下 base; mean; humble

bēizhí 卑職 1. (self-reference) your humble servant 2. a low or humble position

bēi 背

to bear or shoulder (a load, burden, etc.); to carry on the back

bēibāo 背包 a knapsack

bēidài 背帶 suspenders

bēifù 背負 to carry on the back

bēihēiguō 背黑鍋 to take the blame for another person

bēi 盃

a cup; a tumbler

bēi 埤

low-lying

bēi 悲

1. sad; sorrowful; mournful; woeful; rueful; doleful 2. to lament; to deplore; to mourn; to pity; to sympathize

bēicǎn 悲慘 tragic(al); pathetic; miserable

bēicóng zhōnglái 悲從中來 to feel sadness welling up

bēidào 悲悼 to mourn (for or over)

bēifèn 悲憤 1. to lament and resent (an injustice) 2. grief and indignation

bēiguān 悲觀 pessimistic

bēihuān líhé 悲歡離合 the sorrow of parting and the joy of union in life

bēijù 悲劇 a tragedy

bēilián 悲憐 to take pity on (a person)

bēiliáng 悲涼 sad and dreary; somber; dismal

bēimǐn 悲憫 to pity; to have sympathy for

bēiqī 悲戚 rueful; doleful; mournful

bēiqì 悲泣 to sob, or weep, sor-

rowfully

bēishāng 悲傷 sad; sorrowful

bēitàn 悲歎 to lament; to deplore; to sigh over

bēitiān mǐnrén 悲天憫人 to be concerned over the destiny of mankind

bēitòng 悲痛 grieved; deep sorrow

bēitòng 悲慟 to weep loudly for sorrow

bēixǐ jiāojí 悲喜交集 intermingling of sorrow and joy

bēizhuàng 悲壯 tragically heroic

bēi 揹
to carry on the back; to shoulder (a load, responsibility, etc.)

bēihēiguō 揹黑鍋 to be made the scapegoat for somebody

bēi 碑
a stone tablet

bēijié 碑碣 a stone tablet

bēimíng 碑銘 a part of an inscription on a tablet, usually in rhyme

bēiwén 碑文 an inscription on a tablet

bēizhì 碑誌 an inscription on a tablet

běi 北 also **bò**
1. north; northern; northerly 2. northward 3. defeated

Běibànqiú 北半球 the Northern Hemisphere

běibian 北邊 the north; the northern part

Běi Cháoxiǎn 北朝鮮 North Korea

Běidǒu Qīxīng 北斗七星 the Plough; the Big Dipper

Běidǒuxīng 北斗星 the Plough; the Big Dipper

běifāng 北方 1. the northern region; 2. the north

běifāngrén 北方人 a northerner

Běi Fēi 北非 North Africa; North African

Běihǎi 北海 the North Sea

Běi Hán 北韓 North Korea

Běihuíguīxiàn 北回歸線 the Tropic of Cancer

Běijí 北極 1. the North Pole; the Arctic Pole 2. the north magnetic pole

Běijíhǎi 北極海 the Arctic Ocean

Běijíxīng 北極星 Polaris; the North Star

běijíxióng 北極熊 a polar bear

Běijīng 北京 Beijing; Peking

běijīnggǒu 北京狗 a pekingese

Běijīngrén 北京人 1. Peking Man (sinanthropus pekinensis) 2. a native of Beijing

Běi Měizhōu 北美洲 North America

Běi Ōu 北歐 northern Europe

Běipíng 北平 refer to **Běijīng** 北京

běishàng 北上 to go north

Běi Sòng 北宋 the Northern Song Dynasty

běiwěi 北緯 north latitude; northern latitude

bèi 貝
1. shells; cowries (used in ancient China as currency) 2. valuable; precious; treasure 3. (physics) bel 4. a Chinese family name

bèiké 貝殼 seashells; shells

bèi 背
1. the back 2. the reverse side; the back side 3. to cast away; to turn one's back on; to give up 4. to go against; to rebel 5. to remember by rote; to commit to memory in detail 6. (now rarely) to faint; to lapse into a coma

bèibù 背部 the back (of a man or an animal, etc.)

bèidào érchí 背道而馳 to proceed in opposite directions

bèidìlǐ 背地裡 behind one's back; secretly

bèifēng 背風 on the lee side; leeward

bèihòu 背後 behind one's back

bèijǐng 背景 background

bèilí 背離 to deviate from; to depart from

B

bèimiàn 背面 the reverse side; the back side

bèipàn 背叛 to rebel; to betray

bèiqì 背棄 to renounce; to betray

bèishū 背書 1. to recite a lesson 2. to endorse a check 3. endorsement

bèisòng 背誦 to recite

bèixīn 背心 a vest; a waistcoat

bèixìn 背信 to break one's word or promise

bèiyǐng 背影 the sight of one's back

bèiyuē 背約 to break one's promise

bèi 倍
1. double; to double 2. (joined to a numeral) -times; -fold 3. to rebel; to be insubordinate

bèijiā 倍加 to double; double

bèilǜ 倍率 percentage

bèishù 倍數 a multiple

bèizēng 倍增 to double; double

bèi 悖
to go against; to go counter to; to revolt against; contrary to

bèilǐ 悖理 absurd; unreasonable; irrational

bèilǐ 悖禮 uncivil; impolite

bèinì 悖逆 to revolt; to rebel

bèiqì 悖棄 to turn away from something in revolt

bèi 被
1. bedding; a coverlet; a quilt 2. to cover; to shroud 3. to spread; to reach 4. placed before verbs to show a passive voice 5. because of; due to

bèibī 被逼 to be compelled or forced to

bèidān 被單 a bedsheet; a bedspread

bèidòng 被動 passive; to act on order

bèigào 被告 the accused; the defendant

bèihài 被害 to be killed or murdered

bèipò 被迫 to be compelled or forced to

bèirù 被褥 coverlets and mattresses; bedding

bèitào 被套 ticking

bèiwōr 被窩兒 a quilt folded like a sleeve for sleeping

bèizi 被子 a quilt

bèi 焙
to dry or heat near a fire; to toast; to bake

bèi 備
1. a sense of completeness; perfection 2. to be equipped with 3. to get ready 4. to prepare against 5. fully; in every possible way

bèi'àn 備案 to serve as a record

bèi'ér bùyòng 備而不用 keeping for possible future use

bèifù suódéshuì 備付所得稅 provision for income tax

bèimǎ 備馬 to saddle a horse for riding

bèitāi 備胎 a spare tire

bèiwànglù 備忘錄 a memorandum

bèiyòng 備用 reserve; spare; alternate

bèizhàn 備戰 1. to prepare for war 2. to be prepared against war

bèizhì 備至 to the utmost

bèizhù 備注 1. remarks or footnotes 2. space reserved for footnotes

bèi 蓓
a flower bud; a bud

bèilěi 蓓蕾 a flower bud; a bud

bèi 褙
to mount (paintings, or calligraphic works)

bèi 輩
1. rank; a grade 2. a generation

bèifen 輩分 seniority (among relatives); difference in seniority

bèi 憊
tired; exhausted; weary

bèi 臂
refer to **bì** 臂

bēn 奔

1. to move quickly; to run; to hurry 2. to run for one's life; to flee 3. to elope

bēnchí 奔馳 to travel quickly; to move fast

bēnfàng 奔放 1. (said of a horse) galloping 2. (said of a writing or emotional manifestation) expressive and unrestrained

bēnpǎo 奔跑 to run in a great hurry

bēnbō 奔波 to be on the run; to work very hard

bēnsāng 奔喪 to hasten home upon the death of one's parents

bēnzǒu 奔走 1. to solicit help (in trying to land a job, get an appointment, etc.) 2. to do a job on orders; to run errands

běn 本

1. the root of a plant 2. the root; the origin; the source; the basis; the foundation 3. original 4. a book; a copy 5. capital (in business) 6. our; this; the present 7. according to; based on 8. the beginning; the starting point

běn'àn 本案 the present case; this case

běnbān 本班 this (or our) class, squad, team, section, etc.

běnbù 本部 1. headquarters 2. this ministry; our ministry

běnbù 本埠 this city; the local area

běnchū zǐwǔxiàn 本初子午線 the prime meridian

běndāng 本當 should have, or ought to have

běndǎng 本黨 our party; this party

běndì 本地 the local area

běndìrén 本地人 a native

běnfèn 本分 one's part; one's role; one's duty

běnfèng 本俸 the basic salary (exclusive of various additional allowances)

běnguó 本國 one's home country

běnháng 本行 1. one's trade; one's specialty 2. this bank; our bank

běnjiè 本屆 current; this year's

běnjīn 本金 principal as distinct from interest

běnlái 本來 1. originally 2. of course

běnlái miànmù 本來面目 true looks; true colors

bǎnlěipǎo 本壘跑 (baseball) home-run

běnlì 本利 principal and interest

běnlǐng 本領 ability; skill; talent

běnmíng 本名 one's formal name

běnmò dàozhì 本末倒置 to mistake the means for the end

běnnéng 本能 instinct

běnqī 本期 1. this term 2. the present class (of students or cadets)

běnqī 本期 refer to **běnqī** 本期

běnqián 本錢 capital (in business)

běnrén 本人 1. I; me 2. himself; herself; yourself 3. personally

běnrì 本日 today

běnsè 本色 1. the original color 2. the real look

běnshēn 本身 oneself; personally; itself

běnshěng 本省 this province; our province

běnshì 本市 this city; our city

běnshì 本事 a story (or a plot) of a play, movie, etc.

běshì 本事 ability; skill; talent

běntǔ 本土 the mainland; a country proper

běnwèi 本位 1. a basic unit 2. a standard

běnwén 本文 the main body of a writing

běnxiàn 本縣 our (or this) county, prefecture, etc.

běnxiāng 本鄉 our (or this) village

běnxiào 本校 our (or this) school

běnxìng 本性 the real nature

běnxī 本息 principal and interest

běnxí 本息 refer to **běnxī** 本息

běnxīn 本薪 the basic salary (exclusive of various additional allowances)

běnxìng nányí 本性難移 One's nature cannot be altered.

běnyì 本意 the original intention

běnyì 本義 the original meaning

běnyuè 本月 this month

běnzhe 本著 in the light of; in accordance with

běnzhí 本質 refer to **běnzhí** 本質

běnzhǐ 本旨 the real intention or meaning

běnzhí 本質 essence; the intrinsic nature

běnzhōu 本周 this week

běnzi 本子 a book; a notebook

běn 畚

a bamboo or wicker scoop or a basket for carrying earth

běndǒu 畚斗 a dustpan

běnjī 畚箕 a bamboo basket for carrying earth or dirt

bèn 奔(逩)

to go straight forwards; to head for

bèn 笨

1. stupid; dull 2. clumsy; awkward

bèndàn 笨蛋 a fool

bènguā 笨瓜 a fool

bènrén 笨人 a fool; a simpleton; a dullard; an idiot

bènshǒu bènjiǎo 笨手笨腳 all thumbs

bèntóu bènnǎo 笨頭笨腦 stupid; muddleheaded; dull; blockheaded

bènzhòng 笨重 1. cumbersome; too heavy for convenient handling 2. clumsy

bènzhuō 笨拙 unskilled; clumsy; awkward

bènhuó 笨拙 refer to **bènzhuō** 笨拙

bēng 崩

1. to collapse; to disintegrate; to fall 2. (said of an emperor) to die

bēngkuì 崩潰 to collapse; to

break down; to fall to pieces

bēngliè 崩裂 to crack up

bēngtā 崩塌 to crumble; to collapse

bēngtān 崩坍 to crumble; to collapse

bēngxiàn 崩陷 to cave in; to fall in; to collapse

bēng 繃(綳)

to bind

bēngdài 繃帶 a bandage

béng 甭

unnecessary; do not have to

běng 繃(綳)

1. taut; tense 2. to endure or bear

běngzheliǎn 繃著臉 to pull a long face

bèng 迸

1. to scatter; to explode 2. to crack

bèngfā 迸發 to burst forth; to burst out

bèngliè 迸裂 to crack; to split; to dash out

bèng 蹦

to skip; to caper; to trip; to jump; to leap

bèngbèng tiàotiào 蹦蹦跳跳 skipping; capering; tripping; romping; frolicsome

bī 逼

1. to press; to compel; to pressure; to force; to coerce 2. to close in; to draw near 3. to importune; to harass; to annoy 4. narrow; strait

bībù déyǐ 逼不得已 to be compelled or forced to; can't help but

bīgòng 逼供 to force a confession

bījìn 逼近 to draw near; to press

bīpò 逼迫 to compel; to force

bīrén tàishèn 逼人太甚 push someone too hard

bīshàng Liángshān 逼上梁山 to be forced to do something, especially to break the law

bīshì 逼視 to stare at sternly

bīwèn 逼問 to question closely

bīzhài 逼債 to press for payment of debts

bīzhēn 逼眞 (said of acting, performances, etc.) lifelike; almost real

bí 鼻

1. a nose 2. before any others; first

bí'ái 鼻癌 nasopharyngeal cancer

bídòuyán 鼻竇炎 sinusitis

bíkǒng 鼻孔 nostrils

bíqiāng 鼻腔 the nasal cavity

bíqīng liǎnzhǒng 鼻青臉腫 a bloody nose and a swollen face —bruised in the face

bísè 鼻塞 to have a stuffy nose; nasal congestion

bítì 鼻涕 nasal mucus or drips; snivel

bíxī 鼻息 the breath

bíxí 鼻息 refer to bíxī 鼻息

bíxiě 鼻血 refer to bíxuè 鼻血

bíxuè 鼻血 nosebleed; nasal hemorrhage

bíyānhú 鼻煙壺 a snuff bottle

bíyán 鼻炎 nasal catarrh

bíyīn 鼻音 (phonetics) nasal sounds; nasals

bízi 鼻子 a nose

bízǔ 鼻祖 a founder; an originator

bǐ 匕

1. a ladle; a spoon 2. an arrowhead 3. a dagger

bǐshǒu 匕首 a dagger; a short sword

bǐ 比

1. to compare with 2. to liken; to compare to 3. to compete 4. than 5. to (in a score) 6. ratio 7. gesture 8. (also bì) close; next to

bǐbǐ jiēshì 比比皆是 to be found or seen everywhere—very common

bǐduì 比對 to collate

bǐfāng 比方 an example

bǐhua 比畫 1. to gesticulate; to gesture 2. to come to blows

bǐjīní yǒngzhuāng 比基尼泳裝 a bikini

bǐjià 比價 to compare prices or bids

bǐjiān zuòzhàn 比肩作戰 to fight shoulder to shoulder

bǐjiào 比較 1. comparative; relatively 2. to compare

bǐjiàojí 比較級 (grammar) the comparative degree

bǐlì 比例 ratio; proportion

bǐlìchǐ 比例尺 scale (of a map, model, etc.)

bǐlín 比鄰 close neighbors

bǐlǜ 比率 ratio; rate

bǐmùyú 比目魚 a flatfish; a sole

bǐnǐ 比擬 1. to liken; to compare to 2. a parallel

bǐrú 比如 such as; like

bǐsài 比賽 a contest; a match; a tournament

bǐshì 比試 1. have a competition 2. to measure with one's hand or arm

bǐtè 比特 (computer) bit

bǐyì shuāngfēi 比翼雙飛 to fly side by side

bǐyù 比喻 1. a metaphor; a simile 2. to compare to; to liken

bǐzhào 比照 according to; in the light of

bǐzhí 比值 specific value; ratio

bǐzhòng 比重 specific gravity

bǐ 妣

one's deceased mother

bǐ 彼

1. that; those 2. another; the other 3. there

bǐcǐ 彼此 both parties; each other

bǐcǐ bǐcǐ 彼此彼此 We are in similar position.

bǐcǐ zhījiān 彼此之間 between you and me; between two parties

bǐ 筆

1. a writing brush; a pen; a pencil 2. writer's skill or style 3. to write 4. a stroke; a touch 5. a unit of amount 6. (formerly) prose

bǐchù 筆觸 the touch of writing

or drawing

bǐfǎ 筆法 technique of writing, calligraphy or drawing

bǐfēng 筆鋒 1. a penpoint 2. forcefulness of writing

bǐhuà 筆畫 the number of strokes (in a character)

bǐjī 筆跡 one's handwriting

bǐjì 筆記 notes taken (of lectures, speeches, etc.)

bǐjìbù 筆記簿 a notebook

bǐjìxíng diànnǎo 筆記型電腦 a portable computer

bǐjià 筆架 a tubular penrack or penholder

bǐmíng 筆名 a pen name; nom de plume; a pseudonym

bǐshì 筆試 a written examination

bǐtǐng 筆挺 (said of dress) smooth ironed; spick-and-span; trim

bǐtǒng 筆筒 a tubular penrack or penholder

bǐyǒu 筆友 a pen pal

bǐzhí 筆直 perfectly straight

bǐ 鄙 also bǐ

1. mean; base; lowly; despicable 2. superficial; shallow 3. remote 4. to despise; to scorn

bǐlòu 鄙陋 1. mean; base 2. shallow

bǐrén 鄙人 1. I (self-depreciatory); your humble servant 2. a hillbilly

bǐshì 鄙視 to despise; to disdain; to slight; to look down upon; to scorn

bǐsú 鄙俗 vulgar; philistine

bǐyí 鄙夷 to despise; to disdain; to slight; to look down upon; to scorn

bǐ 比

refer to **bǐ** 比 8

bì 必

1. must; necessarily 2. an emphatic particle

bìbèi tiáojiàn 必備條件 the requisitions (for)

bìdé 必得 determined to possess something

bìděi 必得 to have to

bìdìng 必定 most certainly; to be sure to

bìdú 必讀 a must for reading

bìgōng bìjìng 必恭必敬 displaying full courtesy; showing great respect

bìrán 必然 to have to be (like this)

bìrán zhīshì 必然之勢 a natural trend

bìshèng 必勝 will most certainly win

bìsǐ zhīxīn 必死之心 with one's back to the wall

bìxiūkē 必修科 a required course; an obligatory course

bìxū 必須 must; to have to

bìxū 必需 what is essential or indispensable

bìxūpǐn 必需品 daily necessities

bìyào 必要 necessary; need

bì 庇

to hide; to conceal; to harbor; to protect

bìhù 庇護 to give protection to; to harbor

bìhùsuǒ 庇護所 a sanctuary or asylum

bìyìn 庇蔭 to shelter; to harbor

bìyòu 庇祐 (said of a god) to give divine assistance to a mortal

bì 泌

1. swift and easy gushing of water 2. name of a river in Henan Province

bì 拂(弼)

1. to aid; to assist 2. to make correct or right

bìshì 拂士 a straightforward adviser; a wise counselor

bì 祕

refer to **mì** 祕

bì 陛

wide and high steps in the palace; the steps to the throne

bìxià 陛下 Your Majesty; His or Her Majesty

bì 畢
1. to complete; to finish; to end 2. whole; total; complete 3. a Chinese family name

bìjìng 畢竟 after all; in the long run; ultimately

bìshēng 畢生 in one's whole life; throughout one's lifetime; lifelong

bìyè 畢業 to be graduated; to graduate; graduation

bìyèbān 畢業班 the graduating class

bìyè diǎnlǐ 畢業典禮 a commencement

bìyè kǎoshì 畢業考試 a graduation examination

bìyè lùnwén 畢業論文 a thesis

bìyèshēng 畢業生 a graduate

bìyè wénpíng 畢業文憑 a diploma

bìyè zhèngshū 畢業證書 a diploma

bì 閉
1. to close; to shut 2. (said of a conference, etc.) to conclude; to end 3. to block up; to stop; to obstruct 4. to restrain

bìguān zìshǒu 閉關自守 to adopt a policy of exclusion or isolation

bìlù diànshì 閉路電視 closed-circuit television

bìméngēng 閉門羹 to treat someone to a closed door; to close the door on

bìmén sīguò 閉門思過 to reflect on one's faults or misdeeds in private

bìmén zàochē 閉門造車 to do something impractical, useless, or out of one's pure imagination

bìmén zàojū 閉門造車 refer to **bìmén zàochē** 閉門造車

bìmù 閉幕 (said of shows, meetings, etc.) to close or conclude

bìsè 閉塞 1. to block up; to obstruct 2. backward 3. hard to get to

bì 婢
1. a maidservant; a female slave 2. (in old China) a humble term

used by a girl to refer to herself

bì 敝
1. worn-out; broken; tattered 2. exhausted; tired 3. (a self-depreciatory term) my or our

bìguó 敝國 my or our country

bìxǐ 敝屣 worn-out shoes—useless things

bìxìng 敝姓 my family name

bìzhǒu zìzhēn 敝帚自珍 Everyone values things of his own.

bì 裨
1. to aid; to supplement 2. to benefit; to help

bìyì 裨益 to benefit; benefit

bì 辟
1. a monarch 2. to summon; to call 3. to govern; to take the law (to people) 4. to avoid; to escape

bìxié 辟邪 to ward off evils

bì 碧
1. green; blue; verdant; emerald green 2. jasper; emerald

bìcǎo rúyīn 碧草如茵 a carpet of green grass

bìlǜ 碧綠 verdant; emerald green

bìyù 碧玉 jasper; emerald

bì 鄙
refer to **bǐ** 鄙

bì 弊
1. bad; undesirable 2. dishonesty; fraud 3. exhausted; tired 4. disadvantages

bìbìng 弊病 corrupt practices

bìduān 弊端 corrupt practices

bìhài 弊害 harm; damage

bì 幣
1. currency; money 2. a present; an offering

bìbó 幣帛 gifts (in money and silks)

bìzhí 幣值 the purchasing power of a currency

bìzhì 幣制 a currency system

bì 蔽
1. to cover 2. to hide; to conceal; to shelter 3. to screen; to sepa-

rate

bìfēngyǔ 蔽風雨 to shelter from the wind and rain

bìhù 蔽護 to shelter; to protect

bì 壁
1. a partition wall; the walls of a room 2. a military breastwork 3. a cliff

bìbào 壁報 a wall paper; a wall poster

bìchú 壁櫥 a closet; a wall chest

bìhǔ 壁虎 a house lizard or gecko

bìhuà 壁畫 a mural painting; a fresco

bìlěi fēnmíng 壁壘分明 There is no compromise between the contending factions.

bìlú 壁爐 a fireplace

bìtǎn 壁毯 a tapestry

bì 避
1. to avoid; to shun; to evade; to hide 2. to prevent; to keep away; to repel

bìbù jiànmiàn 避不見面 to avoid meeting someone

bìbù zuòdá 避不作答 to parry a question

bìhuì 避諱 (an old Chinese custom) to avoid mentioning the emperor or one's ancestors by name or using any character of it in writing except the family name

bìhui 避諱 to evade

bìkāi 避開 to get out of the way

bìléizhēn 避雷針 a needle gap arrester

bìmiǎn 避免 to avoid; to forestall

bìnàn 避難 to escape a calamity; to avoid disaster; to take refuge

bìrèn 避妊 to avoid pregnancy; contraception

bìshǔ 避暑 to run away from summer heat

bìxián 避嫌 to avoid suspicion

bìxié 避邪 to avoid evil spirits or influences

bìyùn 避孕 to avoid pregnancy;

contraception

bìyùntào 避孕套 a condom

bìzhòng jiùqīng 避重就輕 1. to take the easier way out; to choose the easier of the two alternatives 2. to dwell on the minor points but avoid touching the core of a matter

bì 臂 also **bèi**
the arms (of a human being or a tool, machine, etc.)

bìbǎng 臂膀 the arm

bìzhāng 臂章 an arm badge; a brassard

bì 斃
1. to come to a bad end; decline; destruction 2. to fall; to prostrate 3. dead; to come to the end of life 4. (colloquial) to kill or execute by shooting; to shoot

bìmìng 斃命 to meet violent death; to get killed

bì 璧
1. a round and flat piece of jade with a circular hole in it 2. a general name of all kinds of jade, jade-wares and ornaments

bìhé 璧合 a perfect match

bìrén 璧人 a fine-looking person

bìyù 璧玉 a round and flat piece of jade with a circular hole in it

biān 編
1. to knit; to weave 2. to put together; to organize; to form; to arrange 3. to fabricate; to make up; to invent 4. to compile; to edit 5. a volume

biānduì 編隊 formation (of aircrafts, etc.)

biānhào 編號 1. to arrange under numbers; to number 2. a serial number

biānjí 編輯 1. to edit; to compile 2. an editor

biānjíbù 編輯部 an editorial department; the editorial office

biānjù 編劇 1. to write a play 2. a playwright

biānliè 編列 to list (the expenses for a project in the budget); to compile

biānniánshǐ 編年史 chronicles;

annals

biānpái 編排 1. to arrange in order 2. to write and present (a play, etc.)

biānpài 編派 to libel; to vilify

biānrù 編入 1. to include (in a budget) 2. to enlist; to recruit

biānshěn 編審 1. to edit and screen (textbooks, etc.) 2. a member of the editing and screening committee

biānwǔ 編舞 to choreograph

biānxiě 編寫 1. to compile 2. to compose

biānyì 編譯 1. to translate and compile 2. a translator; an interpreter

biānzào 編造 1. to fabricate 2. to prepare (a budget)

biānzhě 編者 an editor

biānzhī 編織 to knit

biānzhì 編制 1. organization 2. to work out; to draw up

biānzhù 編著 to edit; to compile

biānzhuàn 編撰 to edit; to compile

biānzuǎn 編纂 to compile

biān 蝠 also **biǎn**

     a bat

biānfú 蝙蝠 a bat

biān 鞭

     1. a whip; a lash; to flagellate; to flog 2. an ancient weapon shaped like a whip 3. a string of firecrackers

biāncè 鞭策 1. a horsewhip 2. to urge or goad on; to encourage

biāncháng mòjí 鞭長莫及 beyond one's influence; beyond one's reach; out of range

biāndǎ 鞭打 to flog with a whip; to flagellate

biānpào 鞭炮 (a long string of) firecrackers

biānpì rùlǐ 鞭辟入裡 deep-cutting; incisive; penetrating

biān 邊

     1. an edge; the end of something; a verge; a margin 2. a side 3. a hem; a decorative border 4. the border of a nation's territory; a

boundary 5. limits; bounds 6. nearby; near to

biānchuí 邊陲 a border; a borderland; a frontier

biānfáng 邊防 border defense; frontier defense

biānfú 邊幅 1. the appearance of a person; attire 2. the margin (of a piece of cloth, etc.)

biānjì 邊際 1. a boundary 2. (Buddhism) the extremity of things 3. the substance of one's speech or writing

biānjiāng 邊疆 a borderland; a frontier

biānjiāng mínzú 邊疆民族 tribes living on the borderland

biānjiè 邊界 the national boundary

biānjìng 邊境 the national boundary or border; the frontier

biānsài 邊塞 strategic positions along the frontier; a border pass

biānyuán 邊緣 the edge; the verge

biǎn 扁

     1. flat 2. a tablet

biǎndan 扁擔 a flat carrying pole or shouldering pole

biǎnpíng 扁平 thin and flat

biǎntáoxiàn 扁桃腺 the tonsils

biǎn 匾

     a (wooden) tablet

biǎn'é 匾額 a (wooden) tablet; a horizontal inscribed board

biǎn 貶

     1. to reduce or lower (prices, etc.); to devalue 2. to degrade; to reduce; to demote 3. to disparage; to condemn; to censure 4. to dismiss; to send away

biǎndī 貶低 to belittle; to depreciate; to play down

biǎnyì 貶抑 to debase; to devalue; to belittle; to depreciate

biǎnzhé 貶謫 to demote and exile an official; to relegate

biǎnzhí 貶值 to devalue or debase (especially referring to a currency); devaluation; depreciation

B

biǎn 編
　1. narrow; small; petty 2. small size clothes 3. narrow minded

biǎnjí 褊急 short-tempered; lacking patience

biǎn 蝙
　refer to **biǎn** 編

biàn 弁
　1. a conical cap worn on ceremonious occasions in ancient times 2. in the Qing Dynasty low-ranking military officers

biànyán 弁言 a preface

biàn 便
　1. expedient; convenient; handy 2. fitting; appropriate 3. in that case; even if 4. then 5. advantageous 6. excrement and urine; to relieve oneself 7. informal; at ease; ordinary

biànbì 便秘 constipation

biàncài 便菜 an ordinary dish

biàncān 便餐 an informal and ordinary meal

biàndāng 便當 a box lunch

biàndang 便當 easy; convenient

biànfàn 便飯 a meal; potluck

biànfú 便服 ordinary clothing

biànhú 便壺 a chamber pot

biànjiān 便箋 notepaper; a memo

biànjié 便捷 easy and convenient

biànlì 便利 convenience; facility

biànmào 便帽 a cap or hat for ordinary wear

biànmì 便秘 refer to **biànbì** 便秘

biànmín 便民 to offer greater convenience to the people

biànnì 便溺 to empty the bowels and to urinate

biànsuǒ 便所 a toilet; a rest room

biàntiáo 便條 a note; a memo

biànxié 便鞋 1. cloth shoes 2. slippers

biànyī 便衣 1. ordinary clothes; plain clothes 2. a plainclothesman

biànyí xíngshì 便宜行事 to act as circumstances may require without asking for approval from superiors

biànyú 便於 easy to; convenient to

biàn 遍(徧) also **piàn**
　1. all over; everywhere 2. the whole (world), etc.)

biànbù 遍布 everywhere; all over

biàndì 遍地 everywhere; all places

biànjí 遍及 all over

biàntǐ línshāng 遍體鱗傷 to suffer injuries all over one's body

biàn 辨
　1. to distinguish 2. to identify; to recognize

biànbié 辨別 to distinguish between; to see the difference between

biànmíng shìfēi 辨明是非 to distinguish right from wrong

biànrèn 辨認 to recognize; to identify

biànshí 辨識 to recognize; to identify

biànshì 辨識 refer to **biànshí** 辨識

biàn 辮
　1. to plait; to braid 2. a queue; a pigtail; a braid; a plait

biànzi 辮子 1. a queue; a pigtail; a braid; a plait 2. a mistake or defect that may be exploited by an opponent

biàn 辯
　1. to debate; to argue; to dispute 2. to use specious arguments

biànhù 辯護 1. to speak in defense of; to defend verbally; to defend 2. (law) to plead; to defend; defense

biànhùrén 辯護人 defense counsel; an advocate

biànjiě 辯解 to provide an explanation; to try to defend oneself

biànlùn 辯論 to debate; a

debate

biàn 變

1. to change; to alter; to become different 2. to turn into; to become 3. extraordinary; uncommon 4. an accident; misfortune; tragedy; upheaval; disturbance 5. changeable

biànběn jiālì 變本加厲 to get worse; worsening

biànchéng 變成 to become; to change into

biàndiànsuǒ 變電所 a power substation

biàndòng 變動 1. (said of organizations, arrangements, etc.) to change; to reorganize 2. alteration 3. variation

biàn'gé 變革 (said of an institution, etc.) to change or reform

biàn'gēng 變更 to change (plans, methods, etc.); to alter; to modify

biàngù 變故 an accident; mishap; misfortune

biànguà 變卦 to change one's mind

biànhuà 變化 1. to transform; to transmute 2. to change 3. changeable

biànhuà duōduān 變化多端 changeable

biànhuàn 變幻 to change; to metamorphose

biànhuàn 變換 1. to convert (foreign money, etc.) 2. to change; to vary; to switch

biànhuàn mòcè 變幻莫測 to metamorphose in an unpredictable way

biànjià chūshòu 變價出售 to sell at the current price

biànjú 變局 a critical situation; a crisis

biànmài 變賣 to sell (possessions) to meet an immediate financial need

biànqiān 變遷 evolution; change; vicissitudes

biànsèlóng 變色龍 a chameleon

biànsù 變速 to change in speed; gearshift

biàntài 變態 1. (zoology) metamorphosis 2. abnormality

biàntōng 變通 to adapt oneself to circumstances

biànxīn 變心 to jilt a lover

biànxíng 變形 to transfigure; to transform

biànxìng 變性 1. to change sex by surgical means 2. denaturation

biànyàng 變樣 to change in patterns, style, appearance, etc.

biànzhí 變質 refer to **biànzhì** 變質

biànzhì 變質 1. to change in quality or objectives 2. to deteriorate; to go bad 3. to degenerate

Biāo 杓

name of a constellation—the handle of the Dipper

biāo 彪

1. a tiger cub 2. stripes or streaks on the skin of a tiger 3. tall and big; shining and brilliant; outstanding

biāobǐng 彪炳 brilliant and shining; splendid (achievements, examples, etc.)

biāoxíng dàhàn 彪形大漢 a whale of a man

biāo 標

1. to show; to indicate; to mark; to symbolize 2. a mark; a sign; a symbol; an indication; a label 3. a model; a paragon 4. to bid; to tender

biāobǎng 標榜 1. to glorify 2. to profess 3. to boost

biāoběn 標本 1. a specimen 2. appearance and substance

biāodì 標的 a target; an objective; a purpose; an aim

biāodiǎn 標點 punctuation

biāodiǎn fúhào 標點符號 a punctuation mark

biāogān 標竿 a guidepost

biāogāo 標高 elevation

biāogòu 標購 to buy at public bidding

biāojì 標記 a mark; an indication

biāojià 標價 1. the tag price; the

B

listed price 2. to indicate the price of a commodity on a tag

biāomíng 標明 to label; to indicate; to mark clearly

biāoqiān 標籤 a label; a tag

biāoqiāng 標槍 a javelin; a spear; a lance

biāoshì 標示 to indicate; to mark

biāoshòu 標售 to sell by tender

biāotí 標題 a heading; a title; a headline

biāoxīn lìyì 標新立異 to try to be fanciful

biāoyǔ 標語 a slogan; a motto

biāozhì 標誌 a mark; a sign; a symbol

biāozhi 標致 (said of females) good-looking

biāozhǔn 標準 1. a standard; a criterion 2. typical

biāozhǔngān 標準桿 (golf) par

biāozhǔnhuà 標準化 to standardize

biāozhǔnshí 標準時 standard time

biāozhǔnyǔ 標準語 the standard language

biāo 鏢

1. a dart; a dartlike weapon 2. an escort; a guard; a bodyguard

biāokè 鏢客 (in former times) hired escorts for traveling merchants, etc.

biāo 飆

violent winds; gales

biāochē 飆車 to speed a car or a motorcycle

biǎo 表

1. outside; external; apparent; appearance; exteriors; superficial 2. to announce; to manifest; to show 3. relatives on the side of one's mother's sisters or brothers; relatives on the side of one's father's sisters 4. a report to the emperor 5. a table; a schedule; a chart; a form

biǎobái 表白 to express or state clearly

biǎocéng 表層 a surface layer

biǎodá 表達 to convey or transmit (one's feelings, meaning, etc.); to present; to express; to make known

biǎogé 表格 a form or blank (for filling); a table or chart

biǎojué 表決 to vote; to put to the vote

biǎolǐ bùyī 表裡不一 to think in one way and behave in another

biǎolǐ yīzhì 表裡一致 honest and sincere

biǎolù 表露 to make plain; to express or expose; to voice

biǎomiànshàng 表面上 on the surface; externally; outwardly

biǎomiàn zhānglì 表面張力 surface tension

biǎomíng 表明 to indicate or state clearly or plainly

biǎopí 表皮 1. the epidermis 2. the cuticle (of plants)

biǎoqīn 表親 a cousin

biǎoqíng 表情 facial expression

biǎoshì 表示 to express; to show; to indicate; expression; reaction

biǎoshuài 表率 an example; a paragon

biǎotài 表態 to make known one's position towards an issue

biǎoxiàn 表現 1. to appear 2. to behave 3. to distinguish oneself

biǎoxiōngdì 表兄弟 male first cousins

biǎoyǎn 表演 to perform; to demonstrate; a performance; demonstration; a show

biǎoyáng 表揚 to praise in public; to cite for all to know

biǎozhāng 表彰 to honor; to cite; citation

biǎozǐmèi 表姊妹 female first cousins

biǎo 姻

a prostitute; a whore

biǎo 裱

1. to mount (paintings, calligraphy, etc.) 2. a scarf

biǎobèi 裱褙 to mount (paintings, etc.)

biǎo 錶
a watch; a timepiece
biǎodài 錶帶 a watchband

biē 憋
1. to suppress inner feelings with efforts 2. to feel oppressed
biēqì 憋氣 to suffer breathing obstruction

biē 瘪
a bum; a tramp
biēsān 瘪三 a bum; a tramp

biē 鱉(鼈)
a kind of freshwater turtle, also known as **jiǎyú** 甲魚

bié 別
1. to part 2. to distinguish; to differentiate 3. other; another; different 4. (in imperative expressions) do not
biéchū xīncái 別出心裁 ingenious
biéguǎn 別管 no matter (who, what, etc.)
biéhào 別號 an alias
biéjù yīgé 別具一格 having a unique style
biéjù zhīyǎn 別具隻眼 to have an original view
biékāi shēngmiàn 別開生面 to introduce a novelty
biélí 別離 parting; separation
biémiáotou 別苗頭 (informal) to rival in competition
biémíng 別名 an alias
biéren 別人 other people; others
biéshēng zhījié 別生枝節 to have new complications
biéshù 別墅 a villa; a country house
biéshù yīzhì 別樹一幟 to become independent
biétí 別提 We needn't mention it.
biéyǒu fēngwèi 別有風味 to have a unique flavor
biéyǒu suǒzhǐ 別有所指 to imply another thing
biéyǒu yòngxīn 別有用心 to have a hidden purpose
biézhēn 別針 a safety pin; a pin;

a brooch
biézhì 別致 fresh; new; novel
biézì 別字 1. a word which is not correctly written or pronounced 2. an alias

biě 蹩
to limp
biéjiǎo 蹩脚 1. lame 2. inferior in quality; poor 3. dejected

biě 瘪
flat; sunken; not full
biězuǐzi 瘪嘴子 a person who has lost all teeth

biè 彆
awkward
bièniu 彆扭 1. awkward; refractory 2. an awkward situation
bièqì 彆氣 silently resentful

bīn 彬
intelligent, refined and gentle
bīnbīn yǒulǐ 彬彬有禮 refined and courteous

bīn 斌
equally fine in external accomplishments and internal qualities

bīn 賓
1. a guest; a visitor 2. to treat as a guest 3. to obey; to follow instructions; to submit 4. a Chinese family name
bīnguǎn 賓館 a guesthouse
bīnkè 賓客 guests and visitors
bīnzhì rúguī 賓至如歸 Guests flock to the place like returning home — to feel at home in a place
bīnzhǔ jìnhuān 賓主盡歡 Both the guests and the host are having a great time.

bīn 儐 also **bìn**
1. to entertain guests 2. to set in order; to arrange 3. to guide
bīnxiàng 儐相 1. the best man of a bridegroom 2. a bridesmaid

bīn 濱
1. water's edge; to border on 2. (瀕) near at hand 3. (military) a low, level seacoast

bīnhǎi dìqū 濱海地區 the coastal region; the coast

bīnjìn 濱近 close to; near to

bīn 檳

the areca; the betel; the areca nut; the betel nut

bīnláng 檳榔 the areca (nut); the betel (nut)

bīn 瀕

1. near; close to; to border 2. water's edge

bīnlín 瀕臨 near; on the brink of

bīnsǐ 瀕死 on the brink of death

bīn 繽

1. abundant; plentiful; thriving 2. disorderly; confused

bīnfēn 繽紛 1. flourishing; thriving 2. chaotic

bìn 儐

refer to **bīn** 儐

bìn 擯

1. to expel; to reject; to oust; to get rid of; to discard 2. (儐) an usher

bìnchì 擯斥 to reject; to expel; to repudiate

bìnchú 擯除 to expel; to oust; to eliminate

bìnqì 擯棄 to cast away; to set aside; to discard; to desert

bìn 殯

1. to lay a coffin in a memorial hall 2. to carry to the grave

bìnchē 殯車 a hearse

bìnliàn 殯殮 a funeral

bìnyíguǎn 殯儀館 a funeral parlor

bìn 鬢

hair on the temples

bìnfà 鬢髮 refer to **bìnfà** 鬢髮

bìnfà 鬢髮 hair on the temples

bìnjiǎo 鬢角 temples (beside the ears)

bīng 冰

1. ice; icicles 2. cold; frost

bīngbàng 冰棒 a flavored popsicle

bīngbáo 冰雹 hail; a hailstone

bīngchuān 冰川 a glacier

bīngdāo 冰刀 the blades of ice skates

bīngdiǎn 冰點 the freezing point

bīngdòng 冰凍 to freeze

bīngdòng sānchǐ, fēi yīrì zhīhán 冰凍三尺，非一日之寒 The grudge or animosity has its deep root.

bīngfēng 冰封 icebound

bīnggùnr 冰棍兒 ice-lolly; popsicle; ice-sucker

bīngguǒdiàn 冰果店 a cold drink shop

bīnghé 冰河 a glacier

bīngjiào 冰窖 an icehouse; a glacial vault

bīngjīlíng 冰激凌 ice cream

bīngkuài 冰塊 ice cubes; ice blocks

bīnglěng 冰冷 1. icy cold; cold as ice 2. cold or frosty (expressions, etc.)

bīngliáng 冰涼 icy cold; very cold

bīngqílín 冰淇淋 ice cream

bīngqiāo 冰橇 a sled; a sledge; a sleigh

bīngshān 冰山 an iceberg

bīngshàng yùndòng 冰上運動 ice sports

bīngshì 冰釋 solved; to disappear without a trace

bīngshuāng 冰霜 1. cold and severe 2. incorruptible

bīngshuǐ 冰水 ice water

bīngtáng 冰糖 rock candy

bīngtiān xuědì 冰天雪地 frozen and snow-covered land

bīngxiāng 冰箱 an icebox; a refrigerator

bīngxié 冰鞋 ice skates

bīngxuě cōngmíng 冰雪聰明 very clever; brilliant

bīngyuán 冰原 an ice field

bīngzhèn 冰鎮 to preserve on ice

bīngzhù 冰柱 icicles

bīng 兵

1. arms; weapons 2. a soldier; a serviceman 3. a piece in Chinese chess—a pawn

bīngbiàn 兵變 mutiny; troops in mutiny

bīngbù xiěrèn 兵不血刃 refer to **bīngbù xuèrèn** 兵不血刃

bīngbù xuèrèn 兵不血刃 (to achieve military objective) without firing a shot in anger or without bloodshed

bīngbù yànzhà 兵不厭詐 Trickery is no vice in military operations.

bīngfǎ 兵法 military tactics and strategy

bīnggōngchǎng 兵工廠 an arsenal; an ammunition works

bīnghuāng mǎluàn 兵荒馬亂 disorder caused by continuous military operations

bīngjiā chángshì 兵家常事 a commonplace in military operations

bīnglì 兵力 military strength

bīnglián huòjié 兵連禍結 constantly ravaged by war

bīnglín chéngxià 兵臨城下 The attacking army has reached the city gates.

bīngmǎ 兵馬 troops and horses —armaments

bīngmǎyǒng 兵馬俑 wood or clay figures of soldiers and horses buried with the dead

bīngqì 兵器 weapons; arms

bīngquán 兵權 authority to make military decisions

bīngróng 兵戎 1. arms; weapons 2. warfare

bīngróng xiāngjiàn 兵戎相見 to resort to arms

bīngshì 兵士 a soldier; a foot soldier

bīngshè 兵舍 barracks

bīngtuán 兵團 a large (military) unit; corps

bīngyǐ 兵蟻 a soldier ant

bīngyì 兵役 (compulsory) military service

bīngyìfǎ 兵役法 conscription law

bīngyíng 兵營 barracks

bīngyuán 兵源 manpower as a source of conscription

bīngzhì 兵制 the military system

bīngzhǒng 兵種 intraservice classification of military units according to their equipment and functions

bǐng 丙

1. the third of the ten Celestial Stems (**tiāngān** 天干) 2. another name for fire 3. the tail of a fish

bǐngděng 丙等 roughly equivalent to the C grade; the third grade

bǐng 秉

1. to hold in hand 2. to take charge of; to rule 3. authority 4. an ancient grain measure; a measure for liquid

bǐngchí 秉持 1. to adhere to (one's principles, etc.) 2. to hold in hand (a spear, etc.)

bǐngxìng 秉性 nature; a natural disposition or temperament

bǐng 炳

bright; luminous

bǐng 柄 also **bìng**

1. the handle of something 2. authority; power 3. to operate; to handle; to control 4. a handle

bǐngguó 柄國 to reign over a state

bǐng 屏

to reject; to discard; to dismiss; to get rid of; to abandon

bǐngchì 屏斥 to reproach; to rebuke

bǐngchú 屏除 to get rid of; to banish

bǐngjué 屏絕 to stop having contact or intercourse with

bǐngqì 屏氣 to hold one's breath

bǐngqì 屏棄 to discard; to throw away

bǐngxī 屏息 to hold one's breath

bǐngxí 屏息 refer to **bǐngxī** 屏息

B

bǐng 稟
  1. to report to a superior or one's seniors; to petition; to appeal 2. one's natural endowments or gifts

bǐngbào 稟報 to report to a superior

bǐngfù 稟賦 a natural endowment, gift or disposition

bǐnggào 稟告 to report to a superior

bǐngmíng 稟明 to clarify a matter to a superior or elder

bǐngxìng 稟性 a natural disposition or temperament

bǐng 餅
  1. cakes; biscuits; pastry 2. anything round and flat, as a disc

bìng 並
  1. and; also; at the same time 2. on the same level with; even; equal 3. entirely; completely

bìngbù 並不 really not

bìngfēi 並非 by no means

bìngjià qíqū 並駕齊驅 to keep abreast of; to be equal

bìngjiān 並肩 shoulder to shoulder; side by side; abreast

bìnglì 並立 1. to stand together 2. to exist simultaneously

bìngliè 並列 to stand side by side; to juxtapose

bìngpái 並排 side by side; in the same row

bìngqiě 並且 moreover; furthermore; and

bìngxíng bùbèi 並行不悖 to proceed together or simultaneously without interfering with each other; compatible

bìngzhòng 並重 to lay equal stress on

bìng 并
  1. on a level with; even; equal 2. and; also; or; at the same time

bìng 病
  1. illness; disease; ailment 2. to be ill 3. blemish; fault 4. to injure; to harm 5. to worry 6. to hate 7. to insult

bìngbiàn 病變 pathological changes

bìngchónghài 病蟲害 blight

bìngchuáng 病床 a sickbed

bìngcóng kǒurù 病從口入 Diseases enter by the mouth.

bìngdǎo 病倒 to fall ill; to be confined in bed due to illness

bìngdú 病毒 a virus

bìngfā 病發 to fall ill

bìngfáng 病房 a sickroom; a ward

bìnghuàn 病患 a patient

bìngjià 病假 sick leave

bìngjūn 病菌 germs; bacteria; viruses

bìngjùn 病菌 refer to **bìngjūn** 病菌

bìnglǐxué 病理學 pathology

bìnglì 病例 number of cases of a particular disease

bìnglì 病歷 medical history (of a patient)

bìngmó 病魔 the curse of disease

bìngmò 病歿 to die of illness

bìngqíng 病情 the condition of a patient

bìngrén 病人 a sick man; a patient

bìngróng 病容 a sickly look; an emaciated look

bìngrù gāohuāng 病入膏肓 so advanced in one's disease as to be past remedy

bìngsǐ 病死 to die of an illness

bìngtài 病態 morbid (or abnormal) state

bìngtòng 病痛 slight illness; indisposition

bìngwēi 病危 about to die of an illness

bìngwéi 病危 refer to **bìngwēi** 病危

bìngyīn 病因 the cause of a disease

bìngyù 病癒 to recover from illness; to get well

bìngyuán 病原 the cause of a disease

bìngzhēng 病徵 symptoms of a

disease

bìngzhèng 病症 a disease; an ailment

bìngzhuàng 病狀 the condition of a patient

bìng 併

1. on a level with; even; equal; to go side by side 2. all; entire 3. together 4. to combine; to annex

bìngfā 併發 to begin, explode, erupt, attack, occur, etc. at the same time

bìngfāzhèng 併發症 (medicine) a complication

bìnghé 併合 to unite; to integrate

bìngjiān 併肩 shoulder to shoulder

bìngtūn 併吞 to swallow up entirely

bìng 柄 refer to bǐng 柄

bìng 摒

1. to get rid of; to expel 2. to arrange in order

bìngchú 摒除 to get rid of; to remove

bìngqì 摒棄 to abandon; to get rid of

bō 波 also pō

1. waves; breakers 2. to undulate; undulation; to fluctuate; fluctuations; to affect; to involve; to implicate; to entangle

bōdòng 波動 1. undulation 2. (said of prices) fluctuations

bōduàn 波段 a wave band

Bōduōlígè 波多黎各 Puerto Rico

bōjí 波及 1. to affect; to involve 2. (said of a fire) to engulf; to spread to

Bōlán 波蘭 Poland

bōlán zhuàngkuò 波瀾壯闊 surging forward with great momentum

bōlàng 波浪 billows; breakers; waves

Bōluódìhǎi 波羅的海 the Baltic Sea

bōsījú 波斯菊 coreopsis

bōsīmāo 波斯貓 a Persian cat

Bōsīwān 波斯灣 the Persian Gulf

bōtāo xiōngyǒng 波濤洶湧 to billow—a term used figuratively to describe tumultuous situations

bōzhé 波折 twists and turns of a matter; obstructions or obstacles

bō 玻

glass

bōli 玻璃 glass

bōlibēi 玻璃杯 a glass; a tumbler

bōlichuāng 玻璃窗 a glass window

bāli fànwǎn 玻璃飯碗 an insecure job

bōlipíng 玻璃瓶 a glass bottle

bōliquān 玻璃圈 (slang) the gay circle

Bōlìwéiyà 玻利維亞 Bolivia

bō 般

(Buddhism) intelligence

bōrě 般若 wisdom

bō 剝

to strip; to skin; to make bare; to peel; to peel off; to shell

bōduó 剝奪 to deprive or strip one of (rights, property, etc.)

bōguāng 剝光 stripped naked

bōluò 剝落 to come off; to be peeled off

bōpí 剝皮 to skin; to peel off the skin

bōxuē 剝削 to exploit (people)

bōxuè 剝削 refer to bōxuē 剝削

bō 鉢

1. an earthenware basin or bowl 2. a Buddhist priest's rice bowl

bō 菠

spinach

bōcài 菠菜 spinach

bō 播 also bò

1. to sow; to seed 2. to spread; to propagate 3. to move 4. to cast away; to abandon

bōbào 播報 to broadcast

bōfàng 播放 to broadcast (news,

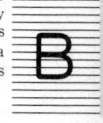
B

etc.) on the air

bōnong 播弄 1. to stir up disputes on purpose 2. to make a mess (of something)

bōsàn 播散 to disseminate

bōsòng 播送 to broadcast (messages, programs, etc.)

bōyīn 播音 to make broadcasts; to transmit

bōyīnyuán 播音員 a broadcaster; an announcer

bōzhǒng 播種 to sow seed; to sow; to seed

bō 撥
1. to dispel; to remove 2. to poke 3. to move; to transfer 4. to distribute; to issue 5. to set aside; to set apart; to appropriate

bōdòng 撥動 1. to move (the minute hand, etc.) by finger 2. to turn (a switch)

bōfù 撥付 to make payment; to appropriate

bōkāi 撥開 to push aside

bōkuǎn 撥款 to issue or appropriate funds; an appropriation

bōlànggǔ 撥浪鼓 a rattle drum

bōnong 撥弄 1. to toy with 2. to move to and fro 3. to stir up (disputes)

bōrǒng 撥冗 to set aside a little time (for a special purpose) out of a tight schedule

bōyòng 撥用 to appropriate

bōyún jiànrì 撥雲見日 to clear up

bó 百
refer to **bǎi** 百

bó 伯 also **bǎi**
1. one's father's elder brother; an uncle 2. a rank of the nobility —a count

bófù 伯父 1. an elder brother of one's father 2. a respectful term for the senior

bójué 伯爵 a count; an earl

bójué fūren 伯爵夫人 a countess

bómǔ 伯母 1. the wife of father's elder brother 2. a respectful term for the senior

bózhòng zhījiān 伯仲之間 almost on a par

bó 帛
(collectively) silk fabrics

bó 泊
1. (also **pò**) to stay; to anchor a ship; to moor 2. (also **pò**) to drift 3. (also **pò**) tranquil and quiet 4. refer to **pō** 泊

bóchuán 泊船 to moor a boat

bó 勃
sudden(ly); quick(ly)

bóqǐ 勃起 to have an erection; erection

bórán biànsè 勃然變色 to show displeasure or bewilderment all of a sudden

bó 柏
refer to **bǎi** 柏

bó 淳
to rise; excited

bórán 淳然 1. rising 2. flourishingly

bó 脖
the neck

bó 舶
an ocean-going ship

bóláipǐn 舶來品 imported goods; foreign goods

bó 渤
(said of water) swelling or rising

Bóhǎi 渤海 Bohai, a gulf of the Yellow Sea

bó 博
1. wide; extensive 2. abundant ample; rich 3. broadly knowledgeable; well-read; learned; erudite 4. to exchange; to barter for 5. to gamble; to play games 6. to win; to gain

bó'ài 博愛 indiscriminate love; fraternity

bódà jīngshēn 博大精深 extensive and profound

bódé 博得 to win; to obtain

bógǔ tōngjīn 博古通今 erudite and informed

bólǎn 博覽 to be well-read

bólǎnhuì 博覽會 a trade fair; an exhibition

bóqǔ 博取 to win; to obtain

bóshì 博士 a doctorate

bówùguǎn 博物館 a museum

bóxué 博學 well-read; erudite

bó 搏

1. to pounce on (or at); to spring upon 2. to grasp; to catch; to arrest; to seize 3. to strike; to box; to engage in a hand-to-hand combat

bódòu 搏鬥 to battle; to wrestle; to fight

bóshā 搏殺 to fight and kill

bó 膊

the shoulders; the upper arms

bó 駁

1. variegated; parti-colored 2. mixed; impure; jumbled 3. to rebut; to dispute; to refute; to disprove 4. to transport; to ship; to load and unload

bóchì 駁斥 1. to refute; to rebut; to disprove 2. to reject (an appeal)

bódǎo 駁倒 to defeat in a debate

bóhuí 駁回 to reject; to turn down; to overrule (an appeal, request, etc.)

bósè 駁色 variegated; parti-colored

bózá 駁雜 mixed; impure

bó 箔

1. foil; gilt 2. a curtain 3. paper tinsel burnt as offerings to the dead

bó 蔔

refer to **bo** 蔔

bó 薄 also **báo**

1. thin; light; slight 2. to despise; to slight; to disdain 3. barren; not fertile 4. to cover; to hide or conceal; to shut 5. a screen 6. a patch of grass 7. to close in; to press near 8. frivolous

bóhǎi ténghuān 薄海騰歡 cheers from all over the country

bólì duōxiāo 薄利多銷 to cut down the profit margin in order

to sell more—commercial tactics

bómìng 薄命 1. star-crossed; ill-fated 2. short-lived

bómù 薄暮 around sunset; dusk

bópiàn 薄片 a thin slice

bóqíng 薄情 heartless; ungrateful

bóruò 薄弱 weak; fragile

bǒ 跛

lame; crippled

bǒzi 跛子 a cripple

bò 北

refer to **běi** 北

bò 柏

refer to **bǎi** 柏

bò 播

refer to **bō** 播

bò 薄

peppermint

bòhe 薄荷 peppermint

bo 蔔 also **bó**

a common name for such edible roots as turnips, carrots, radishes, as in **luóbo** 蘿蔔

bǔ 卜

1. to divine; to consult the oracle 2. to foretell; to predict 3. to choose 4. a Chinese family name

bǔguà 卜卦 to divine by the Eight Diagrams

bǔshì 卜筮 divination

bǔ 捕

1. to arrest; to catch; to seize 2. (formerly) a policeman

bǔfēng zhuōyǐng 捕風捉影 talks that are not substantiated by any evidence or proof

bǔhuò 捕獲 to arrest; to catch

bǔlāo 捕撈 to fish for (aquatic animals and plants); to catch

bǔshā 捕殺 to catch and kill (wild or unlicensed dogs, etc.)

bǔshí 捕食 to catch and feed on; to prey on

bǔshǒu 捕手 (baseball) a catcher

bǔyú 捕魚 to catch fish; to fish

bǔzhuō 捕捉 to chase or hunt

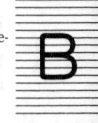

down

bǔ 哺

1. to chew (before swallowing) 2. to feed (a baby, etc.)

bǔrǔ 哺乳 to give suck to; to nurse

bǔrǔlèi 哺乳類 mammals

bǔyù 哺育 1. to feed 2. to nurture

bǔ 補

1. to repair; to patch; to mend; to fill 2. to add to; to supplement; to supply 3. addenda: supplements; complements 4. nutritious; nutrient 5. rich foods; tonics 6. to nourish 7. to make up; to help (finance, etc.); to subsidize 8. to appoint to or fill a post 9. to be of help; benefit

bǔcháng 補償 to compensate; to make up

bǔchōng 補充 to add; to supplement

bǔdīng 補釘 a patch (of a garment, etc.)

bǔfā 補發 to issue or distribute behind schedule

bǔjǐ 補給 (military) provisions; supplies; to supply

bǔjiǎ 補假 a compensatory holiday

bǔjiù 補救 to save the situation

bǔkǎo 補考 to make-up test

bǔkè 補課 a compensatory class

bǔpiào 補票 to buy one's ticket after one gets on a bus, a train, etc.

bǔpǐn 補品 foods or medicines of highly nutritious value; tonics

bǔtiē 補貼 to subsidize; a subsidy; an allowance

bǔxí 補習 private tutoring to supplement regular schooling; to tutor

bǔxíbān 補習班 a class for supplementary schooling

bǔxiéjiàng 補鞋匠 a cobbler

bǔyá 補牙 to fill a tooth cavity; to have a tooth stopped

bǔyào 補藥 tonics

bǔzhù 補助 to subsidize; to help (finance, etc.)

bǔzhù 補注 supplementary notes; to make supplementary notes

bǔzhùjīn 補助金 a grant

bǔzhuì 補綴 to mend; to patch

bǔzú 補足 to make up a deficit; to make complete or whole

bù 不

no; not; negative (Note: When **bù** precedes a 4th-tone sound, it is pronounced as **bú**.)

bù'ān 不安 1. uneasy; disturbed 2. intranquil

bù'ān yúshì 不安於室 (said of women) having extramarital affairs

bùbái zhīyuān 不白之冤 1. a wrong that has not been righted 2. falsely accused

bùbài zhīdì 不敗之地 an invincible position

bùbēi bùkàng 不卑不亢 to conduct oneself properly

bùbǐ 不比 unlike

bùbì 不必 not necessary

bùbiàn 不便 inconvenience; inconvenient

bùcái 不才 without capability

bùcè 不測 1. unpredictable 2. misfortune; disaster; accident

bùchéng 不成 1. will not do 2. an expression used at the end of a question

bùchéng jìngyì 不成敬意 just a little token to show my respect to you

bùchéngqì 不成器 good-for-nothing; useless

bùchéng tǐtǒng 不成體統 (acting or talking) wildly; without regard to common practice

bùchéng wénfǎ 不成文法 unwritten law

bùchǐ xiàwèn 不恥下問 not ashamed to learn from one's inferiors

bùchū suǒliào 不出所料 just as expected

bùcí érbié 不辭而別 to leave without bidding goodbye

bùcí xīnkǔ 不辭辛苦 to work with all-out effort

bùcuò 不錯 1. to be right 2.

granted that; to be sure that 3. not bad

bùdǎ zìzhāo 不打自招 to make a confession without being pressed

bùdàn 不但 not only...

bùdàng 不當 unsuitable; improper; inappropriate

bùdǎowēng 不倒翁 a tumbler

bùdàodé 不道德 immoral; unethical

bùdào Huánghé xīn bùsǐ 不到黃河心不死 to refuse to give up until one reaches one's goal

bùdé 不得 don't; no; must not

bùdébù 不得不 to have to; must

bùdé érzhī 不得而知 no way to know

bùdéliǎo 不得了 1. Good heavens! 2. It's serious!

bùdé rénxīn 不得人心 unpopular

bùdé yàolǐng 不得要領 1. cannot get the gist; pointless 2. don't know the right way

bùdéyǐ 不得已 cannot help but...

bùdēng dàyǎ zhītáng 不登大雅之堂 to be unpresentable

bùděng 不等 differently

bùdí 不敵 no match for; to be defeated

bùdìng 不定 1. not certain 2. indefinite

bùdòngchǎn 不動產 real estate; immovable assets

bùdònggǎng 不凍港 an ice-free port; an open port

bùdòng shēngsè 不動聲色 not showing any feeling or emotion; with composure

bùduàn 不斷 continuous; constant

bùduì 不對 not right; wrong

bùduìjìn 不對勁 not in harmony; listless

bù'èrguò 不貳過 not to repeat a previous mistake

bù'èrjià 不二價 a uniform (or fixed) price

bùfǎ 不法 unlawful; illegal

bùfǎ zhītú 不法之徒 lawless elements

bùfán 不凡 extraordinary; unusual; outstanding

bùfáng 不妨 no harm in (trying doing, etc.)

bùfáng 不防 by surprise; unawares

bùfáng 不妨 refer to **bùfāng** 不妨

bùfèi chuīhuī zhīlì 不費吹灰之力 do not need the slightest effort

bùfēn qīnghóng zàobái 不分青紅皂白 indiscriminately

bùfēn shèngfù 不分勝負 well-matched; a draw; a tie

bùfēn xuānzhì 不分軒輊 well-matched; a draw; a tie

bùfēn zhòuyè 不分晝夜 (to work) day and night

bùfú 不服 to recalcitrate; to disobey

bùfú 不符 do not tally

bùfú zhòngwàng 不孚眾望 not popular with the masses

bùfù suǒtuō 不負所託 to merit someone's trust

bùgān 不甘 unreconciled to

bùgān bùjìng 不乾不淨 not clean; filthy

bùgān jímò 不甘寂寞 refer to **bùgān jìmò** 不甘寂寞

bùgān jìmò 不甘寂寞 eager to seek publicity

bùgǎndāng 不敢當 I don't deserve it.

bùgǎn lǐngjiào 不敢領教 too bad to be accepted (bought, etc.)

bùgōng 不公 unjust; unfair

bùgōng zìpò 不攻自破 to collapse of itself

bùgòng dàitiān 不共戴天 absolutely irreconcilable (with one's enemy)

bùgǒu yánxiào 不苟言笑 strictly adhere to propriety in one's behavior; serious

bùgù 不顧 in disregard of; regardless of; despite; in spite of

bùguān tòngyǎng 不關痛癢 irrelevant; insignificant

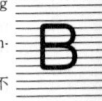

bùguǎn 不管 in disregard of; regardless of

bùguǎn sān qī èrshíyī 不管 三七二十一 regardless of consequences

bùguǐ 不軌 conspiracy, plots, etc.

bùguò 不過 1. only; merely 2. but; nevertheless

bùguò rúcǐ 不過如此 so-so

bùhán érlì 不寒而慄 trembling with fear

bùhǎorě 不好惹 not to be trifled with; not to be pushed around

bùhǎo yìsi 不好意思 to feel embarrassed, shy, bashful or ashamed

bùhé 不合 unsuitable; in disagreement with (rules, etc.)

bùhé 不和 at loggerheads; not on good terms

bùhé shíyí 不合時宜 out of fashion; anachronistic

bùhuái hǎoyì 不懷好意 with evil intention

bùhuān érsàn 不歡而散 to break up in disagreement

bùhuāng bùmáng 不慌不忙 1. leisurely; unhurried 2. with full composure

bùjī 不羈 carefree; not bound by social etiquette, customs, etc.

bùjí 不及 not so (good, tall, early, etc.) as...; to be inferior to

bùjíwù dòngcí 不及物動詞 an intransitive verb

bùjìmíng tóupiào 不記名投 票 secret ballots; secret votes

bùjì qíshù 不計其數 countless; innumerable

bùjì yúshì 不濟於事 to no avail

bùjiǎ sīsuǒ 不假思索 without thinking; without hesitation

bùjiǎ wàichū 不假外出 absent without leave

bùjiàndé 不見得 not likely; not necessarily so

bùjiàn guāncái bù luòlèi 不見棺材不落淚 One refuses to be convinced until one faces the grim reality.

bùjiàn tiānrì 不見天日 1. in total darkness 2. injustice

bùjiéméng guójiā 不結盟國 家 nonaligned nations

bùjiě fēngqíng 不解風情 do not understand implications in love affair

bùjīn 不禁 cannot help...

bùjǐn 不僅 not only

bùjìnrán 不盡然 not exactly so

bùjìn rénqíng 不近人情 unreasonable; inconsiderate

bùjìn zétuì 不進則退 either to keep progressing or retrogressing

bùjīngshì 不經事 inexperienced

bùjīng yīshì, bùzhǎng yīzhì 不經一事，不長一智 Wisdom comes from experience.

bùjīngyì 不經意 inattentive(ly); careless(ly)

bùjiǔ 不久 within a short time; soon

bùjiù jìwǎng 不咎既往 to let bygones be bygones

bùjū 不拘 1. no limit; not to be bound 2. whatever

bùjū xiǎojié 不拘小節 to disregard trifles, niceties, etc.

bùjū yīgé 不拘一格 to follow no set pattern

bùjué rúlǚ 不絕如縷 (said of a situation) critical

bùkān 不堪 cannot suffer; unendurable

bùkān huíshǒu 不堪回首 cannot recall without pain

bùkān shèxiǎng 不堪設想 (said of consequences) serious or unthinkable

bùkě 不可 1. no; negative 2. not allowed 3. cannot

bùkě duōdé 不可多得 hard to come by; scarce

bùkě gàorén 不可告人 not to be divulged; secret or shameful (act, etc.)

bùkě jiùyào 不可救藥 incurable; beyond hope

bùkě lǐyù 不可理喻 unreasonable

bùkě mómiè 不可磨滅 indelible

bùkě shēngshǔ 不可勝數 refer to **bùkě shèngshǔ** 不可勝數

bùkě shèngshǔ 不可勝數 countless; innumerable

bùkě shōushi 不可收拾 pandemonium; hopeless (situation, etc.); out of control

bùkě sīyì 不可思議 mysterious; unimaginable

bùkě xiānliàng 不可限量 limitless (opportunities); very promising

bùkě yīshì 不可一世 to be extremely arrogant

bùkě yúyuè 不可逾越 impassable; insuperable

bùkě zhuōmō 不可捉摸 uncanny; unpredictable

bùkèqi 不客氣 1. impolite; rude; blunt 2. You are welcome.

bùkuài 不快 1. unhappy; uncomfortable 2. slow

bùkuì 不愧 to be worthy of; to deserve to be

bùláo érhuò 不勞而獲 to gain without effort

bùlěng bùrè 不冷不熱 lukewarm

bùlǐ 不理 in disregard of; to ignore

bùlǐ bùcǎi 不理不睬 to ignore completely

bùlì 不利 1. not going smoothly 2. bad; adverse; harmful

bùliáng 不良 bad; harmful; unhealthy

bùliáng dǎotǐ 不良導體 a nonconductor

bùliáng fènzǐ 不良分子 undesirables; scums

bùliáng shàonián 不良少年 juvenile delinquents

bùliǎo liǎozhī 不了了之 to conclude without concrete result or decision

bùliào 不料 unexpectedly; never thought

Bùlièdiān 不列顛 Britain

bùliú qíngmiàn 不留情面 to be very strict; to disregard another's face or feelings

bùliú yúdì 不留餘地 1. without leaving leeway 2. to pursue to

the brutal end

bùlù shēngsè 不露聲色 do not show one's feelings, intentions, motives, etc.

bùlún bùlèi 不倫不類 grotesque; incongruous

bùlùn 不論 no matter; regardless

bùmǎn 不滿 discontent; dissatisfaction

bùmáng 不忙 to take one's time

bùmáo zhīdì 不毛之地 barren land

bùmián bùxiū 不眠不休 without rest; tireless

bùmiǎn 不免 have to; must; unavoidable

bùmiào 不妙 Something is wrong or going badly.

bùmíng fēixíng wùtǐ 不明飛行物體 unidentified flying object (UFO)

bùmíngyù 不名譽 disreputable; scandalous

bùnàifán 不耐煩 impatient

bùnéngbù 不能不 to have to; must; cannot but

bùniàn jiù'è 不念舊惡 to let bygones be bygones

bùpiān bùyǐ 不偏不倚 1. exact; just 2. fair

bùpíng 不平 1. complaint; a grudge 2. unjust

bùpíngděng tiáoyuē 不平等條約 an unequal treaty

bùpíng zémíng 不平則鳴 Those who are discriminated against will complain.

bùqī éryù 不期而遇 to meet by chance

bùqí éryù 不期而遇 refer to **bùqī éryù** 不期而遇

bùqiǎo 不巧 unfortunately

bùqiè shíjì 不切實際 impractical

bùqiú shènjiě 不求甚解 to read casually

bùqiú wéndá 不求聞達 to be uninterested in fame

bùqiú wèndá 不求聞達 refer to **bùqiú wéndá** 不求聞達

B

bùqū 不屈 unyielding; unbending

bùqū bùnáo 不屈不撓 not to be bent or cowed; unswerving

bùrán 不然 1. not so 2. otherwise; or

bùrén 不仁 1. not benevolent 2. paralyzed; numbed

bùrěn 不忍 disturbed (characterized by pity); cannot bear to...

bùróng 不容 1. do not tolerate; do not allow 2. do not welcome

bùrǔ shǐmìng 不辱使命 to have succeeded in carrying out an assignment

bùrù'ěr 不入耳 unpleasant to the ear; not worth listening to

bùsān bùsì 不三不四 grotesque; incongruous

bùshàng bùxià 不上不下 1. on a spot; in an impasse 2. inappropriate

bùshēng 不勝 refer to **bùshèng** 不勝

bùshēng bùxiǎng 不聲不響 stealthily; furtively

bùshēng méijǔ 不勝枚舉 refer to **bùshèng méijǔ** 不勝枚舉

bùshēng qífán 不勝其煩 refer to **bùshèng qífán** 不勝其煩

bùshēng 不勝 1. cannot bear; to be unequal to 2. very; extremely; overwhelmed

bùshèng méijǔ 不勝枚舉 too nemerous to recount

bùshèng qífán 不勝其煩 cannot stand the harassment, nuisance, etc.

bùshí 不時 1. frequently 2. at any time

bùshí dàtǐ 不識大體 to fail to see the important points

bùshí shíwù 不識時務 ignorant of the changes of the times or failing to make use of available chances

bùshí táijǔ 不識抬舉 unappreciative; ungrateful

bùshí Tàishān 不識泰山 to fail to recognize a famous personage when meeting him face to face

bùshí zhīxū 不時之需 occasional needs

bùshì 不是 1. no; not right 2. if... not 3. in the wrong

bùshì 不適 ill; indisposed; unwell

bùshì dàtǐ 不識大體 refer to **bùshí dàtǐ** 不識大體

bùshì shíwù 不識時務 refer to **bùshí shíwù** 不識時務

bùshì táijǔ 不識抬舉 refer to **bùshí táijǔ** 不識抬舉

bùshì Tàishān 不識泰山 refer to **bùshí Tàishān** 不識泰山

bùshì zhīcái 不世之才 a rare talent; a genius

bùsú 不俗 uncommon; not hackneyed

bùsù zhīkè 不速之客 an uninvited guest; an unexpected guest

bùtíng 不停 without stop

bùtóng 不同 different; distinct; difference

bùtóng fánxiǎng 不同凡響 extraordinary; remarkable

bùtuǒ 不妥 not the right way; improper

bùwéi suǒdòng 不為所動 to remain unmoved (by promises of reward, etc.)

bùwén bùwèn 不聞不問 to care nothing about

bùwèn 不問 1. to pay no attention to; to disregard 2. to let go unpunished

bùwú xiǎobǔ 不無小補 It might be of some small help.

bùxī 不惜 to be ready to go to extreme lengths

bùxī gōngběn 不惜工本 to spare no expense

bùxí 不惜 refer to **bùxī** 不惜

bùxí gōngběn 不惜工本 refer to **bùxī gōngběn** 不惜工本

bùxiàyú 不下於 1. as many as; no less than 2. not inferior to; as good as

bùxiāngchèn 不相稱 ill-matched; inharmonious

bùxiānggān 不相干 irrelevant; to have nothing to do with

bùxiāngróng 不相容 incompatible

bùxiāng shàngxià 不相上下

equal; equally matched

bùxiáng 不祥 ominous; unlucky

bùxiáng 不詳 1. unknown 2. not detailed enough

bùxiáng zhīzhào 不祥之兆 a bad (or an ill) omen

bùxiànghuà 不像話 absurd or ludicrous (talks, acts, etc.)

bùxiàngyàng 不像樣 improper (behavior); disreputable (conduct)

bùxiào 不肖 1. a son who is not so good as his father 2. good-for-nothing

bùxiào 不孝 1. not in accordance with filial piety 2. a term referring to oneself in the obituary announcing the death of one's parent

bùxiè 不屑 do not condescend (or deign) to do something; to disdain

bùxiè 不懈 untiring; indefatigable

bùxiè 不謝 Don't mention it.

bùxǐng rénshì 不省人事 in a coma; unconscious

bùxìng 不幸 misfortune; unfortunate

bùxìngzhōng zhī dàxìng 不幸中之大幸 a lucky occurrence in the course of a disaster, such as a priceless painting saved from a fire

bùxiū biānfú 不修邊幅 do not care about details (especially in clothing); slovenly

bùxiǔ 不朽 immortal; immortality

bùxiùgāng 不鏽鋼 stainless steel

bùxū 不需 do not need

bùxū cǐxíng 不虛此行 One gains much on the trip.

bùxǔ 不許 not allowed; must not; prohibited

bùxuān érzhàn 不宣而戰 to fight without a declaration of war

bùxué wúshù 不學無術 unlearned; ignorant

bùxùnyú 不遜於 not worse than

bùyǎguān 不雅觀 ungraceful

bùyàyú 不亞於 not worse than

bùyán éryù 不言而喻 self-evident; to understand without explanation

bùyàn 不厭 do not mind doing something; do not tire of

bùyàn qífán 不厭其煩 to be very patient

bùyào éryù 不藥而癒 to recover (from illness) without medical help

bùyàolián 不要臉 shameless; brazen

bùyī 不一 to vary; to differ

bùyīdìng 不一定 uncertain; not sure

bùyī érzú 不一而足 many; numerous

bùyí 不宜 not suitable; inadvisable

bùyí yúlì 不遺餘力 to spare no effort; to do one's best (or utmost)

bùyǐ wéirán 不以為然 to object to; to take exception to

bùyì érfēi 不翼而飛 missing inexplicably

bùyì lèhū 不亦樂乎 1. What a delight it would be if... 2. extremely; awfully

bùyì zhīcái 不義之財 loot; wealth acquired illicitly

bùyòng 不用 1. not necessary 2. need not

bùyóude 不由得 cannot help; cannot but

bùyóu fēnshuō 不由分說 not waiting for an explanation; unreasonable

bùyóu zìzhǔ 不由自主 can't help; involuntarily

bùyú 不虞 1. unexpected 2. eventuality; contingency 3. do not worry about

bùyù 不育 sterility

bùyuē értóng 不約而同 to accord without consulting each other

bùyuè 不悅 unhappy; displeased

bùzài 不在 1. dead 2. not in; absent

bùzài cǐxiàn 不在此限 not subject to the limits

bùzàn yīcí 不贊一辭 to keep

silent; to make no comment

bùzé shǒuduàn 不擇手段 by fair means or foul

bùzhàn érqū rénzhībīng 不戰而屈人之兵 to subdue the enemy without fighting

bùzhàn érshèng 不戰而勝 to win without fighting a battle

bùzhǎngjìn 不長進 1. without improvement or progress 2. good-for-nothing

bùzhé bùkòu 不折不扣 1. without any discount; net cost 2. absolute; out-and-out

bùzhī 不支 unable to hang on; exhausted

bùzhī bùjué 不知不覺 imperceptibly; unnoticed

bùzhī hǎodǎi 不知好歹 1. unable to tell good from bad 2. stubborn

bùzhī jiùlǐ 不知就裡 do not know the inside story

bùzhī qīngzhòng 不知輕重 muddled or mixed-up

bùzhī qùxiàng 不知去向 disappear without a trace

bùzhī sǐhuó 不知死活 muddled or mixed-up (characterized by rashness or recklessness)

bùzhī suócuò 不知所措 stunned into inaction or stoppage of mental activity

bùzhī suóyún 不知所云 (said of statements) unintelligible

bùzhī tiāngāo dìhòu 不知天高地厚 to think too much of one's abilities

bùzhī zì'ài 不知自愛 to act without self-respect

bùzhí yīqián 不值一錢 worthless

bùzhí yīxiào 不值一笑 extremely ridiculous

bùzhǐ 不止 1. do not stop 2. and more than...; over

bùzhǐ 不只 not only; not merely

bùzhì kěfǒu 不置可否 noncommittal; to make no comment

bùzhìyú 不至於 will not go so far as...; will not be so serious as...

bùzhì zhīzhèng 不治之症 an incurable disease

bùzhōngyòng 不中用 good-for-nothing; useless

bùzhuó biānjì 不著邊際 far-fetched; totally beside the point

bùzhuó hénjì 不著痕跡 without trace

bùzī 不貲 immeasurable; incalculable

bùzìliàng 不自量 without considering one's own capability; overconfident

bùzú 不足 1. not deserving 2. insufficient; not enough

bùzú cǎixìn 不足採信 1. (law) unacceptable as evidence 2. can not be considered as reliable

bùzú qīngzhòng 不足輕重 of little value; of little importance

bùzú wéiqí 不足爲奇 nothing strange, extraordinary or remarkable about it

bùzú wéi wàirén dào 不足爲外人道 no need to let others know

bùzuò dì'èrrén xiǎng 不作第二人想 not content with playing second fiddle

bùzuòshēng 不作聲 to keep silence; to say nothing

bù 布

1. cloth; textiles 2. (佈) to declare, announce or proclaim 3. (佈) to display; to distribute or disseminate; to spread out

bùbó 布帛 (collectively) cloth or textiles

bùdài 布袋 a calico sack (for grains, etc.)

bùdào 布道 (religion) to evangelize

bùdīng 布丁 a pudding

bùfáng 布防 to organize the defense

bùgào 布告 1. a public notice; a bulletin 2. to make a public announcement

bùgàolán 布告欄 a notice board; a bulletin board

bùgǔniǎo 布穀鳥 a cuckoo

bùjǐng 布景 sets; a setting

bùjú 布局 1. overall arrangement

2. the composition (of a picture, a piece of writing, etc.) 3. the position (of pieces on a chessboard)

bùléi 布雷 to lay mines; to mine

bùpǐ 布匹 piece goods; dry goods

bùshāng 布商 dry goods dealers; clothiers

bùshī 布施 (Buddhism) alms-giving; donation

bùyī 布衣 1. dresses made of common cloth 2. commoners

bùzhì 布置 to fix up; to decorate

bù 佈

refer to **bù** 布 2, 3

bù 步

1. a pace; a step 2. to walk; on foot 3. situation; state; degree 4. banks of rivers, ponds, etc. 5. fortune; doom 6. a unit of length in ancient China of about 5. 5 feet

bùbīng 步兵 foot soldiers; infantry

bùbù 步步 1. step by step 2. gradually

bùbù gāoshēng 步步高升 to get promotion step by step or continuously

bùbù wéiyíng 步步爲營 to move carefully every step on the way

bùdào 步道 a sidewalk; a foot-path

bùdiào 步調 marching order; gaits

bùdiào yīzhì 步調一致 to act in unison; to keep in step

bùduì 步隊 a formation of foot soldiers; infantry

bùfá 步伐 steps or paces

bùfǎ 步法 (dancing) footwork

bùlǚ wéijiān 步履維艱 to walk with difficulty

bùqiāng 步槍 a rifle

bùrén hòuchén 步人後塵 to follow in another's footsteps

bùxíng 步行 to walk; to march on foot

bùzǐ 步子 a step; a pace

bùzōu 步驟 procedure, or sequence of doing something

bù 怖

1. terrified; frightened 2. to frighten; to threaten

bù 部

1. a department; a section; a division; a class; a sort 2. a cabinet ministry 3. a volume; a complete work, novel, writing, etc. 4. to lead; to head

bùduì 部隊 troops; a military unit

bùluò 部落 a tribe

bùmén 部門 a class; a section; a department

bùshǒu 部首 radicals of Chinese characters

bùshǔ 部署 to make preparations or arrangements

bùshǔ 部屬 subordinates

bùxià 部下 subordinates

bùzhǎng 部長 1. a cabinet minister 2. (in U.S.) the Secretary (of the army, the navy, the air force, the Defense Department, the Agriculture Department, etc.)

bù 埠

1. a harbor; a port; a pier 2. a mart on the bank of a river or seacoast

bù 簿

1. books 2. to record; to register

bùjì 簿記 bookkeeping

cā 擦

1. to wipe; to mop; to scrub; to polish 2. to spread on; to put on 3. to rub; to graze; to scratch 4. to brush; to shave

cābàngqiú 擦棒球 (baseball) foul tip

cābōlí 擦玻璃 to wipe glass; to wipe windowpanes

cādìbǎn 擦地板 to mop the floor

cāgān 擦乾 to swab up; to wipe dry

cāgānjìng 擦乾淨 to wipe clean

cāhàn 擦汗 to wipe off sweat or perspiration

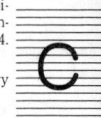

cājiān érguò 擦肩而過 to pass each other so close that they almost rub each other

cāliàng 擦亮 to shine (shoes, utensils, etc.)

cāpíxié 擦皮鞋 to shine shoes

cāqù 擦去 to wipe off

cāshāng 擦傷 a scratch; to suffer a scratch

cāshēn érguò 擦身而過 to pass each other so close that they almost rub each other

cāshì 擦拭 to clean; to cleanse

cāxǐ 擦洗 to scrub

cāxiétóng 擦鞋童 a shoeshine boy; a shoeblack

cāxiéyóu 擦鞋油 shoe polish

cāzi 擦子 a rubber; an eraser

cāi 猜
1. to guess; to suspect; to doubt
2. cruel and suspicious

cāicè 猜測 to guess; to speculate; to conjecture

cāijì 猜忌 to be jealous and suspicious

cāimèir 猜謎兒 1. to solve riddles 2. to guess

cāimí 猜謎 refer to **cāimèir** 猜謎兒

cāiquán 猜拳 to play the finger-guessing game (usually in drinking)

cāitòu 猜透 able to see through (what's on his mind, etc.)

cāixiǎng 猜想 to guess; to speculate; to conjecture

cāiyí 猜疑 suspicion; to suspect; to doubt

cāizháo 猜著 to guess correctly; to make out

cāizhòng 猜中 to guess correctly; to make out

cái 才
1. natural abilities; a gift; talent; a mental faculty 2. a gifted person; a talented person; a brilliant man; a talent 3. people of a certain type 4. certainly; indeed 5. (纔) just; just now

cáidé jiānbèi 才德兼備 to have both talent and virtue

cáigàn 才幹 talent or ability to get things done; competence

cáihuá 才華 brilliance (of mind); a gift; talent

cáihuá chūzhòng 才華出眾 of uncommon brilliance

cáilüè 才略 talent for scheming

cáimào shuāngquán 才貌雙全 (said of women) talented and good-looking

cáinéng 才能 talent; abilities; a gift

cáinǚ 才女 a talented woman

cáiqì 才氣 talent; brilliance

cáiqì yángyì 才氣洋溢 brilliant intelligence

cáiqíng 才情 brilliant expression of emotions (in a writing)

cáishí 才識 ability and insight

cáishì 才識 refer to **cáishí** 才識

cáishū xuéqiǎn 才疏學淺 untalented and unlearned (a polite expression referring to oneself)

cáisī mǐnjié 才思敏捷 to have an agile imagination

cáixué 才學 intelligence and scholarship

cáiyì zhuōjué 才藝卓絕 to stand out in talent and skill

cáiyì zhuójué 才藝卓絕 refer to **cáiyì zhuōjué** 才藝卓絕

cáizhì 才智 intelligence; brilliance

cáizǐ 才子 a talented person; a genius

cáizǐ jiārén 才子佳人 an ideal couple

cái 材
1. materials—especially timber—for building houses, furniture, etc. 2. material in its broadest sense 3. properties of a substance 4. ability; aptitude 5. a coffin

cáiliào 材料 1. raw materials 2. materials (such as data, statistics, figure, information for writing an article, story, novel, etc.) 3. ingredients of a preparation (of food, medicine, etc.) 4. makings; stuff

cái 財
wealth; riches; money

cáibǎo 財寶 money and jewels; valuables

cáichǎn 財產 property; belongings

cáifù 財富 wealth or fortune; riches

cáijīng 財經 finance and economy

cáilì 財力 financial resources

cáimí xīnqiào 財迷心竅 to have one's head turned by greed

cáituán 財團 a consortium

cáituán fǎrén 財團法人 a juridical person

cáiwù 財物 property; belongings

cáiwù 財務 finance; financial affairs

cáiyuán 財源 financial resources

cáizhèng 財政 finance; financial administration

Cáizhèngbù 財政部 Ministry of Finance

cáizhu 財主 a capitalist; a millionaire

cái 裁
1. to cut paper, cloth, etc. with a knife or scissors 2. to diminish; to reduce 3. to delete 4. to consider; to decide; to judge 5. a form; a style 6. sanctions 7. to weight; to measure 8. to kill

cáiféng 裁縫 to tailor; to make dress

cáiféngshī 裁縫師 a tailor; a dressmaker

cáifeng 裁縫 a tailor; a dressmaker

cáijiǎn 裁剪 to tailor; to cut out (a dress)

cáijiǎn 裁減 1. to reduce (personnel, the staff, etc.) 2. reduction

cáijué 裁決 1. to judge and decide 2. a ruling; a judgment; a decision

cáijūn 裁軍 disarmament

cáikāi 裁開 to cut apart with a knife or scissors

cáipàn 裁判 1. a judge; a referee; an umpire 2. a verdict or judg-

ment by law

cáiyuán 裁員 to eliminate unnecessary personnel; to lay off workers

cǎi 采
1. to gather; to collect 2. to pick; to select 3. bright colors

cǎi 彩
1. colors; variegated colors 2. makeup in various Chinese operas 3. special feats or stunts in Chinese operas 4. ornamental; brilliant; gay 5. prize money; stakes in a gambling game

cǎibǐ 彩筆 1. the pen that produces masterpieces 2. color crayons

cǎidài 彩帶 a colored streamer (or ribbon)

cǎihóng 彩虹 a rainbow

cǎihuì 彩繪 a colored drawing or pattern

cǎipái 彩排 a dress rehearsal

cǎipiào 彩票 a lottery ticket; a raffle ticket

cǎisè 彩色 color

cǎisèbǎn 彩色版 chromolithograph printing

cǎisè diànshì 彩色電視 color television

cǎisè ruǎnpiàn 彩色軟片 color film

cǎishì 彩飾 to adorn; to ornament; adornments

cǎitóu 彩頭 good luck; lucky

cǎixiá 彩霞 rosy clouds in the morning or evening

cǎiyún 彩雲 clouds of many hues

cǎi 採
1. to pluck (flowers, etc.); to gather; to collect 2. to select; to adopt 3. (now rarely) to drag 4. (now rarely) to beckon; to take notice of

cǎichá 採茶 to pick tea leaves

cǎifá 採伐 to fell (trees); to open up (a mine)

cǎifǎng 採訪 to cover (a news item or story); to interview

cǎifǎng jìzhě 採訪記者 a news

reporter

căifăng xīnwén 採訪新聞 to cover a news item

căigòu 採購 to purchase

căigòutuán 採購團 a purchase mission

căiguāng 採光 1. lighting 2. to pick or pluck until none is left

căihuāzéi 採花賊 a rapist

căijí 採集 to gather (samples, etc.); to collect (materials, etc.)

căikuàng 採礦 to mine (for minerals)

căimăi 採買 to pick and buy; to purchase

căinà 採納 to accept or adopt (an idea, opinion, proposal, etc.)

căiqŭ 採取 to take or adopt (an attitude, a measure, etc.)

căixìn 採信 to believe; to accept as true

căiyòng 採用 to adopt (a suggestion, new technique, etc.)

căi 睬

1. to look; to watch 2. to notice; to pay attention to

căi 綵

1. varicolored silk; a silk festoon 2. motley; varicolored

căijiào 綵轎 a gaily decorated sedan chair

căiqiú 綵球 a ball wound up from varicolored silk

căi 踩

to tread upon; to trample; to step upon

căigāoqiāo 踩高蹺 to walk on stilts

cài 菜

1. vegetables; greens 2. food eaten with rice or alcoholic drinks 3. a dish; a course

càidān 菜單 a bill of fare; a menu

càidāo 菜刀 a kitchen knife

càiguā 菜瓜 cucumber

càinóng 菜農 a vegetable grower

càipŭ 菜圃 a vegetable garden or field

càishìchăng 菜市場 a grocery market; a vegetable market

càitān 菜攤 a vegetable vendor's stall

càiyáo 菜肴 food eaten with rice or alcoholic drinks

càiyuán 菜園 a vegetable garden or field

cài 蔡

1. a large turtle 2. name of an ancient state in the Epoch of Spring and Autumn 3. a Chinese family name

cān 參

1. to take part in; to get involved in 2. to visit; to interview; to call on 3. to impeach; to censure 4. to recommend 5. to counsel; to consult together 6. to consider; to collate; to compare

cānbàn 參半 half; half-and-half

cānguān 參觀 to visit, inspect or tour (a place, etc.)

cānjiā 參加 to attend; to join

cānkàn 參看 to refer to

cānkăo 參考 1. to consult; to collate 2. reference

cānkăoshū 參考書 a reference book

cānmóu 參謀 the staff; a counselor

cānyìyuán 參議員 a senator

cānyìyuàn 參議院 the upper house of a parliament

cānyù 參與 to take part in; to participate in

cānyuè 參閱 to see; to consult

cānzá 參雜 to mix; to add something of the different nature, quality, color, etc.

cānzhàn 參戰 to participate in a war

cānzhào 參照 in accordance with; with reference to

cānzhèng 參政 to take part in politics or the government

cānzhèngquán 參政權 the right to participate in public affairs

cān 餐

1. a meal 2. to eat 3. food

cānchē 餐車 a diner; a dining car

cānfēng sùlù 餐風宿露 hardships of traveling in old times

cānjīn 餐巾 a napkin

cānjù 餐具 a dinner set; tableware; a dinner service

cānquàn 餐券 a meal coupon; a meal ticket

cāntīng 餐廳 a restaurant; a dining hall; a mess hall

cānyǐnyè 餐飲業 restaurants, bars, coffee houses and tearooms

cán 殘

1. to destroy; to injure; to damage; to spoil 2. to wither 3. cruel and fierce; heartless and relentless 4. crippled; disfigured 5. remnants or residues; the little amount of something left 6. incomplete 7. to kill

cánbào 殘暴 cruel and heartless

cánbīng bàijiàng 殘兵敗將 the remnants of a defeated army

cáncún 殘存 surviving

cán'ér bùfèi 殘而不廢 disabled but useful

cánfèi 殘廢 crippled, maimed, or disabled

cángēng shèngfàn 殘羹剩飯 the remains of a meal; leftovers

cánhái 殘骸 1. incomplete remains 2. the wreckage (of an airplane, ship or truck)

cánhài 殘害 to oppress cruelly; to injure heartlessly; to slaughter

cánhuā bàiliǔ 殘花敗柳 fallen angels; prostitutes

cánjí 殘疾 physical deformity

cánjú 殘局 1. the aftermath of war, revolution or great upheaval 2. an unfinished chess game

cánkù 殘酷 cruelty; heartlessness; cold-bloodedness; savagery

cánliú 殘留 to remain; to be left over

cánpò 殘破 1. damaged; dilapidated 2. not complete; deficient

cánquē 殘缺 incomplete; fragmentary

cánrěn 殘忍 cruel; heartless; brutal; savage

cánshā 殘殺 to massacre; to slaughter

cánshēng 殘生 one's remaining years

cányú 殘餘 remnants; survivals; remains

cánzhàng 殘障 handicapped

cán 慚

ashamed; mortified; humiliated

cánkuì 慚愧 ashamed

cán 蠶

a silkworm

cándòu 蠶豆 a horse bean; a fava bean

cánjiǎn 蠶繭 the cocoon of the silkworm

cánsī 蠶絲 natural silk; silk

cǎn 慘

1. sorrowful; tragic; miserable; sad 2. cruel; merciless; brutal 3. dark; gloomy; dull 4. disastrously

cǎn'àn 慘案 a cruel murder case

cǎnbái 慘白 dreadfully pale; pale

cǎnbài 慘敗 to suffer a crushing or ignominious defeat; crushing defeat

cǎnbù rěndǔ 慘不忍睹 so tragic that one cannot bear to look at it

cǎndàn 慘淡 1. laborious; arduous 2. gloomy; dismal; dim

cǎndàn jīngyíng 慘淡經營 to manage with great pains

cǎnjiào 慘叫 to give a blood-curdling scream or shriek

cǎnjù 慘劇 a tragic event; a calamity

cǎnjué rénhuán 慘絕人寰 a rare tragedy on earth; blood-curdling (atrocities)

cǎnsǐ 慘死 to meet a violent or tragic death

cǎntòng 慘痛 bitter; very painful; agonizing

cǎnwú réndào 慘無人道 inhuman; brutal

cǎnxīxī 慘兮兮 sad-looking

cǎnzāo hènghuò 慘遭橫禍 to

meet a tragic accident

cǎnzhòng 慘重 heavy; grievous; disastrous

cǎnzhuàng 慘狀 a tragic sight; a miserable condition

càn 粲

1. bright and clear; radiant 2. beautiful; splendid; excellent 3. smiling; laughing 4. well-polished rice

càn 璨

bright and brilliant; lustrous and luminous

càn 燦

bright; brilliant

cànlàn 燦爛 resplendent; brilliant; glorious

cāng 倉

1. a granary; a storehouse; a warehouse 2. a cabin, as in the ship 3. green

cāngcù 倉促 in haste; hurriedly

cānghuáng 倉皇 in haste; hurriedly

cāngkù 倉庫 a warehouse; a storehouse

cānglǐn 倉廩 a granary

cāng 傖

1. (said of persons) cheap; vulgar; lowly 2. confused; disorderly

cāng 滄

blue; azure; green

cānghǎi 滄海 the blue sea

cānghǎi sāngtián 滄海桑田 the vicissitudes of life

cānghǎi yīsù 滄海一粟 a grain in the boundless sea—infinitely small

cāngmíng 滄溟 the blue sea

cāngsāng 滄桑 the vicissitudes of life

cāng 蒼

1. green; deep green or blue 2. gray; hoary (hair) 3. old 4. the masses

cāngbái 蒼白 pale; pallid

cānglǎo 蒼老 (said of people) hoary and old

cāngliáng 蒼涼 desolate; bleak

cāngmáng 蒼茫 a vast expanse without a boundary

cāngshēng 蒼生 the ordinary people; the masses

cāngtiān 蒼天 1. the heavens; the sky 2. springtime

cāngyíng 蒼蠅 the fly

cāngyíngpāi 蒼蠅拍 a flyswatter; a flyflap

cāng 艙

the hold or cabin (of a ship)

cāngfáng 艙房 cabins

cáng 藏

1. to hide; to conceal 2. to store; to save; to hoard

cángnì 藏匿 to hide; to harbor (criminals)

cángshēn 藏身 to hide oneself; to conceal

cángshū 藏書 1. to collect books 2. a book collection

cángzhuó 藏拙 to hide one's weak points

cángzhuó 藏拙 refer to **cángzhuó** 藏拙

cāo 操

1. to handle; to manage 2. to hold; to grasp 3. to exercise; to drill 4. to speak

cāochǎng 操場 an athletic ground; a playground

cāochí 操持 to manage; to handle

cāogē 操戈 to take up arms

cāoláo 操勞 1. to work hard 2. to look after

cāoliàn 操練 to drill; to practice

cāoqiāng 操槍 rifle drill

cāoshén 操神 to worry

cāoshǒu 操守 moral fortitude; integrity

cāoxīn 操心 1. to worry about 2. to rack one's brains

cāoxíng 操行 conduct (in the moral sense); behavior or conduct of a student

cāoxìng 操行 refer to **càoxíng** 操行

cāoyǎn 操演 to drill; to exercise

cāozhī guòjí 操之過急 to be

too eager for success

cāozòng 操縱 to manage, control, manipulate or operate

cāozuò 操作 to manipulate or operate (a machine)

cāo 糙
1. coarse or unpolished; rough 2. rude; rough; rash; desultory; careless

cāomǐ 糙米 unpolished rice

cáo 曹
1. a plural particle 2. a Chinese family name

cáo 嘈
noisy; clamorous

cáozá 嘈雜 noisy and confused

cáo 漕
to transport grain by water

cáo 槽
1. a manger 2. a trough; a flume; a chute

cǎo 艸
grass; straw; weeds

cǎo 草
1. grass; straw; a herb; a weed 2. coarse; crude 3. a draft (of writing); to draft 4. the script type of Chinese calligraphy

cǎo'àn 草案 a draft plan; a proposed plan

cǎobāo 草包 a grass bag—a crude fellow

cǎoběn 草本 1. a manuscript 2. herbaceous

cǎocǎo liǎoshì 草草了事 to dispose of a thing carelessly or hastily

cǎochuàng 草創 1. the beginning or initial period (of a project) 2. to make the rough copy

cǎocóng 草叢 a thick growth of grass

cǎodì 草地 a lawn; meadow; pasture

cǎogǎo 草稿 a rough draft

cǎojiān rénmìng 草菅人命 to attach no importance to human life

cǎoliào 草料 fodder; hay

cǎomào 草帽 a straw hat

cǎoméi 草莓 a strawberry

cǎopí 草皮 a young grass cover

cǎopíng 草坪 a lawn; meadow; pasture

cǎoqúnwǔ 草裙舞 a Hawaiian dance; a hulahula

cǎoshéng 草繩 a straw rope; a grass rope

cǎoshū 草書 the script type of calligraphy; script-style characters

cǎoshuài 草率 careless; perfunctory

cǎoxí 草蓆 a straw mat

cǎoxié 草鞋 straw sandals

cǎoyào 草藥 herb medicine

cǎoyuán 草原 a prairie; grassland; a steppe

cè 冊
1. (in ancient China) a register; a book or books in general; volumes 2. a list; statistical tables; to record; records 3. an order to confer nobility titles

cèlì 冊立 to crown an empress

cèzi 冊子 a book; a pamphlet

cè 側
1. the side; sideways 2. to slant; to incline towards 3. low and narrow-minded; prejudiced

cè'ěr qīngtīng 側耳傾聽 to listen attentively

cèmén 側門 a side door

cèmiàn 側面 the side; the flank

cèmiàn xiāoxi 側面消息 sidelights

cèmù 側目 1. a sidelong glance; to look askance 2. to cause raised eyebrows

cèshēn 側身 to sidle; on one's side; sideways

cèwò 側臥 to lie on the side

cèyǐng 側影 a silhouette; a profile

cèzhòng 側重 to place particular emphasis on

cè 惻
to feel anguish

cèyǐn zhīxīn 惻隱之心 innate

mercy; natural compassion

cè 廁
a toilet, lavatory or latrine

cèsuǒ 廁所 a toilet; a lavatory; a latrine; a rest room

cè 策
1. a whip (for goading horses) 2. expository writings on government affairs 3. orders of appointment 4. a plan; a scheme; a stratagem 5. to whip; to spur; to urge; to impel

cèdòng 策動 to machinate; to maneuver; to instigate

cèhuà 策畫 to plan; to make plans

cèlì 策勵 to urge; to impel; to spur

cèlüè 策略 a stratagem; a scheme; tactics

cè 測
to measure; to survey

cèdìng 測定 to determine

cèduó 測度 to speculate; to conjecture; to guess

cèduó 測度 refer to **cèduó** 測度

cèhuǎngqì 測謊器 a lie detector; a polygraph

cèliáng 測量 1. survey 2. to survey

cèliángyuán 測量員 a surveyor

cèyàn 測驗 1. to test; to examine 2. a quiz or test

cēn 參
cēncī 參差 of irregular, different sizes; uneven

cén 涔
1. a puddle 2. tearful

céng 曾
ever; once

céngjǐhéshí 曾幾何時 only a short time ago

céngjīng 曾經 to have had the experience of

céng 層
a layer; a stratum; a story (of a building)

céngchū bùqióng 層出不窮 happen again and again

céngcì 層次 1. order (of importance or priority) 2. the arrangement of ideas (in writing or speech)

céngfēng 層峯 the highest autority

céngluán diézhàng 層巒疊嶂 peaks rising one upon another

chā 叉
a prong; a fork (used in catching fish, etc.)

chāzi 叉子 a fork

chā 差
1. errors; mistakes 2. difference; discrepancy 3. (mathematics) difference

chābié 差別 discrepancy; distinction

chācuò 差錯 1. errors; mistakes 2. accidents

chā'é 差額 the difference between two amounts or figures

chājià 差價 price differences

chājù 差距 gap; disparity; difference

chāqiáng rényì 差強人意 barely satisfactory

chāyǐ háolí, miùyǐ qiānlǐ 差以毫釐，謬以千里 A slight error in the beginning results in a big mistake in the end.

chāyì 差異 1. discrepancy; difference 2. to differ

chā 插
1. to insert; to put in; to stick into 2. to interpose; to get a word in edgeways 3. to plant 4. to take part in

chābō xīnwén 插播新聞 spot news

chāchì nánfēi 插翅難飛 completely surrounded

chāduì 插隊 to cut in; to push in

chāhuā 插花 to arrange flowers

chāhuà 插話 1. to break into a conversation 2. digression

chāhuà 插畫 illustrations (in a book, magazine, etc.)

chākē dǎhùn 插科打諢 (said of clowns in a show) to ad-lib; buf-

C

fooneries; jesting

chākǒu 插口 to interrupt a narration, conversation, etc; to chip in

chāqǔ 插曲 1. a musical interlude 2. songs and tunes used in motion picture dubbing 3. an episode

chārù 插入 to stick into; to insert

chārùjù 插入句 a parenthesis

chāshǒu 插手 to take part in; to meddle

chātóu 插頭 a plug

chātú 插圖 illustrations or plates

chāyāng 插秧 to transplant rice seedlings

chāzuǐ 插嘴 to interrupt a narration, conversation, etc.; to chip in

chāzuò 插座 a receptacle; a socket; an outlet

chā 喳

the sound of chattering

chá 查

1. to investigate; to check; to seek out; to look into 2. (used at the beginning of the official correspondence) It appears....; It seems....; It is known....; It is found that.... 3. a wooden raft

chá'àn 查案 to investigate into a case

chábàn 查辦 to investigate into the irregularities (of an official, etc.) and mete out due punishment

cháchū 查出 to find out; to discover

chádiǎn 查點 to check (the number of prisoners, students, a list of goods, etc.)

cháduì 查對 to check or examine one by one; to verify

cháfǎng 查訪 to go around and make inquiries

cháfēng 查封 the execution of a court order by which all property of a debtor would be placed under legal custody until further action

cháhàotái 查號台 directory information

cháhé 查核 to check and examine

cháhùkǒu 查戶口 census

cháhuò 查獲 to hunt down and seize

chákān 查勘 to survey and examine

chákàn 查看 to investigate; to look into (a matter)

chámíng 查明 to investigate and clarify

chápiào 查票 to examine or check tickets

cháqín 查勤 to make the rounds and check officers, etc. to see if they are doing their duties during office hours

cháshōu 查收 to check the goods delivered and take them over

cháxún 查詢 to inquire about; to inquire

cháyàn 查驗 to investigate; to inspect

cházhàng 查帳 to audit (accounts)

cházhàngyuán 查帳員 an auditor

cházhèng 查證 to investigate and verify

cházìdiǎn 查字典 to look it up in a dictionary

chá 茶

tea

chábēi 茶杯 a teacup

cháchí 茶匙 a teaspoon

chádiǎn 茶點 refreshments

cháfáng 茶房 a waiter; an attendant

cháguǎn 茶館 a tearoom; a teahouse

cháhú 茶壺 a teapot

cháhuā 茶花 camellia

cháhuì 茶會 a tea party; a tea reception

chájī 茶几 1. a teapoy 2. a small table

chájù 茶具 tea utensils; teathings

chálóu 茶樓 a tearoom; a teahouse

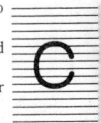

C

cháshì 茶室 1. a tearoom 2. a brothel

cháshui 茶水 tea or boiled water

chásì 茶肆 a tearoom; a teahouse

cháyè 茶葉 tea leaves

cháyuán 茶園 1. a tea plantation 2. (formerly) an opera theater

chá 搽
to rub on (ointment, etc.); to smear; to anoint; to paint

cháfén 搽粉 to powder (the face, etc.)

cháyào 搽藥 to rub on some external medicine, ointment, etc.

chá 察
to examine; to observe; to investigate; to survey; to study; to scrutinize

chábàn 察辦 to investigate a case and determine how to handle it

cháfǎng 察訪 to investigate by visiting the sources of information

cháhé 察核 to investigate a case and then decide what to do

chájué 察覺 to be conscious of; to perceive

chákān 察勘 to survey; to examine

chákàn 察看 to observe; to watch

chǎ 叉
chǎpī 叉劈 (said of the road) divergent

chà 岔
1. to branch; to fork 2. a fork; a branching point

chàdào 岔道 a diverging road

chàkāi 岔開 1. to branch off 2. to change (the subject of conversation) 3. to stagger

chàkǒu 岔口 a fork (in a road)

chàlù 岔路 a diverging road

chàzi 岔子 a trouble; an accident

chà 姹
1. young (girls) 2. charming; attractive; seductive 3. to boast;

to talk big; to lie

chà 刹
a (Buddhist) temple, shrine, monastery or abbey

chà'nà 刹那 a moment; an instant

chà 差
1. to differ 2. wrong 3. to want; to fall short of 4. not up to standard

chàbuduō 差不多 1. almost the same 2. almost; nearly 3. just about enough

chàdiǎnr 差點兒 1. almost; nearly 2. nearly the same 3. not good enough

chàjìn 差勁 disappointing; poor (work, etc.)

chà 詫
1. surprised; to wonder 2. to brag; to boast 3. to cheat; to deceive 4. to inform

chàyì 詫異 to be surprised

chāi 拆 also **chè**
1. to split; to break; to rip open 2. to take down; to tear down (a house, etc.); to destroy; to dismantle 3. to analyze; to scrutinize

chāichú 拆除 to dismantle and get rid of

chāichuān 拆穿 to expose (a secret, etc.)

chāifēng 拆封 to break up a seal; to open a sealed envelope

chāihuǐ 拆毀 to damage; to destroy

chāihuǒ 拆夥 to break up partnership

chāikāi 拆開 to take apart; to dismantle (a machine, etc.)

chāisǎn 拆散 to dismantle

chāisàn 拆散 1. to break up or split apart (a family, a married couple, etc.) 2. refer to **chāisàn** 拆散

chāitái 拆臺 (literally) to pull down the stage—to split up; to pull away a prop

chāixǐ 拆洗 to unpick (a bedspread, etc.) and wash; to take apart (a machine, etc.) for clean-

ing

chāixiè 拆卸 to take apart a large cargo

chāixìn 拆信 to open a letter

chāiyuè 拆閱 to open (a letter, document, etc.) and read

chāi 差

1. a messenger; an errand man 2. to dispatch; to send (a person) 3. one's duty or job 4. an errand

chāiqiǎn 差遣 to dispatch or send (a person on an errand, etc.)

chāirén 差人 an official messenger

chāishǐ 差使 to dispatch or send (a person on an errand, etc.)

chāishì 差事 a job

chāiyì 差役 an official messenger

chái 柴

1. firewood; brushwood; fagots 2. thin; emaciated 3. (now rarely) a fence 4. a Chinese family name

cháihuo 柴火 firewood; fuel

cháimǐ fūqī 柴米夫妻 a couple who live from hand to mouth

cháimǐ yóuyán 柴米油鹽 daily necessities

cháixīn 柴薪 firewood; fuel

cháiyóu 柴油 diesel oil

cháiyú 柴魚 dried bonito

chái 豺

1. a ravenous beast, akin to the wolf 2. cruel; wickedly cunning

cháiláng dāngdào 豺狼當道 (figuratively) wicked persons in power

chái 儕

1. a class; company 2. an adjunct to show plurality 3. to match (as man and wife)

chān 攙

1. to lead (a person) by the hand 2. to mix; to blend

chānfú 攙扶 to lead (a person) by the hand

chānhuo 攙和 to mix; to blend

chānzá 攙雜 to make impure; to add imitation goods or inferior

products to a shipment of merchandise in violation of business ethics

chán 單

the chief of the Huns (a common term during the Han Dynasty)

chányú 單于 the chief of the Huns

chán 孱

weak; feeble; frail

chánfū 孱夫 a coward

chánruò 孱弱 weak; feeble; frail

chán 嬋

graceful; ladylike; attractive; beautiful; pretty

chánjuān 嬋娟 1. graceful 2. the moon; moonlight

chán 潺

the sound of water flowing

chánchán 潺潺 the murmuring of flowing water

chán 禪

1. Zen Buddhism 2. meditation; intense contemplation

chánfáng 禪房 a hermitage; a monastery

chánsì 禪寺 a Buddhist temple

chán 蟬

1. a cicada 2. continuous; uninterrupted

chánlián 蟬聯 to keep on without interruption

chán 蟾

a toad

chánchú 蟾蜍 a toad

chán 纏

1. to wind round; to twine round; to bind; to wrap; to tangle 2. to bother persistently 3. to pester; to worry 4. to deal with

chánmián 纏綿 affectionate; inseparable

chánrǎo 纏繞 1. to wind round; to twine around 2. to bother persistently

chánrǎo 纏繞 refer to **chánrǎo** 纏繞

chánshēn 纏身 to be delayed; to

be held up by or burdened with something

chánzhù 纏住 entangled; to wrap tightly

chán 讒

to misrepresent; to slander; to calumniate; to defame

chánhài 讒害 to incriminate by false charges

chánxiàn 讒陷 to incriminate by false charges

chányán 讒言 malicious, or slanderous talk

chán 饞

piggish; gluttonous; greedy

chánxián yùdì 饞涎欲滴 (said of mouth) to water; to drool over; to covet

chánzuǐ 饞嘴 gluttonous

chǎn 產

1. to bear (offspring); to lay (eggs) 2. to produce; to bring about

chǎndì 產地 a producing center

chǎn'é 產額 the amount of production; output

chǎnfáng 產房 a lying-in room; a maternity room

chǎnfù 產婦 a lying-in woman

chǎnhòu 產後 after childbirth; postnatal

chǎnjiǎ 產假 maternity leave

chǎnliàng 產量 production; output; yield

chǎnluǎn 產卵 to lay eggs; to spawn

chǎnpǐn 產品 products

chǎnpǐn shuōmínghuì 產品說明會 a show and tell

chǎnqī 產期 time of childbirth

chǎnqí 產期 refer to **chǎnqī** 產期

chǎnqián 產前 before childbirth; prenatal

chǎnquán 產權 ownership (of real estate)

chǎnshēng 產生 to produce

chǎnwù 產物 products; outcomes

chǎnxiāo 產銷 production and marketing

chǎnyè 產業 1. property; estate 2. industry

Chǎnyè Gémìng 產業革命 the Industrial Revolution

chǎn 剷

1. a shovel 2. to shovel; to level off; to raze to the ground

chǎnchú 剷除 to root out; to eradicate

chǎnpíng 剷平 to level to the ground; to level

chǎn 諂

to flatter; to fawn; to toady

chǎnmèi 諂媚 to flatter; to fawn; to toady; flattery

chǎn 鏟

1. a shovel; a scoop 2. to shovel; to scoop

chǎn 闡

1. to make clear; to elucidate; to expound 2. evident; clear

chǎnfā 闡發 to expound and promote

chǎnmíng 闡明 to elucidate; to clarify

chǎnshì 闡釋 to explain; to expound

chǎnshù 闡述 to expound; to elaborate

chàn 懺

to confess one's sin; to repent

chànhuǐ 懺悔 to repent of one's sin; to feel repentance

chànhuǐlù 懺悔錄 confessions

chàn 顫 also **zhàn**

to tremble; to shake; to shiver; to quiver; to vibrate

chàndòng 顫動 to shake; to tremble

chàndǒu 顫抖 to quiver; to shiver; to shake; to tremble

chāng 昌

1. proper; good; straight (talk) 2. prosperous; robust; vigorous; to make prosperous; to glorify 3. light; brightness

chāngmíng 昌明 1. to expound and elaborate 2. flourishing; developing 3. glorious

chāngshèng 昌盛 1. prosperous 2. glory

chāng 倡

1. (娼) a prostitute 2. (猖) wild and unrestrained

chāngkuáng 倡狂 profligate

chāng 娼

a prostitute; a whore

chāngjì 娼妓 a streetwalker; a prostitute

chāng 猖

wild; mad; impudent; unruly; reckless

chāngjué 猖獗 rampant; on the rampage

chāngkuáng 猖狂 wild; unrestrained; unbridled

chāng 菖

a sweet flag; a calamus

chāngpú 菖蒲 a sweet flag; a calamus

cháng 長

1. long; length 2. a forte; strong points 3. to be good at; to excel

chángchéng 長城 1. the Great Wall 2. someone who can be trusted

chángchéng 長程 long-term

chángchu 長處 merits; good points; advantages

chángcún 長存 to exist forever; to last forever

chángdèng 長凳 a bench

chángdù 長度 length

chángduǎn 長短 1. long or short 2. length 3. mishaps or accidents which may endanger one's life 4. good or bad; malicious criticism

chángduǎn bùqí 長短不齊 not uniform in length

chángfāngxíng 長方形 a rectangle; an oblong

chánggōng 長工 a regular laborer on a farm; a farm hand; a long-term hired hand

chánghuà duǎnshuō 長話短

說 to make a long story short

Chángjiāng 長江 the Yangtze River

chángjǐnglù 長頸鹿 a giraffe

chángjiǔ 長久 permanent; a very long time

chángkù 長褲 a pair of trousers

chángláng 長廊 a roofed corridor or passage; a gallery

chánglóng 長龍 a long line; a long queue

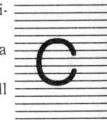

chángnián 長年 yearlong; all the year round

chángnián lěiyuè 長年累月 year in, year out; over the years

chángpáo 長袍 a long gown; a robe

chángpǎo 長跑 a long-distance foot race

chángpiān dàlùn 長篇大論 a harangue or tirade; a lengthy comment; a ponderous talk; a long speech

chángpiān xiǎoshuō 長篇小說 a novel

chángqī 長期 1. a long time 2. long-term; long-range; long-standing

chángqí 長期 refer to **chángqī** 長期

chángqū zhírù 長驅直入 to march in without opposition

chángshé 長舌 to be fond of gossip; long-tongued; loquacious

chángshēng bùlǎo 長生不老 (especially in Taoism) immortality

chángshēngguǒ 長生果 peanuts

chángshíjiān 長時間 a long time

chángshòu 長壽 longevity; a long life

chángtàn 長嘆 to sigh deeply

chángtú 長途 a long distance; a long journey

chángtú diànhuà 長途電話 a long-distance call

chángxiù shànwǔ 長袖善舞 to be resourceful, especially in a dishonest way

chángxū duǎntàn 長吁短嘆

to sigh incessantly; to sigh and groan

chángyīn 長音 a long vowel

chángyuǎn 長遠 for a long time; long-range; long-term

chángyuǎn zhījì 長遠之計 a long-range plan (for the future)

chángzhēng 長征 an expedition (usually military); to take a long journey to a distant place

chángzhì jiǔ'ān 長治久安 a lengthy peaceful reign

chángzú jìnbù 長足進步 marked progress; to come a long way

cháng 徜

going to and fro; lingering; loitering

chángyáng 徜徉 lingering or loitering

cháng 常

1. common; normal 2. long; lasting; eternal 3. regular; frequent; often 4. ordinarily; usually 5. a rule; a principle 6. a Chinese family name

chángbèijūn 常備軍 the standing army

chángcháng 常常 often; frequently

chángchūnténg 常春藤 ivy; bindwood

chángdiǎn 常典 usual rites; regular ceremony

chángguī 常規 ordinary rules or practices

chánghuì 常會 1. regular meetings or conventions 2. to be apt to; to happen often

chángjiàn 常見 to see or to be seen frequently

chángkè 常客 a frequenter

chánglǐ 常理 convention; general consent

chánglǐ 常禮 common or everyday courtesy

chánglì 常例 regular order or procedures

chángliàng 常量 constant

chángnián 常年 all the year round

chángqīng 常青 evergreen

chángqíng 常情 man's natural action or reaction under certain circumstances

chángrén 常人 ordinary people

chángrèn 常任 standing (members of a committee, government organ, etc.)

chángshè 常設 standing; permanent

chángshí 常識 1. general knowledge (as distinct from expertise) 2. common sense

chángshì 常識 refer to **chángshí** 常識

chángshù 常數 constant

chángtài 常態 a normal carriage or manner

chángwù wěiyuán 常務委員 the standing members of a committee

chángyán 常言 a popular saying; a proverb

chángyòng 常用 to use often; used often

chángyǒu 常有 usually; often

chángzhù 常駐 1. standing (members, etc.) 2. (said of policeman, etc.) to be stationed (at a locality, etc.) 3. durable (beauty or youthfulness)

cháng 場

refer to **chǎng** 場

cháng 腸

the intestines; the bowels

cháng'ái 腸癌 bowel cancer

chángwèi 腸胃 intestines and the stomach

chángyán 腸炎 intestinal or bowel catarrh; enteritis

chángzi 腸子 the intestines

cháng 嘗 (嚐)

1. to taste 2. to try 3. to experience

chángshì 嘗試 to try; a try

cháng 裳 also **shāng**

dress; garments; clothing

cháng 嫦

Cháng'é 嫦娥 (Chinese legend) Chang-e, who ascended the moon after secretly eating her

husband's elixir of life

cháng 償

1. to repay 2. to make restitution; to compensate 3. to fulfill (a wish) 4. to offset ·

chángfù 償付 to pay back; to pay

chánghuán 償還 to repay (what one owes)

chángmìng 償命 a life for a life

chángqīng 償清 to clear off

chángzhài 償債 to repay a debt

chǎng 場 also cháng

1. an area of level ground; an open space 2. an act of a play; an act of an opera 3. the stage 4. an arena for drill; a playground 5. a farm 6. a site or place for a special purpose, as an examination, a meeting, etc. 7. (physics) a field

chǎngdì 場地 a playground; a site

chǎnghé 場合 an occasion; a condition

chǎngmiàn 場面 1. pageantry 2. a scene; a spectacle 3. an appearance

chǎngsuǒ 場所 a location; a place; an arena

chǎng 敞

1. open; uncovered 2. spacious; broad

chǎngkāi 敞開 to open; to unfold

chǎngkuài 敞快 straightforward and broad-minded

chǎngpéngchē 敞篷車 an open coach; an open car; a convertible

chǎngxiōng 敞胸 to bare the breast

chǎng 廠

a factory; a plant; a workshop

chǎngfáng 廠房 a factory building

chǎngshāng 廠商 manufacturers

chǎngzhǎng 廠長 a factory manager

chǎngzhǐ 廠址 a factory site or

location

chǎngzhǔ 廠主 a factory owner; a mill owner

chàng 倡

to lead; to introduce; to initiate; to advocate

chàngdǎo 倡導 to lead; to advocate; to promote

chàngyì 倡議 to make a motion; to advocate

chàng 唱

1. to sing; to chant 2. to crow; to cry 3. a song or a singing part of a Chinese opera

chàngfǎndiào 唱反調 to air an opposing view

chànggē 唱歌 to sing songs; to sing

chàngjī 唱機 a record player or phonograph

chàngpán 唱盤 the turntable of a phonograph

chàngpiàn 唱片 a (phonograph) record or a disc

chàngpiào 唱票 to count votes aloud

chàngxì 唱戲 to sing an opera

chàngyóu 唱遊 a recreation class

chàngzhēn 唱針 a phonograph needle; a stylus

chàng 悵

disappointed; frustrated; dissatisfied; sorry

chàngrán 悵然 disappointed

chàngwǎng 悵惘 depressed; in low spirits

chàng 暢

1. smoothly; fluently 2. easily accessible 3. with gusto; to one's heart's content 4. long; expanding 5. luxuriant; luxuriance 6. (to state or elaborate) freely; without restraint; clear 7. very

chàngdá 暢達 clearly and smoothly

chànghuái 暢懷 to one's heart's content

chàngkuài 暢快 cheerful and exuberant

chàngsuǒ yùyán 暢所欲言 to

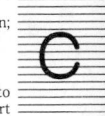

speak one's mind freely

chàngtán 暢談 to talk to one's heart's content

chàngtōng 暢通 unimpeded; unblocked

chàngxiāo 暢銷 a booming sale; to sell well

chàngxiāoshū 暢銷書 a best seller

chàngxíng wúzǔ 暢行無阻 to meet no obstacle wherever one goes

chàngyǐn 暢飲 to drink to one's heart's content

chàngyóu 暢遊 to enjoy a sightseeing tour

chāo 抄

1. to copy; to transcribe; transcription; to plagiarize 2. to confiscate 3. to seize; to take

chāoběn 抄本 a handwritten copy; a transcript

chāogǎo 抄稿 to make a neat copy (of a draft)

chāojiā mièmén 抄家滅門 to confiscate the property and exterminate the family (of an offender)

chāojìnlù 抄近路 to take a shortcut

chāolù 抄錄 to make a copy of; to transcribe

chāoxí 抄襲 1. to plagiarize; to copy off 2. to attack the flank of

chāoxiě 抄寫 to make a copy of; to transcribe

chāoxiěyuán 抄寫員 a copyist

chāo 超

1. to jump over; to leap over 2. to be more than; to exceed 3. to be better than; to excel; to surpass 4. to rise above; to transcend 5. to overtake

chāochē 超車 to overtake a car

chāochū 超出 to exceed; to surpass; to overtake

chāo'é 超額 to exceed a quota or target amount

chāofán rùshèng 超凡入聖 to transcend worldliness and attain holiness

chāoguò 超過 1. to exceed; to be

more than 2. to excel; to surpass; to outweigh

chāojí 超級 super

chāojí míngxīng 超級明星 a superstar

chāojí shìchǎng 超級市場 a supermarket

chāolíng 超齡 to be over the specified age

chāoqián 超前 1. (electricity) lead 2. to overtake

chāoqún 超群 head and shoulders above all others; preeminent; surpassing

chāorén 超人 a superman

chāoshēngbō 超聲波 supersonic waves

chāosù 超速 speeding

chāotuō 超脫 to transcend worldliness; to detach oneself from

chāoyīnbō 超音波 supersonic waves

chāoyuè 超越 1. to excel; to surpass 2. to fly across; to jump over

chāozài 超載 overloading; overload

chāozhī 超支 to overspend; to overdraw

chāozhòng 超重 1. an overload 2. excess; overweight

chāo 鈔

1. to copy; to transcribe 2. (also **chào**) bank notes

chāopiào 鈔票 bank notes; paper money

cháo 巢

1. living quarters in the trees 2. a bird's nest 3. a haunt; a den

cháoxué 巢穴 a den; a lair; a haunt

cháoxuè 巢穴 refer to **cháoxué** 巢穴

cháo 朝

1. an imperial court 2. a dynasty 3. to go to imperial court 4. to face

cháobài 朝拜 1. to worship; to pay respects to (a sovereign) 2. to pilgrimage

cháodài 朝代 a dynasty

cháogāng 朝綱 1. rules of an imperial court 2. the imperial court

cháojiàn 朝見 to be received in audience by a sovereign

cháojìn 朝覲 to be received in audience by a sovereign

cháoshān 朝山 to go on a pilgrimage

cháoshèng 朝聖 to go on a pilgrimage

cháotíng 朝廷 the court (of a sovereign); an imperial court

cháoyě 朝野 the government and the people

cháozhèng 朝政 the affairs of the state

cháo 嘲

to ridicule; to sneer; to mock; to deride

cháofěng 嘲諷 to sneer at; to taunt

cháonòng 嘲弄 to mock; to make fun of

cháoxiào 嘲笑 to laugh at; to jeer at; to sneer at; to deride

cháo 潮

1. the tide 2. damp; moist; wet 3. (now rarely, said of gold, silver, etc.) inferior in skill or fineness

cháoliú 潮流 1. tides 2. a current; a trend

cháoshī 潮濕 humid; damp

cháoshuǐ 潮水 the tide

cháoxī 潮汐 morning tide and evening tide; tides

cháoxì 潮汐 refer to **cháoxī** 潮汐

chǎo 吵

1. to quarrel; to wrangle; to dispute 2. to disturb; to annoy

chǎojià 吵架 to quarrel; to brawl; to argue

chǎonào 吵鬧 to quarrel noisily; to brawl

chǎozuǐ 吵嘴 to dispute

chǎo 炒

to fry; to stir-fry

chǎocài 炒菜 to fry vegetables or meat; fried dishes

chǎodàn 炒蛋 scrambled eggs

chǎodìpí 炒地皮 to engage in land speculation

chǎofàn 炒飯 to fry rice; fried rice

chǎogǔpiào 炒股票 to manipulate stock trading

chǎomǐfěn 炒米粉 to fry rice noodles; fried rice noodles

chǎomiàn 炒麵 to fry noodles; fried noodles

chǎorè 炒熱 1. to jack up the price of stocks by manipulation 2. to make an ordinary news event a top story by sensational reporting

chǎoyóuyú 炒魷魚 (slang) to be fired

chào 鈔

refer to **chāo** 鈔 2

chē 車 also jū

1. a vehicle 2. a wheeled machine 3. to carry in a cart 4. to shape (things) on a lathe; to lathe; to turn 5. to lift water by a watewheel

chēdào 車道 roads or lanes for vehicular traffic

chēdēng 車燈 the headlight of an autombile or a motorcycle or bicycle

chēfū 車夫 a cabman; a chauffeur; adriver; a rickshaw man: a carter

chēháng 車行 1. a vehicle dealer's shop 2. a taxi company

chēhuò 車禍 a traffic a vehicle

chēkù 車庫 a garage; a vehicle barn

chēliàng 車輛 vehiles; rolling stock

chēlún 車輪 wheels of a vehicle

chēlúnzhàn 車輪戰 to fight an enemy by turns in order to wear him down

chēmǎfèi 車馬費 transportation allowances

chēmén 車門 doors of a vehicle

chēpái 車牌 the license plate (on veicle)

chēpiào 車票 a train or bus ticket

chēshuǐ mǎlóng 車水馬龍 (literally) Carts flow like a stream and horses move like a dragon. —Traffic is heavy.

chēsù 車速 the speed of a motor vehicle

chēxiāng 車廂 cars (of a train); railway carriages; compartments

chēzhàn 車站 1. a railway station 2. a bus station; a bus stop; a bus tjrninal

chēzhǎng 車掌 a bus conductress or conductor

chēzhào 車照 a driver's license

chēzī 車資 a fare

chě 扯
1. to tear 2. to pull; to drag; to haul 3. to strain 3. to lump 4. to talk nonsense; to lie; to prevaricate; to digress

chěhòutuǐ 扯後腿 to hinder someone from action

chěhuǎng 扯謊 to tell a lie

chěpò 扯破 to tear to pieces or shreds

chězhù 扯住 to grasp firmly

chě 拆
refer to **chāi** 拆

chě 掣
1. to pull; to drag; to draw 2. to hinder 3. to snatch away

chěhòutuǐ 掣後腿 to hinder

chè 徹
1. penetrating 2. to remove 3. a tax in tithe 4. to manage; to cultivate (farms) 5. to destroy 6. to deprive

chèdǐ 徹底 1. (said of a stream, etc.) to be able to see the bottom 2. to get to the bottom of; thorough

chèdǐ chéngqīng 徹底澄清 to clarify a matter thoroughly

chègǔ 徹骨 penetrating the bone; to the bone

chètóu chèwěi 徹頭徹尾 thoroughly; from beginning to end

chèwù 徹悟 to understand thoroughly

chèyè 徹夜 all through the night

chè 澈
1. thoroughly; completely 2. to understand 3. clear water

chèchá 澈查 to investigate thoroughly

chèdǐ 澈底 thoroughly; completely

chè 撤
to remove; to withdraw; to take back

chèbàn 撤辦 to fire a delinquent official and subject him to disciplinary action

chèchū 撤出 (said of troops) to withdraw or pull out

chèchú 撤除 to abolish; to do away with; to remove; to dismantle

chèhuàn 撤換 to replace

chèhuí 撤回 to take back or withdraw

chèlí 撤離 (said of troops) to move away or withdraw

chèqù 撤去 to withdraw; to remove

chètuì 撤退 (said of troops) to move back or withdraw

chèxiāo 撤銷 to abolish; to do away with

chèzhí 撤職 to remove from office

chèzǒu 撤走 to withdraw; to remove

chēn 嗔
1. to be angry; to take offense; to fly into a temper 2. to be annoyed with

chén 臣
1. a subject; a vassal 2. to subjugate; to conquer 3. a term for "I" used by officials when addressing the king or emperor 4. (in ancient China) a polite term for "I" 5. a minister; an official; a statesman

chénfú 臣服 1. to be conquered or subjugated 2. to serve a king or emperor as his minister

chénliáo 臣僚 officials in a monarchy

chénmín 臣民 subjects of a

kingdom

chénqiè 臣妾 concubines; female attendants

chénzǐ 臣子 a minister of state; officials in ancient China

chén 沈

1. to sink; to submerge 2. to indulge in; to be addicted to 3. (said of sleep) deep; sound; fast 4. for a long time 5. delaying; postponement 6. heavy (in weight) 7. latent; hidden 8. to straighten (one's face); to put on a grave expression 9. to retain (one's composure); to restrain; to contain

chénchuán 沈船 1. a shipwreck 2. to scuttle a ship

chéndiāndiān 沈甸甸 1. (said of swords, etc.) heavy and not easy to wield 2. heavy (at heart); serious (looks)

chéndiàn 沈澱 to precipitate; to settle

chéndiàndiàn 沈甸甸 refer to **chéndiāndiān** 沈甸甸

chéndiànwù 沈澱物 sediment

chénfú 沈浮 1. ups and downs in a person's life 2. to follow or change with prevailing customs, practices, etc.

chénjí 沈寂 refer to **chénjì** 沈寂

chénjì 沈寂 1. newless; traceless 2. quiet; silent 3. to lie low

chénjìn 沈浸 1. to permeate; to submerge; to be steeped in 2. very erudite

chénjìng 沈靜 calm; quiet; placid

chénlún 沈淪 to drown and perish (in water, sins, etc.)

chénluò 沈落 to sink; to fall down

chénmèn 沈悶 1. depressed 2. dull and heavy (atmosphere); hot and humid

chénmí 沈迷 to indulge in; to wallow in

chénmiǎn 沈湎 to wallow in; to be abandoned (or given) to

chénmò 沈沒 to sink

chénmò 沈默 silence; silent; reticent

chénmò guǎyán 沈默寡言 taciturn; reticent

chénmò shìjīn 沈默是金 Silence is golden.

chénnì 沈溺 to be imbibed or to indulge in

chénshuì 沈睡 deep slumber; sound sleep

chénsī 沈思 to ponder; to contemplate; to meditate

chéntòng 沈痛 to be deeply grieved

chénxiāngmù 沈香木 aloeswood; eaglewood

chényín 沈吟 1. to hesitate 2. to ponder

chényú luòyàn 沈魚落雁 (said of women) extremely beautiful

chényuān 沈冤 an unredressed grievance or wrong of long standing

chénzhòng 沈重 1. heavy (in weight) 2. heavy (at heart); serious (looks) 3. calm, steady and graceful

chénzhùqì 沈住氣 Steady (on)!

chénzhuó 沈著 calm and steady; composed

chénzuì 沈醉 1. dead-drunk 2. to become intoxicated

chén 辰

1. the fifth of the Twelve Terrestrial Branches (**dìzhī** 地支) 2. 7:00~9:00 in the morning; early morning 3. a time 4. fortune; luck 5. a heavenly body—the sun, the moon and stars

chén 忱

1. sincere; sincerity 2. to rely on

chénkǔn 忱悃 sincere sentiments

chén 陳

1. a Chinese family name 2. to arrange; to display; to spread out 3. to tell, state, or narrate; to explain 4. old; stale; preserved for a long time 5. name of a dynasty (557-589 AD) 6. to make public

chénchén xiāngyīn 陳陳相因 to copy or follow precedents, old practices, etc.; writing without

new ideas

chénfǔ 陳腐 old or hackneyed (expressions, etc.); stale (food or fruit)

chénguī 陳規 out-of-date conventions

chénhuò 陳貨 old goods; goods from old stock

chénjī 陳跡 relics; vestiges; things of the past; an old trace

chénjiǔ 陳酒 old wine

chénjiù 陳舊 old; worn-out; outmoded; obsolete; shabby

chénliáng 陳糧 old grain

chénliè 陳列 to arrange and display; to set out; to exhibit

chénlièpǐn 陳列品 articles on display; exhibits

chénnián 陳年 of many years' standing

chénnián lǎojiǔ 陳年老酒 alcoholic drinks that have been preserved for a long time; aged wine

chénpímei 陳皮梅 sugar preserved prunes

chénqiāng làndiào 陳腔濫調 hackneyed expressions; cliches; corny statements

chénqíng 陳情 to give a full statement or account of a situation, etc.

chénshè 陳設 to display; to decorate; to exhibit; to set out; to furnish

chénshī 陳屍 to exhibit or expose a corpse

chénshù 陳述 to tell; to narrate; to state

chén 晨

morning; daybreak

chénguāng 晨光 daylight; daybreak

chénhūn 晨昏 morning and evening

chénhūn diāndǎo 晨昏顛倒 to mistake morning for evening and evening for morning

chénxī 晨夕 morning and evening

chénxī 晨曦 morning light; daybreak

chénxī 晨夕 refer to **chénxī** 晨夕

chén 塵

1. dust; dirt 2. trace; trail 3. this world; ways of the world 4. vice; sensual pleasures

chén'āi 塵埃 dust; dirt

chénfēng 塵封 to be laid idle for a long time

chénniàn 塵念 worldly thoughts

chénshì 塵世 this world; this mortal life

chénsú 塵俗 this world; this mortal life

chéntǔ 塵土 dust; dirt

chénxiāo 塵囂 a place filled with a hubbub and an uproar

chényuán 塵緣 worldly passions; mundane desires

chén 橙

refer to **chéng** 橙

chèn 趁

1. to take advantage of; to avail oneself of 2. while

chènhuǒ dǎjié 趁火打劫 (literally) to plunder a house when it is on fire—to try to profit from another's misfortune; to fish in troubled waters

chènrè 趁熱 1. while it is still hot 2. to act before it is too late

chènrén zhīwēi 趁人之危 to take advantage of others' perilous states

chènrén zhīwēi 趁人之危 refer to **chènrén zhīwēi** 趁人之危

chènshì 趁勢 to take advantage of the prevailing circumstances

chènzǎo 趁早 as early as possible

chèn 稱

fit; suitable; in accordance with

chènxīn 稱心 to have something as one's wish

chènxīn rúyì 稱心如意 very gratifying and satisfactory; happy and contented

chèn 襯

1. inner garments; underwear 2. to provide a background 3. a lin-

ing; a liner 4. to line

chènbù 襯布 lining cloth

chènqún 襯裙 a petticoat; an underskirt

chènshān 襯衫 a shirt

chèntuō 襯托 to bring into relief; to set off; to supplement; to embellish; to provide a contrast; a foil

chèn 讖

1. a prophecy; an omen 2. books about omens

chēng 稱

1. to weigh; to measure weight 2. to claim; to report; to declare 3. to call; to name; a name; an appellation 4. to offer as an excuse (as illness) 5. to say; to tell; to state 6. to speak lauda- tory words; to praise 7. to take up (arms, etc.)

chēngbà 稱霸 to become the most powerful nation in the world or part of the world; to hold an undisputed position of strength

chēngchén 稱臣 to be subjugat- ed; to submit to the victor

chēngdào 稱道 to praise or acclaim

chēnghào 稱號 a title; a desig- nation

chēnghu 稱呼 a name by which one addresses another; to address; to name

chēngxiōng dàodì 稱兄道弟 on first-name terms; very inti- mate

chēngxǔ 稱許 to approve and praise; approval and praise

chēngyù 稱譽 to praise; to acclaim; to extol

chēngzàn 稱讚 to praise; to acclaim

chēng 撐

1. to prop; to support 2. to stretch tight; to burst 3. to pole or punt (a raft or a boat) 4. to maintain; to keep up; to go on with 5. to open

chēngcháng zhǔfù 撐腸拄腹 to fill the stomach

chēngchǎngmiàn 撐場面 to

maintain an outward show of prosperity

chēngchí 撐持 to prop up; to sustain

chēngchuán 撐船 to pole (or punt) a boat

chēnggāntiào 撐竿跳 the pole vault

chēngkāi 撐開 to prop open

chēngpò 撐破 to burst

chēngsǎn 撐傘 to prop open an umbrella

chēngyāo 撐腰 to support, or to give backing to someone

chēngzhù 撐住 to prop with a pole; to prop from under

chēng 瞠

to look straight at; to stare at

chēnghū qíhòu 瞠乎其後 far behind, without any hope of catching up

chēngmù jiéshé 瞠目結舌 a- mazed and speechless

chéng 丞

1. to aid; to assist 2. a deputy to an official

chéngxiàng 丞相 the prime minister

chéng 成

1. completed; accomplished; fin- ished; fixed; settled; to accom- plish; to succeed; to complete 2. to achieve 3. to become 4. acceptable; all right 5. able; capable 6. one tenth 7. a Chinese family name

chéngbài 成敗 success or failure

chéngběn 成本 (commerce) cost

chéngcái 成材 to become a use- ful person

chéngduī 成堆 to pile up

chéngfèn 成分 1. an ingredient; a component 2. a factor 3. per- sonal background

chénggōng 成功 success; to suc- ceed

chéngguī 成規 an established practice, rule or regulation; a rut

chéngguǒ 成果 achievements; the fruits (of efforts)

chénghé tǐtǒng 成何體統

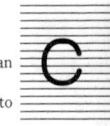

C

What a scandal!

chénghūn 成婚 to get married

chéngjī 成績 records established or set

chéngjīdān 成績單 a report card

chéngjiā 成家 (said of men reaching adulthood) to get married

chéngjiàn 成見 a prejudice; a bias

chéngjiāo 成交 to get accepted by both parties, or to go through a business deal; to strike

chéngjiù 成就 an achievement; an accomplishment; to accomplish

chéngjiùgǎn 成就感 a sense of fulfillment

chénglì 成立 1. to establish; to found; to set up 2. (said of a relation, theory, etc.) to hold good or to be recognized as irrefutable

chéngmíng 成名 to become famous

chéngnián 成年 to reach adulthood; to come of age

chéngnián léiyuè 成年累月 year after year and month after month

chéngpǐn 成品 finished products

chéngqì 成器 to become a useful person

chéngqiān chéngwàn 成千成萬 countless; numerous

chéngqīn 成親 to get married

chéngquán 成全 to help (others) accomplish something

chéngqún 成群 in groups; in large numbers

chéngqún jiéduì 成群結隊 to band together

chéngrén 成人 an adult; a grown-up

chéngrì 成日 the whole day; all day

chéngshú 成熟 to mature; to ripen

chéngshuāng chéngduì 成雙成對 in pairs

chéngtào 成套 to form a complete set

chéngtiān 成天 all day long; the whole day

chéngwéi 成爲 to become; to turn into

chéngwéi pàoyǐng 成爲泡影 to come to nothing

chéngwén 成文 existing writings

chéngxiào 成效 result; effect

chéngxiào zhuōzhù 成效卓著 The achievement is outstanding.

chéngxiào zhuózhù 成效卓著 refer to **chéngxiào zhuōzhù** 成效卓著

chéngxíng 成行 to embark on a journey

chéngxíng 成形 to take shape

chéngyàng 成樣 an established model (of manufactured goods)

chéngyào 成藥 patent medicine

chéngyī 成衣 ready-made clothes; garments

chéngyīn 成因 the cause of formation

chéngyǔ 成語 an idiom; a phrase

chéngyuán 成員 a member

chéngzāi 成災 to cause disaster

chéngzhǎng 成長 to grow up; growth

chéng 呈

1. to submit, present, or hand in (to a superior) 2. to show, manifest, expose, display, disclose, exhibit, etc. 3. a petition or appeal

chéngbào 呈報 to present or submit a report

chéngdì 呈遞 to handle or submit (to higher authorities)

chéngjiāo 呈交 to handle or submit (to higher authorities)

chéngqǐng 呈請 It is requested that....

chéngsòng 呈送 to forward or send (to a higher agency)

chéngwén 呈文 a petition; an appeal

chéngxiàn 呈現 to appear; to emerge

chéngxiàn 呈獻 to present (to a superior)

C

chéngyuè 呈閱 to submit (to a superior or higher agency) for perusal

chéng 承

1. to receive; to inherit; to succeed 2. to undertake; to make it one's responsibility 3. by (order of) 4. to continue; to carry on 5. to hold; to contain; to support; to bear 6. to confess 7. with thanks; obliged 8. to please

chéngbàn 承辦 to handle (a case); to be responsible for (a task); to undertake

chéngbāo 承包 to contract

chéngbāoshāng 承包商 a contractor

chéngdān 承擔 to take or to shoulder (the responsibility, task, etc.)

chéngfèng 承奉 by order of; in compliance with an order

chénggòu 承購 to act as a purchasing agent

chéngguǎn 承管 to take full charge and responsibility (of)

chénghuān xīxià 承歡膝下 to please one's parents by living with them

chéngjiē 承接 to receive and carry on; to continue; to succeed to

chénglǎn 承攬 to take full charge or responsibility (usually under contract)

chéngméng 承蒙 to be obliged to

chéngnuò 承諾 a promise; to promise

chéngpíng 承平 successive peaceful reigns

chéngrèn 承認 1. to confess; to admit 2. to recognize (a nation, etc.)

chéngshòu 承受 to take; to receive; to accept; to bear

chéngxí 承襲 to inherit (a title, etc.)

chéngxiān qǐhòu 承先啟後 to be heir to ancient sages and the teacher of posterity (usually said of a person of profound learning)

chéngzài 承載 to bear the weight of

chéngzū 承租 to rent

chéng 城

1. a city; a town 2. the walls of a city 3. to surround a city with walls

chéngbāng 城邦 a city-state

chéngbǎo 城堡 a fort; a castle

chéngfǔ 城府 a mind; a mental outlook

chénghào 城壕 the moat of a city

chénghé 城河 the moat of a city

chéngmén 城門 the gate of a city wall

chéngqiáng 城牆 the city wall

chéngshì 城市 a city or town

chéng 乘

1. to ride; to mount 2. to avail oneself of; to take advantage of 3. to multiply

chéngchē 乘車 to take an automobile

chéngfǎ 乘法 (arithmetic) multiplication

chéngfāng 乘方 (mathematics) power

chéngfēng pòlàng 乘風破浪 great ambition

chénghào 乘號 the sign of multiplication

chéngjī 乘機 1. to avail oneself of an opportunity; to seize the right time 2. to ride an airplane

chéngjī 乘積 (arithmetic) the product

chéngkè 乘客 a passenger

chéngliáng 乘涼 to cool oneself in the shade

chénglóng kuàixù 乘龍快婿 an ideal son-in-law

chéngmì 乘冪 (mathematics) power

chéngrén zhīwēi 乘人之危 to take advantage of somebody when he is not in a position to resist

chéngrén zhīwéi 乘人之危 refer to **chéngrén zhīwēi** 乘人之危

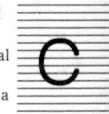

C

chéngshèng zhuíjí 乘勝追擊 to pursue enemy troops in retreat

chéngshèng zhuíjí 乘勝追擊 refer to **chéngshèng zhuíjí** 乘勝追擊

chéngshì 乘勢 to take advantage of circumstances

chéngshù 乘數 multiplicator or multiplier

chéngxìng 乘興 on the spur of the moment

chéngxìng érwǎng, bàixìng érguī 乘興而往，敗興而歸 to go with great enthusiasm and return disappointed

chéngxū érrù 乘虛而入 to take advantage of a weak point

chéng 盛
1. to take (loose material) into a bowl or basin 2. to hold; to contain

chéng 程
1. a form; a pattern 2. degree; extent 3. a schedule; an agenda; order 4. a journey; a road 5. distance 6. a Chinese family name

chéngdù 程度 1. degree; extent 2. standard 3. general achievement in academic studies

chéngshì 程式 1. standard procedures 2. (computer) a program

chéngshì shèjì 程式設計 programing

chéngxù 程序 1. procedures; processes 2. (computer) program

chéng 誠
1. sincere; honest; cordial; sincerity 2. true; real; truly; indeed; actually

chéngfēi suǒliào 誠非所料 It is really unexpected.

chéngfú 誠服 to obey (or submit) willingly

chéngkěn 誠懇 sincere; true-hearted; cordial

chéngshí 誠實 honest; upright; trustworthy; honesty

chéngxīn 誠心 sincerity; whole-heartedness

chéngxīn chéngyì 誠心誠意 earnestly and sincerely

chéngyì 誠意 sincerity; good faith

chéngzhì 誠摯 sincere; true-hearted; cordial

chéng 澄 also **dèng**
1. clear and still (water) 2. to pacify

chéngchè 澄澈 crystal clear

chéngqīng 澄清 1. to set right 2. to clarify 3. clear

chéng 橙 also **chén**
the orange

chénghuángsè 橙黃色 orange (color)

chéngzhī 橙汁 orange juice

chéng 懲
1. to punish; to chastise; to reprimand; to reprove; to warn 2. to stop

chéngbàn 懲辦 to take disciplinary action against

chéng'è quànshàn 懲惡勸善 to punish wickedness and encourage virtue

chéngfá 懲罰 to punish; to penalize; a penalty

chéngjiè 懲戒 to reprimand; to punish

chéngyī jǐngbǎi 懲一儆百 to punish one person as a warning to hundred others

chéngzhì 懲治 to remedy by punishment

chěng 逞
1. to indulge in (pleasures, etc.) 2. to use up; to exhaust 3. to display; to show off 4. fast; speedy 5. to presume on; presumptuous

chěngnéng 逞能 to display or show off one's ability, feat, etc.; boastful

chěngqiáng 逞強 to parade one's superiority; to bully; to throw one's weight around

chěng 騁
1. to go swiftly; to speed 2. to exert; to unfold; to develop 3. to give free play to; to lend wings to

chěngmù 騁目 to look as far as the eyes can see

chèng 秤
  1. (also **píng**) a weighing scale; a balance; a steelyard 2. to weigh with a scale, etc.

chèngchuí 秤錘 the weight used with a steelyard

chèng 稱
  a steelyard; a weighing machine

chī 吃
  1. to eat 2. to sustain 3. (also **jí**) to stammer; to stutter

chībuliǎo, dǒuzhezǒu 吃不了，兜著走 to land oneself in serious trouble

chībuxiāo 吃不消 cannot stand or bear

chībuzhǔn 吃不準 maybe; perhaps; probably

chīchī hēhē 吃吃喝喝 to be interested only in eating and drinking

chīcù 吃醋 to be jealous

chīdexiāo 吃得消 to be able to stand (exertion, fatigue, etc.)

chīdòufu 吃豆腐 (slang) to make advances to a woman without serious intentions

chīfàn 吃飯 to eat, take, or have a meal

chīguānsi 吃官司 to be sued (in a court of law)

chīguāng 吃光 to eat up

chīhē piáodǔ 吃喝嫖賭 a dissipated or dissolute life

chīhē wánlè 吃喝玩樂 to idle away one's time in seeking pleasure

chījiǎozi lǎohǔ 吃角子老虎 a slot machine

chījǐn 吃緊 (usually said of a military situation) hard pressed, or critical

chījīng 吃驚 surprised; frightened; startled

chīkǔ 吃苦 to suffer hardship

chīkǔ nàiláo 吃苦耐勞 diligent; hardworking

chīkǔtou 吃苦頭 to suffer

chīkuī 吃虧 to be at a disadvantage; to suffer a loss

chīlǐ páwài 吃裡扒外 to work

for the interests of an opposing group at the expense of one's own

chīlì 吃力 tired; exhausted

chīlì bùtǎohǎo 吃力不討好 to work laboriously only to earn criticisms

chīnǎi 吃奶 to suck the breast

chīruǎnfàn 吃軟飯 to live on the earnings of a prostitute

chīsù 吃素 to practice vegetarianism

chīxiánfàn 吃閒飯 to live like a parasite

chīxiāng 吃香 to be welcome or valued everywhere; popular

chī yǎbakuī 吃啞巴虧 to be cheated or suffer a loss but unable to talk about it for one reason or another

chīyào 吃藥 to take medicine

chīzhòng 吃重 to play an important role

chī 嗤
  to laugh or chuckle sneeringly

chīdǐ 嗤詆 to laugh at; to mock

chīzhī yìbí 嗤之以鼻 to pooh-pooh

chī 鴟
  1. a kite 2. an owl 3. wine-cups

chīxiāo 鴟鴞 an owl

chī 癡（痴）
  1. idiotic; silly; foolish; stupid 2. to besot

chīdāi 癡呆 stupid; foolish; imbecile; idiotic; dull; silly

chīmí 癡迷 infatuated; besotted

chīqíng 癡情 blind love; blind passion; infatuation

chīrén shuōmèng 癡人說夢 an idiot's gibberish; nonsense

chīxiào 癡笑 to giggle; to titter

chīxīn 癡心 1. blind love; infatuation 2. a silly wish

chīxīn wàngxiǎng 癡心妄想 silly and fantastic notions; daydreaming

chī 魑
  a mountain demon resembling a tiger

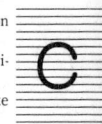

chīmèi wǎngliǎng 魑魅魍魉
all sorts of monsters and goblins

chí 池
1. a pond; a pool; a moat 2. an enclosed space with raised sides

chíshuǐ 池水 pond water

chítáng 池塘 a pond

chíyán 池鹽 lake salt

chíyú zhīyāng 池魚之殃 disasters brought on by others

chízhǎo 池沼 ponds and swamps

chízi 池子 1. a pond 2. orchestra stalls in a theater

chí 弛 also **shǐ**
to unstring; to relax; to neglect

chíhuǎn 弛緩 to relax

chí 治
refer to **zhì** 治 1, 5, 6

chí 持
1. to hold; to grasp 2. to maintain; to support; to keep 3. to manage 4. a tie or stalemate

chídāo 持刀 to hold a knife

chíjiā 持家 1. to run one's home 2. to keep the family estates

chíjiǔ 持久 to hold out; to last for a long time; lasting; durable

chípíng 持平 fair and unbiased

chíqiāng 持槍 1. to hold a gun 2. (military) to port arms

chíxù 持續 continuous; incessant; uninterrupted

chíyǒu 持有 to hold

chízhī yǐhéng 持之以恆 to persevere

chí 匙
a spoon

chí 馳
1. to go swiftly; to fleet; to rush; to speed 2. to exert; to exercise 3. to spread; to propagate

chíchěng 馳騁 1. to rush about on horseback 2. to play an active part in

chímíng 馳名 1. to spread one's fame 2. renowned

chímíng zhōngwài 馳名中外 renowned at home and abroad

chí 踟
to hesitate

chíchú 踟躕 1. linked together 2. to hesitate 3. a comb 4. to be in perplexity

chí 遲
1. late 2. slow; dilatory; tardy 3. to delay 4. (said of a person) dull; stupid 5. a Chinese family name

chídào 遲到 to come or arrive late

chídùn 遲鈍 stupid; awkward; clumsy

chíhuǎn 遲緩 slow; tardy; tardiness

chíyí 遲疑 to hesitate; hesitancy

chízǎo 遲早 sooner or later

chǐ 尺
1. a unit in Chinese linear measurement, equivalent to 1/3 meter 2. a ruler; a rule

chǐcun 尺寸 a small quantity

chǐdú 尺牘 letters; correspondence

chǐdù 尺度 measure; a scale

chǐhàn 尺翰 letters; correspondence

chǐmǎ 尺碼 1. dimensions (of an object) 2. measure; size

chǐ 呎
the foot (a unit of length in English measure)

chǐ 侈
1. wasteful; luxurious; lavish; extravagant 2. to exaggerate; bragging 3. evildoing 4. excessive

chǐmí 侈靡 extravagant; wasteful

chǐyán 侈言 to exaggerate; to swagger

chǐ 恥(耻)
shame; disgrace; humiliation; to feel ashamed

chǐxiào 恥笑 to laugh at; to ridicule

chǐ 褫
1. to strip off; to deprive of 2. to

undress forcibly

chǐduó gōngquán 褫奪公權
to strip or deprive one of one's
civil rights

chǐ 齒

1. teeth 2. age 3. to speak of; to
mention 4. a toothlike part of
anything

chǐgòu 齒垢 tartar (on the teeth)

chǐhán 齒寒 (said of either of
two interdependent beings) to
suffer due to failure of the other

chǐkē 齒科 dentistry

chǐlún 齒輪 a cogwheel; a gear
wheel; a gear

chǐlěng 齒冷 to scorn; to ridicule; to jeer

chǐrú biānbèi 齒如編貝 very
beautiful teeth

chǐwáng shécún 齒亡舌存
The strong is more likely to fall
than the weak.

chǐyá yúlùn 齒牙餘論 to
praise others

chǐyín 齒齦 gums (of the teeth)

chì 叱

to scold; to revile

chìhè 叱喝 to yell at

chìzhà fēngyún 叱吒風雲
(said of a dictator, conqueror,
etc.) to lord it over the world

chì 斥

1. to accuse; to blame; to
reproach; to reprove; to censure
2. to expel; to drive off; to banish; to eject 3. to survey; to
observe; to reconnoiter

chìmà 斥罵 to denounce; to scold

chìzé 斥責 to reprimand; to
rebuke; to censure; to denounce

chì 赤

1. red 2. bare; naked 3. sincere;
loyal; single-hearted

chìbó 赤膊 with the upper half of
the body bared; naked to the
waist

chìchéng 赤誠 sincerity; loyal;
upright

chìdǎn zhōngxīn 赤膽忠心
utter devotion

chìdào 赤道 1. the equator 2.

(astronomy) the celestial equator

chìhuà 赤化 to communize

chìjiǎo 赤腳 1. bare feet 2. barefooted

chìluǒ 赤裸 1. stark-naked;
naked 2. unadorned; frank; plain

chìpín 赤貧 extreme poverty

chìshǒu 赤手 1. bare hands 2.
barehanded

chìshǒu kōngquán 赤手空拳
1. bare hands 2. barehanded

chìzǐ zhīxīn 赤子之心 (literally) a child's heart—man's natural kindness

chìzì 赤字 a deficit

chì 敕(勅)

1. an imperial decree 2. orders
given to demons and spirits by
Taoist priests when they exercise magic powers

chìlìng 敕令 an imperial decree,
edict, command, or ordinance

chì 翅

1. wings 2. fins

chìbǎng 翅膀 wings

chì 飭

1. severe 2. reverent; respectful;
careful 3. to manage; to make
ready; to keep in order 4. to
order; to instruct or direct

chìlìng 飭令 to order; to instruct
or direct

chì 熾

1. intense; vigorous; energetic 2.
burning hot; flaming

chìrè 熾熱 intense heat; intensely
hot

chōng 充

1. full; sufficient 2. to fill 3. to
fake; to cheat; to pretend

chōngchì 充斥 filled with; rife

chōngdāng 充當 to serve as; to
act as

chōngdiàn 充電 to recharge (a
battery)

chōngdiànqì 充電器 a charger

chōng'ěr bùwén 充耳不聞 to
turn a deaf ear to

chōngfēn 充分 fully; sufficient;
enough

chōnggōng 充公 to confiscate

chōngjī 充飢 to satisfy one's hunger

chōngmǎn 充滿 to fill up; full of; filled with

chōngpèi 充沛 brimming (with energy)

chōngqíliàng 充其量 at most; at best

chōngsè 充塞 full of; filled with

chōngshí 充實 1. rich; abundant 2. to fill out 3. to strengthen or improve

chōngshù 充數 to fill a vacancy with an incompetent person

chōngyù 充裕 abundance; sufficiency; rich

chōngzú 充足 plenty; abundant; sufficient

chōng 忡
worried; anxious; uneasy; sad

chōngchōng 忡忡 worried and sad

chōng 沖
1. to wash away; to rinse; to flush 2. to soar; to rise rapidly or shoot up 3. to pour water (to powder, etc.); to infuse 4. empty; void 5. to dash against; to clash with 6. childhood 7. to neutralize; to make void

chōngchá 沖茶 to make tea

chōngdàn 沖淡 1. to dilute 2. to play down 3. to make few demands on life

chōnghūntóu 沖昏頭 to turn someone's head; dizzy

chōngjī 沖積 alluviation

chōngjīshàn 沖積扇 (geology) alluvial fan

chōngjīwù 沖積物 sediment; deposit

chōngkāishuǐ 沖開水 to pour boiled water on

chōngsàn 沖散 to disperse by the use of force

chōngshuā 沖刷 erosion; to scour; to wash out

chōngtiān 沖天 to shoot up to the sky

chōngxǐ 沖洗 1. to flush 2. (photography) to develop or process

negatives

chōng 舂
1. to thresh (grain in order to remove the husk) 2. to pound

chōng 衝
1. to rush; to thrust; to forge ahead; to dash 2. to charge forward; to hit with force 3. a thoroughfare; a hub; a strategic place 4. to offend

chōngchū 衝出 to rush out; to dash out

chōngcì 衝刺 a spurt; a sprint

chōngdòng 衝動 1. an impulse; a sudden urge 2. to be excited

chōngfēng xiànzhèn 衝鋒陷陣 to charge ahead and take enemy positions

chōngjī 衝擊 to strike against; to pound against; to charge

chōngjí 衝擊 refer to **chōngjī** 衝擊

chōngjìn 衝勁 aggressiveness; enterprising spirit; drive

chōnglàng 衝浪 to surf

chōnglì 衝力 impulsive forces; momentum

chōngtū 衝突 a conflict; a fight; a clash

chōngtú 衝突 refer to **chōngtū** 衝突

chōngzhuàng 衝撞 1. to collide; to ram 2. to offend; to treat impolitely

chōng 憧
1. indecisive; irresolute 2. to aspire; to yearn

chōngjǐng 憧憬 to imagine something or a place with yearning or longing

chóng 重
1. to pile one upon another 2. to repeat; to duplicate 3. layers 4. double; manifold 5. numerous

chóngcāo jiùyè 重操舊業 to return to one's old trade

chóngdǎo fùzhé 重蹈覆轍 to follow the same old disastrous road; to fall into the same trap

chóngdào fùchè 重蹈覆轍 refer to **chóngdào fùzhé** 重蹈

chóngdié 重疊 to pile one upon another; to superimpose

chóngfǎn 重返 to go back; to return

chóngfàn 重犯 to repeat (an error or offense)

chóngféng 重逢 to meet again; to have a reunion

chóngfù 重複 1. to repeat; repetition 2. to duplicate

chóngjiàn 重建 to rebuild; to reconstruct

chóngjiàn tiānrì 重見天日 to see daylight again—to regain freedom; to be liberated or emancipated

chónglái 重來 to do a thing over again; to repeat from the start; to return

chóngqǐ lúzào 重起爐灶 to begin all over again

chóngshēn 重申 to reaffirm; to reiterate; to restate

chóngshī gùjì 重施故技 to play the same old trick

chóngwéi 重圍 a many-layered siege; a tight encirclement

chóngwēn jiùmèng 重溫舊夢 to revive an old dream; to reproduce the good old days

chóngxīn 重新 anew; afresh

chóngxiū jiùhǎo 重修舊好 to renew friendly relations; to patch up; to reconcile

chóngyǎn 重演 to repeat the performance of; to repeat

chóngyáng 重洋 the ocean

chóngyóu 重遊 to revisit

chóngzhěng qígǔ 重整旗鼓 to rearm; to make preparations for a comeback

chóng 崇

1. to honor; to respect; to revere; to adore; to worship 2. high; lofty; noble; dignified; exalted

chóngbài 崇拜 to worship; to idolize; to adore

chónggāo 崇高 lofty; sublime; high

chóngjìng 崇敬 to honor; to revere

chóngshān jùnlǐng 崇山峻嶺 lofty and precipitous peaks

chóngshàng 崇尚 1. to uphold; to advocate 2. fashion; a trend

chóngyáng 崇洋 to admire everything of foreign (especially western) origin

chóng 蟲

insects; worms

chónghài 蟲害 damage to farm crops caused by pests; insect pest

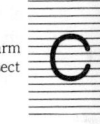

chǒng 寵

1. a concubine 2. to favor; to dote on; to patronize 3. favor or love

chǒng'ài 寵愛 to favor or patronize

chǒng'ér 寵兒 a favored person; a favorite

chǒnghuài 寵壞 to spoil (a child)

chǒngrǔ 寵辱 in favor or out of favor

chǒngwù 寵物 a pet

chǒngxìng 寵幸 to show special favor to a lady or minister

chòng 衝

1. to head or go (south, north, etc.) 2. strong (smell) 3. brave and fierce 4. for (your, his, etc.) sake 5. to direct (one's attack, etc.) toward

chōu 抽

1. to draw out; to pull out; take out 2. to sprout; to put forth shoots; to bud 3. to take away 4. to whip; to lash 5. to smoke (cigarettes, etc.) 6. to shrink

chōuchá 抽查 to investigate, survey or test a part of a group

chōuchū 抽出 to draw out; to pull out

chōudǎ 抽打 to lash; to whip

chōudiào 抽調 to transfer (personnel or material)

chōufēngjī 抽風機 an exhaust fan

chōujiǎng 抽獎 to draw a lottery or raffle

chōujīn 抽筋 to be seized by spasms or cramps

chōukǎo 抽考 1. to select at random a few students from a class for a test 2. an unannounced quiz or test

chōukōng 抽空 to find time (to do something)

chōuqì 抽泣 to sob

chōuqiān 抽籤 to draw (or cast) lots

chōuqǔ 抽取 1. to charge or collect a certain percentage of a sum 2. to take at random from a batch of samples, etc.

chōushēn 抽身 to get away (while one is fully occupied)

chōushuǐ 抽水 to pump water

chōushuǐ mǎtǒng 抽水馬桶 a flush toilet

chōushuì 抽稅 to levy taxes

chōusī bōjiǎn 抽絲剝繭 to make a painstaking investigation or examination

chōuti 抽屜 a drawer

chōuxiàng 抽象 abstract

chōuxiànghuà 抽象畫 abstract painting

chōuxīn zhǐfèi 抽薪止沸 to stop or prevent trouble by removing the cause

chōuxuǎn 抽選 to select from a lot

chōuyān 抽煙 to smoke (a pipe, cigars, cigarets, etc.)

chōuyàng 抽樣 1. a sample 2. sampling

chōuyàng diàochá 抽樣調查 sampling

chōuyē 抽噎 to sob

chóu 仇
1. a foe; an enemy; a rival; an adversary 2. hatred; enmity; antagonism; hostility 3. to hate 4. a Chinese family name

chóudí 仇敵 an enemy

chóuhèn 仇恨 1. hatred; enmity 2. to hate

chóurén 仇人 an enemy; a foe

chóushā 仇殺 a murder committed out of vendetta

chóushì 仇視 to regard with hostility

chóu 惆
1. regretful; rueful; disconsolate; melancholy 2. frustrated; disappointed

chóuchàng 惆悵 rueful; regretful

chóu 稠
1. dense; closely crowded together 2. (said of liquids) thick; viscous

chóumì 稠密 crowded; dense

chóu 酬
1. to toast; to offer or present a cup of spirits 2. to reward; to requite; to reciprocate; reward 3. to fulfill; to realize

chóujīn 酬金 a cash reward; a bounty

chóuláo 酬勞 to reward services

chóuxiè 酬謝 to thank or reward (with money or gifts)

chóu 愁
1. distressed; worried; unhappy; sad; melancholy 2. depressing; saddening; gloomy 3. to worry about; to be anxious about 4. sorrow; woe

chóukǔ 愁苦 distress; misery

chóuméi bùzhǎn 愁眉不展 to wear a sad or distressed expression

chóuméi kǔliǎn 愁眉苦臉 distressed expression

chóuróng mǎnmiàn 愁容滿面 to wear a sad look; to look distressed

chóuxù 愁緒 a sad mood; a gloomy mood

chóu 綢
1. a general name of all silk fabrics 2. fine and delicate 3. (now rarely) to twine and tangle

chóuduàn 綢緞 a general name of silk goods

chóuduànzhuāng 綢緞莊 a mercery

chóu 儔
1. a companion or companions 2.

a class

chóu 疇
1. agricultural land; fields 2. who 3. formerly; previously 4. a class; a category; a rank

chóu 籌
1. chips, tallies, etc. for calculating purposes 2. to plan; to prepare 3. to raise (money) 4. to assess or estimate

chóubàn 籌辦 to plan and sponsor (a show, sports event, school, etc.)

chóubèi 籌備 to prepare and plan; to arrange

chóuhuà 籌畫 to deliberate and plan; a layout

chóujiàn 籌建 to prepare the construction of

chóukuǎn 籌款 to raise funds

chóumǎ 籌碼 chips (in gambling, etc.); a counter

chóumù 籌募 to raise; to collect (funds)

chóu 躊
1. hesitant 2. complacent; confident

chóuchú 躊躇 1. to hesitate; to waver; to falter; to vacillate 2. confident; complacent

chǒu 丑
1. the second of the twelve "Terrestrial Branches" (**dìzhī** 地支) 2. the period of the day from 1 to 3 a.m. 3. a clown

chǒujiǎo 丑角 refer to **chǒujué** 丑角

chǒujué 丑角 a comedian

chǒu 醜
1. ugly; homely 2. abominable; vile; bad 3. shameful; infamous

chǒu'è 醜惡 ugly; repulsive; hideous

chǒuhuà 醜化 to smear; to uglify; to defame

chǒulòu 醜陋 ugly; bad-looking

chǒushì 醜事 scandal

chǒutài 醜態 scandalous behavior; a disgraceful manner

chǒuwén 醜聞 scandal

chòu 臭
1. stinking; smelly 2. notorious; flagrant; disreputable 3. very; much; soundly; sternly 4. (said of friendship, love, etc.) to cool off 5. foul and petty; worthless 6. an odor; a stench

chòuchóng 臭蟲 a bedbug

chòudòufu 臭豆腐 the fermented bean curd (a popular Chinese food item)

chòuliǎn 臭臉 a long face

chòumà 臭罵 a stern scolding; to scold soundly

chòuměi 臭美 presumptuous; smug

chòumíng 臭名 an notorious reputation

chòupí'náng 臭皮囊 the human body

chòuqì chōngtiān 臭氣沖天 a stinking smell assaulting one's nostrils

chòuwèi xiāngtóu 臭味相投 birds of the same feather

chòuxiǎozi 臭小子 a bum; a tramp

chòuyǎngcéng 臭氧層 the ozone layer

chū 出
1. to go out; to come out 2. to produce; to reproduce 3. to beget 4. to happen or occur; to incur 5. to put forth; to bud 6. to divorce (a wife, etc.) 7. to chase away; to banish 8. to expend; to pay out 9. to escape; to leave (one's home, etc.) 10. to appear 11. to take office 12. to vent (one's anger, etc.)

chūbǎn 出版 to publish

chūbǎnwù 出版物 publications

chūbǎnzhě 出版者 a publisher

chūbǎn zìyóu 出版自由 freedom of publication

chūbìn 出殯 to carry a coffin to the grave for burial

chūbīng 出兵 to dispatch troops

chūcāo 出操 to drill; to train (soldiers, etc.)

chūchāi 出差 to go out of town on business

chūchǎn 出產 to produce or grow

chūchǎng 出廠 (said of a product) to leave the factory

chūchāo 出超 a favorable balance of trade

chūchǒu 出醜 to make a scene; to lose face

chūchù 出處 the source of an allusion or a quotation

chūcuò 出錯 to make mistakes

chūdiǎnzi 出點子 to offer advice

chūdòng 出動 to dispatch or send out

chū'ěr fǎn'ěr 出爾反爾 to renege on one's promise

chūfā 出發 to set out; to leave for

chūfādiǎn 出發點 1. the starting point 2. a basis; premises 3. a motive

chūfēngtou 出風頭 to be in the spotlight

chūgǎng 出港 1. to leave (a) port 2. to send (goods) abroad

chūgé 出閣 (said of a girl) to get married

chūguǐ 出軌 to derail

chūguó 出國 to go abroad

chūhǎi 出海 to leave (a) port; to go to sea

chūhǎikǒu 出海口 an estuary

chūhàn 出汗 to perspire; to sweat

chūháng 出航 1. to set sail 2. to set out on a flight

chūhū yìwài 出乎意外 unexpectedly

chūjí 出擊 to leave (a base, camp, position, etc.) to attack or raid (the enemy)

chūjī 出擊 refer to chūjī 出擊

chūjiā 出家 (Buddhism) to leave home and become a monk or nun

chūjià 出嫁 to get married

chūjiè 出界 (sports) out of bounds; outside

chūjìng 出境 to leave a place or country

chūjìngzhèng 出境證 an exit permit

chūjú 出局 (baseball) out

chūkǒu 出口 1. to export 2. to utter; to speak 3. an exit (in a theater, etc.)

chūkǒu chéngzhāng 出口成章 One's tongue is the pen of a ready writer.

chūkǒuhuò 出口貨 exports

chūkǒu shāngrén 出口傷人 to make insulting remarks

chūlái 出來 1. to come out; to appear 2. to make out 3. to bring to pass

chūlèi bácuì 出類拔萃 outstanding; eminent

chūlì 出力 to devote one's efforts to

chūliè 出列 to leave one's place in the ranks

chūlóng 出籠 to become current

chūlù 出路 1. the prospects (of a career, etc.) 2. an outlet

chūmǎ 出馬 to go out and face something

chūmài 出賣 1. to sell 2. to betray

chūmáobìng 出毛病 to be or go out of order; to go wrong

chūmén 出門 to leave one's home; to take a trip

chūmiàn 出面 to assume the responsibility (in mediation, negotiations, etc.)

chūmíng 出名 to become famous; famous

chūmò wúcháng 出沒無常 to appear and disappear at unpredictable places and times

chū'nà 出納 a teller or treasurer

chūpǐn 出品 products

chūqí 出奇 1. extraordinary 2. (to win) by surprise

chūqí bùyì 出其不意 to take by surprise; to catch (someone) off guard

chūqí zhìshèng 出奇制勝 to win by surprise

chūqì 出氣 to vent one's anger

chūqián 出錢 to provide the funds

chūqín 出勤 to take a business

trip

chūqu 出去 1. to go out 2. Get out!

chūràng 出讓 to sell; for sale

chūrén tóudì 出人頭地 to be somebody; to stand out among one's fellows

chūrén yìbiǎo 出人意表 beyond expectation

chūrèn 出任 to take up the post of

chūrù 出入 1. to come and go 2. receipts and expenditures

chūsè 出色 outstanding; remarkable

chūshēn 出身 backgrounds; qualifications

chūshén 出神 1. absorbed in 2. absentminded

chūshén rùhuà 出神入化 superb; out-of-this-world; uncanny (feats, skill, etc.)

chūshēng 出生 to be born

chūshēng 出聲 to make a sound; to speak

chūshēng rùsǐ 出生入死 to risk one's life

chūshī 出師 1. to move soldiers forward for attack 2. to complete one's apprenticeship in a trade and make a debut as a professional

chūshǐ 出使 to be appointed as a diplomatic envoy

chūshì 出示 to show (something to someone)

chūshì 出事 to be in trouble; to have an accident

chūshǒu 出手 1. to sell 2. to take on a job 3. an offer 4. to reach out with one's hand

chūshòu 出售 to sell

chūshū 出書 to publish books

chūtí 出題 1. to set a theme 2. to set questions

chūtíng 出庭 to appear in court

chūtóu 出頭 to make good or to succeed

chūtǔ 出土 to come out of earth

chūwài 出外 to leave for a distant place

chūxí 出席 to attend or to be

present at

chūxi 出息 1. promising 2. profit

chūxiàn 出現 to appear; to emerge

chūxiě 出血 refer to **chūxuè** 出血

chūxuè 出血 bleeding; hemorrhage

chūxún 出巡 to go on an inspection trip

chūyán bùxùn 出言不遜 to utter insulting remarks; to insult

chūyángxiàng 出洋相 to make a fool of oneself (especially in public)

chūyóu 出遊 to go on an excursion

chūyuàn 出院 to leave the hospital

chūzhěn 出診 to be on house call

chūzhēng 出征 to go out to battle

chūzhòng 出衆 outstanding; foremost

chūzhǔyì 出主意 1. to scheme; to provide an idea 2. to incite or instigate

chūzī 出資 to put up capital

chūzǒu 出走 to run away from one's home

chūzū 出租 to let

chūzūchē 出租車 a taxi

chū 初
1. first 2. original 3. junior 4. early; initial

chūbǎn 初版 the first edition (of a book)

chūbù 初步 1. the first or initial step 2. a primer, or the rudimentary knowledge of something

chūchū máolú 初出茅廬 still inexperienced

chūchuàng 初創 newly founded

chūchūn 初春 early spring

chūcì 初次 the first time

chūdōng 初冬 early winter

chūfàn 初犯 1. first offenses 2. a first offender

chūgǎo 初稿 the first draft

chūjí 初級 elementary; primary

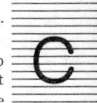

C

chūjí zhōngxué 初級中學 junior middle school

chūjiāo 初交 a new friendship

chūliàn 初戀 first love

chūlù fēngmáng 初露鋒芒 to display one's ability for the first time

chūqī 初期 the first or initial stage

chūqí 初期 refer to **chūqī** 初期

chūqiū 初秋 early autumn

chūsài 初賽 a preliminary competition

chūshěn 初審 1. a first hearing (of a case in court) 2. a preliminary screening (of applications, entries in a contest, etc.)

chūshēng zhīdú bùwèi hǔ 初生之犢不畏虎 Young men fresh from school are uncompromising despite difficulties or pressure from above.

chūshì 初試 1. to try for the first time 2. a preliminary examination or test

chūxià 初夏 early summer

chūxuǎn 初選 a primary election

chūxué 初學 1. in the beginning stage of an effort to learn (a subject) 2. a beginner

chūyè 初葉 the early years (of a century)

chūzhěn 初診 1. the first visit to a doctor 2. to visit a patient for the first time

chūzhōng 初衷 the original longing, aspiration, or intention

chū 齣
1. a chapter (of old-style novels) 2. a numerary adjunct for plays

chú 芻
1. to cut grass; to mow 2. hay; fodder 3. to feed 4. animals that feed on grass

chúliáng 芻糧 fodder for horses and food for men

chú 除
1. (mathematics) to divide; division 2. to remove; to rid of; to wipe out 3. to be appointed to an official rank or office 4. to

subtract; to deduct 5. except; besides; unless 6. to change or turn, as a new year

chúbào ānliáng 除暴安良 to get rid of lawless elements and protect the good

chúcǎo 除草 to weed (in farming); to mow grass or cut weeds

chúchénqì 除塵器 a vacuum cleaner

chúcǐ zhīwài 除此之外 besides this (or these); in addition; except

chúdiào 除掉 to remove; to get rid of

chúfǎ 除法 (mathematics) division

chúfēi 除非 unless

chúhài 除害 to get rid of evils, bad habits, practices, etc.

chújiù bùxīn 除舊布新 to remove the old and introduce the new; to replace the old with the new

chúmíng 除名 to dismiss; to strike one's name off the list; to expel

chúqù 除去 to remove; to except

chúshījī 除濕機 a dehumidifier

chúshù 除數 a divisor

chúwài 除外 except; to, except; in addition

Chúxī 除夕 Lunar New Year's Eve

Chúxì 除夕 refer to **Chúxī** 除夕

chú 廚
1. a kitchen 2. a closet; a chest; a cupboard

chúfáng 廚房 a kitchen

chújù 廚具 kitchen utensils

chúshī 廚師 a chef; a cook

chúzi 廚子 a chef; a cook

chú 鋤
1. a hoe 2. to hoe

chújiān 鋤奸 to wipe out the wicked elements

chútou 鋤頭 a hoe

chú 儲
refer to **chǔ** 儲

chú 雛

1. a chick 2. a very young bird
—a fledgling 3. a small kid or
toddler

chújì 雛妓 a minor prostitute

chúniǎo 雛鳥 a very young bird
—a fledgling

chúxíng 雛形 an embryonic
form

chú 櫥

a closet; a cabinet; a sideboard;
a cupboard, etc.

chúchuāng 櫥窗 a show window; a showcase

chúguì 櫥櫃 a closet; a sideboard; a cupboard; a cabinet,
etc.

chǔ 杵

1. a pestle; a baton used to
pound the laundry 2. to poke

chǔjiù zhījiāo 杵臼之交 true
friendship which disregards discrepancy in wealth, influence,
fame, etc.

chǔ 處

1. to place oneself in; to be faced
with; to live in 2. to get along 3.
to dispose of; to handle 4. to sentence; to punish 5. to dwell; to
live

chǔfá 處罰 to punish

chǔfāng 處方 to prescribe

chǔfēn 處分 1. to take action
against; to punish 2. to deal with
(a matter)

chǔjìng 處境 the position or situation one is in

chǔjué 處決 1. to decide; to
resolve 2. to execute (an
offender)

chǔlǐ 處理 1. to handle; to deal
with 2. to treat by a special
process

chǔnǚ 處女 a virgin

chǔnǚmó 處女膜 the hymen; the
maidenhead

chǔnǚzuò 處女作 a maiden
work

chǔshì 處世 to conduct oneself
in life

chǔsǐ 處死 to punish with death

chǔxīn jīlǜ 處心積慮 to have
in mind for a long time

chǔxíng 處刑 to punish; to execute; to mete out a sentence

chǔzhī tàirán 處之泰然 to
maintain composure

chǔzhì 處置 to dispose of

chǔ 楚

1. name of a powerful feudal
state which existed 740-330 B.C.
2. a Chinese family name 3.
clear; neat 4. distress; suffering

Chǔcái Jìnyòng 楚材晉用
Talents of one country are employed by other countries.

chǔchǔ dòngrén 楚楚動人
(said of a young woman) delicate and attractive

chǔchǔ kělián 楚楚可憐 tender and pathetic

Chǔguǎn Qínlóu 楚館秦樓
brothels

Chǔqiú duìqì 楚囚對泣 to
lament a common misery

chǔ 礎

a plinth

chǔ 儲 also **chú**

1. to save; to store; saving 2. a
deputy; an alternate

chǔbèi 儲備 savings and/or
reserves

chǔcáng 儲藏 1. to store up; to
hoard; to save and preserve 2. a
deposit

chǔcángshì 儲藏室 a storeroom

chǔcún 儲存 1. storage; saving 2.
to store or stockpile

chǔhù 儲戶 a depositor

chǔjīn 儲金 savings

chǔxù 儲蓄 1. to save (money) 2.
savings

chù 怵

1. scared; afraid; frightened; tim-
orous 2. to entice; to induce

chù 畜

1. a dumb creature; an animal 2.
livestock

chùshēng 畜生 dumb creatures;
animals

chù 處

1. a place; a spot; a location; a

C

locality 2. a department in a government agency 3. a special quality

chùchù 處處 1. everywhere 2. in all respects

chùsuǒ 處所 a place; a locality

chù 黜
1. to reject; to dispel 2. to dismiss; to degrade; to demote

chùmiǎn 黜免 to dismiss from office; to remove from office

chùtuì 黜退 to dismiss; to send away

chù 觸
1. to touch; to contact 2. (said of an animal) to ram with the horn; to ram; to butt 3. to move or touch emotionally 4. to offend; to infuriate

chùdiàn 觸電 to get an electric shock

chùdòng 觸動 1. to touch something, and move it slightly 2. to move one's heart

chùfā 觸發 1. to touch off (a war, dispute, etc.) 2. to move or touch (one's feelings)

chùfàn 觸犯 1. to offend; to incur the displeasure of 2. to violate or infringe (regulations, rules, etc.)

chùjī 觸擊 (baseball) a bunt

chùjí 觸擊 refer to **chùjī** 觸擊

chùjiāo 觸礁 1. to strike a submerged reef; to run aground 2. to hit a snag; to meet unexpected difficulty

chùjiǎo 觸角 feelers; tentacles; antennane

chùjué 觸覺 the sense of touch

chùlèi pángtōng 觸類旁通 to draw an analogy; to understand by means of inference processes

chùmù jīngxīn 觸目驚心 frightening; bloodcurdling

chùnù 觸怒 to infuriate; to offend

chùtòng 觸痛 to touch a tender spot

chù 矗
1. rising sharply; steep 2. lofty; upright; straight 3. luxuriant

growth

chùlì 矗立 rising up steeply

chuǎi 揣
1. to measure; to weigh; to estimate; to calculate; to reckon 2. to try; to probe (for possibilities); to put out a feeler

chuǎicè 揣測 to conjecture; to fathom

chuǎiduó 揣度 to speculate; to conjecture

chuǎiduò 揣度 refer to **chuǎiduó** 揣度

chuǎimó 揣摩 1. to learn; to examine 2. to assume; to speculate

chuān 川
1. a river; a stream 2. a flow; a constant flow 3. (cooking) to boil with water 4. Sichuan Province

chuānliú bùxí 川流不息 continuous; a constant flow

chuānliú bùxí 川流不息 refer to **chuānliú bùxí** 川流不息

chuānzé 川澤 marshes; swamps

chuān 穿
1. to wear (clothes, shoes, etc.) 2. to pierce through; to penetrate or bore through; to thread 3. to cross (a street, etc.)

chuānchā 穿插 1. to serve as a go-between 2. the insertion of an episode or interlude

chuāndài 穿戴 to wear (clothes, ornaments, etc.)

chuānsuō 穿梭 1. busy comings and goings of people 2. to shuttle back and forth

chuāntòu 穿透 to penetrate; to pierce through

chuānxiǎoxié 穿小鞋 to avenge a personal wrong in the name of public interests; to abuse public power to retaliate on a personal enemy

chuānxié 穿鞋 to put on shoes

chuānyuè 穿越 to pass through; to cross (a bridge, street, tunnel, etc.)

chuānzáo fùhuì 穿鑿附會 refer to **chuānzuò fùhuì** 穿鑿附會

chuānzhēn yǐnxiàn 穿針引線 to serve as a go-between

chuānzhuó 穿著 1. attire; dress 2. dressed in

chuānzuò fùhuì 穿鑿附會 to offer far-fetched or dubious explanations

chuán 船

a ship; a boat; a vessel; a craft

chúanbǎn 船板 the deck (of a ship)

chuáncāng 船艙 the hold or cabin (of a boat)

chuándào qiáotóu zìrán zhí 船到橋頭自然直 It will take care of itself when the time comes.

chuánfū 船夫 a sailor; a boat-man

chuánjia 船家 a sailor; a boat-man

chuánwéi 船桅 the mast (of a ship)

chuánwù 船塢 a dock (in a shipyard)

chuányuán 船員 the crew (of a ship)

chuányùn 船運 to transport by ship

chuánzhǎng 船長 the captain or skipper (of a boat)

chuánzhī 船隻 ships; boats; crafts; vessels

chuánzhǔ 船主 the owner (of a boat)

chuán 傳

1. to pass (a ball, an order, learning, etc.) on to 2. to propagate; to disseminate 3. to summon 4. to preach

chuánbō 傳播 to disseminate; to spread

chuánbōjiè 傳播界 the media; journalistic circles

chuánbō méitǐ 傳播媒體 a mass medium

chuánbù 傳布 1. to disseminate 2. to preach

chuándá 傳達 1. to forward (a message) 2. to inform, or notify 3. a messenger

chuándān 傳單 handbills; leaf-lets

chuándǎo 傳導 to conduct (heat, electricity)

chuándào 傳道 1. to preach a religion 2. to propagate doctrines of the ancient sages

chuándì 傳遞 to forward; to deliver

chuándòng 傳動 transmission; drive

chuánhūqì 傳呼器 a beeper; a b.b. call

chuánhuà 傳話 to pass on a message

chuánjiābǎo 傳家寶 an heir-loom

chuánjiào 傳教 to preach a religion (especially Christianity)

chuánjiàoshī 傳教士 a missionary

chuánlìng 傳令 to deliver or give orders

chuánlìngbīng 傳令兵 a soldier-messenger

chuánpiào 傳票 1. a voucher 2. a subpoena

chuánqí 傳奇 a legend, saga, romance, etc.

chuánqíng 傳情 to flirt; to coquet

chuánrǎn 傳染 to infect; to be conoagious

chuánrǎnbìng 傳染病 infectious diseases

chuánrè 傳熱 1. heat conduction 2. to communicate heat

chuánshén 傳神 a vivid portrayal

chuánshēngtǒng 傳聲筒 a megaphone

chuánshòu 傳授 to teach; to teach by demonstration

chuánshuō 傳說 hearsay; legends

chuánsòng 傳送 to convey; to deliver

chuánsòng 傳誦 1. to pass from mouth to mouth 2. to be admired and appreciated by all

chuántǒng 傳統 tradition; convention

chuánwéi jiāhuà 傳爲佳話

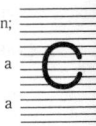

to become a favorite tale

chuánwén 傳聞 hearsay; unconfirmed reports

chuánxùn 傳訊 (law) to summon (someone) for interrogation

chuányán 傳言 1. hearsay; rumor 2. to pass on a message

chuányáng 傳揚 to spread (from mouth to mouth)

chuányībō 傳衣缽 to hand one's trade on to disciples

chuányuè 傳閱 (said of a public notice or circular) to be passed around for perusal; to be circulated

chuánzhēn 傳眞 1. a lifelike portrait by a painter 2. to transmit photos, printed matter, etc.; to facsimile 3. a fax

chuánzhēnjī 傳眞機 a fax machine

chuánzōng jiēdài 傳宗接代 to continue the family line by producing a male heir

chuǎn 舛

1. chaotic; disorderly; messy; confused; mixed up 2. to run counter to; to disobey; to oppose; to deviate from 3. mishap

chuǎn 喘

1. to pant; to gasp; to breathe hard 2. (pathology) asthma

chuǎnqì 喘氣 1. to pant; to gasp 2. to take a break

chuǎnxī 喘息 1. to take breath, or a rest (after strenuous exercise) 2. to pant

chuǎnxí 喘息 refer to **chuǎnxī** 喘息

chuàn 串

1. to string together 2. a string (of coins, etc.) 3. to pour into

chuàngòng 串供 collusion among witnesses or suspects for false confessions

chuànlián 串聯 series connection

chuànménzi 串門子 to visit or gossip from door to door

chuàntōng 串通 to collude or to conspire

chuāng 創

1. a wound 2. (瘡) a sore; a boil; an ulcer

chuāngkǒu 創口 a wound; a cut

chuāngshāng 創傷 a wound; a cut

chuāngtòng 創痛 pains

chuāng 窗

a window; a skylight

chuānghu 窗戶 a window

chuāngkǒu 窗口 1. a window 2. a wicket 3. (computer) window

chuānglián 窗簾 a screen, blind or window curtain

chuāngmíng jījìng 窗明几淨 (said of rooms) neat and bright

chuāng 瘡

1. an ulcer; a sore; a boil 2. a wound

chuāngbā 瘡疤 the scar of an ulcer

chuāngyí mǎnmù 瘡痍滿目 One sees suffering everywhere.

chuáng 床(牀)

1. a bed; a couch 2. the ground under a body of water

chuángdān 床單 bed linen; a bedsheet; sheets

chuángdiàn 床墊 a mattress

chuángpù 床鋪 a bed and bedding

chuángrù 床褥 bedding; bedclothes

chuángwèi 床位 berths or bunks (in a ship or on a train)

chuángzhào 床罩 a bedspread

chuǎng 闖

1. to rush in all of a sudden; to intrude into 2. to be trained by experience; to hew out one's way 3. to cause (a disaster, etc.)

chuǎngguān 闖關 to run a blockade; to try to break into a guarded point

chuǎnghóngdēng 闖紅燈 to run through a red light

chuǎnghuò 闖禍 to cause a disaster

chuǎngjiānghu 闖江湖 to

roam about to make a living

chuǎngkōngmén 闖空門 to break into when the occupants are absent

chuàng 創

1. to start; to begin; to initiate; to create; to establish; to found 2. original; unprecedented

chuàngbàn 創辦 to start; to found

chuàngjìlù 創紀錄 to set a record

chuàngjiàn 創見 1. an original opinion or view 2. an unprecedented thing

chuàngjǔ 創舉 an unprecedented undertaking

chuàngkān 創刊 to put out the first issue (of a periodical)

chuàngkānhào 創刊號 the first issue (of a periodical)

chuànglì 創立 to start, found or establish

chuàngshǐ 創始 to start; to begin; to commence

chuàngxīn 創新 to bring forth new ideas

chuàngyè 創業 to start a business

chuàngyì 創意 creativity

chuàngzào 創造 to create; to produce

chuàngzàolì 創造力 originality; creative ability

chuàngzhìquán 創制權 the initiative

chuàngzuò 創作 1. to write (original works of literature) 2. an original work of literature or art

chuàng 愴

broken-hearted; sad; sorrowful

chuàngrán 愴然 broken-hearted; in anguish of sorrow

chuī 吹

1. to blow; to puff 2. to brag or boast; to praise in exaggerated words 3. to break up

chuīfēngjī 吹風機 a blower; a drier

chuīfú 吹拂 (said of winds, etc.)

to move or wave (grass, branches, etc.); to sway

chuīhuī zhīlì 吹灰之力 strength as little as that needed for blowing dust away

chuīkǒushàor 吹口哨兒 to whistle

chuīlǎba 吹喇叭 to blow the trumpet

chuīmáo qiúcī 吹毛求疵 to engage in faultfinding

chuīniú 吹牛 to brag; to boast

chuīpěng 吹捧 to boast (before equals or inferiors) and to flatter (superiors)

chuīshàozi 吹哨子 to blow the whistle

chuīxū 吹噓 to recommend or praise (a person) in exaggerated words

chuīzòu 吹奏 to play (wind instruments)

chuī 炊

to cook

chuījù 炊具 cooking utensils

chuīshì 炊事 cooking

chuīyān 炊煙 the smoke from a kitchen fire

chuīyān niǎoniǎo 炊煙裊裊 smoke spiraling from kitchens

chuīyān sìqǐ 炊煙四起 cooking smoke all around—It's about mealtime.

chuí 垂

1. to hang down; to let fall 2. to hand down; to leave a name in history 3. nearly; almost; approaching 4. to condescend

chuí'ài 垂愛 to show gracious concern for

chuídiào 垂釣 to go fishing

chuílián 垂憐 to have pity on somebody

chuíliǔ 垂柳 a weeping willow

chuímù zhīnián 垂暮之年 in one's old age

chuíqīng 垂青 to bestow favors

chuísǐ 垂死 at the point of death; dying

chuítóu sàngqì 垂頭喪氣 to be crestfallen; to be downcast

chuíwēi 垂危 (said of an illness or situation) to be in imminent danger

chuíwēi 垂危 refer to **chuíwēi** 垂危

chuíxián 垂涎 to drool; to yearn for; to covet; to crave

chuíxián sānchǐ 垂涎三尺 to drool; to yearn for; to covet; to crave

chuíxián yùdī 垂涎欲滴 to drool; to yearn for; to covet; to crave

chuíyáng 垂楊 a weeping willow

chuízhí 垂直 perpendicular; vertical

chuí 捶(搥)

1. to beat; to thrash; to pound 2. a stick for beating

chuídǎ 捶打 to beat; to thump

chuíxiōng dùnzú 捶胸頓足 to beat one's breast and stamp one's feet—in deep grief

chuí 椎

refer to **zhuī** 椎

chuí 槌

a hammer

chuí 錘(鎚)

1. a weight on a steelyard 2. an ancient unit of weight 3. a kind of ancient weapon 4. to hammer; to pound 5. a hammer

chuíliàn 錘鍊 1. to forge (metal); to temper 2. to polish

chūn 春

1. spring, the first of the four seasons 2. sensuality; lustful; lewd; pornographic 3. alive; vitality; living 4. joyful 5. youth

chūnfēng 春風 1. spring breezes 2. good education 3. sexual intercourse 4. favor; grace 5. happy smiles

chūnfēng déyì 春風得意 to attain a high official rank; to ride on the crest of success

chūnfēng huàyǔ 春風化雨 salutary influence of education

chūnfēng mǎnmiàn 春風滿面 to smile broadly; a cheerful look

chūngōngtú 春宮圖 pornographic drawings

chūnguāng 春光 1. lustful scenes—as a sexual act 2. spring scenes (natural charms in spring)

chūnguāng míngmèi 春光明媚 a sunlit and enchanting scene of spring

chūnhán liàoqiào 春寒料峭 the chill of early spring

chūnhuā qiūyuè 春花秋月 1. the best things at the best time 2. flight of time

chūnhuī 春暉 the light of the spring sun—parental love and care

chūnhuí dàdì 春回大地 Spring returns to the good earth.

chūnjià 春假 spring holidays; the spring vacation

Chūnjié 春節 the Lunar New Year

chūnjuǎn 春捲 spring rolls

chūnléi 春雷 the spring thunder

chūnlián 春聯 New Year's couplets written on strips of red paper and pasted on doors

chūnmèng 春夢 something that is illusory and transient

chūnnuǎn huākāi 春暖花開 During the warmth of spring all the flowers bloom.

chūnqiū 春秋 1. a year 2. spring and autumn 3. age 4. annals of any state during the period of Warring States 5. Spring and Autumn Annals 6. annals; history

chūnqiū dǐngshèng 春秋鼎盛 in the prime of one's life

Chūnqiū Shídài 春秋時代 the Epoch of Spring and Autumn, approximately from 770 to 403 B.C.

chūnsè 春色 1. spring scenery 2. a joyful appearance or expression 3. sensual or carnal scenes

chūntiān 春天 spring; springtime

chūnxiāo 春宵 1. spring nights 2. a wedding night

chūnxiāo kǔduǎn 春宵苦短 The wedding night is always too short (to the newlyweds).

chūnxīn dàngyàng 春心蕩漾
the surging of lustful desire

chūnyào 春藥 aphrodisiac

chūnyì 春意 1. spring in the air
2. thoughts of love

chūnyǔ 春雨 spring rains or
showers

chūnzhuāng 春裝 spring
clothes

chūn 椿
one's father

chūnlíng 椿齡 venerable age;
long life

chūnshòu 椿壽 venerable age;
long life

chūntíng 椿庭 one's father

chūnxuān 椿萱 one's parents

chún 純
1. pure; net (profits, etc.); unal-
loyed 2. sincere; honest; simple;
faithful 3. completely; purely;
entirely 4. (now rare) great;
large

chúnbái 純白 pure white

chúncuì 純粹 1. pure; genuine 2.
completely

chúndù 純度 purity

chúnjié 純潔 innocent; pure and
clean

chúnjīn 純金 pure gold; unal-
loyed gold

chúnjìng 純淨 pure and clean

chúnliáng 純良 kind; honest

chúnmáo 純毛 all-wool; 100%
wool

chúnpú 純樸 refer to **chúnpǔ** 純
樸

chúnpǔ 純樸 simple and sincere

chúnshú 純熟 proficient; very
skillful; adroit

chúnshǔ xūgòu 純屬虛構
being an out-and-out fabrication

chúnzhēn 純眞 pure, sincere
and faithful

chúnzhèng 純正 1. pure and
genuine 2. honest; sincere

chúnzhǒng 純種 thoroughbred;
purebred

chún 唇(脣)
the lips; the labia

chúngāo 唇膏 lipstick

chúnhóng chǐbái 唇紅齒白
red lips and white teeth—very
handsome or beautiful

chúnqiāng shéjiàn 唇槍舌劍
a heated verbal exchange or
debate

chúnshé 唇舌 1. eloquence 2.
explanation

chúnwáng chǐhán 唇亡齒寒
mutual dependency of neighboring countries

chún 淳
1. pure; clean; simple; sincere;
honest 2. a couple or pair (of
chariots) 3. big; great

chúnhòu 淳厚 simple and sincere

chúnliáng 淳良 pure, simple
and honest

chúnpú 淳樸 refer to **chúnpǔ** 淳
樸

chúnpǔ 淳樸 sincere and simple
(villagers, etc.); unsophisticated

chún 醇
1. rich wine; strong wine 2. pure;
unadulterated 3. gentle; gracious
4. ethyl alcohol

chúnměi 醇美 pure and fair

chún 鶉
a quail

chúnyī bǎijié 鶉衣百結 coarse
clothes with many patches

chǔn 蠢
1. to wriggle; to squirm 2. stupid;
foolish; dull; silly

chǔncái 蠢才 a simpleton; a
fool; an idiot

chuō 戳
1. to jab; to poke; to pierce 2. a
chop; a stamp; a seal

chuōjì 戳記 a stamp; a seal

chuōyìn 戳印 1. to stamp 2. a
stamp

chuò 啜
1. to drink; to sip 2. to cry in a
subdued manner; to sob

chuòqì 啜泣 to sob

chuò 綽

chuò 綽 1. spacious; roomy 2. delicate

chuòchuò yǒuyú 綽綽有餘 1. There is enough room to spare. 2. generous feeling

chuòhào 綽號 a nickname; a sobriquet

chuòyuē 綽約 charmingly delicate

chuò 輟 to stop; to halt; to suspend; to cease

chuòxué 輟學 to drop out of school

chuòxuéshēng 輟學生 a school dropout

chuò 齪 1. narrow; small 2. dirty

cī 差 uneven; irregular

cī 疵 also **cí** a defect; a flaw; a mistake

cī 雌 refer to **cí** 雌

cí 祠 1. a temple; a shrine 2. the spring worship

cítáng 祠堂 a shrine; an ancestral hall (or temple); a memorial temple

cí 瓷 porcelain; chinaware

cíqì 瓷器 porcelain; porcelain ware; chinaware; china

cítǔ 瓷土 kaolin(e); porcelain clay

cízhuān 瓷磚 small porcelain tiles used for wall paneling or floor pavement

cí 詞 1. words; phrases; statements; speech; expressions 2. a part of speech in grammar 3. to talk, speak or tell 4. (Chinese literature) a form of poetry

cíbù dáyì 詞不達意 The language cannot convey the ideas intended.

cídiǎn 詞典 a dictionary

cíhuì 詞彙 1. a dictionary 2. a vocabulary

cíjù 詞句 expressions; words and phrases

cíqǔ 詞曲 poems and songs

cíyǔ 詞語 words and expressions; terms

cízǎo 詞藻 ornate terms or expressions

cí 慈 1. kind; benevolent; benignant; charitable; merciful; loving; fond 2. of one's mother; maternal

cí'ài 慈愛 (said of elderly persons) benevolence; affection; love; kindness

cíbēi 慈悲 benevolence; pity; mercy

címéi shànmù 慈眉善目 a benign face

císhàn 慈善 benevolence; charity; philanthropy

císhàn jīgòu 慈善機構 a charity organization

císhànjiā 慈善家 a philanthropist

císhàn shìyè 慈善事業 a charitable enterprise

cíxiáng 慈祥 (said of elderly persons) benevolent; kind; benign

cí 雌 also **cī** 1. female; feminine; womanlike; soft (voice, etc.) 2. weak; retiring 3. to scold 4. (鱦) to expose or show (the teeth)

cíhuáng 雌黃 1. orpiment (As_2S_3) 2. to make changes in writing 3. to criticize without grounds; to malign

círuǐ 雌蕊 a pistil

cíxìng 雌性 female

cíxióng 雌雄 1. the female and the male 2. the victor and the loser

cíxióng mòbiàn 雌雄莫辨 unable to distinguish the sex identity

cí 磁 magnetic; magnetism

cíchǎng 磁場 the magnetic field

cídài 磁帶 a magnetic tape

cídié 磁碟 a magnetic disk

cídiépiàn 磁碟片 (computer) a diskette; a floppy disc

cípiàn 磁片 (computer) a diskette; a floppy disc

cítiě 磁鐵 a magnet; magnetic iron

cítóu 磁頭 a magnetic head

cíxìng 磁性 magnetism

cí 辭

1. language; words; a phrase; an expression 2. to decline; to refuse 3. to leave; to part from; to depart 4. to resign

cíbié 辭別 to bid farewell; to say goodbye; to take one's leave; to make one's adieus

cíchéng 辭呈 a formal notice of resignation; a resignation

cídiǎn 辭典 a dictionary; a lexicon; a thesaurus

cíhǎi 辭海 a collection of words

cíhuì 辭彙 vocabulary

cílìng 辭令 diction appropriate to the occasion

císhì 辭世 to depart from the world; to die; to pass away

cítuì 辭退 1. to remove from office 2. to resign from office

cíxiè 辭謝 to decline with thanks; to ask to be excused

cíxíng 辭行 to take leave of; to say goodbye to

cíyuán 辭源 the origin of a phrase or expression

cízǎo 辭藻 expressions in literary compositions

cízhāng 辭章 1. literary compositions; poetry and prose 2. the art of writing; rhetoric

cízhí 辭職 to resign from one's post; resignation

cǐ 此

1. this; these 2. such; thus 3. if so; in this case 4. here

cǐhòu 此後 from now on; hereafter

cǐjiān 此間 this place; within this; here

cǐjǔ 此舉 this action; this undertaking

cǐkè 此刻 at this moment; at present

cǐlù bùtōng 此路不通 This road is blocked.

cǐqǐ bǐluò 此起彼落 (said of voices) rising and falling; continuously

cǐshí cǐdì 此時此地 here and now; under the present circumstances

cǐshí cǐkè 此時此刻 at the (very) moment

cǐwài 此外 besides; in addition

cǐyīshí, bǐyīshí 此一時，彼一時 Circumstances have changed with the passage of time.

cì 次

1. the next in order; secondary 2. inferior; lower 3. vice or deputy (ministers, etc.) 4. by; at (the feast, table, etc.) 5. a grade; grading; order; sequence 6. time (each occasion of a recurring action or event)

cìděng 次等 a lower or inferior class or category; of the second grade or quality

cìděnghuò 次等貨 seconds; inferior goods; substandard goods

cìdì 次第 1. order; grade; sequence 2. in order; one by one

cìnián 次年 the next year

cìrì 次日 the next day; the following day

cìshù 次數 the number of times

cìxù 次序 order, sequence, succession, etc.

cìyào 次要 secondary; not very important

cìyú 次於 next to...; inferior to...

cìzhǎng 次長 a vice minister; a deputy minister

cìzǐ 次子 the second son

cì 伺

to serve

cìhòu 伺候 to wait, or attend upon; to serve

cì 刺

1. to pierce; to stab; to prick 2. to irritate; to stimulate 3. a thorn; a splinter; small fishbones; a sting 4. to assassinate 5. a

name card

cìbí 刺鼻 to irritate the nose

cìdāo 刺刀 a bayonet

cì'ěr 刺耳 screechy; grating; ear-piercing

cìgǔ 刺骨 1. (said of cold) bone-chilling 2. (said of hatred) bitter or deep

cìjī 刺激 to stimulate; to irritate; exciting

cìjīwù 刺激物 a stimulant

cìjīxìng 刺激性 stimulativeness

cìkè 刺客 an assassin

cìmù 刺目 dazzling

cìqīng 刺青 to tattoo; a tattoo

cìshā 刺殺 1. to assassinate 2. (baseball) to put out (a base runner)

cìtàn 刺探 to spy; to find out secretly

cìwei 刺蝟 a hedgehog

cìxiù 刺繡 to embroider; embroidery

cìyǎn 刺眼 dazzling

cì 賜 also **sì**

1. to bestow or confer on an inferior; to grant 2. favors; benefits 3. to order; to appoint

cìfù 賜覆 Please reply.

cìyǔ 賜予 to bestow or confer upon

cōng 匆(怱)

hasty; hastily; hurriedly

cōngcōng 匆匆 hurriedly

cōngcù 匆促 haste; hastily

cōngmáng 匆忙 haste; in haste; hastily; hurriedly

cōng 囪

a chimney; a flue

cōng 從

1. lax; easy 2. plentiful; abundant 3. to urge

cōngróng 從容 1. unhurried; calm; composed 2. plentiful; plenty of

cōngróng bùpò 從容不迫 in an unhurried or leisurely manner

cōng 葱

1. scallions; onions 2. bright

green

cōng 聰

1. clever; astute; bright; quick of apprehension 2. with a good faculty of hearing

cōngming 聰明 1. clever; bright; intelligent 2. sharp hearing and seeing faculties

cōngming juédǐng 聰明絕頂 extremely clever or intelligent

cōngyǐng 聰穎 clever and bright

cóng 淙

1. the sound of flowing water 2. water flowing

cóngcóng 淙淙 1. the gurgling sound of flowing water—especially a creek 2. the tinkling sound of metals or gems

cóng 從

1. from; by; whence; through 2. to undertake; to manage; to engage in 3. to follow; to yield to; to listen to; to obey 4. (also **zòng**) a follower; an attendant

cóngbù 從不 never

cóngcháng jìyì 從長計議 to take time to make careful deliberations

cóngcǐ yǐhòu 從此以後 from now on; henceforth

cóngfàn 從犯 an accessory

cónghuǎn 從緩 to bide one's time; to postpone

cóngjiǎn 從簡 (said of ceremonies) to be simple; to forgo pageantry

cóngjīn yǐhòu 從今以後 from now on

cóngjūn 從軍 to enlist oneself in military service

cóngkuān 從寬 to be lenient

cónglái 從來 from the beginning

cóngliáng 從良 (said of a prostitute) to get married, or to become a decent woman again

cóngpáng 從旁 (to help, to encourage, etc.) from the side

cóngqián 從前 once upon a time; a long time ago

cóngqīng fāluò 從輕發落 to use leniency in meting out punishment

cóngróng 從戎 to join the armed service

cóngshàn rúliú 從善如流 to forge ahead in doing what is right

cóngshì 從事 to be engaged in (a task); to devote oneself to

cóngshǔ 從屬 subordinate

cóngtiān érjiàng 從天而降 (literally) to descend from heaven—very unexpectedly

cóngtóu zhìwěi 從頭至尾 from beginning to end; throughout

cóngwèi 從未 to have never (happened, etc.)

cóngxiǎo 從小 from one's childhood

cóngxīn zuòrén 從新做人 to start one's life anew

cóngyī érzhōng 從一而終 to be faithful to one husband all her life

cóngyōu 從優 liberally (as of payment); (to pay) according to a higher scale

cóngzǎo dàowǎn 從早到晚 from morning till night

cóngzhèng 從政 to enter politics; to become a government official

cóngzhōng 從中 1. in the process (of doing something) 2. from the inside (of something) 3. in the middle

cóng 叢

1. to crowd together; to meet in large numbers 2. a shrub (plant); a thicket 3. a hideout or den

cónglín 叢林 1. a jungle 2. a Buddhist monastery

cóngshēng 叢生 1. lush growth; dense growth 2. full of (shortcomings)

cóngshū 叢書 a collection of books by an author or on a subject

cōu 湊

1. to put together 2. to raise (fund) 3. to happen by chance 4. to move close to; to press near

cōuhe 湊合 1. to manage to collect or gather together 2. to

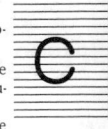

make do with what is available 3. to improvise 4. not too bad; passable

cōujìn 湊近 to get near; to approach

cōuqí 湊齊 1. to manage to line up enough people for a game 2. to manage to collect all the parts to form the whole

cōuqiǎo 湊巧 by chance; by coincidence

cōurè'nào 湊熱鬧 1. to take part in merriment 2. to add trouble to

cōushù 湊數 1. to make up the proper number 2. to play an unimportant role

cōuzài yìqǐ 湊在一起 1. to put together 2. (said of people) to gang up 3. to team up

cōuzú 湊足 to manage to raise enough money for a purpose

cū 粗

1. thick; bulky; big 2. coarse; rough; crude 3. gruff; husky 4. rude; vulgar 5. brief; sketchy

cūbào 粗暴 rude; violent; rough

cūbǐ 粗鄙 vulgar; crude

cūcāo 粗糙 (said of a surface, etc.) coarse; rough; unpolished

cūchá dànfàn 粗茶淡飯 simple food; plain fare

cūdà 粗大 thick and big

cūguǎng 粗獷 1. rough; rude; boorish 2. bold and unconstrained; rugged

cūhuà 粗話 obscene language

cūhuó 粗活 work of a laborer or coolie; work which demands little brains but lots of brawn

cūlǔ 粗魯 rude; impolite; rough

cūlüè 粗略 cursory; rough; sketchy

cūrén 粗人 1. a person of little education 2. a boor; an unrefined person

cūshuài 粗率 1. crude and coarse 2. careless

cūsú 粗俗 coarse; vulgar; unrefined

cūxīn 粗心 careless (in work)

cūxīn dàyì 粗心大意 rash and

C

careless; in advertency

cūyě 粗野 rude; boorish

cūzhī dàyè 粗枝大葉 careless; sketchy (description)

cūzhì lànzào 粗製濫造 to turn out (products) in large quantities without any regard for quality

cūzhòng 粗重 1. bulky (products, etc.) of low value 2. work that needs more muscles than brains

cūzhuàng 粗壯 stout; sturdy; brawny; muscular

cú 徂
1. to go to; to go ahead; to advance 2. the preposition "to" 3. to die 4. past

cú 殂
to die; dead; death

cúluò 殂落 to pass away; to demise

cúmò 殂沒 to die; to perish; death

cúxiè 殂謝 to pass away; to demise

cù 卒
suddenly; abruptly; hurriedly

cù 促
1. close; crowded; near 2. to urge; to hurry; to promote 3. hurried; urgent

cùchéng 促成 to help to materialize

cùjìn 促進 to urge to proceed; to promote

cùshǐ 促使 to impel; to urge; to spur

cùxī tánxīn 促膝談心 to sit side by side and talk intimately

cùxiāo 促銷 sales promotion

cù 猝
sudden; abrupt; hurried; unexpected

cùbù jífáng 猝不及防 to be caught unprepared

cù 醋
vinegar

cùjìn 醋勁 jealousy

cùtánzi 醋罈子 a jealous person

cù 簇
1. a cluster; a crowd; crowded 2. an arrowhead 3. to crowd together; to cluster together

cùxīn 簇新 brand-new

cùyōng 簇擁 attended by a crowd

cù 蹙
1. to contract; to draw together 2. urgent; imminent 3. sad; sorrowful; discomposed

cùméi 蹙眉 to knit the brows; to frown

cuàn 篡
to seize (power, the throne, etc.); to usurp

cuàn'gǎi 篡改 to alter a piece of writing with an evil intent; to tamper (with a document, etc.)

cuànwèi 篡位 to seize the throne

cuàn 竄
1. to escape; to run away; to flee 2. to change or alter (the wording) 3. to banish; to execute

cuàn'gǎi 竄改 to interpolate; to tamper

cuàntáo 竄逃 to flee in disorder

cuī 崔
1. a Chinese family name 2. high and steep

cuī 催
to hasten; to urge; to press; to hurry

cuīcù 催促 to hasten; to urge; to press

cuīgǎn 催趕 1. to urge someone to come or go 2. to hasten to a destination

cuīhuàjì 催化劑 a catalyst

cuīlèidàn 催淚彈 a tear gas bomb

cuīmián 催眠 to hypnotize; to mesmerize

cuīmiánshù 催眠術 hypnotism

cuīshēngjì 催生劑 an axytocic

cuītǎo 催討 to press for repayment of a debt

cuī 摧

cuī 摧
1. to break; to smash; to destroy; to injure; to harm 2. to damp 3. to cause to cease; to extinguish 4. to be sad and sorrowful; to grieve

cuīcán 摧殘 1. to destroy; to ruin 2. to humiliate

cuīhuǐ 摧毀 to destroy (enemy positions, heavy weapons, etc.)

cuīzhé 摧折 to break; to destroy; to smash

cuī 璀
the luster or glitter of jade and gems

cuīcàn 璀璨 the brilliancy and luster of pearls and precious stones

cuì 脆
1. brittle; fragile; hard but easily broken (as glass, porcelain, etc.) 2. crisp 3. light; shallow; thin 4. (said of the operation, etc. of something) easy, quick and convenient; neat

cuìruò 脆弱 weak; fragile; delicate

cuì 悴
1. haggard; worn-out; tired out 2. worried; sad

cuì 淬
1. to temper iron or steel for making swords, etc. (also used figuratively) 2. to dip into water; to soak; to dye

cuìlì 淬勵 to encourage

cuìmiǎn 淬勉 to persuade; to urge and advise

cuì 萃
1. a thick or dense growth of grass 2. a group; a set 3. to gather; to meet; to congregate

cuìqǔ 萃取 (chemistry) extraction

cuì 瘁
1. disease; illness 2. overfatigued; toil

cuì 翠
1. bluish green 2. green jade 3. a kingfisher

cuìyù 翠玉 emerald; blue jade

cuì 粹
1. pure; unmixed; perfect; unadulterated 2. the essence; the best

cuì 橇
refer to **qiāo** 橇

cūn 村
1. a village; the countryside; a hamlet 2. vulgar; coarse 3. simple-minded; naive

cūnfū 村夫 1. a villager 2. a vulgar and naive person

cūnfù 村婦 a village woman

cūngū 村姑 a country girl

cūnluò 村落 a village; a hamlet

cūnzhǎng 村長 the village chief

cūnzhuāng 村莊 a village; a farmstead

cūnzi 村子 a village; a hamlet

cún 存
1. to live; to exist; to survive; to remain 2. to keep; to keep

cún'àn 存案 to put (a legal document, etc.) on public record; to file

cúnchǔqì 存儲器 (computer) storage; memory

cúndǎng 存檔 refer to **cúndàng** 存檔

cúndàng 存檔 to place on file; to file

cúndǐr 存底兒 to keep a file copy

cúnfàng 存放 to deposit (money); to leave (something somewhere) for safekeeping

cúnfàngchù 存放處 a depository

cúngēn 存根 a counterfoil; a stub

cúnhuò 存貨 remaining (still unsold) goods

cúnkuǎn 存款 1. a deposit 2. to make a deposit

cúnkuǎnbù 存款簿 a deposit book

cúnliáng 存糧 to store up grain

cúnmò 存歿 a question of remaining in existence or not

cúnwáng 存亡 life-and-death;

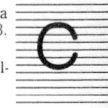

survival and downfall

cúnwáng guāntóu 存亡關頭 at a most critical moment

cúnxīn 存心 intentional; on purpose

cúnyí 存疑 1. a remaining doubt 2. to leave a doubtful point unquestioned

cúnyǒu 存有 being

cúnzài 存在 to exist; to be present

cúnzhé 存摺 a bankbook; a passbook

cún 蹲
refer to **dūn** 蹲

cǔn 忖
to surmise; to consider; to presume; to suppose

cǔnduó 忖度 to suppose; to consider

cǔnduó 忖度 refer to **cǔnduó** 忖度

cǔnsī 忖思 to imagine

cùn 寸
1. a measure of length (equal to about 1/10 foot) 2. as small as an inch; small; tiny; little

cùnbù bùlí 寸步不離 to tag; to follow closely

cùnbù nánxíng 寸步難行 hard to walk even an inch

cùntǔ bìzhēng 寸土必爭 Even an inch of land has to be fought for.

cùn 吋
inch—a unit of length

cuō 搓
1. to rub hands; to rub between the hands 2. to scrub 3. to twist (a thread, etc.) between the hands

cuōbǎn 搓板 a washboard

cuōnòng 搓弄 to rub

cuōróu 搓揉 to rub; to massage

cuō 撮 also **cuǒ**
1. to take with fingers 2. to gather 3. to extract; to summarize 4. a pinch of

cuōhé 撮合 to bring (two persons

or parties) together; to make a match

cuōnòng 撮弄 1. to juggle 2. to incite 3. to make fun of; to kid

cuō 磋
to file; to polish (jade, stone, horn, etc)

cuōshāng 磋商 to exchange views; to hold a discussion or consultation

cuō 蹉
a failure; a miss

cuōtuó 蹉跎 1. to slip and fall 2. to miss a chance; to waste time

cuò 厝
1. to place 2. to place a coffin in a temporary shelter pending burial 3. a gravestone 4. to cut or engrave

cuò 挫
1. to defeat; to frustrate 2. to damp 3. to humiliate; to treat harshly

cuòbài 挫敗 a setback

cuòdí 挫敵 to defeat the enemy

cuòzhé 挫折 a setback; defeat; failure

cuò 措
1. to place 2. to collect; to arrange; to manage; to handle 3. to abandon; to renounce 4. to make plans

cuòcí 措辭 wording (of a letter, diplomatic note, etc.); diction

cuòshī 措施 a (political, financial, etc.) measure; a step

cuòshǒu bùjí 措手不及 to be caught unawares or unprepared

cuò 銼
1. a kind of widemouthed cauldron used in ancient China 2. a file 3. to make smooth with a file; to file

cuòdāo 銼刀 a file (a steel tool)

cuò 撮
refer to **cuō** 撮

cuò 錯
1. wrong; mistaken; erroneous 2. a mistake; an error 3. untidy;

uneven; irregular; intricate 4. a grindstone

cuòbiézì 錯別字 characters wrongly written or mispronounced

cuòguài 錯怪 to blame unjustly or wrongly

cuòguò 錯過 to let (a chance) slip by; to miss

cuòjué 錯覺 a false impression; hallucination; illusion

cuòkāi 錯開 to stagger

cuòluàn 錯亂 disorderly; confused; abnormal deranged

cuòrèn 錯認 to misidentify

cuòwù 錯誤 1. an error; a mistake; a fault 2. erroneous; wrong

cuòwù bǎichū 錯誤百出 full of mistakes; riddled with errors

cuòzì 錯字 misspelling; a misprint

cuòzōng fùzá 錯綜複雜 very complicated; intricate

dā 答

1. to respond 2. to promise

dālǐ 答理 to answer a person; to respond

dāyìng 答應 1. to assent or agree to (a request); to promise (to do something) 2. to answer

dā 搭

1. to attach to; to join together; to add to 2. to hang over 3. to raise; to build (a shed, etc.); to put up; to pitch (a tent, etc.) 4. to travel by; to take (a passage on a bus, train, boat, etc.) 5. to help; to rescue 6. a short garment 7. a cover; to cover

dāchē 搭車 to take a car, bus or train

dāchéng 搭乘 to travel by (air, ship, bus, etc.)

dāchuán 搭船 to board a ship

dādàng 搭檔 1. a partner 2. to cooperate

dāhuǒ 搭夥 to go into partnership; to join

dājī 搭機 to board an airplane

dājiù 搭救 to rescue; to help

dāpèi 搭配 1. to match (colors, etc.) 2. to select (items as a pres-

ent to a person, or dishes for a feast)

dāqiāng 搭腔 1. to answer; to respond 2. to talk to each other

dāqiáo 搭橋 to connect oneself with

dāshàn 搭訕 to strike up a conversation with somebody

dāzài 搭載 to carry (passengers)

dá 打

a dozen

dá 答

1. to answer; to reply 2. to reciprocate; to return

dá'àn 答案 solution, answers (to examination questions, puzzles, etc.)

dábiàn 答辯 to reply (to a verbal attack); to speak in self-defense

dáfēi suǒwèn 答非所問 to give an irrelevant answer

dáfù 答覆 to reply to, or answer (an inquiry, etc.); an answer; a reply

dáhuà 答話 to reply orally

dálǐ 答禮 to return a salute

dálùjī 答錄機 an answering machine

dáxiè 答謝 to convey one's thanks (for a favor, etc.)

dá 達

1. intelligent; smart; understanding; reasonable 2. prominent; successful 3. to reach; to arrive at 4. to inform; to tell 5. openminded

dáchéng 達成 to succeed in (a mission, etc.); to accomplish; to reach (an agreement)

dádào 達到 to reach (a decision or conclusion); to achieve or attain (a goal, etc.)

dáguān 達觀 a kind of wisdom which enables a person to be oblivious of emotions and adversity

dáguān guìrén 達官貴人 prominent officials and eminent personages

Dálài Lǎma 達賴喇嘛 Dalai Lama, the ruler and chief monk

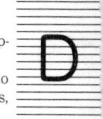

of Tibet

dǎ 打

1. to strike; to beat 2. to attack; to fight 3. to smash 4. to do, make, get, fetch, play, buy, etc. (depending on the object) 5. to; from; toward

dǎ'ànhào 打暗號 to hint; to give a cue

dǎbǎ 打靶 target practice

dǎbài 打敗 1. to defeat 2. to suffer a defeat

dǎbàizhàng 打敗仗 to suffer a defeat

dǎbàn 打扮 to make up

dǎbāo 打包 to pack

dǎbǎopiào 打保票 to vouch for; to guarantee

dǎbǎogér 打飽嗝兒 to belch after a solid meal

dǎbào bùpíng 抱不平 to help the victims of injustice

dǎbiāngǔ 打邊鼓 to incite; to instigate

dǎbuguò 打不過 to be no fighting match for

dǎcǎogǎo 打草稿 to prepare a draft

dǎcǎo jīngshé 打草驚蛇 to cause undesired agitation

dǎchà 打岔 to interrupt another's speech

dǎchéng píngshǒu 打成平手 to fight to a draw

dǎchéng yīpiàn 打成一片 to combine into a whole

dǎchìbó 打赤膊 to bare the upper body

dǎchìjiǎo 打赤脚 to go barefoot (barefooted)

dǎcóng 打從 from; since

dǎdǎ'nàonào 打打鬧鬧 to fight in jest or for fun

dǎdàn 打蛋 to beat, stir or whip eggs

dǎdǎo 打倒 to knock down; to overthrow

dǎdeguò 打得過 able to defeat

dǎde huǒrè 打得火熱 1. to be in the middle of a white-hot battle 2. to be passionately in love with each other

dǎdī 打的 to take a taxi

dǎdìpù 打地鋪 to make a bed on the floor or the ground

dǎdiǎndī 打點滴 to administer intravenous drip

dǎdiànbào 打電報 to telegraph; to cable

dǎdiànhuà 打電話 to make a telephone call; to telephone

dǎdiànnǎo 打電腦 to operate a computer

dǎdian 打點 1. to examine and put in order 2. to bribe

dǎdiào 打掉 to destroy; to knock out; to wipe out

dǎdòng 打動 to move (a person mentally)

dǎdòu 打鬥 a fight; a skirmish; to fight

dǎdǔ 打賭 to make a bet

dǎduàn 打斷 1. to break 2. to interrupt

dǎdǔnr 打盹兒 to doze; to take a nap

dǎduōsuo 打哆嗦 to tremble; to shiver

dǎ'ěrguāng 打耳光 to box somebody's ears

dǎfa 打發 1. to dispatch; to send away 2. to fire; to dismiss 3. to spend (time)

dǎfān 打翻 to overturn; to tip over

dǎfēnshù 打分數 to grade (students' papers); to grade (a performance)

dǎgē 打歌 to promote a new song by singing it frequently in public appearance

dǎgēng 打更 to beat the night watches

dǎgér 打嗝兒 to hiccough

dǎgōng 打工 to do odd jobs as distinct from a regular employment

dǎgōng zuǒyī 打躬作揖 to salute with folded hands again and again

dǎgōng zuòyī 打躬作揖 refer to **dǎgōng zuǒyī** 打躬作揖

dǎgǔ 打鼓 1. to beat a drum 2. to feel uncertain or nervous

dǎgǔ 打穀 to thresh grain

dǎguānqiāng 打官腔 . bureaucratic jargon

dǎguānsi 打官司 to have a lawsuit

dǎguānggùnr 打光棍兒 (said of a man) to remain a bachelor

dǎgǔn 打滾 to roll about

dǎhāha 打哈哈 1. to roar with laughter 2. to have fun; to frolic; to make merry 3. to talk irrelevantly in an apparent effort to avoid touching the real issue

dǎhāqian 打哈欠 to yawn

dǎhān 打鼾 to snore

dǎhuǒjī 打火機 a (cigarette) lighter

dǎjī 打擊 to give a blow to

dǎjīchǔ 打基礎 to lay the foundations

dǎjī yuèqì 打擊樂器 a percussion instrument

dǎjī 打擊 refer to **dǎjī** 打擊

dǎjí yuèqì 打擊樂器 refer to **dǎjī yuèqì** 打擊樂器

dǎjiā jiéshè 打家劫舍 to raid homes and plunder houses; to rob

dǎjià 打架 to have a brawl, a blow, a row or a fight

dǎjiān 打尖 to lodge temporarily

dǎjiāodao 打交道 to associate with; to have dealings with

dǎjiǎo 打攪 to bother; to disturb; to trouble

dǎjié 打劫 to plunder; to loot

dǎjié 打結 to tie a knot; to make a knot

dǎjīng 打更 refer to **dǎgēng** 打更

dǎkǎ 打卡 to record the time of one's presence or departure by punching a time clock

dǎkāi 打開 1. to open 2. to turn on

dǎkāi jiāngjú 打開僵局 to break the impasse

dǎkāi tiānchuāng shuō liànghuà 打開天窗說亮話 to speak frankly

dǎkēshuì 打瞌睡 to doze; to take a nap

dǎkǒng 打孔 to drill a hole; to punch a hole; to perforate

dǎkuǎ 打垮 to strike down

dǎlà 打蠟 to wax

dǎlāo 打撈 to drag sunken things out of water

dǎlàoyìn 打烙印 to brand (cattle)

dǎléi 打雷 to thunder

dǎlěngchàn 打冷顫 refer to **dǎlěngzhan** 打冷顫

dǎlěngzhan 打冷顫 to shudder

dǎliang 打量 to size up; to look someone up and down

dǎliè 打獵 to go hunting

dǎlǐngdài 打領帶 to tie a necktie

dǎ luòshuǐgǒu 打落水狗 to attack someone already down in his luck

dǎmájiàng 打麻將 to play majiang

dǎ mǎhuyǎn 打馬虎眼 to act dumb

dǎmà 打罵 to beat and scold

dǎ máoxiànyī 打毛線衣 to knit a woolen sweater

dǎ'nào 打鬧 to quarrel and fight noisily

dǎpāizi 打拍子 to beat time

dǎpái 打牌 to play a card game, majiang, etc.

dǎpēntì 打噴嚏 to sneeze

dǎpìgu 打屁股 spanking

dǎpò 打破 to smash to pieces; to break

dǎpò jìlù 打破紀錄 to break the record

dǎpò shāguō wèndàodǐ 打破砂鍋問到底 to interrogate persistently

dǎqǐ jīngshen 打起精神 to cheer up

dǎqì 打氣 1. to inflate 2. (figuratively) to pep up

dǎqìtǒng 打氣筒 an air pump

dǎqíng màqiào 打情罵俏 to tease one's lover by showing false displeasure

dǎqiú 打球 to play a ball game

dǎqù 打趣 to make fun of

another; to tease

dǎquán 打拳 to practice boxing

dǎrǎo 打擾 to disturb; to bother; to trouble

dǎ rúyì suànpan 打如意算盤 to expect things to turn out as one wishes

dǎsǎn 打傘 to use an umbrella

dǎsǎn 打散 to break up; to scatter

dǎsàn 打散 refer to **dǎsǎn** 打散

dǎsǎo 打掃 to clean (a room, house, etc.)

dǎshāng 打傷 to wound or injure by beating

dǎshǒushì 打手勢 to gesticulate

dǎshou 打手 thugs hired by men of wealth or power

dǎshuǐ 打水 to draw water (from a well, a spring, etc.)

dǎshuǐpiāo 打水漂 to make ducks and drakes

dǎsǐ 打死 to beat to death; to shoot to death

dǎsuàn 打算 1. to plan; to intend; to prepare 2. a plan; intention

dǎsuànpan 打算盤 1. to use an abacus 2. to reckon 3. calculating; shrewd

dǎsuì 打碎 to smash to pieces; to break to pieces

dǎtàn 打探 to find out

dǎtiě chènrè 打鐵趁熱 Strike while the iron is hot.

dǎtīng 打聽 to inquire; to find out through inquiries

dǎtōng 打通 to establish a connection

dǎtóuzhèn 打頭陣 to lead the attack

dǎ tuìtánggǔ 打退堂鼓 to give up halfway; to back out

dǎxiǎng 打響 1. to start shooting 2. to win initial success

dǎxiāo 打消 to give up (an intention, etc.)

dǎ xiǎobàogào 打小報告 to inform secretly on a colleague, etc.

dǎxìnhào 打信號 to signal

dǎyájì 打牙祭 to have a rare

sumptuous meal

dǎyáng 打烊 to close the store for the night

dǎyē 打噎 to belch; to hiccup

dǎyìnjī 打印機 a printer

dǎyóujī 打游擊 1. to engage in guerrilla warfare 2. (humorously) to use, borrow or take another's belongings without permission

dǎyóují 打游擊 refer to **dǎyóujī** 打游擊

dǎyú 打魚 to catch fish with nets

dǎyuánchǎng 打圓場 to mediate a dispute

dǎzár 打雜兒 to drudge to do odds and ends

dǎzhàng 打仗 to engage in a battle; to fight

dǎzhāohū 打招呼 1.to say hello 2. to use one's influence in other's behalf

dǎzhāomiànr 打照面兒 to meet face to face

dǎzhé 打折 at a discount

dǎzhékòu 打折扣 1. at a discount 2. to detract (from some desirable quality)

dǎzhēn 打針 to give or receive an injection

dǎ zhīmíngdù 打知名度 to seek publicity

dǎzhǒngliǎn chōngpàngzi 打腫臉充胖子 to try to satisfy one's own vanity at any cost

dǎzhòng 打中 to hit the mark

dǎzhǔyì 打主意 1. to decide what to do 2. to scheme for something to which one has no claim

dǎzhù 打住 to stop

dǎzhuàn 打轉 1. to revolve 2. to go round

dǎzì 打字 to do typing work; to typewrite; to type

dǎzìjī 打字機 a typewriter

dǎzìyuán 打字員 a typist

dǎzuò 打坐 (said of a Buddhist) to sit in meditation

dà 大

1. big; large 2. great 3. much 4. very; highly; extremely; greatly 5. (polite expression) your 6. the

dàbáicài 大白菜 a Chinese cabbage

dàbài 大敗 1. to defeat utterly 2. to suffer a severe defeat

dàbān 大班 1. the manager of a foreign firm in China 2. the captain (as of taxi dancers) 3. the senior class in a kindergarten

dàbàn 大半 1. for the most part; mostly 2. probably; likely

dàběnyíng 大本營 headquarters

dàbiàn 大便 1. stool; shit 2. to empty the bowels

dàbó 大伯 1. one's father's elder brother; an uncle 2. an uncle (a polite form of address for an elderly man)

dàbùfen 大部分 for the most part; mainly

dàbù rúqián 大不如前 far worse than it was before

dàbù xiāngtóng 大不相同 entirely or totally different

dàbuliǎo 大不了 1. at the worst 2. serious

dàcái xiǎoyòng 大才小用 to make little use of great talent

dàcháng 大腸 the large intestine

dàchè dàwù 大徹大悟 1. (usually said of oneself) a profound and complete realization 2. (theology) the great revelation

dàchén 大臣 a ranking official

dàchī dàhē 大吃大喝 to eat and drink extravagantly

dàchī yījīng 大吃一驚 to be greatly surprised; to be taken aback

dàchū yángxiàng 大出洋相 to commit a big blunder in public

dàchù zhuóyǎn, xiǎochù zhuóshǒu 大處著眼，小處著手 to make an overall assessment but to start from details

dàchuī dàléi 大吹大擂 refer to **dàchuī dàlèi** 大吹大擂

dàchuī dàlèi 大吹大擂 to brag and blare

dàcí dàbēi 大慈大悲 the great mercy

dàcuò tècuò 大錯特錯 to make a gross error

dàdǎ chūshǒu 大打出手 to get into a free-for-all or a brawl

dàdà xiǎoxiǎo 大大小小 the big and the small—the whole

dàdǎn 大膽 bold; boldness

dàdāo kuòfǔ 大刀闊斧 to act decisively and resolutely

dàdào 大道 1. a wide road 2. the way of virtue and justice

dàdàolǐ 大道理 1. a persuasive argument 2. a major principle

dàdí dāngqián 大敵當前 confronted with a strong opponent

dàdǐ 大抵 generally speaking; for the most part

dàdì 大地 1. the earth 2. the whole territory of a nation

dàdòngmài 大動脈 the main artery

dàdòu 大豆 soybeans

dàdūshì 大都市 a large city; a metropolis

dàdù 大度 magnanimity; generosity

dàdùzi 大肚子 1. pregnant 2. a big eater 3. a potbelly

dàduì rénmǎ 大隊人馬 a large number of soldiers and horses

dàduō 大多 for the most part; mostly

dàduōshù 大多數 the majority

dàér huàzhī 大而化之 careless; slapdash; perfunctory

dàér wúdàng 大而無當 big but useless

dàfā cíwēi 大發雌威 1. (said of a woman) to get very angry 2. (said of a woman athlete) to display great prowess

dàfā léitíng 大發雷霆 to be furious

dàfā lìshì 大發利市 to make big profits

dàfǎguān 大法官 a grand justice

dàfāng 大方 experts; connoisseurs

dàfāng juécí 大放厥辭 to boast

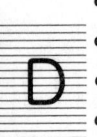

dàfāng yìcǎi 大放異彩 (said of sports performance, etc.) to yield unusually brilliant results

dàfāng 大方 1. generous 2. elegant and composed

dàfèi zhōuzhāng 大費周章 to take great pains

dàfēng dàlàng 大風大浪 great storms

dàfù piánpián 大腹便便 paunchy; potbellied

dàgài 大概 most probably; generally

dàgāng 大綱 a synopsis; a summary

dàgē 大哥 1. the eldest brother 2. elder brother (a polite form of address for a man about one's own age)

dàgēdà 大哥大 a walkie-talkie (a mobile phone); a cellular phone

dàgèr 大個兒 a big man; a giant; a tall guy

dàgōng gàochéng 大功告成 (said of a big or difficult task) to have finally come to completion

dàgōng wúsī 大公無私 all for the public without selfish considerations

dàgūniang 大姑娘 a maiden; a damsel

dàguīmó 大規模 large-scale

dàguō 大鍋 a satellite dish

dàguò 大過 1. a big mistake 2. (said of punishment in school, etc.) a major demerit

dàhǎi 大海 1. a widemouthed bowl or wine cup 2. the ocean

dàhǎi lāozhēn 大海撈針 to look for a needle in a haystack

dàhǎn dàjiào 大喊大叫 1. to shout at the top of one's voice 2. to conduct vigorous propaganda

dàhǎo héshān 大好河山 beautiful rivers and mountains

dàhǎo 大號 1. large-size 2. (music) a tuba; a bass horn

dàhēng 大亨 a bigwig; a tycoon; a magnate

dàhóng dàlù 大紅大綠 gaudy and showy

dàhóng dàzǐ 大紅大紫 to become very popular

dàhòutiān 大後天 two days after tomorrow

dàhù rénjiā 大戶人家 a wealthy and influential family

dàhuāliǎn 大花臉 (Peking opera) a male role of dignified type

dàhuà 大話 boasts; big words

dàhuì 大會 a rally; a conference

dàhuǒr 大夥兒 1. us; we 2. a group of people

dàhuò bùjiě 大惑不解 incomprehensible

dàjí dàlì 大吉大利 very smooth going

dàjiā 大家 1. all of us; we 2. a rich and influential family of long standing 3. a famous expert; a master

dàjiātíng 大家庭 1. a big family 2. a community

dàjià 大駕 1. to your gracious presence 2. the carriage for a sovereign or emperor

dàjiàng 大將 1. an important general; a capable commander 2. a trusted lieutenant 3. a senior general

dàjiē xiǎoxiàng 大街小巷 every street and alley—all over the city

dàjiě 大姊 the eldest sister

dàjīng xiǎoguài 大驚小怪 to make a fuss

dàjiùzi 大舅子 one's wife's elder brothers

dàjú 大局 1. the situation in general 2. the fate of a nation

dàjǔ 大舉 1. large-scale (invasions, etc.) 2. a great undertaking

dàjūn 大軍 a great concentration of troops

dàkāi yǎnjiè 大開眼界 to see something completely new or very strange

dàkǎo 大考 the final examination in school

dàkě bùbì 大可不必 It's unnecessary.

dàkuài rénxīn 大快人心 (usu-

ally said of a wrong being righted, justice prevailed, etc.) to give all a lift of the heart

dàkuàitou 大塊頭 a tall and bulky fellow

dàlǐshí 大理石 marble

dàlǐtáng 大禮堂 an auditorium

dàlìshì 大力士 a hercules

dàliàng 大量 1. a large quantity; mass 2. magnanimous

dàlóu 大樓 a multistoried building

dàlù 大陸 a continent; the mainland

dàlüè 大略 1. brief; generally 2. (a man of) great caliber 3. a general outline

dàmá 大麻 1. hemp 2. marijuana

dàmén 大門 the main door or gate

dàmèng chūxǐng 大夢初醒 the awakening or realization (of past wrongdoings, etc.)

dàmíng 大名 1. your name (used in formal speech) 2. a reputation

dàmíng dǐngdǐng 大名鼎鼎 very famous; celebrated; well-known

dàmú dàyàng 大模大樣 1. with full composure 2. proudly; haughtily

dàmuzhǐ 大拇指 thumb

dà'nàn líntóu 大難臨頭 to be faced with great trouble

dànì bùdào 大逆不道 sedition; treason; traitorous actions

dànián chūyī 大年初一 the first day of the lunar year

Dàniányè 大年夜 on the night of the lunar New Year's Eve

dàpái 大牌 (said of movie stars, etc.) leading or big-name (actors or actresses)

dàpào 大砲 1. a gun; a battery; a cannon 2. (slang) one who talks big

dàpī 大批 a large batch of; a good deal of

dàqì wǎnchéng 大器晚成 A great man will take time to shape and mature.

dàqiān shìjiè 大千世界 the kaleidoscopic world

dàqiántí 大前提 a major premise

dàqiántiān 大前天 three days ago

dàqīngzǎo 大清早 very early in the morning

dàqíngrén 大情人 a Casanova, or ladies' man

dàquán 大全 a complete collection of

dàquán pángluò 大權旁落 Power has fallen into the hands of others.

dàquán zàiwò 大權在握 to hold power unchallenged

dàrén 大人 (in ancient China) a respectful salutation for one's parents, seniors, etc.

dàrénwù 大人物 a VIP; a big shot

dàren 大人 an adult

dàsǎo 大嫂 1. one's eldest sister-in-law 2. a polite name for women of similar age as oneself

dàsǎochú 大掃除 to make a thorough cleanup

dàshà 大廈 a big building; mansion

dàshàoyé 少少爺 1. a term used by a servant to address the eldest son of the family 2. a dandy; a playboy

dàshè 大赦 an amnesty

dàshēng jíhū 大聲疾呼 to urge emphatically

dàshī 大師 1. a master 2. a reverent title for a Buddhist monk 3. maestro

dàshīfu 大師傅 1. a professional master 2. a salutation for a Buddhist monk

dàshī suǒwàng 大失所望 to be greatly disappointed

dàshǐ 大使 an ambassador

dàshǐguǎn 大使館 an embassy

dàshì 大事 important events; serious matters

dàshì huàxiǎo, xiǎoshì huàwú 大事化小，小事化無 to turn big problems into small problems and small problems into no problem at all

dàshì pūzhāng 大事鋪張 to

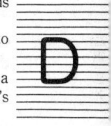

make lavish preparations

dàshì suǒqū 大勢所趨 general trend indicates...; according to the prevailing tendency

dàshì xuānchuán 大事宣傳 to play up; ballyhoo

dàshì yǐqù 大勢已去 The situation is hopeless, etc.

dàshǒubǐ 大手筆 the work or handwriting of a great author or calligrapher

dàsì páoxiāo 大肆咆哮 to roar with rage

dàsuàn 大蒜 garlic

dàtíqín 大提琴 a cello

dàtǐ 大體 1. generally; on the whole 2. the main principle

dàtīng 大廳 the main hall; the parlor

dàtíng guǎngzhòng 大庭廣衆 1. public places where the crowd gather 2. in public

dàtóng shìjiè 大同世界 a political utopia

dàtóng xiǎoyì 大同小異 almost the same

dàtóuzhēn 大頭針 a tack

dàtuányuán 大團圓 a happy ending; a happy reunion

dàtuǐ 大腿 the thigh

dàwáng 大王 1. Your Majesty 2. the chief of brigands

dàwénháo 大文豪 a renowned man of letters

dàwúwèi 大無畏 dauntless; fearless

Dàxīyáng 大西洋 the Atlantic Ocean

dàxǐ guòwàng 大喜過望 to be overjoyed

dàxiǎn shēnshǒu 大顯身手 to display one's skill to the full

dàxiǎn shéntōng 大顯神通 to display one's remarkable skill or abilities to the full

dàxiǎo 大小 1. adults and children 2. sizes (of shoes, etc.) 3. degree of seniority

dàxiǎobiàn 大小便 night soil and urine

dàxiǎo bùyī 大小不一 irregular in size, age, etc.

dàxiǎojie 大小姐 1. a maiden; a Miss 2. a reference to others' elder or eldest daughters

dàxiào 大笑 to laugh heartily

dàxiě 大寫 1. a capital letter 2. the elaborate form of Chinese numerals (used especially in accounting and checks)

dàxīng tǔmù 大興土木 to start a large-scale building project

dàxíng 大型 (said of machines, etc.) large-sized; large-scale

dàxuǎn 大選 1. a presidential election 2. general elections for congressmen

dàxué 大學 1. a university or college 2. *The Great Learning* (one of the *Four Classics*)

dàxuésheng 大學生 a college or university student; a collegian

dàyán bùcán 大言不慚 to boast unabashedly or shamelessly

dàyáng 大洋 1. a silver dollar 2. an ocean

Dàyángzhōu 大洋洲 Oceania; Oceanica

dàyáo dàbǎi 大搖大擺 to swagger

dàyī 大衣 an overcoat

dàyì 大意 1. the general idea; the gist 2. high ambitions

dàyi 大意 negligent

dàyǒu fēnbié 大有分別 poles apart or entirely different

dàyǒu kěwéi 大有可爲 very promising (projects, etc.); very hopeful

dàyǒu rénzài 大有人在 Such people are by no means rare.

dàyǒu wénzhāng 大有文章 There's something behind all this.

dàyú dàròu 大魚大肉 rich food (implying gluttony)

dàyǔ 大雨 heavy rain

dàyuánshuài 大元帥 a marshal; the commander in chief of the armed forces

dàyuē 大約 about; around; probably; likely

dàzáhuì 大雜燴 a hodgepodge

dàzhǎn hóngtú 大展宏圖 to

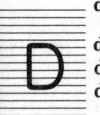

ride on the crest of success

dàzhāng qígǔ 大張旗鼓 1. to make a big show 2. on a grand scale

dàzhāng tǎfá 大張撻伐 to attack with full force

dàzhàngfu 大丈夫 a real man

dàzhì 大致 1. for the most part 2. about

dàzhì ruòyú 大智若愚 The wise man looks dumb.

dàzhòng 大眾 the masses; the public

dàzhòng chuánbō 大眾傳播 mass communications

dàzhòng chuánbō méitǐ 大眾傳播媒體 mass (communications) media

dàzhònghuà 大眾化 to popularize

dàzhòng jiéyùn xìtǒng 大眾捷運系統 mass rapid transit (MRT)

dàzhòng wénxué 大眾文學 popular literature

dàzhǔjiào 大主教 an archbishop

dàzhuān yuànxiào 大專院校 colleges and universities

dàzìbào 大字報 a big-character poster

dàzìrán 大自然 nature

dàzōng 大宗 a large batch; lots of

dàzuò 大作 1. your work, etc. 2. (said of violence, etc.) to erupt; to upheave 3. (said of music, etc.) to come out in ensemble and rather suddenly

dāi 呆(獃) also ái
1. dull; dull-witted; stupid; unintelligent 2. blank; wooden

dāibǎn 呆板 1. boring; dull 2. stiff

dāiruò mùjī 呆若木雞 very dull or stupid

dāizhàng 呆帳 bad debt

dāizhì 呆滯 dull

dāizi 呆子 an idiot; a dullard

dāi 待

1. to stay 2. later

dāibuzhù 待不住 can't or won't stay long

dāidezhù 待得住 able to stay long

dāihuǐr 待會兒 just a little while

dǎi 歹

bad; wicked; depraved; crooked evil; vicious

dǎidú 歹毒 vicious; malicious; malice

dǎiniàn 歹念 evil thoughts

dǎitú 歹徒 a hoodlum; a ruffian; a scoundrel

dǎiyì 歹意 malicious intent; bad intentions

dǎi 逮

to capture; to catch

dǎizhù 逮住 to catch (a thief, a ball, etc.)

dài 大

dàifu 大夫 a doctor

dài 代

1. a generation 2. a dynasty 3. an era 4. to be a substitute or an equivalent; to take the place of

dàibàn 代辦 to manage on behalf of another

dàibǐ 代筆 to write for another

dàibiǎo 代表 1. to represent; to stand for 2. a representative; a delegate; a proxy

dàibiǎoquán 代表權 representation

dàibiǎotuán 代表團 a delegation

dàidǎ 代打 to pinch-hit

dàigōu 代溝 the generation gap

dàihào 代號 a code name

dàihuàn 代換 to replace

dàijià 代價 price; cost; reward

dàikè 代課 to teach on behalf of another teacher

dàiláo 代勞 to labor on behalf of another

dàilǐ 代理 1. an agent 2. to serve as agent of; to act for

dàilǐrén 代理人 an agent; a rep-

D

resentative

dàilǐshāng 代理商 a business agent; an agent

dàimíngcí 代名詞 a pronoun

dàiqiān 代簽 procuration indorsement

dàirén shòuguò 代人受過 to take the blame for others

dàishòu 代售 to be commissioned to sell something

dàishū 代書 a scrivener

dàishù 代數 algebra

dàitì 代替 to take the place of; to substitute

dàiwéi shuōxiàng 代為說項 to intercede or intervene for another person

dàixiāo 代銷 to sell on consignment

dàixiāoshāng 代銷商 a consignee

dàixiè 代謝 1. to express thanks to someone on behalf of others 2. to metabolize

dàiyán 代言 to speak in behalf of

dàiyánrén 代言人 a spokesman; a mouthpiece

dàiyòng 代用 to substitute for something

dàiyòngpǐn 代用品 a substitute; an ersatz

dàizuì gāoyáng 代罪羔羊 a scapegoat

dài 待

1. to treat; to entertain 2. to await; to wait for 3. need 4. until

dàichá 待查 yet to be investigated

dàifā 待發 ready to depart

dàijī 待機 to await the opportune moment (for action)

dàijià érgū 待價而沽 to wait for the right (favorable) price to sell

dàikè 待客 to receive (or entertain) guests

dàilǐng 待領 (said of money, articles) to wait for a claimant

dàimìng 待命 to await orders

dàipìn 待聘 to wait for employ-

ment

dàirén jiēwù 待人接物 the way one treats people

dàirú jǐchū 待如己出 to treat a child as if he were one's own

dàixù 待續 to be continued

dàiyè 待業 to wait for employment

dàiyù 待遇 1. pay, salary, or remuneration 2. the manner of treating people

dàizì guīzhōng 待字閨中 (said of a young woman) not betrothed yet

dài 殆

1. precarious; dangerous; danger; perilous 2. tired 3. afraid 4. nearly; almost 5. only; merely; even

dàiyǐ wúwàng 殆已無望 nearly hopeless

dài 玳

the tortoise shell

dàimào 玳瑁 a hawksbill turtle

dàimèi 玳瑁 refer to **dàimào** 玳瑁

dài 怠

1. idle; remiss; lax; negligent 2. to treat coldly

dàiduò 怠惰 idle and lazy

dàihū 怠忽 to be remiss; to neglect

dàimàn 怠慢 1. to neglect a visitor or guest (often used as a polite expression) 2. lax and crude; idle and remiss

dài 袋

a bag; a sack; a pocket; a pouch

dàishǔ 袋鼠 the kangaroo

dài 帶

1. a girdle; a sash; a belt; a band 2. to wear (a smile, sword, etc.) 3. to bear; to bring along 4. to lead (the way, troops, etc.) 5. to head (an army, etc.) 5. a climatic zone

dàibīng 帶兵 1. to lead troops 2. to carry arms

dàidòng 帶動 to drive; to spur on

dàiduì 帶隊 1. to lead a group 2.

the leader of a group, party or mission

dàihuài 帶壞 to lead astray

dàihuí 帶回 to bring back

dàijìn 帶勁 1. energetic 2. interesting; exciting

dàilai 帶來 to bring here

dàilǐng 帶領 to lead (an army, a party, etc.)

dàilù 帶路 to lead the way

dàiqu 帶去 to bring away; to take along

dàishāng 帶傷 to get wounded or injured

dàishang 帶上 1. to present to you 2. to bring out (the prisoner, etc.) 3. in addition to

dàitóu 帶頭 to pioneer; to initiate; to lead

dàixiào 帶笑 smilingly; wearing a smile

dàixìn 帶信 to take a message

dàiyú 帶魚 ribbonfish; hairtail

dàizi 帶子 1. a ribbon; laces (of shoes, boots, etc.) 2. a tape 3. a belt

dài 逮

1. to reach; to come up to 2. to hunt; to chase and make arrest

dàibǔ 逮捕 to make arrest

dài 貸

1. to loan; to lend or borrow; a loan 2. the credit side in bookkeeping 3. to pardon; to be lenient 4. to shift (responsibility); to shirk

dàikuǎn 貸款 a loan (of money)

dài 黛

1. a bluish-black material used by ancient women to blacken their eyebrows 2. a beauty

dài 戴

1. to wear on the head, the nose, the ear, or the hand; to put on 2. to support; to sustain; to bear 3. a Chinese family name 4. to respect; to honor

dàigāomào 戴高帽 to receive a compliment or flattery; to flatter

dàilǜmào 戴綠帽 to be a cuckold

dàixiào 戴孝 to go into mourning

dàiyǎnjìng 戴眼鏡 to wear glasses or spectacles

dàizuì lìgōng 戴罪立功 to atone for a mistake or failure by meritorious services

dān 丹

1. cinnabar 2. red; scarlet 3. a sophisticated decoction 4. a medical pill, ointment and powder

dānchéng 丹誠 loyalty; devotion

Dānmài 丹麥 Denmark

dāntián 丹田 (Taoism) the region three inches below the navel

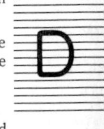

dān 耽(躭)

1. to indulge in; to be addicted to 2. delightful and enduring 3. (said of ears) large and drooping 4. negligent

dān'ge 耽擱 1. to stay; to stop over; a stopover 2. to delay

dānnì 耽溺 to indulge in (evil ways)

dānwù 耽誤 to delay; to hold up

dān 單

1. single; individual 2. alone; only 3. simple 4. of an odd number 5. a slip of paper 6. a list

dānbó 單薄 weak; feeble; flimsy

dānchē 單車 a bicycle

dānchún 單純 1. simple; plain 2. unpretending

dāndǎ 單打 (sports) singles

dāndāo zhírù 單刀直入 (said of action, statement, etc.) straightforward; direct

dāndiào 單調 dull; monotonous; dry; boring

dāndú 單獨 independent; alone

dānfāngmiàn 單方面 one-sided; unilateral

dān'gàng 單槓 (sports) a horizontal bar

dānhào 單號 odd numbers (of seats, ticket, etc.)

dānjià 單價 a unit price

dānjù 單據 a receipt

dānliàn 單戀 one-sided love; unrequited love

dānmiànshǒu 單面手 people who master in one skill only

dānqiāng pǐmǎ 單槍匹馬 refer to **dānqiāng pǐmǎ** 單槍匹馬

dānqiāng pǐmǎ 單槍匹馬 to take on the enemy alone

dānqīn jiātíng 單親家庭 a single-parent family

dānrénchuáng 單人床 a single bed

dānrénfáng 單人房 a single-bed room (in a hotel)

dānshēn 單身 1. alone; unaccompanied 2. unmarried; single

dānshēn guìzú 單身貴族 (colloquial) unmarried gentlemen or ladies

dānshēnhàn 單身漢 a bachelor

dānshēn sùshè 單身宿舍 quarters for single men or women

dānshù 單數 1. an odd number 2. (grammar) singular

dānwèi 單位 1. a unit (in measurement) 2. a military unit or organization

dānxiāngsī 單相思 unrequited love

dānxiàng 單向 one-way; unidirectional

dānxíngběn 單行本 a separate volume

dānxíngdào 單行道 a one-way path, or a one-way street

dānyī 單一 single; unitary

dānyīnjié 單音節 monosyllabic

dānyuánjù 單元劇 a single-episode drama

dānzì 單字 a single character or word

dānzi 單子 a list; a bill; a form

dān 擔

to shoulder; to take upon oneself

dānbǎo 擔保 to guarantee; to pledge

dāndài 擔待 to be lenient

dāndāng 擔當 to take (responsibility) upon oneself, or undertake (a task)

dānfù 擔負 1. a burden; responsibility 2. to assume a responsibility; to undertake

dānjià 擔架 a stretcher

dānrèn 擔任 to take charge of (a task); to hold the post of

dānxīn 擔心 to worry; to feel anxious

dānyōu 擔憂 to be anxious; to worry; to apprehensive

dān 殫 to use up; to exhaust

dānjīng jiélǜ 殫精竭慮 to devote one's entire energy and thought

dǎn 撢 1. to dust; to brush lightly; to whisk 2. a duster

dǎnzi 撢子 a duster

dǎn 膽(胆) 1. the gall 2. courage; bravery; audacity 3. the internal parts, etc. of a vessel 4. the tube of a tire, basketball, etc.

dǎndà bāotiān 膽大包天 recklessly bold; extremely audacious

dǎndà wàngwéi 膽大妄爲 audacious and reckless

dǎn'gǎn 膽敢 so audacious as to; to dare

dǎngùchún 膽固醇 cholesterol; cholesterin

dǎnliàng 膽量 courage; bravery; guts

dǎnqiè 膽怯 frightened; afraid; fainthearted

dǎnquè 膽怯 refer to **dǎnqiè** 膽怯

dǎnshí 膽石 a gallstone

dǎnshí 膽識 courage and wisdom

dǎnshì 膽識 refer to **dǎnshí** 膽識

dǎnxiǎo 膽小 timid; cowardly

dǎnxiǎoguǐ 膽小鬼 a coward

dǎnxiǎo rúshǔ 膽小如鼠 as scared as a mouse

dǎnzhàn xīnjīng 膽戰心驚 tremble with fear

dǎnzhī 膽汁 bile

dǎnzi 膽子 courage; bravery; audacity; nerve

dàn 石

1. a dry measure for grains roughly equivalent to 120-160 pounds; picul 2. a weight measure equivalent to about 110 pounds

dàn 旦

1. daybreak; dawn 2. day; morning 3. a female role in Chinese opera

dànbù bǎoxī 旦不保夕 not knowing how the day will end

dànbù bǎoxī 旦不保夕 refer to **dànbù bǎoxī** 旦不保夕

dànjué 旦角 a female role in Chinese opera

dànxī zhījiān 旦夕之間 within a single day; between morning and evening—a very short time

dànxì zhījiān 旦夕之間 refer to **dànxī zhījiān** 旦夕之間

dàn 但

but; however; yet

dànshǐ 但使 only if; as long as

dànshì 但是 but; however; yet

dànshū 但書 a proviso; a condition

dànshuō wúfāng 但說無妨 Just speak out what is in your mind.

dànshuō wúfāng 但說無妨 refer to **dànshuō wúfāng** 但說無妨

dànyuàn 但願 to wish; to hope

dàn 淡

1. weak or thin (tea, etc.) 2. tasteless; insipid 3. off-season; slack 4. light (in color); slight 5. (澹) without worldly desires 6. (氮) nitrogen

dànbó 淡泊 to lead a tranquil life without worldly desires

dànbó 淡薄 1. thin; weak; light 2. to become indifferent 3. dim; faint

dànbó mínglì 淡泊名利 to be indifferent to fame and wealth

dànhuà 淡化 1. desalination 2. to play down

dànjì 淡季 slack seasons (for business)

dànmò 淡漠 indifference; aloofness

dànrán zhìzhī 淡然置之 to take it easy

dànsǎo éméi 淡掃娥眉 (said of a woman) to apply a light make-up

dànsè 淡色 a light color; light-colored

dànshuǐ 淡水 1. fresh water 2. Danshui (Tamsui), Taiwan

dànshuǐhú 淡水湖 a freshwater lake

dànshuǐyú 淡水魚 fishes grown in fresh water

dànwàng 淡忘 to fade from one's memory

dànyǎ 淡雅 (said of attire, decoration, etc.) light, simple but graceful or elegant

dànyuè 淡月 a slack month (for business, etc.)

dàn 蛋

1. an egg 2. a fellow

dànbái 蛋白 egg white; albumen

dànbáizhì 蛋白質 refer to **dànbáizhì** 蛋白質

dànbáizhì 蛋白質 protein; albumen

dàn'gāo 蛋糕 cake

dànhuáng 蛋黃 yolk

dànké 蛋殼 the eggshell

dànqīng 蛋清 egg white; albumen

dàn 氮

nitrogen

dàn 萏

another name of water lily

dàn 誕

1. birth 2. preposterous; absurd 3. an initial particle

dànchén 誕辰 birthday

dànshēng 誕生 birth

dàn 彈

a pellet; a bullet; a bomb

dàndào fēidàn 彈道飛彈 a ballistic missile

dàngōng 彈弓 a slingshot; a catapult

dànjìn yuánjué 彈盡援絕 The ammunition is gone, and rein-

D

forcements are nowhere in sight.

dànké 彈殼 an empty cartridge case

dàntóu 彈頭 a projectile nose; a warhead

dànwán zhīdì 彈丸之地 a very small piece of land

dànxiá 彈匣 (military) a magazine

dànyào 彈藥 ammunition

dànyàokù 彈藥庫 an ammunition depot; a magazine

dànzifáng 彈子房 a billiard room; a poolroom

D

dàn 擔

1. a load; a burden 2. a unit of weight or capacity

dànzi 擔子 a load or burden upon the shoulder or the back

dāng 當

1. to undertake or assume (responsibilities, etc.); to accept 2. to face 3. equal; well-matched 4. ought to; should; must 5. just at (a time or a place) 6. to work as; to serve as

dāngbān 當班 to be on duty by turns

dāngbīng 當兵 to serve in the army; to be a soldier

dāngchāi 當差 to do a duty; to be on duty

dāngchǎng 當場 on the spot; then and there

dāngchǎng chūchǒu 當場出醜 to suffer embarrassment right before a crowd

dāngchū 當初 at first; in the beginning

dāngdài 當代 in the present age

dāngdào 當道 1. to be in power 2. to block one's way

dāngdì 當地 this place; local

dāngjī lìduàn 當機立斷 to make quick decisions in the face of problems

dāngjí 當即 immediately; right away

dāngjiā 當家 to housekeep; to be the master of a family, an organization, etc.

dāngjiē 當街 in the street

dāngjīn 當今 1. the present time; today 2. the reigning emperor

dāngjú 當局 the authorities

dāngjúzhě mí, pángguānzhě qīng 當局者迷，旁觀者清 The onlooker sees the game more clearly than the players.

dāngmiàn 當面 right in one's face; face to face

dāngmiàn yánmíng 當面言明 to state clearly in one's presence

dāngnián 當年 that year

dāngqián 當前 present; current

dāngquán 當權 to be in power

dāngrán 當然 1. of course; naturally 2. as it should be; only natural

dāngrén bùràng 當仁不讓 do not refuse to accept a reward or position which one deserves

dāngshí 當時 at that time; then

dāngshìrén 當事人 those directly involved

dāngtóu bànghè 當頭棒喝 to arouse a person from stupidity by drastic means

dāngwù zhījí 當務之急 a business or task of the greatest urgency at present

dāngxīn 當心 to be careful; to be cautious

dāngxīn páshǒu 當心扒手 Beware of pickpockets!

dāngxuǎn 當選 to get elected; to be elected; to win an election

dāngzhèng 當政 to be in power (or office)

dāngzhī wúkuì 當之無愧 fully deserve (a title, an honor, etc.); to be worthy of

dāngzhōng 當中 right in the middle

dāngzhòng 當眾 in the presence of all

dāngzhòng xuānbù 當眾宣布 to announce publicly

dāng 噹

a loud, resonant metallic sound

dāng 璫

1. richly ornamented 2. pearls

for filling up ear punctures to prevent the holes from closing 3. ancient headgear

dāng 鐺
1. the sound of striking a gong 2. shackles

dǎng 當
to mistake something for another

dǎngshì 當是 to mistake something for another; to think that...

dǎng 擋
1. to obstruct; to impede; to stop; to resist; to ward off 2. a fender; a blind 3. a gear

dǎngfēng bōli 擋風玻璃 a windshield

dǎngjià 擋駕 to decline to receive visitors

dǎngjiànpái 擋箭牌 1. a shield 2. an excuse; a pretext

dǎnglù 擋路 to be in the way

dǎngníbǎn 擋泥板 a mudguard, or a fender

dǎngzhù 擋住 to block; to impede; to hinder; to obstruct

dǎng 檔
refer to **dàng** 檔

dǎng 黨
1. a party; a faction; a clique; a gang; an association 2. relatives 3. a community of 500 families (in ancient times) 4. to take sides; to associate; to be a partizan 5. the village

dǎngbù 黨部 the headquarters of a political party

dǎnggāng 黨綱 the platform of a political party

dǎngguó 黨國 the party and the nation

dǎngguó yuánlǎo 黨國元老 an elder statesman of the party and the nation

dǎnghuī 黨徽 the emblem of a political party

dǎngjí 黨籍 a party affiliation

dǎngjì 黨紀 party discipline

dǎngkuí 黨魁 a party boss; a party chieftain

dǎnglíng 黨齡 party standing

dǎngpài 黨派 factions; parties; cliques

dǎngqí 黨旗 the flag of a political party

dǎngtóng fáyì 黨同伐異 to unite with those who agree and fight those who differ

dǎngwài 黨外 outside the party

dǎngwù 黨務 party affairs

dǎngyǔ 黨羽 adherents or followers (especially of a condemned leader)

dǎngyuán 黨員 a party member; a partisan

dǎngzhāng 黨章 the constitution of a political party

dǎngzhēng 黨爭 a factional fight; a partisan war

dǎngzhèng 黨政 the party and the government administration

dǎngzhèng 黨證 a membership card of a political party

dàng 當
1. proper; appropriate 2. to pawn; to mortgage; to pledge 3. to take as; to regard as; to consider as 4. to flunk 5. to break down 6. that very same (place, year, day, etc.)

dàng ěrbiānfēng 當耳邊風 to take no serious heed to (advice, etc.)

dàngjī 當機 1. to break down 2. (computer) unexpected failure or shut down

dàngpiào 當票 a pawn ticket

dàngpù 當鋪 a pawnshop

dàngrì 當日 on the same day; on that very day

dàngshí 當時 at that very moment; immediately

dàngtiān 當天 on the same day; on that very day

dàngzhēn 當真 to be serious; no joking

dàngzuò 當做 to regard as; to treat as

dàng 蕩
1. a pond; a pool 2. to cleanse; to wash away 3. to shake; to oscillate; to move to and fro; to loaf

D

about; unsettled; vagrant 4. dissipated; wanton; debauched; licentious; of loose morals 5. agitated; disturbed 6. vast; large; magnificent

dàngfù 蕩婦 a woman of loose morals

dàngqì huícháng 蕩氣迴腸 (said of music or writing) very touching; pathetic

dàngrán wúcún 蕩然無存 to have nothing left

dàngyàng 蕩漾 1. moving, as in ripples 2. agitated or excited 3. to rise and fall like waves; to ripple

dàng 擋
used in the combination of **bìndàng** 摒擋—to arrange in order; to pack up for traveling

dàng 檔 also **dǎng**
1. files 2. shelves; pigeonholes 3. a wooden crosspiece, as the rung of a ladder, etc.

dàng'àn 檔案 archives; offical files (of government offices)

dàng'àn guǎnlǐ 檔案管理 file management

dàngqī 檔期 a schedule for showing motion picture in a theater

dàngqí 檔期 refer to **dàngqī** 檔期

dāo 刀
1. a knife; a blade; a sword 2. knife-shaped coins of ancient China

dāobǎzi 刀把子 the handle of a knife

dāobèi 刀背 the back of a knife

dāochā 刀叉 knives and forks

dāofēng 刀鋒 the blade or edge of a knife

dāokǒu 刀口 1. the blade or edge of a knife 2. an occasion on which money can be spent to advantage

dāomǎdàn 刀馬旦 (Peking opera) the role of a female warrior

dāopiàn 刀片 a razor blade

dāoqiāng 刀槍 swords and spears; weapons

dāoqiào 刀鞘 a sheath

dāorèn 刀刃 1. the blade or edge of a knife 2. an occasion on which money can be spent to advantage

dāoshāng 刀傷 1. knife wound 2. to conflict a wound or injure with a knife

dāozi 刀子 a small knife; a dagger

dāo 叨
talkative; garrulous; fond of talking

dǎo 倒
to fall down; to lie down

dǎobì 倒閉 to close down a shop; to go bankrupt

dǎobì 倒斃 to fall dead

dǎogé 倒閣 the resignation of the cabinet

dǎoméi 倒楣 to be out of luck

dǎotā 倒塌 to collapse

dǎotái 倒臺 to fall from power

dǎowèikǒu 倒胃口 to spoil one's appetite

dǎozhàng 倒帳 1. bad debts 2. to refuse to pay loans under various excuses

dǎo 島
an island; an isle

dǎoguó 島國 an island nation

dǎomín 島民 an islander

dǎoyǔ 島嶼 islands; islets and islands

dǎo 搗
1. to thresh (grains); to hull or unhusk 2. to beat; to pound 3. to drive; to attack 4. to sabotage

dǎodàn 搗蛋 to make trouble; to be mischievous; to sabotage

dǎoguǐ 搗鬼 to play tricks; to sow discord

dǎohuǐ 搗毀 to smash; to sabotage

dǎoluàn 搗亂 to cause disturbance; to sabotage

dǎoluàn fènzǐ 搗亂分子 troublemakers; saboteurs

dǎosuì 搗碎 to pound to pieces

dǎo 導 also **dào**

to guide; to lead; to instruct; to conduct; to direct

dǎoháng 導航 to navigate; navigation

dǎohuǒxiàn 導火線 1. a fuse (for setting off explosives) 2. the direct cause (of a development or event)

dǎolùn 導論 an introducoion

dǎoshī 導師 1. a spiritual guide 2. a tutor

dǎotǐ 導體 an electric conductor

dǎoyǎn 導演 the director

dǎoyóu 導遊 a tourist guide

dǎozhì 導致 to lead to; to cause something to happen

dǎo 蹈 also **dào**

1. to tread; to step; to stamp one's foot 2. to follow; to pursue

dǎo 擣

1. to pound; to beat 2. to attack 3. to harass; to disturb

dǎomǐ 擣米 to hull rice in a mortar

dǎo 禱

to pray; to beseech; to plead; to entreat

dǎogào 禱告 a prayer; to pray

dào 到

to reach; to arrive

dào'àn 到案 to answer a court summons

dàochǎng 到場 to show up; to be present

dàochù 到處 everywhere; far and wide

dàochù wéijiā 到處為家 Everywhere may be one's home.

dàodá 到達 to reach; to arrive

dàodǐ 到底 1. after all; at length; finally 2. to reach the extremity

dàojiā 到家 1. to get home 2. to become proficient, or extremely well-versed

dàoqī 到期 to reach the deadline or date of termination; to expire

dàoqí 到期 refer to **dàoqī** 到期

dàoqí 到齊 Everybody (who is

supposed to be here) has come.

dàorèn 到任 to assume a (high official) post

dàoshǒu 到手 to come into one's hands or possession

dàotóulái 到頭來 after all; in the end

dàozhí 到職 to arrive for a new assignment

dào 倒

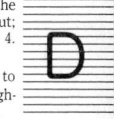

1. to inverse; to place upside down; in reverse order or the wrong direction 2. to pour out; to empty 3. on the contrary 4. after all 5. but; and yet

dàobèi rúliú 倒背如流 to understand something thoroughly by heart

dàoburú 倒不如 1. would rather 2. not better than; even worse than

dàocǎi 倒彩 (Chinese opera) to applaud when a performer slips

dàochē 倒車 to back up a car, locomotive, etc.

dàodúmiǎo 倒讀秒 to count down

dàogē 倒戈 to apostatize or tergiversate; mutiny

dàoguàn 倒灌 to flow backward

dàolì 倒立 1. to stand upside down 2. a handstand

dàoshǔ 倒數 to count from bottom to top

dàoshǔ jìshí 倒數計時 to count down

dàotuì 倒退 1. to retreat; to fall back 2. to retrospect

dàoxíng nìshī 倒行逆施 to go against commonsense rules

dàoxù 倒敘 to narrate an incident in inverted order chronologically

dàoyǐng 倒影 the reflection of something in the water

dàozāicōng 倒栽蔥 to fall headlong

dàozhì 倒置 to place (things, etc.) in wrong order; to place emphasis on the wrong point

dàozhuǎn 倒轉 1. to turn the other way round 2. contrary to reason or one's expectation

dàozhuāng 倒裝 1. to place things in inverted order 2. (rhetoric) hyperbaton

dào 悼
to mourn (for or over); to lament; to regret; to grieve

dàoniàn 悼念 to mourn; to grieve over

dàoshāng 悼傷 to remember (the deceased) with sorrow

dàowáng 悼亡 to be bereaved of one's wife

dào 盜
to steal; to rob; to misappropriate

dàobǎn 盜版 a pirated edition

dàofá 盜伐 to fell trees unlawfully

dàofěi 盜匪 robbers; bandits; brigands

dàohàn 盜汗 (pathology) night sweats

dàoléi 盜壘 base stealing (as of baseball)

dàolù 盜錄 to pirate (records, etc.)

dàomài 盜賣 to misappropriate and sell

dàomù 盜墓 to steal from graves

dàoqiè 盜竊 theft; larceny

dàoqǔ 盜取 to steal; to pilfer

dàoyìn 盜印 to pirate; piracy

dàoyòng 盜用 to embezzle; to usurp

dàozéi 盜賊 a thief; a robber; a bandit

dào 道
1. a road; a path; a street 2. the "way" (in the metaphysical sense) 3. a way; a method 4. Taoism; a Taoist 5. to say; to speak 6. an administrative district in old China 7. a theory; a doctrine 8. to govern; to lead 9. to think; to suppose 10. a skill; an art; a craft

dào bùtóng, bùxiāng wéimóu 道不同,不相爲謀
People adhering to different principles will not map their plan together.

dàodé 道德 morality; morals

dàogāo yìchǐ, mógāo yìzhàng 道高一尺,魔高一丈
The force of evil always manages to beat the force of law.

dàohè 道賀 to congratulate

Dàojiā 道家 the Taoist school

Dàojiào 道教 (religion) Taoism

dàojù 道具 stage properties

dàoli 道理 1. the right way; the proper way 2. reason; rationality

dàolù 道路 a road

dàomào ànrán 道貌岸然 1. to maintain a serene look or dignified appearance 2. to pretend to be a moralist

dàoqiàn 道歉 to make an apology; to apologize

dàoshi 道士 a Taoist priest

dàotīng túshuō 道聽塗說 groundless talk; rumor; hearsay

dàotǒng 道統 orthodoxy of teachings or precepts

dàoxiè 道謝 to thank; to express thanks

dàoxué 道學 1. the emphasis on rationality in learning as advocated by the Song scholars 2. the teachings of Taoism

dàoyì 道義 morals; morality; a sense of righteousness; honor

dào 稻
paddy or rice

dàocǎo 稻草 rice straw

dàocǎorén 稻草人 a scarecrow

dàomǐ 稻米 rice or paddy

dàotián 稻田 a paddy field; a rice field

dàoyāng 稻秧 rice seedlings; rice shoots

dàozi 稻子 unhulled rice

dào 導
refer to **dǎo** 導

dào 蹈
refer to **dǎo** 蹈

dé 得
1. to get; to obtain; to acquire 2. complacent 3. agreement 4. can; may 5. All right! That's enough!

débiāo 得標 to win the contract

débìng 得病 to get sick or ill; to fall sick

débù chángshī 得不償失 not worth the effort

déchěng 得逞 to succeed

déchǒng 得寵 to be favored; to win the favor of

décùn jìnchǐ 得寸進尺 The more one gets, the more one wants.

dédàng 得當 proper; appropriate (ways, arrangements, measures, etc.)

dédào 得到 to succeed in getting or obtaining

dédào duōzhù 得道多助 Those who uphold justice shall not be alone.

défēn 得分 to score; a score

déguò qiěguò 得過且過 to harbor no ambition of achievement; easygoing; to muddle on

déjiǎng 得獎 to win a prize

déjiù 得救 to obtain salvation; to be saved

dékòng 得空 to have spare time

délì 得力 1. capable (assistants, etc.) 2. thanks to 3. to get help from

dé Lǒng wàng Shǔ 得隴望蜀 greedy; avarice; cupidity

dépiào 得票 to gain votes; the votes one obtained in an election

dérénxīn 得人心 to be popular

déshèng 得勝 to win

déshī 得失 gain and loss; success and failure; merits and faults

déshī cānbàn 得失參半 to have both merits and demerits, advantages and disadvantages, gain and loss, etc.

déshì 得勢 to be in a powerful position; to become influential; to be at the helm

déshǒu 得手 to succeed (in performing a task, usually a criminal act)

détǐ 得體 proper (deportment, behavior, conduct, etc.)

détiān dúhòu 得天獨厚 to be particularly favored by nature

déxī 得悉 to have learned; to hear of

déxīn yìngshǒu 得心應手 very smooth operation

déyí 得宜 proper; appropriate; suitable

déyì 得意 to be complacent; to be very satisfied

déyì wàngxíng 得意忘形 to have one's head turned by success; to get dizzy with success

déyì yángyáng 得意洋洋 an appearance of extreme satisfaction; proudly

dézhī 得知 to have learned; to have become acquainted with

dézhì 得志 to have one's ambition fulfilled

dézuì 得罪 1. to offend 2. to violate the law

dé 德

1. morality; decency; virtues 2. favor; kindness 3. behavior; conduct 4. to feel grateful 5. Germany; German

dégāo wàngzhòng 德高望重 (said of a person) of virtue and prestige

Déguó 德國 Germany; Deutschland

Déguó mázhěn 德國麻疹 German measles

déwàng 德望 virtuous conduct and high prestige

Déwén 德文 the German language; German

déxíng 德行 morality and conduct

déxìng 德行 refer to **déxíng** 德行

déxing 德行 (colloquial) manners or appearances

Déyìzhì 德意志 Germany; Deutschland

déyù 德育 moral education

dézé 德澤 the kindness and charity extended to the people

dézhèng 德政 benevolent administration or government

de 地

an adverbial expletive

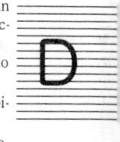

de 的
1. a bound subordinate particle translatable by "s" or with terms interchanged by "of" 2. by "-ly" 3. by an adjectival ending, a prepositional phrase, or a relative

de 得
an adverbial expletive

děi 得
1. must; should; ought to 2. to need; to take

děng 登
1. to ascend; to climb; to rise 2. to record; to register; to enter 3. to take; to employ 4. to board 5. to step on; to tread

dēngbào 登報 to make an announcement in the newspaper

dēngcháng 登場 to be gathered and taken to the threshing ground

dēngchǎng 登場 1. (said of actors, entertainers, etc.) to appear on the stage 2. (said of products) to appear in the market 3. refer to **dēngcháng** 登場

dēngchuán 登船 to take a boat

dēngfēng zàojí 登峰造極 to reach the summit of achievement; to reach the acme

dēnggérè 登革熱 dengue fever

dēngjī 登基 to ascend the throne

dēngjī 登機 to board a plane

dēngjì 登記 to check in; to register

dēngjìbù 登記簿 a register

dēngjìchù 登記處 a registry; a registration office

dēnglóngmén 登龍門 to enter a successful career with the help of an influential person

dēnglù 登陸 to go ashore; to land

dēnglù 登錄 to check in; to register

dēnglùtǐng 登陸艇 landing craft; landing ship tank (LST)

dēnglùzhàn 登陸戰 landing operations

dēngmén bàifǎng 登門拜訪 to make a special call on another at his house; to visit

dēngshān 登山 to climb a mountain; to mountaineer

dēngshānduì 登山隊 a mountaineering party

dēngshān xiéhuì 登山協會 an alpine association

dēngshí 登時 immediately; at once

dēngtáng rùshì 登堂入室 to ascend to the hall and reach the inner room—to master learning or skill

dēngtúzi 登徒子 a lecher; a debauchee

dēngzǎi 登載 (said of a periodical or newspaper) to carry (an article); to publish (a news story)

dēngzài 登載 refer to **dēngzǎi** 登載

dēng 燈
1. a lamp; a lantern; a burner 2. Buddhadharma; the Buddhist doctrine 3. a valve; a tube

dēng'é pūhuǒ 燈蛾撲火 a suicidal act; an act of self-destruction

dēngguāng 燈光 lamplight; lights; illumination

dēnghóng jiǔlǜ 燈紅酒綠 a scene of debauchery

dēnghuǒ 燈火 lamplight; lights illumination

dēnglong 燈籠 a lantern

dēnglongkù 燈籠褲 knickerbockers

dēngmí 燈謎 lantern riddles

dēngpào 燈泡 an electric bulb; a light bulb

dēngruǐ 燈蕊 lampwick; wick

dēngtǎ 燈塔 a lighthouse

dēngyóu 燈油 lamp oil

děng 等
1. rank; grade 2. same; equal 3. to wait 4. when; till 5. and so on, etc.; and the like 6. common

děngdài 等待 to wait for; to await

děngděng 等等 and so forth; et cetera; etc.

děnghào 等號 the equal mark or sign (=)

děnghòu 等候 to wait; to await; to expect

děngjí 等級 grade; rank

děngjùlí 等距離 equal distance; equidistance

děngrén 等人 to wait for someone

děngxián shìzhī 等閒視之 to regard it as of no importance

děngyú 等於 1. to be equal to 2. tantamount to; the same as

dèng 凳
1. a bench 2. a stool

dèngzi 凳子 a stool

dèng 澄
refer to **chéng** 澄

Dèng 鄧
1. a Chinese family name 2. name of an ancient state in what is today's Henan

dèng 瞪
to stare at; to open (one's eyes) wide; to glare at

dèngyǎn 瞪眼 to stare at angrily

dī 氐
1. name of an ancient barbarian tribe to the west 2. (低) low

dī 低
1. low 2. to lower

dīcháo 低潮 a low tide; a low ebb

dīchén 低沈 low and heavy

dīchuí 低垂 to hang low

dīdàng 低檔 refer to **dīdàng** 低檔

dīdàng 低檔 secondary grade

dīgū 低估 to underestimate

dījí 低級 1. elementary; rudimentary 2. vulgar; low

dījí qùwèi 低級趣味 bad taste; vulgar interests

dījí yǔyán 低級語言 low-level language

dījiē yǔyán 低階語言 low-level language

dīlán 低欄 (sports) low hurdles

dīlián 低廉 cheap; low

dīliè 低劣 poor in quality

dīluò 低落 low; downcast

dīmí 低迷 (said of the sky, clouds, etc.) turbid

dīnéng'ér 低能兒 a mentally retarded child

dīqìyā 低氣壓 low atmospheric pressure

dīrén yīděng 低人一等 inferior to others

dīsān xiàsì 低三下四 lowly; mean

dīshēng xiàqì 低聲下氣 to be meek and timid; to be submissive

dītóu 低頭 to bow one's head

dīwā 低窪 low-lying (ground)

dīwēi 低微 1. mean; base; menial 2. humble

dīwéi 低微 refer to **dīwēi** 低微

dīwēn 低溫 1. low temperature 2. (meteorology) microtherm

dīwēn shājùn 低溫殺菌 low temperature sterilization

dīwēn shājùn 低溫殺菌 refer to **dīwēn shājùn** 低溫殺菌

dīxiětáng 低血糖 refer to **dīxuètáng** 低血糖

dīxiěyā 低血壓 refer to **dīxuèyā** 低血壓

dīxuètáng 低血糖 (medicine) hypoglycemia

dīxuèyā 低血壓 low blood pressure

dīyā 低壓 1. low pressure 2. low voltage

dī 提
to hold or take in hand

dīfang 提防 to be on the alert; to guard against

dī 堤(隄) also **tí**
a dike; levee or embankment

dī'àn 堤岸 a dike; levee or embankment

dīfáng 堤防 a dike; levee or embankment

dī 滴
1. water drops 2. to drip

dīdā 滴答 to ticktack; ticktack

D

dīguǎn 滴管 a medicine dropper; a pipette

dīshuǐ chuānshí 滴水穿石 Persistent efforts can overcome any difficulty.

dīxià 滴下 to drip

Dí 狄 1. name of a barbarian tribe to the north of ancient China 2. a Chinese family name

dí 的 accurate; exact; proper

díquè 的確 certainly; surely

dí 迪 1. to advance; to progress 2. to enlighten; to teach

dísīkě 迪斯可 disco

dí 笛 a flute

dízi 笛子 a flute

dí 荻 a kind of reed

dí 嫡 1. the legal wife as opposed to a concubine 2. the sons born of the legal wife

díqī 嫡妻 a legal wife

díqīn 嫡親 blood relatives

dísì 嫡嗣 the eldest son born of the official wife of a man

dí 滌 1. to wash; to cleanse 2. to sweep

díchú 滌除 1. to do away with 2. to sweep away 3. to wash away

díqù 滌去 to wash off; to wash away

dí 敵 1. an enemy; a foe; a rival 2. to oppose; to resist 3. to match; to rival; to equal

díduì 敵對 to be hostile to; to oppose

díjī 敵機 an enemy plane; a hostile plane

díjūn 敵軍 enemy troops; hostile forces

díqíng 敵情 the enemy's situa-

tion

dírén 敵人 an enemy; a foe

díshì 敵視 to regard with hostility

díshǒu 敵手 an opponent; a match; a rival

díyì 敵意 enmity; hostility; antagonism

dízhòng wǒguǎ 敵衆我寡 We are outnumbered by the enemy.

dǐ 氐 1. foundation 2. (抵) on the whole

dǐ 邸 1. the residence of a prince or the nobility; the residence of a high official 2. princes and noblemen 3. (now rarely) a screen 4. the bottom of something 5. a Chinese family name

dǐdì 邸第 residences of lords and the nobility

dǐ 底 1. underside; base; foundation 2. the end

dǐběn 底本 the master copy

dǐbiān 底邊 the base (of a triangle, etc.)

dǐcéng 底層 1. the bottom layer 2. the ground floor

dǐdìng 底定 1. to establish peace in a region after an insurgence is put down 2. to settle (disturbed waters)

dǐgǎo 底稿 a manuscript; MS. or ms.

dǐjià 底價 the floor or minimum price

dǐpái 底牌 cards in one's hand

dǐpiàn 底片 (photography) a negative

dǐxì 底細 1. the unapparent details (of a matter); ins and outs 2. the unknown background (of a person)

dǐxia 底下 the underside; the downward position

dǐxiàrén 底下人 servants; underlings

dǐxiàn 底線 the base line; the

bottom line

dǐxīn 底薪 base pay

dǐzi 底子 1. basis 2. a manuscript 3. a shoe sole

dǐzuò 底座 a support; a base; a stand

dǐ 抵

1. to resist; to oppose 2. to prop; to sustain 3. to offset; to balance 4. to substitute; to give as an equivalent 5. to offer as collateral 6. to arrive at; to reach (a place) 7. to go against; to offend against (the law and regulations)

dǐdá 抵達 to arrive at or reach (a place)

dǐdǎng 抵擋 to resist; to sustain

dǐhuàn 抵換 to substitute (one thing for another)

dǐkàng 抵抗 to resist; to oppose; to withstand

dǐkànglì 抵抗力 the force or power of resistance

dǐlài 抵賴 to deny mistakes or crimes one has committed, or to renege a promise one has given

dǐmìng 抵命 a life for a life

dǐsǐ 抵死 1. to persist 2. excessive

dǐxiāo 抵消 to offset; to counteract

dǐyā 抵押 to mortgage; to collateralize

dǐyù 抵禦 to resist; to oppose; to withstand

dǐzhài 抵債 to pay a debt with goods or by labor

dǐzhàng 抵帳 to repay a debt with goods or articles of equivalent value

dǐzhì 抵制 1. to resist 2. to boycott

dǐzuì 抵罪 to mete out appropriate punishment for a crime committed

dǐ 牴

to gore

dǐchù 牴觸 to contradict; to conflict

dǐ 砥 also zhǐ

1. a whetstone; a grindstone 2. to discipline; to polish

dǐlì 砥礪 to discipline and polish; to encourage

dǐzhù 砥柱 an indomitable person

dǐ 詆

to censure; to slander; to defame

dǐhuǐ 詆毀 to censure; to slander; to defame

dì 地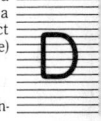

1. the earth 2. land; soil; ground 3. a region; a territory; a belt; a place; a locality 4. a position; a place; a situation 5. an adjunct after a word (usually adjective) to form an adverbial phrase

dìbǎn 地板 floor

dìdài 地帶 a place and its vicinity

dìdào 地道 a tunnel

dìdiǎn 地點 a site; a location; a place

dìdòng 地洞 a hole in the ground; a burrow

dìduàn 地段 the locality of a piece of land (especially referring to the numbered land plots on government file)

dìfāng 地方 1. a locality (in contrast with the central government) 2. local

dìfāng fǎyuàn 地方法院 a district court

dìfāngrén 地方人 the local people

dìfāng rénshì 地方人士 local personalities

dìfāng sècǎi 地方色彩 1. local color 2. provincialism

dìfang 地方 1. a place 2. space; room 3. part; respect

dìguā 地瓜 1. sweet potatoes 2. yam beans

dìjī 地基 the foundation of a building

dìjiào 地窖 a cellar; an underground vault

dìké 地殼 refer to **dìqiào** 地殼

dìláo 地牢 a dungeon

dìlǎo tiānhuāng 地老天荒 (said of love) to outlast even the heaven and the earth

dìléi 地雷 a land mine

dìlǐ 地理 1. geographical characteristics of a place 2. geography

dìmiàn 地面 1. the surface of the earth 2. a region; a territory

dìmíng 地名 the name of a place

dìpán 地盤 1. a region under one's sphere of influence; a domain 2. the foundation of a building or house

dìpéi 地陪 the local tourist guide

dìpí 地皮 land estate; real estate

dìpí liúmáng 地痞流氓 local bullies and loafers

dìpíngxiàn 地平線 the horizon

dìpù 地鋪 a shakedown

dìqì 地契 a title deed for landholdings

dìqiào 地殼 the crust of the earth

dìqiú 地球 the earth

dìqiúyí 地球儀 a terrestrial globe

dìqū 地區 an area; a region; a zone

dìrè 地熱 geothermal

dìshì 地勢 topography; terrain

dìtān 地攤 a stall with goods displaying on the ground for sale

dìtǎn 地毯 a carpet or rug

dìtiě 地鐵 subway

dìtú 地圖 a map

dìwèi 地位 the ranking or position (of a person)

dìxià 地下 1. underground 2. in the grave

dìxiàdào 地下道 an underpass

dìxià qiánzhuāng 地下錢莊 illegal banks

dìxiàshì 地下室 a basement

dìxiàtiě 地下鐵 the subway

dìxià wǔtīng 地下舞廳 unlicensed cabarets

dìxia 地下 on the ground

dìxīn yǐnlì 地心引力 gravity

dìxíng 地形 topography; terrain

dìyù 地域 1. boundaries of a piece of land 2. a district; a region

dìyù 地獄 hell; Hades; the inferno

dìzhèn 地震 earthquakes; seism

dìzhǐ 地質 refer to dìzhǐ 地質

dìzhǐ 地址 the address of a place; a location

dìzhì 地質 geology

Dìzhōnghǎi 地中海 the Mediterranean Sea

dìzhǔ 地主 1. a host 2. a landowner

dìzhǔ zhīyì 地主之誼 refer to dìzhǔ zhīyì 地主之誼

dìzhǔ zhīyì 地主之誼 the friendship or hospitality of a host

dìzū 地租 land rent

dì 弟

1. a younger brother 2. a junior

dìdi 弟弟 a younger brother

dìfù 弟婦 a sister-in-law

dìmèi 弟妹 a sister-in-law

dìxí 弟媳 a sister-in-law

dìxiong 弟兄 1. brothers 2. soldiers

dìzǐ 弟子 1. a disciple; a pupil 2. a youth

dì 的

1. clear; manifest 2. a target; a goal

dì 帝

1. the emperor 2. a god 3. Heaven (as a divine being) 4. imperial

dìguó 帝國 an empire; a monarchy

dìguó zhǔyì 帝國主義 imperialism

dìhào 帝號 the appellation of an emperor

dìwáng 帝王 the emperor; the throne; the king

dìwèi 帝位 the emperor's throne

dìyè 帝業 the reign of an emperor

dìzhì 帝制 monarchy

dìzuò 帝祚 the imperial throne

dì 第

1. sequence; order 2. rank; grade; degree 3. a mansion; a residence

dìliùgǎn 第六感 the sixth sense; extrasensory perception (ESP)

dìyī 第一 first; primary

dìyīcì 第一次 the first time

dìyīliú 第一流 first-rate; first-class

dìyīxiàn 第一線 the first line; the front

dì 蒂
1. a peduncle or footstalk of a flower or fruit; a stem; a base 2. a (cigaret) butt

dì 遞
1. to forward; to transmit; to hand or pass over to 2. to substitute; to alternate

dìbǔ 遞補 to fill a vacancy

dìjiǎn 遞減 to decrease progressively

dìjiāo 遞交 to hand over; to deliver

dìshang 遞上 to forward; to present

dìsòng 遞送 to deliver (a letter, etc.)

dìzēng 遞增 to increase progressively

dì 締
to connect; to join; to unite

dìjiāo 締交 to establish diplomatic ties or friendship

dìjié 締結 to conclude (treaties, agreements, etc.)

dìméng 締盟 to form an alliance

dìzào 締造 to construct; to compose; to build; to found; to create

Diān 滇 also **Tián**
an alternative name of Yunnan

diān 顛
1. (顛) the top; the highest spot; the head 2. to fall; to topple; to upset 3. to jolt; to bump 4. upside down 5. mad; lunatic

diānbǒ 顛簸 to shake; to joggle or jolt; to bump; to toss

diāndǎo 顛倒 1. upside down; to reverse 2. mentally deranged; infatuated

diāndǎo shìfēi 顛倒是非 to confuse justice and injustice; to distort truth; to twist facts

diānfēng 顛峰 a summit; a climax; the zenith

diānfēng zhuāngtài 顛峰狀態 in peak condition

diānfù 顛覆 to topple; to subvert

diānpèi liúlí 顛沛流離 suffering hardships and deprivations; to lead a vagrant life

diānpū bùpò 顛撲不破 irrefutable; absolutely right

diānsān dǎosì 顛三倒四 1. in total disorder; all in confusion 2. lunatic; insane

diān 癲
mentally deranged; insane; mad; crazy; lunatic

diānxián 癲癇 epilepsy

diǎn 典
1. a rule; a statute; a law; a canon 2. a tale or story from the classics; an allusion 3. to pawn; to mortgage

diǎndàng 典當 1. to pawn 2. a pawnshop

diǎnfàn 典範 an example; a paragon

diǎngù 典故 an allusion; an origin

diǎnjí 典籍 ancient books, statute records, etc.

diǎnlǐ 典禮 a ceremony; a rite

diǎnshì wěiyuánhuì 典試委員會 a committee in charge of examination affairs

diǎnxíng 典型 a model; a pattern

diǎnyā 典押 to mortgage

diǎnyǎ 典雅 refined (writing); elegant (style)

diǎnyùzhǎng 典獄長 the warden

diǎnzhāng 典章 institutions

diǎn 碘
iodine

diǎnjiǔ 碘酒 iodine tincture

diǎn 點
1. a dot; a spot; a speck 2. a point 3. a drop; a small amount;

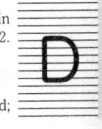

a little 4. snacks; refreshments 5. hours 6. to dot; to mark 7. to instruct; to teach 8. to check; to examine; to investigate; to review 9. to light; to ignite 10. to select; to pick out 11. to nod (the head) 12. to touch; to point at

diǎnbō 點播 (agriculture) dibble seeding; dibbling

diǎncài 點菜 to order dishes at a restaurant

diǎnchàng 點唱 (said of a music audience, etc.) to select one's desired numbers or songs for the performers to sing or play

diǎndào wéizhǐ 點到為止 to go through the motions

diǎndēng 點燈 to light lamps

diǎndī 點滴 1. drops; small amounts; a bit 2. (medicine) an intravenous drip

diǎnhuà 點化 to enlighten; to point out the correct path

diǎnhuǒ 點火 to light a fire

diǎnmíng 點名 1. to call the roll; to make a roll call 2. to mention somebody by name

diǎnmíngbù 點名簿 a roll (of names)

diǎnpò 點破 to unravel (a mystery, etc.); to point out

diǎnqīng 點清 to count accurately

diǎnrán 點燃 to light; to kindle; to ignite

diǎnshí chéngjīn 點石成金 to make a poor writing into a literary masterpiece by skillful retouching

diǎnshōu 點收 to check and accept (articles that are delivered or handed over)

diǎntóu 點頭 to nod

diǎnxin 點心 snacks; refreshments

diǎnxǐng 點醒 to point out someone's errors and make him realize them

diǎnxué 點穴 1. (Chinese boxing) to attack a vital point 2. to select the site of a grave through geomancy, etc.

diǎnxuè 點穴 refer to **diǎnxué**

點穴

diǎnyǎnyào 點眼藥 to apply eye lotion

diǎnzhōng 點鐘 hours; o'clock

diǎnzhuì 點綴 to provide decorative accessories; to embellish

diǎnzì 點字 Braille

diǎnzi 點子 1. a dot; a spot; a speck 2. a little; a bit 3. a key point 4. ideas

diàn 佃

1. a tenant farmer 2. to tenant a farm 3. hunting

diànhù 佃戶 a tenant (of a farm)

diànnóng 佃農 a tenant farmer or sharecropper

diànzū 佃租 land rent

diàn 甸

1. suburbs or outskirts of the capital 2. to govern; to rule 3. farm crops

diàn 店

1. a shop; a store 2. an inn; a hotel

diàndōng 店東 a proprietor (of a store)

diànjiā 店家 a manager (of an inn, shop, etc.)

diànmiàn 店面 a shop front

diànpù 店鋪 a store; a shop

diànxiǎo'ér 店小二 a waiter (in an inn or tavern)

diànyuán 店員 a shop clerk; a shopman

diànzhǔ 店主 a proprietor (of a store)

diàn 玷

1. a flaw or blemish in a piece of jade; a stain; a defect; a spot 2. to stain; to blemish; to disgrace

diànrǔ 玷辱 to disgrace (one's family name, etc.)

diànwū 玷汙 a stain (in one's reputation, etc.)

diàn 惦

to remember; to bear in mind; to miss; to be concerned about; to keep thinking about

diànjì 惦記 to feel concern about

someone far away

diànniàn 恬念 to worry about; to miss (a friend or beloved one)

diàn 奠

1. to settle; to lay (foundation, etc.) 2. to secure; to consolidate 3. to offer libations

diàndìng 奠定 to lay foundation and consolidate it; to settle

diànyí 奠儀 a money gift for a funeral

diàn 殿

1. a palace; a palace hall; a temple; a sanctuary 2. the rear; the rear guard

diànhòu 殿後 the rear, or rear guard (of marching troops)

diànjūn 殿軍 1. the rear guard (of marching troops) 2. the fourth winner in a contest

diàntáng 殿堂 a palace; a sanctuary

diànxià 殿下 Your, His, or Her Highness

diànyǔ 殿宇 a palace; a sanctuary

diàn 電

1. electricity; power 2. short for cable or telegram

diànbào 電報 a cable; a telegram; a wire

diànbiǎo 電表 1. any meter for measuring electricity, such as an ammeter or a voltmeter 2. a kilowatt-hour meter

diànbīngxiāng 電冰箱 a refrigerator; an ice box

diànbō 電波 electric waves

diànchǎng 電廠 a power plant

diànchàngjī 電唱機 a record player; an electric phonograph

diànchē 電車 a tramcar; a streetcar; a trolley car

diànchí 電池 an electric battery; a dry cell

diàncí 電磁 electromagnetism

diàncílú 電磁爐 an induction cooker

diàndēng 電燈 electric lights or lamps

diàndēngpào 電燈泡 1. an elec-

tric bulb 2. (colloquial) an unwanted third party who accompanies a courting pair

diàndòng 電動 powered by electricity

diàndòng wánjù 電動玩具 1. a battery-powered toy 2. a video game; a TV game; a computer game

diàndù 電鍍 electroplate

diànfèi 電費 a power rate; a power bill

diànfēngshàn 電風扇 an electric fan

diànfútī 電扶梯 an escalator

diàngōng 電工 an electrician

diànguāng 電光 electric light; a flash of lightning

diànguāng shíhuǒ 電光石火 anything that vanishes in a flash

diànguō 電鍋 an electric rice cooker

diànhàn 電銲 electric welding; electric soldering

diànhè 電賀 to congratulate by cable

diànhuà 電話 telephone; phone

diànhuàbù 電話簿 a telephone directory; a telephone book

diànhuà dálùjī 電話答錄機 an answering machine; an answer-phone

diànhuà hàomǎ 電話號碼 a telephone number

diànhuàjī 電話機 a telephone set

diànhuàtíng 電話亭 a telephone booth

diànjī 電機 electrical machinery

diànjí 電擊 an electic shock; struck by lightning

diànjīxì 電機系 the department of electrical engineering in a college

diànjí 電擊 refer to diànjī 電擊

diànlǎn 電纜 a cable (usually submarine)

diànlì 電力 electric power

diànlì gōngsī 電力公司 a power company

diànliánchē 電聯車 an electric multiple unit railcar

diànlíng 電鈴 an electric bell; a buzzer

diànliú 電流 an electric current

diànlú 電爐 an electric stove; a hot plate

diànlù 電路 an electric circuit

diànnǎo 電腦 a computer; an electronic computer

diànnǎo chéngshì 電腦程式 a computer program

diànnǎo páibǎn 電腦排版 laser typesetting

diànniǔ 電鈕 a button that controls electric currents

diànqì 電氣 electric

diànqì 電器 electric appliances

diànrèqì 電熱器 a heater

diànshì 電視 television; TV

diànshì dàxué 電視大學 an open university

diànshìjī 電視機 a TV set

diànshì jiémù 電視節目 a TV program

diànshìjù 電視劇 a teleplay

diànshìtái 電視臺 a television station

diànshì yǐngpiàn 電視影片 a telefilm

diànshì yóulèqì 電視遊樂器 a video game

diàntái 電臺 a radio station

diàntǎn 電毯 an electric blanket

diàntàng 電燙 to wave or curl hair by electricity

diàntī 電梯 an electric lift; an elevator

diàntǒng 電筒 a flashlight

diànxiàn 電線 electric wires

diànxiàn zǒuhuǒ 電線走火 a short circuit

diànxìn 電信 telecommunications

diànxìnjú 電信局 a telephone and telegraph office

diànyā 電壓 voltage

diànyǐ 電椅 the electric chair

diànyǐng 電影 movies; motion pictures

diànyǐng míngxīng 電影明星 a movie star

diànyǐngyuàn 電影院 a movie theater; a cinema

diànyuán 電源 the source of electricity

diànyùndǒu 電熨斗 an electric iron

diànzǐ 電子 an electron

diànzǐ jìsuànjī 電子計算機 1. an electronic computer 2. a calculator

diànzǐqín 電子琴 an electronic organ

diànzǐ shāngwù 電子商務 e-commerce

diànzǐ xìnhán 電子信函 an e-mail

diànzǐ yóujiàn 電子郵件 an e-mail

diàn 墊
1. to advance (money); to pay for another and expect to be paid back 2. a cushion; a pad; a bed-mat 3. to cushion 4. to sink into 5. to dig

diànbèi 墊被 a mattress

diànbǔ 墊補 to defray expenses not budgeted

diànjiān 墊肩 a shoulder pad (or padding)

diànjiǎoshí 墊脚石 a stepping-stone

diànzi 墊子 a mat

diàn 澱
1. sediment; dregs; precipitate 2. indigo

diànfěn 澱粉 starch

diāo 刁
low and cunning; crafty; wicked; artful; knavish

diāomán 刁蠻 obstinate

diāonán 刁難 refer to **diāonàn** 刁難

diāonàn 刁難 to (deliberately) make things difficult for others

diāozuān 刁鑽 wily; cunning

diāozuān gǔguài 刁鑽古怪 perverse; mischievous

diāo 叨
to hold in the mouth

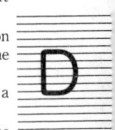

diāo 凋

1. withered; faded 2. exhausted; emaciated

diāolíng 凋零 1. withered 2. to pass away

diāoluò 凋落 1. fallen; withered 2. to pass away

diāowěi 凋萎 1. withered; faded 2. passing away

diāoxiè 凋謝 1. fallen; withered 2. to pass away

diāo 貂

the sable; the marten; the mink

diāopí 貂皮 sable skin or fur; mink

diāopí dàyī 貂皮大衣 a mink (coat)

diāo 碉

a stone chamber

diāobǎo 碉堡 a fort; a pillbox; a blockhouse

diāo 雕

1. to engrave; to carve or cut, as in sculpture 2. an eagle; a hawk 3. to exhaust; to weaken

diāochóng xiǎojì 雕蟲小技 a petty skill or craft; a skill which has no significant value

diāokè 雕刻 1. sculpture 2. to engrave

diāoliáng huàdòng 雕樑畫棟 carved beams and painted rafters—a richly ornamented building

diāosù 雕塑 1. sculpture 2. to cut wood or clay for a statue or idol

diāoxiàng 雕像 a sculptured statue; portrayal of a person

diāozhuó 雕琢 1. to cut and polish (gems) 2. to polish a piece of writing; to write in an ornate style

diāo 鵰

a bird of prey; a vulture

diào 弔 (吊)

1. to condole; to console 2. to mourn 3. to hang; to suspend; suspended

diàochē 弔車 1. a wrecker (or a truck crane) 2. a cable car

diàodài 弔帶 suspenders; garters

diàodēng 弔燈 a low-hanging ceiling lamp, such as a chandelier

diào'ér lángdāng 弔兒郎當 to act or behave irreverently; to do things perfunctorily

diàohuán 弔環 flying rings

diàojì 弔祭 to mourn over (somebody's death)

diàoqǐ 弔起 1. to hang 2. to lift by crane

diàoqiáo 弔橋 1. a suspension bridge 2. a drawbridge over the moat

diàosāng 弔喪 to attend a memorial service

diàosǎngzi 弔嗓子 (Chinese opera) to sing aloud off stage as a vocal training and practice

diàoshàn 弔扇 a ceiling fan

diàosǐ 弔死 to die by hanging

diàosuǒ 弔索 a sling

diàowèi 弔慰 to condole with

diàowèikǒu 弔胃口 to tantalize

diàowén 弔文 a message of condolence; a funeral oration

diàoxiāo 弔銷 to revoke; to withdraw

diàoxiāo zhízhào 弔銷執照 to withdraw a license

diàoyàn 弔唁 to condole

diào 釣

1. to fish (with a hook and line); to angle 2. to lure; to tempt

diào'ěr 釣餌 a bait

diàogān 釣竿 a fishing rod; a fishing pole

diàogōu 釣鉤 a fishhook

diàojù 釣具 fishing gear; fishing tackle

diàoxiàn 釣線 a fishing twine; a fishing line

diàoyú 釣魚 to fish; to angle

diào 掉

1. to turn 2. to fall; to drop; to shed 3. to lose 4. to fall behind; to lag behind 5. to change; to substitute 6. to move; to shake; to wag 7. used as an adverbial particle after verbs expressing

conditions of fulfillment

diàobāo 掉包 to substitute stealthily one thing for another

diàoduì 掉隊 to drop out; to fall behind

diàojià 掉價 to cut a price; a price drop

diàolèi 掉淚 to come to tears; tears falling

diàosè 掉色 refer to **diàoshǎi** 掉色

diàoshǎi 掉色 to discolor; to fade

diàotóu 掉頭 1. to turn one's head (and walk away) 2. to shake one's head 3. to turn back 4. to get beheaded

diàoxià 掉下 to fall down

diàoyǐ qīngxīn 掉以輕心 to lower one's guard; to treat something lightly

diàozhuǎn 掉轉 to turn back; to turn round

diào 調

1. to transfer; to move 2. to collect; to mobilize 3. a tune; a melody; an accent

diàobīng qiǎnjiàng 調兵遣將 (literally) to move troops and despatch generals—to prepare for war

diàochá 調查 to investigate; to study; to probe; to survey; investigation

diàodòng 調動 to transfer; to shift; to move (troops)

diàodù 調度 1. to move (available equipment or manpower) about according to needs 2. a dispatcher

diàohǔ líshān 調虎離山 (literally) to induce the tiger out of the mountain—to use the stratagem of luring the opponent out of his citadel

diàohuàn 調換 to exchange; to replace; to swap

diàopài 調派 to assign

diàorèn 調任 to transfer to a new post

diàotóucùn 調頭寸 to scrape up enough cash

diàozhí 調職 to transfer to a

new post

diē 爹

father

diēniáng 爹娘 father and mother; parents

diē 跌 also **dié**

1. to fall; to drop 2. to stamp 3. a fall

diēdǎo 跌倒 to stumble and fall; to fall down

diēdiēzhuàngzhuàng 跌跌撞撞 to walk unsteadily; to stagger forward

diējià 跌價 to cut a price; a price drop

diējiāo 跌跤 1. to have a fall; to stumble and fall; a fall 2. to make a mistake

diēluò 跌落 to go down; to fall; to drop

diētíngbǎn 跌停板 (stock trading) to fall to the lowest point allowed for a single trading day; to hit the rock bottom

dié 喋

to nag; to chatter; to prattle

diédié bùxiū 喋喋不休 to keep talking; to cackle

dié 跌

refer to **diē 跌**

dié 碟

1. a dish or plate (especially a small one); 2. a disc

diéxíng tiānxiàn 碟形天線 a satellite dish

diézi 碟子 a small dish or plate

dié 蝶

a butterfly

dié 諜

1. glib; garrulous; voluble 2. spying; espionage

diébào 諜報 a spy's report; information obtained through espionage

dié 疊(叠)

1. to fold up 2. to pile up 3. to repeat; to duplicate 4. a stack of (bank notes)

diéluóhàn 疊羅漢 (sports) pyramid

diéqǐ 疊起 1. to fold up 2. to pile up

diéyùn 疊韻 two words of the same rhyme

dīng 丁
1. the fourth of the Ten Celestial Stems (**tiān'gān** 天干) 2. population 3. attendants 4. fourth 5. small cubes of meat or vegetable 6. a Chinese family name

dīngděng 丁等 grade D

dīngkè fūqī 丁克夫妻 DINK, double income no kid

dīngxiāng 丁香 a clove

dīngxiānghuā 丁香花 lilac

dīngyōu 丁憂 bereavement of parents

dīngzìchǐ 丁字尺 a T-square

dīngzìjiē 丁字街 T-shaped road junction

dīng 叮
1. the chimes of a bell 2. to exhort or enjoin repeatedly 3. to sting, as a mosquito, etc.

dīngdāng 叮噹 dingdong (used for the sound of bells)

dīngníng 叮嚀 to exhort repeatedly

dīngzhǔ 叮囑 to enjoin and urge repeatedly

dīng 玎
the jingling or tinkling sound

dīngdāng 玎璫 ding-dong; the jingling or tinkling sound

dīng 盯
to stare at; to gaze at; to fix one's eyes on; to keep a close watch

dīngshāo 盯梢 to tail; to shadow; to trail

dīng 疔
a boil; a carbuncle

dīng 釘
1. nails (for fastening things) 2. to look steadily

dīngxié 釘鞋 boots with nailed soles (for wet weather); track shoes

dǐng 頂
1. the top of anything 2. the crown of the head 3. topmost; extremely; very 4. to carry (a weight) on one's head; to push the head against; to wear on the head 5. to gore; to butt 6. to push up; to prop up 7. to cope with; to stand up to 8. to substitute 9. to equal; to be equivalent to 10. to offend intentionally; to retort; to turn down 11. used as a unit

dǐngdiǎn 頂點 the pinnacle; the topmost

dǐngduān 頂端 the top; the peak; the apex

dǐngduō 頂多 at (the) most; at best

dǐngfēng 頂峰 the peak; the summit; the pinnacle

dǐngguāguā 頂呱呱 topmost; the top; the best; excellent; first-rate

dǐnghǎo 頂好 the best; the first; the topmost; good; excellent; wonderful

dǐngjiān 頂尖 the peak; the highest point; the top; the best

dǐngtì 頂替 1. to assume someone's name with the intent to cheat 2. to represent someone; to take someone's place

dǐngtiān lìdì 頂天立地 independent and indomitable

dǐngtóu shàngsi 頂頭上司 the immediate boss

dǐngzhù 頂住 to support with the head

dǐngzhuàng 頂撞 to talk back; to offend or dispute with words; to contradict

dǐngzuǐ 頂嘴 1. to quarrel 2. to argue with a superior or an elder

dǐngzuì 頂罪 to act as a fall guy

dǐng 鼎
1. a huge tripod of bronze with two ears; a heavy three-legged caldron or sacrificial vessel 2. vigorous; thriving; flourishing 3. involving three parts or things; triangular

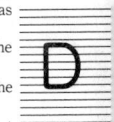

dǐngdǐng dàmíng 鼎鼎大名 renowned; famous; illustrious; celebrated; a great reputation

dǐngfèi 鼎沸 tumultuous; boiling; hubbub; noisy and confused

dǐnglì 鼎力 1. great strength; herculean strength 2. your kind effort

dǐnglì 鼎立 (said of rival groups, etc.) to develop a triangular balance of power

dǐngshèng 鼎盛 in a period of great prosperity; prosperous; thriving; vigorous; flourishing

dǐngzú érsān 鼎足而三 divided into three rival groups; developing into a triangular balance of power

dìng 定

1. to decide; to fix; to settle 2. definite; sure 3. stable 4. to remain

dìng'àn 定案 1. to decide on a verdict 2. a verdict

dìngdān 定單 an order (for goods)

dìngduó 定奪 to decide; to settle

dìngfángjiān 定房間 to make room reservations

dìnggǎo 定稿 1. to finalize a manuscript, text, etc. 2. a final version or text

dìnggòu 定購 to order (goods, etc.)

dìngguàncí 定冠詞 definite article "the"

dìnghūn 定婚 to be betrothed

dìnghuò 定貨 to order goods; to place an order for goods

dìngjià 定價 1. to fix a price 2. a list price

dìngjīn 定金 down payment; earnest money

dìngjū 定居 to settle down

dìngjú 定局 an irreversible situation

dìnglǐ 定理 (mathematics) a theorem

dìnglì 定力 (Buddhism) strength of concentration

dìngliàng 定量 fixed amount

dìnglǜ 定律 (science) a law

dìnglùn 定論 an accepted argument (not questioned any more)

dìngmíng 定名 to give a name; to christen

dìngqī 定期 periodic; regular

dìngqí 定期 refer to **dìngqī** 定期

dìngqīn 定親 to betroth

dìngqíng 定情 to make commitment to one's lover

dìngshén 定神 1. to compose oneself 2. to concentrate one's attention

dìngshí 定時 1. to set time 2. at fixed time

dìngshí zhàdàn 定時炸彈 a time bomb

dìngshù 定數 predestination

dìngwèi 定位 1. a location; orientation 2. to position 3. to make a reservation for seats

dìngxīnwán 定心丸 something capable of setting someone's mind at ease

dìngxíng 定型 to finalize the design

dìngyì 定義 a definition

dìngzé 定則 (science) a rule

dìngzhì 定製 to be made to order; to custom-tailor

dìngzuì 定罪 to declare someone guilty

dìngzuò 定座 to make reservations for seats in theaters, restaurants, etc.

dìngzuò 定做 to be made to order; to custom-tailor

dìng 訂

1. to draw up or conclude (a contract, etc.) 2. to subscribe to (a magazine, etc.) 3. to edit; to collate; to revise 4. to arrange; to settle; to fix 5. to make reservations

dìngbào 訂報 to subscribe to a newspaper

dìngdìng 訂定 1. to fix or arrange beforehand 2. specified in a contract between the two parties concerned

dìnghù 訂戶 1. a subscriber to a newspaper, etc. 2. a person with a standing order for milk, etc.

dìnglì 訂立 to conclude (a contract, etc.)

dìngyuè 訂閱 to subscribe to (a publication)

dìngzhèng 訂正 to revise; to correct

dìng 釘

to fasten (with nails, etc.)

dìngshūjī 釘書機 a stapler

dìng 錠

1. a kind of ancient utensil 2. ingots of gold or silver 3. a spindle 4. a (medical) tablet

dìngjì 錠劑 medicine in tablet form

diū 丟

1. to throw 2. to lose 3. to put (or lay) aside

diūdiào 丟掉 1. to lose 2. to cast away; to throw away

diūkāi 丟開 1. to leave it off; not to mention 2. to throw away

diūliǎn 丟臉 to lose face; to disgrace

diūqì 丟棄 to cast away; to get rid of

diūrén 丟人 to lose face; to disgrace

diūsān làsì 丟三落四 forgetful

diūxià 丟下 to throw down; to lay aside

dōng 冬

1. winter 2. (the lunar calendar) the period from the 10th to the 12th month

dōngguā 冬瓜 a white gourd; a wax gourd

dōnghōng 冬烘 a pedant or a pedagogue

dōngjì 冬季 the winter season

dōnglìng 冬令 winter

dōnglìng jiùjì 冬令救濟 relief of the poor during winter months

dōngmián 冬眠 to hibernate; hibernation

dōngnuǎn xiàliáng 冬暖夏涼 cool in summer and warm in winter

dōngtiān 冬天 winter

dōngzhì 冬至 the winter solstice (22nd solar term)

dōng 東

1. the east; eastern 2. to travel eastward 3. the host; the master

Dōngbànqiú 東半球 the Eastern Hemisphere

dōngběi 東北 1. northeast 2. Manchuria

dōngbēn xīzǒu 東奔西走 to run about busily

dōngbian 東邊 the east side; on the east

dōngchuāng shìfā 東窗事發 to come to light

dōngchuáng kuàixù 東床快婿 a son-in-law

dōngdǎo xīwāi 東倒西歪 1. (said of drunkards) to walk unsteadily 2. (said of a scene, room, village, etc.) dilapidated

dōngdàozhǔ 東道主 the host at a dinner party

dōngfāng 東方 1. the east 2. Oriental 3. a Chinese family name

dōngfēng 東風 an east wind

Dōnghǎi 東海 the East China Sea

Dōng Hàn 東漢 the Eastern Han (25-220 A.D.)

dōngjiā 東家 1. the host 2. the owner of a company or shop

Dōngjīng 東京 1. Tokyo 2. (in the Han Dynasty) Luoyang 3. (in the Song Dynasty) Kaifeng

dōngjīng 東經 longitude east of Greenwich

dōnglā xīchě 東拉西扯 to talk aimlessly or without much thought; to ramble

dōngnán 東南 southeast

dōngnán xīběi 東南西北 (literally) east, south, west and north —all directions

Dōngnányà 東南亞 Southeast Asia

dōngnuó xījiè 東挪西借 to borrow all around

Dōng'ōu 東歐 Eastern Europe

dōngpīn xīcòu 東拼西湊 to scrape (money, etc.) for a pur-

D

chase, project, etc.; to patch up from bits

Dōngshān zàiqǐ 東山再起 (said of a retired person, etc.) to take up official duties again

Dōngshī xiàopín 東施效顰 to imitate awkwardly

dōngxī 東西 1. east and west 2. from east to west

dōngxi 東西 1. things; objects; matters 2. a contemptible fellow

Dōngyáng 東洋 Japan

Dōngyíng 東瀛 Japan

Dōngyìndù Qúndǎo 東印度群島 the East Indies

dōngzhāng xīwàng 東張西望 to look around; to gaze around

dōng 咚

1. the sound of impact caused by a falling object 2. rub-a-dub 3. rat-tat; rat-a-tat

dǒng 董

1. to supervise; to oversee; to rectify; to correct 2. short for directors 3. a Chinese family name

dǒngshìhuì 董事會 a board of directors

dǒngshìzhǎng 董事長 a board director; the chairman of the board of directors

dǒng 懂

to understand; to comprehend; to know

dǒngdàoli 懂道理 to be reasonable

dǒngde 懂得 to understand; to comprehend

dǒngshì 懂事 (said of the young) familiar with human affairs

dòng 洞

1. a cave; a hole 2. to penetrate; to see through

dòngchá 洞察 to see and understand clearly

dòngchuān 洞穿 to pierce through

dòngfáng 洞房 1. an inner chamber 2. a nuptial chamber

dòngfáng huāzhú yè 洞房花燭夜 wedding night

dòngkū 洞窟 a cave; a cavern

Dòngtínghú 洞庭湖 Lake Dong-ting

dòngxī 洞悉 to see clearly and understand thoroughly

dòngxiāo 洞簫 a kind of flute; a bamboo flageolet

dòngxué 洞穴 a cave; a cavern

dòngxuè 洞穴 refer to **dòngxué** 洞穴

dòng 恫

to threaten, intimidate, or scare loudly

dònghè 恫嚇 to threaten; to intimidate

dòng 凍

1. to freeze 2. cold; icy

dòngchuāng 凍瘡 frostbite; chilblains

dòngjiāng 凍僵 to be benumbed with cold

dòngjié 凍結 to freeze (an account, etc.)

dòngshāng 凍傷 to suffer injuries or illness as a result of long exposure to cold weather

dòngsǐ 凍死 to freeze to death

dòng 胴

1. the large intestine 2. the trunk; the body

dòngtǐ 胴體 the trunk; the body

dòng 動

1. to move; to stir 2. to change; to alter 3. to act 4. to touch (one's heart); to arouse; to excite 5. to take up 6. to use 7. to eat or drink 8. movement; action

dòngbǐ 動筆 to start writing

dòngbīng 動兵 to send out troops to fight

dòngbudòng 動不動 to be apt to

dòngchǎn 動產 movable property; movables

dòngcí 動詞 a verb

dòngcū 動粗 to resort to violence

dòngdàng 動盪 uneasy; unstable

dònggōng 動工 to start (construction) work

dònghuà 動畫 an animation picture

dòngjī 動機 motives; intentions

dòngjìng 動靜 signs of action

dònglì 動力 1. power; dynamic force 2. impetus

dòngluàn 動亂 disturbance; commotion

dòngmài 動脈 an artery

dòngmíngcí 動名詞 (grammar) a gerund

dòngnù 動怒 to lose one's temper

dòngqì 動氣 to take offense; to get angry

dòngqíng 動情 to have more than a fleeting interest in a person

dòngrén 動人 1. moving 2. (said of the beauty of a woman) to arouse interest

dòngshēn 動身 to set out (on a trip); to depart

dòngshǒu 動手 1. to start work 2. to use hands; to touch 3.to raise a hand to strike

dòngshǒushù 動手術 1. to operate on a patient 2. to have an operation

dòngtài 動態 1. development 2. the movement

dòngtan 動彈 to budge; to move; to stir

dòngtīng 動聽 appealing to the ear

dòngwǔ 動武 to resort to violence

dòngwù 動物 an animal; a creature

dòngwùyuán 動物園 a zoo

dòngxiàng 動向 trends

dòngxīn 動心 1. to be perturbed mentally 2. to show interest

dòngxíng 動刑 to apply torture; to torture

dòngyáo 動搖 to waver; to shake

dòngyì 動議 a motion; a proposal

dòngyòng 動用 to use or employ

dòngyuán 動員 to mobilize; mobilization

dòngzuò 動作 motions; movements; actions

dòng 棟

1. the main beam of a house 2. a measure word for a building

dòngliáng 棟梁 1. the ridgepole and beams 2. (figuratively) a man of great ability

dòngliáng zhīcái 棟梁之才 a man of tremendous promise

dōu 兜

1. a head-covering; a helmet 2. overalls 3. to solicit 4. to go for a drive around; to move around 5. to surround; to wrap up 6. a small pocket in clothes

dōufēng 兜風 to go joyriding

dōulǎn shēngyi 兜攬生意 to solicit business

dōuquānzi 兜圈子 1. to take a stroll 2. to circle 3. circumlocutory; to beat about the bush

dōushòu 兜售 to peddle

dōu 都

1. all; altogether 2. even 3. already

dǒu 斗

1. Chinese peck (a unite of dry measure for grain) 2. a large container for wine

dǒudǎn 斗膽 great intrepidity or boldness

dǒulì 斗笠 a broad-brimmed rain hat (usually worn by farmers)

dǒupeng 斗篷 a mantle; a cape

dǒushāo zhīrén 斗筲之人 shallow common men (Confucius' description of officials of his times)

dǒushì 斗室 a little room; a small room

dǒu 抖

1. to shiver; to tremble 2. to shake; to jerk 3. to rouse 4. (colloquial) to make good; to become well-to-do

dǒudòng 抖動 to shake; to tremble

dǒulou 抖摟 1. to waste; to squander 2. to expose another's

secrets 3. to catch cold 4. to shake off

dǒusǒu jīngshen 抖擻精神 to pull oneself together or to muster one's energies (for an important task ahead)

dǒu 陡

1. suddenly; abruptly 2. steep; precipitous

dǒupō 陡坡 a steep slope

dǒuqiào 陡峭 steep; precipitous

dòu 豆

1. beans and peas collectively 2. a vessel of wood for containing flesh, sauces, etc. at sacrifices and feasts

dòufu 豆腐 bean curd; tofu

dòufurǔ 豆腐乳 soybean cheese

dòuhuār 豆花兒 soybean jelly

dòukòu niánhuá 豆蔻年華 (said of girls) in their teens

dòushā 豆沙 mashed beans

dòuyár 豆芽兒 bean sprouts

dòuzi 豆子 beans or peas

dòu 鬥 (鬬)

to struggle

dòuhěn 鬥狠 to compete in ferocities

dòujī 鬥雞 a cockfight; cockfighting

dòujīyǎn 鬥雞眼 crossed eyes; convergent strabismus

dòuniú 鬥牛 a bullfight

dòunong 鬥弄 1. to seduce; to flirt with 2. to play jokes on; to make fun of

dòu'ōu 鬥毆 to have a fight; to brawl

dòuqì 鬥氣 to quarrel on emotional grounds

dòuzhēng 鬥爭 struggle; conflict; strife

dòuzhì 鬥志 the determination to compete or fight; pugnacious spirit

dòuzhì bù dòulì 鬥智不鬥力 to fight a battle of wits, not of limbs

dòuzuǐ 鬥嘴 to quarrel; to wrangle

dòu 荳

beans, peas, etc.; legumes

dòu 逗

1. to stay; to linger; to remain; to pause 2. to stir; to rouse; to tickle 3. funny 4. a slight pause in reading

dòudiǎn 逗點 a comma (，)

dòuhào 逗號 a comma (，)

dòuliú 逗留 to stay; to stop over; to linger

dòunong 逗弄 to make fun of; to sport with

dòuqùr 逗趣兒 to amuse; to entertain (with jokes, etc.)

dòurén xǐ'ài 逗人喜愛 (said of a child) to arouse the affection of adults

dòu 痘

smallpox

dòumiáo 痘苗 vaccine

dòu 讀

pauses in a sentence

dū 都

1. a large town; a city; a metropolis 2. the capital of a nation; to make a city the national capital 3. beautiful; elegant; fine

dūhuì 都會 a big city; a metropolis

dūshì 都市 a big city; a metropolis

dūshìhuà 都市化 to urbanize; urbanization

dū 督

1. to oversee; to superintend; to supervise 2. to reprove; to censure 3. a marshal; a general 4. a viceroy or governor-general 5. a Chinese family name

dūchá 督察 1. to superintend and oversee; to act as a watchdog 2. an inspector

dūcù 督促 to urge; to press

dūdǎo 督導 to direct and supervise

dūgōng 督工 1. to oversee working 2. an overseer

dūxué 督學 an inspector of educational establishments

dú 毒

1. poison; toxins 2. poisonous; noxious 3. to poison

dúchóng 毒蟲 a poisonous insect

dúcì 毒刺 a poisonous prick

dúdǎ 毒打 to beat cruelly or savagely

dú'ěr 毒餌 a poison bait

dúhài 毒害 to injure atrociously; to murder

dúhuǐ 毒虺 a venomous snake

dújì 毒計 a malicious scheme

dúlà 毒辣 cruel; malicious; spiteful

dúliú 毒瘤 cancer growth

dúmà 毒罵 to scold ferociously and maliciously; to revil

dúpǐn 毒品 narcotic drugs; narcotics

dúqì 毒氣 poisonous gas; noxious gas

dúshā 毒殺 to poison to death

dúshé 毒蛇 a venomous snake

dúshǒu 毒手 a murderous scheme (or hand)

dúxíng 毒刑 cruel punishment; brutal torture

dúxìng 毒性 toxicity; poisonousness

dúyá 毒牙 a poison fang

dúyào 毒藥 poisonous drugs; poison

dú 獨

1. alone; solitary; single 2. only 3. to monopolize 4. to be old and without a son 5. how; Is it possible?

dúbái 獨白 (dramatics) monologue; soliloquy

dúcái 獨裁 dictatorship; dictatorial

dúchàng 獨唱 singing solo; a vocal recital

dúchǔ 獨處 to stay alone

dúchuàng 獨創 (literally) to create all by oneself—unique; original

dúdāng yīmiàn 獨當一面 to handle a major task or assignment unaided

dúdào 獨到 original

dúdào zhīchù 獨到之處 originality (of ideas); special merits

dúduàn dúxíng 獨斷獨行 to act arbitrarily

dújiā xīnwén 獨家新聞 a scoop; an exclusive news report

dújiǎoshòu 獨角獸 a unicorn (a legendary animal)

dújiǎoxì 獨腳戲 a one-man show

dújū 獨居 to live alone

dújù huìyǎn 獨具慧眼 to have a remarkable view

dújù jiàngxīn 獨具匠心 to have originality

dúlì 獨立 independence; independent

Dúlì Guóxié 獨立國協 Commonwealth of Independent States (reformed after the disintegration of U.S.S.R. in 1992)

dúlì zìzhǔ 獨立自主 1. the independence of sovereignty 2. to act independently and with the initiative in one's own hands

dúmùqiáo 獨木橋 a single-plank bridge

dúmùzhōu 獨木舟 a canoe

dúpái zhòngyì 獨排眾議 to hold one's own opinion against that of the majority

dúshàn qíshēn 獨善其身 to conduct oneself virtuously

dúshēngnǚ 獨生女 the only daughter

dúshēngzǐ 獨生子 the only son

dúshù yīzhì 獨樹一幟 to take a distinctive course or attitude of one's own

dútè 獨特 unique

dútūn 獨吞 to pocket (profit) without sharing (it) with anyone else

dúwǎng dúlái 獨往獨來 (literally) to come and go alone—to act independently without seeking company

dúxíng 獨行 1. to walk alone 2. to insist on one's ways in doing things

dúyī wú'èr 獨一無二 unique

dúzhàn 獨占 to monopolize

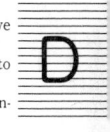

dúzhàn áotóu 獨占鼇頭 1. to emerge first in the civil service examination in former times 2. to come out first

dúzǐ 獨子 the only son

dúzì 獨自 alone; personally

dúzòu 獨奏 (music) a solo performance

dú 瀆
1. a ditch 2. a river 3. to desecrate; to profane; to blaspheme; to be rude and disrespectful 4. to annoy

dúzhí 瀆職 malfeasance

dú 犢
a calf

dú 讀
1. to read 2. to attend school; to go to school, college, etc. 3. to study

dúběn 讀本 a reader (for a language course, etc.)

dúkǎjī 讀卡機 (computers) a card-reader

dúshū 讀書 1. to read books 2. to study

dúwù 讀物 reading matter; reading

dúyīn 讀音 pronunciation (of a word)

dúzhě 讀者 the reader

Dúzhě Wénzhāi 讀者文摘 The Reader's Digest

dú 黷
1. to tarnish 2. to be rash about 3. to corrupt

dúwǔ 黷武 to use military might rashly

dǔ 肚
the stomach

dǔ 堵
1. to stop; to block up; to shut off 2. a wall

dǔsè 堵塞 to stop up; to block up; a jam

dǔzhù 堵住 to block up; to stop

dǔ 睹(覩)
to witness; to see; to look at; to observe; to gaze at

dǔwù sīrén 睹物思人 to see the things one is reminded of the owner

dǔ 賭
1. to gamble; to bet; to wager 2. to compete 3. to swear

dǔběn 賭本 money to gamble with

dǔbó 賭博 to gamble; gambling

dǔchǎng 賭場 a gambling joint; a gambling den or house; a casino

dǔguǐ 賭鬼 a congenital gambler

dǔqì 賭氣 to do something out of spite (or in a rage)

dǔtú 賭徒 a gambler

dǔzhài 賭債 a gambling debt

dǔzhàng 賭帳 a gambling debt

dǔzhù 賭注 stakes

dǔ 篤
1. deep; much; great; profound 2. dangerous; serious 3. generous 4. to consolidate; to make solid 5. to limit

dǔdìng 篤定 (informally) very confident; assured

dǔshí 篤實 1. sincere; honest; candid; faithful 2. solid; sound

dǔxìn 篤信 1. to have sincere faith in 2. honest; trustworthy

dù 杜
1. to plug (a hole, leak, etc.); to stop; to prevent; to put an end to something 2. to shut out; to restrict; to impede 3. the russet pear 4. to fabricate; to practice forgery 5. a Chinese family name

dùbì 杜弊 to prevent corrupt practices

dùjuān 杜鵑 a cuckoo

dùjuānhuā 杜鵑花 azaleas

dùjué 杜絕 1. to stop (a bad practice, etc.) for good; to eradicate 2. to cut off (relations with) 3. irrevocable (contracts, title deeds, etc.)

dùjué hòuhuàn 杜絕後患 to prevent and eliminate possible harmful consequences

dùkǒu 杜口 to shut one's mouth

and say nothing

dùmén xièkè 杜門謝客 to refuse to see visitors

dùzhuàn 杜撰 to fabricate (a story, etc.); to trump up

dù 肚

the belly; the abdomen; the bowels

dùliàng 肚量 capacity for tolerance and forgiveness

dùpí 肚皮 the abdomen; the belly

dùpíwǔ 肚皮舞 a belly dance

dùqí 肚臍 the navel; the belly button

dùzi 肚子 the abdomen; the belly

dù 妒

jealous; envious; jealousy; envy

dù 度

1. an instrument for measuring length 2. a kilowatt-hour 3. a unit of measurement for angles, etc.; a degree 4. (number of) times 5. a system 6. a manner; bearing 7. to pass 8. consideration; careful thought

dùguò nánguān 度過難關 to tide over a difficulty

dùjià 度假 to spend one's holidays (or vacation)

dùliàng 度量 1. an instrument for measuring 2. the capacity for forgiveness

dùliànghéng 度量衡 weights and measures

dùrì 度日 to make a living

dùrì rúnián 度日如年 to pass days as if they were years (because of deep anxiety, worries, or misery)

dùshu 度數 a reading (of a barometer, thermometer, etc.)

dù 渡

1. to cross (a river or ocean) 2. a ferry

dùchuán 渡船 a ferryboat

dùhé 渡河 to cross a river

dùkǒu 渡口 a ferry

dùlún 渡輪 a ferry steamer

dù 鍍

to plate; to gilt

dùjīn 鍍金 to plate with gold

dù 蠹（蠧）

1. a moth 2. moth-eaten; worm-eaten 3. an insect that eats up the resources—(figuratively) an embezzler

dùguó hàimín 蠹國害民 to rob the state and hurt the people

duān 端

1. an extreme; an end 2. a beginning 3. correct; proper; upright 4. leads; a clue 5. to carry carefully 6. cause

duānlài 端賴 to rely entirely upon

duānní 端倪 an outline; a clue; signs

duānshì 端視 to look steadily

Duānwǔjié 端午節 the Dragon-Boat Festival

duānxiáng 端詳 1. to study or examine in detail; to scrutinize 2. details; the whole story 3. dignified and serene

duānzhèng 端正 1. correct; proper 2. to correct; to rectify 3. regular; well-formed; symmetric

duānzhuāng 端莊 sober; dignified

duānzuò 端坐 to sit properly or straight

duǎn 短

1. short; brief 2. to be deficient; to want; to lack; to owe 3. short-comings; faults; mistakes

duǎnbīng xiāngjiē 短兵相接 (military) hand-to-hand combat

duǎnchéng 短程 short distance; short-range

duǎnchu 短處 shortcomings; faults; defects

duǎncù 短促 (said of time) brief; short; transient

duǎndǎ 短打 (baseball) to bunt; a bunt

duǎnjiàn 短見 1. shortsightedness 2. suicide

duǎnjiàn 短劍 a dagger

duǎnkù 短褲 knee pants; shorts; short pants

duǎnlù 短路 (electricity) short

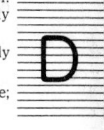

circuit

duǎnmìng 短命 to die early; to die young

duǎnpǎo 短跑 a sprint; a dash

duǎnpǎo jiànjiàng 短跑健将 a sprinter

duǎnpiān xiǎoshuō 短篇小說 short stories

duǎnpiān 短片 a short (film)

duǎnpíng 短評 a short comment or critique

duǎnqī 短期 short-term; a short period

duǎnqí 短期 refer to **duǎnqī** 短期

duǎnquē 短缺 to fall short; deficient

duǎnshǎo 短少 to fall short; deficient

duǎnwà 短襪 socks

duǎnxiǎo 短小 short and small

duǎnxiǎo jīnghàn 短小精悍 short but energetic

duǎnzàn 短暫 (said of time) brief; short; transient

duǎnzhàn 短暫 refer to **duǎnzàn** 短暫

duàn 段

1. a section; a division; a part; a paragraph 2. a stage 3. a Chinese family name

duànluò 段落 1. end (of a paragraph, stage, etc.) 2. a paragraph

duàn 緞

satin

duàndài 緞帶 a satin ribbon

duàn 鍛

1. to smelt; to refine 2. to forge (iron, etc.)

duànliàn 鍛鍊 1. to forge (metal); to temper 2. to train (oneself)

duàn 斷

1. to cut apart; to sever 2. to give up; to abstain from 3. to judge; to decide; to conclude 4. to break; broken 5. absolutely; decidedly; certainly

duàncéng 斷層 (geology) a fault

duàncháng 斷腸 heartbroken

duàndàng 斷檔 to run out of stock

duàndiàn 斷電 power failure; a blackout

duàndìng 斷定 to determine; to conclude

duànduànxùxù 斷斷續續 intermittent; off and on

duàngēn 斷根 to be cured completely (as a disease or addiction)

duànhòu 斷後 1. to cover a retreat 2. to have no offspring

duànjiǎn cánbiān 斷簡殘編 fragmentary works (of a writer)

duànjiāo 斷交 1. to break off relations with someone 2. to sever diplomatic relations

duànjué 斷絕 to break off (relations); to sever

duànjué bāngjiāo 斷絕邦交 to sever diplomatic ties

duànjué guānxi 斷絕關係 to sever relations; to disown (a prodigal son)

duànliáng 斷糧 to run out of food supply

duànnǎi 斷奶 to wean or be weaned

duànqì 斷氣 to breathe one's last

duànrán 斷然 1. absolutely; definitely 2. resolute; drastic

duànshuǐ 斷水 to cut off water supply

duànsòng 斷送 to lose for good

duàntóutái 斷頭臺 a guillotine

duànxiù zhīpǐ 斷袖之癖 male homosexuality

duànyá juébì 斷崖絕壁 broken ridges and steep cliffs

duànyán 斷言 to be absolutely sure; to say with certainty

duànyuán cánbì 斷垣殘壁 broken fences and walls

duànzhāng qǔyì 斷章取義 to interpret a thing out of context

duī 堆

1. to heap up; to pile; to stack 2. a heap; a pile; a mass; a crowd

duīféi 堆肥 compost

duījī 堆積 to store up; to heap up

duīqì 堆砌 1. (composition) allusions, corny expressions, etc. senselessly heaped together 2. to pile up

duì 兌
1. to exchange; to barter 2. (said of wine, etc.) to water; to weaken by adding water

duìhuàn 兌換 exchange; to exchange

duìhuànlǜ 兌換率 exchange rates

duìxiàn 兌現 1. to cash 2. to fulfill; to carry out

duì 隊
1. a group; a team; a batch 2. the troops

duìqí 隊旗 the flag of a team; the team pennant

duìwǔ 隊伍 1. troops in ranks and files 2. a line of (people)

duìxíng 隊形 formation

duìyuán 隊員 members of a team or group

duìzhǎng 隊長 the team leader; the captain of a sports team; the commanding officer of a small military unit

duì 敦
a sort of container

duì 對
1. right; correct; proper 2. parallel; opposing 3. a pair; a couple 4. to check; ascertain 5. to; as to; with regard to 6. to be directed at

duì'àn 對岸 the opposite shore

duìbái 對白 dialogue

duìbàn 對半 a half; one half

duìbǎo 對保 to confirm or verify a guaranty

duìbǐ 對比 contrast; correlation

duìbù gōngtáng 對簿公堂 to face or confront each other in court at a trial

duìbuqǐ 對不起 1. to let a person down 2. I am sorry

duìbuzhù 對不住 1. to let a person down 2. I am sorry

duìcè 對策 a measure (to deal with a problem, etc.); a counter-measure

duìchàng 對唱 a musical dialogue in antiphonal style; antiphonal singing

duìchèn 對稱 symmetry; symmetrical

duìdá 對答 to answer questions

duìdá rúliú 對答如流 to give answers fluently

duìdài 對待 to treat (a person kindly, cruelly, etc.)

duìděng 對等 equal

duìdiào 對調 to exchange positions

duìfāng 對方 the other side (or party)

duìfu 對付 to deal with; to cope with

duìhào 對號 1. to check the number 2. to fit; to tally 3. a check mark

duìhuà 對話 a dialogue; a conversation

duìhuàn 對換 to exchange to barter; to swap

duìjiǎng 對獎 to check the results of a lottery or raffle to see if one holds the winning ticket

duìjiǎngjī 對講機 an interphone; an intercom

duìjìnr 對勁兒 in the right or agreeable condition

duìkāi 對開 folio

duìkàng 對抗 to be opposed to each other

duìkàngsài 對抗賽 a duel meet

duìkǒu 對口 to speak or sing alternately

duìlěi 對壘 to confront each other

duìlì 對立 to be opposed to each other

duìlián 對聯 a Chinese couplet

duìliú 對流 (physics) convection

duìlù 對路 1. to satisfy the need 2. to be to one's liking; to suit one

duìmà 對罵 to call each other names

duìmiàn 對面 on the opposite side

duìnèi 對內 for domestic or internal (consumption, use, etc.)

duìniú tánqín 對牛彈琴 to speak to someone about something completely incomprehensible to him

duǐ'ǒu 對偶 1. to match; to pair 2. verbal parallelism (in poetry)

duìshǒu 對手 an opponent; a match

duìtóu 對頭 an opponent; an adversary

duìwài 對外 for foreign or overseas (consumption, use, etc.)

duìwài màoyì 對外貿易 foreign trade

duìwèir 對味兒 1. to one's taste 2. to seem all right

duìxiàng 對象 the object (of an action); the subject (of consideration)

duìyìng 對應 corresponding; homologous

duìyú 對於 to; as to; with regard to

duìzhào 對照 to compare; to contrast

duìzhàobiǎo 對照表 a contrastive or comparative table

duìzhé 對折 a 50% discount

duìzhèng 對證 to establish evidence through personal confrontation or signed statement

duìzhèng xiàyào 對症下藥 (figuratively) to take the right remedial steps to correct a shortcoming

duìzhì 對質 refer to **duìzhì** 對質

duìzhì 對峙 to face (or confront) each other

duìzhì 對質 to face each other and exchange questions (in order to find out the truth)

duìzhǔn 對準 1. to adjust (a machine part needing adjustment) to the right or proper position 2. to aim at

dūn 敦
1. honest; sincere; candid 2. to deepen or strengthen (relations, etc.) 3. to urge; to press

dūncù 敦促 to urge or press earnestly

dūndǔ 敦篤 honest; sincere

dūnhòu 敦厚 honest; sincere

Dūnhuáng 敦煌 Dunhuang, Gansu Province

dūnmù 敦睦 to have cordial and friendly ties

dūnpǐn lìxué 敦品勵學 upright in character and diligent in the pursuit of knowledge

dūnpìn 敦聘 to cordially invite

dūnqǐng 敦請 to cordially invite

dūn 墩
1. a mound; a heap 2. a block of stone or wood 3. a cluster

dūn 噸 also **dùn**
ton (a unit of weight)

dūnwèi 噸位 tonnage (of a ship)

dūn 蹲 also **cún**
1. to squat; to crouch 2. to stay

dǔn 盹
to doze

dùn 沌
turbid; unclear; chaotic

dùn 盾 also **shǔn**
1. a shield; a buckler 2. a guilder; a monetary unit in Holland

dùnpái 盾牌 1. a shield 2. (figuratively) a pretext; an excuse

dùn 鈍
blunt; dull; obtuse

dùnjiǎo 鈍角 an obtuse angle

dùn 遁
1. to run away; to escape 2. to conceal oneself; to retire

dùncí 遁辭 an excuse; a pretext

dùnshì 遁世 to live incognito

dùnxíng 遁形 to become invisible; to vanish

dùnzǒu 遁走 to flee; to take to one's heels

dùn 頓
1. to stop or halt; to pause 2. to kowtow 3. to stamp (the foot) 4. to arrange; to put in order 5. a time; a turn 6. immediately; promptly 7. to be tired; to fall apart 8. to be broken

dùncuò 頓挫 1. to encounter failure; to receive a setback 2. (said of musical notes) rising and falling

dùnhào 頓號 a punctuation mark "、" indicating a very brief pause in reading

dùnshǒu 頓首 to make a ceremonious nod

dùnwù 頓悟 to realize suddenly; to come to a sudden realization

dùnzú 頓足 to stamp one's foot

dùn 遯

1. to escape; to run off 2. to cheat

dùn 燉

1. to stew; to simmer 2. to warm

dùn 噸

refer to **dūn** 噸

duō 多

1. many; much; too much 2. more than; much more; over 3. greatly; highly 4. to praise 5. only 6. (also **duó**) how, what, etc.—in exclamatory

duōbàn 多半 1. most 2. probably; most likely

duōbāotāi 多胞胎 multiple birth

duōbiānxíng 多邊形 a polygon

duōbìng 多病 constantly ill

duōcái duōyì 多才多藝 versatile; very capable

duōcǎi duōzī 多彩多姿 colorful; many-faceted

duōchóng rén'gé 多重人格 multiple personality

duōchóu shàn'gǎn 多愁善感 sentimental

duōcǐ yījǔ 多此一舉 a superfluous action, etc.

duōcì 多次 many times; time and again

duōdà 多大 1. How big? 2. How old?

duōdǎng zhìdù 多黨制度 the multiparty system

duōduō yìshàn 多多益善 The more, the better.

duōfāngmiàn 多方面 many-sided; in many ways

duōfú duōshòu 多福多壽 happiness and longevity

duōguǎ 多寡 number; amount

duōguǎ bùjū 多寡不拘 It doesn't matter how much or how little (you contribute).

duōguǎn xiánshì 多管閒事 to poke one's nose into others' business; to be a busybody

duōjiǎoxíng 多角形 a polygon

duōjièzhì 多介質 multimedia

duōkuī 多虧 It is fortunate that...; We are lucky to...; Thanks to....

duōme 多麼 how (good, beautiful, etc.); what

duōméitǐ 多媒體 multimedia

duōmiànshǒu 多面手 people who have multiple skills

duōmóu shànduàn 多謀善斷 resourceful and decisive

duōnàn xīngbāng 多難興邦 Foreign aggressions often awaken a nation from its slumbers and thus help make it strong.

Duōnǎohé 多瑙河 the Danube River

duōnián bùjiàn 多年不見 to have not met or seen for many years

duōqíng 多情 passionate; emotional

duōshǎo 多少 more or less; somewhat

duōshao 多少 How much? How many?

duōshí 多時 a long time

duōshì 多事 officious; interfering; meddling

duōshì zhīqiū 多事之秋 troubled times; an eventful year

duōshù 多數 the majority; many

duōtuì shǎobǔ 多退少補 to return the overcharge and demand payment of the shortage, if any

duōxiè 多謝 Thanks a lot.

duōxīn 多心 1. to be very suspicious 2. tricky

D

duōyànghuà 多樣化 to diversify; to make varied

duōyí 多疑 suspicious

duōyú 多餘 unnecessary; superfluous

duōyuán 多元 multiple; plural; poly

duōyún 多雲 cloudy

duōzāi duōnàn 多災多難 to be dogged by bad luck, misfortune, etc.

duōzǐ duōsūn 多子多孫 many children and grandchildren (regarded as a blessing among old Chinese)

duōzuǐ 多嘴 to have a big mouth; to shoot one's mouth off

duō 咄 also **duō**
1. an angry cry 2. to scold in a loud voice

duōduō bīrén 咄咄逼人 1. to browbeat 2. overbearing

duō 哆
to shiver; to tremble

duōsuo 哆嗦 to shiver with cold or tremble with fear

duó 多
refer to **duō** 多 6

duó 度 also **duō**
to consider; to measure; to infer

duó dé liàng lì 度德量力 to act with due consideration of one's own abilities

duó 奪
1. to take by force; to rob 2. to snatch; to grasp 3. to carry away (the first prize, etc.) 3. to settle; to decide

duóbiāo 奪標 to win the first prize—as in a race or contest

duóhuí 奪回 to recapture; to retake

duókuàng érchū 奪眶而出 (said of tears) to break out

duókuí 奪魁 to win a race or tournament

duómén érchū 奪門而出 to force one's way out

duóqǔ 奪取 to take by force; to wrest from

duóquán 奪權 to take over power

duó 踱 also **duò**
to stroll; to walk slowly

duóbù 踱步 to stroll; to walk slowly

duó 鐸
1. a large bell 2. a Chinese family name

duǒ 朵
1. a flower; a cluster of flowers; a bud 2. a lobe of the ear

duǒyí 朵頤 the movement of the jaw in eating—the palate

duǒ 躲
1. to escape; to shun; to avoid 2. to hide

duǒbì 躲避 to dodge; to ward off; to shun

duǒbìqiú 躲避球 dodge ball (a kind of ball game played by children)

duǒcáng 躲藏 to hide oneself; to hide

duǒshǎn 躲閃 1. moving carefully so as to avoid danger 2. bashful; timid; shy

duǒzhài 躲債 to run away from one's creditor; to avoid a creditor

duò 剁
to chop; to mince; to hash

duò 咄
refer to **duō** 咄

duò 度
refer to **duó** 度

duò 舵
a rudder; a helm

duòshǒu 舵手 a helmsman; a steersman

duò 惰
lazy; idle; indolent

duòxìng 惰性 inertia; sloth; laziness

duò 墮
1. to fall; to sink; to let fall 2. to indulge in evil ways 3. lazy; idle

duòluò 墮落 1. to indulge in evil ways; to degenerate 2. the fall (of a nation, family, etc.)

duòtāi 墮胎 abortion; to abort

duò 躱

refer to **duó** 踱

ē 阿

1. to favor; to toady; to assent; to pander to; to play up to 2. to rely on 3. a riverbank 4. the corner or edge 5. a pillar 6. slender and beautiful 7. to discharge (night soil, urine, etc.)

Ēmítuófó 阿彌陀佛 Amitabha, the Buddha of infinite qualities

ēyú 阿諛 to flatter

ē 婀

1. graceful; elegant 2. a Chinese family name

ēnuó duōzī 婀娜多姿 graceful; well-poised

é 俄

1. (also **è**) Russia 2. sudden; suddenly; momentaril

Éguó 俄國 Russia

Éluósī 俄羅斯 Russia

éqing 俄頃 soon

Éyǔ 俄語 Russian (language)

é 娥

1. good; beautiful 2. a common name for a girl 3. a Chinese family name

é 哦

to recite (verses, etc.)

é 訛

1. rumors 2. errors; erroneous; wrong 3. to extort; to swindle; to deceive; to bluff 4. to move about 5. to change

échuán 訛傳 false rumors; wrong information

éwù 訛誤 errors; mistakes

é 蛾

a moth

éméi 蛾眉 long, slender eyebrows arched like the antennae of a moth

é 鵝

a goose; a gander

édànliǎn 鵝蛋臉 an egg-shaped face; an oval face

Éluánbí 鵝鑾鼻 name of the southernmost cape of Taiwan

éluǎnshí 鵝卵石 pebbles

émáo 鵝毛 goose feathers

é 額

1. the forehead 2. a fixed number, amount, value, etc.; a quota 3. a horizontal tablet

éjiǎo 額角 the temples

éshǒu chēngqìng 額手稱慶 to be overjoyed

étou 額頭 the forehead

éwài 額外 extra

éwài shōurù 額外收入 extra income

ě 我

refer to **wǒ** 我

ě 噁(惡)

to disgust; to sicken; to scorn

ěxin 噁心 1. nauseated 2. disgust

è 厄

1. difficulty; adversity; distress; hardship 2. impeded; cramped

èyùn 厄運 bad luck; adversity

è 歹(歺)

(now rarely) the remains of a person

è 阨

1. a strategic position 2. a precarious position 3. to block up or obstruct 4. destitute; difficulty; poverty-stricken

è 呃

to hiccup or hiccough

è 扼

1. to repress; to restrain; to control 2. to clutch; to grasp; to grip 3. to hold and defend (a city, etc.)

èshā 扼殺 to strangle; to throttle

èshǒu 扼守 to hold and defend

èwàn 扼腕 (literally) to seize one's wrist—1. disappointment; regret 2. anger 3. excitement

èyào 扼要 1. to hold a strategic

position 2. in summary

èzhì 扼制 to repress

è 俄

refer to **é** 俄 1

è 愕

startled; astonished; amazed

èrán 愕然 stunned; dumbfounded; astonished

è 惡

1. bad; evil; wickedness; vice; wicked 2. fierce; ferocious

èbà 惡霸 a powerful bully; a local tyrant

èbào 惡報 retribution; evil recompense

èchòu 惡臭 an offensive odor; a bad smell

èdú 惡毒 venomous; vicious; malicious

èguàn mǎnyíng 惡貫滿盈 to reach the limit of crimes (tolerated by Heaven)

ègùn 惡棍 a scoundrel; a rascal; a villain

èguǒ 惡果 undesirable consequences; disastrous effect

èhào 惡耗 news of death or disaster

èhuà 惡化 to get worse; to degenerate

èliè 惡劣 1. of very poor quality; very inferior 2. rude; distasteful 3. vile; satanic

èmèng 惡夢 a nightmare

èmíng 惡名 a bad reputation; ill fame; notoriety

èmíng zhāozhāng 惡名昭彰 notorious

èmó 惡魔 a demon; a fiend; the devil

èmú èyàng 惡模惡樣 a fierce or ferocious appearance

èrén 惡人 a bad man; a scoundrel

èshìlì 惡勢力 vicious power

ètú 惡徒 a scoundrel; a rascal; a villain

èxí 惡習 a bad habit

èxíng 惡行 an evil deed; a wicked act

èxíng 惡形 refer to **èxíng** 惡行

èxìng 惡性 malignant; virulent; vicious

èxìng dǎobì 惡性倒閉 fraudulent insolvency

èxìng xúnhuán 惡性循環 a vicious circle

èyì 惡意 1. malicious; spiteful 2. malice; evil intentions

èyǒu èbào 惡有惡報 Evil will be recompensed with evil.

èyùn 惡運 bad luck; ill luck

èzhào 惡兆 an ill omen

èzuòjù 惡作劇 mischief; a practical joke

è 遏

1. to curb; to stop; to restrain; to prevent 2. to cause one's own extinction; to extinguish; to ruin

èzhǐ 遏止 to check; to hold back; to stop

è 餓

1. hungry; hunger 2. greedy; covetous 3. to starve

èguǐ 餓鬼 1. a person who is always hungry 2. a person who eats piggishly

èsǐ 餓死 to be starved to death

è 噩

1. startling; alarming; dreadful; awesome 2. grave; serious

èhào 噩耗 shocking news (usually news of a person's death)

èmèng 噩夢 a nightmare

è 顎

1. the jowl; jaws 2. high-cheek-boned 3. reverence

ègǔ 顎骨 the jawbones; maxillary bones

è 鱷

a crocodile; an alligator

ēn 恩

favor; grace; gratitude; kindness; benevolence; mercy; charity

ēn'ài 恩愛 (said of a married couple) mutual affection

ēn'ài fūqī 恩愛夫妻 an affectionate couple

ēnchǒng 恩寵 the emperor's affection or favor

ēncì 恩賜 1. a gift of grace from the emperor 2. to bestow (favors)

ēndé 恩德 benevolence; benignity; generosity; bounty

ēndiǎn 恩典 1. (in old China) an imperial favor 2. a favor

ēngōng 恩公 a benefactor

ēnhuì 恩惠 kindness; charity

ēnjiāng chóubào 恩將仇報 to return evil for good; ungrateful

ēnqíng 恩情 loving-kindness; devotion (between friends, teacher and student, husband and wife, etc.)

ēnrén 恩人 a benefactor

ēnshī 恩師 a teacher to whom one is greatly indebted

ēnyuàn 恩怨 1. gratitude and grudges 2. resentment; grievance

ēnzé 恩澤 the pervading benevolence (of the ruler)

ēnzhǔn 恩准 to grant graciously

ér 而

1. accordingly; otherwise 2. and yet; but; nevertheless 3. you 4. on the condition that; supposing that; if 5. and; also

érhòu 而後 then; afterwards; later; thenceforward; thereafter

érjīn 而今 now

érqiě 而且 1. and 2. moreover; furthermore; besides

éryǐ 而已 merely; only; and that is all

ér 兒

1. a child; a baby 2. a son 3. referring to oneself when addressing parents 4. as a particle after noun, pronoun, adjective, adverb, and verb

érgē 兒歌 children's songs

érkē 兒科 pediatrics

érnǚ 兒女 1. sons and daughters; children 2. young men and women

érnǚ qíngcháng 兒女情長 Long is the love between a man and a woman.

érshí 兒時 childhood

érsūn 兒孫 1. children and grand-children 2. offspring; descendants

értóng 兒童 children

értóng dúwù 兒童讀物 juvenile publications

Értóngjié 兒童節 Children's Day

értóng lèyuán 兒童樂園 an amusement park catering to children

értóng wénxué 兒童文學 literary writings for children

értóng xīnlǐxué 兒童心理學 child psychology

érxífur 兒媳婦兒 a daughter-in-law

érxì 兒戲 1. child's play 2. a plaything 3. to treat lightly

érzi 兒子 a son

ěr 耳

1. ears 2. (a phrase-final particle) only; merely

ěrbìn sīmó 耳鬢廝磨 (usually said of childhood lovers) very intimate

ěrchuí 耳垂 an ear lobe; a lobule

ěrduo 耳朵 ears

ěrguāng 耳光 a box on the ear

ěrhuán 耳環 earrings

ěrjī 耳機 an earphone

ěrlóng 耳聾 deaf

ěrmíng 耳鳴 buzzing in the ears; tinnitus aurium

ěrmù 耳目 1. ears and eyes 2. one's attention or notice 3. an informer

ěrmù yīxīn 耳目一新 to have a completely new impression

ěrmù zhòngduō 耳目眾多 There are many spies.

ěrrú mùrǎn 耳濡目染 thoroughly imbued with what one frequently hears and sees

ěrsāi 耳塞 an earplug

ěrshú 耳熟 much heard of

ěrshú néngxiáng 耳熟能詳 so frequently heard about that it can be told (in detail or word by word)

ěrtí miànmìng 耳提面命 to give instructions earnestly

ěrwāzi 耳挖子 an ear pick

ěrwén 耳聞 1. to hear 2. what

one hears about; hearsay

ěryǔ 耳語 to whisper into another's ear

ěr 爾

1. you; thou 2. that; this; those; these; such; so 3. a particle used after adjectives 4. only

ěr'ěr 爾爾 so-so; not so outstanding

ěrhòu 爾後 thereafter; afterwards

ěryú wǒzhà 爾虞我詐 each trying to cheat or outwit the other

ěr 餌

1. to bait; to entice; bait 2. cakes 3. food 4. to eat

èr 二

two; second; twice

èrbā jiārén 二八佳人 a sixteen-year-old beauty

èrbā niánhuá 二八年華 (said of a girl) sixteen years of age

èrbǎiwǔ 二百五 (abuse) a simpleton

èrchóngchàng 二重唱 (vocal) a duet

èrchóngzòu 二重奏 a duet performance on the piano

èrfángdōng 二房東 a person who sublets a house rented from another

èrhú 二胡 a two-stringed Chinese musical instrument

èrlángtuǐ 二郎腿 (to sit) cross-legged

èrlǎo 二老 one's father and mother

èrlèngzi 二愣子 a rash fellow

èrsān qídé 二三其德 inconsistent

èrshǒuhuò 二手貨 a used item; a secondhand commodity

èrshǒuyān 二手煙 passive smoking

èrxīn 二心 disloyalty

èryǎnghuàtàn 二氧化碳 carbon dioxide

èryuè 二月 1. February 2. the second moon of the lunar calendar 3. two months

èr 貳

1. (in ancient China) a deputy; to serve as a deputy 2. to suspect; to doubt; to distrust 3. changeable 4. an elaborate form of 二 (two), used in writing checks, etc. to prevent forgery 5. to repeat 6. doubleness 7. a Chinese family name

èrxīn 貳心 a rebellious mind

èrzhì 貳志 disloyalty

fā 伐

refer to **fá** 伐

fā 發

1. to shoot; to launch 2. to issue; to publish 3. to begin; to start 4. to reveal; to disclose; to uncover 5. to become; to come to be 6. to utter; to express; to speak 7. to set off; to set out 8. to illuminate; to help out

fābái 發白 to turn white; to turn pale

fābǎng 發榜 to publish the result of an examination

fābāo 發包 to contract with a contractor for a construction program

fābào 發報 to transmit messages

fābàojī 發報機 a telegraph transmitter

fābiǎo 發表 to make public; to publish; to announce

fābù 發布 to announce; to promulgate

fācái 發財 to acquire wealth; to become rich

fāchóu 發愁 to worry

fāchū 發出 to send forth; to generate

fācíbēi 發慈悲 to show mercy or pity

fādá 發達 to evolve; developed; prosperous; thriving

fādāi 發呆 to look absent-minded

fādiàn 發電 1. to generate electric power 2. to send a telegram

fādiànchǎng 發電廠 a power plant

fādiànjī 發電機 a generator; a dynamo

fādòng 發動 to start; to launch; to initiate

fādòngjī 發動機 a motor; an engine

fādǒu 發抖 to tremble; to shiver

fāduān 發端 to initiate

fāfàng 發放 1. to issue; to distribute; to provide; to extend 2. to dispose of

fāfěn 發粉 baking powder

fāfèn túqiáng 發憤圖強 (said of a nation) to strive for progress with determination

fāfēng 發瘋 to go mad; to become insane

fāfú 發福 1. to become rich and happy 2. (jocularly) to become fat

fāgǎo 發稿 (journalism) to send out a story or report for publication

fāguāng 發光 to emit light

fāhàn 發汗 1. to perspire or sweat 2. diaphoresis

fāháng 發行 1. to sell wholesale 2. a wholesaler

fāhào shīlìng 發號施令 to issue orders

fāhěn 發狠 1. to exert oneself 2. to show anger

fāhuāng 發慌 to lose one's composure; to feel nervous

fāhuī 發揮 to bring (skill, talent, etc.) into full play

fāhuī zuòyòng 發揮作用 to be effective; (said of effect) to tell

fāhūn 發昏 1. to faint 2. to lose one's head

fāhuǒ 發火 1. to become angry 2. to burst into flames 3. to go off

fājì 發迹 to rise (in business, career, etc.)

fājiào 發酵 to ferment; fermentation

fājiàorǔ 發酵乳 ferment milk; yogurt

fājiǔfēng 發酒瘋 to get drunk and behave irrationally

fājué 發掘 to unearth; to dig out; to excavate

fājué 發噱 refer to **fāxué** 發噱

fājué 發覺 1. to discover; to find 2. (said of crimes, plots, etc.) to be uncovered

fākān 發刊 to start or launch (a magazine, newspaper, etc.)

fāláosāo 發牢騷 to grumble; to complain

fāliàng 發亮 to shine; to glitter

fāluò 發落 to deal with (an offender)

fāmá 發麻 numb; benumbed

fāmáo 發毛 to feel a shudder

fāméi 發霉 to get mildewed; to mildew

fāmíng 發明 1. to invent; to devise 2. an invention

fāmíngjiā 發明家 an inventor

fā'nàn 發難 1. to spearhead a rebellion or revolution 2. to ask difficult questions

fānù 發怒 to burst into anger

fāpái 發排 to send (manuscripts) to the composing room

fāpái 發牌 to deal cards

fāpàng 發胖 to put on (or gain) weight; to get fat

fāpèi 發配 to banish (a criminal) to a frontier garrison

fāpíqi 發脾氣 to lose one's temper; to get angry; to get mad

fāpiào 發票 an invoice; a bill of sale

fāqǐrén 發起人 an originator; an initiator

fāqiú 發球 to serve a ball (in tennis, handball, etc.)

fārè 發熱 to have a temperature; to have a fever

fārén shēnxǐng 發人深省 to stimulate deep thought

fāsàn 發散 to disperse; to dissipate; to scatter

fāshāo 發燒 to have a temperature; to have a fever

fāshè 發射 to launch; to shoot; to catapult

fāshètái 發射臺 a launching pad

fāshénjīng 發神經 to go crazy; to lose sanity

fāshēng 發生 to happen; to occur; to arise

fāshēng chōngtū 發生衝突 to have a conflict

fāshēng guānxi 發生關係 1. to

have something to do with 2. to have an affair with

fāshì 發誓 to swear; to take an oath

fāshòu 發售 to go on sale

fāsòng 發送 1. to send 2. to hold a funeral service

fāsuān 發酸 to become sour; to sour

fātiáo 發條 a spring (of a mechanical device)

fāwèn 發問 to ask questions; to raise questions

fāxiàn 發現 to discover; to find; discovery

fāxiángdì 發祥地 the cradle; a birthplace

fāxiào 發笑 to laugh

fāxiào 發酵 refer to **fājiào** 發酵

fāxiàorǔ 發酵乳 refer to **fā-jiàorǔ** 發酵乳

fāxiè 發泄 to give vent to; to vent; to let out

fāxīnshuǐ 發薪水 to hand out paychecks to employees

fāxìn 發信 to send or post a letter

fāxíng 發行 (said of currency, bonds, books, etc.) to issue; to publish

fāxíngliàng 發行量 the volume of circulation

fāxíngrén 發行人 a publisher

fāxué 發噱 to laugh

fāyá 發芽 to sprout

fāyán 發言 to speak; to voice one's views

fāyán 發炎 to become inflamed; to become infected

fāyánrén 發言人 a spokesman

fāyáng 發揚 to exalt; to enhance

fāyáng guāngdà 發揚光大 to enhance and glorify

fāyǎng 發癢 to itch

fāyīn 發音 to pronounce; pronunciation

fāyù 發育 1. to grow up; to develop 2. to send forth and nourish

fāyù bùliáng 發育不良 maldevelopment

fāyuán 發源 1. an origin; a source 2. to originate

fāyuándì 發源地 (said of rivers, etc.) the place of origin

fāzhǎn 發展 to develop; to grow; to expand

fāzuò 發作 1. to show effect 2. to have a fit (of anger) 3. (said of illness) to have a relapse

fá 乏
1. in want of; deficient; lack 2. exhausted; tired 3. povertystricken; poor

fáshàn kěchén 乏善可陳 to have nothing good to report

fáwèi 乏味 monotonous; dull; insipid

fá 伐 also **fā**
1. to cut (wood) 2. to attack; to smite

fámù 伐木 to fell tress

fá 法
fázǐ 法子 refer to **fǎzi** 法子

fá 筏
a raft

fá 閥
1. a threshold; a doorsill 2. an influential person, family, or clique; a bloc 3. a valve

fá 罰
to punish; to penalize; to fine

fájīn 罰金 to impose a fine; a fine or to be fined cash

fákuǎn 罰款 1. a fine 2. to fine

fǎ 法
1. an institution 2. law; regulations; rules; the statutes; legal 3. methods; ways of doing things 4. to pattern or model after; to emulate 5. (Buddhism) the "way" —doctrines, etc. 6. tricks; magic arts 7. expert or standard (calligraphy, painting, etc.) 8. penalty; punishment 9. (also **fà**) France; French

fǎ'àn 法案 a law; a statute

fǎchǎng 法場 1. an execution ground 2. any place set aside for religious practices

F

fǎdiǎn 法典 1. a code of laws; a statute book 2. the scriptures of Buddhism

fǎdìng 法定 legal

fǎdìng dàilǐrén 法定代理人 a legal representative

fǎguān 法官 a judge (at court); a justice

fǎguī 法規 laws and regulations

Fǎguó 法國 France

fǎhào 法號 the religious name of a Buddhist monk or nun

fǎjì 法紀 law and discipline

Fǎjiā 法家 Legalists, a school of thought in 770-221 B.C.

fǎjǐng 法警 1. the judicial police 2. a bailiff

fǎlánróng 法蘭絨 flannel

Fǎlánxī 法蘭西 France

fǎláng 法郎 franc (a monetary unit of France)

Fǎlǎo 法老 Pharaoh, title of an ancient Egyptian king

fǎlǐ 法理 1. the principle or theory of law 2. the doctrines of Buddhism

fǎlìng 法令 a general term for laws and regulations

fǎlǜ 法律 laws

fǎlǜ chéngxù 法律程序 legal procedure

fǎlǜ gùwèn 法律顧問 a legal advisor

fǎlǜ zhìcái 法律制裁 legal sanctions

fǎmén 法門 the way, or method of learning something

fǎshī 法師 1. a salutation for a Buddhist monk 2. a Taoist high priest

fǎshì 法事 Buddhist rituals performed on special occasions

fǎtiáo 法條 items or articles of law

fǎtíng 法庭 a law court; a tribunal

fǎtǒng 法統 the system of justice

fǎwài shīēn 法外施恩 to be lenient within the limits of the law

fǎwǎng 法網 the dragnet or the arms of law

Fǎwén 法文 French (language)

Fǎwùbù 法務部 the Ministry of Justice

fǎxué 法學 the science of law

Fǎxué Bóshì 法學博士 a Doctor of Laws (LL.D.)

fǎxuéjiā 法學家 a jurist

fǎyī 法醫 an expert in forensic medicine employed by a court of law, such as a coroner

Fǎyǔ 法語 the spoken French; French

fǎyuàn 法院 a court of justice; a court of law

fǎzé 法則 1. a way or method; a pattern or model considered as a standard 2. a formula in mathematics 3. an agreement which has the same binding force as law

fǎzhì 法治 rule of law

fǎzi 法子 a method; a way

fǎ 砝
standard weights used in scales; steelyard weights

fǎmǎ 砝碼 steelyard weights

fà 髮
refer to **fà** 髮

fǎ 法
refer to **fǎ** 法 9

fà 琺
enamel; enamelware

fàlán 琺瑯 refer to **fàláng** 琺瑯

fàláng 琺瑯 enamel

fà 髮 also **fǎ**
1. hair (covering human heads) 2. a hairbreadth; a hair's breadth

fàjì 髮髻 hair tied in a knot

fàjiā 髮夾 a hairpin; a bobby pin

fàjiāo 髮膠 hair spray; fixture for hair

fàqī 髮妻 one's first wife

fàwū 髮屋 a barbershop

fàxíng 髮型 a hair style; a hairdo; a coiffure

fàyóu 髮油 hair oil; pomade

fàzhǐ 髮指 so angry that the hair rises; to boil with anger

fān 帆 also **fán**
canvas; sailcloth

fānbù 帆布 canvas

fānchuán 帆船 a sailboat

fān 番
1. to take turns 2. order in series 3. a time 4. a kind of; a sort of 5. barbarians

fānhào 番號 a numerical designation of a military unit

fānqié 番茄 a tomato

fānqiéjiàng 番茄醬 tomato ketchup

fānqiézhī 番茄汁 tomato juice

fānshíliu 番石榴 a guava

fānshǔ 番薯 a sweet potato

fān 翻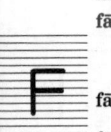
1. to fly; to flutter 2. to turn; to upset; to capsize 3. to rummage 4. to translate 5. to fall out

fān'àn 翻案 to reverse a previous verdict

fānbǎn 翻版 a reprint of a book (with or without proper permission)

fānchuán 翻船 (said of a boat) to capsize

fāngēntou 翻跟頭 1. to turn a somersault 2. (aeronautic) to loop the loop

fāngòng 翻供 to withdraw a confession; to retract a testimony (at a law court)

fāngǔn 翻滾 to roll; to toss; to tumble

fānkāi 翻開 to turn open

fānliǎn 翻臉 to show displeasure; to get angry; to turn hostile

fānliǎn wúqíng 翻臉無情 to turn against a friend and show him no mercy

fānrán huīwù 翻然悔悟 quickly wake up to one's mistakes

fānshān yuèlǐng 翻山越嶺 to travel over mountains and valleys

fānshēn 翻身 1. to turn the body over 2. to rise from poverty to affluence; to have a break of fortune

fānxiū 翻修 to rebuild; to overhaul

fānyì 翻譯 to translate; to interpret

fānyìn 翻印 to reprint (a book with or without proper permission)

fānyuè 翻閱 to browse; to look over

fān 藩 also **fán**
a fence; a hedge; a boundary; a frontier; a barrier

fánlí 藩籬 1. a fence; a hedge 2. anything acting as a hedge 3. a barrier

fánshǔ 藩屬 a vassal state; a protectorate

fán 凡
1. common; ordinary; dull 2. worldly; mortal; earthly 3. generally; every; whenever; wherever 4. altogether

Fán'ěrsài 凡爾賽 Versailles, French city and site of the Versailles Palace built by Louis XIV

fánfū súzǐ 凡夫俗子 the masses; ordinary people

fánjiān 凡間 the material world

fánrén 凡人 an ordinary person

fánshì 凡事 everything

fánshì 凡是 all (who are present, etc. or which are black, heavy, etc.)

fánshìlín 凡士林 vaseline; petrolatum

fánxīn 凡心 worldly desires

fán 帆
refer to **fān** 帆

fán 煩
1. to vex; to annoy; to worry 2. annoying 3. to trouble 4. superfluous and confusing

fánluàn 煩亂 confusing

fánmèn 煩悶 annoyed; downcast; bored; depressed; vexed; worried

fánnǎo 煩惱 worries; cares; worried

fánqǐng 煩請 Would you mind...?

fánxiāo 煩囂 1. the hubbub of a

noisy place 2. cares and worries of this world

fánxīn 煩心 vexation

fánzá 煩雜 petty and varied; confusing and disorderly

fánzào 煩躁 vexed; short-tempered

fán 樊
1. a bird cage 2. disorderly; confused; messy 3. a Chinese family name

fánlóng 樊籠 1. a cage to confine birds or wild beasts 2. (figuratively) the place or condition of confinement

fán 蕃
1. (said of vegetation) flourishing; luxuriant 2. to increase; to multiply; to propagate 3. numerous; plentiful

fányǎn 蕃衍 to propagate rapidly

fán 繁
1. many; numerous; abundant; prolific 2. complex; complicated; intricate

fánduō 繁多 many; numerous

fánfù 繁複 complex; complicated; intricate

fánhuá 繁華 1. pompous; extravagant 2. prosperous; flourishing; booming

fánhuá shìjiè 繁華世界 this vain world

fánmáng 繁忙 very busy; hectic

fánmào 繁茂 (said of vegetation) lush or luxuriant

fánróng 繁榮 prosperous; flourishing; thriving

fánsuǒ 繁瑣 minute and complicated

fánwén rùjié 繁文縟節 excessive ceremony

fánxīng 繁星 numerous stars

fánzá 繁雜 complex; complicated; intricate

fánzhí 繁殖 to propagate; to breed

fánzhòng 繁重 (said of work loads) heavy; arduous

fán 藩

refer to **fān** 藩

fǎn 反
1. reverse; opposite; contrary 2. to return (something); to turn back; to retreat 3. to introspect; to retrospect 4. to rebel; rebellion; to revolt 5. to infer

fǎnbài wéishèng 反敗爲勝 to turn defeat into victory

fǎnbó 反駁 to refute; to retort

fǎnbǔ 反哺 to show filial piety to one's parents

fǎncháng 反常 out-of-the-ordinary; abnormal

fǎnchú 反芻 to ruminate

fǎnchuàn 反串 1. (Peking opera) to play a role other than one's specialty 2. to play the role of the opposite sex

fǎnchún xiāngjī 反唇相稽 to rebut or rebuke with sarcastic remarks

fǎnduì 反對 to oppose; to object

fǎn'ér 反而 unexpectedly; contrarily

fǎnfù 反覆 1. not dependable 2. to relapse 3. repeatedly; again and again

fǎnfù sīliang 反覆思量 to think over and over again

fǎnfù wúcháng 反覆無常 capricious

fǎn'gǎn 反感 antipathy

fǎngōng zìwèn 反躬自問 self-examination

fǎngù 反顧 to look back; to review

fǎnguāng 反光 reflection; reflected light

fǎnhuǐ 反悔 to renege (on a promise)

fǎnjiàn 反間 to alienate the enemy coalition

fǎnkàng 反抗 to counter; to resist; to rebel; to rise up against

fǎnkè wéizhǔ 反客爲主 to exchange the positions of the host and the guest

fǎnmù 反目 to fight

fǎnpài 反派 a villain (in drama, etc.); a negative character

fǎnpàn 反叛 to rebel; to revolt;

F

treason

fǎnpū 反撲 1. to pounce on somebody again after being beaten off 2. a counterattack

fǎnqiú zhūjǐ 反求諸己 to make self-examination

fǎnshè 反射 to reflect; reflection

fǎnshízhōng fāngxiàng 反時鐘方向 counterclockwise

fǎnshìjìng 反視鏡 a rearview mirror

fǎnwèi 反胃 to upset the stomach; nauseating

fǎnwèn 反問 to rebut

fǎnxiàng 反向 the opposite direction

fǎnxǐng 反省 reflection; self-examination

fǎnyán xiāngxiàng 反顏相向 to become hostile

fǎnyǎo yīkǒu 反咬一口 to fabricate a countercharge against one's accuser

fǎnyìzì 反義字 an antonym

fǎnyìng 反映 to reflect

fǎnyìng 反應 1. response 2. chemical reaction

fǎnyìngduī 反應堆 a reactor

fǎnzhèng 反證 the counter-evidence

fǎnzheng 反正 in any case; anyway

fǎnzhuǎn 反轉 1. to turn inside out 2. to return

fǎnzuòyòng 反作用 1. undesirable reactions or results 2. (physics) reaction

fǎn 返

1. to go back; to come back; to return 2. to send back; to give back

fǎnguó 返國 to return from abroad

fǎnháng 返航 to return to a base or port

fǎnlǎo huántóng 返老還童 to regain youth; to rejuvenate oneself

fǎnxiào 返校 to return to school

fàn 氾

1. to spread; to fill everywhere 2.

extensive; vast; boundless 3. floating

fànlàn 氾濫 1. to overflow; in flood 2. to spread far and wide

fàn 犯

1. to violate; to offend; to break (regulations or laws) 2. to commit (crimes, etc.) 3. to invade; to attack 4. a criminal 5. to have a recurrence of

fànbìng 犯病 to fall back into an old illness or a bad habit

fàncuò 犯錯 to make a mistake

fànfǎ 犯法 to violate the law

fànguī 犯規 (sports) to commit a foul

fànjìhuì 犯忌諱 to violate a taboo

fànren 犯人 a criminal; a prisoner

fànshàng zuòluàn 犯上作亂 to rebel against authority

fànzuì 犯罪 to commit (a crime, an offense or a sin)

fàn 泛

1. (氾) to float; to drift 2. not exact or precise; not practical 3. not sincere; not intimate 4. generally (speaking); as a whole; pan- 5. to be suffused with

fànchēng 泛稱 generally called...

fànfàn zhījiāo 泛泛之交 a casual acquaintance

fànzhǐ 泛指 to generally indicate

fànzhōu 泛舟 to row a boat; boating

fàn 范

1. the bee 2. a Chinese family name

fàn 梵

1. clean and pure 2. Sanskrit 3. a Brahman 4. anything pertaining to Buddhism

Fàndìgāng 梵蒂崗 the Vatican

Fànwén 梵文 the written Sanskrit

Fànyǔ 梵語 the spoken Sanskrit

fàn 販

1. to buy and sell; to deal in; to trade in 2. to carry about for

sale; to peddle 3. a seller of goods; a peddler; a monger

fàndú 販毒 to deal in narcotics

fànfū zǒuzú 販夫走卒 people of the lower class

fànmài 販賣 to deal in; to sell; to peddle

fànmàibù 販賣部 a commissary (in barracks, schools, etc.); a store

fàn 飯

1. cooked rice; cooked grain for food 2. a meal 3. to feed 4. a profession; means of living

fàncài 飯菜 1. dishes to go with rice 2. a meal; a repast; food

fàndiàn 飯店 1. a restaurant 2. a hotel

fànguō 飯鍋 a pot for cooking rice

fànhé 飯盒 a lunch box; a rice container

fànjú 飯局 a luncheon or dinner party

fànlái zhāngkǒu 飯來張口 to live an easy life, with everything provided

fànliàng 飯量 an appetite; capacity for eating

fànpiào 飯票 1. a food coupon 2. (slang) a husband

fànqiánjiǔ 飯前酒 aperitif

fàntīng 飯廳 a dining room; a mess hall

fàntǒng 飯桶 1. a tub for storing cooked rice 2. a good-for-nothing; a stupid or clumsy fellow

fànwǎn 飯碗 1. a rice bowl 2. (slang) one's job

fànzhuō 飯桌 a dining table

fàn 範

1. a model; a form; an example; a pattern 2. range; scope; limits 3. to observe the proper rules

fànběn 範本 1. a copy or copybook (for penmanship, calligraphy, painting, etc.) 2. a model; an example

fànchóu 範疇 a domain

fànlì 範例 an example; a model

fànwéi 範圍 range; scope; a

sphere

fāng 方

1. square; rectangular 2. honest; morally upright 3. a region; an area; a place 4. a prescription; a recipe 5. a direction 6. occultism 7. just now; just then 8. (mathematics) power 9. (classifier) short for square meter or cubic meter 10. side; party 11. a method; a way 12. an aspect 13. one side 14. a Chinese family name

fāng'àn 方案 a plan; a project; a design; a scheme; a program

fāngbiàn 方便 1. convenient; handy to do somebody a favor 2. (colloquial) to go to the lavatory

fāngbiànmiàn 方便麵 instant noodles

fāngbiàn shípǐn 方便食品 instant food

fāngcái 方才 just a moment ago

fāngchéngshì 方程式 an equation

fāngchéng zhīzhàn 方城之戰 mah-jong game

fāngfǎ 方法 a method; a way

fānggé 方格 a square (in a checkerboard pattern)

fāngjīn 方今 now; at present; currently

fāngkuòhào 方括號 square brackets([ ])

fānglüè 方略 a general plan

fāngmào 方帽 square caps worn by college graduates

fāngmiàn 方面 1. a direction; a quarter; a district; a sphere; a field 2. (in this or that) respect; (on the one, or other hand); (on this or that) topic, subject, etc.

fāngshì 方式 a mode; a manner; a way

fāngtáng 方糖 cube sugar; sugar cubes

fāngwài zhīrén 方外之人 Buddhist or Taoist priests

fāngwèi 方位 the points of the compass; a direction

fāngxiàng 方向 orientation; a direction; a course

fāngxiàngpán 方向盤 a steer-

F

fāngxīng wèi'ài 方興未艾 to be still growing

fāngxíng 方形 a rectangle

fāngyán 方言 a dialect

fāngyuán 方圓 1. neighborhood 2. squares and circles

fāngzhēn 方針 a principle; a policy

fāngzhèng 方正 irreproachable (conduct)

fāngzi 方子 a medical prescription

fāng 坊
1. a community; a subdivision of a city; a neighborhood; a city quarter; a street; a lane 2. refer to **fáng** 坊 3. an archlike memorial building

fāngjiān 坊間 city quarters; in the streets

fāng 妨
(used in the negative or interrogative, as in **héfāng** 何妨) harm

fāng 芳
1. sweet-smelling; fragrant; aromatic 2. your (used commonly in addressing a young lady) 3. virtuous; honorable; good

fānglín 芳鄰 one's neighbor (a polite expression)

fānglíng 芳齡 age (of a young lady)

fāngmíng 芳名 1. your name (used especially in speaking to a woman) 2. a good reputation

fāngxiāng 芳香 fragrance; aroma

fāngxīn 芳心 the affection, or heart (of a young lady)

fāngzōng 芳蹤 her whereabouts

fāng 肪
refer to **fáng** 肪

fáng 防
1. to defend; defense 2. to prepare for; to take precautions; to prevent

fángbèi 防備 to get ready or prepared (for an incident, etc.); to guard against

fángbù shèngfáng 防不勝防 There's no way of preventing it.

fángchóng 防蟲 pest control; pest prevention

fángdàn 防彈 bulletproof; to protect against bullets

fángdào 防盜 prevention of burglary; to guard against burglary

fángdú 防毒 anti-poison; gas defense

fángdú miànjù 防毒面具 a gas mask; a protective mask

fángfàn 防範 to be alert against; to take precautions; to guard against

fángfēnglín 防風林 a windbreak

fángfǔjì 防腐劑 antiseptic; preservative

fánghóng 防洪 flood control

fánghuàn wèirán 防患未然 to take precautions against a calamity

fánghuǒ 防火 to guard against fire hazards; fireproof

fángkōng 防空 air defense; anti-aircraft

fángkōngdòng 防空洞 an air-raid or bomb shelter

fángláo 防癆 tuberculosis prevention; TB control

fángshēn 防身 to guard personal safety; self-protection

fángshēnshù 防身術 the science (or art) of self-defense

fángshǒu 防守 to defend; to guard

fángshuǐ 防水 1. waterproof; watertight 2. to guard against flood; anti-flood

fángwèi 防衛 to defend; to guard

fángxiàn 防線 a line of defense

fángyù 防禦 to defend; to guard

fángzhèn 防震 shock-resistant; quakeproof

fángzhǐ 防止 to prevent; to guard against; to prohibit

fángzhì 防治 prevention and treatment (of diseases)

fáng 坊 also **fāng**
a workshop of a trade; a mill

fáng 妨

1. to hinder; to impede; to obstruct 2. to undermine; to harm; to damage

fáng'ài 妨礙 to hinder; to hamper

fánghài 妨害 to impair; to be harmful to

fáng 房

1. a house; a building 2. a room; a chamber 3. a compartmentalized structure 4. a wife; a concubine 5. a Chinese family name

fángchǎn 房產 property in the form of a house or houses

fángdìchǎn 房地產 real estates

fángdōng 房東 the landlord (of a house)

fángjiān 房間 a room; a chamber

fángkè 房客 the tenant (of a house); a guest (at a hotel, etc.)

fángmén 房門 a door to a room

fángqì 房契 a house ownership certificate

fángwū 房屋 a house; a building

fángzi 房子 a house; a building

fángzū 房租 a house rental

fáng 肪 also **fāng**

fat

fǎng 仿

to imitate; to copy

fǎngzào 仿造 to manufacture an imitation of something already in market

fǎng 彷

like; similar to; to resemble

fǎngfú 彷彿 1. to seem; as if 2. to be more or less the same; to be alike

fǎng 紡

1. to reel; to spin 2. reeled pongee (a kind of thin silk)

fǎngshā 紡紗 to spin cotton, etc. into yarn

fǎngshājī 紡紗機 a jenny; a spinning jenny

fǎngzhī 紡織 to spin and weave; spinning and weaving

fǎngzhīchǎng 紡織廠 a textile mill

fǎngzhījī 紡織機 a loom

fǎngzhīyè 紡織業 the textile industry

fǎng 訪

1. to visit; to call on 2. to look for; to find out

fǎngchá 訪查 to inquire about and investigate

fǎngkè 訪客 a visitor; a caller

fǎngwèn 訪問 to visit; to call upon

fǎngwèntuán 訪問團 a visiting mission

fàng 放

1. to let go; to release; to free; to liberate; to loosen; to relax 2. to put; to place 3. to put in; to add 4. to dissipate; to debauch; to indulge

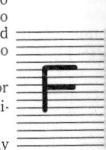

fàngbǎng 放榜 to announce or publish the result of a competitive examination

fàngchàngpiàn 放唱片 to play a phonograph

fàngdà 放大 to magnify; to enlarge

fàngdàjìng 放大鏡 a magnifying glass

fàngdàng 放蕩 dissolute; debauched; dissipated

fàngfēngzheng 放風箏 to fly a kite

fàngguò 放過 to let go

fànghuǒ 放火 to set fire; to commit arson

fàngjià 放假 to have or give a holiday or vacation

fàngkāi 放開 to relax or loosen (a grasp, etc.); to let go

fàngkuān 放寬 to ease or relax (restrictions, etc.); to liberalize

fàngkuǎn 放款 a loan; loaning; to loan

fànglàng xínghái 放浪形骸 to abandon oneself to Bohemianism

fànglǐng 放領 to lease (public land)

fàng mǎhòupào 放馬後砲 to criticize or make comments on something after it is already

over; to second-guess

fàngniú 放牛 to pasture cattle

fàngpì 放屁 1. to let out gas 2. Nonsense!

fàngqì 放棄 1. to give up; to abandon 2. (law) to waive

fàngqíng 放晴 (said of the weather) to clear up

fàngrèn 放任 to let (a person) do as he pleases; to let (a matter) take its own course

fàngshèxìng 放射性 radio activity

fàngshēng 放生 to free or release a captured animal (out of pity)

fàngshēng dàkū 放聲大哭 to cry loudly

fàngshǒu 放手 1. to let go 2. to give up 3. to have a free hand

fàngshǒu qùzuò 放手去做 to act without considering consequences or difficulties

fàngshuǐ 放水 1. to let water out 2. to let the other side win (a game, contest, etc.) purposely

fàngsì 放肆 to take liberties

fàngsōng 放鬆 to relax; to ease; to loosen; to slacken

fàngxià 放下 to put (or lay) down

fàngxīn 放心 to be free from anxiety

fàngxīn bùxià 放心不下 to be kept in suspense

fàngxué 放學 to return home from school at the end of the day's classes

fàngyānhuo 放煙火 to set off fireworks

fàngyìng 放映 to project (on the screen); to show

fàngyìngjī 放映機 a projector

fàngzhì 放置 to place; to put down

fàngzhú 放逐 to exile; to banish

fàngzòng 放縱 1. to debauch; to dissipate; to indulge 2. to break rules of conduct

fēi 妃
1. a wife; a spouse 2. the concubine of a king or an emperor 3.

the wife or spouse of a crown prince

fēi 非
1. negative; not; not to be; non 2. faults; mistakes; evils; wrong 3. to object; to refute; to consider as wrong; to censure; to blame 4. short for Africa

fēicháng 非常 1. extraordinary; unusual; emergency 2. very; terribly

fēicháng shíqī 非常時期 time of emergency

fēicháng shíqī 非常時期 refer to **fēicháng shíqī** 非常時期

fēidàn 非但 not only

fēifǎ 非法 illegal; unlawful; illicit

fēifán 非凡 extraordinary; remarkable

fēifèn 非分 undeserved; beyond the scope of duty or position

fēifèn zhīxiǎng 非分之想 a thought or desire entirely not on a par with or within one's ability, duty, etc. to harbor; an improper thought or desire

fēilǐ 非禮 1. improper 2. to assault a woman sexually

fēimàipǐn 非賣品 items not for sale

fēimìng 非命 1. death by accident or violence 2. a refutation on fatalism

fēinàn 非難 to blame; to dispute; to censure; to criticize; to reproach

fēitóng xiǎokě 非同小可 tremendously important; no small matter; very serious

fēiwǒ mòshǔ 非我莫屬 I, and I alone, deserve (the position, etc.)

fēiwǒ zúlèi 非我族類 not one among us—aliens

fēiyì 非議 to censure; to dispute; to reproach

Fēizhōu 非洲 Africa

fēi 飛
1. to fly; to flit 2. quickly; rapidly 3. high, as a bridge 4. to hang in the air; in the air

fēibēn 飛奔 to run very fast; to fly

fēidàn 飛彈 1. a stray bullet or shell 2. a missile

fēidāo 飛刀 1. to wield the knife 2. a flying knife

fēidié 飛碟 a flying saucer; an unidentified flying object (UFO)

fēiduǎn liúcháng 飛短流長 to spread rumors; to gossip

fēi'é pūhuǒ 飛蛾撲火 to flirt with death; to dig one's own grave

fēihuáng téngdá 飛黃騰達 to make rapid advances in one's career

fēijī 飛機 an airplane; a plane

fēijīchǎng 飛機場 an airport; an airfield; an airdrome

fēijī chéngwùyuán 飛機乘務員 a flight attendant

fēikuài 飛快 1. with lightning speed; at full speed; fast 2. extremely sharp

fēilái hènghuò 來來橫禍 sudden, unexpected calamity or misfortune

fēimáotuǐ 飛毛腿 a fast runner; fleet-footed

fēipán 飛盤 a Frisbee

fēiqín zǒushòu 飛禽走獸 birds and beasts

fēishā zǒushí 飛砂走石 sand and stones flying all about—a very strong wind

fēishēng 飛升 to ascend; to soar

fēiténg 飛騰 1. to fly high (as one's fortune) 2. to soar (as prices)

fēiwěn 飛吻 to throw someone a kiss

fēiwǔ 飛舞 1. to dance in the wind 2. to flutter

fēixiáng 飛翔 to fly; to glide in the air; to hover in the air

fēixíng 飛行 1. to fly, as a plane 2. flight; flying

fēixíngyuán 飛行員 the pilot of a plane

fēiyán zǒubì 飛簷走壁 to fly on eaves and walk on walls —acrobatic feats

fēiyáng 飛揚 to rise up and flutter, as a flag; to float in the air, as music; to fly about, as dust

fēiyáng báhù 飛揚跋扈 unruly and haughty

fēiyuè 飛躍 by leaps and bounds; advancing rapidly

fēizhǎng 飛漲 (said of prices) to soar rapidly; to skyrocket

fēizǒu 飛走 1. birds and beasts 2. to fly away

fēi 啡
a form used in transliterating, as seen in coffee or morphine

fēi 扉
a door leaf

fēiyè 扉頁 a flyleaf; a title page

fēi 菲
1. fragrant 2. the Philippines 3. luxuriant

Fēilùbīn 菲律賓 the Philippines

fēi 緋
scarlet; crimson

fēihóng 緋紅 scarlet; crimson

fēiwén 緋聞 sexy news

fēi 蜚
to fly

fēiduǎn liúcháng 蜚短流長 to spread rumors; to gossip; rumors; gossips

fēi 霏
the falling of snow and rain

féi 肥
1. fat; plump; portly; obese; corpulent 2. fat (of meat) 3. sufficiency; affluence; plenty 4. fertile 5. to fertilize (land) 6. fertilizers 7. baggy

féiliào 肥料 fertilizers; manure

féipàng 肥胖 fat; obese

féiquē 肥缺 a lucrative post

féiròu 肥肉 fat meat

féishuò 肥碩 big and corpulent (persons)

féiwò 肥沃 fertile (land)

féizào 肥皂 soap

féizàofěn 肥皂粉 detergent powder

féizàoshuǐ 肥皂水 suds; soap-suds

féizhuàng 肥壯 husky

fěi 匪

1. a bandit; a rebel; an insurgent 2. not

fěicháo 匪巢 a bandits' lair

fěitú 匪徒 bandits; brigands; robbers

fěiyí suǒsī 匪夷所思 unthinkable

fěi 悱

1. inarticulate; unable to give vent to one's emotion 2. sorrowful

fěicè 悱惻 affected by sorrow; sad at heart; sorrowful

fěi 斐

1. elegant; beautiful 2. a Chinese family name

fěirán chéngzhāng 斐然成章 beautifully composed

fěi 菲

1. a kind of radish 2. thin; trifling; meager 3. frugal; sparing

fěibó 菲薄 1. to slight; to belittle 2. thin; humble; poor 3. frugal; thrifty

fěi 翡

1. a kingfisher 2. emerald

fěicuì 翡翠 1. a kingfisher or halcyon 2. emerald

fěi 誹

to attack; to condemn; to slander

fěibàng 誹謗 to libel; to slander

fèi 吠

(said of a dog) to bark

fèi 沸

1. boiling (water, etc.) 2. to gush; bubbling up

fèidiǎn 沸點 the boiling point

fèidiǎn xīnwén 沸點新聞 the top news

fèishuǐ 沸水 boiling water

fèiténg 沸騰 1. boiling—when liquid turns to steam 2. bubbling and boiling—unrest; seething

fèi 狒

the baboon

fèifèi 狒狒 the baboon

fèi 肺

the lungs

fèi'ái 肺癌 lung cancer

fèifǔ zhīyán 肺腑之言 words from the bottom of one's heart

fèihuóliàng 肺活量 vital capacity; lung capacity

fèijiéhé 肺結核 tuberculosis; consumption

fèiláo 肺癆 tuberculosis; consumption

fèiyán 肺炎 pneumonia

fèizàng 肺臟 lungs

fèi 費

1. expenditure; expenses; fees; dues; charges 2. to waste; to use more than is needed; wasteful; consuming too much 3. to consume; to use; to spend; to cost; to expend 4. a Chinese family name

fèigōngfu 費工夫 to take a lot of time or work

fèijiě 費解 difficult to understand

fèijìn xīnjī 費盡心機 to exhaust all mental efforts

fèilì 費力 1. to need or use great effort 2. difficult (tasks)

fèishén 費神 1. requiring mental exertion 2. Many thanks(for doing this for me).

fèishí 費時 to take, need or waste a lot of time; time-consuming

fèishì 費事 requiring a lot of trouble to accomplish; difficult

fèixīn 費心 1. requiring mental exertion 2. Many thanks (for doing this for me).

fèiyòng 費用 expenditure; expenses; costs

fèi 痱

heat rashes; heat spots; prickly heat

fèizi 痱子 heat rashes; heat spots

fèizifěn 痱子粉 talcum powder; baby powder

fèi 廢

1. to give up; to abandon 2. to

reject 3. useless; disused 4. disabled

fèichí 廢弛 to neglect

fèichú 廢除 to abolish; to annul; to repeal

fèidiào 廢掉 to abolish; to abrogate

fèihuà 廢話 rubbish; nonsense; a meaningless remark

fèiliào 廢料 useless materials; waste materials

fèipiào 廢票 1. an invalidated ballot 2. a used ticket

fèiqì 廢氣 waste gas; exhaust

fèiqì 廢棄 to abandon as useless; to discard

fèiqǐn wàngshí 廢寢忘食 so absorbed (in a pursuit) as to neglect sleep and meals

fèirén 廢人 a disabled person

fèishuǐ 廢水 wastewater; liquid waste

fèitiě 廢鐵 scrap iron

fèiwù 廢物 1. waste material; rubbish 2. a good-for-nothing

fèiwù lìyòng 廢物利用 the utilization of waste material

fèixū 廢墟 ruins (of a city, castle, etc.)

fèizhǐ 廢止 to abolish; to annul; to repeal

fèizhǐ 廢紙 wastepaper

fèizhì bùyòng 廢置不用 to shelve or put aside as useless

fēn 分

1. to divide 2. to part 3. to share 4. to distribute 5. to distinguish 6. one minute 7. one cent 8. one hundredth of a tael 9. a centimeter 10. located separately; a branch

fēnbèi 分貝 a decibel

fēnbēng líxī 分崩離析 to disintegrate and decompose

fēnbiàn 分辨 to distinguish; to tell apart

fēnbiàn 分辯 to make excuses; to explain

fēnbiànlǜ 分辨率 (computer) resolution

fēnbié 分別 1. to part (from a person) 2. to distinguish or tell

apart 3. separately

fēnbù 分布 to be scattered; to spread

fēncéng fùzé 分層負責 delegation of the right authority to the right level of officials

fēncí 分詞 (grammar) a participle

fēncùn 分寸 judgment for propriety (in speech, behavior, etc.)

fēndān 分擔 to undertake different portions of or share the responsibility for

fēndào yángbiāo 分道揚鑣 1. (for two persons) to engage in different pursuits 2. to quit partnership, association, etc.

fēnduì 分隊 a unit of soldiers or policemen corresponding to the platoon or squad

fēnfā 分發 1. to issue 2. to assign

fēn'gē 分割 1. to divide up; to cut apart 2. segmentation

fēn'gé 分隔 to partition

fēngōng hézuò 分工合作 to share out the work and cooperate with one another

fēnháng 分行 a branch office; a branch store

fēnháo 分毫 a modicum; a bit

fēnhào 分號 1. a branch store 2. the semicolon

fēnhóng 分紅 to distribute a dividend

fēnhuà 分化 1. differentiation 2. to disunite

fēnhuì 分會 a branch association

fēnjī 分機 (telephone) an extension

fēnjí 分級 to grade; to classify

fēnjiā 分家 to divide family property

fēnjiě 分解 1. to resolve 2. to dissolve

fēnjiè 分界 1. to have as the boundary; to be demarcated by 2. a line of demarcation

fēnjièxiàn 分界線 a boundary; a borderline

fēnjū 分居 to separate without a legal divorce; to live apart

fēnjú 分局 a police precinct office

fēnjù 分句 (grammar) a clause

fēnkāi 分開 to separate; to set apart

fēnláo 分勞 to help someone do work

fēnlèi 分類 1. to classify 2. taxonomy

fēnlí 分離 to separate; to part; to divide

fēnliè 分裂 to break up; to split; to disunite

fēnmén biélèi 分門別類 to classify systematically

fēnmì 分泌 to secrete; secretion

fēnmiǎn 分娩 to lie in; to give birth

fēnmiǎo bìzhēng 分秒必爭 to make the best of one's time

fēnmíng 分明 clear; distinct; unambiguous

fēnmǔ 分母 the denominator of a fraction

fēnpài 分派 to assign; to allot; to apportion

fēnpèi 分配 1. to distribute; to share out; to allocate 2. distribution

fēnpī 分批 in batches; in turn

fēnqī fùkuǎn 分期付款 payment in installments

fēnqí 分歧 1. difference 2. to diverge

fēnqī fùkuǎn 分期付款 refer to **fēnqí fùkuǎn** 分期付款

fēnqū 分區 to divide into districts; to zone

fēnsàn 分散 to scatter; to disperse

fēnshè 分社 1. a branch office 2. a news bureau

fēnshēn 分身 to handle more than one thing at the same time

fēnshēn fáshù 分身乏術 unable to show up at all the places where one is needed

fēnshén 分神 1. to fail to pay full attention 2. distraction

fēnshǒu 分手 to part; to separate

fēnshù 分數 1. a fraction 2. grades

fēnshùxiàn 分數線 the criterion for selection

fēntān 分攤 to share

fēntíng kànglǐ 分庭抗禮 to rival each other; to compete on equal terms

fēnxī 分析 to analyze; to investigate

fēnxiǎng 分享 to share; to take part in

fēnxiǎo 分曉 the result; the answer

fēnxiào 分校 a branch of a school

fēnxīn 分心 1. to fail to pay full attention 2. distraction

fēnyě 分野 a boundary; a borderline

fēnyōu 分憂 to share sorrows, worries, etc.

fēnzāng 分贓 to share or get a share of loot

fēnzǐ 分子 1. a mumerator 2. a molecule

fēnzǔ 分組 to divide into groups

fēnzǔ tǎolùn 分組討論 group discussion

fēn 吩

to instruct or direct

fēnfu 吩咐 to instruct or direct (someone to do something)

fēn 芬

fragrance; aroma; a sweet smell; perfume

fēnfāng 芬芳 fragrant; aromatic

fēn 氛

air; atmosphere; prevailing mood

fēn 紛

1. confused; disorderly 2. numerous; many; varied

fēnfēi 紛飛 to whirl around in confusion; to fly all over

fēnfēn 紛紛 1. numerous and disorderly 2. (said of people moving) in droves; numerous and in great confusion

fēnluàn 紛亂 confusion; chaotic

fēnrǎo 紛擾 to confuse; turmoil; disturbance

fēnzhēng 紛爭 a dispute; to dispute; to wrangle; to quarrel

fēnzhì tàlái 紛至沓來 to come in a continuous stream; to come thick and fast; to keep pouring in

fén 焚
to burn; to set fire to

fén'gāo jìguǐ 焚膏繼晷 (figuratively) to be very diligent in study

fénhuà 焚化 1. to cremate 2. to burn (offerings, etc.) for the dead 3. to put to fire

fénhuàlú 焚化爐 an incinerator

fénhuǐ 焚毀 to burn up; to destroy by fire

fénshāo 焚燒 to burn; to destroy by burning

fénxiāng 焚香 to burn incense

fén 墳
1. a grave; a mound 2. great; large; big 3. the banks of a river

fénchǎng 墳場 a graveyard; a cemetery

féndì 墳地 a graveyard; a cemetery

fénmù 墳墓 a grave; a tomb

fěn 粉
1. flour 2. powder 3. white (color) 4. to whitewash; to plaster 5. to make up; to doll up; to powder

fěnbǐ 粉筆 chalk

fěncì 粉刺 pimples; acne

fěnhé 粉盒 a powder box; a vanity case

fěnhóng 粉紅 pink

fěnpūr 粉撲兒 a powder puff

fěnshēn suìgǔ 粉身碎骨 (even) at the cost of one's life; great danger or very risky

fěnshì 粉飾 1. to whitewash; to embellish; to touch up 2. to make up

fěnshuā 粉刷 to plaster or whitewash (a wall, etc.)

fěnsuì 粉碎 1. to shatter; to crush up; to smash 2. broken into pieces

fēn 分(份)
1. a role or part (played by a

person in life) 2. a part or portion (of a whole); a component

fènliang 分量 1. an amount 2. (said of statements) weight or impact

fènnèi zhīshì 分內之事 one's due task; a duty

fènwài 分外 1. particularly 2. undeserved

fènzǐ 分子 a member (of some organization)

fèn 奮
1. to rise in force; to arouse; to exert with force 2. (said of a bird) to take wing 3. to advance, promote or invigorate (a cause, etc.)

fènbù gùshēn 奮不顧身 to do something regardless of personal safety

fèndòu 奮鬥 to struggle; to strive

fènfā túqiáng 奮發圖強 to rejuvenate a nation by dedicated work

fènfā yǒuwéi 奮發有為 (often said of a young person) hard-working and promising

fènlì 奮力 to do one's best

fènyǒng 奮勇 courageously; bravely

fènzhàn 奮戰 to fight bravely

fèn 憤(忿)
to resent; indignant; indignation; angry

fènfèn bùpíng 憤憤不平 resentful or indignant because of injustice

fènhèn 憤恨 resentment

fènkǎi 憤慨 anger (especially at injustice); indignation

fènnù 憤怒 anger; wrath; indignation; rage

fènrán 憤然 angrily

fènshì jísú 憤世嫉俗 resentful of the world; misanthropic; cynical

fèn 糞
1. night soil; manure; dung 2. to fertilize the land 3. to sweep

fènbiàn 糞便 excrement; night soil

F

fènduī 糞堆 a dunghill

fènkēng 糞坑 a manure pit; a cesspool

fēng 丰

1. good-looking; buxom 2. appearance and carriage of a person

fēngcǎi 丰采 good-looking

fēngyùn 丰韻 charming appearances or carriage

fēngzī 丰姿 appearances of a person (usually indicating grace and charm)

fēng 封

1. a numerary adjunct for letters 2. to install as a feudal lord or a nobleman 3. to seal; to block 4. a wrapper; an envelope

fēngbì 封閉 to seal; to close completely

fēngdì 封地 a fief; a feud; a manor

fēngjiàn zhìdù 封建制度 the feudal system

fēngkǒu 封口 1. to seal (a letter) 2. to block the entrance (to a passage) 3. to heal

fēngmiàn 封面 the cover (of a book)

fēngmiàn nǚláng 封面女郎 a cover girl

fēngshā 封殺 (baseball) to shut out; force play

fēngsuǒ 封鎖 to blockade (a place)

fēngsuǒ xīnwén 封鎖新聞 to suppress news

fēngtào 封套 an envelope; a wrapper

fēngtiáo 封條 a sealing tape

fēngyìn 封印 (postal service) a seal

fēng 風

1. wind; a breeze; gust; a gale 2. education; influence 3. a fad; customs; practices; fashion; fashionable 4. a scene 5. a style; a manner; deportment; taste 6. fame; reputation 7. rumor 8. ailments supposedly caused by wind and dampness

fēngbào 風暴 a storm; a windstorm

fēngbō 風波 disputes; quarrels; disturbances

fēngcháo 風潮 1. directions of wind and tide 2. disturbance; upheaval 3. a storm

fēngchē 風車 1. a windmill 2. a kind of toy wheel which turns by the power of wind 3. a winnower

fēngchén 風塵 1. confusion of the world 2. hardships of traveling around 3. the world of prostitution

fēngchén nǚláng 風塵女郎 a prostitute; a call girl

fēngchén púpú 風塵僕僕 dust-covered and tired from traveling; to be travel-worn and weary

fēngchí diànchē 風馳電掣 to whip along as fast as wind and lightning

fēngchuī cǎodòng 風吹草動 disquiet; slight disturbance; slight commotion

fēngdù 風度 a manner; poise; bearing

fēngdù piānpiān 風度翩翩 graceful bearing

fēngfān 風帆 a sailboat

fēngfán 風帆 refer to **fēngfān** 風帆

fēngfàn 風範 1. appearance; an air; a manner 2. a model; a paragon

fēngfēngyǔyǔ 風風雨雨 1. storms going on 2. rumors being rife; gossips going the rounds

fēnggé 風格 a style

fēnggǔ 風骨 1. incorruptibility; moral fortitude 2. the vigor of style

fēngguāng 風光 1. scenery 2. elegant style or taste 3. glory; good reputation

fēnghán 風寒 a cold; flu; a chill

fēnghé rìlì 風和日麗 the bright sunshine and gentle breezes; warm and sunny weather

fēnghuā xuěyuè 風花雪月 all ingredients for a gay life; love affairs

fēnghuá 風華 elegance and talent; grace

fēnghuá juédài 風華絕代 unsurpassed elegance and intellectual brilliance

fēnghuà 風化 1. customs and cultural influence; decency 2. (chemistry) efflorescence 3. erosion by the elements

fēnghuàqū 風化區 a district of loose women

fēngjì 風紀 discipline; general moral standards

fēngjǐng 風景 scenery; a landscape

fēngjǐnghuà 風景畫 a landscape

fēngjǐngqū 風景區 scenic spots

fēnglàng 風浪 1. wind and waves at sea 2. a storm

fēnglì 風力 wind power; the force of the wind

fēngliáng 風涼 cool

fēngliánghuà 風涼話 irresponsible and satiric remarks

fēnglíng 風鈴 aeolian bells

fēngliú 風流 1. an elegant style; a refined taste 2. to have a weakness for women

fēngliúshì 風流事 a romance; a romantic episode

fēngliú tìtǎng 風流倜儻 charming; casual and elegant bearing; dashing

fēng mǎ niú bùxiāngjí 風馬牛不相及 things entirely not related; irrelevant

fēngmào 風貌 1. style and features 2. a view; a scene

fēngmǐ yīshí 風靡一時 to become a fad or vogue of the time; to become fashionable for a time

fēngpíng làngjìng 風平浪靜 a calm and unruffled sea

fēngqǐ yúnyǒng 風起雲湧 like rising winds and surging clouds—popular support; an enthusiastic response

fēngqì 風氣 1. customs; a general mood; common practices; traditions 2. air; manner; bearing

fēngqín 風琴 (a musical instrument) an organ

fēngqíng 風情 1. romantic feelings 2. flirtatious expressions 3. fine taste; refined feelings

fēngqù 風趣 interesting; funny; humorous; witty; wit

fēngsāo 風騷 1. seductive; coquettish 2. refinement in literary works

fēngshā 風沙 a sandy wind; a sandstorm

fēngshàn 風扇 1. a fan 2. an electric fan

fēngshàng 風尚 fashion; a custom; a vogue; a fad; taste of the time

fēngshēng 風聲 news; rumor; information

fēngshēng hèlì 風聲鶴唳 to sense danger everywhere

fēngshī 風濕 rheumatism

fēngshuāng 風霜 1. wind and frost—hardships; suffering 2. severe; severity 3. time-honored

fēngshuǐ 風水 the direction and surroundings of a house or tomb, supposed to have an influence on the fortune of a family and their offsprings; a geomantic omen

fēngsú 風俗 customs; accepted practices

fēngsú xíguàn 風俗習慣 customs and habits

fēngsù 風速 wind velocity (or speed)

fēngtiáo yǔshùn 風調雨順 favorable weather (for raising crops); a timely wind and rain

fēngtóu 風頭 the way the wind blows

fēngtou 風頭 1. a situation 2. popularity, distinction or prominence

fēngtǔ rénqíng 風土人情 local customs and practice

fēngwèi 風味 1. the bearing and taste of a person 2. elegance 3. the taste and style of food

fēngwén 風聞 rumored; according to unconfirmed reports; to get wind of

fēngxiǎn 風險 risk; danger

fēngxiàng 風向 the direction of wind

fēngxíng 風行 to become fash-

F

ionable

fēngyǎ 風雅 1. matters pertaining to writing of poems or other literary works; refinement 2. graceful; tasteful

fēngyī 風衣 a thin, usually waterproof, overcoat for warding off wind and rain

fēngyǔ 風雨 wind and rain; the elements—trials and hardships

fēngyǔ tóngzhōu 風雨同舟 to be in the same boat

fēngyǔ wúzǔ 風雨無阻 to take place on schedule regardless of weather changes

fēngyuè 風月 1. matters concerning love 2. easy and random

fēngyún 風雲 1. wind and clouds 2. unpredictable changes 3. imposing; high-positioned; high and exalted

fēngyún biànsè 風雲變色 drastic change of a political situation; catastrophic

fēngyún rénwù 風雲人物 a famed personage; a heroic figure; a man of the hour

fēngyùn 風韻 charms; poise and bearing

fēngyùn yóucún 風韻猶存 (said of a middle-aged woman) to look still attractive

fēngzheng 風箏 a kite

fēngzhú cánnián 風燭殘年 old age; in the closing years of one's life

fēngzī 風姿 looks; graceful bearing

fēng 峰(峯)

1. a peak; a summit 2. a hump

fēngluán 峰巒 peaks and ridges

fēng 烽

(in ancient China) a tall structure (on a city wall, etc.) where fire was made to signal enemy invasion or presence of bandits

fēnghuǒ 烽火 signal fires; beacon fires

fēnghuǒ liánnián 烽火連年 continuous wars

fēngyān sìqǐ 烽煙四起 a land or country beset by war

fēng 蜂

a bee; a wasp

fēngmì 蜂蜜 honey

fēngwō 蜂窩 a beehive; a honeycomb

fēng 楓

a maple

fēngshù 楓樹 a maple

fēngtáng 楓糖 maple sugar

fēng 瘋

insane; crazy; mad; mentally deranged; lunatic; wild

fēngdiān 瘋癲 insane; mentally deranged

fēnggǒu 瘋狗 a mad dog; a rabid dog

fēnghuà 瘋話 gibberish; jargon

fēngkuáng 瘋狂 crazy; mad; insane; wild; irrational

fēngzi 瘋子 a lunatic; a madman; a maniac

fēng 鋒

1. sharp point 2. the vanguard

fēnglì 鋒利 1. sharp-pointed; sharp 2. vigorous; energetic; keen; incisive

fēngmáng 鋒芒 1. sharp point (as of a lance, etc.) 2. dash; mettle; vigor

fēngmáng bìlù 鋒芒畢露 to show one's intelligence, ability, etc. to the full extent

fēng 諷

refer to fēng 諷

fēng 豐

1. abundant; luxuriant; copious; fruitful; plentiful; plenty; thick; big 2. a crop; a harvest

fēngfù 豐富 1. abundant 2. to enrich

fēngmǎn 豐滿 1. rich; affluence; plentiful 2. (said of a woman's figure) plump; buxom 3. full-fledged

fēngpèi 豐沛 copious or plentiful (rainfall, etc.)

fēngráo 豐饒 plentiful; abundant; fertile

fēngshèng 豐盛 luxuriant; sumptuous

fēngshōu 豐收 a rich harvest; a bumper crop

fēngyī zúshí 豐衣足食 well-fed and well-clad

fēngyú 豐腴 plump; buxom and fair

fēngyù 豐裕 abundance; plentiful; high (pay, etc.)

féng 逢
1. to meet; to come across 2. to happen; to fall in with 3. to talk or act in order to please (a superior, etc.)

féngchǎng zuòxì 逢場作戲 to participate in pleasure-seeking as a social activity without being a slave to it

féngnián guòjié 逢年過節 on New Year's Day or other festivals

féngxiōng huàjí 逢凶化吉 to turn bad luck into good fortune

féngyíng 逢迎 1. to receive (guests, visitors, etc.) 2. to ingratiate; to flatter

Féng 馮
a Chinese family name

Féngfù 馮婦 a role one has played before

féng 縫
1. to sew; to stitch 2. to suture

féngbǔ 縫補 to mend (clothes, etc.)

fénghé 縫合 (medicine) to suture; to sew up

féngrèn 縫紉 sewing; needlework

féngrènjī 縫紉機 a sewing machine

féngzhì 縫製 to make or manufacture (sewed products)

fèng 諷 also **fēng**, **fěng**
1. to recite; to chant 2. to satirize 3. to admonish in a roundabout way

fèngcì 諷刺 1. to satirize; to mock 2. irony

fèngyù 諷喻 a parable; an allegory

fèng 奉
1. to receive with respect 2. an expression of respect 3. to offer; to present 4. to admire; to love and respect 5. pay; salary 6. to serve; to wait on

fèngchéng 奉承 1. to receive respectfully 2. to flatter

fènggào 奉告 to let somebody know; to inform

fènggōng shǒufǎ 奉公守法 law-abiding

fènghuán 奉還 respectfully return with thanks

fèngmìng 奉命 to receive orders from above; (to do something) as ordered

fèngpéi 奉陪 (a polite expression) to accompany (you)

fèngquàn 奉勸 May I venture to advise you to...?

fèngsòng 奉送 1. to present respectfully 2. (shop language) to give away as a gift

fèngwéi guīniè 奉為圭臬 to look up to something as a model

fèngxiàn 奉獻 (Christianity) to contribute

fèngxíng 奉行 to act or perform something as ordered

fèngyǎng 奉養 to support (one's parents)

fèngzhào 奉召 to be summoned or recalled

fèngzhǐ 奉旨 on the imperial order

fèng 俸
emoluments; a salary from the government

fènglù 俸祿 a government salary; emoluments

fèng 鳳
a male phoenix

fèngguān xiápèi 鳳冠霞帔 the headgear and dress of a lady or bride in former times

fènghuáng 鳳凰 phoenixes (**fèng** 鳳 being male and **huáng** 凰 being female)

fènghuáng yúfēi 鳳凰于飛 a couple of phoenixes on the wing —happy marriage

fènglí 鳳梨 a pineapple

fèngmáo línjiǎo 鳳毛麟角 rare treasures or talents; something extremely rare

fèngxiānhuā 鳳仙花 a balsam; a garden balsam

fèng 諷

refer to **fèng** 諷

fèng 縫

1. a suture 2. a crack; an opening

fèngxì 縫隙 a chink; a crack; a crevice

fó 佛

1. Buddha (**Shìjiāmóní** 釋迦牟尼) 2. of Buddhism

Fófǎ 佛法 the Buddhist doctrines

Fójiā 佛家 a Buddhist

Fójiào 佛教 Buddhism

Fójiàotú 佛教徒 a Buddhist disciple; a Buddhist

Fójīng 佛經 the Buddhist scriptures; the Sutras

Fómén 佛門 Buddhism; the Buddhist faith

fóshǒu 佛手 bergamot

Fósì 佛寺 a Buddhist temple

Fótáng 佛堂 a Buddhist sanctuary

Fótuó 佛陀 Buddha

Fóxiàng 佛像 a statue of Buddha

Fóxué 佛學 Buddhistic study

Fózǔ 佛祖 1. Buddha 2. Buddhist patriarchs

fóu 浮

refer to **fú** 浮

fǒu 否

1. no; not 2. negative

fǒudìng 否定 1. to deny; to negate; to refute 2. denial; negation

fǒujué 否決 to veto; to vote down

fǒurèn 否認 1. to deny; to reject 2. denial; rejection; repudiation

fǒuzé 否則 otherwise; if not, then...

fū 夫

1. a man; a male adult 2. those eligible for military service 3. a master 4. a husband

fūchàng fùsuí 夫唱婦隨 harmony between husband and wife

fūfù 夫婦 husband and wife; a couple

fūfù hǎohé 夫婦好合 harmony between husband and wife

fūjūn 夫君 1. (in old usage) my husband 2. (Tang Dynasty) a friend

fūqī 夫妻 husband and wife; a couple

fūqī fǎnmù 夫妻反目 the disharmony or discord between husband and wife

fūrén 夫人 1. the wives of high officials 2. Lady; Madame; Mrs.

fūxù 夫婿 a reference to one's own husband

fūzǐ 夫子 1. a title of respect for the elders 2. a master

fū 孵

1. to hatch (eggs); to incubate 2. to emerge from eggs or spawn

fūhuà 孵化 to emerge from eggs; to spawn

fūluǎn 孵卵 to hatch eggs; to incubate

fū 膚

1. the skin; the surface 2. skin-deep; shallow; superficial 3. (now rarely) great, as achievements or merit

fūqiǎn 膚淺 shallow or superficial (views, etc.)

fūsè 膚色 color of the skin

fū 敷

1. to apply or spread over (a surface); to paint 2. to suffice; to be enough 3. to state; to explain; to expound

fūshè 敷設 to install; to arrange; to lay

fūyǎn 敷衍 1. to act in a perfunctory manner 2. to deal with a person insincerely

fūyan liǎoshì 敷衍了事 to carry out a task in a perfunctory manner

fūyào 敷藥 to salve; to apply a salve

fú 夫
1. a demonstrative pronoun — that in most cases 2. a final particle; a particle

fú 弗
not

fúrú 弗如 not as good as

fú 伏
1. to prostrate; to yield 2. to hide; to lie in ambush

fúbīng 伏兵 an ambush

fúdì tǐngshēn 伏地挺身 push-up

fúfǎ 伏法 to plead guilty and be executed

fújī 伏擊 to attack from ambush

fújí 伏擊 refer to **fújī** 伏擊

fúshī biànyě 伏尸遍野 The battlefield is littered with the (enemy) dead.

fútè 伏特 (electricity) a volt

fútiē 伏貼 1. fitting 2. to acknowledge someone's merits, etc. sincerely

fúzhū 伏誅 to plead guilty and be executed

fúzuì 伏罪 1. to admit guilt 2. to be executed

fú 扶
1. to support; to prop up; to aid; to help; to shield; to shelter; to harbor; to protect 2. to lean upon

fúchèn 扶襯 to escort a casket or coffin

fúchí 扶持 to back up; to support

fújiù 扶柩 to escort a casket or coffin

fúlíng 扶靈 to escort a casket or coffin

fúsāng 扶桑 1. (botany) hibiscus 2. Japan 3. where the sun rises

fúshǒu 扶手 a handrail (of a staircase) or any support to be held by the hand

fúshū 扶疏 (said of a plant) luxuriant

fútī 扶梯 a flight of stairs with a handrail or balustrade

fúyǎng 扶養 to provide with means of livelihood

fúyáo zhíshàng 扶搖直上 to rise (in a career) very fast as if to be lifted by a cyclone

fúzhí 扶植 to help grow or develop

fúzhù 扶助 to aid; to help; to assist

fú 拂
1. to brush; to shake; to whisk 2. to dust 3. a duster 4. to oppose; to disobey 5. to expel; to drive away

fúchén 拂塵 1. to shake off dust 2. a duster made of long animal hairs

fúlì 拂戾 1. disagreeable 2. disastrous

fúmiàn 拂面 (said of breezes, leaves, etc.) to brush or caress the face lightly or gently

fúnì 拂逆 1. disagreeable 2. disastrous

fúshì 拂拭 to wipe and clean (a piece of furniture, etc.)

fúshǔ 拂曙 day break; dawn

fúshù 拂曙 refer to **fúshǔ** 拂曙

fúxiǎo 拂曉 daybreak; dawn

fúxiù érqù 拂袖而去 to leave in displeasure or anger

fú 服
1. clothes; dress; garments; costume 2. to wear (clothes) 3. to obey; to be convinced; to yield; to concede

fúcóng 服從 to obey; to follow; to submit to

fúdú 服毒 to take poison

fúqì 服氣 to yield or submit willingly

fúsāng 服喪 to remain in mourning

fúshì 服飾 costume and accessories

fúshi 服侍 to wait upon; to attend on

fúshū 服輸 to concede defeat

fútiē 服帖 obedient; docile

fúwù 服務 1. service 2. to work as an employee

fúwùqì 服務器 (computer) server

fúwùtái 服務臺 a service desk

fúwùyuán 服務員 an attendant; a steward

fúxíng 服刑 to serve a prison term

fúyì 服役 1. to undergo hard labor 2. to undergo military service

fúyīng 服膺 to keep (a teaching, principle, etc.) in mind and stick to (it)

fúyòng 服用 to take (medicine, etc.)

fúzhuāng 服裝 costumes; dress; clothes

fúzuì 服罪 to admit one's crime

fú 芙
a hibiscus

fúróng 芙蓉 a hibiscus

fú 佛
like; similar to; as if

fú 俘
1. prisoners of war 2. to capture

fúhuò 俘獲 to capture

fúlǔ 俘虜 1. to take prisoner 2. a prisoner of war

fú 氟
fluorine

fúhuàwù 氟化物 (chemistry) fluoride

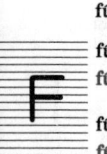

fú 浮 also **fóu**
1. to float; to waft 2. to overflow; to exceed 3. empty; superficial; unsubstantial; unfounded; groundless

fúbiāo 浮標 a buoy

fúbīng 浮冰 floating ice; (ice) floes

fúchén 浮沈 1. rise and fall 2. to follow the trend

fúcí 浮辭 untruthful remarks; unfounded statements

fúdiāo 浮雕 (sculpture) relief

fúdòng 浮動 1. to waft; to float; to drift 2. to be unsteady; to fluctuate

fúguāng lüèyǐng 浮光掠影 1. superficial opinions, descriptions, sketches, etc. 2. hasty and casual

fúhuá 浮華 vanity; superficial beauty

fúlì 浮力 (physics) buoyancy

fúliáng 浮梁 a pontoon bridge

fúmíng 浮名 an empty name or honor

fúpíng 浮萍 duckweed

fúqiáo 浮橋 a pontoon bridge

fúshēng ruòmèng 浮生若夢 Life is like a dream.

fúshī 浮屍 a floating corpse

fúshìhuì 浮世繪 a (Japanese) woodcut

fúshuǐ 浮水 (dialect) to float; to waft

fútǒng 浮筒 a float; a buoy

fútú 浮屠 1. Buddha 2. a pagoda; a stupa

fúxiàn 浮現 (said of memories, etc.) to rise before one's mind

fúyún 浮雲 floating clouds

fúzào 浮躁 restless; impatient; rash

fúzhǒng 浮腫 1. (medicine) dropsy; edema 2. bloated; swollen

fú 匐
1. to lie prostrate; to prostrate 2. to crawl; to creep

fú 符
1. a tally carried for identification, as a warrant, etc.; an identification tag or label 2. an auspicious omen 3. a charm; a talisman; a spell 4. to tally; to correspond; to match; to accord 5. a symbol; a sign

fúhào 符號 a symbol; a sign

fúhé 符合 to correspond; to match; to tally

fúzhòu 符咒 a charm; a spell; an amulet

fú 幅
1. the breadth of cloth; a width (of cloth) 2. a border 3. a numerary adjunct for pictures, scrolls, etc.

fúdù 幅度 1. (said of stocks, com-

modity prices, etc.) the rate of rise or fall 2. a range; an extent

fúyuán 幅員 the territory (of a country)

fú 福

happiness; good fortune; good luck; a blessing; bliss

fúbì 福庇 (a complimentary phrase) your fortunate protection

Fújiàn 福建 Fujian Province

fúlì 福利 welfare

fúlìshè 福利社 a store doing business on the premises of a school, factory, government agency, etc.

fúqì 福氣 good luck

fúxiàng 福相 a countenance of good luck

fúxīng gāozhào 福星高照 to ride the high tide of good luck

fúyīn 福音 1. good news 2. the gospel

fúyìn 福蔭 (a complimentary phrase) your fortunate protection

fúzé 福澤 blessedness; good fortune; happiness

fú 輻

spokes (of a wheel)

fúshè 輻射 to radiate; radiation

fúshèxiàn 輻射線 radiant rays

fú 縛

refer to **fù** 縛

fù 父

a respectful term for an elderly man in ancient times

fǔ 甫

1. (euphemism) a man 2. (euphemism) father 3. then and only then 4. just; immediately after; a short while ago 5. barely

fǔ 斧

1. a hatchet; an ax 2. to chop; to cut; to trim

fǔtou 斧頭 an ax(e); a hatchet

fǔyuè 斧鉞 the executioner's ax —(figuratively) capital punishment

fǔ 府

1. a mansion 2. a government office (or agency) 3. an administrative district in former times; a prefecture 4. your home 5. a treasury; archives

fǔchóu 府綢 poplin

fǔdǐ 府邸 a mansion

fǔdì 府第 a mansion

fǔkù 府庫 a treasury for public funds

fǔshàng 府上 1. your native place 2. your home 3. your family

fǔ 釜

1. a cauldron; a kettle 2. an ancient unit of capacity

fǔdǐ chōuxīn 釜底抽薪 to remove the ultimate cause of trouble

fǔ 俯

1. to face down; to come down; to bow down; to stoop 2. to condescend; to deign

fǔbài 俯拜 to do obeisance to

fǔchōng 俯衝 1. a dive 2. to dive

fǔjiù 俯就 1. to adapt (usually by lowering) oneself to 2. to condescend to accept a job

fǔkàn 俯瞰 to look down at; to overlook

fǔshí jíshì 俯拾即是 It's everywhere.

fǔshì 俯視 to look down at

fǔshǒu 俯首 to bend one's head

fǔshǒu jiùfàn 俯首就範 to submit; to surrender

fǔshǒu tiē'ěr 俯首貼耳 servile; submissive

fǔshǒu wúyán 俯首無言 to admit one's fault or crime without protest

fǔyǎng wúkuì 俯仰無愧 to have done nothing to make one feel ashamed

fǔ 脯

1. dried and seasoned meat 2. preserved fruits

fǔ 腑

F

the bowels; the entrails; the viscera

fǔ 輔

1. human cheeks 2. protective bars on both sides of a cart or carriage 3. to assist; to help; to complement

fǔbì 輔弼 1. to assist 2. a prime minister

fǔdǎo 輔導 1. to assist and guide 2. guidance

fǔzhù 輔助 to assist

fǔ 腐

1. to decay; to rot; rotten; putrid; to disintegrate; stale 2. corrupt; evil 3. old; worn-out; useless or worthless 4. to castrate; castration (as a punishment in ancient China) 5. short for **dòufǔ** 豆腐 —bean curd

fǔbài 腐敗 1. corrupt and rotten (practice, administration, etc.) 2. putrid; decayed; to decay; to decompose

fǔchòu 腐臭 decaying and with a bad odor or stench

fǔlàn 腐爛 to rot or decay

fǔshí 腐蝕 1. to erode; erosion; corrode; corrosion 2. (chemistry) to etch; etching

fǔshíjì 腐蝕劑 a corrodent

fǔxiǔ 腐朽 decayed; rotten

fǔ 撫

1. to stroke; to touch 2. to soothe; to comfort; to console 3. to bring up; to rear; to nurture; to foster

fǔmō 撫摸 to pass one's hand over; to stroke

fǔnòng 撫弄 to stroke; to fondle

fǔwèi 撫慰 to soothe; to comfort; to console

fǔxù 撫恤 to relieve

fǔxùjīn 撫恤金 a pension

fǔyǎng 撫養 to bring up; to rear

fǔyù 撫育 to bring up; to rear

fù 父

1. father 2. a male relative of an elder generation 3. to do father's duties

fùlǎo 父老 elders

fùmǔ 父母 parents; father and mother

fùmǔguān 父母官 a local official; a magistrate

fùqin 父親 father

Fùqinjié 父親節 Father's Day

fùxiōng 父兄 male seniors in a family

fùzǐ 父子 father and son

fù 仆

refer to **pū** 仆

fù 付

1. to pay (money) 2. to consign; to deliver (goods)

fùchū 付出 1. to pay 2. to give

fùkuǎn 付款 to pay (money)

fùkuǎn jiāodān 付款交單 documents against payment

fùqì 付訖 (said of a bill, tax, etc.) paid

fùqián 付錢 to pay (money)

fùqīng 付清 (said of a bill, tax, etc.) paid

fùtuō 付託 to entrust; to commission

fùxiàn 付現 to pay in cash

fùyìn 付印 1. to send to (the) press for publication 2. to turn over to the printing shop (after proofreading)

fùyóu 付郵 to post (a letter); to mail (a parcel)

fùzhàng 付賬 to pay a bill

fùzhī yījù 付之一炬 to burn down

fùzhī yīxiào 付之一笑 to laugh it away (or off)

fùzhū shíshī 付諸實施 to put into effect

fù 咐

refer to **fu** 咐

fù 服

(Chinese medicine) a dose

fù 阜

1. a mound; a small hill 2. the continent; the mainland 3. flourishing; abundant; numerous

fù 附

1. to rely on; to be dependent on; to attach to; to adhere to 2. to enclose; to send along with; to append 3. near or close to 4. to add to; to increase 5. (said of an evil spirit) to be possessed by

fùdài 附帶 1. supplementary 2. to attach 3. in passing

fùhè 附和 to agree without conviction

fùhuì 附會 to twist in making an explanation

fùjiā 附加 1. to add to 2. supplementary

fùjiàn 附件 an enclosure; an accessory; an attachment (of a letter, etc.)

fùjìn 附近 around; nearby; the vicinity

fùkuǎn 附款 appendant provisions in a legal document

fùlù 附錄 an appendix or annex

fùshàng 附上 enclosed herewith

fùshǔ 附屬 accessory; subordinate; to affiliate with; to be attached to

fùtú 附圖 an attached map or drawing; a figure

fùyì 附議 to second a motion; to support a proposal

fùzhù 附註 remarks; notes

fùzhuó 附着 to adhere to; to stick together

fù 訃
an obituary

fùwén 訃聞 an obituary (notice)

fù 赴
to go to; to proceed to

fùhuì 赴會 to go to a meeting

fùrèn 赴任 to proceed to one's new post

fùtāng dǎohuǒ 赴湯蹈火 to go through fire and water; to defy all difficulties and dangers

fùtáng dàohuǒ 赴湯蹈火 refer to **fùtāng dǎohuǒ** 赴湯蹈火

fùyàn 赴宴 to attend a banquet

fùyuē 赴約 to leave for an engagement

fù 負
1. defeat(ed); beaten; to lose; to

fail 2. to bear; to sustain; to shoulder 3. to take refuge in 4. to be proud and complacent 5. to owe 6. negative; minus 7. to turn one's back on; ungrateful 8. to let (someone) down; to disappoint

fùdān 負擔 1. a burden; a load 2. to support (a family, etc.) or pay the expenses 3. liability

fùhào 負號 the negative sign (−)

fùhè 負荷 1. to bear or sustain 2. the load (of electricity, etc.)

fùjīng qǐngzuì 負荊請罪 to offer a modest apology; to apologize

fùqì 負氣 sullen; morose; ill-humored

fùshāng 負傷 to be wounded; to sustain injuries

fùshù 負數 a negative number

fùxīn 負心 ungrateful; heartless

fùyuē 負約 to break a promise, contract, etc.

fùzé 負責 to be responsible

fùzhài 負債 to be in debt; to owe; to incur debts

fù 副
1. to assist 2. secondary; auxiliary; subsidiary 3. deputy; assistant; vice 4. a set

fùběn 副本 a duplicate copy; a copy

fùbiāotí 副標題 a subheading; a subtitle

fùchǎnpǐn 副產品 a by-product

fùcí 副詞 an adverb that modifies an adjective, a verb or another adverb

fùguān 副官 an adjutant; an aide-de-camp

fùjiàshǐ 副駕駛 a copilot

fùjiàoshòu 副教授 an associate professor

fùkān 副刊 a supplement

fùyè 副業 a side job; on the side

fùzǒngtǒng 副總統 a vice-president

fùzuòyòng 副作用 (medicine) side effects; by-effects

fù 婦

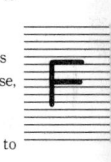

1. a woman; a female 2. the wife of one's son 3. a wife 4. a married woman; a matron

fùchǎnkē 婦產科 the department of gynecology and obstetrics

fùdào 婦道 female virtues, especially chastity

fùdao 婦道 womanhood

fùnǔ 婦女 women; females; womenfolk

fùnǔhuì 婦女會 a women's association

Fùnǔjié 婦女節 Women's Day

fùrén 婦人 1. a woman; a female 2. a married woman

fùrén zhīrén 婦人之仁 womanly kindness

fù 傅

1. a teacher 2. to teach 3. to go together with; to add to; to be attached to 4. a Chinese family name

fù 富

rich; wealthy; affluent; abundant; plentiful

fùguì 富貴 wealth and high position

fùháo 富豪 a man of wealth and influence

fùjiāzǐ 富家子 children of a wealthy family

fùjiǎ tiānxià 富甲天下 the richest in the world

fùlì tánghuáng 富麗堂皇 splendid; gorgeous

fùqiáng 富強 (said of a state) wealthy and powerful

fùráo 富饒 plentiful; abundant; rich

fùshāng 富商 a wealthy merchant

fùshù 富庶 (said of land) plentiful and populous

fùwēng 富翁 a rich man

fùyǒu 富有 1. to abound in; to teem with 2. rich; wealthy

fùyú 富於 rich in (imagination, creative capacity, etc.)

fùyù 富裕 rich; wealthy; prosperous

fùzú 富足 well-off; well-to-do

fù 復

1. to return; to come back 2. to answer; to reply 3. to repeat; again; repeatedly 4. to recover; a recovery 5. to return to a normal state

fùchá 復查 to check; to reexamine

fùchóu 復仇 to avenge; (to) revenge

fùchū 復出 to come out again

fùfā 復發 (said of illness) a relapse; to relapse

fùfǎn 復返 to return

fùgōng 復工 (said of workers on strike, etc.) to go back to work; (said of a plant after work stoppage) to start operations again

fùgǔ 復古 to revive old customs, etc.

fùhé 復合 to reunite

fùhuó 復活 resurrection; to revive

Fùhuójié 復活節 the Easter holiday

fùjiàn 復健 rehabilitation

fùjiàn zhōngxīn 復健中心 a rehabilitation center

fùjiāo 復交 to reestablish diplomatic relations; to resume friendship

fùkān 復刊 to resume publication

fùrèn 復任 to return to one's former office

fùshěn 復審 1. to reexamine 2. (law) to review a case

fùsū 復甦 to come to life again; to revive; recovery

fùwèi 復位 to be restored to the throne

fùxí 復習 to review lessons learned

fùxīn 復新 to make new

fùxīng 復興 to revive; to restore

fùxué 復學 to go back to school (after a prolonged absence)

fùyè 復業 to resume to business again

fùyì 復議 to discuss a project which had been rejected or dis-

carded previously

fùyuán 復元 to have recovered

fùyuán 復員 to demobilize; de-mobilize

fùyuán 復原 to restore

fùzhěn 復診 visits to a doctor, hospital, etc. after the first visit for the treatment of the same disease

fùzhí 復職 to reinstate an official to his former position; reinstatement

fù 腹
1. the belly; under the chest; the abdomen 2. the front part 3. the inside; inner

fùbèi shòudí 腹背受敵 to be attacked from front and rear

fùbù 腹部 the abdomen; the belly

fùdì 腹地 a hinterland; the interior

fùgǎo 腹稿 (literally) a manuscript in the mind—a rough plan or sketch not yet put down in black and white

fùtòng 腹痛 bellyache

fùxiè 腹瀉 diarrhea

fùyì 腹議 to criticize in one's mind

fùyǔ 腹語 ventriloquy, or ventriloquism

fù 複
1. double; overlapping 2. complex (concepts, etc.); compound (interest, etc.) 3. to repeat; to reiterate

fùběn 複本 a duplicate

fùchá 複查 to reinvestigate; to check again

fùhé 複合 compound; complex; composite

fùjù 複句 a complex sentence

fùsài 複賽 (sports) a semifinal; a play-off

fùxiě 複寫 to duplicate or produce copies of writing, etc. with carbon paper, etc.

fùxuǎn 複選 a run-off (election)

fùyìn 複印 duplication

fùzá 複雜 complex; complicated

fùzhì 複製 to make a reproduc-

tion; to reproduce; to duplicate

fù 駙
1. extra horses harnessed by the side of the team 2. swift

fùmǎ 駙馬 1. an ancient official title 2. imperial son-in-law

fù 賦
1. a tax; revenue 2. troops; the army; military levies 3. to bestow; to give 4. natural endowments or gifts 5. to spread; to diffuse 6. to compose or sing (especially poems) 7. one of the Chinese literary forms akin to poetry

fùshuì 賦稅 farm tax and excise tax

fùyǔ 賦予 to give; to endow

fù 縛 also **fú**
to bind; to tie

fùjī zhīlì 縛雞之力 the strength for binding a chicken—very limited strength

fùshǒu fùjiǎo 縛手縛脚 unable to act freely

fù 覆
1. to pour out 2. to overturn; to topple 3. a reply; to reply; to respond 4. to defeat; to destroy 5. to cover; to screen 6. to repeat; a second time; again

fùcháo zhīxià wú wánluǎn 覆巢之下無完卵 If a country is beaten, all its people will suffer.

fùdiàn 覆電 a telegram in reply

fùgài 覆蓋 to cover

fùshěn 覆審 a retrial of a case

fùshì 覆試 1. to test again 2. a second test or examination

fùshuǐ nánshōu 覆水難收 There is no use crying over spilt milk.

fùwén 覆文 an official reply in written form

fùxìn 覆信 1. a letter in reply 2. to reply a letter

fùxuǎn 覆選 1. an election by delegates; an indirect election 2. a run-off (election)

fùyì 覆議 1. to discuss again 2. a renewed discussion

F

fù 馥

fragrant fragrance; aroma

fùyù 馥郁 powerfully fragrant

fu 咐 also **fù**

to tell, bid, or instruct (someone to do something)

gā 咖

a character used in transliterating

gālí 咖哩 curry

gālǐ 咖哩 refer to **gālí** 咖哩

gā 胳 also **gē**

armpits

gāzhiwō 胳肢窩 the armpits

gá 軋

(in the Wu dialect) 1. to crowd 2. to make friends 3. to check

gátóucùn 軋頭寸 (informal) to scramble for cash to meet a payment

gāi 該

1. should; ought to 2. fated to 3. to owe 4. that; the said (person, etc.) 5. to be somebody's turn to do something 6. to deserve 7. inclusive

gāichù 該處 1. that place 2. that department

gāidāng 該當 1. ought to; should 2. to deserve

gāidì 該地 that place; the said place

gāisǐ 該死 to deserve death; Go to hell!

gāixiàng 該項 that item; that matter

gǎi 改

1. to change; to transform; to convert; to alter 2. to correct 3. to revise 4. to switch over

gǎibiān 改編 1. to make a revision (of a book) 2. to reorganize (a military unit, etc.) 3. (said of a movie, stage play, etc.) adapted from or based on (a book, novel, etc.)

gǎibiàn 改變 to change; to alter

gǎibiàn zhǔyì 改變主意 to change one's mind

gǎicháo huàndài 改朝換代 the change of regime

gǎicuò 改錯 to correct mistakes

gǎidào 改道 1. to change the course (of a river) 2. to change one's route

gǎigé 改革 to reform

gǎiguān 改觀 to assume a new look

gǎiguò 改過 to mend one's ways; to correct one's mistakes

gǎiguò qiānshàn 改過遷善 to repent and be good

gǎiguò zìxīn 改過自新 to turn over a new leaf

gǎiháng 改行 to change one's trade, profession or career

gǎihuàn 改換 to replace; to change

gǎijià 改嫁 (said of a woman) to remarry

gǎijiàn 改建 to remodel; to rebuild

gǎijìn 改進 to improve; to better

gǎikǒu 改口 to say something different from what one is expected to say or has been saying

gǎiliáng 改良 to ameliorate; to improve

gǎiqī 改期 to postpone a scheduled event

gǎiqī 改期 refer to **gǎiqī** 改期

gǎirì 改日 some other time; later on

gǎishàn 改善 to ameliorate; to improve

gǎitiān 改天 some other day

gǎitóu huànmiàn 改頭換面 change only the appearance

gǎixián yìzhé 改弦易轍 to change rules and systems

gǎixié guīzhèng 改邪歸正 to give up evil and return to virtue

gǎixiě 改寫 to rewrite; to adapt

gǎixuǎn 改選 to hold a new election

gǎizào 改造 to remodel; to rebuild

gǎizhèng 改正 to correct; to amend

gǎizhì 改制 to change a system

gǎizhuāng 改裝 1. to change dress 2. to convert (a machine, vehicle, etc.) for a new use; to refit; to reequip

gǎizǔ 改組 to reshuffle (an organization); to reorganize

gài 丐

1. to beg for alms 2. a beggar 3. to give

gài 鈣

calcium

gàipiàn 鈣片 a calcium tablet

gàizhí 鈣質 refer to **gàizhì** 鈣質

gàizhì 鈣質 calcium content

gài 溉

1. to water; to irrigate 2. to wash

gài 概

1. general; overall; roughly 2. without exception; categorically 3. the manner of carrying oneself; deportment

gàiguān 概觀 a general view; a conspectus

gàikuàng 概況 a general situation

gàikuò 概括 to summarize; to sum up

gàilüè 概略 an outline; a summary

gàilùn 概論 a general discussion; an outline

gàiniàn 概念 a concept; a conception

gàiyào 概要 a summary; an outline; a synopsis; a resume

gài 蓋

1. to cover; to hide 2. a lid; a covering 3. to build; to construct; to erect 4. to affix (a seal) 5. (an initial particle) now; then; but; because 6. (a particle indicating doubt) for; perhaps; possibly; about 7. to surpass; to excel 8. to brag; to boast

gàiguān lùndìng 蓋棺論定 When one's coffin is covered, one's deserts can be properly judged.

gàishì 蓋世 surpassing one's generation; without a match

gàishì wúshuāng 蓋世無雙 unrivaled; matchless; peerless

gàixiān 蓋仙 a brag

gàiyìn 蓋印 to affix the seal

gàizhāng 蓋章 to affix the seal

gàizi 蓋子 1. a lid; a cover 2. a shell (of a tortoise, etc.)

gān 干

1. to offend; to oppose; to invade 2. to interfere; to intervene 3. to concern; to involve 4. to seek; to beseech 5. the bank (of a river, etc.) 6. a shield 7. (how) many or much; a group 8. a stem

gānbèi 干貝 a dried scallop

gānfàn 干犯 1. to offend 2. to invade

gān'gē 干戈 warfare; armed conflicts

gānlián 干連 to involve; to implicate

gānlù 干祿 1. to seek an official post 2. official emolument

gānmíng cǎiyù 干名采譽 to seek publicity

gānrǎo 干擾 1. to disturb; to interfere 2. (physics) interference; to jam

gānshè 干涉 to interfere; interference

gānxì 干係 involvement; implication

gānxiū 干休 to give up; to bring to an end

gānyù 干預 to intervene; to interfere; intervention

gānzhèng 干政 to interfere in politics

gān 甘

1. tasty; delicious 2. luscious; sweet 3. willing 4. to enjoy 5. pleasant; pleasing 6. a Chinese family name

gānbài xiàfēng 甘拜下風 to admit defeat willingly

gāncǎo 甘草 licorice

gānkǔ 甘苦 1. happiness and suffering 2. hardships and difficulties experienced in work

gānkǔ bèicháng 甘苦備嘗 to have tasted both sweetness and bitterness

G

gānláncài 甘藍菜 a kale; a cabbage

gānlín 甘霖 a seasonable rain; a timely rain

gānlín pǔjiàng 甘霖普降 Seasonable rain has fallen everywhere.

gānlù 甘露 sweet dew

gānměi 甘美 delicious; tasty; palatable

gānshǔ 甘薯 sweet potatoes

Gānsù 甘肅 Gansu Province

gānxīn 甘心 1. willingly; willing 2. joyous; happy

gānxīn qíngyuàn 甘心情願 perfectly willing

gānxiū 甘休 willing to stop or halt

gānyóu 甘油 glycerin(e)

gānyú 甘於 to be willing to; to be happy to

gānyuàn 甘願 willing; willingly; readily

gānzhe 甘蔗 sugarcane

gānzhebǎn 甘蔗板 a bagasse board

gānzhī rúyí 甘之如飴 to be quite content even in adversity

gān 肝
the liver

gān'ái 肝癌 cancer of the liver

gānbìng 肝病 a liver ailment

gāncháng cùnduàn 肝腸寸斷 heartbroken; deep sorrow

gāndǎn xiāngzhào 肝膽相照 to show the deepest sincerity

gānyán 肝炎 hepatitis

gānzàng 肝臟 the liver

gān 竿
a bamboo pole; a bamboo rod

gān 柑
a mandarin orange

gānjú 柑橘 1. oranges and tangerines 2. citruses

gān 乾
1. clean 2. dry; dried 3. exhausted

gānbēi 乾杯 to toast; Bottoms up!

gānbiě 乾癟 dry and withered; shrunken

gānbīng 乾冰 dry ice

gāncǎo 乾草 hay

gānchàng 乾唱 to sing without accompaniment

gāncuì 乾脆 straightforward

gāndèngyǎn 乾瞪眼 to stand by anxiously without doing anything

gāndiànchí 乾電池 a dry battery or cell

gāndiē 乾爹 a man whose position is roughly equivalent to a foster father and godfather

gān'érzi 乾兒子 a nominal foster son

gānfàn 乾飯 cooked rice without gravy

gānguǒ 乾果 dried or preserved fruit

gānhàn 乾旱 drought

gānhé 乾涸 (said of water) to dry up

gānjìng 乾淨 clean

gānjìng lìluo 乾淨俐落 neat and tidy; efficient

gānkū 乾枯 dried up; withered

gānlào 乾酪 cheese

gānliang 乾糧 dry provisions

gānliè 乾裂 dry and cracked (wood, soil)

gānlào 乾酪 refer to **gānlào** 乾酪

gānmiàn 乾麵 dry noodles

gānnǚ'ér 乾女兒 a nominal foster daughter

gānshībiǎo 乾濕表 a psychrometer

gānxǐ 乾洗 dry cleaning

gānxiào 乾笑 to laugh without mirth

gānxīn 乾薪 a salary for a sinecure

gānzào 乾燥 dry

gānzàojì 乾燥劑 a desiccant; a drying agent

gān 尷
embarrassed; ill at ease

gāngà 尷尬 embarrassing; embarrassed

G

gǎn 桿

a wooden pole, cane, stick, or club

gǎnjūn 桿菌 a bacillus; bacilli

gǎnjùn 桿菌 refer to **gǎnjūn** 桿菌

gǎn 敢

1. to dare 2. to have the confidence to; to be sure; to be certain 3. bold; courageous; daring 4. to make bold; to venture

gǎnqǐng 敢請 I venture to request....

gǎnqíng 敢情 1. naturally; of course 2. perhaps; maybe 3. to turn out that...

gǎnsǐduì 敢死隊 a suicide squad; a dare-to-die corps

gǎnwèn 敢問 I venture to ask....

gǎnyú 敢於 to dare to; to be bold in

gǎnzuò gǎndāng 敢作敢當 to have the courage to accept the consequences of one's doing

gǎnzuò gǎnwéi 敢作敢為 to have the courage to do what one believes should be done

gǎn 稈

the stalk of grain; straw

gǎn 感

1. to find; to feel; to sense; to perceive; to respond to 2. to affect, move, or touch 3. feeling; sensation; emotion 4. to be grateful

gǎnchù 感觸 feeling; mental reaction

gǎndào 感到 to feel; to sense

gǎndòng 感動 (mentally) to move, affect, or touch

Gǎn'ēnjié 感恩節 Thanksgiving Day

gǎn'ēn túbào 感恩圖報 to feel grateful for a kind act and plan to repay it

gǎnguān 感官 1. the senses 2. a sensory organ

gǎnguāng 感光 1. to be exposed to light 2. photoreceptive

gǎnhuà 感化 to reform (a person); to influence (a person) by personal examples of moral uprightness

gǎnhuàyuàn 感化院 a reformatory

gǎnhuái 感懷 1. stirred or aroused emotions (often used in titles of old-style poems) 2. to recall with emotion

gǎnjī 感激 to feel grateful

gǎnjué 感覺 1. sense; feeling 2. to feel; to sense

gǎnjué shénjīng 感覺神經 sensory nerves

gǎnkǎi 感慨 emotional excitement; regrets

gǎnkài 感慨 refer to **gǎnkǎi** 感慨

gǎnmào 感冒 1. a cold 2. to catch a cold

gǎnniàn 感念 to remember with gratitude

gǎnqíng 感情 feelings; emotions; devotion (between friends, relatives, etc.)

gǎnqíng yòngshì 感情用事 to appeal to emotions

gǎnrǎn 感染 to be infected with; to affect

gǎnshāng 感傷 sentimental; sentimentality

gǎnshòu 感受 to perceive; to feel

gǎntàn 感嘆 to exclaim

gǎntànhào 感嘆號 the exclamation mark

gǎntóng shēnshòu 感同身受 to feel deeply moved by a kindness (shown to somebody else) as if one were actually the object thereof

gǎnxiǎng 感想 mental reaction; an impression

gǎnxiè 感謝 to thank; gratitude

gǎnxìng 感性 perceptual; sensibility; sentimental

gǎnyìng 感應 1. to feel and respond 2. (physics) induction

gǎnzhào 感召 the inspiration (to do a noble or brave deed) given by religious teachings, great leaders, etc.

G

gǎn 趕

1. to pursue; to catch up with; to overtake 2. to drive; to expel 3. to hurry; to rush 4. to hasten 4. to try to catch; to make a dash for; to rush for

gǎnbují 趕不及 unable to manage to be on time

gǎnchǎng 趕場 (said of actors) after finishing a performance, to hurry to another place for a new one

gǎnchē 趕車 1. to drive a cart or carriage 2. to catch a bus or train

gǎndejí 趕得及 able to manage to be on time

gǎnjí 趕集 to go to market

gǎnjǐn 趕緊 to make haste; quickly; at once; to hurry

gǎnjìn shājué 趕盡殺絕 to injure and oppress to the extreme

gǎnkāi 趕開 to drive away

gǎnkuài 趕快 to make haste; quickly; at once; to hurry

gǎnlù 趕路 to walk hurriedly; to travel in haste

gǎnmáng 趕忙 with haste; hurriedly

gǎnmíngr 趕明兒 some other day; later

gǎnshàng 趕上 1. to catch up with; to overtake; to keep pace with 2. to be in time for 3. to chance upon

gǎnshímáo 趕時髦 to follow the fashion; to try to be in the swim

gǎn 擀

1. to stretch out with a rolling pin 2. to polish; to shine

gǎnmiàn 擀麵 to roll dough

gǎn 橄

an olive

gǎnlǎn 橄欖 an olive

gǎnlǎnqiú 橄欖球 American football; rugby

gǎnlǎnyóu 橄欖油 olive oil

gàn 幹

1. the trunk (of a tree, etc.) 2.

the main part of anything 3. talents; capable; skillful 4. to do; to attend to business; to manage 5. (slang) to kill

gànbù 幹部 a cadre

gàndào 幹道 a trunk (or main) line

gàndiào 幹掉 to kill or eliminate (a person)

gànhuó 幹活 to work; to do a job

gànjìn 幹勁 enthusiasm; drive; vigor

gànliàn 幹練 capable and experienced

gànmá 幹麼 1. Why? Why (are you) doing this? 2. What (do you do)?

gànshì 幹事 1. to manage business or affairs 2. a clerk; a member of an executive committee

gànxiàn 幹線 a trunk (or main) line

gànyuán 幹員 a very capable officer or official

Gàn 贛

1. an alternative name of Jiangxi Province 2. a river in Jiangxi Province 3. a county in Jiangxi Province

gāng 肛

the anus

gāngmén 肛門 the anus

gāng 岡 also **gǎng**

the ridge (of a hill or mountain)

gānglíng 岡陵 a mound

gāng 缸

a cistern; a crock

gāng 剛

1. tough; unyielding; inflexible; hard; firm; strong; indomitable 2. just now 3. just; exactly 4. barely; only

gāngbì zìyòng 剛愎自用 stubborn; obstinate

gāngcái 剛才 just a moment ago; a very short while ago

gānggang 剛剛 1. just now; just a moment ago 2. just; only

Gāngguǒ 剛果 the Congo (Kin-

shasa3

gānghǎo 剛好 exactly; precisely

gāngjiàn 剛健 vigorous; energetic; robust

gāngjìng 剛勁 bold; vigorous; sturdy

gāngliè 剛烈 tough and vehement; violent

gāngqiáng 剛強 tough and strong; staunch

gāngqiǎo 剛巧 exactly; precisely

gāngyì 剛毅 tough and determined; resolute

gāngyì mùnè 剛毅木訥 refer to **gāngyì mùnè** 剛毅木訥

gāngyì mùnè 剛毅木訥 resolute and not eloquent

gāngzhí 剛直 tough and honest; upright

gāng 崗

refer to **gǎng** 崗

gāng 綱

1. the large rope of a net, round which it is netted, and by which it is drawn 2. main points; an outline 3. a principle; discipline

gāngjì 綱紀 1. a principle; discipline; law; order 2. a manager; a magistrate

gānglǐng 綱領 an outline

gāngyào 綱要 main points; an outline

gāng 鋼

steel

gāngbǎn 鋼板 a steel plate

gāngbǐ 鋼筆 a fountain pen

gāngjīn 鋼筋 steel bars; steel rods; wire mesh

gāngjīn shuǐní 鋼筋水泥 reinforced concrete

gāngkuī 鋼盔 a steel helmet; a helmet

gāngqín 鋼琴 a piano

gāngsī 鋼絲 steel wire

gāngtiě 鋼鐵 steel; steel and iron

gāng 繮(韁)

refer to **jiāng** 繮(韁)

gǎng 崗

refer to **gāng** 崗

gǎng 崗 also **gāng**

1. the place where a sentry is posted; a post 2. a position

gǎngshào 崗哨 1. a lookout post 2. a sentry; a sentinel

gǎngtíng 崗亭 a sentry box

gǎngwèi 崗位 one's post; one's duty

gǎng 港

1. a harbor; a seaport 2. a bay; a gulf 3. short for Hongkong

Gǎngbì 港幣 Hongkong currency

gǎngjǐng 港警 the harbor police

gǎngkǒu 港口 a harbor; a seaport; a port

gǎngwān 港灣 1. a harbor 2. a bay; a gulf

gàng 槓

1. a lever; a carrying pole 2. (sports) a bar 3. to sharpen (a knife) 4. to argue; to dispute 5. to cross out

gànggǎn 槓桿 a lever; a pry

gànglíng 槓鈴 (sports) a barbell

gāo 高

1. high; tall 2. of a high level or degree; above the average 3. lofty 4. a Chinese family name

gāo'áng 高昂 (said of prices, morale, etc.) rising high

gāo'ào 高傲 proud; overbearing; haughty

gāobǎozhēn 高保眞 high fidelity (Hi-Fi)

gāobùchéng, dībùjiù 高不成，低不就 unable to find a mate or employment because the object available is either beyond one's reach or below one's minimum expectations

gāobù kěpān 高不可攀 too high to be reached

gāocáishēng 高才生 a bright and excellent student

gāochāo 高超 surpassing; superior; outstanding

gāocháo 高潮 1. a high tide 2. a climax

gāochuánzhēn 高傳眞 high

fidelity (Hi-Fi)

gāodà 高大 tall and big; colossal

gāodànbái 高蛋白 high protein

gāodǎng 高檔 refer to **gāodàng** 高檔

gāodàng 高檔 1. a high grade; a high class; superior 2. advanced (courses)

gāoděng 高等 high or advanced (in the grade)

gāoděng jiàoyù 高等教育 higher education

gāodī 高低 1. height 2. a sense of propriety; discretion 3. (dialect) on any account; simply 4. (dialect) at last; after all 5. relative superiority or inferiority

gāodī bùpíng 高低不平 uneven; rugged; irregular

gāodì 高地 high ground; uplands

gāodiào 高調 1. a high-pitched note 2. high-sounding (but impractical) assertions

gāodù 高度 1. an altitude; a height; an elevation 2. highly; great

gāo'ěrfūqiú 高爾夫球 golf

gāofēiqiú 高飛球 (baseball) fly

gāofēi xīshēngdǎ 高飛犧牲打 (baseball) sacrifice fly

gāofēng 高峰 the peak; the summit; the climax

gāofēng liángjié 高風亮節 noble character and incorruptible principle

gāogāng 高岡 the peak or summit; a high mountain

gāogāo zàishàng 高高在上 (literally) situated high above —(figuratively) lofty; aloof

gāogē 高歌 to sing aloud

gāogēnrxié 高跟兒鞋 high-heeled shoes

gāoguān hòulù 高官厚祿 a high position and a good salary

gāoguì 高貴 noble; exalted

gāohū 高呼 to shout; to call out aloud

gāojí 高級 1. a high grade; a high class; superior 2. advanced (courses)

gāojí zhōngxué 高級中學 a

senior middle (or high) school

gāojìshù 高技術 high-tech; high technology

gāojià 高價 a high price; an exorbitant price

gāojiàqiáo 高架橋 a viaduct

gāojiàn 高見 your esteemed opinion or advice

gāojiù 高就 opportunity for a high or higher position, a good or better employment, etc.

gāojǔ 高舉 1. to raise high; to uplift 2. to become a hermit

gāokàng 高亢 proud and indomitable

gāokōng 高空 high altitude; upper air

gāolíshēn 高麗參 ginseng

gāolìdài 高利貸 usury

gāoliang 高粱 sorghum; kafir

gāoliangjiǔ 高粱酒 gaoliang wine

gāolíng 高齡 advanced age; great age; old age

gāolóu dàshà 高樓大廈 skyscrapers; tall buildings

gāolùn 高論 an outstanding statement; original remarks

gāomàozi 高帽子 flattery; soft soap

gāomíng 高明 1. clever; wise; superior 2. an expert; a master; a qualified person

gāopān 高攀 1. to climb high 2. to cultivate friendship with the socially elevated

gāopéng mǎnzuò 高朋滿座 All the seats are occupied by distinguished guests.

gāoqìyā 高氣壓 high atmospheric pressure

gāoqiáng 高強 surpassing; superior; outstanding

gāorén yīděng 高人一等 a cut above other people

gāoshān jǐngxíng 高山景行 to admire great virtue

gāoshān yǎngzhǐ 高山仰止 (figuratively) A man of virtue is so great that one looks up to him awfully.

gāoshānzhèng 高山症 moun-

tain sickness; altitude sickness

gāoshàng 高尚 1. noble; exalted 2. high-class; refined; respectable

gāoshāo 高燒 a high fever

gāoshèpào 高射砲 an antiaircraft machine; an ack-ack

gāoshēn 高深 recondite; abstruse; profound; advanced; lofty

gāoshēng 高陞 to get a promotion; to be promoted

gāoshǒu 高手 a master; an expert

gāoshòu 高壽 1. advanced age; old age; great age 2. your age

gāosǒng 高聳 to tower; to rise high

gāosù 高速 high speed

gāosù gōnglù 高速公路 a freeway; a motorway; an expressway

gāotái guìshǒu 高抬貴手 (literally) Raise your noble hands. —Please be merciful.

gāotán kuòlùn 高談闊論 to talk freely; to talk in a lively atmosphere

gāotáng 高堂 1. a hall with a high ceiling 2. parents

gāowèi 高位 a high position

gāowēn 高溫 a high temperature

gāoxià 高下 superiority and inferiority

gāoxiěyā 高血壓 refer to gāoxuèyā 高血壓

gāoxīn jìshù 高新技術 high-tech; high technology

gāoxìng 高興 glad; elated; delighted

gāoxuèyā 高血壓 high blood pressure; hypertension

gāoyǎ 高雅 elegant; noble and graceful

gāoyīn 高音 treble

gāoyīn lǎba 高音喇叭 a tweeter

gāoyuán 高原 highlands; plateaus

gāozhān yuǎnzhǔ 高瞻遠矚 farseeing; provident; farsighted

gāozhǎng 高漲 to rise

gāozhěn wúyōu 高枕無憂 to sleep in peace; to be free from worries

gāozú 高足 (an honorific term) your capable student; your brilliant disciple

gāozú 高祖 1. one's ancestor 2. one's great-greatgrandfather 3. the founder of a dynasty

gāo 羔

a lamb

gāoyáng 羔羊 a lamb

gāo 皋(皐)

1. a marsh; a swamp 2. a shore

gāo 睪(睾)

1. the marsh 2. high; lofty 3. the testicle, or testis

gāowán 睪丸 the testis

gāo 膏

1. fat; grease 2. ointment 3. fertile 4. the region just below the heart 5. grace; favors 6. sweet 7. (Chinese medicine) a paste-like preparation for external use 8. plaster 9. (food and fruit) cooked to a very thick or pasty form

gāoyao 膏藥 medicated plaster attached to pieces of cloth or paper

gāoyú zhīdì 膏腴之地 fertile land

gāo 糕

cakes; pastries; steamed dumplings

gāobǐng 糕餅 cakes and biscuits

gāobǐngdiàn 糕餅店 a pastry shop

gāo 篙

the pole for punting a boat; a boat pole

gǎo 搞(攪)

1. to stir up; to cause trouble 2. to do; to carry on; to be engaged in 3. to get; to secure 4. to set up; to start; to organize

gǎobǎxì 搞把戲 to play tricks; to cheat

gǎoguǐ 搞鬼 (said of a person) to cause trouble or pull legs in secret

gǎohuāyàng 搞花樣 to play tricks; to cheat

G

gǎokuǎ 搞垮 to overthrow; to cause to fail

gǎoqīngchu 搞清楚 to make clear

gǎo 槁

withered; dead; rotten

gǎomù sǐhuī 槁木死灰 a person utterly without vitality or ambition

gǎo 稿

1. a manuscript; a sketch; a rough draft or copy 2. a pattern or copy book for drawing 3. straw; a stalk of grain

gǎochóu 稿酬 payment to a writer on a piecework basis

gǎofèi 稿費 payment to a writer on a piecework basis

gǎojiàn 稿件 1. contribution to a publication; writings 2. manuscripts; a sketch

gǎozhǐ 稿紙 manuscript or draft paper

gào 告

1. to tell; to inform; to report 2. to accuse

gàobái 告白 a notice; an announcement

gàobié 告別 to bid farewell; to say good-bye

gàochuī 告吹 to fizzle out; to fail

gàocí 告辭 to take leave; to say good-bye

gàofā 告發 to accuse or charge (someone) in a (written or verbal) report to the authorities

gàojí 告急 in urgent need of help; critical

gàojià 告假 to ask for leave of absence

gàojiè 告誡 to admonish; to warn

gàomì 告密 to tip off; to inform against somebody

gàoráo 告饒 to seek pardon; to apologize

gàoshì 告示 to announce; to proclaim

gàoshi 告示 an official notice, announcement or proclamation

gàosù 告訴 to file a lawsuit

gàosu 告訴 to tell (a person)

gàotuì 告退 1. to resign 2. to withdraw

gàoyù 告諭 to counsel; to advise

gàozhī 告知 to let know; to notify

gàozhuàng 告狀 1. to file a lawsuit 2. to say something bad against a colleague, fellow student, etc. before a superior

gàozuì 告罪 to admit a mistake

gào 膏

1. to lubricate; to grease; to make smooth or glossy 2. to enrich; to freshen

gào 誥

1. to grant; to confer 2. to admonish 3. a written admonition

gàomìng 誥命 a monarch's orders of conferment of titles

gē 戈

1. a spear; a lance 2. a Chinese family name

gēbì 戈壁 Mongolian for "desert"

Gēbì Dàshāmò 戈壁大沙漠 the Gobi Desert

gē 疙

a wart; a pustule; a pimple

gēda 疙瘩 1. a wart; a pustule; a pimple 2. a knot in one's heart; a hang-up

gē 咯 also gé

gēgē 咯咯 1. a low, guttural sound made by a hen when brooding or calling her chicks 2. (laughter) a chuckle

gēzhī 咯吱 to creak

gēzī 咯吱 refer to **gēzhī** 咯吱

gē 哥

an elder brother

gērliǎng 哥兒倆 two brothers

gērmen 哥兒們 1. brothers 2. buddies; pals

gē 胳

1. the arms 2. refer to **gā** 胳

gēbei 胳臂 the upper arm

gēzhiwō 胳肢窝 refer to **gā-zhiwō** 胳肢窝

gē 割

to cut; to sever; to divide

gē'ài 割爱 to give up what one treasures

gēcǎo 割草 to cut grass; to mow grass

gēchú 割除 to cut off or out; to excise

gēduàn 割断 to cut off; to sever by cutting

gēliè 割裂 to split; to slash or rip open

gēràng 割让 to cede (land or territory)

gēshě 割舍 to part with; to give away

gē 歌

1. to sing; to chant 2. to praise 3. a song 4. a ballad

gēběn 歌本 a collection of songs; a songbook

gēchàng 歌唱 to sing; to chant

gēcí 歌词 lyrics or words of a song

gēgōng sòngdé 歌功颂德 1. to praise another (usually one's superior) for his achievements and virtues 2. to flatter

gējí 歌集 a collection of songs; a songbook

gējì 歌妓 (formerly) female entertainers somewhat like the geisha girls in Japan

gējù 歌剧 an opera

gēpǔ 歌谱 song scores

gēqǔ 歌曲 a song; a tune; a ballad

gēshēng 歌声 the singing voice

gēshǒu 歌手 a songster; a vocalist

gēsòng 歌颂 to sing praises

gētái wǔxiè 歌台舞榭 the stage —where songs and dances are performed

gēwǔjù 歌舞剧 a musical; an operetta; a light opera

gēwǔ shēngpíng 歌舞昇平 reign of peace and prosperity (when people can rejoice with singing and dancing)

gēxīng 歌星 a singing star; an accomplished vocalist

gēyáo 歌谣 a ballad; a folk song

gēyǒng 歌咏 to sing praises; to sing; to eulogize

gē 鸽

a pigeon; a dove

gēlóng 鸽笼 a pigeon house

gēzi 鸽子 a pigeon

gē 搁

1. to lay; to leave; to put 2. to file 3. to delay; to put aside

gēqiǎn 搁浅 1. to run aground; to get stranded 2. (said of negotiations) to come to a deadlock

gēxià 搁下 to put aside or lay down (work)

gēzhì 搁置 to shelve or pigeonhole (a plan, proposal, etc.)

gé 咯

refer to **gē** 咯

gé 革

1. hides stripped of hair; skin; leather 2. to get rid of; to eliminate 3. to change; to reform; to renovate 4. (now rarely) human skin 5. Chinese percussion musical instruments 6. armor 7. soldiers 8. one of the Eight Diagrams

géchú 革除 1. to rid; to eliminate (ills, etc.); to abolish 2. to expel; to dismiss

gémìng 革命 a revolution

gémìngdǎng 革命党 a revolutionary political party

géxīn 革新 to reform; to renovate; innovation

gézhí 革职 to fire; a dishonorable discharge; to dismiss

gé 格

1. to correct; to adjust or regulate 2. to reach; to come or go to 3. to influence 4. to resist; to attack; to fight 5. to obstruct; to block 6. to study thoroughly; to search to the very source; to investigate 7. a standard; a form; a rule; a pattern 8. a frame; a

G

trellis 9. squares formed by crossed lines

gédiào 格調 1. literary or artistic style; form; pattern 2. personality

gédòu 格鬥 a brawl; a hand-to-hand fight

gégé bùrù 格格不入 totally incompatible

géjú 格局 structure and form; style; setup

Gélínwēizhì Píngshí 格林威治平時 Greenwich Mean Time (GMT)

Gélínwēizhì Shíjiān 格林威治時間 refer to **Gélínwēizhì Píngshí** 格林威治平時

gélǜ 格律 1. standard; form; pattern 2. the meter of poetry, etc.

géshā wùlùn 格殺勿論 to kill on sight; to shoot on sight

géshi 格式 a form; a pattern

géwài 格外 extraordinary; exceptional; especially

géyán 格言 a proverb; a motto; a maxim

gézi 格子 a trellis; a lattice

gé 蛤
a clam

gé 葛
dolichos (Pueraria thunbergiana), a creeping edible bean whose fibers can be made into linen-like cloth and whose roots are used in herbal medicine

gé 嗝
to hiccup or hiccough; a belch

gé 隔
1. to separate; to divide; to partition 2. blocked; to obstruct; to be veiled 3. at a distance from; at an interval of

gé'àn guānhuǒ 隔岸觀火 to be indifferent; to show no concern

gébì 隔壁 next door

géhé 隔閡 no meeting of minds; a mental barrier

géjiān 隔間 a partition

géjué 隔絕 blocked or obstucted; to separate; to cut off

gékāi 隔開 to separate; to set apart; to partition

gélí 隔離 to separate; to isolate; to segregate; to quarantine

génián 隔年 in the following year; in the year following

géqiáng yǒu'ěr 隔牆有耳 It's difficult to keep a secret.

gérè 隔熱 (construction) heat insulation

gérì 隔日 1. the next day or the day after next 2. every other day

géxuē sāoyǎng 隔靴搔癢 not to the point; having no effect; to attempt an ineffective solution

géyè 隔夜 after a night; last night

géyīn 隔音 soundproof

gé 閣
1. a room; a chamber; a pavilion 2. an attic 3. a cabinet 4. a boudoir

gékuí 閣揆 the premier; the prime minister

gélóu 閣樓 an attic; a garret

géxià 閣下 Your Excellency; you (a polite expression)

géyuán 閣員 cabinet ministers; members of the cabinet

gé 骼
a bone; a skeleton

Gě 葛
a Chinese family name

gè 各
1. each; every 2. all

gèbàn 各半 half-and-half; fifty-fifty

gèbié 各別 individual; isolated (case); separate

gèchí jǐjiàn 各持己見 Each sticks to his own view.

gèdé qísuǒ 各得其所 Each person gets his proper position.

gèdì 各地 various places or localities

gège jīpò 各個擊破 to knock out one adversary after another

gège jípò 各個擊破 refer to **gège jīpò** 各個擊破

gèguó 各國 each and every

G

nation (or country)

gèháng gèyè 各行各業 each and every trade

gèjí 各級 all or different levels

gèjiè 各界 all walks of life; all circles

gèjiù gèwèi 各就各位 1. (military) Man your posts! 2. (athletics) On your marks!

gèlèi 各類 each or every sort, kind, class, species, or order

gèqǔ suǒxū 各取所需 Each takes what he wants.

gèrén 各人 everybody

gèshì gèyàng 各式各樣 all sorts, kinds, or varieties; various

gèshū jǐjiàn 各抒己見 Each airs his own views.

gèwèi 各位 everybody (a term of address)

gèxiǎn shéntōng 各顯神通 Each has his own way.

gèyǒu qiānqiū 各有千秋 Each shows a unique quality.

gèyǒu suǒcháng 各有所長 Each has a unique merit.

gèyǒu suǒhào 各有所好 Each has his likes and dislikes.

gèzhí yīcí 各執一詞 Each (of the disputants) tells a different story.

gèzhǒng 各種 various kinds, species, categories, and

gèzì 各自 each; respective; respectively

gèzì wéizhèng 各自為政 Each (office) administers its affairs in its own way without coordination with others.

gè 個(箇)

1. a numerary adjunct 2. piece 3. single 4. roughly 5. an adjunct to an indefinite pronoun, as this, that

gè'àn 個案 an individual case

gèbǎyuè 個把月 a month or two

gèbié 個別 individual; separately

gègè 個個 (each and) every one

gèr 個兒 size; height; stature

gèrén 個人 1. the individual as contrasted with the group 2. oneself 3. personal

gèrén diànnǎo 個人電腦 a personal computer

gèrénjī 個人機 a personal computer

gèrén zhǔyì 個人主義 individualism; egoism

gètǐ 個體 a matter, etc. having an independent and distinct quality

gètǐhù 個體戶 an individual business or shop

gèwèi 個位 (mathematics) a unit; a digit

gèxìng 個性 personality; individuality

gèzhōng 個中 therein

gèzi 個子 physical size of a person; build

gěi 給

1. to give 2. for; for the benefit of 3. to let; to allow

gēn 根

1. the root of a plant 2. a base; a foundation 3. the beginning, cause, or source of something 4. (mathematics) the root of a number 5. (chemistry) radical 6. a piece (of string, rope, etc.); a (stick, spear or thing of slender shape)

gēnběn 根本 1. a root; a base; a foundation 2. basically

gēnběn bànfǎ 根本辦法 basic methods or measures

gēnběn guānniàn 根本觀念 a radical conception

gēnbù 根部 the root of a plant

gēnchú 根除 thoroughly to do away with

gēnhào 根號 (mathematics) the radical sign

gēnjī 根基 foundation (in learning)

gēnjīng 根莖 a rhizome; a rootstock

gēnjù 根據 1. a basis; grounds 2. in accordance with (the regulation, etc.)

gēnjùdì 根據地 a base (of operations); a home base

gēnjué 根絕 to root out (a problem, vice, etc.)

gēnshēn dìgù 根深蒂固 time-

honored; deep-rooted

gēnyóu 根由 the source, origin or cause of something

gēnyuán 根源 the source, origin or cause of something

gēnzhì 根治 a radical treatment (for a disease, etc.); to cure (a disease) for good

gēn 跟

1. the heel 2. to follow 3. to attend upon 4. and

gēnbān 跟班 an attendant (especially of an official)

gēndìng 跟定 to decide to follow (a leader) for good

gēnjìn 跟進 to follow suit

gēnqián 跟前 the front, side, or presence (of a person)

gēnqian 跟前 used with reference to children in the presence of their parents

gēnshang 跟上 to keep pace with; to catch up with

gēnsuí 跟隨 1. to go closely behind; to follow 2. a retainer; an attendant

gēnzōng 跟蹤 to keep track of; to tail

gēnzōng fúwù 跟蹤服務 after service

gèn 艮

1. (said of food) tough; leathery 2. (said of clothing) simple 3. (said of one's personality) honest; upright

gèn 亙 also **gěng**

to extend (over space or time)

gèngǔ wèiyǒu 亙古未有 unprecedented

gèn 艮

one of the Eight Diagrams for divination

gēng 更

1. (formerly) the watches of the night 2. a night watchman 3. to change; to alter; to shift 4. to experience 5. to alternate

gēngdòng 更動 to shift; to switch; to change

gēngfū 更夫 a night watchman

gēnggǎi 更改 to change (over); to alter

gēnghuàn 更換 to change; to alter

gēnglòu 更漏 an hourglass; a sandglass

gēngniánqī 更年期 (physiology) the menopause

gēngniánqí 更年期 refer to **gēngniánqī** 更年期

gēngtì 更替 to alternate; to take turns

gēngxīn 更新 to renew; to renovate

gēngyī 更衣 to change clothes

gēngyīshì 更衣室 a change-room; a dressing room

gēngzhèng 更正 to correct; to put right

gēng 庚

1. the seventh of the Ten Celestial Stems (**tiāngān** 天干) 2. the age (of a person)

gēng 耕 also **jīng**

to till; to plough; to cultivate

gēngdì 耕地 1. cultivated land 2. to till land

gēngtián 耕田 to till land

gēngyún 耕耘 to till and weed; to cultivate

gēngyúnjī 耕耘機 a power tiller

gēngzhòng 耕種 1. to plough and sow; to cultivate 2. cultivation

gēngzuò 耕作 to cultivate land and grow crops

gēng 羹

thick soup; soup

gēng 埂

1. a pit; a cave 2. an irrigation ditch 3. a low bank of earth between fields

gěng 哽

to choke; to feel a lump in one's throat

gěngsè 哽塞 to choke

gěngyè 哽咽 to be choked with sobs; to sob

gěng 耿

1. bright 2. upright; incorruptible 3. a Chinese family name

gěnggěng yúhuái 耿耿於懷 to keep something anxiously in one's mind

gěngjiè 耿介 1. magnificent 2. upright; just; righteous

gěngzhí 耿直 honest; upright

gěng 梗

1. the branch or stem of a plant 2. to prick or pierce with a thorn; thorny 3. an outline; a synopsis; a summary 4. to block; to obstruct 5. stubborn; stiff 6. fierce and fearless 7. an ailment; bane; distress 8. to straighten 9. honest; straight

gěnggài 梗概 an outline; a summary; a synopsis

gěngsè 梗塞 to obstruct; to block

gěngzhí 梗直 straight and honest; outspoken

gěng 鯁

1. a fishbone stuck in the throat 2. honest; straightforward

gěngzhí 鯁直 honest; straightforward; outspoken

gèng 亙

refer to **gèn** 亙

gèng 更

more; further; to a greater degree

gèngduō 更多 more; still more

gènghǎo 更好 better

gènghuài 更壞 worse; even worse; worse still

gèngjiā 更加 even more

gèngshèng yīchóu 更勝一籌 even better

gōng 工

1. a laborer; a worker 2. a shift 3. work 4. a day's work 5. an engineering or building project 6. a defense work 7. fine; delicate 8. to be skilled in

gōngběnfèi 工本費 the net cost of a product (the cost of raw materials plus labor)

gōngbǐhuà 工筆畫 very fine, delicate drawings

gōngbīng 工兵 1. engineering

corps 2. a serviceman in the engineering corps

gōngchǎng 工場 a workshop; a workplace

gōngchǎng 工廠 a factory; a plant; a workshop

gōngcháo 工潮 a labor strike; sabotage

gōngchéng 工程 an engineering or building project—(figuratively) a job or task

gōngchéngshī 工程師 an engineer

Gōngdǎng 工黨 1. the British Labor Party 2. a labor party

gōngdì 工地 a building site

gōngdú 工讀 to work on a job in order to finance one's study or education

gōngdúshēng 工讀生 a worker-student

gōngfēng 工蜂 a worker or a working bee

gōngfu 工夫 1. time 2. efforts put into a piece of work 3. skill; art

gōnghuì 工會 a labor union; a trade union

gōngjiàng 工匠 a craftsman; an artisan

gōngjù 工具 tools; implements

gōngjùshū 工具書 reference books

gōngjùxiāng 工具箱 a toolbox; a workbox

gōngkē 工科 the engineering department of a college

gōngliáo 工寮 a simple hut for workmen at a construction site

gōngqián 工錢 pay; wages

gōngrén 工人 a laborer; a workman

gōngrén jiējí 工人階級 the working class; labor class

gōngshāngjiè 工商界 the industrial and business circles

gōngshāngyè 工商業 industry and commerce

gōngshí 工時 a man-hour

gōngtóu 工頭 a foreman (of workers)

gōngxuéyuàn 工學院 a college

G

of engineering

gōngyè 工業 industry; industrial

Gōngyè Gémìng 工業革命 Industrial Revolution

gōngyè guójiā 工業國家 industrial nations or powers

gōngyèhuà 工業化 industrialization

gōngyèqū 工業區 an industrial park

gōngyè xuéxiào 工業學校 a technical school

gōngyè yòngshuǐ 工業用水 industrial water

gōngyǐ 工蟻 a worker (ant)

gōngyì 工藝 technology; a craft

gōngyìpǐn 工藝品 handicrafts; handmade products

gōngyǒu 工友 an office boy; an office errand man

gōngyú xīnjì 工於心計 scheming; crafty

gōng yùshàn qíshì, bì xiānlì qíqì 工欲善其事，必先利其器 Good tools are prerequisite to the successful execution of a job.

gōngzhěng 工整 neat (style, calligraphy, etc.)

gōngzī 工資 wages

gōngzuò 工作 1. to work 2. one's job or duty

gōngzuò rényuán 工作人員 workers

gōngzuòtiān 工作天 a man-day

gōng 弓
1. a bow 2. bent; arching; arched 3. a measure of length (equal to five Chinese feet)

gōngjiàn 弓箭 bow and arrow

gōngjiànshǒu 弓箭手 an archer

gōngjiàng 弓匠 a bowyer

gōngnǔshǒu 弓弩手 an archer

gōngshǐ 弓矢 bow and arrow

gōngxián 弓弦 a bowstring

gōngxíng 弓形 (mathematics) a segment of a circle

gōng 公
1. unselfish; unbiased; fair 2. pub-

lic 3. to make public; open to all 4. the first of old China's five grades of the nobility 5. the father of one's husband (one's husband's father) 6. one's grandfather 7. a respectful salutation 8. the male (of animals) 9. office; official duties

gōng'àn 公案 1. a case of law 2. office desks 3. official business

gōngbǎo 公保 government insurance for public servants

gōngbào 公報 an official bulletin; a gazette; a communique

gōngbào sīchóu 公報私仇 to avenge oneself on one's enemies in the name of public interests

gōngbù 公布 to promulgate; to announce

gōngcè 公廁 a public lavatory

gōngchāi 公差 official assignments (usually involving travel)

gōngchǐ 公尺 a meter

gōngchū 公出 to be away on official duties

gōngcùn 公寸 a decimeter

gōngdào 公道 justice

gōngdao 公道 reasonable (prices); just; fair

gōngdé 公德 social morality; social ethics

gōngdéxīn 公德心 public-mindedness

gōngdí 公敵 a public enemy

gōngdūn 公噸 a metric ton

gōngdùn 公噸 refer to **gōngdūn** 公噸

gōng'ér wàngsī 公而忘私 to forget oneself in the discharge of official duties

gōngfǎ 公法 public law

gōngfèi 公費 public funds; government funds

gōngfēn 公分 1. a centimeter (cm.) 2. a gram (g.)

gōngfèn 公憤 public indignation

gōnggàn 公幹 an official assignment or duty

gōnggào 公告 1. a proclamation 2. to make an announcement

gōnggào dìjià 公告地價 a government-assessed land price

gōnggòng 公共 public (relations, health, etc.)

gōnggòng chǎngsuǒ 公共場所 a public place

gōnggòng diànshì 公共電視 public television

gōnggòng guānxi 公共關係 public relations (PR)

gōnggòng qìchē 公共汽車 a bus; an omnibus

gōnggòng shìyè 公共事業 public utilities

gōnggòng wèishēng 公共衛生 public sanitation

gōnggòng xíngzhèng 公共行政 public administration

gōnggòng zhìxù 公共秩序 public order

gōngguǎn 公館 1. an official residence 2. a residence (a polite reference to other's residence)

gōnghǎi 公海 the high seas

gōnghài 公害 social effects of pollution

gōnghán 公函 an official letter

gōngháo 公毫 a centigram

gōnghuì 公會 a union, league, society, federation, etc. of a certain trade

gōngjī 公雞 a cock; a rooster

gōngjì 公祭 a public memorial ceremony

gōngjiào rényuán 公教人員 government employees and staffs of public schools

gōngjīn 公斤 a kilogram (kg)

gōngjué 公爵 a duke

gōngjué fūren 公爵夫人 a duchess

gōngkāi 公開 to make known to the public; to make public

gōngkè 公克 a gram

gōngkuǎn 公款 public funds; public money

gōnglí 公釐 1. a millimeter 2. an area of one square meter

gōnglǐ 公里 a kilometer

gōnglǐ 公理 1. right; justice 2. an axiom

gōnglì xuéxiào 公立學校 a public school

gōngliǎng 公兩 100 grams

gōnglù 公路 a highway

gōnglùn 公論 public opinion

gōngmàijú 公賣局 a government monopoly bureau

gōngmín 公民 citizens

gōngmínkē 公民科 civics

gōngmín tóupiào 公民投票 the referendum; the plebiscite

gōngmǔ 公畝 an area of 100 meters square

gōngmù 公墓 a public cemetery

gōngping 公平 fair; unbiased; just

gōngpó 公婆 the parents of one's husband

gōngpú 公僕 a public servant; an official

gōngqǐng 公頃 a hectare (ha)

gōngquán 公權 civil rights; civic rights

gōngquánlì 公權力 government power or authority

gōngrán 公然 openly; in public

gōngrèn 公認 generally recognized

gōngshěn 公審 a public trial

gōngshēng 公升 a liter

gōngshǐ 公使 (diplomacy) a minister; an envoy

gōngshǐguǎn 公使館 a legation

gōngshì 公式 a formula

gōngshì 公事 official business; public affairs

gōngshì gōngbàn 公事公辦 to discharge official duties strictly according to rules

gōngshìhuà 公式化 stereotyped; formulistic

gōngshǔ 公署 a government office

gōngshuō gōngyǒulǐ, póshuō póyǒulǐ 公說公有理，婆說婆有理 In the presence of a superior, umpire, etc., each of two quarreling parties insists that he is right.

gōngsī 公司 a company; a corporation

gōngsī fēnmíng 公私分明 to be scrupulous in separating pub-

lic from private interests

gōngsī héyíng 公私合營 state and private joint ownership

gōngsù 公訴 public prosecution

gōngtān 公攤 to share (expenditures, capital investment, etc.) equally

gōngtáng 公堂 a court of law

gōngtīnghuì 公聽會 a public hearing

gōngwén 公文 official documents

gōngwù 公物 public or government property

gōngwù 公務 official matters, business, duties, etc.

gōngwùyuán 公務員 government employees; civil servants

Gōngwùyuán Chéngjiè Wěiyuánhuì 公務員懲戒委員會 the Committee on the Discipline of Public Functionaries

gōngxìnlì 公信力 government credibility

gōngxiū 公休 1. an official holiday 2. a holiday for a particular trade

gōngyǎn 公演 to stage shows for public viewing

gōngyì 公益 public interests or welfare

gōngyì 公議 public discussion

gōngyíng 公營 publicly owned

gōngyíng shìyè 公營事業 government-owned enterprises

gōngyòng 公用 public (telephones, etc.)

gōngyòng diànhuà 公用電話 a public telephone

gōngyòng shìyè 公用事業 public utilities

gōngyǒu 公有 publicly-owned; public

gōngyù 公寓 an apartment house

gōngyuán 公元 in the year of our Lord...; the Christian era

gōngyuán 公園 a park; a public garden

gōngyuē 公約 1. a convention; a pact 2. joint pledge

gōngzhài 公債 1. government

bonds 2. the public debt

gōngzhèng 公正 justice; fairness; just; impartial

gōngzhèng 公證 to notarize

gōngzhèng jiéhūn 公證結婚 a court wedding

gōngzhèngrén 公證人 a notary public; a witness

gōngzhí 公職 government offices; official posts or ranks

gōngzhōng tǐguó 公忠體國 to be loyal to one's country

gōngzhòng 公衆 the public

gōngzhǔ 公主 a princess

gōngzǐ 公子 1. (in ancient China) sons of a duke or a ranking official 2. a polite designation for another's son or sons

gōngzǐgēr 公子哥兒 dandies; playboys

gōng 功

1. a merit; an achievement; an accomplishment; an exploit 2. usefulness; effectiveness 3. a function 4. (physics) work

gōngbài chuíchéng 功敗垂成 to fail within reach of success

gōngbù kěmò 功不可沒 The contribution (to success) cannot be left unrecognized.

gōngchén 功臣 one who has made a significant contribution to a specific task

gōngchéng míngjiù 功成名就 to achieve success and acquire fame

gōngchéng shēntuì 功成身退 to retire after achieving success

gōngdé 功德 1. merits and virtues 2. (Buddhism) charitable and pious deeds

gōngdé wúliàng 功德無量 boundless beneficence

gōngfu 功夫 1. efforts (devoted to a task) 2. accomplishments 3. skill

gōngkè 功課 schoolwork; homework

gōngkèbiǎo 功課表 a class schedule (at school)

gōngkuī yīkuì 功虧一簣 failure to achieve success by a very narrow margin

gōnglao 功勞 merits; contribution

gōnglì zhǔyì 功利主義 utilitarianism

gōngmíng 功名 an official rank or an academic title (in former times)

gōngnéng 功能 use; a function; effect

gōngxiào 功效 effectiveness; efficacy

gōngxūn 功勳 distinctive achievements

gōngyòng 功用 use; a function; effect

gōng 攻
1. to attack; to raid; to assault 2. to accuse; to charge; to assail; to criticize; to rebuke 3. to work at; to apply oneself to; to study

gōngdǎ 攻打 to attack; to raid; to invade

gōngdú 攻讀 to apply oneself diligently to study

gōngjí 攻擊 1. to attack 2. to accuse

gōngjí 攻擊 refer to **gōngjí** 攻擊

gōngkè 攻克 to attack and conquer

gōngpò 攻破 to attack and conquer

gōngqǔ 攻取 to attack and capture

gōngshì 攻勢 the offensive

gōngshǒu 攻守 offense and defense

gōngxià 攻下 1. to succeed in capturing (a city, a fort, etc.) by attack 2. to overcome

gōngxiàn 攻陷 to succeed in capturing (a city, a fort, etc.) by attack

gōngzhàn 攻占 to attack and occupy

gōng 供
1. to supply; to contribute to 2. refer to **gòng** 供 1

gōngbù yìngqiú 供不應求 The supply is unable to meet the demand.

gōngdiàn 供電 power supply

gōngguò yúqiú 供過於求 The supply has outstripped the demand.

gōngjǐ 供給 to supply; to equip; to provide

gōngqiú 供求 supply and demand

gōngxiāo 供銷 supply and marketing

gōngyìng 供應 1. to furnish 2. to supply

gōng 紅
work; working

gōng 宮
1. a palace 2. castration

gōngdiàn 宮殿 a palace

gōngnǚ 宮女 a court lady; a lady-in-waiting

gōngquè 宮闕 a palace (as seen from outside)

gōngtíng 宮廷 the living quarters of a monarch in his palace

gōng 恭
respectful; reverent; deferential

gōngdú 恭讀 to read respectfully

gōnghè 恭賀 to congratulate

gōnghè xīnxǐ 恭賀新禧 Happy New Year!

gōnghòu 恭候 to await respectfully

gōngjǐn 恭謹 respectfully serious

gōngjìng 恭敬 respectful; reverent

gōngqǐng 恭請 to invite respectfully; to invite with respect

gōngwéi 恭維 to praise; to flatter

gōngxǐ 恭喜 to congratulate

gōngxǐ fācái 恭喜發財 (a familiar Lunar New Year's greeting) Congratulations and be prosperous.

gōngyíng 恭迎 to welcome respectfully

gōngzhù 恭祝 I, or we, congratulate you upon....

gōng 躬
1. the body; the person 2. in person; personally 3. to bend (the body)

gōngqīn 躬親 in person

gōng 襲

1. reverential 2. a Chinese family name

gǒng 汞 also **hòng**

mercury (an element)

gǒng 拱

1. to fold hands before the breast when making a bow; to salute 2. to encircle with the hands 3. to surround 4. (architecture) arched (doors, windows, etc.) 5. to raise up (in the middle); to hump up; to arch

gǒngláng 拱廊 a cloister

gǒngmén 拱門 an arched door or doorway

gǒngqiáo 拱橋 an arched bridge

gǒngshǒu ràngrén 拱手讓人 to give up something to others without putting up a fight

gǒng 鞏

1. to tie or bind with thongs 2. to guard; to secure; to strengthen

gǒnggù 鞏固 1. strong; well-guarded; secure 2. to consolidate

gòng 共

1. common; same 2. all; collectively 3. to share; to work together 4. together 5. an abbreviation of the word "Communism" or "Communist"

Gòngchǎndǎng 共產黨 the Communist Party

gòngchǎn zhǔyì 共產主義 communism

gòngcún 共存 to coexist; coexistent

gòngcúnwáng 共存亡 (to defend a city or place) to the last man; to live or die together

gòngfàn 共犯 1. collusion 2. an accomplice

gòngfù guónàn 共赴國難 to work together to save the country in time of a national crisis

Gònghédǎng 共和黨 the Republican Party

gònghéguó 共和國 a republic

gòngjì 共計 the sum total; to come to; to add up to

gòngmiǎn 共勉 to encourage each other

gòngmíng 共鳴 1. (physics) resonance or sympathetic vibration 2. (to inspire) the same feeling in others

gòngmóu 共謀 to collaborate; to collude

gòngshì 共事 1. to work together; to be colleagues 2. (said of women) to share the same husband

gòngshì 共識 common consensus

gòngtóng 共同 common; to co-operate in (an undertaking, etc.)

gòngtóng jījīn 共同基金 mutual fund

gòngtóng shìchǎng 共同市場 a common market

gòngxiāng shèngjǔ 共襄盛舉 Let's all work together for this worthy project.

gòngxiǎng 共享 to enjoy together; to share

gòngyǒu 共有 owned by all; common (traits, customs, etc.)

gòng 供

1. (also **gōng**) to give a statement or an account of a criminal act; to give evidence 2. to offer in worship

gòngcí 供詞 a confession to a criminal act

gòngfó 供佛 to make offerings to Buddha

gòngpǐn 供品 offerings

gòngrèn 供認 to confess; a confession

gòngyǎng 供養 to offer provisions

gòngyàng 供養 refer to **gòngyǎng** 供養

gòngzhuō 供桌 the table on which sacrificial offerings are placed

gòng 貢

1. the tribute from a vassal state; to offer tribute 2. to recommend (a person to an office, etc.); to submit 3. (in ancient China) land tax 4. to contribute; to offer

gòngpǐn 貢品 items offered as tribute

gòngxiàn 貢獻 to offer or contribute (oneself to the national cause, etc.); contribution

gōu 勾
1. to mark; to put a check; to mark on 2. to cancel; to cross out (or off) 3. to hook 4. to join; to connect 5. to evoke 6. to entice; to seduce 7. a hook

gōuda 勾搭 1. to have illegitimate relations 2. to conspire with

gōuhuà 勾畫 to delineate; to sketch

gōuhún 勾魂 to bewitch; to enchant

gōujiān dābèi 勾肩搭背 to hold each other's arms while walking side by side

gōujié 勾結 to collude or collaborate

gōuqiàn 勾芡 to thicken (soup, etc.) by means of starch

gōuxiāo 勾消 to liquidate; to cancel

gōuxīn dòujiǎo 勾心鬥角 to intrigue against each other

gōuyǐn 勾引 to entice; to seduce; to tempt; to inveigle

gōu 枸
gōujú 枸橘 a large acid orange

gōu 鉤(鈎)
1. a hook 2. to hook 3. to probe; to investigate 4. to entice; to lure

gōumáoyī 鉤毛衣 to crochet a wool sweater

gōuzhēn 鉤針 a crochet hook; a crochet needle

gōuzhuǎ 鉤爪 talons

gōuzi 鉤子 a hook

gōu 溝
1. a ditch; a waterway; a moat 2. a groove; a rut

gōuhè 溝壑 a valley, gorge, or canyon

gōuqú 溝渠 a ditch; a drain; a gutter; a channel

gōutōng 溝通 to bring about an unobstructed interflow of (feelings, ideas, etc.); to communicate

gǒu 狗
1. a dog 2. (figuratively) a lackey; a footman; a servile person; a follower 3. damned; cursed

gǒují tiàoqiáng 狗急跳牆 A person takes desperate measures in a critical situation.

gǒuná hàozi, duōguǎn xiánshì 狗拿耗子，多管閒事 to poke one's nose into others' business

gǒupì 狗屁 Nonsense! Rubbish!

gǒuròu 狗肉 dog meat

gǒushǐ 狗屎 (literally) dog's droppings—utterly worthless

gǒutóu jūnshī 狗頭軍師 a good-for-nothing adviser

gǒutuǐzi 狗腿子 (figuratively) a hired thug; a henchman

gǒuwō 狗窩 a kennel; a dog-house

gǒuxiě pēntóu 狗血噴頭 refer to **gǒuxuè pēntóu** 狗血噴頭

gǒuxuè pēntóu 狗血噴頭 to be scolded in a very humiliating fashion

gǒuyǎn kànrén dī 狗眼看人低 to act like a snob

gǒuyǎo Lǚ Dòngbīn 狗咬呂洞賓 to mistake a good man for a bad one

gǒuzuǐ tǔbuchū xiàngyá 狗嘴吐不出象牙 A mean fellow never speaks nice things.

gǒu 枸
a medlar

gǒuqǐ 枸杞 Lycium chinense, a Chinese wolfberry

gǒu 苟
1. against principle; illicit; improper 2. careless 3. if

gǒuhé 苟合 1. to join or associate against one's principle 2. an illicit sexual act

gǒuqiě 苟且 1. against one's principle 2. perfunctory 3. illicit (sexual relations)

G

gǒuqiě tōushēng 苟且偷生 to drag out an ignominious existence

gǒutóng 苟同 to agree without giving serious thought

gǒuyán cánchuǎn 苟延殘喘 to prolong one's life only temporarily; to be on one's last legs; to linger on in a steadily deteriorating condition

gòu 勾

1. to manage 2. business; affairs

gòudang 勾當 a plot; an intrigue

gòu 垢

1. dirt; filth; stains 2. shame; disgrace 3. (figuratively) evildoers

gòu 逅

refer to **hòu** 逅

gòu 夠

1. enough; too much; sufficient 2. fully; quite

gòuběn 夠本 enough to cover the cost

gòugé 夠格 to be qualified

gòujìnr 夠勁兒 1. (said of an onerous task) almost too much to cope with 2. strong or hot (in taste, strength, etc.)

gòupéngyou 夠朋友 to be true to friends; to be a friend in need

gòuwèir 夠味兒 enjoyable; pleasant enough

gòuyìsi 夠意思 1. really something; terrific 2. generous; really kind

gòu 詬

1. to insult; to shame 2. to berate; to abuse

gòubìng 詬病 to insult; to criticize; to blame

gòu 搆

1. to pull; to drag 2. to reach

gòu 媾

1. to marry; to wed 2. to negotiate peace; amity 3. to couple; to copulate

gòuhé 媾和 to make peace

gòu 構

to frame; to form; to build; to establish; to constitute; to scheme

gòuchéng 構成 to constitute; to form

gòuhuò 構禍 to bring disaster

gòuluàn 構亂 to stir up disorder

gòusī 構思 1. to weigh something mentally 2. to plot; a plot

gòutú 構圖 composition (in drawing)

gòuxiàn 構陷 to frame a charge against someone

gòuxiǎng 構想 an idea; a plan; a scheme

gòuzào 構造 structure; construction

gòu 購

to buy; to purchase

gòumǎi 購買 to buy

gòumǎilì 購買力 purchasing power

gòuwù 購物 to go shopping

gòuzhì 購置 to buy; to purchase

gū 估

to estimate; to calculate; to evaluate

gūjì 估計 to estimate; to calculate; to reckon; to conjecture

gūjià 估價 to evaluate; to appraise

gūjiàdān 估價單 a list of cost estimate

gūliang 估量 to estimate; to calculate; to reckon; to conjecture

gū 咕

1. to murmur 2. (said of hens) a cluck; (said of turtledoves, etc.) a coo

gūlū 咕嚕 1. a mumbled sound or an indistinct utterance 2. the rumbling sound in the belly

gūnong 咕噥 to murmur

gū 孤

1. solitary; lone; lonely; friendless; helpless; unaided 2. fatherless; orphaned 3. (said of disposition) eccentric 4. negligent in an obligation

gūdān 孤單 solitary; alone

gūdǎo 孤島 an isolated island

G

gūdú 孤獨 solitary; alone

gū'ér 孤兒 an orphan

gū'éryuàn 孤兒院 an orphanage

gūhún 孤魂 a wandering soul

gūjí 孤寂 refer to **gūjì** 孤寂

gūjì 孤寂 lonely; friendless

gūjiā guǎrén 孤家寡人 1. alone 2. a bachelor

gūkǔ língdīng 孤苦伶仃 lonely and helpless

gūlì 孤立 isolation; isolated; unaided

gūlínglíng 孤零零 lonely; friendless

gūlòu guǎwén 孤陋寡聞 ignorant

gūpì 孤僻 (said of a person's disposition) eccentric; idiosyncratic

gūzhǎng nánmíng 孤掌難鳴 to be unable to cope with a situation or accomplish something without help

gū 姑
1. aunts; the sister of one's father 2. the mother of one's husband 3. the sister of one's husband 4. a general term for unmarried women 5. for the time being; meanwhile 6. a nun

gūfù 姑父 an uncle

gūgu 姑姑 an aunt

gūmā 姑媽 an aunt

gūmǔ 姑母 an aunt

gūniang 姑娘 an unmarried girl; a maiden

gūqiě 姑且 for the time being

gūqiě bùtán 姑且不談 to leave something aside for the moment

gūxī 姑息 to spoil (a child); to appease

gūxī yǎngjiān 姑息養奸 To tolerate evil is to encourage evildoers.

gūxí 姑息 refer to **gūxī** 姑息

gùxí yǎngjiān 姑息養奸 refer to **gūxī yǎngjiān** 姑息養奸

gūye 姑爺 a son-in-law

gūzhàng 姑丈 an uncle

gū 呱 also **guā, wā**
1. the cries of an infant 2. to wail

gūgū zhuìdì 呱呱墜地 (said of a baby) to come into this world

gū 沽
1. to buy 2. to sell 3. crude; inferior (quality)

gūjiǔ 沽酒 1. to buy wine 2. spirits or wine bought from stores

gūmíng diàoyù 沽名釣譽 to do something, not for the sake of achievement, but for the sake of fishing for a good reputation or fame

gū 辜
1. sin; crime; guilt 2. to be negligent in an obligation or expectation; to fail 3. a Chinese family name

gūfù 辜負 to fail to live up to (another's expectation, etc.)

gū 菇
mushrooms; a fungus

gū 鈷
cobalt

gú 骨
refer to **gǔ** 骨 1

gǔ 古
1. ancient; antiquated; old; antiquity 2. not following current customs or practices 3. a Chinese family name

Gǔbā 古巴 Cuba

gǔbǎn 古板 1. inactive; dumb 2. out of date; old-fashioned

gǔdài 古代 ancient times

gǔdào rècháng 古道熱腸 honest and upright, and willing to help

gǔdiǎn wénxué 古典文學 classical literature

gǔdiǎn yīnyuè 古典音樂 classical music

gǔdǒng 古董 antiques; curios

gǔdū 古都 an ancient capital

gùguài 古怪 1. anachronistic 2. queer; eccentric; strange; odd

gǔjì 古跡 relics

gǔjí 古籍 ancient books

G

gǔjīn Zhōngwài 古今中外 everywhere and all times

gǔkējiǎn 古柯鹼 cocaine

gǔlǎo 古老 old; antiquated; ancient

gǔrén 古人 ancient people

gǔsè gǔxiāng 古色古香 (usually said of decor, furniture, etc.) in graceful ancient style

gǔshíhou 古時候 in ancient times

gǔshū 古書 ancient books

gǔtóngsè 古銅色 the color of bronze

gǔwán 古玩 antiques; curios

gǔwàn 古玩 refer to **gǔwán** 古玩

gǔwǎng jīnlái 古往今來 from ancient times till today

gǔwù 古物 antiques; curios; relics

gǔzhuāng 古裝 ancient costumes

gǔ 谷
1. a valley; a waterway between two mountains; a ravine 2. a hollow; a pit 3. a dilemma; a difficult situation; a predicament

gǔdǐ 谷底 the bottom of a valley

gǔ 汨
1. to dredge (a channel, etc.) 2. confused; disorderly 3. the sound of waves

gǔluàn 汨亂 to cause disorder

gǔmò 汨沒 to sink; to decline

gǔ 股
1. the thigh; the haunches; the hips 2. a department; a section 3. shares; stock 4. a puff; a blast (of hot air) 5. a bunch or band (of bandits)

gǔdōng 股東 a shareholder or stockholder

gǔfēn 股分 shares or stock

gǔfèn yǒuxiàn gōngsī 股分有限公司 a limited liability company

gǔpiào 股票 stocks

gǔpiào shìchǎng 股票市場 the stock market

gǔquán 股權 the ownership of a share or stock

gǔzhǎng 股長 the head of a subdivision

gǔ 骨
1. (also **gú**) a bone 2. a framework; a frame; a skeleton

gǔ'ái 骨癌 cancer in the bone

gǔdǒng 骨董 curios; antique objects

gǔgàn 骨幹 1. (anatomy) a diaphysis 2. the backbone; a mainstay

gǔgé 骨骼 a frame of the body; a skeleton

gǔhuī 骨灰 bone ashes

gǔjià 骨架 a frame; a framework; a skeleton

gǔkē 骨科 osteopathy

gǔkē yīshēng 骨科醫生 an osteopath

gǔqì 骨氣 fortitude; backbone; pluck

gǔròu 骨肉 one's own flesh and blood—blood relations

gǔshòu rúchái 骨瘦如柴 thin and emaciated; very skinny

gǔsuǐ 骨髓 marrow

gǔzhé 骨折 a bone fracture

gǔ 滑
refer to **huá** 滑 4

gǔ 賈
1. a merchant; a businessman 2. to buy; to trade

gǔ 鼓
1. drums 2. to drum; to beat a drum 3. to vibrate; to quiver 4. to rouse; to stir up; to instigate

gǔchuī 鼓吹 to advocate; to uphold; to promote; to propagate

gǔchuí 鼓槌 a drumstick

gǔchuī 鼓吹 a kind of ancient court music

gǔdòng 鼓動 to instigate; to rouse; to incite; to stir up; to excite

gǔhào yuèduì 鼓號樂隊 a drum and bugle band

gǔlì 鼓勵 to encourage; to hearten

gǔmó 鼓膜 the eardrum

gǔqǐ yǒngqì 鼓起勇氣 to pluck up courage

gǔshé rúhuáng 鼓舌如簧 to wag one's tongue (for honeyed words, malicious gossip, etc.)

gǔshēng 鼓聲 drumbeats

gǔshǒu 鼓手 a drum player; a drummer

gǔwǔ 鼓舞 1. to rouse; to inspire; to stir up; to excite; to spur on 2. to dance for joy; to rejoice

gǔwǔ shìqì 鼓舞士氣 to enhance troop morale; to cheer up troops

gǔzào 鼓譟 to raise an uproar; to be uproarious

gǔzhǎng 鼓掌 to clap the hands; to give applause

gǔ 穀

1. grain; corn; cereals 2. lucky; happy; favorable; good 3. to live; while alive

gǔcāng 穀倉 a barn for storing grain; a granary

gǔlèi 穀類 grain and corn; cereals

gǔzi 穀子 millet; grain

gǔ 膨

to expand; to swell; swollen

gǔzhàng 膨脹 1. expansion; to swell 2. dropsy

gǔ 鵠

a target

gúdì 鵠的 the target; the bull's-eye

gǔ 蠱

1. poison; venom; harm 2. to bewitch; to enchant

gǔhuò 蠱惑 to confuse by magic or witchcraft; to put under a spell; to enchant

gù 估

to sell (used clothing)

gùyīpù 估衣鋪 a secondhand clothes store

gù 固

1. stable; firm; sturdy; secure; solid; hard; strong 2. obstinate; stubborn; insistent; steadfast 3. base; mean; ignorant 4. chronic

5. originally; certainly; as a matter of course; assuredly 6. indeed 7. admittedly; no doubt 8. to become solid; to solidify 9. to strengthen; to guard; to secure; to consolidate

gùdìng 固定 1. to fix 2. fixed; regular

gùdìng huìlǜ 固定匯率 the fixed exchange rate

gùrán 固然 1. of course 2. no doubt; true

gùruò jīntāng 固若金湯 (said of a city, military position, etc.) impregnable

gùshǒu chéngguī 固守成規 to stick to old rules

gùtǐ 固體 solid

gùyǒu 固有 intrinsic; inherent; innate

gùzhí 固執 obstinate; stubborn

gùzhí jǐjiàn 固執己見 to stick to one's opinions

gù 故

1. former; past; earlier; previous; old; ancient 2. intentional; willful; on purpose 3. cause; reason 4. to die 5. an incident; an event; a matter 6. consequently; hence; therefore 7. a friend; an acquaintance

gùbù zìfēng 故步自封 to confine oneself to the old method or traditional way

gùdū 故都 a former capital

Gùgōng Bówùyuàn 故宮博物院 National Palace Museum

gùguó 故國 1. one's fatherland 2. an oldcountry 3. one's hometown

gùjū 故居 one's former residence

gùlǐ 故里 one's hometown

gùnòng xuánxū 故弄玄虛 to puzzle people intentionally

gùrén 故人 an old friend

gùshì 故事 a story; a narrative; a tale

gùtài fùméng 故態復萌 The old (bad) attitude is back.

gùxiāng 故鄉 one's homeland

gùyì 故意 intentional; on purpose

gùyǒu 故友 an old friend

gùzhàng 故障 a bug or break-

G

down (of a machine)

gùzhǔ 故主 the former king or master

gù 雇 (僱)
to employ or hire

gùgōng 雇工 1. a hired laborer 2. to hire a laborer

gùyuán 雇員 an auxiliary employee of very low rank in a government office

gùzhǔ 雇主 the employer

gù 痼
a chronic disease

gùjí 痼疾 an incurable chronic disease

gù 錮
1. to run metal into cracks 2. to confine; to keep in custody; to imprison 3. sturdy; secure

gù 顧
1. to look at; to gaze 2. to turn the head around and look 3. to attend to; to mind; to care for; to concern oneself about; to regard; to look after 4. to visit; to call on 5. however; but; nevertheless 6. indeed; really 7. a Chinese family name

gùcǐ shībǐ 顧此失彼 to take care of one thing and miss the other

gùjí 顧及 to care about; to attend to

gùjì 顧忌 misgivings; scruple; fear

gùkè 顧客 a customer; a patron; a client

gùlǜ 顧慮 to show concern about; misgivings; concern; scruple

gùmiànzi 顧面子 1. to care for one's face or reputation 2. to value friendship; unwilling to embarrass others

gùmíng sīyì 顧名思義 (literally) as a term suggests—self-explanatory

gùniàn 顧念 1. to care for; to be worried about 2. to think of with affection

gùpàn shēngzī 顧盼生姿 to look around charmingly

gùqián bùgùhòu 顧前不顧後 to act with no regard for the consequences

gùquán 顧全 to have consideration for and take care to preserve

gùquán dàjú 顧全大局 in the interest of the whole; for the sake of the country, organization, etc.

gùwèn 顧問 an advisor; a consultant; a counsellor

gùyǐng zìlián 顧影自憐 self-glorification; narcissism; to look at one's shadow and lament one's lot

gùzuǒyòu ér yántā 顧左右而言他 to fudge a question

guā 瓜
melons, gourds, cucumbers, etc.

guādài 瓜代 to relieve or replace (an official) upon the expiration of his term of office

guāfēn 瓜分 to apportion; to partition

guāgé 瓜葛 melon vines—a multitude of relatives

guāpéng 瓜棚 the framework for melon vines

guātián lǐxià 瓜田李下 a position that invites suspicion

guāzǐ 瓜子 melon seeds

guāzǐliǎn 瓜子臉 an oval face

guā 刮
to pare; to shave; to scrape

guādāo 刮刀 a scraper

guāhúzi 刮鬍子 1. to be scolded 2. to shave

guāliǎn 刮臉 to shave (the face)

guāmù xiāngkàn 刮目相看 to marvel at someone's progress

guāpò 刮破 to cut or hurt (the face, etc.) in shaving

guā 呱
refer to **gū** 呱

guā 括
refer to **kuò** 括

guā 䏔
refer to **guǒ** 䏔

guā 蝸

refer to **wō** 蝸

guā 颳
wind blowing; to blow

guāfēng 颳風 wind blowing

guǎ 寡
1. widowed; surviving the spouse 2. lonely; alone; solitary 3. little; few; scant; rare

guǎbù dízhòng 寡不敵衆 to be overpowered by the enemy's larger number

guǎfu 寡婦 a widow

guǎlián xiǎnchǐ 寡廉鮮恥 shameless; unabashed

guǎrén 寡人 (the royal) we

guǎyán 寡言 taciturn; not given to talk

guǎyù 寡欲 having few desires; ascetic

guà 卦
one of the Eight Diagrams of the *Book of Changes*

guà 罣
1. hindrance; obstruction 2. a sieve 3. to be concerned; to be worried

guà'ài 罣礙 hindrance; to block

guàwù 罣誤 to be remiss; to be at fault

guà 掛
1. to hang up; to suspend 2. to ring off 3. to worry; to think of; anxious 4. with one's name registered or listed; recorded 5. to hitch; to get caught

guà'ài 掛礙 to meet many obstacles and obstructions

guàcǎi 掛彩 1. to hang colored silk in celebration of happy occasions 2. to get wounded in action

guàgōu 掛鉤 a hook for hanging clothes, etc. (usually nailed to the wall)

guàhào 掛號 1. registered (mail, etc.); to register a mail 2. to register (at the outpatient department of a hospital)

guàhàochù 掛號處 a register office (of a hospital)

guàhàoxìn 掛號信 a registered letter

guàlǜ 掛慮 to be worried or anxious about

guàmíng 掛名 in name only; nominally; titular

guàniàn 掛念 to be anxious about; to worry about

guàpái 掛牌 (said of lawyers, doctors, etc.) to go into practice

guàshuài 掛帥 to be appointed commander-in-chief

guàxié 掛鞋 to retire from one's career as a sportsman

guàxīn 掛心 to be anxious about; to worry about

guàyī lòuwàn 掛一漏萬 totally incomplete or inadequate

guàyì 掛意 to mind

guàzhàng 掛賬 (to buy) on credit; to owe

guàzhōng 掛鐘 a wall clock

guà 褂
an overcoat; a robe or gown; a jacket

guāi 乖
1. to oppose; to contradict; to be at variance 2. perverse; obstinate; untoward; sulky 3. obedient; well-behaved 4. cunning; artful; crafty; wily

guāiguāi 乖乖 1. submissive; docile; obedient 2. an endearing name for children

guāilì 乖戾 cantankerous; perverse

guāipì 乖僻 unreasonable; eccentric

guāiqiǎo 乖巧 clever; ingenious

guāizhāng 乖張 recalcitrant

guāi 摑 also **guó**
to slap another on his face; to smack; to box

guǎi 拐
1. to kidnap; to abduct 2. to turn or change direction 3. to swindle 4. (枴) a staff for an old person; a cane

guǎijiǎo 拐角 at the corner

guǎipiàn 拐騙 1. to abduct; to kidnap 2. to swindle

guǎiwān 拐彎 to turn the corner

guǎiwān mòjiǎo 拐彎抹角 1. to proceed along a zigzag road 2. a roundabout way of talking; circumlocution

guǎizhàng 拐杖 a staff; a stick

guǎi 枴

a staff for an old person; a cane

guǎizhàng 枴杖 an old person's staff; a cane

guài 怪

1. strange; queer; monstrous; odd; peculiar 2. to be surprised at 3. a ghost; a goblin; an apparition; a monster; an evil spirit 4. uncanny; weird 5. rather; very (interesting, tired, etc.) 6. to blame

guàibude 怪不得 1. No wonder! 2. cannot put the blame on

guàijié 怪傑 an extraordinary person

guàili guàiqì 怪裡怪氣 strange; queer; eccentric

guàimú guàiyàng 怪模怪樣 queer appearance and manner

guàipǐ 怪癖 strange hobbies; eccentricities

guàipì 怪僻 peculiar; eccentric; queer

guàirén 怪人 a peculiar person

guàishì 怪事 strange happenings or things

guàishǒu 怪手 an excavator

guàishòu 怪獸 a rare animal; a monster

guàitán 怪談 weird talks

guàiwu 怪物 1. a monster; a strange creature 2. an eccentric fellow

guàiyì 怪異 eerie; weird

guān 官

1. a government official 2. of, or having to do with, the government or the state 3. (biology) an organ 4. a Chinese family name

guānbàn 官辦 run or operated by the government

guānbīng 官兵 officers and men

guānchāi 官差 1. official business 2. a government messenger

guānchǎng 官場 officialdom

guāndǐ 官邸 an official residence

guānfāng 官方 the government (as opposed to private citizens); official (information, sources, etc.)

guānfèng 官俸 the salary drawn from the government

guānfǔ 官府 1. the local authorities 2. a feudal official

guānjiàzi 官架子 the airs of an official; bureaucratic airs

guānjiē 官階 the rank

guānlì 官吏 a government official

guānliáo 官僚 bureaucrats

guānliáo zhèngzhì 官僚政治 officialism; bureaucracy

guānpài 官派 to be appointed by the government

guānqiāng 官腔 a bureaucratic tone; official jargon

guānshì 官事 1. public affairs 2. a lawsuit

guānshǔ 官署 a government agency

guānsi 官司 a lawsuit

guānxián 官銜 the formal title (of a government official)

guānyìn 官印 an official seal of a government agency

guānyuán 官員 an official

guānyùn 官運 a person's opportunity of official promotion

guānyùn hēngtōng 官運亨通 to have a successful official career

guānzhí 官職 a government post or position

guānzhì 官制 the system of civil service

guān 冠

1. a cap 2. the comb or crest of a bird

guān'gài yúnjí 冠蓋雲集 (usually said of a meeting or gathering) where ranking officials congregate

guānmiǎn tánghuáng 冠冕堂皇 1. elegant and stately 2. high-sounding

G

guān 倌

1. a boy or an assistant in the employ of a teahouse, tavern or restaurant 2. a euphemism for a prostitute 3. the groom

guān 棺

a coffin (usually made of wood in China)

guāncai 棺材 a coffin

guānguǒ 棺槨 inner and outer coffins in ancient times

guānliàn 棺殮 1. coffin and graveclothes 2. to put a shrouded corpse into a coffin

guānmù 棺木 a coffin

guān 關

1. to shut; to close 2. a frontier pass or checkpoint 3. the bar across the door 4. a customs house; a customs barrier 5. a key point; a turning point 6. related; relationship; to involve; to concern 7. to negotiate; to go between 8. to draw (money, or pay) 9. a Chinese family name

guān'ài 關愛 to express solicitude for the well-being of someone

guānbì 關閉 1. to close 2. to close down; to shut down (a store, etc.)

Guāndǎo 關島 Guam

guānfáng 關防 1. the seal of a government agency 2. a military position at a strategic point on the border

guānhuái 關懷 to be concerned about; to show concern; concern

guānjiàn 關鍵 a key (to a problem); an important turning point

guānjié 關節 1. joints in the human body 2. to bribe; a bribe 3. illegal transactions between the examiner and the examinee 4. key links; crucial links

guānjìnbì 關禁閉 (military) to be put in a dark cell as a form of punishment

guānkǎ 關卡 refer to **guānqiǎ** 關卡

guānlián 關聯 related; involved; connection

guānmén 關門 1. to close the door 2. to close a shop 3. to close its door—to go bankrupt

guānmén dàjí 關門大吉 to close down for good

guānqiǎ 關卡 a customs station or barrier

guānqiè 關切 to concern; a concern

guānshuì 關稅 customs duty

guānshuō 關說 to lobby illegally, usually by pedaling one's influence

guānxi 關係 1. relation; connection; ties 2. to matter

guānxīn 關心 to be concerned about; to show concern; concern

guānyú 關於 concerning; with regard to

guānzhào 關照 1. to notify; to inform 2. to take care of; to look after

guān 鰥

1. a kind of huge predatory fish 2. a widower 3. a bachelor

guānfū 鰥夫 1. a widower 2. a bachelor

guānguǎ gūdú 鰥寡孤獨 those who have no wives, husbands, parents or children

guān 觀

1. to see; to observe; to behold; to view; to take a view of; to look; to inspect 2. sights; views 3. to display 4. a point of view; a conception

guāncè 觀測 to observe and survey

guānchá 觀察 to observe; to watch; to inspect

guāndiǎn 觀點 a point of view; one's view on a certain matter

guān'gǎn 觀感 one's feelings or emotional reactions after seeing or reading something

guānguāng 觀光 sightseeing; to see the sights

guānguāngkè 觀光客 a tourist

guānguāng shìyè 觀光事業 tourism; the tourist industry

guānguāngtuán 觀光團 a tour group; a tourist group

guānhùsuǒ 觀護所 a probation

G

office

guānkàn 觀看 to look at; to see

guānlǐ 觀禮 to attend a ceremony

guānmó 觀摩 to emulate the good points of others; to compare notes

guānniàn 觀念 a conception; an idea; a view

guānshǎng 觀賞 to see and enjoy

Guānshìyīn 觀世音 the Goddess of Mercy

guānwàng 觀望 a wait-and-see attitude; to wait and see; to hesitate

Guānyīn 觀音 the Goddess of Mercy

guānzhān 觀瞻 1. the appearance or outward look of something 2. to look at; to see; to view

guānzhàn 觀戰 to witness a battle; to observe a military operation

guānzhòng 觀衆 the audience or spectators

guǎn 管

1. a tube; a pipe; a duct 2. a wind instrument 3. to control; to manage; to take care of; to keep 4. to heed; to pay attention to 5. to provide 6. to guarantee 7. to meddle in; to interfere in; to bother about 8. a key 9. a Chinese family name

guǎndào 管道 1. a pipeline; a conduit 2. a channel (for communication, etc.)

guǎnjiā 管家 to housekeep

guǎnjiāpó 管家婆 1. a housekeeper 2. a nagging woman

guǎnjia 管家 a housekeeper

guǎnjiào 管教 to direct and teach (children, students, etc.)

guǎnkuī lícè 管窺蠡測 restricted in vision and shallow in understanding

guǎnlǐ 管理 to manage; to administer; to handle; to take care of

guǎnlǐyuán 管理員 a keeper; an administrator; a custodian; a

janitor

guǎnshù 管束 to control; to restrain

guǎnxiá 管轄 to have jurisdiction over

guǎnxiányuè 管弦樂 orchestral music

guǎnyòng 管用 useful; effective; to work

guǎnyuèduì 管樂隊 a wind band

guǎnyuèqì 管樂器 wind instruments; the wind

guǎnzhì 管制 to control; control

guǎn 館(舘)

1. a house; a guesthouse; a hotel 2. to stay or lodge 3. an official residence 4. an embassy; a legation; a consulate 5. a place for cultural activities 6. premises 7. a school (in former times) 8. a suffix for a library, teahouse, restaurant, etc.

guǎnzhǎng 館長 a superintendent; a curator; the head of a library or an institute, etc.

guǎnzi 館子 1. a restaurant 2. a theater

guàn 冠

1. at 20 when a young man is capped 2. first-rate 3. to wear a cap

guàncí 冠詞 the article

guànjūn 冠軍 a champion

guànlǐ 冠禮 (in ancient China) a capping ceremony for a young man when he reaches 20

guàn 貫

1. a thread for stringing holed copper coins; to string on a thread 2. a string of 1,000 holed copper coins 3. to see through; throughout; to pass through; to pierce through; thorough 4. to be linked together; to follow in a continuous line 5. to hit the target 6. one's native place

guànchè shǐzhōng 貫徹始終 to remain consistent from the start to the very end

guànchuān 貫穿 1. to run through 2. to penetrate or pierce through 3. to understand thor-

G

oughly

guàntōng 貫通 1. to have a thorough understanding 2. to link up

guàn 慣
1. habitual; customary; usual; accustomed 2. to spoil (a child) 3. to be accustomed to; to be used to

guàncháng 慣常 customary; usual

guànhuài 慣壞 to spoil (a child)

guànlì 慣例 custom; usual (or establish) practice

guànqiè 慣竊 a habitual thief; an incorrigible thief

guànyòng 慣用 commonly used

guànyòng jìliǎng 慣用伎倆 customary tactics; old tricks

guànyú 慣於 accustomed to; to be used to

guàn 盥
1. to wash one's hands 2. to wash

guànxǐ 盥洗 to wash oneself

guànxǐshì 盥洗室 a washroom; a restroom; a lavatory

guàn 灌
1. to water; to fill; to pour (on, into, at); to irrigate 2. to offer a libation 3. shrubs; bushy clumps

guàncháng 灌腸 to give an enema or clyster

guànchàngpiàn 灌唱片 to cut a record

guàn'gài 灌溉 to irrigate; irrigation

guànjiù 灌救 to save life by forcing medicine down the throat of a dying person

guànmǐtāng 灌米湯 to flatter

guànmù 灌木 shrubs

guànshū 灌輸 to instill; to teach; to impart (knowledge to someone); to inculcate

guànshuǐ 灌水 to pour water into something

guànzhù 灌注 1. to pour into 2. to teach 3. to concentrate (attention) on

guànzuì 灌醉 to force someone

to drink until he is drunk

guàn 罐
a vessel; a container; a jar; a jug; a can

guàntou 罐頭 canned goods

guāng 光
1. light; brightness; light rays 2. glossy; smooth 3. glory; glorious; honor 4. to exhaust; to use up 5. alone; only 6. bare; naked; to bare

guāngbiāo 光標 (computer) cursor

guāngbō 光波 light waves

guāngcǎi 光彩 1. luster; splendor; radiance 2. honorable; glorious

guāngcǎi duómù 光彩奪目 the luster that dazzles the eyes

guāngdǎo xiānwéi 光導纖維 optical fiber

guāngdié 光碟 a compact disc

guāngdiéjī 光碟機 an optical disc player

guāngfù 光復 to recover (a lost land)

guānggù 光顧 to patronize; to honor with one's presence

guāngguài lùlí 光怪陸離 strange-looking; fantastic; grotesque

guānggùnr 光棍兒 a bachelor or unmarried man

guānghé zuòyòng 光合作用 photosynthesis

guānghuá 光滑 smooth and glossy

guānghuī 光輝 radiance; brightness

guāngjiǎo 光腳 bare feet; barefooted

guāngjǐng 光景 1. a situation 2. around; about

guāngliàng 光亮 brightness; radiant; light; shiny

guānglín 光臨 Please grace our place with your presence

guāngliūliū 光溜溜 1. smooth and glossy 2. bare; naked

guāngmáng 光芒 rays of light; brilliant rays

G

guāngmáng wànzhàng 光芒萬丈 radiance; radiant

guāngmíng 光明 1. light 2. bright; promising 3. open-hearted; guileless

guāngmíng lěiluò 光明磊落 straightforward and upright

guāngmíng zhèngdà 光明正大 honest, just, and upright

guāngnián 光年 a light-year

guāngpán 光盤 a compact disc

guāngquān 光圈 the diaphragm of a camera

guāngróng 光榮 glory; honor; glorious

guāngshēnzi 光身子 naked

guāngtiān huàrì 光天化日 (in) broad daylight; the light of day

guāngtóu 光頭 a baldhead; bald-headed

guāngtūtū 光禿禿 bare; bald

guāngxiān tōngxùn 光纖通訊 optical fiber communication

guāngxiàn 光線 a ray of light

guāngxué 光學 optics

guāngxué yíqì 光學儀器 optical instruments

guāngyīn 光陰 time

guāngyīn sìjiàn 光陰似箭 Time passes as fast as a flying arrow.

guāngzé 光澤 luster

guāngzōng yàozǔ 光宗耀祖 to glorify one's forebears

guāng 胱
the bladder

guǎng 廣
1. wide; broad; spacious 2. to extend 3. Guangdong or Guangxi

guǎngbō 廣播 1. to broadcast; to telecast 2. a broadcast

guǎngbō diàntái 廣播電臺 a broadcasting station; a radio station

guǎngbō jiémù 廣播節目 1. a radio program; a broadcast 2. a television program; a telecast

guǎngbōjù 廣播劇 a radio drama; a radio play

guǎngbōyuán 廣播員 a broad-caster; a radio announcer

guǎngbó 廣博 wide; extensive

guǎngchǎng 廣場 a square (in a city); a plaza

guǎngdà 廣大 vast

guǎngdà wúbiān 廣大無邊 boundless

Guǎngdōng 廣東 Guangdong Province

guǎng'ér yánzhī 廣而言之 generally speaking

guǎngfàn 廣泛 extensive; wide-spread

guǎnggào 廣告 advertisement

guǎnggào gōngsī 廣告公司 an advertising agency

guǎnggào kèhù 廣告客戶 an advertiser

guǎnggàolán 廣告欄 the ad column

guǎnggàopiàn 廣告片 an advertising film

guǎnggàoyè 廣告業 advertising

guǎngjiāo 廣交 to make friends extensively

guǎngjié shànyuán 廣結善緣 to make friends all around

guǎngkāi cáilù 廣開才路 to open all avenues for people of talent

guǎngkāi yánlù 廣開言路 to encourage freedom of speech

guǎngkuò 廣闊 wide; extensive; vast; spacious

guǎngmò 廣漠 boundless; vast

guǎngpī 廣被 far-reaching (love or benefit)

guǎngtǔ zhòngmín 廣土眾民 (said of a country) having a large territory and a large population

Guǎngxī 廣西 Guangxi Province

guǎngyì 廣義 the broad definition

Guǎngzhōu 廣州 a city in Guangdong

guàng 逛
to stroll; to roam; to ramble; to wander about

guàngjiē 逛街 to stroll down the street; to go window-shopping

guī 圭
a jade tablet with a square base and a pointed top used in official ceremonies in ancient China

guīniè 圭臬 1. ancient timepieces 2. a principle for one to look up to

guī 皈
to follow

guīyī 皈依 to be converted to (Buddhism)

guī 硅
silicon (si)

Guīgǔ 硅谷 Silicium Valley

guī 規
1. regulations; laws; rules; customs or usages 2. a pair of compasses 3. to plan; to scheme 4. to advise so as to correct

guībì 規避 to evade; to shun or avoid

guīdìng 規定 1. to rule; to specify; to stipulate; to regulate 2. rules or regulations

guīfàn 規範 a norm; a standard

guīgé 規格 specifications

guīhuà 規畫 1. to map out or draw up (a plan) 2. a plan or scheme

guījiàn 規諫 to advise or admonish

guījiè 規誡 to admonish

guīju 規矩 1. rules; practices 2. well-behaved; well-disciplined 3. the compass and square

guīlǜ 規律 1. laws, rules or regulations; discipline 2. regular; regularity

guīmó 規模 1. patterns; formulas 2. scale; magnitude; scope; extent

guīquàn 規勸 to admonish; to give friendly advice

guīzé 規則 1. a rule or regulation 2. regular; fixed; inflexible

guī 傀
great; wonderful

guīwěi 傀偉 great and imposing

guī 閨
1. a small door 2. the women's apartment 3. feminine

guīfáng 閨房 a boudoir

guīnǚ 閨女 a maiden; an unmarried girl

guīxiù 閨秀 a well-educated girl brought up in a good family

guī 瑰
1. fabulous; great; extraordinary 2. a stone which is a little less valuable than jade; a kind of jasper

guībǎo 瑰寶 a treasure; a gem

guīlì 瑰麗 fabulously beautiful

guīwěi 瑰瑋 rare and precious; treasurable

guī 龜
a tortoise; a turtle

guījiǎ 龜甲 tortoiseshell

guīshì 龜筮 divination

guīzhào 龜兆 1. marks on seared tortoiseshell used for divination in ancient times 2. omens

guī 鮭
a salmon

guī 歸
1. to come back; to return 2. to return (something to its owner) 3. (said of a woman) to marry 4. to pledge allegiance to 5. to belong; to attribute 6. to turn over to; to put in somebody's charge 7. a Chinese family name

guī'àn 歸案 to arrest a criminal and bring him to court for prosecution

guībìng 歸併 to merge into; to unite with; to put together

guīchéng 歸程 the homeward journey

guīdǎng 歸檔 refer to **guīdàng** 歸檔

guīdàng 歸檔 to return (a document, materials, etc.) back to file; to file away

guīduì 歸隊 to return to the ranks

guīfù 歸附 to pledge allegiance to

guīgēn jiédǐ 歸根結底 fundamentally; basically

G

guīgōngyú 歸功於 to attribute the success to

guīhuà 歸化 1. to be naturalized as a citizen 2. (said of a protectorate state, etc.) to pledge allegiance to

guīhuán 歸還 to return (something to its owner)

guījié 歸結 to sum up

guījiù 歸咎 to lay the blame on...; to impute

guīlèi 歸類 to categorize; to classify

guīnà 歸納 to induct (a theory, natural law, etc.); to sum up

guīníng 歸寧 (said of a woman) to visit her parents after marriage

guīqī 歸期 the date of one's return

guīqí 歸期 refer to **guīqī** 歸期

guīqiáo 歸僑 returned overseas Chinese

guīrù 歸入 to classify; to include

guīshǔ 歸屬 1. ownership 2. to belong

guīshùn 歸順 to yield; to submit; to surrender

guīsù 歸宿 1. a home to return to 2. (said of a woman) marriage 3. conclusions

guītiān 歸天 to pass away

guītú 歸途 on the way home

guīxī 歸西 to pass away

guīxiàng 歸向 1. the direction of movement 2. to turn toward; to incline to

guīxīn sìjiàn 歸心似箭 to be anxious or eager to return home

guīyǐn 歸隱 to retire; retirement

guīyú 歸於 to belong to; to be attributed to

guīzàng 歸葬 to bring back one's remains home for burial

guīzuì 歸罪 to lay the blame on another

guī 環

1. (瑰) a kind of jasper 2. extraordinary; fabulous or admirable

guībǎo 瑰寶 an extraordinary treasure

guǐ 軌

1. the space between the right and the left wheels of a vehicle 2. a rut; a track; a path 3. an orbit 4. a rule; a regulation 5. to follow; to obey

guǐdào 軌道 1. a railway track 2. an orbit 3. laws and conventions 4. a course; a track

guǐjī 軌跡 1. (mathematics) a locus 2. (astronomy) an orbit 3. a track

guǐ 癸

the last of the Ten Celestial Stems

guǐ 鬼

1. spirits; ghosts; demons; devils 2. cunning; crafty; wily; deceitful 3. sinister; evil; a dirty trick, work, etc.

guǐcái 鬼才 a genius in an unorthodox way

guǐdiǎnzi 鬼點子 wicked ideas; tricks

guǐfǔ shéngōng 鬼斧神工 prodigious workmanship

guǐguài 鬼怪 monsters; goblins; bogies

guǐguǐsuìsuì 鬼鬼祟祟 stealthy; sneaky; furtive

guǐhuà 鬼話 false words; lies; nonsense

guǐhuàfú 鬼畫符 1. a very poor work of calligraphy 2. a hypocritical talk

guǐhuà liánpiān 鬼話連篇 to tell a whole series of lies

guǐhún 鬼魂 ghosts; spirits of the dead

guǐhùn 鬼混 to spend days in an idle, slovenly way

guǐhuǒ 鬼火 a jack-o'-lantern; a will-o'-the-wisp

guǐkǔ shénháo 鬼哭神號 to give dreary cries and screams

guǐliǎn 鬼臉 a grimace

guǐmèi 鬼魅 monsters; goblins; bogies

guǐménguān 鬼門關 the gate to the land of ghosts; the gate of hell

guǐmí xīnqiào 鬼迷心竅 to be

possessed

guǐshén 鬼神 ghosts and deities; spirits and gods; spiritual beings

guǐshǐ shénchāi 鬼使神差 to do something inexplicably as if manipulated by supernatural beings

guǐtāi 鬼胎 an evil plot; a dark scheme

guǐzhǔyi 鬼主意 a crafty idea; a dark scheme

guǐ 詭

1. to cheat; to deceive; to feign; to defraud 2. strange; rare; odd; peculiar; uncanny; weird 3. cunning; shrewd; stealthy 4. to urge oneself 5. to go against; to defy; to contradict

guǐjì 詭計 a trick; an artful device or trap

guǐji duōduān 詭計多端 very tricky or crafty

guǐyì 詭異 strange; odd; abnormal; weird

guì 桂

1. a short name of Guangxi Province 2. cassia or cinnamon 3. a Chinese family name

guìguān shīrén 桂冠詩人 a poet laureate, or a laureate

guìhuā 桂花 sweet osmanthus

Guìlín 桂林 capital of Guangxi Province

guìyuán 桂圓 1. a longan 2. dried longan

guì 貴

1. high-placed; high-ranking; honorable; distinguished 2. expensive; costly; high-priced 3. to esteem; to treat with respect 4. to treasure; to value highly; to prize 5. valuable; precious 6. a polite expression referring to another person—you or your 7. a Chinese family name 8. short for Guizhou Province

guìbīn 貴賓 distinguished guests

guìbīnshì 貴賓室 a VIP room; a VIP lounge

guìfù 貴婦 a noblewoman

guìgàn 貴幹 What can I do for you? May I help you?

guìgēng 貴庚 How old are you?

guìguó 貴國 your country

guìkè 貴客 the guest of honor

guìrén 貴人 a distinguished, high-ranking person

guìxìng 貴姓 May I know your distinguished name?

guìzhòng 貴重 precious; expensive; rare; valuable; highly treasured

Guìzhōu 貴州 Guizhou Province

guìzú 貴族 the nobility; an aristocrat

guì 跪

to kneel

guìbài 跪拜 to kowtow

guìdǎo 跪倒 to go on one's knees; to kneel down; to prostrate oneself; to grovel

guìxia 跪下 to kneel down

guìxiè 跪謝 to express thanks on one's knees

guì 會

Guìjì 會稽 Zhejiang Province

guì 創 also kuài

to amputate; to cut off

guìzishǒu 創子手 1. an executioner 2. a hatchet man

guì 檜 also kuài

the Chinese juniper or cypress

guìmù 檜木 timber of a Chinese cypress or juniper

guì 櫃

1. a cabinet; a wardrobe; a cupboard 2. a shop counter

guìtái 櫃檯 the counter in a store

gǔn 滚

1. to turn round and round; to roll; to rotate 2. boiling

gǔnbiān 滚邊 1. an embroidered hem 2. to stitch a hem around a border

gǔnchuqu 滚出去 1. to roll out 2. Get out!

gǔndàn 滚蛋 Get out! Go to hell! Beat it!

gǔndìqiú 滚地球　(baseball)

G

ground ball

gǔndòng 滾動 to roll; to trundle

gǔnguā lànshú 滾瓜爛熟 to recite or to learn very thoroughly

gǔngǔn 滾滾 (said of flowing waters) rolling; torrential; billowing

gǔngǔn érlái 滾滾而來 to come in torrents

gǔnrè 滾熱 piping hot

gǔnshí bùshēng tái 滾石不生苔 A rolling stone gathers no moss.

gǔnshuǐ 滾水 boiling water

gǔntàng 滾燙 boiling; steaming hot

gǔntī 滾梯 an escalator

gùn 棍
　　1. a club; a stick; a cudgel; a truncheon 2. a rascal; a villain; a ruffian

gùnbàng 棍棒 a club; a stick

gùnzi 棍子 a club; a stick

guō 郭
　　1. a town 2. the outer wall of a city 3. the outer part of anything 4. a Chinese family name

guō 聒 also **guā**
　　noisy

guōzào 聒噪 to be uproarious; to be noisy

Guō 渦
　　name of a river

guō 鍋
　　a cooking pot; a pan; a boiler; a caldron

guōbā 鍋巴 burnt rice that sticks to the bottom and sides of the cooking pot

guōgài 鍋蓋 the cover of a cooking pot; a pot cover

guōlú 鍋爐 a boiler (especially of a steam engine)

guōtiēr 鍋貼兒 lightly fried dumpling

guó 國
　　1. a country; a nation; a kingdom; a state 2. national; govern-

mental 3. Chinese

guóbǎo 國寶 a national treasure

guóbīn 國賓 a government guest

guóbù jiānnán 國步艱難 The nation is beset by difficulties.

guócè 國策 national policies

guóchǎn 國產 (said of products) native or locally manufactured

guócuì 國粹 unique cultural features of a nation; national legacies

guódìng jìniànrì 國定紀念日 a national commemoration or memorial day

guódìng jiàrì 國定假日 a national holiday

guódū 國都 the national capital; the capital

guófáng 國防 national defense

guófù 國父 1. the father of a nation 2. Father of the Republic of China—Sun Zhongshan (Dr. Sun Yat-sen)

guógē 國歌 a national anthem

guóhào 國號 1. the name of a dynasty 2. the official name of a nation

guóhuā 國花 the national flower

guóhuà 國畫 a Chinese painting

guóhuī 國徽 the national emblem

guóhuì 國會 parliament, congress, the diet, etc.

guóhuò 國貨 native goods

guójí 國籍 nationality

guójì 國際 international

Guójì Àolínpǐkè Wěiyuánhuì 國際奧林匹克委員會 International Olympic Committee (IOC)

guójì dìwèi 國際地位 international status

guójì diànhuà 國際電話 the overseas telephone

guójì guānxi 國際關係 international relations

guójìhuà 國際化 internationalization

Guójì Huànrìxiàn 國際換日線 International Date Line

guójì màoyì 國際貿易 interna-

G

tional trade; foreign trade

Guójì Yīnbiāo 國際音標 the International Phonetic Alphabet (IPA)

guójiā 國家 a nation; a country

guójiā gōngyuán 國家公園 a national park

guójiā jīmì 國家機密 state secrets

guójiè 國界 border; national boundary

guójìng 國境 border; national boundary

guójù 國劇 Beijing (Peking) opera

guójūn 國君 a sovereign; a monarch

guókù 國庫 the national exchequer

guólì 國力 national power (usually connoting resources and potentialities)

guólì 國立 (said of an institution) nationally supported or operated; national

guólì 國曆 the national (i.e., solar) calendar

guómín 國民 a citizen; the people

guómín píngjūn suǒdé 國民平均所得 per capita income

guómín shēnfenzhèng 國民身分證 an ID card

guómín suǒdé 國民所得 national income

guómín wàijiāo 國民外交 people-to-people diplomacy

guómín xuéxiào 國民學校 a primary school; an elementary school

guómín zhōngxué 國民中學 a junior high school

guónàn 國難 national crises (or calamities)

guónèi 國內 domestic or internal

guópò jiāwáng 國破家亡 The country is defeated and the home is lost.

guóqí 國旗 the national flag

guóqíng 國情 the condition of a country

Guóqìngrì 國慶日 the National Day (of a country)

guósāng 國喪 national mourning

guósè tiānxiāng 國色天香 the beauty of a woman or peony

guóshì 國勢 1. national strength 2. the condition of a country

guóshǒu 國手 (said of athletes, etc.) national representatives, who are the national champions in any lines of activities, especially of sports and games

guóshū 國書 1. credentials (of a diplomat) 2. documents exchanged between nations

guóshù 國術 Chinese martial arts

guótài mín'ān 國泰民安 The country is prosperous and at peace, and the people live in happiness.

guótǔ 國土 territory of a nation

guówài 國外 outside the country; abroad

guówáng 國王 a king; a monarch

guówén 國文 1. the written national language 2. national language and literature 3. Chinese literature (a course in Chinese schools)

guówù huìyì 國務會議 state conference

Guówùqīng 國務卿 Secretary of State (of the U.S. Federal Government)

Guówùyuàn 國務院 1. the Department of State (of the U.S. Federal Government) 2. the Cabinet (of the early Chinese Republican Government) 3. State Council (in mainland China)

guówù zǒnglǐ 國務總理 the premier (of the early Chinese Republican Government)

guóyàn 國宴 state banquet

guóyíng shìyè 國營事業 a state-owned enterprise

guóyǒu 國有 state-owned

guóyǔ 國語 the national language

guóyuè 國樂 Chinese music

guóyùn 國運 the destiny of the nation

guózì 國字 Chinese characters

guó 摑

refer to **guāi** 摑

guǒ 果

1. the fruit of a plant 2. effect (in cause and effect); result; a consequence 3. surely; really; exactly 4. to stuff; to fill 5. to succeed

guǒduàn 果斷 (said of a person) resolute

guǒfù 果腹 to fill one's stomach (usually with poor food); to feed on

guǒgǎn 果敢 having the determination and courage to do something

guǒhé 果核 a kernel; a fruit stone; a pit

guǒjiàng 果醬 jam; marmalade

guǒjué 果決 daring and determined

guǒlǐng 果嶺 (golf) green

guǒpí 果皮 peel; peelings

guǒrán 果然 exactly as one expected

guǒrénr 果仁兒 a kernel

guǒròu 果肉 pulp

guǒshí 果實 fruit

guǒshù 果樹 fruit trees

gāosuān 果酸 tartaric acid

guǒtáng 果糖 fructose, or fruit sugar; levulose

guǒyuán 果園 an orchard

guǒzhēn 果真 really; if really

guǒzhī 果汁 fruit juice

guǒzhījī 果汁機 1. a juicer 2. a blender

guǒ 裹

1. to tie up; to wrap or bind 2. things wrapped, as a parcel 3. to surround; to encompass 4. to close in and force obedience

guǒjiǎo 裹腳 foot-binding

guǒtuǐ 裹腿 leggings; puttees

guǒzú bùqián 裹足不前 to be afraid to move ahead

guò 過

1. to pass; to pass through or by;

to ford 2. across; past; through; over 3. to spend or pass (time) 4. after; past 5. to go beyond the ordinary or proper limits; to surpass 6. too much; excessive 7. a mistake; a demerit 8. a particle indicating the past perfect tense 9. contagious 10. to visit 11. to transfer 12. to die; death 13. to arrive; to get to

guòbàn 過半 more than half

guòbàng 過磅 to weigh

guòbuqù 過不去 1. unable to get through 2. to feel sorry for 3. intentionally to make it difficult for somebody

guòchéng 過程 (in) the process; (in) the course (of)

guòcuò 過錯 mistakes; faults

guòdequ 過得去 1. not too bad; so-so; fair 2. not to embarrass another 3. to be at peace with oneself 4. passable; able to get through

guòdōng 過冬 to pass the winter; to winter

guòdù 過度 1. to go beyond the normal limits; to overdo 2. excessive

guòdù shíqī 過渡時期 a period or stage of transition; a transitional stage or period

guòdù shíqí 過渡時期 refer to **guòdù shíqī** 過渡時期

guòduō 過多 too many or much; excessive

guòfèn 過分 to go beyond the normal or proper limits; to overdo

guòguān 過關 1. to go through a checkpoint 2. to pass a critical test 3. to come up to the standard

guòhé chāiqiáo 過河拆橋 (literally) to destroy the bridge after one has crossed the river —very ungrateful

guòhù 過戶 to transfer the ownership (of bonds, stocks, or property) from one person to another

guòhuó 過活 to make a living

guòhuǒ 過火 to go beyond the proper limits; to overdo; to go too far

guòjì 過繼 1. (said of an heirless

guòjiāng zhījì 過江之鯽 as numerous as a large school of fish migrating in a river

guòjiǎng 過獎 1. to overpraise; to flatter 2. (a polite expression) I don't deserve your praise.

guòjiēqiáo 過街橋 an overhead bridge

guòjié 過節 1. to pass (or celebrate) a festival 2. a grudge

guòjìng 過境 to pass through; in transit

guòkè 過客 a traveler; a passer-by

guòláirén 過來人 a person who has had the experience of something in question

guòlai 過來 Come here.

guòliàng 過量 an overdose; to go beyond the limits

guòlù 過路 to pass by; in transit

guòlǜ 過濾 to filter; to filtrate

guòmén 過門 to get married

guòmén bùrù 過門不入 to act beyond the call of duty

guòmǐn 過敏 allergy

guòmù 過目 to take a look; to go over

guònián 過年 to pass the New Year

guònián 過年 next year

guòqī 過期 to have passed the deadline; (said of permits, etc.) to have passed the date of expiration; overdue

guòqī 過期 refer to **guòqī** 過期

guòqù 過去 1. in the past; formerly; once 2. to die; to pass away

guòqu 過去 1. to go over 2. to pass; to pass by

guòrén 過人 to supass others

guòrìzi 過日子 1. to practice economy 2. to live

guòshēngri 過生日 to celebrate a birthday

guòshèng 過剩 a surplus

guòshī 過失 errors committed

unintentionally; faults

guòshí bùhòu 過時不候 The deadline (appointed time, or specified date) will not be extended.

guòshì 過世 to pass away; to die; dead

guòtóu 過頭 to go beyond the norm or the set goal; to overdo

guòwǎng 過往 1. comings and goings 2. social contacts

guòwèn 過問 1. to make inquiry about; to ask about 2. to interfere with 3. to care

guòyǎn yānyún 過眼煙雲 (literally) ephemeral

guòyè 過夜 1. to pass the night; to overnight 2. to spend a whole night with a prostitute (as distinct from "short-time quickies")

guòyì bùqù 過意不去 1. very much obliged; unable to express one's thanks adequately 2. to feel sorry

guòyǐn 過癮 1. to do something to one's heart's content 2. to satisfy the urge of an addiction

guòyóu bùjí 過猶不及 Too much is as bad as not enough.

hā 哈

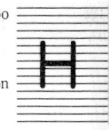

1. a form used in transliteration 2. a sound of hearty laughter

Hā'ěrbīn 哈爾濱 Harbin

Hāfó Dàxué 哈佛大學 Harvard University

hāhā dàxiào 哈哈大笑 to laugh heartily

Hāléi Huìxīng 哈雷彗星 Halley's Comet

hāmìguā 哈密瓜 a honey dew melon

hāqian 哈欠 a yawn

há 蛤

a toad

háma 蛤蟆 a toad

hǎ 哈

hǎbagǒu 哈巴狗 1. a Pekingese or Pekinese (dog) 2. toady; sycophant

hāi 咳 also **hài**

hāi 咳
an interjection of regret or remorse

hái 孩
1. a child; an infant; a baby 2. young; small

háití 孩提 an infant; childhood

háitóng 孩童 a child

háizi 孩子 a child

háiziqì 孩子氣 childish; childishness

hái 骸
1. the shinbone 2. a skeleton

hái 還
1. yet; still 2. passably; fairly; quite 3. also 4. even 5. at the same time 6. or 7. had better

háihǎo 還好 1. passable; so-so; not bad 2. fortunately

háishì 還是 1. still; nevertheless 2. again 3. had better 4. or (showing doubt)

háiyǒu 還有 1. There are still some left. 2. furthermore; in addition

háizài 還在 1. still here 2. still (working, gambling, etc.)

háizǎo 還早 still early

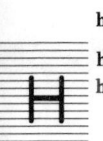

hǎi 海
1. the sea; the ocean 2. a great number of people, etc. coming together—(figuratively) a huge gathering 3. an area; a field 4. great; unlimited

hǎi'àn 海岸 the coast; the seaside; the seashore

hǎi'ànxiàn 海岸線 the coastal line

hǎibá 海拔 the elevation or height above sea level

hǎibào 海豹 a seal

hǎibào 海報 a poster

hǎibiān 海邊 the seashore; the seaside; the beach

hǎibīn 海濱 the seashore; the beach

hǎichǎn 海產 marine products; seafood

hǎicháo 海潮 ocean tides

hǎidài 海帶 kelp; a sea tangle

hǎidǎn 海膽 a sea urchin

hǎidǎo 海島 an island (in the sea)

hǎidào 海盜 a pirate; a sea rover

hǎidī 海堤 a sea embankment

hǎidǐ 海底 the bed or bottom of the sea

hǎidǐ lāoyuè 海底撈月 to strive in vain

hǎidǐ lāozhēn 海底撈針 to make a futile search

hǎidiào 海釣 offshore angling

hǎifáng 海防 coastal defense

hǎifáng bùduì 海防部隊 coastal defense forces

hǎifēng 海風 a sea wind; a sea breeze

hǎigǎng 海港 a seaport; a harbor

hǎigǒu 海狗 a fur seal; an ursine seal

hǎiguān 海關 the customs; a custom house

hǎiguān rényuán 海關人員 customs officers

hǎiguī 海龜 a green turtle

hǎihán 海涵 broad-mindedness; forgiveness

hǎijiǎ 海岬 a cape

hǎijiǎo tiānyá 海角天涯 the farthest end of the earth

hǎijǐng 海景 the seascape

hǎijūn 海軍 the navy; naval

hǎijūn guānxiào 海軍官校 a naval academy

hǎijūn lùzhànduì 海軍陸戰隊 the marine corps

hǎijūn shàngjiàng 海軍上將 an admiral

hǎijūn zǒngsīlìng 海軍總司令 the commander in chief of the navy; (in the U.S.) the chief of naval operations

hǎikǒu 海口 1. a seaport 2. bragging

hǎikū shílàn 海枯石爛 (I will remain faithful to you) even if the sea dries and stones roll

hǎikuò tiānkōng 海闊天空 endlessly vast; boundless

hǎilàng 海浪 seas; sea waves

hǎilí 海狸 a sea otter; a beaver

hǎilǐ 海里 nautical mile, a unit of distance

hǎiliàng 海量 1. magnanimous 2. great capacity for alcoholic drinks

hǎiliú 海流 the ocean current

hǎilù 海路 a sea route; a seaway

hǎilún 海輪 a seagoing (or oceangoing) ship

hǎiluó 海螺 a sea univalve; a conch

hǎiluòyīn 海洛因 heroin

hǎimǎ 海馬 a hippocampus; a sea horse

hǎimán 海鰻 a conger pike; a sea eel

hǎimián 海綿 sponge

hǎimiándiàn 海綿墊 a foam-rubber cushion

hǎimiàn 海面 the sea surface

Hǎinándǎo 海南島 Hainan (an island off South China)

hǎinán 海難 a wreck

hǎinèi 海內 within the four seas; within the country

hǎiniǎo 海鳥 a seafowl; a sea-bird

hǎi'ōu 海鷗 a sea gull

hǎipánchē 海盤車 an asteroid; a starfish

hǎipíngmiàn 海平面 sea level

hǎipǔ xīnshēngdì 海埔新生地 the tidal land

hǎishàn 海扇 a scallop

hǎishēn 海參 a trepang; a sea cucumber; a sea slug

hǎishī 海獅 a sea lion

hǎishì shānméng 海誓山盟 to vow eternal love

hǎishì shènlóu 海市蜃樓 a mirage

hǎishuǐ wūrǎn 海水污染 sea-water pollution

hǎishuǐyù 海水浴 sea bathing

hǎitǎ 海獺 a sea otter; a beaver

hǎitǎ 海獺 refer to **hǎitǎ** 海獺

hǎitān 海灘 the seashore; the beach

hǎitáng 海塘 a sea embankment

hǎitāo 海濤 sea waves; billows

hǎití 海堤 refer to **hǎidī** 海堤

hǎitún 海豚 a dolphin

hǎiwài 海外 overseas; abroad

hǎiwài qiáobāo 海外僑胞 overseas Chinese

hǎiwān 海灣 a bay; a gulf

Hǎiwángxīng 海王星 the planet Neptune

hǎixiá 海峽 straits; a channel

hǎixiān 海鮮 fresh seafood; marine delicacies

hǎixiào 海嘯 a tsunami; a tidal wave

hǎixīng 海星 an asteroid; a starfish

Hǎiyá 海牙 The Hague

hǎiyàn 海燕 a petrel

hǎiyàn héqīng 海晏河清 time of peace and calm

hǎiyáng 海洋 seas and oceans; the ocean

hǎiyáng zīyuán 海洋資源 marine resources

hǎiyú 海隅 remote regions by the sea

hǎiyù 海域 a sea area; a marine area

hǎiyuán 海員 a sailor; a seaman; a mariner

hǎiyùn 海運 marine transportation

hǎizàng 海葬 burial at sea

hǎizǎo 海藻 seaweed

hǎizhé 海蜇 a sea blubber; a jellyfish

hài 亥 1. the last of the Twelve Terrestrial Branches 2. the hours between 9 and 11 p.m.

hài 咳 refer to **hāi** 咳

hài 害 1. to injure; to hurt; to damage; to destroy 2. to kill 3. damage; injury; harm; detriment 4. a vital point

hàibìng 害病 to get sick; to fall ill

hàichóng 害蟲 injurious or nox-

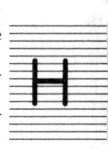

ious insects

hàichu 害處 shortcomings; harm disadvantages

hàipà 害怕 to be afraid of; to fear

hàiqún zhīmǎ 害群之馬 a black sheep; a public nuisance

hàirén 害人 to harm or injure others

hàirénjīng 害人精 a mischief-maker

hàisào 害臊 shy; bashful

hàixǐ 害喜 the sickness during the early pregnancy

hàixiū 害羞 shy; bashful

hài 駭

1. to terrify; to frighten; to startle; to scare; to amaze; to surprise 2. to marvel; to wonder

hàikè 駭客 a hacker

hàipà 駭怕 scared; frightened

hàirén tīngwén 駭人聽聞 (said of crimes, atrocities, etc.) frightening; bloodcurdling; shocking (news)

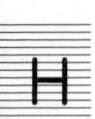

hān 酣

1. to enjoy intoxicants; to drink wine 2. to one's heart's content; as much as one wants; without inhibition

hānshuì 酣睡 to sleep soundly

hānyǐn 酣飲 to drink as much as one can; to drink like a fish

hānzuì 酣醉 deeply intoxicated by alcoholic beverages

hān 憨

1. silly; stupid; foolish 2. naive; straightforward

hānhou 憨厚 simple and honest

hānxiào 憨笑 to giggle; to titter; to smile foolishly

hānzhí 憨直 honest and straightforward

hān 鼾

to snore

hānshēng 鼾聲 sound of snoring

hānshēng rúléi 鼾聲如雷 to snore terribly

hānshuì 鼾睡 a heavy sleep with snoring

hán 汗

as in **kèhán** 可汗—a khan

hán 含

1. to hold in the mouth 2. to contain; to include 3. to bear

hánhèn 含恨 to cherish resentment, disappointment, etc.

hánhu 含糊 (said of a statement, manners, etc.) vague; ambiguous

hánhu qící 含糊其詞 to talk ambiguously

hánlèi 含淚 with tears in the eyes

hánliàng 含量 content

hánnù 含怒 in anger

hánqíng mòmò 含情脈脈 full of tenderness (in silent communication of affection or love, especially said of young girls)

hánxiào 含笑 to smile; to grin

hánxiào jiǔquán 含笑九泉 to die with satisfaction

hánxiě pēnrén 含血噴人 refer to **hánxuè pēnrén** 含血噴人

hánxīn rúkǔ 含辛茹苦 to undergo all sorts of hardships and deprivations

hánxiū 含羞 to blush

hánxiūcǎo 含羞草 sensitive plant

hánxù 含蓄 with concealed or implied deep meanings

hánxuè pēnrén 含血噴人 to bring false accusations against others

hányì 含義 a meaning; an implication

hányuān 含冤 to be the victim of an unjust charge

hányuān mòbái 含冤莫白 unable to clear oneself of a false accusation

hán 函

1. a letter; correspondence 2. armor 3. to contain; to envelop 4. a sheath, as for a sword 5. an envelope

hán'gòu 函購 to purchase by mail order

hánshòu 函授 teaching by mail or correspondence

hánshù 函數 (mathematics) function

hán 涵

1. wet, damp and marshy 2. to contain 3. lenient ·and broad-minded

hányǎng 涵養 1. capability to be kind, lenient, patient, or broad-minded under all circumstances 2. to cherish and nourish

hán 寒

1. cold; chilly; wintry 2. poor

háncāng 寒傖 refer to **hánchen** 寒傖

hánchen 寒傖 1. ugly; unsightly 2. shabby; disgraceful

hándài 寒帶 the Frigid Zone

hánfēng 寒風 a cold wind

hánfēng cìgǔ 寒風刺骨 The cold wind chilled one to the bone.

hánjià 寒假 the winter vacation

hánlěng 寒冷 cold; chilly; chilling

hánliú 寒流 1. a cold current; polar currents 2. a scholar of little means

hánmao 寒毛 downy hair (on human body)

hánqì 寒氣 chilly air; cold air

hánshè 寒舍 (a self-depreciatory term) my poor house

hánshǔbiǎo 寒暑表 a thermometer

hánsuān 寒酸 1. poverty 2. unpresentable (dress, gifts, etc.)

hánxīn 寒心 bitterly disappointed

hánxuān 寒暄 to talk about the weather (in a conversation)

hánzhàn 寒顫 to tremble with cold or fear

hán 韓

1. a fence 2. name of two feudal states in the late Zhou Dynasty 3. short for the Republic of Korea 4. a Chinese family name

Hánguó 韓國 Korea

hǎn 罕

rare; few; seldom

hǎnjiàn 罕見 rarely found; rare

hǎnshì 罕事 a rare thing or event

hǎn 喊

1. to shout; to scream; to cry; a loud call or cry; a shout or scream 2. to call

hǎnjiào 喊叫 to shout, scream, or cry loudly

hǎnjiù 喊救 to call for help; to cry for help

hǎnyuān 喊冤 to shout out one's grievance in the streets (when a high official is passing) or in court

hàn 汗

sweat; perspiration

hàn'gòu 汗垢 sweat mixed with dirt

hànjīn 汗巾 a girdle; a sash

hànliú jiābèi 汗流浹背 to perspire all over

hànliú jiábèi 汗流浹背 refer to **hànliú jiābèi** 汗流浹背

hànmǎ gōngláo 汗馬功勞 distinguished services in war

hànmao 汗毛 fine hair on the human body

hànniú chōngdòng 汗牛充棟 (said of books, etc.) overabundant; numerous

hànrú yǔxià 汗如雨下 to sweat profusely

hànshān 汗衫 a T-shirt

hànxiàn 汗腺 a sweat gland

hànyán 汗顏 to perspire from shame

hàn 旱

1. drought; dry 2. (by) land route (as opposed to waterway)

hànbīngchǎng 旱冰場 a skating rink

hànbīngxié 旱冰鞋 skates

hànjì 旱季 a dry season

hànlào 旱澇 droughts and floods

hànxiàng 旱象 the signs of drought

hànzāi 旱災 a drought

hàn 和

refer to **hé** 和 6

hàn 捍

to defend; to guard; to ward off

hànwèi 捍衛 to defend (a nation's territory, etc.); to protect

hànyù 捍禦 to ward off

hàn 悍

1. violent; fierce; cruel 2. audacious; brave 3. stubborn

hànjiàng 悍將 1. a brave general 2. a recalcitrant general

hànrán 悍然 outrageously; rudely; unreasonably

hànrán bùgù 悍然不顧 to ignore (advice) stubbornly

hàn 菡

another name of water lily or lotus flower

hàndàn 菡萏 another name of water lily

hàn 漢

1. of the Han Dynasty (206 B.C. - 220 A.D.) 2. of the Chinese people or language 3. a man; a fellow 4. name of a tributary of the Changjiang (Yangtze) River

Hànbǎo 漢堡 Hamburg, Germany

hànbǎo 漢堡 a hamburger

Hàncháo 漢朝 the Han Dynasty (206 B.C.- 220 A.D.)

Hànchéng 漢城 Seoul, capital of South Korea

Hànhuà 漢化 sinicized; assimilated by the Chinese

Hànjiān 漢奸 a traitor (to China)

Hànxué 漢學 Sinology

Hàn Yīng cídiǎn 漢英詞典 a Chinese-English dictionary

hànzi 漢子 1. a man 2. a husband

hàn 銲

to solder; to weld

hànjiē 銲接 to join with solder; to weld; to solder

hàn 撼

to shake; to rock; to jolt; to joggle

hàndòng 撼動 to shake; to rock

hàntiān dòngdì 撼天動地 to

shake both the heaven and the earth—to cause a great sensation

hàn 翰

1. a white horse 2. a long and hard feather 3. a piece of writing

hànlín 翰林 1. the literary circles 2. a scholar with a high literary degree in old China

hàn 頷

1. the chin; the jaws 2. a slight nod of the head

hànshǒu 頷首 to nod the head —a sign of approval

hànshǒu zhījiāo 頷首之交 a nodding acquaintance

hàn 憾

regret; remorse; dissatisfaction

hànshì 憾事 a regrettable thing

hàn 瀚

vast; expansive

háng 行

1. a row; a line; a series 2. a business firm; a company 3. a trade; a line; a profession 4. order of brothers (and sisters) according to seniority 5. a generation

hángháng chū zhuàngyuan 行行出狀元 Every trade has its master. One may distinguish himself in any trade.

hánghào 行號 shops; stores; business establishments

hángjia 行家 a professional; an expert

hánglièe 行列 the rank and file; rows and columns

hángqíng 行情 1. market prices of certain commodities; a quotation; market 2. general standing of a person in terms of finance, influence, popularity, etc.

hángyè 行業 a trade; an occupation

háng 杭

1. Hangzhou 2. (航) to sail; to cross a stream; to navigate

Hángzhōu 杭州 Hangzhou, capital city of Zhejiang Province

háng 航

1. a ship; a boat; a vessel 2. to navigate

hángchéng 航程 the distance of an air or a sea trip; sail

hánghǎi 航海 maritime navigation; a voyage; to sail on the seas

hángkōng 航空 aviation; aeronautics

hángkōng gōngsī 航空公司 airlines

hángkōng mǔjiàn 航空母艦 an aircraft carrier; a flattop

hángkōngxìn 航空信 airmail

hángtài gōngyè 航太工業 aerospace industry

hángtiān 航天 spaceflight

hángtiān fēijī 航天飛機 a space shuttle; a shuttle

hángtiānzhàn 航天站 space station

hángxiàn 航線 routes (of an airline or shipping company)

hángxíng 航行 1. to sail 2. to fly

hàng 沆

1. a vast expanse of water 2. mist 3. flowing

hàngxiè yīqì 沆瀣一氣 (to talk, think, etc.) in the same vein; the meeting of minds

háo 毫

1. fine hair 2. a measure of length 3. a writing brush 4. a dime 5. a measure of weight

háobù xiānggān 毫不相干 totally unrelated

háobù zàihu 毫不在乎 do not mind or care at all

háofà 毫髮 refer to háofà 毫髮

háofà 毫髮 extremely little

háokè 毫克 milligram (mg.)

háolí 毫釐 extremely small space; an iota

háomǐ 毫米 millimeter (mm.)

háoshēng 毫升 milliliter (ml.)

háowú jiàzhí 毫無價值 good for nothing

háowú yíwèn 毫無疑問 There

is no doubt.

háo 號

to cry; to shout; to howl; to wail

háo 豪

1. a person outstanding in intelligence or talent; a heroic person 2. a leader; a ringleader 3. a proclivity to the use of force, bullying ways, etc.

háofàng 豪放 vigorous and unrestrained

háohuá 豪華 luxurious; swanky; plush

háojié 豪傑 a man of outstanding intelligence and courage

háomài 豪邁 straightforward and carefree

háomén 豪門 a rich and powerful family

háoshuǎng 豪爽 bold and generous; chivalrous

háoyǔ 豪雨 a downpour; to rain cats and dogs

háoyǔ 豪語 big talk

háo 嘷(噑)

to howl; to yelp; the frantic barks or howls of dogs or wolves

háo 嚎

to cry loudly; to howl; to wail

háotáo dàkū 嚎啕大哭 to cry loudly with abandon

háo 濠

a moat; a trench or ditch

háogōu 濠溝 a trench

háo 壕

1. the ditch around a city wall; a moat 2. a trench

háogōu 壕溝 a trench (in warfare); a ditch

háo 蠔

an oyster

háoyóu 蠔油 oyster sauce

háo 鶴

refer to **hè** 鶴

hǎo 好

1. good; nice; fine 2. pleasing (looks, taste, etc.); easy (to deal

with, etc.) 3. to finish (dressing, eating, etc.) 4. very; much 5. so that 6. Wonderful! 7. an exclamatory expression 8. a friendly meeting 9. fit; suitable; proper

hǎobàntiān 好半天 quite a while; a long time

hǎobǐ 好比 to be like

hǎobù róngyì 好不容易 1. very difficult 2. after all the trouble

hǎochī 好吃 good to eat; tasty; delicious

hǎochu 好處 1. good points; advantages 2. profit

hǎodǎi 好歹 1. emergency; an accident 2. by hook or by crook 3. good and bad 4. anyhow; in any case

hǎoduō 好多 1. How much or many? 2. a good deal; so much; so many

hǎogǎn 好感 a favorable impression

hǎohàn bùchī yǎnqiánkuī 好漢不吃眼前虧 A wise man knows how to avoid being beaten.

hǎojiāhuo 好傢伙 1. The scoundrel! 2. Fine thing indeed! 3. What a powerful blow!

hǎojǐng bùcháng 好景不長 Good fortune won't last forever.

hǎojiǔ 好久 1. How long? 2. a long time

hǎokàn 好看 good-looking; beautiful; nice

Hǎoláiwū 好萊塢 Hollywood

hǎopíng 好評 favorable comment

hǎoqiú 好球 1. a good shot 2. a strike

hǎorén 好人 1. a beauty 2. a person of virtue 3. a person who gets along very well with everyone

hǎorén nánzuò 好人難做 It's difficult to please everybody.

hǎorìzi 好日子 1. an auspicious day 2. a wedding day 3. a happy life

hǎoshì 好事 1. good things 2. charity 3. marriage

hǎoshì duōmó 好事多磨 The realization of good things is usually preceded by rough going.

hǎoshǒu 好手 an expert

hǎoshuō dǎishuō 好說歹說 to try every possible way to persuade somebody

hǎotīng 好聽 pleasant to hear

hǎowánr 好玩兒 interesting; full of fun

hǎoxì 好戲 1. (sarcastic) great fun 2. good play

hǎoxiàng 好像 to seem; to look like

hǎoxiāoxi 好消息 good news

hǎoxiǎozi 好小子 a smart guy; a wise guy

hǎoxiào 好笑 laughable; funny; ridiculous

hǎoxiē 好些 1. a little better 2. many (people, etc.)

hǎoxīn 好心 kind-hearted

hǎoyì 好意 goodwill; kindness

hǎozài 好在 fortunately; luckily

hǎozhuǎn 好轉 to take a turn for the better

hǎozì wéizhī 好自為之 to do one's best (to keep a job, run a business, etc.)

Hǎo 郝 also **hè**
1. name of an ancient place in today's Shanxi Province 2. a Chinese family name

hào 好
1. to love to; to like to; to be fond of 2. to be addicted to 3. what one likes or prefers

hàochī lǎnzuò 好吃懶做 lazy

hàodà xǐgōng 好大喜功 to love to brag and show off

hàodòng 好動 (said of one's disposition) very active or restless

hàodǔ 好賭 fond of gambling

hàogāo wùyuǎn 好高騖遠 to aim high but care nothing about the fundamental; unrealistic

hàokè 好客 to be hospitable

hàoqí 好奇 to be curious; curiosity

hàoqiáng 好強 to be eager to do well in everything

hàosè 好色 lewd; libidinous; lustful

hàoshèng 好勝 to love to win; emulative

hàoshì zhītú 好事之徒 a meddler; a busybody

hàowèn 好問 inquisitive

hàowù 好惡 likes and dislikes

hàoxué 好學 to be fond of studying

hàoyì wùláo 好逸惡勞 to love ease and hate work; pleasure-seeking

hàoyǒng dòuhěn 好勇鬥狠 combative

hàozhàn 好戰 hawkish; warmongering

hào 昊

1. summer time 2. the sky; the heavens

hàotiān wǎngjí 昊天罔極 (said of parental love) as vast as the boundless heavens

hào 浩

1. massive; great; vast 2. much; many

hàohàn 浩瀚 vast

hàohào dàngdàng 浩浩蕩蕩 (said of an army in march) moving in an imposing manner

hàojié 浩劫 a catastrophe; a calamity

hàomiǎo 浩渺 (said of a body of water) vast or extensive

hàorán 浩然 great; overwhelming

hàotàn 浩歎 to heave a deep sigh

hào 耗

1. to expend; to use up; to waste; to squander; to consume 2. news; a report

hàofèi 耗費 to expend; to squander

hàojìn 耗盡 to exhaust; to use up

hàosǔn 耗損 to diminish by expending

hàozi 耗子 a mouse; a rat

hào 涸

refer to **hé** 涸

hào 皓

white and bright

hàochǐ 皓齒 white teeth; sparkling teeth

hàohào 皓皓 gleaming; brilliant; glistening; bright

hàoyuè dāngkōng 皓月當空 The bright moon hangs in the sky.

hào 號

1. a designation; a title 2. sizes 3. a call 4. a number 5. a mark; a sign 6. a store; a shop 7. a bugle 8. date

hàochēng 號稱 1. to claim; to profess 2. to be known as

hàojiǎo 號角 a bugle; a horn

hàolìng 號令 a command; an order

hàowài 號外 an extra

hàozhào 號召 a call; to summon

hàozhì 號誌 a signal; a sign

hàozi 號子 (slang) a stock exchange

hē 呵

1. (詞) to scold in a loud voice 2. to yawn

hēchì 呵斥 to scold in a loud voice

hēhē dàxiào 呵呵大笑 to roar with laughter

hēhù 呵護 divine protection

hēqiàn 呵欠 to yawn and to stretch

hēzé 呵責 to scold in a loud voice

hē 喝

to drink

hējiǔ 喝酒 to drink (alcoholic beverages)

hē xīběifēng 喝西北風 to have nothing to eat

hēzuì 喝醉 to get drunk

hé 禾

1. grains still on the stalk 2. the rice crop

hégǎn 禾稈 the stalk of a rice plant

hémiáo 禾苗 rice seedlings

H

hé 合

1. to combine; to unite; to gather; to collect 2. to close; to shut 3. to suit

hébàn 合辦 to operate, or run jointly

hébìng 合併 to combine; to unite; to conjoin; to consolidate

hébulái 合不來 cannot get along with (somebody)

héchàng 合唱 to sing in chorus

héchàngtuán 合唱團 a chorus; a choir

hédelái 合得來 to get along well; to be congenial

hédìngběn 合訂本 a bound volume

héfǎ 合法 lawful; legal; legitimate

hégé 合格 qualified; up to the standard

hégǔ 合股 to pool capital; to enter into partnership

héhū 合乎 to qualify; to tally with

héhuì 合會 a mutual help loan association

héhūn 合婚 to be united in wedlock

héhuǒ 合夥 to enter into partnership

héhuǒrén 合夥人 (accounting) partners

héjī 合擊 to make a joint attack on

héjí 合擊 refer to **héjī** 合擊

héjì 合計 a total; to add up to

héjiāhuān 合家歡 a family reunion

héjīn 合金 an alloy

hékān 合刊 a combined issue (of a periodical)

hélǐ 合理 reasonable; logical; rational

héliú 合流 1. confluence 2. to flow together; to merge

hélǒng 合攏 to close up

hémóu 合謀 to conspire together

héqíng hélǐ 合情合理 fair and reasonable

héqún 合群 to be gregarious

héshēn 合身 to fit

héshí 合時 timely; seasonable

héshì 合適 suitable; fitting

hésuàn 合算 1. to reckon up 2. worthwhile

hétong 合同 an agreement; a contract

héwèikǒu 合胃口 to suit one's taste

héyǎn 合眼 to close the eyes

héyí 合宜 fitting; suitable; proper

héyì 合意 (said of a thing) to suit one's fancy

héyīn 合音 (music) combination tone

héyǐng 合影 to have a group photo

héyuē 合約 an agreement; a contract

hézàng 合葬 to bury (husband and wife) in one grave

hézhù 合著 to coauthor

hézòu 合奏 (music) a united performance of the full number of players

hézuò 合作 to cooperate; to collaborate

hézuò jīnkù 合作金庫 a cooperative bank

hézuòshè 合作社 a co-op

hé 何

1. what; how; where; why 2. a Chinese family name

hébì 何必 why should; why is it necessary

hébù 何不 why not

hécháng 何嘗 How (could it be an exception)?

héchù 何處 where; in what place

héděng 何等 1. how 2. what sort of

héfáng 何妨 There is no harm (trying, doing, etc.)

hégān 何干 What has that got to do with...?

hégù 何故 why; for what reason

hékǔ 何苦 Why take the trouble?

hékuàng 何況 much less; not to mention; let alone

hélè bùwéi 何樂不為 Why not do it gladly?

héqù hécóng 何去何從 what to do

héshí 何時 when; at what time

héshì 何事 What (do you want)?

héwèi 何謂 what is meant by

hézài 何在 1. Where is (that particular thing)? 2. What is (that particular reason)?

hézhě 何者 which one

hézhǐ 何止 far more than

hézhìyú 何至於 How could it have turned out (like that)? How come?

hézú guàchǐ 何足掛齒 Don't mention it. (used in formal speech)

hé 和

1. harmony; harmonious 2. peace(ful) 3. to be affable 4. the sum or aggregate 5. of Japan 6. (also **hàn**) and

hé'ǎi 和藹 amiable; benign

hécài 和菜 a fixed menu in a restaurant

héfēng 和風 a gentle breeze

héfú 和服 a (Japanese) kimono

héhǎo 和好 1. to be on friendly terms 2. to make up

héhuì 和會 a peace conference

héjiě 和解 to be reconciled; reconciliation

héjú 和局 (said of a contest) a tie or a draw

hémù 和睦 to be on friendly terms

hépán tuōchū 和盤托出 to reveal the whole truth

hépíng 和平 1. peaceful; mild (such as the weather, etc.) 2. peace

héqì 和氣 gentle; affable friendly; cordial

héshàn 和善 kind and gentle; genial

héshang 和尚 a Buddhist monk

héshēng 和聲 (music) harmony

héshìlǎo 和事佬 a mediator; a peacemaker

hétán 和談 peace talks

héxián 和弦 (music) a chord

héxié 和諧 in harmony; harmony

héyán yuèsè 和顏悅色 a peaceful and happy look

héyuē 和約 a peace treaty

hézhōng gòngjì 和衷共濟 to be united and to work in concert

hé 河

1. a general name for rivers, streams, and waterways 2. the Huanghe (Yellow) River in northern China, 4,450 km long

hé'àn 河岸 the riverbanks; the riverside; the waterfront

hébà 河壩 embankments; levees; dikes

Héběi 河北 Hebei Province

hébiān 河邊 the riverside

hébīn 河濱 the riverbanks; the riverside; the waterfront

héchuáng 河床 the riverbed; the floor of a river

hédào 河道 the course of a river; a waterway

hédī 河堤 embankments; levees; dikes

Hédōng shīhǒu 河東獅吼 the display of shrewishness

hégōu 河溝 a brook

hégǔ 河谷 a river valley

Héhàn 河漢 the Milky Way

hékǒu 河口 a river mouth; a stream outlet

héliú 河流 streams, rivers or channels of water

hémǎ 河馬 a hippopotamus, or a hippo

Hén'án 河南 Henan Province

hépàn 河畔 the riverbanks; the river side; the waterfront

héqīng hǎiyàn 河清海晏 halcyon days; time of peace and prosperity

héqū 河曲 meander

héqú 河渠 a reservoir; waterways

héshān 河山 rivers and mountains—the territory of a country

héshuǐ bùfàn jǐngshuǐ 河水

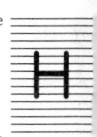

H

不犯井水 Everyone minds his own business.

hétí 河堤 refer to **hédī** 河堤

hétún 河豚 the globefish; a blowfish; a Puffer

héxīn 河心 the middle of a river

hézhōu 河洲 a sand bar or islet in a river

hé 劾
to accuse; to charge; to impeach

hé 曷
1. what 2. why not 3. how

hégù 曷故 why; what for

hé 核
1. a kernel; a fruit stone; a walnut; a pit 2. to investigate; to examine; to verify; to check 3. a nucleus; nuclear 4. a hard lump

hébàn 核辦 to study and examine (a case, etc.) and act accordingly

hédìng 核定 1. to decide after examination 2. to check and ratify

héduì 核對 to verify; to check (the facts)

héfù 核覆 to make a reply after thorough investigation

héjì 核計 to examine and calculate

hé'néng 核能 nuclear energy

hé'néng diànchǎng 核能電廠 a nuclear power station

hérén 核仁 1. a nucleolus 2. the kernel (of a fruit stone)

hésuàn 核算 to examine and calculate

hétao 核桃 a walnut

héxīn 核心 1. the core (of a matter, etc.) 2. the inner circle (of a political party, government, etc.)

héyì 核議 to decide after consideration

hézhǔn 核准 to approve; approval

hézǐ 核子 a nucleus; a nucleon

hézǐ wǔqì 核子武器 nuclear weapons

hézǐ zhànzhēng 核子戰爭 nuclear war

hé 盍
1. what 2. why not 3. to get together

hé 荷
a lotus; a water lily

hébao 荷包 a purse; a pouch (carried with oneself)

hébaodàn 荷包蛋 fried eggs

hé'érméng 荷爾蒙 hormone

héhuā 荷花 a lotus flower

Hélán 荷蘭 Holland; the Netherlands

hé 盒
a small box; a case

hé 涸 also **hào**
drying up; dried-up; exhausted

hé 闔
1. to close (doors) 2. whole; all

hé 褐
refer to **hè** 褐

hé 闔
1. a leaf of a door 2. to shut or close 3. all; the whole 4. Why? Why not?

hédì guānglín 闔第光臨
Please come with your whole family.

héfǔ 闔府 your whole family

héfǔ píng'ān 闔府平安 Hope your whole family is doing well.

héjiā 闔家 the whole family

hé 覈
1. to test; to examine; to investigate 2. deep; deeply 3. the stone (of a fruit)

héshí 覈實 to examine or investigate the fact or truth

hè 和
1. to match; to harmonize 2. to write a poem in reply

hè 郝
refer to **hǎo** 郝

hè 荷
1. a load; a burden 2. to bear; to carry; to shoulder 3. to receive

hè 黑
refer to **hēi** 黑

hè 喝

to shout; to call out aloud

hècǎi 喝彩 to shout "Bravo!"; to applaud

hēdàocǎi 喝倒彩 to hoot; to hiss

hèlìng 喝令 to shout an order

hè 賀

1. to congratulate; to send a present in congratulation 2. a Chinese family name

hècí 賀詞 greetings; congratulations

hèdiàn 賀電 a congratulatory cable or telegram

hèlǐ 賀禮 a congratulatory present

hènián 賀年 to offer congratulations on New Year's Day

hèsuì 賀歲 to offer congratulations on New Year's Day

hèxǐ 賀喜 to congratulate; to felicitate

hè 褐 also **hé**

1. coarse woolen cloth; coarse cloth; haircloth; rough cloth 2. the poor or destitute 3. brown

hèsè 褐色 brown

hè 赫

1. bright; glowing 2. brilliant; glorious 3. angry; indignant 4. a Chinese family name

hèhè yǒumíng 赫赫有名 illustrious; far-famed

hè 嚇

1. to intimidate; to threaten 2. the sound of laughter

hèzǔ 嚇阻 to stop (someone) by threat

hè 壑 also **huò**

1. a gully; a channel for water 2. a narrow ravine at the foot

hè 鶴 also **háo**

a crane

hèfǎ tóngyán 鶴髮童顏 refer to **hèfà tóngyán** 鶴髮童顏

hèfà tóngyán 鶴髮童顏 a hoary head with a youthful face

hèlì 鶴立 to expect (or await) eagerly

hèlì 鶴唳 the cries of cranes

hèlì jīqún 鶴立雞群 (literally) a crane standing among chickens —far surpassing the others; to stand head and shoulders over others

hēi 黑 also **hè**

1. black; dark 2. evil; sinister; gloomy

hēi'àn 黑暗 darkness; dark

hēibái 黑白 black and white —right and wrong, good and bad, etc.

hēibái fēnmíng 黑白分明 1. right and wrong clearly distinguished 2. the sharp contrast between black and white

hēibān 黑斑 dark spots; black specks

hēibǎn 黑板 a blackboard

hēibǎncā 黑板擦 an eraser; a wiper

hēibāng 黑幫 a reactionary gang

hēidào rénwù 黑道人物 a gangster; an underworld figure

hēidiàn 黑店 an inn that kills and robs lodgers

hēidòng 黑洞 (astronomy) a black hole

Hēihǎi 黑海 the Black Sea

hēihézi 黑盒子 a cockpit voice recorder

Hēilóngjiāng 黑龍江 1. the name of the river in the north east China 2. Heilongjiang Province

hēimíngdān 黑名單 a blacklist

hēipíjiǔ 黑啤酒 dark beer; stout

hēiqīqī 黑漆漆 pitch-dark; very dark

hēirén 黑人 a Negro; a black

hēisè 黑色 black

hēishèhuì 黑社會 underworld society; the underworld; gangsterdom

hēishì 黑市 a black market

hēishǒu 黑手 a vicious backstage manipulator

Hēishǒudǎng 黑手黨 the Black Hand; the Mafia

Hēisǐbìng 黑死病 the Black

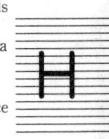

Death

hēitǐzì 黑體字 boldface type

hēixīn'gān 黑心肝 an ungrateful person

hēixīngxīng 黑猩猩 a chimpanzee

hēiyāyā 黑壓壓 extremely crowded; a dense or dark mass of

hēiyān 黑煙 1. black smoke 2. opium

hēiyè 黑夜 a dark night; night

hēi 嘿

an interjection

hén 痕

a mark; a scar; a trace

hénjī 痕跡 a trace

hěn 狠

1. vicious; cruel; atrocious 2. severe(ly); extreme(ly)

hěndú 狠毒 atrocious; malicious

hěnmìng 狠命 to make a desperate effort

hěnxīn 狠心 heartless; pitiless

hěn 很

1. very; quite 2. fierce; cruel 3. disobedient; quarrelsome 4. dispute; quarrel

hèn 恨

1. to resent; to hate; hatred; hate 2. to regret

hènbude 恨不得 to wish that one could (do something which is not proper to do)

hèntòule 恨透了 to hate to the utmost degree

hēng 亨

to go through smoothly

hēngtōng 亨通 to go well

hēng 哼

1. to croon; to hum 2. to groan; to moan 3. the grunt of disapproval or contempt

héng 恆

1. constant; regular; persevering 2. lasting; continual; continually

héngchǎn 恆產 immovable property—real estate

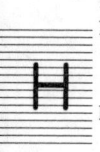

héngcháng 恆常 1. permanent; constant 2. regular; common (practices, etc.)

héngchǐ 恆齒 (anatomy) permanent teeth

Hénghé shāshù 恆河沙數 innumerable; countless

héngjiǔ 恆久 constancy; lasting; forever

héngxīn 恆心 perseverance

héngxīng 恆星 fixed stars

héng 衡

1. to weigh; to measure; to assess; to consider 2. horizontal 3. railings 4. a beam 5. the beam of a steelyard

héngliáng 衡量 to weigh; to measure; to consider

héng 橫

1. horizontal; crosswise; lateral 2. east to west or vice versa 3. by the side of; sideways 4. to move crosswise; to traverse 5. unrestrainedly; turbulently

héngchén 橫陳 to lie down with limbs fully stretched

héngchōng zhízhuàng 橫衝直撞 (said of a bull, car, truck, etc.) to bump; to jostle and elbow one's way right and left

héngdāo duó'ài 橫刀奪愛 to take away another's lover

héngdù 橫渡 to cross (a river, ocean, etc.)

héngduì 橫隊 a rank; a row

hénggémó 橫膈膜 the diaphragm

hénggèn 橫亙 crosswise; horizontal to span; to traverse

héngguàn gōnglù 橫貫公路 1. any highway that runs from east to west 2. the Cross-Island or East-West Highway in Taiwan

héngkuà 橫跨 to stretch over or across

hénglèxīn 橫了心 to steel one's heart (as a result of anger; an indication of determination, etc.); in desperation

héngliè 橫列 to arrange in a horizontal line

héngliú 橫流 (said of a river) to

overflow

héngqī shùbā 橫七豎八 in total disorder or disarray

héngsǎo 橫掃 to sweep away; to roll back

héngshēng zhījié 橫生枝節 1. side issues or new problems that come or appear unexpectedly 2. to raise obstacles, to complicate an issue deliberately

héngshù 橫豎 1. in any case; anyway 2. horizontal and perpendicular; in every direction

héngxiě 橫寫 to write horizontally

héngxíng 橫行 1. to run wild 2. to move sideways—as crabs

héngxíng bàdào 橫行霸道 to bully; to terrorize; to act tyrannically

héngyì 橫溢 1. brimming; overflowing 2. to brim; to overflow

héngzuòbiāo 橫坐標 (mathematics) an abscissa

hèng 橫

1. cross-grained; perverse 2. presumptuous and unreasonable 3. unexpected; uncalled for 4. violent; cross

hèngcái 橫財 a windfall; illegal gains

hènghuò 橫禍 unexpected misfortune or disaster

hèngsǐ 橫死 a violent death; to meet with a sudden death

hōng 哄

(said of a group of people) to make a roaring noise

hōngtái wùjià 哄抬物價 to rig prices

hōngtáng dàxiào 哄堂大笑 The hole room rocks with laughter.

hōng 烘

1. to bake; to roast 2. to dry or warm near a fire

hōngbèi 烘焙 to dry (herbal medicine) over a fire

hōnggān 烘乾 to dry beside or over a fire

hōnggānjī 烘乾機 a clothing dryer

hōngkǎo 烘烤 to bake; to roast; to warm or dry by the fire

hōngtuō 烘托 to make conspicuous by contrast

hōng 轟

1. noise of a number of vehicles 2. noise; an uproar 3. grand; magnificent 4. to bombard; to blast

hōngdòng 轟動 1. to cause an uproar; to create a sensation 2. to excite (the public)

hōnghōng lièliè 轟轟烈烈 in a grand fashion; on a grand and spectacular scale

hōngzhà 轟炸 to bomb (from an airplane)

hóng 弘

1. great; capacious 2. to enlarge; to broaden

hóngdà 弘大 great; immense

hóngyáng 弘揚 to propagate; to promote; to develop

hóngyuǎn 弘遠 far and wide

hóngyuàn 弘願 great ambition

hóng 宏

great; vast; wide; ample

hóngdà 宏大 great; grand; vast; immense

Hóngdūlāsī 宏都拉斯 Honduras

hóngliàng 宏亮 (said of a voice) loud and clear

hóngtú 宏圖 an ambitious plan

hóngwěi 宏偉 magnificent; grand

hóngyáng 宏揚 to disseminate

hóngyuàn 宏願 an ambition

hóngzhǐ 宏旨 the main theme

hóng 泓

1. clear, deep water; limpid water 2. the ancient name of a stream in Henan Province

hóng 虹

a rainbow

hóngní 虹霓 a rainbow and its reflection

hóng 洪

1. great; immense; magnificent 2. floods; turbulent waters; torrents 3. a Chinese family name

hóngcái dàlüè 洪才大略 a great mind with great schemes

hóngdà 洪大 great; massive

hóng'ēn 洪恩 great kindness

hóngfú qítiān 洪福齊天 boundless bliss

hónghuāng 洪荒 primitive; chaotic

hóngliàng 洪亮 loud and clear; sonorous

hóngliú 洪流 1. a torrent 2. a powerful current

hóngshuǐ 洪水 a flood; a deluge

hóngshuǐ měngshòu 洪水猛獸 disaster; calamity

hóngzhōng 洪鐘 1. a large bell 2. (said of a voice) stentorian; very loud or powerful

hóng 紅

1. red; vermilion; rosy 2. to blush; to redden 3. eminent; influential; (said of players) very popular 4. specially favored; a favorite

hóngbāo 紅包 1. a red paper bag containing money as a gift 2. a bribe or kickback

hóngbǎoshí 紅寶石 a ruby

hóngchá 紅茶 black tea

hóngchén 紅塵 the mundane world; the world of mortals

hóngdòu 紅豆 1. Abrus precatorius, the red bean—a love pea 2. Ormosia

hóngfěn jiārén 紅粉佳人 a young beauty

hóngfěn zhījǐ 紅粉知己 a girlfriend; a mistress

hóngguāng mǎnmiàn 紅光滿面 a healthy and hearty look

Hónghǎi 紅海 the Red Sea

hónglì 紅利 a net profit; a bonus

hónglǜdēng 紅綠燈 red and green lights; traffic lights

hóngluánxīng dòng 紅鸞星動 a wedding being imminent

hóngluóbo 紅蘿蔔 a radish

hóngniáng 紅娘 a nonprofit-

making woman go-between for lovers

hóngqíshǒu 紅旗手 a model worker

hóngrén 紅人 the trusted lieutenant of the boss

hóngrùn 紅潤 (said of the skin, cheeks, etc.) glowing, tender and rosy

hóngsè 紅色 red color

Hóngshízìhuì 紅十字會 Red Cross Society

hóngtáng 紅糖 brown sugar

hóngtōngtōng 紅通通 glowing; aglow; bright red

hóngwàixiàn 紅外線 infrared rays

Hóngwèibīng 紅衛兵 the Red Guards

hóngxiěqiú 紅血球 refer to **hóngxuèqiú** 紅血球

hóngxīn 紅心 the bull's-eye (of a target)

hóngxìng chūqiáng 紅杏出牆 (said of a married woman) to have a lover; to commit adultery

hóngxuèqiú 紅血球 red blood cells; erythrocyte

hóngyán 紅顏 1. young beauties 2. youths 3. rosy cheeks

hóngyán bómìng 紅顏薄命 a popular Chinese saying) Beauties are often ill-fated.

hóngyàoshuǐ 紅藥水 mercurochrome

hóngyùn 紅暈 a blush; a flush

hóngzhǒng 紅腫 a red swelling of the skin

hóngzhuān 紅磚 red bricks

hóng 鴻

1. a wild swan; a wild goose 2. great; huge; large

hóngfú qítiān 鴻福齊天 One's vast happiness is as high as the heaven.

hónghú zhīzhì 鴻鵠之志 great ambition

hóngmáo 鴻毛 swan's down —something very light or insignificant

hóngtú 鴻圖 1. a great plan; a great enterprise; a great under-

hóngyàn chuánshū 鴻雁傳書 to deliver messages by wild swans

hóngzhuǎ 鴻爪 traces that one leaves behind

hǒng 哄

to beguile; to cheat; to defraud

hǒngháizi 哄孩子 to coax a child

hǒngpiàn 哄騙 to defraud; to cheat; to swindle; to take in

hòng 汞

refer to **gǒng** 汞

hóu 侯

1. (in ancient China) the second of the five grades of the nobility 2. the target in archery 3. a marquis; a nobleman or a high official 4. a Chinese family name

hóujué 侯爵 a marquis

hóujué fūren 侯爵夫人 a marchioness

hóu 喉

the throat; the gullet; guttural

hóujié 喉結 Adam's apple

hóulóng 喉嚨 the throat; the gullet

hóu 猴

1. the monkey 2. naughty or impish (child)

hóují 猴急 very impatient

hǒu 吼

(said of beasts) to roar or howl

hòu 后

1. an empress 2. the god of the earth 3. (後) after; behind

hòutǔ 后土 the earth; the god of the earth

hòu 厚

1. thick; thickness 2. deep friendship 3. to treat kindly; generous 4. substantial 5. kind; considerate; virtuous

hòu'ài 厚愛 to treat very kindly and generously

hòucǐ bóbǐ 厚此薄彼 to treat with partiality

hòudao 厚道 kind; virtuous; sincere

hòudù 厚度 thickness

hòulǐ 厚禮 lavish gifts; liberal presents

hòuliǎnpí 厚臉皮 brazen-faced; shameless

hòuwàng 厚望 high hopes; high expectations

hòuyán wúchǐ 厚顏無恥 impudent; shameless

hòuzàng 厚葬 an elaborate funeral

hòu 後

1. behind; at the back of 2. afterwards; to come after 3. descendants; posterity 4. an auxiliary to indicate "then" or "afterwards"

hòubànbù 後半部 the latter portion of a book

hòubànshēng 後半生 the latter half of one's life

hòubèi 後輩 1. juniors; inferiors 2. descendants

hòubèi jūnrén 後備軍人 military reservists

hòubèi rényuán 後備人員 backup personnel

hòubǔ 後補 1. to make amends 2. to replenish

hòubù 後部 behind; the back of

hòudài 後代 descendants or posterity

hòudùn 後盾 a support; a backing

hòufāng 後方 the rear (as contrasted to the war front)

hòufú 後福 the blessings to follow; the good days to come

hòugēn 後跟 the heel

hòugù zhīyōu 後顧之憂 the worries behind

hòuguǒ 後果 consequences

hòuhuàn 後患 the lurking dangers which will become manifest afterward

hòuhuàn wúqióng 後患無窮 an endless flow of disastrous aftermath

hòuhuǐ 後悔 to regret; remorse

hòuhuǐ bùyǐ 後悔不已 to be

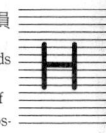

overcome with regret

hòuhuǐ mòjí 後悔莫及 It will be too late to regret.

hòuhuǐ yǒuqī 後會有期 See you again.

hòuhuì yǒuqí 後會有期 refer to **hòuhuì yǒuqī** 後會有期

hòujì wúrén 後繼無人 There is no successor (capable of continuing the task).

hòujìn 後進 juniors; the rising generation

hòulái 後來 then; afterwards

hòulái jūshàng 後來居上 The latecomer (or newcomer) ends up in front.

hòulì bùjì 後力不繼 to lack the strength to continue

hòulù 後路 1. the route of retreat 2. room for a maneuver; a road for retreat

hòulún 後輪 a rear wheel

hòumén 後門 the back door

hòumian 後面 1. behind 2. afterwards

hòumǔ 後母 one's stepmother

hòunián 後年 the year after next

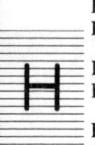

hòupái 後排 a back row

hòuqī 後期 1. to be behind schedule 2. the latter part of an era

hòuqí 後期 refer to **hòuqī** 後期

hòuqǐ zhīxiù 後起之秀 a remarkable young person

hòuqín 後勤 logistic service in the rear

hòurén 後人 1. one's descendants or posterity 2. to be behind others (in doing good things, charity work, etc.)

hòurèn 後任 the successor to an office after the incumbent quits

hòushēng kěwèi 後生可畏 The young hold potentials for greatness.

hòushēng xiǎozi 後生小子 naive youths; young greenhorns

hòushì 後事 matters calling for immediate attention after a person's death—as funerals, etc.

hòushìjìng 後視鏡 a rearview mirror

hòusì 後嗣 descendants or posterity

hòutái 後臺 1. a backstage 2. (usually in politics) one's backing or backers

hòutiān 後天 1. the day after tomorrow 2. acquired; postnatal

Hòutiānxìng Miǎnyì Bùquán Zhènghòuqún 後天性免疫不全症候群 AIDS (Acquired Immune Deficiency Syndrome)

hòutou 後頭 1. behind 2. in the future

hòutuì 後退 to retreat; to withdraw; retreat

hòuwèi 後衛 1. the rear guard (in military operations) 2. the fullback (in football); the guard (in basketball)

hòuxiàndài 後現代 post-modern

hòuxù 後序 an epilog(ue)

hòuxù 後續 follow-up

hòuyízhèng 後遺症 (pathology) aftereffect; sequela

hòuyì 後裔 descendants

hòuyuán 後援 reinforcement from the rear; support

hòuyuán tóushǒu 後援投手 (baseball) relief pitcher

hòuyuàn 後院 a backyard

hòuzhě 後者 the latter

hòuzhī hòujué 後知後覺 to know afterwards

hòuzuòlì 後坐力 recoil

hòu 候

1. to wait; to expect 2. a period; time; a season

hòubǔ 候補 waiting to fill a vacancy, such as an alternate member of a committee, etc.

hòuchēshì 候車室 a waiting room (at a railway station or bus terminal)

hòujīshì 候機室 a lounge or waiting room (at an airport terminal building)

hòujià 候駕 to await (your) gracious presence

hòuniǎo 候鳥 migratory birds

hòushěn 候審 (law) to await trial

hòuxuǎnrén 候選人 a candidate

hòuzhěn 候診 to wait to see the doctor

hòu 逅 also **gòu**

to meet unexpectedly; to come across; to run into

hū 乎

1. at; in; from; than 2. an interrogative particle 3. an exclamatory particle

hū 忽

1. suddenly; abruptly 2. to disregard; to be indifferent; to neglect 3. to forget 4. one millionth of a tael

hūdì 忽地 abruptly; unexpectedly

hūlěng hūrè 忽冷忽熱 1. now hot, now cold—abrupt changes of temperature 2. sudden changes in one's affection, attitude, enthusiasm, etc.

hūlüè 忽略 to overlook; to neglect

hūqǐ hūluò 忽起忽落 1. sudden rise and sudden fall 2. the erratic fluctuation of market prices, etc. 3. sudden changes (of mood); now..., now...

hūrán 忽然 suddenly; unexpectedly

hūshì 忽視 to disregard; to overlook; to neglect

hū 呼

1. to call; to cry 2. to exhale

hūfēng huànyǔ 呼風喚雨 1. (said of immortals with divine power) to summon wind and rain 2. to stir up trouble

hūhǎn 呼喊 to yell; to shout

hūháo 呼號 to cry; to wail

hūhào 呼號 to call the sign (of a message sent by radio)

hūhuàn 呼喚 to call; to shout; to cry out

hūjiào 呼叫 to shout; to cry out; to yell

hūjiàoqì 呼叫器 a pager; a beeper

hūjiù 呼救 to cry for help; to call for help

hūkǒuhào 呼口號 to shout slogans

hūpéng yǐnbàn 呼朋引伴 to call friends and fellows together

hūqì 呼氣 to expire; to exhale

hūtiān chuǎngdì 呼天搶地 refer to **hūtiān qiāngdì** 呼天搶地

hūtiān qiāngdì 呼天搶地 to cry bitterly and loudly in excessive grief

hūxī 呼吸 to breathe

hūxī qìguān 呼吸器官 the respiratory organs

hūxiào 呼嘯 to roar or howl

hūyìng 呼應 to act in coordination with each other; to echo

hūyù 呼籲 to appeal; to petition

hūzhī yùchū 呼之欲出 obvious; almost certain

hū 戲

alas; oh; o; ah

hú 囫

entire; whole

húlún tūnzǎo 囫圇吞棗 to read hastily without thinking

hú 狐

the fox

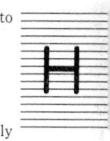

húchòu 狐臭 an armpit odor

hújiǎ hǔwēi 狐假虎威 to bully the weak because of one's association with the powerful

húli 狐狸 a fox

húligǒu 狐狸狗 a spitz

húlijīng 狐狸精 an enchantress

húli wěiba 狐狸尾巴 a fox's tail—something that reveals one's true form or evil intentions

húmèi 狐媚 to charm by flattery; to be sycophantic

húqún gǒudǎng 狐群狗黨 a gang of scoundrels

húyí 狐疑 suspicious; doubt; suspicion

hú 弧

1. a wooden bow 2. a segment of a circle

húdù 弧度 circular measure

húxíng 弧形 an arc; a curve

hú 胡
1. to blunder; reckless; wildly; disorderly 2. stupidly; blindly; confusedly 3. (in ancient China) a general name of the northern tribes 4. (an interrogative particle) How? Why? When? 5. (now rarely) long and lasting 6. a Chinese family name

húchě 胡扯 1. random talk 2. wild talk; lies

húgǎo 胡搞 to cause confusion or a disturbance recklessly

húguā 胡瓜 a cucumber

húhùn 胡混 to fool around

hújiāo 胡椒 pepper

húlái 胡來 to proceed (with a matter, etc.) recklessly and without thought

húluàn 胡亂 1. at random 2. not choosy

húluóbo 胡蘿蔔 the carrot

hú'nào 胡鬧 reckless, irresponsible words or actions

húqín 胡琴 the two-stringed Chinese violin

húshuō 胡說 wild talk; to talk nonsense

húshuō bādào 胡說八道 to talk nonsense; wild talk; lies

húsī luànxiǎng 胡思亂想 to daydream; to give one's thoughts free rein

hútáo 胡桃 walnuts

hútóngr 胡同兒 refer to **hútòngr**

hútòngr 胡同兒 a lane

hútu 胡塗 confused; muddle-headed; stupid

húyán luànyǔ 胡言亂語 to talk nonsense; to gibber; lies or wild talk

húzhōu 胡謅 wild talk; nonsensical talk; to invent (something false); to lie

húzōu 胡謅 refer to **húzhōu** 胡謅

húzuò fēiwéi 胡作非爲 to bully others as if the law were nonexistent; to do as one pleases

hú 壺
1. a pot; a jug 2. any potbellied

container with a small opening

hú 湖
1. a lake 2. a Chinese family name

Húběi 湖北 Hubei Province

húbiān 湖邊 the shore of a lake; beside the lake

húbīn 湖濱 the shore of a lake; beside the lake

húbó 湖泊 refer to **húpō** 湖泊

húguāng shānsè 湖光山色 the natural beauty of lakes and mountains

Hú'nán 湖南 Hunan Province

húpàn 湖畔 the shore of a lake; beside the lake

húpō 湖泊 lakes

húshuǐ 湖水 lake water

húxīn 湖心 the middle of a lake

húzé 湖澤 lakes

húzhǎo 湖沼 lakes and marshes

hú 葫
a bottle gourd or a calabash

húlu 葫蘆 a bottle gourd or a calabash

hú 瑚
coral

hú 糊
1. paste 2. to paste 3. scorched 4. not clear; blurred; confused; ambiguous; unintelligible

húkǒu 糊口 to make a living; to live from hand to mouth

húli hútu 糊裡糊塗 (to do something) without thinking; confused or mixed-up

hútu 糊塗 1. mixed-up; confused 2. stupid; foolish

hútuchóng 糊塗蟲 a blunderer; a bungler

hú 蝴
a butterfly

húdié 蝴蝶 a butterfly

hú 餬
1. congee; porridge; gruel 2. paste

húkǒu 餬口 just to make ends meet; to make a bare living

hú 鵠
1. a swan 2. standing quietly; standing erect

húlì 鵠立 to stand on the lookout

húmiàn jiūxíng 鵠面鳩形 emaciated from hunger

hú 鬍
beard

húxū 鬍鬚 beard

hǔ 虎
1. a tiger 2. fierce; savage; vigorous; brave

hǔbèi xióngyāo 虎背熊腰 heavy and muscular build of the body

hǔfù wú quǎnzǐ 虎父無犬子 There will be no laggard among the children of a brave or talented man.

hǔkǒu 虎口 1. a tiger's mouth —a dangerous place 2. the part of a hand between the thumb and the index finger

hǔkǒu yúshēng 虎口餘生 to have a narrow escape

hǔpí 虎皮 1. a tiger skin 2. seeming bravery

hǔshì dāndān 虎視眈眈 to gaze with the cruel greed of a tiger

hǔtóu shéwěi 虎頭蛇尾 to start doing something with vigor but fail to see it through

hǔ 唬
1. to intimidate; to scare 2. the roar of a tiger

hǔrén 唬人 to intimidate people; to bluff

hǔ 琥
1. a jade ornament in the shape of a tiger 2. amber

hǔpò 琥珀 amber

hǔ 滸
waterside; shore

hù 互
each other; mutually; reciprocally

hùbǔ 互補 complementary

hùbù qīnfàn 互不侵犯 to refrain from invading each other

hùfǎng 互訪 to exchange visits

hùhuàn 互換 to exchange

hùhuì 互惠 mutually beneficial

hùtōng yǒuwú 互通有無 to supply each other's needs

hùwéi yīnguǒ 互為因果 to interact as both cause and effect

hùxiāng 互相 mutually; each other; one another

hùxiāng qiēcuō 互相切磋 to improve each other by active discussion

hùzhēng xióngzhǎng 互爭雄長 to fight for leadership

hùzhù 互助 to help each other; mutual help

hùzhùhuì 互助會 slate club

hù 戶
1. a door 2. a household; a family

hùjí 戶籍 a domicile

hùkǒu 戶口 households

hùkǒu míngbù 戶口名簿 a household identification book

hùkǒu pǔchá 戶口普查 census taking; a census

hùmíng 戶名 a depositor (in banking)

hùnèi 戶內 indoor; indoors

hùnèi yùndòng 戶內運動 indoor games

hùtóu 戶頭 an account; a depositor (in banking)

hùwài 戶外 outdoor; outdoors

hùwài yùndòng 戶外運動 outdoor games

hùzhǎng 戶長 the household head

hùzhèng 戶政 the administration with regard to residents and residence

hù 戽
a pail; a bucket

hù 怙
1. to rely on 2. one's father 3. things or persons that one relies on

hù'è bùquān 怙惡不悛 incorrigible; obdurate and irreclaimable

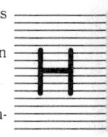

hù'è língrén 怙惡凌人 to intimidate and oppress others

hùshì 怙恃 1. those one relies on (as troops, gangsters, etc.) 2. one's parents—father (怙 **hù**) and mother (恃 **shì**)

hù 護

1. to protect; to guard; to defend; to shield 2. to take sides; to be partial to

hùduǎn 護短 to conceal one's faults

hùhuā shǐzhě 護花使者 a protector of women

hùjià 護駕 to guard (or escort) the emperor

hùháng 護航 1. to escort another vessel 2. to help another illicitly during an examination

hùlǐ 護理 1. to act for a senior official 2. nursing

hùmùjìng 護目鏡 (computer) screen shield

hùshēnfú 護身符 1. an amulet 2. anything which one uses as a protective shield

hùshi 護士 a nurse

hùsòng 護送 to guard; to escort; to convoy

hùwèi 護衛 to guard; to escort; to convoy

hùzhào 護照 a passport

huā 花

1. a flower 2. a flowering plant 3. a prostitute 4. varicolored 5. fireworks 6. to spend 7. a Chinese family name

huābàn 花瓣 the petal (of a flower or blossom)

huābāo 花苞 a bud

huābiān 花邊 1. lace; an embroidered hem (of a garment) 2. fancy borders (in printing)

huābiān xīnwén 花邊新聞 a sidebar

huācǎo 花草 flowers and grass

huāchē 花車 a float; a decorated vehicle in parade

huādēng 花燈 a fancy lantern (made for the Lantern Festival)

huādiāo 花雕 rice wine of the best quality from Shaoxing

(**shàoxīng** 紹興)

huāfèi 花費 to spend; to expend

huāfěn 花粉 pollen

huāgāngyán 花岡岩 granite

huāhǎo yuèyuán 花好月圓 perfect conjugal bliss

huāhuā gōngzǐ 花花公子 a beau; a fop; a playboy

huāhuālǜlǜ 花花綠綠 varicolored; colorful

huāhuā shìjiè 花花世界 the gay and material world

huāhuì 花卉 flowering plants

huājiǎ 花甲 (said of a person) 60 years old

huālán 花籃 a flower basket

huāliǔbìng 花柳病 a venereal disease; V.D.

huāpén 花盆 a flower pot

huāpíng 花瓶 a vase

huāpǔ 花圃 a flower bed

huāqián 花錢 to spend money

huāquān 花圈 a garland; a wreath; a lei

huāróng yuèmào 花容月貌 (said of a woman) fair as a flower and the moon

huāruǐ 花蕊 pistils and stamens

huāsè 花色 varieties; patterns

huāshēng 花生 a peanut plant

huāshēngjiàng 花生醬 peanut butter

huāshēngmǐ 花生米 a peanut

huāshì 花市 a flower market

huāshù 花束 a bouquet; a bunch of flowers

huātóng 花童 a bridal page

huātuán jǐncù 花團錦簇 1. a conglomeration of splendid and beautiful things 2. a group of richly attired women

huāwén 花紋 a decorative design or pattern

huāxiāng 花香 fragrance of a flower

huāxīn 花心 unfaithful

huāyán qiǎoyǔ 花言巧語 honeyed words

huāyàng 花樣 a pattern; a style; a model

huāyuán 花園 a flower garden; a garden

huāzhāo 花招 a sly trick

huāzhī zhāozhǎn 花枝招展 (said of beautifully dressed women) like a flowering branch attracting people's attention

huā 嘩

an onomatopoeia, such gurgle, clang, crack, etc.

huá 划

to oar; to row

huáchuán 划船 to row a boat

huáquán 划拳 a finger-guessing game

huásuàn 划算 1. to calculate; to weigh 2. profitable

huá 華

1. Cathay; China 2. splendid; majestic; gorgeous; colorful; brilliant; bright; fine; beautiful; luxurious 3. prosperous; thriving

huádēng chūshàng 華燈初上 (descriptive of urban scenes at dusk) Colorful lamps are beginning to light up.

huá'ěrzīwǔ 華爾茲舞 waltz

Huáfǔ 華府 Washington D.C.

huálì 華麗 magnificent; resplendent; gorgeous

Huáqiáo 華僑 overseas Chinese

Huáxià 華夏 Cathay

Huáyì 華裔 foreign citizens of Chinese origin

Huáyǔ 華語 the Chinese language; Chinese

huá 猾

cunning; shrewd; crafty

huá 滑

1. to slip; to slide; to glide 2. smooth; slippery 3. insincere; dishonest; cunning 4. (also **gǔ**) funny; comical; ridiculous

huábǎn 滑板 1. (machinery) a slide 2. (table tennis) feint play 3. a skateboard

huábīng 滑冰 ice-skating

huácǎo 滑草 grass skiing

huádǎo 滑倒 to slip and fall

huádòng 滑動 (physics) to slide

huáji 滑稽 funny; comical; ridiculous

huájiāo 滑跤 to slip and fall down

huálěi 滑壘 (baseball) base sliding

huálún 滑輪 1. a roller 2. a pulley

huáshǔ 滑鼠 (computer) a mouse

huáshuǐ 滑水 water skiing

huátī 滑梯 a slideway (for children's amusement)

huátóu 滑頭 a crafty person; a cunning person

huátóu huá'nǎo 滑頭滑腦 sly; crafty; guile

huáxiáng 滑翔 to glide

huáxiángjī 滑翔機 a glider

huáxiángyì 滑翔翼 a hang glider

huáxíng 滑行 to slide; to coast; to taxi

huáxuě 滑雪 to ski; to slide or travel on skis

huá 劃

to cut

huá 譁(嘩)

noise; tumult; hubbub; clamor; uproar

huárán 譁然 uproarious; boisterous; tumultuous

huázhòng qǔchǒng 譁衆取寵 to practice demagogy; to make seditious speeches

huà 化

1. to change; to convert; to transform; to influence 2. short for "chemistry" 3. to melt

huàchú 化除 to dissolve to nothing; to dispel

huàdí wéiyǒu 化敵爲友 to convert an enemy into a friend

huàfēnchí 化糞池 a cesspool or cesspit

huàgōng 化工 1. Nature's work; operations of Nature 2. chemical engineering

huàhé 化合 to combine (chemically)

huàhéwù 化合物 a (chemical)

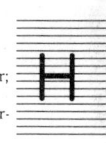

H

compound

huàjiě 化解 to settle (disputes)

huàmíng 化名 to assume a pseudonym; a pseudonym

huàshēn 化身 an incarnation; an embodiment

huàshí 化石 a fossil

huàwéi wūyǒu 化爲烏有 to disappear completely

huàxiǎn wéiyí 化險爲夷 to turn peril into safety

huàxué 化學 chemistry

huàxué féiliào 化學肥料 chemical fertilizer

huàxué xiānwéi 化學纖維 synthetic fiber

huàyàn 化驗 to subject to chemical analysis

huàyànshì 化驗室 a laboratory

huàyuán 化緣 to solicit alms

huàzhěng wéilíng 化整爲零 to break up the whole into parts

huàzhuāng 化妝 to make up; to apply cosmetics

huàzhuāng 化裝 to masquerade

huàzhuāngpǐn 化妝品 cosmetics

huàzhuāng wǔhuì 化裝舞會 a masquerade

huà 畫

1. to paint or draw (a picture); a painting; a drawing 2. to mark off; to delimit 3. to plan; to design; a plan 4. a stroke in a Chinese character

huàbǎn 畫板 a drawing board

huàbǐ 畫筆 a painting brush

huàbǐng chōngjī 畫餅充飢 (literally) to try to satisfy hunger by drawing cakes—to value empty names

huàbù 畫布 a canvas (for painting)

huàcè 畫冊 a picture or painting album

huàfǎ 畫法 a method of painting or drawing

huàfēn 畫分 to mark off; to divide; to demarcate

huàfēng 畫風 style of painting

huàgǎo 畫稿 drafts for paintings

or drawings

huàhǔ lèiquǎn 畫虎類犬 to fail because of undue ambition

huàjiā 畫家 a painter; an artist

huàjià 畫架 an easel

huàjiè 畫界 to delimit; to mark boundaries; to demarcate

huàjù 畫具 articles used for painting; painting tools

huàkān 畫刊 a pictorial magazine

huàkuāng 畫框 refer to **huàkuāng** 畫框

huàkuāng 畫框 a picture frame

huàláng 畫廊 a gallery (for paintings)

huàlóng diǎnjīng 畫龍點睛 to add the punch line; to add the finishing touch

huàméiniǎo 畫眉鳥 the thrush

huàmiàn 畫面 general appearance of a picture; tableau

huàshé tiānzú 畫蛇添足 to make undesirable additions; superfluous

huàshī 畫師 a painter; an artist

huàshì 畫室 an artist's studio

huàtú 畫圖 to draw pictures

huàxiàng 畫像 1. to paint a portrait 2. a portrait

huàyī 畫一 to make uniform

huàyì 畫意 the mood of a painting

huàzhǎn 畫展 an art exhibition

huà 華

1. luster; brilliancy; glory; splendor 2. a Chinese family name

Huàshān 華山 Mountain Hua, a sacred mountain in Shaanxi Province

huà 話

1. words; sayings 2. to speak; to talk; to converse; to say 3. language

huàbié 話別 to bid farewell; to say good-bye

huàbǐng 話柄 words or behavior as material for others' gossip

huàbù tóujī 話不投機 not seeing eye to eye in conversation or talk

huàjiācháng 話家常 to chitchat

huàjiù 話舊 to talk over old times

huàjù 話劇 a play or drama (as distinct from opera)

huàtí 話題 the topic of conversation or discussion

huàtŏng 話筒 1. a microphone 2. a telephone transmitter 3. a megaphone

huàxiázi 話匣子 1. a phonograph 2. a chatterbox

huàzhōng yǒuhuà 話中有話 overtones in conversation

huà 劃

1. to unify 2. to lay boundaries 3. to draw a line; to mark; to delineate 4. to plan or design 5. to set aside; to divide 6. a stroke (of a Chinese character)

huàbō 劃撥 to deposit money under the account of a seller in payment of goods purchased; to transfer funds

huàdìng 劃定 to delimit; to mark out

huàfēn 劃分 to differentiate

huàqīng 劃清 to draw a clear line of demarcation

huàshídài 劃時代 epoch-making; epochal

huàyī 劃一 to make uniform

huà 樺

a birch

huái 徊 also huí

1. hesitating; irresolute; indecisive 2. to move to and fro; to walk around

Huái 淮

name of a river flowing from West China into the Gulf of Bohai

Huáinán 淮南 the region south of the Huai River

Huáihé 淮河 the Huai River

huái 懷

1. bosom; breast 2. to hold; to harbor 3. to think of; to recollect 4. to conceive (a child)

huáibào 懷抱 an embrace; a hug; to embrace; to hug

huáibiǎo 懷錶 a pocket watch

huáicái bùyù 懷才不遇 to have talent but no opportunity to use it

huáichūn 懷春 (usually said of young girls) to begin to think of love, or become sexually awakened

huáiguǐtāi 懷鬼胎 to harbor an evil scheme

huáihèn 懷恨 to bear a grudge

huáijiù 懷舊 1. to yearn for the past; nostalgia 2. to think of old friends

huáiniàn 懷念 to have a sweet memory of

huáitāi 懷胎 to become pregnant; to conceive

huáixiāng 懷鄉 homesick

huáixiǎng 懷想 to remember with fondness; to yearn for

huáiyí 懷疑 to doubt; to suspect

huáiyùn 懷孕 to become pregnant; to conceive

huáizhōng 懷中 1. in the arms 2. in the mind

huài 壞

1. broken-down; decaying; rotten; out of order; useless 2. bad; poor (scores, etc.) 3. vicious; mean; evil (persons, etc.)

huàichu 壞處 bad points; shortcomings

huàidàn 壞蛋 a bad fellow; a villain

huàidōngxi 壞東西 a bad person or thing

huàihuà 壞話 slander

huàipēizi 壞坯子 a bad egg; a lout

huàiqiú 壞球 (baseball) ball

huàirén 壞人 a bad guy; an evil person

huàishì 壞事 1. a bad thing; an evil deed 2. to make things worse

huàisǐ 壞死 a necrosis

huàixiěbìng 壞血病 refer to **huàixuěbìng** 壞血病

huàixīnyǎnr 壞心眼兒 ill-intentioned; malicious

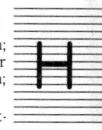

huàixuèbìng 壞血病 scurvy; scorbutus

huàizhàng 壞帳 bad debt

huàizhǔyì 壞主意 a wicked or crooked idea

huān 歡
1. pleased; glad; jubilant 2. pleasures; joys 3. a lover 4. in full swing; active and energetic; quick

huāndù jiājié 歡度佳節 to celebrate a festival with jubilation

huānhū 歡呼 to cheer with jubilation; to hurrah

huānjù 歡聚 1. a happy reunion; a joyful meeting 2. to gather together happily

huānlè 歡樂 joy; happiness; gaiety

huānshēng léidòng 歡聲雷動 to cheer thunderously; roaring applause

huānsòng 歡送 to send off; to give a farewell party

huāntiān xǐdì 歡天喜地 overjoyed

huānxǐ 歡喜 joyful; happy

huānxiào 歡笑 cheer and laughter—great joy; jubilation

huānxīn 歡心 (to win another's) favor or heart; love

huānxīn gǔwǔ 歡欣鼓舞 to be overjoyed; to be filled with exultation

huānyán 歡顏 happy looks or appearances

huānyíng 歡迎 to welcome; a welcome

huán 寰
a large domain; a vast space

huányǔ 寰宇 the world; the earth

huán 還
1. to return; to come back; return 2. to repay; to pay back; to restore

huánbào 還報 to repay; repayment

huánjī 還擊 1. to fight back; to return fire 2. (fencing) a riposte

huánjí 還擊 refer to **huánjī** 還擊

huánjià 還價 to haggle over a price

huánlǐ 還禮 1. to return a salute 2. to send a present in return

huánqīng 還清 to settle an account; all paid—as an account or debt

huánshǒu 還手 to strike back; to retaliate

huánxiāng 還鄉 to return to one's hometown

huányuán 還原 1. to return to normal or original status 2. (chemistry) reduction

huányuàn 還願 to fulfil a vow —to thank god for answering one's prayers

huánzhài 還債 to repay a debt

huán 環
1. a jade ring or bracelet; a ring; a bracelet 2. earrings for women; ear-ornaments 3. around; round; to surround 4. a link 5. (sports) a ring

Huánbǎoshǔ 環保署 the Environmental Protection Agency (EPA) in the Central Government

huánbào 環抱 to surround; to encircle

huándǎo 環島 around-the-island

huángù 環顧 1. to look around 2. to review

huángù sìzhōu 環顧四周 to look around

huánjié 環節 a segment; a link

huánjìng 環境 surroundings; environment

huánjìng bǎohù 環境保護 environmental protection

huánjìng wèishēng 環境衛生 environmental sanitation

huánjìng wūrǎn 環境汙染 environmental pollution

huánliè 環列 to surround on all sides

huánliú 環流 1. to flow or travel around in circles 2. circulation; circumfluence

huánqiú 環球 around the globe

huánrǎo 環繞 to surround; to move round; to circle

huánrǎo 環繞 refer to **huánrǎo** 環繞

huányóu shìjiè 環遊世界 to take a round-the-world tour

huán 鍰
1. an ancient unit of weight 2. money; cash

huán 浣
refer to **huàn** 浣

huán 緩
1. slow; gradual; tardy; leisurely; unhurried 2. to delay; to slacken; to put off; to postpone; to defer 3. to revive; to refresh

huánbīng zhìjì 緩兵之計 delaying tactics

huǎnchōng 緩衝 to serve as a buffer; to buff

huǎnhé 緩和 1. to subside; to relax; to alleviate 2. calm; mild

huǎnmàn 緩慢 slow

huǎnxíng 緩刑 1. to suspend a sentence; to reprieve 2. a reprieve; probation

huǎnyì 緩議 to defer the discussion

huàn 幻
1. illusion; hallucination; magic; fantasy 2. illusory; changeable; unreal

huàndēngjī 幻燈機 a slide projector

huàndēngpiàn 幻燈片 a slide

huànjǐng 幻景 a mirage; Fata Morgana

huànjìng 幻境 a dreamland

huànjué 幻覺 hallucination; a phantasm; a fantasy

huànmèng 幻夢 a daydream; a fantasy; a fantasm

huànmiè 幻滅 disillusionment

huànxiǎng 幻想 to daydream; reverie; a vision

huànxiǎngqǔ 幻想曲 a fantasia or fantasy

huànxiàng 幻象 a vision; an illusion; a phantasm or fantasm

huànyǐng 幻影 an unreal and visionary image

huàn 宦
1. a government official; the government service 2. castrated

huànguān 宦官 a eunuch

huànhǎi fúchén 宦海浮沈 the ups and downs in officialdom

huàn 浣 also **huǎn, wǎn**
1. to wash; to rinse 2. ten days; any of the three ten-day divisions of a month

huàndí 浣滌 to wash; to rinse

huànxióng 浣熊 a racoon

huàn 患
1. suffering; adversity; disaster; peril 2. trouble; worry 3. to be troubled by; to be worried about

huànbìng 患病 to be ill

huànbù 患部 (said of wounds or skin diseases) the infected part

huànchù 患處 the wounded part

huàndé huànshī 患得患失 to worry about worldly gain and loss

huànnàn 患難 suffering; distress; adversity; trouble

huànnàn zhījiāo 患難之交 friendship cemented in adversity

huànzhě 患者 a patient (at a hospital)

huàn 換
to exchange; to change; to alter; to substitute

huànbān 換班 (said of factory workers) to change a shift; to relieve (guard or sentry duties)

huànbiān 換邊 (sports) to change sides

huàndǎng 換擋 to shift gears

huàn'gǎng 換崗 refer to **huàn-gǎng** 換崗

huàn'gǎng 換崗 to relieve a guard or sentry

huànjì 換季 1. the change of seasons 2. to change clothing or uniforms according to the season

huànqì 換氣 to breathe; to take breath (in swimming)

huànqián 換錢 1. to change money (into small change) 2. to convert one currency to another 3. to barter goods for money

huànqǔ 換取 to change; to

H

exchange

huànrén 換人 substitution (of players)

huànsuàn 換算 to convert (one system of measurement into another)

huànsuànbiǎo 換算表 a conversion table

huàntāng bù huànyào 換湯不換藥 a change in form but not in content

huànxīn 換新 to change something for a new one

huànyánzhī 換言之 in other words

huànyīfu 換衣服 to change dresses

huàn 渙

1. scattered; dispersed 2. name of a river

huànrán 渙然 scattered; dispersed

huànrán bīngshì 渙然冰釋 (said of a grudge, misunderstanding, etc.) to vanish

huànsàn 渙散 1. lacking concentration or organization 2. (said of morale) to collapse

huàn 喚

1. to call 2. to summon 3. to arouse

huànqǐ 喚起 1. to arouse to action 2. to call; to evoke

huànxǐng 喚醒 to arouse; to awaken

huàn 煥

1. bright; brilliant; lustrous; luminous 2. (said of an appearance) shining; vigorous and elegant

huànfā 煥發 scintillating; shining; radiant

huànrán yīxīn 煥然一新 brand-new

huàn 瘓

paralysis

huāng 荒

1. uncultivated; desolate; wild; waste; deserted; barren 2. absurd; ridiculous 3. famine; scarcity; deficiency 4. to neglect

huāngdàn 荒誕 absurd; nonsensical

huāngdǎo 荒島 an uninhabited island; a barren island

huāngdì 荒地 uncultivated land; waste land; the wilderness

huāngfèi 荒廢 to neglect; to leave completely unattended to

huāngliáng 荒涼 desolate; deserted; wild

huāngmiù 荒謬 grossly absurd; ridiculous; preposterous

huāngnián 荒年 a year of bad crops; a year of famine

huāngqiāng zǒudiào 荒腔走調 out of tune

huāngtang 荒唐 absurd; nonsensical

huāngtǔ 荒土 uncultivated land; waste land; the wilderness

huāngwú 荒蕪 deserted and desolate; desolation

huāngyě 荒野 the wilderness

huāngyín 荒淫 dissipated; dissolute; profligate

huāng 慌

to lose self-possession; to lose one's head; panic; confused

huāngluàn 慌亂 in a hurry and confusion

huāngmáng 慌忙 hurried and flustered; hurry-scurry

huāngzhang 慌張 flustered; nervous and confused

huáng 皇

1. imperial; royal 2. an emperor 3. beautiful; brilliant 4. uneasy; anxious 5. a term of respect for an ancestor

huángchú 皇儲 refer to **huángchǔ** 皇儲

huángchǔ 皇儲 the crown prince

huángdì 皇帝 an emperor

huáng'ēn 皇恩 imperial favor or kindness

huánggōng 皇宮 an imperial palace

huángguān 皇冠 an imperial crown

huánghòu 皇后 an empress

huángjiā 皇家 the imperial family (or house)

huánglíng 皇陵 an imperial mausoleum

huángqīn guóqī 皇親國戚 relatives of the emperor

huángshang 皇上 His Majesty

huángshì 皇室 the imperial household; the royal household

huángtàihòu 皇太后 the empress dowager

huángtiān hòutǔ 皇天后土 Heaven and Earth

huáng 凰

the female phoenix, a legendary bird in Chinese mythology

huáng 惶

1. afraid; fearful; apprehensive 2. anxious; uneasy 3. flurried; hurried

huánghuáng 惶惶 1. anxious; uneasy 2. hurried; hasty

huángkǒng 惶恐 apprehensive; fearful; afraid

huáng 黃

1. yellow 2. a Chinese family name

huángbāochē 黃包車 a ricksha(w)

huángchéngchéng 黃澄澄 refer to **huángdēngdēng** 黃澄澄

huángdǎn 黃疸 jaundice; icterus

huángdào jírì 黃道吉日 a lucky day

huángdēngdēng 黃澄澄 glistening yellow; golden

Huángdì 黃帝 the Yellow Emperor, a legendary ruler

huángdòu 黃豆 soybean

huángfà chuítiáo 黃髮垂髫 refer to **huángfà chuítiáo** 黃髮垂髫

huángfà chuítiáo 黃髮垂髫 the aged and the young

huángfēng 黃蜂 a wasp

huángguā 黃瓜 a cucumber

Huánghǎi 黃海 the Huanghai (Yellow) Sea

Huánghé 黃河 the Huanghe (Yellow) River

Huánghé Liúyù 黃河流域 the Huanghe (Yellow) River Valley

huánghuā guīnǚ 黃花閨女 a virgin

huánghūn 黃昏 dusk

huángjīn 黃金 gold

huángjīn shídài 黃金時代 the golden age

Huáng Lǎo 黃老 1. Huang Di and Laozi 2. Taoism

huánglíniǎo 黃鸝鳥 the oriole

huángli 黃曆 (colloquial) an almanac

huángliǎnpó 黃臉婆 the yellow-faced woman—my wife

huángmá 黃麻 jute

huángmáo yātou 黃毛丫頭 a fledgling little girl

huángméidiào 黃梅調 a popular folk melody

huángniú 黃牛 1. a common Chinese ox 2. a scalper of tickets, etc. 3. (slang) to fail to appear on an appointment

huángniúpiào 黃牛票 scalped tickets

huángpáo 黃袍 1. high-ranking Buddhist monks (marked by their yellow robes) 2. the imperial robe

huángquán 黃泉 Hades

huángrèbìng 黃熱病 yellow fever

huángsè 黃色 1. yellow 2. decadent; obscene; pornographic

huángsè shūkān 黃色書刊 pornographic books and periodicals

huángsè zhàyào 黃色炸藥 TNT

huángshǔláng 黃鼠狼 a weasel

huángtāng 黃湯 wine

huángtóng 黃銅 brass

huángtǔ 黃土 loess

huángyīng 黃鶯 an oriole

huángyú 黃魚 a yellow croaker

huángzhǒngrén 黃種人 the yellow race; the Mongolian race

huáng 徨

1. agitated; alarmed 2. irresolute

huánghuáng 徨徨 agitated and indecisive; alarmed and anxious

huáng 遑
1. hurry; to hurry 2. disturbed anxious 3. leisurely 4. not to

huánglùn 遑論 not to mention...

huáng 潢
a lake or a pond

Huángchí nòngbīng 潢池弄兵 to disregard a disaster

huáng 蝗
a locust

huángchóng 蝗蟲 a locust

huáng 磺
sulfur; brimstone

huáng 簧
1. a reed; the metal tongue in a reed organ 2. a reed organ 3. a spring or catch in a machine

huángpiàn 簧片 the metal tongue in a reed organ

huǎng 恍
1. absent-minded; unconscious 2. all of a sudden; suddenly 3. seem; as if

huǎnghū 恍惚 1. in a trance; absent-minded 2. dimly; faintly

huǎngrán dàwù 恍然大悟 to come to understand suddenly

huǎngrú géshì 恍如隔世 so different that it is as if a generation has passed

huǎng 晃
1. brightness 2. dazzling; glaring 3. a flash; to flash past; to appear and disappear very quickly

huǎng 幌
a curtain; a cloth screen; a strip of cloth

huǎngzi 幌子 something to dazzle or cheat another with, as boasts or swashbuckling ways; a facade

huǎng 謊
1. a lie 2. to lie

huǎngbào 謊報 to report a falsehood

huǎnghuà 謊話 a lie

huǎngyán 謊言 a lie

huàng 晃
to rock; to sway; to shake

huàngdang 晃蕩 to sway; to oscillate

huàngdòng 晃動 to rock; to sway

huī 灰
1. ashes; dust 2. lime 3. gray (color) 4. disheartened; disappointed or discouraged 5. (now rarely) to break into tiny pieces or particles

huī'àn 灰暗 murky gray; gloomy

huībái 灰白 pale; ashen

huīchén 灰塵 dust

huīgūniang 灰姑娘 Cinderella

huījìn 灰燼 ashes; embers

huīmēngmēng 灰蒙蒙 dusky; overcast

huīméngméng 灰蒙蒙 refer to **huīmēngmēng** 灰蒙蒙

huīsè 灰色 gray color

huīxīn 灰心 disappointed; discouraged; disheartened

huī 恢
1. great; immense; enormous; vast; extensive 2. to recover; to restore; to regain

huīfù 恢復 to restore; to regain; to recover

huīfù yuánzhuàng 恢復原狀 to restore the original condition

huīhóng 恢宏 extensive; magnanimous

huī 揮
1. to wield (a sword, pen, etc.); to move; to shake; to wave; to brandish; to make a light or rapid stroke 2. to conduct; to direct (troop movements, a concert, a course of action, etc.) 3. to wipe away (sweat, tears, etc.) 4. to scatter; to sprinkle 5. to squander (money, etc.) 6. to swing (fists)

huīdòng 揮動 to wield (a sword, etc.); to swing (fists, etc.)

huīfā 揮發 to volatilize; to evaporate

huīfāyóu 揮發油 benzine

huīháo 揮毫 (said of calligraphers) to wield the writing brush —to write

huīhuò 揮霍 to spend freely; to squander

huījūn 揮軍 to march troops to war

huīsǎ 揮灑 to write or paint freely

huīshǒu 揮手 to wave one's hand (in greeting or bidding farewell)

huīwǔ 揮舞 to wave; to wield; to brandish

huī 暉
1. the sunshine 2. bright; radiant

huīyìng 暉映 bright and brilliant

huī 詼
1. funny; humorous 2. to ridicule; to joke

huīxié 詼諧 funny; humorous; comical

huī 輝
brightness; splendor; light; luster; luminosity; brilliance

huīhuáng 輝煌 magnificent; splendid; glorious; brilliant

huīyìng 輝映 to emit and reflect light

huī 麾
1. a flag; a banner; a standard 2. to command; to lead

huījūn 麾軍 to lead an army

huīxià 麾下 1. under a general's command 2. sir (in addressing a general)

huī 徽
1. honorable 2. stops on a lute 3. a streamer, flag, pennant, etc.; a flag-sign 4. an emblem; a badge 5. Anhui Province

huīzhāng 徽章 a badge

huí 回
1. to return; to go back; to bring back; to turn back 2. to reply; to answer 3. to turn round 4. the number of times 5. a kind; a sort 6. chapters in a novel 7. of Mo-

hammedanism; Moslems 8. the Hui nationality

huíbào 回報 1. to bring back a report 2. to repay (a favor or an injury)

huíbǐng 回稟 to report back (to one's superior)

huíchéng 回程 the return trip

huídá 回答 to reply; to answer; a reply

huídiàn 回電 1. a cable or telegram sent in reply 2. to wire back

huífǔ 回府 to return home

huífù 回覆 to reply; to answer; a reply

huígù 回顧 to look back

huíguāng fǎnzhào 回光返照 the transient reviving of the dying

huíháng 回航 to sail or fly back

huíhé 回合 an encounter; a round; a bout

huíhuà 回話 1. to bring back word; to report 2. a reply (usually one conveyed by a messenger)

huíjī 回擊 to fight back; to counterattack

huíjí 回擊 refer to huíjī 回擊

Huíjiào 回教 Mohammedanism; Islam

Huíjiàotú 回教徒 a Muslim

huíjìng 回敬 1. to give a gift in return 2. tit for tat

huíjué 回絕 to decline; to refuse

huíkòu 回扣 a commision on sales

huíkuì 回饋 to feedback

huílai 回來 to come back; to return

huílǐ 回禮 1. to return a salute 2. to send a present in return

huílìqiú 回力球 pelota; jai alai

Huí Lù zhīzāi 回祿之災 a fire disaster

huímóu 回眸 (said of a woman) to glance back

huíqu 回去 1. to go back 2. to return

huíshēng 回升 to rise again (after a fall)

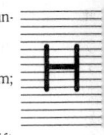

huíshēng 回聲 an echo

huíshōu 回收 1. to retrieve; to recover; to reclaim 2. to recycle

huítiān fáshù 回天乏術 Nothing can be done to revive the dead or to save the dying.

huítiáo 回條 a receipt

huítóu 回頭 1. to turn back 2. after a while; later 3. to return 4. to repent

huítóukè 回頭客 a regular customer; an old customer

huítóu shì'àn 回頭是岸 Repentance is salvation.

huíwèi 回味 to ponder over

huíxiāng 回鄉 to return to one's home village

huíxiǎng 回想 to recollect; to recall

huíxiǎng 回響 response

huíxīn zhuǎnyì 回心轉意 1. to decide to return from sin to virtue 2. to change one's mind

huíxìn 回信 1. a letter in reply 2. to write back 3. a reply

huíyì 回憶 to recollect; to recall

huíyìlù 回憶錄 memoirs; recollections

huíyīn 回音 1. to echo; an echo 2. a response

huíyóu 回郵 return mail

huízhuǎn 回轉 to turn round

huízuǐ 回嘴 to talk back; to retort

huí 徊

refer to **huái** 徊

huí 洄

(said of water) whirling

huílán 洄瀾 eddies

huí 迴

1. to turn; to rotate; to revolve 2. to zigzag; to wind 3. (回) to return

huíbì 迴避 1. to avoid meeting (another person) 2. (law) to withdraw; withdrawal 3. to decline an offer, or resign from a job, in order to avoid likely suspicion of favoritism

huícháng dàngqì 迴腸盪氣 (said of music, poetry, etc.) to

deeply affect one's emotions; very touching

huíláng 迴廊 a winding corridor

huíwénzhēn 迴紋針 a paper clip

huíxuán 迴旋 to turn round and round; to circle

huízhuǎn 迴轉 to turn round

huí 蛔

an ascarid; a roundworm

huíchóng 蛔蟲 a roundworm

huǐ 悔

to regret; to repent; remorse

huǐbù dāngchū 悔不當初 to regret a previous mistake

huǐgǎi 悔改 to repent of (a sin); to be repentant of

huǐguò 悔過 to show penitence; to be repentant

huǐguòshū 悔過書 a written statement of repentance pledging not to commit the same offense again (a form of punishment)

huǐhèn 悔恨 to feel remorse for; to regret; remorse

huǐwù 悔悟 to awake from sin; to repent

huǐzhī yīwǎn 悔之已晚 It is too late to repent or regret.

huǐ 賄

refer to **huì** 賄

huǐ 毀

1. to destroy; to ruin; to damage; to injure 2. to libel; to slander; to abuse; to revile; to defame

huǐbàng 毀謗 to libel; to slander; to malign

huǐhuài 毀壞 to destroy; to injure; to damage

huǐmiè 毀滅 to demolish; to ruin; to destroy

huǐqì 毀棄 to abrogate; to repeal; to dissolve; to annul; to rescind

huǐróng 毀容 to disfigure

huǐsǔn 毀損 to damage; to injure; to disfigure

huǐyú yīdàn 毀於一旦 to be ruined or destroyed in one day

huǐyù cānbàn 毀譽參半 to draw both praises and criticisms

huǐyuē 毀約 to break one's promise

huì 會
refer to **huì** 會 10

huì 誨
refer to **huì** 誨

huì 燬
1. fire; a blaze 2. to destroy by fire; to burn away; to burn down

huì 卉
1. a general term for grasses 2. myriads of

huì 晦
1. the last day of every month in the lunar calendar 2. night; evening; dark 3. obscure; indistinguishable 4. unlucky; bad luck

huì'àn 晦暗 dark; gloomy

huìqì 晦氣 unlucky; bad luck

huìsè 晦澀 hard to understand

huì 彗
1. a broom 2. a comet 3. to expose to sunlight

huìxīng 彗星 a comet

huì 喙
1. a beak; a bill; a snout 2. a mouth

huì 惠
1. to benefit; benefit; to profit; profit; to favor; a favor 2. kind; benevolent; gracious 3. gentle and yielding

huìcì 惠賜 to be kind enough to give (me something)

huìcún 惠存 to be so kind as to keep (my gift)

huìgù 惠顧 1. to patronize (my business establishment) 2. your kindness, favor or patronage

huìlín 惠臨 (honorific expression) to favor with one's presence

huìsì 惠賜 refer to **huìcì** 惠賜

huìzé 惠澤 benevolence; favor

huì 賄 also **huì**
1. to bribe; bribery 2. money; wealth

huìlù 賄賂 to bribe; bribery

huìxuǎn 賄選 to try to win in an election by means of bribery

huì 彙
1. a category; a class; a series 2. to categorize 3. to collect

huìbào 彙報 to collect (all information) and report

huìbiān 彙編 to edit (data, etc.)

huìjí 彙集 to collect (materials, etc.)

huìzhù 彙注 a collection of footnotes, etc., for expounding a book, etc.

huì 會
1. to meet 2. to assemble; to gather; to converge 3. a meeting; a convention; a conference 4. an association; a society 5. a private banking cooperative 6. to be able to 7. to understand; to comprehend; to realize 8. shall; will 9. a chief city; a capital 10. (also **huì**) a brief period of time; a moment

huìcān 會餐 to dine together

huìchǎng 會場 the place of a meeting; the site of a conference

huìcuì 會萃 to converge

huìhé 會合 to assemble; to gather; to meet

huìhuà 會話 a conversation; a dialogue

huìjiàn 會見 to meet (a person)

huìkè 會客 to receive callers (or visitors)

huìkè shíjiān 會客時間 visiting hours

huìkèshì 會客室 a reception room

huìmiàn 會面 to meet face to face

huìqí 會期 1. the time of a meeting 2. the duration of a meeting

huìqí 會期 refer to **huìqí** 會期

huìshāng 會商 to negotiate; to consult

huìshěn 會審 to review or try jointly

huìshī 會師 to join forces

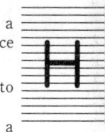

huìtán 會談 talks

huìtóng 會同 together with

huìwù 會晤 to meet

huìwù 會務 the business of a meeting, conference, convention, association, etc.

huìxīn 會心 to come to an understanding without explanations

huìyì 會意 1. to understand the meaning 2. associative compounds, one of six categories under which Chinese characters are grouped

huìyì 會議 a conference; a meeting

huìyuán 會員 a member of an association, society, etc.

huìyuánguó 會員國 a member nation (or state)

huìzhāng 會章 the charter of an association or organization

huìzhǎng 會長 the president of an association or organization

huì 匯

1. to remit money 2. to converge 3. to flow into

huìduì 匯兌 (commerce) exchange

huìfèi 匯費 the remitting charge or fee

huìhé 匯合 to converge; to join

huìjí 匯集 to gather in one place

huìjù 匯聚 to gather in one place

huìkuǎn 匯款 1. a remittance 2. to remit money

huìlǜ 匯率 the exchange rate

huìpiào 匯票 a money order; a draft; a bill of exchange

huì 誨 also huì

1. to teach; to instruct 2. instructions 3. to admonish 4. to induce

huìrén bùjuàn 誨人不倦 to teach without weariness

huì 慧

intelligent; bright; wise

huìgēn 慧根 (Buddhism) the root of wisdom that can lead one to truth

huìxiá 慧黠 (literary language) clever and artful; astute

huìyǎn 慧眼 1. insight 2. (Buddhism) the eye of religious insight

huìyǎn shí yīngxióng 慧眼識英雄 Discerning eyes can tell greatness from mediocrity

huìyǎn shì yīngxióng 慧眼識英雄 refer to **huìyǎn shí yīngxióng** 慧眼識英雄

huì 諱

1. to conceal; to hide 2. to shun; to avoid; taboo 3. name of a deceased elder member of the family

huìjí jìyī 諱疾忌醫 to conceal one's ailment and refuse to consult the doctor—to refuse to face a harsh reality

huìmò rúshēn 諱莫如深 kept as a top secret; to avoid mentioning something completely

huìyán 諱言 to avoid mentioning something

huì 蕙

1. a species of fragrant grass with red flowers and black seeds in early fall 2. a species of fragrant orchid

huìzhí lánxīn 蕙質蘭心 refer to **huìzhì lánxīn** 蕙質蘭心

huìzhì lánxīn 蕙質蘭心 (said of a lady) beautiful and intelligent

huì 薈

1. a luxuriant growth of vegetation 2. to cover or conceal

huìcuì 薈萃 1. flourishing or thriving 2. (said of distinguished people) to gather; to assemble

huì 燴

1. to put (a variety of materials) together and cook; to braise 2. to serve (noodles, rice, etc.) with a topping of meat, vegetables, etc., in gravy

huì 穢

1. vile; wicked 2. dirty; filthy 3. obscene; wanton (ways or conduct) 4. ugly and abominable 5. weeds on a farm

huìwù 穢物 filth

huì 繪
to draw (pictures)

huìhuà 繪畫 painting; drawing

huìshēng huìyǐng 繪聲繪影
to give a very vivid description

huìtú 繪圖 1. to draw pictures 2. to prepare (engineering) drawings

hūn 昏
1. dusk; dark 2. confused; muddled; mixed-up; demented 3. unclear of sight; dizzy 4. (婚) to marry

hūn'àn 昏暗 dim; dusky

hūndǎo 昏倒 to faint; to swoon

hūnhuā 昏花 poor of vision

hūnhuáng 昏黃 twilight; dim

hūnhūnchénchén 昏昏沈沈
dizzy and sleepy; slumberous

hūnhūn yùshuì 昏昏欲睡
drowsy; sleepy

hūnjué 昏厥 to faint; to swoon

hūnkuì 昏聵 muddled, confused and stupid

hūnluàn 昏亂 stupid and confused

hūnmèi 昏昧 stupid; stupidity

hūnmí 昏迷 in a coma; delirious; stupor

hūnshuì 昏睡 deep slumber; lethargic sleep

hūntiān hēidì 昏天黑地 1. very dark (as before a storm) 2. stupid or ignorant 3. dizzy

hūntóu hūnnǎo 昏頭昏腦 to feel dizzy, confused, and mixed-up

hūnxuàn 昏眩 dizzy; faint; giddy

hūnyōng 昏庸 muddle-headed; stupid; imbecile

hūn 婚
1. to wed; to marry 2. marriage

hūnjià 婚假 a wedding leave

hūnjià 婚嫁 to wed; marriage

hūnlǐ 婚禮 a wedding (ceremony)

hūnqī 婚期 the date of a wedding

hūnqī 婚期 refer to **hūnqī** 婚期

hūnshì 婚事 marriage

hūnyīn 婚姻 marriage

hūnyuē 婚約 a marriage contract; betrothal

hūn 葷
1. a meat and fish diet; meat-eating (as opposed to what vegetarians are practicing) 2. strong smelling foods or spices—such as onions, leeks, garlic, etc. 3. obscene or dirty language, narration, films, etc.

hún 混
turbid; muddy; not clear

húndàn 混蛋 Bloody fool!

hún 渾
1. entire; complete 2. to blend; to merge 3. muddy; turbid

húndàn 渾蛋 "rotten egg"—(abusive language) a blackguard

húnhòu 渾厚 1. (said of one's character) simple and honest 2. (said of writing, painting, etc.) simple and vigorous

húnhún'e'è 渾渾噩噩 muddle-headed; ignorant

húnqiú 渾球 a zany

húnrán 渾然 completely

húnrán yītǐ 渾然一體 a unified entity

húnshēn 渾身 one's entire body; from head to toe

húnshēn jiěshù 渾身解數
every means of solution

húnshēn shìdǎn 渾身是膽
very daring; fearless

húnshuǐ 渾水 muddy water

húntiānyí 渾天儀 (astronomy) an armillary sphere

húnyuán 渾圓 1. tactful; sophisticated 2. a sphere 3. perfectly round

húnzhuó 渾濁 turbid; muddy

hún 魂
a soul; a spirit

húnbù fùtǐ 魂不附體 frightened out of one's wits

húnfēi pòsàn 魂飛魄散 1. frightened out of one's senses; frightened out of one's wits 2. as good as dead

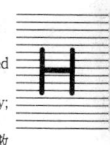

húnpò 魂魄 a soul

hún 餛

    stuffed dumplings with delicate flour wrapping; ravioli

húntun 餛飩 stuffed dumplings with delicate flour wrapping; ravioli

hǔn 混

    refer to **hùn** 混 1

hùn 混

    1. (also **hǔn**) disorderly; confused 2. to mix; mixed; to mingle or blend 3. to fool around; just to get along 4. to do things at random or without purpose

hùndùn 混沌 1. the chaotic world in prehistoric times 2. ignorant and dumb

hùndùn chūkāi 混沌初開 at the dawn of civilization

hùnfànchī 混飯吃 just to make ends meet

hùnhé 混合 to mix, mingle or blend together

hùnhé shuāngdǎ 混合雙打 mixed doubles

hùnhéwù 混合物 a mixture; a blend

hùnhùn 混混 1. dark; opaque 2. to drift through (life) 3. a hoodlum; a rascal

hùnjìn 混進 to infiltrate; to sneak into

hùnluàn 混亂 confusion; chaos

hùnníngtǔ 混凝土 concrete

hùnrìzi 混日子 just to make a living

hùnrù 混入 to mix oneself inside a body of people, an organization

hùnshì mówáng 混世魔王 a fiendish person who causes an upheaval in the world

hùntóng 混同 to merge; to combine

hùnwéi yītán 混爲一談 to lump together

hùnxiáo 混淆 mixed, confused and indistinguishable

hùnxiě'ér 混血兒 refer to **hùnxuè'ér** 混血兒

hùnxuè'ér 混血兒 a human hybrid; a mixed-blood

hùnyáo 混淆 refer to **hùnxiáo** 混淆

hùnzá 混雜 1. to mix 2. motley; heterogeneous 3. disorderly; confused

hùnzhàn 混戰 a melee; a wild battle

hùnzhàng 混帳 Scoundrel! Rascal!

hùn 溷

    1. dirty 2. messy

hùnjī 溷跡 to conceal

hùnzhuó 溷濁 dirty; muddy

hùn 諢

    ridicule; derision; a joke; a jest

hùnmíng 諢名 a nickname; a sobriquet

huō 豁

    1. a crack; a break; a breach 2. to crack; to break open; to split 3. to give up; to sacrifice; to risk one's life for

huōchuqu 豁出去 to forge ahead in disregard of the consequence

huó 和 also **huò**

    to mix with water, etc.

huómiàn 和麵 to knead flour

huó 活

    1. to live; to survive; to be alive 2. to save the life of 3. active; lively; vivacious 4. movable; mobile; flexible 5. work

huóbàn 活瓣 a valve

huóbǎo 活寶 one who behaves clownishly

huódàolǎo, xuédàolǎo 活到老，學到老 One is never too old to learn.

huódòng 活動 1. activities 2. active; lively 3. to lobby; to canvass 4. movable; mobile 5. loose 6. to exercise

Huófó 活佛 (Lamaism) a Buddha incarnate

huógāi 活該 It serves you (him, them) right.

huóhuǒshān 活火山 an active

volcano

huójiānguǐ 活見鬼 absurd; preposterous

huókǒu 活口 1. a captive; a prisoner 2. to support a dependent or dependents

huólì 活力 vitality; vigor

huólóng huóxiàn 活龍活現 vividly

huólù 活路 1. an unblocked passage 2. a way out 3. a way to make a living

huóluò 活絡 1. loose 2. indefinite

huómén 活門 a valve

huómìng 活命 1. to survive; to live 2. life

huópo 活潑 active; lively; sprightly

huóqī cúnkuǎn 活期存款 a current deposit

huóqí cúnkuǎn 活期存款 refer to **huóqī cúnkuǎn** 活期存款

huósāi 活塞 a piston

huóshēngshēng 活生生 alive and kicking

huóshòuzuì 活受罪 to feel as if one were just living to suffer

huóxiàng 活像 to be quite like

huóyè 活頁 loose or detachable leaves (of notebooks, etc.)

huóyòng 活用 to use or apply knowledge with imagination or ingenuity

huóyuè 活躍 active; actively

huózhuō 活捉 to catch alive; to capture alive

huǒ 火

1. fire; flames; to burn with fire 2. fury; anger; temper 3. urgency; urgent; imminent; pressing 4. (Chinese herbal medicine) the latent "heat" in human body

huǒbǎ 火把 a torch

huǒbào 火爆 (dialect) fiery; irritable

huǒbìng 火併 an intramural fight

huǒchái 火柴 a match

huǒcháihé 火柴盒 a matchbox

huǒchǎng 火場 the scene of a fire

huǒchē 火車 a train

huǒchēpiào 火車票 train tickets

huǒchē shíjiānbiǎo 火車時間表 a train schedule

huǒchēzhàn 火車站 a railway station

huǒfū 火夫 a kitchen assistant; (military) a cook

huǒguāng 火光 the light or glow of fire

huǒguō 火鍋 a chafing pot; a chafing dish

huǒhǎi 火海 a great fire; a conflagration

huǒhóng 火紅 red as fire; fiery; flaming

huǒhou 火候 1. the time used in cooking a certain food 2. scholastic achievement 3. Taoist alchemy

huǒhuā 火花 sparks

huǒhuà 火化 to cremate; cremation

huǒjī 火雞 a turkey

huǒjí 火急 very urgent; imminent

huǒjiàn 火箭 a rocket

huǒjǐng 火警 a fire alarm

huǒjù 火炬 a torch

huǒkēng 火坑 1. a situation of extreme hardship or difficulty 2. prostitution

huǒlàlà 火辣辣 burning

huǒlàlà 火辣辣 refer to **huǒlàlà** 火辣辣

huǒlì 火力 1. firepower 2. thermal

huǒlì fādiànchǎng 火力發電廠 a thermoelectric plant

huǒlú 火爐 a stove

huǒmiáo 火苗 flames

huǒqì 火氣 1. (Chinese medicine) internal heat 2. temper

huǒrè 火熱 passionate; enthusiastic; intimate

huǒsǎn gāozhāng 火傘高張 the scorching sunshine in summer—like a fully spread umbrella of fire

huǒshān 火山 a volcano

huǒshāng 火傷 a burn

huǒshàng jiāyóu 火上加油 (literally) to pour oil on the flame—to make things worse

huǒshāo méimao 火燒眉毛 very urgent or imminent

huǒshé 火舌 tongues of flame

huǒshì 火勢 the intensity and scope of a fire

huǒshǒu 火首 one whose house is the first to catch fire

huǒsù 火速 urgently; imminent; urgent

huǒtuǐ 火腿 Chinese ham; ham

huǒtuǐ sānmíngzhì 火腿三明治 a ham sandwich

huǒxīng 火星 1. the planet Mars 2. sparks

huǒyàn 火焰 flames

huǒyào 火藥 gunpowder

huǒyàokù 火藥庫 a powder magazine; an ammunition depot

huǒyàowèi 火藥味 the smell of gunpowder—a tense situation which can easily erupt into open hostilities

huǒzāi 火災 a fire disaster

huǒzāi bǎoxiǎn 火災保險 fire insurance

huǒzàng 火葬 to cremate; cremation

huǒzàngchǎng 火葬場 a crematory; a crematorium

huǒzhǒng 火種 1. tinder; embers kept for starting a new fire 2. any burning object which causes a fire disaster

huǒzhú 火燭 1. candlelight 2. an inflammable substance

huǒ 伙

1. a companion; a colleague 2. household goods

huǒbàn 伙伴 a companion; a colleague

huǒfáng 伙房 a kitchen

huǒfū 伙夫 a cook (in military troops)

huǒjì 伙計 a shop clerk

huǒshí 伙食 meals

huǒshítuán 伙食團 a mess

huǒtóng 伙同 in league with

huǒ 夥

1. many; much; lots of 2. a partner; a company 3. a waiter 4. a crowd

huǒbàn 夥伴 a companion; a partner

huǒjì 夥計 1. a waiter; a clerk 2. buddy

huǒtóng 夥同 in league with; to gang up with

huò 和

1. to blend; to mix 2. refer to **huó** 和

huò 或

1. a certain; some 2. perhaps; probably 3. or

huòduō huòshǎo 或多或少 more or less

huòxǔ 或許 perhaps; probably; maybe

huòzǎo huòwǎn 或早或晚 sooner or later

huòzhě 或者 1. or 2. perhaps

huò 貨

1. commodities; goods; products; freight; cargo 2. money; currency; property 3. to bribe; bribery 4. to sell 5. used as a term of reviling with an abusive suffix

huòbì 貨幣 currency; money

huòcāng 貨艙 the hold of a freighter; the cargo bay (of a plane)

huòchē 貨車 a freight car; a lorry; a cargo truck

huòchuán 貨船 a freighter; a cargo boat

huòdān 貨單 a manifest; an invoice

huòguì 貨櫃 a container

huòjī 貨機 an air freighter

huòkuǎn 貨款 payment for goods

huòlún 貨輪 a cargo tanker; a cargo vessel

huòsè 貨色 kinds, material or quality of goods; stock in trade; stuff

huòwù 貨物 commodities; goods

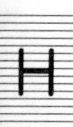

huòwùshuì 貨物稅 commodity tax

huòyùn 貨運 transportation service

huòzhēn jiàshí 貨眞價實 (a commercial slogan) goods of high quality sold at reasonable prices

huò 惑
1. to confuse; to perplex; to delude; to beguile; to mislead; to misguide; to puzzle 2. to doubt; to suspect

huò 禍
1. calamity; disaster; misfortune; evil 2. to bring disaster upon; to harm; to injure; to do evil to 3. to punish

huòbù dānxíng 禍不單行 Misfortunes never come singly (or single).

huòcóng kǒuchū 禍從口出 Careless talks may land one in trouble.

huòduān 禍端 the cause of a misfortune or disaster

huògēn 禍根 the cause of a misfortune or disaster

huòguó yāngmín 禍國殃民 to bring disaster upon the state and the people

huòhai 禍害 harm; injury; evil

huòhuàn 禍患 misfortune; disaster; harm; evil

huòluàn 禍亂 disturbances; disastrous disorder

huòshuǐ 禍水 a woman who is often the source of troubles

huò 霍
1. very rapidly; in a flash; suddenly 2. a Chinese family name

huòluàn 霍亂 cholera

huò 豁
1. to open up; clear 2. to exempt from (duties, etc.)

huòdá 豁達 1. open and clear 2. open-minded

huòmiǎn 豁免 to exempt from (taxes, military service, etc.); immunity

huò 獲

1. to get; to obtain; to incur; to capture; to catch; to reap 2. can; able

huòdé 獲得 to get or obtain; to acquire

huòjiǎng 獲獎 to win a prize

huòjiù 獲救 to be rescued or saved

huòshèng 獲勝 to triumph; to obtain victory; to win

huòyì 獲益 to get profit

huò 蒦
refer to hè 蒦

huò 穫
to reap or harvest; to cut grain

jī 几 also jǐ
a small table

jī 占
to divine; to resolve doubts by an application to spiritual beings

jītóng 乩童 a person who does planchette writing

jī 肌
1. tissue; muscles; flesh 2. the skin

jīfū 肌膚 1. the skin and flesh 2. the intimate relation between man and woman

jīròu 肌肉 muscles

jī 圾 also sè
garbage; refuse; waste

jī 奇
odd (numbers)

jīshù 奇數 an odd number

jī 迹
footprints; traces; tracks

jīxiàng 迹象 signs; marks; indications

jī 飢
hungry; hunger; starving; famine

jībù zéshí 飢不擇食 When one is hungry, one is not particular about what he is going to eat.

jīcháng lùlù 飢腸轆轆 to feel very hungry

jī'è 飢餓 hunger; hungry; starvation

J

jīhán jiāopò 飢寒交迫 to suffer from hunger and cold

jīhuang 飢荒 famine

jījǐn 飢饉 famine

jīkě 飢渴 hungry and thirsty

jīmín 飢民 starved people; famished people

jī 唧 also **jí**
1. a pump 2. the buzzing sound 3. to squirt

jījizhāzhā 唧唧喳喳 to chirp

jī 姬
1. a beautiful lady; a charming girl 2. a concubine 3. a Chinese family name

jī 基
1. a foundation; a base 2. an origin; a basis; a root 3. on the basis of; according to; on the strength of 4. the base of a chemical compound

jīběn 基本 1. a root, foundation or base 2. fundamental; basic; elementary 3. basically; on the whole; by and large

jīběn gōngzī 基本工資 basic wages

jīcéng 基層 basic level; a grass-roots unit

jīchǔ 基礎 1. the foundation of a building 2. the basis of an argument, etc.

jīdì 基地 a base (of operations)

Jīdūjiào 基督教 Christianity

jījīn 基金 a reserve fund

jījīnhuì 基金會 foundation

jīyīn 基因 a gene

jīyú 基於 because of; in view of

jīzhǔn 基準 a pattern; a standard; a model

jī 幾
1. small; tiny; slight 2. nearly an omen; a portent

jīdài 幾殆 in great danger

jīhū 幾乎 almost; nearly

jī 犄
a horn

jījiǎo 犄角 a corner

jījiao 犄角 a horn

jī 期
one year

jīfú 期服 one-year mourning

jīnián 期年 the first anniversary

jī 畸
1. fields with irregular boundaries 2. malformed; misshapen; deformity 3. fractional remainders

jījiǎo 畸角 a corner

jīxíng 畸形 malformation; abnormality; deformity

jī 跡
traces; tracks; relics; a print

jī 箕
1. a winnowing basket; a sieve 2. a dust basket; a dustpan 3. non-spiral lines on a fingertip

jījù 箕踞 (said of a person) to sit with legs sprawled out

jī 緝 also **qī**
1. to arrest; to capture 2. to twist and join (cords) 3. to continue 4. to hem clothing

jībǔ 緝捕 to search and arrest; to capture

jīhuò 緝獲 to arrest; to capture; to seize

jīsī 緝私 to arrest smugglers

jī 畿 also **qí**
areas near the capital; the royal domain

jī 稽
1. to investigate; to examine; to inspect; to verify 2. to stay; to delay or procrastinate

jīchá 稽查 to examine and investigate

jīhé 稽核 to examine and audit

jīkǎo 稽考 to examine; to verify

jī 嘰
1. to talk indistinctly in a low voice 2. to chirp

jīgu 嘰咕 to grumble

jījizhāzhā 嘰嘰喳喳 1. to chirp; to twitter 2. to jabber

jī 機

1. mechanics; machinery 2. opportune; an opportunity 3. a crucial point; a pivot 4. tricky; cunning 5. an aircraft; a plane; an airplane

jīcāng 機艙 the cockpit of a small airplane; the cabin of an airliner

jīchǎng 機場 an airport; an airfield

jīchē 機車 1. a motorcycle 2. a locomotive

jīdòngxìng 機動性 (military) mobility

jīfáng 機房 1. a storage for textile machinery 2. an engine room

jīgòu 機構 an organization

jīguān 機關 1. an organization; an institution 2. a machine 3. a stratagem; an intrigue

jīguānqiāng 機關槍 a machine gun

jīhuì 機會 an opportunity

jījǐng 機警 alert

jīlíng 機靈 clever; smart; sharp; intelligent

jīlíngguǐr 機伶鬼兒 a quick-witted or clever fellow

jīlǜ 機率 the probability

jīmì 機密 secret; confidential; classified

jīmì wénjiàn 機密文件 secret or confidential documents

jīnéng 機能 functions; functional

jīqì 機器 machinery; a machine

jīqìrén 機器人 a robot

jīqún 機群 an air armada; a fleet of airplanes

jīshēn 機身 the fuselage

jīwù rényuán 機務人員 1. maintenance personnel 2. ground crew

jīxiè 機械 1. a machine 2. mechanical 3. (said of persons) cunning or shrewd

jīxièhuà 機械化 mechanization

jīxíng 機型 1. the type (of an aircraft) 2. the model (of a machine)

jīyào 機要 confidential and important

jīyào mìshū 機要祕書 a confidential secretary

jīyí 機宜 a matter and its arrangements; a line of action; guidelines; a policy

jīyì 機翼 wings of an airplane

jīyóu 機油 lubricating oil; lubricant

jīyù 機遇 a chance; an opportunity; luck

jīyuán 機員 a member of an aircraft crew

jīyuán 機緣 a chance and an opportunity

jīyùn 機運 luck; fate

jīzhǎng 機長 an aircraft (or crew) commander

jīzhì 機智 alertness; quick wit; tact

jīzuò 機座 machine base; machine foundation

jī 積

1. to accumulate; to store up; to amass 2. long (time); old; deep-rooted; longstanding 3. (mathematics) product

jīfēn 積分 1. accumulated points 2. integral calculus

jījí 積極 active(ly); positive(ly); persistent(ly)

jīláo chéngjí 積勞成疾 to fall sick from persistent overwork

jīnián lěiyuè 積年累月 for years and months—a long time

jīqiàn 積欠 accumulated debts; outstanding debts; arrears

jīshǎo chéngduō 積少成多 Economy in trifles will ensure abundance.

jīshuǐ 積水 to accumulate water; accumulated water (in low-lying areas after a shower)

jīxí 積習 a deep-rooted practice; an old habit

jīxù 積蓄 savings

jīyā 積壓 to neglect handling official papers, legal cases, etc.

jī 激

1. to stir up; to rouse; to arouse; to urge; to excite 2. sudden; great; very 3. heated (debate,

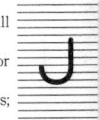

battle, etc.); fierce; angry; vexed 4. abnormal; unusual; drastic 5. to turn back the current—as a dike

jī'áng 激昂 high-spirited; tremendously excited

jīdàng 激盪 to surge; turmoil; stirring

jīdòng 激動 aroused; excited; agitated

jīfā 激發 to stir up; to arouse

jīfèn 激憤 wrathful; indignant

jīguāng 激光 laser

jīguāng chàngjī 激光唱機 a compact disc player

jīguāng dǎyìnjī 激光打印機 a laser printer

jīguāng shìpán 激光視盤 an optical disc player

jīguāng zhàopái 激光照牌 laser typesetting

jījiàngfǎ 激將法 urging or prodding somebody by derision, sarcasm, etc.

jījìn fēnzǐ 激進分子 radicals; extremists

jīlì 激勵 to arouse and encourage; to impel

jīliè 激烈 heated (debates, battles, etc.)

jīliú 激流 rapids

jīnù 激怒 to irritate; to infuriate; to provoke; to enrage

jīqǐ 激起 to arouse; to excite; to stir up

jīqíng 激情 fervor; ardor; passion

jīshǎng 激賞 to heap high praise on (a work, person, etc.)

jīzhàn 激戰 a fierce combat

jī 績
1. to spin; to twist 2. merit; achievements; exploits; meritorious labor

jīxiào 績效 results; effects; achievements

jī 擊 also **jí**
to beat; to strike; to attack

jībài 擊敗 to defeat; to beat; to conquer

jīchén 擊沈 to sink (vessels by torpedoing, bombing, or bombarding)

jīdǎo 擊倒 to knock down

jīhuǐ 擊毀 to wreck; to destory

jīkuì 擊潰 1. to knock to pieces 2. to rout (the enemytroops)

jīluò 擊落 to shoot down (aircraft)

jīsuì 擊碎 to knock (or smash) to pieces

jītuì 擊退 to beat back; to drive back

jīzhòng 擊中 to hit (the target)

jīzhòng yàohài 擊中要害 to hit somebody's vital point

jī 雞
a chicken; a hen; a cock; a fowl

jīdàn 雞蛋 a hen's egg

jīdàn'gāo 雞蛋糕 sponge cake

jīdànli tiāo gǔtou 雞蛋裡挑骨頭 to look for a flaw where there is none; to find fault on purpose; to nitpick

jīdàn pèng shítou 雞蛋碰石頭 like an egg hitting a rock—to attack someone much stronger than oneself

jīguān 雞冠 the cockscomb

jīkǒu niúhòu 雞口牛後 It's better to be the boss of a small group than the top lieutenant in a large organization.

jīmáo dǎnzi 雞毛撢子 a chicken-feather duster

jīmáo suànpí 雞毛蒜皮 petty or trifling things

jīmíng gǒudào 雞鳴狗盜 small tricks; various kinds of talent or skill useful in emergency

jīpí gēda 雞皮疙瘩 goose pimples; goose flesh

jīpí hèfà 雞皮鶴髮 refer to **jīpí hèfà** 雞皮鶴髮

jīpí hèfà 雞皮鶴髮 (said of the aged) with shriveled skin and hoary-headed

jīquǎn bùníng 雞犬不寧 great disturbance; a pandemonium

jīquǎn shēngtiān 雞犬升天 the rise of a powerful person's underlings

jīquǎn xiāngwén 雞犬相聞 to

J

live nearby or in the neighborhood

jīròu 雞肉 chicken (as food)

jītí 雞啼 the crowing of cocks

jītuǐ 雞腿 drumsticks; chicken's legs

jīwěijiǔ 雞尾酒 cocktail

jī 譏
1. to ridicule; to jeer; to sneer 2. to inspect

jīfěng 譏諷 to ridicule; to deride; to satirize

jīxiào 譏笑 to laugh at; taunts; sneers

jī 饑
1. a year of famine 2. hunger; hungry

jīhán jiāopò 饑寒交迫 to suffer from both the cold and hunger

jīhuāng 饑荒 starvation; famine

jījǐn 饑饉 starvation; famine

jī 鷄(雞)
fowls

jī 齋
1. to present; to offer 2. to harbor; to have in one's mind; to entertain

jīzhì 齋志 to cherish unfulfilled ambitions

jī 羈
to travel; to be on a tour or trip

jīlǚ 羈旅 a traveler

jī 羈
1. a bridle 2. to confine; to restrain; to bind 3. to lodge at another's house

jībàn 羈絆 to restrain; to confine

jīliú 羈留 1. to detain (an offender) 2. to stop over

jīyā 羈押 to take into custody

jí 及
1. to reach; to attain; to come up to 2. and; as well as; with 3. just at the moment; timely; when 4. as long as; up to; until 5. to continue 6. to extend

jídì 及第 (in ancient China) to pass the civil examinations

jígé 及格 to pass an examination; to be qualified

jíguàn zhīnián 及冠之年 (said of a young man) to reach the age of 20

jíguàn zhīnián 及冠之年 refer to **jíguàn zhīnián** 及冠之年

jíshí 及時 in time

jízǎo 及早 as soon as possible; before it is too late

jízǎo huítóu 及早回頭 to repent before it is too late

jízhì 及至 until; up to a given point

jí 吃
refer to **chī** 吃 3

jí 吉
good; lucky; auspicious; propitious; favorable; fortunate

jílì 吉利 good luck; propitiousness

jípǔchē 吉普車 a jeep

Jípǔsài 吉普賽 the Gypsies

jírén tiānxiàng 吉人天相 Heaven helps a good man.

jítā 吉他 a guitar

jíwū zhāozū 吉屋招租 a house for rent

jíxiáng 吉祥 propitious; auspicious

jíxīng gāozhào 吉星高照 The lucky star shines bright.

jíxiōng wèibǔ 吉凶未卜 No one knows how it will turn out.

jízhào 吉兆 a good omen

jí 汲
to draw water or liquid

jíjí 汲汲 anxious; avid; restless(ly); to crave

jíqǔ 汲取 to draw; to derive

jíshuǐ 汲水 to draw water

jíyǐn 汲引 to employ people of talent

jí 岌
1. (said of a peak) rising high above others 2. perilous; hazardous

jíjí kěwēi 岌岌可危 in a very critical situation

jíjí kěwēi 岌岌可危 refer to **jíjí**

kěwēi 发发可危

jí 即

1. promptly; immediately; now 2. then; accordingly 3. even if—indicating supposition or sequence

jíjiāng 即將 to be about to

jíkè 即刻 immediately; promptly; now

jíshí 即時 immediately; at once

jíshǐ 即使 even if

jíwèi 即位 to ascend the throne

jíxìng 即興 impromptu; extemporaneous

jíxìng zhīzuò 即興之作 an improvisation

jí 急

1. quick; quickly; with expedition 2. urgent; hurried; hasty 3. anxious; very eager; worried

jíbìng 急病 a sudden illness

jícù 急促 1. urgently; hastily; hurriedly 2. (said of time) short

jídiàn 急電 1. an urgent cable 2. to call urgently

jígōng hàoyì 急公好義 to be enthusiastic about charity work

jígōng jìnlì 急功近利 so eager to be successful that one sees only the immediate advantages

jíjiàn 急件 an urgent document; a dispatch

jíjiù 急救 first-aid; first aid

jíjiùxiāng 急救箱 a first-aid kit

jíjù 急遽 quick (falls, rises, etc.)

jíliú 急流 swift currents; rapids

jíliú yǒngtuì 急流勇退 to retire when one has ridden the crest of success

jímáng 急忙 urgently; hastily; hurriedly; quickly; in a hurry

jí'nàn 急難 1. a crisis; an emergency 2. to offer help in an emergency

jípò 急迫 urgent; pressing

jíqǐ zhízhuī 急起直追 to rise and make a hot chase; to make amends as quickly as possible

jíqiè 急切 1. urgent; anxiously (awaiting, etc.) 2. in a hurry; in haste

jíshì 急事 an urgent matter

jísù 急速 hurriedly; hastily

jítuān 急湍 a swift flow of water; angry torrents

jíxìng lánwěiyán 急性闌尾炎 acute appendicitis

jíxìngzi 急性子 impatient; rash; quick-tempered

jíxū 急需 to need urgently

jíyòng 急用 (for) urgent use or need

jíyú 急於 to be in a hurry or anxious to (finish the task, conclude the war, etc.); eager

jízào 急躁 rash and impatient

jízhěn 急診 (medicine) emergency treatment

jízhěnshì 急診室 emergency room; ER

jízhì 急智 quick-witted

jízhōng shēngzhì 急中生智 suddenly hit upon a way out of a predicament

jí 亟

urgently; pressingly

jíyù 亟欲 very anxious to do something

jí 脊

refer to jǐ 脊

jí 疾

1. disease; suffering 2. to hate; to detest 3. swift; rapid; quick; fast

jíbìng 疾病 diseases

jí'è rúchóu 疾惡如仇 to hate evil as much as one hates an enemy

jífēng zhī jìngcǎo 疾風知勁草 Adversity tests the character of a man.

jíkǔ 疾苦 suffering (especially under an oppressive government)

jíshǐ 疾駛 to move swiftly; to dart; to fleet

jíyán lìsè 疾言厲色 (literally) to speak fast with a harsh look—to lecture severely

jízǒu 疾走 to walk quickly; to run

jí 級

1. a grade; a class (at school) 2. a level; a degree; a mark of

merit; a rank 3. a step (of a flight of steps) 4. a decapitated head

jíbié 級別 ranks; levels; grades; scales

jífèng 級俸 a scale of salaries

jírèn dǎoshī 級任導師 a home-room teacher

jí 唧
refer to **jī** 唧

jí 寂
refer to **jì** 寂

jí 棘
1. buckthorns; thorny brambles 2. urgent

jíshǒu 棘手 difficult to handle

jí 集
1. to assemble; to collect; to gather together; to concentrate 2. a collection of works by one or more authors; to compile; to edit 3. achievements 4. a fair; a periodical market

jídàchéng 集大成 a theory, etc. representing a generalization of many views or ideas; eclectic

jíhé 集合 to assemble; to gather together; to muster

jíhuì 集會 a meeting; a conference; an assemblage; an assembly

jíjié 集結 to concentrate (troops)

jíjǐn 集錦 a collection of homogeneous passages from various literary pieces

jíquán 集權 centralization of authority; concentration of power

jísī guǎngyì 集思廣益 to canvass various opinions and benefit from them

jítǐ 集體 collective

jítuán 集團 a bloc; a faction; a clique

jítuán jiéhūn 集團結婚 a mass wedding

jíxùn 集訓 to train many people at the same place and the same time

jíyóu 集郵 philately; stamp collection

jízhōng 集中 1. to concentrate; to center; to centralize 2. to gather

jízhōngyíng 集中營 a concentration camp

jí 極
1. to exhaust 2. extreme(ly); utmost; highest; topmost; farthest 3. poles 4. to reach; to arrive at

jídà 極大 maximum

jídì 極地 the polar regions

jídù 極度 extremely; exceedingly

jíduān 極端 an extreme; extremely

jíjìn 極盡 to use to the utmost

jíkǒu chēngzàn 極口稱讚 to praise lavishly

Jílè Shìjiè 極樂世界 (Buddhism) Paradise

jílì 極力 to make the utmost effort

jípǐn 極品 a thing of the highest grade

jíqí 極其 very; exceedingly; highly

jíquān 極圈 the polar circles

jíquán guójiā 極權國家 a dictatorial nation

jíshèng 極盛 the heyday; the prime; the zenith; the acme

jíxiàn 極限 (mathematics) limit

jíxíng 極刑 death penalty; capital punishment

jízhì 極致 the ultimate attainment; the acme

jí 嫉
1. jealous; envious; jealousy 2. to hate; to dislike

jídù 嫉妒 jealous; envy; jealousy

jí'è rúchóu 嫉惡如仇 not to compromise with evil deeds or evil persons

jíhèn 嫉恨 to hate out of jealousy

jí 瘠
1. thin; lean; meager 2. (said of land) sterile, infertile, or unproductive

jíshòu 瘠瘦 emaciated; lean and weak

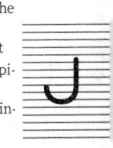

jítǔ 瘠土 sterile soil; infertile soil

jí 輯
1. friendly 2. to collect; to compile; to gather

jí 擊
refer to jī 擊

jí 藉
disorder; confusion

jí 籍
1. books; volumes; reading materials 2. one's hometown or native place

jíguàn 籍貫 one's native place or hometown

jǐ 几
refer to jī 几

jǐ 己
1. self; one's own; oneself 2. the sixth of the Ten Celestial Stems (tiān'gān 天干)

jǐrèn 己任 one's duty or obligation

jǐsuǒ bùyù, wùshī yúrén
己所不欲，勿施於人 Do not do to others what you don't want to be done to you.

Jǐ 紀 also **Jì**
a Chinese family name

jǐ 脊 also **jí**
1. the spine; the spinal column 2. the ridge

jǐliang 脊梁 1. the back　2. (construction) a ridgepole

jǐsuǐ 脊髓 the spinal cord

jǐzhuī 脊椎 the vertebrae

jǐzhuīgǔ 脊椎骨 a vertebra; the spine

jǐ 幾
1. how many (or much) 2. a few; some 3. which; when

jǐdù 幾度 1. several times 2. how many times　3. how many degrees 4. several degrees

jǐfēn 幾分 a bit; somewhat; rather

jǐhé 幾何 1. how much 2. geometry

jǐhéxué 幾何學 geometry

jǐnián 幾年 1. several years 2. how many years

jǐshí 幾時 what time; when

jǐtiān 幾天 1. several days 2. how many days

jǐxǔ 幾許 how many; how much

jǐ 給
1. to provide; provisions; to supply; supplies 2. to award; to approve; to grant 3. sufficiency; affluence 4. glib; eloquent

jǐjià 給假 to grant a leave of absence

jǐjiǎng 給獎 to award prizes

jǐshuǐ 給水 a water supply

jǐyǔ 給與 to give

jǐ 擠
1. to push; to jostle 2. to wring; to squeeze; to twist; to press 3. to crowd; to throng; to pack

jǐduì 擠兌 a run on a bank

jǐmǎn 擠滿 to pack (a place, car, etc.) to capacity

jǐméi nòngyǎn 擠眉弄眼 to make eyes; to wink

jǐyā 擠壓 extruding

jì 濟
1. various; varied; numerous 2. elegant and dignified 3. name of various counties and a river

jìjì yītáng 濟濟一堂 to gather together or congregate in this hall

jì 伎
talent; ability; skill

jìliǎng 伎倆 dexterity; skill; craft

jì 忌
1. jealous; to envy 2. to fear; a fear 3. to shun 4. to prohibit; (to) taboo 5. death anniversaries of one's parents, etc.

jìchén 忌辰 death anniversaries of one's parents, etc.

jìdàn 忌憚 (to) dread; (to) scruple

jìdu 忌妒 to be jealous of; to envy

jìhèn 忌恨 jealousy; to envy and hate

jìhui 忌諱 1. a taboo 2. to avoid

J

as taboo 3. to avoid as harmful
4. vinegar

jìkǒu 忌口 to be on a diet

jìrì 忌日 death anniversaries of
one's parents, etc.

jì 技

skill; ingenuity; dexterity; special
ability; tricks

jìgōng 技工 a skilled worker

jì'néng 技能 skill; technical ability

jìqiǎo 技巧 ingenuity; dexterity;
adroitness; skill

jìshī 技師 an engineer or a tech-
nician

jìshù 技術 techniques; technology; skill

jìshù gāochāo 技術高超 in
possession of superb skills or
superb techniques

jìshù rényuán 技術人員 tech-
nicians; technical personnel

jìshù shuǐzhǔn 技術水準 technological standards

jìshù xuéxiào 技術學校 a
technical school

jìshù zhuǎnràng 技術轉讓
technical transfer

jìshù zhuǎnyí 技術轉移 technical transfer

jìyǎng 技癢 anxious or itching
to demonstrate some skill

jìyì 技藝 skill; art; craft

jì 妓

1. a prostitute; a whore 2. a
young woman who sings or
dances to amuse her customers

jìnǚ 妓女 a prostitute; a whore

jì 季

1. a season; a quarter of a year
2. the last (month of a season) 3.
the youngest (of brothers) 4. a
Chinese family name

jìfēng 季風 (meteorology) the
monsoon

jìjié 季節 a season

jìjūn 季軍 the second runner-up
in a contest

jì 紀

1. a historical record; annals;

chronicles 2. a period of 12 years
3. a century 4. to arrange; to put
in order 5. institutions; laws and
regulations; discipline 6. the age
of a person 7. a geological
period 8. refer to **Jǐ** 紀

jìlù 紀錄 a record; to take notes

jìlùpiàn 紀錄片 a documentary
film

jìlǜ 紀律 discipline; laws and regulations

jìniàn 紀念 to remember; to
commemorate

jìniànbēi 紀念碑 a monument; a
memorial

jìniàncè 紀念冊 an autograph
book

jìniànpǐn 紀念品 a souvenir; a
memento

jìniànrì 紀念日 a commemoration day; a memorial day; an
anniversary

jìyuán 紀元 in the year of our
Lord...; the Christian era

jìyuánhòu 紀元後 A.D. (anno
Domini)

jìyuánqián 紀元前 B.C. (before
Christ)

jì 計

1. a scheme; a plot; a trick 2. a
plan; a program; to discuss or
plan 3. to calculate; to count 4. a
mechanical measuring device

jìcè 計策 a scheme; a device

jìchéngchē 計程車 a taxi

jìfēn 計分 1. to count scores or
points 2. divided or classified as
follows

jìhuà 計畫 a plan; a program; to
plan; to devise

jìhuàshū 計畫書 a prospectus

jìjiàn 計件 to reckon by the
piece

jìjiào 計較 1. to haggle; to fuss
about 2. to negotiate 3. to care
4. to plan

jìliàng 計量 to calculate; to
weigh; to estimate

jìlüè 計略 to scheme; to deliberate; a scheme

jìmóu 計謀 a scheme; to scheme

jìshí 計時 to count time to see

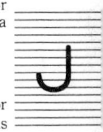

how long something lasts

jìsuàn 計算 1. to calculate; to count 2. to consider

jìsuànjī 計算機 a calculating machine; a computer

jìsuànqì 計算器 a caculator

jì 記

1. to remember; to call to mind; to keep in mind 2. to record; to register 3. a book recording anecdotes, etc. 4. seals or chops; a sign; a mark

jìchóu 記仇 to bear a grudge

jìde 記得 to remember

jìfēn 記分 1. to record scores or points 2. to register a student's mark

jìfēnyuán 記分員 a scorer; a marker

jìgōng 記功 to record a merit

jìguà 記掛 to remember and be anxious about

jìguò 記過 to record a demerit

jìhao 記號 a mark; a sign; a symbol

jìhèn 記恨 to bear a grudge

jìláo 記牢 to commit to memory firmly

jìlù 記錄 1. to record; to note down 2. a note-taker 3. a record

jìlùpiàn 記錄片 a documentary film

jìrù 記入 to enter... in; to make an entry

jìshù 記述 to record and narrate

jìxialai 記下來 to take down (dictation, etc.)

jìxìng 記性 memory

jìxùwén 記敘文 narrative writing

jìyì 記憶 memory or recollection

jìyìlì 記憶力 a retentive faculty

jìyìtǐ 記憶體 (computer) memory

jìyì yóuxīn 記憶猶新 The memory is still fresh.

jìzǎi 記載 to record; an account

jìzhàng 記帳 1. to buy or sell on credit 2. to record buying, selling, etc. in books

jìzhě 記者 a reporter; a journalist

jì 寄

1. to send; to transmit; to mail 2. to entrust; to consign; to commit; to deposit

jìcún 寄存 to place or leave (a thing) in (another's) custody

jìfàng 寄放 to place or leave (a thing) in (another's) custody

jìjiànrén 寄件人 the sender

jìjū 寄居 to live temporarily (with a family, in a place, etc.)

jìmài 寄賣 to consign (goods, etc.) for sale

jìqíng 寄情 to give expression to one's feelings (through writing, etc.)

jìrén líxià 寄人籬下 to live in another's house

jìshēngchóng 寄生蟲 a parasite

jìshòu 寄售 to consign (goods, etc.) for sale

jìsù 寄宿 to lodge (at another's house)

jìtuō 寄託 to consign or commit (one's soul to God, emotions to writing, etc.)

jìxìn 寄信 to send or mail a letter

jìyǎng 寄養 to send a child to another family for temporary care

jì 寂 also jí

1. the death of a Buddhist monk or nun 2. quiet; still; serene; peaceful; desolate

jìjìng 寂靜 quiet; still

jìliáo 寂寥 lonely; deserted; desolate;still

jìmò 寂寞 lonely; lonesome

jì 祭

1. to worship; to offer sacrifices to; to honor by a rite or service 2. to wield

jìdiǎn 祭典 services or ceremonies of offering sacrifices

jìpǐn 祭品 offerings; sacrificial articles; sacrifices

jìsì 祭祀 to worship; to offer sacrifices to; to honor by a service or rite

jìtán 祭壇 an altar

jìzǔ 祭祖 to perform rites in honor of ancestors

jì 悸

1. palpitation of the heart 2. fear

jìdòng 悸動 to palpitate with terror

jì 既

1. since; as 2. already 3. to finish 4. all

jìchéng shìshí 既成事實 a fact already accomplished

jìdé lìyì 既得利益 vested interests

jìdìng 既定 already decided or fixed

jìláizhī, zé'ānzhī 既來之，則安之 Since we (or you) are already here, let's make ourselves (or yourself) at home.

jìrán 既然 since (it is so, etc.); this being the case

jìrán rúcǐ 既然如此 this being the case; since it is so

jìwǎng bùjiù 既往不咎 Let bygones be bygones.

jì 際

1. (to occur) at the time or on the occasion of 2. a border or boundary; an edge 3. by the side of; beside 4. in the middle; between; among 5. an opportunity; fortune or luck

jìhuì 際會 1. to meet; to encounter 2. a happenstance

jìyù 際遇 1. an opportunity; a chance 2. what one has experienced in one's life

jì 稷

panicled millet

jì 髻

a coiffure with a topknot

jì 暨

1. and 2. to reach; to attain; to overtake 3. up to; till

jì 劑

1. a dose (of medicine) 2. prepared medicines or drugs 3. to prepare (medicines and drugs)

jì 冀

1. to hope 2. another name for Hebei Province

jì 覬

to covet; to desire something belonging to others

jìyú 覬覦 to covet; to desire something belonging to others

jì 濟

1. to relieve; to aid 2. to cross a stream 3. to succeed; to be up to standard 4. to benefit; benefits 5. a ford

jìkùn fúwēi 濟困扶危 (literally) to relieve the less privileged and help the endangered

jìkùn fúwēi 濟困扶危 refer to **jìkùn fúwēi** 濟困扶危

jì ránméi zhījí 濟燃眉之急 to help meet an urgent need

jìruò fúqīng 濟弱扶傾 to help the weak and aid the needy

jìshì 濟世 to benefit the world

jì 騎

refer to **qí** 騎 2

jì 繫

to bind; to tie; to hang up

jì 繼

1. to continue; to carry on 2. then; afterwards 3. to follow; to inherit; to succeed to

jìchéng 繼承 to inherit; to succeed to

jìchéngrén 繼承人 a successor; an heir

jìfù 繼父 a stepfather

jìmǔ 繼母 a stepmother

jìrèn 繼任 to succeed to an office

jìwèi 繼位 to succeed to the throne

jìxù 繼續 to continue; to last; to go on

jì 鯽

a gold carp

jì 霽

1. to stop raining; to clear up after rain or snow 2. to stop being angry

jìyuè 霽月 1. a clear moon after rain 2. open-minded

jì 驥
1. a very fast horse 2. a man of outstanding ability; a great man

jiā 加
1. plus; to add 2. to increase; to augment 3. to append

jiābān 加班 to work overtime

jiābèi 加倍 to double; to redouble

jiāfǎ 加法 (arithmetic) addition

jiāgōng 加工 to process (goods)

jiāgōng chūkǒuqū 加工出口區 an export processing zone

jiāguān jìnjué 加官晉爵 to advance in rank and position; promotion

jiāhài 加害 to do somebody harm

jiāhào 加號 the plus symbol (+)

jiāhù bìngfáng 加護病房 an intensive care unit (ICU)

jiājiǎn chéngchú 加減乘除 addition, subtraction, multiplication and division

jiājǐn 加緊 to intensify; to step up

jiākuài 加快 to speed up; to accelerate

jiākuān 加寬 to broaden; to widen

jiālún 加侖 a gallon

jiāméng 加盟 to join an alliance, a fraternity or a secret society

jiāmiǎn 加冕 to crown; to coronate

jiāqiáng 加強 to strengthen; to reinforce

jiāquán zhǐshù 加權指數 the weighted index number in stock trading

jiārè 加熱 to heat; to warm

jiārù 加入 1. to join; to accede to 2. to add into

jiāshēn 加深 1. to deepen 2. to become more severe

jiāsù 加速 to step up; to accelerate

jiāxīn 加薪 to give a pay raise

jiāyóu 加油 1. to oil 2. to refuel 3. to step up effort

jiāyóuzhàn 加油站 a gas station

jiāzhòng 加重 to increase work loads, burdens, etc.

jiā 夾 also **jiá, jià**
1. to be wedged between; to be sandwiched 2. to squeeze; to press; to occupy both sides of 3. pincers 4. of two or more layers; lined (garments, etc.) 5. a folder to keep sheets of paper, etc. 6. to carry secretly 7. to mix; to mingle

jiācéng 夾層 a double layer; a false bottom (of a trunk, etc.)

jiāchí 夾持 to hold in between

jiādài 夾帶 1. to smuggle 2. things brought in secretly such as contraband 3. a crib

jiādào huānyíng 夾道歡迎 to line the street to welcome

jiāfèng 夾縫 a crack; a loophole (in the law)

jiāgōng 夾攻 to attack from both sides

jiājí 夾擊 to attack from both sides

jiājí 夾擊 refer to **jiājī** 夾擊

jiāzá 夾雜 mixed-up

jiāzhútáo 夾竹桃 an oleander

jiāzi 夾子 folders for keeping documents, papers, pictures, etc; clips

jiā 佳
1. beautiful; good; fine 2. auspicious 3. distinguished

jiābīn 佳賓 distinguished or honored guests

jiājié 佳節 a festival; a carnival

jiājù 佳句 a quotable qutoe

jiā'ǒu 佳偶 a happily married couple

jiā'ǒu tiānchéng 佳偶天成 an ideal couple

jiāqī 佳期 the wedding or nuptial day

jiāqī 佳期 refer to **jiāqī** 佳期

jiārén 佳人 a beauty

jiāyáo 佳餚 a delicacy

jiāyīn 佳音 good news

jiāzuò 佳作 an excellent (literary) work

jiā 枷

a cangue; a pillory—worn by prisoners in former times

jiāsuǒ 枷鎖 1. the cangue and lock 2. (figuratively) bondage; shackles

jiā 痂

scab over a sore

jiā 家

1. home; house; household; family; of a household; domestic 2. a specialist

jiāchǎn 家產 family property

jiācháng biànfàn 家常便飯 1. an ordinary plain meal (such as one normally gets at home); pot-luck 2. routine

jiāchánghuà 家常話 an ordinary conversation

jiāchǒu bùkě wàiyáng 家醜不可外揚 Don't wash your dirty linen in public.

jiāchù 家畜 livestock; domestic animals

jiāchuán mìfāng 家傳祕方 a secret recipe handed down in the family

jiādang 家當 the belongings of a family

jiādào zhōngluò 家道中落 to suffer a fall in one's family fortune

jiādiàn yòngpǐn 家電用品 home appliances

jiādīng 家丁 a servant (in a family)

jiāfǎ 家法 domestic discipline

jiāfù 家父 my father (used in a polite conversation)

jiāhé wànshì xīng 家和萬事興 Harmony in the family is the basis for success in any undertaking.

jiājì 家計 a family livelihood

jiājiāhùhù 家家戶戶 every family and household

jiājiào 家教 1. family education 2. a tutor

jiājìng 家境 the financial condition of a family

jiāju 家具 furniture

jiājuàn 家眷 one's family; one's dependents

jiālěi 家累 a family burden

jiāmǔ 家母 my mother

jiāpín rúxǐ 家貧如洗 to be in extreme poverty

jiāpò rénwáng 家破人亡 with one's home in ruins and family members dead or scattered

jiāpǔ 家譜 a family pedigree

jiāqín 家禽 domestic fowls; poultry

jiārén 家人 the members of one's family

jiāshì 家世 one's family background

jiāshì 家事 housekeeping; housework

jiāshū 家書 a letter from home or addressed to a member of the family

jiāshǔ 家屬 one's family or dependents

jiātíng 家庭 a home; a household

jiātíng bèijǐng 家庭背景 family background

jiātíng fǎngwèn 家庭訪問 a visit to the parents of schoolchildren or young workers

jiātíng jìhuà 家庭計畫 family planning—birth control

jiātíng jiàoyù 家庭教育 home education

jiātíng shēnghuó 家庭生活 home life; family life

jiātíng zhǔfù 家庭主婦 a housewife

jiātíng zuòyè 家庭作業 homework

jiātú sìbì 家徒四壁 extremely poor

jiāwù 家務 household affairs; housework

jiāxiāng 家鄉 one's hometown

jiāxué yuānyuán 家學淵源 (from) a family of scholars

jiāxùn 家訓 family precepts

jiāyè 家業 family property

jiāyòng 家用 domestic expenses

jiāyù hùxiǎo 家喻戶曉 well-known; widely known

jiāyuán 家園 hometown; native heath

jiāzhǎng 家長 the head of a family or household

jiāzhèng 家政 1. housekeeping 2. home economics

jiāzú 家族 a family; a clan

jiā 袈

the cassock or robe of a Buddhist monk

jiāshā 袈裟 a kasaya or cassock, the robe of a Buddhist monk

jiā 傢

1. furniture 2. a tool or tools

jiāhuo 傢伙 1. (comically) a character 2. a tool

jiā 嘉

1. to praise; to commend; to admire 2. good; fine; excellent

jiābīn 嘉賓 an honored guest

jiāhuì 嘉惠 to benefit

jiājiǎng 嘉獎 to commend (as an encouragement)

jiāmiǎn 嘉勉 to praise and encourage

jiāniánhuáhuì 嘉年華會 a carnival

jiá 夾

refer to **jiā** 夾

jiá 莢

a pod—the shell or case in which plants like beans and peas grow their seed

jiáguǒ 莢果 a pod; legume

jiá 頰

the cheeks

jiágǔ 頰骨 the cheekbone

jiǎ 甲

1. the first of the Ten Celestial Stems 2. armor; shell; crust 3. most outstanding 4. a measure of land in Taiwan (equal to 0.97 hectare)

jiǎbǎn 甲板 the deck (of a ship)

jiǎchóng 甲蟲 a beetle

jiǎděng 甲等 grade A

jiǎgǔwén 甲骨文 oracle bone inscriptions

jiǎkélèi 甲殼類 the crustacea

jiǎyú 甲魚 a green turtle

jiǎzhòu 甲胄 armor; a panoply

jiǎzhuàngxiàn 甲狀腺 thyroid

jiǎ 岬

a cape; a promontory; a headland; a point

jiǎjiǎo 岬角 a cape; a promontory

jiǎ 夏

jiǎchǔ 夏楚 a ferule; a rod for punishing pupils

jiǎ 假

1. false; not real; phony; artificial; fake; bogus; sham 2. supposing; if 3. to borrow; to avail oneself of

jiǎbàn 假扮 to disguise; to masquerade

jiǎchōng 假充 to counterfeit; to pretend

jiǎdào 假道 via; by way of

jiǎdìng 假定 1. if; supposing 2. postulate

jiǎdòngzuò 假動作 (sports) dummy play

jiǎfǎ 假髮 refer to **jiǎfà** 假髮

jiǎfà 假髮 a wig

jiǎfēnshù 假分數 an improper fraction

jiǎgōng jìsī 假公濟私 to attain private or personal ends in the name of official duties

jiǎhuà 假話 a lie; a falsehood

jiǎjiè 假借 to borrow

jiǎjiè míngyì 假借名義 in the name of

jiǎmào 假冒 1. to counterfeit 2. to assume the identity of somebody else

jiǎmèi 假寐 to take a nap; a catnap; a doze

jiǎmiànjù 假面具 a mask—a false front

jiǎmíng 假名 1. a pseudonym 2. kana (the Japanese syllabary)

jiǎrén jiǎyì 假仁假義 to be a

wolf in sheep's clothing; to shed crocodile tears

jiǎrú 假如 if; in case; supposing

jiǎruò 假若 if; in case; supposing

jiǎsǎngzi 假嗓子 falsetto

jiǎshān 假山 a small artificial hill

jiǎshè 假設 a hypothesis; a supposition

jiǎshǐ 假使 if; in case; supposing

jiǎshì 假釋 to parole; parole

jiǎshǒu 假手 to do something by means of (an agent)

jiǎtuō 假託 a pretext; a subterfuge

jiǎxì zhēnzuò 假戲真做 to do something seriously after starting it as a joke, urse, etc.

jiǎxiǎng 假想 1. a hypothesis 2. imaginary

jiǎxiǎngdí 假想敵 a hypothetical enemy

jiǎxiàng 假相 false appearances

jiǎxīngxing 假惺惺 to pretend; to shed crocodile tears

jiǎxìng jìnshì 假性近視 pseudomyopia

jiǎyá 假牙 a false tooth; a denture

jiǎyǐ shírì 假以時日 to give sufficient time

jiǎyì fèngcheng 假意奉承 false flattery

jiǎzào 假造 1. to counterfeit 2. to fabricate

jiǎzào zuìmíng 假造罪名 to cook up a false charge against; to frame up

jiǎzhèngjing 假正經 hypocritical

jiǎzhuāng 假裝 to pretend; to assume the appearance of

Jiǎ 賈

a Chinese family name

jiǎ 鉀

potassium

jiǎ 夾

refer to jiā 夾

jiázhútáo 夾竹桃 refer to **jiāzhútáo** 夾竹桃

jià 架

1. a prop; a stand; a rack; a frame 2. to prop up; to set up; to support 3. a framework or scaffold 4. to frame up (a charge, etc.); to fabricate 5. to lay something on 6. a quarrel

jiàqǐ 架起 to set up; to prop up

jiàqiáo 架橋 to build a bridge

jiàshè 架設 to build over something

jiàshi 架式 a style; a manner; a pose

jiàzi 架子 1. a rack; a stand; a frame; a scaffold 2. a skeleton; an outline

jià 假

a holiday

jiàqī 假期 a vacation; a holiday

jiàqí 假期 refer to **jiàqī** 假期

jiàrì 假日 a holiday

jiàtiáo 假條 1. an application for leave 2. a leave permit

jià 嫁

1. (said of a woman) to get married; to marry a man 2. to marry off a daughter 3. to impute (blame, a crime, etc.) to another

jiàhuò 嫁禍 to impute blame, a crime, punishment, etc. (to another person)

jiàqǔ 嫁娶 marriage

jiàzhuang 嫁妝 a bride's trousseau; a dowry

jià 稼

1. to farm, plant, sow or cultivate 2. grain; crops

jià 駕

1. to ride; to drive; to pilot 2. to excel; to surpass 3. to yoke; to put the horses to the carriage 4. vehicles 5. an honorific epithet 6. to control; to reign or rule 7. the emperor

jiàbēng 駕崩 (said of the emperor) to pass away

jiàjī 駕機 to pilot a plane

jiàlín 駕臨 to give (our humble place) the honor of your visit

jiàqīng jiùshú 駕輕就熟 to do

a task with ease

jiàshǐ 駕駛 1. to drive (automobiles); to pilot (aircraft); to steer (boats) 2. a driver

jiàshǐyuán 駕駛員 a driver; a pilot

jiàshǐ zhízhào 駕駛執照 a driver's license

jiàyù 駕馭 1. to drive (horse-drawn vehicles) 2. to control; to tame

jià 價

1. prices; cost; value 2. (chemistry) valence

jiàgé 價格 prices

jiàlián wùměi 價廉物美 (literally) excellent quality at low prices—a good bargain

jiàmǎ 價碼 the price of a commodity

jiàmù 價目 prices; quotations

jiàmùdān 價目單 a price (or quotation) list

jiàqian 價錢 prices

jiàzhí 價值 value

jiàzhí liánchéng 價值連城 invaluable; priceless

jiān 尖

sharp; acute; pointed; keen

jiānbīng 尖兵 (military) a point

jiānduān kējì 尖端科技 high-tech; high technology

jiānduān kēxué 尖端科學 the frontiers of science

jiānruì 尖銳 1. sharp-pointed 2. sharp; keen 3. shrill; piercing 4. intense; acute

jiānsuān 尖酸 (said of words, speech, etc.) sarcastic; petty; mean

jiānsuān kèbó 尖酸刻薄 unsympathetic; merciless; pitiless

jiān 奸

1. false 2. selfish 3. disloyal 4. crafty; wicked; villainous; cunning; evil 5. adultery; fornication; licentiousness 6. a traitor; a villain

jiānchén 奸臣 (formerly) a selfish, disloyal and cunning minister; a traitor

jiānjì 奸計 a wicked scheme

jiānshāng 奸商 unethical merchants; profiteers

jiānxi 奸細 a spy (from the enemy side); a stool pigeon

jiānxiǎn 奸險 crafty, mean and malicious

jiānyín 奸淫 1. adultery 2. lecherous 3. to rape

jiānzéi 奸賊 a scoundrel; a traitor

jiānzhà 奸詐 crafty; cunning

jiān 肩

1. shoulders 2. to shoulder (responsibility, etc.); to sustain 3. to employ; to appoint

jiānbǎng 肩膀 1. the shoulder 2. a sense of responsibility

jiānfù 肩負 to take on; to undertake; to shoulder; to bear

jiānjiǎgǔ 肩胛骨 the scapula

jiān 戔

small; little; tiny

jiānjiān zhīshù 戔戔之數 an insignificant amount (of money)

jiān 姦

1. adultery; debauchery; licentiousness 2. to debauch; to ravish; to attack (a woman) sexually 3. a crook

jiānfū 姦夫 1. an adulterer 2. a man who acts criminally

jiānfù 姦婦 an adulteress

jiānyín 姦淫 debauchery; adultery; to rape

jiānyín lǜlüè 姦淫擄掠 rape and rapine

jiān 兼

1. to unite in one; to connect; to annex 2. and; also; together with; both; equally; concurrently

jiān'ài 兼愛 love without distinction

jiānbèi 兼備 to be in possession of both

jiānbìng 兼併 to annex (another country, etc.)

jiānchāi 兼差 to take two or more jobs concurrently; a part-time job

jiānchéng 兼程 to proceed on one's trip on the double

jiāngù 兼顧 to look after both sides

jiānkè 兼課 1. to do some teaching besides one's main occupation 2. to hold two or more teaching jobs concurrently

jiānrèn 兼任 to serve concurrently as

jiānrèn jiàoshī 兼任教師 a part-time teacher

jiānróng 兼容 (computer) compatible

jiānróng bìngxù 兼容並蓄 tolerant; open-minded

jiānshàn tiānxià 兼善天下 to benefit all the people in the world

jiānzhí 兼職 to take two or more jobs concurrently; a part-time job

jiān 堅

1. strong and durable 2. solid; firm 3. to dedicate to; to devote to 4. calm; steady; stable; determined 5. close; intimate 6. armor, etc. 7. the strongest position or point of enemy troops 8. steadfastly; resolutely

jiānbù kěcuī 堅不可摧 invulnerable; impregnable

jiānbù tǔshí 堅不吐實 to refuse to tell the truth

jiānchí 堅持 to insist on; to persist in

jiānchí dàodǐ 堅持到底 to stick it out

jiāndìng 堅定 determined; steadfast; staunch

jiāndìng bùyí 堅定不移 unswerving; unshakable

jiāngù 堅固 solid; firm; stable

jiānguǒ 堅果 nuts

jiānjiǎ lìbīng 堅甲利兵 ready for combat

jiānjué 堅決 firmly (opposed to, etc.)

jiānkǔ zhuójué 堅苦卓絕 to endure all the hardships; firm

jiānkǔ zhuójué 堅苦卓絕 refer to **jiānkǔ zhuójué** 堅苦卓絕

jiānláo 堅牢 strong; durable

jiānqiáng 堅強 strong; staunch

jiānrěn 堅忍 fortitude; firmness; dedication

jiānrěn bùbá 堅忍不拔 invincible; indomitable

jiānrèn 堅韌 great strength or durability

jiānshǒu 堅守 1. to firmly stand by (one's promise, principle, etc.) 2. to defend (a place) resolutely

jiānyì 堅毅 fortitude; dedication

jiānyìng 堅硬 hard and solid

jiānzhēn 堅貞 chaste

jiān 菅

a coarse grass (used for making brushes, brooms, etc.)

jiān 湔

to wash

jiānxuě 湔雪 to wipe away (disgrace, etc.)

jiān 間

1. between two things; the space between; among 2. a numerical adjunct for rooms 3. within a definite time or space

jiān 煎

1. to fry in fat or oil 2. to decoct 3. (figuratively) to torment; to kill

jiān'áo 煎熬 1. to decoct until almost dry 2. to torture; to torment

jiānbing 煎餅 pancakes

jiānchǎo 煎炒 to fry; to stir-fry

jiāndàn 煎蛋 1. to fry eggs 2. fried eggs

jiānyào 煎藥 to make a decoction of herbal medicines

jiānyú 煎魚 to fry fish

jiān 犍

a castrated bull

jiān 監

1. to supervise; to superintend; to oversee; to direct; to inspect 2. to confine; to keep in custody; to imprison

jiānchá 監察 to supervise; to control; control

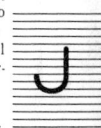

jiānchá wěiyuán 監察委員 a member of the Control Yuan

Jiāncháyuàn 監察院 Control Yuan (one of the five major branches of the government of the Republic of China)

jiāndū 監督 to supervise; to superintend; to oversee

jiānhù 監護 custody; to act as the guardian

jiānhùrén 監護人 a guardian (of a minor)

jiānjìn 監禁 1. to confine; to imprison 2. custody; confinement

jiānkǎo 監考 to proctor or invigilate an examination

jiānkǎoyuán 監考員 a proctor; an invigilator

jiānláo 監牢 a prison; a jail

jiānpiào 監票 (in elections) to scrutinize a ballot

jiānpiàoyuán 監票員 a ballot supervisor; a scrutineer

jiānshì 監視 1. to keep a watchful eye on 2. to monitor

jiānshìqì 監視器 a watchdog; a monitor

jiāntīng 監聽 to monitor

jiānyā 監押 to keep (a person) in custody

jiānyù 監獄 a prison; a jail

jiānzhì 監製 to direct or supervise the manufacture of

jiān 箋
1. a commentary; a note 2. fancy note paper, letter paper, or stationery

jiān 漸
1. to soak; to permeate 2. (said of the territory) to reach

jiānrǎn 漸染 to soak; to imbue

jiān 緘
1. to seal; to close 2. a letter

jiānmò 緘默 to keep silence

jiān 艱
1. difficult; hard 2. mourning for one's parents

jiānjù 艱鉅 hard; arduous; laborious

jiānkǔ 艱苦 trying; hard; priva-

tion

jiānkùn 艱困 difficult

jiānnán 艱難 difficulty; distress; hardship

jiānsè 艱澀 abstruse; difficult

jiānshēn 艱深 abstruse; difficult

jiānxiǎn 艱險 difficult and dangerous

jiānxīn 艱辛 hard; arduous; laborious

jiān 鶼
a fabulous bird having only one wing so that a pair must unite in order to fly

jiāndié 鶼鰈 birds and fishes that move in pairs—a devoted couple

jiān 殲
to annihilate; to exterminate; to destroy

jiāndí 殲敵 to destroy the enemy

jiānmiè 殲滅 to annihilate; to wipe out

jiǎn 柬
1. a letter; an invitation or visiting card 2. to select; to pick

jiǎntiě 柬帖 1. an invitation card 2. (in old China) a red visiting card

jiǎn 剪
1. to cut or clip with scissors; to shear; to trim 2. to annihilate; to destroy completely 3. scissors; clippers; shears

jiǎnbào 剪報 a newspaper cutting (or clipping)

jiǎncái 剪裁 to tailor clothing materials for a dress

jiǎncǎi 剪綵 to cut the ribbon

jiǎndāo 剪刀 scissors; clippers

jiǎnfà 剪髮 refer to **jiǎnfà** 剪髮

jiǎnfà 剪髮 to cut hair

jiǎnjí 剪輯 1. (movie) montage; film editing 2. editing and rearrangement

jiǎnjiē 剪接 to edit or cut a film

jiǎnpiào 剪票 to punch a ticket

jiǎntiē 剪貼 1. to clip and paste (something out of a newspaper, etc.) in a scrapbook or on cards

2. cutting out (as a school children's activity)

jiǎntiēbù 剪貼簿 a scrapbook

jiǎnzhījia 剪指甲 to trim one's nails

jiǎnzhǐ 剪紙 (art and crafts) paper-cut

jiǎnzhǐjiǎ 剪指甲 refer to **jiǎnzhījia** 剪指甲

jiǎn 減

to decrease; to reduce; to lessen; to diminish; to subtract; to cut

jiǎnbàn 減半 to reduce to a half

jiǎnchǎn 減產 to cut production or output

jiǎndī 減低 to decrease; to diminish; to lessen; to reduce

jiǎnfǎ 減法 (arithmetic) subtraction

jiǎnféi 減肥 to reduce (weight)

jiǎnfèng 減俸 a pay cut

jiǎnhào 減號 the minus sign(−)

jiǎnhuǎn 減緩 to retard; to slow down

jiǎnjià 減價 to cut down prices; to mark down; to reduce prices

jiǎnmiǎn 減免 1. to mitigate or annul (a punishment) 2. to reduce or remit (taxation, etc.)

jiǎnqīng 減輕 to lighten; to lessen; to mitigate

jiǎnruò 減弱 to weaken; to subside

jiǎnshǎo 減少 to decrease; to diminish; to lessen; to reduce

jiǎnsù 減速 to slow down; to decelerate

jiǎntuì 減退 to fall; to abate; to decrease

jdǎnxīn 減薪 a pay cut

jiǎnxíng 減刑 1. to commute a sentence 2. a commutation of sentence

jiǎnzī 減資 the reduction of captial

jiǎn 揀

1. to select; to choose; to pick 2. to pick up (something another has left behind, etc.)

jiǎnxuǎn 揀選 to choose; to select; to pick

jiǎn 儉 also **jiàn**

1. frugal; economical; thrift 2. meager 3. a poor harvest

jiǎnpú 儉樸 refer to **jiǎnpú** 儉樸

jiǎnpú 儉樸 to be thrifty in daily spending

jiǎnshěng 儉省 thrift; frugal; economical

jiǎnyǐ yǎnglián 儉以養廉 Frugality makes honesty.

jiǎnyuē 儉約 thrifty and temperate

jiǎn 翦(剪)

to trim; to clip; to cut with scissors

jiǎn 撿

to pick up; to collect

jiǎnchái 撿柴 to collect firewood

jiǎnpòlànr 撿破爛兒 to collect junk

jiǎn 檢

1. a book label 2. to sort; to gather 3. to inspect; to check up; to collate 4. to discuss thoroughly 5. a form; a pattern 6. to restrict; to regulate

jiǎnchá 檢查 to inspect; to examine; to test

jiǎncháguān 檢察官 a court prosecutor; a procurator

jiǎnchá rényuán 檢查人員 an inspector (as a customs officer, etc.)

jiǎndiǎn 檢點 1. to behave (oneself) 2. to inspect and arrange; to check

jiǎndìng 檢定 1. to inspect and approve (or sanction) 2. inspection

jiǎnjǔ 檢舉 to inform the authorities of an unlawful act, plot, etc.

jiǎnshù 檢束 to discipline; to restrain

jiǎntǎo 檢討 to review and discuss (past performances, etc.); to make self-examination

jiǎnxiū 檢修 to examine and repair; to overhaul

jiǎnyàn 檢驗 to inspect and

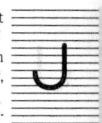

J

examine

jiǎnyì 檢疫 quarantine

jiǎnyìsuǒ 檢疫所 the quarantine office

jiǎnyuè 檢閱 to inspect or review (troops)

jiǎn 簡

1. brief; succinct; terse; simple 2. (in ancient China) a slip or tablet of bamboo for writing 3. a letter; a note 4. to designate or appoint (an official) 5. a Chinese family name

jiǎnbào 簡報 a briefing

jiǎnbiàn 簡便 simple and convenient

jiǎnchēng 簡稱 to be called or known as... for short

jiǎndān 簡單 1. simple; brief 2. ordinary

jiǎnduǎn 簡短 brief; terse; succinct; short

jiǎn'ér yánzhī 簡而言之 in short; briefly; in a word

jiǎnhuà 簡化 to simplify; simplification

jiǎnjié 簡潔 (said of a piece of writing) brief and to the point; succinct

jiǎnjiè 簡介 a brief introduction; a synopsis

jiǎnlì 簡歷 biographical notes; a resume

jiǎnlòu 簡陋 simple and crude

jiǎnlüè 簡略 brief; sketchy

jiǎnmíng 簡明 brief and clear; concise

jiǎnyào 簡要 brief and concise

jiǎnyì 簡易 simple; easy

jiǎnyuē 簡約 brief; terse; succinct; short

jiǎnzhāng 簡章 a brief and concise statement of regulations, procedures, etc.

jiǎnzhí 簡直 1. simply; outright; at all 2. honest; unaffected

jiǎn 繭

1. cocoons; a chrysalis 2. a callus

jiǎn 鹼

lye; alkali

jiǎnxìng 鹼性 alkalinity

jiàn 件

an auxiliary noun applied to things, clothes, etc.

jiàn 見

1. to see; to perceive; to understand; to observe or examine 2. to visit; to see; to call on or at; to meet 3. to receive (visitors, etc.); to come face to face with

jiànbào 見報 to appear in the newspapers

jiànbùdérén 見不得人 too ashamed to show up in public

jiàndào 見到 1. to meet; to see 2. to perceive or think of

jiànduō shíguǎng 見多識廣 experienced and knowledgeable

jiànduō shìguǎng 見多識廣 refer to **jiànduō shíguǎng** 見多識廣

jiànfāng 見方 square, as a foot square

jiànfēng zhuǎnduò 見風轉舵 to go with the tide

jiànguài 見怪 to take offense; to blame; to mind

jiànjī xíngshì 見機行事 to act as the circumstances dictate; to do as one sees fit

jiànjiě 見解 one's views, ideas or observations or opinions about something

jiànkè 見客 to receive guests

jiànlì wàngyì 見利忘義 to forget one's integrity under the temptation of personal gain

jiànliàng 見諒 to pardon me; to forgive me; to excuse me

jiànmiàn 見面 to come face to face; to see; to meet

jiànmiànlǐ 見面禮 gift(s) given at one's first meeting, especially with a relative of a junior generation

jiànqì 見棄 to be cast away or rejected

jiànshìmiàn 見世面 to see the world; to enrich one's experience

jiànshi 見識 1. knowledge and experience; scope; sense 2. to experience (something new)

jiànsǐ bùjiù 見死不救 to see someone in mortal danger without lifting a finger to save him

jiànwài 見外 to treat as an outsider

jiànwén 見聞 what one has seen and heard—experience; knowledge

jiànxí 見習 apprenticeship; probation

jiànxián sīqí 見賢思齊 to see the virtuous and think of equaling or emulating them

jiànxiào 見笑 1. to be laughed at 2. to incur ridicule (by one's poor performance)

jiànxiào 見效 effective; efficacious

jiànyì sīqiān 見異思遷 easily moved by what one sees or hears

jiànyì yǒngwéi 見義勇為 to have the courage to do what is right regardless of consequences; to act heroically

jiànzhèng 見證 to bear witness

jiàn 建

1. to establish; to build 2. to propose; to suggest

jiàndǎng 建黨 to found a political party

jiàndū 建都 to select a city as the capital (of the empire)

jiànguó 建國 1. to found (or establish) a state 2. to build up a country

jiànjiāo 建交 to establish diplomatic relations

jiànjiāo hézuò 建教合作 a work study program

jiànlì 建立 to establish; to build; to set up; to found

jiànpíng 建坪 the floor space of a building in ping (equivalent to 36 square feet)

jiànshè 建設 to construct; to build; construction

jiànshèxìng 建設性 constructive

jiànshù 建樹 an achievement; contribution

jiànyì 建議 to propose; to suggest

jiànyì'àn 建議案 a proposal

jiànzào 建造 to build; to construct; to frame

jiànzhú 建築 refer to **jiànzhù** 建築

jiànzhúshī 建築師 refer to **jiànzhùshī** 建築師

jiànzhúwù 建築物 refer to **jiànzhùwù** 建築物

jiànzhù 建築 1. to build; to construct 2. a building or structure

jiànzhùshī 建築師 an architect

jiànzhùwù 建築物 a building; a structure

jiàn 健

1. healthy; strong 2. vigorous; capable 3. fond of; inclined to; liable to 4. to strengthen; to toughen

jiànkāng 健康 1. health 2. healthy

jiànměi 健美 healthy and handsome

jiànquán 健全 in good condition

jiànshēncāo 健身操 calisthenics

jiànshēnfáng 健身房 a gymnasium; a gym

jiàntán 健談 brilliant conversation

jiànwàng 健忘 forgetful; liable to forget

jiànwàngzhèng 健忘症 (pathology) amnesia

jiànxíng 健行 to hike; hiking

jiànzài 健在 to be in good health; alive

jiànzhuàng 健壯 healthy and robust

jiàn 間

1. a crevice; a leak; space in between 2. to divide; a division of a house; to separate 3. to put a space between; to drive a wedge between; to part friends 4. to change; to substitute 5. to block up 6. (said of illness) to get a little better 7. occasionally

jiànbù róngfǎ 間不容髮 refer to **jiànbù róngfǎ** 間不容髮

jiànbù róngfǎ 間不容髮 1. very close; imminent 2. precari-

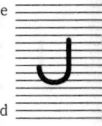

ous

jiàndié 間諜 a spy; a secret agent

jiànduàn 間斷 suspended; interrupted

jiàn'gé 間隔 1. separated; spaced at intervals 2. distance; intervals

jiànjiē 間接 indirect; vicariously

jiànxiē 間歇 1. intermittent; sporadic 2. short intervals or stops; a pause

jiàn 毽

a shuttlecock

jiànzi 毽子 a shuttlecock

jiàn 監

1. an official position in former times 2. a government establishment (such as a school) in former times 3. a eunuch

jiàn 僭

to assume; to usurp; to overstep one's authority

jiànwèi 僭位 to usurp the throne

jiànyuè 僭越 to assume (a title or powers)

jiàn 漸

gradually; little by little; by degrees

jiàncì 漸次 gradually

jiànjiàn 漸漸 gradually

jiànjìn 漸進 to advance little by little

jiànrù jiājìng 漸入佳境 to get better and better

jiàn 儉

refer to **jiǎn** 儉

jiàn 劍

a sword; a dagger; a saber

jiànbá nǔzhāng 劍拔弩張 ready to fight

jiànjí lǚjí 劍及履及 to perform a task with full vigor and urgency

jiànkè 劍客 a swordsman

jiànlán 劍蘭 (botany) a gladiolus

Jiànqiáo 劍橋 Cambridge, England

jiànshù 劍術 swordsmanship; fencing

jiàn 澗

a mountain stream

jiànhè 澗壑 a valley; a ravine

jiànhuò 澗壑 refer to **jiànhè** 澗壑

jiànxī 澗溪 a stream in a valley

jiàn 箭

1. an arrow 2. a sign which is like an arrow

jiànbǎzi 箭靶子 a target for archery

jiàntǒng 箭筒 a quiver

jiànzài xiánshàng 箭在絃上 1. imminent action expected 2. There can be no turning back.

jiànzhú 箭竹 a variety of bamboo

jiànzú 箭鏃 an arrowhead

jiàn 踐

1. to tread upon; to trample 2. to fulfill; to carry out; to perform 3. to ascend; to occupy

jiàntà 踐踏 1. to trample; to tread on 2. to abuse

jiàn 賤

1. cheap; inexpensive; low cost 2. lowly; humble; inferior in position 3. low-down; base; ignoble; despicable 4. to slight; to look down on 5. my, a self-derogatory expression

jiànhuò 賤貨 1. (a term of revile) a tramp 2. worthless goods

jiànjià 賤價 a low price; low-priced

jiànrén 賤人 a slut or tramp

jiàn 諫

to admonish; to remonstrate

jiànyán 諫言 admonition

jiàn 餞

1. a farewell dinner or luncheon 2. to send off; to convoy 3. to present as a gift 4. preserves; jam

jiànbié 餞別 to entertain a parting friend with a feast

jiànxíng 餞行 to entertain a parting friend with a feast

jiàn 薦(荐)

1. to recommend; to offer; to present 2. fodder for animals; grass 3. a straw mat 4. food and dishes 5. to repeat; repeatedly

jiànjǔ 薦舉 to propose; to introduce

jiàn 鍵

a key (to a door or on a musical instrument, etc.)

jiànpán 鍵盤 a keyboard (on a piano, typewriter, etc.)

jiàn 檻

railings; bars, as window or door bars

jiàn 濺

to splash; to sprinkle; to spray; to spill

jiànluò 濺落 to splash down

jiàn 艦

a warship; a man-of-war; a naval vessel

jiànduì 艦隊 a fleet; a naval task force

jiàntǐng 艦艇 naval vessels

jiànzhǎng 艦長 the captain or skipper of a naval vessel

jiàn 鑑

1. a mirror 2. to mirror; to reflect 3. to study or examine; to scrutinize 4. an example serving as a rule or warning

jiànbié 鑑別 to distinguish (the genuine from an imitation); to judge or identify; to discriminate

jiàndìng 鑑定 to examine and determine; to judge; to make an appraisal

jiànshǎng 鑑賞 to examine and appreciate

jiànwǎng zhīlái 鑑往知來 to foresee the future by reviewing the past

jiàn 鑒

to examine, etc.

jiāng 江

1. a large river 2. the Changjiang (Yangtze) River

jiānghé rìxià 江河日下 to go

jiānghú 江湖 1. rivers and lakes 2. wandering; vagrant

jiānghu 江湖 1. sophisticated and shrewd 2. practicing quackery; a quack

Jiāngláng cáijìn 江郎才盡 to have used up one's literary talent or energy

jiānglún 江輪 a river steamship

jiāngpàn 江畔 the riverbank; beside the river

jiāngshān 江山 the mountains and rivers of a country—the land; the throne

jiāngshān měirén 江山美人 the throne and the beauty

jiāngshān yìgǎi, běnxìng nányí 江山易改，本性難移 Changing one's nature is harder than changing mountains and rivers.

Jiāngsū 江蘇 Jiangsu Province

Jiāngxī 江西 Jiangxi Province

jiāngxīn bǔlòu 江心補漏 to try to prevent a disaster when it is too late

jiāngyáng dàdào 江洋大盜 a notorious bandit leader

jiāng 姜

1. a Chinese family name 2. ginger

jiāng 將

1. (used with a verb expressing future action) going to; about to 2. used with a noun functioning as a direct object 3. to nourish

jiāngcuò jiùcuò 將錯就錯 to accept the consequences of a mistake and try to adapt oneself thereto

jiānggōng shúzuì 將功贖罪 to atone for mistakes by meritorious service

jiāngjì jiùjì 將計就計 to deal with an opponent by taking advantage of his scheme

jiāngjìn 將近 approximately; close to; nearly

jiāngjiu 將就 to manage with something unsatisfactory

jiāngjūn 將軍 1. a general or

admiral 2. a call to indicate a checkmate (in Chinese chess) 3. to challenge

jiānglái 將來 the future; the days to come

jiāngxìn jiāngyí 將信將疑 half in doubt; skeptical

jiāng 僵

1. to lie flat 2. to be inactive; stiff; rigid; numb 3. to be at a stalemate; deadlocked

jiāngchí 僵持 to come to a deadlock

jiānghuà 僵化 1. heading toward a deadlock 2. to become rigid; to ossify

jiāngjú 僵局 a deadlock; a stalemate

jiānglì 僵立 to stand rigidly

jiāngshī 僵屍 1. a stiff corpse 2. a zombie

jiāngyìng 僵硬 rigid; stiff

jiāng 漿

1. thick fluid; starch 2. to starch

jiāngguǒ 漿果 a berry

jiāng 殭

dead and stiff

jiāngyìng 殭硬 stiff

jiāng 薑

ginger

jiāng 疆

1. the boundary; the border; the frontier 2. a limit

jiāngjiè 疆界 borders; frontiers

jiāngtǔ 疆土 territory

jiāngyù 疆域 territory

jiāng 繮(韁) also **gāng**

reins; a bridle; a halter

jiāngsheng 繮繩 reins; a bridle; a halter

jiǎng 獎

1. to encourage; to exhort 2. to praise; to commend 3. to cite or give a prize or reward (for a merit, etc.) 4. a prize or reward

jiǎngbēi 獎杯 a cup (as a prize)

jiǎngjīn 獎金 prize money; a bounty; a bonus

jiǎnglì 獎勵 to encourage by rewards

jiǎngpái 獎牌 a medal given as an award

jiǎngpǐn 獎品 prizes or rewards

jiǎngquàn 獎券 a lottery ticket or raffle ticket

jiǎngshǎng 獎賞 1. rewards in money, etc. 2. to reward

jiǎngxuéjīn 獎學金 a scholarship; a fellowship

jiǎngzhāng 獎章 a medal

jiǎngzhuàng 獎狀 a citation of meritorious services, etc.

jiǎng 槳

an oar

Jiǎng 蔣

a Chinese family name

jiǎng 講

1. to speak; to talk 2. to pay particular attention to; to be particular about 3. to explain; to explicate 4. as to; when it comes to 5. to have recourse to

jiǎngdào 講道 to preach; to give sermons

jiǎnggǎo 講稿 the manuscript of a prepared speech; lecture notes

jiǎnggùshi 講故事 to tell stories

jiǎnghé 講和 to make peace; to conclude peace

jiǎnghuà 講話 to talk; to speak; to address

jiǎngjià 講價 to haggle over prices; to bargain

jiǎngjiě 講解 to discuss and explain

jiǎngjiu 講究 1. to be particular or elaborate (about something); to have regard for 2. (said of dress, etc.) tasteful

jiǎngkè 講課 to teach; to lecture

jiǎnglǐ 講理 1. to have regard for reason 2. to argue with someone in order to convince him that he is wrong

jiǎngpíng 講評 to review (a literary work, a game, etc., especially in speech)

jiǎngqiú 講求 1. to investigate; to study 2. to strive for; to be

elaborate about

jiǎngshī 講師 a lecturer; an instructor

jiǎngshòu 講授 to teach; to lecture; to instruct

jiǎngshù 講述 to explain and discuss (subjects, problems, etc.)

jiǎngtái 講臺 a platform; a dais; a podium

jiǎngtáng 講堂 a lecture hall; a lecture room

jiǎngtí 講題 the topic (of a speech)

jiǎngxí 講習 short-term training or instruction

jiǎngxué 講學 to lecture; to discourse on an academic subject

jiǎngyǎn 講演 to speak or lecture; a speech

jiǎngyì 講義 1. teacher's handouts at school; (mimeographed or printed) teaching materials 2. commentaries on classics

jiǎngzuò 講座 a lectureship; a professorship; a chair

jiàng 匠

a craftsman; an artisan; a skilled workman

jiàngxīn 匠心 originality; craftsmanship

jiàngxīn jīngyíng 匠心經營 to use the original thought in any creation

jiàng 降

1. to descend 2. to lower 3. to condescend; to deign 4. to drop; to decline 5. to surrender

jiànggé 降格 to lower the scale, standard, standing or status

jiàngjí 降級 to degrade; to downgrade; to demote

jiànglín 降臨 1. to come down; to fall 2. to condescend (to visit)

jiàngluò 降落 1. to land; landing; descent; to descend 2. to drop; to rain down

jiàngluòsǎn 降落傘 a parachute

jiàngqí 降旗 to lower the flag

jiàngshēng 降生 to be born into the world

jiàngshì 降世 to come down to

the world

jiàngwēn 降溫 1. to lower the temperature (as in a workshop) 2. to drop in temperature

jiàngyǔliàng 降雨量 rainfall

jiàng 將

1. a general; an admiral; a military leader of high rank 2. to lead (soldiers)

jiàngcái 將才 the talent as a field commander

jiàngmén hǔzǐ 將門虎子 a capable young man from a distinguished family

jiàngshì 將士 officers and men

jiàngshuài 將帥 a general

jiàng 強

inflexible; obstinate; stubborn

jiàngpíqi 強脾氣 an obstinate disposition

jiàng 糨

1. paste; to paste together; to starch; starched 2. thick

jiànghu 糨糊 paste; glue

jiàng 醬

1. soybean sauce; soy 2. food in the form of paste; jam

jiàngcài 醬菜 cabbages, etc. pickled in soybean sauce

jiàngguā 醬瓜 cucumbers, etc. pickled in soybean sauce

jiàngyóu 醬油 soybean sauce; soy; soy sauce

jiāo 交

1. to submit; to hand in or over 2. to meet 3. to exchange 4. to intersect

jiāobáijuàn 交白卷 to turn in a blank examination paper

jiāobān 交班 to hand over to the next shift

jiāobǎo 交保 to release (a suspect) on bail

jiāobì 交臂 very close or near

jiāobīng 交兵 to fight (between nations)

jiāochā 交叉 to cross each other; to intersect

jiāochādiǎn 交叉點 a point of intersection

jiāochāi 交差 to report what one has done in the line of duty

jiāochū 交出 to surrender; to hand over

jiāocuò 交錯 to interlock

jiāodài 代代 1. to hand over responsibility 2. to give an explanation

jiāofēng 交鋒 to engage in battle

jiāofù 交付 1. to hand over 2. to make payment

jiāogē 交割 a business transaction

jiāogěi 交給 to hand to; to give to

jiāohù zuòyòng 交互作用 interaction; interplay

jiāohuán 交還 to hand back; to return

jiāohuàn 交換 to exchange

jiāohuò 交貨 to deliver goods; delivery

jiāojí 交集 (said of different feelings) to be mixed

jiāojì 交際 social intercourse

jiāojìfèi 交際費 entertainment fees

jiāojìwǔ 交際舞 a social dance

jiāojiā 交加 to act upon (something) or to hit (someone) simultaneously by two or more forces

jiāojiē 交接 1. to make contact with each other 2. to adjoin each other 3. to hand over and to take over (duties)

jiāojiè 交界 a border (between two areas)

jiāojuàn 交卷 1. to hand in the examination paper 2. to complete an assignment

jiāokǒu chēngzàn 交口稱讚 to praise somebody or something unanimously

jiāoliú 交流 to flow across each other

jiāoliúdiàn 交流電 an alternating current

jiāopèi 交配 1. (biology) copulation 2. to mate

jiāopò 交迫 beleaguered; beset

jiāoqíng 交情 friendship

jiāoshè 交涉 to negotiate; negotiation

jiāoshǒu 交手 to exchange blows (in a fight)

jiāotán 交談 to converse

jiāotì 交替 to alternate

jiāotōng 交通 1. traffic 2. communication

Jiāotōngbù 交通部 Ministry of Communications

jiāotōng jǐngchá 交通警察 traffic police

jiāotóu jiē'ěr 交頭接耳 to whisper in each other's ears

jiāowǎng 交往 to have friendly relations

jiāowěi 交尾 (said of birds) to mate

jiāowù 交惡 to be on unfriendly terms

jiāoxiǎngyuè 交響樂 a symphony; symphonic music

jiāoxiǎng yuètuán 交響樂團 an orchestra

jiāoxīn 交心 to be frank with others; to open one's heart to

jiāoyí 交誼 refer to jiāoyì 交誼

jiāoyì 交易 a trade; business transaction; to trade

jiāoyì 交誼 friendly relations; amity

jiāoyìsuǒ 交易所 a stock exchange; a bourse

jiāoyì wùpǐn 交易物品 barter

jiāoyóu 交遊 1. to have friendly contact with 2. friends

jiāoyǒu 交友 to make friends

jiāozhàn 交戰 to wage war against each other

jiāozhànguó 交戰國 a belligerent state

jiāozhī 交織 to interlace; to interweave

jiāo 郊

1. suburbs of a city 2. a ceremony for offering sacrifices to Heaven and Earth

jiāoqū 郊區 suburban districts; suburbs; outskirts; a suburban area

jiāowài 郊外 suburbs

jiāoyóu 郊遊 an outing; an excursion

jiāo 姣 also **jiāo**
1. handsome; pretty; beautiful 2. coquettish

jiāohǎo 姣好 pretty; pleasant (looks); good-looking

jiāo 教
to teach; to guide

jiāoshū 教書 to teach (usually for a living)

jiāo 焦
1. scorched or burned; charred 2. the smell or stench of things burned 3. worried and anxious 4. a Chinese family name

jiāodiǎn 焦點 1. focus 2. a burning point; a focal point

jiāodiǎn xīnwén 焦點新聞 breaking news; top story or news

jiāohuáng 焦黃 1. pale yellow 2. scorched

jiāojí 焦急 very anxious; in deep anxiety

jiāojù 焦距 (physics) focus

jiāolǜ 焦慮 deeply worried and anxious

jiāolǜ bù'ān 焦慮不安 to be on pins and needles

jiāotàn 焦炭 coke

jiāozào 焦躁 worried, anxious and getting impatient

jiāo 椒
1. pepper 2. mountaintops

jiāo 跤
a stumble; a fall

jiāo 嬌
1. tender; delicate; beautiful; lovely 2. spoiled; pampered; coddled

jiāochēn 嬌嗔 (said of women) to get angry

jiāodīdī 嬌滴滴 fascinatingly beautiful

jiāoměi 嬌美 beautiful and graceful

jiāomèi 嬌媚 beautiful; handsome

jiāonèn 嬌嫩 delicate and soft; tender

jiāoqī 嬌妻 a beloved wife

jiāoróu 嬌柔 beautiful and frail

jiāoshēng guànyǎng 嬌生慣養 to live a sheltered life

jiāowá 嬌娃 a beauty

jiāoxiǎo 嬌小 dainty and little

jiāoxiǎo línglóng 嬌小玲瓏 delicate and refined

jiāoxiū 嬌羞 bashful; modest and retiring

jiāozòng 嬌縱 to pamper

jiāo 膠
1. glue; gum 2. resin; sap 3. anything sticky 4. rubber; plastics 5. to stick on or together; to adhere 6. stubborn; obstinate

jiāobù 膠布 rubber cloth; plastic cloth

jiāodài 膠帶 an adhesive tape

jiāojuǎn 膠捲 unexposed film

jiāonáng 膠囊 a medical capsule

jiāopiàn 膠片 film

jiāoshuǐ 膠水 glue; size

jiāoxié 膠鞋 rubber shoes; galoshes

jiāozhuó 膠著 stalemated; at a stalemate; a standstill

jiāo 澆
1. to water (plants, flowers, etc.) 2. to sprinkle water on 3. perfidious; faithless; ungrateful

jiāobó 澆薄 rash and perfidious; faithless and ungrateful

jiāoguàn 澆灌 to water (plants, etc.)

jiāohuā 澆花 to water flowers

jiāo 蕉
1. the banana 2. the plantain

jiāo 礁
a reef

jiāo 驕
1. untamed; intractable; disobedient 2. proud; haughty; arrogant; overbearing 3. severe; harsh; intense

jiāo'ào 驕傲 proud; haughty; disdainful

jiāojīn 驕矜 puffed up; conceited; self-important; proud; haughty

jiāokuā 驕誇 to boast; to brag

jiāoqì 驕氣 overbearing airs; arrogance

jiāoshē yínyì 驕奢淫佚 pride, luxury, dissolute and self-indulgence

jiāotài 驕態 proud bearing; haughty manner; an overbearing attitude

jiāoyáng 驕陽 the intense sunshine; the hot sunshine

jiāozhě bìbài 驕者必敗 Pride goes before a fall.

jiāozòng 驕縱 disregardful of all authority; proud and unruly

jiáo 嚼 also **jué**

to chew; to masticate; to munch

jiǎo 角

1. the horn of an animal 2. a direction; a corner 3. an angle 4. a tenth of a dollar; a 10-cent piece 5. something in the shape of a horn 6. a cape; a promontory

jiǎodù 角度 1. an angle 2. angular measure

jiǎomó 角膜 (anatomy) cornea

jiǎo 佼

1. beautiful; handsome; attractive; charming 2. outstanding

jiǎohǎo 佼好 pretty; pleasant

jiǎojiǎozhě 佼佼者 an outstanding person

jiǎo 狡

1. cunning; crafty; sly; wily; artful; shrewd 2. suspicion; to suspect

jiǎobiàn 狡辯 to defend oneself in a devious way; to quibble

jiǎohuá 狡猾 cunning; crafty; sly; wily; artful

jiǎolài 狡賴 to prevaricate

jiǎoshì 狡飾 to deceive; to lie

jiǎozhà 狡詐 deceitful; cunning; swindling

jiǎo 姣

refer to **jiāo** 姣

jiǎo 皎

1. white; clean 2. bright; lustrous; brilliant ·

jiǎojié 皎潔 brightly clean

jiǎorú rìxīng 皎如日星 as bright as the heavenly bodies

jiǎo 絞

1. to twist; to twine; to wring 2. to hang (a criminal) 3. rudeness 4. to mix up

jiǎojià 絞架 gallows

jiǎojìn nǎozhī 絞盡腦汁 to cudgel one's brains

jiǎoròujī 絞肉機 meat mincer

jiǎotòng 絞痛 an acute or gripping pain caused by cholera, appendicitis, etc.

jiǎo 腳(脚) also **jué**

1. the feet 2. the leg or base of something

jiǎoběn 腳本 the script of a play, an opera, etc.

jiǎobù 腳步 steps; paces; strides; footsteps

jiǎofū 腳夫 a porter or coolie

jiǎogēn 腳跟 1. the heel of the foot 2. (figuratively) foothold

jiǎosè 腳色 1. a character; a role 2. personal background of examinees under the old civil service examination system 3. a talented or resourceful person

jiǎotàbǎn 腳踏板 1. a footboard 2. a pedal

jiǎotàchē 腳踏車 a bicycle

jiǎotà shídì 腳踏實地 to do a job honestly and with dedication

jiǎoyìn 腳印 footprints; footmarks; footsteps

jiǎozhǎng 腳掌 the sole (of the foot)

jiǎozhījia 腳趾甲 toenails

jiǎozhítou 腳趾頭 toes

jiǎozhíjia 腳趾甲 refer to **jiǎozhījia** 腳趾甲

jiǎo 較

refer to **jiào** 較

jiǎo 剿

to exterminate; to stamp out; to destroy; to put down

jiǎofěi 剿匪 to launch attacks against the bandits

jiǎomiè 剿滅 to exterminate

jiǎo 餃

stuffed dumplings; Chinese ravioli

jiǎo 僥

luck; lucky

jiǎoxìng 僥倖 by luck or chance

jiǎo 鉸

1. scissors; shears 2. hinges 3. to shear

jiǎoliàn 鉸鏈 hinges

jiǎo 徼

to be lucky; fortunate

jiǎoxìng 徼幸 lucky; (said of happy events) beyond one's expectations

jiǎo 矯

1. to straighten; to correct; to rectify 2. to falsify; to forge 3. strong and powerful; vigorous 4. to raise (one's head) high

jiǎojiàn 矯健 strong and vigorous

jiǎojié 矯捷 agile; vigorous and nimble

jiǎoqíng 矯情 to be affectedly unconventional

jiǎoróu zàozuò 矯揉造作 to behave in an affected manner

jiǎowǎng guòzhèng 矯枉過正 to be overstrict in correcting mistakes, faults, etc.

jiǎozhèng 矯正 to correct or rectify

jiǎo 繳

1. to surrender (articles); to submit 2. to pay (taxes, tuition, etc.)

jiǎofèi 繳費 to pay fees

jiǎojuǎn 繳卷 to hand in examination papers

jiǎokuǎn 繳款 to make payments

jiǎonà 繳納 to pay (taxes, tuition, etc.)

jiǎoshuì 繳稅 to pay taxes

jiǎoxiè 繳械 to disarm; to hand over weapons

jiǎo 攪

1. to stir; to mix 2. to agitate; to disturb; to annoy

jiǎobàn 攪拌 to stir or churn; to mix

jiǎobànqì 攪拌器 a mixer; an agitator

jiǎodòng 攪動 to stir or churn; to mix

jiǎohuo 攪和 1. to mingle 2. to confuse

jiǎojú 攪局 to spoil; to disturb

jiǎoluàn 攪亂 to disturb; to ruffle; to disarrange

jiào 叫

1. to be called or known as 2. to cry; to scream; a shout or scream 3. to call; to summon 4. to cause

jiàocài 叫菜 to order dishes

jiàohǎn 叫喊 to shout; to yell; to scream; to cry

jiàohǎo 叫好 to cheer; to applaud

jiàohuāzi 叫化子 a beggar

jiàohuan 叫喚 1. to call; to summon 2. to shout

jiàohuò 叫貨 to order goods

jiàokǔ 叫苦 to complain of hardship

jiàokǔ liántiān 叫苦連天 to be full of complaints

jiàomà 叫罵 to scream and use foul language like a fishwife

jiàomài 叫賣 to hawk

jiàoqū 叫屈 to cry out for justice; to complain of unfair treatment

jiàoxiāo 叫囂 to shout and yell; clamor

jiàoxǐng 叫醒 to waken; to wake up

jiàozuò 叫座 (said of plays, dramas, etc.) to have appeal to the audience

jiàozuò 叫做 to be called; to be known as

jiào 校

1. to compare 2. to proofread; proofs 3. to revise (books, etc.); to collate

jiàodìng 校訂 to revise

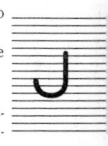

jiàoduì 校對 1. to proofread 2. a proofreader 3. to calibrate

jiàoyuè 校閱 1. to collate 2. to inspect troops, honor guards, etc.

jiàozhèng 校正 to correct; to correct proofs

jiào 教
1. a religion 2. an order; a directive 3. to educate 4. to urge; to incite; to bid; to instigate 5. to instruct; instruction(s); to advise; advice 6. to have; to let; to make

jiàocái 教材 teaching materials

jiàodǎo 教導 1. to instruct 2. guidance

jiàodǎo yǒufāng 教導有方 skillful in teaching and providing guidance

jiàofù 教父 godfather

jiàoguān 教官 a military instructor; a drill master

jiàohuà 教化 1. culture 2. to bring enlightenment to the people by education

Jiàohuáng 教皇 the Pope; the Pontiff

jiàohuì 教誨 refer to jiàohuì 教誨

jiàohuì 教會 the church

jiàohuì 教誨 to teach and admonish

jiàohuì xuéxiào 教會學校 a church school

jiàokēshū 教科書 the textbook

jiàoliàn 教練 1. a coach (of athletes); an instructor 2. to train

jiàomíng 教名 one's Christian name or forename

jiàopài 教派 religious sects

jiàoshī 教師 a teacher

Jiàoshījié 教師節 Teacher's Day

jiàoshì 教士 an evangelist; a priest; a clergyman

jiàoshì 教室 a classroom

jiàoshòu 教授 a professor

jiàosuō 教唆 to instigate; to incite; to abet

jiàotáng 教堂 a church; a mosque

jiàotiáo 教條 a doctrine

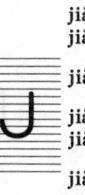

Jiàotíng 教廷 the Holy See; the Vatican

jiàotú 教徒 a (religious) believer or follower

jiàowùchù 教務處 the office of the dean of studies

jiàowù zhǔrèn 教務主任 the dean of studies (of a primary or secondary school)

jiàoxué 教學 1. instruction; teaching 2. to teach and to learn

jiàoxun 教訓 1. a lesson 2. to admonish; teachings

jiàoyǎng 教養 to bring up; to rear

jiàoyì 教義 a creed

jiàoyǒu 教友 a fellow believer (of a religion)

jiàoyù 教育 1. to educate 2. education

Jiàoyùbù 教育部 Ministry of Education

jiàoyù bùzhǎng 教育部長 a minister of education

jiàoyù chéngdù 教育程度 the level of education

jiàoyùfèi 教育費 the cost of education

jiàoyùjiā 教育家 an educator or educationist

jiàoyùjiè 教育界 educational circles

jiàoyù zhìdù 教育制度 the educational system

jiàoyuán 教員 a member of the teaching profession; a teacher

jiàozhí 教職 the occupation of teaching

jiàozhíyuán 教職員 the teaching and administrative staff of a school

jiàozhǔ 教主 a religious leader

Jiàozōng 教宗 the Pope; the Pontiff

jiào 窖
1. a cellar; a vault; a pit 2. to store things in a cellar, etc.

jiào 較 also **jiǎo**
1. to compare 2. in a greater or lesser degree; more or less; earlier or later 3. clear; conspicuous; obvious; marked 4. to com-

jiàojìn 較勁 to have a trial of strength

jiàoliàng 較量 to compare (strength, etc.) in a contest

jiào 酵 also **xiāo**
yeast; leaven

jiàomǔ 酵母 yeast; leaven

jiàomǔjūn 酵母菌 a yeast fungus

jiàomǔjùn 酵母菌 refer to **jiàomǔjūn** 酵母菌

jiàosù 酵素 an enzyme

jiào 徼
1. frontiers 2. to take an inspection trip

jiào 轎
a chair; a sedan chair; a palankeen or a palanquin

jiàochē 轎車 a sedan (a kind of automobile)

jiàozi 轎子 a chair; a sedan chair

jiào 覺
a sleep; a nap

jiē 皆
all; every; entire

jiēdà huānxǐ 皆大歡喜 Everybody is satisfied.

jiēkě 皆可 all acceptable

jiē 接
1. to receive; to accept 2. to welcome; to meet 3. to join; to connect 4. to graft 5. to come close to; to make contact with 6. to succeed to

jiēbān 接班 to relieve another in work

jiēbàn 接辦 to succeed another in managing a task

jiēchù 接觸 1. (said of nations) to wage war against each other 2. to make contact with

jiēdài 接待 to receive (a guest); reception

jiēdài rényuán 接待人員 reception personnel

jiē'ěr liánsān 接二連三 one after another; continuously

jiēgǔ 接骨 to set broken bones

jiēguǎn 接管 to take over (the management of)

jiēhé 接合 to connect; to assemble

jiējì 接濟 to give financial or material assistance to

jiējiàn 接見 to receive (a visitor, etc.)

jiējìn 接近 to come close; to approach

jiēkè 接客 1. (said of a hotel, etc.) to receive lodgers or guests 2. (said of prostitutes) to receive patrons in boudoirs

jiēkǒu 接口 (computer) interface

jiēlì sàipǎo 接力賽跑 a relay race

jiēlián 接連 repeatedly; to continue

jiēlián bùduàn 接連不斷 continuously; incessantly

jiēnà 接納 to accept (a proposal, advice, etc.)

jiēqià 接洽 to contact, discuss or negotiate

jiērǎng 接壤 adjoining boundary; adjacent to

jiērèn 接任 to take over an office; to succeed

jiēshēng 接生 to practice midwifery

jiēshēngpó 接生婆 a midwife

jiēshōu 接收 to take over; to receive

jiēshōu tiānxiàn 接收天線 a receiving antenna

jiēshǒu 接手 1. to carry on the task of the predecessor 2. assistants or aides 3. (baseball) a catcher

jiēshòu 接受 to accept (an invitation, an assignment, etc.)

jiēsòng 接送 1. to receive and send off (guests or visitors) 2. transportation to and from a certain place

jiētì 接替 to relieve; to succeed (a predecessor)

jiētōng 接通 to put through

jiētóu 接頭 1. to have a firm grasp of the situation so that

one can manage a matter by oneself 2. to make contact with (the responsible person)

jiētóur 接頭兒 a joint

jiēwěn 接吻 to kiss; a kiss

jiēxiànshēng 接線生 a switchboard operator

jiēxù 接續 to continue; to connect

jiēyìng 接應 to stand ready for assistance; to come to somebody's aid

jiēzhe 接著 1. then; shortly afterwards 2. to follow; to add 3. to catch

jiēzhī 接枝 (botany) to graft; a graft

jiēzhǒng érzhì 接踵而至 to follow at the heels of

jiēzhù 接住 to catch (a flying object)

jiē 偕

refer to **xié** 偕

jiē 揭

1. to lift up or off; to raise high 2. to unveil, uncover or unearth; to expose 3. to announce; to publicize

jiēchuān 揭穿 to expose (a conspiracy, trick, etc.)

jiēchuāngbā 揭瘡疤 to reopen old wounds (in order to put someone to shame)

jiēduǎn 揭短 to expose the blemishes (or faults) of others

jiēfā 揭發 to expose (a plot, scandal, etc.)

jiēgān érqǐ 揭竿而起 to start a revolution or an uprising

jiēkāi 揭開 1. to pull apart or separate 2. to uncover

jiēlù 揭露 to uncover or expose (another's secret, etc.)

jiēmù 揭幕 to raise or lift the curtain (of a meeting, exhibition, etc.); to unveil—to inaugurate

jiēshì 揭示 to announce; to reveal

jiēxiǎo 揭曉 to make public; to publish

jiēzhù 揭櫫 to announce (goals,

objectives, etc. of a movement, cause, etc.); to proclaim; to publish

jié 結

1. to stutter; to stammer 2. tough; strong; durable 3. (also **jié**) to bear (fruit); to form (seed)

jiēba 結巴 to stutter; to stammer

jiēguǒ 結果 (said of plants) to bear fruit

jiēshi 結實 1. strong; sturdy 2. tough; durable; solid

jiē 街

a street; a road in a city; a thoroughfare

jiēdào 街道 streets; roads in a city or town

jiētóu xiàngwěi 街頭巷尾 throughout the city; in every nook and corner of the city

jiē 階

1. a way leading to the main hall 2. a flight of steps or stairs 3. a grade or a rank 4. to rely on

jiēcéng 階層 subdivisions within a class of people; a class of people

jiēduàn 階段 a stage or phase

jiējí 階級 a rank; a class (of people)

jiētī 階梯 1. a flight of stairs or steps 2. (figuratively) a way, ladder or step leading to success

jiēxiàqiú 階下囚 a prisoner; a captive

jié 孑

1. the larvae of mosquitoes 2. solitary; unaccompanied; lonely

jiéjué 孑孓 the larvae of mosquitoes

jiérán yīshēn 孑然一身 alone

jié 劫

1. to rob; to plunder; to take by force 2. sufferings; misfortunes; disasters

jié'àn 劫案 a case of robbery

jiéchí 劫持 1. to threaten 2. to hijack

jiéhòu yúshēng 劫後餘生 life after surviving a disaster

jiéjī 劫機 to skyjack; to hijack a plane

jiénàn 劫難 a destined calamity

jiéshù 劫數 ill luck; ill fortune

jié 杰
a hero; an outstanding person

jié 拮
laboring hard; occupied

jiéjū 拮据 1. troubles or difficulties 2. in financial straits

jié 桔
a well sweep

jiégěng 桔梗 a Chinese bellflower

jié 桀
1. ferocious and cruel 2. name of the last ruler of the Xia Dynasty 3. (傑) outstanding and brave

jié'áo bùxún 桀驁不馴 obstinate and unruly

jié 捷
1. to win; to triumph; the prizes of a victory 2. swift; quick; rapid; agile

jiébào 捷報 a report of success in an examination; a war bulletin announcing a victory

jiéjìng 捷徑 a shortcut; a snap course

Jiékè 捷克 Czech

jiéyùn 捷運 rapid transit

jiéyùn xìtǒng 捷運系統 a rapid transit system

jiézú xiāndēng 捷足先登 The first prize will go to the nimblest.

jié 傑
1. outstanding; remarkable; extraordinary 2. a hero

jiéchū 傑出 outstanding; extraordinary

jiézuò 傑作 a masterpiece

jié 結
1. to tie; to knot; to weave 2. a knot 3. to unite; to join; to connect 4. to congeal; coagulation 5. to form; to found; to constitute 6. a result; an outcome 7. to pay, or settle (as an account, etc.) 8. a node 9. refer to jiē (結) 1

jiébā 結疤 to heal up; to scar

jiébài 結拜 sworn (brothers, or sisters); to pledge in a sworn brotherhood

jiébàn 結伴 to accompany

jiébīng 結冰 to freeze; to form ice

jiécǎi 結綵 to festoon (for celebration)

jiéchóu 結仇 to contract ill will or animus of

jiécún 結存 the credit balance; (said of government finance) foreign exchange reserves

jiégòu 結構 1. structure 2. (said of a piece of writing) the arrangement of ideas; presentation

jiéguǒ 結果 1. refer to jiēguǒ 結果 2. the result, outcome or consequence 3. in the end; finally

jiéhé 結合 1. to get united; to combine with 2. to get married; to marry

jiéhébìng 結核病 tuberculosis

jiéhuì 結匯 to sell foreign exchange to (or to buy it from) banks; foreign exchange settlement

jiéhūn 結婚 marriage; to get married

jiéhūn zhèngshū 結婚證書 a marriage certificate

jiéhuǒ 結夥 to gang up; to collude

jiéjí 結集 to concentrate (troops, etc.); concentration (of troops, etc.)

jiéjiāo 結交 to associate with; to befriend; to make friends with

jiéjīng 結晶 to crystallize; crystallization; crystal

jiéjú 結局 the outcome; the result; the end

jiélí 結縭 to be married

jiélùn 結論 the conclusion (of a meeting, argument, etc.)

jiéméng 結盟 to ally with; align-

J

ment

jiéshí 結石 (pathology) stone; calculus

jiéshí 結識 to know or associate with

jiéshì 結識 refer to **jiéshí** 結識

jiéshù 結束 to conclude; to end; to wind up

jiésuàn 結算 to settle accounts; settlement of accounts

jiéwǎng 結網 to make a net

jiéwěi 結尾 the conclusion; the end

jiéyè 結業 to graduate; to conclude or complete a training course

jiéyú 結餘 a cash surplus; a surplus

jiéyuán 結緣 to associate on good terms

jiéyuàn 結怨 to arouse ill will or dislike; to incur hatred

jiézā 結紮 (medicine) ligation; to ligature

jiézhàng 結帳 to settle accounts; to pay up

jié 詰

1. to question; to ask 2. to punish 3. to prohibit

jiéqū áoyá 詰屈聱牙 (said of writings) hard and difficult to read

jiéwèn 詰問 to demand an explanation angrily

jié 睫

1. eyelashes 2. to blink; to wink

jiémáo 睫毛 eyelashes

jié 截

1. to cut; to section; to truncate 2. a slice; a division; a section 3. to detain; to withhold 4. to keep; to set in order 5. to stop; to close; to end

jiécháng bǔduǎn 截長補短 to even up scarcity and superabundance

jiéduàn 截斷 to disrupt; to cut off

jiéhuò 截獲 to capture by interception

jiéjī 截擊 to intercept

jiéjí 截擊 refer to **jiéjī** 截擊

jiéjiǎo 截角 to cut off or tear off a corner (of an envelope, a ticket, etc.); to truncate

jiérán 截然 distinctly

jiézhī 截肢 amputation

jiézhǐ 截止 to close (application, registration, etc.) upon reaching the deadline

jié 竭

1. to exhaust; to use up 2. to devote, or put forth (efforts, etc.)

jiéchéng 竭誠 wholeheartedly; with all sincerity

jiéjìn 竭盡 to exhaust; to use up

jiélì 竭力 to do one's best

jié 節

1. a node; a knot; a joint 2. a passage; a paragraph; a section 3. principles; integrity; fidelity; constancy; uprightness 4. a festival; a holiday 5. seasons 6. (music) beats; rhythm; time 7. to restrain; to control; to restrict 8. to curtail; to economize

jié'āi shùnbiàn 節哀順變 to restrain grief and accept the change (common advice to the bereaved)

jiécāo 節操 constancy; fidelity; integrity

jiégǔyǎn 節骨眼 a critical moment

jiéjiǎn 節儉 to be frugal; to practice austerity; to economize

jiélìng 節令 festivals

jiélù 節錄 1. to excerpt 2. an excerpt

jiémù 節目 a program; items on a program

jiémùdān 節目單 a program (of a concert, show, etc.)

jiépāi 節拍 (music) beats, rhythm or time

jiérì 節日 a festival; a holiday

jiéshěng 節省 to economize; to save

jiéwài shēngzhī 節外生枝 to bring about extra complications; to hit a snag

jiéyuē 節約 to economize; to save

jiéyù 節育 birth control

jiézhì 節制 to restrict; to hold down; to limit; to control

jiézhì shēngyù 節制生育 birth control

jié 潔

1. clean; spotless; pure; stainless; immaculate 2. to clean; to keep clean

jiébái 潔白 clean and white; immaculate

jiéjìng 潔淨 clean; untainted; stainless

jiépǐ 潔癖 mysophobia

jiéshēn zì'ài 潔身自愛 to exercise self-control so as to protect oneself from immorality

jié 櫛

refer to **zhì** 櫛

jié 擷

refer to **xié** 擷

jiě 姊

refer to **zǐ** 姊

jiě 姐

1. (姊) one's elder sister or sisters 2. a general term for women, usually young

jiěfu 姐夫 the husband of one's elder sister; a brother-in-law

jiějie 姐姐 one's elder sister

jiěmèi 姐妹 sisters

jiě 解

1. to unfasten; to untie; to loosen 2. to solve (difficult problems, etc.) 3. to explain; to clarify 4. to understand 5. ideas; views 6. to break up, separate or disperse 7. to take off; to strip 8. to relieve; to alleviate (pain, etc.) 9. to cut apart; to dissect 10. to dissolve 11. to discharge (water, etc.); to defecate

jiěchán 解饞 to satisfy a desire for delicious food

jiěchú 解除 1. to annul or cancel (a contract, agreement, etc.) 2. (law) to restore to the original status 3. to relieve (a person of his duties, etc.) 4. to remove; to get rid of

jiědá 解答 1. explanations or answers to certain questions 2. to answer or explain

jiědòng 解凍 1. to thaw 2. to unfreeze (funds, assets, etc.)

jiědú 解毒 to detoxify; to antidote

jiěfàng 解放 to untie or set free; to liberate

jiěgù 解雇 to get fired; to fire; to dismiss or discharge

jiěhuò 解惑 to remove doubts

jiějiǎ guītián 解甲歸田 to be demobilized

jiějiǔ 解酒 to neutralize the effect of alcoholic drinks; to alleviate a hangover

jiějiù 解救 to deliver (the people from tyranny, etc.); to rescue

jiějué 解決 1. to settle (a dispute, fight, etc.); to solve (a problem) 2. to dispose of; to finish off

jiěkāi 解開 to untie; to unbind; to loosen; to undo

jiěkě 解渴 to quench thirst; to allay thirst

jiěmǎqì 解碼器 a decoder

jiěmèn 解悶 to kill time; to dispel loneliness

jiěpìn 解聘 to relieve one of his duties; to dismiss or discharge a person from his post

jiěpōu 解剖 1. anatomization; to dissect; dissection 2. to analyze; analysis

jiěpǒu 解剖 refer to **jiěpōu** 解剖

jiěsàn 解散 to dismiss; to disband

jiěshì 解釋 to explain; explanation

jiětǐ 解體 disintegration; dissolution

jiětuō 解脫 to extricate

jiěwēi 解危 to head off danger

jiěwéi 解危 refer to **jiěwēi** 解危

jiěwéi 解圍 1. to resolve difficulties for others; to save others from embarrassment; etc. 2. to raise a siege

jiěxīdù 解析度 (computer) resolution

jiěyōu 解憂 to alleviate sorrow;

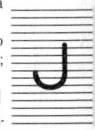

to relieve worries

jiěyuē 解約 to annul a contract or agreement

jiè 介

1. a shelled aquatic animal 2. to lie between 3. (said of one's character) upright 4. great and honorable 5. to aid; to benefit 6. tiny

jiècí 介詞 a preposition

jièké 介殼 refer to **jièqiào** 介殼

jièqiào 介殼 the shell

jièrù 介入 to get involved; to interfere with

jièshào 介紹 to introduce (a person to another)

jièshàorén 介紹人 an introducer; a matchmaker

jièyì 介意 to mind; to heed

jièyú 介於 to lie in between

jiè 戒

1. to warn; to admonish; to caution 2. to abstain from; to refrain from; to give up 3. to guard against; to avoid 4. a commandment; Buddhist monastic discipline

jièbèi 戒備 on guard (against enemy attacks, natural disasters, etc.)

jièbèi sēnyán 戒備森嚴 to be heavily guarded

jièchǐ 戒尺 a ferule

jièchú 戒除 to abstain from; to give up

jièdiào 戒掉 to abstain or give up (a bad habit)

jièdǔ 戒賭 to abstain from gambling

jièjù 戒懼 to be afraid and watchful

jièlǜ 戒律 don'ts; (Buddhism) the rules; commandments

jiètiáo 戒條 don'ts; (Buddhism) the rules; commandments

jièxīn 戒心 watchfulness; on one's guard

jièyān 戒煙 to give up smoking

jièyán 戒嚴 to impose a curfew

jièyánlìng 戒嚴令 martial law

jièzhi 戒指 a ring (on a finger)

jiè 屆

a numerary adjunct for periodic terms or events

jièmǎn 屆滿 (said of a term) to expire

jièqī 屆期 (said of an appointed time) to arrive

jièqí 屆期 refer to **jièqī** 屆期

jièshí 屆時 at the appointed time

jiè 芥

1. a mustard plant 2. tiny

jiècài 芥菜 a mustard plant

jièdì 芥蒂 1. remorse; a grudge 2. a barrier which mars friendship

jièmo 芥末 ground mustard

jiè 疥

scabies

jièchuāng 疥瘡 sores from scabies

jièxiǎn 疥癬 refer to **jièxuǎn** 疥癬

jièxuǎn 疥癬 scabies; the itch; mange; ringworm

jiè 界

1. a boundary 2. to limit; to demarcate; to define; to delimit 3. world

jièbēi 界碑 a landmark; a boundary stone

jièmiàn 界面 interface

jièwàiqiú 界外球 (sports) out-of-bounds

jièxiàn 界限 1. a border 2. to limit; to restrict

jièxiàn 界線 a boundary; a borderline

jiè 借

1. to lend 2. to borrow 3. to avail oneself of; to make use of; to resort to 4. to make a pretext of 5. if; supposing

jièdài 借貸 1. to ask for a loan 2. debit and credit

jièdāo shārén 借刀殺人 to kill one's enemy by another's hands

jièdiào 借調 to transfer temporarily; loan

jiègǔ fěngjīn 借古諷今 to use the past to disparage the present

jièhuā xiànfó 借花獻佛 to get things from another person to entertain one's own guest

jièjiàn 借鑑 to learn a lesson from another person's experience

jièjìng 借鏡 to learn a lesson from another person's experience

jièjiǔ jiāochóu 借酒澆愁 to drown one's worries or anxieties by drinking

jièjù 借據 an I.O.U.

jièkuǎn 借款 to borrow money; a loan

jièshūzhèng 借書證 a library card

jièsù 借宿 to stay overnight in another's place (or hotel, etc.)

jiètí fāhuī 借題發揮 to seize a pretext (to air one's own complaints, to attack others, etc.)

jièwèn 借問 Will you please tell me...?

jièyòng 借用 to borrow

jièzhòng 借重 to rely on; to seek the assistance (of)

jièzhǔ 借主 the creditor

jièzhù 借助 to have the aid of; to draw support from

jiè 械
refer to **xiè** 械

jiè 誡
1. to warn; to admonish 2. a commandment

jiè 藉
1. a mat, pad, or cushion of grass (or straw) 2. to rely on; to lean on; on the strength of; to avail oneself of; by means of

jiègù 藉故 to avail oneself of a certain excuse or pretext

jièkǒu 藉口 an excuse; a pretext

jīn 巾
1. a napkin or towel 2. a headgear

jīnguó yīngxióng 巾幗英雄 a heroine

jīnpà 巾帕 1. a napkin or kerchief 2. a headwrapper

jīn 斤
1. a catty 2. an ax 3. discerning; keen in observation

jīnjīn jìjiào 斤斤計較 to be particular about every point, detail, or trifle

jīnliǎng 斤兩 weight

jīn 今
1. present; recent; modern 2. now; currently; presently; nowadays 3. immediately; right away

jīnfēi xībǐ 今非昔比 Time has changed and the good old days are gone.

jīnfēi xíbǐ 今非昔比 refer to **jīnfēi xíbǐ** 今非昔比

jīnhòu 今後 hereafter; henceforward; from now on

jīnnián 今年 this year

jīnrì 今日 today

jīnshēng 今生 this present life

jīnshì 今世 1. the present era 2. this present life

jīntiān 今天 today

jīnyè 今夜 tonight

jīnzhāo 今朝 today; this morning

jīn 金
1. gold 2. metal 3. wealth; money 4. weapons; arms 5. excellent; precious; fine 6. golden 7. durable 8. a Chinese family name

jīnbǎng tímíng 金榜題名 to emerge successful from a competitive examination

jīnbàng 金鎊 pound sterling

jīnbì 金幣 gold coins

jīnbì huīhuáng 金碧輝煌 (said of a building) resplendent; gorgeous; grand; splendid; magnificent

jīnchāi 金釵 a gold hairpin

jīnchán tuōké 金蟬脫殼 refer to **jīnchán tuōqiào** 金蟬脫殼

jīnchán tuōqiào 金蟬脫殼 to escape by a cunning maneuver

jīn'é 金額 the amount of money

jīn'gāng 金剛 1. hard metal 2. a Buddhist god sometimes identified with Indra

Jīn'gāngjīng 金剛經 The Dia-

mond Sutra

jīn'gāngshí 金剛石 diamond

jīnguāngdǎng 金光黨 swindlers; racketeers

jīnguāng shǎnshǎn 金光閃閃 glittering; glistening

jīnguīxù 金龜婿 a fine (or a rich) son-in-law

jīnguīzǐ 金龜子 a tumblebug

jīnhuángsè 金黃色 bright yellow; golden

jīnhūn 金婚 a golden wedding; the 50th wedding anniversary

jīnjiàng 金匠 a goldsmith

jīnkē yùlǜ 金科玉律 the golden rule; an immutable law

jīnkù 金庫 coffers; a treasury

jīnkuài 金塊 gold bullion; a gold ingot

jīnkuàng 金礦 a gold mine

jīnlán 金蘭 sworn brotherhood; harmonious friendship

jīnlǚyī 金縷衣 a gold-threaded robe

jīn mù shuǐ huǒ tǔ 金木水火土 metal, wood, water, fire and earth—the five elements in ancient Chinese philosophy and fortunetelling

jīnpái 金牌 a gold medal

jīnqì 金器 a gold vessel

jīnqián 金錢 money; cash; riches; wealth

jīnqiánbào 金錢豹 a spotted leopard

jīnqián wànnéng 金錢萬能 Money is almighty.

jīnróng 金融 finance; banking; a monetary situation

jīnróngkǎ 金融卡 a fiscard; ATM card

jīnshí 金石 1. metal and stone—a symbol of durability 2. gold and precious stones 3. weapons; arms 4. bronze and stone inscriptions

jīnshí wéikāi 金石爲開 Sincerity can make metal and stone crack.

jīnshǔ 金屬 metals

jīnsīquè 金絲雀 a canary bird; a canary

jīntóng yùnǚ 金童玉女 young boys and girls attending upon an immortal

jīnwén 金文 ancient inscriptions on bronze

jīnwū cángjiāo 金屋藏嬌 to build a magnificent house for a beloved woman (especially a concubine or mistress)

Jīnxiàngjiǎng 金像獎 an Oscar (award)

Jīnxīng 金星 (astronomy) Venus

jīnyín cáibǎo 金銀財寶 treasures; wealth

jīnyú 金魚 goldfish

jīnyù liángyán 金玉良言 a wise saying; good counsel

jīnyù mǎntáng 金玉滿堂 to have one's house filled with riches

jīnyù qíwài, bàixù qízhōng 金玉其外，敗絮其中 a rotten interior beneath a fine exterior

jīnzhī yùyè 金枝玉葉 a term referring to the members of the royal family

jīnzìtǎ 金字塔 a pyramid

jīnzì zhāopái 金字招牌 (literally) a signboard with gilded inscriptions—a good reputation; high prestige

jīnzi 金子 gold

jīn 津

1. a ferry 2. juicy; tasty 3. saliva 4. to sweat; to perspire

jīnjīn lèdào 津津樂道 to talk with great relish

jīnjīn yǒuwèi 津津有味 1. (to do something) with great relish or interest; with gusto 2. very tasty

jīntiē 津貼 an allowance; to subsidize

jīnyào 津要 1. key places or locations 2. key posts

jīn 矜

1. to feel sorry for; to pity; to be sympathetic with; to compassionate 2. to brag; to boast 3. self-esteem; self-control; dignified; self-discipline 4. to emulate

jīnchí 矜持 to carry oneself with dignity and reserve

jīnshì 矜飾 to brag and pretend

jīn 筋
1. tendons; sinews; muscles 2. veins that stand out under the skin 3. plant fibers resembling a tendon

jīndǒu 筋斗 a somersault

jīngǔ 筋骨 1. bones and muscles—physique; build (of one's body) 2. strength

jīnpí lìjié 筋疲力竭 to be completely exhausted

jīn 禁
to endure; to bear; to withstand; to stand

jīnbuqǐ 禁不起 unable to endure

jīnbuzhù 禁不住 1. unable to endure; unable to withstand 2. can not help

jīndeqǐ 禁得起 able to withstand; able to stand

jīndezhù 禁得住 able to withstand; able to stand

jīn 襟
1. the lapel or collar of a garment or robe 2. aspiration; ambition; the mental outlook 3. (said of waters) to converge

jīnhuái 襟懷 one's feelings, ambitions, aspirations, bosom, (breadth of) mind, etc.

jǐn 僅
1. only 2. barely; scarcely; almost

jǐnjǐn 僅僅 only; hardly enough; barely

jǐnróng xuánmǎ 僅容旋馬 narrow space

jǐnyǒu 僅有 to have only...; there is (or are) only...

jǐn 緊
1. tight; firm; fast; secure; taut; tense; close 2. urgent; critical; pressing

jǐnbēng 緊繃 to stretch taut

jǐnbī 緊逼 1. to press hard; to close in on 2. (basketball) press

jǐncòu 緊湊 1. compact 2. (said

of an entertainment program, a show, a composition, etc.) one climax after another

jǐnjí 緊急 urgent; critical

jǐnjiēzhe 緊接著 to follow close behind

jǐnjǐn 緊緊 tightly; firmly; closely

jǐnlín 緊鄰 a close neighbor

jǐnmì 緊密 1. rigidly precise; rigorous 2. compact and orderly 3. to close together 4. rapid and intense

jǐnpò 緊迫 urgent; pressing

jǐnqiào shāngpǐn 緊俏商品 commodities in great demand; goods in short supply

jǐnsuō 緊縮 to retrench; to curtail

jǐnwò 緊握 to grasp firmly

jǐnyào guāntóu 緊要關頭 a critical moment

jǐnzhāng 緊張 nervous; taut; tight; tension

jǐn 瑾
fine jade

jǐnyú 瑾瑜 a fine piece of jade

jǐn 錦
1. brocade; tapestry 2. brilliant and beautiful 3. glorious

jǐnbiāo 錦標 1. a championship (in a tournament) 2. a trophy; a cup

jǐnduàn 錦緞 brocade

jǐnnáng miàojì 錦囊妙計 a clever scheme yet to be revealed

jǐnqí 錦旗 an embroidered flag; a pennant

jǐnshàng tiānhuā 錦上添花 to give someone or something additional splendor; to cap it all

jǐnxiù héshān 錦繡河山 land of splendor—one's fatherland

jǐnxiù qiánchéng 錦繡前程 a glorious or promising future; a bright or rosy future

jǐnyī yùshí 錦衣玉食 to lead a luxurious life; to live in luxury

jǐn 儘
1. the utmost; the extreme 2. to let (someone do it)

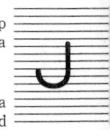

jǐnguǎn 儘管 1. even if; no matter 2. not hesitate to

jǐn 謹

1. cautious; prudent; careful; attentive 2. sincerely; reverent; deferential

jǐnfáng 謹防 to guard carefully against; to take precautions against

jǐnfáng jiǎmào 謹防假冒 Beware of imitations!

jǐnfáng páshǒu 謹防扒手 Beware of pickpockets!

jǐnjì 謹記 to remember with reverence

jǐnshèn 謹慎 prudent; cautious

jǐnyán 謹嚴 strict; rigorous

jǐnyán shènxíng 謹言慎行 to be prudent in making statements and careful in personal conduct

jǐn 饉

1. a year of famine 2. hunger; hungry

jìn 近

1. near or close (in space) 2. near or close (in time); immediate; recent 3. near or close (in abstract relation); intimate 4. to approach; to approximate

jìndài 近代 modern times; recent times

jìndàishǐ 近代史 modern history

jìnhǎi 近海 near the sea; coastal; offshore

jìnjiāo 近郊 suburbs; outskirts

jìnkuàng 近況 a recent situation; how things stand

jìnlái 近來 recently; lately

jìnlín 近鄰 a close neighbor

jìnlù 近路 a shortcut

jìnnián 近年 in recent years

jìnqī 近期 in the near future

jìnqī 近期 refer to jìnqī 近期

jìnqīn 近親 close relatives

jìnrì 近日 recently; lately

jìnshi 近視 nearsightedness; myopia

jìnshuǐ lóutái xiāndé yuè 近水樓臺先得月 A waterfront

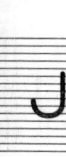

pavilion gets the moonlight first —the advantage of being in a favorable position

jìnyīn 近因 an immediate cause

jìnzài yǎnqián 近在眼前 very near as if located right before one's eyes; right under one's nose

jìnzài zhíchí 近在咫尺 very near as if just a few feet away

jìnzhūzhě chì, jìnmòzhě hēi 近朱者赤，近墨者黑 Good companions have good influence while bad ones have bad influence.

jìn 勁

1. vigor; energy; strength 2. spirit 3. an air; manner

jìn 浸

1. to dip; to immerse; to soak; to permeate; to percolate 2. gradual; gradually

jìnpào 浸泡 to soak; to immerse

jìnrǎn 浸染 to be contaminated gradually

jìnrùn 浸潤 to pass in gradually; to soak

jìnshī 浸濕 to soak

jìnshí 浸蝕 erosion; to erode

jìnshuǐ 浸水 to immerse or dip in water; deluged

jìnzì 浸漬 to soak or be soaked

jìn 晉

1. to advance; to flourish; to increase 2. Jin (a state during the Epoch of Spring and Autumn, occupying parts of today's Shanxi and Hebei provinces) 3. another name for Shanxi Province 4. the Jin Dynasty (265–420 A.D.) 5. a Chinese family name

jìnjí 晉級 promotion; to promote

jìnjiàn 晉見 to have an audience with

jìnshēng 晉升 to rise in rank; to promote

jìnyè 晉謁 to visit or call on (a superior)

jìn 進

1. to go ahead; to move forward;

to proceed; to advance 2. to improve; improvement; progress 3. to recommend; to introduce 4. to offer (advice, presents, etc.) 5. a generation 6. income 7. rooms in a house divided by a courtyard; a courtyard 8. to enter 9. to eat; to take; to have

jìnbù 進步 to improve; to progress; improvement; progress; progressive

jìnchǎng 進場 to get into an examination room, a sports arena, etc.

jìnchū 進出 1. to get in and out; incoming and outgoing 2. (business) a turnover

jìnchūkǒu 進出口 1. imports and exports 2. exits and entrances

jìndù 進度 (said of work) degree of progress

jìngōng 進攻 to attack; attack; offensive

jìnhuà 進化 to evolve; evolution

jìnkǒu 進口 1. to import; importation 2. an intake (for liquid or gaseous matters)

jìnlai 進來 to come in; to enter

jìnqǔ 進取 1. to be aggressive, as in jockeying for position, etc. 2. to forge ahead with effort; to advance

jìnrù 進入 to enter; to get in; to reach

jìnshí 進食 to eat; to take food

jìnshuǐ 進水 (said of a house) to get flooded; water flowing in

jìntuì 進退 1. to advance or retreat 2. to stay or quit a job 3. to employ or fire a person 4. a sense of propriety

jìntuì liǎngnán 進退兩難 difficult either to proceed or retreat; in a dilemma

jìnxíng 進行 1. to advance; to march forward 2. to proceed (with one's business, plan, etc.); to carry on

jìnxiū 進修 to advance in study; to engage in advanced studies

jìnyán 進言 to offer advice

jìnyíbù 進一步 to take one step ahead; to move further ahead

jìnzhǎn 進展 progress; headway

jìn 禁
1. to prohibit; to forbid; to ban 2. to confine; to imprison; to detain 3. a secret 4. a royal residence

jìnbì 禁閉 1. to prohibit entry into government services 2. to imprison; to confine

jìndì 禁地 a forbidden ground

jìngù 禁錮 1. to prohibit entry into government services 2. to imprison; to confine

jìnguǒ 禁果 the forbidden fruit

jìnjì 禁忌 1. a taboo; to taboo 2. to avoid; to abstain from

jìnlìng 禁令 a prohibition; a ban

jìnluán 禁臠 1. a forbidden thing; one's exclusive domain 2. a precious thing

jìnpǐn 禁品 contraband

jìnqū 禁區 1. a forbidden region; a restricted zone 2. a preserve

jìnshí 禁食 to fast; to fast

jìnshū 禁書 banned books

jìnzhǐ 禁止 to forbid; to prohibit; to ban

jìnzhǐ rùnèi 禁止入內 No admittance.

jìnzhǐ tíngchē 禁止停車 No parking.

jìnzhǐ xīyān 禁止吸煙 No smoking.

jìnzú 禁足 to forbid a soldier to leave the barracks on holidays as a form of punishment

jìn 盡
1. to exhaust; to use up 2. to put to the best use 3. to complete; to finish; to accomplish 4. all; entirely; totally; completely; wholly 5. the utmost

jìnběnfèn 盡本分 to do what one is supposed to do, no more and no less

jìnfù dōngliú 盡付東流 all in vain

jìnhuān érsàn 盡歡而散 to leave only after each has enjoyed himself to the utmost

jìnlì 盡力 to make efforts; to exert oneself; to do one's best

jìnlì érwéi 盡力而爲 to do one's

best

jìnliàng 盡量 as much as possible

jìnqíng 盡情 to one's heart's content

jìnrénshì yǐ tīngtiānmìng 盡人事以聽天命 One does one's best and leaves the rest to Heaven.

jìnshàn jìnměi 盡善盡美 flawless; perfect

jìnshì 盡是 all are; without exception; to be full of

jìntóu 盡頭 the extremity; the end

jìnxiào 盡孝 to do one's filial duty

jìnxīn 盡心 to devote all one's energies

jìnxìng 盡興 to enjoy to one's heart's content

jìnzhí 盡職 to do one's duty

jìnzhōng bàoguó 盡忠報國 to devote oneself to one's country

jìn 噤

to keep the mouth shut; to shut up

jìnruò hánchán 噤若寒蟬 to say or reveal nothing (especially out of fear)

jìn 燼

1. embers; ashes; cinders 2. victims of disasters

jīng 京

1. the capital (of a country); a metropolis 2. great; greatness

jīngchéng 京城 the capital

jīngjī 京畿 the capital and vicinity

Jīngjù 京劇 Beijing opera

jīngshī 京師 the capital

Jīngxì 京戲 Beijing opera

jīng 耕

refer to **gēng** 耕

Jīng 涇

name of a river in Shaanxi Province

Jīng Wèi fēnmíng 涇渭分明 to be entirely different

jīng 莖

a stalk; a stem

jīng 旌

1. a kind of flag, banner, standard, etc. ornamented with feathers 2. to cite (one's merits, virtues, etc.); to make manifest

jīngqí 旌旗 a general name for flags and banners

jīngqí bìrì 旌旗蔽日 (literally) There are so many flags that they cover the whole sky (or darken the sun)—a very large army

jīng 菁

1. the flower of the leek 2. the rape turnip 3. luxuriant; lush

jīnghuá 菁華 essence

jīng 荊

1. a kind of bramble; a thorn 2. a cane for punishment used in ancient China 3. (a polite expression) my wife 4. (in ancient China) name of one of the nine political regions 5. a Chinese family name

jīngjí 荊棘 1. thorns; thorny 2. a difficult situation

jīng 晶

1. crystal 2. bright; clear; brilliant; radiant

jīngpiàn 晶片 a chip

jīngtǐ 晶體 a (radio) crystal

jīngyíng 晶瑩 sparkling

jīng 睛

1. the pupil of the eye 2. eyes

jīng 經

1. classic books; religious scriptures; books of significant value 2. the warp of a fabric; things running lengthwise 3. common or customary ways, rules, regulations, etc. 4. to plan; to arrange; to regulate; to rule; to manage; to deal in; to engage in 5. menses 6. human arteries, etc. 7. as a result; after 8. to pass through or by 9. longitude

jīngcháng 經常 frequently; often; constantly

jīngdiǎn 經典 1. religious scrip-

tures 2. classics

jīngdù 經度 degrees of longitude

jīngfèi 經費 a budget; funds

jīngguò 經過 to pass by or through

jīngjì 經濟 1. economy; economic 2. economical; to economize

jīngjì jīchǔ 經濟基礎 an economic base

jīngjì mìngmài 經濟命脈 the economic lifeline

jīngjìrén 經紀人 1. a manager (of entertainers, boxers, etc.) 2. a broker; an agent

jīngjì xiāotiáo 經濟蕭條 economic stagnation

jīngjìxué 經濟學 economics

jīngjìxuéjiā 經濟學家 an economist

jīngjiǔ nàiyòng 經久耐用 (said of goods) durable

jīnglǐ 經理 1. a manager (of a company) 2. to manage, direct, regulate, etc.

jīnglì 經歷 1. one's past experiences 2. to undergo; to go through

jīngmài 經脈 blood vessels

jīngnián léiyuè 經年累月 for months and years

jīngshāng 經商 to go into business

jīngshì jìmín 經世濟民 to govern and benefit the people

jīngshǒu 經手 to handle; to deal with

jīngshū 經書 classic books

jīngwěi 經緯 1. longitude and latitude 2. the warp and the woof

jīngwén 經文 classical text

jīngxiàn 經線 longitude; the meridian

jīngxiāo 經銷 to sell as a consignee

jīngyàn 經驗 experience; empirical

jīngyíng 經營 to operate or manage (a shop, a business, etc.)

jīngyóu 經由 by (a person); through or via (a place)

jīng 兢

to fear; to dread; apprehensive; cautious

jīngjīngyèyè 兢兢業業 cautious and attentive

jīng 精

1. polished rice; unmixed rice 2. the essence; the essentials 3. energy; spirits 4. the male sperm; semen 5. fine and delicate; exquisite 6. dedicated; intensive 7. very; completely; extremely 8. keen; smart; sharp; clever 9. skilled; to specialize in 10. a goblin; a spirit; a demon

jīngcǎi 精彩 1. the highlight or climax (of a play, etc.); the most attractive or wonderful part (of something) 2. Wonderful! Bravo! Excellent!

jīngchéng tuánjié 精誠團結 to unite together with utmost sincerity; esprit de corps

jīngchún 精純 1. pure 2. to refine

jīngcuì 精萃 cream; pick

jīngcuì 精粹 the essence or essentials; refined and pure

jīngdǎ xìsuàn 精打細算 calculate carefully and budget strictly

jīnghuá 精華 the essence; the essentials

jīngjiǎn 精簡 to simplify

jīngjìn 精進 to devote oneself to improvement

jīnglì 精力 stamina; vitality; energy

jīnglì wàngshèng 精力旺盛 to be full of vitality

jīngliàn 精煉 to rectify; to refine; refined

jīngliáng 精良 exquisite; fine; excellent

jīnglíng 精靈 an elf; a fairy

jīngměi 精美 exquisite; delicate and beautiful

jīngmì 精密 minute or detailed; precise

jīngmíng 精明 keen or sharp; clever

jīngpí lìjié 精疲力竭 exhausted; worn-out

jīngpǐn 精品 an exquisite article

jīngqiǎo 精巧 exquisite; fine and delicate (workmanship, etc.)

jīngquè 精確 precise; accurate; precision; accuracy

jīngruì 精銳 crack; picked

jīngshēn 精深 profound; profundity

jīngshén 精神 1. one's spirit 2. mental

jīngshénbìng 精神病 mental illness

jīngshénbìngyuàn 精神病院 an asylum

jīngshén fēnlièzhèng 精神分裂症 schizophrenia

jīngshén huǎnghū 精神恍惚 absent-minded

jīngshén shīcháng 精神失常 mental disorder

jīngshen 精神 lively; vigorous

jīngshen bǎomǎn 精神飽滿 in high spirits; vigorous and energetic

jīngshen dǒusǒu 精神抖擻 high-spirited; sprightly

jīngsuǐ 精髓 the marrow; the essence; the pith

jīngtiāo xìxuǎn 精挑細選 very choosy

jīngtōng 精通 well versed in; good at; expert at

jīngxì 精細 1. fine (materials, etc.); delicate and painstaking (workmanship, handicraft, etc.); exquisite 2. very careful and attentive

jīngxīn jiézuò 精心傑作 a masterpiece; a brainchild

jīngxuǎn 精選 to pick the best; to hand-pick; to select

jīngyán 精鹽 refined salt; purified salt

jīngyì 精義 the essential significance

jīngyì qiújīng 精益求精 Second best is not good enough. —to try for the best

jīngzhàn 精湛 consummate; exquisite; perfect

jīngzhì 精製 specially picked and baked (tea, etc.); highly finished; refined

jīngzhì 精緻 fine; exquisite; delicate

jīngzhōng bàoguó 精忠報國 to serve one's fatherland with unreserved loyalty

jīngzhuāngběn 精裝本 a deluxe edition

jīngzǐ 精子 spermatozoa

jīng 鯨
a whale

jīngtūn cánshí 鯨吞蠶食 aggression by engulfing and nibbling processes

jīngyóu 鯨油 whale oil

jīng 驚
1. to startle; to surprise; to amaze; to astound; to alarm; to flabbergast; to dumbfound; to terrify; to frighten 2. afraid; frightened; scared; fearful; terrified 3. to marvel; to be surprised; to be amazed

jīngdòng 驚動 1. to astonish; to startle; to stir up; to alarm 2. to bother; to disturb

jīng'è 驚愕 to be astonished

jīnggōng zhīniǎo 驚弓之鳥 a person seized with fear because of some frightening experience encountered in the past

jīnghài 驚駭 frightened; terrified

jīnghóng yīpiē 驚鴻一瞥 to have a fleeting glimpse of a beauty

jīnghuāng 驚慌 to lose one's head from terror; to be frightened and confused

jīnghuāng shīcuò 驚慌失措 to lose one's head from fear; terrified and not knowing what to do; to panic

jīnghún wèidìng 驚魂未定 not yet become calm or normal from a fright

jīngjì 驚悸 quickened heartbeat due to fear

jīngjiào 驚叫 to cry in fear; to scream

jīngjù 驚懼 scared; afraid; fearful

jīngkǒng 驚恐 scared; fearful; afraid

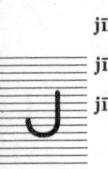

jīngpà 驚怕 scared; fearful; afraid

jīngqí 驚奇 to be surprised; to be amazed; to marvel

jīngrǎo 驚擾 to disturb

jīngrén 驚人 surprising; astounding; astonishing; startling; amazing; sensational

jīngshì hàisú 驚世駭俗 to astound the world with an extraordinary idea, etc.

jīngtàn 驚嘆 to marvel; to exclaim

jīngtànhào 驚嘆號 an exclamation mark; an exclamation point

jīngtāo hàilàng 驚濤駭浪 (said of the sea) churning; furious; choppy; mountainous waves

jīngtiāndì, qìguǐshén 驚天動地，泣鬼神 to startle the universe and move the gods

jīngtiān dòngdì 驚天動地 to startle even the universe; world-shaking; earthshaking

jīngxǐ 驚喜 pleasantly surprised

jīngxià 驚嚇 to frighten; to scare; to alarm suddenly

jīngxiǎn 驚險 breathtaking; alarmingly dangerous; thrilling

jīngxīn dòngpò 驚心動魄 heart-shaking; horrified; soul-stirring

jīngxǐng 驚醒 to cause to wake up with a startle

jīngyà 驚訝 to marvel; to be surprised; to be amazed

jīngyì 驚異 to marvel; to be surprised; to be amazed

jǐng 井
a well

jǐngdǐwā 井底蛙 a person of very limited outlook and experience

jǐngjǐng yǒutiáo 井井有條 systematic; orderly

jǐngrán 井然 orderly

jǐngshuǐ bùfàn héshuǐ 井水不犯河水 not to interfere with each other's affairs

jǐngyán 井鹽 well salt

jǐng 阱
a trap; a snare

jǐng 景
1. scenery; views 2. prospects; circumstances; situations 3. (in motion pictures, stage shows, etc.) settings; background scenes 4. big and strong 5. great 6. high 7. bright and luminous 8. to admire; to respect 9. a Chinese family name

jǐngguān 景觀 (geography) landscape

jǐngqì 景氣 (economics) booming; prosperity

jǐngsè 景色 scenery; landscapes

jǐngwù 景物 scenery; landscapes

jǐngxiàng 景象 appearances; scenes; conditions; outlooks; sights

jǐngyǎng 景仰 to admire and respect

jǐngzhì 景致 scenes; views; a vista

jǐng 儆
1. to be on guard 2. to warn; to caution

jǐng 頸
the neck; the throat

jǐng 警
1. to guard; to keep watch 2. to warn; to alert 3. an alarm 4. quick; alert; agile 5. the police

jǐngbào 警報 an alert; an alarm; a warning

jǐngbàoqì 警報器 a siren

jǐngbào xìnhào 警報信號 a warning signal

jǐngchá 警察 a policeman; a cup

jǐngchájú 警察局 county (or city) police headquarters

jǐngchá pàichūsuǒ 警察派出所 a police substation; a station house

jǐngchá xuéxiào 警察學校 a police school; a police academy

jǐngchē 警車 a squad car; a police car

jǐnggào 警告 1. to warn; to caution; to admonish 2. a warning

jǐngguān 警官 a police officer

jǐngguān xuéxiào 警官學校 a police academy

jǐngjiè 警戒 1. to be on the alert 2. to warn and admonish

jǐngjù 警句 an epigram

jǐngjué 警覺 vigilant; alert; watchful

jǐnglíng 警鈴 a warning bell; an alarm bell

jǐngquǎn 警犬 a police dog

jǐngtàn 警探 a police detective

jǐngtì 警惕 1. to be wary; to be alert; to be watchful 2. a warning

jǐngwèi 警衛 1. to guard 2. a guard

jǐngyǔ 警語 an epigram

jǐngyuán 警員 a policeman; a cop

jìng 勁

strong; tough; powerful; sturdy

jìngdí 勁敵 a powerful enemy

jìnglǚ 勁旅 a powerful army; crack troops

jìng 徑

1. a narrow path; a byway; a shortcut 2. a diameter 3. direct; straight 4. already—implying a sense of surprise

jìngsài 徑賽 (sports) track events

jìng 竟

1. to come to an end; to terminate; to go through the whole course; to finish; to complete 2. rather unexpectedly; somewhat to one's surprise; in a way thought to be rather unlikely

jìnggǎn 竟敢 to dare (somewhat to one's surprise); to have the audacity

jìngrán 竟然 somewhat unexpectedly; somewhat to one's surprise

jìngyè 竟夜 all night; the whole night

jìng 淨

1. clean; pure; to cleanse; to purify 2. empty; vain 3. a role in Chinese opera with a heavily painted face 4. completely;

totally 5. only; merely; nothing but 6. net (income, etc.)

jìnghuà 淨化 to purify

jìngjià 淨價 a net price

jìnglì 淨利 net profit

jìngshēn 淨身 to castrate; castration

jìngshuǐ 淨水 clean water

jìngtǔ 淨土 sukhavati; the land of the pure

jìngzhí 淨值 net value

jìngzhòng 淨重 net weight

jìngzhuàn 淨賺 net earnings

jìng 逕

1. a path 2. direct

jìngtíng 逕庭 very unlike; quite different; poles apart

jìng 痙

spasm; convulsions

jìngluán 痙攣 convulsions; spasm; cramp; a jerk

jìng 敬

1. to respect; to revere; to honor; to esteem 2. to present; to offer

jìng'ài 敬愛 to respect and love

jìngchēng 敬稱 an honorific appellation

jìngchéng 敬呈 to present with respect

jìngfèng 敬奉 1. to receive respectfully 2. to present (or offer) respectfully

jìnggào 敬告 to tell respectfully

jìnghè 敬賀 to congratulate with respect

jìnghòu 敬候 1. to inquire after respectfully 2. to await respectfully

jìngjiǔ 敬酒 to drink a toast; to toast

jìnglǎo zūnxián 敬老尊賢 to revere the aged and honor the wise

jìnglǐ 敬禮 to salute

jìngpéi mòzuò 敬陪末座 to sit below the salt

jìngpèi 敬佩 to admire; to esteem; to respect

jìngqǐ 敬啓 to state with respect (a conventional phrase in corre-

(spondence)

jìngqǐng 敬請 to invite respectfully

jìngqǐng zhǐjiào 敬請指教 I humbly request your advice.

jìngwèi 敬畏 to hold in awe; to venerate

jìngxiāng 敬香 to offer incense

jìngxiè 敬謝 to thank respectfully

jìngyǎng 敬仰 to admire; to esteem; to respect

jìngyì 敬意 respects; regards

jìngzèng 敬贈 to present respectfully

jìngzhòng 敬重 to respect; to esteem

jìngzhù 敬祝 to wish respectfully (a conventional phrase used at the end of a letter)

jìng 靖
1. peaceful; still; tranquil; quiet 2. to pacify; to quell (an uprising, etc.); to tranquilize 3. to order 4. to praise in public

jìng 境
1. a boundary; a frontier; a border 2. a place; an area 3. a state; a situation; circumstances

jìngjiè 境界 1. a boundary 2. a situation 3. a state (of mind); a realm

jìngkuàng 境況 a situation; a condition

jìngnèi 境內 within the border; in the country

jìngyù 境遇 circumstances; conditions

jìng 靚
1. to ornament; to doll up 2. still; quiet; tranquil

jìngzhuāng 靚妝 (said of a woman) fully dressed and ornamented

jìng 靜
1. still; motionless; tranquility; quiet(ly); calm; silent 2. peaceful; harmonious; serene 3. virtuous; chaste

jìngdiàn 靜電 static electricity

jìngdiàn zhàoxiàng yìn-

shuājī 靜電照相印刷機 a laser printer

jìngguān zìdé 靜觀自得 Everything comes to one who waits.

jìngjí sīdòng 靜極思動 When one remains idle for too long, he thinks of taking an active role in life.

jìngmài 靜脈 veins

jìngmò 靜默 1. silence; to become silent 2. to mourn in silence

jìngqiāoqiāo 靜悄悄 quietly; stealthily; very quiet

jìngqiǎoqiāo 靜悄悄 refer to jìngqiāoqiāo 靜悄悄

jìngruò chǔnǚ, dòngruò tuōtù 靜若處女，動若脫兔 Deliberate in counsel, prompt in action.

jìngtài 靜態 a motionless state; the state of stillness; a stationary state

jìngyǎng 靜養 to rest or convalesce without disturbance; to recuperate in quiet surroundings

jìngzhǐ 靜止 motionless; static; rest

jìngzuò 靜坐 to sit still with a peaceful mind; to sit still as a form of therapy

jìng 鏡
1. a mirror 2. lenses; spectacles; glasses 3. to mirror 4. to take warning (from a past failure)

jìnghuā shuǐyuè 鏡花水月 things appealing but unreal

jìngkuàng 鏡框 refer to jìngkuàng 鏡框

jìngkuàng 鏡框 a picture frame

jìngpiàn 鏡片 a lens

jìngtóu 鏡頭 1. the lens of a camera 2. a scene captured by the camera

jìng 競
to compete; to vie

jìngjì 競技 a race; a contest; a tournament

jìngsài 競賽 a race; a contest

jìngxuǎn 競選 to campaign; to run for

jìngzhēng 競爭 to compete; to

vie; competition

jìngzhēngzhě 競爭者 a competitor

jiǒng 炯

bright; brightness; clear

jiǒngjiè 炯戒 a clear warning

jiǒng 迥

1. far away 2. widely different

jiǒngrán bùtóng 迥然不同 not in the least alike; diametrically different

jiǒng 窘

1. hard-pressed; poverty-stricken 2. to embarrass 3. afflicted; distressed

jiǒngjìng 窘境 a predicament; a plight

jiǒngtài 窘態 an embarrassed look

jiū 究 also **jiǔ**

1. to examine; to study; to investigate exhaustively; to dig into 2. finally; in the end; after all 3. actually; really

jiūjìng 究竟 1. the very source; the outcome 2. after all; finally; actually; exactly

jiū 糾 also **jiǔ**

1. to supervise; to inspect; to investigate 2. to correct; to censure; to impeach; to discipline 3. to collaborate; to band together; to entangle; to bind together; to involve; involved

jiūchá 糾察 1. to discipline; to investigate; to picket 2. a disciplinary officer

jiūchán 糾纏 1. to tangle; to involve; entanglement 2. to pester

jiūfēn 糾紛 disputes; quarrels; entanglements

jiūgé 糾葛 an endless involvement; a dispute

jiūhé 糾合 to band together

jiūhé 糾劾 to censure and impeach

jiūjié 糾結 to band together; to collaborate

jiūzhèng 糾正 to correct; to check; to discipline; to rectify

jiū 赳 also **jiǔ**

valiant; gallant

jiū 揪

1. to clutch; to grasp with one's hand 2. to pull; to drag 3. to pick on

jiūchū 揪出 to uncover; to ferret out

jiū'ěrduo 揪耳朵 to hold (another) by the ear

jiūxīn 揪心 1. anxious 2. heartrending

jiū 鳩

1. a pigeon; a dove 2. to collect; to assemble

jiūzhàn quècháo 鳩占鵲巢 enjoying the fruits of others' without having worked hard; to usurp what is another's

jiǔ 九

nine; ninth

jiǔchéng 九成 ninety percent

jiǔdà xíngxīng 九大行星 the nine planets in the solar system —Mercury, Venus, Earth, Mars, Jupiter, Saturn, Uranus, Neptune, and Pluto

jiǔjiǔbiǎo 九九表 the multiplication table up to nine times nine

jiǔliàn chénggāng 九鍊成鋼 Mastery is the result of long practice or training.

jiǔniú èrhǔ 九牛二虎 a herculean effort

jiǔniú yīmáo 九牛一毛 an iota from a vast quantity

jiǔquán 九泉 Hades; the underworld

jiǔsǐ yīshēng 九死一生 grave danger

jiǔxiāo yúnwài 九霄雲外 beyond the farthest limits of the sky—far, far away

jiǔyuè 九月 1. September 2. the ninth month of the lunar calendar 3. nine months

Jiǔzhōu 九州 1. another name for ancient China 2. Kyushu, an island of Japan

jiǔ 久

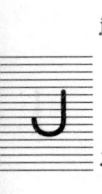

1. long 2. for a long time 3. to detain someone long

jiǔbié 久別 long separation

jiǔbìng chéng liángyī 久病成良醫 Long illness makes the patient a good doctor.

jiǔ'ér jiǔzhī 久而久之 over a long period of time

jiǔhòu 久候 to wait for a long time

jiǔjīng fēngshuāng 久經風霜 to have experienced all sorts of hardships

jiǔjiǔ 久久 for a long, long time

jiǔjū rénxià 久居人下 to remain in a subordinate position for a long period

jiǔliú 久留 to stay for a long time

jiǔwéi 久違 the literary form of "Long time no see."

jiǔyǎng 久仰 Glad to meet you.

jiǔyǎng dàmíng 久仰大名 I've heard of your illustrious name for a long time.

jiǔyuǎn 久遠 a long time; forever; perpetual

jiǔ 玖

1. a black jade stone 2. an elaborate form of **jiǔ** 九, nine, used in checks, etc. to prevent fraud

jiǔ 灸

(Chinese medicine) to cauterize by burning moxa; moxa cautery; moxibustion

jiǔ 糾

refer to **jiū** 糾

jiǔ 韭(韮)

scallions; leeks; Chinese chives

jiǔcài 韭菜 leeks or scallions

jiǔhuáng 韭黃 yellow, tender leeks or scallions

jiǔ 赳

refer to **jiū** 赳

jiǔ 酒

alcoholic drinks (brewed or distilled); wine; liquor; spirits

jiǔbā 酒吧 a bar (for alcoholic drinks)

jiǔbǎo 酒保 a bartender; a waiter

jiǔbēi 酒杯 winecups

jiǔchǎng 酒廠 a brewery; a winery; a distillery

jiǔdiàn 酒店 a tavern; a saloon

jiǔféng zhījǐ qiānbēi shǎo 酒逢知己千杯少 One can drink far more than usual with a bosom friend.

jiǔguǎn 酒館 a tavern; a pub; a saloon; a bar

jiǔguǐ 酒鬼 1. a drunkard; a sot 2. a toper; a wine bibber

jiǔhān ěrrè 酒酣耳熱 The enlivening effect of alcohol is just at its height.

jiǔhú 酒壺 a wine pot or jar

jiǔjiā 酒家 1. a tavern; a bar; a wineshop 2. the Chinese version of the geisha house in Japan; a girlie restaurant

jiǔjiānǚ 酒家女 a barmaid; a bargirl

jiǔjiào 酒窖 a wine cellar

jiǔjīng 酒精 alcohol

jiǔkè 酒客 a drinker

jiǔliàng 酒量 one's capacity for drinking

jiǔlóu 酒樓 a tavern; a pub; a saloon; a bar

jiǔpǐn 酒品 decorum in drinking

jiǔpíng 酒瓶 a bottle for alcoholic drinks

jiǔròu péngyou 酒肉朋友 friends in one's revels (not in one's need); fair-weather friends

jiǔsè cáiqì 酒色財氣 wine, women, wealth, and power—four main temptations to a man

jiǔsè zhītú 酒色之徒 a libertine; a debauchee

jiǔtǒng 酒桶 a wine barrel or cask

jiǔwō 酒窩 dimples on one's cheeks

jiǔxí 酒席 a feast; a banquet

jiǔyàn 酒宴 a feast; a banquet

jiǔyǐn 酒癮 addiction to alcohol

jiǔyǒu 酒友 a bottle companion

jiǔzuì 酒醉 drunk; intoxicated;

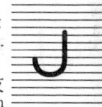

tipsy

jiŭzuì fànbǎo 酒醉飯飽 having drunk and eaten to one's heart's content

jiù 臼

1. a mortar for unhusking rice 2. a socket at a bone joint

jiù 究

refer to **jiū** 究

jiù 咎

1. a disaster; a calamity 2. a fault; a mistake 3. to blame; to punish; to censure

jiùyóu zìqǔ 咎由自取 a trouble of one's own making

jiù 疚

1. prolonged illness 2. mental discomfort 3. a guilty conscience

jiù 柩

a coffin with a corpse in it

jiù 救

to save; to relieve; to rescue; to aid; to help

jiùbīng 救兵 relieving troops; reinforcements

jiùhù 救護 to relieve and nurse (the wounded, etc.); to rescue

jiùhùchē 救護車 an ambulance

jiùhuó 救活 to resuscitate; to revive

jiùhuǒ 救火 1. to try to extinguish a fire 2. firefighting

jiùjí 救急 1. to give help in emergency 2. to apply first aid

jiùjì 救濟 to relieve (the suffering, the poor, etc.)

jiùjìjīn 救濟金 relief funds

jiùjìyuàn 救濟院 a poorhouse; a workhouse

jiùmìng 救命 1. to save one's life 2. Help!

jiùmìng ēnrén 救命恩人 the savior of one's life

jiùshēnghé 救生盒 a first-aid kit

jiùshēngquān 救生圈 a life ring; a life buoy

jiùshēngtǐng 救生艇 a lifeboat

jiùshēngyī 救生衣 a life jacket

jiùshēngyuán 救生員 a lifeguard; a lifesaver

Jiùshìzhǔ 救世主 the Savior; the Messiah

jiùxīng 救星 a savior

jiùyuán 救援 to help or aid (the distressed)

jiùyuán tóushǒu 救援投手 (baseball) a relief pitcher

jiùzāi 救災 to relieve victims of a disaster

jiùzhì 救治 to treat and cure (the sick); to remedy

jiùzhù 救助 to relieve or help (persons)

jiù 就

1. to receive 2. to undergo 3. to assume 4. to follow 5. to come or go to 6. to suit; to fit 7. forthwith; right away 8. exactly; precisely 9. namely 10. even if

jiùcǐ 就此 then; thereupon; thereafter

jiùdì 就地 on the spot

jiùdì qǔcái 就地取材 1. to acquire necessary material locally 2. to employ local talents

jiùdì zhèngfǎ 就地正法 to execute an offender summarily right on the spot

jiùfàn 就範 to give up; to be subdued; to yield

jiùjìn 就近 at the nearest convenient place

jiùqǐn 就寢 to go to bed

jiùrèn 就任 to take office

jiùshì 就是 1. exactly 2. namely; that is 3. even if; even though 4. only; but

jiùshì lùnshì 就事論事 to confine the discussion to the matter at issue

jiùsuàn 就算 (colloquial) even though; even if; granted that

jiùxù 就緒 to be complete; to be all set; ready

jiùxué 就學 to go to school

jiùyào 就要 to be about to; to be going to

jiùyè 就業 to get employment; to get a job

jiùyè fǔdǎo 就業輔導 place-

ment or appointment service

jiùyè kōngbái 就業空白 an unattractive job

jiùyī 就醫 to receive or undergo medical treatment

jiùyì 就義 to become a martyr to a worthy cause or principle

jiùzhí 就職 to be sworn in; to be inaugurated

jiùzuò 就座 to take one's seat

jiù 舅

1. a maternal uncle (one's mother's brother) 2. a brother-in-law (one's wife's brother) 3. a woman's father-in-law 4. a man's father-in-law

jiùfù 舅父 a maternal uncle

jiùmā 舅媽 a maternal aunt

jiù 廐

a stable

jiù 舊

1. old; past; former 2. ancient; antique 3. longstanding

jiùbìng fùfā 舊病復發 to have a relapse of an old ailment

jiùdì chóngyóu 舊地重遊 to revisit a place

jiùguān 舊觀 the former appearance

jiùguānniàn 舊觀念 old ideas

jiùhuò 舊貨 secondhand goods; junk

jiùhuòtān 舊貨攤 a junk store

jiùjiāo 舊交 an old friend

Jiùjīnshān 舊金山 San Francisco

Jiùlìnián 舊曆年 the Lunar New Year

jiùrì 舊日 bygone days; former times

jiùshì 舊式 out-of-date; old-style; old-fashioned

jiùshū 舊書 1. a used book 2. ancient books

jiùshūdiàn 舊書店 a second-hand bookstore

jiùshūtān 舊書攤 a secondhand bookstand

jiùyǔ xīnzhī 舊雨新知 old friends and new acquaintances

jiùzhàng 舊賬 old debts; old bills

jiùzhǐ 舊址 a former site; a former address

jiùzhǔ 舊主 one's former master

jū 車

1. name of a chessman in a kind of Chinese chess 2. refer to **chē** 車 1

jū 拘

1. to apprehend; to detain; to arrest 2. inflexible; to adhere rigidly to (conventions, etc.) 3. confined

jūbǔ 拘捕 to detain or arrest (a suspect)

jūjǐn 拘謹 restrained and cautious—implying social timidity

jūjìn 拘禁 to detain; to imprison

jūlǐ 拘禮 strict adherence to social etiquette

jūliú 拘留 to detain; detention

jūliúsuǒ 拘留所 a detention house to keep criminal suspects pending a court decision

jū'ná 拘拿 to arrest

jūnì 拘泥 to be tied down by conventions

jūnì xiǎojié 拘泥小節 to be punctilious

jūshù 拘束 1. to tie (someone) down; to restrain 2. timid and awkward

jūyā 拘押 to take into custody

jū 狙

1. a monkey; an ape 2. to lie in ambush

jūjī 狙擊 to attack by surprise; to snipe

jūjīshǒu 狙擊手 a shiper

jūjí 狙擊 refer to **jūjī** 狙擊

jūjíshǒu 狙擊手 refer to **jūjīshǒu** 狙擊手

Jū 沮

name of a river in Shandong Province; name of a river in Shanxi Province

jū 居

1. to dwell; to reside; to inhabit; to occupy 2. an abode; a dwell-

ing 3. to stay put; to be at a standstill

jūduō 居多 to be the majority; mostly

jūgāo línxià 居高臨下 1. to overlook 2. to enjoy a strategic advantage by holding a high ground overlooking the enemy position

jūgōng 居功 to take credit (for a success, achievement, etc.)

jūjiā 居家 to lead one's life at home

jūliúquán 居留權 the right of permanent residence (in a foreign country)

jūmín 居民 residents or inhabitants

jūrán 居然 incredibly; to my surprise

jūshì 居士 1. a retired scholar 2. a secular Buddhist devotee

jūshǒu 居首 to be at the head

jūsuǒ 居所 a residence (usually a temporary one)

jūxīn 居心 to harbor (evil) intentions

jūxīn pǒcè 居心叵測 There is no way of telling his (or her) real intentions.

jūzhōng 居中 situated in the middle

jūzhōng tiáotíng 居中調停 to mediate (between two quarreling parties)

jūzhōng wòxuán 居中斡旋 to mediate (between two quarreling parties)

jūzhù 居住 to dwell; to inhabit; to live

jūzhù xiǎoqū 居住小區 a community; a residential area

jū 俱

refer to **jù 俱**

jū 据

stiff joints in the hand, used most often to describe financial stringency or short of money

jū 駒

1. a young and fleet-footed horse; a foal; a colt 2. (figuratively) the sun

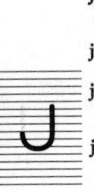

---

jū 鞠 also **jú**

1. to bow; a bow (as a gesture of respect) 2. a leather ball 3. to nourish; to raise or rear 4. young; tender 5. high 6. to exhaust 7. to admonish; to warn; to caution 8. to make judicial investigation

jūgōng 鞠躬 to bow; a bow

jūgōng jìncuì, sǐ'ér hòuyǐ 鞠躬盡瘁，死而後已 to devote oneself to the task until one's death

jú 局

1. an office; a bureau 2. a situation; a state of affairs 3. an inning 4. a game

júbù 局部 having to do with only a part; partial; local

júmiàn 局面 an aspect; a situation

jú'nèirén 局內人 an insider

júshì 局勢 an aspect; a situation

júwàirén 局外人 an outsider

júxiàn 局限 to limit; to confine

jú 侷

narrow; cramped; confined

júchǔ yīyú 侷處一隅 to be confined to a small place or corner

júcù 侷促 1. cramped; confined 2. fidgeting; restless

júcù bù'ān 侷促不安 fidgeting; uneasy

jú 桔

an abbreviated form of **jú 橘**, a mandarin orange or tangerine

júzi 桔子 a small mandarin orange

jú 菊

a chrysanthemum

júhuā 菊花 a chrysanthemum

jú 橘

the mandarin (or the Chinese) orange; a tangerine

júhóng 橘紅 tangerine (color)

júhuáng 橘黃 an orange color

júzhī 橘子汁 orange juice

jú 鞠

refer to **jū** 鞠

jǔ 沮
1. to stop; to abate 2. to lose; to be defeated 3. to spoil; to injure; to destroy or damage

jǔsàng 沮喪 despondent; crest-fallen; downcast

jǔ 咀
to chew; to masticate

jǔjué 咀嚼 to chew; to masticate

jǔ 矩
1. a carpenter's square 2. a rule; a regulation; a pattern 3.to carve

jǔxíng 矩形 a rectangle; rectangular

jǔzhèn 矩陣 (mathematics) a matrix

jǔ 莒
1. taros 2. name of an ancient state 3. name of a county in Shandong Province

jǔ 舉
1. to lift; to raise 2. to recommend; to commend; to praise 3. entire; all; whole 4. manner; deportment 5. to give birth to a child

jǔbàn 舉辦 to sponsor, organize, or initiate

jǔchū 舉出 to enumerate; to itemize

jǔdòng 舉動 1. manner; behavior 2. movement

jǔfā 舉發 to expose (a secret or conspiracy)

jǔguó shàngxià 舉國上下 the entire nation regardless of classes

jǔjiā 舉家 the whole family

jǔjiàn 舉薦 to recommend (a person)

jǔlì 舉例 to give examples

jǔlì shuōmíng 舉例說明 to illustrate

jǔmù wúqīn 舉目無親 There is not a single friend or relative around.—to have no one to turn to (for help)

jǔqí búdìng 舉棋不定 indecisive; irresolute

jǔqǐ 舉起 to lift; to raise

jǔshì wénmíng 舉世聞名 to be known to the whole world; world-renowned

jǔshì wúshuāng 舉世無雙 without a match in the world —unique

jǔshǒu 舉手 to raise one's hand

jǔshǒu zhīláo 舉手之勞 (literally) the trouble involved in raising a hand—little effort

jǔxíng 舉行 to hold (examinations, rallies, parties, etc.); to take place

jǔyī fǎnsān 舉一反三 to infer the rest from what is already known

jǔzhèng 舉證 to give proof or evidence

jǔzhǐ 舉止 deportment; conduct

jǔzhòng 舉重 weightlifting

jǔzú qīngzhòng 舉足輕重 so important is the role one plays in a matter that each step one takes may affect it in a significant way

jǔ 齟
irregular teeth

jǔyǔ 齟齬 1. irregular teeth 2. to have discord; to disagree

jù 巨
1. great; big 2. very

jùbò 巨擘 1. the thumb 2. the foremost figure (in a field)

jùdà 巨大 giant (size); mammoth

jù'é 巨額 a great deal of

jùfù 巨富 a multimillionaire

jùkuǎn 巨款 a huge sum of money

jùliú 巨流 a mighty current

jùrén 巨人 a giant

jùtóu 巨頭 a national leader; a big chief

jùwúbà 巨無霸 (figuratively) giant

jùxì mǐyí 巨細靡遺 not to leave out any detail

jùxīng 巨星 1. a giant star 2. a superstar

jùxíng 巨型 a large model (of cars, etc.)

jùzhù 巨著 a great book; a monumental literary work

jùzǐ 巨子 1. a business tycoon 2. a master; a maestro

jù 句
a sentence

jùdiǎn 句點 a full stop or period

jùfǎ 句法 sentence structure; syntax

jùhào 句號 a full stop or period

jùxíng 句型 a sentence pattern

jù 拒
1. to defend; to ward off; to resist 2. to refuse; to reject

jùbǔ 拒捕 to resist arrest

jùfù 拒付 to refuse to pay; to dishonor (a check)

jùjiǎo 拒繳 to refuse to pay (taxes or money one is obliged to pay)

jùjué 拒絕 to refuse

jùjué láiwǎng 拒絕來往 to sever communications, intercourse or relations

jùmǎ 拒馬 an abatis

jùrén yú qiānlǐ zhīwài 拒人於千里之外 (literally) to keep people a thousand miles away —extremely indifferent and cool

jù 具
1. an appliance, implement, utensil, tool, etc. 2. talent; capability 3. to prepare; to equip 4. complete; all

jùbèi 具備 1. all complete; all ready 2. to have (qualifications or advantages)

jùjié 具結 1. to submit a pledge or guarantee to a government office for fulfilling of all obligations agreed upon 2. (law) to sign an affidavit

jùmíng 具名 1. to sign 2. to publish a writing, letter, etc. with a byline

jùtǐ 具體 concrete

jùwén 具文 1. to prepare a document, etc. for presenting to higher authorities 2. empty words

jùyǒu 具有 to be provided with

jù 沮
a damp, low-lying land; marshy

jùrù 沮洳 a damp, lowlying land

jù 炬
1. a torch 2. fire

jù 俱 also **jū**
1. altogether; all 2. to accompany

jùbèi 俱備 all made ready; all complete

jùlèbù 俱樂部 a club

jùquán 俱全 to be available in all varieties

jùzài 俱在 all present

jù 倨(据)
arrogant; haughty

jù'ào 倨傲 arrogant

jù 距
1. a bird's spur 2. distance

jùlí 距離 distance

jù 詎
an interjection indicating surprise

jùliào 詎料 unexpectedly

jù 鉅
1. (巨) great 2. steel

jùkuǎn 鉅款 a large sum of money

jùzǐ 鉅子 a great man; a tycoon; a magnate

jù 聚
to come or put together; to gather; to assemble; to collect

jùcān 聚餐 to get together for luncheon or dinner

jùdǔ 聚賭 to assemble for gambling

jùhuì 聚會 to assemble; to gather

jùjī 聚積 to accumulate

jùjí 聚集 to gather; to assemble

jùjīng huìshén 聚精會神 concentrate oneself

jùjū 聚居 to live together

jùlǒng 聚攏 to gather; to assemble

jùluò 聚落 a village; a town

jùshā chéngtǎ 聚沙成塔 Accumulation of small amounts results in a huge quantity.

jùshǒu 聚首 to get together; to meet

jù 劇

1. a drama; a theatrical work; a play 2. intense; strenuous; acute; severe 3. to play

jùběn 劇本 a play; a scenario

jùchǎng 劇場 a theater

jùdú 劇毒 deadly poison

jùfāng 劇坊 a theater workshop

jùliè 劇烈 strenuous; intense; hard; fierce

jùmù 劇目 a repertoire

jùqíng 劇情 the plot

jùqíng jiǎnjiè 劇情簡介 a synopsis

jùtuán 劇團 an opera troupe; a troupe; a theatrical company

jùwù 劇務 1. stage management 2. a stage manager

jùyuàn 劇院 a theater

jùzhào 劇照 a stage photo; a still

jùzhōng 劇終 the end; a curtainfall

jùzuòjiā 劇作家 a playwright; a dramatist

jù 據(据)

1. according to; on the basis of; on the grounds of 2. to depend on 3. to occupy; to take possession of; to seize 4. proof; evidence 5. a Chinese family name

jùchēng 據稱 according to reports, assertions, or claims

jùcǐ 據此 (a conventional phrase in official correspondence) on these grounds

jùdiǎn 據點 a base (for operations or activities)

jùlǐ lìzhēng 據理力爭 to argue vigorously on the basis of sound reason or justice

jùshí 據實 according to the fact

jùshǒu 據守 to hold a position against attack; to make a stand

jùshuō 據說 It is said that....; according to hearsay

jùwéi jǐyǒu 據為己有 to take possession of (what does not belong to oneself)

jùwǒ kànlái 據我看來 as I see it; in my opinion

jùwǒ suǒzhī 據我所知 as far as I know

jùxī 據悉 It is reported that....

jù 鋸

1. a saw 2. to saw; to cut with a saw 3. to amputate

jùchǐ 鋸齒 teeth of a saw

jùkāi 鋸開 to saw asunder

jùzi 鋸子 a saw

jù 颶

a hurricane; a gale; strong gusts at sea; a cyclone

jùfēng 颶風 a hurricane; a gale; a cyclone

jù 遽

1. suddenly; abruptly; hastily; hurriedly 2. scared; frightened; agitated; agitation 3. a stagecoach

jù 懼

1. to fear; to dread; to be afraid of 2. to frighten

jùgāozhèng 懼高症 acrophobia

jùnèi 懼內 henpecked

jùpà 懼怕 to fear; to dread; to be afraid of

juān 捐

1. tax; duty; charge; dues 2. to donate; to contribute; to subscribe 3. to buy or purchase (an official rank) 4. to give up (one's life for a cause, etc.) 5. to remove

juānkuǎn 捐款 1. to donate money 2. donations

juānqì 捐棄 to renounce; to reject

juānqián 捐錢 to donate money; donations

juānqū 捐軀 to die for one's country or duty

juānxiàn 捐獻 to contribute; contributions

juānxiě 捐血 refer to **juānxuè** 捐血

juānxuè 捐血 1. to donate blood 2. blood donation

juānzèng 捐贈 to donate or contribute

juānzhù 捐助 to contribute; to donate (to help the poor, relief work, etc.)

juān 涓
a small stream; a rivulet; a brook

juāndī guīgōng 涓滴歸公 (said of an honest official) to hand over every cent of public money to the government treasury

juānjuān 涓涓 trickles; a small stream

juān 娟
pretty; good-looking; graceful; attractive

juān 鵑
as in **dùjuān** 杜鵑—1. the cuckoo 2. an azalea

juān 鐫
1. to carve; to engrave 2. (said of an official) to be demoted

juānkē 鐫刻 refer to **juānkè** 鐫刻

juānkè 鐫刻 to carve; to engrave

juǎn 捲（卷）
1. to roll up 2. to curl (hair, etc.); curly (hair) 3. to sweep off 4. a roll

juǎnchǐ 捲尺 a tape measure or tapeline

juǎnfǎ 捲髮 refer to **juǎnfà** 捲髮

juǎnfà 捲髮 1. to curl hair (at a hairdresser's, etc.) 2. curly hair

juǎnrù 捲入 to be drawn into

juǎntáo 捲逃 to clear up everything and run away; to abscond

juǎntǒng 捲筒 a reel

juǎntǔ chónglái 捲土重來 to stage a comeback; resurgence

juàn 卷
1. painting which can be easily folded or rolled up 2. a book 3. a division of a book; a volume 4. a test paper 5. files; filed documents

juànzi 卷子 a test paper

juànzōng 卷宗 filed documents, especially in public offices; files

juàn 倦
tired; weary

juàndài 倦怠 to be tired; worn out; languor

juànniǎo zhīhuán 倦鳥知還 to return home after years of wandering far away

juàn 圈
an enclosure or a pen for keeping livestock

juàn 眷
1. to look back—to regard; to care for; to concern 2. to admire; to love 3. relatives; dependents

juàncūn 眷村 a military dependents' village

juàngù 眷顧 to care for; to concern

juànliàn 眷戀 to be attached to someone

juànniàn 眷念 to think of or remember with affection

juànshǔ 眷屬 dependents; family

juàn 絹
1. a kind of thick, loosely-woven raw silk fabric 2. a handkerchief

juànshàn 絹扇 a fan made with silk

juàn 雋
1. fat meat 2. meaningful

juànyǒng 雋永 very interesting or intriguing; meaningful

jué 撅
1. to break; to snap 2. to stick up; to protrude

juézuǐ 撅嘴 to pout

jué 孑
the larvae of mosquitoes

jué 角
1. to compete; to contest; to wrestle 2. a corner 3. a dramatic role; a character 4. one of the five musical notes in ancient Chinese music

juésè 角色 a role; a character

juézhú 角逐 to contest (for a post, etc.)

jué 抉
1. to choose; pick; to select 2. to gouge; to dig

juézé 抉擇 choice; to choose

jué 決
1. to decide; to conclude; to judge 2. (said of a dike) to burst; to break 3. certain; definite 4. to execute a person

juécè 決策 an adopted policy; a decision

juédìng 決定 to determine; to decide

juédìngquán 決定權 the say; the power to make decisions

juédòu 決鬥 a duel; to fight a duel

juéduàn 決斷 to decide; to conclude; to make a decision

juékǒu 決口 a rupture; an opening

juéliè 決裂 1. to burst open 2. a rupture

juérán 決然 resolutely; firmly

juésài 決賽 the final (of a contest, race, etc.)

juéshèng 決勝 1. certain to bring victory 2. to decide a contest

juésǐ 決死 life-and-death

juésuàn 決算 a final financial statement

juétí 決堤 the collapse of a dike

juéxīn 決心 to make up one's mind; to resolve

juéxuǎn 決選 a runoff (election)

juéyì 決議 1. a resolution (reached at a meeting) 2. to decide; to resolve

juézhàn 決戰 a decisive battle; to fight a decisive battle

jué 玨(珏)
two pieces of jade fastened together

jué 倔
intransigent; hard; obstinate; stubborn

juéjiàng 倔強 obstinate; stubborn

jué 訣
1. to part; to separate 2. sorcery; an occult art 3. a formula of doing something; the secret of doing things

juébié 訣別 1. to say good-bye; to bid farewell 2. to part forever

juéqiào 訣竅 the secret or knack of doing something

jué 掘
to dig; to excavate; to make a hole or cave

juéchuān 掘穿 to dig through

juéjǐng 掘井 to dig a well

juézáo 掘鑿 excavation

jué 崛
to rise abruptly

juéqǐ 崛起 to rise suddenly

jué 厥
1. to faint 2. a personal and possessive pronoun

jué gōng shènwěi 厥功甚偉 to have made great contribution to the successful conclusion of a task

jué 絕
1. to sever; to break off; to cut 2. to renounce; to decline 3. to run out of; exhausted 4. without match; peerless 5. isolated; to separate 6. to discontinue; to stop; to cease 7. without posterity 8. extremely; utmost; absolutely 9. to destroy 10. leaving no leeway 11. a poem of four lines

juébǎn 絕版 out-of-print (books)

juébǐ 絕筆 1. one's last writing (before death) 2. to discontinue writing

juébì 絕壁 cliffs

juébù 絕不 never

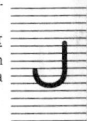

J

juédài jiārén 絕代佳人 a matchless beauty

juédǐng cōngming 絕頂聰明 extremely bright, intelligent or clever

juéduì 絕對 absolute(ly); definite(ly)

juéhòu 絕後 1. heirless 2. probably cannot be repeated again

juéjī 絕跡 to vanish completely

juéjì 絕技 a feat or stunt

juéjiā 絕佳 extremely good; excellent

juéjiāo 絕交 to cut off or sever friendship, diplomatic relations, etc.

juéjìng 絕境 the end of one's rope; an impasse

juékǒu 絕口 1. never to mention again 2. to stop talking about

juéliáng 絕糧 to run out of food supplies

juélù 絕路 a dead end; an impasse

juélún 絕倫 without match; peerless

juémiào 絕妙 extremely good or wonderful

juémiào hǎocí 絕妙好辭 quotable quotes; the last say in (wisecracks, quotes, etc.)

juémìng 絕命 to die; death

juésè 絕色 an incomparably beautiful girl

juéshí 絕食 to fast

juésì 絕嗣 without heir or posterity

juéwàng 絕望 hopeless; desperate; despair

juéwú jǐnyǒu 絕無僅有 very rare; unique

juéxiǎng 絕響 1. lost arts 2. (said of a great musician) cannot be heard again

juéyì 絕藝 a unique feat, stunt or performance

juéyuántǐ 絕緣體 an insulator

juézhāo 絕招 1. unique skill 2. an unexpected tricky move (as the last resort) 3. a masterstroke

juézhèng 絕症 an incurable disease; a fatal illness

juézhǒng 絕種 (said of species of animals, etc.) extinction; extinct

jué 腳
refer to jiǎo 腳

jué 蕨
the bracken

jué 噱 also **xué**
loud laughter

jué 爵
1. a degree or a title of nobility; peerage; the rank or dignity of a peer 2. an ancient wine pitcher with three legs and a loop handle

juéshì 爵士 Sir (a title of nobility)

juéshì yīnyuè 爵士音樂 jazz; jazz music

juéwèi 爵位 a degree of nobility

jué 嚼
refer to jiáo 嚼

jué 譎
1. to cheat; to deceive; to swindle 2. wily; artful; crafty; cunning; tricky

juézhà 譎詐 cunning; crafty

jué 覺
1. to wake up from sleep 2. senses 3. to be conscious of; to sense 4. to awaken; to realize; to discover 5. to tell; to feel

juéde 覺得 1. to be conscious of; to realize; to sense 2. to feel 3. to think; to be of the opinion

juéwù 覺悟 to become aware; to realize

juéxǐng 覺醒 to wake up

jué 攫
to seize; to take hold of; to snatch; to catch

juéduó 攫奪 to seize; to snatch; to grab

juéqǔ 攫取 to take by force; to seize

juè 倔
gruff; surly; rude in manner or speech

jūn 君

1. a sovereign; a monarch; a king; a lord 2. you (used in addressing a male in formal speech)

jūnquán 君權 sovereign power

jūnwáng 君王 a sovereign; a ruler; a monarch

jūnzhǔ 君主 a sovereign; a ruler; a monarch

jūnzǐ 君子 a perfect or true gentleman

jūnzǐ xiédìng 君子協定 a gentlemen's agreement

jūn 均

1. equal; equally; even; level 2. to be fair 3. all; also; too 4. a potter's wheel 5. an ancient musical instrument

jūnděng 均等 equality; equal; impartial; fair

jūnfēn 均分 to divide equally

jūnhéng 均衡 equality; balance equilibrium

jūnkě 均可 all can; either will do; also can

jūntān 均攤 to share equally

jūnyún 均勻 even (blending, etc.); uniform

jūn 軍

1. the military; forces; of national defense 2. corps (as a military unit) 3. an armed service

jūnbèi 軍備 armaments; arms

jūnbù 軍部 the war ministry; the defense department

jūnduì 軍隊 troops; the armed forces

jūnfá 軍閥 the militarist; the warlord

jūnfá 軍法 military law

jūnfāng 軍方 the military authorities

jūnfèi 軍費 a defense budget; military expenses

jūnfú 軍服 (military) uniform

jūngǎng 軍港 a naval harbor; a naval port

jūngē 軍歌 a war song; a martial chant

jūnguān 軍官 (military) an officer

jūnguó zhǔyì 軍國主義 militarism

jūnhuǒ 軍火 arms; munitions

jūnhuǒkù 軍火庫 an arsenal

jūnjī 軍機 1. a military secret 2. a military aircraft

jūnjì 軍紀 military laws; military discipline

jūnjiàn 軍艦 a war vessel; a warship; a man-of-war

jūnjiē 軍階 (military) a rank; a grade

jūnjiè 軍界 the military circles; the military

jūnjǐng 軍警 the military and the police

jūnjuàn 軍眷 a soldier's dependants

jūnlǐ 軍禮 military rites; a military salute

jūnlì 軍力 military strength (or power)

jūnlìng rúshān 軍令如山 Military orders cannot be disobeyed or revoked.

jūnlǜ 軍律 military laws; military discipline

jūnmín 軍民 soldiers and civilians

jūnqíng 軍情 a military (or war) situation

jūnrén 軍人 a soldier; a serviceman

jūnshì 軍事 military affairs

jūnshì dìqū 軍事地區 a military area; a military scope; a military district

jūnshì jīdì 軍事基地 a military base

jūnshì yǎnxí 軍事演習 military maneuvers; military exercises; war games (or exercises)

jūntuán 軍團 1. an army (a unit consisting of a number of corps) 2. any large unit of troops; a legion

jūnxiǎng 軍餉 pay and allowances for soldiers; military payroll

jūnxiào 軍校 a military school

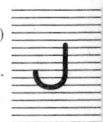

jūnxùn 軍訓 military training

jūnyī 軍醫 (military) a surgeon; a medic

jūnyíng 軍營 a military camp

jūnyòng 軍用 for military use; military

jūnyuán 軍援 military aid

jūnyuèduì 軍樂隊 a military band

jūnzhèng 軍政 1. a military government 2. the administration of the armed forces

jūnzhí 軍職 a military (as opposed to civilian) office or post; a military appointment

jūnzhōng wú xìyán 軍中無戲言 (literally) There are no jokes in the armed forces.—A military pledge or order must be carried out.

jūnzhǒng 軍種 branches of the armed forces; the armed services

jūn 菌 also jùn

1. fungi; mushrooms 2. bacteria

jūn 鈞

1. a unit of weight (equal to 30 catties) in former times 2. (in addressing a superior in a letter) you; your

jūn'ān 鈞安 May you enjoy peace.—a form of complimentary close in a letter to a superior

jūn 龜

chapped; cracked

jūnliè 龜裂 chapped; cracked

jùn 俊

1. talented; capable; superior; refined; smart; bright 2. good-looking; handsome; 3. big; huge

jùnjié 俊傑 a brave and superior person

jùnměi 俊美 good-looking; handsome

jùnqiào 俊俏 good-looking and smart

jùnwěi 俊偉 superior and great

jùnxiù 俊秀 handsome and refined

jùn 峻

1. high; lofty 2. steep 3. severe; harsh; rigorous

jùnlǐng 峻嶺 a lofty range (of mountains)

jùnqiào 峻峭 1. precipitous 2. strict; severe

jùnxíng 峻刑 severe punishment or penalty

jùn 郡

a political division in ancient China; a county

jùnshǒu 郡守 the magistrate of a prefecture

jùnxiàn 郡縣 prefectures and counties; administrative districts smaller than a province

jùnzhǔ 郡主 a princess

jùn 浚

1. to dredge 2. deep

jùnníchuán 浚泥船 a dredger

jùn 竣

accomplished; completed

jùngōng 竣工 (said of a construction project) to be completed

jùn 畯

1. the official in charge of farmland in ancient times 2. rustic; crude

jùn 菌

refer to jūn 菌

jùn 雋

1. good-looking 2. outstanding; talented; extraordinary

jùnbá 雋拔 outstandingly talented

jùn 濬

1. to dredge a waterway; to dig or wash (a well, etc.) 2. deep; profound

jùnzhé 濬哲 profound wisdom

jùn 駿

1. a fine horse; a swift horse 2. great; large 3. swift; speedy 4. (峻) rigorous; stringent 5. outstanding

jùnmǎ 駿馬 a fine horse

jùnyì 駿逸 distinguished; outstanding

J

kā 咖

a character used in transliterating

kāfēi 咖啡 coffee

kāfēiguǎn 咖啡館 a cafe; a coffee shop

kāfēitīng 咖啡廳 a cafe; a coffee shop

kāfēiyīn 咖啡因 coffeine

kā 喀

1. (also **kà**) a character used for transliterating 2. noise made in coughing or vomiting

kāchā 喀嚓 to crack; to snap

kǎ 卡

1. a card, as a visiting card; cardboard 2. an abbreviated form for "calorie" 3. a guardhouse 4. a customs barrier; a roadblock; a checkpoint 5. to block; to check

kǎbīnqiāng 卡賓槍 a carbine

kǎchē 卡車 a truck; a lorry

kǎdài 卡帶 a cassette tape

kǎjièmiáo 卡介苗 BCG (Bacillus Calmette-Guerin), a TB vaccine

kǎlùlǐ 卡路里 a calorie

kǎpiàn 卡片 a card; a calling card

kǎqíbù 卡其布 khaki

kǎtōng 卡通 a cartoon; animation

kǎ 咯 also **luò**

to cough; a cough

kǎ 咳

to cough up

kǎtán 咳痰 to cough up phlegm

kà 喀

refer to **kā** 喀 1

kāi 開

1. to open 2. to drive 3. to begin; to start 4. to reveal; to disclose 5. to state; to explain 6. to found; to expand 7. to eliminate 8. to divide into 9. to write down; to list 10. to undo; to unfold; to wind off 11. a carat 12. to run (a shop or business)

kāibàn 開辦 to start or open (a shop, school, business, etc.)

kāicǎi 開採 to excavate; to mine

kāichǎng 開場 the beginning of a show or anything

kāichǎngbái 開場白 a prologue; a speech that opens a show or a meeting

kāichē 開車 to drive a car

kāichéng bùgōng 開誠布公 to wear one's heart on one's sleeve

kāichú 開除 to dismiss; to fire

kāichuán 開船 to set sail; to weigh anchor

kāichuàng 開創 to found (a nation, big business, etc.); to start

kāidāo 開刀 1. to operate on (a patient); an operation 2. to punish 3. to behead

kāidǎo 開導 to educate and enlighten

kāidàochē 開倒車 1. to back a car, train, etc. 2. to be old-fashioned or anachronistic 3. to turn back the clock; to retrograde

kāidēng 開燈 to turn on the light

kāiduān 開端 the beginning or start

kāi'ēn 開恩 to have mercy on; to grant special favor

kāifā 開發 to develop; development (of natural resources, industry, etc.)

kāifàn 開飯 time to eat

kāifàng 開放 1. to open (to trade, traffic, etc.); to be open 2. to liberalize or hand over a government monopoly to private operations 3. to lift a ban 4. to come into bloom

kāigōng 開工 to go into operation; to start work; to begin a building project

kāiguān 開關 1. a switch or similar device to put on or shut off an electric current, etc. 2. to open and close

kāiháng 開航 1. to open up for navigation 2. to set sail

kāihù 開戶 to open a bank

K

account

kāihuā 開花 1. to flower; to blossom 2. (said of shells) to burst

kāihuà 開化 civilized

kāihuái 開懷 joyful; jubilant; happy

kāihuì 開會 to hold a meeting; to attend a meeting or conference

kāihuǒ 開火 to open fire; to engage in battle

kāijià 開價 to ask for a price; to quote; the price quoted

kāijiǎng 開獎 to draw the winning numbers of a lottery

kāijiǎng 開講 to begin a speech or lecture; to begin telling a story

kāijiè 開戒 to break one's resolution

kāijuàn yǒuyì 開卷有益 Reading is always beneficial.

kāikěn 開墾 to open up wasteland for farming

kāikǒu 開口 to open one's mouth; to speak

kāikuàichē 開快車 1. (said of a car, etc.) to speed; speeding 2. to hasten up with one's work

kāikuò 開闊 1. spacious; open; wide 2. broad-minded

kāilǎng 開朗 1. to clear up, as weather 2. open and clear 3. broad-minded and outspoken

kāilù 開路 to pioneer; to cut the way, as in a jungle

kāilù xiānfēng 開路先鋒 a pioneer; a trailblazer; to blaze a trail

kāimàilā 開麥拉 1. a camera 2. (a movie director's command) Camera!

kāimén jiànshān 開門見山 to talk or write right to the point

kāimíng 開明 enlightened; open-minded

kāimù 開幕 1. to raise the curtain 2. to open; to begin a meeting

kāipán 開盤 (said of a market) the opening quotation

kāipào 開砲 1. (said of a field-piece, battery, or artillery) to open fire 2. to launch a verbal attack

kāipì 開闢 to open up or develop (a new market, farm plot, etc.); to start

kāipiào 開票 1. to count ballots or votes 2. to make out an invoice

kāiqǐ 開啓 to open

kāiqiāng 開槍 to shoot; to fire

kāiqiào 開竅 to open one's eyes to

kāishān zǔshī 開山祖師 the founder of a religion or a sect of religion

kāishè 開設 to establish; to set up

kāishǐ 開始 to begin; to commence; to start

kāishì 開市 to start trading; to open the market

kāishì 開釋 to release (a prisoner, etc.); to set free

kāishuǐ 開水 boiled water

kāitiānchuāng 開天窗 1. to open up a skylight 2. open space in a newspaper

kāitiān pìdì 開天闢地 1. to open or develop 2. creation of the world

kāitíng 開庭 to start a court trial; to hold a court session

kāitōng 開通 to do away with all obstructions

kāitong 開通 modern-minded; enlightened

kāituò 開拓 to open up, enlarge or expand (new frontiers, territory, etc.)

kāiwài 開外 upwards of; over or more than

kāiwánxiào 開玩笑 to play a joke; to joke

kāiwǎng 開往 1. (said of a train, ship, etc.) to leave for; to be bound for 2. (said of troops, etc.) to move; to set out

kāiwèi 開胃 1. appetizing; to whet or stimulate one's appetite 2. to make fun of; to tease

kāixiao 開銷 1. expenses; (an) expenditure 2. to pay expenses

K

kāixīn 開心 1. happy; to have a great time 2. to play a joke on; to amuse oneself at somebody's expense

kāixīnguǒ 開心果 a pistachio

kāixué 開學 The school starts.

kāiyǎnjiè 開眼界 to expand one's experience and horizon

kāiyè 開業 to start doing business; to start practicing (law, medicine, etc.)

kāiyèchē 開夜車 to burn the midnight oil; to stay up late at night

kāiyuán jiéliú 開源節流 to open more sources of income and cut down expenses

kāizáo 開鑿 to dig (a well, canal, etc.); to drill

kāizhǎn 開展 to expand; to spread out; to develop

kāizhàn 開戰 to declare war; to do battle

kāizhāng 開張 1. to open a shop; to start doing a business 2. to expand, spread out or develop

kāizhī 開支 expenses; (an) expenditure

kāizhīpiào 開支票 to write a check

kāizuì 開罪 to offend another with what one says, writes or does

kāi 揩
to wipe; to scrub; to rub; to dust; to clean

kāiyóu 揩油 to make some (usually small) outside gains not included in a deal

kǎi 凱
1. peace; joy 2. balmy; soothing; tender 3. victory—a triumphant return of an army

kǎigē 凱歌 a song of victory

kǎixuán 凱旋 to return in triumph

kǎixuánmén 凱旋門 1. the Arc of Triumph (in Paris, France) 2. a triumphal arch

kǎi 楷
1. regular; standard 2. a model; a norm 3. (calligraphy) standard script

kǎimó 楷模 a model (for imitation)

kǎishū 楷書 model-style characters

kǎi 慨 also **kài**
1. to sigh emotionally 2. generous; magnanimous

kǎitàn 慨歎 to deplore or lament with sighs

kǎi 嘅 also **kài**
the sound of sighing

kǎi 鎧
armor; a coat of mail

kǎijiǎ 鎧甲 armor

kài 咳
refer to **ké** 咳

kài 慨
refer to **kǎi** 慨

kài 嘅
refer to **kǎi** 嘅

kān 刊
1. to hew; to cut 2. to engrave 3. a publication 4. to publish

kāndēng 刊登 1. to publish 2. to carry (an article)

kānwù 刊物 a periodical; a publication

kānzǎi 刊載 1. to publish 2. to carry (an article)

kān 看
1. to watch; to mind; to look after 2. to guard; to keep under surveillance

kānguǎn 看管 1. to take into custody; to guard; to safeguard 2. a custodian

kānhù 看護 1. to nurse; to take care 2. a nurse (in hospital)

kānjiā 看家 1. to stay at home and look after the house 2. a houseguard 3. (money, etc.) saved for a rainy day

kānjiā běnlǐng 看家本領 one's specialty or special skill

kānjiāgǒu 看家狗 a watchdog

kānmén 看門 1. a doorkeeper or gatekeeper 2. to watch or guard

K

the door

kānshǒu 看守 1. to watch or guard 2. to detain

kānshǒusuǒ 看守所 a detention house for prisoners awaiting trials

kān 勘 also **kàn**

1. to investigate; to explore; to examine; to check 2. to collate; to compare critically

kāncè 勘測 to survey

kānchá 勘察 to investigate; to inspect

kānwù 勘誤 to collate; to correct errors

kānwùbiǎo 勘誤表 corrigenda; errata

kān 堪 1. to sustain; to bear; to stand 2. may; can

kānchēng jiāzuò 堪稱佳作 may be rated as an excellent piece of writing or a fine work of art

kāndāng zhòngrèn 堪當重任 to be capable of shouldering important tasks

kān 戡 1. to subdue; to suppress; to put down 2. to kill

kānluàn 戡亂 to suppress a rebellion

kān 龕 a niche for an idol

kǎn 坎 1. a pit; a hole; a depression 2. one of the Eight Diagrams in the *Book of Changes* 3. the sound of percussion 4. a snare; a danger; a crisis

kǎnkě yīshēng 坎坷一生 a lifetime of frustrations

kǎn 侃 1. straightforward; frank; bold; open 2. amiable; pleasant 3. with confidence and composure

kǎndàshān 侃大山 to chat

kǎnjià 侃價 to bargain

kǎnkǎn értán 侃侃而談 to talk with confidence and compo-

sure

kǎn 砍 1. to chop; to hack; to fell (trees, etc.); to cut down 2. to throw at

kǎnchái 砍柴 to chop or cut firewood

kǎnduàn 砍斷 to break apart by chopping

kǎnfá 砍伐 to fell (trees, etc.)

kǎnshāng 砍傷 to wound by hacking or cutting

kǎnsǐ 砍死 to hack to death

kǎntóu 砍頭 to behead; to decapitate

kǎn 檻 a doorsill; a threshold

kàn 看 1. to see; to look at; to observe; to watch; to read 2. to examine; to consider; to think 3. to visit; to call on 4. to present (tea, wine, etc.) 5. to depend on

kànbìng 看病 1. to see a doctor 2. to examine the patient

kànbuguàn 看不慣 to detest; to disdain

kànbuqǐ 看不起 to look down upon

kànbushàng 看不上 1. to detest; to disdain 2. not up to one's standard

kànchéng 看成 to look upon as; to regard as

kànchū 看出 to make out; to see

kànchuān 看穿 to see through (a trick)

kàncuò 看錯 1. to mistake someone or something for another 2. to misjudge someone's ability, character, etc.

kàndài 看待 to treat (another, a child, friend, etc.); treatment

kàndào 看到 to see; to catch sight of

kàndeqǐ 看得起 to think highly of

kànfǎ 看法 an opinion; a viewpoint

kànguò 看過 1. to take a look at 2. to make a perusal of 3. to have seen or read

K

kànjian 看見 to see; to catch sight of

kànlai 看來 it looks as if; evidently

kànpò 看破 1. to see through a thing 2. to be resigned to what is inevitable

kànpò hóngchén 看破紅塵 to see through the vanity of life (and to become a Buddhist monk or nun)

kànqí 看齊 1. (military) to dress 2. to emulate (someone)

kànqīng 看輕 to despise; to underestimate

kànqíngxing 看情形 depending on circumstances

kànshū 看書 to read a book

kàntái 看臺 (sports) bleachers

kàntòu 看透 1. to see through (a trick, conspiracy, etc.) 2. to be resigned to what is inevitable

kàntou 看頭 that which is worth seeing or reading

kànxì 看戲 to watch a show

kànyàngzi 看樣子 it seems; it looks as if

kànyīshēng 看醫生 to consult a doctor or physician

kànzhòng 看中 to feel satisfied with; to prefer; to like

kànzhòng 看重 to esteem; to regard as important; to value

kànzuò 看作 to regard as; to consider to be

kàn 勘

refer to **kān** 勘

kāng 康

1. healthy 2. peaceful 3. abundant 4. level, even and smooth (road, etc.)

kāngfù 康復 recovery (from illness)

kāngjiàn 康健 in good health; healthy

kānglè 康樂 1. (wholesome) recreation 2. peace and happiness

kāngníng 康寧 healthy and undisturbed

kāngtài 康泰 healthy and free from trouble

kāngzhuāng dàdào 康莊大道 a level and easy thoroughfare leading to many places

kāng 慷 also **kǎng**

1. ardent; impassioned 2. generous; liberal; magnanimous; unselfish

kāngkǎi 慷慨 1. generous 2. (usually said of a hero) vehement; fervent

kāngkǎi jī'áng 慷慨激昂 (said of speech or conduct) impassioned; arousing

kāngkǎi jiěnáng 慷慨解囊 to make generous contributions (of funds)

kāng 糠

1. husks of rice; rice bran or chaff 2. of inferior quality; not sturdy; empty inside; things of no value 3. spongy

káng 扛

to lift (especially when only a single person is involved)

kǎng 慷

refer to **kāng** 慷

kàng 亢

1. proud 2. indomitable 3. excessive

kàngfèn 亢奮 stimulated; excited

kàngjìn 亢進 hyperfunction

kàng 伉

a spouse

kànglì 伉儷 a married couple

kàng 抗

1. to resist; to oppose 2. to reject; to refute; to rebuke; to defy 3. high and virtuous 4. to raise; to set up 5. to hide; to conceal; to screen; to secrete

kàngbào 抗暴 to oppose tyranny

kàngdí 抗敵 1. to resist or fight enemy troops 2. to equal or match

kànghéng 抗衡 to compete; to match

kàngjù 抗拒 to resist; to oppose

kànglì 抗力 (physics) resistance

or resistance strength

kàngmìng 抗命 to disobey orders

kàngshēngsù 抗生素 antibiotics

kàngtǐ 抗體 an antibody

kàngyì 抗議 to protest

kàngyì yóuxíng 抗議遊行 a protest march

kàngzhàn 抗戰 1. to fight the invading army 2. the War of Resistance against Japan (1937-1945)

kàngzhēng 抗爭 to contend; to oppose; to resist

kàng 炕

1. dry; to dry 2. hot 3. a brick bed warmed by a fire underneath (in North China)

kǎo 考

1. one's deceased father 2. to test; to examine 3. to check; to investigate; to study

kǎobǐ 考妣 one's deceased father and mother

kǎochá 考察 to inspect; to examine

kǎochǎng 考場 an examination hall or site

kǎogǔ 考古 to study the life and culture of ancient people

kǎohé 考核 to review or assess (a plan, proposal, etc.); to evaluate

kǎojī 考績 to grade the service

kǎojiu 考究 1. to examine and consider 2. elaborate; beautiful 3. tasteful; elegant; choosy; particular

kǎojù 考據 to search for proofs (in textual research)

kǎojuàn 考卷 an examination paper

kǎolǜ 考慮 to consider; to weigh; to think over

kǎoqín 考勤 to check on work attendance

kǎoqū 考區 an examination district

kǎoqǔ 考取 to pass an examination (for admission to employment, a school, etc.)

kǎoshang 考上 to pass an examination (for admission to employment, a school, etc.)

kǎoshēng 考生 an examinee

kǎoshì 考試 an examination; a test; a quiz

kǎoyàn 考驗 1. to test; to try 2. a test; a trial

kǎo 拷

to flog, whip or torture (in order to get a confession, etc.)

kǎobèi 拷貝 a copy

kǎodǎ 拷打 to flog; to whip; to torture

kǎowèn 拷問 to extort information or confessions by means of torture

kǎo 烤

1. to roast; to bake; to toast 2. to warm by a fire 3. scorching

kǎomiànbāo 烤麵包 to toast bread

kǎomiànbāojī 烤麵包機 a toaster

kǎoròu 烤肉 1. to barbecue 2. barbecue

kǎoxiāng 烤箱 an oven for baking

kǎoyā 烤鴨 1. to roast duck 2. roasted duck

kào 銬

manacles; handcuffs

kào 犒

to reward (soldiers, laborers, etc.)

kàojūn 犒軍 to cheer troops with material gifts

kàoshǎng 犒賞 to reward (one for contributions) with money or gifts

kàoshī 犒師 to cheer troops with material gifts

kào 靠

1. to rely on; to depend on 2. to lean on 3. near to; bordering on; to keep to (the left or the right), as in driving 4. (Chinese opera) make-believe armor worn by actors

kào'àn 靠岸 to draw alongside

the shore, quay or pier; to pull in to the shore

kàobèi 靠背 the back of a chair

kàobiān 靠邊 1. to keep to the right or left side (of the road) 2. reasonable

kàobuzhù 靠不住 not dependable; not reliable

kàodezhù 靠得住 dependable; can be trusted

kàodiàn 靠墊 a (back) cushion

kàojìn 靠近 1. near to; in the neighbor hood 2. to approach; to draw nearer

kàolǒng 靠攏 1. to shorten the distance; to sit or stand closer 2. to tergiversate; to shift allegiance to a new master

kàoshān chīshān, kàoshuǐ chīshuǐ 靠山吃山，靠水吃水 to make a living in one's given circumstances

kàoshān 靠山 a person from whom one draws his influence

kàotiān chīfàn 靠天吃飯 to depend on heaven for food—to leave everything to fate

kē 刻

refer to **kè** 刻 1

kē 苛

harsh; severe; rigorous; caustic

kēkè 苛刻 harsh; pitiless; relentless; merciless; unkind; coldhearted

kēqiú 苛求 to be very exacting

kēzé 苛責 to criticize severely; to rebuke; to excoriate

kēzhèng 苛政 despotic rule; despotism; tyranny

kē 科

1. a department 2. a section 3. a class; a variety; a family (of plants or animals) 4. rules; laws 5. the action in Chinese opera 6. a subject in the civil service examination of former times 7. a branch of academic or vocational studies 8. to mete out (prison terms, etc.); to levy (taxes, etc.); to fine someone

kēbān 科班 1. a Chinese operatic company which operates a class

to train young pupils 2. very formal or orthodox training one received when young

kēhuàn xiǎoshuō 科幻小說 science fiction

kējì 科技 science and technology

kēmù 科目 1. subjects, courses, classifications of academic studies 2. the civil examination system in former times

Kēwēitè 科威特 Kuwait

kēxué 科學 science

kēxuéjiā 科學家 scientists

kēxuéjiè 科學界 1. the world of science 2. the community of scientists

kēyuán 科員 a junior government employee

kē 柯

1. a tall evergreen tree 2. the handle of an ax 3. the stalk or the trunk of a plant 4. a Chinese family name

Kēdá 柯達 Kodak, a brand name

kē 棵

a numerary adjunct for trees

kē 窠

1. a den; a burrow 2. a nest 3. a hole for people 4. a dwelling for people

kējiù 窠臼 a set pattern or rule; a stereotype

kē 蝌

a tadpole

kēdǒu 蝌蚪 a tadpole

kē 瞌

to be tired and to doze off

kēshuì 瞌睡 to doze off while sitting

kē 磕

to strike; to bump; to knock; to collide

kētóu 磕頭 to kowtow

kē 顆

a drop or droplet; a grain; a pill; a numerary adjunct for bombs, bullets, etc

ké 咳 also **kài**

to cough

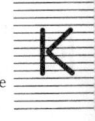

K

késou 咳嗽 to cough; a cough

ké 殼

refer to **qiào** 殼

kě 可

1. may; can; to be able to 2. around; estimated at 3. an auxiliary 4. but; however 5. a Chinese family name

kě'ài 可愛 lovable; likable

kěbēi 可悲 sad; lamentable

kěchéng zhījī 可乘之機 an opportunity that can be exploited to somebody's advantage

kěchǐ 可恥 shameful

kěfóu 可否 can; may (used at the beginning of a question)

kěgē kěqì 可歌可泣 (said of bravery or fortitude in serving the nation) very moving; very touching

kěguān 可觀 1. to be worth seeing 2. considerable (sum of money, losses, etc.)

kěguì 可貴 valuable; praiseworthy

kěhèn 可恨 hateful; detestable; abominable

kějiàn 可見 1. that can be seen 2. to be perceived

kěkào 可靠 reliable (sources, etc.); dependable

kěkàoxìng 可靠性 reliability

kěkě 可可 cocoa

kěkǒu 可口 tasty; pleasant to the palate

Kěkǒu Kělè 可口可樂 Coca Cola or Coke

kělián 可憐 pitiful; pitiable; poor; miserable

kěliánchóng 可憐蟲 a poor creature; a poor guy

kě'néng 可能 probable; possible

kě'néngxìng 可能性 possibility; probability

kěpà 可怕 dreadful; frightening; terrible

kěqiǎo 可巧 by coincidence; coincidently

kěqīn 可親 kindly; friendly; amiable

kěqǔ 可取 worth having

kěquān kědiǎn 可圈可點 1. (said of a writing) very good 2. (said of the manner in doing something) very laudable

kěrén 可人 1. enjoyable; lovable 2. a person with many admirable qualities

kěshì 可是 1. to be (in a more emphatic sense); will really be 2. but; however

kěwàng érbù kějí 可望而不可即 can be looked at but not touched

kěwèi 可謂 one may well say; it may be called

kěwù 可惡 detestable; hateful

kěxī 可惜 It's a pity that....

kěxí 可惜 refer to **kěxī** 可惜

kěxiǎng érzhī 可想而知 to be obvious; one can well imagine

kěxiào 可笑 laughable; ridiculous

kěxìndù 可信度 (sociology) the confidence level

kěxíng 可行 feasible; can be carried out

kěxíngxìng 可行性 feasibility

kěyí 可疑 1. suspicious 2. doubtful

kěyǐ 可以 1. can; may 2. Yes, you can. 3. Okay. That will do.

kěyòng 可用 1. serviceable 2. employable

kěyǒu kěwú 可有可無 dispensable; not essential

kěyù érbù kěqiú 可遇而不可求 (something) considered to be uncertain

kě 坷

1. bad luck; unfortunate 2. rugged, uneven (roads, etc.)

kě 渴

1. thirsty 2. to long; to crave; to pine

kěqiú 渴求 to crave for; to search for earnestly

kěsǐ 渴死 extremely thirsty

kěwàng 渴望 to long for; to crave for; to aspire after

kè 可
as in **kèhán** 可汗—a khan

kè 克
1. to be able to 2. to win; to overcome; to conquer 3. love of superiority 4. a gram 5. to limit

kèdí zhìshèng 克敵致勝 to defeat the enemy and win the battle

kèfú 克服 1. to overcome 2. to put up with

kèlā 克拉 a carat

kèqín kèjiǎn 克勤克儉 diligent and frugal

kèzhì 克制 to restrain; to control

kè 刻
1. (also **kē**) to carve; to engrave; to cut 2. a quarter (of an hour) 3. cruel; heartless; unfeeling; cutting; harshly; acrimonious; biting 4. moment

kèbǎn 刻板 1. to engrave (for printing) 2. monotonous; dull; stereotyped

kèbó 刻薄 cold-hearted; acrimonious

kèbó guǎ'ēn 刻薄寡恩 to treat harshly and to give rare generosity

kèbù rónghuǎn 刻不容緩 Not a moment is to be lost.

kèdāo 刻刀 a burin; a graver

kègǔ míngxīn 刻骨銘心 to permanently imprint (another's favor, etc.) on the mind

kèhuà 刻畫 to depict; to portray

kèhuà rùwēi 刻畫入微 vivid portrayal of details

kèhuà rùwéi 刻畫入微 refer to **kèhuà rùwēi** 刻畫入微

kèjǐ dàirén 刻己待人 self-sacrificing

kèkǔ 刻苦 1. assiduous; hard-working 2. simple and frugal

kèkǔ nàiláo 刻苦耐勞 to work hard without complaint

kètúzhāng 刻圖章 to make a chop by carving

kèyì 刻意 to do something with intensive attention

kèyìn 刻印 to make a chop by

carving

kèzhōu qiújiàn 刻舟求劍 to be stubbornly unimaginative

kèzì 刻字 to engrave words (on stone, blocks, etc.)

kè 恪
also **què**
respectful; reverent; to respect; respectfully

kèshǒu 恪守 to observe (rules) strictly

kèzūn 恪遵 to obey or follow (orders, rules, etc.) with respect

kè 客
1. a guest 2. a stranger; an alien; a foreigner 3. a customer 4. a spectator; an audience 5. foreign; strange; alien 6. an adventurer 7. a Chinese family name

kèchuàn 客串 (said of an amateur actor or actress, etc.) to be a guest performer; (said of an established actor or actress) to play unimportant roles for a promotional purpose

kèdiàn 客店 an inn; a hotel

kèfáng 客房 a guest room

kèguān 客觀 objective

kèhù 客戶 a client

kèjī 客機 a passenger plane; an airliner

Kèjiāhuà 客家話 Hakka

kèmǎn 客滿 (said of theater tickets, etc.) sold out; a full house

kèqi 客氣 polite; courteous; sticking to the proprieties

kèqìhuà 客氣話 polite remarks

kèrén 客人 a guest

kètào 客套 civilities

kètīng 客廳 a parlor; a living room

kèyùn 客運 passenger transportation

kèzhàn 客棧 an inn

kèzuò jiàoshòu 客座教授 a visiting professor

kè 剋
1. to overcome 2. to cut down 3. to limit 4. to engrave; to imprint 5. can; to be able to

kèfū 剋夫 to be fated to mourn

one's husband's death

kèkòu 剋扣 to withhold (military supplies, etc.) for personal gain

kèqī 剋妻 to be fated to mourn one's wife's death

kèxīng 剋星 a person who always bars another person from success; a jinx

kè 溘

sudden; abrupt; unexpected

kèshì 溘逝 to die suddenly

kè 嗑

to crack something between the teeth

kè 課

1. a class meeting 2. a course (of study) 3. a lesson 4. to impose; to levy; to tax 5. a session at divination 6. a suboffice or bureau 7. to supervise

kèběn 課本 a textbook

kèbiǎo 課表 a school timetable

kèchéng 課程 a curriculum

kèchéngbiǎo 課程表 a school schedule; a class schedule

kèhòu 課後 after school or class

kèshí gōngzī 課時工資 hourly pay (for the teacher)

kèshuì 課稅 to levy taxes; to impose taxes

kètáng 課堂 a classroom

kètí 課題 1. a task or problem (for students) 2. a theme; a question for study

kèwài 課外 outside class; extra-curricular

kèwài huódòng 課外活動 extracurricular activities

kèwén 課文 the text or contents of a lesson

kèyè 課業 schoolwork; lessons

kèyú 課餘 after school or class

kèzhǎng 課長 a section chief

kěn 肯 also kěng

to be willing; to approve of; to consent to; to permit; to agree

kěndìng 肯定 affirmative; positive; sure; definite

kěn 啃

to bite; to gnaw; to nibble

kěn 墾

to open new land for farming, etc.; to reclaim land

Kěndìng Gōngyuán 墾丁公園 Kending (Kenting) Park, Ping-dong (Pingtung), Taiwan

kěnhuāng 墾荒 to open up bar-ren land for farming

kěnzhí 墾殖 to reclaim land and cultivate it

kěn 懇

cordial; sincere; earnest

kěnqiè 懇切 very sincere; ear-nest

kěnqīnhuì 懇親會 PTA (parent-teacher association or meeting)

kěnqǐng 懇請 to ask earnestly; to implore; to entreat

kěnqiú 懇求 to implore; to plead

kěntán 懇談 to talk in a sincere manner

kēng 坑

1. a pit; a hole in the ground 2. to bury alive 3. to entrap

kēngdào 坑道 a tunnel; a pit

kēngpiàn 坑騙 to cheat by tricks

kēngrén 坑人 to entrap, ensnare or harm someone

kēng 傾

kēngrén 傾人 to frame or implicate a person

kēng 鏗

1. the clang of metal; clatter 2. the twang of a string

kēngqiāng 鏗鏘 1. a tinkle; a clang 2. (figuratively) sonorous and forceful

kěng 肯

refer to **kěn** 肯

kōng 空

1. empty; hollow; void 2. to empty; to exhaust; to reduce to extremity 3. fictitious; unreal; impractical 4. vain and useless (efforts, etc.); ineffective; fruit-less 5. high and vast 6. the sky; space 7. (Buddhism) sunyata;

empty; void; vacant; nonexistent 8. merely; only

kōngchéngjì 空城計 1. a bluff 2. nobody left behind to guard the house

kōngdàngdàng 空蕩蕩 empty; deserted

kōngdòng 空洞 1. vast and empty 2 .(said of writings, thought, etc.) shallow

kōngfáng 空防 air defense

kōngfúyuán 空服員 a flight attendant

kōngfù 空腹 on an empty stomach

kōnghuānxǐ 空歡喜 joy that ends in disappointment

kōngjiān 空間 space

kōngjiān jìshù 空間技術 space technology

kōngjūn 空軍 the air force

kōngkǒu wúpíng 空口無憑 (said of a promise or pledge) Mere verbal statement has no binding force.

kōngkuàng 空曠 expansive; vast and boundless

kōngmén 空門 Buddhism

kōngnàn 空難 a plane crash or collision

kōngqì 空氣 air or atmosphere (also used figuratively)

kōngqì wūrǎn 空氣汚染 air pollution

kōngqián juéhòu 空前絕後 (said of a remarkable achievement, masterpiece, etc.) not equaled before or after

kōngshǒu 空手 empty-handed; unarmed

kōngshǒudào 空手道 karate, a type of Oriental boxing

kōngtán 空談 empty talks; idle chatter

kōngtóu zhīpiào 空頭支票 1. a dishonored check; a check that bounces 2. an empty promise

kōngxí 空襲 an air raid; an air attack

kōngxīncài 空心菜 a water convolvulus

kōngxū 空虛 empty; void; emptiness

kōngxué láifēng 空穴來風 (said of news, or information) groundless or baseless

kōngxué láifēng 空穴來風 refer to **kōngxué láifēng** 空穴來風

kōngyùn 空運 air freight; to transport by air

kōngzhōng bāshì 空中巴士 an air bus

kōngzhōng dàxué 空中大學 an open university

kōngzhōng fēirén 空中飛人 a trapeze artist; trapezist

kōngzhōng shàoye 空中少爺 (informal) a male flight attendant

kōngzhōng xiǎojie 空中小姐 a stewardess (of a passenger plane); an air hostess

kǒng 孔

1. a hole; an orifice; an opening; an aperture 2. very; exceedingly 3. of or pertaining to Confucius or Confucianism 4. urgent; badly 5. a Chinese family name

kǒngjí 孔急 urgent; urgently

Kǒng Mèng 孔孟 Confucius and Mencius

Kǒngmiào 孔廟 a Confucian temple

kǒngque 孔雀 a peacock

kǒngwǔ yǒulì 孔武有力 (said of a man) very strong and brave; herculean

Kǒngzǐ 孔子 Confucius

kǒng 恐

1. to fear; to dread 2. I am afraid....

kǒngbù 恐怖 terror; horror; fear

kǒngbù fènzǐ 恐怖分子 terrorists

kǒnghè 恐嚇 to intimidate; to threaten; to menace; to blackmail

kǒnghèxìn 恐嚇信 a blackmailing letter

kǒnghuāng 恐慌 1. panic; panicky 2. (economic) depression or crises

kǒngjù 恐懼 fear; dread; fright

kǒnglóng 恐龍 a dinosaur

kǒngpà 恐怕 1. perhaps; I think; maybe 2. I'm afraid that....

kòng 空
1. leisure; free time; spare time 2. blank (space); vacant; vacancy; to leave blank or vacant 3. spacious—implying a sense of awe 4. a chance; an opportunity 5. wanting; deficient; impoverished

kòngbái 空白 a blank in a paper or form

kòngbái zhīpiào 空白支票 a blank check

kòngdǎng 空檔 1. vacant space in a movie theater schedule 2. free time

kòngdì 空地 a vacant area; a vacant lot; a vacancy

kòngfáng 空房 an unoccupied house or room

kòngquē 空缺 1. a vacant position; a vacancy 2. scarcity

kòngwèi 空位 a vacant or un-occupied seat

kòngxì 空隙 a crevice; a gap; a loophole

kòngxiá 空暇 leisure; spare time

kòngxián 空閒 leisure; spare time

kòng 控
1. to accuse; to charge; to sue 2. to control; control 3. to draw (a bow)

kòngcí 控詞 a charge; a complaint

kònggào 控告 to accuse

kòngsù 控訴 1. to appeal to a higher court 2. to accuse before an authority

kòngsùzhuàng 控訴狀 a written appeal

kòngzhì 控制 to control; to dominate

kǒu 口
1. the mouth 2. a person 3. a certain article (as a cistern, a big jar, etc.) 4. the edge or blade of a knife 5. an opening 6. a gate (especially in the Great Wall or city walls) 7. a crack

kǒubēi 口碑 public praise

kǒubù zéyán 口不擇言 to talk without considering the consequences of what one says

kǒucái 口才 eloquence; eloquent

kǒuchī 口吃 to stammer; to stutter

kǒuchǐ língli 口齒伶俐 glib and suave

kǒuchòu 口臭 halitosis; bad breath

kǒudài 口袋 a pocket

kǒudé 口德 propriety in one's remarks

kǒu'ěr xiāngchuán 口耳相傳 to teach orally

kǒufú 口福 enjoyment of the palate

kǒufú yìmiáo 口服疫苗 oral vaccine

kǒufù zhīyù 口腹之欲 the desire for good food

kǒugòng 口供 a confession

kǒuhào 口號 1. a slogan 2. (military) an oral command

kǒuhóng 口紅 a lipstick

kǒují 口吃 refer to **kǒuchī** 口吃

kǒují 口技 oral stunts

kǒujiǎo 口角 a quarrel; to quarrel

kǒujìng 口徑 the caliber (of a gun, etc.)

kǒujué 口訣 a pithy formula

kǒukě 口渴 thirsty

kǒuliáng 口糧 food rations; grain rations

kǒulìng 口令 1. a military password 2. a verbal instruction

kǒuméi zhēlán 口沒遮攔 irresponsible talk; to talk through one's hat

kǒumì fùjiàn 口蜜腹劍 sweet words but a wicked heart

kǒuqì 口氣 1. the meaning (usually hidden) of words said 2. the way of speaking

kǒuqiāng 口腔 the cavity of the mouth

kǒuqín 口琴 a harmonica

kǒuruò xuánhé 口若懸河 glib; eloquent

kǒushàor 口哨兒 a whistle

kǒushé 口舌 quarrels, bickerings, squabbles, dispute, argument, etc.

kǒushí 口實 1. an excuse; a pretext 2. something which makes one to be ridiculed or criticized by others

kǒushì 口試 an oral test

kǒushì xīnfēi 口是心非 to mean contrary to what is spoken

kǒushù 口述 to narrate; to dictate

kǒushuǐ 口水 saliva

kǒushuō wúpíng 口說無憑 An oral agreement cannot serve as evidence.

kǒutóu 口頭 verbally; orally

kǒutóuchán 口頭禪 platitudes; pet phrases

kǒutóu shēngmíng 口頭聲明 an oral statement

kǒuwèi 口味 taste

kǒuwěn 吻 a tone

kǒuxiāngtáng 口香糖 chewing gum

kǒuxìn 口信 a verbal message

kǒuyǔ 口語 1. plain, spoken language 2. to slander

kǒuzhào 口罩 a mouth-muffle

kòu 叩

1. to knock; to hit 2. to ask 3. to kowtow

kòujiàn 叩見 to interview or visit a superior

kòumén 叩門 to knock at a door

kòuxiè 叩謝 to thank politely

kòuyè 叩謁 to interview or visit a superior

kòu 扣

1. to tap; to strike; to rap; to pull 2. to fasten; to button; to buckle 3. to detain; to confine 4. to deduct 5. a button; a hook; a buckle 6. to impound; to withhold 7. to cover on top

kòuchú 扣除 to deduct

kòujǐn 扣緊 to button (or fasten) tightly

kòuliú 扣留 to keep in custody

kòumàozi 扣帽子 to put a label

on someone

kòumén 扣門 to knock at a door

kòuqǐlai 扣來 1. to button up (one's coat, etc.) 2. to take (a person) into custody

kòurén xīnxián 扣人心弦 (said of music, writing, etc.) very touching

kòuwèn 扣問 to stop and ask

kòuxīn 扣薪 to deduct a certain amount from an employee's pay

kòuyā 扣押 to detain; to keep in custody

kòuzhù 扣住 held or fastened (by a button, hook, etc.); to hook

kòuzi 扣子 a button; a buckle; a hook

kòu 寇

1. bandits; enemies; robbers 2. to invade; to pillage; to plunder 3. a Chinese family name

kòufěi 寇匪 insurgents

kòu 釦

buttons (on garments)

kòu 蔻

cardamon seeds

kòudān 蔻丹 red nail polish (a transliteration of the trade name "Cutex")

kū 枯

1. withered; dry 2. dried wood 3. ill health; emaciated

kūgān 枯乾 dry (branches, or fruit)

kūgǎo 枯槁 1. (said of a person's appearance) pale, dry and emaciated; haggard 2. withered and dry

kūhuáng 枯黃 withered and yellow

kūjié 枯竭 (said of source of supply) exhausted; dried up

kūjǐng 枯井 a dried-up well; a dry well

kūsǐ 枯死 to wither; to dry up and die

kūwēi 枯萎 refer to **kūwěi** 枯萎

kūwěi 枯萎 withered

kūxiǔ 枯朽 dry and decayed; rot-

K

ten

kūyè 枯葉 dried leaves

kūzào 枯燥 1. dry 2. uninteresting; dull

kūzào wúwèi 枯燥無味 dry and tasteless—uninteresting; monotonous

kū 哭

to weep; to cry; to sob; to wail; to whimper

kūkutítí 哭哭啼啼 to whimper; to blubber

kūqì 哭泣 to sob; to weep

kūsangzhe liǎn 哭喪著臉 to look sad or mournful

kūsù 哭訴 to complain tearfully

kūxiào bude 哭笑不得 to be at a loss whether to cry or to laugh

kū 窟

1. a hole; a cave; a pit 2. to dig the ground and build underground living quarters

kūlong 窟窿 holes

kū 骷

a human skeleton

kūlóu 骷髏 a human skeleton

kǔ 苦

1. bitter 2. painful; hard; difficult; laborious; miserable 3. strenuous; earnest; diligent 4. to abhor 5. to feel miserable about

kǔbù kānyán 苦不堪言 painful or miserable beyond description

kǔchǔ 苦楚 pain; suffering

kǔchu 苦處 the cause of pain; difficulty

kǔgàn 苦幹 1. to make a strenuous effort 2. to do something against great odds

kǔgōng 苦工 toil; hard labor

kǔguā 苦瓜 a bitter gourd

kǔjìn gānlái 苦盡甘來 The happy sunny days are coming after all the hardships endured.

kǔkǒu póxīn 苦口婆心 to exhort or remonstrate with earnest words prompted by a kind heart

kǔlì 苦力 1. strenuous efforts;

hard work 2. a coolie; a laborer

kǔmèn 苦悶 boredom; bored; distressed; low-spirited; depressed; dejected

kǔmìng 苦命 a hard lot

kǔ'nàn 苦難 privation; suffering; hardship

kǔ'nǎo 苦惱 misery; distress; trouble

kǔquàn 苦勸 earnest exhortation; to exhort or advise earnestly

kǔròujì 苦肉計 a trick of securing another's faith by intentionally injuring oneself; acting the underdog to win sympathy

kǔsè 苦澀 1. bitter and astringent 2. agonized; pained; anguished

kǔtòng 苦痛 pain; suffering

kǔtou 苦頭 hardship(s)

kǔwèi 苦味 a bitter taste

kǔxiào 苦笑 to force a smile; a forced smile

kǔxīn 苦心 great pains taken for something

kǔxíngzhě 苦行者 an ascetic

kǔxué 苦學 to study or learn under adversity

kǔzhàn 苦戰 to fight against heavy odds

kǔzhōng 苦衷 a reason for doing something not easily understood by others

kǔzhōng zuòlè 苦中作樂 to find joy amid hardship; to enjoy in adversity

kù 庫

1. a storeroom; a granary 2. a treasury

kùcáng 庫藏 the contents of a storeroom

kùcún 庫存 a stock; reserve

kùfáng 庫房 a storeroom; a warehouse

kù 袴

trousers; drawers; breeches; pants; panties

kù 酷

1. (said of intoxicants) strong 2. (said of fragrance) very stimulating 3. cruel; brutal; harsh 4.

exceedingly

kù'ài 酷愛 to be very fond of (a thing)

kùhán 酷寒 severe cold

kùrè 酷熱 torturing heat; extremely hot

kùsì 酷似 to resemble very closely

kùxíng 酷刑 to torture; torture

kù 褲
drawers; trousers; pants

kùwà 褲襪 pantyhose

kuā 夸
1. big; large 2. lavish; luxurious 3. good-looking; pleasant 4. to brag

kuādàn 夸誕 boastful; bragging

kuā 誇
1. to exaggerate; to boast; to brag 2. big; great 3. to show off 4. to praise

kuādà 誇大 1. to exaggerate 2. arrogant

kuādà qící 誇大其詞 to exaggerate

kuājiǎng 誇獎 to praise; to acclaim; to extol

kuākǒu 誇口 to boast; to brag; to talk big

kuāyào 誇耀 to flaunt; to show off

kuāzàn 誇讚 to praise; to extol

kuāzhāng 誇張 to exaggerate; to overstate

kuǎ 垮
1. to topple; to collapse 2. to wear down 3. to put to rout 4. to fall (out of power)

kuǎtái 垮臺 the fall (of a government, project, person, etc.); collapse

kuà 胯
space between the legs; the groin

kuàbù 胯部 the crotch

kuà 跨
1. to take a stride; to stride 2. to sit astride on; to straddle; to ride 3. to cut across; to go beyond; to extend across

kuàguó gōngsī 跨國公司 a multinational corporation

kuàhǎi 跨海 to cross the sea; to sail across the ocean

kuàniándù 跨年度 to go beyond the year

kuàyuè 跨越 to stride over (a ditch, etc.)

kuǎi 舀
refer to **yǎo** 舀

kuài 快
1. quickly; fast; hasty; soon 2. nearly; near 3. to hurry up; to make haste 4. quick-witted; ingenious 5. sharp (blades, etc.); keen 6. pleasant; happy 7. honest; straightforward

kuàibǎn 快板 quick tempo

kuàibào 快報 a dispatch; a bulletin

kuàibù 快步 a half step; a trot

kuàicān 快餐 a quick meal; a snack

kuàicān shípǐng 快餐食品 instant food

kuàichē 快車 an express train

kuàichēdào 快車道 a speedway

kuàidāo zhǎn luànmá 快刀斬亂麻 to straighten up a complicated or messy situation by taking drastic steps and with dispatch

kuàidì 快遞 express delivery

kuàidiǎn 快點 Make it snappy. Be quick!

kuàigānqī 快乾漆 quick-drying paint

kuàigǎn 快感 a pleasant feeling

kuàigōng 快攻 a quick attack (in ball games)

kuàiguō 快鍋 a pressure cooker

kuàihuo 快活 happy; joy

kuàijié 快捷 speedy; fast; nimble

kuàilè 快樂 happy; joy

kuàimǎ jiābiān 快馬加鞭 to proceed as quickly as possible; posthaste

kuàimàn 快慢 speed

kuàimén 快門 a camera shutter

kuàipǎo 快跑 to run fast; Go

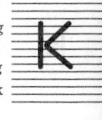

quick! On the double!

kuàirén kuàiyǔ 快人快語 the straightforward talk of a straightforward person

kuàishuō 快說 Speak up! Be quick!

kuàisù 快速 fast; quick; prompt

kuàitǐng 快艇 a speedboat; a motorboat

kuàiwèi 快慰 happy; satisfying; to be pleased

kuàixiē 快些 Hurry! faster than

kuàizhào 快照 a snapshot

kuàizǒu 快走 Hurry, let's go. Beat it!

kuàizuǐ kuàishé 快嘴快舌 quick of tongue

kuài 塊

1. a lump (or clod) of earth 2. a lump; a piece; a cube 3. a piece of (land, bread, etc.) 4. alone; to be all by oneself

kuàigēn 塊根 a root tuber

kuàitou 塊頭 stature; build

kuài 會

to add; to compute

kuàijì 會計 1. accounting 2. an accountant; a treasurer

kuàijìshī 會計師 C.A. (a chartered accountant); C.P.A. (a certified public accountant)

kuàijìxué 會計學 accounting

kuài 筷

chopsticks

kuàizi 筷子 chopsticks

kuài 儈

a middleman; a go-between; a broker

kuài 劊

refer to **guì** 劊

kuài 膾

minced meat

kuàizhì rénkǒu 膾炙人口 (said of interesting things, good writings, etc.) to be talked about by everyone

kuài 檜

refer to **guì** 檜

kuān 寬

1. broad; wide; spacious; vast 2. magnanimous; lenient; tolerant; liberal; forgiving; indulgent 3. to loosen; to widen 4. well-off

kuānchang 寬敞 spacious; roomy

kuāndà 寬大 lenient; magnanimous

kuāndà wéihuái 寬大為懷 magnanimous; benignant; liberal; open-hearted

kuāndù 寬度 width; breadth

kuānguǎng 寬廣 vast; broad; spacious; wide

kuānhóng dàliàng 寬宏大量 magnanimous; benignant; broadminded

kuānhòu 寬厚 tolerant and generous

kuānkuò 寬闊 roomy; wide; spacious

kuānróng 寬容 to forgive; to pardon

kuānshù 寬恕 to forgive; to pardon

kuānsōng 寬鬆 loose and comfortable

kuānxiàn 寬限 1. to extend a time limit 2. a moratorium

kuānxīn 寬心 to feel at rest; to set one's mind at ease

kuānxīnwán 寬心丸 something capable of setting someone's mind at ease

kuānyī 寬衣 1. a loose garment 2. to remove the upper coat (for relaxation)

kuānyī jiědài 寬衣解帶 to undress

kuānyù 寬裕 well-to-do; well-off; ample

kuānzhǎi 寬窄 width; breadth

kuǎn 款

1. sincerity; sincere; sincerely 2. an article, an item, etc. (in a contract, treaty, etc.) 3. to entertain; to treat well 4. slowly; slow 5. to knock (at a door) 6. a fund; a sum of money; money 7. empty (words, etc.)

K

kuǎndài 款待 to entertain with courtesy and warmth; hospitality

kuǎn'é 款額 the amount of money involved

kuǎnkuǎn 款款 1. sincerely 2. slowly

kuǎnqū 款曲 1. heartfelt feelings 2. to conduct oneself with great tact in social gatherings

kuǎnshì 款式 fashions; styles; patterns

kuǎnxiàng 款項 a sum of money; a fund; money

kuāng 匡
1. to rectify; to correct 2. to deliver from 3. a Chinese family name

kuāngjì 匡濟 to relieve distress

kuāngzhèng 匡正 to rectify; to correct; to reform

kuāngzhù 匡助 to rectify; to correct

kuāng 框
refer to **kuàng** 框

kuāng 筐
a rectangular chest or box woven from bamboo strips (or wicker); a shallow basket

kuáng 狂
1. crazy; mad; mentally deranged 2. violent 3. unrestrained; uninhibited; wild 4. haughty

kuáng'ào 狂傲 unreasonably haughty

kuángbào 狂暴 wild; fierce; ferocious; brutal

kuángbēn 狂奔 to run about wildly; to run about madly

kuángbiāo 狂飆 a hurricane

kuángfēng bàoyǔ 狂風暴雨 a violent storm

kuánghuān 狂歡 to revel; to rejoice with wild excitement

kuánglán 狂瀾 1. violent waves 2. violent disturbances

kuángluàn 狂亂 wild; frenzied; frantic; mad

kuángquǎnbìng 狂犬病 rabies; hydrophobia

kuángrè 狂熱 1. fanatical; fever-ish 2. a fad

kuángrén 狂人 1. a lunatic 2. an extremely conceited fellow

kuángwàng 狂妄 1. wild; irrational; crazy 2. extremely conceited

kuángxiǎngqǔ 狂想曲 (music) a rhapsody

kuàng 況
1. moreover; in addition; not to mention... 2. to compare; comparative 3. situations; conditions 4. to visit; to call on

kuàngqiě 況且 moreover; besides; furthermore

kuàng 框 also **kuāng**
1. a frame 2. to frame 3. the skeleton (of a lantern, etc.)

kuàng 曠
1. open; wide; broad; vast; spacious 2. free from worries and petty ideas 3. to neglect

kuàngfèi 曠廢 to neglect

kuànggōng 曠工 to neglect work

kuàngkè 曠課 to cut school; to truant

kuàngshì zhīcái 曠世之才 a man of brilliance unequaled by his contemporaries

kuàngyě 曠野 wild plains; a prairie

kuàngzhí 曠職 1. to be absent from the office without leave 2. to neglect official duties

kuàng 礦(鑛)
1. a mineral; ore 2. mining 3. a mine

kuànggōng 礦工 a miner

kuàngkēng 礦坑 a mining shaft; a pit

kuàngqū 礦區 a mining district; an ore field

kuàngquánshuǐ 礦泉水 mineral water

kuàngshí 礦石 a mineral; ore

kuàngwù 礦物 a mineral

kuī 盔
1. a helmet 2. a basin; a pot

kuījiǎ 盔甲 helmets and mail;

armor

kuī 窺

to watch or see in secret; to spy; to peep; to pry into

kuīcè 窺測 to watch and assess (a situation, development, etc.)

kuīshì 窺視 to peep at; to spy on

kuīsì 窺伺 to watch and wait (for a chance to attack, etc.)

kuītàn 窺探 to spy on; to peep; to pry into

kuī 虧

1. to lose; to damage; to have a deficit 2. to lack; to want; short; deficient 3. to treat unfairly; to be unfair to 4. fortunately; luckily 5. used in a mocking sense 6. the waning; to wane

kuīdài 虧待 to maltreat

kuīkong 虧空 1. to spend more than one makes 2. a loss; a deficit

kuīqiàn 虧欠 1. a deficit 2. insufficiency 3. to owe

kuīsǔn 虧損 1. a deficit; a loss; to deplete 2. enfeebled or weakened by illness

kuīxīnshì 虧心事 something which gives one a guilty conscience

kuí 葵

a sunflower

kuíhuā 葵花 a sunflower

kuíhuāyóu 葵花油 sunflower oil

kuí 暌

1. in opposition 2. to separate; to part

kuíwéi 暌違 (said of friends) separated; parted; separation

kuí 魁

1. the chief; the head; the leader 2. tall; big; great

kuíwú 魁梧 tall and robust; husky

kuí 睽

1. (暌) separated 2. in opposition 3. to squint 4. to stare at 5. unusual; strange

kúikúi 睽睽 to stare; to gaze

kuǐ 傀

a puppet

kuǐlěi 傀儡 a puppet

kuǐlěixì 傀儡戲 a puppet show

kuì 喟

to sigh heavily

kuìrán chángtàn 喟然長嘆 to sigh deeply

kuì 愧

ashamed; conscience-stricken; shameful; abashed

kuìbù gǎndāng 愧不敢當 (an expression used to show humbleness and politeness) ashamed to accept (an honor); do not deserve (a gift, compliment, etc.)

kuìjiù 愧疚 to feel the discomfort of shame

kuìnǎn 愧赧 to redden from shame

kuìzuò 愧怍 to feel shame; ashamed

kuì 匱

to lack; deficient

kuìfá 匱乏 1. lack 2. a chest or cabinet 3. exhausted

kuì 憒

muddleheaded; confused in one's mind

kuìluàn 憒亂 confused in one's mind; at a loss

kuì 潰

1. a river overflowing its banks 2. broken up; scattered 3. (military) defeated 4. (said of a dike or dam) to burst

kuìbài 潰敗 (military) defeated and scattered; a rout

kuìbù chéngjǔn 潰不成軍 completely routed

kuìlàn 潰爛 bursting of an abscess; inflamed

kuìsàn 潰散 defeated and dispersed

kuìtáo 潰逃 to escape in disorder; to flee pell-mell

kuìyáng 潰瘍 an ulcer

kuì 饋

1. to offer food to a superior 2.

K

to send someone a present; to present as a gift

kuìzèng 饋贈 to present (a gift); to make a present of something

kūn 昆
1. an elder brother 2. descendants; posterity 3. multitudes 4. together; in unison

kūnchóng 昆蟲 insects

Kūnmíng 昆明 the capital city of Yunnan Province

Kūnqǔ 昆曲 1. Kun opera 2. melodies for Kun opera

kūnyù 昆玉 (a polite expression) your brothers

kūnzhòng 昆仲 brothers

kūn 坤
1. one of the Eight Diagrams —earth 2. compliance; obedience 3. female; feminine

kūnjuér 坤角兒 an actress of Beijing opera

kūnlíng 坤伶 an actress of Beijing opera

kūnyú 坤輿 another name of the earth

kūn 琨
fine rocks next to jade in quality

kǔn 捆
1. to bind; to tie up 2. a bundle

kǔnbǎng 捆綁 to bind

kǔnqǐlái 捆起來 to tie up (a prisoner, etc.)

kǔnyā 捆押 to tie up and escort

kǔn 綑
1. a bundle; to make a bundle; to tie up; to bundle up 2. to weave

kǔnbǎng 綑綁 to bind; to tie up

kǔnjǐn 綑緊 to bind tight; to tighten the rope

kùn 困
1. difficult; hard 2. poor 3. fatigued; weary; tired 4. to trouble; to worry; to harass; to be stranded; to be hard pressed

kùndùn 困頓 1. tired; exhausted; fatigued 2. in financial straits

kùnhuò 困惑 to perplex; to confuse

kùnjìng 困境 a predicament; straits

kùnjiǒng 困窘 embarrassment; to embarrass

kùnkǔ 困苦 in great distress; poverty-stricken

kùnnán 困難 difficulty; hardship

kùnnan chóngchóng 困難重重 to be beset with difficulties

kùnrǎo 困擾 to perplex; to confuse

kùnshòu zhīdòu 困獸之鬥 a desperate fight

kùn 睏
drowsy; sleepy

kuò 括 also **guā**
1. to include; to embrace 2. to seek; to search for 3. to come; to arrive 4. to bound; to tie 5. to restrain

kuòhào 括號 (mathematics) the sign of aggregation

kuòhú 括弧 brackets; braces; parentheses—[]; {}; ( )

kuò 廓
1. open; wide 2. empty

kuòqīng 廓清 to liquidate; to clean up; to wipe out

kuòrán 廓然 1. spacious 2. vast; boundless 3. unprejudiced; unbiased

kuòtǔ 廓土 an open ground

kuò 闊
1. broad; wide; width 2. separated; widely apart 3. rich; loaded; wealthy; extravagant

kuòbié 闊別 separated for a long time

kuòbù 闊步 to walk with big strides; to stride

kuòchuò 闊綽 extravagant; throwing money around; lavish

kuòlǎo 闊佬 a rich man

kuòqi 闊氣 extravagant in spending; lavish

kuò 擴
to enlarge; to magnify; to expand; to extend

kuòchōng 擴充 to expand; to enlarge

kuòdà 擴大 1. to enlarge; to expand 2. to swell; to distend

kuòjiàn 擴建 to extend (a factory, mine, etc.)

kuòsàn 擴散 1. (physics) to diffuse; diffusion 2. to scatter about

kuòxiāo 擴銷 sales promotion

kuòyīnqì 擴音器 a megaphone; a loudspeaker

kuòzhǎn 擴展 to stretch; to extend; to spread

kuòzhāng 擴張 1. to extend; to spread; to expand 2. to dilate; dilation

lā 垃 also **lè**

    garbage; refuse; waste

lājī 垃圾 garbage; refuse

lājīchǎng 垃圾場 a rubbish heap

lājīchē 垃圾車 a collection truck

lājīduī 垃圾堆 a rubbish heap

lājītǒng 垃圾桶 a dustbin; a garbage can

lā 拉

    1. to pull; to drag; to hold; to draw 2. to discharge (especially stool, urine, etc.) 3. to lengthen; to elongate 4. to play

lābá 拉拔 to help (a protege) advance

lācháng 拉長 1. to prolong (business, voice, etc.) 2. to draw

lāchē 拉車 to pull or haul a cart (or ricksha)

lāche 拉扯 1. to pull and drag 2. to implicate or involve 3. to talk a lot outside of one's topic

lādǎo 拉倒 1. Never mind. 2. to pull down

Lādīng Měizhōu 拉丁美洲 Latin America

Lādīngwén 拉丁文 Latin (language)

lādùzi 拉肚子 to suffer from diarrhea

lāguānxi 拉關係 to seek special favor or help from somebody by elaborating on one's relationship with him

lājǐn 拉緊 1. to draw or pull tight 2. to hang on firmly

lājìn 拉近 to draw close or near

lājù 拉鋸 1. to cut with a saw 2. to be locked in a seesaw struggle

lājùzhàn 拉鋸戰 a seesaw battle; stalemate

lākai 拉開 1. to pull open; to draw aside 2. to increase the distance between

lāliàn 拉鍊 a zipper

lālong 拉攏 1. to befriend another person with a view to winning him over 2. to make two persons or parties become friends

lāniào 拉尿 to urinate

lāpiào 拉票 to solicit votes; to canvass

lāpíng 拉平 to even up; to end up in a draw

lāshēngyi 拉生意 to solicit business; to tout

lāshǐ 拉屎 to go to stool; to empty the bowels; to move one's bowels

lāshǒu 拉手 1. to hold another's hands 2. to pull by the hand

lāzá 拉雜 1. rambling; jumbled 2. (said of a room, etc.) untidy

lāzhù 拉住 to hold on firmly

lā 啦

    (onomatopoeia) the sound of water, rain, etc.

lāladuì 啦啦隊 a cheer squad

lā 喇

    a character used for its sound

lā 邋 also **lá**

lāta 邋遢 dirty; untidy

lá 邋

    refer to **lā** 邋

lǎ 喇

    1. a horn; a trumpet; a bugle 2. a lama 3. a character used in transliteration

lǎba 喇叭 1. a trumpet 2. a loudspeaker

lǎbahuā 喇叭花 (botany) morning glory

lǎbakù 喇叭褲 bell-shaped pants

lǎma 喇嘛 a lama (a priest of Lamaism)

Lǎmajiào 喇嘛教 Lamaism

là 剌

to go against; to contradict; perverse; disagreeable; rebellious

là 辣

1. pungent; piquant; hot 2. (said of smell or taste) to burn; to bite 3. vicious; ruthless

làjiàng 辣醬 thick chilli sauce

làjiāo 辣椒 capsicum; chilli

làmèi 辣妹 a sexy girl

làzi 辣子 chilli

là 癩

favus

làlìtóu 癩痢頭 a head made bald by favus

là 臘

1. sacrifice at the end of the lunar year 2. the end of the lunar year 3. salted and smoked meat, fish, chicken, etc. 4. the age of a Buddhist monk

làcháng 臘腸 a sausage

làchánggǒu 臘腸狗 a dachshund

làméi 臘梅 plum flowers

làròu 臘肉 salted and dried meat

làwèi 臘味 preserved meat

làyuè 臘月 the 12th moon of the lunar year

là 蠟

1. wax 2. a candle

làbǐ 蠟筆 a crayon

làlèi 蠟淚 wax guttering; drips from a burning candle

làxiàng 蠟像 a wax figure; a waxwork

làzhú 蠟燭 a candle

la 啦

a phrase final particle

lái 來

1. to come; coming; to arrive 2. to return; to come back; returning

láibīn 來賓 a guest; a visitor

láibùjí 來不及 unable to make it in time

láidào 來到 to arrive; to come

láidejí 來得及 there is time for...

láifàn 來犯 to come to attack us

láifǎng 來訪 to come to visit

láifúqiāng 來福槍 a rifle

láihán 來函 your letter

láihuí 來回 coming and going; to come and go

láihuípiào 來回票 a round-trip ticket

láijiàn 來件 the communication received

lái wǎngwǎng 來來往往 coming and going in great numbers

láilì 來歷 past history; origin; background

láilì bùmíng 來歷不明 of questionable antecedents, source, origin, background, etc.

láilín 來臨 to arrive; to approach; to come

láilóng qùmài 來龍去脈 the beginning and subsequent development of (an incident, etc.)

láilù 來路 incoming road

láilu 來路 source; (personal) background

láilu bùmíng 來路不明 of questionable origin

láinián 來年 the next year; the years to come

láirén 來人 1. the person or persons who came or are coming 2. the incoming envoy, messenger, etc.

láirì 來日 1. tomorrow 2. the future

láirì fāngcháng 來日方長 There is a long time ahead.

láishēng 來生 the next life or incarnation

láishì 來世 1. later generations 2. (Buddhism) the future life

láishì 來勢 oncoming force

láishì xiōngxiōng 來勢洶洶 to move threateningly towards

láitou 來頭 personal connections

láiwǎng 來往 coming and going

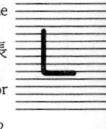

láiwang 來往 social intercourse or connection

láiwén 來文 incoming documents, letters, etc.

láixìn 來信 1. your letter 2. to send a letter here

láiyì 來意 the purpose of a personal call

láiyóu 來由 reason; cause

láiyuán 來源 the source; the origin

láizhě bùjù 來者不拒 to grant favors to whoever asks for it

lái 萊
1. fields lying fallow 2. wild weeds 3. to weed

Láiyīnhé 萊因河 the Rhine River

lài 賴
1. to rely on; to depend on 2. to accuse without grounds or evidence; to put the blame on somebody else 3. to repudiate (a debt); to disavow; to deny something which one has said or done 4. to postpone or procrastinate intentionally 5. no good; poor; bad 6. lazy 7. a Chinese family name

làipí 賴皮 1. a person without any sense of shame; a rogue 2. shameless

làizhàng 賴賬 1. to repudiate accounts 2. to go back on one's word

lài 癩
1. leprosy; favus; scabies 3. bad

làichuāng 癩瘡 scabies

làiháma 癩蝦蟆 the toad

làipígǒu 癩皮狗 1. a mangy dog 2. a disgusting creature

lán 婪
covetous; greedy; avarice

lán 嵐
mountain vapor; mist

lán 闌
1. a door curtain or screen 2. a fence 3. to block up; to cut off 4. the end of (a year, etc.); late (in the night, etc.) 5. weakened; withered

lán'gān 闌干 1. a fence; banisters; a balustrade; railings 2. the eye sockets 3. a crisscross

lánshān 闌珊 withered; declining; waning

lánwěi 闌尾 the appendix

lán 藍
1. blue; indigo 2. an indigo plant 3. a Chinese family name

lánbǎoshí 藍寶石 sapphire

lánběn 藍本 the original; a blueprint

lánlǐng jiējí 藍領階級 blue-collar

lántú 藍圖 a blueprint; an outline of a project

lán 襤
1. ragged garments; clothes without a hem 2. shabbily dressed

lánlǚ 襤褸 (said of clothes) tattered

lán 瀾
a great wave; a huge billow

lán 籃
a basket

lánqiú 籃球 basketball

lánqiúsài 籃球賽 a basketball game

lán 攔
to impede; to obstruct; to hinder; to block

lánchē 攔車 to stop a vehicle

lánjí 攔擊 to intercept and attack; to volley

lánjí 攔擊 refer to **lánjí** 攔擊

lánjié 攔劫 to intercept and rob

lánjié 攔截 to intercept; to attack or stop on the way

lánzhù 攔住 to obstruct; to block; to hinder

lánzǔ 攔阻 to impede; to obstruct

lán 欄
1. a railing; a balustrade; a fence 2. a pen for domesticated animals

lán'gān 欄杆 1. a railing; a balustrade 2. silk trimming for girls

lánwèi 欄位 (computer) field

lán 蘭
an orchid

lánhuā 蘭花 an orchid; a cymbidium

lǎn 懶
lazy; indolent; idle; inactive; listless

lǎnchóng 懶蟲 lazybones; a lazy person

lǎnduò 懶惰 lazy; idle; indolent

lǎnsǎn 懶散 indolent; inactive

lǎsàn 懶散 refer to **lǎnsǎn** 懶散

lǎnyāngyāng 懶洋洋 indolent; sluggish

lǎnyángyáng 懶洋洋 refer to **lǎnyāngyāng** 懶洋洋

lǎn 覽
1. to look at; to sightsee 2. to read

lǎnshèng 覽勝 to tour a resort; to see or visit a scenic spot

lǎn 攬
1. to be in full possession of 2. to take into one's arms 3. to make a selective collection of 4. to take on; to undertake 5. to grasp; to monopolize 6. to round up

lǎnjìng zìzhào 攬鏡自照 to hold a mirror to watch one's own reflection

lǎnquán 攬權 to grasp full authority

lǎn 檻
the olive

lǎn 纜 also **làn**
a hawser; a cable

lǎnchē 纜車 a cable car

lǎnshéng 纜繩 cordage; a thick rope

làn 濫
1. to overflow; to flood; to inundate; inundation 2. to do things without plans; reckless 3. to practice no self-restraint; to give way to unbridled license 4. to abuse (one's power, influence, etc.) 5. false; not true 6. superfluous words or expressions

lànfá 濫伐 excessive felling of trees

lànjiāo 濫交 to befriend at random

lànkěn 濫墾 to cultivate farms in areas where soil conservation should be maintained

lànshā 濫殺 to kill at random

lànshāng 濫觴 the very origin or source (of a practice, tradition, etc.)

lànyòng 濫用 1. to spend excessively 2. to abuse

lànyú chōngshù 濫竽充數 to hold a post without the necessary qualifications just to make up the number

làn 瀾
1. overflowing; dripping wet; a vast expanse of water 2. thin rice paste

lànmàn 瀾漫 1. overflowing; inundating 2. wet through 3. sprightly

làn 爛
1. overripe; rotten; to rot; to fester 2. cooked soft; well cooked 3. bright; brilliant 4. to scald; to burn; to scorch 5. worn-out 6. dissolute

lànhǎorén 爛好人 one who cannot say no to requests for help or favor

lànhuò 爛貨 worthless goods

lànmàn 爛漫 1. resplendent 2. dissipated; debauched 3. fast asleep 4. naive

lànshú 爛熟 1. very ripe 2. thoroughly familiar

làntānzi 爛攤子 a shambles

lànzhàng 爛脹 uncollectable debts

lànzuì rúní 爛醉如泥 dead drunk

làn 纜
refer to **lǎn** 纜

láng 郎
1. an official rank in ancient times 2. a man 3. the husband;

the beau 4. the master (as opposite to servants) 5. a Chinese family name

lángcái nǔmào 郎才女貌 a perfect match between a man and a woman

lángjūn 郎君 1. a term of address for a man 2. your son (a polite expression) 3. the husband

lángzhōng 郎中 1. an official rank in ancient China 2. a physician 3. a card shark

láng 狼

1. a wolf 2. a heartless, cruel person; cruel and heartless; cunning and crafty 3. name of a constellation

lángbèi 狼狽 1. desperate in 2. in a difficult position 3. embarrassed 4. heartless and cruel persons

lángbèi bùkān 狼狽不堪 to be in utter disorder

lángbèi wéijiān 狼狽為奸 to work hand in glove

lánggǒu 狼狗 1. a German shepherd 2. a wolfhound

lángquǎn 狼犬 1. a German shepherd 2. a wolfhound

lángrén 狼人 a wolf man; a werewolf

lángtūn hǔyàn 狼吞虎嚥 to gobble up; to wolf down

lángxīn gǒufèi 狼心狗肺 heartless and cruel

láng 浪

flowing; fluent

láng 琅

1. a kind of stone resembling jade 2. clean and white; pure; spotless

láng 廊

a portico; a corridor; a hallway

lángmiào 廊廟 the court (of a monarch)

lángmiào zhīzhì 廊廟之志 political aspiration

láng 榔

1. a betel palm 2. a betel nut

lángtou 榔頭 a hammer

láng 鋃

1. chains for prisoners 2. the tolling of a bell

lángdāng rùyù 鋃鐺入獄 to be shackled and imprisoned; to be jailed

lǎng 朗

1. bright; clear 2. resonant; sonorous

lǎngdú 朗讀 to read aloud

lǎngsòng 朗誦 to read aloud

làng 浪

1. waves; billows; breakers 2. dissolute; debauched; rash; unrestrained

làngcháo 浪潮 1. tide; waves 2. (figuratively) tide; tendency

làngdàng 浪蕩 to debauch; to dissipate

làngfèi 浪費 to waste; to lavish; waste

lànghuā 浪花 spray of breaking waves

làngjī tiānyá 浪跡天涯 to wander about far away from home

làngmàn 浪漫 1. debauched 2. romantic

làngrén 浪人 1. a vagrant 2. a dismissed courtier 3. a jobless person

làngtou 浪頭 the crest of a wave

làngzǐ 浪子 a prodigal; a debauchee; a loafer

lāo 撈 also **láo**

1. to pull or drag out of the water 2. to fish up; to get by improper means

lāoběn 撈本 1. to win back money (lost in gambling) 2. to recover invested capital

lāoqǐ 撈起 to recover from water, the riverbed, etc.

lāoqǔ 撈取 to fish for; to gain

lāoyībǎ 撈一把 to reap some profit; to profiteer

lāoyīpiào 撈一票 to make money, legally or otherwise

láo 牢

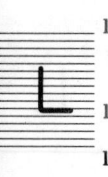

1. a pen; a stable; a cage 2. a jail; a prison 3. secure; stable; firm; fast 4. worried; concerned 5. sacrifice

láobù kěpò 牢不可破 unbreakable; invulnerable

láogù 牢固 secure; firm

láojì 牢記 to keep firmly in mind

láokao 牢靠 1. sturdy; stable; secure; firm 2. reliable; trustworthy; dependable

láolóng 牢籠 1. to cover; to include a cage; a prison

láosāo 牢騷 grumbling; complaint

láoyù 牢獄 a jail; a prison

láo 勞

1. to labor; to take the toil; to work 2. to trouble; to worry; to bother 3. meritorious deeds; services 4. (also **lào**) to comfort or entertain (the tired)

láodòng 勞動 1. to toil; to labor 2. to trouble

Láodòngjié 勞動節 Labor Day

láodùn 勞頓 fatigue; exhaustion

láofāng 勞方 labor (in contrast to capital or management)

láogōng 勞工 laborers; workers

láogōng bǎoxiǎn 勞工保險 labor insurance

láojià 勞駕 to be sorry to have to trouble someone to do something

láojūn 勞軍 to cheer or entertain troops

láokǔ 勞苦 1. to labor; to toil 2. toil

láokǔ gōnggāo 勞苦功高 meritorious service

láolèi 勞累 to fatigue, tire or exhaust

láolì 勞力 1. labor 2. to labor physically

láolù 勞碌 to work hard; to drudge

láolùmìng 勞碌命 a born laborer

láomín shāngcái 勞民傷財 to tire the people and waste the resources

láoshī dòngzhòng 勞師動眾

1. to waste manpower 2. to involve too many people

láoxīn 勞心 1. to labor mentally 2. to be worried; to be anxious

láoyàn fēnfēi 勞燕分飛 (said of people) to separate or part (like birds flying in different directions)

láoyì 勞役 hard labor (as punishment)

láozī 勞資 labor and management

láozuò 勞作 1. manual work or training (at school) 2. manual labor

láo 嘮

loquacious; garrulous; voluble

láodao 嘮叨 to nag; to din

láo 撈

refer to **lāo 撈**

láo 癆

tuberculosis; consumption

láobìng 癆病 tuberculosis; consumption

lǎo 老

1. old; aged 2. always 3. the youngest 4. very 5. a particle indicating ordinal numbers to designate order of birth 6. parents 7. a particle used before a man's family name to indicate familiarity and friendship 8. (said of meat, etc.) tough; over cooked 9. to treat with the reverence to the aged 10. (said of color) dark

lǎobǎixìng 老百姓 the people; the common people

lǎobǎn 老闆 1. a boss; a master 2. a keeper; a proprietor

lǎobǎnniáng 老闆娘 1. a proprietress; proprietor's wife 2. boss's wife; a mistress

lǎobàntiān 老半天 quite a while

lǎobàng shēngzhū 老蚌生珠 a son born in one's old age

lǎobǎo 老鴇 a procuress

lǎoběn 老本 1. a principal; a capital; the original investment 2. an old edition

lǎobīng 老兵 an old soldier; a veteran

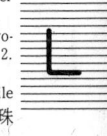

lǎobùxiū 老不修 an old lecher

lǎochéng 老成 sophisticated; experienced

lǎochǔnǚ 老處女 an old maid; a spinster

lǎocū 老粗 a rude fellow; a boor

lǎodādàng 老搭檔 an old partner

lǎodà 老大 1. old 2. the eldest child 3. the leader of a gang 4. extremely; exceedingly

lǎodà bùxiǎo 老大不小 to have come of age

lǎodāng yìzhuàng 老當益壯 to gain vigor with age

lǎodiào chóngtán 老調重彈 to play the same old tune

lǎodiàoyá 老掉牙 old-fashioned; outdated; obsolete

lǎodiē 老爹 1. one's father 2. an intimate address for an aged man

lǎofū 老夫 1. (used by an old man) I; me 2. an old husband

lǎofū lǎoqī 老夫老妻 an old couple

lǎofùrén 老婦人 an old woman

lǎogē 老哥 my dear friend (used among males)

lǎogōng 老公 1. an old man 2. (slang) one's husband

lǎogǔdǒng 老古董 1. antiques; curios 2. an ultraconservative

lǎogùkè 老顧客 a regular customer; an old customer

lǎoguīju 老規矩 old rules; old practices

lǎohǎorén 老好人 a soft-hearted person

lǎohúli 老狐狸 1. an old fox 2. a cunning old man

lǎohútu 老糊塗 a dotard

lǎohǔ 老虎 a tiger

lǎohǔqián 老虎鉗 pincer pliers

lǎohuāyǎn 老花眼 presbyopia

lǎohuà 老化 ageing

lǎojiā 老家 1. one's original home 2. hell

lǎojiān jùhuá 老奸巨猾 shrewd and crafty

lǎojiāoqíng 老交情 old friend-

ship

lǎojiù 老舊 old-style; old-fashioned

lǎoliàn 老練 experienced; skilled; expert

lǎomǎ shítú 老馬識途 experienced and capable of leading others wisely

lǎomǎ shítú 老馬識途 refer to **lǎomǎ shítú** 老馬識途

lǎomáobìng 老毛病 1. an old ailment 2. old weakness

lǎomìng 老命 1. the life of an old person 2. one's dear life

lǎomóu shēnsuàn 老謀深算 experienced and astute

lǎonián 老年 old age; old life; late years

lǎonián chīdāizhèng 老年痴呆症 (pathology) senile dementia

lǎoniáng 老娘 1. one's old mother 2. self-reference of a virago in a quarrel

lǎopái 老牌 1. an old brand 2. a veteran (actor or actress)

lǎopo 老婆 (vulgar usage) wife

lǎoqì 老氣 1. an experienced air or style 2. old-fashioned 3. (said of colors) plain or dark

lǎoqiān 老千 a swindler

lǎoqiánbèi 老前輩 a term used to address one's senior or an aged person

lǎorén 老人 an old person

lǎoruò cánbīng 老弱殘兵 1. old and weak surviving soldiers 2. incompetent workers

lǎoshào xiányí 老少咸宜 suitable for both the old and the young

lǎoshēng chángtán 老生常談 a cliche

lǎoshī 老師 a teacher

lǎoshí 老實 honest; truthful

lǎoshǒu 老手 an old hand; an old stager

lǎoshǔ 老鼠 a rat; a mouse

lǎotài lóngzhōng 老態龍鍾 the appearance of senility and dotage of the aged

lǎotàipó 老太婆 an old woman

lǎotàitai 老太太 an old lady

lǎotàiyé 老太爺 1. (in addressing an aged man) venerable sir 2. an old gentleman

lǎotāo 老饕 a glutton

lǎotiānyé 老天爺 Heaven

lǎotóuzi 老頭子 1. an old chap; an old fellow 2. one's husband

lǎowài 老外 (slang) a foreigner

lǎowángu 老頑固 a stubborn person

lǎoxiānsheng 老先生 1. (in addressing an aged man) venerable sir 2. an old gentleman

lǎoxiōng 老兄 my dear friend (used among males)

lǎoxiū chéngnù 老羞成怒 to be angry as a result of embarrassment

lǎoxuéjiū 老學究 an old pedant

lǎoyǎn hūnhuā 老眼昏花 the blurred vision of an old person

lǎoyàngzi 老樣子 the way a thing or person used to look

lǎoyāo 老么 1. the youngest child of a family 2. the youngest one in a group

lǎoye 老爺 1. sir 2. an old man

lǎoyībèi 老一輩 the older generation

lǎoyīng 老鷹 the eagle

lǎoyóutiáo 老油條 a sleeky fellow

lǎoyǒu 老友 an old friend

lǎoyuǎn 老遠 a very long way; very far

lǎozǎo 老早 1. very early 2. long ago

lǎozhàng 老賬 1. old debts 2. old scores

lǎozhǔgù 老主顧 an old customer

lǎozǔzōng 老祖宗 ancestors; forefathers

lǎo 佬
1. a fellow; a man; a guy 2. a vulgar person; a hillbilly

lǎo 姥
1. one's maternal grandmother 2. an old woman

lǎo 潦
a puddle

lào 烙 also **luò**
1. to burn 2. to brand; to iron 3. to bake in a pan

làotie 烙鐵 an iron; a branding iron

làoyìn 烙印 to brand; a brand

lào 絡
a fine thread basket

lào 勞
refer to **láo** 勞 4

lào 酪 also **luò**
1. alcoholic drinks 2. animal milk 3. cheese 4. fruit jam 5. junket 6. thick fruit juice; fruit jelly

làonóng 酪農 a dairy farmer

lànóngchǎng 酪農場 a dairy farm

lào 落
1. to fall or drop (in prices, etc.) 2. (said of a bird, etc.) to land; to perch 3. to get 4. a net income; a surplus

làojià 落價 to come down in prices

lào 潦
to flood; floods

lè 肋
refer to **lèi** 肋

lè 垃
refer to **lā** 垃

lè 捋
refer to **luō** 捋 3

lè 勒
1. to force; to compel 2. to reign or rule; to control; to command 3. to engrave; to carve 4. a bridle 5. (calligraphy) a horizontal stroke

lèjièsuǒ 勒戒所 a clinic where addicts are treated and made to kick the habit

lèlìng 勒令 to compel by an order or injunction

lèlìng tuìxué 勒令退學 suspended indefinitely

lèshú 勒贖 to kidnap a person for ransom

lèsuǒ 勒索 to blackmail; to extort

lèzhù 勒住 to halt by pulling in reins

lè 樂

1. happy; glad; joyful; joyous; cheerful; elated; content; pleased; delighted; willing 2. pleasant; agreeable; enjoyable; pleasing; comfortable

lèbù kèzhī 樂不可支 to be overwhelmed with joy

lèbù sī Shǔ 樂不思蜀 too happy to think of home

lècǐ bùpí 樂此不疲 to delight in a thing and never get tired of it

lè'ér wàngfǎn 樂而忘返 to be a slave of pleasure

lèguān 樂觀 optimistic

lèjí shēngbēi 樂極生悲 Happiness is followed by sorrow when it reaches an extreme.

lèjuān 樂捐 to donate voluntarily

lèqù 樂趣 delight; pleasure; joy; fun

lèshàn hàoshī 樂善好施 willing to do good and give help to the poor; charitable

lèshì 樂事 a pleasant thing or matter

lètáotáo 樂陶陶 cheerful; happy; joyful

lètiān zhīmìng 樂天知命 to be content with what one is; happy-go-lucky

lètǔ 樂土 a land of no comfort; a paradise

lèyè 樂業 to like one's job or trade

lèyǐ wàngyōu 樂以忘憂 to seek pleasure in order to free oneself from care

lèyì 樂意 1. willing 2. pleased

lèyú 樂於 to like or love (doing something)

lèyuán 樂園 a paradise; Elysium

lèzi 樂子 joy; fun

le 了

an expletive in the Chinese language

léi 勒

to tighten

léisǐ 勒死 to strangle; to throttle

léi 累

1. a nuisance 2. to fasten; to bind

léizhui 累贅 1. a nuisance; a burden; a troublesome thing 2. wordy; verbose

léi 雷

1. thunder 2. a mine (an explosive)

léidá 雷達 a radar

léidiàn 雷電 lightning and thunder

léidiàn jiāojiā 雷電交加 It's thundering and lightening.

léigōng 雷公 the thunder god

léilì fēngxíng 雷厲風行 to enforce a law or rule with speed and great determination

léimíng 雷鳴 1. roars of thunder; thunderpeal 2. very loud sounds; thunderous

léishè 雷射 a laser

léishè chàngjī 雷射唱機 a compact disc player

léishè chàngpiàn 雷射唱片 a compact disc (CD)

léishè yìnbiǎojī 雷射印表機 a laser printer

léishēng 雷聲 a thunderclap; thunder

léishēng dà, yǔdiǎn xiǎo 雷聲大，雨點小 to talk a great deal about something with little or no follow-up action

léitíng wànjūn 雷霆萬鈞 overwhelming or overpowering (power, strength, etc.)

léitóng 雷同 similar; identical; exactly the same

léiyǔ 雷雨 a thunderstorm

léizhènyǔ 雷陣雨 a thundershower

léi 擂

1. to grind; to pestle 2. refer to **lèi** 擂 2

léi 贏

1. lean; emaciated 2. weak; feeble 3. to entangle; to bind

léiruò 羸弱 emaciated and weak

léi 纍
1. strung together 2. a heavy rope 3. to tie; to bind; to twine around; to wind round

léiléi 纍纍 1. strung together 2. tired; exhausted 3. despondent

lěi 累
1. to accumulate through a length of time 2. to pile up 3. to repeat; repeatedly; successively 4. (also **lèi**) to involve; involvement; to implicate

lěicì 累次 repeatedly; many times

lěidài 累代 generation after generation

lěifàn 累犯 1. to offend or violate the law repeatedly 2. a recidivist

lěijī 累積 to accumulate; to pile up

lěijí tārén 累及他人 to involve or implicate others

lěijí wúgū 累及無辜 to involve the innocent

lěijì 累計 to include previous figures in the calculation

lěijiā 累加 to acculate; to increase

lěilěi 累累 1. repeatedly; successively 2. piling up 3. countless

lěi 磊
1. a heap of stones 2. great; massive

lěiluò 磊落 1. a lot of 2. openhearted; candid

lěi 蕾
a flower bud; an unopened flower

lěi 儡
1. a puppet 2. sickly and thin 3. dilapidated

lěi 壘
1. a military wall; a rampart 2. to pile up 3. a base

lěiqiú 壘球 softball

lèi 肋 also **lè**
the ribs; the sides

lèigǔ 肋骨 the ribs

lèi 累
1. refer to **lěi** 累 4 2. to owe; to be in debt 3. tired; weary; fatigue 4. (said of eyes) to strain 5. a family burden

lèibìng 累病 to become sick owing to hard work

lèidǎo 累倒 to become sick owing to hard work

lèihuài 累壞 to become ill as a result of backbreaking toil

lèirén 累人 to wear down; to be tiring

lèi 淚
tears

lèidī 淚滴 teardrops

lèihén 淚痕 traces of tears

lèirú quányǒng 淚如泉湧 tears welling up like a fountain

lèirú yǔxià 淚如雨下 The tears come down like rain

lèiwāngwāng 淚汪汪 tearful; brimming with tears

lèiyǎn 淚眼 teary eyes

lèizhū 淚珠 teardrops

lèi 擂
1. a ring for martial contests 2. (also **léi**) to beat; to hit

lèigǔ 擂鼓 to beat a drum

lèitái 擂臺 a platform for contests in martial arts; an arena

lèi 類
1. a species; a kind; a class; a race; a group; a category 2. similar; alike 3. (now rarely) good; virtue 4. a kind of wildcat 5. (now rarely) biased; prejudiced

lèibǐ 類比 (logic) analogy

lèibié 類別 classification; categorization

lèisì 類似 to resemble; similar to; like

lèituī 類推 to reason by analogy; to draw analogies

lèixíng 類型 a type; a category

léng 稜(棱)
1. a corner; an angle; an edge 2. a square piece of wood 3. an awe-inspiring air

léngjiǎo 稜角 1. an angle; a cor-

ner 2. pointedness

lěng 冷

1. cold 2. (said of business, farming, etc.) off- season

lěngbǎndèng 冷板凳 1. a post which has little or no authority 2. a cold reception

lěngbīngbīng 冷冰冰 icy cold; cold as ice

lěngbufáng 冷不防 unexpectedly

lěngcáng 冷藏 to preserve by means of refrigeration

lěngchǎng 冷場 temporary suspension of a show, party, etc. occasioned by inefficient management

lěngcháo rèfěng 冷嘲熱諷 sarcasm and mockery

lěngdàn 冷淡 cold (expressions); indifferent (attitudes)

lěngdòng 冷凍 freezing

lěngdòngkù 冷凍庫 a freezer

lěngdòng shípǐn 冷凍食品 frozen foods

lěngfēng 冷鋒 a cold front

lěnghàn 冷汗 1. a cold sweat 2. clammy perspiration

lěngjiàn 冷箭 an unexpected attack or a pot shot

lěngjìng 冷靜 calm or composed

lěngkù 冷酷 merciless; heartless

lěngluò 冷落 1. cold and lonely 2. cold reception; to cold-shoulder

lěngmén 冷門 not popular or not in great demand

lěngmiàn 冷麵 cold noodles

lěngmò 冷漠 indifferent; apathetic

lěngnuǎn 冷暖 the degree of cold or heat

lěngnuǎn zìzhī 冷暖自知 One knows what it's like without being told.

lěngpán 冷盤 a dish of assorted cold meats

lěngpì 冷僻 1. out-of-the-way or secluded (places) 2. big or hard (words)

lěngqì 冷氣 1. air conditioning 2. cold air

lěngqìjī 冷氣機 an airconditioner

lěngqìtuán 冷氣團 a cold air mass

lěngqīng 冷清 desolate; lonely; deserted

lěngquè 冷卻 to get cold; to cool off

lěngquèjì 冷卻劑 a coolant

lěngruò bīngshuāng 冷若冰霜 as cold as an iceberg—aloof

lěngshuāng 冷霜 cold cream

lěngshuǐ 冷水 cold water; unboiled water

lěngsōusōu 冷颼颼 frosty; chilly

lěngxiào 冷笑 a sarcastic smile or grin; to sneer

lěngxiě dòngwù 冷血動物 refer to lěngxuě dòngwù 冷血動物

lěngxuě dòngwù 冷血動物 1. cold-blooded animals 2. a heartless or ruthless person

lěngyán lěngyǔ 冷言冷語 sarcastic remarks

lěngyǎn pángguān 冷眼旁觀 1. to look on coldly 2. to look on with a critical eye

lěngyǐn 冷飲 cold drinks

lěngzhàn 冷戰 cold war

lèng 愣(楞)

1. dumbfounded 2. reckless; rash; irresponsible; rude 3. outspoken

lèngtóu lèngnǎo 愣頭愣腦 1. rash; reckless 2. stupid; in a stupor

lèngxiǎozi 愣小子 a little fool; a rash young fellow

lèngzhù 愣住 to be taken aback

lī 哩

to speak indistinctly

līliluōluō 哩哩囉囉 verbose and unclear in speech

lí 狸

1. a fox 2. a racoon dog

límāo 狸貓 a kind of wild cat

lí 犁

1. to till; to plough 2. a plough

lítián 犁田 to plough (or plow) a field

lí 梨
1. a pear 2. Chinese opera

líshù 梨樹 the pear tree

líwō 梨渦 dimples

líyuán 梨園 the operatic circle

líyuán zǐdì 梨園子弟 operatic players

lí 璃
glass; a glassy substance

lí 犛
1. a black ox 2. a yak

líniú 犛牛 a yak

lí 黎
1. many; numerous 2. black; dark 3. a Chinese family name

Líbā'nèn 黎巴嫩 Lebanon

límíng 黎明 dawn; daybreak

lí 罹
1. sorrow; grief 2. to meet (disaster, misfortune, etc.); to be stricken by

lí'nàn 罹難 to fall victim to a disaster

lí 釐
1. a unit of linear measure equal to one thousandth of the Chinese foot 2. a unit of weight equal to one thousandth of the tael 3. to manage; to administer; to arrange 4. to revise; to reform; to correct 5. a widow

lídìng 釐定 to formulate (rules, etc.)

límǐ 釐米 centimeter

lí 離
1. to leave; to depart; to separate; separation 2. to defy; to go against 3. distant from; apart from 4. to run into; to meet with 5. (said of light) bright

líbié 離別 to say good-bye; to leave; to separate

líchóu 離愁 parting sorrow or grief; sadness at separation

líhūn 離婚 to divorce; a divorce

líjiā 離家 to leave home; to be away from home; to depart from home

líjiàn 離間 to drive a wedge between; to alienate (allies, etc.); to saw discord

líjīng pàndào 離經叛道 to rebel against orthodox teachings

líjìng 離境 to leave a country or place

líkāi 離開 to separate from; to leave; to depart; to keep away from

lípǔ 離譜 too far away from what is normal or acceptable

líqí 離奇 odd; fantastic; strange

líqì 離棄 to abandon; to desert

líqù 離去 to leave; to go away; to depart

líqún suǒjū 離群索居 to leave one's friends and live alone

lísàn 離散 separated and scattered; dispersed

lítí 離題 to depart from the topic

líxí 離席 to leave or withdraw a dinner party, conference, etc.

líxiāng bèijǐng 離鄉背井 to travel to a distant land; to stay far away from home

líyì 離異 to separate; to divorce

lízhí 離職 1. to leave or resign from one's office 2. to retire from one's office

lí 黧
dark yellow; sallow

líhēi 黧黑 (said of a complexion) dark

lí 蠡
1. a calabash 2. a calabash shell serving as a dipper; a dipper

lícè 蠡測 to be very naive (like one trying to measure the ocean with a calabash)

lí 籬
a bamboo fence; a hedge

líba 籬笆 a bamboo fence

lí 驪
1. a black horse 2. to drive a carriage drawn by two horses

lígē 驪歌 a song of farewell

lǐ 里
1. a neighborhood, or community, of 25 families (in ancient times); a neighborhood 2. a unit

of linear measure about one third of a mile

lǐchéng 里程 1. mileage 2. the course of development; course

lǐchéngbēi 里程碑 a milestone; a milepost

lǐxiàng 里巷 streets

lǐxiàng zhītán 里巷之談 idle talk in the street; gossip

lǐzhǎng 里長 the head of a subdivision of the district, or borough, in a city or county

lǐ 李

1. plums 2. (now rarely) a judge; a justice 3. a Chinese family name

lǐdài táojiāng 李代桃僵 to substitute this for that

lǐshù 李樹 the plum tree

lǐxià zhīxián 李下之嫌 a position that invites suspicion

lǐzi 李子 plums

lǐ 俚

1. vulgar; rustic; unpolished; unrefined 2. a small town or village; a tribe (aborigines, etc.)

lǐgē 俚歌 folk songs; country songs

lǐsú 俚俗 vulgar; unrefined

lǐyǔ 俚語 slang; rustic expressions

lǐ 哩

a mile

lǐ 浬

(a unit of distance used chiefly in navigation) a nautical mile; a geographic mile; a sea mile

lǐ 理

1. reason; logic; cause; truth; right 2. law; principles; doctrine; theory; science 3. to arrange 4. to govern; to operate; to regulate; to manage; to run 5. to reply or answer; to respond 6. texture; grain (in wood, skin, etc.) 7. name of a religious sect

lǐcái 理財 to manage finances

lǐcǎi 理睬 to pay attention to; to heed

lǐdāng 理當 ought to; to be obliged to

lǐfǎ 理髮 refer to lǐfǎ 理髮

lǐfǎdiàn 理髮店 refer to lǐfǎdiàn 理髮店

lǐfàshī 理髮師 refer to lǐfàshī 理髮師

lǐfàtīng 理髮廳 refer to lǐfàtīng 理髮廳

lǐfǎ 理髮 to cut the hair; to have a haircut

lǐfàdiàn 理髮店 a barbershop

lǐfàshī 理髮師 a barber; a hairdresser

lǐfàtīng 理髮廳 a barbershop

lǐgōngkē 理工科 departments of natural sciences and engineering in a college

lǐhuì 理會 1. to understand; to comprehend 2. to heed; to pay attention to

lǐjiě 理解 to comprehend; to understand

lǐjiělì 理解力 understanding; perception

lǐkuī 理虧 to be on the wrong side

lǐlùn 理論 1. theory 2. to argue

lǐniàn 理念 a rational concept; an idea

lǐpéi 理賠 (insurance) adjustment

lǐqū 理屈 to be on the wrong side

lǐshìhuì 理事會 the board of directors

lǐshìzhǎng 理事長 the board chairman

lǐsuǒ dāngrán 理所當然 as a matter of course; naturally

lǐxiǎng 理想 1. ideal 2. ideas; thought

lǐxìng 理性 (philosophy) reason; rationality

lǐyīng 理應 duty-bound to; ought to

lǐyóu 理由 reasons; grounds

lǐyù 理喻 to appeal with reason

lǐzhí qìzhuàng 理直氣壯 with confidence for one knows that he is in the right

lǐzhì 理智 intellect; reason

lǐ 裡(裏)

1. within; inside 2. used to indicate time of day, night, a season,

etc. 3. the lining of a dress or clothes

lǐlǐwàiwài 裡裡外外 inside and outside

lǐmiàn 裡面 inside; within

lǐtou 裡頭 inside

lǐyìng wàihé 裡應外合 the joining of forces within and without

lǐzi 裡子 the lining of a garment, a hat or shoes

lǐ 禮

1. courtesy; propriety; decorum; politeness; civility; etiquette 2. rites; ceremony 3. a gift; a present

lǐbài 禮拜 1. church service; worship 2. a week

lǐbàitáng 禮拜堂 a chapel; a church

lǐbàitiān 禮拜天 Sunday

lǐchéng 禮成 Ceremony is over.

lǐdān 禮單 a list of presents

lǐfú 禮服 ceremonial dress

lǐjiào 禮教 ethical education

lǐjié 禮節 etiquette

lǐjīn 禮金 a cash gift

lǐmào 禮帽 a ceremonial hat or cap

lǐmào 禮貌 etiquette; politeness; civility

lǐpào 禮砲 a gun salute; a salvo

lǐpǐn 禮品 a gift; a present

lǐpìn 禮聘 to cordially invite the service of

lǐquàn 禮券 gift coupons sold by a shop, which the recipient can convert into goods (or cash) at the shop in question

lǐràng 禮讓 to make way humbly or modestly

lǐshàng wǎnglái 禮尚往來 Courtesy emphasizes reciprocity.

lǐsú 禮俗 manners and custom

lǐtáng 禮堂 1. an auditorium 2. a hall decorated for a wedding ceremony or funeral service

lǐwù 禮物 a gift; a present

lǐyí 禮儀 etiquette; protocol; decorum

lǐyù 禮遇 to treat with courtesy

lǐzàn 禮讚 to adore; to glorify

lǐ 鯉

1. a carp 2. letters; epistles

lǐyú 鯉魚 a carp

lǐyú tiào lóngmén 鯉魚跳龍門 to succeed in the civil service examination in former times

lì 力

1. strength; force; power; ability; vigor 2. vigorously; earnestly 3. to do one's best

lìbù cóngxīn 力不從心 to have too little power to do as much as one wishes

lìdà wúbǐ 力大無比 without a match in physical prowess

lìjiàn 力薦 to recommend (someone) strongly

lìliang 力量 strength; force; power

lìpái zhòngyì 力排眾議 to refute the consensus

lìqi 力氣 1. physical strength or power 2. an effort

lìqiú 力求 to do one's best to; to strive to

lìtú 力圖 to try hard; to strive to

lìwǎn kuánglán 力挽狂瀾 (figuratively) to do one's best to reverse the course of events

lìxíng 力行 to practice or perform energetically

lìzhēng 力爭 to struggle hard

lìzhēng shàngyóu 力爭上游 to try to excel by strenuous efforts

lì 立

1. to stand 2. to establish; to found; to build; to erect; to create; to start 3. to stand on one's own feet; to live 4. immediately; at once

lì'àn 立案 to accredit (a school, etc.)

lìbēi 立碑 to erect a monument

lìchǎng 立場 a position; a stand; an attitude

lìdìng 立定 (word of command) Halt!

lìfǎ 立法 to legislate; to make laws

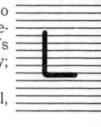

lìfǎ jīguān 立法機關 the legislative body

lìfāng 立方 (mathematics) cube

lìgān jiànyǐng 立竿見影 The outcome may be known immediately.

lìjí 立即 at once; immediately; promptly; right away

lìkè 立刻 at once; immediately; promptly; right away

lìshēn chǔshì 立身處世 to establish oneself and manage to get along in the world

lìshì 立誓 to take an oath; to vow; to swear

lìsì 立嗣 to adopt an heir

lìtǐ 立體 1. three-dimensional 2. a solid

lìyè 立業 to establish a business

lìyízhǔ 立遺囑 to make one's will

lìzhèng 立正 to stand at attention

lìzhì 立志 to make up one's mind to pursue some object; to resolve

lìzhuī zhīdì 立錐之地 space just enough for the point of a drill—very small space

lìzú 立足 1. to have a foothold somewhere 2. to base oneself upon

lìzúdiǎn 立足點 a footing; a foothold

lì 吏
a civil officer

lìyuán 吏員 a minor official

lì 利
1. profit; benefit; advantage; gain 2. sharp 3. to benefit; to serve

Lìbǐyà 利比亞 Libya

lìbì 利弊 advantages and disadvantages

lìhài 利害 interest and disinterest

lìlìng zhìhūn 利令智昏 blinded or dulled by greed

lìlǜ 利率 the interest rate

lìlù 利祿 wealth and position

lìniào 利尿 diuresis

lìrùn 利潤 profit; gain; net profit

lìshì bǎibèi 利市百倍 to make an enormous profit

lìxī 利息 interest

lìxī 利息 refer to **lìxī** 利息

lìyì 利益 benefit; profit; advantage

lìyì jūnzhān 利益均霑 to let everybody have his hands on the pie

lìyòng 利用 to utilize; to make use of

lìyòu 利誘 to tempt with money or material gain

lìyù xūnxīn 利慾薰心 lured by profits; blinded or dulled by greed

lì 例
1. a regulation; a rule; a custom 2. a precedent 3. an example; an instance 4. regular; routine

lìjiǎ 例假 a statutory holiday; a customary holiday; a legal holiday

lìjù 例句 a sentence serving as an example

lìrú 例如 for example; for instance; such as

lìtí 例題 an example; an instance

lìwài 例外 an exception

lìxíng gōngshì 例行公事 official routine; routine

lìzhèng 例證 an antecedent used to clarify or explain a point

lìzi 例子 an example; an instance

lì 俐
1. facile; easy and quick 2. sharp; clever 3. in good order; tidy; neat

lìluo 俐落 well-executed

lì 栗
1. a chestnut tree 2. strong and firm; tough; durable 3. respectful; fearful; awe-inspiring 4. to tremble 5. majestic; dignified 6. a Chinese family name

lìsè 栗色 chestnut color; maroon

lìshǔ 栗鼠 a squirrel

lìzi 栗子 a chestnut

lì 荔
a lichee

lìzhī 荔枝 a lichee

lì 鬲
a kind of caldron

lì 笠
1. a bamboo hat 2. a bamboo shade or covering

lì 唳
the cry of a crane, wild goose, etc.

lì 粒
1. a grain (of rice, etc.) 2. to get grain to eat 3. a pill; a bead

lì 莉
white jasmine

lì 痢
dysentery; diarrhea

lìji 痢疾 dysentery; diarrhea

lì 涖
to arrive

lìlín 涖臨 to be present; to arrive

lì 厲
1. a coarse whetstone 2. harsh; violent; severe; stern; serious 3. to persuade; to urge; to encourage 4. bad; evil 5. an epidemic 6. to oppress; oppressive; cruel

lìbīng mòmǎ 厲兵秣馬 to make military preparations

lìguǐ 厲鬼 a fierce ghost; a malicious spirit

lìhai 厲害 1. fierceness; ferociousness 2. very (ill, etc.); serious (damage, destruction, etc.)

lìshēng 厲聲 to talk harshly; to shout angrily

lìxíng 厲行 to enforce

lì 歷
1. to pass; to elapse 2. to undergo; to go through; to experience 3. things or duration that had come to pass 4. all previous (occasions, sessions) 5. through; throughout; successive 6. to last (a certain period of time)

lìchéng 歷程 process; course

lìdài 歷代 successive generations; the dynasties in their successive order

lìjié 歷劫 to experience many mishaps and misfortunes

lìjiè 歷屆 successive (or all) previous

lìjìn jiānnán 歷盡艱難 to have gone through all kinds of hardships and difficulties

lìjīng 歷經 to have experienced, undergone or encountered many times

lìjiǔ bùshuāi 歷久不衰 long-lasting

lìjiǔ míjiān 歷久彌堅 to remain unshakable and become even firmer as time goes by

lìlái 歷來 hitherto; till now; heretofore

lìlǎn 歷覽 to travel and see; to visit

lìlì rúhuì 歷歷如繪 vividly; distinctly

lìlì zàimù 歷歷在目 as if it were taking place right before one's eyes; vividly

lìliàn 歷練 to practice and experience

lìnián 歷年 in the years past

lìrèn 歷任 to have held the following posts

lìshí 歷時 to last (a certain period of time)

lìshǐ 歷史 history

lìshǐjiā 歷史家 a historian

lìxiǎn 歷險 to undergo or experience adventures and dangers

lì 曆
1. a calendar 2. an era; an age 3. to calculate; to count

lìshū 曆書 an almanac

lì 勵
1. to incite; to encourage; to rouse (to action) 2. to exert oneself

lìjīng túzhì 勵精圖治 (said of a government or a national leader) to pursue the task of a national buildup with determination and dedication

lìxíng 勵行 to enforce or practice with determination

lìzhì 勵志 to pursue a goal with determination

lì 隸

1. to be subordinate to; inferior; to belong or attach to 2. slaves; servants; underlings 3. a type of Chinese calligraphy

lìshū 隸書 clerical-style characters

lìshǔ 隸屬 to be attached to

lì 瀝

1. to fall down by drops; to drip; to trickle 2. remaining drops of wine 3. to strain water or liquids

lìqīng 瀝青 1. asphalt; pitch 2. another name of resin

lì 麗

1. beautiful; elegant; fine; magnificent 2. to hang 3. (儷) dual; double

lìrén 麗人 a beauty; a belle; a beautiful woman

lìzhí 麗質 refer to **lìzhì** 麗質

lìzhì 麗質 beauty (especially feminine)

lì 礪

1. a whetstone 2. to sharpen (a knife)

lì 礫

gravel; a pebble; shingle

lìshí 礫石 gravel; a pebble; shingle

lì 儷

1. a pair; a couple 2. husband and wife; a married couple

lìyǐng 儷影 the heart-warming sight of a couple in love

li 哩

a sentence particle which cannot be used in the interrogative sentence

li 裡(裏)

a nominal suffix used to indicate location, time, domain, etc.

liǎ 倆

two; a pair; a couple

liǎkǒuzi 倆口子 husband and wife

lián 帘

1. a flag sign of a winehouse or tavern 2. a door or window screen

liánzi 帘子 a screen for a door or a window

lián 連

1. to connect; to join; to unite 2. in succession 3. a company (of soldiers) 4. together with 5. even; and; including 6. a Chinese family name

liánchuàn 連串 to string together; a string (of events, etc.); a series of

liándài 連帶 joint (responsibility, obligation, etc.)

liánguàn 連貫 1. to link up; to piece together; to hang together 2. coherent

liánhuán túhuà 連環圖畫 comics; a comic strip

liánjiē 連接 1.continuously 2.to adjoin

liánlèi 連累 to involve; to get someone into trouble

liánlěi 連累 refer to **liánlèi** 連累

liánlǐ 連理 1. trees whose branches interlock or join together 2. a couple very much in love

liánlián 連連 1. continuously; unceasingly; again and again 2. one after another

liánluò 連絡 liaison; to make contact with

liánmáng 連忙 promptly; quickly; immediately; at once

liánmián bùjué 連綿不絕 in endless succession; continuously

liánrèn 連任 to continue in one's office for another term; to be reappointed or reelected

liánrì 連日 for consecutive days

liánshǒu 連手 1. to take concerted action 2. (gambling) to gang up on cheating

liánshǔ 連署 to sign jointly; joint signatures

liánsuǒdiàn 連鎖店 a chain store

liántiān 連天 1. to stab deep into the sky 2. incessantly; continuously 3. to shake the sky 4. for several days in a row 5. to merge with the sky

liántóng 連同 together with; in addition to; along with

liánxì 連繫 to keep in contact; contact

liánxīn 連心 the meeting of minds; bosom (friends)

liánxù 連續 successive; continuous; incessantly

liánxùjù 連續劇 (television) a soap opera; a drama series

liányè 連夜 all through the night

liánzǎi 連載 to publish serially in a newspaper or magazine

liánzhàn jiējié 連戰皆捷 to win one victory after another

liánzhǎng 連長 a company commander

liánzhūpào 連珠炮 1. a rapid-fire gun 2. continuous firing; drumfire

lián 廉

1. incorrupt; upright 2. inexpensive; cheap 3. to examine; to inspect

liánchá 廉察 to inspect; to investigate

liánchǐ 廉恥 the integrity of character and a sense of honor

liánjià 廉價 a low price

liánjiàpǐn 廉價品 a bargain; cheap goods

liánjié 廉潔 incorrupt; incorruptible

liánlì 廉吏 an incorrupt official

liánmíng 廉明 incorruptible and intelligent

liánràng 廉讓 to sell (property) at a low price

liánshòu 廉售 to sell at a low price

lián 漣

1. ripples 2. weeping

liányī 漣漪 ripples

lián 蓮

1. the lotus, or water lily 2. the clean land—Buddhist Paradise

liánhuā 蓮花 lotus blossoms or water lilies

lián'ǒu 蓮藕 the lotus root

liánpeng 蓮蓬 the cupule of a lotus

liánpengtóu 蓮蓬頭 a finely perforated nozzle for a shower bath

liánwù 蓮霧 the wax apple

lián 憐(怜)

1. to sympathize; to pity 2. to feel tender regard for 3.touching

lián'ài 憐愛 to feel pity and love for

liánmǐn 憐憫 to pity; to take compassion on; to commiserate

liánxī 憐惜 to feel tender regard for

liánxí 憐惜 refer to **liánxī** 憐惜

liánxiāng xíyù 憐香惜玉 to have a tender heart for the fair sex

liánxiāng xíyù 憐香惜玉 refer to **liánxiāng xíyù** 憐香惜玉

lián 聯

1. to unite; to ally; to connect; to join; to make an alliance with 2. allied (forces, etc.); joint (effort, etc.); mutual (guaranties, etc.) 3. a couplet

liánbāng 聯邦 a federal union; a federal state

liánbō 聯播 a radio hookup

liánguàn 聯貫 to link or string together; connection

liánhé 聯合 to unite; to form an alliance of some kind; joint (effort, etc.)

Liánhéguó 聯合國 United Nations

liánhé shēngmíng 聯合聲明 a joint statement or declaration

liánhuānhuì 聯歡會 a get-together; a social gathering; a gay party

liánjié 聯結 to join together or gang up

liánjūn 聯軍 allied forces

liánluò 聯絡 to communicate with; to contact

liánméng 聯盟 an alliance; a union; to form an alliance, etc.

liánmíng 聯名 to sign together

liánshǒu 聯手 to join hands (with someone); to gang up

liánshǔ 聯署 to sign jointly

liánxì 聯繫 1. to unite; to link; to relate 2. to get in touch with

liánxiǎng 聯想 association of ideas; to associate

liányí huódòng 聯誼活動 refer to **liányì huódòng** 聯誼活動

liányì huódòng 聯誼活動 activities for promoting fellowship

liányīn 聯姻 connections through marriage

liányíng 聯營 (said of two or more business setups) joint operation; a pool

lián 簾
1. a loose hanging screen for a door or window, usually made of stringed beads, bamboo slabs, etc.; blinds; a curtain 2. a flag as a shop sign

lián 鐮
a sickle

liándāo 鐮刀 a sickle

liǎn 臉
the face (used both in its physical and figurative senses)

liǎndànr 臉蛋兒 the shape of a woman's face

liǎnhóng 臉紅 a blush; to blush

liǎnjiá 臉頰 cheeks

liǎnkǒng 臉孔 the face

liǎnpén 臉盆 a washing basin

liǎnpíhòu 臉皮厚 shameless; brazen

liǎnsè 臉色 1. facial expression 2. a complexion

liǎn 斂(歛) also **liàn**
1. to draw together; to contract 2. to hold back; to restrain 3. to collect; to gather

liǎncái 斂財 to collect wealth illegally or immorally

lián 煉
1. to smelt; to refine; to condense (milk); to temper (a metal) with fire 2. (Chinese medicine) to keep herbs, etc. boiling for a long time 3. to train; to form

character by hardship

liàn'gāng 煉鋼 to refine steel; steelmaking

liàn'gāngchǎng 煉鋼廠 a steel refinery; a steel mill

liànrǔ 煉乳 condensed milk

liànyóu 煉油 1. oil refining 2. to extract oil by heat 3. to heat edible oil

liànyóuchǎng 煉油廠 an oil refinery

liànyù 煉獄 the purgatory

liànzhì 煉製 to refine

liàn 練
1. to practice; to train; to exercise 2. skilled; experienced 3. to soften and whiten raw silk by boiling

liàndá 練達 experienced; sophisticated

liànxí 練習 1. to train; to practice (so as to gain skill) 2. exercises

liànxíshēng 練習生 a trainee; an apprentice

liàn 鍊
1. to smelt; to refine; to forge; to temper 2. to polish 3. a chain

liàndān 鍊丹 to make pills of wonder; to practice alchemy

liàn'gāng 鍊鋼 to refine steel

liànzi 鍊子 a chain

liàn 斂(歛)
refer to **liǎn** 斂

liàn 殮
to prepare a body for the coffin; to encoffin

liànzàng 殮葬 to shroud and bury

liàn 鏈
a chain

liànqiú 鏈球 (sports) 1. a hammer 2. hammer throw

liàn 戀
1. to love (one of the other sex); to be in love 2. to feel a persistent attachment (for a thing)

liàn'ài 戀愛 tender passions; to be in love

L

liànfù qíngjié 戀父情結 Electra complex

liànjiā 戀家 to be reluctant to leave home

liànjiù 戀舊 to yearn for the past

liànmǔ qíngjié 戀母情結 Oedipus complex

liànqíng 戀情 love between man and woman

liànrén 戀人 a sweetheart

liànzhàn 戀棧 reluctant to give up a position (particularly a public post) one is holding

liáng 良

1. good; fine; desirable 2. very 3. instinctive; inborn; innate

liángbàn 良伴 a good companion

liángchén měijǐng 良辰美景 a pleasant day coupled with a fine landscape

liángfāng 良方 1. a good remedy; a good prescription 2. a good course of action

liángjī 良機 a good chance

liángjiā zǐnǔ 良家子女 children of good parentage

liángjiǔ 良久 for a very long time

liángrén 良人 1. a good person 2. one's husband

liángshī yìyǒu 良師益友 good teachers and helpful friends

liángxīn 良心 conscience

liángyào kǔkǒu 良藥苦口 Good advice is never pleasant to the ear.

liángyǒu bùqí 良莠不齊 some good, some bad

liángyǒu bùqí 良莠不齊 refer to **liángyǒu bùqí** 良莠不齊

liángyuán 良緣 a harmonious union

liáng 涼

1. cool; chilly 2. thin 3. discouraged; disappointed 4. name of one of the 16 states during the Eastern Jin

liángbàn 涼拌 (said of food) cold and dressed with sauce

liángfēng 涼風 a cool breeze

liángkuai 涼快 1. cool and comfortable 2. to cool oneself

liángle bànjié 涼了半截 to be greatly disappointed

liángmiàn 涼麵 cold noodles

liángshuǎng 涼爽 cool and comfortable

liángsōusōu 涼颼颼 chilly

liángtái 涼臺 a balcony; a veranda

liángtíng 涼亭 a shed along a highway to provide a place of rest for travelers

liángxí 涼蓆 a sleeping mat (usually made of straw or bamboo) used in summer

liángxié 涼鞋 sandals; summer shoes; slippers

liáng 梁

1. a bridge 2. beams of a house 3. a ridge; a swelling 4. Liang, name of a dynasty (502 to 557 A. D.) 5. a state during the Epoch of Warring States, also known as Wei 6. a Chinese family name

liáng 量

to measure

liángbēi 量杯 a graduated cylinder; a measuring glass or cup

liángduó 量度 to measure; to estimate

liángbuó 量度 refer to **liangduó** 量度

liáng 梁

maize; grain; sorghums

liáng 糧

1. grain; food; provisions; rations 2. farm or land taxes

liángcāng 糧倉 a granary

liánghéng 糧行 a store selling grain and provisions

liángshi 糧食 foodstuffs; provisions

liángxiǎng 糧餉 army provisions and payroll

liǎng 兩

1. two; a pair; a couple 2. both; either 3. a tael (a unit of weight) 4. (in ancient China) a piece of cloth, etc. of about 44 feet

liǎngbài jùshāng 兩敗俱傷 Both are hurt.

liǎngbànr 兩半兒 two halves

liǎngbèi 兩倍 double; twice

liǎngbiān 兩邊 both sides; two sides

liǎngbiān tǎohǎo 兩邊討好 to please both sides

liǎngdǎngzhì 兩黨制 the bipartisan system

liǎnghài xiāngquán qǔqí qīng 兩害相權取其輕 to accept the lesser of two evils

liǎnghǔ xiāngdòu bì yǒu yīshāng 兩虎相鬥必有一傷 When two powers battle, one is going to get hurt.

liǎnghuíshì 兩回事 two entirely different things

liǎngjí 兩極 the opposing poles

liǎngjiǎo shūchú 兩脚書櫥 1. a two-legged bookcase 2. a bookworm

liǎnglì 兩立 to coexist; coexistence

liǎngmiàn 兩面 1. two sides 2. double; dual

liǎngmiàn jiāgōng 兩面夾攻 to make a pincers drive

liǎngmiàn jiágōng 兩面夾攻 refer to **liǎngmiàn jiāgōng** 兩面夾攻

liǎngmiàn zuòzhàn 兩面作戰 to fight on two fronts

liǎngnán 兩難 indecisive

liǎngpáng 兩旁 bothsides; two sides

liǎngqī bùduì 兩棲部隊 amphibious force

liǎngqī zuòzhàn 兩棲作戰 amphibious operations

liǎngqì 兩訖 (said of a purchase) paid and delivered; (said of an account) both sides clear

liǎngqīng 兩清 (said of a purchase) paid and delivered; (said of an account) both sides clear

liǎngqíng qiánquǎn 兩情繾綣 deeply in love with each other

liǎngquán 兩全 to be satisfactory to both parties

liǎngquán qíměi 兩全其美 to profit both parties or attain two objectives by a single act

liǎngtóu 兩頭 both ends; either end

liǎngxiānghǎo 兩相好 two lovers

liǎngxiāng qíngyuàn 兩相情願 Both parties are willing.

liǎngxiǎo wúcāi 兩小無猜 living and playing together in childhood innocence

liǎngxìng 兩性 1. both sexes 2. amphoteric

liǎngxiù qīngfēng 兩袖清風 (usually said of an honest public servant) to attain high official ranks without money in the bank

liǎngyì 兩翼 (a military term) two flanks or wings

liǎngyòng 兩用 1. serving two purposes 2. (said of a coat) reversible

liǎngyuànzhì 兩院制 the bicameral system (of a parliament)

liǎng 倆
craft; ability

liàng 亮
1. bright; lustrous; brilliant; luminous; radiant; clear 2. to display; to show

liàngdù 亮度 brightness; luminosity

liàngguāng 亮光 bright light; flash

liàngjīngjīng 亮晶晶 dazzling; glistening; radiant

liàngxiàng 亮相 to pose for the audience's admiration on the stage

liàng 晾
1. to dry in the air; to air; to hang in the wind to dry 2. to dry in the sun

liànggān 晾乾 to dry in the air

liàngyīfu 晾衣服 to hang clothes in the wind to dry

liàngyīshéng 晾衣繩 a clothesline

liàng 量

1. quantity 2. capacity 3. to estimate

liàngcí 量詞 a classifier

liànglì érwéi 量力而為 to estimate one's resources or strength before acting

liàngrù wéichū 量入為出 to regulate one's expenses according to one's income

liàng 輛
a numeracy adjunct for vehicles

liàng 諒
1. honest; sincere 2. to forgive; to excuse 3. to guess; to infer 4. stubborn

liàngjiě 諒解 to forgive; to be understanding

liāo 撩
1. to raise; to hold up 2. to sprinkle

liáo 聊
1. somehow; somewhat; a little 2. to rely; to depend 3. to chat; a chat 4. interest 5. for the time being

liáoshèng yīchóu 聊勝一籌 to surpass only a little bit

liáoshèng yúwú 聊勝於無 It's better than nothing.

liáotiānr 聊天兒 to chat; a chat

liáoyǐ zìwèi 聊以自慰 just to console oneself

liáo 寥
1. few; sparse 2. deserted; desolate; empty

liáoliáo wújǐ 寥寥無幾 few; not many

liáo 僚
1. a companion; a friend 2. a colleague; subordinates 3. officials

liáo 撩
1. to provoke; to excite; to stir up; to tease; to tantalize 2. disorderly; confused

liáobō 撩撥 to provoke; to entice

liáodòng gānhuǒ 撩動肝火 to stir up anger

liáoluàn 撩亂 confused; disorderly

liáorén 撩人 to make one excited

liáo 潦
refer to **liǎo** 潦

liáo 獠
1. (said of one's looks) fierce 2. nocturnal hunting 3. a monster; a wicked person

liáo 嘹
(said of voice) resonant

liáoliàng 嘹亮 loud and clear; resonant

liáo 遼
1. distant; far 2. the Liao River in Manchuria 3. the Liao Dynasty (916-1125) founded by the Kitan Tartars in the greater part of northern China

liáokuò 遼闊 vast; distant

liáo 燎 also **liǎo, liāo**
1. to burn over a wider and wider area; to set fire to 2. to be brilliant

liáoyuán 燎原 to set the prairie ablaze

liáo 療
to treat (a disease); to relieve; to heal

liáofǎ 療法 a cure; a therapy

liáoxiào 療效 curative effect

liáoyǎng 療養 to recuperate; to convalesce

liáoyǎngyuàn 療養院 a sanatorium; a sanitarium

liáozhì 療治 to treat (a disease)

liáo 繚
to wind round

liáoluàn 繚亂 intricate; tangled; disorderly; confused

liáorào 繚繞 winding round and round

liáorǎo 繚繞 refer to **liáorǎo** 繚繞

liǎo 鐐
refer to **liào** 鐐

liǎo 了
1. to finish; to end; to complete 2. intelligent; remarkable 3.

entirely; wholly 4. to understand

liǎo'àn 了案 to conclude a case

liǎobude 了不得 Wonderful! Excellent!

liǎobuqǐ 了不起 Wonderful!

liǎocǐ cánshēng 了此残生 to end this miserable life

liǎoduàn 了断 1. to settle (a case) 2. to commit suicide

liǎojié 了結 to get through with; to bring to conclusion

liǎojiě 了解 to understand

liǎojú 了局 the end; the conclusion

liǎorán 了然 to understand clearly

liǎoshì 了事 to finish up a matter

liǎowù 了悟 to comprehend

liǎo 潦 also **liáo**

1. disheartened; disappointed 2. without care

liǎocǎo 潦草 1. perfunctory 2. (said of handwriting) hasty and careless; illegible

liǎodǎo 潦倒 disappointed ; down in luck

liǎo 燎 refer to **liáo** 燎

liǎo 瞭

1. to understand 2. clear and bright

liǎojiě 瞭解 to comprehend; to understand

liǎorán 瞭然 clear and evident; plain and fully understandable

liǎorú zhǐzhǎng 瞭如指掌 to know thoroughly

liào 料

1. to conjecture; to reckon; to estimate 2. to infer; to anticipate; to foresee 3. to consider; to calculate 4. to manage; to handle; to care 5. material; stuff; makings

liàodào 料到 to foresee; to expect

liàolǐ 料理 1.to manage; to dispose of 2. a dish

liàoshì rúshén 料事如神 to

foresee with divine accuracy

liàoxiǎng 料想 to reckon; to imagine; to expect; to presume

liàozhòng 料中 to guess correctly

liàozi 料子 cloth; fabric; material

Liào 廖 a Chinese family name

liào 燎 refer to **liáo** 燎

liào 瞭 to look down from a higher place

liàowàng 瞭望 to look down from a higher place

liàowàngtái 瞭望臺 a watchtower; a lookout (post)

liào 鐐 also **liáo** shackles; fetters; manacles

liě 咧 also **lié** to babble

liěliě 咧咧 to babble

lié 咧 refer to **liě** 咧

liě 咧 to stretch (the mouth) horizontally

liè 劣 inferior; mean; bad; of low quality

lièděng 劣等 of inferior quality; low-grade

liègēnxìng 劣根性 a depravity

lièshēn 劣紳 evil gentry

lièshì 劣勢 inferior strength or position

lièzhí 劣质 refer to **lièzhí** 劣質

lièzhí 劣質 of poor (or low) quality; inferior

liè 列

1. to arrange in a line; to line up 2. to enumerate 3. to display 4. a line; a series

lièchē 列車 a train

lièchēyuán 列車員 a conductor

lièdǎo 列島 an archipelago

lièjǔ 列舉 to enumerate

lièqiáng 列強 the various powers

lièxí 列席 to be present (at a meeting as an observer)

lièzhuàn 列傳 collected biographies

lièzǔ lièzōng 列祖列宗 an array of ancestors

liè 烈

1. fiery; acute; vehement; fierce; strong; violent 2. honest and virtuous; just and straightforward; chaste 3. merits; achievements

lièhuǒ 烈火 a blazing fire; a fierce fire

lièjiǔ 烈酒 strong drink; a stiff drink

liènǚ 烈女 a girl of virtuous upbringing

lièrì 烈日 the scorching sun

lièrì dāngkōng 烈日當空 the scorching sun high up in the sky

lièshì 烈士 martyrs

lièyàn 烈焰 blazing flames; a violent or fierce fire

liè 裂

1. to crack; to break; a crack 2. to split or divide up (profits, etc.); to rend; to sever

lièfèng 裂縫 a crack; a breach; a crevice

lièhén 裂痕 1. a chasm (in friendship, etc.) 2. a fissure; a split

lièkāi 裂開 to split, rip or break apart

lièkǒu 裂口 a crack; a chink

liè 獵

to hunt; to chase; field sports

lièqiāng 獵槍 a hunting gun; a shotgun

lièqǔ 獵取 to chase after; to hunt

lièquǎn 獵犬 a hunting dog; a hound

lièrén 獵人 a hunter; a huntsman

lièshí 獵食 to hunt for food

lièwù 獵物 game; a quarry

lièyàn 獵艷 to chase after pretty women

lièyīng 獵鷹 a falcon

lièzhuāng 獵裝 hunting dress

lín 林

1. a forest; a grove; a copse 2. a collection of books, works, literary extracts, etc. 3. circles; numerous; many; a great body of (capable persons, etc.) 4. a Chinese family name

línchǎng 林場 1. wooded land; a forest 2. a logging station

líndì 林地 forest land; woodland

línlì 林立 (literally) to stand up like a forest—a great many; a forest of (stacks, derricks, etc.)

línlínzǒngzǒng 林林總總 numerous; multitudinous

línmù 林木 a forest; woods

línqū 林區 a forest zone; a forest region; a forest

línyè 林業 the forestry industry

línyīn dàdào 林蔭大道 an avenue; a boulevard

línzi 林子 a grove; a forest

lín 淋

1. to soak with water; to drip 2. gonorrhea

línbāxiàn 淋巴腺 lymphatic glands

línbìng 淋病 refer to **línbìng** 淋病

línlí jìnzhì 淋漓盡致 (to narrate, describe, argue, etc.) thoroughly; completely

línshī 淋濕 to be soaked, splashed wet

línyǔ 淋雨 to get wet in the rain

línyù 淋浴 a shower; a shower bath

lín 琳

a fine piece of jade; a gem

línláng mǎnmù 琳琅滿目 (literally) Good gems fill the eyes. —a vast array of beautiful and fine things

lín 鄰

1. neighboring; adjoining; contiguous 2. neighborhood; a community 3. a neighbor 4. a basic community unit which consists of a number of families in the same neighborhood

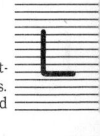

línbāng 鄰邦 a neighboring state or country

línguó 鄰國 a neighboring country

línjìn 鄰近 1. located nearby; located in the vicinity 2. neighborhood

línjū 鄰居 neighbors; people next-door

línlǐ 鄰里 neighborhood; a community

lín 嶙
(said of mountains) rugged

línxún 嶙峋 1. (said of mountain rocks) rugged; craggy 2. (said of a person) upright

lín 霖
a copious rain falling continuously; a continuous heavy rain

línyǔ 霖雨 1. a pouring rain 2. graces; favors; benevolence

lín 遴
to choose or select carefully

línxuǎn 遴選 to choose or pick (a person); to select

lín 臨
1. to look down from above—preside over 2. to approach; to descend; to come to; to reach; to visit 3. on the point of; near to; during; at; whilst; while 4. to copy; to imitate 5. temporary; provisional 6. a Chinese family name

línbié 臨別 at the time of parting; on departure

línchuáng 臨床 clinical

línjǐ yìngbiàn 臨機應變 to make changes or adjustments as the situation demands

línjìn 臨近 close by; close to; close on

línmó 臨摹 to copy or imitate (paintings or calligraphy)

línpén 臨盆 parturition; childbirth

línshí 臨時 for the time being; temporary; provisional

línshí bàofójiǎo 臨時抱佛腳 to do something too late and without preparation

línshígōng 臨時工 a short-term worker

línshí yǎnyuán 臨時演員 an extra

línsǐ 臨死 at one's deathbed; just before dying

línwēi shòumìng 臨危授命 to give a very important assignment in time of a national emergency

línwēi shòumìng 臨危授命 refer to **línwēi shòumìng** 臨危授命

línxíng 臨行 on the point of departure

línzhèn móqiāng 臨陣磨鎗 to make preparations at the last moment

línzhèn tuōtáo 臨陣脫逃 to absent oneself when one's presence counts

línzhōng 臨終 at one's deathbed; just before dying

línzǒu 臨走 on the point of departure

lín 磷
1. phosphorus 2. water flowing between stones

lín 鱗
scales (of fish etc.)

línjiǎ 鱗甲 hard scales (of crocodiles, etc.)

línpiàn 鱗片 1. scales (of fish, etc.) 2. a bud scale

línzhǎo 鱗爪 (literally) scales and claws—minutiae; trifles

lín 麟
the female of a fabulous animal resembling the deer

lín'ér 麟兒 a fine son

línjiǎo 麟角 rare things

lǐn 凜
1. cold; bleak 2. imposing; awe-inspiring

lǐnliè 凜冽 very cold; cold to the marrow

lǐnrán 凜然 a stern, repellent appearance arousing fear, reverence

lìn 吝

stingy; niggardly; parsimonious

lìnsè 吝嗇 stingy; miserly; niggardly

lìnxī 吝惜 to be stingy about

lìnxī 吝惜 refer to **lìnxī** 吝惜

lìn 淋
to filter; to strain

lìnbìng 淋病 gonorrhoea

lìn 賃
1. to rent; to hire 2. a hireling

lìnwū 賃屋 to rent a house

lìnzū 賃租 to rent

līng 拎
to haul; to take; to carry; to lift

líng 令
refer to **lǐng** 令

líng 伶
1. a drama performer; a theatrical performer; an actor; an actress 2. lonely; solitary 3. (伶) clever; intelligent

língdīng 伶仃 lonely; solitary

línglì 伶俐 clever; intelligent; smart

língyá lìchǐ 伶牙俐齒 eloquent

líng 泠
1. clear sounds 2. mild and comfortable 3. (伶) a drama performer; an actor; an actress

língliè 泠冽 clear

línglíng 泠泠 1. gurgling sound 2. cool 3. clear and crisp sound

líng 囹
a prison; a jail

língyǔ 囹圄 a prison; a jail

líng 玲
the tinkling of jade pendants

línglóng 玲瓏 1. pleasing; delicate; cute; fine; regular 2. bright 3. tinkling of jades

línglóng tītòu 玲瓏剔透 1. exquisitely carved 2. (said of a person) very bright

líng 凌 (淩)
1. accumulated ice 2. to insult; to maltreat; to throw one's weight around 3. to rise; to ride; to soar

4. to traverse

língchén 凌晨 the wee hours

língjià 凌駕 to rise above others; to outstrip

língluàn 凌亂 in total disorder

língrǔ 凌辱 1. to insult; to maltreat 2. to assault

líng 陵
1. a high mound 2. the tomb of an emperor; a mausoleum 3. to offend; to insult 4. to usurp 5. to climb; to scale

língmù 陵墓 a tomb; a grave; a mausoleum

língqǐn 陵寢 the tomb of an emperor or king; a mausoleum

língyí 陵夷 to deteriorate; to decay

líng 聆
to listen; to hear

língtīng 聆聽 to listen to

líng 羚
an antelope

líng 菱
a water chestnut

língjiao 菱角 a water chestnut

língxíng 菱形 a rhomb or rhombus; rhombic

líng 鈴
(jingling) bells

língshēng 鈴聲 the tinkle of bells

líng 零
1. zero; nil; nought 2. a fraction; fractional; remainder 3. to flow down 4. a light rain; drizzle

língdīng gūkǔ 零丁孤苦 solitary; lonely

língdù 零度 zero; nought degrees

língfēn 零分 1. (grading examination papers) zero; no marks 2. (sports) scoreless

línggōng 零工 1. odd jobs; short-term hired labor 2. an odd-job man; a casual laborer

língjiàn 零件 component parts; spare parts

língluàn 零亂 disorderly; in confusion; indisorder

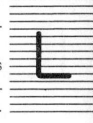

língluò 零落 desolate and scattered; dilapidated; run-down 2. withered and fallen

língmài 零賣 1. retail sales 2. to sell by the piece or in small quantities

língqián 零錢 small change; petty cash; odd change

língsan 零散 scattered

língshí 零食 snacks; refreshments

língshòu 零售 retail sales; to sell by retail

língshòushāng 零售商 a retailer

língsuì 零碎 fragments; fragmentary; fractions

língtóu 零頭 oddments

língxīng 零星 1. fragmented; fractional; not as a whole 2. scattered

língyòng 零用 1. (said of money) for everyday expenses of a nondescript nature 2. pocket money

língyòngqián 零用錢 pocket money

língzuǐ 零嘴 snacks; refreshments

líng 綾

very fine silk cloth; damask silk

língluó 綾羅 silk gauze

líng 齡

age; years

líng 靈

1. the spirit; the soul 2. a fairy; an elf 3. anything pertaining to the deceased 4. wonderful; a wonder 5. mysterious; supernatural; divine 6. clever; nimble; sharp; with quick reflexes 7. good; excellent; efficacious; effective; to work 8. witchcraft

língchē 靈車 a hearse; a funeral carriage

língdān miàoyào 靈丹妙藥 a wonder drug; a panacea

línggǎn 靈感 1. inspiration 2. the faculty of telepathy

línggǔtǎ 靈骨塔 a pagoda-shaped ossuary or ossuarium

línghún 靈魂 the soul; the spirit

línghuó 靈活 energetic, active and clever; quick-witted; quick-minded; flexible; nimble

língjī yīdòng 靈機一動 to have a brainstorm; to have a brain wave

língjiù 靈柩 a bier; a coffin containing a corpse

língméi 靈媒 spirit mediumship

língmǐn 靈敏 adroitness; dexterity; sensitive; clever; skillful; active; acute; nimble

língpái 靈牌 a spirit tablet; an ancestral tablet

língqì 靈氣 (said of beautiful mountains) spiritual influence

língqiǎo 靈巧 1. clever; ingenious; nimble 2. cute; lovable

língtáng 靈堂 a hall where the body of the deceased is placed during the funeral service; a mourning hall

língtōng 靈通 1. (said of news, messages, etc.) to spread fast; to pass with great speed 2. having quick access to information; well-informed

língwèi 靈位 a tablet inscribed with the name of the deceased

língxī yīdiǎntōng 靈犀一點通 a meeting of minds; mental rapport

língxìng 靈性 intelligence, or a natural gift

língxiù 靈秀 refined, elegant and exquisite

língyàn 靈驗 1. (said of a prediction, or prophecy) to come true; with unbelievable accuracy 2. (said of a drug, etc.) with uncanny

língyào 靈藥 panacea

língyì 靈異 strange; mysterious; occult

língzhī 靈芝 Ganoderma lucidum

lǐng 令 also **líng**

a ream (of paper)

lǐng 領

1. the neck 2. the collar; the neckband 3. a piece of clothing 4. to lead; to head; to guide 5. to

receive; to get 6. to understand 7. (now rarely) to manage; to operate

lǐngbān 領班 the leader of a team; a headman; a foreman

lǐngbīng 領兵 1. to lead troops 2. a military officer

lǐngdài 領帶 1. a necktie 2. to lead

lǐngdàijiā 領帶夾 a tie clip

lǐngdàijiá 領帶夾 refer to lǐngdàijiā 領帶夾

lǐngdǎo 領導 1. to lead; leadership 2. a guide

lǐngdǎo yǒufāng 領導有方 to lead correctly; wise leadership

lǐngdì 領地 territory

lǐngduì 領隊 1. the leader of a group or team 2. to lead a group

lǐnghǎi 領海 territorial waters or seas

lǐnghuì 領會 to understand; to appreciate

lǐngjiǎng 領獎 to receive an award or prize

lǐngjiào 領教 1. to be taught; to get instruction 2. (a polite expression) to have received your reply

lǐngjié 領結 the loop of a necktie; a bow tie

lǐngjīn 領巾 a scarf

lǐngkōng 領空 territorial air; an aerial domain

lǐngkǒu 領口 the collar of a garment; the neckband

lǐngkuǎn 領款 to receive funds; to draw money

lǐnglù 領路 to lead the way

lǐnglüè 領略 to understand; to taste; to experience; to appreciate

lǐngqíng 領情 to appreciate favors given; to feel grateful to somebody

lǐngqǔ 領取 to get; receive

lǐngshǎng 領賞 to receive a reward

lǐngshì 領事 (diplomacy) a consul

lǐngshòu 領受 to receive

lǐngtǔ 領土 territory

lǐngwù 領悟 to understand; to comprehend

lǐngxiān 領先 1. to lead; to walk ahead 2. the lead; the first place or position

lǐngxián 領銜 1. the first to sign in a list of signatures 2. to be the first on a name list 3. to play the lead in a film

lǐngxīnshuǐ 領薪水 to receive pay; to get salary

lǐngxiù 領袖 a leader; the leading figure

lǐngyǎng 領養 to adopt (a child)

lǐngyù 領域 1. the territory of a nation; a realm; a domain; a sphere; a field

lǐngzi 領子 the collar or neck of a garment

lǐng 嶺

1. the ridge of a mountain; a mountain range 2. a mountain

Lǐngnán 嶺南 the area south of the Five Ridges (i.e., Guangdong)

lìng 另

1. another; extra; in addition; besides 2. to separate; separation (as of a couple); to divide

lìnghán 另函 a separate letter

lìngqǐ lúzào 另起爐灶 1. to start a new trade or line of business 2. to start all over again

lìngqǐng gāomíng 另請高明 to find someone better qualified (than myself)

lìngwài 另外 besides; in addition

lìngyǎn kàndài 另眼看待 to give favored treatment

lìngyǒu gāojiù 另有高就 to have found better employment elsewhere

lìng 令

1. a directive; an order 2. to order 3. to cause; to make 4. nice; excellent

lìng'ài 令嬡 your daughter

lìngchū rúshān 令出如山 Orders must be obeyed implicitly.

lìngláng 令郎 your son

lìngrén fǎzhǐ 令人髮指 refer

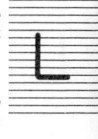

to **lìngrén fàzhǐ** 令人髮指

lìngrén fàzhǐ 令人髮指 to make one's blood boil

lìngrén mǎnyì 令人滿意 to make people contented

lìngtáng 令堂 your mother

lìngzūn 令尊 your father

liū 溜

1. to go secretly and quietly 2. to slip; to slide

liūbīng 溜冰 to skate; skating

liūbīngchǎng 溜冰場 a skating rink

liūbīngxié 溜冰鞋 a pair of skates

liūda 溜達 to stroll; to ramble

liūzhī dàjí 溜之大吉 to leave stealthily; to slip out

liú 流

1. to flow; to discharge 2. to wander; to stray 3. a branch; a division 4. a class; a rank 5. unsettled; unfixed; mobile

liúbì 流弊 long accumulated evil effect; abuses

liúchǎn 流產 1. abortion 2. to prove abortive; to fail to materialize

liúchàng 流暢 (usually said of the style of writing) fluent; smooth

liúchéng 流程 1. technological process 2. (mining) circuits

liúchuán 流傳 to transmit, or be transmitted, from person to person, or from generation to generation; to spread

liúcuàn 流竄 (said of bandits or rebel troops) to roam about

liúdàn 流彈 a stray bullet

liúdòng 流動 1. to be in flowing motion 2. on the move 3. mobile; itinerant

liúdòng hùkǒu 流動戶口 the registered temporary domicile

liúdòngxìng 流動性 mobility; fluidity

liúfāng bǎishì 流芳百世 to hand down a fine reputation through generations

liúfàng 流放 to exile; to banish

liúhàn 流汗 to perspire; to sweat

liúkòu 流寇 wandering bandits

liúlǎn 流覽 1. to take a comprehensive look 2. to skim over

liúlàng 流浪 to wander about; to rove

liúlànghàn 流浪漢 a vagabond; a bum; a drifter

liúlèi 流淚 to shed tears

liúlí shīsuǒ 流離失所 homeless and wandering from place to place

liúlǐtái 流理台 a set of kitchen units including such items as a kitchen sink, a range, etc.

liúlì 流利 fluent

liúlǐliúqì 流里流氣 rascally

liúlián 流連 reluctant to leave; to tarry; to linger on

liúlián wàngfǎn 流連忘返 to forget to go home because of pleasures elsewhere

liúlù 流露 to reveal unknowingly; to manifest

liúluò 流落 to become an outcast in a strange land

liúmáng 流氓 a hoodlum; a hooligan; a villain; a rascal

liúmín 流民 refugees

liúnián 流年 1. years that flow by one after another 2. the change of one's fortune in a given year

liúnián bùlì 流年不利 to have a year of ill luck

liúshā 流沙 1. sediment (in rivers) 2. the quicksand

liúshēng 流生 a school dropout

liúshī 流失 to run off; to be washed away

liúshì 流逝 (said of time) to elapse; to pass; passage

liúshuǐ 流水 flowing water; current

liúshuǐzhàng 流水賬 running account; journal account

liúsū 流蘇 tassels (of flags)

liúsù 流速 current velocity

liútǐ 流體 fluid

liútì 流涕 to shed tears

liútōng 流通 in circulation; to

circulate; to ventilate

liúwáng 流亡 to be exiled; to wander in a strange land

liúxǐ 流徙 to exile; to banish

liúxiànxíng 流線型 streamlined

liúxiě 流血 refer to **liúxuè** 流血

liúxīng 流星 (astronomy) a meteor

liúxíng 流行 1. to be in vogue; fashionable; prevalent 2. (said of a contagious disease) to spread, rage, or be rampant

liúxíngxìng gǎnmào 流行性感冒 influenza; flu

liúxuè 流血 to shed blood; to bleed

liúyán 流言 idle talk; rumor; hearsay

liúyīng 流鶯 a streetwalker

liúyíng 流螢 a firefly

liúyù 流域 drainage basin; drainage area

liúzhí 流質 refer to **liúzhì** 流質

liúzhì 流質 liquid

liú 留

1. to remain; to stay; to be at a standstill 2. to ask somebody to stay 3. to detain; to obstruct; to keep; to delay 4. to leave 5. to preserve; to reserve

liúbù 留步 (Please) do not trouble yourself by accompanying me to the door

liúbuzhù 留不住 unable to detain; unable to make someone stay

liúdài 留待 to wait until

liúdé qīngshān zài, bùchóu méichái shāo 留得青山在,不愁沒柴燒 As long as there is life, there is hope.

liúhòulù 留後路 to leave a way out

liújí 留級 to fail to get promoted to the next grade at school

liúkè 留客 to detain a guest

liúlián 留連 reluctant to leave; unwilling to part with

liúlián wàngfǎn 留連忘返 so enchanted as to forget about

home

liúliàn 留戀 reluctant to leave; unwilling to part with

liúmíng 留名 to leave behind a good reputation

liúqíng 留情 to show mercy; to relent

liúrèn 留任 to stay in a position for another term

liúshén 留神 to pay attention; to be careful

liúshēngjī 留聲機 a phonograph

liúshǒu 留守 (said of troops) to remain stationed at a camp in the rear

liúsù 留宿 to keep (a guest) overnight

liúxià 留下 1. to leave 2. to detain; to stop 3. to remain; to stay 4. to preserve

liúxīn 留心 to pay attention; to take heed

liúxué 留學 to study abroad

liúxuéshēng 留學生 a student studying abroad

liúyán 留言 to leave a message

liúyīshǒu 留一手 to hold back a trick or two

liúyì 留意 to pay attention; to be careful; to be cautious

liúyǐng 留影 to take a photo as a memento

liúyúdì 留餘地 to refrain from going to extremes

liúzhí tíngxīn 留職停薪 leave without pay

liúzhì 留置 to detain; to put aside

liúzhì 留滯 to remain at a standstill; to stay

liúzhù 留住 to succeed in making someone stay

liú 琉

1. a glossy and bright stone 2. glazed

liúli 琉璃 1. glass 2. porcelain 3. colored glaze 4. glossy gems

liúliwǎ 琉璃瓦 encaustic tiles; glazed tiles

Liúqiú 琉球 Ryukyu

liú 硫

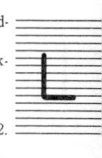

sulphur, or sulfur

liúhuáng 硫磺 sulphur, or sulfur

liúsuān 硫酸 sulfuric acid

liú 榴
a pomegranate

liúlián 榴蓮 (botany) a durian

liú 劉
1. a Chinese family name 2. to kill

liú 瘤
a tumor; a swelling; a lump

liú 瀏
1. (said of water) clear; bright and clear; the appearance of a clear stream 2. a fast-blowing wind; a cool wind 3. to get away secretly; to take French leave

liúhǎir 瀏海兒 bangs; fringe

liúlǎn 瀏覽 to glance over; to skim through

liǔ 柳
1. a willow tree 2. name of one of the 28 Constellations 3. (figuratively) a singsong house; the red-light district 4. a tumor; a swelling; a lump 5. a Chinese family name

liǔ'àn huāmíng 柳暗花明 an enchanting sight in springtime

liǔchéng 柳橙 an orange

liǔméi 柳眉 the eyebrows of a beautiful woman

liǔtiáo 柳條 a withe; a willow branch

liǔxiàng huājiē 柳巷花街 the red-light district

liǔxù 柳絮 willow catkins

liǔyāo 柳腰 a willowy waist; a slender waist

liǔyè 柳葉 willow leaves

liù 六
six

Liùfǎ Quánshū 六法全書 The Complete Volume of Six Laws

liùgēn qīngjìng 六根清淨 (said of a Buddha) free from human desires and passions

liùjiǎoxíng 六角形 a hexagon

liùshén wúzhǔ 六神無主 shocked; stunned out of one's wits

liùyuè 六月 1. June 2. the sixth month of the lunar calendar 3. six months

liù 陸
an elaborate form of **liù** 六 used in documents or checks to prevent forgery

liù 溜
1. rapids 2. a row; a column 3. surroundings; neighborhood

liù 遛
to stroll; to walk slowly; to roam

liùda 遛達 to take a walk; to stroll as an exercise

liù 餾
1. to steam 2. distilled (water)

lo 咯
a phrase-final particle

lóng 隆
1. prosperous; flourishing; brisk (business, etc.); booming 2. lofty; eminent; glorious 3. abundant; ample; generous 4. the rumble (of thunder, vehicles, artillery fire, etc.)

lóngdōng 隆冬 (in) the depth of winter; winter at its coldest

lónglóng 隆隆 1. flourishing; booming 2. (said of sound) roaring, booming or rumbling

lóngqǐ 隆起 to rise up; to swell up; to bulge

lóngqíng hòuyí 隆情厚誼 refer to **lóngqíng hòuyì** 隆情厚誼

lóngqíng hòuyì 隆情厚誼 great kindness, hospitality and friendship

lóngzhòng 隆重 impressive, grand and solemn

lóng 龍
1. a dragon 2. of the emperor; imperial 3. a huge extinct reptile 4. a Chinese family name

lóngfēi fèngwǔ 龍飛鳳舞 vivid and vigorous flourishes in calligraphy

lóngfèng 龍鳳 1. fine offspring; excellent children 2. men of wisdom 3. a noble look 4. man and woman 5. dragon and phoenix

lóngfèng chéngxiáng 龍鳳呈祥 prosperity brought by the dragon and the phoenix—in extremely good fortune

lónggān fèngsuǐ 龍肝鳳髓 rare delicacies

lóngjǐngchá 龍井茶 a kind of green tea produced at Hangzhou, Zhejiang

lóngjuǎnfēng 龍捲風 a tornado; a cyclone; a twister

lóngmén 龍門 fame; success; glory

lóngpán hǔjù 龍蟠虎踞 like a dragon that coils and a tiger that crouches—impressive terrain

lóngpáo 龍袍 an imperial robe

lóngshé hùnzá 龍蛇混雜 the wise and the unwise huddled together

lóngshēnglóng, fèngshēngfèng 龍生龍，鳳生鳳 Like father, like son.

lóngtán hǔxué 龍潭虎穴 places of extreme danger

lóngtán hǔxuè 龍潭虎穴 refer to **lóngtán hǔxué** 龍潭虎穴

lóngtào 龍套 1. a kind of costume in Chinese opera 2. a character in such a costume in Chinese opera—a role that requires neither acting nor singing 3. a very insignificant role

lóngténg hǔyuè 龍騰虎躍 dragons rising and tigers leaping —a scene of bustling activity

lóngtóu 龍頭 1. a faucet; a tap; a cock 2. the top successful candidate in the imperial examination under the former civil service examination system 3. the leader of a sect, secret society, etc.

Lóngwáng 龍王 the sea god

lóngxiā 龍蝦 a lobster

lóngxíng hǔbù 龍行虎步 the dignified manner of an emperor

lóngyán 龍顏 the noble face of the emperor

lóngyǎn 龍眼 longan

lóngzhēng hǔdòu 龍爭虎鬥 a fierce battle between giants

lóngzhōu 龍舟 a dragon-shaped racing boat

lóngzhōu jìngdù 龍舟競渡 a dragon-boat race

lóng 窿
a hole; a cavity

lóng 聾
1. deaf; hard of hearing 2. deaf —stupid and ignorant

lóngyǎ xuéxiào 聾啞學校 a deaf-and-dumb school

lóngzi 聾子 a deaf person

lóng 籠
1. a cage; a coop 2. a basket; a container

lóngzhōngniǎo 籠中鳥 restricted and confined

lóngzi 籠子 a cage; a coop

lǒng 隴
1. another name of Gansu Province 2. (壟) a mound 3. prosperous

lǒngmǔ 隴畝 a rural community; the farm

lǒng 壟
1. a grave; a mound of earth 2. a high place in a field

lǒngduàn 壟斷 a monopoly; to monopolize

lǒng 籠
to include; to encompass

lǒngluò 籠絡 1. to entice, tempt, ensnare or cajole 2. to befriend another with a view to winning him over

lǒngtǒng 籠統 general; indiscriminate

lǒngzhào 籠罩 to cover completely; to permeate; to shroud

lòng 弄
1. lane; alley 2. refer to **nòng** 弄

lōu 摟
1. to hold up; to tuck up 2. to squeeze or extort (money, etc.) 3. to gather up; to collect; to rake

together

lóu 嘍
a bandit's lackey or follower

lóuluo 嘍囉 a bandit's lackey or follower; the rank and file of a band of outlaws

lóu 樓
a building of two stories or more; a tower

lóudǐng 樓頂 the top of a tall building

lóufáng 樓房 a building of two stories or more

lóugé 樓閣 a tower

lóushàng 樓上 upstairs

lóutái 樓臺 a tower

lóutī 樓梯 a staircase

lóuxià 樓下 downstairs

lǒu 摟
to hold in the arms; to embrace; to hug

lǒubào 摟抱 to hold in the arms; to embrace

lǒu 簍
a basket made by weaving bamboo slats, wickers or twigs

lòu 陋
1. narrow and small 2. ugly 3. vile; low; mean; humble 4. ignorant; crude; simple-minded 5. poor (performances, knowledge, etc.); inferior; superficial; shallow 6. stingy; tight-fisted

lòuguī 陋規 bad practices

lòushì 陋室 a crude abode; a humble room

lòusú 陋俗 vile customs; vulgar customs

lòuxí 陋習 bad habits; corrupt practices

lòuxiàng 陋巷 a narrow, dirty alley; slums

lòu 漏
1. to divulge; to disclose 2. leak; to leak 3. to slip or omit unintentionally; to neglect 4. a water clock; an hourglass

lòudiàn 漏電 electric leakage

lòudiào 漏掉 to be missing or

left out

lòudòng 漏洞 a shortcoming; a loophole

lòudǒu 漏斗 a funnel

lòufēng 漏風 not airtight

lòufēngshēng 漏風聲 to disclose a secret

lòujiē 漏接 (baseball) passed ball

lòuqì 漏氣 (said of air) to leak out

lòushuǐ 漏水 (said of containers, holds, etc.) leaking

lòushuì 漏稅 to evade tax payment

lòuwǎng zhīyú 漏網之魚 a fish that has escaped the net—a criminal who has escaped punishment

lòuyè 漏夜 in the dead of night

lòu 鏤
to engrave; to carve

lòuhuā 鏤花 ornamental engraving

lòukōng 鏤空 to hollow out; hollowed-out

lòu 露
refer to **lù** 露 2

lòubái 露白 to show money, valuables, etc. one carries unintentionally

lòucái 露財 to show wealth unintentionally

lòuchū mǎjiao 露出馬腳 to reveal one's true form or character; to show the cloven hoof

lòuchū pòzhàn 露出破綻 to show one's slip; to belie

lòufēngmáng 露鋒芒 to make one's aggressiveness or talent felt

lòuliǎn 露臉 1. successful; with flying colors 2. to show one's face; to appear

lòumiàn 露面 to show up; to appear in public; to show one's face; to make an appearance

lòuxiàng 露相 to show one's true form or colors

lòuyīshǒu 露一手 to make an exhibition of one's skills

lou 嘍

a phrase-final partical

lú 盧

1. black 2. a Chinese family name

Lúsēnbǎo 盧森堡 Luxemburg, Europe

lú 廬

1. a thatched cottage 2. Mt. Lu (in Jiangxi)

Lúshān zhēnmiànmù 廬山眞面目 the real appearance (of a thing or person in disguise)

lúshè 廬舍 a cottage; a hut

lú 爐

a stove; an oven; a fireplace; a hearth

lúhuǒ chúnqīng 爐火純青 The skill is mature.

lútái 爐臺 a mantel

lúzào 爐灶 1. a cooking stove 2. (figuratively) a stat; an enterprise

lúzi 爐子 a stove; a furnace; a kiln

lú 蘆

1. reeds; rushes 2. gourds

lúhuì 蘆薈 aloes

lúsǔn 蘆筍 (botany) asparagus

lúwěi 蘆葦 reeds

lú 顱

1. the skull 2. the head 3. the forehead

lúgǔ 顱骨 the skull; the parietal bone

lú 鱸

a perch; a bass

lúyú 鱸魚 the sea bass

lǔ 鹵

1. alkaline or saline soil 2. natural salt 3. (魯) rude; unrefined 4. (擄) to capture; to seize

lǔmǎng 鹵莽 rude; rash; foolhardy

lǔwèi 鹵味 1. pot-stewed fowl, meat, etc. served cold 2. a salty taste; saltiness

lǔ 虜 also **luǒ**

1. a captive; a prisoner 2. (擄) to

take prisoner; to capture alive

lǔhuò 虜獲 1. to capture 2. men and arms captured

lǔlüè 虜掠 to plunder; to rob; to pillage

lǔrén lèshú 虜人勒贖 to kidnap a person for ransom

lǔ 滷

1. gravy; broth; sauce 2. salty; salted

lǔdàn 滷蛋 a marinated egg

lǔwèi 滷味 pot-stewed fowl, meat, etc. served cold

lǔ 魯

1. stupid; dull 2. vulgar 3. name of an ancient kingdom in what is today's Shandong; an alternative name of Shandong 4. a Chinese family name

lǔdùn 魯鈍 dull; slow-witted

lǔmǎng 魯莽 1. rude; disrespectful; uncivil; ill-mannered; discourteous 2. rash; careless

lǔ 櫓

1. an oar; a scull; a sweep 2. (in ancient warfare) a big shield; a long spear

lǔfū 櫓夫 an oarsman

lù 陸

1. land; the shore; a continent 2. by way of land; land transportation 3. a Chinese family name

lùdì 陸地 land

lùhǎikōng 陸海空 land, sea and air

lùjūn 陸軍 the army; the land force

lùlù 陸路 by land; a highway or railway; by way of land

lùqiáo 陸橋 1. an overpass 2. a land bridge

lùxù 陸續 continuous; one by one; one after another

lùzhànduì 陸戰隊 the marines; the Marine Corps

lù 鹿

a deer; a stag; a doe

lùjiǎo 鹿角 antlers

lùpí 鹿皮 deerskin

lùróng 鹿茸 young antlers

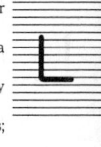

(regarded as a very valuable medicine)

lùsǐ shuíshǒu 鹿死誰手 (literally) Who is to kill the deer? —Who will win?

lù 祿

1. happiness; prosperity 2. official pay; salary

lùwèi 祿位 official salary and rank

lù 碌

1. mediocre; common 2. busy; occupied 3. a kind of stone roller

lùlù 碌碌 1. mediocre; commonplace 2. busy

lù 勠

1. to unite or join (forces) 2. to kill; to slay

lùlì tóngxīn 勠力同心 to work together with the same objective in mind

lù 賂

1. to send a gift 2. to bribe

lù 路

1. a way; a road; a path 2. a sort; a kind; a gang 3. a way; means 4. directions; courses 5. province (an administrative division during the Song Dynasty) 6. a Chinese family name

lùbiāntān 路邊攤 street venders; sidewalk pedlers

lùbiāo 路標 a road sign; a signpost

lùchéng 路程 a journey; traveling distance

lùdēng 路燈 a streetlamp

lùduàn 路段 a section of a highway or railway

lùguò 路過 to pass by or through (a place)

lùjī 路基 a road base

lùjiān 路肩 the shoulder of the road

lùjìng 路徑 a way; a road; a route

lùkǒu 路口 an entrance to a road or street; a street intersection; a street crossing

lùmiàn 路面 a road surface

lùpáng 路旁 the roadside

lùrén 路人 1. a wayfarer 2. a stranger

lùshàng 路上 on the way; along the way; en route

lùtú 路途 a way; a road

lùxiàn 路線 a route; a road; a course

lùzhàng 路障 a roadblock

lù 綠

lùlín háojié 綠林豪傑 1. heros of the greenwood 2. brigands

lùlín hǎohàn 綠林好漢 1. heros of the greenwood 2. brigands

lù 戮

1. to slay; to massacre; to slaughter 2. to unite or join

lùlì 戮力 to join forces; to cooperate

lùlì tóngxīn 戮力同心 to join forces and work for a common cause

lù 錄

1. to take down; to copy; to record 2. to accept (applicants) 3. a record

lùfàngyǐngjī 錄放影機 a videocassette recorder

lùqǔ 錄取 to accept

lùxiàng 錄像 vedio tape recording

lùxiàngjī 錄像機 a video recorder

lùyīn 錄音 1. to record 2. recording

lùyīndài 錄音帶 a recording tape

lùyīnjī 錄音機 a tape recorder; a recorder

lùyǐng 錄影 to video tape

lùyǐngdài 錄影帶 a videotape

lùyòng 錄用 to accept for employment

lù 麓

the foot of a hill or mountain

lù 露

1. dew 2. (also **lòu**) uncovered; exposed; to show; to reveal; to

betray 3. a cold, soothing and aromatic drink; beverages distilled from flowers, fruit or leaves

lùgǔ 露骨 without reserve or tact; candid; outspoken; thinly veiled

lùshuǐ 露水 dew

lùshuǐ fūqī 露水夫妻 a couple living together without being married

lùtǐ 露體 naked; in the nude; in the altogether

lùtiān 露天 open air; outdoor

lùtóujiǎo 露頭角 (said of a young person) beginning to show ability or talent; budding

lùyíng 露營 1. to camp; to bivouac 2. an open-air camping; a jamboree; a camporee

lùzhū 露珠 dewdrops

lù 鷺

an egret

lùsī 鷺鷥 an egret

lǘ 閭

1. a community of 25 families in ancient China 2. the gate of a village 3. to meet; to gather together

lǘlǐ 閭里 alleys or lanes—1. one's neighbors; one's neighborhood 2. one's native village

lǘ 驢

an ass; a donkey

Lǚ 呂

a Chinese family name

lǚ 侶

1. a companion; a mate 2. to associate with

lǚ 旅

1. to travel; to lodge 2. a traveler; a passenger 3. a multitude; people 4. (military) a brigade; troops 5. to proceed together; to do things together

lǚchéng 旅程 the route a traveler takes from one place to another

lǚdiàn 旅店 a tavern; an inn

lǚfèi 旅費 traveling expenses

lǚguǎn 旅館 a hotel; a hostel; an inn

lǚjū 旅居 to stay in a place for a while

lǚkè 旅客 a traveler; a passenger

lǚshè 旅社 a hotel; a hostel; an inn

lǚtú 旅途 on one's way (to a destination); during one's trip

lǚxíng 旅行 to travel

lǚxíngchē 旅行車 a station wagon

lǚxíngdài 旅行袋 a traveling bag

lǚxíngshè 旅行社 a travel agency; a travel bureau

lǚxíngtuán 旅行團 a traveling party; a tourist group

lǚxíng zhīpiào 旅行支票 a traveler's check

lǚyóu 旅遊 a tour; tourism

lǚ 捋

to stroke (one's beard, etc.)

lǚhúxū 捋鬍鬚 to stroke one's beard

lǚ 屢

frequently; repeatedly; again and again

lǚcì 屢次 repeatedly; frequently

lǚjiàn bùxiān 屢見不鮮 not rare; nothing new

lǚlǚ 屢屢 frequently; again and again

lǚshì bùshuǎng 屢試不爽 to have the same result or reaction (usually positive result or reaction) after each try

lǚ 鋁

alumin(i)um

lǚbó 鋁箔 alumin(i)um foil

lǚ 履

1. shoes 2. to step on; to tread on; to follow

lǚlì 履歷 one's personal history

lǚlìbiǎo 履歷表 a biographic sketch

lǚrèn 履任 to take or assume one's new office or post

lǚxiǎn rúyí 履險如夷 to go through danger as if there were

no danger at all

lǚxīn 履新 to take or assume one's new office or post

lǚxíng 履行 to fulfill or carry out

lǚyuē 履約 to keep or fulfill an agreement

lǚ 褸
1. the collar or lapel of a garment 2. (said of clothes) tattered; in rags

lǚ 縷
1. a thread; yarn 2. a wisp; a strand; a lock 3. detailed; in detail

lǚlǚ 縷縷 continuous; endlessly

lǚxī 縷析 to analyze in detail

lǜ 律
1. a law; a rule; a regulation; a statute 2. to bind by law; to control or restrain; to discipline 3. a series of standard bamboo tuning pitch pipes used in ancient music 4. a form in Chinese poetry—a stanza of eight lines

lǜlìng 律令 1. laws and regulations 2. a Taoist incantation

lǜshī 律師 1. a lawyer; a barrister

lǜshī shìwùsuǒ 律師事務所 a lawyer's office

lǜ 率
1. (mathematics) ratio 2. a suffix used to indicate a measure or rate 3. calculate

lǜ 氯
chlorine

lǜhuà'nà 氯化鈉 sodium chloride

lǜ 綠
green (color)

lǜbǎoshí 綠寶石 emerald; beryl

lǜchá 綠茶 green tea

lǜdēng 綠燈 1. (transportation) the green light 2. permission to go ahead with some project; the green light

lǜdòu 綠豆 the green beans; green lentils

lǜhuà 綠化 to plant trees, build

parks, or lay out lawns in deserts or urban areas

lǜkǎ 綠卡 a green card, permanent residence permit issued by the U.S. government

lǜyīn 綠蔭 a green shade; the shade of trees

lǜyōuyōu 綠油油 bright green

lǜzǎo 綠藻 algae; chlorophyceae; chlorella

lǜzhōu 綠洲 an oasis

lǜ 慮
1. to consider; to take into account 2. to worry about; anxious about

lǜ 濾
to filter; to strain out

lǜguòxìng bìngdú 濾過性病毒 virus

lǜshuǐchí 濾水池 a depositing reservoir

luán 孿
twin

luánshēng 孿生 born as twins; to bear twins

luán 鑾
1. bells around the neck of a horse 2. the imperial carriage

luán 鸞
1. a fabulous bird related to the phoenix 2. the bells at horses' bits

luánfèng 鸞鳳 1. a married couple 2. a fabulous bird and a phoenix—(figuratively) good beings 3. handsome; gallant

luánfèng hémíng 鸞鳳和鳴 harmony in marriage

luǎn 卵
1. an egg; an ovum 2. roe 3. the testicles

luǎncháo 卵巢 ovaries

luǎnshēng 卵生 oviparous

luǎnzǐ 卵子 1. an ovum 2. testes; testicles

luàn 亂
1. chaos; confusion; distraction; anarchy 2. rebellion; revolt; insurrection 3. confused; per-

plexed; agitated; disarranged; raveled 4. out of order; out of sorts

luànchén zéizǐ 亂臣賊子 ministers or generals who rebel against their monarch or collaborate with the enemy

luànchéng yītuán 亂成一團 topsy-turvy; in great confusion

luàndǎng 亂黨 a rebel party or faction

luànfá 亂罰 to mete out unjustified punishment

luànfēnfēn 亂紛紛 disorderly; chaotic; tumultuous

luànhǎn luànjiào 亂喊亂叫 to clamor; to talk wildly

luànhōnghōng 亂烘烘 noisy and disorderly

luànlái 亂來 to act foolishly or recklessly

luànlún 亂倫 incest

luànmín 亂民 rioters; mobsters

luànqī bāzāo 亂七八糟 in confusion; topsy-turvy

luànshì 亂世 times of anarchy and disorder

luànshì 亂視 astigmatism

luànshuō 亂說 to say what should not be said; to lie

luànzāozāo 亂糟糟 1. chaotic 2. confused

luànzi 亂子 disturbance

lüè 掠
1.to take by force; to rob; to plunder; to pillage 2. to brush; to pass lightly on the side; to sweep past 3. to whip; to flog 4. a long stroke to the left in Chinese calligraphy

lüèduó 掠奪 to seize or rob by force

lüèguò 掠過 to skim over

lüèqǔ 掠取 to take by force; to rob

lüèshí 掠食 to hunt for food

lüè 略
1. approximate; rough; brief 2. slight; small in extent 3. to scheme; to plan 4. strategy 5. to invade; to seize 6. to omit; to leave out 7. to survey the bound-

aries

lüèkě 略可 acceptable in general

lüèqù 略去 to omit; to leave out; to delete

lüèshèng yīchóu 略勝一籌 slightly better

lüèshí zhīwú 略識之無 only slightly literate

lüèshì zhīwú 略識之無 refer to **lüèshí zhīwú** 略識之無

lüèshù 略述 to describe briefly; to outline

lüèshuō 略說 to say a few words about; briefly refer to

lüètóng 略同 about the same; similar

lüèwēi 略微 slightly; a little; somewhat

lüèwéi 略微 refer to **lüèwēi** 略微

lüèyǒu suǒwén 略有所聞 to have heard something (about it)

lüèzhī yī'èr 略知一二 to know or understand just a little

lūn 掄
1. to turn or spin with hands or arms 2. to brandish 3. to squander

lūndāo 掄刀 to swing a knife

lún 倫
1. normal relationships among people 2. comparison 3. classification 4. order; logic 5. regular; ordinary 6. to choose; choice

lúncháng 倫常 normal and accepted ways and relationships of people

Lúndūn 倫敦 London

lúnlǐ 倫理 moral principles; ethics

lúnlǐxué 倫理學 ethics

lún 掄
to select; to choose

lúnxuǎn 掄選 to select (competent persons, adequate materials, etc.)

lúnyuán 掄元 to come out first in examinations

lúnzé 掄擇 to select (competent persons, adequate materials, etc.)

lún 淪

1. to sink into ruin, etc.; to fall; submerged 2. ripples; eddying water

lúnluò 淪落 to get lost (in a strange land, etc.)

lúnsàng 淪喪 to be lost or ruined

lúnwáng 淪亡 lost or ruined

lúnxiàn 淪陷 occupied by or lost to the enemy

lún 圇

entire; whole

lún 論

an alternative of **lùn** 論 for some phrass

Lúnyǔ 論語 The Analects of Confucius, one of the Four Books

lún 輪

1. a wheel 2. to recur; to alternate 3. majestic; stately 4. to take turns; by turns; in relays

lúnbān 輪班 to go on duty by rotation; to take turns; in relays; in rotation

lúnbào 輪暴 to gang-rape; gang rape

lúnchàng 輪唱 1. (singing) to troll 2. to chant Buddhist prayers 3. a canon (a form of musical composition)

lúnchuán 輪船 a steamship; a steamer

lúnfān 輪番 to assume duties in turn

lúnhuí 輪迴 1. to recur successively; to move in a cycle 2. transmigration (of the soul); metempsychosis

lúnkuò 輪廓 an outline; a silhouette

lúnliú 輪流 to take turns; by turns

lúntāi 輪胎 the tire (of a wheel)

lúnxiū 輪休 to rest by turns; to take a day off by turns

lúnyǐ 輪椅 a wheelchair

lúnzhí 輪值 to go on duty in turn; to take turns

lùn 論

1. to discuss; to comment on; to

talk about 2. to debate; to dispute 3. a theory; an essay 4. to regard; to consider 5. in terms of; by

lùndiǎn 論點 the point at issue; an issue; a thesis

lùndiào 論調 the tone or argument (of a speech, etc.)

lùnduàn 論斷 to discuss and judge

lùngōng xíngshǎng 論功行賞 to evaluate services and grant rewards accordingly

lùnjí 論及 to touch upon

lùnjù 論據 grounds or bases (of an argument)

lùnshù 論述 to discuss; to expound

lùnshuō 論說 a theory, or thoughts (advanced in a treatise)

lùnshuōwén 論說文 an argumentative treatise

lùnwén 論文 a treatise; a thesis; an essay

lùnzhàn 論戰 controversy; debate; argument

lùnzhēng 論爭 controversy; debate; argument

lùnzhèng 論政 to discuss politics; to make comments on politics

lùnzhèng 論證 demonstration; to expound and prove

lùnzhù 論著 a treatise; a discourse; a work

luō 捋

1. to rub one's palm along (something long) 2. to squeeze with hands 3. (also **lè**) to pluck; to gather in the fingers

luōhǔxū 捋虎鬚 to offend the powerful

luō 囉

to chatter

luōsuo 囉唆 vexingly verbose or wordy

luó 螺

1. a spiral shell; a conch 2. an alias of wine cups 3. a spiral

luósī 螺絲 a male screw; an external screw; a screw

luósīdīng 螺絲釘 a male screw; an external screw; a screw

luóxuán 螺旋 a screw; a spiral

luó 羅
1. thin, light silk 2. a net; a snare 3. to arrange over a wide space 4. a Chinese family name

luóliè 羅列 to arrange for display; to spread out

Luómǎníyà 羅馬尼亞 Romania

luómàndìkè 羅曼蒂克 romantic

luómànshǐ 羅曼史 a romance; a love affair

luópán 羅盤 a compass

luówǎng 羅網 a net; a snare

luó 騾
a mule

luózi 騾子 1. a mule 2. a stubborn person

luó 囉
1. noisiness 2. a band of outlaws 3. used as a slightly argumentative final particle

luó 邏
to patrol; to inspect

luóji 邏輯 logic

luó 蘿
1. a kind of creeping plant; a wistaria 2. a radish; a turnip

luóbo 蘿蔔 a radish; a turnip

luóbogān 蘿蔔乾 a dried radish or turnip

luóbogāo 蘿蔔糕 turnip pudding

luó 籮
1. a bamboo basket with a square or rectangular bottom and a round top 2. a piece of sievelike ware with a broad edge

luókuāng 籮筐 a large basket made of bamboo

luó 鑼
a gong

luógǔ xuāntiān 鑼鼓喧天 noisy celebration of a festival or carnival

luó 虜
refer to **lǔ** 虜

luǒ 裸
bare; nude; naked

luǒchéng 裸裎 naked; undressed

luǒlù 裸露 uncovered; exposed

luǒtǎn 裸袒 bare or naked

luǒtǐ 裸體 nude; naked; without a stitch on

Luò 洛
name of a river

Luòyáng 洛陽 Luoyang, in Henan

Luòyáng zhǐguì 洛陽紙貴 to become a best seller

luò 咯
refer to **kǎ** 咯

luò 烙
refer to **lào** 烙

luò 絡
1. to wrap around; to encompass 2. a net; a web 3. a cellulose structure in fruits, as melons 4. to associate; to connect 5. a halter 6. (said of blood vessels) capillaries 7. to unreel silk 8. cotton fiber 9. hemp

luòsāihú 絡腮鬍 whiskers

luòyì bùjué 絡繹不絕 (said of people) to come one after another; continuous

luò 酪
refer to **lào** 酪

luò 落
1. to fall; to decline; to wither; weakened; fallen 2. to lose 3. few and far-spaced; to stand apart; loose and scattered 4. a village; a hamlet 5. to put (pen to paper) 6. to settle down 7. a pile; a heap

luòbǎng 落榜 to flunk (or fail in) a competitive examination for a job or school admission

luòchā 落差 the drop in elevation

luòchéng 落成 completion (of a new building, etc.)

luòdì 落地 1. to be born 2. to fall to the ground

luòdì 落第 to flunk (or fail in) a competitive examination for a job or school admission

luòdìchuāng 落地窗 a French window

luòdiǎn 落點 1. (in tennis, badminton, handball, etc.) placement 2. (military) the point of a fall

luòhòu 落後 to fall behind; to lag behind

luòhuāshēng 落花生 a groundnut, or peanut

luòhuāng értáo 落荒而逃 to be defeated and run away the battlefield

luòjiǎo 落脚 to stay at; to stop at

luòjǐng xiàshí 落井下石 to beat a person when he's already down

luòkōng 落空 to come to nothing

luòlèi 落淚 to cry or weep; to shed tears

luòluò dàfāng 落落大方 natural; unaffected; easy

luòmò 落寞 desolate and scattered; lonely

luònàn 落難 to encounter difficulty, disaster, calamity, etc.; to be out of luck

luòrì 落日 the setting sun

luòshí 落實 1. practicable 2. to carry out

luòshuǐ 落水 to fall into water

luòtāngjī 落湯雞 dripping wet; drenched and bedraggled

luòtuò 落拓 jobless and listless; down in one's luck; out of luck

luòwǎng 落網 (said of a criminal) to be caught; to be captured

luòwǔ 落伍 anachronistic; to outdate

luòxià 落下 to fall down; to drop

luòxuǎn 落選 to fail in an election

luòyīng bīnfēn 落英繽紛 fallen flowers scattering and flying around like snow flakes

luò 駱

1. a white horse (or steed) with black mane 2. a camel

luòtuo 駱駝 a camel

mā 媽

1. one's mother 2. a woman servant

māma 媽媽 mama; mother

Māzǔ 媽祖 Goddess of the Sea

má 麻

1. hemp; jute; ramie; sisal; flax 2. sesame 3. numb; torpid 4. a tingle; to tingle 5. (痳) pockmarked 6. rough 7. pitted; spotty 8. (痳) measles 9. (痳) leprosy 10. (痳) to paralyze

mábì 麻痺 paralysis; palsy; numbness

mábù 麻布 linen; gunny; hempen fabrics

mádài 麻袋 a jute bag; a hemp bag

máfan 麻煩 1. troublesome 2. trouble 3. to bother

máhuā 麻花 a fried dough twist

májiàng 麻將 mahjong, Chinese gambling game

májiàng 麻醬 sesame paste

máliǎn 麻臉 a pockmarked face

mámù 麻木 paralyzed; numbed; palsied

mámù bùrén 麻木不仁 numbed; paralyzed; unsympathetic; unfeeling

máquè 麻雀 a sparrow

máquè suīxiǎo, wǔzàng jùquán 麻雀雖小，五臟俱全 small but complete

máshéng 麻繩 hemp cordage; hemp rope

máyào 麻藥 1. an anesthetic 2. narcotics; drugs; dopes

máyóu 麻油 sesame oil

mázhěn 麻疹 (medicine) measles

mázi 麻子 1. a pockmarked person 2. pockmarks

mázuì 麻醉 1. to anesthetize 2. to dope; to drug

mázuìjì 麻醉劑 1. an anesthetic 2. narcotics; drugs; dopes

má 嘛

a particle used in the phrase **gànmá** 幹嘛 why

mǎ 馬
a horse

mǎ'ān 馬鞍 a saddle

mǎbèi 馬背 horseback

mǎbiān 馬鞭 a horsewhip

mǎbiǎo 馬錶 a pocket watch; a stopwatch

mǎbù tíngtí 馬不停蹄 to do something without stop or a single halt

mǎchē 馬車 a carriage; a coach; a landau

mǎchǐ túzēng 馬齒徒增 having accomplished nothing despite one's advanced age

mǎdá 馬達 a motor

mǎdào chénggōng 馬到成功 to be accomplished quickly and easily; with immediate success

Mǎ'ěrdìfū 馬爾地夫 the Maldive Islands

mǎfáng 馬房 a stable

mǎfū 馬夫 a groom

mǎguà 馬掛 the ceremonial jacket of a mandarin

mǎhòupào 馬後砲 1. belated action 2. I-told-you-so remarks

mǎhu 馬虎 1. careless; perfunctory; sloppy; slovenly 2. not very good; so-so

majiù 馬廄 a stable

Mǎkè 馬克 a Deutsche mark; an ostmark

mǎlāsōng 馬拉松 marathon

Mǎláixīyà 馬來西亞 Malaysia; Malaysian

mǎlì 馬力 horsepower

mǎlíngshǔ 馬鈴薯 a potato

mǎlù 馬路 a street; a highway; a road

mǎlù rú hǔkǒu 馬路如虎口 The street is as dangerous as a tiger.—Beware of traffic accidents.

mǎlù shìchǎng 馬路市場 street venders; sidewalk peddlers

mǎpìjīng 馬屁精 a flatterer; a toady

mǎqiú 馬球 polo

mǎshàng 馬上 1. on horseback 2. right away; at once; immedi-ately; without delay

mǎshǒu shìzhān 馬首是瞻 to follow someone; to look on someone as an example

mǎshù 馬術 horsemanship

mǎtí 馬蹄 1. hoofs of a horse 2. a horseshoe

mǎtíxíng 馬蹄形 the shape of a hoof; U-shaped

mǎtǒng 馬桶 1. a toilet 2. a chamber pot; a close-stool

mǎxì 馬戲 a circus show; a circus

mǎxìtuán 馬戲團 a circus troupe; a circus

mǎxuē 馬靴 jackboots; riding boots

Mǎzǔ 馬祖 the Mazu Islands

mǎ 嗎
a character used in transliterating

mǎfēi 嗎啡 morphine

mǎ 瑪
agate; cornelian

mǎnǎo 瑪瑙 agate; cornelian

mǎ 碼
1. yard (a measure of length) 2. a symbol; a code; a sign or thing indicating number

mǎtou 碼頭 a dock; a quay; a wharf; a pier

mǎtou gōngrén 碼頭工人 a stevedore

mǎ 螞
1. an ant 2. a kind of leech

mǎyǐ 螞蟻 an ant

mà 罵
to call names; to swear; to curse; to revile

màrén 罵人 to call names; to scold

ma 嗎
a phrase-final particle used in questions

ma 嘛
a final interrogative particle

mái 埋
1. to bury 2. to secrete; to lie in

wait
máicáng 埋藏 to hide; to conceal
máifu 埋伏 an ambush; to ambush
máimò 埋沒 to bury (one's talents, etc.)
máitóu kǔgàn 埋頭苦幹 to bury one's head (in studying); to work with all-out effort
máizàng 埋葬 to bury (a corpse)

mǎi 買
1. to buy; to purchase 2. to win over (usually with a promise of favors in return)
mǎifāng 買方 the buyer
mǎijìn 買進 to buy
mǎikōng màikōng 買空賣空 to speculate (on the stock, etc. markets)
mǎimài 買賣 a line of business; trade
mǎimai 買賣 to buy and sell
mǎirù 買入 to buy
mǎitōng 買通 to offer bribes to facilitate one's operations; to buy off
mǎizhǔ 買主 the buyer
mǎizuì 買醉 to buy drinks

mài 脈 also **mò**
1. the blood vessels; the veins or arteries; the circulation system 2. the pulse 3. a mountain range 4. things that are related and form a system of some kind 5. stipules or stems of a leaf
màibó 脈搏 the pulse; pulsation
màiluò 脈絡 things that are related and form a system of their own

mài 麥 also **mò**
1. wheat; barley; oats 2. a Chinese family name
màibǐng 麥餅 wheaten cake
màifěn 麥粉 flour
màifū 麥麩 wheat bran
Màijiā 麥加 Mecca, Saudi Arabia
màijiǔ 麥酒 beer
màikèfēng 麥克風 a microphone
màilàng 麥浪 the wavy motion of wheat, etc., in the field when winds blow
màimiáo 麥苗 young wheat, barley, etc.
màipiàn 麥片 oatmeal
màisuì 麥穗 ears of wheat, etc.
màitián 麥田 wheatland; a wheat field
màiyá 麥芽 malt
màiyátáng 麥芽糖 malt sugar; maltose
màizi 麥子 wheat; barley

mài 賣
1. to sell 2. to betray; to harm another in order to benefit oneself 3. to show off; to flaunt
màichàng 賣唱 to live on singing
màifāng 賣方 the seller
màiguāng 賣光 sold out
màiguózéi 賣國賊 a traitor
màijià 賣價 the selling price
màijìnr 賣勁兒 to exert all one's strength
màilì 賣力 to work hard willingly
màimìng 賣命 1. to work oneself to the bone for somebody 2. to die (unworthily) for
màinong 賣弄 to flaunt; to show off
màiwán 賣完 sold out
màizhǔ 賣主 the seller
màizuò 賣座 1. (said of a theater, etc.) to draw large audiences 2. (said of a restaurant, etc.) to attract large numbers of customers

mài 邁
1. to surpass or exceed 2. to stride; to step 3. to go on a long journey 4. old (age) 5. to pass
màijìn 邁進 to forge ahead
màixiàng 邁向 to march toward

mán 埋
mányuàn 埋怨 to grumble; to complain

mán 漫

refer to **màn** 漫 7

mán 瞞

1. to hide the truth; to fool others by lying; to deceive 2. dim-sighted; poor vision

mánhǒng 瞞哄 to hide (the truth) and cheat

mánpiàn 瞞騙 to deceive and lie

mántiān guòhǎi 瞞天過海 very clever and daring in deceiving others

mán 蹣

1. to jump over 2. refer to **pán** 蹣

mán 饅

steamed buns; steamed bread; stuffed or unstuffed dumplings

mántou 饅頭 steamed buns; steam bread

mán 鰻

an eel

mán 蠻

1. barbarous; savage; barbarians in the south 2. quite; pretty; very; fairly

mánhèng 蠻橫 barbarous; savage

mánzú 蠻族 barbarian tribes; savage tribes; primitive people

mǎn 滿

1. full; filled 2. plentiful; abundant 3. proud; haughty 4. to expire 5. completely; entirely; perfectly 6. Manchu

mǎnbēi 滿杯 a full cup

mǎnbù zàihu 滿不在乎 do not care at all

mǎnchǎng 滿場 1. the whole assembly 2. Tickets sold out!

mǎnchéng fēngyǔ 滿城風雨 widespread excitement over a scandal, an incident, etc.

mǎndì 滿地 everywhere; all over the world

mǎnfēn 滿分 a perfect score; full marks

mǎnfù húyí 滿腹狐疑 to be filled with suspicion

mǎnfù jīnglún 滿腹經綸 very erudite

mǎnfù láosāo 滿腹牢騷 to have a heart full of discontents, grievances, complaints, etc.

mǎnhuái 滿懷 a heart full of (enthusiasm, sorrow, etc.)

mǎnjiē 滿街 all over the street

mǎnkǒu chēngzàn 滿口稱讚 to praise unreservedly

mǎnkǒu dāying 滿口答應 to promise with great readiness

mǎnkǒu húshuō 滿口胡說 to talk nonsense

mǎnlěi 滿壘 bases loaded

mǎnliǎn tōnghóng 滿臉通紅 The face reddens all over.

mǎnmén 滿門 the whole family

mǎnmén táolǐ 滿門桃李 a lot of students

mǎnmiàn chūnfēng 滿面春風 looking happy and cheerful; all smiles

mǎnmù chuāngyí 滿目瘡痍 Misery and suffering greets the eye everywhere.

mǎnnǎozi 滿腦子 to have one's mind stuffed with

mǎnqiāng rèxiě 滿腔熱血 refer to **mǎnqiāng rèxuè** 滿腔熱血

mǎnqiāng rèxuè 滿腔熱血 full of patriotic fervor

Mǎnqīng 滿清 the Qing Dynasty (1644-1911)

mǎnshēn 滿身 the whole body

mǎntiānxià 滿天下 everywhere; all over the world

mǎntiānxīng 滿天星 1. (botany) *Serissa foetida* 2. the sky filled with stars

mǎntóu dàhàn 滿頭大汗 with one's brow bead

mǎnxīn huānxǐ 滿心歡喜 to be filled with joy

mǎnyì 滿意 satisfied; content

mǎnyuè 滿月 1. a full moon 2. (of a baby) to be one month old

mǎnzài 滿載 fully laden

mǎnzài érguī 滿載而歸 to return home fully laden with riches, gifts, etc.

mǎnzhāosǔn, qiānshòuyì 滿招損，謙受益 Haughtiness invites losses while modesty brings profits.

Mǎnzhōu 滿洲 Manchuria

mǎnzú 滿足 to satisfy or be satisfied; content

mǎnzuǐ 滿嘴 to have a mouthful of (food, honeyed words, etc.)

mǎnzuò 滿座 1. all the audience; all the attendants 2. a capacity audience

màn 曼 also **wàn**
1. delicately beautiful; graceful 2. long; vast; prolonged

Màngǔ 曼谷 Bangkok, capital of Thailand

màntuólín 曼陀林 (music) a mandolin

màn 慢
1. slow; sluggish 2. negligent 3. haughty; rude; disrespectful; arrogant; supercilious 4. to postpone; to defer

mànchē 慢車 a local train; a slow train

mànchēdào 慢車道 slow-traffic lanes

màndòngzuò 慢動作 slow motion

màngōng chū xìhuó 慢工出細活 Fine products come from slow work.

mànpǎo 慢跑 to jog; jogging

màntiáo sīlǐ 慢條斯理 unhurried; leisurely

màntūntūn 慢吞吞 irritatingly slow

mànxìng 慢性 1. chronic (disease, etc.) 2. slow (in taking effect)

mànxìngbìng 慢性病 a chronic disease

mànzǒu 慢走 1. Don't go yet! Halt! 2. (polite formula) Goodbye!

màn 漫
1. overflowing 2. uncontrolled; uninhibited 3. reckless; wild 4. unsystematic; aimless 5. to spread or extend over 6. all over the place; everywhere 7. (also

mán) (said of expanse of water) vast or endless

mànbù 漫步 to ramble; to stroll

mànbù jīngxīn 漫不經心 heedless; unmindful; inattentive; unconcerned

màncháng 漫長 endless; infinite

mànhuà 漫畫 a cartoon; a caricature

mànhuàjiā 漫畫家 a cartoonist; a caricaturist

mànmà 漫罵 to abuse or slander with abandon

mànmàn chángyè 漫漫長夜 a long, long night which seems to have no end

mànshān biànyě 漫山遍野 so numerous as to cover the mountains and the plains

màntiān dàhuǎng 漫天大謊 a monstrous lie

màntiān yàojià 漫天要價 to quote an exorbitant price in anticipation of haggling

mànwú biānjì 漫無邊際 1. boundless 2. rambling

mànwú mùbiāo 漫無目標 aimless; at random

mànyóu 漫遊 to travel about for pleasure

màn 蔓
plants with creeping tendrils or vines

mànyán 蔓延 to spread; to creep

màn 謾
1. to scorn; to disdain 2. disrespectful; rude

mànmà 謾罵 to revile scornfully; to rail

máng 忙
1. busy; short of time; fully occupied 2. hurried; in haste; to make haste

mánglǐ tōuxián 忙裡偷閒 to steal a moment of leisure under the pressure of heavy workload

mánglù 忙碌 1. busy; fully occupied 2. hurriedly; in great haste

mángluàn 忙亂 busy and flurried

M

mángzhōng yǒucuò 忙中有錯 Errors are likely to occur in haste.

máng 芒
1. a kind of grass whose leaves can be used to make sandals 2. a sharp point 3. (botany) beards of wheat 4. rays (of stars)

mángcì zàibèi 芒刺在背 ill at ease

mángguǒ 芒果 a mango

máng 盲
1. blind; to blind 2. deluded

mángcháng 盲腸 the cecum, or caecum

mángchángyán 盲腸炎 appendicitis

mángcóng 盲從 to follow blindly

mángmù 盲目 1. blind 2. lacking insight or understanding 3. reckless; aimless

mángrén 盲人 a blind person

mángyǎ xuéxiào 盲啞學校 a school for the blind and the mute

máng 氓
a rascal; a vagabond

máng 茫
1. vast; boundless 2. vague; uncertain

mángmáng dàhǎi 茫茫大海 the boundless ocean

mángrán 茫然 vague; blank; uncertain

mángwú tóuxù 茫無頭緒 1. (said of things) to be all in a jumble 2. not knowing where or how to start

mǎng 莽
1. bushy; weedy 2. a poisonous bushy plant 3. rude; uncultured; impolite; reckless

mǎngfū 莽夫 a rude fellow; a rough

mǎngzhuàng 莽撞 rude; rough; uncultured

mǎng 蟒
a python; a boa

mǎngshé 蟒蛇 a python; a boa

māo 摸
refer to **mō** 摸

māo 貓
the cat

māokū hàozi jiǎcíbēi 貓哭耗子假慈悲 to shed crocodile tears

māotóuyīng 貓頭鷹 the owl

māoxióng 貓熊 (animal) a panda

máo 毛
1. hair; fur; feathers; down 2. vegetation 3. ten cents; a dime 4. gross; untouched; unpolished 5. flurried; panicstricken; scared; 6. very young; little 7. a Chinese family name

máobǐ 毛筆 a writing brush; a hair pencil

máobing 毛病 1. fault; defects; shortcoming; blemish 2. trouble; disorder 3. disease; illness

máogǔ sǒngrán 毛骨悚然 to shudder with fear; to be horror-stricken

máojīn 毛巾 a towel

máokǒng 毛孔 pores (of the skin)

máoliào 毛料 woolen material

máomaochóng 毛毛蟲 a caterpillar

máomaoyǔ 毛毛雨 drizzle

máopí 毛皮 fur; pelt

máoróngróng 毛茸茸 hairy; downy

máoróngróng 毛茸茸 refer to **máoróngróng** 毛茸茸

máoshǒu máojiǎo 毛手毛腳 1. restless; uneasy 2. to take liberties with a woman by the actions of one's hands

Máo Suì zìjiàn 毛遂自薦 to recommend oneself

máotǎn 毛毯 a woolen blanket

máowà 毛襪 woolen stockings

máoxìguǎn 毛細管 a capillary tube; a capillary

máoxiàn 毛線 woolen yarn; knitting wool

máoxiànyī 毛線衣 a sweater; wool

máoyī 毛衣 woolen sweaters; sweaters

máozao 毛躁 1. irritable 2. rash and restless

máozhān 毛氈 1. a woolen carpet 2. felt

máozhīwù 毛織物 woolen textiles

máo 矛

a lance; a spear

máodùn 矛盾 to contradict; contradiction; inconsistency

máotóu 矛頭 a spearhead

máo 茅

1. couch grass 2. a Chinese family name

máocè 茅廁 refer to **máosi** 茅廁

máofáng 茅房 1. a thatched house 2. a latrine

máosè dùnkāi 茅塞頓開 to come to an understanding all of a sudden

máoshè 茅舍 1. a straw hut; a thatched house 2. my humble cottage

máosi 茅廁 a latrine; a lavatory; a water closet

máowū 茅屋 a thatched house; a straw hut

máo 髦

1. a children's hair style with front hair covering the forehead 2. the mane 3. a man of talent

máo 錨

1. to anchor 2. an anchor

mǎo 卯

1. the fourth of the 12 Terrestrial Branches 2. the period from 5 to 7 a.m. 3. a roll call

mǎoshí 卯時 the period of the day from 5 to 7 a.m.

mào 冒

1. incautious; imprudent; rash 2. to risk; to brave; to be exposed to (hardships) 3. to put forth; to issue forth; to go up (as fire, smoke, etc.)

màochēng 冒稱 to claim falsely

màochōng 冒充 to pretend to be somebody else

màodú 冒瀆 to bother or annoy (a superior)

màofàn 冒犯 to offend (a superior, elder, etc.)

màofù 冒富 to become rich all of a sudden

màohào 冒號 the colon

màohuǒ 冒火 to become angry

màolǐng 冒領 to get or take something by posing as someone else for whom it is intended

màomèi 冒昧 to make bold; to presume

màomíng 冒名 to assume another's name

màomíng dǐngtì 冒名頂替 to assume the identity of another person

màopái 冒牌 a fake; an imitation

màorán 冒然 reckless; rashly; rash

màoshi 冒失 hasty; reckless; rash

màoshiguǐ 冒失鬼 a rash fellow; a reckless guy

màosǐ 冒死 to risk death

màoxiǎn 冒險 to take risks

màoxiǎn fànnán 冒險犯難 to do something despite the dangers and difficulties involved

màoyān 冒煙 to belch smoke

màoyǔ 冒雨 to brave the rain

mào 茂 also **mòu**

1. exuberant; lush; luxuriant; flourishing; healthy; vigorous; strong 2. fine; fair; excellent

màoshèng 茂盛 luxuriant; flourishing; lush; exuberant

mào 貿

1. to trade; to barter 2. mixed 3. rashly

màorán 貿然 rashly; blindly

màoyì 貿易 trade; to trade

màoyì gōngsī 貿易公司 a trading company or firm

màoyìshāng 貿易商 a trader

mào 帽

1. a hat; a headwear 2. a cap (of a fountain pen, screw, etc.)

M

màodài 帽帶 hat strings

màohuī 帽徽 insignia on a cap

màojià 帽架 a hatrack; a hat tree

màoshé 帽舌 a visor

màoyán 帽簷 the brim of a hat

màozi 帽子 1. a hat; a cap 2. a label; a tag

mào 貌
1. a facial appearance; features 2. a general appearance; a manner; form; bearing 3. to appear or pretend to be like 4. a ceremonious manner

màohé shénlí 貌合神離 to appear united outwardly but divided at heart

màoměi 貌美 (said of a woman) beautiful

màosì 貌似 to look like

me 麼
a particle used in the interrogative phrase, as in **shénme** 什麼 (what)

méi 沒
1. none; nothing; no 2. not yet; negative

méicuòr 沒錯兒 1. I'm quite sure. 2. can't go wrong

méidà méixiǎo 沒大沒小 ill-mannered or rude to one's elders

méiduōshǎo 沒多少 not much; not many

méifázi 沒法子 refer to **méifǎzi** 沒法子

méifǎzi 沒法子 no way out; no alternative (but...)

méiguānxi 沒關係 It does not matter. Never mind.

méijìnr 沒勁兒 1. to have no interest in, or desire for anything 2. listless

méijīng dǎcǎi 沒精打彩 listless; dispirited

méiláiyóu 沒來由 without any cause or reason; uncalled for

méiliángxīn 沒良心 without conscience

méimìng 沒命 1. with one's all-out effort 2. to die; dead

méiqù 沒趣 1. uninteresting 2.

rebuke; snub; rebuff

méishéme 沒什麼 refer to **méishénme** 沒什麼

méishénme 沒什麼 1. Nothing! Never mind! 2. not difficult, bad, etc.

méishìr 沒事兒 1. all right; O.K. 2. without anything to do

méishì zhǎoshì 沒事找事 1. to ask for trouble 2. to cavil

méitóu méinǎo 沒頭沒腦 (to utter, do, etc. something) all of a sudden; illogical

méiwán 沒完 1. continuous; without end 2. There will be no end to it.

méiwángfǎ 沒王法 lawless; without justice

méiwèikǒu 沒胃口 1. to have lost one's appetite 2. to have no interest in something

méixiàba 沒下巴 irresponsible talk; to talk through one's hat

méixiǎngdào 沒想到 unexpectedly; to have not thought about

méixīncháng 沒心腸 no heart for

méixīnyǎnr 沒心眼兒 1. careless 2. frank

méiyìsi 沒意思 weary; bored

méiyòng 沒用 useless; of no use

méiyǒu 沒有 no; not; without

méizàohua 沒造化 unlucky; out of luck

méizhé 沒轍 Nothing can be done about it.

méizhǒng 沒種 cowardly

méizhǔyì 沒主意 to lose one's head; cannot make up one's mind

méi 玫
1. the rose 2. another name of black mica—a sparkling red gem

méigui 玫瑰 1. the rose (blossoms) 2. black mica—a sparkling red gem

méiguihóng 玫瑰紅 1. rose red 2. rose-red

méi 枚
1. the stalk; the trunk as opposed to branches 2. a numer-

ary auxiliary (used in connection with coins, fruits, stamps, bombs, etc.) 3. a gag for troops marching at night when silence means a lot

méijǔ 枚舉 to enumerate; to recount one by one

méi 眉

1. eyebrows 2. the side 3. the top margin of a printed page in a book 4. a rare Chinese family name

méibǐ 眉筆 an eyebrow pencil

méifēi sèwǔ 眉飛色舞 to be overjoyed; to be exultant

méijié 眉睫 1. very close, imminent or urgent 2. eyebrows and eyelashes

méikāi yǎnxiào 眉開眼笑 very happy, joyful or jubilant

méilái yǎnqù 眉來眼去 (between a man and a woman) to converse with eyes

méimao 眉毛 the eyebrows

méimù 眉目 a general facial appearance

méimù chuánqíng 眉目傳情 to make sheep's eyes at (someone)

méimu 眉目 a general sketch or idea of things

méiqīng mùxiù 眉清目秀 good-looking; pleasant facial features

méishāo 眉梢 the ends of the eyebrows

méiyǔ 眉宇 1. a facial appearance 2. the forehead

méi 梅

1. prunes 2. a Chinese family name

méidú 梅毒 syphilis

méihuā 梅花 1. plum blossoms 2. a wintersweet

méihuālù 梅花鹿 sika; a spotted deer

méiqī hèzǐ 梅妻鶴子 the life of a hermit

méiyǔ 梅雨 the rainy season in early summer when plums are ripening

méizi 梅子 plums

méi 莓

1. berries 2. moss; lichen

méi 湄

shore; bank; the margin (of the water)

méi 媒

1. a marriage go-between; a matchmaker 2. a medium

méijiè 媒介 1. a go-between 2. a medium

méirén 媒人 a matchmaker

méishuò 媒妁 a matchmaker

méitǐ 媒體 a medium

méi 楣

the lintel (over a door)

méi 煤

1. coal; charcoal; coke 2. carbon; soot

méikuàng 煤礦 1. a coal mine 2. a coal shaft

méikuàng gōngrén 煤礦工人 a coal miner

méiqì 煤氣 gas (for lighting or heating)

méiqì zhòngdú 煤氣中毒 gas poisoning

méitàn 煤炭 coal; anthracite

méiyóu 煤油 kerosene

méi 霉

1. musty; moldy; mil-dewed 2. mildew; mold

méijūn 霉菌 mold; mildew

méijùn 霉菌 refer to **méijūn** 霉菌

méiqì 霉氣 1. a moldy smell; musty 2. bad luck or fortune

méi 黴

1. mold; mildew; must 2. germs; bacteria 3. fungi 4. dirty; dingy

méijūn 黴菌 1. fungi; mold fungi 2. germs; bacteria

méijùn 黴菌 refer to **méijūn** 黴菌

měi 每

every; each; per

měichù 每處 everywhere

měicì 每次 every time; each time

měidāng 每當 whenever; every time

M

měiféng 每逢 every time or whenever

měigé 每隔 every (three hours, five days, two feet, etc.)

měikuāng yùxià 每況愈下 getting worse and worse

měiměi 每每 repeatedly; often

měinián 每年 every year; annually; yearly

měirén 每人 everybody; everyone; each one

měitiān 每天 every day; daily

měiyuè 每月 every month; monthly

měi 美
1. beautiful; pretty; fine; fair 2. good; excellent; exquisite; nice 3. to be pleased with oneself 4. to praise

měibù shèngshōu 美不勝收 refer to **měibù shèngshōu** 美不勝收

měibù shèngshōu 美不勝收 (said of landscape, etc.) too many beautiful or excellent things to be fully appreciated

měidé 美德 virtue

měigǎn 美感 the esthetic sense

měigōng 美工 1. art designing 2. an art designer

měiguān 美觀 pleasant to the eye

měiguān dàfang 美觀大方 beautiful and dignified

Měiguó 美國 the United States; the United States of America; America

měihǎo 美好 exquisite; fine

měihuà 美化 1. to beautify 2. Americanized

Měijīn 美金 the (American) dollar

měilì 美麗 beautiful; pretty; fair

Měilìjiān Hézhòngguó 美利堅合衆國 the United States; the United States of America; America

měilún měihuàn 美輪美奐 splendid and magnificent

měimào 美貌 a beautiful face

(of a woman); beauty

měimèng 美夢 a fond dream; a beautiful dream

měimiào 美妙 exquisite; very pleasant

měimíng 美名 high prestige; a good reputation

měinánzǐ 美男子 a handsome man; an Adonis

měinǚ 美女 a beautiful woman; a beauty

měirén 美人 a beauty; a belle

měirényú 美人魚 a mermaid

měiróng 美容 to apply make-up or undergo plastic surgery

měiróngshī 美容師 a beautician

měiróngyuàn 美容院 a beauty parlor

měishù 美術 the fine arts

měishùguǎn 美術館 an art museum (or gallery)

měiwèi 美味 delicious; tasty

měiyán 美言 1. a fine saying 2. commending remarks

měiyì 美意 a kind intention; goodwill

měizhōng bùzú 美中不足 a flaw that mars perfection

Měizhōu 美洲 the Americas

měi 浼
1. to stain; to soil; to contaminate; to defile 2. full of water 3. to entrust

měiwū 浼污 to soil; to besmirch

měi 鎂
magnesium

měiguāngdēng 鎂光燈 a magnesium light

mèi 妹
a younger sister

mèifu 妹夫 the husband of one's younger sister; a brother-in-law

mèimei 妹妹 a younger sister

mèi 昧
1. obscure; dark 2. to hide; to pocket 3. to ignore (one's conscience, etc.) 4. blind; ignorant 5. to faint; fainting

mèiliángxīn 昧良心 to ignore one's conscience

mèiyú shìlǐ 昧於事理 to be ignorant of good reason, judgment, common practice, etc.

mèi 昧
dim-sighted; poor-visioned

mèiyú 昧於 blind to

mèi 寐
a sound sleep; a deep sleep; to doze; to sleep

mèi 媚
1. to fawn on; to flatter 2. to please 3. to love 4. attractive; fascinating; seductive 5. to coax

mèiwài 媚外 to fawn on a foreign power

mèi 瑁
a tortoise shell

mèi 魅
1. a mischievous spirit; a goblin; an elf 2. to charm; to mislead

mèihuò 魅惑 to bedevil; to bewitch

mèilì 魅力 glamor; sexiness; attractiveness; spell; charm; charisma

mèi 謎
refer to **mí** 謎

mēn 悶
1. (said of weather, rooms, etc.) oppressive or suffocating; stuffy 2. (said of a sound) muffled 3. to shut oneself or somebody indoors 4. to cover the tea pot for a while when one makes tea with boiling water

mēnrè 悶熱 sticky; sultry; sweltering

mēnshēng bùxiǎng 悶聲不響 to keep one's mouth shut; to remain silent; to remain quiet

mēnsǐ 悶死 to die of suffocation

mēn 燜
refer to **mèn** 燜

mén 門
1. a door; a gateway 2. a clan; a family 3. a sect; a school 4. a class; a category 5. the key; the

turning point 6. a piece of (artillery); a (cannon) 7. gatekeeping 8. a Chinese family name

ménbǎ 門把 refer to **ménbà** 門把

ménbà 門把 a doorknob; a door handle

méndāng hùduì 門當戶對 families of equal standing; well-matched

méndì 門第 family standing or reputation; family status

ménfáng 門房 1. a gatekeeper; a janitor; a doorman 2. a gate-house

ménfèng 門縫 crevices or cracks in the door

ménhù 門戶 1. a family 2. a strategic position 3. a sect; a bloc 4. a door

ménhù kāifàng 門戶開放 an open-door policy

ménhù zhījiàn 門戶之見 prejudiced or biased views of a particular sect, bloc, gang, etc.

ménjìn 門禁 a checkpoint at the gate

ménjìn sēnyán 門禁森嚴 The gate is strictly guarded.

ménkě luóquè 門可羅雀 (said of a store, fallen family, etc.) where visitors are few and far between; deserted

ménkǒu 門口 a gate; a doorway; an entrance

ménlián 門簾 a door curtain or screen

ménlíng 門鈴 the doorbell

ménlù 門路 1. one's means of approach, contacts, connections, etc. 2. a key or tip to a beginner in the pursuit of a certain skill; a knack

ménméi 門楣 1. a beam over a doorway 2. family standing

ménmiàn 門面 1. the front of a store 2. the outward appearance; a facade

ménpái 門牌 a doorplate

ménpài 門派 a sect

ménpiào 門票 an admission ticket; an entrance ticket

ménshēng 門生 pupils or disciples

M

ménshì 門市 to sell by retail; to sell over the counter

ménshìbù 門市部 a retail department; a sales department

ménshuān 門閂 a latch; a door bolt

méntíng ruòshì 門庭若市 1. (said of a store, etc.) doing booming business 2. (said of a household) swarmed with visitors; much visited

méntú 門徒 one's students, pupils, followers, or disciples

ménxià 門下 pupils or disciples

ményá 門牙 front teeth; incisors

ménzhěn 門診 to treat patients at the OPD; the outpatient service

mén 們

refer to men 們

mén 捫

to feel or touch with hands; to hold

ménxīn wúkuì 捫心無愧 to examine oneself and find nothing to be ashamed of

ménxīn zìwèn 捫心自問 to examine oneself; introspection

mèn 悶

melancholy; depressed; bored; in low spirits

mènmèn bùlè 悶悶不樂 depressed; sulky; unhappy

mènqì 悶氣 the sulks; pent-up sorrow or resentment

mèn 燜 also **mēn**

to cook with mild heat in a closed vessel; to cook in a casserole

men 們 also **mén**

an adjunct to a pronoun or noun to indicate plurality

mēng 矇

1. to deceive; to cheat 2. lucky

mēnghùn 矇混 to fake and cheat

mēngpiàn 矇騙 to deceive; to cheat

méng 氓

the people; the populace

ménglì 氓隸 people who are engaged in laborious work

méng 萌

1. to bud; to sprout; to germinate; to shoot forth 2. to harbor (a thought) 3. the beginning; initiation; initial

méngyá 萌芽 1. the initial stage of something 2. to sprout; to be in bud

méng 盟

1. a covenant; an oath; a vow; to covenant; to ally 2. a Mongol league

méngbāng 盟邦 an allied country; allies

méngguó 盟國 allied powers; allies

méngjūn 盟軍 allied troops; allied forces

méngyuē 盟約 a treaty of alliance

méng 蒙

1. to cover (up); to wrap 2. naive; childish 3. ignorant; gullible; stupid 4. to cheat; to deceive; to fool 5. to bear; to take 6. refer to **Měng** 蒙

méngbì 蒙蔽 to deceive; to swindle; to fool

ménghùn 蒙混 to hoodwink; to deceive and swindle

méngnàn 蒙難 to suffer disaster; to be in distress

méngpiàn 蒙騙 to fool with the intention to cheat

méngxiū 蒙羞 to suffer shame or insult

méngzài gǔlǐ 蒙在鼓裡 to be deceived

méng 濛

misty; drizzly

méngméng xìyǔ 濛濛細雨 drizzle; to drizzle

méng 檬

1. a kind of locust or acacia 2. lemon

méng 朦

1. the state of the moon just

before setting 2. dim; vague; hazy 3. to deceive; to swindle

ménglóng 朦朧 1. the appearance of the moon just before setting 2. dim; vague

méng 懵

refer to **měng** 懵 2

méng 矇

1. blind 2. (figuratively) ignorant; stupid and obstinate

méngbì 矇蔽 to hide the truth from a superior

ménglóng 矇矓 1. hazy; sight-blurred 2. half-asleep; drowsy; somnolent

měng 猛

1. bold; brave; fierce; violent 2. sudden and quick (strikes, thrusts, etc.) 3. severe; strict; stringent 4. a Chinese family name

měnggōng 猛攻 to attack in full force or savagely; a furious assault

měnghǔ 猛虎 a ferocious tiger

měnghuǒ 猛火 a raging fire

měngjiàng 猛將 a brave or courageous general

měngliè 猛烈 fierce; violent and savage

měngrán 猛然 suddenly; abruptly

měngshòu 猛獸 fierce wild beasts

měngzhuàng 猛撞 to ram or bump suddenly and with force

měngzhuī 猛追 to be in hot pursuit of

Měng 蒙 also **Méng**

short for Mongolia

Měnggǔ 蒙古 Mongolia; Mongolian

Měnggǔ dàifū 蒙古大夫 a medical quack

měng 錳

manganese

měng 懵

1. muddleheaded; confused 2. (also **méng**) ignorant

měngdǒng 懵懂 1. muddle-headed 2. ignorant

mèng 孟

1. a Chinese family name 2. the eldest of children 3. rude; rough 4. of or having to do with Mencius 5. the first month of a season

Mèngjiālā 孟加拉 Bengal

mènglàng 孟浪 rude; rough; rash

Mèngzǐ 孟子 Mencius

mèng 夢

1. a dream 2. to dream 3. wishful thinking; wishful

mènghuà 夢話 1. an absurd and unthinkable speech 2. somniloquy

mènghuàn 夢幻 illusion; a dream; reverie

mèngjian 夢見 to dream

mèngjìng 夢境 dreamland

mèngmèi yǐqiú 夢寐以求 to long for something day and night

mèngxiāng 夢鄉 asleep; dreamland; slumber

mèngxiǎng 夢想 1. a daydream 2. to dream of

mèngxióng zhīxǐ 夢熊之喜 to give birth to a son

mèngyǎn 夢魘 a nightmare; a bad dream

mèngyí 夢遺 nocturnal emission

mèngyì 夢囈 1. somniloquy 2. nonsense

mèngyóu 夢遊 to somnambulate

mèngzhào 夢兆 a prognostic from a dream

mèngzhōngrén 夢中人 a sweetheart

mī 咪

1. a meow (meou, miaow, miaou) 2. smiling

mí 迷

1. indistinct; vague; dim 2. to enchant; to be crazy about; to charm; to fascinate 3. a fiend; a fan

mígōng 迷宮 a labyrinth; a maze

míhu 迷糊 1. vague; dim; indistinct 2. unconscious; half awake and half asleep 3. dazzled 4. muddleheaded

míhuànyào 迷幻藥 a hallucinogenic

míhuo 迷惑 1. to misguide; to delude; to confuse; to mislead 2. confused; puzzled; bewildered

mílù 迷路 to go astray; to get lost

mínǐ 迷你 mini

mínǐqún 迷你裙 a miniskirt

mírén 迷人 charming; fascinating; enchanting

míshī 迷失 to get lost; to lose (one's way, etc.)

mítāng 迷湯 flatteries; honey words

mítú 迷途 1. to go astray; to get lost 2. a wrong path

mítú zhīfǎn 迷途知返 able to return to the proper path after going astray; able to correct one's own mistake

míwǎng 迷惘 bemused

míxìn 迷信 to believe blindly; superstition

mí 麋
a kind of deer

mílù 麋鹿 1. (animal) the elk and the deer 2. (figuratively) a rude person

mí 糜
1. congee; porridge; rice gruel 2. rotten; mashed; corrupted 3. to waste

mílàn 糜爛 1. rotten; corrupt debauchery 2. to oppress and destroy the people (through devious means)

mí 謎 also **mèi, mǐ**
a riddle; a puzzle; a conundrum; an enigma

mídǐ 謎底 an answer to a riddle; a truth

míyǔ 謎語 a riddle; a conundrum

mí 彌
1. to fill 2. more

míbǔ 彌補 to stop or fill up (a gap); to supplement

mífēng 彌封 to seal examinee's name on an examination paper

míliú 彌留 on the point of death from a serious disease

mímàn 彌漫 to be present all over; to fill the air

Mísa 彌撒 (Catholic) a Mass

míyuè 彌月 the completion of the first month after birth of a child

mí 靡
1. to waste; extravagant 2. to rot

mífèi 靡費 wasteful; extravagant; to waste

mí 瀰
(said of water) brimming; overflowing

mímàn 瀰漫 1. brimming or overflowing water 2. to permeate

mí 獼
a rhesus monkey

míhóu 獼猴 a rhesus monkey; a macaque

mǐ 米
1. hulled or husked rice; uncooked rice 2. a shelled or a husked seed 3. meter (the fundamental unit of length in the metric system)

mǐfàn 米飯 cooked rice

mǐfěn 米粉 1. rice flour 2. thin noodles made of rice flour

mǐjiǔ 米酒 rice wine; rice beer

mǐkāng 米糠 rice bran; paddy chaff

mǐshí 米食 a rice diet

mǐ 弭
1. to stop; to end 2. the ends of a bow

mǐbīng 弭兵 to stop war

mǐluàn 弭亂 to stop disturbance of a civil war

mǐ 靡
1. to disperse; to scatter; to divide; blown away by the wind 2. to lean with pressure 3. not; no; negative 4. tiny; petty; small 5. wonderful; good; excellent

mǐmǐ zhīyīn 靡靡之音 lewd music or songs

Mì 汨
name of a river in Hunan Province

mì 泌
to seep out; to excrete; to secrete

mìniàokē 泌尿科 the urological department

mìniào qìguān 泌尿器官 urinary organs

mì 祕 also **bì**
secret; confidential; hidden; unknown mysterious

mìfāng 祕方 a secret recipe

mìjué 祕訣 a knack; secrets (of success, etc.); the key (to the solution of a problem)

mìmì 祕密 secret; confidential; hidden; clandestine

mìmì wénjiàn 祕密文件 a classified document

mìshū 祕書 a secretary

mì 密
1. dense; tight; thick 2. close; intimate 3. secret; confidential; hidden

mìbào 密報 to send a secret message (or report)

mìbì 密閉 airtight; hermetic

mìbù 密布 closely or densely spread over; (with secret agents, guards, etc.) everywhere

mìbù tòufēng 密不透風 tightly shut; hermetically sealed

mìdù 密度 density

mìfǎng 密訪 1. to pay a secret visit 2. to make investigation by traveling incognito

mìfēng 密封 to seal tightly or securely

mìgào 密告 to tip off

mìhán 密函 a secret letter; a confidential letter

mìjí 密集 concentrated; crowded together

mìjiàn 密件 confidential or secret documents

mìmǎ 密碼 a secret code

mìmìmámá 密密麻麻 very dense

mìmóu 密謀 1. to plot 2. a secret scheme

mìqiè 密切 (said of relations, contact, etc.) close or intimate

mìqiè zhùyì 密切注意 to pay close attention to

mìshāng 密商 to hold private counsel (or secret talks)

mìshǐ 密使 a secret emissary

mìshì 密室 a secret chamber

mìtán 密談 to have a secret or close conversation

mìtàn 密探 a secret detective; a spy

mìyī 密醫 an unlicensed doctor; a quack

mìyǒu 密友 a close friend; an intimate

mìyuē 密約 a secret engagement or appointment

mì 覓
to seek; to search or look for

mìbǎo 覓保 to find a guarantor

mì 蜜
1. honey; nectar (in a flower) 2. sweet; syrupy; honeyed

mìfēng 蜜蜂 a honeybee; a bee

mìyuè 蜜月 a honeymoon

mì 冪
1. to cover with cloth 2. a cloth cover 3. (mathematics) power

mì 謐
silent; quiet; serene; still

mìjìng 謐靜 quiet; calm; tranquil; serene; silent

mí 謎
refer to **mí** 謎

mián 眠
1. to sleep; sleep 2. to hibernate; hibernation

mián 棉
cotton

mián'ǎo 棉襖 a cotton-padded Chinese jacket

miánbèi 棉被 a cotton quilt

miánbù 棉布 a cotton cloth

miánpáo 棉袍 a cotton-wadded long gown

miánshā 棉紗 cotton yarn

miánshéng 棉繩 cotton cord

miánxiàn 棉線 cotton thread; cotton

miánxù 棉絮 fluffed cotton; cotton batting

miánzhīpǐn 棉織品 cotton (piece) goods

mián 綿
1. cotton 2. everlasting; endless 3. weak

miánbó 綿薄 (a polite expression) my feeble strength, limited power, or poor abilities

mián'gèn 綿亙 to stretch in an unbroken chain

miánmián bùjué 綿綿不絕 to last forever

miányán 綿延 to stretch over a long distance

miányáng 綿羊 sheep

miǎn 免
1. to avoid; to escape; to evade 2. to forego; to spare; to excuse; to exempt 3. to dismiss (from office)

miǎnbuliǎo 免不了 unavoidable; to have to

miǎnchú 免除 1. to prevent 2. to exempt

miǎnde 免得 to save (the trouble of); to avoid; so as not to

miǎnfèi 免費 free of charge; gratuitous

miǎnkāi zūnkǒu 免開尊口 You might as well save your breath.

miǎnlǐ 免禮 (usually ordered by a superior) to forego formalities

miǎnpiào 免票 1. a free ticket; a free pass 2. free of charge

miǎnshì shēngxué 免試升學 to enter a school without taking an entrance examination

miǎnshuì 免稅 free of duty; duty-free

miǎnshuì shāngdiàn 免稅商店 a duty-free shop

miǎnsú 免俗 to forego customary routines, formalities, etc.

miǎntán 免談 You might just as well save your breath.

miǎnyàn 免驗 to be exempt from customs examination

miǎnyì 免役 exemption from military service

miǎnyì 免疫 immunity

miǎnzhí 免職 to be dismissed from office

miǎn 勉
1. to urge; to encourage 2. to strive; to make efforts; to exert oneself to

miǎnlì 勉勵 to encourage; to urge

miǎnqiǎng 勉強 1. involuntarily; reluctantly 2. barely 3. to force 4. unconvincing

miǎnwéi qí'nán 勉為其難 to take on some difficult job reluctantly

miǎn 娩
to give birth to a child

miǎn 冕
1. a ceremonial cap for high ministers in ancient China 2. a crown

miǎn 湎
1. drunk 2. unaware 3. changing

miǎn 惽
to remember; to give thought to

miǎnhuái 惽懷 to think of; to remember

miǎn 腼(靦)
1. shy; bashful 2. (said of girls) quiet and graceful

miǎntian 腼腆 shy; bashful

miǎn 緬
1. distant; far; remote 2. to think of something or somebody in the past

Miǎndiàn 緬甸 Burma

miǎnhuái 緬懷 to think of; to remember

miàn 面

1. the face of a person 2. the surface; the top; the face 3. a side; a direction; an aspect 4. extent; range; scale; scope 5. to face or confront; to look 6. face-to-face; in or to one's face; personally; directly 7. (mathematics) a plane 8. to indicate some thing flat

miànbù 面部 the face; facial

miànbù gǎisè 面不改色 not to change color; without batting an eyelid

miànduì 面對 to face; to confront; opposite; facing

miànduìmiàn 面對面 face-to-face; vis-a-vis

miàn'é 面額 (economics) denomination

miànhóng ěrchì 面紅耳赤 to blush; to flush

miànhuáng jīshòu 面黃肌瘦 thin and sickly in appearance; an emaciated look

miànji 面積 area

miànjīn 面巾 a face towel

miànjù 面具 a mask

miànkǒng 面孔 the face (of a person)

miànmào 面貌 appearance; face; looks

miànmiàn jùdào 面面俱到 well considered in every respect

miànmù 面目 face; features; looks; appearance; countenance

miànmù kězēng 面目可憎 abominable (in looks); ugly; repulsive in appearance

miànmù quánfēi 面目全非 Everything's changed beyond recognition

miànmù yīxīn 面目一新 a brand-new look

miànmù zhēngníng 面目爭獰 sinister in appearance

miànpáng 面龐 facial appearance; facial features

miànpào 面皰 pimples; acne; comedos

miànqià 面洽 to meet and talk it over

miànqián 面前 before; in front

of; in the presence of

miànróng 面容 countenance; face

miànshā 面紗 a veil (for women)

miànshàn 面善 1. to look familiar 2. to look kind-hearted

miànshàn xīn'è 面善心惡 a wolf in sheep's clothing

miànshàng wúguāng 面上無光 loss of prestige

miànshēng 面生 unfamiliar; to have not met before

miànshì 面試 an oral quiz; an audition; an interview

miànshòu jīyí 面授機宜 personally instruct somebody on the line of action to pursue

miànshú 面熟 to look familiar

miànshuāng 面霜 cream

miàntán 面談 to talk face-to-face; to take up a matter with somebody personally

miànwú rénsè 面無人色 to look ghastly pale; to look extremely scared

miànxiàng 面向 to face

miànyāo 面邀 to invite in person

miànyì 面議 face-to-face negotiations; to negotiate face to face

miànyǒu nánsè 面有難色 to look reluctant

miànzhào 面罩 a face guard

miànzhǐ 面紙 face tissues

miànzi 面子 1. honor; one's face (in the figurative sense) 2. the outside or facing of a garment

miàn 瞑

to throw into a state of confusion

miàn 麵

1. flour 2. dough 3. noodles

miànbāo 麵包 bread

miànbāodiàn 麵包店 a bakery

miànbāoshù 麵包樹 a breadfruit tree

miànbāoxiè 麵包屑 crumbs of bread

miànchá 麵茶 porridge made by mixing roasted flour in boiling

M

water

miànfěn 麵粉 flour

miànjīn 麵筋 gluten of flour

miànshí 麵食 wheaten foods; pastry

miàntiáo 麵條 noodles; spaghetti; vermicelli

miàntuán 麵團 dough

miáo 苗

1. a sprout 2. descendants; posterity 3. (said of children) peevish or disobedient 4. the Miao tribe in southwestern China 5. summer hunting 6. a Chinese family name 7. a beginning or omen

miáopǔ 苗圃 a seedbed; a nursery

miáotiao 苗條 (said of a woman) slim

miáotou 苗頭 the first sign of success

miáo 描

1. to trace; to draw; to sketch 2. to describe; to depict

miáohuì 描繪 to paint; to sketch; to describe

miáomó 描摹 to imitate (an old painting, etc.); to copy

miáoshù 描述 to describe

miáoxiě 描寫 to describe; to portray

miáo 瞄

to aim at; to take aim; to look at attentively

miáozhǔn 瞄準 to take aim

miǎo 眇

1. tiny; fine; small 2. blind in one eye

miǎomiǎo hūhū 眇眇忽忽 indistinct; too small to identify

miǎo 秒

1. (said of time or a degree) a second 2. the beard of grain

miǎozhēn 秒針 the second hand

miǎo 渺

1. endlessly long or vast 2. tiny; infinitesimal 3. indistinct; blurred

miǎománg 渺茫 1. boundless 2.

indistinct

miǎomiǎo 渺渺 blurred; indistinct

miǎorán 渺然 vast; boundless; endless

miǎowú rénjī 渺無人跡 remote and uninhabited

miǎoxiǎo 渺小 very small; tiny; infinitesimal

miǎo 淼

(said of water) extensive or overwhelming

miǎo 藐

1. to slight; to despise; to belittle; to treat with disdain 2. small; petite

miǎoshì 藐視 to disdain; to slight; to despise

miǎo 邈

1. distant; remote 2. (藐) to slight; to look down upon

miǎoshì 邈視 to despise; to look down upon

miào 妙

1. wonderful; excellent 2. very interesting; intriguing 3. clever; subtle; ingenious

miàobù kěyán 妙不可言 ingenious beyond description

miàojíle 妙極了 wonderful

miàojì 妙計 a wonderful idea

miàolíng 妙齡 young; in one's youth

miàonián 妙年 young; in one's youth

miàoqù héngshēng 妙趣橫生 full of wit and humor

miàoshǒu huíchūn 妙手回春 the hands that cure—used to praise a good physician

miàoshǒu kōngkōng 妙手空空 1. a wheeler-dealer 2. a pickpocket

miàoyòng 妙用 ingenious uses; (serving unexpected) subtle effects

miàoyǔ rúzhū 妙語如珠 sparkling discourse

miào 廟

a temple; a shrine

miàohào 廟號 the posthumous title of an emperor

miàohuì 廟會 a fair held at the site of a temple when the faithful converge to worship the deity

miàotáng 廟堂 1. the ancestral temple of the royal family 2. the court (of a monarch)

miàoyǔ 廟宇 a temple; a shrine

miàozhù 廟祝 a temple attendant

miē 乜

miēxié 乜斜 to glance sideways

miē 咩

the cries of sheep

miè 滅

1. to destroy; to ruin; to wipe out; to exterminate 2. to put out; to extinguish; to go out

mièdǐng 滅頂 to be drowned

mièhuǒqì 滅火器 a fire extinguisher

mièjī 滅跡 to destroy evidence

mièjìn tiānliáng 滅盡天良 to destroy utterly one's conscience

mièjué 滅絕 to exterminate; to annihilate; to wipe out

mièkǒu 滅口 to kill a person to prevent him from disclosing a secret

mièmén 滅門 to put a whole family to death

mièwáng 滅亡 to perish

mièzhǒng 滅種 to commit genocide

miè 蔑

1. to disdain; to slight; to despise; to neglect; to disregard; to feel contempt for 2. without; none; no 3. to cast away 4. tiny; small

mièshì 蔑視 to disdain; to slight; to flout or disregard (rules, etc.); to defy (orders, etc.)

mín 民

1. the people; the subject; the populace; the public 2. civilians 3. a Chinese family name

mínbāo wùyǔ 民胞物與 to be

kind to people and animals

mínbīng 民兵 1. a militiaman 2. a militia force

mínbù liáoshēng 民不聊生 The people cannot live in peace.

mínfǎ 民法 the civil law; the civil code

mínfáng 民房 a civilian house

mínfēng 民風 popular customs

mín'gē 民歌 a folk song; a ballad

mínhángjī 民航機 an airliner; a civil airplane (or aircraft)

Mínhángjú 民航局 Civil Aeronautics Administration (CAA)

mínjiān 民間 among the people

mínqíng 民情 the condition of the people

mínqióng cáijìn 民窮財盡 The means of the people have been used up.

mínquán 民權 civil rights; people's rights

mínshēng 民生 the people's livelihood

mínshēng wèntí 民生問題 problems of the people's livelihood

mínshēng wùzī 民生物資 daily necessities

mínsú 民俗 folkways

mínxīn 民心 popular sentiments; popular support

mínxuǎn 民選 popularly elected

mínyáo 民謠 a folk song

mínyì 民意 public opinion; popular sentiments

mínyì cèyàn 民意測驗 a poll; polltaking

mínyì dàibiǎo 民意代表 people's representatives

mínyì jīguān 民意機關 the people's representative body

mínyíng 民營 privately owned

mínyuàn fèiténg 民怨沸騰 Discontent among the people is boiling.

mínyùn 民運 1. civil transport 2. democratic movement

mínzhī mín'gāo 民脂民膏 the hard-won possessions of the people

mínzhì 民治 government by the people

mínzhòng 民眾 the people; the multitude; the masses; the populace

mínzhòng tuántǐ 民眾團體 a civic organization

mínzhǔ 民主 democratic; democracy

mínzhǔ cháoliú 民主潮流 the tide of democracy

Mínzhǔdǎng 民主黨 Democratic Party (of the United States)

mínzhǔ zhèngzhì 民主政治 democracy

mínzhǔ zhǔyì 民主主義 democratism

mínzú 民族 a nation; a people

mínzú wǔdào 民族舞蹈 race dance

mínzúxìng 民族性 national character

mínzú yìshí 民族意識 national consciousness

mínzú yìshì 民族意識 refer to mínzú yìshí 民族意識

mínzú yīngxióng 民族英雄 a national hero

mín 閩 refer to mǐn 閩

mǐn 皿 also míng a shallow container (such as a dish, plate, saucer, etc.)

mǐn 泯 to destroy; to eliminate; to put an end to; to vanish

mǐnjué 泯絕 to be lost for ever; extinguished

mǐnmiè 泯滅 to vanish without a trace

mǐnmò 泯沒 to vanish without a trace

mǐn 抿 1. to smooth (hair); to stroke; to caress 2. to purse up (lips); to contract; to tuck 3. to sip; a sip

mǐnzuǐxiào 抿嘴笑 to smile with mouth closed

mǐn 敏 1. quick; agile; speedy; clever; smart; nimble; sensitive 2. diligent; industrious; earnest; eager

mǐn'gǎn 敏感 1. sensitive 2. (medicine) allergic

mǐnjié 敏捷 agile; adroit; quick; nimble

mǐnruì 敏銳 keen; sharp; sharp-witted; acute

mǐn 黽 to strive; to endeavor

mǐnmiǎn 黽勉 to strive; to endeavor; to exert oneself

mǐn 愍 to pity; to commiserate

mǐnxù 愍恤 to feel pity; to show kindness (toward people)

Mǐn 閩 also mín 1. another name for Fujian Province 2. name of a river and an ancient tribe in today's Fujian Province

Mǐnnányǔ 閩南語 the southern Fujian dialect

mǐn 憫 1. to pity; to commiserate; to feel concerned over 2. to sorrow; to grieve

míng 名 1. a name; a designation; a title; rank 2. position; honor; fame; renown; reputation 3. famous; noted; distinguished; renowned; valuable; precious; noble; rare; great 4. to name; to describe

míngbù xūchuán 名不虛傳 The reputation is well supported by fact.

míngcè 名冊 a roster; a roll

míngchǎn 名產 a noted product or special product (of a place)

míngchēng 名稱 the name or designation (of a thing)

míngchuí qīngshǐ 名垂青史 to go down in history

míngcí 名詞 1. a noun 2. a term

míngcì 名次 one's position or standing

míngcún shíwáng 名存實亡 (said of established institutions) to exist in name only

míngdān 名單 a name list; a roster; a roll

míng'é 名額 the number of openings, or quota (for employees, students, etc.)

míngfèn 名分 a role or duties proper to one's title

míngfù qíshí 名副其實 to be worthy of the name or reputation

míngguì 名貴 valuable; precious; rare

míngguò qíshí 名過其實 to have an exaggerated reputation

mínghuā yǒuzhǔ 名花有主 The beauty has already been won by somebody.

míngjié 名節 honor and integrity

mínglì 名利 fame and gain

mínglì shuāngshōu 名利雙收 to achieve both fame and wealth

míngliè qiánmáo 名列前茅 to head the list of successful candidates

mínglíng 名伶 a renowned actor or actress

míngliú 名流 a celebrity; a notable

míngluò Sūn Shān 名落孫山 to fail in an examination

míngmǎn tiānxià 名滿天下 to be world-famous

míngmén guìxiù 名門閨秀 a daughter of an illustrious family

míngmù 名目 a name

míngpái 名牌 1. a famous brand 2. a nameplate

míngpiàn 名片 a calling card

míngqì 名氣 fame; reputation; renown

míngrén 名人 a celebrity; a notable

míngrénlù 名人錄 who's who

míngshēng 名聲 fame; reputation; renown

míngshèng 名勝 a scenic spot; a resort

míngshèng gǔjī 名勝古跡 places of historic interest and scenic beauty

míngshī 名師 a great teacher; a master

míngtáng 名堂 1. a dignified name or designation 2. a result that is worth mentioning

míngwàng 名望 fame; reputation; renown

míngxià 名下 1. under (one's) account 2. to (one's) account

míngyán 名言 a maxim; an adage

míngyáng sìhǎi 名揚四海 to become famous all over the world

míngyī 名醫 a famous doctor

míngyì 名義 1. the name 2. the outward reason

míngyù 名譽 1. honor; reputation 2. honorary

míngyù bóshì 名譽博士 an honorary doctorate

míngyuàn 名媛 a young lady of note

míngzào yīshí 名噪一時 (said of writers, artists, etc.) very famous at one time

míngzhèng yánshùn 名正言順 valid in name and in reasoning; to deserve

míngzhù 名著 a literary masterpiece

míngzi 名字 the name (of a person, etc.)

míng 明

1. light; bright; brilliant 2. clear; understandable; to clarify; to understand; obvious; evident 3. intelligent; clever 4. eyesight; the seeing faculty 5. day; daybreak; dawn 6. to state; to assert; to show 7. next (day or year) 8. the Ming Dynasty (1368-1644 A.D.) 9. aboveboard; honest 10. a Chinese family name

míng'àn 明暗 brightness and darkness

míngbai 明白 1. to understand; to know (a trick, secret, etc.) 2. clever and bright; smart 3. obvi-

míngbiàn shìfēi 明辨是非 to know distinctly what is right and what is wrong

míngchá 明察 to be sharp and

M

perspicacious

míngchá ànfǎng 明察暗訪 to investigate openly and secretly

míngchá qiūháo 明察秋毫 able to examine the tiniest things (as the tip of a hair) —sharp discerning intelligence

míngfán 明礬 alum

míngjiàn 明鑑 1. a clear mirror 2. (your) penetrating judgment

míngjìng gāoxuán 明鏡高懸 transcending or perspicuousness intelligence in judgment

míngkuài 明快 1. lucid and lively (style, etc.) 2. straightforward

mínglǎng 明朗 1. open-minded; straightforward 2. to become clear; to clarify

mínglǐ 明理 understanding; reasonable

míngliàng 明亮 bright (eyes, etc.); will-illuminated (rooms, etc.)

míngliǎo 明瞭 1. to understand 2. clear and evident

mínglìng 明令 a written order; a government order or decree

míngmèi 明媚 fair and enchanting, or bright and charming

míngmíng 明明 obviously; plainly

míngmóu hàochǐ 明眸皓齒 (said of a woman) with bright eyes and sparkling teeth

míngmù zhāngdǎn 明目張膽 (to do some shameful or unlawful acts) openly or shamelessly

míngnián 明年 next year; the coming year

míngqiāng ànjiàn 明槍暗箭 overt and covert attack

míngqiāng yìduǒ, ànjiàn nánfáng 明槍易躲，暗箭難防 It's easy to dodge an open attack but difficult to escape from a clandestine one.

míngquè 明確 clear and definite; unequivocal

míngrì 明日 1. tomorrow 2. one of these days; some day

míngrì huánghuā 明日黃花 1. outmoded; obsolete 2. what has already taken place

míngshì 明示 to express clearly

míngshuō 明說 to speak frankly; to speak up

míngtiān 明天 tomorrow

míngwén guīdìng 明文規定 clearly stipulated in regulations, laws, agreements, contracts, etc.

míngxiā 明蝦 a prawn

míngxiǎn 明顯 evident; obvious; clear

míngxìnpiàn 明信片 a postcard; a postal card

míngxīng 明星 1. a bright star 2. a movie star

míngxiū zhàndào, àndù Chéncāng 明修棧道，暗渡陳倉 to feign action in one place and to make the real move in another

míngyǎnrén 明眼人 a man of clear mind and high intelligence

míngzhé bǎoshēn 明哲保身 (often said of people living under tyranny) A wise person who knows what's best for himself can safeguard his personal security.

míngzhēng àndòu 明爭暗鬥 (often said of intramural fights) to fight overtly and covertly

míngzhī 明知 to know perfectly well; to be fully aware

míngzhī gùwèn 明知故問 to ask about something one already knows

míngzhì 明智 sensible; sagacious; wise

míngzhì zhījǔ 明智之舉 a wise move; an intelligent or sensible act

míng 冥

1. dark; obscure; dim; dusk 2. stupidity; stupid 3. far and high 4. deep 5. the unseen world; Hades 6. night

míngfǔ 冥府 the underworld; Hades

míngmíng zhīzhōng 冥冥之中 (said of divine influence) imperceptibly but inexorably

míngsī kǔxiǎng 冥思苦想 to cudgel one's brains

M

míngwán bùlíng 冥頑不靈 stupid and stubborn

Míngwángxīng 冥王星 the planet Pluto

míngxiǎng 冥想 deep meditation

míng 茗 also **mǐng**
tea; a tea plant

míngjù 茗具 a tea set

míng 溟
1. drizzle 2. vast; boundless 3. the sea; the ocean

míng 銘
1. to engrave; to inscribe; to imprint 2. inscriptions

míngjì zàixīn 銘記在心 to imprint on one's mind

míngwén 銘文 inscription; epigraph

míngxiè 銘謝 to show gratefulness

míng 鳴
1. (said of birds) to sing; to chirp; to warble; (said of cocks) to crow 2. the notes of birds 3. to make sounds; to sound

míngdí 鳴笛 to blow a whistle; to signal with a siren

míngfàng 鳴放 the airing of views (through posters, meetings or other media)

mínggǔ érgōng 鳴鼓而攻 to attack while beating the drum

míngjīn shōubīng 鳴金收兵 to beat the gong to call back the troops

míngqiāng 鳴槍 to fire rifles into the air

míngyuān 鳴冤 to complain of unfairness; to air grievances

míngzhōng 鳴鐘 to strike or toll a bell

míng 瞑 also **mǐng**
to close the eyes

míngmù 瞑目 1. to close the eyes 2. to die without regret or in peace

míng 酩
refer to **mǐng** 酩

míng 螟
snout moth's larva

mínglíng 螟蛉 1. corn earworm 2. adopted son

mǐn 皿
refer to **mǐn** 皿

mǐn 茗
refer to **míng** 茗

mǐng 酩 also **míng**
drunk; intoxicated; inebriety; inebriate; tipsy

mǐngdǐng 酩酊 drunk; intoxicated; dead drunk; tipsy

mǐng 瞑
refer to **míng** 瞑

mìng 命
1. life 2. a fate; destiny; a lot 3. the ordinances of Heaven 4. orders; a command

mìng'àn 命案 a case of murder or homicide

mìngbù gāijué 命不該絕 not destined to die

mìnglìng 命令 to order; to command

mìnglìngháng 命令行 (computer) command line

mìnglìngliè 命令列 (computer) command line

mìngmài 命脈 a lifeline

mìngmíng 命名 to name, christen, baptize, or dub

mìngtí 命題 1. a proposition (in logic) 2. to prepare examination questions

mìngyùn 命運 a fate; destiny; a lot; fortune

mìngzài dànxī 命在旦夕 Death may come (to a person) any minute.

mìngzài dànxì 命在旦夕 refer to **mìngzài dànxī** 命在旦夕

mìngzhōng zhùdìng 命中注定 (said of individuals) predestined

mìngzhòng 命中 to hit the target

miù 謬 also **niù**
1. incorrect; wrong; mistaken 2.

absurd; unreasonable

miùlùn 謬論 an absurd statement; a fallacious argument

miùwù 謬誤 an error; inaccuracy; fallacy

mō 摸 also **māo**

1. to feel or touch lightly with fingers; to caress 2. to grope 3. to try to find out; to feel out 4. to seek after; to try to get at

mōbuzháo tóunǎo 摸不著頭腦 to be at a loss

mōcǎi 摸彩 to draw lots to determine the prize winners in a raffle or lottery

mōhēir 摸黑兒 to do something in the dark

mōsuo 摸索 1. to do things slowly 2. to grope (in the dark, the meaning of, etc.); to feel (in one's pocket, etc.)

mōyú 摸魚 to idle; to loaf on a job

mó 模

1. a model; a norm 2. to imitate; to copy 3. (糢)blurred; indistinct

mófàn 模範 an example; a model

mófànshēng 模範生 a model student

mófǎng 模仿 to imitate; to copy

móhu 模糊 1. dim; vague; ambiguous 2. to obscure

móléng liǎngkě 模稜兩可 equivocal; ambiguous

mónǐ 模擬 to simulate; to imitate

móshì 模式 a model; a formula; a miniature; a pattern

mótèr 模特兒 1. a model (for artists, photographers, etc.) 2. a manikin

móxíng 模型 a model; a formula; a miniature; a pattern

mó 摹

1. to copy; to make an exact copy 2. to model or pattern after; to imitate

móběn 摹本 a facsimile

mófǎng 摹仿 to copy; to model or pattern after; to imitate; to ape

mónǐ 摹擬 to model or pattern

after

mó 摩

1. to chafe; to scour; to rub; to scrape 2. friction 3. to feel with the hand 4. (now rarely) to work and encourage each other (especially in study) 5. to learn from long and constant study

mócā 摩擦 1. to chafe; to scour 2. friction

módēng 摩登 modern; fashionable

Mójiézuò 摩羯座 (astronomy) Capricorn

Mónàgē 摩納哥 Monaco

móquán cāzhǎng 摩拳擦掌 1. to get ready for a fight 2. to be eager to start on a task

mósuō 摩挲 to caress, touch, rub, etc. with the hand

mótiān dàlóu 摩天大樓 skyscrapers

mótuōchē 摩托車 a motorcycle

mó 膜

1. to kneel and worship 2. (also **mò**) membrane 3. (also **mò**) a film; a thin coating

móbài 膜拜 to worship

mó 磨

1. to dawdle; to waste time; to while away 2. to rub; to grind; to polish; to wear 3. sufferings; obstacles; setbacks

mócā 磨擦 1. to rub 2. friction

móceng 磨蹭 to be tardy; to be slow; to dawdle

móchǔ chéngzhēn 磨杵成針 Persistent efforts can achieve difficult things.

módāo 磨刀 to sharpen a knife

móguāng 磨光 to polish; to burnish

móliàn 磨鍊 to train; to harden; to discipline

mómiè 磨滅 1. to wear out 2. to obliterate

mómò 磨墨 to rub down an ink stick

mónàn 磨難 sufferings; obstacles; difficulties

móshízidì 磨石子地 terrazzo

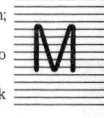

floor

mósǔn 磨損 wear and tear; to wear away

mó 魔

a wizard; a witch; a demon; a devil

mófǎ 魔法 witchcraft; wizardry; sorcery; magic

móguǐ 魔鬼 devils; demons; evil spirits

mólì 魔力 magic power; wizardly ability; charm; spell

móshù 魔術 witchcraft; wizardry; sorcery; magic

móshù fāngkuài 魔術方塊 a magic square

móshùshī 魔術師 a magician

Mówáng 魔王 the Devil; Satan; Prince of Darkness

mózhǎng 魔掌 devil's clutches; evil hands

mózhǎo 魔爪 devil's talons

mǒ 抹

1. to wipe; to rub; to mop 2. to smear; to apply to 3. to obliterate; to blot out

mǒbù 抹布 a dish cloth; a mopper; a cleaning rag

mǒdiào 抹掉 to wipe out

mǒpiàn 抹片 a smear (for microscopic examination)

mǒqù 抹去 to wipe out

mǒshā 抹殺 to withhold recognition for; do not give credit to

mǒshā 抹煞 to withhold recognition for; do not give credit to

mò 末

1. last; final 2. late; recent 3. unimportant; insignificant 4. the end; the tip 5. the four limbs

mòbān 末班 the last scheduled train, bus, ship, or airplane in a day

mòdài 末代 the last reign (of a dynasty)

mòliǎo 末了 in the end; finally

mònián 末年 the declining years of one's life, a dynasty, etc.

mòrì 末日 1. the last day; doom 2. (Christianity) Doomsday; Judgment Day

mòshāo 末梢 the tip; the end

mòshì 末世 the last years (of a dynasty)

mòwěi 末尾 the end

mòyè 末葉 1. posterity; descendants 2. the last part of a dynasty 3. the latter part of a century

mò 沒

1. to sink; to submerge 2. to overflow; to rise beyond 3. to disappear 4. to go into oblivion 5. none; exhausted 6. eliminated 7. completed finished 8. to take property away from another; to confiscate 9. to die

mòchǐ nánwàng 沒齒難忘 to remember (a favor) as long as one lives

mòluò 沒落 1. to sink 2. the decline (of an empire, etc.)

mòshōu 沒收 to confiscate; confiscation

mò 沫

1. tiny bubbles on the surface of water; froth; suds; lather 2. saliva

mò 歿

to die; death

mòshì bùwàng 歿世不忘 shall never forget

mò 抹

1. to plaster 2. a tight undergarment 3. to turn

mò 陌

paths in the rice field

mòshēng 陌生 unfamiliar; strange; inexperienced

mòshēngrén 陌生人 a stranger

mò 茉

white jasmine

mòlì 茉莉 white jasmine

mò 脈

refer to **mài** 脈

mòmò hánqíng 脈脈含情 (said of eyes) quietly sending the message of love

mò 麥

refer to **mài** 麥

M

mò 莫
1. not 2. a Chinese family name

mòcè gāoshēn 莫測高深 unfathomable; inscrutable

mòdà 莫大 greatest; utmost

mòfēi 莫非 1. certainly; surely 2. all; all-inclusive; the whole amount of 3. Can it be that...?

mòmíng qímiào 莫名其妙 1. incomprehensible; mysterious; baffling 2. impossible (as in an impossible person)

mònì zhījiāo 莫逆之交 close friendship; bosom friends

Mòsīkē 莫斯科 Moscow

mòxūyǒu 莫須有 a trumped-up charge; false accusation

mò 寞
still; silent; quiet; lonely

mò 漠
1. a desert 2. unconcerned; indifferent 3. quiet; silent

mòbù guānxīn 漠不關心 to pay no attention at all; do not care at all

mòrán 漠然 1. indifferent; unmoved 2. completely ignorant

mòshì 漠視 1. to despise 2. to ignore 3. to underestimate

mò 膜
refer to **mó** 膜 2, 3

mò 墨
1. black; dark 2. a black dye 3. a Chinese inkstick; ink 4. calligraphy 5. literate; letters; learning 6. statutes; institutions 7. greedy; covetous 8. to tattoo the face —one of the five punishments in ancient China

mòbǎo 墨寶 treasured calligraphic works

mòhé 墨盒 an ink box

mòjìng 墨鏡 sunglasses

mòlǜ 墨綠 blackish green

mòshǒu chéngguī 墨守成規 to stick to old rules; conservative

mòshuǐ 墨水 1. ink 2. learning; letters

mòyú 墨魚 the squid; the cuttle-fish

mòzhī 墨汁 1. ink 2. learning; letters

mò 默
1. speechless; silent 2. quiet; still

mò'āi 默哀 to stand in silent tribute

mòbù zuòshēng 默不作聲 to keep silence; to keep quiet; to refuse to speak

mòjì 默記 silently remember

mòjù 默劇 pantomime

mòmò 默默 1. quietly; silently 2. secretly; in one's heart

mòmò wúwén 默默無聞 obscure; unknown to the public

mòmò wúyán 默默無言 wordless; speechless; silent; in silence

mòniàn 默念 1. to repeat (a passage, etc.) silently inside the mind 2. to ponder or think

mòqì 默契 a tacit understanding; an implicit agreement; a secret agreement

mòrèn 默認 tacit consent, confession or approval

mòshū 默書 to write from memory

mòxiǎng 默想 to meditate; to contemplate

mòxiě 默寫 to write from memory

mòxǔ 默許 tacit permission

mò 磨
1. a mill 2. to turn around 3. to grind (grain, etc.)

mòfāng 磨坊 a mill (referring to the building)

mò 驀
1. sudden; abrupt 2. to mount the horse

mòdì 驀地 suddenly; all of a sudden

mòrán 驀然 suddenly; all of a sudden

móu 牟
1. to seek 2. to bellow (or low)

móulì 牟利 to seek profits

móu 眸

the pupil of the eye—the eyes

móu 謀

1. to scheme; to plan; to design 2. a scheme; a stratagem; a conspiracy 3. astute; resourceful 4. to consult 5. to seek; to try to get

móucái hàimìng 謀財害命 to commit murder out of greed; to murder somebody for his money

móufǎn 謀反 to plot a revolt; to conspire against the state

móuhài 謀害 1. to plot against someone 2. to murder

móuhuà 謀畫 to scheme; to plot; to plan; to design; to devise

móulì 謀利 to seek profit

móulüè 謀略 1. a strategy; a plot; a scheme 2. (said of a person) resourceful; astute

móumiàn 謀面 to meet each other; to see each other

móuqiú 謀求 to try to get; to seek

móushā 謀殺 to murder

móushēng 謀生 to make a living; to get a livelihood

móushì 謀士 a strategist; a resourceful man; an adviser; a counselor

móushì zàirén, chéngshì zàitiān 謀事在人，成事在天 Man proposes, but God disposes.

móuzhí 謀職 to try to find employment; to hunt for a job

mǒu 牡

refer to **mǔ** 牡

mǒu 某

1. a certain person or thing 2. formerly used in place of "I"

mǒuchù 某處 a certain place; somewhere

mǒumǒu 某某 so-and-so; a certain person

mǒunián 某年 a certain year

mǒurén 某人 1. a certain person 2. a pronoun used in place of one's own name

mǒurì 某日 a certain day

mǒushíhòu 某時候 sometime; a certain time

mǒuxiē 某些 certain (things, people, etc.)

mǒuzhǒng 某種 certain (reasons, results, etc.)

mòu 茂

refer to **mào** 茂

mú 模

a mold; a form; a matrix

múyàng 模樣 appearances; looks

mǔ 母

1. one's mother 2. mother—(figuratively) the origin 3. female

mǔ'ài 母愛 maternal love

mǔgǒu 母狗 a bitch

mǔjī 母雞 a hen

mǔjiěhuì 母姊會 a mother-sister conference

mǔlǎohǔ 母老虎 1. a shrew; a termagant 2. a tigress

mǔlù 母鹿 a roe deer; a roe

mǔmǎ 母馬 a mare

mǔniú 母牛 a cow

mǔqīn 母親 mother

Mǔqīnjié 母親節 Mother's Day

mǔshī 母獅 a lioness

mǔxiào 母校 one's alma mater; Alma Mater

mǔyèchā 母夜叉 1. an ugly female devil 2. an ugly and fierce woman

mǔyīn 母音 a vowel

mǔyǔ 母語 1. one's native language 2. a parent language

mǔzhū 母豬 a sow

mǔzǐ 母子 1. mother and son 2. principal and interest

mǔ 牡 also **mǒu**

a male animal

mǔdān 牡丹 a peony

mǔlì 牡蠣 an oyster

mǔlù 牡鹿 a stag

mǔmǎ 牡馬 a stallion

mǔ 姆

1. (in old China) a governess; a woman tutor 2. a matron who looks after small children

mǔ 拇
1. the thumb 2. the big toe

mǔzhǐ 拇指 the thumb

mǔ 畝
a Chinese land measure (equal to 733 1/2 square yards)

mù 木
1. a tree 2. wood; timber 3. made of wood; wooden 4. simple; honest 5. senseless; numbed 6. a coffin

mùbǎn 木板 planks; boards

mùbàng 木棒 a wooden club

mùcái 木材 lumber; timber

mùchái 木柴 firewood

mùfá 木筏 a wooden raft

mùgōng 木工 1. a carpenter; a woodworker 2. carpentry

mùguā 木瓜 papaya

mùgùn 木棍 a wooden club

mùjī 木屐 clogs; pattens

mùjiang 木匠 a carpenter; a woodworker

mùmián 木棉 silk cotton

mùnà 木訥 refer to **mùnè** 木訥

mùnǎiyī 木乃伊 a mummy

mùnè 木訥 honest and slow-witted

mù'ǒu 木偶 a puppet

mù'ǒuxì 木偶戲 a puppet show

mùtàn 木炭 charcoal

mùtou 木頭 1. wood 2. a stupid fellow

mùtóurénr 木頭人兒 a stupid fellow; an idiot

mùwū 木屋 a log cabin

mùxiāng 木箱 a wooden box; a wooden trunk

mùyǐ chéngzhōu 木已成舟 (literally) The timber has been turned into a boat already.—It is irrevocable.

mùzhà 木柵 a stockade

mùzhuāng 木樁 a wooden post or pile

mù 目
1. the eye 2. to look; to regard; to see 3. a table of contents; a category

mùbiāo 目標 1. an objective; a target; to target 2. an aim; a goal

mùbù shídīng 目不識丁 completely illiterate

mùbù shídīng 目不識丁 refer to **mùbù shídīng** 目不識丁

mùbù xiágěi 目不暇給 So many things come into sight that the eyes are kept fully occupied.

mùbù xiájiē 目不暇接 So many things come into sight that the eyes are kept fully occupied.

mùbù xiéshì 目不斜視 to look straight ahead

mùbù zhuǎnjīng 目不轉睛 to look attentively

mùdèng kǒudāi 目瞪口呆 dumbfounded; stupefied

mùdì 目的 a purpose; an objective; an end; an aim

mùdìdì 目的地 a destination

mùdǔ 目睹 to see directly; to witness

mùguāng 目光 insight; vision; sight

mùguāng jiǒngjiǒng 目光炯炯 to have eyes with a piercing gleam

mùguāng ruìlì 目光銳利 sharp-sighted; sharp-eyed

mùjī 目擊 to witness

mùjí 目擊 refer to **mùjī** 目擊

mùjīn 目今 now; the present

mùkōng yīqiè 目空一切 to look down on everyone or everything

mùlù 目錄 1. contents 2. a list; a catalogue

mùqián 目前 now; the present

mùsòng 目送 to gaze after; to follow with the eyes

mùwú fǎjì 目無法紀 to disregard all laws and regulations; lawless

mùwú zūnzhǎng 目無尊長 to show no respect to elders and superiors

mùxuàn 目眩 dazzled

mùzhōng wúrén 目中無人 to be supercilious; to be overweening

mù 沐

1. to shampoo; to wash; to bathe; to cleanse 2. a holiday; a leave; to take a leave 3. to receive favor

mùhóu érguàn 沐猴而冠 Clothes do not make the man.

mùyǔ jiéfēng 沐雨櫛風 refer to **mùyǔ zhìfēng** 沐雨櫛風

mùyǔ zhìfēng 沐雨櫛風 to work and toil

mùyù 沐浴 1. to bathe 2. to steep in or receive favor 3. to soak in

mù 牧

1. to pasture; to shepherd 2. a pasture 3. to govern 4. a magistrate

mùcǎo 牧草 herbage; pasture

mùchǎng 牧場 a pasture; a ranch

mùdí 牧笛 a shepherd's pipe

mùmǎ 牧馬 to pasture horses

mùniú 牧牛 to pasture cattle; to herd cows

mùshi 牧師 a preacher; a clergyman

mùtóng 牧童 a cowboy; a shepherd boy

mùyáng 牧羊 to pasture sheep; to tend sheep

mùyángquǎn 牧羊犬 a shepherd dog; a collie

mùyángrén 牧羊人 a shepherd

mù 睦

friendly; amiable; to befriend; to be on friendly terms

mù 募

1. to recruit or enlist (personnel) 2. to raise (funds); to collect

mùjí 募集 to recruit; to raise; to collect

mùjuān 募捐 to collect contributions

mùkuǎn 募款 to raise funds

mù 墓

a grave; a tomb; a mausoleum

mùbēi 墓碑 a gravestone; a tomb stone

mùdì 墓地 the site of a grave or tomb; a cemetery

mùxué 墓穴 the vault of a tomb

mùxué 墓穴 refer to **mùxué** 墓穴

mùyuán 墓園 a cemetery ground

mù 幕

1. a screen; a curtain 2. a tent 3. an advisor; staffs 4. an act 5. to cover

mùhòu 幕後 behind the scenes; backstage

mùhòu cāozòng 幕後操縱 to pull strings behind the scenes

mùhòu rénwù 幕後人物 behind-the-scenes personalities; string-pullers

mùhòu xīnwén 幕後新聞 behind-the-scenes news

mùliáo 幕僚 staffs; secretaries; advisors

mù 慕

1. to yearn for; to long for 2. to adore; to admire

mùmíng 慕名 1. eager for fame 2. to admire another's reputation

mùmíng érlái 慕名而來 1. to be attracted to a place by its reputation as a scenic spot, etc. 2. to visit a stranger far away because of his or her reputation as a hero, great beauty, etc.

mù 暮

1. sunset; evening; dusk 2. closing (years); late

mùchūn 暮春 late spring

mùgǔ chénzhōng 暮鼓晨鐘 1. (literally) evening drums and morning bells—used in Buddhist temples to tell time 2. ringing statements or remarks which arouse the public from degeneracy or warn against lurking danger, etc.

mùnián 暮年 closing years of one's life

mùqì chénchén 暮氣沈沈 1. (said of a person) despondent and dejected; lethargy 2. (said of atmosphere) dead and dull; gloomy

mùsè 暮色 dusk; twilight; the gloaming

mù 穆

1. peaceful; serene 2. respectful; reverent 3. profound 4. majestic; solemn 5. the right side of an ancestral shrine 6. a Chinese family name

mùrán 穆然 peaceful and respectful

ná 拿

1. to hold in one's hand; to grasp; to take 2. to arrest; to apprehend; to capture 3. to use; to employ (a method, device, etc.) 4. with; in 5. (now rarely) to be confined or restrained

náchū 拿出 to take out

nádeqǐ, fāngdexià 拿得起, 放得下 able to advance or retreat, to attack or withdraw, etc. as the occasion demands; flexible

nádìng zhǔyi 拿定主意 to make up one's mind

nájī 拿緝 to search and arrest

nániē 拿捏 1. deliberately make things difficult for others 2. to pretend to observe rules of propriety

náqī 拿緝 refer to **nájī** 拿緝

náqù 拿去 to take away

náshǒu 拿手 to be particularly good or dexterous at

náshǒu hǎoxì 拿手好戲 one's specialty

náwěn 拿穩 1. to hold steadily 2. to predict with confidence

nǎ 哪 also **něi**

(an interrogative particle) how; where; what; which

nǎge 哪個 1. Which one? 2. Who is it?

nǎli 哪裡 where

nǎpà 哪怕 even if

nǎr 哪兒 where

nǎxiē 哪些 which; who; what

nà 那 also **nè, nèi**

1. that; those 2. then; in that case

nàge 那個 1. that one 2. embarrassing 3. funny 4. too much, too far, too hot, etc.

nàli 那裡 that place; there; over there

nàme 那麼 1. so; that; in that way 2. then; such being the case 3. about; or so

nàxiē 那些 those

nà 吶

1. to shout 2. to speak hesitatingly

nàhǎn 吶喊 to give a whoop, or to shout (in a battle, etc.)

nà 納

1. to receive; take; to accept; to admit; to adopt 2. to offer as tribute 3. to enjoy; to feel 4. to repress; to restrain 5. to patch old clothes 6. a Chinese family name

nàhuì 納賄 1. to offer bribes 2. to receive bribes

nàjiàn 納諫 to accept an admonition

nàliáng 納涼 to enjoy the cool air

nàmènr 納悶兒 1. to feel depressed 2. to feel curious

nàrù 納入 to bring into

nàshuì 納稅 to pay duties or taxes

nàshuìrén 納稅人 the taxpayer

nà 娜

a word used in the transliteration of a western female name

na 哪

a phrase-final partical

nǎi 乃

1. to be 2. but; however 3. and also; moreover 4. so; therefore 5. you; your 6. then 7. if

nǎizhì 乃至 1. so that; so... as to; leading to 2. hence; consequently

nǎi 奶

1. the breasts of a woman 2. milk 3. grandma 4. to feed with milk; to breast-feed 5. a term of respect for married women

nǎichá 奶茶 tea with milk

nǎifěn 奶粉 milk powder

nǎimā 奶媽 a wet nurse

nǎinai 奶奶 1. a term of respect for older women 2. grandma

nǎipíng 奶瓶 a milk bottle

nǎishuǐ 奶水 milk

nǎiyóu 奶油 butter

nǎizuǐ 奶嘴 the nipple (of a nursing bottle)

nǎi 奈

1. what; how; but 2. to bear; to endure

nàihé 奈何 What to do now? What can we do now? What then? Why?

nài 耐

to bear; to endure; to stand; to resist

nàijiǔ 耐久 lasting a long time; durable

nàilì 耐力 endurance; staying power; stamina

nàimó 耐磨 (said of metals) wearproof

nàirè 耐熱 heat-proof

nàirén xúnwèi 耐人尋味 intriguing; perplexing

nàixīn 耐心 patience; perseverance

nàixìng 耐性 patience; perseverance

nàiyòng 耐用 durable; sturdy

nán 男

1. a human male; a man; a boy; a son 2. a baron

nánbàn nǚzhuāng 男扮女裝 disguised as a woman

nánbīnxiàng 男儐相 a best man (at a wedding)

náncèsuǒ 男廁所 men's room

nándīyīn 男低音 (music) bass

nán'gāoyīn 男高音 (music) tenor

nánhuān nǚ'ài 男歡女愛 The couple are enraptured with love.

nánjué 男爵 a baron

nánjué fūrén 男爵夫人 a baroness

nánnǚ guānxi 男女關係 relations between the two sexes

nánnǚ píngděng 男女平等 equal rights for both sexes

nánnǚ yǒubié 男女有別 Males and females should be distinguished.

nánpéngyou 男朋友 a boyfriend

nánpú 男僕 a male servant

nánrén 男人 a man

nánshēng 男生 a boy

nánxìng 男性 1. the male sex 2. the masculine gender

nánzhōngyīn 男中音 (music) baritone, or barytone

nánzhuāng 男裝 male costume; men's clothing

nánzǐ 男子 a man

nánzǐhàn 男子漢 a manly man

nán 南

1. south; southward 2. a type of ancient music played in the south of China 3. a Chinese family name

Nánbànqiú 南半球 the Southern Hemisphere

nánběi 南北 1. north and south 2. from north to south 3. (in ancient China) a man

nánběihuò 南北貨 sundry goods

nánbian 南邊 1. the south; the southern side 2. the southern provinces of China

nánbù 南部 southern part; south

Náncháo 南朝 the Southern Dynasties

nánfāng 南方 the south; the South

nánfāngrén 南方人 a southerner

Nán Fēi 南非 South Africa

nánguā 南瓜 a pumpkin; a cushaw

nánhú 南胡 the two-stringed Chinese viola

Nánhuíguīxiàn 南回歸線 the Tropic of Capricorn

Nánjí 南極 the South Pole; the Antarctic Pole

Nánjíquān 南極圈 the Antarctic Circle

Nánjízhōu 南極洲 Antarctica

Nánjīng 南京 Nanjing

Nánkē yīmèng 南柯一夢 a dream

Nán Měizhōu 南美洲 South America; Latin America

nánqiāng běidiào 南腔北調 to speak with a mixed accent

Nánshā Qúndǎo 南沙群島 Nansha Qundao; the Spratly Islands

nánwěi 南緯 latitudes south of the equator

nánxià 南下 to go down south

mányuán běichè 南轅北轍 refer to **nányuán běizhé** 南轅北轍

nányuán běizhé 南轅北轍 practice diametrically opposed to preaching

nánzhēng běizhàn 南征北戰 to participate in battles everywhere

nán 喃

1. the cries of a swallow 2. to murmur; to mumble; to mutter

nánnán zìyǔ 喃喃自語 to murmur to oneself

nán 難

1. difficult; not easy; hard 2. unable; not in a position to 3. unpleasant; not good

nánchán 難纏 hard to deal with

nánchǎn 難產 1. (medicine) difficult labor; dystocia 2. hard to come into being or materialize

nánchī 難吃 unbearable to palate; unpalatable; tasting bad

nánchǔ 難處 hard to get along with

nánchu 難處 difficult points; problems

nándǎo 難倒 to confound; to daunt

nándào 難道 Is it possible...? Do you really mean to say...?

nándé 難得 1. rare; hard to get; hard to come by 2. fortunate; lucky 3. rarely; seldom

nándǒng 難懂 hard to understand

nándù 難度 degree of difficulty; difficulty

nánfēn nánshě 難分難捨 (said of a couple in love) very reluctant to separate

nánguài 難怪 1. cannot hold responsible for 2. no wonder that; it's understandable that

nánguān 難關 an impasse; an obstacle or obstruction difficult to overcome; a difficult situation; a crisis

nánguò 難過 1. to feel uneasy; to feel bad; to feel sorry 2. hard to endure or bear; uncomfortable 3. difficult; hard

nánjiǎng 難講 hard to say; difficult to predict

nánjiě nánfēn 難解難分 1. difficult to separate 2. to be locked together (in a struggle)

nánkān 難堪 1. to embarrass; embarrassment 2. intolerable; unbearable

nánkàn 難看 1. bad-looking; not pleasant to the eye；ugly; offensive; repulsive 2. embarrassing; awkward

nánmiǎn 難免 can hardly avoid; inescapable

nánnài 難耐 unable to endure; unbearable

nánnéng kěguì 難能可貴 rare and commendable

nánsè 難色 an expression of reluctance

nánshì 難事 a difficult task; something not easy to manage; a difficult matter

nánshòu 難受 1. to feel bad; to feel sorry 2. unbearable; intolerable 3. to suffer pain; to feel unwell

nánshuō 難說 1. hard to say or predict 2. difficult to speak out 3. not easy to express with words

nántáo fǎwǎng 難逃法網 It's hard to escape the dragnet of law. Crime does not pay.

nántí 難題 a hard nut to crack; a tough problem; a puzzle

nántīng 難聽 1. unpleasant to hear; to grate on the ear 2. offensive; coarse 3. scandalous

nánwàng 難忘 difficult to forget; unforgettable

nánwéiqíng 難爲情 to feel ashamed, uneasy or embarrassed; bashful

nányán zhīyǐn 難言之隱 secrets or problems one doesn't want to reveal

nányǐ 難以 difficult; hard to

nányǐ wéijì 難以爲繼 hard to carry on; difficult to continue

nányǐ xiāngchǔ 難以相處 hard to get along with

nányǐ xiāngxìn 難以相信 incredible; difficult to believe; hard to believe

nányǐ xíngróng 難以形容 indescribable; beyond description

nǎn 赧
to turn red from shame or embarrassment; to blush

nǎnkuì 赧愧 to blush; to be ashamed

nàn 難
1. disaster; calamity; misfortune 2. to rebuke; to reprove; to reprimand 3. to discountenance

nànmín 難民 refugees

nànxiōng nàndì 難兄難弟 fellow sufferers

náng 囊
1. a bag; a sack; a purse 2. to put in a bag

nángkōng rúxǐ 囊空如洗 to be dead broke; to be penniless

nángkuò 囊括 to encompass; to include; to comprise

nángzhōngwù 囊中物 (figuratively) a thing very easy to get

nǎng 曩
past; former

nǎngshí 曩時 in the past; in former times

nǎngxī 曩昔 in the past; in former times

nángxī 曩昔 refer to **nángxī** 曩昔

náo 撓
1. to bend; to daunt; to subjugate 2. to hinder; to obstruct 3. to scratch; to rub

náo 鐃

1. a kind of bell used in the army in ancient times 2. cymbals

nǎo 惱
1. to anger; to exasperate; to trouble; to irritate; to vex; to annoy 2. angered; offended; annoyed; vexed

nǎohèn 惱恨 to be angry at; to be vexed at

nǎohuǒ 惱火 to become irritated; annoyed

nǎonù 惱怒 angry; indignant; anger; rage; indignation

nǎorén 惱人 irritating

nǎoxiū chéngnù 惱羞成怒 to be moved to anger by the feeling of shame

nǎo 瑙
agate; cornelian

nǎo 腦
the brain

nǎodai 腦袋 the head

nǎohǎi 腦海 the mind

nǎojīn 腦筋 brains; mentality; mental capacity

nǎokù 腦庫 a brain trust; a think tank

nǎoliúshī 腦流失 the brain drain

nǎomǎn chángféi 腦滿腸肥 heavy-jowled and potbellied-the idle rich

nǎoshénjīng 腦神經 cranial nerves

nǎoyán 腦炎 encephalitis

nǎoyìxiě 腦溢血 refer to **nǎoyìxuè** 腦溢血

nǎoyìxuè 腦溢血 a stroke; apoplexy

nǎozhèndàng 腦震盪 brain concussion

nǎozhòngfēng 腦中風 (pathology) stroke

nǎozi 腦子 1. the brain 2. mental capability

nào 淖
slush; mud

nàonìng 淖濘 slushy mud

nào 鬧

nào 鬧 1. to disturb; to agitate; to trouble 2. to have or experience (disasters, sickness, etc.) 3. noisy; uproarious; stormy; clamorous

nàobièniu 鬧彆扭 to act peevishly; to show resentment; to be dissatisfied

nàodùzi 鬧肚子 to have loose bowels

nàofān 鬧翻 to fall out with somebody

nàofāntiān 鬧翻天 to raise a hell of a noise; to raise a rumpus

nàoguǐ 鬧鬼 1. haunted 2. to play tricks behind somebody's back

nàohōnghōng 鬧轟轟 1. arousing intense excitement; sensational 2. noisy; uproarious; clamorous

nàojīhuang 鬧飢荒 to have a famine

nàojiǔ 鬧酒 to start a drinking bout; to engage in a drunken brawl

nàojù 鬧劇 a farce

nàoqíngxù 鬧情緒 to be in a bad mood; to be in low spirits

nàoshì 鬧市 a busy shopping district

nàoshì 鬧事 to cause trouble or uproar

nàoxiàohuà 鬧笑話 to arouse ridicule; to make oneself a laughingstock

nàoxīnfáng 鬧新房 rough horseplay at a wedding

nàozhewánr 鬧著玩兒 to raise hell just for fun or joke

nàozhōng 鬧鐘 an alarm clock

nè 那

refer to **nà** 那

ne 呢

an interrogative or emphatic particle used after a sentence

něi 哪

refer to **nǎ** 哪

něi 餒

1. to starve; hungry 2. decay or decomposition of fish 3. lacking in confidence, courage, etc.; disheartened; dispirited

nèi 內

1. inside; within; inner; interior 2. wife 3. the palace of an emperor

nèibù 內部 the interior; the internal parts

nèichūxiě 內出血 refer to **nèichūxuè** 內出血

nèichūxuè 內出血 internal bleeding

nèidì 內地 the hinterland; the inland

nèidì 內弟 younger brothers of one's wife

nèidìng 內定 to have already decided, but yet to be officially announced

nèifēnmì 內分泌 internal secretion; endocrines

nèifúyào 內服藥 drugs taken orally or internally

nèigé 內閣 the cabinet

nèihǎi 內海 inland seas; continental seas

nèihán 內涵 (logic) intension; connotation

nèiháng 內行 a specialist; an expert

nèihé 內河 inland rivers

nèihòng 內訌 an intramural fight

nèijiān 內奸 a spy within; a traitor

nèijǐng 內景 indoor scenes

nèijiù 內疚 deep regret; remorse

nèikē 內科 internal medicine

nèikē yīshēng 內科醫生 a physician

nèilù 內陸 inland; interior

nèilùguó 內陸國 a landlocked country

nèiluàn 內亂 rebellion; a civil war

nèiluànzuì 內亂罪 treason

nèimù xiāoxi 內幕消息 inside information

nèiqīn 內親 relatives of one's wife

nèiqín 內勤 desk work

nèiqíng 內情 an inside story

nèiránjī 內燃機 an internal-combustion engine

nèirén 內人 my wife

nèiróng 內容 1. the meaning, theme, etc. of a literary work 2. content

nèishāng 內傷 internal injury

nèiwù 內務 1. domestic affairs; internal affairs 2. (in ancient China) affairs within the palace 3. family affairs

nèixiàn 內線 inside contacts; a stool pigeon

nèixiàng 內向 introversion; introverted

nèixiāo 內銷 (said of local products) for domestic sale or market

nèixīn 內心 heart

nèiyī 內衣 underwear; undergarments

nèiyìng 內應 an inside help; a planted agent

nèiyōu wàihuàn 內憂外患 (said of countries) troubles within and without

nèizài 內在 inherent; intrinsic; internal

nèizàiměi 內在美 inner beauty

nèizàng 內臟 internal organs; viscera

nèizhài 內債 internal debts

nèizhàn 內戰 a civil war

nèizhèng 內政 internal (or domestic) affairs

nèizǐ 內子 my wife

nèi 那

refer to **nà** 那

nèn 嫩

1. tender; delicate 2. young; immature 3. (of color) light

nènyá 嫩芽 a tender shoot

nènyè 嫩葉 a young leaf; a tender leaf

néng 能

1. can; to be able to 2. capability; talent; competence 3. energy, as atomic energy

néngfǒu 能否 can or can't; may or may not

nénggàn 能幹 capable; able; very competent and efficient

nénggòu 能夠 able to; capable of; can; may

néngjiàndù 能見度 visibility

nénglì 能力 1. power, as the power of the Almighty, etc. 2. a faculty; ability; capability

néngliàng 能量 1. (physics) energy 2. capabilities

néngnài 能耐 skill; ability; capability

nénggū néngshēn 能屈能伸 adaptable; flexible

néngshǒu 能手 a capable or competent person; an expert

néngyán shànbiàn 能言善辯 eloquent and glib in argument

néngyuán 能源 the sources of energy

néngyuán wēijī 能源危機 the energy crisis

néngyuán wēijī 能源危機 refer to **néngyuán wēijī** 能源危機

néngzhě duōláo 能者多勞 The capable are usually the busy ones.

nèng 濘

pasty; soft and mashy

nèngní 濘泥 mire; mud

ní 尼

a nun

Níbó'ěr 尼泊爾 Nepal

nígū 尼姑 a nun

nígū'ān 尼姑庵 a nunnery

nígǔdīng 尼古丁 nicotine

Níjiālā Dàpùbù 尼加拉大瀑布 Niagara Falls

nílóng 尼龍 (textile) nylon

Níluóhé 尼羅河 the Nile River; the Nile

ní 泥

1. mud; mire; earth; soil; clay 2. to paste; to plaster 3. mashed vegetables or fruit; paste

níbā 泥巴 mud; clay; earth; soil

níjiāng 泥漿 mire

ní'nào 泥淖 mud; quagmires

nínìng 泥濘 muddy

níniú rùhǎi 泥牛入海 like a clay ox entering the sea—gone

forever

níqiū 泥鰍 a loach; a mudfish

níshā 泥沙 1. mud and sand; silt 2. something worthless

níshuǐjiàng 泥水匠 a bricklayer; a plasterer

nísù 泥塑 a clay sculpture

nítǔ 泥土 mud; clay; earth; soil

níwáwa 泥娃娃 a clay doll

nízhǎo 泥沼 mire; swamp; morasses

nízhuān 泥磚 sun-dried mud bricks

ní 呢

1. a woolen fabric 2. a murmur

ní'nán 呢喃 1. the chirps of the swallows 2. to murmur; to twitter

níróng 呢絨 woolen goods; wool fabric

ní 霓

a rainbow; a colored cloud

níhóngdēng 霓虹燈 the neon light

nǐ 你

you (singular)

nǐhǎo 你好 How do you do? How are you?

nǐmen 你們 you (plural)

nǐsǐ wǒhuó 你死我活 (to fight) until either of the combatants is killed

nǐ 擬

1. to plan; to intend; to decide; to determine 2. to draft; to draw up; to design 3. to imitate

nǐdìng 擬定 to draw up or map out (a plan); to draft

nǐgǎo 擬稿 to prepare manuscripts or write copies (for publication)

nǐqǐng 擬請 to intend to ask or request

nǐrénfǎ 擬人法 (rhetoric) personification

ní 泥

1. to be tied down by conventions, old practices; very conservative 2. to request with sweet words 3. inapplicable

nìgǔ 泥古 to stick to ancient ways and thoughts

nì 逆

1. to meet; to welcome 2. to oppose; to go against 3. beforehand; in advance 4. inverse; converse; adverse

nìchā 逆差 (commerce) an adverse balance of trade; a deficit

nìfēng 逆風 1. a head wind 2. against the wind

nìjìng 逆境 adverse circumstances; adversity

nìlái shùnshòu 逆來順受 to accept adversity philosophically; to be resigned to one's fate

nìshuǐ xíngzhōu 逆水行舟 a boat going against the stream

nìxiàng 逆向 in the opposite direction

nì 匿

to hide; to conceal

nìmíngxìn 匿名信 an anonymous letter

nì 溺

1. to drown 2. to indulge

nì'ài 溺愛 to lavish one's love upon (a child)

nìbì 溺斃 to be drowned

nìsǐ 溺死 to be drowned

nì 暱

intimate; close

nì'ài 暱愛 love or affection (between opposite sexes)

nì 膩

1. fatty or greasy (food) 2. smooth 3. dirty 4. bored; tired; weary 5. intimate (friends)

nìrén 膩人 1. boring; tiresome 2. too greasy

nìyǒu 膩友 bosom friends

niān 拈 also **nián**

1. to take or hold with fingers 2. to draw (lots)

niānhuā rěcǎo 拈花惹草 to fool around with women; lewd and prurient

niānxiāng 拈香 to offer

incense; to burn joss sticks

nián 年

1. a year 2. one's age 3. a Chinese family name

niánbiǎo 年表 a chronicle

niáncài 年菜 food and dishes prepared for the Lunar New Year

niánchū 年初 the beginning of the year

niándài 年代 1. an age, era, generation, etc. 2. years in a decade

niándǐ 年底 the end of a year

niándù 年度 a year fixed arbitrarily for convenience, a better administrative purpose, etc., as a fiscal year, a school year, etc.

niándù juésuàn 年度決算 (accounting) annual closing

niánfen 年份 age; time

niánfù lìqiáng 年富力強 the prime of one's life

nián'gāo 年糕 New Year's cake

nián'gāo déshào 年高德劭 advanced in years and virtue

niánguān 年關 the end of a year when all accounts and debts must be settled

niánhào 年號 the title of an emperor's reign

niánhuá 年華 time; years; age

niánhuá xūdù 年華虛度 to have spent one's best years without any achievements

niánhuì 年會 an annual meeting or convention

niánjí 年級 (in school) a grade

niánjì 年紀 years; age

niánjià 年假 New Year's holidays or vacation

niánjiàn 年鑑 an almanac; a yearbook

niánjié 年節 the three major festivals of the year—the Dragon Boat, the Mid-Autumn and the Lunar New Year festivals

niánjīn 年金 an annuity

niánjiǔ shīxiū 年久失修 worn down by the years without repair

niánlǎo 年老 to get old; aged

niánlǐ 年禮 New Year's presents

niánlì 年利 annual interest (rate)

niánlì 年曆 a calendar with the whole year printed on one sheet

niánlíng 年齡 age

niánlún 年輪 annual rings (indicating the age of a tree)

niánmài 年邁 to get old; aged

niánnián 年年 every year; year after year

niánpǔ 年譜 a biography arranged in chronological order

niánqián 年前 before the turn of the year

niánqīng 年輕 young; youthful; youth

niánqīng màoměi 年輕貌美 young and pretty

niánshào 年少 young

niánshēn rìjiǔ 年深日久 after a long lapse of time

niánshì 年事 the age of a person

niánsuì 年歲 1. the age of a person 2. years; an age 3. harvests

niánwěi 年尾 the end of a year

nianxī 年息 annual interest (rate)

niánxí 年息 refer to **niánxī** 年息

niánxiàn 年限 a service life

niánxīn 年薪 an annual salary

Niányè 年夜 New Year's Eve

niányèfàn 年夜飯 the dinner for the whole family on the eve of the Lunar New Year

niányòu wúzhī 年幼無知 ignorance for being young of age

niányú bùhuò 年逾不惑 to have passed 40

niánzhǎng 年長 old or aged; older

niánzhōng 年終 the end of a year

niánzī 年資 1. the years one spends in an endeavor or job 2. seniority

nián 拈

refer to **niān** 拈

nián 粘

to paste up; to attach to; to stick up; to glue

niántiē 粘貼 to paste; to stick

nián 黏
1. to stick 2. sticky; glutinous; gluey; adhesive; clammy; viscid

niándù 黏度 (chemistry) viscosity

niánlì 黏力 adhesive power; viscosity

niánmó 黏膜 the mucous membrane

niántiē 黏貼 to glue; to paste; to stick

niántǔ 黏土 clay

niánxìng 黏性 viscosity

niányè 黏液 viscous liquid; mucus

niánzhù 粘住 to stick; to adhere

niǎn 捻
1. to nip with fingers 2. the Nian Bandits 3. to twist 4. something made by twisting

niǎndēng 捻燈 to turn up the wick of a lamp

niǎn 撚
to twist with fingers; to toy with

niǎnxiāng 撚香 to burn joss sticks in worship

niǎn 碾
1. a stone roller 2. to mill; to roll; to crush

niǎnmǐchǎng 碾米廠 a rice-husking mill

niǎnsuì 碾碎 to pulverize

niǎn 輾(碾)
to grind; to run over

niǎnbì 輾斃 to be run over by a vehicle and got killed

niǎn 攆
1. to expel; to oust; to drive 2. to catch up

niǎnchuqu 攆出去 to throw (someone) out; to drive away

niǎnzǒu 攆走 to drive (someone) away; to dismiss

niàn 念
1. to think of; to miss; to remember 2. to read out aloud; to chant 3. to study; to attend

school 4. twenty

niànfó 念佛 to call out Buddha's name aloud as an expression of devotion

niànjīng 念經 to chant or intone scriptures

niànjiù 念舊 to remember old friends

niànniàn bùwàng 念念不忘 to have (somebody or something) always in one's mind

niànniàn yǒucí 念念有詞 to mumble; to mutter

niànshū 念書 1. to read a book aloud 2. to study 3. to receive an education

niàntou 念頭 an idea; a thought

niànzhòu 念咒 to chant or intone charms

niànzhū 念珠 a Buddhist rosary

niàn 唸
to read; to chant; to recite

niànniàn yǒucí 唸唸有詞 to mumble to oneself

niáng 娘
1. mother 2. girls or women

niángjia 娘家 one's wife's family

niángniangqiāng 娘娘腔 sissy; womanish

niàng 釀
1. to brew; to ferment 2. to take shape or form slowly 3. wine

niàngchéng 釀成 to bring about slowly; to lead slowly to; to breed; to form gradually

niàngjiǔ 釀酒 to brew wine

niàngzào 釀造 to brew

niǎo 鳥
a bird

niǎocháo 鳥巢 a bird's nest

niǎodàn 鳥蛋 bird's eggs

niǎojìn gōngcáng 鳥盡弓藏 to discharge a worthy official in times of peace

niǎokàn 鳥瞰 1. to have a bird's-eye view 2. an aerial view; a bird's-eye view

niǎolóng 鳥籠 a birdcage

niǎoshòu 鳥獸 birds and beasts

niǎowéi shíwáng, rénwèi cáisǐ 鳥為食亡，人為財死 Birds die in pursuit of food, and human beings die in pursuit of wealth.

niǎowō 鳥窩 a bird's nest

niǎoyǔ huāxiāng 鳥語花香 birds singing and flowers radiating fragrance—the joyous scene in spring

niǎoyuán 鳥園 an aviary

niǎozhuǎ 鳥爪 1. bird's talons 2. fine, delicate human finger tips

niǎozhī jiāngsǐ, qímíng yěbēi 鳥之將死，其鳴也悲 (figurative) A man's last words are sincere.

niǎo 裊
1. curling up (as smoke, etc.); wavering gently 2. around; all around, as sound of music or voices of spring

niǎoniǎo 裊裊 1. curling up 2. continuous (sound of music, etc.)

niǎo 嫋
delicate; graceful

niǎoniǎo 嫋嫋 1. (said of a willow) waving gracefully 2. (said of a young woman) appealingly slender and delicate

niào 尿
1. urine 2. to urinate

niàobù 尿布 a diaper; a napkin; a nappy

niàochuáng 尿床 (said of a child) to wet the bed

niàodào 尿道 a urethra; a urinary canal

niàohú 尿壺 a bedpan; a chamber pot

niàopén 尿盆 a chamber pot; a urinal

niē 捏(揑)
1. to knead; to pinch; to squeeze or press with fingers 2. to mold (mud, etc.) 3. to fabricate; to trump up; to make up

niēbào 捏報 to fabricate a report or charge

niēshǒu niējiǎo 捏手捏腳 stealthily; to pussyfoot

niēsù 捏塑 to mold (mud) into a statue, etc.

niē yìbǎhàn 捏一把汗 to be breathless with anxiety or tension

niēzào 捏造 to fabricate (evidence, etc.); to trump up (charges, etc.)

niè 涅(湼)
1. to blacken; to dye black 2. to block up

Nièpán 涅槃 Nirvana

niè 鎳
nickel

nièbì 鎳幣 nickel coins

Niè 聶
a very rare Chinese family name

niè 孽
1. the son of a concubine 2. a monster 3. sin; evil 4. calamity

nièzǐ 孽子 1. a son born of a concubine 2. a sinner

niè 囁
to speak haltingly

nièrú 囁嚅 to speak haltingly

niè 齧
to gnaw; to bite

nièhé 齧合 1. to clench the teeth 2. (said of gears) to mesh; to engage

nièshì 齧噬 to bite; to gnaw

niè 躡
1. to tread on; to step over 2. to follow; to pursue 3. to walk lightly; to tiptoe

nièshǒu nièjiǎo 躡手躡腳 walking with light steps; walking stealthily

niè 鑷
1. tweezers; pincers; forceps 2. to pull out; to nip

nièzi 鑷子 a pair of tweezers

nín 您
a deferential form of "**nǐ** 你" (you)

níng 寧
1. peace; repose; serenity; tran-

quility 2. refer to **nìng** 寧

níngjìng 寧靜 quiet; tranquil; serene; placid; calm

níng 凝

1. to freeze 2. to congeal; to coagulate 3. to form; to take shape 4. to concentrate; to cohere

nínggù 凝固 (said of liquid) to congeal; to solidify

níngjié 凝結 to condense; to curdle

níngjù 凝聚 to concentrate; to curdle

níngshén 凝神 to concentrate

níngshén dìtīng 凝神諦聽 to listen attentively

níngshì 凝視 to gaze (lovingly)

níngxiǎng 凝想 to meditate

níngzhòng 凝重 dignified

níng 獰

an awe-inspiring look; a fierce appearance

níngxiào 獰笑 to grin hideously

níng 嚀

to enjoin; to instruct

níng 擰

to twist; to pinch; to wring

níng 檸

lemon

níngméng 檸檬 lemon

níngméngshuǐ 檸檬水 lemonade

níngméngsuān 檸檬酸 citric acid

nǐng 擰

1. to wrench; to twist; to screw 2. wrong; mistaken 3. to differ; to disagree

nǐngkāi 擰開 to wrench apart

nìng 佞

1. eloquent; persuasive; gifted with a glib tongue 2. obsequious; fawning 3. to believe (in superstition) 4. one given to flattery

nìngchén 佞臣 a flattering courtier

nìng 寧 also **níng**

1. would rather; had rather; would sooner 2. could there be

nìngquē wúlàn 寧缺毋濫 It is better to leave a deficiency uncovered than to have it covered without discretion.

nìngsǐ bùqū 寧死不屈 would rather die than submit (or surrender)

nìngwéi yùsuì, bùwéi wǎquán 寧為玉碎，不為瓦全 would rather die for justice than live in disgrace

nìngyuàn 寧願 would rather; would sooner

nìng 擰

pigheaded; stubborn

nìng 濘

muddy; miry

niū 妞

a girl; a little girl

niú 牛

1. an ox; cattle; a cow; a bull 2. a Chinese family name 3. (said of a person) stubborn; headstrong

niúchē 牛車 an oxcart; an ox-drawn cart

niúdāo xiǎoshì 牛刀小試 1. to try to kill a fly with a long spear 2. the first small display of a master hand

niúdòu 牛痘 cowpox; vaccinia

niúfèn 牛糞 cow dung

niúguǐ shéshén 牛鬼蛇神 1. absurdities 2. forces of evil

niújiǎo 牛角 horns of cattle

Niúláng Zhīnǚ 牛郎織女 the Cowherd and the Weaving Maid —lovers who can rarely see each other

niúnǎi 牛奶 (cow's) milk

niúnǎitáng 牛奶糖 butter candy; toffee; taffy

niúnǎn 牛腩 sirloin; tenderloin

niúpái 牛排 steak; beefsteak

niúpéng 牛棚 a cattle pen, shed, or yard

niúpíqi 牛脾氣 stubbornness; obstinacy

niúpízhǐ 牛皮紙 kraft paper; brown paper

niúqún 牛群 a herd of cattle

niúròu 牛肉 beef

niúròugān 牛肉乾 dried roast beef

niúròumiàn 牛肉麵 noodles served with stewed beef

niúshè 牛舍 a cattle pen, shed, or yard

niútóu bùduì mǎzuǐ 牛頭不對馬嘴 irrelevant; unconnected

niúwā 牛蛙 a bullfrog

niúyǐn 牛飲 to drink heavily; to drink like a fish

niúyóu 牛油 butter

niúzǎi 牛仔 a cowboy

niúzǎikù 牛仔褲 blue jeans; jeans

niǔ 扭
1. to wrench; to twist; to turn; to wring 2. to seize; to grasp

niǔdǎ 扭打 to have a grapple or to grapple with somebody

niǔduàn 扭斷 to dislocate (the bones) by twisting or wrenching

niǔgān 扭乾 to wring (a towel, clothes, etc.) dry

niǔnie 扭捏 1. to mince 2. to do things in an unmanly way

niǔqū 扭曲 to twist

niǔqū zuòzhí 扭曲作直 to distort the fact

niǔshāng 扭傷 a sprain; to wrench

niǔyāo 扭腰 1. to twist the hip or the waist 2. to sprain one's back

niǔzhuǎn 扭轉 1. to wring; to wrench; to twist 2. to turn (the tide of a war or contest) for the better 3. to turn round

niǔzhuǎn qiánkūn 扭轉乾坤 to retrieve a hopeless situation

niǔ 忸 also **nǔ**
1. to be accustomed to; to be inclined to (evils, etc.) 2. bashful; ashamed

niǔní 忸怩 blush; ashamed; bashful; coyly

niǔ 紐
1. a knot; a tie; a cord 2. a hold (of a vessel) or handle 3. a button

niǔkòu 紐扣 a button

Niǔxīlán 紐西蘭 New Zealand

niǔ 鈕
buttons

niǔkǒng 鈕孔 a buttonhole

niù 拗 also **ào**
stubborn; obstinate; difficult

niùbuguò 拗不過 unable to dissuade; fail to talk someone out of doing something

niù 糅
refer to **róu** 糅

niù 謬
refer to **miù** 謬

nóng 農
1. agriculture; farming 2. to farm 3. a farmer; a peasant

nóngchǎnpǐn 農產品 farm products; agricultural products

nóngchǎng 農場 a farm

nóngcūn 農村 farm village

nóngdì 農地 agricultural fields; farmland

nóngfū 農夫 a husbandman; a farmer

nóngfù 農婦 a farm woman

nónghuì 農會 a farmers' association (or cooperative)

nóngjiā 農家 a farming family

nóngjù 農具 farm tools; agricultural implements

nónglì 農曆 the lunar calendar

nóngmín 農民 farmers; peasants; the farming population

nóngshè 農舍 a farmhouse

nóngshí 農時 the seasons for farming—spring for plowing, summer for weeding, and autumn for reaping

nóngshì 農事 farming; agricultural operations

nóngtián 農田 agricultural fields; farmland

nóngxué 農學 science of agriculture

nóngyào 農藥 pesticide; agricultural chemicals

nóngyè 農業 agriculture; farming

nóngzuòwù 農作物 farm products; crops

nóng 儂

1. (in old usage) I; me 2. (Shanghai dialect) you 3. he; she

nóng 濃

1. (said of drinks, liquids, etc.) thick; strong; heavy; concentrated 2. (said of colors) deep; dark 3. dense 4. (said of a smell) strong; heavy

nóngdàn 濃淡 1. (said of color) deep or light 2. (said of drinks) strong or weak 3. (said of make-up) heavy or light 4. (said of liquid generally) concentrated or diluted

nóngdù 濃度 1. (chemistry) concentration 2. density

nónghòu 濃厚 1. (said of material things) thick and dense 2. (said of feelings, interest, etc.) deep; great

nóngméi dàyǎn 濃眉大眼 heavy features

nóngmì 濃密 (said of the growth of vegetation, beard, hair, etc.) dense; thick

nóngqíng mìyì 濃情蜜意 strong affection and deep love

nóngsuō 濃縮 1. to enrich 2. to condense; to concentrate

nóngtāng 濃湯 thick soup

nóngwù 濃霧 heavy fog; dense mist

nóngyān 濃煙 thick smoke; heavy smoke

nóngyàn 濃豔 rich and gaudy

nóngyù 濃郁 strong; heavy; thick

nóngyún mìbù 濃雲密佈 Dark clouds stretch all over the sky. —a sign of an impending storm

nóngzhuāng yànmǒ 濃妝艷抹 to wear heavy make-up

nóng 膿

pus or purulent matter

nóngbāo 膿包 1. a pustule; an abscess 2. a good-for-nothing; a

useless person

nóngchuāng 膿瘡 an abscess; a boil

nóngzhǒng 膿腫 purulent swellings

nóng 穠

luxuriant growth of plants

nóngxiān hédù 穠纖合度 (said of a girl's figure) well-proportioned

nòng 弄 also lòng

1. to play with 2. to make fun of; to mock 3. to handle; to do

nòngcháo'ér 弄潮兒 1. a seaman 2. a beach swimmer

nòngcuò 弄錯 to make a mistake

nònghǎo 弄好 1. to get or put into (good) shape 2. to finish doing something 3. to do well

nònghútu 弄糊塗 to puzzle; to confuse

nònghuài 弄壞 to bungle; to spoil

nòngjiǎ chéngzhēn 弄假成眞 to turn simulation into reality unintentionally

nòngjiāng 弄僵 to bring to a deadlock

nòngqiǎo chéngzhuō 弄巧成拙 to bungle an ingenious scheme

nòngqiǎo chéngzhuó 弄巧成拙 refer to **nòngqiǎo chéngzhuō** 弄巧成拙

nòngqīng 弄清 to make clear; to clarify; to understand fully

nòngquán 弄權 to abuse one's power

nòngtōng 弄通 to get a good grasp of

nòngwǎ 弄瓦 to give birth to a daughter

nòngzāo 弄糟 to mess up; to bungle; to spoil

nòngzhāng 弄璋 to give birth to a son

nú 奴

1. a slave; a servant 2. a self-derogatory expression used by a girl to refer to herself in former

N

times 3. a despicable yes-man

núbì 奴婢 slaves; servants

núcai 奴才 1. a slave; a serf; a bondman 2. a good-for-nothing; a useless fellow; a yes-man

núlì 奴隸 a serf; a slave

núyán bìxī 奴顏婢膝 fawning; obsequious

núyì 奴役 to enslave

nú 駑

1. an old, worn-out horse; a jade; a hack 2. incompetent; stupid; good-for-nothing

núdùn 駑鈍 incompetent; incapable

númǎ 駑馬 a hack; a jade; an old, worn-out horse

nǔ 努

1. to exert oneself; to make an effort 2. to protrude

nǔlì 努力 to make efforts; to strive

nù 怒

1. temper; anger; rage; angry; furious 2. to put forth with vigor (as plants, etc.); to sprout; to spring up 3. forceful and vigorous

nùchì 怒叱 to shout in rage; angry shouts

nùfà chōngguān 怒髮衝冠 refer to **nùfà chōngguān** 怒髮衝冠

nùfà chōngguān 怒髮衝冠 intense anger; to bristle with anger

nùfàng 怒放 1. in full bloom 2. (figuratively) wild with joy

nùháo 怒號 (said of winds) howling; roaring

nùhǒu 怒吼 to roar; roars

nùhuǒ 怒火 flames of fury; fury

nùmà 怒罵 to curse in rage

nùmù xiāngshì 怒目相視 to look black at each other

nùqì 怒氣 anger; wrath; rage; fury

nùqì chōngchōng 怒氣沖沖 furious; angry; in a great rage

nùshì 怒視 to look at someone angrily

nǚ 女

1. a daughter; a girl; a maiden; a lady 2. a woman; a female

nǚbàn nánzhuāng 女扮男裝 a woman disguising herself as a man

nǚbīnxiàng 女儐相 a bridesmaid

nǚcèsuǒ 女廁所 a women's lavatory; a ladies' room

nǚ'ér 女兒 1. one's daughter 2. a girl

nǚfúwùyuán 女服務員 1. an air hostess; a stewardess 2. a waitress

nǚgōng 女工 women labor

nǚgōng 女紅 needlework

nǚhái 女孩 a girl

nǚhuáng 女皇 an empress

nǚláng 女郎 a maiden; a young woman; a young girl

nǚlíng 女伶 an actress

nǚpéngyou 女朋友 a girlfriend

nǚpú 女僕 a female servant; a maid

nǚqiángrén 女強人 a successful career woman

nǚquán zhǔyì 女權主義 feminism

nǚrén 女人 a woman

nǚshēng 女生 a girl

nǚshēng sùshè 女生宿舍 a women's dormitory

nǚshì 女士 Ms.; a lady

nǚwáng 女王 a queen regnant

nǚwū 女巫 a witch

nǚxìng 女性 female; the fair sex

nǚxìnghuà 女性化 feminization; to feminize

nǚxu 女婿 a son-in-law

nǚzhǔjiǎo 女主角 refer to **nǚzhǔjué** 女主角

nǚzhǔjué 女主角 a leading lady; a heroine

nǚzhǔren 女主人 a hostess

nǚzhuāng 女裝 a woman dress

nǚzǐ 女子 a woman; a girl

nǚ 忸

refer to **niǔ** 忸

nuǎn 暖
 warm or genial (weather)

nuǎnfáng 暖房 a hothouse; a greenhouse

nuǎnhuo 暖和 1. warm 2. to warm up

nuǎnliú 暖流 1. (geography) warm ocean currents 2. (meteorology) warm air currents

nuǎnlú 暖爐 a brazier

nuǎnqì 暖氣 warm vapor; warm air

nuǎnqìlú 暖氣爐 a gas heater

nuǎnqì zhuāngzhì 暖氣裝置 central heating installation; a heater

nüè 虐
 1. cruel; ferocious; atrocious 2. to tyrannize over; to oppress

nüèdài 虐待 to maltreat; to torture

nüè 瘧
 malaria

nüèji 瘧疾 malaria

nüèwén 瘧蚊 an anopheles

nüè 謔
 refer to **xuè** 謔

nuó 娜
 the word used in a female name

nuó 挪
 to move; to shift; to transfer

nuódòng 挪動 to move

nuójiè 挪借 to borrow from the public funds

Nuówēi 挪威 Norway

nuóyí 挪移 1. to move 2. to borrow from the public funds

nuóyòng 挪用 to use money for a purpose not originally intended

nuóyòng gōngkuǎn 挪用公款 to embezzle public money

nuò 娜
 tender, slender and graceful

nuò 諾
 1. to assent 2. to promise; to pledge

Nuòbèi'ěrjiǎng 諾貝爾獎 Nobel prizes

nuòyán 諾言 a promise; a pledge

nuò 懦
 timid; cowardly; weak

nuòfū 懦夫 a coward

nuòruò 懦弱 weak; cowardly

nuò 糯
 glutinous rice

nuòmǐ 糯米 polished glutinous rice

ō 喔
 an exclamation

ó 哦
 (an interjection) oh; ah

ōu 嘔
 refer to **ǒu** 嘔

ōu 歐
 1. Europe; European 2. (嘔) to vomit 3. (毆) to beat 4. (謳) to sing 5. (electricity) ohm, the SI unit of electrical resistance 6. a Chinese family name

Ōuhuà 歐化 Europeanization

Ōu Měi 歐美 Europe and America

Ōu Yà 歐亞 Europe and Asia; Eurasia

Ōuzhōu 歐洲 Europe

Ōuzhōu Gòngtóng Shìchǎng 歐洲共同市場 European Common Market (ECM)

ōu 毆
 to beat; to hit; a blow

ōudǎ 毆打 to fisticuff

ōushāng 毆傷 to injure by beating

ōu 謳
 to sing; to chant

ōugē 謳歌 to glorify; to eulogize

ōu 鷗
 a gull

ōulù wàngjī 鷗鷺忘機 (said of a hermit) so much in harmony with nature that the water birds are not frightened away by his presence

ǒu 偶
1. an idol; an image 2. coincidentally; accidentally 3. once in a while; occasionally 4. not to be taken for granted 5. an even number 6. a counterpart 7. a mate; to mate 8. one's company; fellows; buddies

ǒu'ér 偶而 occasionally

ǒu'ěr 偶爾 occasionally

ǒufā 偶發 to happen accidentally

ǒufàn 偶犯 1. a casual offense 2. a casual offender

ǒurán 偶然 1. by chance 2. un-expectedly

ǒushù 偶數 an even number

ǒuxiàng 偶像 an idol; an image

ǒu 嘔 also **ōu**
to vomit; to throw up

ǒutù 嘔吐 to vomit; to disgorge

ǒuxīn lìxiě 嘔心瀝血 refer to **ǒuxīn lìxuè 嘔心瀝血**

ǒuxīn lìxuè 嘔心瀝血 to work one's heart out

ǒu 藕
rhizomes, or rootstocks of the lotus

ǒuduàn sīlián 藕斷絲連 The ties are severed but not completely.

òu 慪
to annoy on purpose

òuqì 慪氣 to be angry but refrain from showing it

òu 慪
1. (嘔) to irritate; to exasperate 2. to be stingy about something

òuqì 慪氣 to become exasperated; to be difficult and sulky

pā 趴
1. to prostrate oneself; to lie face downwards 2. to bend over

pāxià 趴下 1. to prostrate oneself; to lie face downwards 2. to fall flat on the ground

pāzhe 趴著 lying flat on the ground; prostrate

pá 扒
1. to gather up; to rake up 2. to stew; to braise 3. to scratch; to claw

páqiè 扒竊 to pick pockets and steal

páshǒu 扒手 a pickpocket

pá 爬
1. to creep; to crawl 2. to climb; to clamber 3. to scratch 4. to lie face downwards

páchóng 爬蟲 a reptile

páqǐlai 爬起來 to get up

páqiáng 爬牆 to climb a fence

páshān 爬山 to climb mountains

páxíng 爬行 1. to crawl; to creep 2. a crawl

pá 耙 also **bà**
1. a harrow; a drag 2. to rake

pázi 耙子 a rake

pá 琶
a four-stringed guitar or balloon-guitar

pà 怕
1. to fear; to dread; afraid; scared apprehensive 2. maybe; perhaps; I am afraid....; I suppose....

pàshēng 怕生 to be shy with strangers

pàshì 怕事 to be timid and over-cautious

pàsǐ 怕死 to be afraid of death

pàxiū 怕羞 shy; bashful

pà 帕
1. a turban 2. to wrap and bind 3. a handkerchief 4. a veil 5. a curtain made of cloth

pāi 拍 also **pò**
1. to strike with the hand; to slap; to clap; to pat; to swat 2. the time or beat of a piece of music 3. to fawn; to flatter

pāi'àn jiàojué 拍案叫絕 to show extreme surprise or admiration by pounding the table

pāida 拍打 to pat; to slap or tap lightly

pāidiànyǐng 拍電影 to shoot a film

pāifā diànbào 拍發電報 to cable

pāimǎpì 拍馬屁 to flatter; to soft-soap; to claw (or curry) favor

pāimài 拍賣 to auction off; an auction

pāipiàn 拍片 to shoot a film

pāishè 拍攝 to take (a picture)

pāishǒu 拍手 to clap hands

pāizhǎng 拍掌 to clap hands

pāizhào 拍照 to take a picture or photo

pāizi 拍子 (music) time; rhythm

pái 排

1. a row; a line; a rank 2. to arrange; to put in order 3. (military) a platoon 4. to clear out 5. to expel; to exclude 6. to rehearse 7. a raft 8. to push

páibǎn 排版 (printing) to set type

páibiàn 排便 defecation; the evacuation of the bowels

páichang 排場 1. ostentation and extravagance 2. a person's social position

páichì 排斥 to discriminate against; to expel

páichú 排除 to get rid of; to remove

páidǎng 排檔 a gear (in an automobile engine)

páiduì 排隊 to line up; to stand in a queue

páigǔ 排骨 1. ribs of animals; spareribs 2. (slang) a skinny person

páiháng 排行 one's seniority among brothers and sisters

páijǐ 排擠 1. to expel somebody out of an inner circle or clique, etc. 2. to push aside; to elbow out

páijiě 排解 to resolve (disputes); to mediate

páikāi 排開 to spread out

páiliàn 排練 to rehearse for a show

páiliè 排列 to arrange in series, rows, etc.

páiluǎn 排卵 (biology) to ovulate

páimíng 排名 to list names according to the order of senior-

ity or position

páiniào 排尿 to urinate; to micturate

páiqìguǎn 排氣管 an exhaust pipe

páiqiǎn 排遣 (said of a disappointed person) to find comfort in

páiqiú 排球 volleyball

páishān dǎohǎi 排山倒海 overwhelming or sweeping

páishuǐ 排水 to drain water; drainage

páishuǐgōu 排水溝 a discharge ditch; a drainage ditch

páishuǐguǎn 排水管 a drainpipe

páishuǐliàng 排水量 1. the volume of water displacement 2. displacement (of a ship)

páishuǐ xìtǒng 排水系統 a drainage system

páitóu 排頭 to stand first in the line

páiwài 排外 antiforeign; chauvinistic

páixì 排戲 to rehearse for a show

páixiè 排泄 to excrete; to discharge; excretion

páixièwù 排泄物 excreta; excrement

páiyìn 排印 to set type and print

páizhǎng 排長 a platoon leader

pái 徘

1. hesitating; irresolute; indecisive 2. to walk to and fro; to move around

páihuái 徘徊 1. to linger; to walk to and fro 2. hesitating 3. to fluctuate

páihuái liúlián 徘徊流連 walk to and fro hesitatingly with reluctance to leave

pái 牌

1. a bulletin board 2. a tablet; a signboard; a plate 3. a card; a tag; a label 4. a trademark; a brand

páifāng 牌坊 an honorific arch or portal

páijiǔ 牌九 Chinese dominoes

páijú 牌局 a gambling game

páiwèi 牌位 an ancestral tablet

páizhào 牌照 a license plate; a license

páizi 牌子 1. a bulletin board 2. a card; a label 3. a brand 4. a signboard; a plate

pài 派

1. a tributary; a branch 2. a division; a school (of philosophy, art, etc.); a party 3. a faction 4. to assign; to dispatch; to send 5. pie

pàibié 派別 1. factions 2. schools (of thought)

pàibīng qiǎnjiàng 派兵遣將 to dispatch troops and send generals

pàichūsuǒ 派出所 a police station

pàiduì 派對 a party (for social entertainment)

pàifā 派發 to distribute

pàiqiǎn 派遣 to dispatch

pàitóu 派頭 manner; air

pàixì 派系 1. factions (within a political party, etc.) 2. affiliation with (a school or party)

pài 湃

billowy; turbulent

Pān 番

a county in Guangdong province

pān 潘

1. a Chinese family name 2. water in which rice has been washed

pān 攀

1. to hold to; to climb; to hang on; to clamber 2. to involve

pāndēng 攀登 to climb; to scale

pānfù 攀附 to hang on or to attach oneself to (power, glory, etc.)

pānlóng fùfèng 攀龍附鳳 to establish oneself by riding on the coattails of a brilliant master

pāntán 攀談 to drag another into conversation

pānyán 攀岩 rock climbing

pānyuán 攀緣 1. (Buddhism) to be affected by one's environment

2. to climb

pānzhé 攀折 to injure (a plant) by picking or breaking

pán 胖

comfortable

pán 槃

1. a wooden tray 2. great

pán'gēn cuòjié 槃根錯節 1. very complicated; difficult to solve or explain 2. (said of old social forces) deep-rooted

pán 盤

1. a tray; a plate; a dish 2. twisted; entangled; entwined; intricate; winding; to entangle; to entwine 3. to investigate; to interrogate 4. (said of a chess match, etc.) a round

pánchá 盤查 to question; to cross-examine

pánchan 盤纏 traveling expenses

pándiǎn 盤點 to check; to make an inventory of

pán'gēn cuòjié 盤根錯節 very complicated

pánhuò 盤貨 to make an inventory of stock

pánjié 盤詰 to interrogate closely

pánjù 盤踞 1. to occupy 2. to squat with the legs crossed

pánjù 盤據 (usually said of enemy troops, rebels or bandits) to occupy and hold a place

pánníxīlín 盤尼西林 penicillin

pánnòng 盤弄 1. to tamper with 2. to provoke

pánrǎo 盤繞 to twine; to wind round

pánrào 盤繞 refer to **pánrǎo** 盤繞

pánsuan 盤算 to make a mental calculation

pánwèn 盤問 to interrogate closely

pánxuán 盤旋 to circle; to hover around

pánzi 盤子 a tray; a plate; a dish

pán 磐

1. a massive rock 2. to linger

around 3. to league together

pánshí 磐石 a massive rock

pán 蟠
1. to coil; to curl up 2. to occupy

pánjù 蟠踞 to occupy

pán 蹣 also **mán**
to limp

pánshān 蹣跚 to walk haltingly; to limp; to hobble

pàn 判
to judge; to conclude

pànbié 判別 to distinguish; to tell apart

pànchǔ 判處 to sentence; to condemn

pàndìng 判定 to judge; to decide

pànduàn 判斷 judgment, decision or conclusion

pànguān 判官 a fierce-looking judge in the afterlife court of law

pànjué 判決 a verdict; a sentence

pànjuéshū 判決書 a verdict in writing

pànlì 判例 (said of court decisions) a precedent

pànruò liǎngrén 判若兩人 to become a completely different person

pànzuì 判罪 to declare guilty

pàn 拚
1. to go all out 2. at the risk of 3. to reject

pànmìng 拚命 to risk one's life

pàn 叛
to rebel; to revolt

pànbiàn 叛變 a mutiny; to revolt

pànguó 叛國 sedition

pànjūn 叛軍 the rebels

pànlí 叛離 to betray; to desert

pànluàn 叛亂 a rebellion; revolt; sedition

pànnì 叛逆 1. to revolt; sedition 2. one who rebels against his country or superiors

pàntú 叛徒 a rebel; an insurgent

pàn 盼
1. to look 2. (descriptive of the black and white of the eyes) well defined 3. to hope; to expect

pànwàng 盼望 to hope; to wish

pàn 畔
1. a boundary between fields 2. a side; a bank 3. (叛) to rebel; to betray

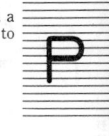

pāng 乓
used for the sound

pāng 滂
torrential; overwhelming

pāngpài 滂湃 surging; overwhelming; torrential

pāngtuó 滂沱 1. (said of rain) torrential 2. (said of tears) streaming

pāng 磅
refer to **páng** 磅

páng 彷
hesitating; unsettled

pánghuáng 彷徨 to hesitate; undecided

páng 旁(傍)
1. side 2. by the side of; nearby 3. other; else

pángbái 旁白 (drama) aside

pángbiān 旁邊 1. the side; by the side of 2. nearby; in the vicinity of

pángguān 旁觀 to look on

pángguānzhě 旁觀者 an onlooker; a bystander; a spectator

pángguānzhě qīng 旁觀者清 The onlooker is clear-headed (because he can see what's going on with detachment).

pángmén zuǒdào 旁門左道 heresy; unorthodox ways

pángqiāo cèjī 旁敲側擊 to ask seemingly irrelevant questions or speak aimlessly with a hidden purpose

pángqiāo cèjí 旁敲側擊 refer to **pángqiāo cèjī** 旁敲側擊

pángrén 旁人 1. bystanders; onlookers; outsiders 2. the others

pángruò wúrén 旁若無人 to act as if there weren't any bystanders

pángtīng 旁聽 to audit

pángtīngshēng 旁聽生 an auditor (at a class)

pángxì qīnshǔ 旁系親屬 collateral relatives

pángzhēng bóyǐn 旁徵博引 to quote widely or extensively

páng 徬

anxious, agitated and indecisive

pánghuáng 徬徨 to be anxious, agitated and not knowing what to do

páng 磅 also **pāng**

the noise of stone crashing

pángbó 磅礴 boundless; majestic; extensive

páng 膀

the bladder

pángguāng 膀胱 the bladder

pángguāng jiéshí 膀胱結石 a calculus of the bladder

pángguāngyán 膀胱炎 cystitis

páng 螃

a crab

pángxiè 螃蟹 a crab

páng 龐

1. disorderly; confused 2. enormous 3. a face

pángdà 龐大 immense; huge; enormous

pángrán dàwù 龐然大物 1. a huge object 2. a mammoth animal

pángzá 龐雜 disorderly; confused

pàng 胖

obese; fat; corpulent

pàngzi 胖子 a fat or corpulent person; a fatty

pāo 泡

1. loose and soft; spongy 2. an amount of excrement or urine

pāo 拋

1. to throw; to cast; to hurl 2. to abandon; to reject; to give up 3. to cast aside; to leave behind

pāochū 拋出 1. to throw out; to cast away 2. (especially in the stock market) to sell

pāogē qìjiǎ 拋戈棄甲 to throw away weapons and armor—to be routed

pāomáo 拋錨 1. to cast anchor 2. to break down

pāoqì 拋棄 to abandon; to throw away; to give up

pāotóu lùmiàn 拋頭露面 (said of women in old China) to go out and be seen in public; to hold a job which involves a lot of exposure to the public (considered unbecoming to a decent woman)

pāowùxiàn 拋物線 a parabola

pāoxiùqiú 拋繡球 to throw an embroidered ball—to choose a husband

pāozhí 拋擲 refer to **pāozhì** 拋擲

pāozhì 拋擲 1. to cast; to throw; to hurl 2. to throw away; to abandon

pāozhuān yǐnyù 拋磚引玉 (literally) to throw a brick and to get a piece of jade in return

páo 刨

to dig; to excavate

páo 咆

to roar

páoxiāo 咆哮 1. (said of a tiger, etc.) to roar 2. (said of winds, etc.) to bluster 3. (said of a person) to rage

páo 庖

the kitchen; the cuisine

páochú 庖廚 a kitchen

páodài 庖代 to act for another

páodīng 庖丁 a cook

páo 炮

to refine medicinal herbs

páo 袍

a long gown; a robe

páozé 袍澤 comrades in arms

pǎo 跑

1. to run 2. to run away; to flee

pǎobù 跑步 to run; on the double

pǎochē 跑車 a racer; a sports car

pǎodào 跑道 1. a track 2. a runway

pǎolěi 跑壘 (baseball) base running

pǎolóngtào 跑龍套 to play an insignificant role

pǎolù 跑路 to travel on foot

pǎotángrde 跑堂兒的 a waiter

pǎotuǐr 跑腿兒 to run errands

pǎoxié 跑鞋 spiked shoes (of a sprinter)

pào 泡

1. bubbles; suds; froth; foam 2. a blister 3. to steep; to soak; to dip; to infuse (tea, etc.) 4. (slang) to dawdle; to fool around (especially with women)

pàocài 泡菜 vegetables preserved in salted water

pàochá 泡茶 to infuse tea; to make tea

pàomò 泡沫 suds; foam; froth

pàopàotáng 泡泡糖 bubble gum

pàoshuǐ 泡水 to soak in water

pàotāng 泡湯 1. to make soup by infusing in hot water 2. (said of a dream) busted; (said of money) wasted; (said of hope) dashed 3. to take a bath in the hot spring

pàoyǐng 泡影 the shadow of bubbles—unreality

pào 炮

a big gun, cannon, etc.

pào 疱

acne

pàozhěn 疱疹 1. a bleb 2. herpes

pào 皰

pimples

pào 礮(砲)

1. a catapult 2. an artillery piece; a cannon; a gun

pàobīng 礮兵 1. an artilleryman; a gunner 2. artillery

pàodàn 礮彈 a cannon ball or shot; a shell

pàohōng 礮轟 to cannonade

pàohuī 礮灰 cannon fodder

pàohuǒ 礮火 artillery fire; gunfire

pàojí 礮擊 to bombard; to shell

pàojí 礮擊 refer to pàojí 礮擊

pàojiàn 礮艦 a gunboat

pàoshēng 礮聲 the thunder of cannonade

pàotái 礮臺 a gun emplacement; a battery; a fort

pàotǐng 礮艇 a gunboat

pēi 披

refer to pī 披

pēi 胚

1. a three-month-old fetus; three months of pregnancy 2. things in the embryonic stage; unfinished moldings 3. the tender sprouts of plants

pēitāi 胚胎 1. the origination or beginning of things 2. an embryo

pēiyá 胚芽 a sprout; to germinate

péi 陪

1. to accompany; to keep company 2. to assist

péibàn 陪伴 to keep company; to accompany

péichèn 陪襯 to serve as a background in order to bring out the subject with greater brilliance; to serve as a prop

péijià 陪嫁 the dowry given to a daughter on her marriage

péijiǔ 陪酒 (said of a bar girl, etc.) to accompany a patron in drinking

péikè 陪客 1. to receive guests; to keep guests company 2. (said of girls in gay establishments) to attend on patrons

péike 陪客 a guest invited to keep the guest of honor company

péishěn 陪審 1. to act (or serve) as an assessor (in a law case) 2. to serve on a jury

péixiào 陪笑 to put up a smiling face in order to please or pla-

P

cate someone

péizàng 陪葬 to bury (a person or thing) along with the deceased

péizuì 陪罪 to ask forgiveness; to apologize

péi 培

1. to bank up with earth 2. to nourish; to strengthen; to cultivate

péiyǎng 培養 1. to grow (plants) 2. to raise (kids) 3. to foster

péiyù 培育 to raise; to breed

péizhí 培植 1. to plant 2. to educate

péi 裴

1. the look of a flowing gown 2. a Chinese family name

péi 賠

1. to compensate or indemnify; to make up for a loss due to one's fault; to pay for 2. to offer (an apology) 3. to lose money

péiběn 賠本 to lose money in business

péibùshì 賠不是 to apologize

péicháng 賠償 compensation; indemnity; to recompense; to make amends for

péikuǎn 賠款 an indemnity; a compensation; reparations

péilǐ 賠禮 to offer an apology

péiqián 賠錢 1. to make a pecuniary compensation 2. to lose money in business

péizuì 賠罪 to apologize

pèi 沛

1. copious; abundance; full of 2. quickly; rapidly; sudden 3. to fall prostrate 4. to reserve water for irrigation 5. tall; high; great

pèi 佩

1. to wear; to carry 2. to admire; to adore 3. to be grateful 4. something worn on a girdle or clothing; a pendant

pèidài 佩帶 to wear; to carry

pèifu 佩服 to admire; to respect

pèixūnzhāng 佩勳章 to wear medals

pèi 珮

jade pendants

pèi 配

1. to join in marriage 2. to mate 3. to pair; to match 4. to fit; to suit; to be a match for; to match; to equal 5. to dispense (medicines); to prepare (according to a demand) 6. to exile 7. a spouse; a partner 8. subordinate; supplementary; supporting; attached 9. to deserve; to be worthy of

pèibèi 配備 1. an outfit; equipment 2. to provide; to fit out

pèiduì 配對 to pair; to be a pair

pèifāng 配方 to dispense prescriptions

pèihé 配合 to be in tune with; to be adapted to

pèijǐ 配給 1. to distribute in rations; to allocate 2. allocation

pèijiàn 配件 accessories

pèijué 配角 1. to appear with another leading player; to costar 2. a supporting role; a minor role

pèi'ǒu 配偶 a spouse; a mate

pèisè 配色 refer to **pèishǎi** 配色

pèishǎi 配色 to blend (or match) colors

pèiyào 配藥 to dispense medicines; to fill a prescription

pèiyīn 配音 (movies) to dub; dubbing; to synchronize; synchronization

pèiyuè 配樂 to dub in background music; incidental music

pèizhì 配製 to prepare or concoct according to a recipe or prescription

pèizhǒng 配種 (animal husbandry) breeding

pèi 轡

reins; a bridle

pèitóu 轡頭 a bridle

pēn 噴

1. to spurt; to gush 2. to spray; to sprinkle

pēnqī 噴漆 to spray paint (or lacquer)

pēnquán 噴泉 a fountain

pēnsǎ 噴灑 to spray; to sprinkle

pēnshèshì kèjī 噴射式客機 a jet airliner

pēnshuǐchí 噴水池 a fountain

pēntì 噴嚏 sneezing; a sneeze

pén 盆
a bowl; a basin; a tub

péndì 盆地 (geology) a basin

pénjǐng 盆景 a potted plant; a bonsai

pénzāi 盆栽 1. a potted plant; a bonsai 2. to plant in a pot

pēng 抨
to impeach; to censure

pēngjī 抨擊 to criticize; to lash

pēngjí 抨擊 refer to **pēngjī** 抨擊

pēng 怦
eager; anxious; impulsive

pēngpēng 怦怦 1. eager and anxious (to do something) 2. faithful and upright 3. with quick beating; pit-a-pat

pēngrán 怦然 with a sudden shock

pēng 砰
1. the sound of crashing stones 2. Bang!

pēngrán 砰然 loud; deafening; roaring

pēng 烹
1. to cook; to boil; to decoct 2. (cooking) to add bean sauce and dressing after frying 3. (slang) to frighten (away)

pēngrèn 烹飪 to cook or prepare (food); cooking

pēngtiáo 烹調 to cook or prepare (food); cóoking

pēngzhǔ 烹煮 to cook; to boil

péng 澎
the roaring of colliding billows

péngpài 澎湃 the roaring of billows; to surge

péng 朋
1. a friend; a companion 2. a group; a clique

péngbǐ wéijiān 朋比爲奸 to

gang up for evil doings

péngbì wéijiān 朋比爲奸 refer to **péngbì wéijiān** 朋比爲奸

péngdǎng 朋黨 a faction; a clique

péngyou 朋友 a friend

péng 棚
a tent; a shed; a (mat) awning

péng 彭
1. big 2. longevity 3. proud

péng 硼
1. borax 2. (chemistry) boron

péngshā 硼砂 borax

péngsuān 硼酸 boric acid

péng 蓬
1. Erigeron acer, a species of raspberry 2. tangled 3. disheveled (hair) 4. flourishing; prospering

péngbì shēnghuī 蓬蓽生輝 (Your gracious presence) has added glitter to my humble house.

péngbó 蓬勃 booming; vigorously

Pénglái xiānjìng 蓬萊仙境 a fairyland; a paradise

péngsōng 蓬鬆 disheveled; very loose

péngtóu gòumiàn 蓬頭垢面 disheveled hair and a dirty face —very untidy in appearance

Péng 澎
the Pescadores

Pénghú 澎湖 the Penghus, or the Pescadores, in the Taiwan Straits

péng 膨
to expand; to swell; to inflate

péngzhàng 膨脹 inflation; bloated; to swell

péng 篷
1. a covering; an awning; a tent 2. a sail; a boat

péngchē 篷車 a wagon

péng 鵬
Peng, a fabulous bird supposed to be the greatest of all kinds,

comparable to the roc

péngchéng wànlǐ 鵬程萬里 (literally) a journey of 10,000 miles faced by the roc—of great promise

péngtú 鵬圖 great ambition

pěng 捧

1. to hold something in both hands 2. to boost; to flatter; to treat as a VIP 3. to support, cheer or render assistance by one's presence

pěngchǎng 捧場 to render support or assistance (by one's presence, endorsement, etc.)

pěngfù dàxiào 捧腹大笑 to hold one's sides with laughter

pèng 碰

1. to collide; to hit; to touch; to bump 2. to meet unexpectedly; to run into 3. to take one's chance

pèngbì 碰壁 1. to meet rejection 2. to encounter difficulties

pèngdǎo 碰倒 to tumble down after being hit by something

pèngdīngzi 碰釘子 to be rebuked

pèngjiàn 碰見 to meet or encounter someone unexpectedly; to run into

pèngmiàn 碰面 to meet

pèngqiǎo 碰巧 by coincidence; accidentally

pèngtóu 碰頭 to meet

pèngyùnqì 碰運氣 1. to try one's luck 2. sheer luck

pèngzhuàng 碰撞 to hit; to run into

pī 匹

refer to **pǐ** 匹 4

pīsà 匹薩 pizza

pī 丕

1. great; distinguished 2. in observance of (a ruling, etc.)

pīxiǎn 丕顯 great and distinguished; splendid

pī 批

1. to comment; to judge; to criticize 2. a whole batch (of things or people); a large quantity or

number 3. to slap

pīdòu 批鬥 to criticize and denounce someone

pīfā 批發 wholesale

pīfājià 批發價 a wholesale price

pīfāshāng 批發商 a wholesale dealer; a wholesaler

pīgǎi 批改 to correct (students' papers)

pīpàn 批判 to appraise; to judge

pīpíng 批評 to criticize; criticism; comment

pīpíngjiā 批評家 a critic

pīshì 批示 to instruct or direct (usually by writing on the paper carrying a message from a subordinate)

pīyuè 批閱 to read (a message from a subordinate) and write down comments or instructions

pīzhù 批註 to write commentaries

pīzhǔn 批准 to approve; to ratify

pī 披 also **pēi**

1. to open (a book, scroll, etc.); to unroll 2. to spread out; to disperse 3. to thumb through or read casually 4. to throw on (a garment, etc.); to wear untidily

pīfēng 披風 a cape

pīgān lìdǎn 披肝瀝膽 to talk without reserve; to have a heart-to-heart talk

pīguà shàngzhèn 披掛上陣 to wear full battle dress and go into battle

pījiān 披肩 a shawl

pījīng zhǎnjí 披荊斬棘 1. to cultivate land as a pioneer 2. to travel through thick bushes and dense jungles

pīmá dàixiào 披麻帶孝 to put on mourning apparel (especially said of sons or daughters of the deceased)

pīmǐ 披靡 1. (said of grass, etc.) blown about by the wind 2. (said of an army) beaten and scattered; routed

pītóu sǎnfà 披頭散髮 disheveled hair (often referring to an untidy woman)

pítóu sànfǎ 披頭散髮 refer to pítóu sànfǎ 披頭散髮

pīxīng dàiyuè 披星戴月 1. to travel by night 2. to toil night and day

pīyuè 披閱 to read

pī 砒
arsenic

pīshuāng 砒霜 arsenic trioxide (As₂O₃)

pī 被
1. to put on or throw on (garments, etc.) without buttoning up 2. to disperse or spread out

pīfà zuǒrèn 被髮左衽 refer to pīfà zuǒrèn 被髮左衽

pīfà zuǒrèn 被髮左衽 hair unbound and coats buttoned on the left side—to become a barbarian

pī 紕
1. errors; mistakes; blunders 2. (said of cloth, thread, etc.) to become unwoven or untwisted

pīlòu 紕漏 errors or mistakes; something going wrong

pī 劈
1. to cleave; to split; to rive; to rend 2. a wedge

pīchái 劈柴 to split or chop firewood

pīlipālā 劈哩啪啦 a descriptive sound of firecrackers, guns, etc.

pītóu 劈頭 1. right in the face 2. at the very start

pī 霹
thunders; a sudden peal of thunder

pīlì 霹靂 a thunderclap; a thunderbolt

pí 皮
1. skin; fur; hide; leather; rind; peltry; bark 2. a thin sheet 3. naughty 4. a Chinese family name

pí'ǎo 皮襖 a fur coat; a leather coat

píbāo 皮包 a handbag or purse

píbāogǔ 皮包骨 skinny

píchǐ 皮尺 a tape measure; a tape

pídài 皮帶 a leather belt

pídàn 皮蛋 duck's eggs preserved in lime

pífá 皮筏 a kayak

pífūbìng 皮膚病 skin disease

pífūkē 皮膚科 dermatology

pígé 皮革 leather

píhuò 皮貨 furs

píjiākè 皮夾克 a leather jacket; windbreaker

píjiāzi 皮夾子 a wallet

píjiákè 皮夾克 refer to píjiākè 皮夾克

píjiázi 皮夾子 refer to píjiāzi 皮夾子

pímáo zhījiàn 皮毛之見 a superficial view or opinion

pí'náng 皮囊 a leather bag

píqiú 皮球 a rubber ball

pítiáokè 皮條客 a pimp

píxiāng 皮箱 a suitcase or valise (especially of leather)

píxiào ròu bùxiào 皮笑肉不笑 treacherous; crafty; putting on a false smile

píxié 皮鞋 leather shoes

píxuē 皮靴 leather boots

píyī 皮衣 fur clothing

píyǐngxì 皮影戲 the shadow show

pí 枇
loquats

pípa 枇杷 loquats

pípagāo 枇杷膏 condensed loquat extract

pí 毗
1. to assist 2. to adjoin

pílián 毗連 (said of lands) adjacent to

pí 疲
weary; tired; fatigued; exhausted

píbèi 疲憊 fatigued; tired; weary

píbèi bùkān 疲憊不堪 extremely tired

pífá 疲乏 tired; exhausted; weary

píjuàn 疲倦 tired; exhausted; weary

píláo 疲勞 fatigue; exhaustion;

P

weariness

píláo guòdù 疲勞過度 excessive fatigue

píláo hōngzhà 疲勞轟炸 1. harassing air raids 2. a long and tedious harangue

píruǎn 疲軟 1. tired and feeble 2. (said of commodities) to decrease in demand 3. (said of finance) to weaken

píyú bēnmìng 疲於奔命 tired from running around

pí 啤
a character used in transliterating

píjiǔ 啤酒 beer

pí 埤
1. a low wall; a parapet 2. an increase; increasingly; to add to

píyì 埤益 to increase

pí 脾
1. the spleen 2. a temper; a disposition

píwèi 脾胃 1. the stomach 2. appetite 3. one's temperament or natural inclination

pízàng 脾臟 the spleen

pí 琶
the four-stringed guitar or the balloon-guitar

pípa 琵琶 a short-necked fretted lute of Chinese origin

pípa biébào 琵琶別抱 to marry another husband

pí 罷
tired; exhausted; weary

píbì 罷弊 exhausted; weary

pǐ 匹
1. a bolt (of cloth) 2. to match 3. equal 4. (also **pī**) a numerary particle for horses

pǐdí 匹敵 to match or equal (in a contest)

pǐfū zhīyǒng 匹夫之勇 foolhardiness

pǐpèi 匹配 1. to match 2. matching

pǐ 疋
a roll (of cloth); a bolt (of cloth)

pǐ 仳
to part company

pǐlí 仳離 to part (from one's spouse); to divorce

pǐ 否
evil; bad

pǐjí tàilái 否極泰來 Adversity, after reaching its extremity, is followed by felicity.

pǐ 痞
1. dyspepsia; a spleen infection 2. a ruffian; a scoundrel

pǐgùn 痞棍 a rascal; a scoundrel

pǐzi 痞子 a rascal; a scoundrel

pǐ 劈
to split; to chop

pǐchai 劈柴 firewood

pǐ 癖
1. chronic swelling of the spleen 2. addiction; a habitual inclination

pì 屁
1. a fart 2. the hip

pìgu 屁股 the hip; the buttocks; the rump; the bottom

pìgǔn niǎoliú 屁滾尿流 to be frightened out of one's wits

pìhuà 屁話 Baloney!

pì 僻
1. biased 2. not easily accessible; out-of-the-way; secluded 3. not common; not ordinary; unusual

pìjìng 僻靜 out-of-the-way; secluded

pìyuǎn 僻遠 distant and out-of-the-way

pì 譬
1. to liken; to compare 2. a simile; an example 3. to tell 4. to understand

pìrú 譬如 for instance; for example

pìruò 譬若 for instance; for example; to suppose

pìyù 譬喻 a simile or metaphor

pì 闢
1. to open up; to develop 2. to

rid; to do away with 3. to refute

pìdì 闢地 to open up land for cultivation

pìxié 闢邪 to refute heresy

pìyáo 闢謠 to refute rumors; to clarify rumored reports

piān 片 also **piàn**
1. a photograph 2. a phonograph record

piānzi 片子 1. a film; a movie 2. a roll of film

piān 扁
small

piānzhōu 扁舟 a small boat; a skiff

piān 偏
1. biased; not fair; prejudiced; partial 2. leaning; inclined to one side 3. an auxiliary verb indicating a sense of contrariness or determination

piān'ài 偏愛 to love someone or something in particular

piānchā 偏差 errors; deviation

piānfāng 偏方 an informal recipe or prescription

piānfáng 偏房 a concubine

piānfèi 偏廢 1. crippled 2. to emphasize one thing and neglect others

piānhào 偏好 a hobby

piānhù 偏護 partial; to favor one side against the other

piānjī 偏激 extreme; radical

piānjiàn 偏見 prejudice; bias

piānláo 偏勞 1. to let one person take on the work of the whole team 2. Thanks for the good work.

piānlí 偏離 to deviate; to diverge

piānpì 偏僻 out-of-the-way; secluded

piānpiān 偏偏 unfortunately it happened that...

piānpō 偏頗 partial; biased; not fair

piānpǒ 偏頗 refer to **piānpō** 偏頗

piānqiǎo 偏巧 it so happened; as luck would have it

piānshí 偏食 to eat certain dishes only

piāntǎn 偏袒 partiality; partial

piāntí 偏題 a catch question (in an examination)

piāntóutòng 偏頭痛 (medicine) hemicrania

piānxiàng 偏向 to lean or to be inclined toward

piānxīn 偏心 partiality; bias

piānyuǎn 偏遠 remote; faraway

piānzhí 偏執 strong inclination toward

piānzhòng 偏重 1. to give undue emphasis to 2. to have extraordinary faith in (somebody)

piān 篇
1. a numerary adjunct for compositions, poems, etc. 2. a chapter; a section; a part 3. a page 4. books; volumes

piānfú 篇幅 1. the length (of a piece of writing) 2. space (of a periodical or newspaper)

piānmù 篇目 titles; headings

piān 翩
to fly swiftly

piānpiān 翩翩 1. to fly swiftly; to flutter 2. (descriptive of movement) lightly and swiftly 3. complacent 4. elegant

pián 便
cheap; inexpensive

piánnìng 便佞 a glib-tongued man

piányi 便宜 1. cheap; inexpensive 2. to gain advantage

pián 胼
calluses

piánshǒu zhīzú 胼手胝足 calluses on the hands and feet—to toil or work hard

piánzhī 胼胝 calluses on the hands and feet—to toil or work hard

pián 駢
1. a pair of horses 2. to stand, lie, or go side by side

piánjiān 駢肩 shoulders by

shoulders—crowded

piántǐwén 骈體文 a euphuistically antithetic style of writing

pián 片

1. a piece; a slice; a fragment; a chip 2. refer to **piàn** 片

piàncháng 片長 the length of a motion picture in terms of showing time

piànchóu 片酬 remuneration for a movie actor or actress for starring in a film

piànduàn 片段 1. passages or fragments of a writing 2. parts; fragments

piànjiǎ bùliú 片甲不留 to wipe out the enemy to a man

piànjiǎmíng 片假名 katakana

piànkè 片刻 a little while; a moment

piànmiàn 片面 1. unilateral 2. unfair

piànmiàn zhīcí 片面之詞 one-sided remarks

piànmíng 片名 title of a motion picture

piànpiàn 片片 in pieces; in fragments

pián 遍

refer to **biàn** 遍

pián 騙

1. to cheat; to defraud; to swindle; to deceive 2. to get by fraud

piànjú 騙局 a fraud; a swindle; a trick; a chicanery; a deception; a hoax

piànqǔ 騙取 to obtain by fraud; to cheat

piànshù 騙術 a trick; a ruse; a stratagem

piànzi 騙子 a swindler; a cheat; a confidence man; a racketeer; an impostor

piāo 剽 also **piào**

1. to plunder; to rob; to steal 2. agile; fast

piāoqiè 剽竊 1. to purloin 2. to plagiarize

piāo 漂

to drift; to float; to be tossed about

piāobó 漂泊 to drift; to wander

piāodàng 漂蕩 1. to drift about; to be tossed (by waves) 2. to wander; to ramble about

piāofú 漂浮 to drift; to float

piāoliú 漂流 to drift

piāoyáo 漂搖 to wave; to flutter

piāo 縹 also **piǎo**

1. light-blue silk 2. light blue 3. dim; misty; indistinct

piāomiǎo 縹緲 distant and dim; far and indistinct

piāo 飄

1. to blow (in the air); to waft; to move with the wind 2. a cyclone; a whirling wind 3. to float; to drift

piāobó 飄泊 to drift about—with no fixed lodging place

piāodàng 飄蕩 to drift along without fixed lodging; to float

piāohū 飄忽 1. to float in the air hither and thither 2. to have no fixed address 3. light and speedy

piāohū bùdìng 飄忽不定 to drift from place to place

piāolíng 飄零 1. (said of leaves and plants) falling and withering 2. to drift about alone; wandering; homeless

piāoliú 飄流 1. to drift; to float 2. to knock about; to wander aimlessly

piāoluò 飄落 to fall down slowly in the air

piāopiāo yùxiān 飄飄欲仙 light, airy, comfortable, and complacent

piāosǎ 飄灑 to float; to drift

piāosa 飄灑 (of a person) suave; (of calligraphy) facile and graceful

piāosàn 飄散 dispersed and flying about

piāoxuě 飄雪 snowflakes falling

piāoyáng 飄洋 to take a sea voyage

piāoyáng 飄揚 to be blown about in the wind; to flutter

piāoyáo 飄搖 1. to dance and toss about in the wind 2. precari-

ous; unsteady

piāoyì 飄逸 elegant; high, stately and graceful

piáo 嫖

to patronize whorehouses; to visit prostitutes; to go whoring

piáodǔ 嫖賭 to patronize whorehouses and gambling houses—to lead a life of debauchery

piáo 瓢

a ladle (often made of a dried calabash)

piáochóng 瓢蟲 a ladybug; a ladybird

piǎo 漂

to bleach

piǎobái 漂白 to bleach

piǎobáijì 漂白劑 a decolorant

piǎo 縹

refer to **piāo** 縹

piào 票

1. a bill; a note 2. a ticket 3. a ballot 4. a hostage 5. amateur performance

piào'é 票額 face value

piàofànzi 票販子 a scalper of tickets

piàofáng 票房 1. a box office; a ticket window 2. a club of amateur Peking opera actors 3. box office—(figuratively) the power of a show or performer to attract an audience

piàogēn 票根 a ticket stub; a counterfoil

piàojià 票價 the price of a ticket

piàojù 票據 bills; notes; receipts

piàoshù 票數 the number of votes or ballots

piàotíng 票亭 ticket stands

piàoxuǎn 票選 to elect by casting ballots

piào 剽

refer to **piāo** 剽

piào 漂

pretty; nice; sleek

piàoliang 漂亮 1. pretty; handsome 2. wise in worldly ways 3.

brilliant; beautiful

piào 驃

1. a horse with a yellowish white color 2. valiant 3. galloping

piàojì 驃騎 refer to **piàoqí** 驃騎

piàoqí 驃騎 an ancient title of general rank

piē 撇

1. to cast away; to throw away; to abandon 2. to skim

piēkai 撇開 to dismiss or exclude (from discussion or consideration); to set aside

piēqīng 撇清 to pretend innocence

piē 瞥

to have a casual and short glance; to catch a glimpse of

piējiàn 瞥見 to catch sight of; to catch a glimpse of

piě 撇

1. (calligraphy) a stroke made in the lower left direction 2. to purse the mouth (in contempt or to resist an impulse to cry)

piězuǐ 撇嘴 to purse the mouth

pīn 姘

to make love without a formal wedding; illicit intercourse

pīnfū 姘夫 a man one cohabits with

pīn 拼

1. to join together; to incorporate; to put together; to make a whole 2. to spell (a word) 3. to risk

pīncòu 拼湊 1. to put bits together to make a whole 2. (machinery) to cannibalize 3. to raise money here and there

pīnfǎ 拼法 spelling

pīnmìng 拼命 1. to risk one's life 2. with all one's might

pīnpán 拼盤 assorted cold dishes

pīnyīn 拼音 to spell phonetically

pín 貧 1. poverty; poor; destitute; impoverished 2. deficiency; deficient; lack 3. garrulous

pínbìng jiāopò 貧病交迫 to be

beset by poverty and illness

pínfá 貧乏 wanting; destitute; insufficient

pínjí 貧瘠 (said of land) poor and barren

pínkǔ 貧苦 poor; destitute; poverty-stricken

pínkùn 貧困 impoverished; in straitened circumstances; poor

pínmín 貧民 poor people; a pauper

pínmínkū 貧民窟 a slum area; a shantytown

pínqióng 貧窮 penury; poor; needy; destitution; poverty; impoverishment

pínxiě 貧血 refer to **pínxuè** 貧血

pínxuè 貧血 anaemia; anaemic

pínzuǐ 貧嘴 talkative; garrulous

pín 頻 1. incessant; successive; continuous; frequently or repeatedly 2. urgent; precarious 3. (蹙) to knit the brows 4. frequency

píndào 頻道 (television) a channel

pínfán 頻繁 frequent; incessant; busy

pínlǜ 頻率 frequency

pínnián 頻年 years in a row; year after year

pínpín 頻頻 incessantly; repeatedly; continuously

pǐn 品 1. personality; character 2. an article; a commodity 3. a rank or grade in the government service in former times 4. to appraise; to rate 5. to find out

pǐncháng 品嘗 to taste (food) in order to appraise, rate or grade its worth

pǐndé 品德 personal character

pǐn'gé 品格 one's moral character

pǐnguǎn 品管 Q.C. (quality control)

pǐntóu lùnzú 品頭論足 to make critical remarks about a person's physical appearance

pǐnwèi 品味 taste; a savor

pǐnxìng 品性 one's moral character

pǐnxué jiānyōu 品學兼優 to excel in morals as well as academic performances

pǐnzhí 品質 refer to **pǐnzhì** 品質

pǐnzhì 品質 quality

pǐnzhǒng 品種 a species or variety

pìn 牝 female of an animal

pìnjī sīchén 牝雞司晨 a woman usurping man's power

pìn 聘 1. to invite for service; to employ; to engage 2. to be betrothed; to be engaged 3. to pay respect by sending an envoy 4. to ask; to inquire

pìnjīn 聘金 money paid at a betrothal

pìnqǐng 聘請 to engage; to appoint

pìnshū 聘書 the letter of appointment

pìnyòng 聘用 to employ; to engage

pīng 乒 used for the sound

pīngpāngqiú 乒乓球 table tennis

pīng 娉 good-looking; elegant; charming; graceful

pīngtíng 娉婷 graceful and charming

píng 平 1. level; even 2. equal 3. peaceful 4. to conquer; to quell (a revolt); to calm down 5. to control; to regulate 6. (said of prices) to go back to normal after sharp rises 7. (sports) to make the same score 8. to pacify; to bring peace to 9. short for Beiping

píng'ān 平安 safe and sound; peace

píng'ān wúshì 平安無事 All is well.; safe and without any mishaps; safe and sound

píngbái 平白 without reason or

cause; without provocation

píngbái wúgù 平白無故 without reason or cause; without provocation

píngbèi 平輩 of the same generation

píngbù qīngyún 平步青雲 (said of a career or social position) a meteoric rise

píngcháng 平常 1. normal; natural 2. usual(ly) 3. ordinary; so-so

píngchángxīn 平常心 the absence of excitement, expectation, etc.; composure

píngdàn 平淡 commonplace; insipid; ordinary

píngděng 平等 equality; equal

píngděng hùlì 平等互利 equality and mutual benefit

píngdì 平地 1. a piece of level ground; the plain 2. suddenly

píngdìng 平定 1. (said of situations, etc.) settled 2. to quell (rebellions, etc.)

píngfán 平凡 common; ordinary; usual

píngfǎn 平反 to reverse or redress a miscarriage of justice

píngfāng 平方 (mathematics) a square

píngfáng 平房 a one-storied house; a bungalow

píngfēn 平分 to divide equally

píngfēn qiūsè 平分秋色 (said of two sides) to share (fame, etc.); to equal each other in (achievements, etc.)

píngfu 平復 1. (said of situations, social order, etc.) to calm down; to subside 2. to recover from an illness, etc.

pínghéng 平衡 equilibrium; balance

pínghénglì 平衡力 equilibrant

pínghuá 平滑 even and smooth

pínghuǎn 平緩 1. gently 2. mild; gentle

píngjià 平價 1. a fair price 2. to lower prices

píngjiāodào 平交道 a level crossing

píngjìng 平靜 quiet; calm

píngjú 平局 a draw; a tie

Píngjù 平劇 Beiping opera; Peking opera

píngjūn 平均 the average

píngjūn niánlíng 平均年齡 composite life

píngjūn shòumìng 平均壽命 mean life

píngkōng 平空 to occur without any reason or cause; to fabricate or invent

píngluàn 平亂 to suppress a rebellion or revolt

píngmiàn 平面 a plane, or plane surface

píngmín 平民 a commoner; a civilian

píngmín zhèngzhì 平民政治 popular government; democracy

píngpíng 平平 average; common; so-so

píngpù zhíxù 平鋪直敍 straight reporting; factual description

píngqǐ píngzuò 平起平坐 1. to treat another as one's equal 2. to show no deference

píngrì 平日 on usual days; ordinarily

píngshēng 平生 in all one's life; throughout one's life

píngshēng 平聲 level tone—the first tone in classical Chinese phonetics

píngshí 平時 ordinarily; in normal times

píngshí bù shāoxiāng, línshí bào fójiǎo 平時不燒香，臨時抱佛腳 Last minute efforts are useless if no preparatory work has been done beforehand.

píngshǒu 平手 (in a competition, etc.) to draw; to tie another

píngsù 平素 usually; ordinarily

píngtái 平臺 1. a flat-top building 2. a stadium-like building 3. balcony, open porch or portico

píngtǎn 平坦 level, even and smooth (going, roads, etc.)

píngtiān 平添 to add something unexpectedly

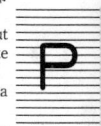

píngwěn 平穩 steady and smooth; stable

píngxí 平息 to come to an end; to subside

píngxí 平息 refer to **píngxī** 平息

píngxīn érlùn 平心而論 to discuss something fairly; to be fair

píngxīn jìngqì 平心靜氣 to be calm and fair (in resolving a dispute, etc.)

píngxìn 平信 ordinary mail

píngxíng 平行 1. parallel 2. of equal rank

píngyě 平野 an open field

píngyì jìnrén 平易近人 (said of one's personality) easy to approach; easy to get along with

píngyōng 平庸 commonplace; dull

píngyuán 平原 a plain; a steppe

píngzhěng 平整 1. to level 2. neat; smooth

píngzhí 平直 fair and frank

píngzhuāng 平裝 paperback; paperbound

píng 坪

1. a level piece of ground 2. (in Japanese measurement) an area of 6 feet square

píng 屏

1. a shield; a screen 2. to shield; to guard

Píngdōng 屏東 Pingdong (Pingtung) county in Taiwan

píngfēng 屏風 a screen

píngmù 屏幕 a screen

píngmù wénzì 屏幕文字 subtitle

píngzhàng 屏障 1. a barrier 2. to shield; to guard

píng 秤

refer to **chèng** 秤 1

píng 萍

1. duckweed 2. moving about rootlessly; traveling or wandering

píngshuǐ xiāngféng 萍水相逢 to meet by accident

píng 評

1. to comment; to criticize; to review 2. comments; reviews 3. to judge

píngdìng 評定 to examine, judge and decide

píngduàn 評斷 to decide; to arbitrate

píngfēn 評分 marks or points given by a judge

píngjià 評價 1. to appraise 2. an objective assessment of the worth or merit of a person, a piece of writing, etc.

pínglǐ 評理 to ask a third party to judge which side is right

píngliáng 評量 to weigh; to evaluate

pínglùn 評論 to comment; to review

píngpàn 評判 to criticize; to judge or decide, as in a beauty contest, etc.

píngxuǎn 評選 to choose through public appraisal

píngyǔ 評語 comments; criticism

píng 瓶

a bottle; a pitcher; a jug; a vase

píngjǐng 瓶頸 a bottleneck

píngsāi 瓶塞 a bottle stopper or plug; a cork

píngzhuāng 瓶裝 bottled

píngzi 瓶子 a bottle

píng 憑

1. to rely upon 2. to lean on 3. to be based on; to go by; to base on; to take as a basis 4. a proof; evidence 5. no matter (what, how, etc.)

píngdān 憑單 a certificate; a receipt

píngdiào 憑弔 1. to pay homage to (the deceased) 2. to contemplate (a ruin, relics, etc.) with emotion

píngjiè 憑藉 1. by means of 2. to rely on 3. something on which one relies

píngjù 憑據 a basis (for belief or supposition); grounds; reasons; proof

píngkōng 憑空 without substantial support or proof

píngshì 憑恃 to rely upon; to depend upon

píngtiào 憑眺 to look far from an eminence

píngzhàng 憑仗 to rely upon; to depend upon

píngzhèng 憑證 a voucher; proof; evidence

píng 蘋
an apple

píngguǒ 蘋果 an apple

pō 坡
a slope; a bank; a hillside

pōdì 坡地 hillside fields; sloping fields

pōdù 坡度 the degree of a slope; grade

pō 泊 also **bó**
a lake; a body of water

pō 波
refer to **bō** 波

pō 頗 also **pǒ**
1. somewhat 2. quite; very; fairly; considerably

pōbiǎo tóngqíng 頗表同情 rather sympathetic

pōwéi mǎnyì 頗為滿意 rather or much satisfied

pōzhī yī'èr 頗知一二 (literally) to know it rather well

pō 潑
1. to pour; to sprinkle; to spill 2. ferocious; fierce; spiteful; villainous

pōfù 潑婦 a virago; a shrew; a termagant

pōla 潑辣 1. ferocious; spiteful 2. pungent

pōlěngshuǐ 潑冷水 (figuratively) to dampen the enthusiasm of

pó 婆
1. an old woman 2. the mother of one's husband 3. one's grandmother

pójia 婆家 one's husband's family

pópo 婆婆 1. the mother of one's husband 2. a term of respect for an old lady

pópo māmā 婆婆媽媽 1. sissy 2. mawkish; oversentimental 3. nagging

pósuō qǐwǔ 婆娑起舞 to start dancing

póxí 婆媳 a woman and her daughter-in-law

pǒ 叵
unable; improbable

pǒcè 叵測 unfathomable; unpredictable

pǒ 頗
refer to **pō** 頗

pò 朴
saltpeter

pò 泊
refer to **bó** 泊

pò 迫
1. to press; to force; to compel 2. pressing; urgent; imminent 3. distressed; pressed

pòbù déyǐ 迫不得已 to have no alternative (but to)

pòbù jídài 迫不及待 too impatient to wait

pòhài 迫害 to persecute; to oppress cruelly

pòjiàng 迫降 a forced landing; a distress landing

pòqiè 迫切 urgent; pressing; imperative

pòshǐ 迫使 to force or compel (one to do a thing)

pòyú 迫於 to have no other alternative because of...

pòzài méijié 迫在眉睫 1. extremely urgent and near 2. imminent

pò 拍
refer to **pāi** 拍

pò 珀
amber

pò 破
1. to break 2. dilapidated; destroyed; ruined 3. to defeat; to beat (the enemy); to capture (enemy territory) 4. to expose; exposed; (to see) through; to lay bare 5. to spend (money, etc.) 6.

to solve or break (a murder case, etc.); to analyze 7. to come to an end 8. paltry

pò'àn 破案 to break a criminal case; to solve a case

pòbài 破敗 ruined; dilapidated; tumbledown

pòcái 破財 to lose money

pòcái xiāozāi 破財消災 to suffer unexpected financial losses and forestall calamities

pòchǎn 破產 bankruptcy

pòchú 破除 to eliminate; to get rid of

pòfèi 破費 to spend money

pòfǔ chénzhōu 破釜沈舟 to cut off all means of retreat

pòhuài 破壞 to ruin; to destroy; to violate

pòhuò 破獲 to break (into a secret hideout) and capture (criminals, loots, etc.)

pòjìlù 破紀錄 to break a record

pòjiè 破戒 1. (usually said of monks, nuns, etc.) to break the rules 2. to make an exception

pòjìng chóngyuán 破鏡重圓 (said of a divorced or separated couple) reunion and reconciliation

pòjiù 破舊 shabby; worn-out; dilapidated

pòkǒu dàmà 破口大罵 to abuse freely and loudly

pòlàn 破爛 wastes or refuse; junk

pòlì 破例 to make an exception

pòliè 破裂 1. to break off; rupture; severance 2. broken; cracked

pòmǎqì 破碼器 a decoder

pòmén érrù 破門而入 to break into a house

pòmiè 破滅 to come to nil

pòpòlànlàn 破破爛爛 tattered; tumble-down; dilapidated

pòshāngfēng 破傷風 tetanus

pòsuì 破碎 1. to come to pieces 2. broken (heart, hope, etc.)

pòsǔn 破損 broken or damaged; ruined

pòtì wéixiào 破涕為笑

smile through tears

pòtiānhuāng 破天荒 never before—for the first time; unprecedented

pòtǔ diǎnlǐ 破土典禮 a ground-breaking ceremony

pòxiǎo 破曉 daybreak; dawn

pòzhàn 破綻 a slip, flaw or weak point; a loophole

pòzhéhào 破折號 a dash

pòzhú zhīshì 破竹之勢 overwhelming force; irresistible

pò 魄

1. (Taoism) vigor; animation; life 2. form; shape; body 3. the dark part of the moon

pòlì 魄力 guts; decisiveness; the ability to make major decisions promptly

pōu 剖 also pǒu

1. to cut, rip or tear open 2. to explain; to analyze; to dissect

pōubái 剖白 to dispel suspicion by explanation

pōufù 剖腹 to cut the belly open

pōufù zìshā 剖腹自殺 (to commit) hara-kiri

pōujiě 剖解 1. to dissect; to anatomize 2. to analyze

pōukāi 剖開 to cut or rip open

pōumiàn 剖面 a section

pōuxī 剖析 to analyse; dissect

pǒu 剖

refer to **pōu** 剖

pū 仆 also fū

1. to prostrate 2. to fall

pū 扑

to beat; to strike

pūjī 扑擊 to hit; to strike

pūjí 扑擊 refer to **pūjī** 扑擊

pūtà 扑撻 to whip; to lash; to flog

pū 鋪

to lay in order; to spread; to arrange; to pave

pūchén 鋪陳 1. to state in detail; to elaborate 2. to arrange for display

pūchuáng 鋪床 to make the bed

pūgai 鋪蓋 bedding

pūlù 鋪路 to surface a road; to pave a road

pūshè 鋪設 to lay in order; to arrange

pūxù 鋪敘 to state in detail

pūzhāng 鋪張 1. to arrange; to lay in order 2. to make an ostentatious or vain show; to be pompous

pū 撲

1. to beat; to strike; to pound 2. to dash; to smash 3. to throw oneself on; to spring at 4. to flap; to flutter

pūbí 撲鼻 to assail the nostrils

pūdǎ 撲打 to beat; to pat; to swat

pūfěn 撲粉 1. to powder (one's face) 2. face powder

pūguolai 撲過來 to come in a dash

pūjiù 撲救 to fight (a fire)

pūkè 撲克 poker (a gambling game)

pūkèpái 撲克牌 playing cards

pūkōng 撲空 1. to fail to meet a person one intended to meet 2. to do a thing in vain

pūmǎn 撲滿 a savings box; a piggy bank

pūmiàn 撲面 to blow on (against) one's face

pūmiè 撲滅 to exterminate (vermins); to extinguish (a fire)

pūshā 撲殺 to kill

pūshí 撲食 to seize for prey

pūshuò mílí 撲朔迷離 1. (said of a person) to look both like a man and a woman 2. vague or ambiguous

pūtōng 撲通 a plop; a splash; a thump

pú 匍

1. to crawl; to creep 2. to lie prostrate; to prostrate

púfú 匍匐 1. to prostrate 2. to crawl; to creep

pú 脯

flesh or meat in the general area of the chest or breast

pú 菩

1. a fragrant herb 2. the sacred tree of the Buddhists

Púsà 菩薩 1. Bodhisattva 2. Buddha

Púsà xīncháng 菩薩心腸 kind-hearted; compassionate

pútíshù 菩提樹 1. a peepul tree 2. (Buddhism) a bo tree

pú 葡

1. a grape; a vine 2. short for Portugal

Pútáoyá 葡萄牙 Portugal

pútao 葡萄 grapes

pútaogān 葡萄乾 raisins

pútaojiǔ 葡萄酒 grape wine; port wine; a vintage; wine

pútaotáng 葡萄糖 glucose

pútaoyòu 葡萄柚 a grapefruit

pú 僕

1. a servant 2. a modest term referring to oneself 3. (formerly) to act as a driver; to drive

púcóng 僕從 retinue; a group of retainers

púpú fēngchén 僕僕風塵 to be travel-worn and weary

púrén 僕人 a servant

púyì 僕役 servants

púzòng 僕從 refer to **púcóng** 僕從

pú 蒲

1. various kinds of rush from which mats, bags, etc. are made; vines of the rushes 2. a Chinese family name

púgōngyīng 蒲公英 the dandelion

púshàn 蒲扇 a rush-leaf fan

pú 樸

refer to **pǔ** 樸

pú 璞

1. an uncarved or unpolished jade 2. (figuratively) natural; unadorned

pǔ 浦

1. the shore; the beach; the river-

Q

side 2. a Chinese family name

pǔ 埔
1. a plain; an arena 2. a port; a mart

pǔ 圃
1. a vegetable garden (or plot); a nursery; an orchard; a plantation 2. a planter; a gardener

pǔ 普
universal; all; widespread; everywhere; general

pǔbiàn 普遍 universal; general; widespread

pǔbiànxìng 普遍性 universality

pǔchá 普查 a general survey

pǔdù zhòngshēng 普渡眾生 (Buddhism) to deliver or save all beings

pǔjí 普及 1. universal; available to all 2. to popularize; to disseminate

pǔjíběn 普及本 a paperback edition

pǔjiàng gānlín 普降甘霖 timely rain for all drought areas

pǔtiān tóngqìng 普天同慶 The whole world joins in the rejoicing, celebration or congratulations.

pǔtiān zhīxià 普天之下 all over the world

pǔtōng 普通 ordinary; common; plain

pǔtōnghuà 普通話 the common dialect of the Chinese language; Mandarin

pǔxuǎn 普選 universal suffrage; general elections

pǔzhào 普照 (said of sunshine, God's grace, etc.) to shine upon all

pǔ 溥
1. great; wide; vast 2. universal 3. a Chinese family name

pǔtiān tóngqìng 溥天同慶 universally celebrated

pǔtiān zhīxià 溥天之下 everywhere under the sun

pǔ 樸 also **pú**
1. (said of dress, clothing, literary style, etc.) plain; simple 2.

the substance of things; things in the rough 3. honest; sincere; simple

pǔshí 樸實 1. simple; plain (said of dresses, style, etc.) 2. honest; sincere

pǔsù 樸素 (said of dresses, etc.) simple and plain

pǔzhí 樸直 honest and straightforward

pǔzhuō 樸拙 simple and naive

pǔzhuō 樸拙 refer to **púzhuō** 樸拙

pǔ 譜
1. a register; a table; a list 2. (music) a score 3. to compose (a song) 4. a general idea; a rough picture 5. a manual; a guide

pǔqǔ 譜曲 to compose a song

pǔzi 譜子 music score; music

pù 暴
refer to **bào** 暴 2

pù 鋪(舖)
a store; a shop; a grocery

pùmiàn 鋪面 the shop front; the facade of a store

pùwèi 鋪位 a bunk

pùzi 鋪子 a shop; a store

pù 瀑
a waterfall; a cascade; a cataract

pùbù 瀑布 a waterfall; a cataract

pù 曝
to expose to sunlight; to sun

pùguāng 曝光 (photography) exposure

pùlù 曝露 to expose oneself to the weather

pùshài 曝曬 to expose to sunlight; to sun

qī 七
the number seven (Note: when **qī** 七 precedes a 4th-tone sound, its pronunciation should be changed to the second tone, i.e. **qí**.)

qīcháng bāduǎn 七長八短 of various lengths

qīchǐ zhīqū 七尺之軀 men's average height (referring to a

full-grown man)

qījiǎoxíng 七角形 a heptagon

qīlíng bāluò 七零八落 scattered here and there; in confusion

qīpīn bācòu 七拼八湊 1. to cannibalize 2. to piece together

qīpíng bāwěn 七平八穩 balanced; stable

qīqiào shēngyān 七竅生煙 to fume with anger; to foam with rage

qīqíng liùyù 七情六欲 (Buddhism) the seven emotions and the six sensory pleasures

qīshàng bāxià 七上八下 an unsettled state of mind

Qīxī 七夕 the seventh evening of the seventh moon (when according to legend the Cowherd and the Weaver Maid meet in Heaven)

Qìxì 七夕 refer to **Qīxī** 七夕

qīyánshī 七言詩 verses with seven characters to a line

qīyuè 七月 1. July 2. the seventh month of the lunar year; the seventh moon

qīzhé bākòu 七折八扣 1. big discounts (in a bargain sale) 2. to make allowance for exaggeration in a statement

qīzuǐ bāshé 七嘴八舌 everybody talking at the same time

qī 沏

1. to infuse 2. (said of the flowing water) rapidly; turbulently

qīchá 沏茶 to infuse tea; to make tea

qī 妻

one's formal or legal wife

qīlí zǐsàn 妻離子散 The family breaks up.

qīqiè 妻妾 one's wife and concubine(s)

qīzǐ 妻子 one's wife and children

qīzi 妻子 one's wife

qī 柒

another form of 七 (seven), used in writing checks, etc. to prevent fraud

qī 戚

1. relatives by marriage 2. sad; woeful; mournful 3. a battle-ax 4. a Chinese family name

qīqī 戚戚 1. mournful 2. touched

qī 悽

1. grieved; sorrowful; afflicted 2. tragic; pathetic; pitiful; grievous

qīcǎn 悽慘 tragic; heartrending

qīchuàng 悽愴 1. pathetic; pitiful 2. cold; dreary; desolate

qīcè 悽惻 sad; sorrowful

qīchǔ 悽楚 pathetic; pitiful

qīkǔ 悽苦 suffering tragically

qīliáng 悽涼 dreary; desolate

qīqī 悽悽 pathetic; pitiful; grievous

qīqī huánghuáng 悽悽惶惶 hurriedly; hastily

qīqiè 悽切 pathetic; pitiful

qīrán 悽然 sad; sorrowful

qī 凄

1. cloudy and rainy 2. cold and chilly 3. sorrow; sorrowful; miserable; desolate

qīcǎn 凄慘 heartrending; heartbreaking

qīchuàng 凄愴 heartrending; heartbreaking

qīfēng kǔyǔ 凄風苦雨 chilly winds and cold rains that inspire sadness in a person's mind

qīlěng 凄冷 desolate; bleak

qīlì 凄厲 1. sad and sorrowful 2. bleak and harsh

qīliáng 凄涼 desolate and sorrowful; lonely; lonesome

qīmí 凄迷 1. (said of sights) desolate 2. (said of the mood) despondent

qīrán 凄然 very sorrowful

qī 棲(栖) also **xī**

1. to rest; to stay; to perch; to settle 2. the place one stays 3. (now rarely) a bed

qīchǔ 棲處 to stay (at a place)

qīchù 棲處 an abode (usually temporarily)

qījū 棲居 to dwell; to live

qīshēn 棲身 to live; to stay; to dwell

qīxī 棲息 to rest; to stay; to perch

qīxí 棲息 refer to **qīxī** 棲息

qī 萋
1. luxuriant foliage; a dense growth of grass 2. many; crowded

qīqī 萋萋 luxuriant

qī 期 also **qí**
1. periods; times 2. a designated time; a time limit 3. to expect; to hope; to wait

qīdài 期待 to expect; to hope

qīfáng 期房 soon to be available housing

qījiān 期間 a period; a term

qīkān 期刊 a periodical

qīmǎn 期滿 The term (or period) has expired.

qīmò kǎoshì 期末考試 the final examination of a school term; the final

qīqī ài'ài 期期艾艾 stammering

qīwàng 期望 to expect; to hope

qīxiàn 期限 a time limit; a deadline

qīxǔ 期許 to expect; expectation

qīzhōng kǎoshì 期中考試 a midterm examination

qī 欺
1. to cheat; to deceive; to swindle; to impose on; to take advantage of 2. to disregard the dictates of one's own conscience 3. to insult; to bully

qīfu 欺負 to insult or oppress; to bully

qīlíng 欺凌 to mistreat; to insult; to bully

qīmán 欺瞞 to deceive; to cheat

qīpiàn 欺騙 to cheat; to deceive; to swindle

qīrén tàishèn 欺人太甚 You have insulted me beyond the limit.

qīshàn pà'è 欺善怕惡 to oppress the good and timid and fear the wicked

qīshàng mánxià 欺上瞞下 to deceive one's superiors and delude one's subordinates

qīshì dàomíng 欺世盜名 to win fame by cheating the world

qīwǔ 欺侮 to insult or ridicule; to bully

qīyā 欺壓 to cheat and oppress

qīzhà 欺詐 to swindle; to defraud; to cheat

qī 溪
refer to **xī** 溪

qī 漆
1. a varnish tree; a lacquer tree 2. varnish; lacquer 3. to varnish; to lacquer; to paint 4. (also **qù**) pitch-black

qīgōng 漆工 a varnisher; a painter

qīhēi 漆黑 pitch-dark; pitch-black

qīqì 漆器 lacquer wares

qī 緝
to sew in close and straight stitches

qī 慼
1. mournful; woeful 2. ashamed

qīqī 慼慼 sorrowful; sad; rueful

qīróng 慼容 a sad look; a sorrowful expression

qí 歧
1. a path branching out from the main road; a forked road 2. forked; divergent; strayed 3. anything that goes astray

qíjiàn 歧見 different opinions or interpretations

qílù 歧路 1. a path branching out from the main road 2. the wrong way

qílù wángyáng 歧路亡羊 One who seeks truth is apt to get lost when confronted with too many choices.

qíshì 歧視 to act biasedly; to discriminate against

qítú 歧途 1. a path branching out from the main road 2. the wrong way

qí 枝

qízhǐ 枝指 a forked finger; an additional finger

qí 祇

1. the god of the earth 2. peace; serenity; to be at rest

qí 其

1. a pronoun—he, she, it, they; his, her, its, their 2. this; that; the 3. an interrogative used to introduce a question

qícì 其次 secondly; besides

qíjiān 其間 in; among; in between; between

qílái yǒuzì 其來有自 It did not happen by accident.

qílè wúqióng 其樂無窮 The joy is boundless.

qímào bùyáng 其貌不揚 ugly in appearance

qíshí 其實 in fact; as a matter of fact

qítā 其他 the others; the rest

qíyú 其餘 the others; the rest

qízhōng 其中 in; among; in the midst

qí 奇

1. strange; uncanny; occult; rare 2. wonderful 3. to feel strange about

qícái 奇才 a rare talent; a genius

qíchǐ dàrǔ 奇恥大辱 great shame or disgrace; great insult or humiliation

qíguài 奇怪 strange; unusual; odd

qíguān 奇觀 a spectacular or wonderful sight or phenomenon

qíhuò kějū 奇貨可居 (literally) rare commodities which can be hoarded for better prices

qíjī 奇蹟 miracles; wonders

qíjǐng 奇景 wonderful scenes

qímiào 奇妙 wonderful; rare

qítán 奇談 a strange story

qítè 奇特 unique; outstanding; strange

qíwén 奇聞 something unheard-of

qíxíng guàizhuàng 奇形怪狀 of strange, bizarre or grotesque shapes and sizes

qíyì 奇異 strange; unusual; odd

qíyìguǒ 奇異果 kiwi; Chinese gooseberries

qíyù 奇遇 an unexpected encounter

qízhuāng yìfú 奇裝異服 strange or queer clothing

qí 祈

1. to pray 2. to beg; to entreat; to beseech; to supplicate; to request respectfully

qídǎo 祈禱 to pray; to offer a prayer

qíqiú 祈求 to pray for; to appeal for

qí 耆

to be in one's sixties; old

qínián shuòdé 耆年碩德 aged and virtuous

qísù 耆宿 a respected old person

qí 崎

1. the banks of a winding river 2. rugged; uneven; rough

qíqū 崎嶇 (said of terrain) uneven; rolling; rugged

qí 畦 also xī

a plot, piece or parcel of land

qí 期

refer to **qī** 期

qí 琪

a piece of jade; a white gem

qí 棋

1. any piece used in the game of chess 2. chess or other similar games

qíféng díshǒu 棋逢敵手 a good match; to be well-matched in a contest

qígāo yīzhāo 棋高一著 to be superior in intelligence, stratagem, skill, etc. than one's opponent

qíjú 棋局 1. the chessboard with the pieces arranged 2. a game of chess

qípán 棋盤 a chessboard

qíshǒu 棋手 a high-graded chess player

qíwáng 棋王 a chess champion

qízǐ 棋子 chess pieces

Q

qí 齊

1. equal; uniform; to be on a level 2. name of an ancient feudal state 3. name of a dynasty 4. to set in order 5. a Chinese family name

qíbèi 齊備 everything ready; everything complete

qíbù 齊步 in step; uniform steps

qíjí 齊集 all assembled

qíjiā 齊家 to govern one's family

qíméi 齊眉 respect between husband and wife

qímíng 齊名 equally well-known; equal in fame

qínián 齊年 of the same age

qíqū 齊驅 to advance abreast—to be equal in ability

qíquán 齊全 everything complete; nothing missing; all in readiness

Qírén zhīfú 齊人之福 to have more than one wife; to have a concubine

qíshēng 齊聲 in unison; with one voice

qítóu bìngjìn 齊頭並進 to go ahead together; to march together

qíxīn 齊心 of one mind

qíyī 齊一 uniform; equal

qí 旗

1. a flag; a pennant; a banner; a streamer 2. a sign; an insignia; an emblem 3. an administrative division of Mongolia and Qinghai 4. the Manchus

qígān 旗杆 a flagstaff

qígān 旗竿 a flagstaff

qígǔ xiāngdāng 旗鼓相當 of approximately equal strength, ability, etc.

qíkāi déshèng 旗開得勝 to win in the first battle, game or match

qípáo 旗袍 traditional costume for women, which is a close fitting dress with high neck and slit skirt

qíyú 旗魚 spearfish

qízhì 旗幟 flags, pennants, streamers, etc.

qí 畿

refer to **jī** 畿

qí 騎

1. to ride (a horse, etc.); to sit astride on 2. (also **jì**) cavalry; a rider; a jotckey

qíbīng 騎兵 cavalry; mounted troops

qíhǔ nánxià 騎虎難下 in a position from which there is no easy retreat; unable to stop or quit

qílóu 騎樓 an arcade (a covered avenue)

qímǎ zhǎomǎ 騎馬找馬 to hold a temporary position while seeking a better job

qíshī 騎師 a jockey

qíshì 騎士 1. a knight 2. a horse-back rider

qíshù 騎術 equitation; horsemanship

qí 臍

1. the navel; the umbilicus 2. the underside of a crab

qídài 臍帶 the umbilical cord

qí 麒

the male of a fabulous animal resembling the deer

qílín 麒麟 a fabulous animal resembling the deer said to appear only in time of peace and prosperity

qí 鰭

fins

qǐ 乞

to ask for alms; to beg

qǐgài 乞丐 a beggar

qǐlián 乞憐 to beg for pity and charity

qǐqiú 乞求 to beg for; to supplicate; to implore

qǐtǎo 乞討 to beg for food, money, etc.

qǐxiáng 乞降 to negotiate for surrender on the part of the defeated

qǐyuán 乞援 to ask for assistance

qǐ 企 also **qì**
1. to stand on tiptoe 2. to hope; to long; to expect

qǐ'é 企鵝 a penguin

qǐguǎn 企管 business management

qǐhuà 企劃 to design; to lay out; to plan

qǐpàn 企盼 to expect or hope with eagerness

qǐqiú 企求 to desire; to hanker for

qǐtú 企圖 1. to intend; to attempt 2. a plan

qǐtúxīn 企圖心 enterprising spirit

qǐwàng 企望 to hope for; to look forward to

qǐyè 企業 an enterprise

qǐyèjiā 企業家 an entrepreneur

qǐ 杞
1. a species of willow 2. a medlar 3. name of a state in the Zhou Dynasty in today's Henan Province

Qǐrén yōutiān 杞人憂天 A man entertains imaginary or groundless fears.

qǐ 起
1. to begin; to start 2. to rise; to get up 3. to stand up; to go up 3. to happen; to take place 4. to unfold; to uncover 5. to build; to establish 6. a numerary adjunct for incidents

qǐcǎo 起草 to prepare a draft; to draft

qǐchéng 起程 to start on a journey; to set out

qǐchuáng 起床 to get out of bed; to get up

qǐdiǎn 起點 a starting point

qǐdòng 起動 to start (a machine, etc.)

qǐfēi 起飛 to take off; a takeoff

qǐfú 起伏 1. to undulate; undulation 2. ups and downs; the rise and fall

qǐhòng 起鬨 to create disturbances

qǐhuǒ 起火 1. to catch fire; to be

on fire 2. to lose one's temper 3. to cook meals

qǐjìn 起勁 (said of actions, performances, etc.) showing much zeal; eager; energetic; vigorous; with gusto

qǐjū 起居 one's everyday life at home

qǐlái 起來 to stand up; to rise; to get up

qǐlì 起立 to stand up

qǐluò 起落 rising and falling

qǐmǎ 起碼 at least

qǐmáo 起錨 to weigh anchor

qǐqì 起訖 the beginning and the end

qǐsè 起色 1. a sign of improvement 2. a sign of recovery

qǐshēn 起身 1. to set out; to leave; to get off 2. to get up

qǐsǐ huíshēng 起死回生 to revive the dead; to come back to life

qǐsù 起訴 (said of a prosecutor) to file a formal indictment

qǐtiào 起跳 (sports) to take off

qǐtóu 起頭 1. the origin; the beginning 2. at first; in the beginning

qǐwǔ 起舞 1. to rise and dance 2. to be excited with joy

qǐxiān 起先 at first; in the beginning

qǐyǎn 起眼 to attract attention

qǐyí 起疑 to begin to suspect; to become suspicious

qǐyì 起意 to conceive a design; to have an idea of (doing something)

qǐyì 起義 to start an uprising (in a righteous revolution); to revolt

qǐyīn 起因 a cause

qǐyuán 起源 the origin; the source; the beginning

qǐzi 起子 1. (dialect) baking powder; leaven 2. (dialect) a screwdriver 3. a bottle opener

qǐ 豈
an interrogative particle implying a conflicting or dissenting view or answer—how; what

qǐgǎn 豈敢 (a term implying

humbleness or sarcasm) How dare I...? would not dare...

qǐ'néng 豈能 How can...?

qǐyǒu cǐlǐ 豈有此理 What kind of reasoning is that? How absurd!

qǐzhǐ 豈只 not only that... (but)

qǐ 啓

1. to open 2. to begin; to start 3. to explain 4. to inform; to state 5. a letter

qǐchéng 啓程 to start on a journey; to set out

qǐchǐ 啓齒 to open the mouth to say something

qǐdí 啓迪 to prompt mental development

qǐdòng 啓動 to start (a machine, etc.)

qǐfā 啓發 to prompt mental development

qǐháng 啓航 to set sail; to weigh anchor

qǐméng 啓蒙 to enlighten

qǐshì 啓示 revelation

qǐshì 啓事 a notice; an announcement (in writing)

qǐxíng 啓行 to start on a journey; to set out

qǐyòng 啓用 to start using

qǐ 綺

1. beautiful; magnificent; fine; fair; gorgeous; resplendent; elegant 2. twilled silk cloth

qǐlì 綺麗 beautiful; fair; resplendent; enchanting

qǐnián yùmào 綺年玉貌 (said of a girl) young and beautiful

qǐ 稽

to kowtow; to bow to the ground

qǐ 企

refer to **qǐ** 企

qì 汽

gas; steam; vapor

qìchē 汽車 an automobile

qìchē lǚguǎn 汽車旅館 a motel

qìchuán 汽船 a steamship; a

steamboat; a steamer

qìdí 汽笛 a steam whistle; a siren

qìgāng 汽缸 cylinders (in automobiles, etc.)

qìguō 汽鍋 a (steam) boiler

qìhuà 汽化 vaporization; to vaporize

qìmén 汽門 a steam valve

qìshuǐ 汽水 soda water; soft drinks or soda pop

qìtǐng 汽艇 a motorboat; a steam launch

qìyóu 汽油 gasoline; gas

qìyóudàn 汽油彈 1. a napalm bomb 2. a fire bomb or Molotov cocktail

qì 迄

up to; down to; so far; till

qìjīn 迄今 up to now; until now; so far; to this day

qì 妻

to marry one's daughter to someone

qì 泣

to weep; to come to tears without crying

qìbù chéngshēng 泣不成聲 to choke with sobs

qìsù 泣訴 to tell one's sorrows or grievances in tears

qìxiě 泣血 refer to **qìxuè** 泣血

qìxuè 泣血 to weep blood (an expression used especially after one's name in a mourning notice for one's parents)

qì 砌

1. to lay (bricks, etc.); to pave; to raise in layers; to build 2. steps

qìqiáng 砌牆 to build a wall

qì 契

1. a contract; an agreement; a bond 2. a divining instrument in ancient China 3. to be compatible, harmonious in thought and aspiration 4. to adopt 5. to cut 6. to carve

qìhé 契合 to be in agreement; harmony

qìjī 契機 1. (philosophy) a

moment 2. a turning point; a critical point of time

qìjù 契據 a contract; an agreement

qìyuē 契約 a written contract or agreement

qì 訖

1. to come to an end; to conclude; cleared or settled 2. (迄) until

qì 氣

1. air; gas; vapor; the atmosphere 2. breath 3. spirit; morale 4. influence 5. bearing; manner 6. smells; odors 7. to be angry; to be indignant; rage; anger 8. to provoke; to goad; to make angry; to annoy 9. weather

qìchōngchōng 氣沖沖 furious; to fly into a rage

qìchuǎn 氣喘 1. to pant; to gasp 2. asthma

qìchuǎn rúniú 氣喘如牛 to pant like an ox

qìdù 氣度 1. spirit; air; bearing 2. capacity for tolerance

qìfēn 氣氛 atmosphere; mood

qìfèn 氣忿 to be angry, furious, enraged or indignant

qìfèn 氣憤 to be angry, furious, enraged or indignant

qìgài 氣概 spirit; air; bearing; manner

qìgōng 氣功 (Chinese boxing) a system of deep breathing exercises

qìguǎn 氣管 trachea; windpipe

qìguǎnyán 氣管炎 tracheitis

qìhòu 氣候 1. climate; weather 2. situations

qìhuà 氣化 to evaporate; to vaporize

qìhūn 氣昏 to be driven mad by anger

qìjí bàihuài 氣急敗壞 desperate and low-spirited

qìjué 氣絕 to breathe one's last

qìkǒng 氣孔 pores (on the skin); stomas (on a leaf); the spiracle or blow hole (of a whale); vesicles (of the igneous rock)

qìliàng 氣量 tolerance

qìliú 氣流 an airflow; an air current

qì'nǎo 氣惱 to be sulky; to be sullen

qì'něi 氣餒 despondent; crestfallen

qìpài 氣派 a dignified air

qìpào 氣泡 air bubbles

qìpò 氣魄 spirit; vigor; moral strength

qìqiú 氣球 a balloon

qìsè 氣色 complexion; color

qìshì 氣勢 vehemence; fervor

qìshì pángbó 氣勢磅礴 of great momentum

qìshù 氣數 destiny; fate; fortune

qìsǐrén 氣死人 infuriating; exasperating

qìtǐ 氣體 gas; the gaseous body; vapor

qìtǒng 氣筒 an air pump; an inflator

qìtóushang 氣頭上 right in the middle of one's fit of rage

qìtuán 氣團 a mass of cold or hot air

qìwèi 氣味 smacks; smells; odors

qìwèi xiāngtóu 氣味相投 having the same tastes and temperament; congenial

qìwēn 氣溫 the temperature

qìxī 氣息 breath

qìxí 氣息 refer to qìxī 氣息

qìxiàng 氣象 1. weather; climates 2. atmosphere

qìxiàng bàogào 氣象報告 a weather forecast

qìxiàngjú 氣象局 a weather bureau

qìxiàngtái 氣象臺 a weather station

qìxiàng wànqiān 氣象萬千 Nature abounds in changes.

qìyā 氣壓 air pressure

qìyǔ xuānáng 氣宇軒昂 dignified; exalted

qìzhí 氣質 refer to qìzhì 氣質

qìzhì 氣質 dispositions; temperament

qì 棄

1. to discard; to cast aside 2. to reject; to abandon; to desert 3. to forget 4. to throw away one's own life

qì'àn tóumíng 棄暗投明 to renounce a bad cause and join the camp of justice

qìguān 棄官 to give up one's office

qìjiǎ yèbīng 棄甲曳兵 (said of military troops) to throw away their armor and trail their weapons behind them—to be totally defeated

qìjiǎ yìbīng 棄甲曳兵 refer to **qìjiǎ yèbīng** 棄甲曳兵

qìjiù yíngxīn 棄舊迎新 to reject the old and welcome the new—as in the case of taking a second wife

qìjuān 棄捐 to reject; to abandon

qìquán 棄權 (in voting) to abstain; a waiver

qìshì 棄世 to die

qìwù 棄物 trash; discarded useless things

qìxié guīzhèng 棄邪歸正 to reject evil ways and start on the right track

qìyīng 棄嬰 a foundling

qìzhì 棄置 to cast aside

qì 葺

1. to repair 2. thatched 3. to pile up; to heap together

qìbǔ 葺補 to repair and mend

qì 緝

refer to **jī** 緝

qì 憩

to rest; to repose

qìxī 憩息 to rest; to take a rest

qìxí 憩息 refer to **qìxī** 憩息

qì 器

1. an instrument; an implement; a utensil; a tool; a piece of apparatus 2. magnanimity 3. talent; ability 4. to think highly of (a person)

qìcái 器材 implements and mate-

rials

qìguān 器官 the apparatus; the organs

qìjù 器具 tools; instruments

qìliàng 器量 the capacity for magnanimity; tolerance

qìmǐn 器皿 food containers

qìyǔ xuānáng 器宇軒昂 of dignified bearing

qìzhòng 器重 to think highly of

qì 磧

1. gravel and sand in shallow waters 2. a desert

qiā 掐

1. to dig the nail into 2. to cut with fingernails; to nip; to pinch; to give a pinch 3. to hold; to grasp; to clutch; to gather with the hand

qiāduàn 掐斷 to break; to nip

qiāsǐ 掐死 to choke to death by strangling with hands

qiāzhù 掐住 to seize; to grasp; to hold

qiá 卡

refer to **qiǎ** 卡 2

qiǎ 卡

1. to choke; to be choked 2. (also **qiá**) to be squeezed in between; to be sandwiched

qià 恰

proper; appropriate; suitable

qiàdàng 恰當 appropriate; fitting; apt; apposite

qiàdào hǎochu 恰到好處 neither too much nor too little; just right

qiàhǎo 恰好 1. just; exactly 2. by coincidence

qiàqiǎo 恰巧 by coincidence; by chance

qiàrú qífèn 恰如其分 just suited or becoming to one's importance

qiàsì 恰似 just like; just as if; just as though

qiàzhí 恰值 just at the time of

qià 洽 also **xiá**

1. to spread; to diffuse 2. har-

mony; agreement 3. to negotiate; to consult

qiàbàn 洽辦 to handle an assignment through negotiation

qiàshāng 洽商 to discuss (details of a contract, etc.)

qiàtán 洽談 to discuss or consult (problems) together

qiān 千

1. thousand 2. many; numerous

qiānbiàn wànhuà 千變萬化 countless changes

qiānchuí bǎiliàn 千錘百鍊 1. (to undergo) severe training and hammering 2. (to write) with the utmost care

qiāndāo wànguǎ 千刀萬剮 to hack someone to pieces

qiāndīngníng wànzhǔfu 千叮嚀萬囑咐 to exhort repeatedly

qiānfāng bǎijì 千方百計 a thousand schemes—by hook or by crook

qiāngǔ 千古 1. a long, long time 2. (used in mourning) in eternity

qiāngǔ qíwén 千古奇聞 a forever strange tale

qiānhè 千赫 kilohertz

qiānhuí bǎizhé 千迴百折 innumerable twists and turns

qiānjiāo bǎimèi 千嬌百媚 the beauty of beauties

qiānjīn 千金 1. a courteous expression referring to another's daughter 2. a thousand pieces of gold

qiānjīndǐng 千斤頂 a jack

qiānjīn xiǎojiě 千金小姐 a young lady of a wealthy family

qiānjūn wànmǎ 千軍萬馬 a large number of mounted and foot soldiers

qiānjūn yīfà 千鈞一髮 refer to qiānjūn yīfà 千鈞一髮

qiānjūn yīfà 千鈞一髮 very precarious

qiānlǐ 千里 a long distance

qiānlǐmǎ 千里馬 a winged steed

qiānlǐ tiáotiáo 千里迢迢 from afar

qiānlǐyǎn 千里眼 1. farsightedness 2. (mythology) name of a

god whose eyesight that can reach the heaven 3. another name for telescope or binoculars

qiānnián 千年 a thousand years

qiānpiān yīlǜ 千篇一律 without changes; dull; monotonous

qiānqí bǎiguài 千奇百怪 grotesque or weird shapes

qiānqiū wànsuì 千秋萬歲 a long, long time

qiānshān wànshuǐ 千山萬水 distant (places, etc.); (a journey from) afar

qiāntóu wànxù 千頭萬緒 (said of a problem or task) very complicated or confused

qiānwàn 千萬 1. a huge amount 2. an expression used to emphasize an injunction

qiānxīn wànkǔ 千辛萬苦 to suffer or undergo all conceivable hardships (to accomplish something)

qiānyán wànyǔ 千言萬語 many, many words in one's heart (but one doesn't know where to begin)

qiānzǎi nánféng 千載難逢 once in a lifetime; a very rare chance

qiānzhēn wànquè 千真萬確 very real; absolutely true

qiān 仟

1. leader of one thousand men 2. thousand

qiān 阡

1. paths on farms; a footpath between fields, running north and south 2. the path leading to a grave

qiānmò 阡陌 paths on farmland

qiānmò zònghéng 阡陌縱橫 crisscross paths on farmland

qiān 牽

1. to lead along; to drag; to pull; to tug; to haul 2. to involve; to affect 3. to control; to restrain

qiāncháng guàdù 牽腸掛肚 to be very worried about

qiānchě 牽扯 complication (of a matter); to involve; to implicate

qiāndòng 牽動 to influence

Q

qiānguà 牽掛 to be concerned for; to worry about

qiānlěi 牽累 to drag (into trouble); to involve; to implicate

qiānlián 牽連 to drag (into trouble); to involve; to implicate

qiānniàn 牽念 to feel anxious about

qiānniúhuā 牽牛花 morning glory

qiānqiǎng 牽強 forced; far-fetched; unnatural

qiānqiǎng fùhuì 牽強附會 to give a forced interpretation; to distort the meaning

qiānshè 牽涉 to involve; to implicate

qiānshǒu 牽手 1. to lead by the hand 2. one's wife

qiānxiàn 牽線 to build a bridge; bridging; to exploit the connection; wire-pulling

qiānyǐn 牽引 1. to involve (in trouble) 2. to draw

qiānzhì 牽制 1. to restrain; to curb 2. to divert (enemy attention)

qiān 嵌

refer to **qiàn** 嵌

qiān 愆

1. a fault; a mistake; a misdemeanor 2. to lose 3. a malignant disease

qiānguò 愆過 a fault; a mistake

qiānqī 愆期 to fail to meet a deadline

qiānqī 愆期 refer to **qiānqī** 愆期

qiān 鉛

lead (a metal)

qiānbǐ 鉛筆 a pencil; a lead pencil

qiānhuá 鉛華 cosmetics; face powder

qiānkuàng 鉛礦 lead ore

qiānqiú 鉛球 a shot (thrown in the shot put)

qiānzì 鉛字 lead type (in printing)

qiān 慳

1. stingy; niggardly; parsimonious; close 2. deficient

qiānlìn 慳吝 stingy; niggardly; miserly

qiān 搴

to pull or pluck up

qiānqí zhǎnjiàng 搴旗斬將 to defeat the enemy decisively

qiān 遷

1. to move; to remove 2. to change 3. (said of officials, etc.) to get transferred 4. to be banished

qiāndiào 遷調 to get transferred to another post

qiāndū 遷都 to move the national capital

qiānjiù 遷就 to compromise

qiānjū 遷居 to move into a new residence

qiānnù 遷怒 1. to blame a person for one's own blunder, failure, etc. 2. to shift or transfer one's anger from one person to another

qiānshàn 遷善 to reform one's ways

qiānxǐ 遷徙 to move; to remove

qiānyí 遷移 to move (to a new address)

qiān 謙

modest; humble; retiring; self-effacing

qiānbēi 謙卑 humble; self-depreciating

qiāncí 謙辭 1. modest speech; a humble remark 2. to decline out of humbleness

qiāngōng 謙恭 respectful; unassuming

qiānqiān jūnzǐ 謙謙君子 a modest gentleman

qiānràng 謙讓 to yield from modesty

qiānxū 謙虛 1. modest; unassuming; self-effacing 2. to make modest remarks

qiānxùn 謙遜 humble; modest; unassuming

qiān 簽

1. to sign one's name; to put down one's signature; to sub-

scribe; to endorse 2. bamboo slips used for drawing lots or divination 3. a label

qiāndào 簽到 to sign on an attendance book of an office, firm or factory

qiāndìng 簽訂 to conclude and sign (a treaty, etc.)

qiānmíng 簽名 to sign; a signature

qiānshōu 簽收 to sign after receiving something

qiānshǔ 簽署 to sign or initial (a document)

qiāntiáo 簽條 1. a label 2. an office note; a memo

qiānyuē 簽約 to sign a contract, treaty, etc.

qiānzhèng 簽證 a visa; to visa

qiānzìbǐ 簽字筆 a felt pen; a felt-tip pen

qiān 籤

1. a slip of bamboo engraved with signs to be used in gambling or divination; a lot 2. a label 3. a small sharp-pointed stick

qiān 鞦

a swing

qián 前

1. front; forward; before 2. previous; former; preceding; past; of earlier times 3. future 4. to advance; to proceed; to progress; to precede

qiánbèi 前輩 a senior

qiánbian 前邊 1. the front 2. ahead; in front

qiánchē zhījiàn 前車之鑒 a lesson from the failure of one's predecessor

qiánchéng 前程 1. a future 2. a career

qiánchéng sìjǐn 前程似錦 to have brilliant prospects

qiánchéng wànlǐ 前程萬里 to have the prospect of a very successful career

qiáncì 前次 the previous occasion; last time

qiándǎo 前導 the guide or motorcade

qián'é 前額 the forehead

qiánfāng 前方 1. the front (in war) 2. the forward direction

qiánfēng 前鋒 the vanguard; the van

qiángōng jìnqì 前功盡棄 to nullify all the previous efforts

qiánhòu 前後 1. the front and the rear; before and after 2. (indicating time) around; about 3. from beginning to end; altogether

qiánhòu máodùn 前後矛盾 inconsistent; contradictory

qiánhū hòuyōng 前呼後擁 (said of VIPs) with a large retinue

qiánjìn 前進 to advance; to proceed; to go forward; to progress

qiánkē 前科 a previous criminal record

qiánkēfàn 前科犯 an ex-convict

qiánlì 前例 a precedent

qiánmén 前門 the front door or gate

qiánmian 前面 1. the front; the front side 2. ahead; in front

qiánnián 前年 the year before last

qiánpái 前排 the front row

qiánpú hòujì 前仆後繼 Behind the fallen is an endless column of successors.

qiánqián hòuhòu 前前後後 the ins and outs

qiánqū 前驅 the forerunner; the vanguard

qiánrén zhòngshù, hòurén chéngliáng 前人種樹, 後人乘涼 to profit from the labor of one's forefathers

qiánrèn 前任 a predecessor

qiánrì 前日 the day before yesterday

qiánshào 前哨 (military) a sentry; an outpost

qiánshēn 前身 the forerunner

qiánshēng 前生 the former life or lives

qiánshì 前世 1. the previous generation 2. the previous life

qiánshì bùwàng, hòushì

zhīshì 前事不忘，後事之師 To remember past errors insures one against repetition of the same errors.

qiánsī hòuxiǎng 前思後想 to turn over (a problem) in one's mind; to ponder

qiánsuǒ wèiwén 前所未聞 to have never heard of before

qiánsuǒ wèiyǒu 前所未有 unprecedented

qiántái 前臺 the stage; the proscenium

qiántí 前提 1. a premise 2. a prerequisite

qiántiān 前天 the day before yesterday

qiántīng 前廳 an antechamber

qiántú 前途 the prospect

qiántú mángmáng 前途茫茫 One's future is indefinite.

qiántú wúliàng 前途無量 to have boundless prospects

qiánwǎn 前晚 the evening before last

qiánwǎng 前往 to go to (a place); to visit

qiánwèi 前衛 1. front line troops 2. a forward 3. vanguard; avant-garde

qiánxī 前夕 the eve (of an event)

qiánxì 前夕 refer to **qiánxī** 前夕

qiánxiàn 前線 the front line (in war); the front

qiányán 前言 a foreword; a preface

qiányè 前夜 the night before last

qiányīn hòuguǒ 前因後果 cause and effect

qiánzhào 前兆 an omen; a premonition

qiánzhě 前者 the former

qiánzhìcí 前置詞 a preposition

qiánzòu 前奏 a prelude; a harbinger

qián 虔

reverence; reverent; respectful; pious

qiánchéng 虔誠 devout; piety; sincerity; pious

qiánjìng 虔敬 reverent; reverently

qián 掮

to bear a load on the shoulder

qiánkè 掮客 a broker

qián 乾

1. the first of the Eight Diagrams (**bāguà** 八卦) 2. heaven; male; a father; a sovereign

qián 鉗

1. pincers; forceps; tweezers; tongs; pliers 2. chains put around a prisoner's neck 3. to hold with tongs, etc.

qiánzhì 鉗制 to keep under control with force; to tie down or pin down

qiánzi 鉗子 1. tweezers; pincers; forceps; tongs 2. a convict; a prisoner

qián 箝

1. tongs; pincers; tweezers 2. to tweeze

qiánjǐn 箝緊 to clasp tightly

qiánzhì 箝制 to use pressure upon; to force; to pin down

qiánzi 箝子 tongs; tweezers; pincers

qián 潛

1. to hide; to conceal 2. to dive 3. hidden; secret; latent

qiáncáng 潛藏 to be in hiding

qiánfú 潛伏 1. to lie hidden 2. latent; hidden

qiánfúqī 潛伏期 a latent period

qiánfúqī 潛伏期 refer to **qiánfúqī** 潛伏期

qiánlì 潛力 potential; hidden force

qiánrù 潛入 1. to enter secretly; to slip in 2. to dive into (water)

qiánshuǐ 潛水 to dive

qiánshuǐtǐng 潛水艇 a submarine

qiántáo 潛逃 to flee secretly; to slip away

qiánxīn yánjiū 潛心研究 to study diligently with a quiet mind

qiányí mòhuà 潛移默化 to change and influence un-

obtrusively and imperceptibly

qiányìshí 潛意識 subconsciousness

qiányìshí 潛意識 refer to **qiányìshí** 潛意識

qiánzài 潛在 latent

qián 錢

1. money; cash 2. a unit of weight (equal to 1/10th of a tael) 3. a Chinese family name

qiánbāo 錢包 a wallet; a purse

qiánbì 錢幣 1. coin 2. currency; money

qiáncái 錢財 wealth; riches

qiáncái shēnwàiwù 錢財身外物 Money is not an inherent part of the human being.

qiánguì 錢櫃 a cash box

qiánpù 錢鋪 a banking house (in former times)

qiánzhuāng 錢莊 a banking house (in former times)

qián 黔

1. black 2. Guizhou province (an alternative name)

qiánlí 黔黎 the common people

Qiánlǘ jìqióng 黔驢技窮 the Guizhou donkey at the end of its resourcefulness—a person who has exposed his limited ability

qiǎn 淺

1. shallow; superficial 2. easy; simple 3. (color) light 4. (said of land) narrow and small

qiǎnbó 淺薄 superficial; shallow; meager

qiǎncháng zhézhǐ 淺嘗輒止 do not study further or deeper

qiǎn'ér yìjiàn 淺而易見 apparent; obvious; easily understood

qiǎnhǎi 淺海 a shallow sea; an epeiric sea

qiǎnjiàn 淺見 1. a shortsighted view 2. (a polite expression) my shallow view

qiǎnjiāo 淺交 not on intimate terms

qiǎnjìn 淺近 simple; easy to understand

qiǎnlòu 淺陋 vulgar; crude; shallow

qiǎnsè 淺色 light colors

qiǎntān 淺灘 a shoal

qiǎnxiǎn 淺顯 apparent; obvious; easily understood

qiǎnxiào 淺笑 a smile; to smile

qiǎn 遣

1. to dispatch; to send 2. to kill (time); to forget (one's sorrow); to divert 3. to banish 4. to release

qiǎncí zàojù 遣詞造句 the choice of words and building of sentences

qiǎnfǎn 遣返 to send back; to send home

qiǎnsàn 遣散 to disband

qiǎnsòng 遣送 to send away; to deport

qiǎn 繾

entangled

qiǎnquǎn 繾綣 entangled

qiǎn 譴

1. to reproach; to reprimand; to upbraid 2. punishment

qiǎnzé 譴責 to reprimand; to reproach

qiàn 欠

1. to owe; to owe money 2. deficient; lacking 3. to raise slightly (a part of the body) 4. to yawn

qiànjiā 欠佳 not satisfactory

qiànjiǎo 欠繳 to have not paid (one's due, tax, etc.)

qiànkuǎn 欠款 1. to owe money 2. debts

qiànqián 欠錢 1. to owe money 2. to be short of money

qiànquē 欠缺 1. to lack; deficient; short of 2. shortcomings

qiànshēn 欠身 to get ready to stand up as a gesture of courtesy

qiànshuì 欠稅 tax arrears

qiànzhài 欠債 to be in debt; to owe money

qiànzhàng 欠賬 1. to owe money; to buy on credit 2. overdue bills

qiànzī yóupiào 欠資郵票 a postage due stamp

Q

qiàn 倩
1. pretty dimples of a smiling woman 2. handsome 3. a son-in-law 4. to ask somebody to do something for oneself

qiànyǐng 倩影 the beautiful image of a woman

qiàn 嵌 also **qiān**
to inlay; to set in

qiànjīn 嵌金 to inlay with gold

qiàn 慊
to resent

qiàn 歉
1. deficient; insufficient; deficiency 2. a poor crop or harvest 3. to regret; sorry 4. an apology; apologetic

qiànshōu 歉收 a bad harvest

qiànyì 歉意 regrets; apologies

qiàn 塹
1. the moat around a city 2. a pit; a hole or cavity in the ground

qiāng 戕 also **qiáng**
1. to slay; to kill; to destroy 2. to be injurious

qiānghài 戕害 to slay

qiāng 腔
1. the cavity—especially referring to the chest and belly 2. a cavity in any vessel 3. a tune 4. an accent of one's pronunciation; a tone of one's voice 5. a manner

qiāngdiào 腔調 1. a tune; the melody of a tune 2. an accent 3. a manner or style of behavior

qiāng 搶
1. head (winds); adverse 2. to strike; to hit; to knock

qiāng 嗆
1. to peck 2. stupid; foolish 3. to cough because of a temporary blockade of the nasal passage

qiāng 槍
1. a spear; a lance; a javelin 2. a rifle; a pistol; a gun

qiāngbì 槍斃 to execute by shooting

qiāngdàn 槍彈 a cartridge; a shell; a bullet

qiāngfǎ 槍法 1. marksmanship 2. art of using spears

qiānggǎn 槍桿 1. the shaft of a spear 2. a rifle; arms

qiāngjué 槍決 to execute by shooting

qiāngkǒu 槍口 a muzzle (of a rifle, pistol, etc.)

qiānglín dànyǔ 槍林彈雨 a fierce battle (in which one faces a rain of bullets and artillery shells)

qiāngpào 槍炮 firearms; guns

qiāngshā 槍殺 to shoot

qiāngshāng 槍傷 bullet (or gunshot) wounds

qiāngshēng 槍聲 the report or crack of a gun; a shot

qiāngshǒu 槍手 a rifleman; a gunman

qiāngshou 槍手 1. a substitute examinee 2. a ghost writer

qiāngtuō 槍托 the rifle butt; the gun stock

qiāngxiè 槍械 weapons

qiāngzhàn 槍戰 a gun battle; a shoot-out

qiāngzhī 槍枝 rifles

qiāng 鎗
firearms; guns; pistols; rifles

qiāngbǎ 鎗靶 the target for shooting

qiāngbì 鎗斃 execution by a firing squad; execution by shooting

qiāngdàn 鎗彈 bullets

qiānggǎn 鎗桿 rifles; firearms

qiāngjué 鎗決 execution by a firing squad; execution by shooting

qiāngkǒu 鎗口 the muzzle of a gun

qiānglín dànyǔ 鎗林彈雨 heavy gunfire; a hail of bullets

qiāngshǒu 鎗手 a gunman

qiāngshou 鎗手 a substitute writer in an examination

qiāngzhàn 鎗戰 gun battle

qiāng 鎗
a tinkle; a clang

qiáng 戕
refer to **qiāng 戕**

qiáng 強
1. strong; powerful; vigorous 2. better 3. violent

qiángbào 強暴 1. violent; fierce; ferocious; atrocious 2. rape

qiángdà 強大 powerful and strong

qiángdào 強盜 a robber; a bandit

qiángdí 強敵 a powerful foe or enemy

qiángdiào 強調 to emphasize; to stress

qiángdù 強度 intensity (of light, etc.)

qiángfēng 強風 (meteorology) strong breeze

qiángguó 強國 a powerful country; a power

qiánghàn 強悍 fierce; truculent

qiánghèng 強橫 tyrannical; despotic; dictatorial

qiánghuà 強化 to strengthen; to intensify

qiángjiā 強加 to impose; to force

qiángjiān 強姦 to rape; to violate

qiángjìng 強勁 powerful; forceful

qiánglìjiāo 強力膠 glue

qiángliè 強烈 violent; strong; intense; severe; acute; keen

qiángquán 強權 brute force; might

qiángrén 強人 1. robbers 2. a strongman

qiángrèn 強韌 strong; tough; tenacious

qiángshēn 強身 to strengthen the body

qiángshèng 強盛 strong and prosperous

qiángxīnjì 強心劑 a heart stimulant

qiángxíng 強行 to force

qiángyìng 強硬 1. hard; strong 2. defiant

qiángzhàn 強佔 to occupy forcibly; to take (property, one's wife, etc.) by force

qiángzhì 強制 compulsory; to compel; to force

qiángzhì zhíxíng 強制執行 forcible execution; to execute forcibly

qiángzhuàng 強壯 strong; vigorous; virile; energetic; robust

qiáng 薔
the rose

qiángwēi 薔薇 the rose

qiáng 牆
a wall; a fence

qiángbì 牆壁 a wall (of a building)

qiángjiǎo 牆角 a corner between two walls

qiǎng 強
1. to force 2. to make an effort; to strive

qiǎngbī 強逼 to force (one to do something)

qiǎngbiàn 強辯 to obstinately stick to false reasoning or a lame excuse

qiǎngcí duólǐ 強詞奪理 to argue irrationally

qiǎngpò 強迫 to force (one to do something)

qiǎngqiú 強求 to demand; to extort; to exact; to impose

qiǎngqǔ 強取 to take by force

qiǎngrén suǒnán 強人所難 to force someone to do something against his will

qiǎngyán huānxiào 強顏歡笑 to assume a joyous mood reluctantly

qiǎng 搶
1. to take by force; to snatch; to rob; to loot 2. to do something in haste, as in an emergency; to rush 3. to oppose 4. to try to beat others in a performance

qiǎng'àn 搶案 (law) a case of robbery

qiǎngduó 搶奪 to rob; to loot;

Q

to plunder

qiǎnggòu 搶購 to try to beat others in making purchases (as in time of war, etc.)

qiǎngjié 搶劫 to rob; robbery

qiǎngjìngtóu 搶鏡頭 1. to outshine others 2. (said of cameramen) to fight for a vantage point in taking news pictures

qiǎngjiù 搶救 to make emergency rescue

qiǎngshōu 搶收 to get the harvest in quickly

qiǎngshǒuhuò 搶手貨 a commodity in great demand; popular products

qiǎngtān 搶灘 to make a forced beach landing

qiǎngxiān 搶先 to rush ahead; to try to be the first

qiǎngxiū 搶修 to race against time in making a repair job

qiǎng 襁

swaddling clothes for an infant; a broad bandage for carrying an infant on the back

qiǎngbǎo 襁褓 1. swaddling clothes or carrying band for an infant 2. infancy

qiàng 嗆

(said of smoke, smell, etc.) to irritate the throat or nose; to suffocate

qiāo 敲

1. to rap; to strike; to tap; to beat; to knock 2. a truncheon 3. to extort; to blackmail; to overcharge

qiāobiāngǔ 敲邊鼓 to speak for someone in order to help him

qiāoda 敲打 to rap; to knock; to beat

qiāojī 敲擊 to rap; to knock; to beat

qiāojí 敲擊 refer to **qiāojī** 敲擊

qiāoluó 敲鑼 to beat a gong

qiāomén 敲門 to knock at (or on) the door

qiāopò 敲破 to smash; to shatter

qiāozhà 敲詐 to blackmail

qiāozhōng 敲鐘 to toll a bell

qiāozhúgàng 敲竹槓 to extort money; to fleece

qiāo 橇 also **cuì**

a sledge for transportation over mud or snow; a sleigh

qiāo 蹺

1. to raise one's feet 2. on tiptoe 3. stilts

qiāobān 蹺班 to play hooky

qiāobiànzi 蹺辮子 to die

qiāojiā 蹺家 (slang) to run away from home

qiāokè 蹺課 (slang) to avoid attending classes

qiāoqiāobǎn 蹺蹺板 a seesaw; a teeterboard

qiáo 喬

1. tall 2. to disguise; to pretend 3. a Chinese family name

qiáoqiān 喬遷 to move into a new and better house

qiáoqiān zhīxǐ 喬遷之喜 Best wishes for your new home.

qiáozhuāng 喬裝 to disguise oneself

qiáozǐ 喬梓 father and son

qiáo 僑

to sojourn; a sojourn

qiáobāo 僑胞 overseas Chinese

qiáojū 僑居 to reside in a town or country other than one's own

qiáomín 僑民 alien residents

qiáoshēng 僑生 children of overseas Chinese who attend schools in China

Qiáowù Wěiyuánhuì 僑務委員會 the Overseas Chinese Affairs Commission

qiáo 憔

emaciated; haggard; worn

qiáocuì 憔悴 1. to look haggard 2. to suffer distress, worries, etc. 3. (said of plants) withered

qiáo 橋

1. a bridge; any bridgelike structure 2. beams of a structure 3. tall; high; elevated

qiáodūn 橋墩 the buttresses of a bridge

qiáogǒng 橋拱 a bridge arch

qiáoliáng 橋梁 any material which forms the span of a bridge

qiáopái 橋牌 (card games) bridge

qiáoshàng 橋上 on the bridge

qiáotóu 橋頭 either end of a bridge

qiáoxià 橋下 below the bridge

qiáo 樵
1. firewood; fuel 2. to gather fuel or firewood 3. a woodcutter 4. to burn 5. a tower; a lookout

qiáofū 樵夫 a woodcutter

qiáosǒu 樵叟 an old woodcutter

qiáoxīn 樵薪 to gather fuel or firewood

qiáo 瞧
1. to see; to look at 2. to steal a glance; to glance quickly

qiáobuqǐ 瞧不起 to look down upon; to despise

qiáobu shàngyǎn 瞧不上眼 not worth seeing

qiáodeqǐ 瞧得起 to think much of somebody

qiáojian 瞧見 to see; to catch sight of

qiáo 翹
1. long tail feathers 2. to raise 3. outstanding

qiáochǔ 翹楚 an outstanding person

qiáoqǐ 翹企 to long eagerly

qiáoqǐ 翹企 refer to **qiáoqǐ** 翹企

qiáoshǒu 翹首 to long eagerly

qiǎo 巧
1. clever; witty 2. ingenious; artful 3. a clever feat; a stunt 4. pretty; cute 5. coincidence; coincidental

qiǎobiàn 巧辯 an ingenious argument

qiǎoduó tiāngōng 巧奪天工 ingenuity that rivals the work of God

qiǎohé 巧合 a coincidence

qiǎokèlìtáng 巧克力糖 chocolate

qiǎolì míngmù 巧立名目 to fabricate various excuses

qiǎomiào 巧妙 ingenuity; ingenious; skillful

qiǎoqǔ háoduó 巧取豪奪 to rob others by hook or by crook

qiǎoshǒu 巧手 a skillful person; a dab

qiǎoyù 巧遇 a chance encounter

qiǎo 悄
quiet

qiǎoqiǎode 悄悄地 stealthily; secretly; in a clandestine way

qiǎorán 悄然 1. quietly 2. sorrowfully

qiǎo 雀
refer to **què** 雀

qiǎo 愀
1. anxious-looking 2. to show a sudden change of expression

qiǎochuàng 愀愴 rueful; doleful; sad; sorrowful

qiǎorán 愀然 1. turning pale or red suddenly 2. anxious; sorrowful

qiǎo 鵲
refer to **què** 鵲

qiào 俏
1. like; similar; to resemble; to be like 2. pretty and cute; good-looking 3. (commodities) enjoying brisk sale at higher prices; in great demand 4. (said of stocks) bullish

qiàolì 俏麗 good-looking

qiàopí 俏皮 1. pretty and cute 2. sarcastic

qiàopihuà 俏皮話 a wisecrack; a jibe

qiàoyuānjiā 俏冤家 (my) pretty but naughty lover

qiào 峭
1. steep; precipitous 2. harsh; unkind; sharp; severe

qiàobá 峭拔 1. high and steep 2. (said of penmanship or calligraphic style) vigorous

qiàobì 峭壁 a precipice; a cliff

qiàozhí 峭直 stern; strict

Q

qiào 殻 also **ké, què**

shells; husks; coverings

qiào 撬

to pry; to prize

qiàokāi 撬開 to open by prying

qiào 鞘

a scabbard; a sheath

qiào 翹

to project upward; to stick up; to turn upward

qiàobiànzi 翹辮子 to die

qiào 竅

1. a hole; a cavity 2. apertures 3. the crux, key points, gist of a matter; a knack

qiàomén 竅門 the key to something; a knack

qiē 切

to cut; to mince; to slice; to carve

qiēchú 切除 1. to cut out; to resect 2. excision; resection

qiēcuō 切磋 to improve oneself through discussions with another

qiēduàn 切斷 to sever; to cut asunder

qiēfù zìshā 切腹自殺 to commit hara-kiri

qiēkāi 切開 to cut open

qiēpiàn 切片 1. section 2. to microtome

qiēpiàn jiǎnchá 切片檢查 the microscopic examination of the affected tissue cut into very thin pieces

qié 茄

an eggplant; an aubergine

qiě 且

1. moreover; still; further 2. just; for the time being 3. both...and... 4. even

qiěmàn 且慢 Hold it!

qiè 切

to be close to

qièfū 切膚 very close to oneself

qièjǐ 切己 very close to oneself

qièjì 切忌 to be sure to avoid; to

forbid

qièjì 切記 to keep or to bear in mind

qièshēn 切身 personal (interests)

qièshí 切實 1. thoroughly 2. sure; certain

qiètí 切題 to the point

qièwù 切勿 do not by any means

qiè 怯 also **què**

1. lacking in courage; cowardly 2. nervous; socially timid; fright; fear; afraid

qièchǎng 怯場 stage fright

qiènuò 怯懦 cowardice

qièruò 怯弱 timid, weak and cowardly; cowardice

qiè 妾

1. a concubine 2. (in old China) a polite term used by a woman to refer to herself when speaking to her husband

qiè 契

to be separated from

qièkuò 契闊 to be separated from one another

qiè 挈

1. to lead 2. to rise above; to raise

qièlǐng 挈領 to make a summary

qiè 愜

cheerful; satisfied; contented

qièyì 愜意 satisfied; contented

qiè 慊

contented; gratified; pleased; satisfied

qiè 鍥

to carve

qiè'ér bùshě 鍥而不捨 to carve without rest—to make steady efforts

qiè 竊

1. to steal; to burglarize 2. a thief; a burglar 3. to usurp 4. stealthy

qiè'àn 竊案 a theft or larceny case

qièjù 竊據 the occupation of an

area, or a city by rebels

qièqiè sīyǔ 竊竊私語 to talk stealthily or in a very low voice; to whisper

qièqǔ 竊取 to steal

qiètīng 竊聽 to eavesdrop; eavesdropping

qiètīngqì 竊聽器 a listening-in device; a bug

qièxiào 竊笑 to laugh in secret

qièzéi 竊賊 a thief; a burglar

qīn 侵

1. to raid; to aggress 2. to encroach upon; to use force stealthily 3. to proceed gradually 4. a bad year; a year of famine or disaster

qīnduó 侵奪 to seize by force

qīnfàn 侵犯 (law) to encroach upon other's rights; to violate; to invade

qīnhài 侵害 to infringe or encroach upon

qīnlüè 侵略 1. to invade 2. aggression

qīnrǎo 侵擾 to harass

qīnrén fànguī 侵人犯規 (sports) a personal foul

qīnrù 侵入 to intrude

qīnshí 侵蝕 erosion; to encroach; to erode

qīntūn 侵吞 to misappropriate; to embezzle

qīnxí 侵襲 to attack stealthily

qīnzhàn 侵占 to take (the property, the land, etc. of another) illegally

qīn 衾 also **qín**

1. a large coverlet or quilt 2. garments or dress for the deceased

qīnzhěn 衾枕 quilts and pillows

qīn 欽

1. to respect; respectful; to admire 2. a term used to address a monarch in ancient China —Your Majesty

qīnchāi dàchén 欽差大臣 imperial inspector generals

qīncì 欽賜 granted or bestowed by the emperor

qīnmù 欽慕 to admire; to look up to

qīnpèi 欽佩 to admire; to respect

qīnyǎng 欽仰 to admire and respect; to look up to

qīn 嶔

(said of a mountain) lofty

qīnqí lěiluò 嶔崎磊落 honest and upright

qīn 親

1. parents 2. relatives 3. to love; intimate; near to; dear 4. personally; personal; in person 5. to kiss

qīn'ài 親愛 love; affection; dear

qīnbǐ 親筆 one's own handwriting; to write personally

qīngǔròu 親骨肉 one's own flesh and blood

qīnhélì 親和力 1. (chemistry) affinity 2. affability; amiability

qīnjìn 親近 to be near to or intimate with; to be close to

qīnkǒu 親口 (said of words, etc.) right from one's own mouth; to state or tell personally

qīnlì qíjìng 親歷其境 to be on the spot or scene in person; to experience personally

qīnlín 親臨 to arrive personally

qīnmì 親密 intimate; intimacy; close

qīnnì 親暱 intimate; very dear to

qīnpéng 親朋 relatives and friends

qīnqī 親戚 relatives

qīnqiè 親切 intimately; cordially; kind

qīnrén 親人 close relatives—as one's parents, brothers, spouse, children, etc.

qīnshēn 親身 personally; in person

qīnshì 親事 marriage

qīnshǒu 親手 personally; with one's own hands

qīnshǔ 親屬 relatives; family members

qīnshǔ guānxi 親屬關係 kinship

qīntòng chóukuài 親痛仇快

(said of a mistake, blunder, etc.) to pain one's friends and please one's enemies

qīnwáng 親王 a prince

qīnwěn 親吻 to kiss

qīnxìn 親信 a confidant

qīnxiōngdì míngsuànzhàng 親兄弟明算賬 Financial matters should be settled clearly even between brothers.

qīnyǎn kànjian 親眼看見 to witness; to see with one's own eyes

qīnyǒu 親友 friends and relatives

qīnzǐ guānxi 親子關係 parent-child relations

qīnzì 親自 personally; in person

qīnzì chūmǎ 親自出馬 to go out and take care of something in person; to confront the enemy, etc.) personally

qīnzú 親族 one's kinsmen; members of the same clan

qīnzuǐ 親嘴 to kiss

qín 芹
celery

qíncài 芹菜 celery

qín 衾
refer to **qīn** 衾

Qín 秦
1. the feudal state of Qin (879-221 B.C.) in the Zhou Dynasty, which later unified the whole country 2. the Qin Dynasty (221-206 B.C.) 3. another name of Shaanxi Province 4. the ancient name of China as known to the people of the Western Region 5. a Chinese family name

Qínlóu Chǔguǎn 秦樓楚館 brothels

Qínshǐhuáng 秦始皇 the First Emperor of Qin, 259-210 B.C.

qín 琴
1. a Chinese fretted instrument with seven or five strings somewhat similar to the zither 2. a musical instrument

qínjiàn 琴鍵 a key

qínsè héming 琴瑟和鳴 marital harmony

qínshī 琴師 a player of the stringed instrument; a pianist

qínxián 琴弦 the string of a stringed instrument

qín 禽
1. birds; fowls 2. (擒) to catch; to capture

qínshòu 禽獸 1. dumb creatures 2. birds and beasts

qín 勤
1. diligent; industrious; sedulous; hardworking 2. frequently; regularly

qínfèn 勤奮 diligent; assiduous; industrious

qínjiǎn 勤儉 diligent and frugal

qínkuai 勤快 diligent; assiduous; industrious

qínláo 勤勞 to toil or labor sedulously

qínmiǎn 勤勉 diligent; hardworking

qínnéng bǔzhuō 勤能補拙 Stupidity can be remedied by diligence.

qínnéng bǔzhuó 勤能補拙 refer to **qínnéng bǔzhuō** 勤能補拙

qínxué 勤學 to study diligently

qín 擒
to arrest; to capture

qínhuò 擒獲 to arrest; to capture

qínná 擒拿 to arrest; to capture

qǐn 寢
1. to sleep; to rest 2. a tomb 3. a residence 4. stop; end

qǐnjù 寢具 bedding

qǐnmèi nán'ān 寢寐難安 restless sleep (from worries)

qǐnshì 寢室 a bedroom

qìn 沁
to soak; to seep; to percolate; to ooze; to exude

qìnrén xīnpí 沁人心脾 to affect people deeply

qìnrù 沁入 to soak into; to permeate

qīng 青

1. green; blue; black 2. green grass 3. not ripe 4. young; youth; youthful 5. the skin of bamboo 6. the white of an egg 7. short for Qinghai Province or Qingdao City

qīngcài 青菜 vegetables; the greens

qīngcǎo 青草 green grass

qīngchū yúlán 青出於藍 to surpass one's master or teacher in learning

qīngchūn 青春 1. one's youth; young adulthood 2. age (in asking a youth)

qīngchūndòu 青春痘 acne

qīngchūnfàn 青春飯 jobs for the young

qīngchūnqī 青春期 adolescence; puberty; teens

qīngchūnqí 青春期 refer to **qīngchūnqī** 青春期

qīngcuì 青翠 fresh green; verdant

Qīngdǎo 青島 a port-and-resort city in Shandong Province

qīngguāngyǎn 青光眼 glaucoma

Qīnghǎi 青海 1. Qinghai Province 2. Koko Nor, a lake in Qinghai

qīnghóng zàobái 青紅皂白 right and wrong; the truth about an event

qīnghuáng bùjiē 青黃不接 a period of insufficiency to tide over; temporary shortage

qīngjiāo 青椒 green cayenne pepper

qīnglài 青睞 a look of joy; favor; preference

qīnglóu 青樓 1. the abode of a beauty 2. a brothel—(figuratively) prostitutes 3. a mansion in ancient times

qīngméi zhúmǎ 青梅竹馬 the innocent affection between a boy and a girl in their childhood

qīngmiàn liáoyá 青面獠牙 to have a fierce look on one's face

qīngnián 青年 youths; young people

Qīngniánhuì 青年會 YMCA (Young Men's Christian Association)

qīngshān 青山 green hills

qīngshān lǜshuǐ 青山綠水 blue mountains and green water —a charming natural scene

qīngshàonián 青少年 teenagers; youngsters

qīngsī 青絲 black hair (of a woman or girl)

qīngtái 青苔 green moss (lichen)

qīngtiān báirì 青天白日 blue sky and white sun—a fine day; in broad daylight

qīngtóng 青銅 bronze

qīngwā 青蛙 a frog

qīngyún zhíshàng 青雲直上 to soar higher and higher in one's career

qīng 氫

hydrogen

qīngdàn 氫彈 hydrogen bombs

qīnghuàwù 氫化物 the hydride

qīng 清

1. pure; clean; clear 2. brief; scarce 3. virtuous; honest 4. to arrange; to place in order 5. to conclude; to terminate; to settle 6. clear, simple and easily understandable 7. the Qing Dynasty (1644-1911) 8. to clean

qīngbái 清白 (said of a person's character, etc.) clean; innocent

qīngchá 清查 to check, investigate, survey thoroughly

qīngcháng 清償 to pay off all one's debts

qīngchǎng 清場 (said of movie theaters) to have every moviegoer out before the next show starts

qīngchàng 清唱 to sing without accompaniment; to sing Chinese opera without wearing costume or makeup

Qīngcháo 清朝 the Qing Dynasty (1644-1911)

qīngchè 清澈 limpid (water); crystal-clear

qīngchén 清晨 early in the morning; dawn

Q

qīngchú 清除 1. to eliminate, rid of, clear away, liquidate, or remove 2. to clean or tidy up (a house)

qīngchu 清楚 1. clear; without ambiguity 2. to understand

qīngcuì 清脆 clear and crisp (note, sound, etc.); sharp and loud

qīngdān 清單 a detailed list of items which serves as a receipt, statement, etc.

qīngdàn 清淡 1. not enthusiastic; calm 2. slack 3. (said of food) simple; without grease or heavy seasoning

qīngdàofū 清道夫 a scavenger

qīngdiǎn 清點 to check; to make an inventory

qīngdùn 清燉 to stew or steam meat without seasoning

qīngfēng míngyuè 清風明月 (literally) the soothing wind and the bright moon—aloof

qīngfú 清福 an easy and care-free life

qīnggāo 清高 morally lofty or upright

qīnggǎo 清稿 a fair copy

qīngguān 清官 honest officials

qīngguī 清規 Buddhist rules

qīngguī jièlǜ 清規戒律 restrictions and fetters

qīnghán 清寒 1. poor but clean and honest 2. (said of weather, etc.) cold and crisp 3. (said of moonlight) cold and bright

Qīngjiàotú 清教徒 the Puritans

qīngjié 清潔 clean; sanitary

qīngjiéduì 清潔隊 a cleaning squad

qīngjié gōngrén 清潔工人 street cleaners; sanitation workers

qīngjiéjì 清潔劑 a detergent

qīngjìng 清淨 clean and pure

qīngjìng 清靜 quiet (houses, surroundings, etc.)

qīngkǔ 清苦 poor but clean and honest

qīnglǎng 清朗 1. clear and loud (sound, voice, etc.) 2. clear and crisp (weather)

qīnglǐ 清理 1. to settle (accounts, etc.); clearance (of sales, etc.) 2. to arrange; to tidy up

qīnglián 清廉 clean, honest and capable (officials, etc.)

qīngliáng 清涼 refreshing (weather, water, etc.); nice and cool

qīngliáng yǐnliào 清涼飲料 a cold drink; a cooler

qīngliè 清冽 clear and cold (water)

qīngliú 清流 1. a clear stream 2. virtuous scholars

qīngmíng 清名 an unimpeachable reputation

qīngmíng 清明 1. clean and just (administration) 2. one of the 24 solar periods in a year which falls on April 5 or 6 when people visit their ancestral tombs, also known as Tomb-Sweeping Day

qīngpíng 清平 1. peace and justice 2. (said of a disposition) pure, honest and peace-loving

qīngqú 清癯 thin but healthy

qīngquán 清泉 a crystal-clear fountain

qīngshòu 清瘦 thin and lean

qīngshuǎng 清爽 1. sober 2. quiet and comfortable 3. clear and easy to understand 4. to have everything (debts, etc.) settled; relieved

qīngshuǐ 清水 clear (or fresh) water

qīngsuàn 清算 1. to liquidate; liquidation 2. to purge

qīngtāng 清湯 consomme; clear soup

qīngxī 清晰 1. loud and clear (in radio reception, talking, listening, etc.) 2. clearly

qīngxǐ 清洗 to wash; to clean

qīngxián 清閒 at leisure

qīngxiāng pūbí 清香撲鼻 A sweet scent assails one's nostrils.

qīngxīn 清新 refreshing (style, fashion, etc.); fresh

qīngxīn guǎyù 清心寡慾 to purge one's mind of desires and ambitions

qīngxǐng 清醒 1. to come to;

wide awake 2. clear-minded; sober

qīngxiù 清秀 good-looking; well-shaped

qīngyǎ 清雅 neat and refined (taste, adornment, etc.); graceful

qīngyàng 清樣 final proofs

qīngyīsè 清一色 uniformly; homogeneous

qīngyōu 清幽 quiet and secluded

qīngzǎo 清早 early in the morning; dawn

qīngzhēng 清蒸 (cooking) steamed; to steam

qīngzhēnsì 清眞寺 a mosque

qīng 卿
1. (in ancient China) a salutation of an emperor to his ministers 2. used in addressing one's wife—Honey, Darling, Dear, etc. 3. (in ancient China) a nobleman; a high official rank

qīngqīng wǒwǒ 卿卿我我 to be very much in love

qīng 傾 also **qǐng**
1. to slant; to bend 2. to collapse; to fall flat; to upset; to subvert 3. to pour out 4. to exhaust (one's wealth, etc.); to exert oneself to do (something) 5. to admire; to be fascinated or intrigued

qīngdǎo 傾倒 1. to fall for (a woman) 2. to collapse

qīngdào 傾倒 to dump

qīngfù 傾覆 1. to topple 2. to overturn

qīngjiā dàngchǎn 傾家蕩產 to go bankrupt

qīngmù 傾慕 to admire; admiration

qīngnáng xiāngzhù 傾囊相助 to exhaust (or give) all one has to help

qīngpén dàyǔ 傾盆大雨 to rain hard; to rain cats and dogs

qīngsù 傾訴 to pour out (one's heart, troubles, etc.)

qīngtán 傾談 to have a good, heart-to-heart talk

qīngtīng 傾聽 to listen carefully

qīngtǔ 傾吐 to get (something) off one's chest

qīngxiàng 傾向 1. to be inclined to 2. a tendency; a trend

qīngxiāo 傾銷 a cutthroat sale; dumping

qīngxié 傾斜 1. to slant 2. the angle formed by a stratum with the level; to slope

qīngxīn 傾心 1. to admire wholeheartedly 2. heart-to-heart

qīng 蜻
a dragonfly

qīngtíng 蜻蜓 a dragonfly

qīng 輕
1. light 2. simple; easy; facile 3. mild; gentle; soft; tender; lightly 4. mean; base; lowly; unimportant 5. frivolous; flippant; fickle; rash; reckless 6. to slight; to neglect; to ignore

qīngbiàn 輕便 handy; convenient; light; portable

qīngbó 輕薄 1. frivolous; flippant 2. disrespectful; irreverent 3. to insult

qīng'ér yìjǔ 輕而易舉 easy to accomplish

qīngfú 輕浮 flippant; frivolous; playful

qīnggōngyè 輕工業 light industry

qīngjǔ wàngdòng 輕舉妄動 to act rashly and blindly; to do something foolish

qīngkuài 輕快 1. agile; brisk; spry; nimble; sprightly 2. lighthearted 3. lively

qīngmiáo dànxiě 輕描淡寫 to describe in a light, moderate tone

qīngmiè 輕蔑 to despise; to disdain; to contemn; to slight

qīngpiāopiāo 輕飄飄 very light; lightly

qīngqí 輕騎 1. a light cavalryman; light cavalry 2. a sprightly horse

qīngqiǎo 輕巧 1. light and efficient; handy 2. dexterous(ly)

qīngqǔ 輕取 to beat easily; to win an easy victory

qīngróu 輕柔 soft; gentle

qīngshāng 輕傷 a slight injury;

a minor wound

qīngshēng 輕生 to commit suicide

qīngshì 輕視 to make light of; to slight

qīngshuài 輕率 1. to make light of; to neglect; to slight; to ignore 2. careless

qīngshuǎng 輕爽 relaxed; easy; comfortable

qīngsōng 輕鬆 1. to lighten; to relax 2. easy; comfortable

qīngtiāo 輕佻 frivolous; flippant; capricious

qīngwēi 輕微 light; slight; little

qīngwéi 輕微 refer to **qīngwēi** 輕微

qīngxìn 輕信 credulous; to believe lightly

qīngyì 輕易 1. easy; facile; effortless 2. reckless; rash

qīngyīnyuè 輕音樂 light music

qīngyíng 輕盈 (said of a woman) nimble and shapely

qīngzhòng 輕重 1. weight; light and heavy 2. degree of seriousness; of relative importance 3. propriety

qīngzhuāng 輕裝 light and simple luggage

qíng 情

1. feelings; emotions; sentiments 2. fact; detail; situation; condition 3. love; affection; passion 4. nature; reason

qíngbào 情報 information; intelligence reports

qíngbàoyuán 情報員 a secret agent; an intelligence agent

qíngbù zìjìn 情不自禁 to feel an irresistible impulse

qíngcāo 情操 1. sentiment (connoting highbrow and complicated sentiment) 2. noble thoughts and feelings

qíngdí 情敵 a rival in a love affair

qíngdiào 情調 1. a mood; taste 2. (psychology) affective feeling tone

qíngdòu chūkāi 情竇初開 (said of girls) to reach puberty; first awaking of love

qíngfen 情分 1. friendship 2. good intentions; good will; solicitude

qíngfū 情夫 the paramour of a married woman

qíngfù 情婦 a mistress; the other woman

qínggǎn 情感 emotions; feelings; affection

qínggē 情歌 a love song

qínghuà 情話 whispers of love; lovers' prattle

qínghuà miánmián 情話綿綿 occupied with endless whispers of love

qínghuái 情懷 a mood; feelings

qíngjié 情節 1. a plot (of a play, novel, etc.) 2. details (of an affair or event); circumstances

qíngjǐng 情景 a scene; a sight

qíngjìng 情境 circumstances; a situation

qíngkuàng 情況 a situation; circumstances

qíngláng 情郎 a girl's lover

qínglǐ 情理 reason; common sense

qínglǚ 情侶 lovers

qíngmian 情面 1. friendship; regard for others 2. face (self-respect; reputation)

qíngqù 情趣 sentiment; interest

qíngrén 情人 a paramour, sweetheart or lover

Qíngrénjié 情人節 St. Valentine's Day

qíngshāng 情商 to ask for a favor as a friend

qíngshēn sìhǎi 情深似海 Love is as deep as the sea.

qíngshì 情勢 a situation; the state of affairs

qíngshū 情書 a love letter; a billet-doux

qíngsù 情愫 innermost feelings

qíngtóng shǒuzú 情同手足 to be attached to each other like brothers

qíngtóu yìhé 情投意合 to be congenial

qíngwǎng 情網 the cobweb of love

qíng 情

qíngwén bìngmào 情文並茂 (said of a composition) rich in feelings and eloquent in expression

qíngxíng 情形 a situation; circumstances; conditions

qíngxù 情緒 1. emotions; a mood 2. depression; the sulks

qíngyí 情誼 refer to **qíngyì** 情誼

qíngyì 情意 feeling; sentiment; affection

qíngyì 情義 friendship; amity

qíngyì 情誼 friendship; amity

qíngyóu 情由 reason; cause

qíngyǒu kěyuán 情有可原 pardonable; excusable

qíngyuàn 情願 1. to be willing 2. would rather

qíng 晴

1. (said of the weather) fine; fair; bright; clear 2. when the rain stops

qíngkōng wànlǐ 晴空萬里 a clear and boundless sky

qínglǎng 晴朗 (said of the sky) fine and cloudless

qíngtiān 晴天 a fine day; a cloudless day

qíngtiān pīlì 晴天霹靂 a bolt from the blue

qíngyǔbiǎo 晴雨表 a barometer

qíng 傾

refer to **qīng** 傾

qíng 擎

to lift; to support

qíng 黥

ancient punishment of tattooing the face; branding

qíngmiàn 黥面 ancient punishment of tattooing the face

qíngshǒu 黥首 ancient punishment of tattooing the face

qǐng 頃

1. a moment; an instant; just; just now 2. a hundred mu (**mǔ** 畝) —10,000 square meters 3. to lean toward one side; to incline

qǐngkè 頃刻 in a short moment

qǐng 請

1. to request; to ask; to beg 2. please 3. to hire; to seek the service of; to engage

qǐng'ān 請安 to pay respects; to inquire after (an elder)

qǐngbiàn 請便 as you please

qǐngcí 請辭 to request permission to resign

qǐngjià 請假 to ask for leave of absence

qǐngjiǎn 請柬 an invitation card

qǐngjiào 請教 to request advice; to consult

qǐngkè 請客 to invite guests; to give a party

qǐngqiú 請求 to request; to ask; to beg

qǐngshì 請示 to ask for instructions

qǐngtiě 請帖 an invitation card

qǐngtuō 請託 to ask for a favor

qǐngwèn 請問 Please tell me...; May I ask you...?

qǐngwù 請勿 please don't

qǐngyuàn 請願 to petition

qǐngyuànshū 請願書 a written petition

qǐngzuì 請罪 1. to ask for punishment 2. to appeal for leniency

qǐngzuò 請坐 Please have a seat.

qìng 慶

1. festivity; blessing; felicity; joy 2. to celebrate; to congratulate; to rejoice

qìngdiǎn 慶典 national festivities and celebration ceremonies

qìnggōngyàn 慶功宴 a celebration party

qìnghè 慶賀 to celebrate; to rejoice; to offer congratulations

qìngshēnghuì 慶生會 a birthday party

qìngxìng 慶幸 to congratulate or rejoice oneself

qìngzhù 慶祝 to celebrate; celebration

qìng 親

relatives by marriage

qìngjia 親家 1. relatives as a result of marriage 2. parents of the married couple

qìng 罄
to exhaust; to use up; to empty

qióng 穹
refer to **qióng** 穹

qióng 穹 also **qīong**
1. high and vast 2. the sky

qióngcāng 穹蒼 the sky; the firmament

qióng 窮
1. poor; impoverished; destitute 2. distress; affliction 3. the extreme; the farthest; an end 4. thoroughly

qióngguāngdàn 窮光蛋 a destitute fellow; a pauper

qiónggguǐ 窮鬼 a poverty-stricken fellow

qióngjí wúliáo 窮極無聊 1. to do very foolish things in desperation 2. to be utterly bored 3. absolutely senseless

qióngkāixīn 窮開心 to enjoy moments of happiness even in poverty

qióngkǔ 窮苦 destitute; poverty; poverty-stricken

qióngkùn liǎodǎo 窮困潦倒 to be penniless and frustrated

qióngrén 窮人 destitute people; the poor

qióngsuān 窮酸 (said of a scholar) poor, jealous and pedantic

qióngxiāng pìrǎng 窮鄉僻壤 out-of-the-way regions

qióngxiǎozi 窮小子 a poor bum (a contemptuous expression)

qióngxiōng jí'è 窮凶極惡 extremely violent and wicked; atrocious

qióngzhuī bùshě 窮追不捨 to pursue relentlessly

qióng 瓊
1. fine jade or agate 2. excellent;

beautiful

qióngjiāng 瓊漿 good wine

qiónglóu yùyǔ 瓊樓玉宇 1. the Palace of the Moon 2. a magnificent or splendid building

qióngmá 瓊蔴 sisal

qióngyáo 瓊瑤 1. fine jade 2. your letter 3. a literary piece written for others

qióngzhī yùyè 瓊枝玉葉 lineal imperial descendants

qiū 丘
1. a hillock or mound 2. big; elder 3. empty 4. first name of Confucius 5. a surname

qiūhè 丘壑 (literary) hills and ravines—a wooded place for retirement

qiūhuò 丘壑 refer to **qiūhè** 丘壑

qiūlíng 丘陵 mounds; craggy terrains; hills

qiū 邱
1. (丘) a hill 2. name of a county in Shandong Province 3. a Chinese family name

qiū 秋
1. autumn; fall 2. time; a period 3. a season 4. a year 5. a harvest; ripening of grains

qiūgāo qìshuǎng 秋高氣爽 the clear and crisp autumn climate

qiūhǎitáng 秋海棠 (botany) a begonia

qiūháo 秋毫 1. trifles 2. a writing brush

qiūjì 秋季 autumn (season)

qiūlǎohǔ 秋老虎 scorching heat in early autumn

qiūqiān 秋千 a swing

qiūshōu 秋收 the autumn harvest

qiūshuāng 秋霜 1. autumn frost —(figuratively) snowy hair 2. severity; sternness

qiūtiān 秋天 autumn; fall

qiū 蚯
an earthworm

qiūyǐn 蚯蚓 an earthworm

qiū 鞦

1. a swing 2. a crupper 3. traces

qiūqiān 鞦韆 a swing

qiú 囚

1. a prisoner; a convict 2. to imprison

qiúchē 囚車 a prison cart

qiúfàn 囚犯 a prisoner; a convict; a jailbird

qiúfáng 囚房 a prison; a jail; a cell

qiújìn 囚禁 to imprison; to jail; to confine

qiúláo 囚牢 a jail; a cell

qiú 求

1. to ask for; to pray for; to beg 2. demand 3. to seek 4. to covet; to desire

qiú'ài 求愛 to woo; to court

qiúcái 求才 positions vacant

qiúdài 求貸 to ask for loan

qiúhé 求和 to seek peace with an enemy

qiúhūn 求婚 to propose (to a woman)

qiújiàn 求見 to seek an interview

qiújiào 求教 to seek instruction; to seek advice

qiújiě 求解 1. to seek help in distress 2. to seek the solution to a mathematical problem

qiújiù 求救 to seek relief; to ask for rescue

qiú'ǒu 求偶 to seek a spouse

qiúqiān 求籤 to seek divine guidance by drawing lots

qiúqīn 求親 1. to seek a marriage alliance 2. to ask for help from relatives

qiúqíng 求情 to ask for mercy; to plead

qiúquán 求全 1. to seek a satisfactory result 2. to try to preserve oneself

qiúquán zébèi 求全責備 to criticize so that everything will become perfect

qiúráo 求饒 to ask for forgiveness; to seek pardon

qiúrén 求人 1. to ask for help 2.

to look for talents

qiúrén dérén 求仁得仁 to seek for virtue and get virtue—to want something and succeed in getting it

qiúshén wènbǔ 求神問卜 to seek divine advice

qiúshēng 求生 to try to remain alive

qiúshèng 求勝 to strive for victory

qiúxián ruòkě 求賢若渴 to seek talent with eagerness

qiúxué 求學 to receive education; to study

qiúyuán 求援 to seek relief; to ask for help

qiúzhèng 求證 to seek verification or confirmation

qiúzhī 求知 to seek knowledge

qiúzhī bùdé 求之不得 to be exactly what has been sought eagerly

qiúzhīyù 求知慾 a thirst (or craving) for knowledge

qiúzhí 求職 positions wanted

qiúzhù 求助 to resort to; to seek help

qiú 泅

to swim

qiúdù 泅渡 to swim across

qiú 酋

1. the chief of a clan or tribe; a chieftain 2. to end

qiúzhǎng 酋長 1. a chieftain; the chief of a tribe 2. a sheik(h); an emir

qiú 球

1. a ball or anything shaped like a ball 2. the globe; the earth

qiúchǎng 球場 a playground for ball games

qiúduì 球隊 teams for playing ball games

qiúmén 球門 the goal (in football, etc.)

qiúmí 球迷 fans of ball games

qiúpāi 球拍 rackets (for tennis, etc.)

qiúsài 球賽 a ball game

Q

qiútóng 球僮 a caddy

qiúwǎng 球網 a net (for ball games)

qiúxié 球鞋 tennis shoes; sneakers

qiúxíng 球形 spherical; globular; bulbous

qiúyī 球衣 the jacket for a ball-player

qiúyuán 球員 a ballplayer

qiú 裘
furs; any garments, robes, etc. of fur

qiú 遒
1. strong; powerful; vigorous 2. to come to an end; to close 3. to gather; to concentrate

qiú 糗
parched grain, rice, etc.; dry food; dry rations

qū 曲
1. bent; crooked; twisted; winding 2. little known; obscure 3. wrong; unjustifiable

qūchǐ 曲尺 a (carpenter's) square

qūgùnqiú 曲棍球 1. hockey 2. a hockey ball

qūjiě 曲解 to misinterpret; to distort

qūliú 曲流 a meander

qūxiàn 曲線 curved line; curve

qūyì féngyíng 曲意逢迎 to try in every way to flatter someone

qūzhé 曲折 1. bends; curves 2. complicated

qūzhí 曲直 right and wrong

qū 泇
to drench with water

qū 屈
1. to bend; to flex; to bow; to crook 2. to humiliate; to humble 3. wrong; injustice 4. in the wrong 5. to be in an inferior or uncomfortable position 6. a Chinese family name

qūcóng 屈從 to submit to; to yield to

qūdǎ chéngzhāo 屈打成招 to confess under torture to a crime

one hasn't committed

qūfú 屈服 to succumb, yield, or submit to (power, a threat, etc.); to give in

qūjiù 屈就 to accept a job too humble for one's position or ability

qūrǔ 屈辱 humiliation; disgrace

qūxī 屈膝 to kneel down

qūzhǐ kěshǔ 屈指可數 can be counted on one's fingers—very few

qūzhǐ yīsuàn 屈指一算 to count on one's fingers

qū 祛
to dispel; to expel; to remove

qūzāi 祛災 to dispel disasters

qū 區
1. to distinguish; to discriminate 2. a district; an area; a zone 3. a border 4. little; few

qūbié 區別 to discriminate; to distinguish

qūfēn 區分 to set apart; to consider

qūgōngsuǒ 區公所 a district office

qūjiānchē 區間車 a bus traveling merely part of its normal route

qūqū 區區 small or unimportant; trifling

qūyù 區域 a district; a zone

qūyù guīhuà 區域規劃 regional planning

qūyùxìng 區域性 regional

qūzhǎng 區長 a district magistrate

qū 嶇
rugged; uneven; irregular

qū 趨
1. to go quickly; to hasten; to hurry 2. to be inclined; to tend; to follow

qūlì 趨利 to go after material gain

qūshì 趨勢 1. a trend; a tendency 2. to go after men of power

qūxiàng 趨向 1. a tendency; a trend 2. to tend to; to incline to

qūyán fùshì 趨炎附勢 to hang on men of influence

qūzhī ruòwù 趨之若鶩 to go after in a swarm

qū 麴 also **qú**
a ferment for brewing

qū 軀
1. the body; the trunk 2. a child in the womb

qūgàn 軀幹 1. (anatomy) the trunk 2. the body; the physical build

qū 驅
1. to go before others 2. to drive; to urge 3. to expel 4. to command

qūcè 驅策 1. to urge; to spur 2. to order (a person) about

qūchú 驅除 to drive out; to get rid of; to expel; to eliminate

qūpò 驅迫 to force; to be driven; to compel

qūqiǎn 驅遣 1. to send away (a person so as to get rid of him) 2. to order (a person) about

qūsàn 驅散 to disperse by force; to scatter; to dispel

qūshǐ 驅使 to order (a person) about

qūxié 驅邪 to expel evil; to keep evil spirits away

qūzhú 驅逐 to drive out; to get rid of; to expel; to eliminate

qú 劬
labor; toil; diligent; to labor incessantly

qú 渠
1. a drain; a channel; a ditch 2. great; deep 3. he; she

qúdào 渠道 1. an irrigation ditch 2. a channel

qú 麴
refer to **qū** 麴

qú 衢
a thoroughfare; a highway junction

qúdào 衢道 a side street; crossroads

qǔ 曲

1. a type of verse for singing, which emerged in the Southern Song and Jin dynasties and became popular in the Yuan Dynasty 2. a piece of music; a song

qǔdiào 曲調 tunes; melodies

qǔgāo hèguǎ 曲高和寡 caviare to the general

qǔzhōng rénsàn 曲終人散 The music is over and the people are gone.——the sadness one feels after a fanfare

qǔ 取

1. to take; to receive; to fetch; to obtain; to take hold of 2. to select; to choose 3. to summon; to recall 4. to marry; to take a wife

qǔcái 取材 to select material

qǔcháng bǔduǎn 取長補短 to learn from others' strong points to make up for one's weaknesses

qǔdài 取代 to replace; to substitute

qǔdào 取道 to go by way of

qǔdé 取得 to gain; to acquire; to obtain

qǔdì 取締 to prohibit; to punish the violator

qǔ'ér dàizhī 取而代之 to usurp another's (usually higher, and better) position

qǔjǐng 取景 to find a view (to photograph, paint, etc.)

qǔjué 取決 It's up to (someone else to make the decision).

qǔkuǎn 取款 to take money or draw money

qǔlè 取樂 to make merry

qǔmíng 取名 to name; to christen

qǔnuǎn 取暖 to warm oneself (by a fire, etc.)

qǔqiǎo 取巧 to take a snap course

qǔshě 取捨 to accept or refuse

qǔshèng 取勝 to win a victory

qǔxiāo 取消 to cancel; to nullify

qǔxiào 取笑 to laugh at; to make fun of

qǔxìn yúrén 取信於人 to

establish credibility among others

qǔyàng 取樣 sampling

qǔyuè 取悅 to please

qǔzhī bùjìn 取之不盡 The supply is inexhaustible.

qǔ 娶

to take a wife

qǔqī 娶妻 (said of a man) to take a wife

qǔqīn 娶親 (said of a man) to take a wife

qǔ 齲

tooth decay

qǔchǐ 齲齒 a decayed tooth; a carious tooth

qù 去

1. to go away; to depart 2. to get rid of; to remove 3. to be apart 4. past; gone 5. an auxiliary verb 6. the fourth of the four tones in Chinese phonetics 7. (Beijing opera) to play the part of

qù'è cóngshàn 去惡從善 to shun the evil and follow the good

qùliú 去留 to go or to stay

qùlù 去路 the way along which one is going

qùnián 去年 last year; the year past

qùshì 去世 to die; to leave the world

qùshì 去勢 to castrate; to emasculate

qùwú cúnjīng 去蕪存菁 to keep the good and get rid of the bad

qùxiàng 去向 whereabouts

qù 漆

refer to **qī** 漆 4

qù 趣

interest; fun; interesting; funny

qùshì 趣事 an amusing incident; an interesting episode

qùwèi 趣味 fun; interest; taste

qùwén 趣聞 an amusing report; interesting news

qù 闃

quiet; without people around

qùjí 闃寂 refer to **qùjì** 闃寂

qùjì 闃寂 still; quiet

quān 圈

1. a circle; a ring 2. with a return to the starting point; round 3. to circle 4. a circle—a number of persons bound together by having the same interests

quānr 圈兒 a circle

quāntào 圈套 a snare; a trap; a trick

quānzi 圈子 a circle

quán 全

1. perfect 2. complete; whole; total; intact; all; entire; absolute 3. to keep whole or intact

quánbān 全班 the whole class

quánbù 全部 the whole; completely; total

quáncái 全才 a versatile person

quánchǎng 全場 the whole audience

quánchéng 全程 the whole course

quánfù wǔzhuāng 全副武裝 to be armed to the teeth

quánguó 全國 the whole country or nation

quánguóxìng 全國性 nationwide; countrywide

quánjí 全集 the complete works of (Shakespeare, etc.)

quánjiā 全家 the whole family

quánjiāfú 全家福 a family photo

quánjǐng 全景 a full view; a whole scene

quánjú 全局 the overall situation

quánjūn 全軍 the whole (or entire) army

quánjūn fùmò 全軍覆沒 The whole army was lost.

quánkāi 全開 standard-sized; full-size

quánlěidǎ 全壘打 a home run

quánlì 全力 (with) all-out effort

quánlì yìfù 全力以赴 to spare no efforts

quánmào 全貌 the overall appearance

quánmiàn 全面 overall; comprehensive

quánmiàn gōngjī 全面攻擊 an all-out offensive

quánmiàn gōngjí 全面攻擊 refer to **quánmiàn gōngjī** 全面攻擊

quánmín 全民 the whole (or entire) people

quánnéng 全能 1. omnipotence 2. all-round

quánnián 全年 the whole year; all the year round

quánpán 全盤 total; overall

quánpán jìhuà 全盤計劃 an overall program or plan

quánpéi 全陪 a national tour guide

quánqiú 全球 the globe; the world

quánquán dàibiǎo 全權代表 an envoy plenipotentiary

quánrán 全然 completely (ignorant, etc.); totally

quánshēn 全身 the whole body

quánshēn guànzhù 全神貫注 to concentrate on

quánshèng shíqī 全盛時期 the heyday; the zenith; the prime

quánshèng shíqí 全盛時期 refer to **quánshèng shíqī** 全盛時期

quánshí 全蝕 a total eclipse

quánsù 全速 full (or maximum) speed

quántào 全套 the whole set

quántǐ 全體 all; everybody

quántiānhòu 全天候 all-weather

quánwén 全文 a full text

quánxiàn 全線 all fronts; the whole line

quánxīn quányì 全心全意 wholeheartedly

quánxiū 全休 a complete rest

quánzhī nǎifěn 全脂奶粉 whole milk powder

quán 泉
1. a spring; a fountain 2. money

(archaic) 3. a Chinese family name

quánlín 泉林 1. natural scenery 2. the abode of a recluse

quánshuǐ 泉水 spring water

quányuán 泉源 a fountainhead; a springhead; a source; a well-spring

quán 拳
1. a fist 2. sparring feats; various forms of boxing 3. strength

quándǎ jiǎotī 拳打腳踢 to beat up; to strike and kick

quánjī 拳擊 boxing; the boxing art

quánjīshǒu 拳擊手 a boxer; a pugilist

quánjí 拳擊 refer to **quánjī** 拳擊

quánjíshǒu 拳擊手 refer to **quánjīshǒu** 拳擊手

quánquán fúyīng 拳拳服膺 to adhere to faithfully

quánsài 拳賽 a boxing match

quántou 拳頭 a fist

quánwáng 拳王 a boxing champion

quán 痊
healed; cured; recovery

quányù 痊癒 to have been cured; to have recovered from illness

quán 詮
1. to explain; to expound 2. the truth or core of something 3. to weigh; to assess; to rate; to appraise

quánshì 詮釋 to interpret; to explain

quán 銓
1. to weigh 2. to evaluate qualifications in selecting officials

quánxù 銓敘 to select and appoint officials

quánxuǎn 銓選 to select (officials) after evaluating qualifications

quán 蜷
to wriggle; to be coiled; to be curled up

quánfú 蜷伏 to curl up; to hud-

dle up; to lie with the knees
drawn up

quán 鬈
1. fine hair 2. curled hair

quánfǎ 鬈髮 refer to **quánfà**
鬈髮

quánfà 鬈髮 crimps

quánqū 鬈曲 to crinkle; to curl

quán 權
1. to weigh (the significance,
etc.); to assess 2. power; authority; inherent rights; jurisdiction;
influence 3. an expedient way;
expediency 4. temporarily; temporarily; for the time being

quánbiàn 權變 adaptability in
tactics; tact

quánbǐng 權柄 authority; power

quánchén 權臣 powerful court-
iers

quándài 權代 to act in another's
place temporarily

quánguì 權貴 ranking officials;
influential figures

quánhéng 權衡 to weigh, consider or assess

quánlì 權力 power; authority

quánlì 權利 rights

quánmóu 權謀 schemes and
power; the use of schemes and
power

quánnéng 權能 1. authority;
powers and functions 2. (law) the
exercise of one's rights

quánshì 權勢 power and influence

quánshù 權術 political trickery;
shifts in politics

quánwēi 權威 1. an authority (in
certain sphere of knowledge) 2.
power and prestige

quánxiàn 權限 limitation of
power or authority

quányào 權要 1. bigwigs; powerful persons 2. confidential matter

quányí 權宜 expedient; temporary (measures, etc.)

quányí zhījì 權宜之計 an
expedient; a makeshift

quányì 權益 rights and interests

quǎn 犬

a dog; a canine

quǎnchǐ 犬齒 a cuspid; a canine
tooth

quǎnmǎ zhīláo 犬馬之勞
one's own service (a self-
depreciatory term)

quǎnyá 犬牙 a cuspid; a canine
tooth

quǎnyá jiāocuò 犬牙交錯
interlocking

quǎnzǐ 犬子 my son (a self-
depreciatory term)

quǎn 綣
to make tender love

quàn 券
1. a ticket 2. a certificate 3. a
bond

quàn 勸
to exhort; to urge; to advise; to
persuade

quàndǎo 勸導 to exhort and
guide

quàngào 勸告 to advise; to
counsel; to exhort

quànhé 勸和 to reconcile a quarrel or dispute

quànjià 勸架 to mediate a quarrel

quànjiàn 勸諫 to remonstrate
(with a superior)

quànjiě 勸解 to mediate; to
exhort to peace

quànjiè 勸戒 to admonish; to
dissuade

quànshì 勸世 to admonish

quànshuō 勸說 to persuade; to
advise

quànwèi 勸慰 to console; to
soothe

quànxiáng 勸降 to induce to
surrender

quànzhǐ 勸止 to dissuade

quànzǔ 勸阻 to dissuade

quē 缺
1. deficient; lacking; short; incomplete; defective 2. a vacancy;
an opening

quēdé 缺德 deficient in the sense
of morality; mischievous

quēdéguǐ 缺德鬼 a mean fellow

quēdiǎn 缺點 a defect; a short-coming; a flaw

quē'é 缺額 vacancies waiting to be filled

quēfá 缺乏 to lack; to be short of

quēhàn 缺憾 a defect; a short-coming; a flaw

quēhuò 缺貨 (merchandise) to run out of stock

quēkè 缺課 to be absent from class

quēkǒu 缺口 1. a breach; a gap 2. a notch

quēshǎo 缺少 to lack; to be short of

quēxí 缺席 to be absent (from a meeting, etc.)

quēxiàn 缺陷 a defect; a short-coming; a handicap; inadequacy

quēyǎng 缺氧 oxygen deficit

quē 闕
1. faults; errors; mistakes; defects 2. to lack; deficient

quērú 闕如 lacking; wanting; deficient

quēshī 闕失 a mistake; an error

qué 瘸
1. a cripple; a lame man 2. to be lame

quétuǐ 瘸腿 crippled; lame

què 怯
refer to **qiè** 怯

què 恪
refer to **kè** 恪

què 卻
1. still; but; yet 2. to refuse to accept 3. to retreat; to withdraw

quèbù 卻步 to retreat or with-draw; to shrink back

quèzhī bùgōng 卻之不恭 It's not polite to refuse (an offer, present, etc.).

què 雀 also **qiǎo**
1. a general name of small birds, as sparrows, chickadees, etc. 2. freckled

quèbān 雀斑 freckles

quèpíng zhòngxuǎn 雀屏中選 to be selected as someone's

son-in-law

quèyuè 雀躍 to jump up with joy; greatly excited with joy

quèzhàn 雀戰 to play a game of mah-jong

què 殼
refer to **qiào** 殼

què 榷
1. to monopolize 2. to levy taxes

què 確
1. sure; certain; secure; real; true; valid 2. firm; firmly

quèdìng 確定 1. to decide; to fix; to settle; to determine 2. certain; sure

quèlì 確立 to establish firmly

quèqiè 確切 accurate; exact; precise

quèrèn 確認 to certify; to affirm; to confirm

quèshí 確實 real; true; certain

quèxìn 確信 to be convinced; to believe firmly

quèzáo 確鑿 refer to **quèzuò** 確鑿

quèzhī 確知 to know for sure

quèzuò 確鑿 accurate; precise

què 闕
1. a watchtower outside the palace gate in ancient China 2. a palace

què 鵲 also **qiǎo**
a magpie

quècháo jiūzhàn 鵲巢鳩佔 to usurp other's position, property, etc.

qún 裙
a skirt; a petticoat; an apron

qúnzi 裙子 a skirt

qún 群
a group; a multitude; a host; a crowd; a swarm; a large number

qúncè qúnlì 群策群力 to pool the wisdom and efforts of every-one

qúndǎo 群島 an archipelago

qúnjū 群居 to live as a group; gregarious

qúnlóng wúshǒu 群龍無首 a multitude without a leader; leaderless

qúnqíng 群情 public sentiment; feelings of the masses

qúnzhòng 群眾 a crowd; a mob

rán 然
1. yes; most certainly; permission; right; correct 2. however; but; still; nevertheless; on the other hand 3. really; if so 4. (燃) to burn

rán'ér 然而 however; but; nevertheless

ránhòu 然後 then; afterward; later

R

rán 髯
1. whiskers 2. a heavily bearded man

rán 燃
to burn; to ignite; to light

ránfàng 燃放 to set off (fireworks, etc.)

ránliào 燃料 fuel

ránméi zhījí 燃眉之急 a matter as urgent as if the eyebrows had caught fire

ránshāo 燃燒 to burn; to be on fire; to be in flames; combustion

rǎn 冉
1. gradually 2. tender; weak 3. the outer edge of a turtle's shell

rǎnrǎn shàngshēng 冉冉上升 to rise gradually

rǎn 苒
(said of flowers and grass) lush or delicate

rǎnrěn 苒荏 time passing gradually

rǎn 染
1. to dye 2. to soil; to pollute 3. to get infected; to catch a disease; infectious 4. to have an affair with 5. (in Chinese painting and calligraphy) to make strokes

rǎnbìng 染病 to get infected; to catch a disease; to fall ill

rǎndú 染毒 1. to be infected with venereal disease 2. to use narcotics

rǎnfāng 染坊 refer to **rǎnfáng** 染坊

rǎnfáng 染坊 a dyeing mill

rǎnliào 染料 dyestuff; dye

rǎnsè 染色 to dye

rǎnsètǐ 染色體 (genetics) a chromosome

rěnzhǐ 染指 to encroach on

rāng 嚷

rāngrang 嚷嚷 1. to shout; to yell 2. to make widely known

ráng 攘
refer to **rǎng** 攘 1, 2, 3

ráng 壤
1. loose soil 2. earth 3. a region; a place; a land 4. rich; abundant

rǎng 攘
1. (also **ráng**) to take by force 2. (also **ráng**) to eliminate; to repel; to resist 3. (also **ráng**) to shake 4. confused; disorderly

rǎngchú 攘除 to rid; to eliminate; to dispel

rǎngduó 攘奪 to take by force

rǎngrǎng 攘攘 in a state of confusion

rǎng 嚷
to shout; to cry; to call out loudly

rǎngjiào 嚷叫 to bellow; to howl

ràng 讓
1. to give way; to make a concession; to back down; to yield; to give ground 2. to allow; to let; to permit 3. to turn over; to transfer; to surrender; to cede 4. by 5. to step aside; to make way; to let by

ràngbù 讓步 to give way; to yield

ràngdù 讓渡 to turn over; to transfer

ràngkai 讓開 to make way; to step aside

rànglù 讓路 to get out of the way

ràngwèi 讓位 1. to yield the

throne; to abdicate the throne 2. to yield to

ràngzǎo tuīlí 讓棗推梨 to show brotherly love

ràngzuò 讓座 to yield a seat

ráo 饒
1. abundant; plentiful; full of; fertile 2. to give something extra as a gift; to let somebody have something into the bargain 3. to forgive; to spare; to have mercy; to let somebody off 4. lenient; liberal 5. (now rarely) even though; in spite of the fact that; whatever

ráofù 饒富 abundant; plentiful

ráomìng 饒命 to spare a life

ráoshé 饒舌 loquacious; talkative; garrulous

ráoshù 饒恕 to forgive; to pardon

rǎo 擾
1. to disturb; to agitate; to harass 2. to trespass on somebody's hospitality 3. disorder

rǎoluàn 擾亂 to disturb; to agitate

rǎorǎng 擾攘 tumult; hustle and bustle

rào 遶
to surround

rào 繞
1. to go around; to make a detour 2. to march round; to circle

ràodào 繞道 to make a detour; to detour

ràoguò 繞過 to pass over a point by a detour

ràokǒulìng 繞口令 a tongue twister

ràolù 繞路 to make a detour; to detour

ràoquānzi 繞圈子 1. to go round and round 2. to talk in a roundabout way

ràowānr 繞彎兒 to take a stroll

ràoxíng 繞行 1. to detour 2. to orbit; to revolve around

rě 若

as in **bōrě** 般若—(Buddism) prajna, wisdom

rě 惹
to provoke; to rouse; to induce; to attract; to cause; to bring upon oneself; to offend; to incur

rěhuǒ shāoshēn 惹火燒身 to ask for trouble

rěhuò 惹禍 to bring disaster or misfortune

rěmáfan 惹麻煩 to excite trouble; to invite trouble

rěqǐ 惹起 to incite; to provoke; to incur

rěrén zhùmù 惹人注目 to attract attention

rěshì 惹事 to create trouble

rěshì shēngfēi 惹是生非 to incur unnecessary trouble; to stir up ill will

rè 熱
1. hot; heated; burning; to heat 2. fever 3. earnest; ardent; zealous; enthusiastic; passionate

rè'ài 熱愛 to love passionately

rèbìng 熱病 fever

rèchén 熱忱 enthusiasm; sincerity; earnest

rèchéng 熱誠 earnestness; sincerity

rèdài 熱帶 the tropics

rèdàiyú 熱帶魚 tropical fish

rèdù 熱度 1. heat; temperature 2. enthusiasm

règǒu 熱狗 a hot dog

rèhōnghōng 熱烘烘 red-hot; white-hot

rèhuò 熱貨 popular products

rèlàng 熱浪 a heat wave; a hot wave

rèlèi yíngkuàng 熱淚盈眶 tearful; eyes moistening

rèliàn 熱戀 to be passionately in love

rèliàng 熱量 the quantity of heat; calories

rèliè 熱烈 fervent; passionate; vehement

rèluò 熱絡 on friendly terms; very intimate

rèmài 熱賣 to be in great

rèmén 熱門 something very much in vogue or fashion; a craze

rènao 熱鬧 1. bustling; populous; noisy 2. prosperous; thriving 3. lively; merry

rèqì 熱氣 hot vapor; hot gas; hot air; heat

rèqiè 熱切 fervent; earnest; sincerely

rèqíng 熱情 passion; ardor; fervor

rèshēn yùndòng 熱身運動 warm-up exercise

rèshuǐpíng 熱水瓶 a thermos (bottle)

rèshuǐqì 熱水器 a water heater

rètāng 熱湯 hot soup

rèténgténg 熱騰騰 piping hot; steaming hot

rèténgténg 熱騰騰 refer to **rètēngtēng** 熱騰騰

rèxiāo 熱銷 to be in great demand; to sell well; to have a ready market

rèxiě 熱血 refer to **rèxuè** 熱血

rèxiě fèiténg 熱血沸騰 refer to **rèxuè fèiténg** 熱血沸騰

rèxīn 熱心 zealous; warm-hearted

rèxuè 熱血 hot-blooded; fiery-spirited; fervent; zealous

rèxuè fèiténg 熱血沸騰 to see the with fervor

rèyǐn 熱飲 hot drinks

rén 人

a human being; a person; people

rénběn zhǔyì 人本主義 humanism

rén bùkě màoxiàng 人不可貌相 A man's worth cannot be measured by his looks.

rénbùzhī guǐbùjué 人不知鬼不覺 without the knowledge of anybody else

réncái 人才 a man of ability; a talent

réncái bèichū 人才輩出 Great talents appear successively (or continuously).

réncái jǐjǐ 人才濟濟 There is a wealth of talents.

réncái wàiliú 人才外流 the brain drain

rénchén 人臣 a vassal

rénchēng 人稱 1. (grammar) the first, second or third person 2. a nickname by which one is known

rénchēng dàimíngcí 人稱代名詞 a personal pronoun

réncún zhèngjǔ, rénwáng zhèngxī 人存政舉，人亡政息 The policies and regulations of an organization shift with the change of the person in charge.

réncún zhèngjǔ, rénwáng zhèngxī 人存政舉，人亡政息 refer to **réncún zhèngjǔ, rénwáng zhèngxī** 人存政舉，人亡政息

réndào 人道 philanthropy; humanitarianism

réndì shēngshū 人地生疏 to have trouble getting about in a strange land because of unfamiliarity with the local people and their customs

réndìng shèngtiān 人定勝天 Man's determination will conquer nature.

rénduō zuǐzá 人多嘴雜 Agreement is difficult if there are too many people.

rénfàn 人犯 a criminal; a suspect (in a criminal case)

rén'gé 人格 character; personality

réngōng 人工 1. human labor 2. man-made

réngōng hūxī 人工呼吸 artificial respiration

réngōng zhìhuì 人工智慧 artificial intelligence

réngōng zhìnéng 人工智能 artificial intelligence

rénhǎi fúchén 人海浮沈 the vicissitudes of life

rénhǎi zhànshù 人海戰術 human-sea tactics

rénjì guānxi 人際關係 human relation

rénjiā 人家 a human abode

rénjiān 人間 the world of mortals

rénjiàn rén'ài 人見人愛 loved by all

rénjié dìlíng 人傑地靈 The birth (or presence) of heroes brings glory to a place.

rénjìn kěfū 人盡可夫 (said of women) promiscuous

rénkǒu 人口 population

rénlèi 人類 man; mankind; the human race

rénlì 人力 human power or strength

rénmǎ 人馬 1. traffic (consisting of people and horses) 2. troops (consisting of soldiers and horses)

rénmǎn wéihuàn 人滿為患 trouble of overpopulation

rénmiàn shòuxīn 人面獸心 a wolf in sheep's clothing

rénmín 人民 people

rénmìng guāntiān 人命關天 Human life is of utmost importance.

rénpà chūmíng zhūpà féi 人怕出名豬怕肥 Fame portends trouble for people.

rénpǐn 人品 character (of a person); personality

rénqíng 人情 human sentiment, emotion or feeling

rénqíng shìgù 人情世故 the ways of the world

rénqíngwèi 人情味 friendliness; hospitality

rénqióng zhìduǎn 人窮志短 Poverty stifles ambition.

rénquán 人權 human rights

rénqún 人群 a crowd, throng or multitude (of people)

rénrén 人人 everybody

rénrén zìwēi 人人自危 Everyone feels insecure.

rénrén zìwéi 人人自危 refer to **rénrén zìwēi** 人人自危

rénruì 人瑞 a very old man or woman, considered a happy omen for the whole human race

rénshān rénhǎi 人山人海 a large crowd

rénshēn 人參 ginseng

rénshēng 人生 human life; life

rénshēngguān 人生觀 a view of life; an outlook on life

rénshēng rúmèng 人生如夢 Life is but a dream.

rénshī 人師 a paragon

rénshì 人士 personages (usually plural)

rénshì 人世 the world

rénshì 人事 1. human affairs 2. personnel affairs 3. human endeavors

rénshì guānxi 人事關係 personal connections

rénshǒu 人手 1. manpower 2. a human hand

rénshòu bǎoxiǎn 人壽保險 life insurance

réntǐ 人體 a human body

rénwéi 人為 man-made; artificial; imitation

rénwéi wànwù zhīlíng 人為萬物之靈 The human being is the most intelligent among creatures.

rénwén 人文 1. humanities 2. human affairs

rénwén dìlǐ 人文地理 human geography

rénwén huìcuì 人文薈萃 (said of culture centers) gathering of talents

rénwù 人物 1. a personage or figure 2. people and things

rénwùhuà 人物畫 portrait painting

rénxiàng 人像 a portrait; an image

rénxiǎo guǐdà 人小鬼大 young but tricky

rénxīn 人心 human heart, will or feeling

rénxīn bùgǔ 人心不古 Public morality is not what it used to be.

rénxīn bùtóng, gèrú qímiàn 人心不同，各如其面 Individual thinking is as varied as individual looks.

rénxīn huánghuáng 人心惶惶 jittery or panicky

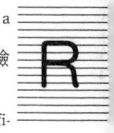

rénxíngdào 人行道 a sidewalk; a footpath

rénxìng 人性 human nature

rénxuǎn 人選 candidates (for certain jobs)

rényān 人煙 signs of a human settlement

rényán kěwèi 人言可畏 Criticisms should be feared.

rényán zézé 人言嘖嘖 There are plenty of criticisms.

rényǎng mǎfān 人仰馬翻 to suffer an utter defeat

rényǐngr 人影兒 a human shadow

rényuán 人員 the personnel; the staff

rényuán 人猿 an ape

rényuánr 人緣兒 relations with others

rényún yìyún 人云亦云 metooism; me-too

rénzāng bìnghuò 人贓並獲 (a thief or robber) caught together with the loot

rénzào 人造 man-made; artificial; imitation

rénzào wèixīng 人造衛星 a satellite

rénzhèng 人證 witnesses

rénzhī chángqíng 人之常情 what is natural in human relationships

rénzhì 人質 a hostage

rénzhōng 人中 philtrum

rénzhǒng 人種 human races

rén 壬
1. the ninth of the Ten Celestial Stems 2. artful and crafty 3. great 4. pregnant

rén 仁
1. benevolence; humanity; mercy; kindness; charity 2. kernel

rén'ài 仁愛 humanity; philanthropy

réncí 仁慈 charity; kindness

rénhòu 仁厚 benevolent and generous

rénmín àiwù 仁民愛物 to love all people and animals

rénrén jūnzǐ 仁人君子 kind-hearted gentlemen

rényì dàodé 仁義道德 virtue and morality

rénzhèng 仁政 humanitarian rule

rénzhì yìjìn 仁至義盡 Everything to be expected in the light of benevolence and duty has been done.

Rén 任
a surname

rěn 忍
1. to endure; to bear; to tolerate; to put up with; to suffer 2. merciless; truculence 3. to forbear; to repress

rěnbuzhù 忍不住 1. cannot stand it any more 2. can not help (laughing, etc.)

rěnjī āi'è 忍飢挨餓 refer to **rěnjī āi'è** 忍飢挨餓

rěnjī āi'è 忍飢挨餓 to suffer hunger

rěnjùn bùjīn 忍俊不禁 refer to **rěnjùn bùjìn** 忍俊不禁

rěnjùn bùjìn 忍俊不禁 cannot help smiling or laughing

rěnnài 忍耐 patience; forbearance; patient

rěnqì tūnshēng 忍氣吞聲 to keep quiet and swallow the insults

rěnràng 忍讓 to be forbearing and conciliatory

rěnrǔ fùzhòng 忍辱負重 to suffer all disgrace and insults in order to accomplish a task

rěnshòu 忍受 to endure; to bear; to suffer

rěntòng 忍痛 1. to bear pain with dignity 2. (to give up or sell something) reluctantly

rěnwú kěrěn 忍無可忍 beyond one's endurance; can not stand (insults or provocation) any longer

rěnxīn 忍心 hardhearted; to steel one's heart

rěnzhù 忍住 to hold back the manifestation of feelings by the force of will

rěn 荏

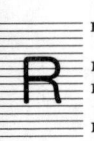

1. Perilla frutescens, whose seeds are birds' feed 2. soft; weak; fragile

rěnrǎn 荏苒 (said of time) to elapse imperceptibly; to slip by

rěn 稔

1. the ripening of paddy or rice; a harvest 2. a year 3. to accumulate; to hoard 4. to be familiar with somebody

rèn 刃

1. the blade or edge of a knife 2. to kill

rèn 任

1. a duty 2. to let (one act at will) 3. to employ (one for a job) 4. to bear (a burden) 5. an official post; office

rènhé 任何 any; whatever

rènláo rènyuàn 任勞任怨 to do something without complaint despite hardships and criticisms

rènmiǎn 任免 employment and discharge

rènmìng 任命 to appoint; appointment

rènpíng 任憑 without restriction; (to allow someone to do something) at will

rènqī 任期 the tenure of office

rènqí 任期 refer to **rènqī** 任期

rènrén wéixián 任人唯賢 to appoint a person according to his ability and virtue

rènwu 任務 duty; responsibility

rènxìng 任性 doing as one pleases; unrestrained

rènyì 任意 arbitrary; at will

rènyòng 任用 to employ; to hire; to engage

rènzhí 任職 to hold a post; to be in office

rènzhòng dàoyuǎn 任重道遠 The load is heavy, while the way is long.

rèn 妊

pregnant; to be expecting

rènshēn 妊娠 to be pregnant; pregnancy

rèn 紉

1. to sew; to stitch 2. to tie; to wear 3. to feel deeply 4. to thread a needle

rèn 韌

soft but tough; pliable but strong

rènxìng 韌性 tenacity

rèn 飪

to cook

rèn 認

1. to recognize; to know; to make out 2. to admit; to acknowledge 3. to accept; to resign oneself to 4. to adopt 5. to promise to do something

rèncuò 認錯 1. to admit a fault or mistake 2. to make identification in correctly

rènde 認得 to know; to recognize

rèndìng 認定 1. to conclude or decide; to believe firmly 2. to set one's mind on

rèn'gòu 認購 to offer to buy; to subscribe

rènkě 認可 to sanction; to approve

rènlǐng 認領 1. to identify and claim (a child, etc.) 2. (said of a man) to adopt a child born out of wedlock

rènmíng 認明 to see clearly; to recognize

rènmìng 認命 to resign oneself to destiny

rènqīng 認清 to see or know clearly (which is which)

rènshi 認識 1. to know 2. to understand

rènshū 認輸 to concede defeat; to give up

rèntóng 認同 to identify; identification

rènwéi 認爲 to think that...; to consider that...

rènzhàng 認賬 1. to acknowledge a debt 2. to admit a mistake

rènzhēn 認眞 to be serious; to be earnest

rènzhī 認知 cognition

rènzuì 認罪 to plead guilty

rēng 扔

1. to throw; to hurl 2. to abandon; to discard

rēngdiào 扔掉 to throw away

rēngxia 扔下 to throw down; to put aside

réng 仍
still; yet

réngjiù 仍舊 still; yet

réngrán 仍然 still; yet

rì 日
1. the sun 2. a day 3. every day; daily 4. Japan; Japanese 5. time 6. day; daytime

rìbān 日班 the day shift (in factories, etc.)

rìbào 日報 a daily newspaper

Rìběn 日本 Japan

rìbó xīshān 日薄西山 declining rapidly; old age; approaching one's grave; one's days are numbered

rìbù xiájǐ 日不暇給 too many things to do in a day

rìcháng 日常 common; usually; ordinarily; daily

rìcháng shēnghuó 日常生活 daily life

rìchéng 日程 1. an itinerary 2. the agenda on a specific day (of a conference)

rìchū 日出 sunrise

rìfù yīrì 日復一日 day after day

rìguāng 日光 sunshine; the light of the sun

rìguāngdēng 日光燈 a fluorescent lamp

rìguāngyù 日光浴 a sunbath

rìguǐ 日晷 a sundial

rìhòu 日後 in the days to come; in the future

rìjī yuèlěi 日積月累 gradual accumulation over a long time

rìjì 日記 a diary

rìjiàn 日見 with each passing day

rìjiàn 日漸 with each passing day

rìjiǔ jiàn rénxīn 日久見人心 Time reveals a person's heart.

rìjiǔ qíngshēng 日久情生

Having been together for a long time, people come to have a tender feeling for each other.

rìlǐ wànjī 日理萬機 (literally) to manage 10,000 things in a day —very busy

rìlì 日利 daily interest (rate)

rìlì 日曆 a calendar

rìmù túqióng 日暮途窮 at the end of one's rope

Rìnèiwǎ 日內瓦 Geneva, Switzerland

rìqī 日期 date

rìqí 日期 refet to **rìqī** 日期

rìqián 日前 a few days ago; recently

rìqū 日趨 gradually; day by day

rìshàng sān'gān 日上三竿 rather late in the morning —about 9 a.m. (often used to describe someone who gets up late)

rìshí 日食 solar eclipse

rìshí 日蝕 solar eclipse

Rìwén 日文 the Japanese (language)

rìxī 日息 daily interest (rate)

rìxí 日息 refer to **rìxī** 日息

rìxīn 日薪 day wages

rìxīn yuèyì 日新月異 continuous improvement; ever newer

rìxíng yīshàn 日行一善 to do one good deed a day

rìyè 日夜 day and night

rìyǐ jìyè 日以繼夜 day and night; continuously

rìyòngpǐn 日用品 daily necessities

rìyǒu jìnbù 日有進步 to show improvements or progress day by day

rìyǒu suǒsī, yèyǒu suǒmèng 日有所思,夜有所夢 One dreams at night what one thinks in the day.

Rìyǔ 日語 the Japanese (language)

rìyuè rúsuō 日月如梭 How fast time flies!

Rìyuètán 日月潭 Sun Moon Lake, Taiwan

rìzhì 日誌 a daily record

R

rìzi 日子 1. time; duration 2. life; living

rìzuò chóuchéng 日坐愁城 to be in deep worry every day

róng 戎

1. war; fighting 2. arms; the apparatus of war 3. military affairs; army 4. barbarians to the west

róngmǎ shēngyá 戎馬生涯 an army life; a military career

róngwǔ 戎伍 the ranks; the army

róngyī 戎衣 military dress

róngzhuāng 戎裝 military dress

róng 容

1. a face; an expression; a countenance 2. to contain; to hold 3. to allow; to permit 4. to forgive; to pardon 5. to forbear; forbearance

róngguāng huànfā 容光煥發 to have a face radiant with well-being

róngliàng 容量 the capacity

róngmào 容貌 looks; a countenance; features

róngnà 容納 1. to contain 2. to tolerate

róngqì 容器 a container

róngrěn 容忍 to endure; to bear; to tolerate

róngshēn 容身 to find living space

róngxǔ 容許 to allow; to permit

róngyán 容顏 a facial appearance

róngyì 容易 1. easy 2. apt to; liable to

róng 絨

1. fine wool; woolen; velvety; velvet 2. any kind of woolen goods or fabric with a feltlike surface 3. fine; furry; flossy

róngbù 絨布 flannel; felt

róngkù 絨褲 sweat pants

róngmáo 絨毛 down

róng 溶

1. to dissolve; to melt 2. (said of rivers) having much water

róngdiǎn 溶點 the melting point

rónghuà 溶化 to dissolve; to melt

róngjì 溶劑 a dissolvent; a solvent

róngjiě 溶解 to dissolve; to melt

róngjiědù 溶解度 solubility

róngrù 溶入 to dissolve into

róng 榮

1. glory; honor 2. luxuriant; lush; teeming

róngguī 榮歸 1. (said of a high official) to retire in glory 2. to return home in triumph

rónghuá fùguì 榮華富貴 honor and wealth

rónghuò 榮獲 to get or win the honor

róngmín 榮民 retired servicemen; veterans

róngrèn 榮任 to have the honor of being appointed (to a post)

róngrǔ 榮辱 honor and dishonor

róngxìng 榮幸 honored; to have the honor of

róngyào 榮耀 glory; honor; splendor

róngyīng 榮膺 to have the honor of being appointed (to a post)

róngyù 榮譽 honor

róngzōng yàozǔ 榮宗耀祖 to bring glory to one's family and ancestors

róng 蓉

the hibiscus

róng 榕

a banyan tree

róng 熔

to smelt; to weld or fuse metals

rónghuà 熔化 to smelt; to melt

róngjiě 熔解 to smelt; to melt; to fuse

rónglú 熔爐 a smelting furnace; a melting pot

róngyán 熔岩 lava

róngzhù 熔鑄 founding; casting

róng 融
1. very bright; glowing; burning 2. to melt 3. to melt into; to blend; to harmonize 4. cheerful; happy; joyful

rónghé 融合 to blend; to fuse

rónghuà 融化 to melt; to fuse; to thaw

rónghuì guàntōng 融會貫通 well digested and completely understood

róngjiě 融解 to melt; to thaw

róngqià 融洽 (said especially of human relations) harmonious

róng 鎔
1. to melt; to smelt; to fuse 2. a mold 3. a kind of spear

rónghuà 鎔化 to melt; to fuse

róngjiě 鎔解 to melt; to fuse

rónglú 鎔爐 a smelting furnace; a cupola

róngzhù 鎔鑄 to cast (metal)

rǒng 冗
1. redundant; superfluous 2. disorderly

rǒngcháng 冗長 1. superfluous 2. (said of writing) verbose 3. tediously long

rǒngyuán 冗員 a supernumerary

róu 柔
1. soft and tender 2. amiable; pliant; yielding; submissive; gentle; supple 3. the new grass budding in spring

róucháng cùnduàn 柔腸寸斷 broken-hearted

róudào 柔道 judo

róuhe 柔和 soft; gentle; amiable; tender

róuměi 柔媚 amiable, pliant and yielding

róunèn 柔嫩 soft and tender

róunéng kègāng 柔能克剛 Soft and subtle approach can disarm a man of hot temper.

róuqíng sìshuǐ 柔情似水 tender and soft as water

róuruǎn 柔軟 soft; yielding; lithe

róuruǎn tǐcāo 柔軟體操 calisthenics

róuruò 柔弱 weak (physique); low and gentle (voice, etc.)

róushùn 柔順 gentle and yielding

róu 揉
1. to rub; to knead 2. to crumple by hand 3. to massage 4. to subdue; to make smooth or peaceful 5. mixed-up; confused

róucuo 揉搓 1. to rub; to massage 2. to tease or play jokes on

róuhé 揉合 to combine; to blend

róuyǎnjing 揉眼睛 to rub eyes

róu 糅 also **niù, rǒu**
to mix; mixed

róuhé 糅和 to mix together; to blend

róu 蹂
1. to tread upon; to trample 2. to tread out grain

róulìn 蹂躪 1. to trample 2. to devastate; rapacious acts

rǒu 糅
refer to **róu 糅**

ròu 肉 also **rù**
1. flesh 2. physical; carnal 3. meat of animals; meat or pulp of fruits, etc. 4. flesh and blood-dearest, as one's children 5. slow-motion

ròubāozi 肉包子 steamed dumplings stuffed with meat

ròubó 肉搏 hand-to-hand combat

ròujiàng 肉醬 meat pulp

ròukuài 肉塊 chopped meat; meat chops

ròumá 肉麻 a creepy feeling; disgusting

ròupiào 肉票 a hostage kidnapped for a ransom

ròupù 肉鋪 a butcher's shop

ròusè 肉色 flesh-colored; yellowish pink

ròushí 肉食 to eat meat; meat-eating; carnivorous

ròusī 肉絲 shredded meat

ròusōng 肉鬆 fried shredded meat; meat fluff

R

ròutǐ 肉體 flesh and blood; physical

ròuwánzi 肉丸子 meatballs

ròuyǎn 肉眼 1. a layman's eyes 2. the naked eye

rú 如
1. like; as 2. if; supposing 3. as if 4. as good as; equal to 5. to follow (advice); to listen to 6. to go to; to arrive at 7. should; ought to 8. on or in (time)

rúcè 如厠 to go to the toilet

rúcháng 如常 as usual

rúchū yīchē 如出一轍 refer to **rúchū yīzhé** 如出一轍

rúchū yīzhé 如出一轍 (said of events) very similar; almost the same

rúcǐ 如此 thus; like this

rúcǐ éryǐ 如此而已 That's what it all amounts to.

rúduò wǔlǐ wùzhōng 如墮五里霧中 utterly being mystified

rúfǎ páozhì 如法炮製 to do something exactly as others have done

rúguǒ 如果 if; supposing

rúhé 如何 1. How (can we deal with...)? 2. What do you think of it? How about it? 3. What to do now? How is it?

rúhǔ tiānyì 如虎添翼 with added strength

rúhuā sìyù 如花似玉 (said of a girl) young, beautiful and pure

rúhuǒ rútú 如火如荼 (troops) in an imposing array; luxuriant (growth, etc.)

rúhuò zhìbǎo 如獲至寶 to get what one has wished or desired for a long time

rújiàn zàixián 如箭在弦 ready to go or start; imminent

rújiāo sìqì 如膠似漆 very much in love; inseparable

rújīn 如今 now; nowadays

rújiù 如舊 as it has always been; as usual

rúléi guàn'ěr 如雷貫耳 (one's

famous name) has long been known to people

rúlín dàdí 如臨大敵 very careful or cautious; to take all possible precautions

rúmèng chūxǐng 如夢初醒 to come to a sudden realization

rúniǎo shòusàn 如鳥獸散 to flee helter-skelter

rúqī 如期 on time; punctually

rúqī 如期 refer to **rúqī** 如期

rúrì zhōngtiān 如日中天 1. to ride on the crest of success 2. very influential

rúshàng suǒshù 如上所述 as mentioned above

rúshì zhòngfù 如釋重負 to feel greatly relieved (after discharging a duty)

rúshǔ jiāzhēn 如數家珍 to describe distinctly and in good order

rúshù chánghuán 如數償還 to pay back in full

rúxià 如下 as follows; as below

rúxū 如須 if (you) want to; if (you) have to

rúyì 如意 as one wishes

rúyì suànpán 如意算盤 wishful thinking

rúyǐng suíxíng 如影隨形 (said of two persons) inseparable; to tag after

rúyú déshuǐ 如魚得水 (said of friends, newlyweds, the king and the ministers, etc.) very satisfied and pleased

rúyuàn yǐcháng 如願以償 to have one's wish fulfilled

rúzuì rúchī 如醉如癡 to be drunk with; to be crazy about

rúzuò zhēnzhān 如坐針氈 very anxious; in a state of agitation

rú 茹 also **rù**
1. entangled roots 2. to eat; to taste; to mouth 3. (figuratively) to experience 4. stinking

rúmáo yǐnxiě 茹毛飲血 refer to **rúmáo yǐnxuè** 茹毛飲血

rúmáo yǐnxuè 茹毛飲血 (said of primitive people) to eat birds and beasts uncooked

rú 儒
1. the learned; scholars collectively 2. Confucian; Confucianism 3. weak; shrinking from hardship

Rújiā 儒家 Confucianists; the Confucian school

Rújiào 儒教 Confucianism

Rúxué 儒學 the teachings of Confucius

rúyǎ 儒雅 scholarly and refined; elegant

rú 濡
1. to moisten; to immerse; to wet 2. to linger; to procrastinate 3. glossy; smooth 4. to tolerate; to endure

rú 孺
a young child; an infant

rúzǐ 孺子 a child; a boy

rú 蠕
wriggle; squirm

rúchóng 蠕蟲 worm; helminth

rúdòng 蠕動 1. wriggle; squirm 2. peristalsis

rǔ 汝
you; thou; thee; thy

rǔbèi 汝輩 (plural) ye; you

rǔ 乳
1. breasts; the nipple 2. milk 3. any milk-like liquid 4. the young of animals, birds, etc. 5. to give birth 6. to triturate

rǔái 乳癌 cancer of the breast

rǔbái 乳白 milky white; cream color

rǔchǐ 乳齒 milk teeth; deciduous teeth

rǔchòu wèigān 乳臭未乾 very young and inexperienced like a sucking child

rǔfáng 乳房 the udders; the breasts

rǔlào 乳酪 junke; curds

rǔluò 乳酪 refer to rúlào 乳酪

rǔmíng 乳名 a pet name given to a child

rǔmǔ 乳母 a wet nurse

rǔniáng 乳娘 a wet nurse

rǔniú 乳牛 the dairy cattle; a milch cow

rǔsuān 乳酸 lactic acid

rǔtáng 乳糖 lactose; milk sugar

rǔtóu 乳頭 a nipple; a teat

rǔxiù wèigān 乳臭未乾 refer to rǔchòu wèigān 乳臭未乾

rǔyùn 乳暈 mammary areola

rǔzhào 乳罩 a brassiere; a bra

rǔzhī 乳汁 milk

rǔzhìpǐn 乳製品 dairy products

rǔzhìpǐn gōngyè 乳製品工業 the dairy industry

rǔ 辱 also rù
1. disgrace 2. to disgrace; to insult; to dishonor 3. to condescend; to design 4. undeservingly

rǔmà 辱罵 to abuse and insult

rù 入
1. to enter; to come into 2. to join; to come into the company of 3. to arrive at; to reach 4. to put in 5. receipts; income 6. to get out of sight; to disappear 7. to get (inside, picked, elected, etc.) 8. to agree with; to conform to 9. one of the four tones of a character

rùbù fūchū 入不敷出 cannot make both ends meet

rùchǎng 入場 1. to enter a meeting place 2. to take part in an examination

rùchǎngquàn 入場券 an admission ticket

rùchāo 入超 excess of import

rùdǎng 入黨 to join a political party

rùgǎng 入港 to enter a harbor (or port)

rùgǔ 入股 to become a shareholder

rùgǔ 入骨 deep (hatred, love, etc.); to the marrow

rùhǎikǒu 入海口 an estuary

rùhuà 入畫 picturesque

rùhuǒ 入伙 1. to join in an enterprise 2. to join a mess

rùhuǒ 入夥 1. to join a gang 2. to join in an undertaking or enterprise

rùjí 入籍 to naturalize; to be naturalized

rùjìng 入境 to entry a country

rùjìng wènsú 入境問俗 to learn the customs of a new place when one goes there

rùjìngzhèng 入境證 an entry permit

rùkǒu 入口 an entrance

rùliàn 入殮 to put a corpse in a coffin; to coffin

rùliè 入列 to take one's place in the ranks; to fall in

rùmén 入門 to have an elementary knowledge of

rùmèng 入夢 1. to fall asleep 2. to appear in one's dream

rùmí 入迷 to be captivated or fascinated

rùmù sānfēn 入木三分 1. (said of Chinese calligraphy) a forceful style 2. (comments, analyses, etc.) incisive; penetrating

rùqīn 入侵 to invade; to intrude

rùqíng rùlǐ 入情入理 fair and reasonable

rùshén 入神 captivated; bewitched; fascinated; spellbound

rùshēng 入聲 (traditional Chinese phonetics) the fourth tone

rùshuì 入睡 to go to sleep; to fall asleep

rùtǔ 入土 to bury; to be buried

rùwéi 入圍 1. to be selected as one of the few 2. to enter a trapped area

rùwèi 入味 1. tasty 2. interesting

rùwǔ 入伍 to become a soldier (usually under the conscription system)

rùxí 入席 to be properly seated at a gathering, meeting or feast

rùxuǎn 入選 to be selected

rùxué 入學 to enter school

rùxué kǎoshì 入學考試 an entrance examination

rùyǎn 入眼 pleasing to the eye; agreeable to look at

rùyè 入夜 at night; in the evening

rùyíng 入營 to enter the barracks—to join the army

rùyù 入獄 to be imprisoned

rùyuàn 入院 to be hospitalized

rùzhuì 入贅 to marry into the family of one's wife

rùzuò 入座 properly seated

rù 肉
refer to **ròu** 肉

rú 茹
refer to **rú** 茹

rù 辱
refer to **rǔ** 辱

rù 溽
moist; humid

rùshǔ 溽暑 sweltering summer weather

rù 褥
bedding; quilts or coverlets; a mattress; cushion; bedclothes

ruǎn 阮
1. name of an ancient state in today's Gansu Province 2. an ancient musical instrument 3. a Chinese family name

ruǎnnáng xiūsè 阮囊羞澀 short of cash; poor

ruǎn 軟
1. soft; pliable; tender 2. gentle; soft; mild 3. weak; cowardly 4. poor in quality, ability, etc. 5. easily moved or influenced

ruǎndàikuǎn 軟貸款 low interest loan; soft loan

ruǎngāo 軟膏 ointment

ruǎnjiàn 軟件 (computer) software

ruǎnjiànbāo 軟件包 (computer) software package

ruǎnjìn 軟禁 to put under house arrest; to confine informally

ruǎnmiánmián 軟綿綿 1. soft 2. (said of songs) sentimental 3. weak

ruǎnmùsāi 軟木塞 a cork stopper; a cork

ruǎnpiàn 軟片 (photographic) film; roll film

ruǎnruò 軟弱 weak; feeble; flabby

ruǎntáng 軟糖 a fondant; fudge

ruǎntǐ 軟體 (computer) software

ruǎnyìng bùchī 軟硬不吃 to yield to neither the carrot nor the stick

ruǎnyìng jiānshī 軟硬兼施 to use both hard and soft tactics

ruǐ 蕊

1. a flower bud; an unopened flower 2. the stamens or pistils of a flower

ruì 瑞

1. something portending good luck or fortune; good omen; signs of good luck 2. lucky; auspicious 3. a jade tablet given to feudal princes on their investiture, as a sign of authority and rank

Ruìdiǎn 瑞典 Sweden

Ruìshì 瑞士 Switzerland

ruì 睿

1. to understand thoroughly 2. wise and clever 3. the profoundest (learning)

ruìzhì 睿智 superior intelligence

ruì 銳

1. sharp; acute; keen 2. quickwitted; intelligent; clever 3. energetic; vigorous

ruìbù kědāng 銳不可當 too sharp to resist; too powerful to stop

ruìjiǎn 銳減 to decline sharply; to drop markedly

ruìjiǎo 銳角 an acute angle

ruìlì 銳利 sharp; pointed

ruìqì 銳氣 dash; mettle; vigor; virility; aggressiveness

rùn 閏

1. with surplus or leftover 2. usurped; deputy or substitute 3. extra, inserted between others, as a day, or a month; to intercalate

rùnnián 閏年 a leap year; an intercalary year

rùnyuè 閏月 an intercalary moon or month

rùn 潤

1. moist; glossy; fresh 2. to moisten; to freshen 3. to enrich; to benefit 4. to embellish

rùnbǐ 潤筆 remuneration (or fee) for writing or painting

rùnhuá 潤滑 1. to lubricate 2. smooth

rùnhuájì 潤滑劑 a lubricant

rùnhuáyóu 潤滑油 lubricating oil

rùnsè 潤色 to embellish or polish a writing

rùnshì 潤飾 to embellish or polish a writing

rùnzé 潤澤 1. moist and glossy 2. to invigorate; to moisten

ruò 若

1. if; suppose; supposing; assuming; provided that 2. you 3. similar to; like

ruòfēi 若非 unless; if not

ruògān 若干 some; a few; several

ruòjí ruòlí 若即若離 to keep at arm's length

ruòshì 若是 if; suppose

ruòwú qíshì 若無其事 as if nothing had happened; to remain calm

ruòyào 若要 if...has (have) to...

ruòyǐn ruòxiàn 若隱若現 half-hidden; discernible at one moment and gone the next (like a will-o'-the-wisp)

ruò 弱

1. weak; fragile; feeble; tender 2. inferior 3. young 4. a little less than

ruòbù jīnfēng 弱不禁風 so weak as to have inadequate strength to withstand the wind

ruòdiǎn 弱點 a weak point; a weakness

ruòguàn 弱冠 a twenty-year-old man; a youth

ruòròu qiángshí 弱肉強食 the weak falling victim to the strong —the law of the jungle

ruòshì 弱視 amblyopia

ruòxiǎo 弱小 small and weak

ruòxiǎo mínzú 弱小民族 a small nation

ruòzhě 弱者 the weak and the timid

ruò 偌 so (used as an adverb to modify an adjective)

sā 仨 three (Beijing colloquialism)

sā 撒 1. to relax; to ease 2. to loosen; to unleash 3. to exhibit; to display; to show

Sādàn 撒旦 Satan

Sāhālā Shāmò 撒哈拉沙漠 the Sahara Desert

sāhuǎng 撒謊 to tell a lie; to lie

sājiāo 撒嬌 1. to show pettishness, as a spoilt child 2. (said of a woman) to pretend to be angry or displeased

sāniào 撒尿 to urinate; to piss; to pee; to pass urine

sāshǒu chénhuán 撒手塵寰 to pass away

sāshǒujiān 撒手鐧 the climaxing act; one's specialty

sāshǒujiān 撒手鐧 refer to sāshǒujiān 撒手鐧

sāyě 撒野 to act boorishly

sǎ 洒 1. I; me 2. to pour; to sprinkle

sǎjiā 洒家 I; me

sǎsǎo 洒掃 to sprinkle water and sweep away the dirt; to clean up

sǎ 撒 to scatter; to sprinkle; to disperse

sǎsàn 撒散 to spread; to scatter about

sǎshuǐ 撒水 to sprinkle or spray water

sǎ 灑 1. to splash; to sprinkle (liquids) 2. to wash

sǎsǎo 灑掃 to sprinkle water and sweep

sǎshuǐ 灑水 to spill water; to sprinkle water

sǎtuō 灑脫 casual and carefree

sà 颯 1. the sound of wind; rustling 2. weakened; failing; declining

sà 薩 a general name of Buddhist gods or immortals; Buddha

sāi 塞 (usually used in the spoken language) 1. refer to **sè** 塞 2. a cork or stopper; to cork; to seal

sāimǎn 塞滿 to stuff full; to fill up

sāizhù 塞住 to stop up; to block up

sāizi 塞子 a cork; a stopper

sāi 腮 the cheeks

sāibāngzi 腮幫子 (colloquial) the cheek

sāi 鰓 gills (of fish)

sài 塞 strategic points along the frontiers

Sàiwēng shīmǎ, yānzhī fēifú 塞翁失馬，焉知非福 A loss may turn out to be a gain.

sài 賽 1. to compete; to contest; to rival; to contend for superiority 2. a race; a tournament; a match; a game 3. to surpass 4. a Chinese family name

sàichē 賽車 a car race; to race cars

sàimǎ 賽馬 a horse race

sàimǎchǎng 賽馬場 a race course (or ground)

sàipǎo 賽跑 to run a race on foot; a foot race

sān 三 three; third; thrice

sānbǎi liùshí háng 三百六十行 all trades and professions

sānbāotāi 三胞胎 triplets

sānbùguǎn 三不管 a district not within the jurisdiction of any of the neighboring magistrates

sānbùqǔ 三部曲 a trilogy

sānbùxiǔ 三不朽 the three imperishables—one's virtue, achievements and teachings

sāncān 三餐 three meals—breakfast, lunch and supper

sānchà lùkǒu 三叉路口 a junction where three roads meet

sāncháng liǎngduǎn 三長兩短 unforeseen disasters or accidents

sāncháo yuánlǎo 三朝元老 a veteran statesman who had served under three emperors in a row

sāndádé 三達德 the three virtues—wisdom, benevolence and courage

sāndài 三代 1. three generations 2. the three ancient Chinese dynasties—Xsia, Shang and Zhou

sāndài tóngtáng 三代同堂 three generations living under the same roof (under the big family system in old China)

sānděng 三等 1. three grades 2. the third grade

sāndiǎnshì yǒngzhuāng 三點式泳裝 a bikini (suit)

sāndú 三讀 the third reading of a bill in a legislative session

sāndù kōngjiān 三度空間 three-dimensional space

sānfān liǎngcì 三番兩次 time and again; over and over again

sānfútiān 三伏天 dog days

sānge chòupíjiang, shèngguò yīge Zhūgě Liàng 三個臭皮匠，勝過一個諸葛亮 The wisdom of the masses exceeds that of the wisest individual.

sān'gēng bànyè 三更半夜 late at night

sānhébǎn 三合板 plywood; a three-ply board

sānjí tiàoyuǎn 三級跳遠 hop, step, and jump

sānjiān qíkǒu 三緘其口 to remain silent

sānjiǎo 三角 1. trigonometry 2. three angles

sānjiǎobǎn 三角板 a triangle; a set square

sānjiǎojià 三腳架 a tripod

sānjiǎokù 三角褲 panties; briefs

sānjiǎo liàn'ài 三角戀愛 a love triangle

sānjiǎotiě 三角鐵 (construction) angle iron

sānjiào jiǔliú 三教九流 people of all walks of life

sānjù bùlí běnháng 三句不離本行 to talk shop frequently when conversing with people outside one's own profession

sānjūn 三軍 the three armies; the armed forces

sānlúnchē 三輪車 a pedicab; a tricycle

Sānmín Zhǔyì 三民主義 the Three Principles of the People —nationalism, democracy and livelihood

sānmíngzhì 三明治 a sandwich

sānnián wǔzǎi 三年五載 three to five years

sānnián yǒuchéng 三年有成 Three years' hard work is crowned with success.

sānqī èrshíyī 三七二十一 1. Three sevens are twenty-one. 2. the true story of a matter or happening

sānquán fēnlì 三權分立 separation of the legislative, executive and judicial functions of a government

sānquēyī 三缺一 (mah-jong) one more player still needed

sānrénxíng bìyǒu wǒshī 三人行必有我師 If three of us are walking together, at least one of the other two is good enough to be my teacher.

sānsān liǎngliǎng 三三兩兩 by twos and threes

sānshēng 三牲 three sacrificial offerings—ox, sheep and hog

sānshēng yǒuxìng 三生有幸 the greatest fortune in three incarnations (to make friends with worthy persons or to marry a virtuous and beautiful wife, etc.)

sānshí érlì 三十而立 thirty

years of age when a man should stand on his own feet

sānshí'èr kāi 三十二開 thirty-twomo; 32mo

sānshíliù jì 三十六計 all the possible schemes or stratagems

sānshíliù jì, zǒuwéi shàng-cè 三十六計，走爲上策 The best thing to do now is to go away.

sānsī érhòu xíng 三思而後行 Look before you leap.

sāntiān dǎyú, liǎngtiān shàiwǎng 天天打魚，兩天曬網 (figuratively) to work off and on

sāntóu liùbì 三頭六臂 a resourceful and capable man who, figuratively speaking, has three heads and six arms to use

sāntóu zhèngzhì 三頭政治 the triumvirate

sānwéi 三圍 chest measurement, waist measurement and hip measurement

sānwèi yìtǐ 三位一體 the Trinity; three-in-one

sānwēnnuǎn 三溫暖 sauna bath

sānwǔ chéngqún 三五成群 in groups of three or five

Sānxiá 三峽 the Three Gorges of the Changjiang (Yangtze) River

sānxīn èryì 三心二意 hesitating; irresolute; vacillating

sānyán liǎngyǔ 三言兩語 a brief talk, discussion, conversation, description, etc.

sānyáng kāitài 三陽開泰 a surge of good luck

sānyuè 三月 1. March 2. the third moon of the lunar calendar 3. three months

sānzhèn chūjú 三振出局 to strike out; a strikeout

sānzhīshǒu 三隻手 a pickpocket

sān 參
an elaborate form of **sān** 三 (three) used in documents or checks to prevent forgery

sǎn 傘
1. an umbrella 2. a parachute

sǎnbīng 傘兵 paratroopers

sǎn 散
1. loose; loosened 2. idle; leisurely 3. powdered medicine

sǎnbīng 散兵 1. skirmishers 2. stragglers

sǎndàn 散彈 a grapeshot; a pellet

sǎnguāng 散光 astigmatism; astigmatic

sǎnjì 散記 random notes

sǎnjū 散居 to live in scattered places

sǎnwén 散文 prose

sǎnzhuāng 散裝 not in a package; bulk

sàn 散
1. to scatter; to disperse 2. to end; to be over; to stop 3. to disseminate; to give out

sànbō 散播 to disseminate; to spread

sànbù 散布 1. to scatter; to sprinkle 2. to spread

sànbù 散步 to take a walk, a stroll, or a ramble

sànchǎng 散場 (said of a show, a meeting, etc.) to be over

sànfā 散發 1. to send out; to emit 2. to distribute; to issue; to give out

sànhuì 散會 to dissolve a meeting

sànhuǒ 散夥 (said of a group) to disband

sànkai 散開 spread out or apart

sànluàn 散亂 confused; in disorder

sànluò 散落 to be strewn or scattered

sànrè 散熱 to dissipate heat

sànshī 散失 to get scattered and lost; missing

sànxīn 散心 to have some recreation

sāng 桑
the mulberry tree

sāngcán 桑蠶 a silkworm

sāngjiān púshàng 桑間濮上 a place notorious for profligacy

sāngshèn 桑葚 a mulberry; mulberry fruit

sāngtián 桑田 a plantation of mulberry trees

sāngyè 桑葉 mulberry leaves

sāngyú 桑榆 1. the west 2. the closing years of one's life

sāngyuán 桑園 mulberry fields

sāng 喪
1. death; dying 2. to mourn 3. funeral

sāngfú 喪服 mourning dress or costume

sānglǐ 喪禮 funeral rites

sāngqī 喪期 a mourning period

sāngqí 喪期 refer to **sāngqī** 喪期

sāngshì 喪事 funeral affairs

sāngzàng 喪葬 funeral service and burial

sǎng 嗓
1. the throat (as the source of one's voice) 2. one's voice

sǎngménr 嗓門兒 1. one's voice 2. the vocal organs

sǎngzi 嗓子 1. the throat 2. one's voice

sàng 喪
1. to lose; to be deprived of 2. to be defeated 3. to decline; to go down

sàngdǎn 喪膽 to be much afraid

sàngjiā zhīquǎn 喪家之犬 an outcast

sàngjìn tiānliáng 喪盡天良 to have no conscience

sàngmìng 喪命 to lose one's life; to die

sàng'ǒu 喪偶 to be deprived of one's spouse, especially one's wife

sàngqì 喪氣 dejected; despondent

sàngshī 喪失 to lose; to be deprived of

sàngxīn bìngkuáng 喪心病狂 out of one's right mind

sāo 搔
1. to scratch lightly 2. to irritate;

to annoy

sāorǎo 搔擾 to annoy; to harass

sāoshǒu nòngzī 搔首弄姿 (said of women) to act coquettishly to attract men's attention; to flirt

sāoyǎng 搔癢 to scratch the itching place

sāozháo yǎngchù 搔著癢處 1. to touch somebody to the quick 2. to say something exactly to the point

sāo 艘
refer to **sōu** 艘

sāo 臊
a bad odor or smell, as that of decaying fish, meat, fox, sheep, etc.

sāo 騷
1. to disturb; to agitate 2. to worry; to feel concerned 3. illsmelling; stinking 4. (colloquial) amorous; erotic

sāodòng 騷動 disturbance; upheaval; unrest

sāoluàn 騷亂 disturbance; tumult; agitation

sāorǎo 騷擾 to disturb; to harass; to agitate

sāorén mòkè 騷人墨客 a poet; a bard

sǎo 掃
1. to sweep with a broom; to clear away; to clean 2. to wipe out; to weed out; to exterminate; to mop up 3. sweepingly; totally 4. to paint (the eyebrows, etc.)

sǎochú 掃除 1. to sweep up; to clean 2. to eliminate

sǎodàng 掃蕩 to make a clean sweep of (enemy troops, rebels, etc.); a mop-up operation

sǎodì 掃地 1. to sweep the floor 2. (said of reputation) to soil

sǎohēi 掃黑 to crack down on crime

sǎohuáng 掃黃 to crack down on pornography

sǎomiáo 掃描 (electricity) scanning

sǎomù 掃墓 (literally) to sweep the tomb—to pay respects to

one's ancestor at his grave

sǎopíng 掃平 to quell an uprising, etc.; to put down

sǎoshè 掃射 1. to strafe (with machine gun fire) 2. to look around

sǎoxìng 掃興 1. to throw cold water on; to spoil pleasure 2. to feel disappointed or discouraged

sǎo 嫂

the wife of one's elder brother

sǎosao 嫂嫂 a sister-in-law

sào 掃

a broom

sàozhou 掃帚 a broom

sàozhouxīng 掃帚星 1. (astronomy) a comet 2. a jinx

sào 臊

1. ashamed; bashful 2. minced meat

sè 色

1. (also **shǎi**) color; a tinge; a tint; a hue 2. facial expression; a look; an appearance 3. sensuality; lust; lewdness; carnal pleasure 4. worldly things 5. a kind; a sort

sècǎi 色彩 a tinge; a color; a hue; a sort

sèdǎn bāotiān 色膽包天 extremely daring in lewdness

sèláng 色狼 (slang) a lecherous person

sèmáng 色盲 color-blind; achromatopsy

sèqíng 色情 sexual passion; lust

sèsù 色素 pigment

sèzé 色澤 a tinge; a color; a hue; a tint

sèzhǐ 色紙 colored paper

sè 圾

refer to **jī** 圾

sè 瑟

1. a large horizontal musical instrument 2. varied and many 3. elegant and stately; majestic 4. bright and clear; pure and clean 5. alone; lonely; solitary

sèsè 瑟瑟 the heaving sound of wind

sèsuō 瑟縮 1. stiff and numb—as from cold 2. timid and trembling 3. the heaving sound of wind

sè 嗇

stingy; parsimonious; miserly

sè 塞 also **sāi**

(usually used in the written language) 1. to block; to stop up; to clog 2. to stuff; to squeeze in; to fill

sècāyīn 塞擦音 affricate

sèyīn 塞音 plosive

sèzé 塞責 not to do one's job conscientiously

sè 澀

1. rough; harsh; not smooth 2. a slightly bitter taste that numbs the tongue—as some unripened fruits; puckery 3. (said of writing, reading, etc.) difficult or jolting 4. slow of tongue

sèwèi 澀味 astringent taste

sēn 森

1. luxuriant vegetation or luxuriant growth of trees 2. dark and obscure; severe 3. serene; majestic

sēnbāwǔ 森巴舞 samba, originated in Brazil

sēnlín 森林 forest

sēnlínyù 森林浴 a green shower

sēnluó wànxiàng 森羅萬象 the phenomena of the universe

sēnrán 森然 awe-inspiring; trembling

sēnyán 森嚴 stern and severe

sēng 僧

a Buddhist; a priest; a monk

sēngduō zhōushǎo 僧多粥少 not enough (gifts, positions, etc.) to go around because there are too many people on the waiting list

Sēnglǚ 僧侶 Buddhist monks

sēngyuàn 僧院 a monastery

shā 沙

1. sand; tiny gravel or pebbles 2. the land around water; a beach; a sandbank; a desert 3. to pick, select or sift 4. (said of fruit,

especially melons) overripe 5. hoarse 6. sandy—not glossy or smooth; granular 7. a kind of clay for making utensils, etc.

shābāo 沙包 1. sandbags 2. a porcelain vessel shaped like a small jug

shāchǎng 沙場 a battlefield

shādài 沙袋 sandbags

shādīngyú 沙丁魚 a sardine

shāduī 沙堆 a sand dune; a sand hill

shāfā 沙發 a sofa

shāguō 沙鍋 1. an earthenware cooking pot 2. food cooked and served in such a pot

shāhuáng 沙皇 a czar or a tsar (of Russia)

shājīn 沙金 alluvial gold

shākēng 沙坑 a sand pit

shālā 沙拉 salad

shālājiàng 沙拉醬 salad dressing

shālāyóu 沙拉油 salad oil

shālì 沙礫 pebbles; gravel; grit

shālóng 沙龍 a salon

shālòu 沙漏 1. an hourglass 2. a sand filter

Shāmí 沙彌 a Buddhist novice

shāmò 沙漠 a desert

shāmò zhīzhōu 沙漠之舟 the ship of the desert—the camel

shā'ōu 沙鷗 a sea gull

shāqiū 沙丘 a sand dune; a sand hill

shāshā shēngxiǎng 沙沙聲響 a rustle

shāshí 沙石 gravel sandstone

shāshì 沙士 sarsaparilla

shātān 沙灘 a sandbank; a sandy beach

shātáng 沙糖 crystal sugar; granular sugar

shātǔ 沙土 sandy soil

shāwén zhǔyì 沙文主義 chauvinism

Shāwūdì Ālābó 沙烏地阿拉伯 Saudi Arabia

shāyǎ 沙啞 (said of the voice) hoarse; husky

shāyǎn 沙眼 trachoma

shāzhǐ 沙紙 sandpaper; emery paper

shāzhōu 沙洲 a shoal; a sand bar; a sandbank

shāzi 沙子 1. sand; grit 2. small grains; pellets

shā 杉

refer to **shān** 杉

shā 砂

1. sand; coarse sand; gravel 2. coarse—not smooth 3. infinitesimal

shābù 砂布 emery cloth; abrasive cloth

shājīn 砂金 gold dust; placer gold; alluvial gold

shālì 砂礫 gravel; pebbles

shātáng 砂糖 crude sugar; brown sugar

shātǔ 砂土 sandy soil

shāyǎn 砂眼 (medicine) trachoma

shāzhǐ 砂紙 sandpaper; emery paper

shā 紗

1. gauze; thin silk or cloth 2. yarn, as cotton yarn

shābù 紗布 1. gauze 2. a bandage

shāchuāng 紗窗 a window screen

shā 殺

1. to kill; to put to death; to slaughter 2. extremely; exceedingly 3. to weaken; to deflate 4. to fight

shāchóngjì 殺蟲劑 the insecticide

shādí 殺敵 to fight the enemy

shāfēngjǐng 殺風景 to spoil or ruin happiness

shāhài 殺害 to murder; to kill

shājī 殺雞警猴 to punish somebody as a warning to others

shājī qǔluǎn 殺雞取卵 to kill the hen to get eggs—a very foolish act

shājià 殺價 to reduce prices; to cut price down

S

shājùn 殺菌 disinfect; sterilize

shājùn 殺菌 refer to **shājùn** 殺菌

shālù 殺戮 to kill; to slay

shālüè 殺掠 to kill and plunder

shāqì 殺氣 1. (said of a sight or scene) a very severe or chilling appearance 2. a murderous atmosphere

shārén 殺人 to kill a person; to murder

shārén bù zhǎyǎn 殺人不眨眼 cold-blooded, hard-hearted, or very cruel

shārénfàn 殺人犯 a murderer; a homicide

shārén rúmá 殺人如麻 to have killed many people

shārén wèisuì 殺人未遂 an attempted murder

shārén yuèhuò 殺人越貨 to kill and rob

shārénzuì 殺人罪 homicide; murder

shāshāng 殺傷 to kill and wound

shāshēn chéngrén 殺身成仁 to sacrifice one's own life for justice

shāshēn zhīhuò 殺身之禍 a fatal disaster

shāshēng 殺生 killing

shāshǒu 殺手 a hit man; a killer

shātóu 殺頭 to behead

shātuì 殺退 to put to flight; to rout

shā 莎
a kind of insect

Shāshìbǐyà 莎士比亞 William Shakespeare

shā 煞
1. to tighten; to bind 2. to offset; to reduce; to mitigate 3. an auxiliary particle in old usage 4. to brake; to stop; to bring to a close

shāchē 煞車 1. to fasten goods on a truck or cart with ropes 2. to brake

shā 裟
a cassock or robe of a Buddhist monk

shā 鯊
a shark

shā 鎩
1. a lance 2. to shed (feathers)

shāyǔ 鎩羽 1. having shed feathers 2. discouraged; crestfallen; disheartened; defeated

shá 啥
refer to **shà** 啥

shǎ 傻
1. stupid; foolish; dumb 2. naive 3. stunned; stupefied; terrified 4. to think or work mechanically

shǎguā 傻瓜 a fool; a silly; a blockhead

shǎhēhē 傻呵呵 likable but stupid; silly appearance; simple-minded

shǎhuà 傻話 foolish talk; nonsense

shǎjìnr 傻勁兒 1. stupidity; foolishness 2. sheer enthusiasm; doggedness

shǎlishǎqi 傻裡傻氣 foolish-looking or acting foolishly

shǎtóu shǎ'nǎo 傻頭傻腦 1. foolish-looking 2. muddle-headed

shǎxiào 傻笑 to smirk; to laugh for no conceivable reason

shǎyǎn 傻眼 to be dumbfounded

shǎzi 傻子 an idiot; a blockhead

shà 啥 also **shá**
what

shàrén 啥人 (Shanghai dialect) who are you? Who is it (or there)?

shà 廈 also **xià**
a tall building; an edifice

shà 煞
1. a fierce god; a malignant deity; an evil spirit; a goblin 2. very; much; extremely 3. to bring to an end; to conclude

shàfèi kǔxīn 煞費苦心 to have made painstaking effort

shàfēngjǐng 煞風景 to spoil pleasure

shàshì 煞是 very (interesting, encouraging, etc.)

shàxīng 煞星 a malignant star —(usually said of a person) that brings wars, deaths, calamities, disasters

shāi 篩

1. a sieve; a screen; a sifter; a strainer 2. to sieve; to screen; to sift; to strain

shāixuǎn 篩選 screening; sieving; sifting

shāizi 篩子 a sieve; a sifter

shǎi 色

refer to **sè** 色 1

shǎi 骰 also **tóu**

1. dice 2. to dice

shài 殺

to degrade; to decline; to diminish; to abate

shài 曬

to expose to sunlight; to dry in the sun

shàigān 曬乾 to dry in the sun

shàihēi 曬黑 (said of skin) darkened by overexposure to the sun

shàitàiyáng 曬太陽 to be exposed to the sun

shàitú 曬圖 to make a blueprint; a blueprint

shān 山

a mountain; a hill

shān'ài 山隘 a mountain pass

shānbēng 山崩 a landslide; a landslip

shānbōshǔ 山撥鼠 a marmot

shānchuān 山川 mountains and rivers

shāndì 山地 a mountainous region

shāndiān 山巔 a mountaintop; a hilltop

shāndǐng 山頂 a mountaintop; a hilltop

Shāndōng 山東 Shandong Province

shāndòng 山洞 a cave; a tunnel; a grotto

shānfēng 山峰 a mountaintop

shānfù 山腹 the mid slope of a mountain

shān'gāng 山岡 a ridge; a mountain ridge

shān'gāo shuǐcháng 山高水長 (descriptive of the virtues of a great man) to be like lofty mountains and mighty streams

shān'gē 山歌 a mountaineers' song

shān'gōu 山溝 a gully; a ravine; a valley

shāngǔ 山谷 a dale; a ravine; a gorge

Shānhǎiguān 山海關 Shanhai Pass

shānhé 山河 mountains and rivers—(figuratively) the territory of a nation

shānhóng 山洪 mountain torrents

shānhóng bàofā 山洪暴發 A flood is unleashed from the mountains all of a sudden.

shānjī 山雞 a pheasant

shānjí 山脊 refer to **shānjǐ** 山脊

shānjǐ 山脊 a mountain ridge; a ridge

shānjiàn 山澗 mountain creeks

shānjiǎo 山脚 the foot of a mountain

shānlín 山林 1. a mountain forest 2. the place where a hermit lives

shānlíng 山陵 1. a plateau 2. an imperial tomb

shānlù 山路 a mountain path

shānlù 山麓 the foot of a mountain

shānluán 山巒 the chain of mountains with pointed peaks

shānmài 山脈 a mountain range; mountains

shānmāo 山貓 a wildcat; a lynx

shānméng hǎishì 山盟海誓 a vow between lovers that their mutual love will last as long as the mountain and the sea

shānmíng shuǐxiù 山明水秀 The mountains are bright and

the waters are fair. (descriptive of scenic beauty)

shānpō 山坡 a mountainside; a hillside

shānqióng shuǐjìn 山窮水盡 in a desperate situation

shānqiū 山丘 mountains and hills

shānqū 山區 a mountain area

shānquán 山泉 a mountain spring

shānrén 山人 a hermit; a recluse

shānshuǐ 山水 1. mountains and rivers 2. natural scenery; a landscape

shānshuǐhuà 山水畫 a landscape painting

Shānxī 山西 Shanxi Province

shānyá 山崖 a cliff

shānyáng 山羊 a goat

shānyāo 山腰 the mid-slope of a mountain

shānyě 山野 mountain villages and the remote wilderness

shānyuè 山岳 mountains

shānzhā 山楂 a hawthorn

shānzhài 山寨 a mountain fortress

shānzhēn hǎiwèi 山珍海味 a sumptuous repast

shānzhuāng 山莊 a country house, or villa, built in the mountains

shān 杉 also **shā**

the various species of fir and pine; a China fir

shān 刪

to delete; to take out; to erase

shānchú 刪除 to delete; to strike out

shāndìng 刪訂 to revise (an edition)

shān'gǎi 刪改 to remove superfluities and correct errors (in a writing)

shānjiǎn 刪減 to abridge or condense

shānjié 刪節 to abridge or condense

shānjiéhào 刪節號 ellipsis (a punctuation mark)

shān 姍

1. to ridicule; to laugh at 2. (said of a woman) to walk slowly

shānshān láichí 姍姍來遲 to walk or proceed slowly (and keep others waiting)

shān 衫

a shirt; a garment; a gown

shān 舢

a sampan

shānbǎn 舢板 a sampan

shānbǎn 舢舨 a sampan

shān 珊

1. coral 2. the tinkling of pendants

shānhújiāo 珊瑚礁 coral reefs

shān 扇

to fan; to instigate; to incite

shāndòng 扇動 to incite; to instigate

shānhuò 扇惑 to instigate and mislead; to agitate

shān 搧

1. to fan 2. to stir up; to incite 3. to slap on the face

shāndòng 搧動 to stir up; to incite; to agitate

shānfēng 搧風 to fan

shān 煽

1. to stir up; to instigate; to incite; to fan 2. flaming; blazing; to flame

shāndòng 煽動 to incite; to stir up (a strike, uprising, etc.)

shānhuǒ 煽火 to fan the fire

shān 潸

tears flowing; to weep

shānrán 潸然 tears falling

shān 羶(膻)

the odor of a sheep or goat

Shǎn 陝

short for Shaanxi Province

Shǎnxī 陝西 Shaanxi Province

shǎn 閃

1. to flash; a flash, as of lightning; a very brief glimpse 2. to

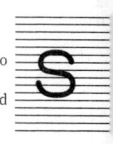

dodge; to evade; to avoid 3. to twist, strain or sprain (one's back, etc.) 4. to cast away; to leave behind

shǎnbì 閃避 to dodge quickly

shǎndiàn 閃電 1. to lighten 2. lightning 3. with lightning speed

shǎndòng 閃動 to move fast; to shine off and on

shǎnguāng 閃光 1. sparks; a flash 2. to flash; to sparkle

shǎnguāngdēng 閃光燈 a flashlight; a blinker

shǎnkai 閃開 to dodge quickly; to avoid (a hit, collision, etc.)

shǎnshēn 閃身 1. to dodge 2. sideways

shǎnshī 閃失 1. errors or mistakes 2. an accident

shǎnshuò 閃爍 1. to twinkle; twinkling; to scintillate 2. vague; evasive

shǎnshuò qící 閃爍其詞 to speak evasively

shǎnyāo 閃腰 to strain a muscle on the waist

shǎnyào 閃耀 to glint; to twinkle; to sparkle

shān 汕

a basket for catching fish

shàn 疝

hernia

shànqì 疝氣 hernia

shàn 扇

1. a fan 2. a numerary auxiliary for door or gate leaves

shànxíng 扇形 fan-shaped; a sector (of a circle)

shànzi 扇子 a fan

shàn 訕

1. to sneer at 2. to abuse 3. embarrassed; shamefaced

shànxiào 訕笑 to laugh or sneer at; to ridicule; to mock; to deride

shàn 善

1. good; virtuous; goodness; virtue 2. to be good at; to be skilled in 3. to perfect; to make a success of 4. to remedy; to

relieve 5. properly

shànbà gānxiū 善罷甘休 to stop quarrelling, fighting, etc. with others

shànbiàn 善變 changeable; fickle; capricious

shàndài 善待 to treat (a person) well

shàn'è 善惡 good and evil; virtue and vice

shàn'è bùfēn 善惡不分 to be unable to tell good from evil

shànhòu 善後 rehabilitation (after a disaster, a tragedy, etc.)

shànjǔ 善舉 a good deed

shànliáng 善良 (said of a person) kindhearted; well-disposed

shànnán xìnnǚ 善男信女 devotees of Buddha

shànshì 善事 good deeds; philanthropic acts

shànxīn 善心 a compassionate heart; kindness

shànxíng 善行 a good deed

shànyì 善意 1. good or kindly intentions 2. well-meaning

shànyǒu shànbào 善有善報 Kind deeds pay rich dividends to the doer.

shànyú 善於 to be good at; to be skilled in

shànzhōng 善終 to die a natural death

Shàn 單

a Chinese family name

shàn 擅

1. unauthorized; arbitrary 2. to monopolize; to take exclusive possession 3. to be good at; to be expert in

shàncháng 擅長 to excel in; to be good at

shàn'gǎi 擅改 to change or revise without authorization

shànyòng 擅用 to use without permission

shànzì 擅自 to do something without authorization

shànzì xíngdòng 擅自行動 to act presumptuously

shànzì zuòzhǔ 擅自作主

take an unauthorized action

shàn 禪

to abdicate (the throne)

shànràng 禪讓 to abdicate (the throne)

shàn 膳

meals; food; provisions

shànshí 膳食 meat; victuals

shànsù 膳宿 food and lodging

shànsùfèi 膳宿費 boarding charges

shàn 繕

1. to mend; to repair 2. to copy; to transcribe

shànxiě 繕寫 to transcribe; to copy neatly

shànxiū 繕修 to repair; to mend

shàn 贍

1. to provide; to supply 2. adequate; abundance; plenty

shànyǎng 贍養 to provide with means of support; to support

shànyǎngfèi 贍養費 alimony

shāng 商

1. commerce; trade; business 2. a merchant; a trader; a businessman 3. to discuss; to exchange views; to confer 4. (arithmetic) the quotient

shāngbiāo 商標 a trademark

shāngbiāocài 商標菜 brand dish

shāngbù 商埠 a commercial port

shāngchǎng 商場 a market place; a bazaar

shāngchuán 商船 a merchant-man

shāngdiàn 商店 a store; a shop

shāngdìng 商定 to decide or settle through discussions

shānggǎng 商港 a commercial port

shāngháng 商行 1. name of a shop or firm 2. a business firm

shānghào 商號 1. name of a shop or firm 2. a business firm

shāngjiè 商界 business circles

shāngkē 商科 a department of

commerce (in a college or university)

shāngliáng 商量 to exchange opinions or views; to confer

shāngpǐn 商品 merchandise; goods

shāngquè 商榷 to discuss and consider

shāngrén 商人 a merchant; a businessman

shāngshù 商數 (arithmetic) the quotient

shāngtán 商談 to exchange views

shāngtǎo 商討 a discussion; to discuss

shāngwù dàibiǎo 商務代表 a commercial representative

shāngxuéyuàn 商學院 the college of commerce

shāngyè 商業 commerce

shāngyì 商議 to discuss and debate

shāngzhǎn 商展 a trade fair

shāngzhuó 商酌 to exchange opinions or views; to confer

shāng 湯

(said of water) flowing

shāng 傷

1. a cut, wound, or injury 2. to cut or injure 3. grief; to grieve; distressed 4. to impede; an impediment 5. to hurt (feelings) 6. to make sick

shāngbā 傷疤 a scar; a bruise

shāngbēi 傷悲 grief; distress

shāngbīng 傷兵 wounded soldiers

shāngcán 傷殘 the wounded and disabled

shāngfēng 傷風 to catch cold; to have a cold

shāngfēng bàisú 傷風敗俗 to act immorally

shānggǎn 傷感 to be deeply moved or touched

shānggǎnqíng 傷感情 to hurt the feelings

shānghài 傷害 to hurt; to injure; to harm

shānghàizuì 傷害罪 (law)

S

injury

shānghán 傷寒 typhoid fever; typhus

shānghén 傷痕 a scar; a bruise

shānghuái 傷懷 a distressing mood; grief

shānghuàn 傷患 the sick and wounded

shāngkǒu 傷口 a wound

shāngnǎojīn 傷腦筋 1. to beat one's brains; to have a nut to crack 2. troublesome

shāngshén 傷神 1. to beat one's brains out 2. deeply hurt

shāngshì 傷勢 the condition of an injury (or a wound)

shāngtiān hàilǐ 傷天害理 to commit crimes

shāngtòng 傷痛 to mourn

shāngwáng 傷亡 casualties

shāngxīn 傷心 1. to hurt one's feelings; to break one's heart 2. very sad

shāng 裳

refer to **cháng** 裳

shāng 殤

1. to die young; to die prematurely 2. national mourning

shāng 觴

1. a general name of all sorts of wine vessels 2. to offer drinks to others

shǎng 上

shǎngshēng 上聲 falling-rising tone, one of the four tones in classical Chinese and the third tone in modern standard Chinese phonetics

shǎng 晌

1. high noon 2. a certain duration or interval of time 3. (Northeast China dialect) a day's work

shǎngwu 晌午 midday; (colloquial) high noon

shǎng 賞

1. to reward; to award; to bestow; to grant; to give to an inferior 2. a reward; an award 3. to appreciate; to enjoy; to

admire 4. (a polite expression) to be given the honor of...

shǎngcì 賞賜 to bestow money or presents on an inferior or junior

shǎngfá 賞罰 reward and punishment

shǎngguāng 賞光 (a polite expression) to honor me with your gracious presence or company

shǎngjīn 賞金 reward money; a bonus

shǎngqián 賞錢 tips (for waiters, servants, etc.)

shǎngshí 賞識 to appreciate the virtues in a person or thing

shǎngshì 賞識 refer to **shǎngshí** 賞識

shǎngwán 賞玩 to enjoy or appreciate the sight of; to delight in

shǎngxīn yuèmù 賞心悅目 to flatter the heart and please the eye—beautiful and restful

shǎngyuè 賞月 to enjoy moonlight

shàng 上

1. above 2. upper; upward; up 3. better; superior 4. previous; before 5. top; summit; on 6. to ascend; to mount; to board 7. to go to court

shàngbān 上班 to go to office; to go on duty

shàngbànchǎng 上半場 the first half (of a game)

shàngbànshēn 上半身 the upper part of the body

shàngbàntiān 上半天 the morning; the forenoon

shàngbànyè 上半夜 before midnight

shàngbànyuè 上半月 the first half of a month

shàngbǎng 上榜 to have one's name included in the name list of successful candidates of an examination

shàngbào 上報 1. to be published in newspapers 2. to report to a higher body; to report to one's boss

shàngbì 上臂 the upper arm

shàngbian 上邊 1. the upper side 2. up there

shàngbīn 上賓 distinguished guests

shàngcài 上菜 1. the best dishes 2. to place dishes on the table

shàngcāng 上蒼 Heaven; God

shàngcè 上策 the best stratagem (or plan)

shàngcéng 上層 the upper layer, level or stratum

shàngchǎng 上場 1. (drama) to go on stage; to enter 2. (sports) to enter the court

shàngchē 上車 to get on or into (a car, bus, truck or train)

shàngchuán 上船 to board a ship; to embark

shàngchuáng 上床 to go to bed

shàngcì 上次 last time; the previous occasion

shàngdàng 上當 to be taken in

shàngděng 上等 first-class; superior quality

shàngděngbīng 上等兵 private first class (PFC)

Shàngdì 上帝 God

shàngdiào 上弔 to commit suicide by hanging; to hang oneself

shàngduān 上端 the upper end

shàng'è 上顎 the palate

shàngfātiáo 上發條 to wind a watch, clock, mechanical toy, etc.

shàngfāng 上方 1. the place above 2. the celestial realm

shàngfén 上墳 to visit somebody's grave

shàngfēng 上風 1. the upper hand; advantage 2. windward

shànggōng 上工 to begin work

shànggōu 上鉤 1. (fishing) to be caught by the hook 2. to fall into the snare; to be tricked into doing something

shànggǔ 上古 prehistoric times

shàngguǐdào 上軌道 to get on the right track—to begin to work smoothly

shànghǎo 上好 superior; excellent; the best

shànghuí 上回 the previous occasion; last time

shànghuò 上貨 to load (ships, trucks, etc.)

shàngjí 上級 higher-ups; superiors

shàngjiāng 上漿 to starch (the laundry, etc.)

shàngjiàng 上將 (army, marine, and air force) full general; (navy) full admiral

shàngjiē 上街 1. to go into (or on) the street 2. to go shopping

shàngjiè 上屆 the previous (election, congress, conference, tour of duty, etc.)

shàngjìn 上進 to make progress; to advance

shàngjìngtóu 上鏡頭 1. photogenic 2. to appear in a movie

shàngkè 上課 (said of students) to attend class; (said of teachers) to conduct class

shàngkōngzhuāng 上空裝 a topless suit

shàngkǒu 上口 easy to read

shànglà 上蠟 waxing

shànglai 上來 Come up! Come out!

shànglěi 上壘 (baseball) to touch the base

shànglǐbài 上禮拜 last week

shàngliú 上流 1. the upper part of a stream 2. belonging to the upper circles

shàngliú shèhuì 上流社會 the upper class; the high society

shànglóu 上樓 to go upstairs

shànglù 上路 1. to start a journey 2. (slang) good; well-behaved

shàngmǎ 上馬 1. to mount a horse 2. to start (a project, etc.)

shàngmén 上門 to visit

shàngmian 上面 1. the top; above 2. the higher authorities

shàngniánjì 上年紀 getting on in years

shàngpǐn 上品 goods of superior quality

shàngpō 上坡 to climb a slope

shàngpōlù 上坡路 an ascending

road

shàngpù 上鋪 the upper berth

shàngqì bùjiē xiàqì 上氣不接下氣 to be out of breath

shàngqián 上前 to come forward

shàngqu 上去 to go up; to ascend

shàngrèn 上任 to take up an official appointment

shàngshān 上山 to go up a hill; to go to the mountains

shàngshàng xiàxià 上上下下 1. up and down 2. all; the whole

shàngshēn 上身 1. the torso; the upper part of the body 2. a blouse; a jacket 3. to wear 4. to contract a disease

shàngshēng 上升 to soar or rise

shàngshèng 上乘 1. a carriage drawn by a team of four horses 2. (Buddhism) the Great Conveyance 3. the best in quality

shàngshì 上士 (military rank) first sergeant

shàngshì 上市 (said of new products) to go on the market

shàngshū 上書 to present a petition

shàngshù 上述 the aforementioned

shàngsi 上司 a boss; a superior official

shàngsù 上訴 1. to appeal to a higher court 2. to state one's case to a superior

shàngsuàn 上算 a profitable deal; economical

shàngsuǒ 上鎖 to lock

shàngtái 上臺 1. to go on the stage 2. to assume office

shàngtáng 上膛 (said of a gun) to be loaded

shàngtiān 上天 1. Heaven; Providence; God 2. to go up into the sky

shàngtou 上頭 1. the top; above; up 2. the authorities

shàngwèi 上尉 (navy) lieutenant; (army and air force) captain

shàngwén 上文 the foregoing paragraphs or chapters

shàngwǔ 上午 forenoon; A.M.

shàngxià qíshǒu 上下其手 to distort facts to suit one's private ends

shàngxiàwén 上下文 the context

shàngxià yīxīn 上下一心 of one heart and mind

shàngxiàn 上限 the upper limit

shàngxiāng 上香 to offer incense

shàngxiào 上校 (army, marine, and air force) colonel; (navy) captain

shàngxīngqí 上星期 last week

shàngxīngqí 上星期 refer to **shàngxīngqí** 上星期

shàngxíngchē 上行車 the up train

shàngxíng xiàxiào 上行下效 The doings of superiors are imitated by inferiors.

shàngxuǎn 上選 the choicest

shàngxué 上學 to go to school

shàngxún 上旬 the first ten days of a month

shàngyǎn 上演 to perform; to stage (a play)

shàngyī 上衣 upper garments; jackets

Shàngyìyuàn 上議院 the Upper House; the Senate

shàngyǐn 上癮 to become addicted to a certain drug or habit

shàngyìng 上映 to show (a movie)

shàngyóu 上游 1. the upper reaches (of a river) 2. advanced position

shàngyuán 上元 the fifteenth of the first lunar month (which is the Lantern Festival in China)

shàngyuè 上月 last month

shàngzhǎng 上漲 (said of commodity prices or flood waters) to rise

shàngzhèn 上陣 1. to pitch into the work 2. to go to battle

shàngzhī 上肢 the upper limbs

shàngzhōu 上週 last week

shàngzhuāng 上裝 to make up (for a theatrical performance);

dress up (as an actor or a bride)

shàngzuò 上座 the seat of honor

shàng 尚
1. yet; still 2. to uphold; to honor; to esteem

shàngjiā 尚佳 passable; not too bad

shàngkě 尚可 1. passable; acceptable 2. still permissible; still possible

shàngqí 尚祈 I hope....; I pray....

shàngqiě 尚且 1. yet; still 2. even

shàngyǒu kěwéi 尚有可爲 still retrievable

shang 裳
refer to **cháng** 裳

shāo 捎
1. to carry; to take or bring along at one's convenience 2. to brush over lightly 3. to wipe out

shāo 梢
1. the tip of a branch or things of similar shape 2. the end of something—the result, etc. 3. the rudder

shāo 稍
1. slightly; a little; slight 2. somewhat; rather 3. gradually

shāoděng 稍等 to wait for a while (or moment)

shāohòu 稍後 shortly (or soon) afterward

shāohòu 稍候 to wait for a while (or moment)

shāowēi 稍微 slightly; a little; a bit

shāowēi 稍微 refer to **shāowēi** 稍微

shāoxí 稍息 At ease!

shāoxī 稍息 refer to **shāoxí** 稍息

shāoxǔ 稍許 slightly; a little; a bit

shāozòng jíshì 稍縱即逝 transient; fleeting

shāo 燒
1. to burn 2. to roast; to stew 3. to boil; to heat 4. to run a fever 5. a fever

shāobēi 燒杯 a beaker

shāobing 燒餅 a sesame seed cake

shāohuǐ 燒燬 to burn down; to destroy in fire

shāojiāo 燒焦 to scorch; to sear; to singe

shāojiǔ 燒酒 white spirits

shāokǎo 燒烤 to roast

shāoshā 燒殺 burning and killing; atrocities committed by enemy troops, bandits, etc.

shāoshāng 燒傷 burns

shāoshuǐ 燒水 to boil water; to heat water

shāosǐ 燒死 to burn to death

shāoxiāng 燒香 to burn joss sticks in worship

sháo 勺(杓)
a ladle; a spoon; a scoop

sháozi 勺子 a ladle; a spoon; a scoop

sháo 芍 also **shuò**
a peony

sháoyao 芍藥 a Chinese herbaceous peony

sháo 韶
1. the music during the time of the sage emperor Shun (**Shùn** 舜) 2. beautiful; excellent; harmonious 3. continuous

sháoguāng 韶光 1. beautiful scenes in the spring 2. best years of one's life—youth

shǎo 少
1. small or little (in number, quantity, or duration) 2. missing; lost 3. to stop; to quit

shǎobuliǎo 少不了 1. indispensable; cannot do without 2. unlikely to be lost

shǎoguǎn xiánshì 少管閒事 Mind your own business.

shǎojiàn 少見 seldom seen; unique; rare

shǎojiàn duōguài 少見多怪 to wonder much because one has seen little

shǎolái zhèyītào 少來這一套 Let's have no more of this.

shǎoliàng 少量 a small amount (or quantity); a little; a few

shǎoqǐng 少頃 a little while; a short while; a short time

shǎoshù 少數 1. a few; a small number (of) 2. minority

shǎoxǔ 少許 a little bit; a little; a sprinkling of

shǎoyǒu 少有 rare; scarce

shào 少

young; youthful; junior; juvenile

shàobù gēngshì 少不更事 young and inexperienced

shàofù 少婦 a young woman

shàojiàng 少將 major general (in the army, air force and marine corps); rear admiral (in the navy)

shàonǎinai 少奶奶 the wife of the young lord or master

shàonián 少年 1. a boy; a juvenile; a youth 2. young

shàonián fànzuì 少年犯罪 juvenile delinquency

shàonián lǎochéng 少年老成 young but competent

shàonǚ 少女 a young girl; a damsel

shàowèi 少尉 second lieutenant (in the army, air force or marine corps); ensign (in the navy)

shàoxiào 少校 major (in the army, air force and marine corps); lieutenant commander (in the navy)

shàoye 少爺 a young master (of a rich family); a young lord

shàozhuàng 少壯 young and energetic

shào 劭

1. to encourage; to urge 2. graceful; excellent; admirable; respectable

shào 邵

1. advanced, as age 2. a Chinese family name

shào 哨

1. a whistle 2. to patrol 3. an outpost; a guard station

shàobīng 哨兵 a sentinel or sentry

shàozi 哨子 a whistle

shào 紹

1. to bring together; to connect 2. to hand down; to continue

Shàoxīngjiǔ 紹興酒 the Shao-xing wine

shē 奢

1. extravagant; wasteful; lavish 2. excess; excessive 3. to exaggerate; to brag

shēchǐ 奢侈 luxury; wasteful; prodigal

shēhuá 奢華 showy; to be indulgent in luxurious and expensive habits

shēmí 奢靡 wasteful; lavish spending (of money)

shēwàng 奢望 to entertain hopes beyond one's ability to realize; a wild hope

shē 賒

1. to buy or sell on credit 2. distant; faraway 3. slow; slowly 4. to put off or postpone 5. luxurious or extravagant

shēdài 賒貸 credit

shēqiàn 賒欠 to buy on credit

shēzhàng 賒賬 to buy on account or credit

shé 舌

the tongue

shétāi 舌苔 fur (on the tongue)

shétou 舌頭 the tongue

shézhàn 舌戰 to debate with verbal confrontation

shé 折

1. to lose money; to fail in business 2. to break; to snap

shé 甚(什)

refer to **shén** 甚(什)

shé 蛇

a snake; a serpent

shéxiē 蛇蠍 snakes and scorpions—things to be dreaded

shéxíng 蛇行 1. to take a zigzag course 2. to creep along; to crawl

shě 舍(捨)

to throw away

shě 捨

1. to reject; to give up; to abandon; to relinquish; to renounce; to part with; to forsake; to let go 2. to give alms

shěběn zhúmò 捨本逐末 to concentrate on details but forget the main purpose or objective

shěbude 捨不得 reluctant to give up, let go, etc.

shěde 捨得 to be willing to part with (a person, thing, etc.)

shějǐ wèirén 捨己爲人 to give up one's own interests for the sake of others

shějìn qiúyuǎn 捨近求遠 to reject what is near at hand and seek for what is far away

shěmìng 捨命 in disregard of one's safety or life

shěqì 捨棄 to give up or renounce

shěshēn 捨身 to give up one's life

shěshēng qǔyì 捨生取義 to sacrifice oneself for righteousness

shè 社

1. the god of land 2. an association; an organization; a corporation; an agency 3. society; a community

shèhuì 社會 society; a community

shèhuì dìwèi 社會地位 social status; social position

shèhuì fúlì 社會福利 social welfare

shèhuì xīnwén 社會新聞 human interest stories or crime stories

shèjì 社稷 the god of land and the god of grain—a country

shèjiāo 社交 social intercourse; sociality

shèjiāowǔ 社交舞 social dancing; ballroom dancing

shèlùn 社論 an editorial

shèpíng 社評 an editorial

shèqū 社區 a community

shètuán 社團 an association; a corporation

shèyuán 社員 a member

shèzhǎng 社長 the president or director (of an association, newspaper, etc.)

shè 舍

1. a house 2. an inn 3. to halt; to stop; to rest 4. a self-depreciatory possessive pronoun for the first person singular in formal speech

shèjiān 舍間 my humble house

shèjiān 舍監 a dormitory superintendent

shèxià 舍下 my humble house

shè 拾

to go up; to ascend

shè 射

1. (also **shí**) to shoot 2. (also **shí**) to send out (light, heat, etc.) 3. archery 4. (also **yì**) Chinese musical term 5. (also **yè**) as in **púyè** 僕射, an official title in the Tang Dynasty

shèchéng 射程 a range (of the projectile)

shèjī 射擊 to shoot; shooting

shèjīchǎng 射擊場 a shooting range

shèjí 射擊 refer to **shèjī** 射擊

shèjíchǎng 射擊場 refer to **shèjīchǎng** 射擊場

shèjiàn 射箭 to shoot an arrow; archery

shèliè 射獵 hunting

shèmén 射門 (in soccer, etc.) to shoot or kick the ball toward the goal

shèshǒu 射手 an archer; a shooter

shèxiàn 射線 (physics) a ray

shèzhòng 射中 to hit (with a shot) the target

shè 涉

1. to wade 2. to cross 3. to experience 4. to involve; to entangle

shèjí 涉及 to involve; to relate to

shèliè 涉獵 to dabble in; to browse

shèshì wèishēn 涉世未深 inexperienced in affairs of the world

shèxián 涉嫌 to be involved (in a crime)

shèxiǎn 涉險 to adventure

shèzú 涉足 to set foot in

shèzú qíjiān 涉足其間 to set foot there

shè 赦

to pardon; to excuse; to forgive; an amnesty

shèmiǎn 赦免 to pardon (an offender)

shè 設

1. to lay out; to display 2. to establish; to set up; to found 3. to furnish; to provide 4. to arrange; to plan or devise 5. supposing that; in case of

shèbèi 設備 1. equipment 2. defense works

shèfǎ 設法 to think up a method; a way

shèfáng 設防 to fortify; to garrison

shèjì 設計 1. to map out a scheme 2. to design

shèjìzhě 設計者 the designer

shèlì 設立 to establish; to set up

shèshēn chǔdì 設身處地 to put oneself in another's position

shèshī 設施 1. to plan and execute 2. installations; facilities

shèxià quāntào 設下圈套 to set a snare

shèxiǎng 設想 1. an idea 2. to imagine; to think

shèyàn 設宴 to throw a banquet

shèzhì 設置 1. to establish; to set up; to found 2. establishment; installations

Shè 葉

used in names of places

shè 麝

a musk deer

shèxiāng 麝香 musk

shè 攝

1. to take in; to absorb 2. to attract 3. to take a photograph (or a shot) of 3. to regulate 4. to represent

shèqǔ 攝取 to take in; to absorb

shèshì wēndùjì 攝氏溫度計 a centigrade thermometer

shèyǐng 攝影 photography; to take a photograph of

shèyǐngjī 攝影機 a camera

shèyǐngpéng 攝影棚 a sound stage; a (movie) studio

shè 懾 also zhé

fearful; awe-struct

shèfú 懾服 to yield from fear

shéi 誰 also shuí

1. who 2. anyone; someone

shéishì shéifēi 誰是誰非 Who is right and who is wrong?

shēn 申

1. the ninth of the Twelve Terrestrial Branches 2. to appeal; to plead 3. to state; to set forth; to explain; to explicate 4. to extend; to expand 5. to inculcate (especially repeatedly) 6. a brief name of Shanghai

shēnbào 申報 to declare; to file (tax returns)

shēnbào hùkǒu 申報戶口 to report one's address for the domiciliary register

shēnbiàn 申辯 to argue; to contend

shēnchì 申斥 to reprimand; to rebuke

shēnfù 申覆 to reply to a superior

shēn'gào 申告 to appeal to a court of law

shēnjiè 申誡 a reprimand; a rebuke

shēnmíng 申明 to explain; to expound

shēnqǐng 申請 application

shēnqǐngrén 申請人 an applicant

shēnqǐngshū 申請書 an application form; a written request

shēnshí 申時 3-5 p.m.

shēnshù 申述 to state; to explain in detail

shēnsù 申訴 to appeal; to lodge a complaint

shēnyuān 申冤 to appeal for justice regarding a false charge

shēn 身
1. a body; a trunk 2. one's own person; oneself 3. a child in the womb 4. in person; personally

shēnbài mínglìe 身敗名裂 to lose both one's fortune and honor

shēnbiān 身邊 1. at (by) one's side; 2. (to have something) on one; with one

shēnbù yóuzhǔ 身不由主 unable to act according to one's own will; involuntarily

shēncái 身材 physique; physical build; figure

shēnduàn 身段 1. physique; a figure 2. postures (of a dancer, etc.)

shēnfen 身分 1. status; capacity; identity 2. dignity

shēnfenzhèng 身分證 a citizenship card; an identity card; an ID card

shēn'gāo 身高 stature; height

shēnhòu 身後 after one's death

shēnhuái liùjiǎ 身懷六甲 to be pregnant

shēnjiā diàochá 身家調查 the investigation of one's family background

shēnjiā qīngbái 身家清白 of respectable descent or parentage

shēnjià 身價 one's social position or prestige

shēnjià bǎibèi 身價百倍 to receive a tremendous boost in one's social position or prestige

shēnjiào 身教 to teach by personal example

shēnjīng bǎizhàn 身經百戰 have fought a hundred battles

shēnlín qíjìng 身臨其境 to experience personally; to be personally on the scene

shēnqū 身軀 a body; stature

shēnshang 身上 1. on one's body 2. (to have something) with one

shēnshì 身世 experiences in one's lifetime

shēnshǒu 身手 agility; dexterity; artistic skill

shēntǐ 身體 1. the body 2. health

shēntǐ jiǎnchá 身體檢查 a physical examination; a physical checkup

shēntǐ lìxíng 身體力行 to carry out by actual efforts

shēnwài zhīwù 身外之物 (literally) things that are not part of one's body—money; material wealth

shēnxīn jiànkāng 身心健康 sound in body and mind; physically and mentally healthy

shēnyùn 身孕 pregnancy

shēnzài fúzhōng bùzhī fú 身在福中不知福 Living in happiness, one often fails to appreciate what happiness really means.

shēnzi 身子 a body

shēn 伸
1. to stretch; to extend; to straighten 2. to report

shēnchū 伸出 to stretch outward

shēnkāi 伸開 to stretch out; to extend

shēnlǎnyāo 伸懶腰 to stretch and yawn

shēnshǒu 伸手 to reach out one's hand

shēnsuō 伸縮 to expand and contract

shēnsuōxìng 伸縮性 flexibility; elasticity

shēntóu tànnǎo 伸頭探腦 to crane, or stretch the neck in an effort to find out

shēnzhǎn 伸展 to stretch; to spread out

shēnzhāng 伸張 to expand (power)

shēn 呻
to groan; to moan

shēnyín 呻吟 to groan; to moan

shēn 莘 also **xīn**
1. long 2. numerous

shēnshēn xuézǐ 莘莘學子 students in large numbers

shēn 紳
1. the middle class as a group or individuals; the gentry; a gentle-

man 2. a sash; a girdle 3. to tie

shēnshāng 紳商 the gentry and merchant class

shēnshì 紳士 a gentleman; an esquire

shēn 深

1. deep; depth 2. profound; mysterious; difficult 3. close; intimate 4. very

shēn'àn 深黯 dark; dark and obscure

shēn'ào 深奧 deep; abstruse; profound

shēnbiǎo tóngqíng 深表同情 to express deep sympathy

shēnbù kěcè 深不可測 extremely abstruse; unfathomable

shēncáng bùlù 深藏不露 Real knowledge is not showy.

shēncháng 深長 profound meaning (significance, etc.)

shēnchén 深沈 1. dark 2. (said of a person) impenetrable; unfathomable; calm

shēnchóu 深仇 deep animosity or hatred

shēnchóu dàhèn 深仇大恨 a deep-seated hatred

shēnchù 深處 the deep, inner or obscure part (of woods, heart, etc.)

shēndé mínxīn 深得民心 to win strong popular support; well-received

shēndù 深度 1. depth (of a river, box, tank, etc.) 2. profundity (of learning, etc.) 3. understanding (of the ways of the world); sophistication

shēn'gǎn 深感 to feel keenly or deeply

shēn'gēng bànyè 深更半夜 deep in the night; midnight

shēngōng 深宮 the forbidden palace; the harem

shēnhòu 深厚 1. long and close (friendship, relationship, etc.) 2. profound (learning, training, etc.) 3. deep-seated; solid

shēnhūxī 深呼吸 to breathe deeply

shēnjiāo 深交 long, intimate

friendship

shēnjiū 深究 to study, deliberate, search or delve into something deeply

shēnjiù 深究 refer to **shēnjiū** 深究

shēnjū jiǎnchū 深居簡出 to lead a secluded life

shēnkè 深刻 1. profound significance 2. penetrating (views, comments, etc.)

shēnmíng dàyì 深明大義 to forget self-interest in the face of an event of great significance

shēnmóu yuǎnlǜ 深謀遠慮 to think and plan far ahead; foresight

shēnqiǎn 深淺 1. deep or shallow; depth 2. (said of colors) deep or light 3. (good or evil) intentions

shēnqiè 深切 deeply; sincerely; intensely

shēnqíng 深情 deep affection or love

shēnqiū 深秋 late fall; late autumn

shēnrù 深入 (to research, study, delve, etc.) deeply or thoroughly into something; to reach or penetrate deep (into enemy territory)

shēnrù qiǎnchū 深入淺出 to explain in everyday language the results of a profound study, etc.

shēnrù rénxīn 深入人心 to impress deeply upon everyone's mind

shēnshān 深山 deep in the mountain

shēnsī 深思 deep thought; contemplation; to think deeply

shēnsī shúlǜ 深思熟慮 to think and contemplate thoroughly; to ponder

shēnsuì 深邃 deep and far; profound and abstruse

shēnxìn 深信 to believe strongly; firmly convinced

shēnxìn bùyí 深信不疑 to believe without a shadow of doubt

shēnxǐng 深省 to make a thorough self-examination

shēnyè 深夜 deep in the night

shēnyì 深意 deep or abstruse meaning

shēnyuān 深淵 an abyss

shēnyuǎn 深遠 deep and far (in meaning, significance, etc.)

shēnzào 深造 to pursue advanced study

shēnzhī 深知 to know thoroughly; to realize fully

shēnzhì 深摯 close or intimate (friendship, etc.); deep (affection); sincere

shēn 參

1. name of a star 2. a ginseng

shén 甚(什) also shé

what

shénme 甚麼 what

shén 神

1. gods; deities; immortals; spiritual beings 2. soul; mind; spirit 3. appearances; looks; expressions; airs 4. supernatural; marvelous; wondrous; miraculous; mysterious; mystical 5. smart; clever

shénbù shǒushè 神不守舍 out of one's wits; delirious

shénbùzhī, guǐbùjué 神不知, 鬼不覺 extremely stealthy

shéncǎi 神采 a countenance; a look; an expression

shéncǎi yìyì 神采奕奕 1. in high spirits 2. glowing with health and radiating vigor

shénchū guǐmò 神出鬼沒 to appear and disappear quite unpredictably like gods and demons

shéndiàn 神殿 a sanctuary

shénfu 神父 a Catholic father

shénhuà 神化 to deify

shénhuà 神話 a myth; mythology

shénhún diāndǎo 神魂顛倒 to be held spell-bound; to be infatuated

shénjī miàosuàn 神機妙算 1. stratagems so wonderful that they seem to be conceived by divine beings 2. wonderful foresight

shénjīng 神經 nerve

shénjīngbìng 神經病 1. neurosis; mental disorder 2. a neurotic

shénjīng cuòluàn 神經錯亂 mental disorder

shénjīng guòmǐn 神經過敏 1. excessively sensitive 2. (medicine) hyperaesthesia

shénjīngzhí 神經質 refer to **shénjīngzhì** 神經質

shenjīngzhì 神經質 nervosity

shénkān 神龕 a sanctuary

shénmì 神祕 mysterious; mystical; mystery

shénmiào 神妙 marvelous; wondrous

shénmiào 神廟 a temple of the gods

shénmíng 神明 the gods; deities; divinities

shénqí 神奇 marvelous; miraculous

shénqí 神祇 the gods; the spirits

shénqi 神氣 1. divine atmosphere 2. dignified; imposing 3. to put on airs

shénqi huóxiàn 神氣活現 as proud as a peacock

shénqiāngshǒu 神槍手 a sharpshooter; a marksman

shénqíng 神情 an appearance; an air

shénsè zìruò 神色自若 to look unperturbed

shénshèng 神聖 holy; sacred; divine

shénsì 神似 lifelike; to be alike in spirit

shénsù 神速 marvelously fast

shénsuǐ 神髓 essence; quintessence

shéntài 神態 looks; appearances; facial expressions

shéntōng guǎngdà 神通廣大 possessing marvelous abilities

shéntóng 神童 a child prodigy

shénwǎng 神往 to have one's thoughts or imagination absorbed in some wonderful thing or place

shénxian 神仙 an immortal; a celestial being

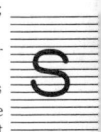

S

shénxiàng 神像 1. an image of a dead person 2. an idol

shénxiào 神效 marvelous effect

shénxuéyuàn 神學院 a seminary (for training priests or ministers)

shényī 神醫 a marvelous physician

shényǒng 神勇 extraordinarily brave

shényóu 神遊 to tour (a place) by imagination

shényùn 神韻 1. (said of a person) an appearance and a carriage; an air 2. (said of paintings or calligraphic works) poetic quality

shénzhí rényuán 神職人員 the clergy

shénzhì bùqīng 神志不清 unconscious; in a state of a coma

shénzhì bùqīng 神智不清 muddleheaded

Shěn 沈
a Chinese family name

shěn 審
1. to examine; to review; to investigate 2. to know; to discern; to appreciate 3. cautious 4. really; indeed

shěn'àn 審案 to hold court trial

shěnchá 審查 to examine; to review

shěnchá 審察 to examine; to review

shěndìng 審定 to authorize (a publication, etc.)

shěndìng 審訂 to examine and revise

shěnhé 審核 to examine and consider

shěnjì 審計 1. an audit 2. to audit

Shěnjìbù 審計部 Ministry of Audit

shěnlǐ 審理 to try; to hear

shěnměiguān 審美觀 esthetic sense (or notions)

shěnpàn 審判 1. to try (a case or person in a law court) 2. a trial

shěnshèn 審慎 cautious; careful

shěnwèn 審問 to hold a hearing (on a legal case); to interrogate a prisoner

shěnxùn 審訊 to hold a hearing (on a legal case); to interrogate a prisoner

shěnyì 審議 consideration; deliberation

shěnyuè 審閱 to examine; to review

shěn 嬸
1. an aunt (the wife of one's father's younger brother) 2. a sister-in-law (the wife of one's husband's younger brother)

shěn 瀋
1. juice; fluid; liquid; water 2. short for Shenyang (Mukden), capital of Liaoning Province

Shěnyáng 瀋陽 Mukden (Shenyang), capital of Liaoning Province

shèn 甚
1. to a great extent; to a high degree; very; exceedingly 2. more than

shèn'ér 甚而 so much so that...

shènwéi bùjiě 甚為不解 much perplexed; completely at a loss

shènxiāo chénshàng 甚囂塵上 widely reported or speculated

shènyú 甚於 (to be worse, harder, better, etc.) than...

shènzhì 甚至 even to the extent that...; even; to go so far as...

shèn 腎
1. the kidneys 2. the testicles

shènjiéshí 腎結石 (pathology) kidney stone; nephrolithiasis

shènzàng 腎臟 the kidneys

shènzàngbìng 腎臟病 a kidney ailment or disease

shèn 慎
cautious; careful; scrupulous; prudent

shènmì 慎密 meticulous

shènzhòng 慎重 cautious; careful; prudent; discreet

shènzhòng qíshì 慎重其事 to do something in a serious man-

shèn 滲

to permeate; to percolate; to infiltrate; to seep; to ooze

shènchū 滲出 to seep out; to ooze out

shènrù 滲入 1. to permeate; to seep into 2. (said of influence, etc.) to penetrate

shèntòu 滲透 to seep through; to permeate

shēng 升

1. to rise; to raise; to ascend 2. to advance; to promote 3. a unit of volume measurement (especially for grain)

shēngdǒu xiǎomín 升斗小民 those who live from hand to mouth

shēnggé 升格 to promote; to upgrade

shēngguān fācái 升官發財 to attain high ranks and acquire great wealth

shēngjí 升級 1. (said of an official) to be promoted 2. (school) to advance to a higher grade

shēngjiàng 升降 to rise and fall

shēngjiàngjī 升降機 an elevator; a lift

shēngpíng 升平 peace and prosperity

shēngqí 升旗 to hoist a flag

shēngqiān 升遷 promotion

shēngtiān 升天 1. to ascend to heaven—to die 2. (Christianity) the Ascension

shēngxué 升學 to enter a higher school

shēngxué kǎoshì 升學考試 an entrance examination for a higher school

shēngzhí 升值 (economics) 1. to revalue 2. to appreciate

shēng 生

1. to live; life; living; alive 2. to be born; to come into being or existence 3. to breed; to bear; to beget; to produce 4. unripe; raw; uncooked 5. unfamiliar; strange 6. savage; untamed; barbarian 7. a pupil; a student 8. the male

character type in Chinese opera 9. creatures

shēngbìng 生病 to get sick; to fall ill

shēngbù féngchén 生不逢辰 to be born at a wrong time; unlucky

shēngcái yǒudào 生財有道 to be expert in making money

shēngcài 生菜 raw vegetables; salad

shēngchǎn 生產 1. to produce 2. to give birth to

shēngchǎn jìshù 生產技術 production technique

shēngchǎnlì 生產力 productivity

shēngchǎnlǜ 生產率 the production rate

shēngchǎnxiàn 生產線 production line

shēngchén 生辰 birthday

shēngchī 生吃 to eat (something) raw

shēngcún 生存 to survive; survival; existence

shēngcún kōngjiān 生存空間 living space; lebensraum

shēngdòng 生動 vivid; lively; lifelike

shēng'ér yùnǚ 生兒育女 to give birth to children and rear them

shēngfàyóu 生髮油 refer to **shēngfàyóu** 生髮油

shēngfàyóu 生髮油 hair tonic

shēnghuā miàobǐ 生花妙筆 ability for exquisite writing

shēnghuán 生還 to come back alive; to survive

shēnghuánzhě 生還者 a survivor

shēnghuó 生活 1. life 2. to live

shēnghuó bìxūpǐn 生活必需品 necessities of life

shēnghuó fāngshì 生活方式 the ways of living

shēnghuófèi 生活費 living expenses

shēnghuó shuǐzhǔn 生活水準 the standard of living

shēnghuǒ 生火 to make a fire;

to build a fire

shēngjī 生機 1. liveliness 2. the chance of survival

shēngjì 生計 livelihood; living

shēngjiāng 生薑 green ginger

shēnglái 生來 by nature; inborn

shēnglěng 生冷 (said of food) uncooked and cold

shēnglí sǐbié 生離死別 separation in life and parting at death —the bitterest sorrows to man

shēnglǐ 生理 physiological functions and processes; physiology

shēnglǐ shízhōng 生理時鐘 biological clock

shēnglìjūn 生力軍 a vital new force

shēnglíng tútàn 生靈塗炭 The people are suffering from extreme privation (during wartime).

shēnglóng huóhǔ 生龍活虎 (like) a live dragon or a live tiger—full of vigor and vitality

shēnglù 生路 1. a way to make a living; a way to survive 2. a strange road

shēngmǐ zhǔchéng shúfàn 生米煮成熟飯 What is done cannot be undone.

shēngmìng 生命 life

shēngmìnglì 生命力 vitality

shēngmìngxiàn 生命線 a lifeline (in a figurative sense)

shēngpà 生怕 very anxious; very apprehensive

shēngpíjiǔ 生啤酒 draught beer

shēngpíng 生平 1. one's brief biographical sketch 2. in the course of life

shēngqì 生氣 1. vitality; liveliness 2. to get angry; to get mad

shēngqì péngbó 生氣蓬勃 vigorous; active; lively

shēngqián 生前 before one's death

shēngqù 生趣 the pleasure of life

shēngri 生日 birthday

shēngsè 生澀 (said of a piece of writing) difficult to read or understand

shēngshēn fùmǔ 生身父母 real parents (as distinct from foster parents)

shēngshēng bùxī 生生不息 to breed in endless succession

shēngshēng bùxí 生生不息 refer to **shēngshēng bùxī** 生生不息

shēngshǒu 生手 a beginner; a novice

shēngshū 生疏 unfamiliar; unskilled

shēngshuǐ 生水 unboiled water

shēngsī 生絲 raw silk

shēngsǐ guāntóu 生死關頭 life-and-death crisis

shēngsǐ zhījiāo 生死之交 deep friendship

shēngtài 生態 the relations and interactions between organisms and their environment, including other organisms

shēngtiě 生鐵 pig iron; crude iron

shēngtūn huóbō 生吞活剝 to use someone's ideas without fully understanding them

shēngwù 生物 1. a living thing 2. biology

shēngwùjiè 生物界 the biological world

shēngwùxué 生物學 biology

shēngwùzhōng 生物鐘 biological clock

shēngxiào 生效 to go into effect

shēngxìng 生性 natural disposition; nature

shēngxiù 生銹 to rust

shēngyá 生涯 1. a career; a life 2. livelihood

shēngyí 生疑 to become suspicious

shēngyì 生意 vitality

shēngyi 生意 business; trade

shēngyù 生育 to give birth to; to bear

shēngzhǎng 生長 to grow; to develop; growth

shēngzhí 生殖 (biology) reproduction

S

shēngzhíqì 生殖器 reproductive organs; genitals

shēngzì 生字 a new word; an unfamiliar word

shēng 昇

1. to ascend 2. peace; peaceful

shēnggé 昇格 to elevate status; elevation of status

shēnghuá 昇華 1. (chemistry) to sublime 2. the rising of things to a higher level

shēngjí 昇級 to promote

shēngjiàng 昇降 promotion and demotion

shēngjiàngjī 昇降機 an elevator

shēngpíng 昇平 time of peace

shēng 牲

1. domestic animals 2. animal sacrifice

shēngchù 牲畜 livestock

shēng 笙

a kind of panpipe with 13 reeds

shēnggē 笙歌 music and songs

shēng 甥

1. a nephew (son of a sister) 2. a son-in-law who assumes one's own name and lives under one's own roof

shēngnǚ 甥女 a niece (daughter of a sister)

shēng 勝

refer to **shèng** 勝 6

shēng 聲

1. sound; voice; a tone 2. music 3. language; a tongue 4. reputation; fame 5. to make known

shēngchēng 聲稱 to assert; to declare

shēngdài 聲帶 vocal cords

shēngdiào 聲調 1. tone; note 2. the tone of a Chinese character

shēngdiéjī 聲碟機 a compact disc player

shēngdōng jīxī 聲東擊西 (literally) to make noise in the east while striking in the west—feigning tactics

shēngdōng jíxī 聲東擊西 refer to **shēngdōng jīxī** 聲東擊西

shēnglèi jùxià 聲淚俱下 to cry while speaking

shēngmíng 聲明 to announce; to declare

shēngmíng lángjí 聲名狼藉 a notorious reputation

shēngshì hàodà 聲勢浩大 an impressive display of power or influence

shēngsī lìjié 聲嘶力竭 The voice gets husky as a result of exhaustion.

shēngtǎo 聲討 to condemn or attack (a rebel, traitor, etc.) by words

shēngwàng 聲望 fame; reputation; prestige

shēngxiǎng 聲響 1. sound; noise 2. reputation

shēngyīn 聲音 a sound; a voice

shēngyuán 聲援 to give moral support

shēngyuè 聲樂 vocal music

shēngyuèjiā 聲樂家 a vocalist

shēngzhāng 聲張 to make known; to announce

shéng 繩

1. a rope; a cord; a line 2. to restrain 3. to rectify; to correct

shéngsuǒ 繩索 a rope; a line; a cord

shéngtī 繩梯 a rope ladder

shéngzhī yǐfǎ 繩之以法 to prosecute according to the law

shéngzi 繩子 a rope; a line; a cord

shěng 省

1. a province; provincial 2. economical; frugal; to economize 3. to save 4. to omit; to reduce; to abridge

shěngchī jiǎnyòng 省吃儉用 frugal and thrifty

shěngdào 省道 a provincial highway

shěngde 省得 1. lest 2. to avoid; to save (trouble, etc.)

shěngfèn 省份 a province

shěnghuì 省會 a provincial capital

S

shěngjiè 省界 provincial boundaries

shěnglì 省力 to save energy or labor

shěnglì xuéxiào 省立學校 a provincial school

shěnglüè 省略 to omit; to abridge; omission

shěngqián 省錢 to save money; economical

shěngquè 省卻 to avoid (trouble, etc.); to save (time, etc.)

shěngshí 省時 to save time; timesaving

shěngshì 省事 1. to save trouble 2. easy

shěngxià 省下 to save (money)

shěngyìhuì 省議會 the provincial assembly

shěngyìyuán 省議員 a provincial assemblyman

shěngzhèngfǔ 省政府 the provincial government

shěngzhǔxí 省主席 the governor of a province

shèng 乘

1. historical records 2. an ancient carriage 3. Buddhist teaching—a conveyance to bring the truth to men and help them 4. a team of four horses

shèng 盛

1. abundant; rich; exuberant; flourishing; prosperous 2. (said of fire, storm, etc.) to rage

shèngchǎn 盛產 to abound in; to be rich in

shèngdà 盛大 grand; magnificent; majestic

shèngdiǎn 盛典 a grand occasion; a big ceremony

shènghuì 盛會 a grand gathering; a magnificent assembly

shèngjí yīshí 極盛一時 to be in vogue for a time

shèngkāi 盛開 in full bloom

shèngkuàng kōngqián 盛況空前 unprecedented in grandeur, festivity, etc.

shèngmíng 盛名 a glorious name; great reputation

shèngmíng zhīlěi 盛名之累 the trouble of being a famous personality

shèngnù 盛怒 in great anger; wrath

shèngqì língrén 盛氣凌人 to treat others rudely through arrogance

shèngqíng 盛情 warm thoughtfulness; utmost sincerity

shèngqíng nánquè 盛情難卻 It is hard to turn down the offer made with such warm-heartedness.

shèngshì 盛世 a prosperous age or period

shèngshuāi róngrǔ 盛衰榮辱 prosperity and decline; glory and humiliation

shèngxià 盛夏 midsummer

shèngxíng 盛行 to be popular or in vogue

shèngyàn 盛宴 a grand banquet

shèngzhuāng 盛裝 in full dress; in rich attire

shèng 剩

to remain; to be left over; in excess; residues; remainder; surplus; remains

shèngfàn 剩飯 leftover rice

shènghuò 剩貨 leftover goods; leftovers

shèngxia 剩下 the remainder; to be left over

shèngyú 剩餘 the surplus

shèng 勝

1. to win; to excel; to triumph; to surpass; to get the better of 2. victory; success 3. (sports) a win 4. a scenic view; a place of natural beauty 5. excellent; distinctive; wonderful 6. (also **shēng**) to be competent enough (for a task)

shèngdì 勝地 famous scenic spot

shèngfù 勝負 victory and defeat; the outcome (of a contest); success or failure

shèngguò 勝過 to excel; to surpass

shènglì 勝利 1. victory 2. successfully

shèngrèn 勝任 competent; quali-

fied; equal to

shèngsù 勝訴 to win a lawsuit

shèngsuàn 勝算 to be sure of success; odds or advantages (in a contest)

shèngzhàng 勝仗 a victorious battle; a victory

shèng 聖
1. a sage 2. sacred; holy

shèngdànhóng 聖誕紅 a poinsettia

Shèngdànjié 聖誕節 Christmastide; Christmastime

Shèngdànkǎ 聖誕卡 a Christmas card

Shèngdàn Lǎorén 聖誕老人 Santa Claus

Shèngdànshù 聖誕樹 a Christmas tree

shèngdì 聖地 a holy ground

shèngjié 聖潔 holy and immaculate

Shèngjīng 聖經 the Bible

shèngrén 聖人 a sage; a saint

Shèngshàng 聖上 His Majesty

shèngtú 聖徒 an apostle; a saint

shèngxián 聖賢 sages and virtuous men; saints

shèngzhǐ 聖旨 an imperial decree

shī 尸
1. a corpse 2. to preside; to direct

shīwèi sùcān 尸位素餐 to neglect the duties of an office while taking the pay

shī 失
1. to let slip; to neglect; to miss 2. to lose 3. an omission; a mistake

shībài 失敗 to fail; a failure; a defeat

shīcè 失策 poor tactic or strategy

shīcháng 失常 off form; to perform below one's normal capacity

shīchǒng 失寵 to be in disgrace

shīchuán 失傳 lost (arts, skills, etc.)

shīdàng 失當 improper; improperly

shīdiào 失掉 to lose (a chance, confidence, etc.)

shī'ér fùdé 失而復得 to be lost and found again

shīhé 失和 (said of a couple) to be on bad terms; to be at loggerheads

shīhù 失怙 to lose one's father; to be orphaned

shīhún luòpò 失魂落魄 despondent; listless

shīhuǒ 失火 to catch fire

shījìn 失禁 incontinence

shījìng 失敬 Excuse me for being disrespectful.

shīkòng 失控 out of control; runaway

shīlǐ 失禮 to be impolite; impropriety

shīlì 失利 to suffer a defeat (or setback)

shīliàn 失戀 to be jilted; to lose one's love

shīlíng 失靈 (said of a machine, instrument, etc.) to be out of order

shīluò 失落 to lose

shīmián 失眠 to suffer from insomnia; insomnia

shīmíng 失明 to become blind; blind

shīpéi 失陪 Please excuse me for not being able to keep you company for the moment.

shīqiè 失竊 to be stolen

shīqù 失去 to lose

shīsàn 失散 lost and scattered

shīsè 失色 to lose color; to turn pale

shīshēn 失身 1. to lose chastity 2. to incur danger

shīshēng 失聲 to lose one's voice for crying too much

shīshì 失事 an accident; to meet with an accident

shīshì 失恃 to lose one's mother

shīshì 失勢 to lose one's position, authority, influence, etc.

shīshǒu 失手 to break something or hurt somebody by acci-

S

dent; to slip

shīshǒu 失守 1. to fail to fulfill one's duty 2. (said of a city, territory, etc.) to fall into the hands of the enemy

shīsuàn 失算 to miscalculate

shītài 失態 to misbehave

shītiáo 失調 1. maladjustment 2. to be careless about one's health, etc.

shīwàng 失望 disappointment

shīwù 失誤 an error; an omission

shīwù zhāolǐng 失物招領 lost items or articles (found by others) kept for claimants

shīxiàn 失陷 (said of cities, territory, etc.) to fall to the enemy

shīxiào 失效 1. (law) to be invalidated; null and void 2. (said of medicines, etc.) to lose potency or efficacy

shīxiào 失笑 cannot help laughing

shīxiě 失血 refer to **shīxuè** 失血

shīxìn 失信 to break one's word or promise

shīxué 失學 to lack formal schooling or education

shīxuè 失血 to lose blood

shīyán 失言 to say what should not be said; an improper pronouncement, remark, etc.

shīyè 失業 to lose one's job; jobless

shīyì 失意 disappointed; frustrated

shīyuē 失約 1. to break one's promise 2. to break a date or an appointment

shīzhī háolí, chāzhī qiānlǐ 失之毫釐，差之千里 A slight mistake will result in a great error in the end.

shīzhī jiāobì 失之交臂 to miss (a person or chance) at very close range

shīzhí 失職 to be delinquent

shīzhǔ 失主 (law) the owner of lost property or the victim of a robbery, burglary, etc.

shīzōng 失蹤 missing

shīzú 失足 1. to slip; to lose one's

footing 2. to commit a mistake

shī 虱

a louse

shīmùyú 虱目魚 a milkfish

shī 施

1. to act; to do; to make 2. to bestow; to grant; to give (alms, etc.) 3. to apply 4. a Chinese family name

shī'ēn 施恩 to give favors to others

shīfàng 施放 to discharge; to fire

shīféi 施肥 to apply fertilizers

shīgōng 施工 to start construction or building

shījiā 施加 to exert; to bring to bear on

shījiù 施救 to rescue and resuscitate

shīshě 施捨 to give to charity

shīxǐ 施洗 to baptize

shīxíng 施行 1. (law) to enforce; to execute 2. to perform

shīxíng xìzé 施行細則 bylaws

shīyòng 施用 to use; to employ

shīyǔ 施與 to give to the poor; to give to charity

shīzhǎn 施展 to display (one's feat, talent, skill, etc.)

shīzhèng 施政 (government) to administer; to govern

shī 屍

a corpse; a carcass

shīgǔ 屍骨 the skeleton of a corpse

shīshēn 屍身 a corpse; remains

shītǐ 屍體 a corpse; remains

shī 師

1. a divison in the Chinese army 2. an army 3. a model; an example 4. a teacher; a tutor 5. to teach 6. to pattern or model after another 7. a specialist (of painting, music, etc.) 8. a local administrative chief

shībiǎo 師表 a model worthy of emulation

shīchéng 師承 to have learned under (especially referring to a

particular school of learning)

shīchū wúmíng 師出無名 to fight a war without a just cause

shīfǎ 師法 1. to pattern after; to imitate 2. methods taught by one's teacher

shīfàn dàxué 師範大學 a normal university

shīfàn jiàoyù 師範教育 normal education

shīfàn xuéyuàn 師範學院 a normal college

shīfù 師父 1. tutors; masters; teachers 2. a respectful term of address for monks, nuns, etc.

shīfu 師傅 1. (collectively) teachers; masters; tutors 2. the tutors of a king 3. a polite term of address for an artisan as a carpenter, cook, etc.

shīmén 師門 a school or sect founded by a master

shīmǔ 師母 the wife of one's tutor, teacher or master

shīniáng 師娘 the wife of one's tutor, teacher or master

shīqí gùzhì 師其故智 to copy an old method

shīshēng 師生 teachers and students

shīshì 師事 to serve and respect (another) as one's teacher

shītú 師徒 the master and his student(s)

shīxīn zìyòng 師心自用 conceited; opinionated

shīzhǎng 師長 1. one's teachers; faculty members 2. a division commander

shīzhàng 師丈 the husband of one's teacher

shīzī 師資 1. teachers 2. the qualifications of a teacher

shī 獅

the lion

shīzi 獅子 a lion

shīzibí 獅子鼻 a snub nose

shīzigǒu 獅子狗 a poodle

Shīzihuì 獅子會 International Association of Lions Clubs

shīzitóu 獅子頭 stewed meatballs

Shīzizuò 獅子座 (astronomy) Leo

shī 詩

1. poetry; poems; poetic 2. anything or quality as an offspring of pure imagination 3. short for *The Book of Odes* edited by Confucius

shīgē 詩歌 1. poems and songs collectively 2. poetry

shījí 詩集 a collection of poems

shījù 詩句 a stanza or line in a poem

shīpiān 詩篇 poems

shīqíng huàyì 詩情畫意 (said of a landscape) idyllic

shīrén 詩人 a poet

shīxuǎn 詩選 a selection of poems

shīyì 詩意 the poetic quality; the romantic atmosphere

shīyùn 詩韻 1. rhyme of verses 2. a rhyme book

shī 濕

damp; moist; wet; humid; to get wet

shīdù 濕度 humidity

shīlínlín 濕淋淋 dripping wet; drenched

shīqì 濕氣 humidity; dampness; moisture

shīrùn 濕潤 damp; to moisten

shīzhěn 濕疹 eczema

shí 十

1. ten; the tenth 2. complete; completely; perfect; perfectly; extremely

shí'è bùshè 十惡不赦 guilty of unpardonable evil

shí'èryuè 十二月 1. December 2. twelve months 3. the twelfth month of the lunar calendar

shí'èr zhǐcháng 十二指腸 a duodenum

shífēn 十分 1. completely 2. very 3. 10 points

shíliùkāi 十六開 sixteenmo

shíná jiǔwěn 十拿九穩 to be very sure of

shíquán shíměi 十全十美 perfect; complete

S

shísāndiǎn 十三點 (slang) silly

shísìhángshī 十四行詩 (Western poetry) the sonnet

shíwàn bāqiān lǐ 十萬八千里 to be poles apart

shíwàn huǒjí 十萬火急 1. to be in posthaste 2. Most Urgent (as a mark on dispatches)

shíwèi 十位 (arithmetic) the tens place

shíxiàng yùndòng 十項運動 decathlon

shíxiàng quánnéng yùndòng 十項全能運動 decathlon

shíyīyuè 十一月 1. November 2. the eleventh month of the lunar calendar 3. eleven months

shíyǒu bājiǔ 十有八九 most probably; very likely

shíyuè 十月 1. October 2. the tenth month of the lunar calendar 3. ten months

shízìjià 十字架 1. the Cross 2. a yoke one has to take

Shízìjūn 十字軍 the Crusaders

shízì lùkǒu 十字路口 1. the junction of crossroads 2. a point of decision

shízú 十足 extremely; completely

shí 什

1. sundry; miscellaneous 2. ten 3. a squad (of ten soldiers, in former times)

shíjǐn 什錦 multiple ingredients (for a dish); assorted

shí 石

1. rocks; stones; minerals, etc. 2. a calculus, as a kidney calculus (commonly known as a kidney stone) 3. stone tablets 4. medicines 5. barren, as a barren woman 6. name of an ancient musical instrument 7. a Chinese family name

shíbǎnhuà 石版畫 a lithograph

shíbēi 石碑 a stone tablet; a stele

shíbì 石壁 a stone wall; a precipice

shíchén dàhǎi 石沈大海 no news at all; to disappear forever

shídiāo 石雕 1. stone carving 2. carved stone

shígāo 石膏 gypsum; plaster

shígāoxiàng 石膏像 a plaster bust; a plaster statue

shíhuī 石灰 lime

shíjiang 石匠 a stonemason

shíjiē 石階 stone steps

shíkū 石窟 a grotto

shíkuài 石塊 a piece of stone or rock; a pebble; a boulder

shílì 石礫 gravel

shíliu 石榴 a pomegranate

Shímén Shuǐkù 石門水庫 the Shi-men Reservoir in northern Taiwan

shímiánwǎ 石綿瓦 an asbestos tile

shímò 石墨 graphite; plumbago

shímò 石磨 a millstone; a grindstone

shípò tiānjīng 石破天驚 world-shaking; sensational

shíqì 石器 stoneware; stone implements

Shíqì Shídài 石器時代 the Stone Age

shítou 石頭 stones; rocks

shíxiàng 石像 a statue or bust of stone

shíyīng 石英 quartz

shíyóu 石油 crude oil; petroleum

shíyóu gōngyè 石油工業 petroleum industry

shízhù 石柱 a stone pillar

shízǐ 石子 pieces of stone; pebbles

shízǐlù 石子路 a graveled path; a macadam road

shí 食

1. to eat 2. food; meal 3. livelihood; living 4. (an old usage) salary; pay 5. (蝕) eclipse

shíbù zhīwèi 食不知味 to eat food but without knowing its taste—deep anxiety, grief, etc.

shídào 食道 1. the ways of eating; table manners 2. the route for transporting foodstuffs 3. the gullet; the esophagus

shígǔ bùhuà 食古不化 to read a lot of classics without diges-

S

tion; to be pedantic

shíjù 食具 a table service (such as bowls, etc.)

shíkè 食客 dependent-advisors under a leader in ancient times, especially during the Epoch of Warring States

shíliáng 食糧 foodstuffs; food grain; provisions

shíliàng 食量 the quantity of food one consumes; appetite

shípǐn 食品 foods; food items; foodstuffs

shípǐndiàn 食品店 a store for selling food items; a food store; a confectionary

shípǐn fángfǔjì 食品防腐劑 food disinfectant

shípǔ 食譜 a cookbook; a collection of recipes

shísù 食宿 board and lodging; bed and board

shítáng 食堂 a mess hall; the restaurant

shíwù 食物 eatables; provisions; foodstuffs

shíwù guòmǐn 食物過敏 food allergy

shíwùliàn 食物鏈 a food chain

shíwù zhòngdú 食物中毒 food poisoning

shíyán 食鹽 kitchen salt; table salt

shíyán érféi 食言而肥 to grow fat by eating one's words—to break a promise

shíyòng 食用 1. edible 2. living expenses

shíyù 食慾 appetite

shíyù bùzhèn 食慾不振 a poor appetite; lack of appetite

shízhǐ hàofán 食指浩繁 many mouths to feed

shí 拾
1. to pick up; to collect 2. to put away 3. a formal form of the figure ten used to prevent fraud in a document or check 4. an armlet used by archers

shíduo 拾掇 1. to tidy up 2. (colloquial) to punish 3. to repair

shíhuāng 拾荒 to glean and collect scraps (to eke out an existence)

shíqǐ 拾起 to pick up

shíqǔ 拾取 to collect; to pick up

shírén yáhuì 拾人牙慧[*] to plagiarize

shísuì 拾穗 to glean

shí 時

1. a season 2. an era; an epoch; an age; a period 3. time; fixed time 4. hours 5. often; frequently 6. fashionable 7. proper and adequate 8. opportune (moments); opportunity 9. timely; seasonable 10. now... now...; sometimes... sometimes...

shíchā 時差 1. (astronomy) the equation of time 2. the time difference of two places located on different longitudes or time zones

shícháng 時常 often; frequently

shíchen 時辰 1. the 12 divisions of a day named after the 12 Terrestrial Branches 2. the time for...

shídài 時代 an era; an epoch; a period

shí'ér 時而 from time to time; sometimes

shífèn 時分 1. seasons; periods 2. time

shíguāng 時光 time

shíguò jìngqiān 時過境遷 Things have changed with the passage of time.

shíhou 時候 time; hour; juncture; moment

shíjī 時機 opportunity

shíjī chéngshú 時機成熟 The right time has come. The opportune moment is here.

shíjià 時價 current prices; prevailing prices

shíjiān 時間 1. time; the hour 2. time—as opposed to space

shíjié 時節 a period of the year; season

shíjú 時局 the national situation; the world situation

shíkè 時刻 1. time; hour 2. always; constantly; continually

shíkèbiǎo 時刻表 a timetable; a

S

schedule

shílái yùnzhuǎn 時來運轉 to get a break (after a long period of bad luck)

shílìng 時令 time of year; seasons

shímáo 時髦 fashionable; modern; up-to-date

shíqī 時期 1. times; a period 2. duration

shíqī 時期 refer to **shíqī** 時期

shírì 時日 1. time 2. an auspicious time 3. this day

shíshàng 時尚 a fad

shíshí kèkè 時時刻刻 constantly; always

shíshì 時事 current events

shíshì 時勢 the time and the circumstances

shísù 時速 speed per hour

shítài 時態 (grammar) tense

shíxià 時下 nowadays; in these days

shíxiàn 時限 a time limit; a deadline

shíxiào 時效 (law) prescription; the duration of validity

shíxīng 時興 fashionable or seasonable

shíyí 時宜 proper at the time

shíyù bùjì 時遇不濟 to be out of luck

shíyùn hēngtōng 時運亨通 to be lucky

shízhēn 時針 the hour hand of a clock or watch

shízhí 時值 the time being...

shízhì jīnrì 時至今日 up to now

shízhōng 時鐘 a clock

shízhuāng 時裝 1. fashionable dresses 2. (in show biz) modern dresses

shízhuāng zhǎnlǎn 時裝展覽 a fashion show

shí 實

1. real; true 2. practically 3. honest; faithful 4. concrete; substantial 5. fact; reality 6. fruit; seed

shídì diàochá 實地調查 an on-the-spot investigation

shíhuà 實話 the truth

shíhuà shíshuō 實話實說 to tell the truth (without adding or withholding anything)

shíhuì 實惠 a real benefit; substantial

shíjì 實際 1. actual; real 2. practical; realistic 3. reality; practice

shíjì qíngkuàng 實際情況 the actual situation

shíjiàn 實踐 to practice (a principle); to put in practice

shíkuàng 實況 factual conditions

shíkuàng zhuǎnbō 實況轉播 a live broadcast; a live telecast

shílì 實力 strength

shílì 實例 a living example; an example

shílì xiāngdāng 實力相當 to be well-matched in strength

shíqíng 實情 the real picture or real story (of a case)

shíshī 實施 to put (regulations, plans, etc.) into effect; to implement

shíwù 實物 goods or produce (as opposed to money)

shíxí 實習 to practice what one has been taught

shíxíshēng 實習生 a trainee

shíxí yīshēng 實習醫生 an intern(e)

shíxiàn 實現 to realize (a plan, etc.); (said of a dream, etc.) to come true

shíxiào 實效 real effect; effect

shíxíng 實行 to practice (a principle)

shíyàn 實驗 1. to experiment; to test 2. an experiment; a test

shíyàn jùchǎng 實驗劇場 an experimental theater

shíyànshì 實驗室 a laboratory

shíyè 實業 industry; business

shíyèjiè 實業界 the business world or circles; industry

shíyòng 實用 1. practical use 2. useful

shízài 實在 1. really; truly 2. real; concrete

shízai 實在 well-done

shízhí 實質 refer to **shízhì** 實質

shízhí 實值 net value; intrinsic value

shízhì 實質 essence; substance

shízhì míngguī 實至名歸 Where there is real ability, there is fame.

shí 碩

refer to **shuò** 碩

shí 蝕

1. to eclipse; an eclipse 2. to erode; to eat up slowly

shí 識 also **shì**

1. to know, to recognize; to discern 2. an opinion; a view 3. knowledge

shíbié 識別 1. to discern; to distinguish 2. identification

shíbiézhèng 識別證 an I.D. card

shíhuò 識貨 to appreciate; able to evaluate wares correctly

shípò 識破 to see through

shíqù 識趣 to have tact; tactful

shítú lǎomǎ 識途老馬 an old horse which knows the way—an experienced person

shíxiàng 識相 to know noe's own limitations

shízì 識字 able to read; literate

shǐ 矢

1. an arrow; a dart 2. to vow; to take an oath; to pledge 3. to display

shǐkǒu fǒurèn 矢口否認 to deny flatly

shǐliàng 矢量 vector

shǐzhì bùyí 矢志不移 to take an oath not to change one's mind

shǐ 史

1. history; chronicles; annals 2. a Chinese family name

shǐjī 史跡 1. historic events 2. historic relics

shǐjī 史蹟 1. historic events 2. historic relics

shǐjiā 史家 a historian

shǐqián shídài 史前時代 the prehistoric age

shǐshī 史詩 an epic

shǐshū 史書 a book of history; an annal

shǐwú qiánlì 史無前例 without precedent in history

shǐxué 史學 history (as a science)

shǐ 弛

refer to **chí** 弛

shǐ 使

1. to use; to employ; to apply 2. to make; to act 3. to indulge in 4. (also **shì**) to send as diplomatic personnel; diplomatic envoys 5. (also **shì**) an envoy; an emissary; a minister 6. if

shǐchū 使出 to exert

shǐchū húnshēn jiěshù 使出渾身解數 to do one's best (in order to please or impress somebody)

shǐde 使得 1. all right; can be done or used 2. to make; to cause

shǐguǎn 使館 a legation; an embassy

shǐhuài 使壞 1. to be up to mischief; to play a dirty trick 2. to destroy

shǐhuan 使喚 1. to run errands for 2. to order others to do something

shǐjìn 使勁 to exert effort

shǐlǐngguǎn 使領館 embassies and consulates

shǐmìng 使命 a mission

shǐnǚ 使女 a maidservant; a housemaid

shǐxìngzi 使性子 to lose one's temper

shǐyǎnsè 使眼色 to make eyes at

shǐyòng 使用 to use; to employ

shǐyòng niánxiàn 使用年限 the tenure of use

shǐzhě 使者 an envoy; an emissary; a messenger

shǐ 始

1. the beginning; the start; the first 2. to start; to begin; to be the first

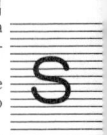

shǐluàn zhōngqì 始亂終棄 to desert a girl after robbing her of her chastity

shǐmò 始末 1. from beginning to end—throughout 2. the ins and outs (of an incident, story, etc.)

shǐzhōng 始終 throughout; from beginning to end

shǐzhōng rúyī 始終如一 consistent; unremitting

shǐzǔ 始祖 1. the founder 2. the first ancestor

shǐzuò yǒngzhě 始作俑者 the originator (usually of a bad practice, etc.)

shǐ 屎

excrement

shǐ 駛

1. (said of vehicles) to run; (said of vessels) to sail 2. fast; fleeting

shì 士

1. a scholar; a man of learning; a gentleman 2. an official rank in ancient China; an officer 3. a noncommissioned officer 4. a person 5. name of a chessman in Chinese chess

shìbīng 士兵 soldiers; privates; enlisted men

shìdàfū 士大夫 1. an official 2. a general 3. a scholar

shìqì 士氣 1. the morale of a fighting force 2. the trends and temperaments of scholars in a given era

shìshēn 士紳 the gentry

shìzú 士卒 soldiers; privates; enlisted men

shì 氏

1. family name; surname 2. a character placed after a married woman's maiden name; nee 3. the title of a government position in former times

shìzú 氏族 a family; a clan

shì 世

1. a generation 2. a person's life span 3. an age 4. the world

shìbó 世伯 a designation for the male friends of one's father

shìchóu 世仇 family feud; blood feud

shìchuán 世傳 hereditary; to be handed down through generations

shìdài 世代 1. a generation 2. the times 3. from generation to generation

shìdài jiāotì 世代交替 (biology) metagenesis; alternation of generations

shìdào rénxīn 世道人心 the ways of the world and the time

shìfēng jiāobó 世風澆薄 There are scarcely public morals to speak of these days.

shìfēng rìxià 世風日下 The moral degeneration of the world is getting worse day by day.

shìgù 世故 the ways of the world

shìgu 世故 shrewd; worldly

shìjì 世紀 a century

shìjiā 世家 a family holding official ranks for generations

shìjiān 世間 on earth; in the world

shìjiāo 世交 families closely related or associated for generations

shìjiè 世界 the world

shìjiè cháoliú 世界潮流 world trends

shìjiè dàtóng 世界大同 universal brotherhood

shìjiè dàzhàn 世界大戰 a world war

shìjiè mòrì 世界末日 the end of the world; doomsday

shìmiàn 世面 the various facets of human activities

shìrén 世人 people of the world

shìshì 世事 affairs of the world

shìshì dàidài 世世代代 generation after generation; from generation to generation

shìsú 世俗 customs and traditions

shìsú zhījiàn 世俗之見 common views

shìtài yánliáng 世態炎涼 snobbish; inconstancy of human relationships

shìwài táoyuán 世外桃源

S

Shangri-la; a secluded paradise

shìxí 世襲 hereditary (title, rank, etc.)

shìxì 世系 a family tree; a pedigree

Shìyùn 世運 the Olympiad

shìzhí 世姪 one's close friend's son

shìzǐ 世子 the crown prince

shìzú 世族 a powerful family that has great political influence for generations

shì 示

1. to show; to indicate 2. to make known; to notify; a notice 3. to instruct 4. to demonstrate

shì'ài 示愛 to show one's tender feeling to one of the opposite sex

shìfàn 示範 to set an example

shìfàn biǎoyǎn 示範表演 demonstration (of a skill)

shìjǐng 示警 to give a warning

shìwēi 示威 to demonstrate (by a mass meeting or parade)

shìwēi yóuxíng 示威遊行 demonstration

shìyì 示意 to drop a hint; to motion

shìzhòng 示眾 to exhibit to the public

shì 市

1. a market (place) 2. a city 3. to buy or sell

shìchǎng 市場 a market (place)

shìchǎng diàochá 市場調查 a market survey

shìgōngsuǒ 市公所 a city or town office

shìjí 市集 a market (place)

shìjià 市價 market prices; the current price (of a commodity)

shìjiāo 市郊 suburbia

shìjǐng wúlài 市井無賴 the scoundrels of the marketplace

shìjǐng zhītú 市井之徒 vulgar people who place money before anything else in life

shìkuài 市儈 1. a broker 2. a crafty businessman

shìlì 市立 municipal

shìmiàn 市面 1. market conditions 2. the sights and splendors in big cities

shìmín 市民 citizens

shìnèi 市內 in the city

shìqū 市區 1. the area within the city limits 2. the downtown area

shìróng 市容 the appearance of a city

shìyìhuì 市議會 a city council

shìzhǎng 市長 the mayor of a city

shìzhèn 市鎮 small towns; towns

shìzhèng 市政 municipal administration

shìzhèngfǔ 市政府 a city government

shì 仕

1. an official 2. to enter government service

shìhuàn 仕宦 to be an official

shìnǚ 仕女 1. young men and women 2. a painting portraying beautiful women

shìtú 仕途 the career in government service

shì 式

1. fashion; style 2. a pattern; a type 3. a system 4. a ceremony

shìwēi 式微 the decline (of a nation, etc.)

shìwéi 式微 refer to **shìwēi** 式微

shìyàng 式樣 1. a type; a model 2. a mode; a style

shì 事

1. an affair; a matter; business 2. a job; an occupation; a task 3. a service 4. duties; functions 5. a subject 6. to serve; to attend 7. to manage a business

shìbàn gōngbèi 事半功倍 to achieve maximum results with little effort

shìbèi gōngbàn 事倍功半 to achieve little result despite herculean effort

shìbì gōngqīn 事必躬親 to attend to everything personally

shìbiàn 事變 an incident

shìbù yíchí 事不宜遲 One must lose no time in doing something.

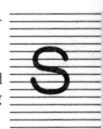

shìchū yǒuyīn 事出有因 not entirely devoid of truth

shìdào rújīn 事到如今 as things have come to such a pass

shìduān 事端 a trouble

shìfēi déyǐ 事非得已 There is no other choice.

shìgù 事故 an accident

shìguò jìngqiān 事過境遷 Things change with the passage of time.

shìhòu 事後 after an event; afterward

shìjì 事跡 a vestige

shìjī 事蹟 the accomplishments, exploits, etc. of a person during his or her life time

shìjià 事假 private affair leave

shìjiàn 事件 an incident; an event

shìlì 事例 an example; a precedent

shìqián 事前 beforehand

shìqīn zhìxiào 事親至孝 to treat one's parents with great respect and tender affection

shìqíng 事情 a matter

shìshí 事實 a fact; truth; reality

shìshí hūnyīn 事實婚姻 to cohabit; a de facto marriage; a companionate marriage

shìshíshang 事實上 in fact; in reality

shìshí shèng yú xióngbiàn 事實勝於雄辯 Facts are more convincing than eloquent theories.

shìshì 事事 everything

shìtài 事態 the situation

shìwù 事物 things; articles; objects

shìwù 事務 business; work; general affairs

shìwùsuǒ 事務所 an office

shìwùyuán 事務員 an office clerk

shìxiān 事先 beforehand

shìyè 事業 1. an enterprise 2. a career

shìyí 事宜 1. affairs; matters 2. the necessary arrangements

shìyǐ rúcǐ 事已如此 things being so

shìyóu 事由 1. the origin of a matter 2. the subject (of a business letter)

shìyǔ yuànwéi 事與願違 Things do not turn out as one wishes.

shìzài rénwéi 事在人為 Human effort can achieve everything.

shìzhǔ 事主 the victim in a criminal case

shǐ 使

refer to shǐ 使 4, 5

shì 侍

1. to serve; to wait upon 2. to accompany one's elder or superior 3. a designation for oneself when addressing an elder or a senior 4. an attendant

shìcóng 侍從 attendants; servants; retinue

shìfèng 侍奉 to serve; to attend on

shìhòu 侍候 to wait upon; to serve

shìnǚ 侍女 a maid; a maidservant

shìqīn 侍親 to attend one's parents

shìwèi 侍衛 bodyguards

shìzhě 侍者 attendants, waiters, etc.

shì 是

1. yes; right; positive (as contrasted to negative) 2. the verb to be (for all persons and numbers) 3. this, that, or which

shìde 是的 yes; right; That's it.

shìfēi 是非 1. right and wrong; yes and no 2. gossip; scandal 3. discord

shìfēi diāndǎo 是非顛倒 to confound right and wrong

shìfēi qūzhí 是非曲直 right and wrong, proper and improper

shìfēití 是非題 a true-or-false problem

shìfēi zhīdì 是非之地 a place where one is apt to get into trouble

shìfǒu 是否 Is it...? Are you...? Is he...?

shìgù 是故 therefore

shìhé jūxīn 是何居心 What evil intention is this!

shìshì fēifēi 是是非非 gossip(s); scandal(s)

shì 恃
to rely on; to depend on; to presume upon

shìcái àowù 恃才傲物 to be arrogant because of one's talents or ability

shìchǒng 恃寵 to presume on being a favorite (of a high-placed personality)

shìqiáng língruò 恃強凌弱 to use one's strength (or power) to bully the weak

shì 拭
1. to wipe; to rub (eyes, etc.) 2. to dust; to clean

shìlèi 拭淚 to wipe tears

shìmù yǐdài 拭目以待 to wait for the result anxiously; to wait and see

shì 室
1. a room; an apartment; a home 2. wife

shìnèi 室內 indoor

shìnèi shèjì 室內設計 interior design

shìnèi yùndòng 室內運動 indoor sports

shìnèi zhuānghuáng 室內裝潢 interior decoration

shìwài 室外 outdoor (as opposed to indoor)

shìwài yùndòng 室外運動 outdoor activities

shìwēn 室溫 room temperature

shì 柿
the persimmon

shìzi 柿子 the persimmon fruit

shì 舐
to lick

shìdú qíngshēn 舐犢情深 very affectionate toward one's children (like a cow caressing her calves with the tongue)

shì 逝
1. to pass; to be gone; to depart 2. to pass on; to die

shìshì 逝世 to pass away; to die

shì 視
1. to look at; to observe; to inspect; to see; to watch 2. to consider or regard as; to take it for 3. to compare; to be equivalent to

shìchá 視察 to inspect

shìchuāng 視窗 (computer) window

shì'ér bùjiàn 視而不見 (literally) to look but see nothing —absent-minded; to ignore

shìjué 視覺 the sense of sight

shìlì 視力 the visual faculty; eyesight

shìlì bǎohù píngmù 視力保護屏幕 (computer) screen shield

shìrú bìxǐ 視如敝屣 to regard as worn-out shoes

shìruò wúdǔ 視若無睹 to be undisturbed by what one has seen

shìshì 視事 1. to administer; to govern or rule 2. to be installed or inaugurated; to be sworn in

shìsǐ rúguī 視死如歸 to look upon death as going home—fearless and dauntless

shìtīng 視聽 1. what one saw and heard 2. public opinion 3. audio-visual

shìtóng érxì 視同兒戲 to take it lightly; to regard it as unimportant

shì 弒
to kill or murder one's superior, senior, etc.

shìfù 弒父 patricide; to commit patricide

shìjūn 弒君 regicide; to commit regicide

shìmǔ 弒母 matricide; to commit matricide

shì 試
1. to try; to test; to experiment 2. to use 3. to examine 4. to sound out; to put up a trial bal-

loon 5. to compare

shìbàn 試辦 to do something on an experimental basis

shìchǎng 試場 an examination place

shìchuān 試穿 to try on (a garment, etc.)

shìfēi 試飛 to test a new airplane in flight; a trial flight

shìguǎn 試管 a test tube

shìguǎn yīng'ér 試管嬰兒 a test-tube baby

shìjuàn 試卷 a test paper; an examination paper

shìtàn 試探 to test; to sound out; to probe

shìtí 試題 questions in a test or examination

shìtú 試圖 to attempt; to try

shìwèn 試問 May we ask...?

shìxiǎng 試想 to think it over; just think

shìxíng 試行 to try out something

shìyǎn 試演 a dress rehearsal; a preview

shìyàn 試驗 an experiment; to experiment

shìyìng 試映 to give a preview; a preview (of a movie)

shìyòng 試用 to use on a trial basis

shìyòng rényuán 試用人員 probational personnel

shì 飾

1. to ornament; to decorate; to polish (writing) 2. ornamentation; decorations 3. to excuse oneself on a pretext, etc.; to fake 4. clothing and dresses 5. to whitewash; to deceive; to cover up 6. to play the role of; to act the part of

shìfēi 飾非 to hide and gloss over one's faults or mistakes

shìguò 飾過 to hide and gloss over one's faults or mistakes

shìwù 飾物 adornments; decorations

shì 嗜

to delight in; to be fond of; to relish; to like

shìhào 嗜好 one's liking, hobby, or weakness for something

shì 勢

1. power; force; influence 2. a tendency 3. the natural features 4. a situation 5. signs; gestures 6. male genitals

shìbì 勢必 certainly; to be bound to

shìbù liǎnglì 勢不兩立 unable to coexist; incompatible

shìjūn lìdí 勢均力敵 evenly matched; well-matched

shìlì 勢力 force; power; influence

shìlì 勢利 snobbish

shìlì fànwéi 勢力範圍 the sphere of influence

shìlìyǎn 勢利眼 a snob

shìrú pòzhú 勢如破竹 to advance with irresistible force

shìzài bìxíng 勢在必行 to be imperative, urgent, or essential (under the circumstances)

shì 誓

1. to pledge; to vow; to swear 2. to take an oath (of allegiance, office, etc.)

shìbù gānxiū 誓不甘休 to vow never to let the offender get away with it

shìbù liǎnglì 誓不兩立 to vow to fight till oneself or the other party falls

shìcí 誓詞 an oath; a pledge

shìyán 誓言 a vow; an oath

shìyuē 誓約 a vow; an oath

shì 適

1. to go; to arrive at; to reach 2. just right; exactly; appropriate; fit; just 3. comfortable; at ease with oneself 4. (said of a girl) to marry 5. to follow; to be faithful to 6. only 7. by chance; accidentally 8. just now

shìdàng 適當 proper; appropriate; fit

shìdé qífǎn 適得其反 to get exactly the opposite

shìdù 適度 appropriate; within limits

shìhé 適合 suitable or suitable

for; to fit

shìkě érzhǐ 適可而止 to stop at the right moment or point

shìshí 適時 at the right time

shìyí 適宜 fit; suitable; proper

shìyìng 適應 to adapt; adaptation (to environment, etc.)

shìyòng 適用 fit or suitable for use

shìzhě shēngcún 適者生存 the survival of the fittest

shìzhōng 適中 proper; adequate; appropriate

shì 謚

a posthumous title

shì 螫

refer to **zhē** 螫

shì 識

refer to **shí** 識

shì 釋

1. to explain; to interpret 2. to set free 3. to relieve 4. to disperse; to dispel 5. of Buddha or Buddhism

Shìjiāmóuní 釋迦牟尼 Sakyamuni

shìrán 釋然 1. at ease; relaxed 2. having all the misunderstandings cleared up

shìyì 釋義 expatiation; interpretation

shì 匙

a key

shōu 收

1. to draw together; to gather; to collect 2. to contain 3. to receive; to accept; to take 4. to end; to come to a close 5. to retrieve; to take back

shōubàojī 收報機 a telegraph receiver

shōucáng 收藏 to collect and keep

shōucángjiā 收藏家 a collector

shōuchǎng 收場 1. conclusion 2. to wind up; to end up

shōucheng 收成 harvest

shōudào 收到 to receive; to obtain

shōufā 收發 to receive and send out (official papers, documents, etc.)

shōufèi 收費 to collect fees; to charge

shōufèizhàn 收費站 a toll station

shōufù 收復 to recover (lost territory)

shōugē 收割 to reap; to harvest

shōugōng 收工 to end the day's work

shōugòu 收購 to buy up; to purchase

shōuhuí 收回 to recover; to recall; to retrieve

shōuhuì 收賄 to accept bribes; bribery

shōuhuò 收穫 1. harvest; fruits (of efforts) 2. to reap

shōují 收集 collection; to collect; to gather

shōujiànrén 收件人 an addressee; a consignee

shōujù 收據 a receipt

shōukàn 收看 to watch (television)

shōukuǎnrén 收款人 a recipient (of remittance); a payee

shōulǎn 收攬 to collect extensively 2. to win (the people's hearts)

shōuliǎn 收斂 1. to collect (taxes, grains, etc.) 2. to contract 3. to weaken or disappear 4. to pull in one's horns

shōuliàn 收斂 refer to **shōuliǎn** 收斂

shōuliú 收留 to take somebody in

shōulǒng 收攏 to draw something in

shōulù 收錄 1. to employ; to recruit 2. to include (in a list, etc.)

shōumǎi 收買 1. to bribe 2. to buy up 3. to win (support, people's hearts, etc. by less than honorable means)

shōupán 收盤 the closing quotation (of a stock or commodity) for the day

shōupiàoyuán 收票員 a ticket

collector

shōuqǐ 收起 to pack up

shōuqì 收訖 received

shōuqián 收錢 to collect payments

shōuróng 收容 to give shelter to; to accommodate

shōurù 收入 1. to take in; to include 2. income; earnings; revenue; receipts

shōushi 收拾 1. to clear away; to tidy 2. to manage 3. to punish

shōusuō 收縮 1. to shrink; to contract 2. systole

shōusuōyā 收縮壓 systolic pressure

shōutānr 收攤兒 to pack up the stall or booth (after a day's business is over)

shōutīng 收聽 to tune in; to listen to (the radio)

shōuxia 收下 to accept; to receive

shōuxiào 收效 to get the desired result or effect

shōuxīn 收心 to concentrate attention

shōuyā 收押 to take (a criminal suspect) into custody; to detain

shōuyǎng 收養 to adopt (a child)

shōuyì 收益 to get benefit; to benefit

shōuyīn 收音 (radio) reception

shōuyīnjī 收音機 a radio receiving set; a radio

shōuyínjī 收銀機 a cash register

shōuzhī 收支 income and expenditure

shóu 熟

refer to **shú** 熟

shǒu 手

1. hand; of the hand; having to do with the hand 2. to have in one's hand; to hold 3. a skilled person; a person 4. action 5. personally

shǒubǎ 手把 a handle

shǒubèi 手背 1. the back of the hand 2. (gambling) having bad luck

shǒubei 手臂 the arm from the wrist up

shǒubǐ 手筆 1. a literary work or handwriting 2. the courage of spending money on a grand scale

shǒubiān 手邊 at hand; handy

shǒubiǎo 手錶 a wrist watch

shǒucè 手冊 a handbook; a manual

shǒuchāoběn 手抄本 a hand-copied book

shǒuchíshì jìsuànjī 手持式計算機 a portable computer

shǒudào qínlái 手到擒來 to capture an enemy easily

shǒudiàntǒng 手電筒 a flashlight; an electric torch

shǒuduàn 手段 1. the means (as opposed to the end) 2. a devious way of dealing with people

shǒufǎ 手法 workmanship; artistry; skill; technique

shǒufēngqín 手風琴 an accordion

shǒugǎo 手稿 manuscript

shǒugōng 手工 handwork; handiwork

shǒugōngyè 手工業 a manual trade

shǒugōngyì 手工藝 handicrafts; handiwork

shǒugōngyìpǐn 手工藝品 fancy works; handicraft articles

shǒujī 手機 a cellular phone

shǒujiǎo 手腳 1. hand and foot 2. motion; action 3. tricks; juggles

shǒujiǎo lìluo 手腳俐落 nimble; agile

shǒujin 手巾 a towel

shǒukào 手銬 handcuffs

shǒulāshǒu 手拉手 hand in hand

shǒuliúdàn 手榴彈 a hand grenade

shǒumáng jiǎoluàn 手忙腳亂 to be in a flurry

shǒumiàn kuòchuò 手面闊綽 extravagantly generous or lib-

eral; lavish

shǒupà 手帕 a handkerchief

shǒuqì 手氣 (gambling) luck

shǒuqiāng 手槍 a pistol; a revolver; a gun

shǒuqiǎo 手巧 dexterous; skillful

shǒuqiú 手球 (sports) handball

shǒurèn 手刃 to kill someone personally with a sword

shǒushì 手勢 a gesture; a sign; to sign

shǒushù 手術 a surgical operation; surgery

shǒutào 手套 gloves; gauntlets; mittens

shǒutídài 手提袋 a valise; a Boston bag

shǒutíxiāng 手提箱 an attache case; a suitcase

shǒutóu 手頭 1. on hand; at hand; in hand 2. financial conditions

shǒutóujǐn 手頭緊 1. short of cash (or money) 2. closefisted

shǒutuīchē 手推車 a handcart; a wheelbarrow

shǒuwàn 手腕 1. the wrist 2. skill; tact; tricks; ability

shǒuwén 手紋 the lines on the palm

shǒuwú cùntiě 手無寸鐵 totally unarmed

shǒuwǔ zúdǎo 手舞足蹈 to caper beyond oneself with joy

shǒuxià 手下 1. a subordinate 2. under the leadership of

shǒuxià bàijiàng 手下敗將 one who has suffered defeat at (my, your, etc.) hands

shǒuxià liúqíng 手下留情 to show leniency or mercy

shǒuxiàng 手相 the lines of the palm by which fortunetellers tell one's fortune

shǒuxīn 手心 1. the center of the palm 2. (figuratively) control

shǒuxù 手續 procedures; red tape

shǒuyǎng 手癢 1. an itch on one's hands 2. to have an itch to do something

shǒuyì 手藝 handicrafts; a trade

shǒuyìn 手印 an impression of the thumb as a signature

shǒuyǔ 手語 dactylology; sign language

shǒuzhá 手札 a personally hand-written letter

shǒuzhǎng 手掌 the palm (of the hand)

shǒuzhǎngjī 手掌機 hand-held electronic video game

shǒuzhàng 手杖 a cane; a walking stick

shǒuzhǐtóu 手指頭 1. a fingertip 2. a finger

shǒuzhǐ 手指 1. a finger 2. to point at something with the index finger

shǒuzhuó 手鐲 a bracelet

shǒuzú 手足 brothers

shǒuzú qíngshēn 手足情深 The love between brothers is deep.

shǒuzú wúcuò 手足無措 to be at a loss what to do

shǒu 守

1. to guard; to protect; to defend; to watch 2. to wait 3. to keep (a secret, etc.) 4. to stick to; to maintain 5. to abide by

shǒubèi 守備 to be on garrison duty

shǒucáinú 守財奴 a miser

shǒuchéng bùbiàn 守成不變 holding to existing custom

shǒufǎ 守法 to abide by the law

shǒufèn 守分 to stick to what one is suited for

shǒugēng 守更 to keep watch during the night

shǒuguǎ 守寡 to remain in widowhood

shǒuhòu 守候 to wait; to bide one's time

shǒuhù 守護 to guard; to protect

shǒujìlǜ 守紀律 to observe the rules

shǒujié 守節 1. to remain a widow forever although one is still young 2. to stick to principle

shǒujiù 守舊 sticking to old

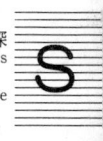

S

shǒukǒu rúpíng 守口如瓶 to keep one's mouth shut

shǒumìmì 守祕密 to keep a secret

shǒusāng 守喪 to remain in mourning for one's parent

shǒushēn rúyù 守身如玉 to keep one's integrity intact in adversity

shǒushí 守時 punctual

shǒusuì 守歲 to see the old year out and the new year in by staying up on the Lunar New Year's Eve

shǒuwàng xiāngzhù 守望相助 (said of neighbors in a community) to help each other in guarding against enemies

shǒuwèi 守衛 1. to guard 2. a guard

shǒuxiào 守孝 to be in mourning for one's parent

shǒuxìnyòng 守信用 to keep promises; to honor one's words

shǒuyè 守夜 to keep night watch

shǒuyuē 守約 to keep a promise; to honor a pledge

shǒuzé 守則 a rule; a regulation

shǒuzhūdàitù 守株待兔 stupid and unimaginative in doing things

shǒu 首

1. the head 2. the king; the emperor; the chief; the leader 3. the first; the beginning 4. a (poem, song, etc.)

shǒuchuàng 首創 to found; to start; to initiate

shǒucì 首次 the first time

shǒudāng qíchōng 首當其衝 the first to bear the brunt of

shǒudū 首都 the (national) capital

shǒufǔ 首府 the capital city

shǒují 首級 the human head

shǒujiè 首屆 the first (conference, assembly, etc.)

shǒukěn 首肯 to nod one's head in approval; to approve

shǒulǐng 首領 1. the leader; the chief 2. head and neck

shǒunǎo rénwù 首腦人物 the chief; the boss; the key member; the mastermind

shǒuqū yīzhǐ 首屈一指 foremost; second to none; the best

shǒurèn 首任 the first to be appointed to an office

shǒurú fēipéng 首如飛蓬 disheveled hair

shǒushì 首飾 jewelry; ornaments; trinkets

shǒutuī 首推 to consider (a person) first

shǒuwěi 首尾 1. the head and the tail; the beginning and the end 2. from beginning to end

shǒuwěi xiāngyìng 首尾相應 head and tail (or beginning and end) corresponding with each other

shǒuwèi 首位 1. the place of honor 2. the first place

shǒuxí 首席 the highest-ranking or high-estpositioned; the senior

shǒuxiān 首先 the very first; at first; first of all

shǒuxiàng 首相 the prime minister; the premier

shǒuyào 首要 of the first importance; first of all; chief

shǒuyào tiáojiàn 首要條件 a prerequisite; the number one condition

shǒuyìng 首映 the premiere (of a movie)

shǒuzhǎng 首長 the chief; the leading cadre

shòu 受

1. to receive; to accept; to get 2. to take; to stand; to suffer; to tolerate; to endure 3. to be pleasant to (the ears, etc.) 4. preceding a verb to form a passive voice

shòubuliǎo 受不了 1. cannot stand it 2. very much

shòucháo 受潮 to be affected with damp

shòuchǒng ruòjīng 受寵若驚 to receive much more favor than one expected

shòucuò 受挫 to be frustrated;

ways; conservative

to suffer·a setback

shòufá 受罰 to be punished or penalized

shòuhài 受害 to be victimized

shòuhàirén 受害人 the victim

shòuhuàqì 受話器 a telephone receiver

shòuhuì 受惠 to be benefited

shòuhuì 受賄 to be bribed; to receive bribes

shòujiào 受教 1. to receive education 2. to receive instructions or guidance

shòujīng 受精 to be fertilized

shòujīng 受驚 to be frightened

shòujīngluǎn 受精卵 a zygote

shòukǔ 受苦 to suffer (hardships)

shòulěi 受累 to be involved

shòulǐ 受理 to accept (a petition, complaint, etc.)

shòumìng 受命 to accept an order

shòunàn 受難 to be in distress

shòupiàn 受騙 to be cheated or swindled; to be fooled; to be tricked

shòupìn 受聘 to accept a job offer

shòuqì 受氣 to be a punching bag; to suffer indignities

shòuqū 受屈 to suffer a grievance or indignity

shòurén zhītuō 受人之託 to be entrusted by someone to do a job

shòurǔ 受辱 to be humiliated

shòushāng 受傷 to be injured; to get hurt; to be wounded

shòushěn 受審 to stand trial; to be on trial

shòutāi 受胎 to conceive; fertilization; to be impregnated

shòutuō 受託 to be entrusted with

shòuxǐ 受洗 to be baptized

shòuxiáng 受降 to accept a surrender

shòuxíng 受刑 to be tortured; to be punished (by law)

shòuxùn 受訓 to receive training

shòuyì 受益 to benefit from; to benefit by

shòuyìrén 受益人 a beneficiary

shòuyòng 受用 1. to enjoy; enjoyable 2. to get the benefit

shòuyong 受用 comfortable; to feel good

shòuyùn 受孕 to be impregnated

shòuzhī wúkuì 受之無愧 to deserve (a reward, gift, etc.)

shòuzuì 受罪 to suffer hardships

shòu 狩

1. to hunt in winter 2. an imperial tour

shòuliè 狩獵 hunting; to hunt or trap game

shòu 售

to sell

shòuhòu fúwù 售後服務 after service

shòuhuòyuán 售貨員 a salesman; a salesgirl; a salesclerk

shòujià 售價 the (retail) price (of a commodity)

shòupiào 售票 to sell tickets

shòupiàochù 售票處 a ticket office; a box office

shòupiàokǒu 售票口 a wicket

shòu 授

1. to give; to hand over to; to confer (a degree, prize, etc.) 2. to teach; to tutor 3. to give up (one's life, etc.)

shòujiǎng 授獎 to award a prize

shòujīng 授精 to inseminate; insemination

shòukè 授課 to teach; to tutor

shòumìng 授命 to sacrifice one's life

shòuquán 授權 1. to authorize 2. to license

shòutú 授徒 to teach students or pupils

shòuyè 授業 to teach; to tutor

shòuyì 授意 to intimate; to inspire

shòuyǔ 授與 to confer; to give

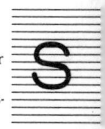

S

shòuzhí 授職 to give an official job to

shòu 壽
1. the life span 2. old age; a long life; longevity 3. birthday 4. to die of old age 5. to present another with gold, silk, etc. 6. to toast an elder

shòubǐ Nánshān 壽比南山 May your life be as lofty as the Southern Mountain Ranges.

shòuchén 壽辰 birthday

shòudàn 壽誕 a birthday anniversary

shòukǎo 壽考 long life

shòulǐ 壽禮 birthday gifts or presents

shòumìng 壽命 the life span of a person

shòutáo 壽桃 longevity peaches

shòuxing 壽星 1. a reference to a person on his birthday 2. the God of Longevity 3. Canopus

shòuzhōng zhèngqǐn 壽終正瘦 to die a natural death; to die of old age

shòu 瘦
thin; lean; slim; meager; scrawny; emaciated

shòucháng 瘦長 skinny and tall; tall and lean

shòugǔ línxún 瘦骨嶙峋 very skinny

shòuròu 瘦肉 lean meat

shòuruò 瘦弱 thin and weak; emaciated and frail

shòuxiǎo 瘦小 thin and small

shòu 獸
1. a general name for quadruped; a beast or animal 2. bestial; beastly

shòujiān 獸檻 a pen or cage for animals

shòupí 獸皮 animal skin or hide

shòuxìng 獸性 1. bestiality 2. animal passions or desires

shòuxìng dàfā 獸性大發 to raise one's animal disposition

shòuyī 獸醫 a veterinarian

shòuyù 獸欲 carnal desire; lust (especially referring to rape)

shū 抒
1. to give expression to; to express 2. to relieve; to ease; to lighten; to unburden

shūfā 抒發 to express; to voice; to give expression to

shūhuái 抒懷 to relieve the heart of emotions

shūqíng 抒情 to express one's feelings

shūqíngshī 抒情詩 a lyric; a lyric poem; lyric poetry

shūqíngwén 抒情文 lyrical writing

shū 叔 also **shú**
1. a younger brother of one's father; a paternal uncle 2. a younger brother of one's husband 3. a general designation for members of one's father's generation who are younger than one's father 4. declining

shūbái 叔伯 a relationship among cousins born of the same grandfather

shūfù 叔父 a younger brother of one's father; uncle

shūmǔ 叔母 the wife of one's father's younger brother; aunt

shūzhí 叔姪 an uncle and a nephew

shū 紓
1. to relax; to slacken; to slow down; to mitigate 2. to extricate from; to remove (causes of difficulties, poverty, etc.); to free from

shū'nàn 紓難 to extricate from trouble or danger

shū 書
1. writings; a book 2. to write 3. a letter 4. a document; a certificate 5. the style of the calligraphy; script

shūbāo 書包 a satchel; a schoolbag

shūbào 書報 books and newspapers

shūchú 書櫥 a bookcase

shūdāizi 書獃子 a pedant; a bookworm

shūdān 書單 a booklist

S

shūdiàn 書店 a bookstore

shūdù 書蠹 a bookworm

shūfǎ 書法 calligraphy

shūfǎjiā 書法家 a calligrapher

shūfáng 書房 a study

shūguì 書櫃 a bookcase

shūhán 書函 letters; correspondence

shūhuà 書畫 works of calligraphy and painting

shūhuàjiā 書畫家 a master in calligraphy and painting

shūjí 書籍 books

shūjiguān 書記官 a clerk of a law court

shūjiā 書夾 a bookend

shūjiá 書夾 refer to **shūjiā** 書夾

shūjià 書架 a bookshelf; a bookrack

shūjiǎn 書簡 a letter

shūjú 書局 a bookstore

shūjuànqì 書卷氣 bookishness

shūkān 書刊 books and magazines

shūkù 書庫 stack room

shūméi 書眉 the upper margin of a book page

shūmiàn dáfù 書面答覆 a written reply

shūmíng 書名 the title of a book

shūmù 書目 a book catalogue

shūpíng 書評 a book review

shūqiān 書籤 1. a book label pasted on the cover 2. a bookmark

shūshēng 書生 a student; a scholar

shūtān 書攤 a bookstand; a bookstall

shūtào 書套 a book jacket; a slipcase

shūxiāng méndì 書香門第 a literary family

shūxiě 書寫 to write

shūxìn 書信 letters; correspondence

shūyè 書頁 a page

shūzhāi 書齋 a study

shūzhuō 書桌 a desk

shū 殊

1. different; special; strange 2. distinguished; outstanding 3. extremely; very 4. really; indeed 5. still; yet 6. exceed; over

shūchǒng 殊寵 special favor

shūróng 殊榮 special honors

shūsǐzhàn 殊死戰 a life-or-death battle

shūtú tóngguī 殊途同歸 to reach the same destination (or goal) by different routes

shūyì 殊異 special; extraordinary

shū 倏 also **shù**

hastily; suddenly

shūhū 倏忽 all of a suddn; quickly

shū 梳

1. a comb; a coarse comb 2. to comb

shūlǐ 梳理 1. combing 2. (textile) carding

shūxǐ 梳洗 to comb one's hair and wash up

shūzhuāng 梳粧 (said of a woman) to doll up; to dress and make up

shūzhuāng dǎbàn 梳粧打扮 to dress smartly; to be dressed up

shūzhuāngtái 梳粧臺 a dressing table where cosmetics, toilet requisites, etc. are laid out for use

shūzi 梳子 a comb

shū 淑 also **shú**

1. good; pure; virtuous 2. (said of women) beautiful or charming 3. clear

shūnǚ 淑女 a gentlewoman; a lady

shūshèn 淑慎 (said of women) gentle and respectful

shūyuàn 淑媛 1. a rank of court ladies in ancient China 2. a lady; a gentlewoman

shū 疏

1. thin; sparse; few 2. unfamiliar; distant; unfriendly 3. careless; neglectful 4. to channel; to remove obstructions 5. coarse

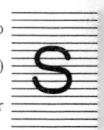

shūcái zhàngyì 疏財仗義 to give generously and be a champion of justice

shūdǎo 疏導 1. to channel 2. to enlighten

shūhu 疏忽 careless; remiss; negligent; oversight; to neglect

shūjùn 疏濬 to clean or dredge (waterways)

shūlòu 疏漏 careless omissions; slips; oversights

shūmì 疏密 1. looseness and density 2. neglect and watchfulness

shūsàn 疏散 to disperse; dispersion

shūshī 疏失 remiss; at fault; negligent

shūsōng 疏鬆 1. loose 2. puffy

shūtōng 疏通 to clean or dredge (a waterway)

shūyú fángfàn 疏於防範 to fail to take precautions

shūyú zhíshǒu 疏於職守 to neglect one's duty

shūyuǎn 疏遠 (said of relations) not close

shū 舒

1. to unfold; to stretch; to open; to relax 2. slow; unhurried; leisurely 3. a Chinese family name

shūchàng 舒暢 1. pleasant; comfortable 2. leisurely and harmonious

shūfu 舒服 comfortable; cosy; comfort

shūhuǎn 舒緩 leisurely; relaxed; to relax

shūméi 舒眉 to show pleasure

shūshì 舒適 comfortable; cosy; snug

shūtǎn 舒坦 happy; comfortable

shūzhǎn 舒展 to limber up; to unfold; to relax; to stretch

shū 蔬

1. vegetables; greens 2. a vegetarian diet; vegetable food

shūcài 蔬菜 vegetables

shū 樞

a hinge; a pivot

shūjī zhǔjiào 樞機主教 a cardinal of the Catholic Church

shūniǔ 樞紐 the vital point; the key; the pivot

shū 輸

1. to transport; to convey; to haul 2. to hand in; to contribute; to donate; to submit 3. to be beaten; to lose (a game, contest, etc.)

shūbuqǐ 輸不起 1. to display ill humor after losing a game, etc.; to lack sportsmanship 2. cannot afford to lose

shūchū 輸出 1. export (of goods); to export 2. (computers) output

shūjiā 輸家 the loser

shūqián 輸錢 to lose money in gambling

shūrù 輸入 1. import (of goods); to import 2. (computers) input

shūsòng 輸送 to transport; to convey

shūxiě 輸血 refer to **shūxuè** 輸血

shūxuè 輸血 1. (medicine) blood transfusion 2. to give aid and support; to give somebody a shot in the arm

shūyíng 輸贏 losses and gains (in gambling, etc.); defeat or victory (in a game, etc.)

shú 叔

refer to **shū** 叔

shú 孰

1. (in literary texts) what; which 2. who; whom

shúshì shúfēi 孰是孰非 Which is right and which is wrong?

shú 淑

refer to **shū** 淑

shú 塾

1. an anteroom or vestibule 2. a family school; a village school; a private primary school

shú 熟 also **shóu**

1. cooked or well-done (as opposed to raw); prepared or processed 2. ripe (fruit); to ripen 3. very familiar; well versed; experienced; conversant 4. careful or painstaking (survey, study,

inspection, etc.) 5. deep or sound (sleep)

shú'ān 熟諳 to be well versed in; to be an expert in

shúdú 熟讀 to read thoroughly; to memorize by rote

shújì 熟記 to learn by heart; to memorize

shúkè 熟客 an old customer or patron; a frequent visitor

shúliàn 熟練 experienced, skilled or dexterous

shúlù 熟路 a familiar route

shúmiànkǒng 熟面孔 a familiar face

shú'néng shēngqiǎo 熟能生巧 Practice makes perfect.

shúrén 熟人 an old acquaintance

shúshì 熟視 to look carefully and for a long time

shúshì 熟識 very familiar with

shúshǒu 熟手 an experienced or skilled hand

shúshuì 熟睡 a sound sleep; to sleep soundly

shúxī 熟悉 very familiar with

shúxí 熟習 to be skilled in

shúzhī 熟知 well acquainted or familiar with; to know well

shú 贖

1. to redeem; to ransom 2. to atone for; to expiate

shúhuí 贖回 to recover by paying money; to redeem; to ransom

shújīn 贖金 a ransom

shúkuǎn 贖款 a ransom

shúshēn 贖身 to redeem oneself

shúzuì 贖罪 1. to atone for a sin; to expiate a sin 2. to buy freedom from punishment 3. (Christianity) redemption

shǔ 黍

a variety of millet

shǔjì 黍稷 a variety of millet

shǔ 暑

1. hot; heat; the heat of summer 2. midsummer; summer

shǔjià 暑假 summer vacation

shǔqī 暑期 1. summer 2. the summer vacation

shǔqībān 暑期班 a summer class or school

shǔqī 暑期 refer to **shǔqī** 暑期

shǔqībān 暑期班 refer to **shǔqībān** 暑期班

shǔqì 暑氣 the scorching heat; the heat of summer

shǔqì pòrén 暑氣迫人 The summer heat is very oppressive.

shǔrè 暑熱 the scorching heat; the heat of summer

shǔrù 暑溽 hot and humid

Shǔ 蜀

1. an ancient kingdom in what is Sichuan Province today 2. an alternative name of Sichuan Province

shǔ 鼠

a mouse; a rat

shǔbèi 鼠輩 a mean fellow

shǔcuàn 鼠竄 to run away like frightened rats

shǔmù cùnguāng 鼠目寸光 shortsighted; lacking foresight

shǔxī 鼠蹊 the groin

shǔyá quèjiǎo 鼠牙雀角 (figuratively) to carry on a lawsuit; to litigate

shǔ 署

1. (also **shù**) to arrange 2. (also **shù**) to write down; to put down 3. (also **shù**) to be a deputy 4. a public office

shǔmíng 署名 to sign one's name

shǔ 數

1. to count; to enumerate 2. to count (as best, etc.); to be reckoned as exceptionally (good, bad, etc.)

shǔbuqīng 數不清 innumerable; countless

shǔdiǎn wàngzǔ 數典忘祖 to forget one's origin; ungrateful

shǔluo 數落 to blame; to reprove

shǔshùr 數數兒 to name numbers; to count

shǔyī shǔ'èr 數一數二 either the best or second only to the best

shǔ 薯

a yam; a potato

shǔtiáo 薯條 French fries

shǔ 曙 also **shù**

down; daybreak

shǔguāng 曙光 the first light of morning; light at dawn

shǔsè 曙色 light at daybreak

shǔ 屬

1. a category; a class; a kind 2. to belong to; to be subordinate to

shǔdì 屬地 a territory; a colony

shǔshí 屬實 true

shǔxià 屬下 one's subordinate

shǔyú 屬於 to belong to

shù 戍

to guard; to defend

shùbiān 戍邊 to guard the border or the frontier

shùshǒu 戍守 to be stationed as garrison troops at (a fortified place, the border, etc.)

shùzú 戍卒 garrison soldiers; a frontier guard

shù 束

1. to bind 2. a bunch; a bundle 3. to control; to restrain; restraint

shùfú 束縛 refer to **shùfù** 束縛

shùfù 束縛 restrictions; to restrain; to bind up

shùshǒu dàibì 束手待斃 (literally) to wait for one's death with hands tied—to be a sitting duck

shùshǒu jiùqín 束手就擒 to put up no fight and allow oneself to be caught

shùshǒu wúcè 束手無策 no way out; at the end of the rope

shùxiū 束脩 (literally) ten pieces of dried meat—tuition

shùzhī gāogé 束之高閣 (literally) to place (something) high in the attic—to shelve it and forget about it

shù 述

1. to give an account of; to explain; to expound 2. to follow (precedents); to carry forward

shùzhí 述職 to report in person the performance of one's official duties

shù 恕

1. to forgive; to excuse 2. Excuse me. 3. benevolence

shùbù fèngpéi 恕不奉陪 I am sorry but I cannot keep you company.

shùbù yuǎnsòng 恕不遠送 I am sorry I cannot escort you farther.

shùzuì 恕罪 to forgive a fault; to pardon an offense

shù 倏

refer to **shū** 倏

shù 庶

1. born of a concubine 2. numerous 3. general; common 4. the common people; the commoners 5. almost

shùjī 庶幾 1. almost; nearly 2. probably 3. the capable and the virtuous

shùmín 庶民 the commoners; the multitude; the populace

shùwù 庶務 general affairs

shùxiū 庶羞 the various kinds of delicacies

shùzhèng 庶政 the numerous affairs of the state

shùzǐ 庶子 1. the son of a concubine 2. an ancient official title

shù 術

1. a skill; a feat 2. a way or method to do something

shùyǔ 術語 professional jargon; terminology; technical terms

shù 疏

1. to present point by point 2. to explicate; to annotate

shù 署

refer to **shǔ** 署 1, 2, 3

shù 漱 also **sòu**

1. to rinse; to gargle 2. to wash

shùkǒu 漱口 to gargle the throat

shùkǒubēi 漱口杯 a mouth

washing cup; a mug

shùkǒushuǐ 漱口水 a gargle; a mouthwash

shù 墅

a villa; a country house

shù 豎

1. to erect; to set up; to stand 2. upright; perpendicular; vertical 3. a young servant 4. petty officers in the palace 5. a downward, perpendicular stroke in calligraphy

shùdí 豎笛 a clarinet

shùlì 豎立 to erect

shùqǐ dàmuzhǐ 豎起大拇指 thumbs up

shùqín 豎琴 the harp

shù 數

1. number; quantity; amount; sum 2. (mathematics) numbers 3. several; a few 4. a plan; an idea 5. fate; destiny 6. art

shùbèi 數倍 several times; manifold

shù'é 數額 number; sum

shùjù 數據 data

shùliàng 數量 quantity; amount

shùmù 數目 number; sum

shùnián 數年 several years; a few years

shùnián rú yīrì 數年如一日 with perseverance and consistency

shùtiān 數天 several days; a few days

shùxué 數學 mathematics

shùyǐ wànjì 數以萬計 by tens of thousands; numerous

shùzhí 數值 numerical value

shùzì 數字 a numeral; a figure; a digit

shù 樹

1. a tree 2. to plant 3. to erect; to establish

shùbēi 樹碑 to erect a memorial tablet

shùcóng 樹叢 a grove of trees

shùdà zhāofēng 樹大招風 Famous persons attract criticisms easily.

shùdǎng 樹黨 to form a clique, gang, faction, party, etc.

shùdé 樹德 to exemplify one's integrity

shùdí 樹敵 to make an enemy of; to make enemy; to antagonize

shùgàn 樹幹 the trunk of a tree

shùgēn 樹根 the root of a tree

shùjiāo 樹膠 resin; gum

shùlì 樹立 to establish (a reputation, etc.)

shùlín 樹林 a forest; woods

shùmiáo 樹苗 a seedling; a sapling

shùmù 樹木 a tree

shùpí 樹皮 bark

shùshang 樹上 on the tree; above the tree

shùshāo 樹梢 the tip of a tree

shùxià 樹下 under the tree

shùyè 樹葉 the leaf of a tree; foliage

shùyìn 樹蔭 the shade of a tree

shùyǐng 樹影 the shadow of a tree

shùzhī 樹枝 the branch of a tree

shùzhī 樹脂 resin

shù 曙

refer to **shǔ** 曙

shuā 刷

1. to brush; to scrub; to clean; to daub 2. a brush 3. to eliminate

shuāxǐ 刷洗 to scrub

shuāxīn 刷新 1. to make like new; to renovate 2. to make (a new sports record)

shuāyá 刷牙 to brush the teeth

shuāzi 刷子 a brush

shuǎ 耍

to play; to sport

shuǎbǎxì 耍把戲 to juggle; to play tricks

shuǎdàpái 耍大牌 to act like a prima donna

shuǎhuāzhāo 耍花招 1. to show off some special skill 2. to play tricks

shuǎlài 耍賴 to act shamelessly; to be perverse

shuǎliúmáng 耍流氓 to behave like a hooligan; to act rudely

shuǎnòng 耍弄 to make a fool of; to deceive

shuǎpíqi 耍脾氣 to lose one's temper

shuǎwēifēng 耍威風 to throw one's weight about; to be overbearing

shuǎwúlài 耍無賴 to be perverse

shuǎ zuǐpízi 耍嘴皮子 to brag; to talk big

shuà 刷

shuàxuǎn 刷選 to choose; to pick; to select

shuāi 衰

1. to decline; weakening; failing (health, etc.) 2. declining or falling (nations, etc.)

shuāibài 衰敗 to decline and disintegrate

shuāijié 衰竭 exhaustion; prostration

shuāilǎo 衰老 senile; senility

shuāiluò 衰落 the decline and fall

shuāiruò 衰弱 to debilitate; weak; sickly; not healthy

shuāituì 衰退 failing (energy, strength, etc.)

shuāiwáng 衰亡 the decline and fall

shuāiwēi 衰微 to decline; to wane; declining

shuāiwéi 衰微 refer to **shuāiwēi** 衰微

shuāi 摔

1. to throw to the ground; to fling; to break 2. to get rid of; to shake off (a tail, etc.) 3. to fall down; to tumble; to lose one's balance

shuāijiāo 摔跤 to fall down; to suffer a fall

shuāijiǎo 摔角 to wrestle; wrestling

shuāipò 摔破 1. to suffer bruises or in juries in a fall 2. to break something by dashing it on the ground

shuāishāng 摔傷 to get hurt in a fall

shuāisǐ 摔死 to fall to death

shuǎi 甩

1. to throw away; to discard; to cast away 2. to leave (somebody) behind 3. to swing

shuǎidiào 甩掉 to get rid of

shuài 帥 also **shuò**

1. commander-in-chief 2. to lead; to command 3. to follow (with orders) 4. (slang) dashing; smart looking

shuàilǐng 帥領 to command

shuài 率

1. to lead (troops, a team, etc.); to command 2. to follow; to act in accordance with 3. rash and hasty 4. generally; in general; usually 5. simple and candid; frank; straightforward; to the point 6. (said of men) dashing

shuàilǐng 率領 to lead (troops, a team, etc.); to head (a mission, etc.)

shuàishī 率師 to lead troops

shuàitóng 率同 accompanied by; to lead all the others in (visiting, inspecting, etc.)

shuàixiān 率先 to be the first; to take the lead

shuàixìng 率性 1. one's natural disposition 2. to act according to the dictates of one's conscience

shuàiyóu jiùzhāng 率由舊章 to follow old practices or precedents

shuàizhēn 率眞 candid; frank; honest; straight

shuàizhí 率直 candid; frank; honest; straight

shuàizhòng 率衆 to lead a crowd

shuān 拴

1. to tie up; to fasten 2. to drive a wedge between two parties

shuānshang 拴上 to fasten (the door, window, etc.)

shuānzhe 拴著 tied up; fastened

shuān 閂

1. to fasten with a bolt or latch

2. the latch of a door

shuān 栓
1. a wooden pin; a peg 2. a bolt; a plug 3. a stopper; a cork

shuàn 涮
1. to rinse (a container, etc.) 2. to boil in a chafing pot 3. to cheat with lies

shuànguōzi 涮鍋子 mutton cooked in a chafing pot

shuànxǐ 涮洗 to rinse

shuànyángròu 涮羊肉 mutton cooked in a chafing pot

shuāng 霜
1. frost; hoarfrost 2. white and powdery—like hoarfrost 3. coolness; indifference; grave 4. virtuous; pure and clean

shuāngbìn 霜鬢 hoary hair on the temples

shuānghài 霜害 damage to farm crops caused by frost; frostbite; frost injury

shuāngqílín 霜淇淋 soft ice cream

shuāngxuě 霜雪 1. frost and snow 2. snow-white

shuāng 雙
1. a pair; a brace; a couple; persons or things that come in pairs 2. two; both; even (as distinct from odd)

shuāngbāotāi 雙胞胎 twins

shuāngbèi 雙倍 double; twofold; twice the amount or number

shuāngbiān huìtán 雙邊會談 bilateral talks

shuāngcéng 雙層 double layers; double decks

shuāngchóng 雙重 double; dual; twofold

shuāngdǎ 雙打 to play in doubles (as tennis); doubles

shuāngfāng 雙方 both parties or sides

shuāngguān 雙關 ambiguous; subject to two different interpretations

shuāngguānyǔ 雙關語 a double entendre; a pun

shuāngguǎn qíxià 雙管齊下 1. to do two things simultaneously in order to attain an objective; a double-barreled move 2. ambiguous; subject to two different interpretations

shuānghào 雙號 an even number

shuāngliào 雙料 articles, products built with added strength, durability, etc. by using better and more raw materials

shuāngmiàn 雙面 two-sided; double-faced; reversible; double-edged

shuāngqīn 雙親 one's parents

shuāngrénchuáng 雙人床 a double bed

shuāngrénfáng 雙人房 a double room; a twin room

shuāngshā 雙殺 (baseball) double play

shuāngshēng 雙生 twin; twins

shuāngshǒu 雙手 the two hands; both hands

shuāngshǒu wànnéng 雙手萬能 With two hands, one can work miracles.

shuāngshuāng duìduì 雙雙對對 in pairs and couples

shuāngsù shuāngfēi 雙宿雙飛 to live like man and wife; to sleep and move together

shuāngxǐ línmén 雙喜臨門 to have simultaneously two happy events in a family

shuāngxiàbā 雙下巴 a double chin

shuāngxiǎng 雙餉 double pay for soldiers

shuāngxiàng gōutōng 雙向溝通 two-way communication

shuāngyǎngshuǐ 雙氧水 hydrogen peroxide

Shuāngyúzuò 雙魚座 Pisces

Shuāngzǐzuò 雙子座 Gemini

shuāng 孀
a widow

shuāngjū 孀居 to remain in widowhood; to live as a widow

shuǎng 爽

1. refreshing; bracing; pleasant; crisp; agreeable; brisk 2. to feel well 3. frank; straightforward; open-hearted 4. to fail; to miss; to lose 5. to be in error

shuǎngkǒu 爽口 palatable; tasty

shuǎngkuai 爽快 1. straightforward; open-hearted 2. readily and briskly 3. comfortable; pleasant

shuǎnglǎng 爽朗 1. (said of weather, etc.) refreshing 2. straightforward; open-minded

shuǎngshēnfěn 爽身粉 talcum powder

shuǎngyuē 爽約 to fail to keep a promise

shuǎngzhí 爽直 outspoken; straightforward

shuí 誰
refer to **shéi** 誰

shuǐ 水
1. water 2. a general term for seas, lakes, rivers, etc. 3. liquid; juice 4. flood disaster; flood 5. a Chinese family name

shuǐbà 水壩 a dam

shuǐbīn 水濱 the shore

shuǐbō 水波 ripples of water

shuǐcǎi 水彩 watercolor

shuǐcǎihuà 水彩畫 a watercolor painting; a watercolor

shuǐcáo 水槽 a water trough; a water tank

shuǐcǎo 水草 1. waterweeds 2. water and grass

shuǐchǎn 水產 marine products

shuǐchē 水車 1. a water wheel 2. a water cart

shuǐchí 水池 a pool; a pond

shuǐdào 水道 1. a watercourse; a waterway 2. (by) water

shuǐdào 水稻 aquatic rice (as opposed to hill rice)

shuǐdào qúchéng 水到渠成 The thing takes care of itself.

shuǐdī 水滴 water drops

shuǐdǐ 水底 at the bottom of water

shuǐdiàn 水電 water and electricity

shuǐdiànfèi 水電費 charges for water and electricity

shuǐdòu 水痘 chicken pox; varicella

shuǐfèn 水分 moisture; water content

shuǐgāng 水缸 a large pottery jug for holding water

shuǐgōu 水溝 a ditch; a drain; a gutter

shuǐguǎn 水管 a water pipe

shuǐguǐ 水鬼 1. a water goblin 2. (slang) a frogman

shuǐguǒ 水果 fruit

shuǐhú 水壺 a canteen

shuǐhuā 水花 foam; froth; spray

shuǐhuàn 水患 floods; flood disaster

shuǐhuǒ bù xiāngróng 水火不相容 Water and fire can not coexist—(figuratively) incompatible

shuǐjiǎo 水餃 Chinese ravioli; boiled dumplings

shuǐjīng 水晶 crystal; crystallized quartz

shuǐjīngqiú 水晶球 a crystal ball

shuǐjīngtǐ 水晶體 1. (anatomy) the lens (of eyes) 2. the crystalline lens

shuǐjǐng 水井 a well

shuǐjiǔ 水酒 diluted wine

shuǐjūn 水軍 (formerly) the navy; naval units

shuǐkēng 水坑 a water hole; a pool

shuǐkù 水庫 a reservoir

shuǐlái tǔyǎn 水來土掩 to attempt to stop any onslaught

shuǐléi 水雷 a mine (against the ship)

shuǐlì 水力 water power

shuǐlì 水利 water conservancy

shuǐlì fādiàn 水力發電 hydraulic power generation

shuǐlì fādiànchǎng 水力發電廠 a hydraulic power plant

shuǐlì gōngchéng 水利工程 hydraulic engineering

shuǐliàng 水量 water volume; amount of water

shuǐliú 水流 water current; water flow

shuǐlóngtóu 水龍頭 a faucet; a cock; a tap

shuǐlù 水陸 land and water

shuǐlù 水路 1. a watercourse; a waterway 2. (by) water

shuǐluò shíchū 水落石出 The truth comes into light eventually.

shuǐmén 水門 a floodgate; a sluice

shuǐmìtáo 水蜜桃 a honey peach

shuǐmiàn 水面 the water surface; the water level

shuǐmǔ 水母 a jellyfish

shuǐní 水泥 cement

shuǐniǎo 水鳥 water birds; waterfowls

shuǐnéng 水能 hydraulic power generation

shuǐniú 水牛 a water buffalo

shuǐpào 水泡 1. a bubble 2. a blister

shuǐpào 水疱 a blister

shuǐpén 水盆 a basin

shuǐpíng 水平 horizontal

Shuǐpíngzuò 水瓶座 (astrology) Aquarius (or Water Carrier)

shuǐqì 水汽 water vapor; moisture; steam

shuǐqiāng 水槍 a squirt gun

shuǐqiú 水球 (sports) water polo

shuǐróngxìng 水溶性 solubility

shuǐshàng rénjiā 水上人家 boat dwellers

shuǐshàng yùndòng 水上運動 water sports; aquatic sports

shuǐshēn 水深 the depth of water

shuǐshēn huǒrè 水深火熱 an abyss of suffering

shuǐshì 水勢 1. the flow of the water 2. the direction of flowing water

shuǐshǒu 水手 a sailor; a mariner

shuǐtǎ 水塔 a water tower

shuǐtǎ 水獺 an otter

shuǐtǎ 水獺 refer to **shuǐtǎ** 水獺

shuǐtán 水潭 a pool; a pond

shuǐtáng 水塘 a pool; a pond

shuǐtǒng 水桶 a bucket; a pail

shuǐtǔ bǎochí 水土保持 soil conservation

shuǐtǔ bùfú 水土不服 one's system disagreeing with a new natural environment

shuǐwāngwāng 水汪汪 (said of women's eyes) bright and attractive

shuǐwèi 水位 the water stage; the water level

shuǐwūrǎn 水污染 water pollution

shuǐxiānhuā 水仙花 a narcissus; a daffodil

shuǐxiāng 水箱 a water tank

shuǐxiè bùtōng 水泄不通 so crowded

Shuǐxīng 水星 the planet Mercury

shuǐxìng yánghuā 水性楊花 (said of women) fickle and lascivious

shuǐyā 水鴨 a teal

shuǐyā 水壓 water pressure

shuǐyín 水銀 mercury (an element)

shuǐyíndēng 水銀燈 a mercury lamp

shuǐyù 水域 waters; a water area

shuǐyuán 水源 1. the riverhead; the waterhead 2. a source of water

shuǐyùn 水運 transportation by water

shuǐzāi 水災 flood disaster; floods

shuǐzhá 水閘 a floodgate; a sluice

shuǐzhēngqì 水蒸氣 water vapor; steam; vapor

shuǐzhí 水質 refer to **shuǐzhì** 水質

shuǐzhì 水蛭 a leech

shuǐzhì 水質 properties of par-

ticular specimens of water

shuǐzhōng lāoyuè 水中撈月 to make obviously futile efforts

shuǐzhǒng 水腫 dropsy; hydrophilic swelling

shuǐzhǔn 水準 a standard; a level

shuǐzúguǎn 水族館 an aquarium

shuì 稅

taxes; duties on commodities

shuìdān 稅單 1. a tax invoice 2. a tax form

shuìjīn 稅金 tax money

shuìjuān 稅捐 taxes and surtaxes

shuìkuǎn 稅款 tax money

shuìlǜ 稅率 tax rates; duty rates

shuìshōu 稅收 tax revenue

shuìwù jīguān 稅務機關 tax offices

shuì 蛻

refer to **tuì** 蛻

shuì 睡

to sleep; to rest with eyes closed

shuìdài 睡袋 a sleeping bag

shuìjiào 睡覺 to sleep; to go to bed

shuìlián 睡蓮 a water lily

shuìmào 睡帽 a nightcap

shuìmián 睡眠 sleep

shuìpáo 睡袍 a sleeping gown; pajamas

shuìwǔjiào 睡午覺 to take a siesta or afternoon nap

shuìxǐng 睡醒 to wake up from sleep

shuìyǎn xīngsōng 睡眼惺忪 to have a drowsy look

shuìyī 睡衣 a sleeping gown; pajamas

shuìyì 睡意 sleepiness; drowsiness

shuìzháo 睡著 to have fallen asleep

shuì 說

to persuade; to influence

shuìfú 說服 to persuade; to convince

shuìkè 說客 a professional commissary in ancient times sent by one monarch to another with a view to convincing him

shǔn 吮

to suck; to lick

shǔn 盾

refer to **dùn** 盾

shùn 順

1. to follow; to submit to; obedient 2. in the same direction as 3. agreeable; favorable; comfortable 4. to arrange; to put in order 5. convenient; smooth 6. to take the opportunity to

shùnbiàn 順便 at one's convenience; without taking extra trouble

shùnchā 順差 favorable balance; surplus

shùnchàng 順暢 smooth; unhindered

shùncóng 順從 1. to obey; obedient 2. (psychology) submission

shùndang 順當 without a hitch; easy and smooth

shùndào 順道 1. to obey good reasons 2. to do something on the way to a place, which requires no additional travel

shùn'ěr 順耳 pleasant to the ear

shùnfēng 順風 1. to move with the wind 2. good luck 3. a favorable wind; a tail wind

shùnfēng zhuǎnduò 順風轉舵 to trim one's sails; to take one's cue from changing conditions

shùnjìng 順境 in easy circumstances; in favorable circumstances

shùnkǒu 順口 1. to speak without much thought; to slip out of one's tongue 2. easy to speak, read or sing 3. to suit one's taste

shùnkǒuliū 順口溜 doggerel; a jingle

shùnlǐ chéngzhāng 順理成章 as a matter of course

shùnlì 順利 (going) smoothly; having no trouble; easy (going); encountering no difficulties

shùnlù 順路 in passing; while on the way

shùnqí zìrán 順其自然 to let nature take its course; in accordance with its natural tendency

shùnshì 順勢 to take advantage of an opportunity (as provided by an opponent's reckless move)

shùnshǒu 順手 1. smooth (operation); easy (going) 2. to do something without extra trouble 3. handy; conveniently

shùnshǒu qiānyáng 順手牽羊 to steal something in passing; to pick up something on the sly

shùnshuǐ rénqíng 順水人情 to do someone a favor without causing oneself any trouble

shùnshuǐ tuīzhōu 順水推舟 to approve something that is sure to succeed

shùnsuì 順遂 without a hitch or obstruction; very smooth or easy going; in satisfactory circumstances

shùnxīn 順心 satisfactorily; gratifying

shùnxù 順序 according to right order

shùnyán 順延 to postpone

shùnyǎn 順眼 to please the eye; pleasant to the eye

shùnyìng 順應 to adjust

shùnyìng cháoliú 順應潮流 to conform to modern trends

Shùn 舜

a legendary ruler said to have ruled ancient China around 2200 B.C.

shùn 瞬

1. to blink, wink or twinkle 2. a very short time; in the twinkling of an eye

shùnjiān 瞬間 in an instant

shùnxī wànbiàn 瞬息萬變 many changes within a short time

shùnxí wànbiàn 瞬息萬變 refer to **shùnxī wànbiàn** 瞬息萬變

shuō 說

1. to speak; to talk; to say 2. to

explain; to clarify 3. a description; a narration; a statement 4. a theory 5. to scold

shuōbù chūkǒu 說不出口 unutterable

shuōbude 說不得 1. unspeakable; indescribable 2. unfit for mention 3. unavoidable

shuōbudìng 說不定 maybe; perhaps; probably

shuōbu guòqù 說不過去 unacceptable to one's sense of propriety or justice

shuō Cáo Cāo, Cáo Cāo jiù dào 說曹操，曹操就到 Talk of the devil and the devil appears.

shuōcháng dàoduǎn 說長道短 to criticize others

shuōchū 說出 to speak out; to reveal; to utter

shuōchuān 說穿 to unravel or expose by some remarks; to tell what something really is

shuōcí 說詞 excuses; pretexts

shuōcuòhuà 說錯話 to speak what should not have been uttered

shuōdàhuà 說大話 to brag

shuōdào 說到 to speak of; to mention

shuōdào zuòdào 說到做到 to do what one says

shuōde guòqù 說得過去 acceptable; passable; excusable

shuōdehǎo 說得好 well said

shuōde hǎotīng 說得好聽 to make an unpleasant fact sound attractive

shuōde yǒulǐ 說得有理 to sound reasonable

shuōfǎ 說法 to preach Buddhism

shuōfa 說法 the way of reasoning; an argument

shuō fēngliánghuà 說風涼話 to talk like an unconcerned person

shuōhǎo shuōdǎi 說好說歹 to speak both well and ill in an attempt to influence or induce

shuōhe 說合 to help arrange a union

shuōhe 說和 to act as a mediator

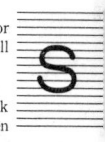

S

shuōhuà 說話 1. to speak; to talk; to say 2. to tell stories 3. a chat; a talk 4. gossip; talk

shuōhuǎng 說謊 to tell a lie; to lie

shuōjiào 說教 to preach; to deliver a sermon

shuōlái huàcháng 說來話長 It is a long story....

shuōlái shuōqù 說來說去 to say the same thing over and over again

shuōlǐ 說理 1. to give a sermon; to preach 2. to be reasonable; to argue

shuōliūzuǐ 說溜嘴 to have a slip of the tongue; to blurt out something

shuōméi 說媒 to propose a marriage as a matchmaker

shuōmènghuà 說夢話 1. to talk in one's sleep 2. to talk nonsense

shuōmíng 說明 1. to explain; to clarify; to expound 2. expository writing

shuōmíngshū 說明書 a written explanation

shuōqǐ 說起 1. to start talking about; to bring up (a subject) 2. with reference to; as for

shuōqīn 說親 to propose a marriage as a matchmaker

shuōqíng 說情 to solicit a favor or to ask for mercy on behalf of others

shuōshū 說書 to tell stories

shuōxiánhuà 說閒話 to gossip; to criticize

shuōxiàng 說項 to speak favorably of another

shuōxiàohuà 說笑話 to tell jokes

shuōxiào 說笑 to joke; to talk and laugh

shuōyī bù'èr 說一不二 to be a man of his word; to keep one's promise; to stand by one's word

shuōzǒu jiùzǒu 說走就走 to announce the intention to leave and really mean it

shuó 芍
refer to **sháo** 芍

shuò 帥
refer to **shuài** 帥

shuò 朔
1. to begin 2. north 3. the first day of the month of the lunar calendar

shuòwàng 朔望 the first and the 15th days of the lunar month

shuò 碩 also **shí**
great; large

shuòguǒ jǐncún 碩果僅存 the only one of its kind to have survived

shuòshì 碩士 a holder of the master's degree

shuò 數
often; frequently

shuòjiàn bùxiān 數見不鮮 not uncommon; nothing new

shuòjiàn bùxiǎn 數見不鮮 refer to **shuòjiàn bùxiān** 數見不鮮

shuò 爍
1. to glitter; to glisten; to sparkle 2. to melt

sī 司
1. to have charge of; to preside over 2. a (government) department

sīfǎ 司法 judicature; judiciary

sīfǎguān 司法官 a legal officer; a judge

sīfǎ jīguān 司法機關 judicial organs

sījī 司機 a driver; a chauffeur

sīkōng jiànguàn 司空見慣 something quite usual

sīlìng 司令 a commander

sīlìngbù 司令部 headquarters

sīlìngtái 司令臺 a review stand

sīyí 司儀 an M.C.; an emcee

sī 私
1. private; personal; person-to-person 2. secret; clandestine 3. to have illicit relations or an affair with 4. contraband 5. prejudice; biased; to favor 6. selfish; selfishly 7. reproductive organs of both sexes

S

sībēn 私奔 to elope; elopement

sīcáng 私藏 1. private collection 2. to keep something against the law

sīchǎn 私產 private property

sīchù 私處 private parts; reproductive organs of both sexes

sīdìng zhōngshēn 私定終身 (in old China) to pledge to marry without the permission of parents

sīfangqián 私房錢 private savings

sījiā zhēntàn 私家偵探 a private detective

sījiāo 私交 personal friendship

sījiǔ 私酒 bootleg; moonshine

sīlì 私立 (usually said of schools, hospitals, etc.) established and operated by private funds

sīrén 私人 individual; personal; private

sīshēnghuó 私生活 one's private life

sīshēngzǐ 私生子 an illegitimate child; a bastard

sīshì 私事 personal affairs; private affairs

sītōng 私通 1. to collaborate with enemy forces or a foreign country 2. to have an illicit affair with parties other than one's spouse; adultery

sīxià 私下 privately; secretly

sīxīn 私心 selfishness; favoritism

sīyíng 私營 privately-operated

sīyǒu 私有 privately-owned

sīyù 私欲 1. personal or selfish desires 2. greediness

sīzhāng 私章 a personal seal; a private chop

sīzì 私自 personally; privately

sī 思

1. to think; to contemplate; to consider 2. memory; remembrance; to remember; to recall; to think of 3. to mourn; to grieve 4. to admire 5. to pine for 6. a final particle to sound off an expression

sīcháo 思潮 1. the prevailing trend of thought 2. the changing tides of one's thought

sīchūn 思春 (usually said of girls) to pine for the opposite sex

sīcǔn 思忖 to think; to consider; to ponder

sīkǎo 思考 to ponder; to think; contemplation

sīkǎolì 思考力 the power to think, analyze and speculate

sīliang 思量 to think; to consider; to ponder

sīlù 思路 (usually said of writing) the clarity of thinking, or the lack of it

sīlǜ 思慮 consideration; contemplation; to think carefully

sīmù 思慕 1. to admire (a girl, etc.) 2. to remember (old days, etc.)

sīniàn 思念 to remember (old days, friends, etc.); to recall

sīsuǒ 思索 to study; to ponder over

sīwéi 思維 thought; thinking

sīxiāngbìng 思鄉病 homesickness; nostalgia

sīxiǎng 思想 1. thought; ideas; mentality 2. to think of; to recall

sīxiǎngjiā 思想家 a thinker

sīxiǎng luòwǔ 思想落伍 old-fashioned in thinking; outdated ideas

sīxù 思緒 a train of thought

sī 絲

1. silk 2. very fine thread, fiber, etc. as those making a spider's web 3. a general name of silk fabrics or goods 4. strings of musical instruments 5. infinitesimal; a trace; a thread; a tiny bit

sīchóu 絲綢 silk cloth; silk

sīdài 絲帶 silk ribbons

sīguā 絲瓜 the sponge gourd (the fruit of a loofah); towel gourds

sīháo 絲毫 the tiniest, slightest, or least bit

sīháo bùshuǎng 絲毫不爽 very reliable or accurate

sīróng 絲絨 velvet

sīsī rùkòu 絲絲入扣 ingenious and touching; right on the beat

sīwà 絲襪 silk stockings; silk socks

sīzhīpǐn 絲織品 silk fabrics; silk goods

sī 斯

1. this; these; such; here 2. a connecting particle—then; thus

Sīlǐlánkǎ 斯里蘭卡 Sri Lanka

sīwén 斯文 cultured; gentle; elegant; refined

sī 廝

1. a servant 2. a fellow; a guy 3. each other; together

sīdǎ 廝打 to have a melee; to fight

sīhùn 廝混 1. to mingle 2. to fool around together 3. to make trouble

sīnào 廝鬧 to have a spree

sīshā 廝殺 to slaughter one another (as in a battle); to fight at close quarters

sīshǒu 廝守 to take care of each other

sī 撕

to tear; to rip

sīdiào 撕掉 to tear up; to tear off

sīhuǐ 撕毀 to tear; to rip

sīkāi 撕開 to tear open; to rip open

sīpiào 撕票 to kill a hostage

sīpò 撕破 to tear; to rip

sīsuì 撕碎 to tear or rip to pieces

sī 嘶

1. the neighing of a horse 2. (said of voice) hoarse

sī 鷥

an egret

sǐ 死

1. to die; to die for; dead; death 2. used as an intensive or superlative; very; extremely 3. condemned (persons whose deaths are numbered, as criminals on the death row) 4. inanimate; dull and stupid; inert; insensible; lifeless 5. obstinate or stubborn; persevering; resolute; resolutely 6. rigid, fixed or unchangeable

(regulations, etc.); immovable (drawers, etc.) 7. impassable; closed

sǐbǎn 死板 wooden (persons); rigid (regulations); fixed and unchangeable (methods, etc.)

sǐbié 死別 to be parted by death; death-partings

sǐbù míngmù 死不瞑目 to be unwilling to die (because of some unfinished tasks, unfulfilled wishes, intensive grudges, etc.)

sǐbù rèncuò 死不認錯 stubbornly refuse to admit one's guilt or mistake

sǐbù zúxī 死不足惜 Death is not to be regretted (if it serves a purpose).

sǐbù zúxí 死不足惜 refer to **sǐbù zúxī** 死不足惜

sǐdǎng 死黨 sworn confederates; sworn followers

sǐdé qísuǒ 死得其所 to die a worthy death

sǐdúshū 死讀書 to read (a book) without thinking

sǐduìtou 死對頭 arch enemies or rivals

sǐhòu 死後 after death; postmortem

sǐhútòng 死胡同 refer to **sǐhútòng** 死胡同

sǐhútòng 死胡同 a dead-end alley

sǐhuī fùrán 死灰復燃 (said of emotion, especially love, crushed rebellious force, dormant ideas, etc.) rekindled; rejuvenated

sǐhuó 死活 dead or alive

sǐhuǒshān 死火山 an extinct volcano

sǐjí 死寂 refer to **sǐjì** 死寂

sǐjì 死記 to memorize by rote

sǐjì 死寂 deathly stillness

sǐjiǎo 死角 a dead angle; the defiladed space

sǐjié 死結 1. a fast knot (as opposed to slip knots) 2. an impasse

sǐjìnr 死勁兒 all one's strength

sǐlǐ táoshēng 死裡逃生 to escape death by a narrow mar-

gin

sǐlù 死路 1. a blind alley; a dead end 2. a fatal route

sǐlù yītiáo 死路一條 no way out; doomed

sǐnǎojīn 死腦筋 a one-track mind

sǐpí làiliǎn 死皮賴臉 brazen-faced and unreasonable

sǐqī 死期 the time of death; the hour of doom

sǐqí 死期 refer to sǐqī 死期

sǐqì chénchén 死氣沈沈 hopeless and gloomy; a dead atmosphere

sǐqiú 死囚 a death convict

sǐqù huólái 死去活來 half dead

sǐrén 死人 a dead person

sǐshāng 死傷 the dead and wounded

sǐshī 死屍 a corpse

sǐshǒu 死守 to defend (a position, city, etc.) to the last

sǐshuǐ 死水 stagnant (or stagnating) water

sǐwáng 死亡 to die; death

sǐwánglǜ 死亡率 death rate; mortality

sǐwáng zhèngshū 死亡證書 a death certificate

sǐwú duìzhèng 死無對證 to lack evidence because of the death of a principal witness

sǐwú zàngshēn zhīdì 死無葬身之地 to die without a place for burial (a phrase usually used as a warning to somebody)

sǐxiàng 死巷 a dead-end alley

sǐxīn 死心 to think no more of something

sǐxīn tādì 死心塌地 wholeheartedly; unreservedly

sǐxīnyǎnr 死心眼兒 obstinate and simple-minded

sǐxíng 死刑 a death penalty

sǐxùn 死訊 news of someone's death

sǐyào miànzi 死要面子 to try to preserve one's face at all costs

sǐyīn 死因 the cause of death

sǐyìngpài 死硬派 die-hards

sǐyǒu yúgū 死有餘辜 Death will not expiate all his crimes.

sǐyú fēimìng 死於非命 to die an unnatural death

sǐzhě 死者 the dead; the deceased

sǐzuì 死罪 the capital punishment

sì 巳
1. the sixth of the Twelve Terrestrial Branches 2. 9 to 11 a.m.

sìshí 巳時 the period of the day from 9 a.m. to 11 a.m.

sì 四
1. four; fourth 2. all around

sìbì xiāotiáo 四壁蕭條 as poor as a church mouse

sìbiānxíng 四邊形 a quadrilateral or tetragon

sìchóngzòu 四重奏 (instrumental) a quartet

sìchù 四處 everywhere; all around

Sìchuān 四川 Sichuan Province

sìfāng 四方 1. the four directions (east, west, north, and south) 2. every direction; all sides; everywhere

sìfēn wǔliè 四分五裂 to fall to pieces; to be all split up

sìhǎi wéijiā 四海爲家 1. (said of emperors) to make the country a big family 2. to lead a wandering life

sìjì 四季 the four seasons

sìjìdòu 四季豆 string beans; kidney beans

sìjiǎo cháotiān 四脚朝天 to fall on one's back

sìkāi 四開 quarto

sìmiàn 四面 four sides; all sides

sìmiàn bāfāng 四面八方 on every side; all directions; all around

sìmiàn Chǔgē 四面楚歌 facing hostility, difficulty, or frustration on all sides

sìpíng bāwěn 四平八穩 completely stable and safe

sìsàn 四散 to disperse everywhere

sìtōng bādá 四通八達 (said of

a communication network) leading everywhere

sìyuè 四月 1. April 2. the fourth month of the lunar calendar 3. four months

sìzhī 四肢 the four limbs

sìzhōuwéi 四周圍 all around; on all sides

sì 寺

a temple; a mosque; a shrine; a monastery

sì 伺

to spy; to reconnoiter; to watch

sìjī 伺機 to wait for one's chance

sìjī érdòng 伺機而動 to wait for a favorable moment to make a move

sìtàn 伺探 to investigate secretly

sì 祀

to worship; to offer sacrifices to

sìdiǎn 祀典 religious rites or services

sìfèng 祀奉 to worship; to offer sacrifices to

sì 似

1. to resemble; to seem 2. like; as if

sìhu 似乎 it seems, appears, or looks as if or as though

sìshì érfēi 似是而非 seemingly correct but really incorrect

sì 飼

to feed; to raise (domesticated animals)

sìliào 飼料 animal feed; fodder; forage

sìyǎng 飼養 to raise; to breed

sì 嗣

1. to inherit; to succeed to 2. a descendant 3. to continue; to follow

sìhòu 嗣後 thereafter

sìlì 嗣立 to appoint or to be appointed as heir

sìwèi 嗣位 to succeed to the throne

sì 肆

1. to let loose; to indulge in; to behave without restraint 2. a

shop; a marketplace; a place to display goods 3. to exhibit; to display 4. to execute a criminal and expose his corpse in the market 5. to extend; to expand 6. to assault; to attack suddenly 7. to use to the utmost; to exhaust 8. an elaborate form of four to prevent forgery

sìnüè 肆虐 1. to do damage unhinderedly 2. reckless and oppressive rampant

sìwú jìdàn 肆無忌憚 indulgent and reckless

sì 駟

1. a team of four horses 2. horses 3. four 4. name of a star

sìmǎ nánzhuī 駟馬難追 Even with a team of four horses, it is difficult to overtake carelessly uttered words.

sì 賜

refer to **cì** 賜

sōng 忪

used in the phrase **xīngsōng** (惺忪)—(said of eyes) not yet fully open on waking up

sōng 松

pines; firs

sōngbǎi 松柏 1. the pine and the cypress 2. the conifers

sōngbǎi chángqīng 松柏長青 (a congratulatory expression on someone's birthday) May you live long and remain strong like the evergreen pine and cypress！

sōngbǎi jiécāo 松柏節操 honest and virtuous conduct; fortitude

sōngbó 松柏 refer to **sōngbǎi** 松柏

sōngbó chángqīng 松柏長青 refer to **sōngbǎi chángqīng** 松柏長青

sōngbó jiécāo 松柏節操 refer to **sōngbǎi jiécāo** 松柏節操

sōngguǒ 松果 a strobile

sōnghè xiálíng 松鶴遐齡 longevity

Sōnghuājiāng 松花江 the Songhua River

sōngjiéyóu 松節油 turpentine

sōnglín 松林 a pinery

sōngshǔ 松鼠 the squirrel

sōngshù 松樹 a pine

sōngtāo 松濤 the soughing of the wind in the pines which sounds like roaring waves

sōng 嵩

1. Mountain Song 2. lofty

sōng 鬆

1. loose; lax; slack 2. to relax 3. to loosen 4. soft; light

sōngchí 鬆弛 1. relaxed; flabby 2. lax; slack

sōngdong 鬆動 1. to become less crowded 2. not hard up; well-off 3. to become relaxed or flexible

sōngjǐndài 鬆緊帶 an elastic string, band, etc.

sōngkāi 鬆開 to loosen

sōngkǒuqì 鬆口氣 to relax for a while; to get a breathing spell

sōngruǎn 鬆軟 loose and soft

sōngsǎn 鬆散 incompact; loosely arranged

sōngshǒu 鬆手 to let go the hands; to relax the hold

sōngxiè 鬆懈 to relax efforts, attention, etc.

sǒng 悚

fearful; terrified; frightened

sǒngjù 悚懼 to tremble with fear; frightened; terrified

sǒnglì 悚慄 to tremble with fear; frightened; terrified

sǒngrán 悚然 in terror; terror-stricken

sǒng 竦

1. respectful 2. awed

sǒngrán 竦然 fearful; scared

sǒng 慫

to instigate; to incite

sǒngyǒng 慫恿 to instigate; to incite

sǒng 聳

1. to alarm; to alert; to warn; to be sensational 2. to rise up; to stretch up erect or at full length

3. to be born deaf 4. to urge; to egg on

sǒngdòng 聳動 1. to urge; to egg on 2. to be moved or alarmed

sǒngjiān 聳肩 to shrug shoulders

sǒnglì 聳立 to tower aloft; to rise up steeply

sǒngrán 聳然 cliffy; rising in sharp elevation

Sòng 宋

1. the Song Dynasty (960-1279 A.D.); of, or having to do with, the Song Dynasty 2. a state in the Warring States period 3. a Chinese family name

sòng 送

1. to send; to dispatch; to deliver; to convey 2. to present; to give 3. to see someone off; to send off; to wish Godspeed to

sòngbàoshēng 送報生 a news-boy

sòngbié 送別 to see someone off; to give a send-off; to wish Godspeed to

sòngdá 送達 1. to deliver to; to dispatch to; to send to 2. (law) to serve (a writ on a person)

sòngjiù yíngxīn 送舊迎新 1. to bid farewell to those departing and greet the arrival of new comers 2. to send off the old year and usher in the new year

sònghuán 送還 to send back; to return

sònghuò 送貨 to deliver goods

sòngkè 送客 1. to escort a visitor on his way out 2. to speed a parting guest

sònglǐ 送禮 to give presents; to send gifts

sòngsǐ 送死 1. to prepare for the burial of one's parents 2. to bring death upon oneself

sòngxìnr 送信兒 to carry letters; to deliver letters

sòngxíng 送行 to see someone off; to give a send-off; to wish Godspeed to

sòngzàng 送葬 to attend a funeral; to take part in a funeral

procession

sòngzhōng 送終 to prepare for the burial of one's parents

sòng 訟

1. a lawsuit; litigation 2. to argue over the right and wrong of something; to dispute; to demand justice 3. publicly; in public

sòng'àn 訟案 a case at law

sòng 頌

1. to praise; to acclaim; to extol; to eulogize; to laud 2. a hymn to something; a composition in praise of some achievements, etc.; an ode; a eulogy; a paean; an accolade 3. a section in *The Book of Poetry*

sòngshēng zàidào 頌聲載道 praises all along the way—popular support

sòngyáng 頌揚 to praise; to acclaim; to eulogize

sòng 誦

1. to recite; to intone; to chant 2. poetry; poems; songs

sòngjīng 誦經 to recite passages from scriptures

sōu 搜

1. to search; to seek 2. to inquire into; to investigate

sōubǔ 搜捕 to search and arrest

sōuchá 搜查 to search (a house, a person, etc.)

sōuchulai 搜出來 to search out; to find

sōugòu 搜購 to collect or select for purchase

sōuguā 搜括 1. to search 2. to extort; to loot; to plunder

sōují 搜緝 to search for (a criminal, etc)

sōují 搜集 to seek and gather; to collect

sōujiù 搜救 to search for and rescue

sōuluó 搜羅 1. to seek and invite (men of ability, specialists, etc.) 2. to collect (rare stamps, antiques, etc.) 3. to scratch the bottom (for money, materials, etc.)

sōuná 搜拿 to hunt for (a fugitive)

sōuqì 搜緝 refer to **sōují** 搜緝

sōuqiú 搜求 to seek; to find; to look for

sōushēn 搜身 to frisk

sōusuǒ 搜索 to search; to reconnoiter

sōusuǒ kūcháng 搜索枯腸 to cudgel (or rack) one's brains (for new ideas, etc.)

sōusuǒzhuàng 搜索狀 a search warrant

sōuxún 搜尋 to search for; to seek and find

sōu 溲

1. to urinate 2. to immerse; to soak; to drench

sōu 蒐

1. to gather; to collect 2. to hunt or search for; hunting

sōují 蒐集 to collect or gather

sōuluó 蒐羅 to search and collect

sōu 艘 also **sāo**

a numerary adjunct for ships

sōu 餿

1. decayed; rotten; stale 2. foul; lousy

sōuzhǔyì 餿主意 a lousy idea

sǒu 嗾

1. to give vocal signals to a dog 2. to instigate

sǒushǐ 嗾使 to instigate; to incite

sòu 嗽

to cough; to clear the throat

sòu 漱

refer to **shù** 漱

sū 酥

1. brittle; fragile 2. crunchy; crisp 3. lustrous

sūbǐng 酥餅 a kind of crisp biscuit; shortcake

sūmá 酥麻 frail and numb

sūruǎn 酥軟 lacking strength; feeble

sūtáng 酥糖 crunchy candy;

sugar cakes

sūxiōng 酥胸 the soft and smooth skin of a woman's bosom

sū 甦

to come back to life; to rise from the dead; to revive; to resurrect; to regain consciousness

sūxǐng 甦醒 to come back to life; to revive; to come to

sū 穌

1. to mow grass 2. to revive; to come to; to rise again

sū 蘇

1. purple perilla 2. to revive; to come back to life; to resurrect 3. to awake 4. to rest 5. short for Jiangsu Province or Suzhou 6. a Chinese family name

sūdá 蘇打 soda

sūdá 蘇打 refer to **sūdá** 蘇打

sūxǐng 蘇醒 to come to; to awaken; to revive

sú 俗

1. customs or customary 2. vulgar; unrefined 3. common; popular 4. lay (as distinguished from clerical); worldly; secular 5. tasteless; trite

súbù kě'nài 俗不可耐 unbearably vulgar

súchēng 俗稱 commonly called...

súhuà 俗話 a common saying; a proverb

súlèi 俗累 worldly troubles

súniàn 俗念 worldly thoughts

súqì 俗氣 1. vulgarity 2. hackneyed

súrén 俗人 1. a layman as opposed to 2. the clergy a vulgarian

súshì 俗世 earthly life

súshì 俗事 mundane affairs

sútào 俗套 social conventions

súwù 俗物 philistines; a vulgar

súwù 俗務 chores; routines

súyàn 俗諺 a common saying; a proverb

sù 夙

1. the early morning 2. old

(desires, etc.)

sùchóu 夙仇 an old enemy

sùxí 夙昔 1. past times; in the past 2. day and night

sùxīng yèmèi 夙興夜寐 to rise early and sleep late—very diligent

sùyè fěixiè 夙夜匪懈 to work diligently day and night

sùyuàn 夙願 a long-cherished wish

sù 素

1. pure white silk 2. white (color) 3. plain; simple 4. mourning 5. vegetable food; a vegetarian diet 6. heretofore; up to the present 7. usually; generally 8. the original constitution of things; matter; elements

sùbù xiāngshí 素不相識 to have never met or seen before

sùbù xiāngshì 素不相識 refer to **sùbù xiāngshí** 素不相識

sùchēng 素稱 usually called; reputed to be

sùjìng 素淨 1. simple, or plain (clothes) 2. simple, or not greasy (food)

sùlái 素來 heretofore; always; up to the present

sùmèi píngshēng 素昧平生 to have never known, met or seen before; to be a total stranger

sùmiáo 素描 (said of writing or painting) a sketch

sùrěn 素稔 to have known or been familiar with

sùrì 素日 usually; commonly; daily; regularly; frequently

sùshí 素食 vegetarian food

sùxíng 素行 daily conduct or behavior

sùyǎ 素雅 simple but elegant

sùyǎng 素養 one's general capacity and disposition as a result of long and regular self-discipline; accomplishments

sùzhí 素質 refer to **sùzhì** 素質

sùzhì 素質 1. one's natural talent 2. white

sù 速

1. quick; speed; speedy; prompt

2. to invite

sùchéng 速成 to attain goals within a short time

sùcìkāng 速賜康 pentazocine

sùdú 速讀 speed-reading

sùdù 速度 1. velocity; speed 2. (music) a tempo

sùjì 速記 speedwriting; shorthand

sùshí 速食 fast food; instant food

sùshídiàn 速食店 a fast food restaurant

sùshímiàn 速食麵 instant noodles

sùzhàn sùjué 速戰速決 a blitzkrieg strategy

sù 宿

1. to stay overnight; to lodge; to sojourn 2. long-harbored; long-cherished 3. of the former life; inborn; innate; destined 4. veteran; old

sùjí 宿疾 a chronic disease

sùmìng 宿命 predestination

sùmìnglùn 宿命論 fatalism

sùrú 宿儒 a learned scholar

sùshè 宿舍 a dormitory

sùxí 宿昔 1. the past 2. long-standing

sùyuàn 宿怨 an old grudge; an old feud

sùyuàn 宿願 a cherished hope

sùzuì 宿醉 hangover

sù 粟

1. grain; paddy 2. millet 3. goose flesh; goose pimples; goose bumps; goose skin

sùmǐ 粟米 millet; grain

sù 訴

1. to tell; to inform 2. to accuse; to charge 3. to appeal 4. to resort to

sùkǔ 訴苦 to complain about one's grievances

sùshuō 訴說 to tell; to relate; to recount

sùsòng 訴訟 a lawsuit; to go to law; litigation

sùzhū wǔlì 訴諸武力 to resort to force

sùzhuàng 訴狀 a plaint; a petition

sù 溯(泝)

1. to go upstream; to go against a stream 2. to trace; to recall

sùjiāng érshàng 溯江而上 to go upstream in a boat

sùyóu 溯游 to go upstream

sùyuán 溯源 to trace back to the source

sùzì 溯自 ever since

sù 肅

1. respectful; reverential; to pay respects; to salute 2. solemn; serious; majestic; awe-inspiring 3. to usher in 4. neat and quiet 5. to withdraw; to shrink (as in cold weather, etc.) 6. a Chinese family name

sùjìng 肅敬 respectful

sùjìng 肅靜 1. a solemn silence 2. peaceful

sùlì 肅立 to stand upright as a mark of respect

sùmù 肅穆 1. solemn 2. peaceful

sùqīng 肅清 to wipe out or eliminate (rebels, etc.)

sùrán qǐjìng 肅然起敬 great respect rising in one's heart

sù 塑

1. to mold (in clay, etc.); to sculpt 2. a figure; a model 3. plastics

sùjiāo 塑膠 plastics

sùjiāobù 塑膠布 plastic cloth

sùjiāodài 塑膠袋 a plastic bag

sùxiàng 塑像 1. to make an idol, image or statue 2. a statue

sùzào 塑造 to mold; to make by molding

sù 縮

refer to **suō** 縮

suān 痠

muscular pains

suānténg 痠疼 (said of bones, muscles, etc.) to ache

suāntòng 痠痛 (said of bones, muscles, etc.) to ache

suān 酸

1. sour; acid; tart 2. stale; spoiled

3. sad; grieved; sorrowful 4. (痠) aching; a tingle; an ache 5. jealous; envious 6. stingy 7. (chemistry) acid

suānlàtāng 酸辣湯 a kind of soup seasoned with vinegar and pepper

suānliūliū 酸溜溜 1. sour 2. tingle; ache

suānméi 酸梅 sour plums

suānniúnǎi 酸牛奶 yoghurt; sour milk

suānpútao 酸葡萄 something scorned because it cannot be had

suānténg 酸疼 (said of muscles) to ache from overexertion

suāntián kǔlà 酸甜苦辣 sour, sweet, bitter, and hot—the sweets and bitters (of life)

suāntòng 酸痛 (said of muscles) to ache from overexertion

suānwèi 酸味 acid; a sour taste

suàn 蒜
garlic

suànní 蒜泥 mashed garlic

suàntóu 蒜頭 the garlic head

suàn 算
1. to count; to figure; to reckon; to compute; to calculate 2. to plan; to scheme 3. to infer; to guess; to foretell

suànji 算計 1. to consider; to plan 2. to plot against someone

suànle 算了 1. Forget about it. 2. settled; (said of a case) concluded

suànmìng 算命 to tell one's fortune

suànmìng xiānsheng 算命先生 a fortune-teller

suànpan 算盤 an abacus

suànqilai 算起來 in total; all told

suànqīng 算清 to find out the sum, ratio, etc. of

suànshù 算術 arithmetic

suànshù 算數 to count; to stand; to mean what one says

suànzhàng 算帳 1. to settle an account 2. to get even (with a person)

suí 綏
refer to **suí** 綏

suí 雖 also **suī**
1. although; even though; even if; supposing 2. to push away; to dismiss 3. only 4. (now rarely) a lizard-like reptile

suíbài yóuróng 雖敗猶榮 to feel proud even in defeat

suīrán 雖然 even though; although; in spite of; even if

Suí 隋
name of a dynasty (581-618 A.D.)

suí 遂
refer to **suì** 遂

suí 綏 also **suī**
1. to repose; to pacify; to appease; to soothe; to tranquilize 2. to retreat

suíjìng 綏靖 to pacify; pacification

suí 隨
1. to follow; to trace; to come after 2. to listen to; to submit to; to comply with 3. to let (it go, it be, etc.) 4. to accompany 5. to resemble; to look like

suíbǐ 隨筆 to write as one's thought rambles; literary rambles

suíbiàn 隨便 1. as you like; as you see fit; as you please 2. casual; careless

suíbō zhúliú 隨波逐流 1. to follow the currents in sailing 2. to speak and behave as others do without views of his own

suícóng 隨從 an entourage; aides; attendants

suídài 隨帶 to carry about; to take along

suídì 隨地 anywhere; everywhere

suíhe 隨和 easygoing; amiable

suíhòu 隨後 immediately afterward; right off; in no time at all; right after

suíjī cúnqǔ chǔcúnqì 隨機存取儲存器 (computer) internal memory; RAM (random access memory)

S

suíjī cúnqǔ jìyìtǐ 隨機存取記憶體 (computer) internal memory; RAM (random access memory)

suíjī yìngbiàn 隨機應變 to adapt oneself quickly to the changing circumstances

suíjiào suídào 隨叫隨到 to arrive as soon as it is ordered by telephone call; to be on call at any hour

suíkǒu 隨口 to slip out of one's tongue without much thought

suíshēn 隨身 to carry something with one; to take something with one; carry about

suíshēntīng 隨身聽 a walkman

suíshí 隨時 at all times; anytime

suíshí suídì 隨時隨地 at all times and places; anytime and anyplace; wherever and whenever

suíshǒu 隨手 at hand; readily; immediately

suísú 隨俗 to act according to the prevailing customs or practices

suítóng 隨同 to follow or accompany; together with

suíxīn suóyù 隨心所欲 to do anything one's heart dictates

suíxíng 隨行 to follow or accompany someone on a trip

suíyì 隨意 according to your wish; as you like it; as you please

suíyù ér'ān 隨遇而安 to feel at ease under all circumstances

suízhe 隨著 along with; in the wake of; in pace with

suízǒng 隨從 refer to **suícóng** 隨從

suí 雖

refer to **suī** 雖

suǐ 髓

marrow; pith; essence

suì 祟

1. the evil influence of gods or demons 2. (said of ghosts or evil spirits) to haunt

suì 碎

1. broken; smashed; torn; to break to pieces; to smash 2. trivial; unimportant; trifling 3. garrulous; gabby

suìbù 碎步兒 short quick steps

suìliè 碎裂 torn or broken to pieces

suìpiàn 碎片 fragments; splinters; shreds; chips

suìshī wànduàn 碎屍萬段 to inflict severe punishment

suìshízi 碎石子 gravel; macadam

suì 遂 also **suí**

1. to have one's will; to satisfy; to fulfill 2. successful; to succeed 3. to proceed to; to reach 4. then; consequently; thereupon 5. to flee

suìxīn 遂心 to have one's will; to satisfy

suì 歲

1. a year; age (of a person) 2. harvest

suìbù wǒyǔ 歲不我與 Time and tide wait for no one.

suìchū 歲出 annual expenditures

suìhán sānyǒu 歲寒三友 the pine, the bamboo, and the plum, which do not wither in winter

suìmù 歲暮 1. the late season of a year 2. the closing years of one's life

suìrù 歲入 the annual income

suìshōu 歲收 the annual income

suìshu 歲數 age (of a person); years

suìyuè 歲月 times and seasons; time

suìyuè rúliú 歲月如流 Time and tide wait for no man. Time flies!

suì 隧

1. an underground passage; a tunnel 2. (in ancient China) a tower on the wall to watch signal fires

suìdào 隧道 a tunnel

suì 穗

1. fruits or grains in a cluster grown at the tip of a stem or

stalk 2. the ear of grain 3. another name of Guangzhou 4. a candle snuff; a candlewick

suì 燧
1. flint 2. a beacon

suìshí 燧石 flint

sūn 孫
1. a grandchild; a descendant 2. a Chinese family name

sūnnǚ 孫女 a granddaughter

Sūn Yìxiān 孫逸仙 Dr. Sun Yat-sen, Chinese political and revolutionary leadr

sūnzi 孫子 1. a grandchild 2. a grandson

sǔn 筍
bamboo shoots or sprouts

sǔn 損
1. to detract; to damage; to injure; to destroy; harm; damage 2. to lose; loss 3. to reduce; to decrease 4. weak; emaciated 5. to ridicule; to jeer at 6. wicked and mean; cruel 7. (Chinese medicine) long-term emaciation

sǔnhài 損害 to impair; to injure; damages or losses

sǔnhào 損耗 to deplete; to exhaust (supply); to weaken (strength); loss

sǔnhuài 損壞 to damage; damage

sǔnrén lìjǐ 損人利己 to harm others to benefit oneself

sǔnshāng 損傷 losses; to hurt (another's feelings, etc.)

sǔnshī 損失 losses; casualties

sǔn 榫
tenon and mortise

sǔntou 榫頭 a tenon

sùn 遜
refer to **xùn** 遜

suō 唆
to instigate; to incite

suōshǐ 唆使 to instigate; to incite

suō 娑
to dance

suō 梭
1. a weaver's shuttle 2. to move to and fro 3. swift

suōxún 梭巡 to patrol to and fro

suō 蓑
a raincoat or cloak of straw, rushes, coir, etc.

suōyī 蓑衣 a coir raincoat

suō 縮 also **sù**
1. to contract; to shorten; to reduce; to decrease; to shrink 2. to draw back; to recoil; to wince 3. to bind

suōduǎn 縮短 to shorten; to cut down; to shrink

suōhuí 縮回 to draw back; to wince; to flinch

suōjiǎn 縮減 to reduce; to lessen; to decrease

suōshuǐ 縮水 1. dehydration 2. (said of fabrics) to shrink after washing

suōtóu suōnǎo 縮頭縮腦 to cower or shrink from fear; to be hesitant

suōxiǎo 縮小 to reduce; to lessen; to shrink

suōxiě 縮寫 abbreviation; to abbreviate

suōyī jiéshí 縮衣節食 to practice austerity

suōyǐng 縮影 a miniature; an epitome

suǒ 索
refer to **suǒ** 索 7

suǒ 所
1. a place; a location; a position 2. a building; an office 3. that which

suǒcháng 所長 one's specialty

suǒdào zhīchù 所到之處 wherever one goes

suǒdé 所得 1. income 2. what one gets or receives

suǒdéshuì 所得稅 income tax

suǒfèi bùzī 所費不貲 to have spent a fortune

suǒhào 所好 one's hobbies or likes

suǒshǔ 所屬 subordinates; subor-

S

dinate agencies

suǒwèi 所謂 so-called

suǒxiàng pīmí 所向披靡 (said of an invincible army) victorious wherever it goes

suǒxiàng pīmí 所向披靡 refer to **suǒxiàng pīmí** 所向披靡

suǒxiàng wúdí 所向無敵 undefeatable; invincible

suǒxū 所需 needs or requirements (in doing something)

suǒxué 所學 one's specialty; what one has majored in

suǒyǐ 所以 therefore; so; consequently

suǒyǒu 所有 1. belongings 2. to own 3. all; every

suǒyǒuquán 所有權 ownership

suǒyǒurén 所有人 an owner; a proprietor

suǒyuàn 所願 one's wishes

suǒzài 所在 1. where one dwells 2. a place; a location

suǒzàidì 所在地 a seat

suǒzhǎng 所長 the head or director of an office

suǒzhī 所知 1. what one knows 2. an acquaintance

suǒzhì 所致 as a result of

suǒzuò suǒwéi 所作所爲 actions; behavior; conduct

suǒ 索

1. a thick rope; a cable 2. solitary; alone; lonely 3. to search or inquire into 4. laws and regulations; rules 5. to demand; to ask; to exact 6. to need 7. (also **suǒ**) to decide to go ahead and do something without any more consideration

suǒjià 索價 to demand a price; to quote a price

suǒmìng 索命 (usually referring to a ghost, a victim of injustice) to demand one's life

suǒpéi 索賠 to demand compensation; to claim

suǒqiú 索求 to seek (persons, jobs, etc.)

suǒqǔ 索取 1. to ask for 2. to extort

suǒrán wúwèi 索然無味 not

interesting; tasteless

suǒxìng 索性 directly; to go all the way

suǒyǐn 索引 1. the index (of a book) 2. to bring together

suǒ 嗩

a trumpet-like wind instrument

suǒnà 嗩吶 a trumpet-like wind instrument

suǒ 瑣

1. trifles; petty; frivolous; trifling 2. troublesome; annoying 3. a jade chain 4. a palace gate

suǒshì 瑣事 trifles; trivial matters

suǒsuì 瑣碎 1. trifling; petty and varied 2. a slight indisposition or ailment

suǒxiè 瑣屑 petty; unimportant; insignificant; small

suǒ 鎖

1. a lock 2. fetters; chains 3. to lock 4. to confine 5. to lockstitch

suǒjiang 鎖匠 a locksmith

suǒliàn 鎖鏈 chains

tā 他

1. he; him 2. other; another 3. future

tāfāng 他方 the other party (to a transaction, dispute, etc.)

tāmen 他們 they; them

tārén 他人 other people; somebody else

tārì 他日 1. another day 2. some time in the past

tāshā 他殺 homicide (as opposed to suicide)

tāshān zhīshí, kěyǐ gōngyù 他山之石，可以攻玉 Advice from others may help one overcome one's defects.

tāxiāng 他鄉 other lands or strange lands

tāxiāng yù gùzhī 他鄉遇故知 to run across an old friend in a distant land

tā 它 also **tuō**

it; that; this

tāmen 它們 they

tā 她
she

tā 牠 also **tē, tuō**
it

tā 塌
1. to cave in; to fall in ruins; to collapse 2. to sink; to droop

tābí 塌鼻 a snub nose

tāshí 塌實 1. steady and sure; dependable 2. free from anxiety

tāxiàn 塌陷 to sink; to cave in; to subside

tǎ 塔
1. a pagoda 2. a tower 3. a lighthouse

tǎdǐng 塔頂 the top of a pagoda

tǎtái 塔臺 a control tower

tǎ 獺 also **tà**
an otter

tà 拓
to copy characters from an ancient tablet or tomb by rubbing over a paper placed on its surface

tà 沓
1. repeated; reiterated 2. joined or connected; piled up 3. lax 4. talkative

tàtà 沓沓 1. lax 2. chattering and talkative 3. running quickly

tàzá 沓雜 crowded and mixed; confused

tà 榻
a couch; a bed

tàtàmǐ 榻榻米 (Japanese) tatami

tà 踏
1. to step upon; to tread upon; to trample 2. to go to the spot (to make an investigation or survey)

tàbǎn 踏板 1. a footboard; a footrest; a footstool 2. a pedal; a treadle

tàjiǎoshí 踏腳石 a stepping-stone

tàqīng 踏青 to go hiking on a spring day; a spring outing

tà 獺
refer to **tǎ** 獺

tāi 苔
fur (on the tongue)

tāi 胎
1. a fetus; an embryo 2. an unpolished, semiprocessed molding of something

tāi'ér 胎兒 a fetus; an unborn baby; an embryo

tāijì 胎記 a birthmark

tāipán 胎盤 the placenta

tāisǐ fùzhōng 胎死腹中 (literally) death in the womb—(said of a plan, or operation) to fail or be discarded before it gets started; abortive

tāiwèi 胎位 the position of a fetus

tái 台
1. a raised platform 2. a polite expression of addressing

táiduān 台端 you (an honorific in addressing one's equal)

táijiàn 台鑒 a form used after the name in the salutation of a business letter

táishì jìsuànjī 台式計算機 a desktop computer

táizhào 台照 a form used after the name in the salutation of a business letter

tái 苔
moss; lichen

táixiǎn 苔蘚 moss and lichen

tái 跆
to trample

táiquándào 跆拳道 tae kwon do

tái 颱
a typhoon; a hurricane

táifēng 颱風 a typhoon; a hurricane

tái 臺(台)
1. a lookout; an observatory; a tower 2. a terrace; an elevated platform; a stage; a stand 3. a title of respect 4. short for Taiwan 5. a Chinese family name

Táibì 臺幣 Taiwan currency

táicí 臺詞 actor's lines

táidì 臺地 a tableland; a plateau

táifēngr 臺風兒 the deportment of an actor or actress on stage

táijiē 臺階 1. brick or stone steps 2. a means to save face or resolve a dispute

Táiwān 臺灣 Taiwan (Formosa)

Táiwān Hǎixiá 臺灣海峽 Taiwan Strait

táizhùzi 臺柱子 a mainstay

tái 擡(抬)
to lift; to raise; to carry

táigàng 擡槓 to argue for the sake of arguing

táiju 擡舉 to do a good turn or favor

táitóu 擡頭 1. to raise one's head 2. (said of the price) an upsurge; (said of fortune) a turn for the better 3. a bank's salutation for a client

táitóu tǐngxiōng 擡頭挺胸 (literally) chin up and chest out —full of confidence or pride

tái 檯(枱)
a table

táibù 檯布 a tablecloth

táidēng 檯燈 a table lamp

tài 太
1. very big or large 2. much; too; over; excessively; extremely; very 3. a term of respect, used in titles 4. a Chinese family name

tàibǎo 太保 1. a very high official in ancient 2. China juvenile delinquents

Tàigōng diàoyú, yuànzhě shànggōu 太公釣魚, 願者上鉤 A victim letting himself be caught of his own will.

tàigǔ 太古 prehistoric times

tàihòu 太后 the empress dowager

tàijíquán 太極拳 taichichuan; shadowboxing

tàijiàn 太監 a eunuch

tàikōng 太空 space

tàikōngchuán 太空船 a spacecraft; a spaceship

tàikōng kējì 太空科技 space technology

tàikōngrén 太空人 an astronaut; a cosmonaut

tàikōngsuō 太空梭 a space shuttle; a shuttle

tàikōng tōngxìn 太空通信 space communication

tàikōngyī 太空衣 a space suit

tàikōngzhàn 太空站 a space station

tàimèi 太妹 a girl delinquent; a tomboy

tàipíng 太平 peace; peaceful

tàipíngjiān 太平間 a mortuary

tàipíngmén 太平門 (in public buildings, especially in theaters) exits, especially those leading to fire escapes

tàipíng shèngshì 太平盛世 a reign of peace, order, and prosperity

Tàipíngyáng 太平洋 the Pacific Ocean

tàishànghuáng 太上皇 1. the emperor's father 2. (colloquial) a person who exercises supreme powers

tàisuì tóushang dòngtǔ 太歲上動土 to offend or provoke the most powerful

tàitai 太太 1. a madame 2. one's wife

tàixū huànjìng 太虛幻境 an illusory scene

tàiyáng 太陽 the sun

tàiyángnéng 太陽能 solar energy

tàiyángxì 太陽系 the solar system

tàiyángxué 太陽穴 the temples (of a human being)

tàiyángxué 太陽穴 refer to tàiyángxué 太陽穴

tàiyáng yǎnjìng 太陽眼鏡 sunglasses

tàiyīn 太陰 1. the moon 2. lunar

tàizǐ 太子 the crown prince

tàizuǒ 太座 one's wife (a joking expression connoting the dominating position of a wife in the family)

tài 汰
1. excessive 2. to sift; to eliminate; to remove

tàijiǎn 汰揀 to wash and polish

tài 泰
1. great; big 2. quiet; calm; peace; ease 3. Thailand 4. good luck 5. (太) very; much; too; excessive

tàibàn 泰半 more than half; the greater part; the majority

tàidǒu 泰斗 1. Mountain Tai and the Dipper 2. a leading authority (in certain field or discipline)

Tàiguó 泰國 Thailand

tàirán 泰然 unperturbed

tàirán zìruò 泰然自若 unperturbed

tàishān 泰山 1. Mountain Tai (in Shandong) 2. (figuratively) great importance 3. one's wife's father; father-in-law 4. Tarzan

Tàishān yādǐng 泰山壓頂 (literally) It is like Mountain Tai crushing an egg—overwhelming force

Tàiwùshìhé 泰晤士河 the Thames River

tài 態
1. an attitude; a position 2. a manner; carriage; deportment; bearing 3. a situation; a condition; circumstances 4. (physics) state of matter

tàidu 態度 1. an attitude 2. a manner

tān 坍
sliding of earth (as in a landslide); to fall into ruins; to collapse; to tumble

tānfāng 坍方 a landslide; to collapse

tāntā 坍塌 to collapse; to cave in

tān 探
to try; to tempt; to test

tān 貪
1. to desire for more than one's rightful share 2. to hope or wish for; to probe or search for

tānchī 貪吃 gluttonous; piggish

tāndé wúyàn 貪得無饜 never satisfied with what one has got

tānguān wūlì 貪官污吏 corrupt officials

tānlán 貪婪 avaricious; greedy

tānqiú 貪求 to desire or long for (usually more than one's rightful share)

tānshēng pàsǐ 貪生怕死 cowardly; cowardice

tāntú 貪圖 to hanker after; to covet

tānwán 貪玩 to be fond of playing or fooling around

tānwū 貪污 corruption; graft

tānxīn 貪心 avarice; cupidity; greed

tānzāng 貪臟 to take bribes; to practice graft

tānzuǐ 貪嘴 gluttonous; piggish

tān 灘
a beach; a sandbank; a shoal

tāntóubǎo 灘頭堡 a beachhead

tāntóu zhèndì 灘頭陣地 a beachhead

tān 攤
1. to spread; to open 2. to divide equally; to apportion 3. a booth; a stand; a stall 4. a collection of liquid; a pool of (water, mud, blood, etc.)

tānfàn 攤販 a vender or stallkeeper

tānhuán 攤還 to amortize

tānkāi 攤開 to spread out; to unfold

tānpái 攤牌 a showdown; to have a showdown

tānpài 攤派 to apportion

tānwèi 攤位 a stall or booth (especially a fixed one in a market)

tānzi 攤子 a stand; a booth; a stall

tān 癱
paralysis

tānhuàn 癱瘓 paralyzed; standstill

tānruǎn 癱軟 (said of arms, legs, etc.) weak and limp

tán 覃

1. to spread to; to involve 2. deep and vast; profound

tán 痰

phlegm; expectoration; sputum

tánguàn 痰罐 a spittoon

tányú 痰盂 a spittoon

tán 潭

1. deep water; a deep pool 2. deep; profound

tán 彈

1. to rebound 2. to play 3. to impeach

tánhé 彈劾 to impeach

tánhéquán 彈劾權 impeachment power

tánhuáng 彈簧 a spring

tánhuángdāo 彈簧刀 a switchblade

tánhuángdiàn 彈簧墊 a trampoline

tánlì 彈力 elasticity; elastic force

tánqín 彈琴 to play (stringed instruments)

tánxìng 彈性 elasticity; resilience

tánxìng pífá 彈性疲乏 elastic fatigue

tánzhǐ zhījiān 彈指之間 a very brief space of time

tánzòu 彈奏 to play

tán 談

1. to talk; to converse; to chat 2. what is said or talked about; a talk

tánhé róngyì 談何容易 How easy it is just to talk about it! (But it is easier said than done.)

tánhǔ sèbiàn 談虎色變 (literally) to turn pale at the mention of a tiger—to turn pale when something horrible is mentioned

tánhuà 談話 a statement; a talk; a chat; to talk

tánlùn 談論 to discuss; to talk about

tánpàn 談判 negotiation; to negotiate

tánqíng shuō'ài 談情說愛 (said of a couple in love) to chat intimately

tántiān 談天 to chat idly

tántiān shuōdì 談天說地 to chat about all sorts of subjects

tántǔ 談吐 the way a person talks; the manner of speaking

tánxiào fēngshēng 談笑風生 to talk cheerfully and humorously

tánxīn 談心 to have a tete-a-tete

tán 壇

1. a platform for sacrificial rites; an altar 2. a hall for important meetings and ceremonies in ancient China

tán 曇

clouds

tánhuā 曇花 the epiphyllum

tánhuā yīxiàn 曇花一現 to appear and then quickly disappear

tán 檀

sandalwood

Tándǎo 檀島 the Hawaiian Islands

tánxiāng 檀香 1. incense made of sandalwood 2. Santalum album

tán 罎

an earthenware jar or jug for wine

tán 譚

1. (談) to talk 2. a Chinese family name

tǎn 忐

1. timid; apprehensive 2. indecisive; vacillating

tǎntè 忐忑 1. indecisive 2. apprehensive 3. a fidget; to fidget 4. honesty

tǎn 坦

1. wide and smooth; level 2. self-possessed; composed; calm 3. frank; straightforward 4. a son-in-law

tǎnbái 坦白 frank; honest; to tell the truth

tǎnchéng 坦誠 to open one's heart to

tǎndàng 坦蕩 1. contented and composed 2. (said of a road) broad and level

tǎnfū dōngchuáng 坦腹東床 1. an ideal son-in-law 2. to lie in bed with a bare belly

tǎnkèchē 坦克車 a tank

tǎnrán 坦然 calm; unperturbed

tǎnshuài 坦率 frank; straightforward; blunt

tǎn 袒
1. to bare; to strip; bared 2. to protect or screen (with an implication of prejudice)

tǎnhù 袒護 to shield; to protect; to screen; to side with; to be partial

tǎnlù 袒露 to expose

tǎn 毯
a rug; a carpet; a blanket

tǎnzi 毯子 blanket

tàn 炭
1. charcoal 2. coal 3. (碳) (chemistry) C-carbon

tànbǐ 炭筆 charcoal for drawing

tàn 探
1. to find; to search; to prospect; to feel (in a pocket or bag) 2. to spy; to investigate 3. a spy; a detective; a secret agent 4. to try; to venture; to tempt 5. to explore 6. to visit; to inquire about

tàncè 探測 to survey; to sound

tànfǎng 探訪 to investigate; to make inquiries

tàn'gē 探戈 (dancing) tango

tànjiān 探監 to visit a prisoner

tànjiū 探究 to investigate; to probe

tànjiù 探究 refer to **tànjiū** 探究

tànkān 探勘 to prospect

tànnáng qǔwù 探囊取物 as easy as taking things out of one's own pocket

tànqīn 探親 to visit one's relatives

tànqiú 探求 to seek; to search for; to find out

tànshì 探視 to visit (a patient, etc.)

tànsuǒ 探索 to probe; to search for; to look into

tàntǎo 探討 to investigate; to study; to explore (possibilities, etc.); to approach (a problem, etc.); to discuss (causes or effects, etc.)

tàntīng 探聽 to investigate secretly

tàntīng xūshí 探聽虛實 to try to find out about an opponent or adversary

tàntóu tànnǎo 探頭探腦 to act stealthily

tànwàng 探望 1. to visit 2. to look about

tànwèn 探問 to inquire about or after

tànxiǎn 探險 to undertake an exploratory trip; exploration

tànxiǎnduì 探險隊 an expedition team; an exploration party

tànxiǎnjiā 探險家 an explorer

tànxìn 探信 to make inquiries

tànxún 探詢 to make inquiries

tànzhàodēng 探照燈 a searchlight

tàn 碳
carbon

tànshuǐ huàhéwù 碳水化合物 carbohydrate

tàn 歎
to sigh in wonderment or lamentation; to exclaim

tànqì 歎氣 to sigh

tànshǎng 歎賞 to praise and admire

tànwéi guānzhǐ 歎為觀止 the most magnificent sight of all; an unrivaled sight

tànxī 歎息 1. to sigh in lamentation; to lament 2. to exclaim 3. a sigh

tànxí 歎息 refer to **tànxī** 歎息

tāng 湯
1. hot water 2. soup; broth 3. a Chinese family name

tāngchí 湯匙 a spoon

tāngmiàn 湯麵 noodles with soup

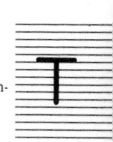

tāngsháo 湯勺 a soup ladle

tāngshuǐ 湯水 1. name of a river in Henan 2. soup

tāngtóu 湯頭 a prescription of herbal medicines

tāngwǎn 湯碗 a large bowl for holding soup

tāngyào 湯藥 decoction of Chinese medicine

tāngyuán 湯圓 balls of glutinous rice

táng 唐
1. the Tang Dynasty 2. a Chinese family name 3. abrupt; rude; preposterous; impertinent

Tángdài 唐代 the Tang Dynasty (618-907 A.D.)

Tángrénjiē 唐人街 the China-town

tángtū 唐突 abrupt; rude; brusque; blunt

tángtú 唐突 refer to **tángtū** 唐突

táng 堂
1. a hall; an office; a reception room 2. a meeting place; a court of justice 3. a salutation for another's mother 4. an open level place on the hill 5. relatives born of the same grandfather 6. venerable; grave; imposing

tánghuáng 堂皇 1. imposing; impressive; grand; stately 2. openly and legally

tángtáng zhèngzhèng 堂堂正正 dignified and imposing

tángxiōngdì 堂兄弟 one's male first cousins on the father's side

tángzǐmèi 堂姊妹 one's female first cousins on the father's side

táng 棠
the sweet pear tree; the wild plum

táng 搪
1. to ward off; to keep out 2. to parry

tángcí 搪瓷 enamel

tángsè 搪塞 to stall somebody off; to parry something

táng 塘
1. an embankment; a bund; a bank; a dike 2. a square pool; a pond; a tank

táng 膛
1. the breast; the chest 2. a cavity 3. the chamber of a firearm

táng 糖
sugar

tángchǎng 糖廠 a sugar mill; a sugar refinery

tángguǒ 糖果 candy; sweets

tángjiāng 糖漿 syrup; molasses

tángniàobìng 糖尿病 diabetes

tángshuǐ 糖水 sweetened water; sugar solution

táng 螳
a mantis

tángláng 螳螂 a mantis

tǎng 倘
if; supposing; in the event of

tǎngruò 倘若 if; in case

tǎng 淌
to flow down; to trickle; to drip

tǎnghàn 淌汗 to perspire

tǎngyǎnlèi 淌眼淚 to shed tears; to be in tears

tǎng 躺
to be in a lying position; to lie down

tǎngyǐ 躺椅 a couch; a deck chair; a divan

tàng 趟
an auxiliary noun for verbs meaning "to walk", "to journey" etc.

tàng 燙
1. to scald; to burn 2. to heat; to warm 3. very hot 4. to iron

tàngfǎ 燙髮 refer to **tàngfà** 燙髮

tàngfà 燙髮 to have a permanent wave

tàngjīn 燙金 gilding; bronzing

tàngshāng 燙傷 a burn; a scald

tàngshǒu 燙手 1. to scald one's hand 2. difficult to handle or manage

tàngyīfu 燙衣服 to iron clothes

tāo 叨

to be favored with; to get the benefit of

tāojiāo 叨教 to trouble you by requesting your instructions

tāorǎo 叨擾 Thanks for the wonderful entertainment (which has put you to great trouble)

tāo 掏

1. to take out; to pull out 2. to dig; to scoop out

tāo'ěrduo 掏耳朵 to pick or clean ears

tāoqián 掏錢 to take out money; to spend money

tāoyāobāo 掏腰包 (colloquial) to shell out; to spend one's own money

tāo 滔

1. fluent 2. to fill; to prevail

tāotāo 滔滔 flowing smoothly; fluent

tāotāo bùjué 滔滔不絕 talking fluently and endlessly

tāotāo xióngbiàn 滔滔雄辯 a torrent of eloquence

tāotiān dàzuì 滔天大罪 heinous crimes

tāo 濤 also **táo**

a big wave; a billow; a heavy swell

tāo 韜

1. scabbards or sheaths for blades or swords 2. military strategy; tactics 3. to conceal 4. to idle

tāoguāng yǎnghuì 韜光養晦 to conceal one's ability and bide one's time

tāo 饕

1. name of a legendary ferocious animal 2. a fierce person 3. a greedy and gluttonous person

tāotiè 饕餮 gluttons; greedy persons

táo 桃

a peach

táohóng 桃紅 pink; light red

táohóng liǔlǜ 桃紅柳綠 a

description of the beautiful scenes of spring

táohuā 桃花 the peach blossom

táohuāliǎn 桃花臉 the peach-blossom face of a beauty; rosy cheeks

táohuāxīnmù 桃花心木 mahogany

táohuāyùn 桃花運 luck in love; a romance

táolǐ mǎnmén 桃李滿門 to have many pupils

táolǐ mǎn tiānxià 桃李滿天下 (said of a master or teacher) His students have spread throughout the world.

táosè xīnwén 桃色新聞 news of illicit love

táoshù 桃樹 a peach tree

táo 逃

1. to run away; to flee; to fly; to abscond; to escape 2. to dodge; to evade; to avoid; to shirk

táobì 逃避 to run away from; to shirk; to evade; to dodge

táobīng 逃兵 a deserter; a fugitive soldier

táofàn 逃犯 a fugitive from the law; a jailbreaker; a wanted criminal

táojiā 逃家 to run away from home

táomìng 逃命 to flee for one's life

táonàn 逃難 to seek refuge from calamities

táopǎo 逃跑 to run away; to flee; to escape

táoshēng 逃生 to flee for one's life

táoshuì 逃稅 to avoid tax payment; tax evasion

táotuō 逃脫 to escape from; to free oneself from; to succeed in escaping from

táowáng 逃亡 to run away; to escape; to flee

táoxué 逃學 to play truant; to cut class; to truant

táozhài 逃債 to run away from the creditor

táozǒu 逃走 to run away; to flee;

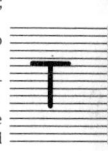

to escape

táo 淘
1. to wash (especially rice); to wash in a sieve 2. to dredge; to scour 3. to eliminate the inferior (by exams, contests, etc.)

táojīn 淘金 1. to pan gold 2. to make quick bucks or high profits

táojīnzhě 淘金者 a gold digger

táomǐ 淘米 to wash rice

táoqì 淘氣 naughty, or annoying (children)

táoqìguǐ 淘氣鬼 a mischievous imp

táotài 淘汰 1. to eliminate inferior contestants, goods, etc. 2. elimination

táotàisài 淘汰賽 elimination series

táo 陶
1. to make pottery or earthenware; pottery or earthenware 2. happy; joyful 3. to move and influence a person 4. a Chinese family name

táocí 陶瓷 pottery and porcelain

táoqì 陶器 pottery; earthenware

táoyě 陶冶 1. to mold (pottery) and smelt (metals) 2. to cultivate or shape (taste, character, etc.)

táoyě xìngqíng 陶冶性情 to shape or cleanse one's spirit

táozhù 陶鑄 to educate and mold persons of talent

táozuì 陶醉 to be intoxicated (with success, etc.); very happy; highly gratified

táo 萄
grapes

táo 濤
refer to **tāo** 濤

tǎo 討
1. to quell; to put down; to suppress 2. to denounce; to condemn 3. to marry (a wife or concubine) 4. to demand; to beg for; to get 5. to study; to examine into; to research 6. (rarely) to govern; to administer

tǎofá 討伐 to quell (an uprising,

etc.)

tǎofàn 討飯 to beg for food; to be a beggar

tǎohǎo 討好 1. to curry favor; to please; to fawn on 2. to be rewarded with a fruitful result

tǎojià huánjià 討價還價 to haggle over prices; to bargain

tǎojiào 討教 May I ask for your advice?

tǎojiùbīng 討救兵 to seek help

tǎolùn 討論 to discuss; discussion

tǎolùnhuì 討論會 a forum; a symposium

tǎoráo 討饒 to ask for mercy

tǎorén xǐhuan 討人喜歡 likable; delightful

tǎoshēnghuó 討生活 to make a living

tǎoxífù 討媳婦 to get a wife for one's son

tǎoyàn 討厭 troublesome; nasty; to dislike

tǎozhài 討債 to demand repayment of a loan

tào 套
1. a case; an envelope 2. a trap 3. to wear or slip on (a sweater, etc.) 4. to trap or trick a person (into telling the truth) 5. to harness 6. to pattern or model after 7. convention; a formula 8. a suit (of clothes)

tàofáng 套房 a suite (of rooms)

tàofú 套服 a suit

tàohuà 套話 to trap a person into telling the truth

tàoláo 套牢 lockup; to lock up

tàoyòng 套用 to use indiscriminately

tàozhuāng 套裝 an ensemble

tàozhuāng ruǎntǐ 套裝軟體 (computer) software package

tē 牠
refer to **tā** 牠

tè 特
1. special; unique; peculiar; particular; extraordinary; unusual; outstanding; distinguished; exclusive 2. just; merely; only

tèbié 特別 special; peculiar; particular

tèchǎn 特產 unique or special products (of a place)

tècháng 特長 special merits; a specialty

tèdà 特大 exceptionally big; the most

tèdàhào 特大號 king-size; extra large size

tèdì 特地 on purpose; specially

tèdiǎn 特點 characteristics; peculiarities

tèdìng 特定 1. specially designated 2. specific; given

tèjí 特級 superfine

tèjì 特技 special skills; stunts; aerobatics

tèjià 特價 a specially reduced price

tèjiǎng 特獎 a special prize; a grand prize

tèkān 特刊 the extra edition, special edition or special supplement (of a newspaper or magazine)

tèkuàichē 特快車 a special express

tèlì 特例 a special case; an exceptional case

tèlì dúxíng 特立獨行 to be self-reliant

tèpài 特派 specially dispatched or appointed

tèpài jìzhě 特派記者 an accredited journalist

tèpàiyuán 特派員 a correspondent of a news agency, newspaper, etc.

tèquán 特權 privileges

tèsè 特色 special features; characteristics

tèshè 特赦 special pardon; an amnesty

tèshǐ 特使 a special envoy

tèshū 特殊 special; unusual; unique

tèwù 特務 a secret agent

tèxiàoyào 特效藥 a specific; a wonder drug

tèxiě 特寫 1. a feature story (in a news paper or magazine) 2. a close-up (in a movie)

tèxìng 特性 characteristics; peculiarities

tèxuǎn 特選 carefully chosen; hand-picked

tèyuē 特約 1. a special agreement or contract 2. specially or exclusively engaged

tèyuē zhěnsuǒ 特約診所 a clinic exclusively engaged by an organization

tèzhēng 特徵 distinctive features; characteristics

tèzhí 特質 refer to **tèzhì** 特質

tèzhì 特製 manufactured for a specific purpose

tèzhì 特質 special qualities; characteristics; peculiarities

tèzhǒng bùduì 特種部隊 special forces

tèzhǒng yíngyè 特種營業 special business operations (such as cabarets, bars, winehouses, etc.)

tèzhǔn 特准 to permit as a special case

téng 疼
1. to ache; to hurt; pain; sore 2. to dote on; to be fond of (a child)

téng'ài 疼愛 to be fond of (a child)

téng 謄
to transcribe; to copy

téngběn 謄本 a transcript; a copy

téngxiě 謄寫 to copy; to transcribe

téng 藤(籐)
a rattan; a vine

téngtiáo 藤條 a rattan

téngyǐ 藤椅 a rattan chair; a cane chair

téng 騰
1. to prance; to rear; to leap; to jump 2. to go up; to rise; to fly; to soar 3. to turn over; to surrender; to transfer

téngdá 騰達 to prosper; to thrive

téngkōng 騰空 to fly in the sky; to soar

T

téngyún jiàwù 騰雲駕霧 1. to sail clouds and ride mist (as immortals do) 2. fast; quick

tī 剔

1. to separate bones from meat; to scrape meat off bones 2. to pick out inferior materials; to scrape off 3. a rising stroke in Chinese characters

tīchú 剔除 to eliminate

tīyá 剔牙 to pick the teeth

tī 梯

1. a ladder; steps; stairs 2. something to lean or depend on 3. terraced 4. private; intimate 5. a phase

tīcì 梯次 phases (in the induction of military draftees)

tījiē 梯階 1. steps of a ladder 2. keys to accomplish something

tītián 梯田 terraced paddies on a slope

tīxíng 梯形 1. (geometry) trapezoid 2. a flat raised piece of land in gardens

tī 踢

1. to kick 2. to play (football)

tījiànzi 踢毽子 the game of repeatedly bouncing a shuttlecock off a foot

tīkāi 踢開 1. to kick open (a door) 2. to kick (something) out of the way

tīpíqiú 踢皮球 1. to kick a ball 2. to shirk (reponsibility, etc.)

tītàwǔ 踢踏舞 tap dance

tīzhèngbù 踢正步 to march in goose steps

tí 堤(隄)

refer to **dī** 堤

tí 提

1. to lift by hand; to pull up 2. to cause to rise or happen 3. to mention; to bring forward; to suggest 4. to obtain; to make delivery; to draw out 5. a rising stroke (in Chinese calligraphy)

tí'àn 提案 a motion; a proposal

tíba 提拔 to promote (a person); to elevate

tíbāo 提包 a handbag; a valise

tíbǐ 提筆 to lift one's pen—to write

tíchàng 提倡 to promote (a cause, etc.); to advocate

tíchū 提出 to raise (a question, etc.); to put forth

tídào 提到 to mention

tífáng 提防 refer to **dīfang** 提防

tígāng 提綱 an outline

tígāo 提高 to lift (morale, etc.); to raise (prices, etc.)

tígāo jǐngjué 提高警覺 to be on the ball

tígōng 提供 1. to offer (proposals, opinions, etc.); to provide (assistance, etc.) 2. to sponsor (a TV or radio program, etc.)

tíhuò 提貨 to make delivery of goods or cargo

tíjí 提及 to mention

tíjiāo 提交 1. to hand over to the custody of 2. to submit to another body for discussion

tíkuǎn 提款 to draw money from a bank

tíkuǎndān 提款單 a withdrawal slip

tílán 提籃 a handbasket

tíliàn 提鍊 to refine (crude oil, etc.); to extract

tímíng 提名 to nominate

tíqǐ 提起 1. to lift up; to arouse (oneself to action, etc.) 2. to mention

tíqǐ jīngshen 提起精神 to cheer up

tíqián 提前 1. to give precedence or priority to 2. (to complete a task, etc.) ahead of schedule

tíqiè 提挈 to help; assistance

tíqīn 提親 a matchmaking

tíqín 提琴 a violin

tíqǐng 提請 to submit something (for approval, etc.)

tíqǔ 提取 1. to draw (deposits from the bank) 2. to pick up

tíshén 提神 1. to watch out 2. to stimulate; to elate; to refresh

tíshěn 提審 to bring forward for trial

tíshēng 提升 to promote (an officer, etc.); to elevate

tíshì 提示 1. to hint; a hint 2. (drama) to prompt; to give a cue

tíxī 提攜 refer to **tíxié** 提攜

tíxiāng 提箱 a suitcase

tíxié 提攜 help; assistance; to help; to aid

tíxīn diàodǎn 提心弔膽 cautious and anxious; jittery

tíxǐng 提醒 to remind

tíxùn 提訊 to arraign

tíyào 提要 1. to bring forth the main points 2. a synopsis; a summary

tíyì 提議 to propose a proposal, suggestion, etc.

tízǎo 提早 ahead of schedule; in advance

tí 啼

(especially said of birds) to crow; to cry

tíjiào 啼叫 to scream; to screech

tíkū 啼哭 to cry; to weep and wail

tíxiào jiēfēi 啼笑皆非 unable to cry or laugh

tí 蹄

1. (zoology) a hoof 2. the feet of beasts

típǎng 蹄膀 (dialect) the uppermost part of legs of pork

tí 題

1. the forehead 2. a sign; a signal 3. a subject; the title of a composition or speech 4. commentaries; notes 5. to sign; to write; to inscribe 6. the end; the top 7. the ornamental woodwork under the eaves of public buildings

tícái 題材 material constituting the main theme of an article, composition, etc.

tíjiě 題解 1. explanatory notes on the title or background of a book 2. keys to exercises or problems

tímíng 題名 to name a work; to entitle

tímù 題目 1. the subject or title of a composition or speech; a theme or heading 2. a question or problem

tíshī 題詩 to write verses on something

tízì 題字 to write on something; an inscription; an autograph

tǐ 體

1. the body 2. shape; form 3. an entity; a unit 4. a style; a fashion; a system 5. substance; essence 6. theory (as opposed to practice)

tǐcái 體裁 a form or a style (of writing)

tǐcāo 體操 gymnastics; calisthenics

tǐcāo xuǎnshǒu 體操選手 a gymnast

tǐchá 體察 1. to examine or investigate with intensive personal attention 2. to be understanding or sympathetic toward

tǐdà sījīng 體大思精 (said of a book) extensive in scope and penetrating in thought

tǐfá 體罰 corporal punishment

tǐgé 體格 physique

tǐgé jiǎnchá 體格檢查 a physical examination

tǐhuì 體會 to understand through something beyond the intellect

tǐjī 體積 volume (of a solid)

tǐlì 體力 stamina; physical agility

tǐlì 體例 general form

tǐliàng 體諒 to be understanding or sympathetic toward; to be considerate of

tǐmiàn 體面 1. honor; dignity; face 2. appearing good; looking elegant

tǐnéng 體能 stamina; physical agility

tǐniàn 體念 to be understanding

tǐpò 體魄 the human body as the source of strength

tǐrèn 體認 to perceive intuitively

tǐtài 體態 1. outward form; an exterior look 2. a manner, deportment, or a carriage

tǐtiē 體貼 kind; considerate; thoughtful

tǐtǒng 體統 1. a system; an organized whole 2. propriety in conduct

tǐwèi 體味 to appreciate; to savor

tǐwēn 體溫 body temperature

tǐwēnjì 體溫計 a clinical thermometer

tǐwú wánfū 體無完膚 injured all over the body (often used figuratively for damage inflicted by verbal attacks)

tǐxì 體系 a system; orderliness

tǐxíng 體型 an external physical appearance; (physical) build

tǐxù 體恤 to be considerate of and sympathize with

tǐyàn 體驗 to experience firsthand; firsthand experience

tǐyù 體育 1. physical education 2. athletics

tǐyùchǎng 體育場 a stadium; a play ground

tǐyùguǎn 體育館 a gymnasium

tǐyù jìzhě 體育記者 a sportswriter

tǐyù yòngpǐn 體育用品 sports goods; sports requisites

tǐzhì 體質 refer to **tǐzhì** 體質

tǐzhì 體制 a system of rules; a system

tǐzhì 體質 a bodily constitution; a physical make-up

tǐzhòng 體重 body weight

tì 剃
to shave

tìdāo 剃刀 a razo

tìdù 剃度 to cut off hair and join a monastery; to tonsure

tìtóu 剃頭 to shave the head

tì 倜
1. to raise high 2. unrestrained; unoccupied

tìtǎng 倜儻 free and easy of manner

tì 涕
1. tears 2. snivel

tìlíng 涕零 to shed tears

tìqì 涕泣 to weep; to cry

tìqì zhānjīn 涕泣沾襟 to wet the front part of one's garment with tears

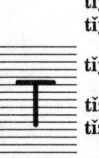

tì 悌（弟）
to show brotherly love; love and respect for one's elder brother

tì 屜
a drawer

tì 惕
1. cautious; watchout; prudent; careful; to be on the alert 2. afraid 3. anxious

tìlì 惕厲 to exercise caution and discipline

tì 替
1. to take the place of; to replace; to substitute 2. to decay; to decline 3. to neglect 4. for; on behalf of

tìbǔ tóushǒu 替補投手 (baseball) relief pitcher

tìdài 替代 to replace; to substitute

tìhuan 替換 to replace; to substitute

tìkǎo 替考 a substitute examinee

tìshēn 替身 a double; an understudy

tìshēn yǎnyuán 替身演員 a stunt man

tìsǐguǐ 替死鬼 a scapegoat

tì 嚏
sneezing; a sneeze

tiān 天
1. the sky; the heavens 2. Nature; God; Heaven 3. nature; natural 4. a day 5. seasons; weather 6. father or husband 7. something indispensable

Tiān'ānmén 天安門 Tian An Men (the Gate of Heavenly Peace)

tiānbēng dìliè 天崩地裂 deafening sounds—as the falling of heaven and cracking of earth

tiānbiān 天邊 the ends of the earth; remotest places

tiān bùpà, dì bùpà 天不怕, 地不怕 to fear nothing and no one

tiāncái 天才 a genius; natural talent

tiāncái értóng 天才兒童 a

child prodigy

tiāncháng dìjiǔ 天長地久 (literally) as old as heaven and earth—a very long time

tiānchuāng 天窗 a skylight

Tiānchèngzuò 天秤座 Libra

tiāncóng rényuàn 天從人願 What man hoped to happen has come to pass.

tiāndìxià 天底下 in this world; under the sun

tiāndì 天地 1. the world; the universe 2. a field of activity 3. the upper and lower margins of a scroll 4. a world of difference

tiāndì liángxīn 天地良心 from the bottom of my heart

tiāndìng 天定 preordained; predestined

tiān'é 天鵝 a swan

tiānfān dìfù 天翻地覆 in total disorder or disarrangement

tiānfèn 天分 natural endowments; talent

tiānfǔ zhīguó 天府之國 a country with rich natural resources

tiānfù 天賦 1. inherent and inborn 2. natural endowments

tiānfù rénquán 天賦人權 inborn human rights

tiāngān 天干 the Ten Celestial Stems

tiāngāo qìshuǎng 天高氣爽 (usually said of the crisp air in autumn) The sky is high and the weather is fine.

Tiānguó 天國 the Kingdom of Heaven

tiānhuā 天花 (pathology) the smallpox

tiānhuābǎn 天花板 the ceiling (of a room)

tiānhuā luànzhuì 天花亂墜 exaggerated description

tiānhūn dì'àn 天昏地暗 dark above and below

tiānjià 天價 the highest price

Tiānjīn 天津 Tianjin

tiānjīng dìyì 天經地義 a matter of course

tiānkōng 天空 the sky; the fir-

mament

tiānlài 天籟 the sounds of nature

tiānlánsè 天藍色 sky blue

tiānlǐ 天理 natural law

tiānlǐ zhāozhāng 天理昭彰 The law of Heaven always prevails.

tiānliáng 天良 one's conscience

tiānliàng 天亮 daybreak

tiānlún zhīlè 天倫之樂 family love and joy

tiānluó dìwǎng 天羅地網 the dragnet of justice surrounding on all sides; envelopment

tiānmǎ xíngkōng 天馬行空 (said of calligraphic writing or works) an unrestrained and vigorous style that brims with talent

tiānmíng 天明 daybreak; dawn

tiānmìng 天命 1. a heavenly mandate 2. fate 3. one's life span

tiānnán dìběi 天南地北 1. poles apart 2. (to chat or talk casually about) discursive

tiānnù rényuàn 天怒人怨 (to incur) the wrath of Heaven and opposition of man

tiānpíng 天平 scales

tiānqì 天氣 weather

tiānqì yùbào 天氣預報 a weather forecast

tiānqiǎn 天譴 God's punishment—fire-and-brimstone

tiānqiáo 天橋 an overhead bridge or elevated passage

tiānrán 天然 natural

tiānrǎng zhībié 天壤之別 vastly different; poles apart

tiānsè 天色 the color of the sky

tiānshēng 天生 natural; to be born with; congenital; inborn

tiānshí 天時 weather, or climates

tiānshǐ 天使 1. an angel 2. an emissary from the emperor

tiāntáng 天堂 heaven; a paradise

tiāntǐyíng 天體營 a nudist camp

tiāntiān 天天 every day

Tiānwángxīng 天王星 the

tiānwéntái 天文臺 an astronomical observatory

tiānwénxué 天文學 astronomy

tiānwú juérén zhīlù 天無絕人之路 Heaven will always leave a door open.

tiānxià 天下 the world

tiānxià wéigōng 天下爲公 The world is for all.

tiānxià wūyā yìbān hēi 天下烏鴉一般黑 Evil people are bad all over the world.

tiānxià yìjiā 天下一家 All people under the sun are one family.

tiānxiǎn 天險 impregnable natural barriers (for defense)

tiānxiàn 天線 an antenna (for radio, TV, etc.)

tiānxiǎode 天曉得 God knows! Heaven knows!

Tiānxiēzuò 天蠍座 Scorpio

tiānxìng 天性 natural disposition

tiānyá hǎijiǎo 天涯海角 far-away, remote or distant places

tiānyī wúfèng 天衣無縫 without a trace; perfect (jobs); flawless (lies)

tiānyì 天意 the will of Heaven; God's will

tiānyǒu bùcè fēngyún, rényǒu dànxī huòfú 天有不測風雲,人有旦夕禍福 Human fortunes are as unpredictable as the weather.

tiānyǒu bùcè fēngyún, rényǒu dànxī huòfú 天有不測風雲,人有旦夕禍福 refer to **tiānyǒu bùcè fēngyún, rényǒu dànxī huòfú** 天有不測風雲,人有旦夕禍福

tiānyuān zhībié 天淵之別 vastly different

tiānzāi 天災 a natural disaster

tiānzāi rénhuò 天災人禍 natural disasters and man-made calamities

tiānzào dìshè 天造地設 1. (said of a couple) matched by Heaven and Earth 2. a natural creation; heavenly

tiānzhēn 天眞 naive; innocent

tiānzhēn lànmàn 天眞爛漫 innocent and carefree—lovely like a child

tiānzhī jiāozǐ 天之驕子 to be extraordinarily blessed

tiānzhí 天職 bounden duty

tiānzhū dìmiè 天誅地滅 to be damned by Heaven and Earth

Tiānzhú 天竺 the ancient name of India

tiānzhúshǔ 天竺鼠 a guinea pig; a cavy

Tiānzhǔjiào 天主教 Catholicism

tiānzī 天資 natural endowments

tiānzǐ 天子 the emperor

tiānzòng yīngmíng 天縱英明 (said of a ruler) born with wisdom and farsightedness

tiānzuò zhīhé 天作之合 a match blessed by God

tiān 添

1. to add to; to increase; to replenish (stock, etc.) 2. to have a baby

tiānbu 添補 to make complete; to complete what is lacking

tiāndīng 添丁 to beget a son

tiānfàn 添飯 to have another helping (or bowl) of rice

tiānfú tiānshòu 添福添壽 (a well-wishing expression) to add to your happiness and your longevity

tiānfù 添附 to enclose; to supplement; to add to; additional

tiāngòu 添購 to purchase; to make additional purchase of

tiānhuò 添貨 (said of a store) to replenish stock

tiānjiā 添加 to add to; to increase

tiānjiājì 添加劑 (chemistry) an additive

tiānshang 添上 1. to add to 2. besides; in addition to

tiānshè 添設 to set up additionally

tiānyóu jiācù 添油加醋 to embellish or blow up a story or report with something which is

usually not true

tiānzào 添造 to expand; to construct; to build more

tiānzhì 添置 to purchase; to make additional purchase of

tián 田

1. agricultural land; cultivated land; a field; a rice field; farmland; cropland 2. to hunt game 3. a Chinese family name

tiánchǎn 田產 real estate

tiándì 田地 1. agricultural land 2. position; condition; a plight

tiángěng 田埂 ridges between plots of farmland

tiánjī 田雞 a frog

tiánjiān 田間 in the field

tiánjìngsài 田徑賽 track and field events

tiánluó 田螺 a mud snail; a pond snail

tiánqì 田契 a title deed for agricultural land

tiánshè 田舍 a farmhouse

tiányě 田野 fields; cultivated lands

tiányuán 田園 fields and gardens

tiányuán shīrén 田園詩人 a pastoral poet; an idyllist

tiánzhǔ 田主 a landlord (of agricultural land)

tiánzhuāng 田莊 a farmhouse; a farmstead

tiánzū 田租 the land rental paid by a tenant farmer

tián 恬

quiet; peaceful; undisturbed

tiándàn 恬淡 contented; indifferent to worldly gain

tiánjìng 恬靜 undisturbed; having peace of mind; tranquil

tián 畋

1. to cultivate land 2. to hunt game

tián 甜

1. sweet; luscious 2. agreeable; pleasant

tiándiǎn 甜點 sweet; dessert

tiánměi 甜美 1. sweet; luscious

2. pleasant; refreshing

tiánmì 甜蜜 sweet as honey; honeyed; affectionate; fond; happy

tiánshí 甜食 sweet food; sweetmeats

tiántou 甜頭 1. sweet taste 2. good; benefit

tiánwèi 甜味 sweet taste

tiánxīn 甜心 a sweetheart

tiányán mìyǔ 甜言蜜語 honeyed words; cajolery

tiányùmǐ 甜玉米 sweet corn; sugar corn

tián 填

1. to fill up; to fill in; to stuff 2. the sound of drumbeats

tiánbǔ 填補 to fill (vacancies, etc.); to make up a deficiency

tiánchōng 填充 1. (a form of testing) filling the blanks 2. to fill up; to stuff

tiánfáng 填房 a second wife one marries after the death of the first

tiánpíng 填平 to fill up the depressions or holes on the ground

tiánxiě 填寫 to fill in (a blank, form, etc.)

Tián 滇

refer to **Diān** 滇

tiǎn 忝

1. ashamed; to disgrace 2. a depreciatory expression referring to oneself 3. to be unworthy of the honor

tiǎnbù zhīchǐ 忝不知恥 shameless

tiǎnrǔ jiāmén 忝辱家門 to disgrace one's family

tiǎnwéi zhījǐ 忝爲知己 As an intimate friend of yours, I....; (I'm sure you'll forgive me) since we have been good friends.

tiǎn 殄

1. to end; to terminate 2. to exterminate; to extirpate; to weed out; to wipe out 3. to waste

tiǎnmiè 殄滅 to exterminate

thoroughly; to extirpate

tiǎn 舔
to lick; to taste

tiāo 挑
1. to carry things with a pole on one's shoulder; to shoulder 2. to select; to choose; to pick 3. to pick by pitchfork

tiāocuò 挑錯 to find fault; to pick flaws

tiāodàliáng 挑大樑 to play the leading role; to shoulder the main responsibility

tiāodàn 挑擔 to carry a load with a carrying pole

tiāofū 挑夫 a coolie; a bearer; a porter

tiāojiǎn 挑揀 to pick; to choose; to select

tiāokāi 挑開 to brush aside with a poker or stick

tiāosān jiǎnsì 挑三揀四 to be choosy

tiāoti 挑剔 1. to be very particular in making selection 2. to nitpick

tiāoxuǎn 挑選 to select; to choose

tiáo 迢
far; distant; remote

tiáotiáo 迢迢 faraway; far and remote

tiáo 條
1. an article, section, clause, etc. of an agreement, pact, treaty, law, etc. 2. in good order; (to present) one by one 3. a numerary adjunct for something narrow and long, as roads, fish, ropes, dogs, snakes, etc. 4. stripes

tiáofú 條幅 a vertical hanging scroll of calligraphy or painting

tiáoguī 條規 rules and regulations

tiáojiàn 條件 1. terms; conditions 2. articles, clauses, etc. in an agreement, etc.

tiáokuǎn 條款 an article of laws; a section, chapter, or clause of agreements, regulations, etc.

tiáolǐ 條理 1. reasonable; logical 2. orderly; in good order

tiáolǐ jǐngrán 條理井然 in good order and with good reasoning

tiáolì 條例 rules, regulations, or laws

tiáoliè 條列 to list item by item

tiáomǎ yuèdújī 條碼閱讀機 a barcode reader

tiáotiáo dàdào tōng Luómǎ 條條大道通羅馬 Every road leads to Rome.

tiáowén 條文 the text of a treaty, regulation, law, etc.

tiáowén 條紋 stripes; streaks; the grain (of wood)

tiáoxíngmǎ dúchūqì 條形碼讀出器 a barcode reader

tiáoyuē 條約 a treaty (between nations)

tiáo 調
1. to mix; to blend 2. to regulate; to adjust 3. balance; regular 4. to make fun of; to tease 5. to mediate

tiáofú 調幅 (radio) amplitude modulation (AM)

tiáohe 調和 1. to mix; to blend 2. to harmonize 3. to adjust; to tune 4. to mediate; to reconcile

tiáojì 調劑 1. to prepare drugs 2. to adjust; to make adjustments

tiáojié 調節 1. to regulate; to adjust 2. to moderate

tiáokǎn 調侃 to scoff; to mock; to jeer

tiáolǐ 調理 1. to train; to teach 2. to nurse impaired health 3. to take care of

tiáopèi 調配 1. to mix; to blend 2. to coordinate; to arrange

tiáopí 調皮 1. naughty 2. sly; treacherous; unruly; tricky

tiáopí dǎodàn 調皮搗蛋 making troubles; mischievous; ungovernable

tiáopín 調頻 (electricity) frequency modulation (FM)

tiáoqíng 調情 to flirt; to play at love

tiáosè 調色 refer to **tiáoshǎi** 調

色

tiáoshǎi 調色 to mix colors; to mix paints

tiáotíng 調停 to mediate

tiáowèi 調味 to season foods; to mix flavors

tiáowèipǐn 調味品 seasoning; spice; dressing material; condiment

tiáoxì 調戲 to flirt with (women)

tiáoxiào 調笑 to tease; to make fun of

tiáoyǎng 調養 to nurse one's health; to take care of oneself

tiáoyīn 調音 tuning

tiáozhěng 調整 to adjust; to tune up

tiáozhì 調製 to prepare or concoct

tiáo 齠
to shed the milk teeth

tiáonián 齠年 the age of shedding the milk teeth—childhood

tiǎo 挑
1. to stir; to provoke; to arouse 2. to dally; to make a pass at; to seduce

tiǎobō 挑撥 to instigate; to cause dispute

tiǎobō líjiàn 挑撥離間 to stir up ill will or bad feelings; to sow discord

tiǎodēng yèzhàn 挑燈夜戰 to continue working by lamplight

tiǎodòng 挑動 1. to arouse; to seduce 2. to instigate; to incite

tiǎodòu 挑逗 to seduce; to arouse amorous desires

tiǎonòng shìfēi 挑弄是非 to stir up one side against the other

tiǎosuo 挑唆 to stir up something with mischievous intentions

tiǎoxìn 挑釁 to provoke

tiǎozhàn 挑戰 to challenge to a duel; a challenge

tiǎo 窕
1. slender 2. quiet and modest; charming and attractive 3. good; beautiful; wonderful

tiào 眺
to look far away; to take a look at faraway things; to look far into the distance

tiàowàng 眺望 to look far away

tiào 跳
1. to jump; to leap; to bounce; to spring 2. to throb; to pulsate; to beat 3. to skip (over); to make omissions

tiàobǎn 跳板 1. a gangplank 2. a diving board; a springboard 3. a steppingstone

tiàocáo 跳槽 to abandon one occupation in favor of another; to get new employment

tiàodòng 跳動 to throb; to pulsate; to beat

tiàogāo 跳高 (sports) high jump (in track and field)

tiàoguò 跳過 to jump over or across; to succeed in jumping over or across

tiàojí 跳級 (education) to skip a grade

tiàojiǎo 跳腳 to stamp one's foot

tiàolán 跳欄 (sports) hurdle race; the hurdles

tiàopiào 跳票 a bounced check; a check that bounced

tiàoqí 跳棋 Chinese checkers

tiàosǎn 跳傘 to parachute

tiàoshéng 跳繩 rope jumping

tiàoshuǐ 跳水 to dive; to jump into the water; to dive from a diving board (or a springboard)

tiàowǔ 跳舞 to dance; dancing

tiàoyuǎn 跳遠 (sports) the broad jump; the long jump

tiàoyuè 跳躍 to jump; to leap; to hop

tiàozǎo 跳蚤 a flea

tiē 帖
1. submissive or obedient 2. proper

tiē'ěr 帖耳 (literally) to droop one's ears like a dog—submissive

tiē 貼

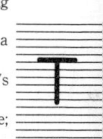

1. to paste; to stick; to glue 2. to keep close to; to nestle closely to 3. to make up the deficiency; to subsidize; subsidies; an allowance 4. proper; appropriate; comfortable 5. attached to

tiēbǔ 貼補 to make up a deficiency; to supplement

tiējìn 貼近 nearby; close to; to press close to; to nestle up against

tiēqiè 貼切 proper or appropriate; apt

tiēshēn 貼身 1. personal servants 2. closely attached, as children, undergarments, concubines, etc.

tiēxiàn 貼現 (banking) discount

tiēxīn 貼心 intimate; close

tiě 帖

1. an invitation card 2. a label; a document 3. a copybook (of calligraphy) 4. a medical prescription

tiězi 帖子 1. an invitation letter or card 2. a money order

tiě 鐵

1. iron 2. firm; indisputable; unyielding (like iron) 3. cruel; merciless; unfeeling 4. arms; weapons

tiěbǎn 鐵板 1. an iron plate; sheet iron 2. a kind of percussion instrument

tiěbàng 鐵棒 an iron club

tiěbǐng 鐵餅 a discus

tiěchǔmózhēn 鐵杵磨針 Steady efforts can work miracles.

tiěchuāng 鐵窗 1. a window with metal gratings 2. a prison

tiěchuí 鐵鎚 an iron hammer; a hammer

tiědīng 鐵釘 iron nails

tiědìng 鐵定 definitely; ironclad; unalterable; not subject to change

tiěfànwǎn 鐵飯碗 a very secure job

tiěgōngjī 鐵公雞 a stingy person

tiěguānyīn 鐵觀音 a variety of oolong tea

tiěguǐ 鐵軌 iron rails (of a rail-way)

tiějiǎ 鐵甲 steel armor

tiějiang 鐵匠 an ironsmith; a blacksmith

tiěkuàng 鐵礦 1. iron ore 2. an iron mine

tiěliàn 鐵鏈 an iron chain

tiělù 鐵路 a railroad; a railway

tiěmǎ 鐵馬 1. strong cavalry 2. (colloquial) a bicycle 3. armored horses

tiěmén 鐵門 1. a metal security door 2. name of a county in Henan

tiěmiàn wúsī 鐵面無私 inflexibly just and fair

tiěpí 鐵皮 iron sheet

tiěqì 鐵器 ironware

tiěqīng 鐵青 livid; bluish black

tiěrén 鐵人 1. an iron man 2. a man of great physical strength

tiěshāzhǎng 鐵沙掌 a Chinese version of karate

tiěshí xīncháng 鐵石心腸 a cold heart; an unfeeling heart; iron-hearted; hardhearted

tiěshù kāihuā 鐵樹開花 something that very rarely happens

tiěsī 鐵絲 iron wire

tiěsīwǎng 鐵絲網 1. wire netting; wire meshes 2. barbed-wire entanglements

tiětǎ 鐵塔 an iron or steel tower

tiěwàn 鐵腕 iron hand; iron fist

tiěxiàn 鐵線 iron wire

tiěxiù 鐵銹 rust

tiězhèng rúshān 鐵證如山 irrefutable, decisive evidence

tīng 汀

1. a low, level land along a river 2. a shoal

tīngzhōu 汀洲 an islet in a stream; a shoal

tīng 聽

1. to hear; to listen 2. to obey; to follow 3. to wait for 4. a hall 5. (also **tìng**) to allow; to let 6. (also **tìng**) to manage; to govern; to rule

tīngcóng 聽從 to listen to (another's advice, etc.); to listen

tīng 聽 and follow

tīnghòu 聽候 to wait for

tīnghuà 聽話 1. to obey; obedient 2. to wait for word or a reply

tīngjian 聽見 to hear

tīngjiǎng 聽講 to listen to a talk; to attend a lecture

tīngjué 聽覺 hearing; the sense of hearing

tīngkè 聽課 to attend class teaching or lectures

tīnglì 聽力 1. hearing 2. aural comprehension (in language teaching)

tīngmìng 聽命 to follow orders

tīngqí zìrán 聽其自然 to let things take their own course; to let matters slide

tīngqǔ 聽取 to listen (with due attention); to hear (a report)

tīngshuō 聽說 1. It is reported that.... It is said that.... 2. to hear

tīngtiān yóumìng 聽天由命 to resign oneself to fate

tīngtǒng 聽筒 a telephone receiver

tīngxì 聽戲 to see an operatic show

tīngxìn 聽信 1. to listen to and believe (what others said) 2. to wait for news, messages, information, etc.

tīngzhěnqì 聽診器 a stethoscope

tīngzhòng 聽衆 an audience; listeners

tīng 廳 1. a central or main room of a house 2. a hall 3. a government agency

tīngfáng 廳房 a central room open to a number of other rooms; a hall

tīngtáng 廳堂 the central room of a house; a hall

tīngzhǎng 廳長 the director of a department under a provincial government

tíng 廷 the imperial court; the court

tíngyì 廷議 a discussion at imperial court

tíng 亭 1. a booth; a pavilion; a garden house or rest house 2. slim and erect 3. exactly during

tíngtíng yùlì 亭亭玉立 slim and graceful

tíng 庭 1. a hall 2. a yard 3. the imperial court 4. a court of justice

tíngshàng 庭上 1. in court (of justice) 2. at (imperial) court

tíngwéi 庭闈 1. parents' abode 2. parents

tíngxùn 庭訓 exhortation or admonition from one's father

tíngyuán 庭園 a garden

tíngyuàn 庭院 a courtyard; a garden

tíngzhǎng 庭長 a chief justice; a presiding judge

tíng 停 1. to stop; to pause; to halt; to stay 2. to suspend; to delay 3. percentage

tíngbǎi 停擺 to suspend work

tíngbàn 停辦 to suspend; to stop handling something

tíngbó 停泊 to anchor; to berth; to dock

tíngchē 停車 to park a car

tíngchēchǎng 停車場 a parking lot

tíngdiàn 停電 1. blackout 2. to cut off power supply

tíngdùn 停頓 to grind to a halt

tíngfàng 停放 to park; to place

tíngfēi 停飛 the grounding of aircraft

tínggōng 停工 to suspend work

tíngháng 停航 to suspend air or shipping service

tínghuǒ 停火 to cease fire

tíngjīpíng 停機坪 an apron (at an airfield)

tíngkān 停刊 to stop publication

tíngkào 停靠 (of a train) to stop; (of a ship) to berth

tíngkè 停課 to suspend class

tíngliú 停留 to stay

tíngshījiān 停屍間 a mortuary

tíngshuǐ 停水 to cut off the water supply

tíngtuǒ 停妥 1. ready 2. to have been parked in a proper place

tíngxī 停息 to stop; to cease

tíngxí 停息 refer to **tíngxī** 停息

tíngxiē 停歇 to stop for a rest

tíngxīn 停薪 to stop or suspend payment to an employee

tíngyè 停業 to stop doing business; to close down

tíngzhàn 停戰 1. to stop fighting 2. a truce

tíngzhí 停職 to suspend a person from office

tíngzhǐ 停止 to stop; to cease

tíngzhì 停滯 1. to be held up 2. indigestion

tíng 婷
pretty; attractive; graceful

tǐng 町
the boundary between agricultural land

tǐng 挺
1. to stand straight (or upright); to square; to straighten; rigid 2. to pull up 3. unyielding; tough 4. outstanding; remarkable 5. to thrust forward (as one's breast) 6. to sustain; to endure; to stand; to hold out 7. very 8. the number of machine guns

tǐngbá 挺拔 independent, eminent and outstanding

tǐng'ér zǒuxiǎn 挺而走險 1. to risk danger in desperation 2. to be forced to break the law

tǐnglì 挺立 to stand upright; to stand erect

tǐngshēn 挺身 to straighten one's back

tǐngshēn érchū 挺身而出 to thrust oneself out to face a challenge

tǐngxiōng 挺胸 to thrust out one's chest

tǐngzhí 挺直 straight and upright; erect

tǐng 艇
a long, narrow boat

tǐng 鋌
to rush

tǐng'ér zǒuxiǎn 鋌而走險 to be forced to break the law; to risk danger in desperation

tìng 聽
refer to **tīng** 聽 5, 6

tōng 恫
pain

tōng 通
1. to go, move, or flow unobstructed 2. to communicate; to interchange 3. to lead to; to reach 4. to understand thoroughly; to be versed in 5. to let through; through 6. smooth; fluent 7. open; passable 8. all; general; overall; throughout 9. thorough 10. common; popular 11. (said of a sentence) well-constructed; containing no fallacy

tōngbào 通報 to notify

tōngbìng 通病 common ills; common deficiencies; common faults

tōngcái 通才 an all-round talent; a versatile scholar

tōngcháng 通常 normally; usually; generally

tōngchàng 通暢 1. (said of writings) smooth; easy to read; highly readable 2. passing freely or smoothly

tōngchē 通車 (said of roads, etc.) to be open (to vehicular traffic)

tōngchēng 通稱 a popular name; popularly (or generally) known as...

tōngdá 通達 1. to understand clearly 2. unobstructed 3. (said of a road) to lead to

tōngdào 通道 a passage; a way

tōngdí 通敵 to collaborate with the enemy secretly

tōngfēng 通風 1. to let the wind through; ventilation 2. to let out news or secrets

tōnggào 通告 1. to notify 2. a public notice; an announcement

tōngguò 通過 1. to pass through

2. (said of a motion or bill) to be passed 3. (said of a nomination or appointment) to be confirmed or approved

tōngháng 通航 air or sea navigation

tōnghuà 通話 to communicate by telephone or radio

tōnghūn 通婚 to marry (said of members of two families, tribes, etc.); to intermarry

tōnghuò péngzhàng 通貨膨脹 (economics) inflation

tōngjīfàn 通緝犯 a criminal wated by the law

tōngjiān 通姦 adultery; illicit intercourse

tōnglì hézuò 通力合作 to make a concerted effort; to join forces with

tōnglù 通路 a thoroughfare; a passageway; a route

tōngqì 通氣 1. sympathetic to each other 2. breathing freely 3. not airtight

tōngqìfàn 通緝犯 refer to **tōngjīfàn** 通緝犯

tōngqíng dálǐ 通情達理 sensible; reasonable

tōngrong 通融 1. departure from principles for convenience; compromise; to accommodate; to compromise 2. to accommodate somebody with a short-term loan

tōngshāng 通商 to have commercial intercourse; to trade

tōngshùn 通順 (said of writings) fluent; smooth

tōngsú 通俗 popular; common

tōngtōng 通通 wholly; altogether

tōngxiāo 通宵 all night; the whole night

tōngxiāo dádàn 通宵達旦 all night long; till daybreak

tōngxiāo diànyǐng 通宵電影 movie marthon

tōngxiǎo 通曉 to be familiar with; to understand

tōngxìn 通信 in correspondence with

tōngxíng 通行 1. to travel through (a road, etc.) 2. common

practice

tōngxíngzhèng 通行證 a safe-conduct; a pass

tōngxué 通學 to commute

tōngxuésheng 通學生 a non-resident student

tōngxùn 通訊 correspondence; communication

tōngxùnlù 通訊錄 an address book

tōngyòng 通用 1. (said of words or characters) interchangeable 2. in common use 3. practicable; usable 4. (said of currency) in circulation

tōngyóu 通郵 postal communication

tōngyùn 通運 to transport; to ship

tōngzhī 通知 to inform; to notify; a notification

tōngzhīdān 通知單 a notification

tóng 同

1. same; equal; identical; similar; common 2. to share; to agree 3. together

tóngbān 同班 a classmate

tóngbàn 同伴 a companion

tóngbāo 同胞 a compatriot

tóngbèi 同輩 of the same generation; a peer; one's equal (in seniority)

tóngbìng xiānglián 同病相憐 Fellow sufferers have mutual sympathy.

tóngbù 同步 synchronism; to synchronize

tóngchái 同儕 contemporaries

tóngchóu díkài 同仇敵愾 to share the same hatred and fight against a common enemy

tóngchuāng 同窗 a classmate or schoolmate

tóngchuáng yìmèng 同床異夢 to have different dreams in the same bed

tóngděng 同等 of the same rank or class

tóngděng xuélì 同等學力 (said of persons without a diploma in comparison with those who have

it) with the same intellectual capacity and scholastic achievements

tóngfáng 同房 to share the same room

tóngfù yìmǔ 同父異母 having the same father but different mothers

tónggān gòngkǔ 同甘共苦 to share bliss and adversity together

tónggǎn 同感 to have the same feeling

tóngguī yújìn 同歸於盡 to die together

tóngháng 同行 in the same trade, line, occupation, or profession

tónghào 同好 people with the same hobby

tónghuà 同化 to assimilate; assimilation

tónghuǒ 同夥 a member of the same group

tóngjū 同居 to cohabit; a de facto marriage; a companionate marriage

tónglèhuì 同樂會 a party

tónglèi 同類 the same kind, class, or species

tóngliáo 同僚 colleagues

tóngliú héwū 同流合污 to follow the bad example of others

tóngmén 同門 a fellow disciple

tóngméng 同盟 an alliance; a league

tóngmíng 同名 a namesake

tóngmíng tóngxìng 同名同姓 having the same given name and family name

tóngmóu 同謀 to conspire

tóngnián 同年 of the same age

tóngpáo 同袍 1. comrades in arms 2. to share the same robes with

tóngqì xiāngqiú 同氣相求 People with the same ideals have an affinity for one another.

tóngqíng 同情 to sympathize

tóngqíngxīn 同情心 sympathies; compassion; pity

tóngrén 同仁 a colleague

tóngrì éryǔ 同日而語 to mention in equal terms

tóngshēng xiāngyìng 同聲相應 to act in unison

tóngshí 同時 at the same time; simultaneously

tóngshì 同事 colleagues

tóngshì cāogē 同室操戈 (especially said of brothers) to engage in internal strife

tóngwèiyǔ 同位語 (English grammar) an appositive

tóngxiāng 同鄉 the people from the same province, county, town, etc.

tóngxīn xiélì 同心協力 to work in cooperation

tóngxíng 同行 to go together

tóngxìng 同姓 members of the same clan

tóngxìng 同性 of the same sex

tóngxìngliàn 同性戀 homosexuality

tóngxìngliànzhě 同性戀者 a gay; a homosexual

tóngxué 同學 a fellow student; a schoolmate

tóngxuéhuì 同學會 an alumni association

tóngyàng 同樣 1. in the same way, manner, or fashion; likewise 2. the same

tóngyè 同業 the people of the same trade or occupation

tóngyè gōnghuì 同業公會 a guild; a trade union

tóngyì 同意 to agree; to consent; to concur

tóngyìshū 同意書 a written consent; a letter of authorization

tóngzhì 同志 a comrade

tóngzhōu gòngjì 同舟共濟 to show the mutual concern of the people in the same boat

tóngzōng 同宗 of the same clan

tóng 桐 a paulownia

tóngshù 桐樹 a tung tree

tóngyóu 桐油 tung oil

tóng 筒

refer to **tóng** 筒

tóng 童
1. a child; a minor; a virgin 2. (said of land, etc.) bare; barren 3. a Chinese family name

tónggōng 童工 child labor; a child laborer

tónghuà 童話 nursery stories; fairy tales

tóngnián 童年 childhood; youth

tóngpú 童僕 a boy servant

tóngshān zhuózhuó 童山濯濯 1. an unforested mountain 2. baldheaded

tóngxīn wèimǐn 童心未泯 to retain a childish heart

tóngyáo 童謠 nursery rhymes; nursery songs

tóngzhēn 童貞 virginity; chastity

tóngzhuāng 童裝 children's garments

tóngzǐ 童子 a minor; a child; a boy; a lad

tóngzǐjūn 童子軍 a boy scout

tóng 銅
copper; bronze; brass

tóngbǎn 銅板 copper coins

tóngkuàng 銅礦 1. copper ore 2. copper mine

tóngluó 銅鑼 a copper gong

tóngpái 銅牌 a bronze medal

tóngqì 銅器 bronze utensils

tóngqián 銅錢 copper coins

tóngqiáng tiěbì 銅牆鐵壁 impregnable like walls of brass and iron

tóngxiàng 銅像 a bronze image; a bronze statue

tóng 僮
1. a servant 2. a boy

tóng 瞳
1. the pupil of the eye 2. ignorant

tóngkǒng 瞳孔 the pupil of the eye

tǒng 桶
a bucket; a tub; a pail; a barrel

tǒng 統
1. to govern; to rule; to control 2. to unify; to unite 3. wholly; totally; all; completely; generally 4. succession; from generation to generation

tǒngchēng 統稱 known together as

tǒngchóu 統籌 to plan as a whole

tǒngjì 統計 1. statistics 2. to count

tǒngjìxué 統計學 statistics (as a science)

tǒnglǐng 統領 a commanding officer

tǒngshuài 統帥 the commander in chief

tǒngshuài 統率 to lead (troops, a mission, etc.); to rule; to govern

tǒngyī 統一 to unify; uniform; unitary

tǒngyī fāpiào 統一發票 a uniform invoice

tǒngyù 統馭 to reign; to rule

tǒngzhì 統治 to reign; to rule; to govern

tǒngzhìzhě 統治者 the ruler

tǒng 筒 also **tóng**
a tube; a pipe; a cylinder

tǒngzi 筒子 a tube or tube-shaped object

tòng 痛
1. painful; aching 2. sorrowful; sad; bitter; poignant; bitterly 3. heartily; to one's heart's content

tòngbù yùshēng 痛不欲生 to grieve to the extent of wishing to die

tòngchì 痛斥 to scold severely; scathingly denounce

tòngchǔ 痛楚 pain; anguish

tòngdǎ 痛打 to beat soundly; to give a severe thrashing

tòngdìng sītòng 痛定思痛 to feel pangs over a past defeat, failure, mistake, etc.

tòngfēng 痛風 gout (a disease)

tònggǎi qiánfēi 痛改前非 to repent past mistakes

tònghèn 痛恨 to detest; to hate deeply

tòngjī 痛擊 to give a hard blow

tòngjí 痛擊 refer to **tòngjī** 痛擊

tòngkū 痛哭 to weep bitterly

tòngkū liútì 痛哭流涕 to shed tears of anguish

tòngkǔ 痛苦 painful; suffering; pain; anguish

tòngkuai 痛快 very happy; delighted

tòngkuai línlí 痛快淋漓 satisfying in every respect

tòngmà 痛罵 to berate; to revile; to vituperate

tòng'ōu 痛毆 to beat savagely

tòngxī 痛惜 to regret deeply

tòngxí 痛惜 refer to **tòngxī** 痛惜

tòngxīn 痛心 heartbroken; very sorry

tòngxīn jíshǒu 痛心疾首 to hate deeply; to feel bitter about...

tòngyǐn 痛飲 to drink to one's heart's content

tòngzé 痛責 to scold severely

tòng 慟
extreme grief

tòngkū 慟哭 to weep bitterly

tōu 偷
1. to steal; to filch; to burglarize; to pilfer 2. to do something without others' knowledge; stealthily; surreptitiously

tōu'ān 偷安 to seek temporary ease

tōudù 偷渡 to stow away

tōudùzhě 偷渡者 a stowaway

tōugōng jiǎnliào 偷工減料 to jerry-build

tōukàn 偷看 to steal a look

tōukòng 偷空 to avail oneself of a leisure moment

tōulǎn 偷懶 to be lazy

tōulěi 偷壘 (baseball) base stealing

tōuqiè 偷竊 to steal; to thieve

tōuqíng 偷情 to carry on a clandestine love affair

tōushēng 偷生 to live in disgrace

tōushuì 偷稅 to evade tax payment

tōutiān huànrì 偷天換日 to commit a big cheat, fraud, etc.

tōutīng 偷聽 to eavesdrop

tōutōu 偷偷 stealthily; secretly; covertly

tōutōu mōmō 偷偷摸摸 stealthily; surreptitiously

tōuxí 偷襲 to attack by surprise

tóu 投
1. to throw; to pitch; to toss 2. to present as a gift 3. to lodge; to stay 4. to head (west, etc.) 5. agreeable; congenial; harmonious; to fit in with; to cater to 6. to join; to submit to 7. to project; to cast 8. to deliver (mail, etc.); to send (letters, etc.)

tóu'àn 投案 to surrender oneself to justice or the police

tóubǎo 投保 to take out an insurance policy

tóubèn 投奔 1. to flee (to freedom) 2. to seek employment or protection from somebody

tóubǐ cóngróng 投筆從戎 (said of a student or intellectual) to join the army voluntarily

tóuchéng 投誠 (said of enemy troops, bandits, etc.) to voluntarily surrender to the government forces

tóudì 投遞 to send or deliver (letters, etc.); delivery

tóufàng 投放 1. to throw in 2. to put (money) into circulation; to put (goods) on the market

tóugǎo 投稿 1. a contributed article 2. to contribute an article

tóuhé 投合 to see eye to eye; to agree with

tóuhuái sòngbào 投懷送抱 (said of a woman) overtly aggressive in love affairs; acting like a man-chaser

tóujī 投機 1. to speculate 2. to see eye to eye

tóujī fènzǐ 投機分子 an oppor-

tunist; a speculator

tóujī qǔqiǎo 投機取巧 to speculate and take advantage of an opportunity

tóujī shìyè 投機事業 speculative business

tóujǐng 投井 to drown oneself in a well

tóukǎo 投考 to go in for an examination

tóukǎo 投靠 to go and seek refuge with somebody

tóulán 投籃 (basketball) to shoot

tóupiào 投票 to cast a vote

tóupiàoquán 投票權 the ballot; the right to vote

tóupiàosuǒ 投票所 a polling place; polls

tóuqí suǒhào 投其所好 to cater to another's pleasure

tóuqì 投契 meeting of minds (between friends)

tóuqīn 投親 (said of an orphan, etc.) to go and live with one's relatives

tóurù 投入 1. to throw in 2. to join (the army, revolutionaries, etc.)

tóushè 投射 1. to project; to shoot 2. to harvest profit from speculation

tóushēn 投身 1. to give oneself to (the revolutionary cause, a military career, etc.) 2. to find employment or shelter

tóushí wènlù 投石問路 (said of burglars) to throw a stone into a house to find out if the occupants are awake

tóushǒu 投手 (baseball) a pitcher

tóushū 投書 to send a letter to (a newspaper editor, etc.)

tóusù 投宿 to stay or check in (at a hotel, etc.) for the night

tóutāi 投胎 to get into the cycle of reincarnation

tóutáo bàolǐ 投桃報李 to return a favor with a favor

tóuxià 投下 1. to throw down; to drop 2. to invest (capital)

tóuxián zhìsǎn 投閒置散 to stay idle

tóuxiáng 投降 to surrender; to capitulate

tóuxiào 投效 to offer one's services to

tóuyǐng 投影 1. (mathematics) projection 2. (art) cast shadow 3. to project

tóuyuán 投緣 to be on intimate terms at once

tóuzhàdàn 投炸彈 to throw bombs

tóuzhí 投擲 refer to **tóuzhì** 投擲

tóuzhì 投擲 to throw (a discus, etc.)

tóuzī 投資 to invest; investment

tóuzī gōngsī 投資公司 an investment company

tóu 頭
1. the head 2. the top; the first; first; the beginning 3. the chief; the boss; the leader; the head (of a group) 4. the two ends (of anything); an aspect 5. a head (of cattle, etc.) 6. an auxiliary, as a suffix

tóubǎn 頭版 1. the front page (of a newspaper) 2. the first edition

tóubù 頭部 the head

tóucùn 頭寸 cash; money supply

tóuděng 頭等 first class; the best quality

tóuděngcāng 頭等艙 a first-class cabin

tóudǐng 頭頂 1. the top of one's head 2. to wear or support with one's head

tóufa 頭髮 hair on the head

tóuhūn 頭昏 dizzy; giddy

tóuhūn nǎozhàng 頭昏腦脹 to feel dizzy and have a headache

tóuhūn yǎnhuā 頭昏眼花 dizzy

tóujiā 頭家 the operator of a gambling joint

tóujiǎng 頭獎 the first prize

tóujiǎo 頭角 1. a lead or clue 2. looks of a promising youth; brilliance (of a young person); talent

tóujīn 頭巾 a turban; a kerchief

tóukuī 頭盔 a helmet

tóulú 頭顱 the head

tóulù 頭路 1. a clue; a main thread 2. one's occupation; one's job 3. access

tóumù 頭目 a chief; a leader; a ringleader; a chieftain

tóunǎo 頭腦 1. brains; mind 2. main threads; clues 3. the chief or boss

tóupí 頭皮 the scalp

tóupíxiè 頭皮屑 dandruff

tóupò xièliú 頭破血流 refer to **tóupò xuèliú** 頭破血流

tóupò xuèliú 頭破血流 with one's head broken and bleeding

tóutāi 頭胎 the firstborn

tóutào 頭套 an actor's headgear

tóutiáo xīnwén 頭條新聞 the leading story in a paper; headline news

tóutòng 頭痛 a headache

tóutòng yītóu, jiǎotòng yījiǎo 頭痛醫頭，腳痛醫腳 to treat only where the pain is—not to find the source of a disease

tóutóu shìdào 頭頭是道 logically (arranged and narrated); systematically and orderly (stated)

tóuwěi 頭尾 head and tail —beginning and end

tóuxián 頭銜 the official title of a person

tóuxù 頭緒 1. (said of a complicated affair) leads or clues; main clues 2. ways or means 3. sequence; systematical

tóuyīhuí 頭一回 for the first time

tóuyūn 頭暈 dizzy; giddy; dizziness

tóuzhòng jiǎoqīng 頭重腳輕 top-heavy

tóuzi 頭子 1. the best; the winner 2. the leader (of bandits, rebels, etc.)

tóu 骰

refer to **shǎi** 骰

tòu 透

1. to pass through; to penetrate 2. to let out or through 3. thorough; quite; complete 4. to appear; to show

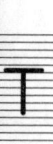

tòufēng 透風 1. to let the wind through 2. to divulge a secret; to let out a secret

tòuguāng 透光 1. diaphaneity 2. to let the light pass through

tòuguò 透過 1. to pass through; to penetrate 2. through the intermediary of

tòujìng 透鏡 lenses

tòulù 透露 (said of something) to come to light; to divulge; to reveal; to let out

tòumíng 透明 transparent

tòuqì 透氣 1. to let air through 2. to give vent to a pent-up feeling of discontent 3. to relax from strain

tòushì 透視 1. to see through; to penetrate 2. to observe what is behind a solid covering (by X-ray, etc.) 3. to gain a perspective of; perspective

tòuzhī 透支 to overdraw; to spend more than the budgeted fund

tou 頭

1. a suffix indicating positions or directions 2. as a suffix to certain verbs to indicate the worthiness

tū 凸 also **tú**

1. protuberant; convex 2. to protrude; to jut

tūchū 凸出 bulging out; to protrude

tūtòujìng 凸透鏡 a convex lens

tū 禿

bald; bare

tūtóu 禿頭 baldheaded; bald; a bald head

tūzi 禿子 a baldhead; a baldpate

tū 突 also **tú**

1. abrupt; sudden; unexpected; suddenly; unexpectedly 2. to offend; to go against 3. to break through (enemy encirclement) 4. to project or jut out 5. a chimney

tūbiàn 突變 1. an unexpected change 2. mutation

tūchū 突出 1. outstanding; remarkable 2. to jut out

tūfēi měngjìn 突飛猛進 to progress rapidly

tūjī 突擊 to attack (or assault) suddenly; to raid

tūjí 突擊 refer to **tūjī** 突擊

tūpò 突破 1. to break or smash (old records, etc.) 2. to break through

tūqǐ 突起 1. to rise up all of a sudden 2. to break out; suddenly appear

tūrán 突然 suddenly; unexpectedly

tūrú qílái 突如其來 suddenly; abruptly

tūwéi 突圍 to break through enemy encirclement or siege

tūxí 突襲 surprise attack

tú 凸

refer to **tū** 凸

tú 突

refer to **tū** 突

tú 徒

1. disciples; followers; pupils; apprentices 2. a crowd; a gang; a group of people 3. to go on foot 4. a punishment 5. only; merely; in vain 6. empty, as empty-handed 7. convicts; infantry

túbù 徒步 to go on foot

túdì 徒弟 an apprentice; a disciple; a pupil

túfèi kǒushé 徒費口舌 to waste one's breath

túláo 徒勞 futile effort

túláo wúgōng 徒勞無功 to labor in vain

túrán 徒然 in vain; useless; meaningless

túshǒu 徒手 barehanded

túshǒu zhìfù 徒手致富 from rags to riches

túxíng 徒刑 a prison term; imprisonment

túyōng xūmíng 徒擁虛名 to have an undeserved reputation

túzēng 徒增 to increase (cost, trouble, age, etc.) without gaining advantage of any kind

túzhòng 徒眾 a gang; a group of followers

túzǐ túsūn 徒子徒孫 followers

tú 途

a way; a road

tújìng 途徑 a way; a road

túzhōng 途中 on the way; en route

tú 荼

1. a kind of bitter-tasting vegetable; sow thistle 2. to harm; to poison

túdú shēnglíng 荼毒生靈 to injure the people

tútàn 荼炭 suffering of the common people

tú 屠

to slaughter; to butcher; to massacre

túdāo 屠刀 a butcher's knife

túfū 屠夫 a butcher

túlù 屠戮 to massacre

túshā 屠殺 to massacre

túzǎi 屠宰 to slaughter (livestock)

túzǎichǎng 屠宰場 a slaughterhouse; an abattoir

tú 塗

1. to smear; to apply; to spread (ointment on a wound, etc.) 2. to scribble; to scrawl 3. to erase; to blot out; to efface; to obliterate 4. mud; mire

túgǎi 塗改 to erase and change the wording of an article, etc.; to alter

túliào 塗料 paint; coating

túmǒ 塗抹 1. to erase; to obliterate 2. to scribble

túyā 塗鴉 1. to scribble 2. graffiti

tú 圖

1. a picture; a map; a portrait; a chart; a diagram 2. to seek; to pursue 3. to plan; to scheme; to conspire 4. intention; aim; purpose 5. a Chinese family name

tú'àn 圖案 (fine arts) patterns

túbǎo sīnáng 圖飽私囊 to try to enrich oneself (from public services)

túbiǎo 圖表 charts, diagrams and tables—used in statistics

túdīng 圖釘 thumbtacks; a drawing pin

túhuà 圖畫 1. a drawing; a picture 2. painting 3. to plot; to plan

tújiě 圖解 illustrations

túlì 圖利 to desire to make money or profit

túlì 圖例 a brief explanation or key to an illustration, map, etc.

túmóu 圖謀 to plan; to conspire

túmóu bùguǐ 圖謀不軌 to harbor evil intentions

túpiàn 圖片 pictures; photographs

túqióng bǐxiàn 圖窮匕見 The real intention is revealed in the end.

túshūguǎn 圖書館 a library

túxíng 圖形 a graph; a figure

túyàng 圖樣 (architecture) a design

túzhāng 圖章 a seal; a chop

tǔ 土

1. earth; soil 2. land; territory; domain 3. local; native; indigenous 4. unrefined; unenlightened 5. rustic; countrified 6. opium 7. an abbreviation for Turkey

tǔbāozi 土包子 a hillbilly; a country bumpkin

tǔbēng wǎjiě 土崩瓦解 in total disorder or confusion

tǔbōshǔ 土撥鼠 a marmot; a ground hog

tǔchǎn 土產 local products

tǔdì 土地 land

Tǔdì 土地 the God of Earth

Tǔdigōng 土地公 the God of Earth

Tǔdimiào 土地廟 the temple of the God of Earth

tǔdòu 土豆 1. peanuts 2. potatoes

tǔdòutiáo 土豆條 French fries

tǔduī 土堆 a mound

Tǔ'ěrqí 土耳其 Turkey

tǔfěi 土匪 bandits; brigands

tǔfēngwǔ 土風舞 folk dance

tǔháo lièshēn 土豪劣紳 local ruffians and the oppressive gentry

tǔlǐ tǔqi 土裡土氣 rustic; countrified; hillbilly

tǔmù gōngchéng 土木工程 civil engineering

tǔrǎng 土壤 soil

tǔshēng tǔzhǎng 土生土長 to be born and grow up in the local community

Tǔxīng 土星 the planet Saturn

tǔzàng 土葬 a burial in the ground

tǔzhí 土質 refer to **tǔzhǐ** 土質

tǔzhǐ 土質 the condition or nature of the soil

tǔzhù 土著 a native; an aborigine

tǔ 吐

to spit; to utter

tǔchū 吐出 to spit out; to utter

tǔlù 吐露 to confess; to disclose

tǔqì 吐氣 to give vent to pent-up feelings

tǔtán 吐痰 to spit phlegm; to spit

tù 吐

to vomit; to throw up; to spew

tùxiě 吐血 refer to **tùxuè** 吐血

tùxuè 吐血 to vomit blood; hematemesis

tù 兔

1. a hare; a rabbit 2. a young boy kept for sexual perversion

tùchún 兔唇 a harelip, or a cleft lip

tùsǐ húbēi 兔死狐悲 sympathy with one of its kind

tùzǎizi 兔崽子 a brat; a bastard

tùzi 兔子 a hare; a rabbit

tuān 湍

rapidly flowing

tuānjí 湍急 (said of water) swift; rapid

tuānliú 湍流 rapids; torrent; swift current

tuán 團

1. a sphere; something shaped like a ball 2. a mass; a lump 3. a group; a party; a mission; an organization; a society 4. (infantry) a regiment, consisting of three battalions of foot soldiers

5. to unite

tuánduì jīngshén 團隊精神 team spirit

tuánjié 團結 union; solidarity; to unite

tuánjù 團聚 (said of a family, etc.) to congregate; a reunion; a gathering

tuántǐ 團體 an organization; group (action, etc.)

tuántǐcāo 團體操 callisthenics done by a large group of people

tuántǐsài 團體賽 a team competition

tuántuán wéizhù 團團圍住 to be completely surrounded (by rows of enemy troops)

tuányuán 團員 a member

tuányuán 團圓 a union or reunion (especially of a family)

tuánzhǎng 團長 a regiment commander

tuī 推

1. to push; to shove 2. to look into; to find out; to ponder; to infer; to deduce 3. to shirk; to shift (responsibility, etc.); to refuse 4. to elect; to recommend; to praise; to esteem 5. to move along; to change in succession (as seasons) 6. to extend; to enlarge

tuīběn sùyuán 推本溯源 to trace the origins

tuībō zhùlán 推波助瀾 to add fuel to the fire; to incite

tuīcè 推測 to infer; to deduce; to predict; to conjecture

tuīchén chūxīn 推陳出新 to find new ways of doing things from old theories

tuīchóng 推崇 to respect; to praise highly

tuīchū 推出 1. to push out 2. to present (a picture, a show, etc.)

tuīcí 推辭 to decline (an offer, invitation, etc.); to reject

tuīdǎo 推倒 1. to overturn 2. to shove

tuīdòng 推動 to push (a sales project, etc.)

tuīduàn 推斷 to infer; inference

tuīfān 推翻 1. to overthrow (a

government, etc.); to topple 2. to stultify (a theory, principle, etc.)

tuīguǎng 推廣 to propagate; to popularize

tuījǐ jírén 推己及人 to put oneself in another's position

tuījiàn 推薦 to recommend (somebody for a job, etc.)

tuījiànshū 推薦書 a letter of recommendation

tuījìn 推進 to push forward; to advance

tuījìnqì 推進器 a propeller

tuījiū 推究 to study; to investigate

tuījiù 推究 refer to **tuījiū** 推究

tuījǔ 推舉 1. to recommend for a post 2. (weightlifting) to press

tuīlǐ 推理 to reason (out); to infer

tuīlǐ xiǎoshuō 推理小說 detective stories

tuīlùn 推論 to infer; inference

tuīná 推拿 1. to massage 2. to fix a dislocated bone by massage

tuīqiāo 推敲 1. to weigh or consider words in writing 2. to investigate or examine carefully

tuīqiú 推求 to ascertain; to analyze and study (for a solution, an answer, etc.)

tuīquè 推卻 to decline (an invitation, offer, etc.)

tuīràng 推讓 to yield to someone as a token of deference to the other party

tuīsān zǔsì 推三阻四 to make numerous excuses

tuīshì 推事 (court) a judge

tuīsuàn 推算 to calculate; to reckon

tuītǔjī 推土機 a bulldozer

tuītuō 推託 to make excuses

tuīwěi 推諉 to make excuses; to shirk (responsibility, etc.)

tuīxiǎng 推想 to infer; to deduce

tuīxiāo 推銷 to promote sales; to sell

tuīxiāoyuán 推銷員 a salesman or saleswoman

tuīxiè 推卸 to be irresponsible

tuīxīn zhìfù 推心置腹 to treat

others with the utmost sincerity

tuīxíng 推行 to promote (a cause, movement, etc.)

tuīxǔ 推許 to praise; to approve (a performance)

tuīxuǎn 推選 to elect

tuí 頹

1. to crumble; to collapse; disintegrated; ruined; dilapidated 2. weakened; withered; emaciated; declining; decadent 3. bald 4. to descend; to cascade down 5. a Chinese family name

tuífèi 頹廢 1. ruined; weakened; decadent 2. low-spirited; depressed

tuífēng 頹風 depraved or decadent customs; moral degeneracy

tuísàng 頹喪 beaten; ruined; discouraged

tuíshì 頹勢 a declining tendency

tuǐ 腿

the leg and the thigh

tuì 退

1. to retreat; to withdraw; to recede; to regress; to retrogress 2. to recoil; to shrink 3. to bow out; to retire 4. to send back; to give back; to return

tuìbì 退避 to withdraw and avoid

tuìbì sānshè 退避三舍 (literally) to retreat ninety *li* (里) —to retreat as far as possible in the face of a strong adversary or contestant

tuìbù 退步 1. to fall off; to regress; to retrogress; to fall backwards; to suffer a relapse 2. to retreat

tuìchǎng 退場 to leave the stage; an exit

tuìcháo 退潮 (said of the tide) to ebb

tuìchū 退出 to withdraw or retreat (from a city or position)

tuìdí 退敵 to repel the enemy

tuìér qiú qícì 退而求其次 to seek what is less attractive than one's original objective

tuìhòu 退後 to fall backward; to move backward

tuìhuà 退化 to degenerate; to atrophy

tuìhuán 退還 to return (a gift, defective merchandise, etc.)

tuìhuàn 退換 to return (merchandise) in exchange for another; to exchange a purchase

tuìhuí 退回 1. to return (a gift, defective merchandise, etc.); to send back 2. to retreat; to turn back

tuìhūn 退婚 to break off a marital engagement

tuìhuò 退貨 to return goods already purchased

tuìkuǎn 退款 to reimburse

tuìlù 退路 1. a retreat 2. something to fall back on

tuìpiào 退票 1. (said of theaters, music halls, etc.) to refund; to return the ticket and get the money back 2. (said of checks) to be dishonored; to bounce

tuìquè 退卻 1. to retreat 2. to decline

tuìshāo 退燒 to reduce or remove fever

tuìshuì 退稅 drawback

tuìsuō 退縮 to shrink; to recoil; to flinch

tuìwǔ 退伍 to retire or to be discharged from military service

tuìwǔ jūnrén 退伍軍人 a retired soldier; veterans

tuìxí 退席 to withdraw (from the presence of others)

tuìxiū 退休 to retire from active life

tuìxiūjīn 退休金 a retiring allowance; a pension

tuìxué 退學 to withdraw from a school; to drop out of a school

tuì 蛻 also **shuì**

1. to slough; to exuviate 2. exuviae; a slough

tuìbiàn 蛻變 1. to undergo transformation 2. decay

tuìpí 蛻皮 to exuviate; to slough

tuì 褪 also **tùn**

1. to take off one's clothing; to strip 2. to fall off; to fade, as color

tuìsè 褪色 color fading

tūn 吞
to swallow; to engulf; to gulp

tūnbìng 吞併 to annex (a foreign territory); to take possession of (another's property)

tūnfú 吞服 to swallow or take (medicine)

tūnmò 吞沒 1. to take possession of (another's property) 2. to engulf

tūnshí 吞食 to swallow; to devour

tūnshì 吞噬 1. (said of beasts) to swallow or devour (the prey) 2. (said of fire, etc.) to devour; to engulf

tūntūn tǔtǔ 吞吞吐吐 to hum and haw

tūnyún tǔwù 吞雲吐霧 to puff; to take puffs

tún 屯
1. to station (an army) 2. to stockpile

túnjī 屯積 to hoard up

túnjù 屯聚 to assemble; to gather together

túnliáng 屯糧 to hoard up or stockpile grains

tún 囤
to store up; to hoard; to stockpile

túnjī 囤積 to hoard commodities for speculation; to corner

tún 飩
stuffed dumplings

tún 臀
1. the buttocks; the behind; the bottom; the rump 2. (now rarely) the bottom of a ware or vessel

túnbù 臀部 the buttocks; the bottom; the rump

tùn 褪
1. refer to **tuì** 褪 2. to retreat; to move backward

tuō 它
refer to **tā** 它

tuō 托
1. to hold, or lift, on the palm 2. to entrust; to charge 3. a tray; a pad

tuōbìng 托病 on the pretext of sickness

tuōbō 托鉢 (Buddhism) to beg for alms

tuōcí 托辭 1. to make excuses 2. a pretext; an excuse

tuō'érsuǒ 托兒所 a nursery school

tuōfú 托福 Thanks. (used in reply to others' congratulations on a success, a narrow escape, etc.)

tuōfú cèyàn 托福測驗 Test of English as a Foreign Language (TOEFL)

tuōfù 托付 to entrust; to charge; to consign

tuōguǎn 托管 trusteeship; mandate

tuōmèng 托夢 (said of a spirit or deity) to convey a message to a mortal through his dream

tuōpán 托盤 a tray

tuōyùn 托運 to consign for shipment; to check

tuō 牠
refer to **tā** 牠

tuō 拖
1. to drag along, after or out 2. to procrastinate; to drag out; to delay 3. to involve; to implicate

tuōbǎ 拖把 a mop

tuōcháng 拖長 1. to lengthen 2. to drag on (or out)

tuōchē 拖車 a trailer

tuōchuán 拖船 a tugboat

tuōdài 拖帶 1. to drag along 2. to involve

tuōjiā dàijuàn 拖家帶眷 to have a family burden

tuōkuǎ 拖垮 to be worn down

tuōlěi 拖累 1. to involve or implicate 2. a drag

tuōní dàishuǐ 拖泥帶水 confused, sloppy and muddled (style of writing or acting); unable to make a decision

tuōqiàn 拖欠 to owe and delay payment for a long time; arrears

tuōshíjiān 拖時間 to stall for

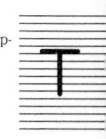

time; to delay

tuōxié 拖鞋 slippers

tuōyán 拖延 to procrastinate; to delay

tuōyì 拖曳 to drag; to pull; to tow

tuōyóupíng 拖油瓶 a woman's children by previous marriage

tuō 託

1. to commission; to entrust to 2. to ask; to request 3. to consign 4. to use as an excuse or pretext 5. to send (messages, etc.) indirectly

tuōcí 託辭 to make excuses; pretexts or excuses

tuō'érsuǒ 託兒所 a public nursery

tuōfù 託付 to entrust to; to commission

tuōgù 託故 to make an excuse

tuōguǎn 託管 to trust; to mandate

tuōmèng 託夢 (said of a dead person) to appear in one's dream

tuōrén 託人 to ask somebody to do something for oneself

tuōyùn 託運 to consign for shipment; to check

tuō 脫

1. to strip; to undress; to take off 2. to abandon; to renounce; to cast off 3. to leave; to escape from; to get out of 4. to omit; omission; to miss out 5. to slip off 6. if; in case; perhaps

tuōchǎn 脫產 to quit one's job

tuōdàng 脫檔 to run out of stock

tuōguāng 脫光 to strip nude

tuōguǐ 脫軌 to derail

tuōjiāng zhīmǎ 脫韁之馬 (literally) an unbridled wild horse—forceful and unrestrained

tuōjié 脫節 1. disconnected; irrelevant or incoherent 2. luxation; to dislocate

tuōjiù 脫臼 dislocation (of the joints)

tuōkǒu érchū 脫口而出 to speak without thinking of the consequence

T

tuōlí 脫離 1. to break away 2. away from; out of

tuōluò 脫落 to drop; to fall off

tuōmào 脫帽 to take off one's hat (in respect)

tuōpí 脫皮 1. (said of some kinds of reptiles or insects) ecdyses; to molt 2. to cast off the skin; to peel

tuōshēn 脫身 to get away from; to escape

tuōshǒu 脫手 1. (said of goods or stock at hand) to sell out 2. to slip off one's hands

tuōshòu 脫售 to sell out

tuōshuǐ 脫水 to dehydrate; dehydration

tuōshuǐjī 脫水機 a hydroextractor; a whizzer

tuōtāi huàngǔ 脫胎換骨 1. to disembody (and become immortal) 2. to change oneself inside out

tuōtáo 脫逃 to escape from; to withdraw or run away

tuōxià 脫下 to take off

tuōxiǎn 脫險 to be out of danger

tuōxié 脫鞋 to take off shoes

tuōxiè 脫卸 to relinquish or shirk (one's responsibility)

tuōyīwǔ 脫衣舞 a striptease

tuōyǐng érchū 脫穎而出 (in a race, competition, etc.) to overtake others or outscore rival teams

tuōzhī 脫脂 de-fat; degrease

tuōzuì 脫罪 to exonerate someone from a charge

tuó 陀

craggy; rugged terrain

tuóluó 陀螺 a top

tuó 馱

to carry (a load) on the back

tuóchù 馱畜 a pack animal

tuó 駝

1. a camel 2. hunchbacked 3. to carry on the back 4. to pay

tuóbèi 駝背 hunchbacked; humpbacked

tuó 鴕
an ostrich
tuóniǎo 鴕鳥 an ostrich

tuǒ 妥
1. firm; safe; secure 2. appropriate 3. ready; set; to settle

tuǒdàng 妥當 1. appropriate or secure 2. ready

tuǒshàn 妥善 proper; appropriate

tuǒshàn ānpái 妥善安排 to make appropriate arrangements

tuǒxié 妥協 1. amity 2. a compromise; a reconciliation 3. appeasement (in international relations)

tuǒ 橢
oval; oblong; elliptical

tuǒyuán 橢圓 (mathematics) an ellipse

tuò 拓
1. to expand; to aggrandize; to open up (new frontiers, etc.); to develop 2. to push with hands

tuòhuāng 拓荒 to open up virgin soil

tuòzhǎn 拓展 to expand (business, etc.); to realize (great ambitions, etc.)

tuò 唾
1. saliva 2. to spit

tuòmà 唾罵 to spit out; to revile

tuòqì 唾棄 to show contempt for

tuòshǒu kědé 唾手可得 (to accomplish) with extreme ease

tuòyè 唾液 saliva

tuò 魄
as in luòtuò 落魄—dispirited; out of luck

wā 呱
refer to gū 呱

wā 挖
1. to scoop out; to dig out 2. to engrave with a knife; to cut or gouge

wādòng 挖洞 to make a hole or cave

wā'ěrduo 挖耳朵 to pick ears

wājiǎo 挖角 refer to wājué 挖角

wājué 挖角 to lure away the employees of another company or organization by making attractive offers

wājué 挖掘 to dig; to excavate

wākōng xīnsī 挖空心思 to cudgel (or rack) one's brains

wāku 挖苦 1. to ridicule 2. a dig

wāméi 挖煤 to mine for coal

wāròu bǔchuāng 挖肉補瘡 to make up for a deficit by raising loans

wā 哇
1. to vomit 2. the sound of crying by a child

wāwā dàkū 哇哇大哭 to cry very loudly

wā 蛙
a frog

wārén 蛙人 a frogman

wāyǒng 蛙泳 (swimming) the breaststroke

wā 窪
1. deep; hollow; low-lying 2. a pit; a hole; a hollow; a depression

wādì 窪地 marsh land; low-lying land

wá 娃
1. a beautiful woman 2. a baby; a child 3. exquisite; fine

wáwa 娃娃 a baby; a young child

wáwachē 娃娃車 a baby car or carriage

wáwaliǎn 娃娃臉 a baby face; baby-faced

wǎ 瓦
1. earthenware; pottery 2. a tile 3. watt

wǎfáng 瓦房 a tiled house

wǎfǔ léimíng 瓦釜雷鳴 an unworthy man creating sensations and enjoying popularity

wǎguàn 瓦罐 an earthen jar

wǎjiě 瓦解 to fall apart; to collapse; to disintegrate

wǎjiě bīngxiāo 瓦解冰銷 to disintegrate like tiles and to dis-

solve like ice

wǎléngzhǐ 瓦楞紙 corrugated paper

wǎlì 瓦礫 1. rubble; ruin 2. worthless things

wǎsī 瓦斯 gas; poisonous gas used in war

wǎsītǒng 瓦斯筒 a gas cylinder

wà 瓦
to cover a roof with tiles; to tile

wà 襪
stockings; socks

wàdài 襪帶 garters

wa 哇
phrase-final particle

wāi 歪
1. aslant; askew; crooked; tilted; awry 2. depraved; evil 3. to lie down on one side for a brief nap 4. to shirk one's responsibility and try to involve others

wāidǎ zhèngzháo 歪打正著 to hit the mark by a fluke

wāifēng 歪風 an unhealthy trend

wāiqī niǔbā 歪七扭八 aslant; askew; to twist around

wāiqū 歪曲 to twist or confuse (things, facts, etc.) intentionally

wāiqū shìshí 歪曲事實 to twist or distort facts

wāixié 歪斜 aslant; askew; crooked

wāizhǔyì 歪主意 evil ideas

wài 外
1. out; outside 2. foreign; alien 3. diplomatic 4. besides 5. to alienate

wàibì 外幣 foreign currency

wàibian 外邊 1. out; outside 2. faraway or distant places 3. a border region

wàibiǎo 外表 an outward appearance; an exterior

wàibīn 外賓 foreign visitors; foreign guests

wàibù 外部 the external of anything; outside

wàichū 外出 to go out

wàichūxiě 外出血 refer to **wài-**

chūxuè 外出血

wàichūxuè 外出血 external hemorrhage

wàichuán 外傳 rumors are circulating...

wàidài 外帶 1. a tire (cover) 2. as well; besides

wàidì 外地 parts of the country other than where one is

wàidiàn 外電 dispatches from foreign news agencies

wàidiào 外調 to transfer (materials or personnel) to other places

wàifàng 外放 1. to send an official in the capital for a provincial post 2. to send an official for an overseas assignment

wàigōng 外公 one's maternal grandfather

wàiguān 外觀 an outward appearance

wàiguó 外國 a foreign country

wàiguóhuò 外國貨 commodities of foreign make

wàiguórén 外國人 a foreigner; an alien

wàiguóyǔ 外國語 a foreign language

wàiháng 外行 1. a greenhorn 2. unskilled

wàihánghuà 外行話 layman's language

wàihào 外號 a nickname

wàihuàn 外患 foreign invasion, aggression, or intrusion

wàihuì 外匯 foreign exchange

wàihuì jiāoyì 外匯交易 foreign exchange transactions

wàihuì shìchǎng 外匯市場 a foreign exchange market

wàijí rénshì 外籍人士 a foreigher; an alien

wàijiā 外加 plus; in addition (to)

wàijiāo 外交 diplomacy; diplomatic

Wàijiāobù 外交部 Ministry of Foreign Affairs

Wàijiāo Bùzhǎng 外交部長 Minister of Foreign Affairs

wàijiāo cílìng 外交辭令 tactful remarks; euphemisms

wàijiāoguān 外交官 diplomatic officials; diplomats

wàijiāojiā 外交家 skillful diplomats

wàijiāo zhèngcè 外交政策 foreign policy

wàijiè 外界 1. outsiders 2. the outside 3. one's environment

wàijǐng 外景 a location; an exterior

wàikē 外科 surgery

wàikē yīshēng 外科醫生 a surgeon

wàiké 外殼 a shell; a case

wàikuài 外快 extra income; perquisites

wàilái 外來 outside; external; foreign

wàiláiyǔ 外來語 foreign terms

wàiliú 外流 to flow outward; the outflow

wàimào 外貿 foreign (or external) trade

wàimào 外貌 an outward appearance

wàimiàn 外面 an outward appearance

wàimian 外面 outside

wàipó 外婆 one's maternal grandmother

wàiqiáng zhōnggān 外強中乾 a paper tiger

wàiqiáo 外僑 a foreign resident

wàiqín 外勤 work done outside the office

wàirén 外人 1. an outsider; a stranger 2. a foreigner

wàishāng 外商 foreign businessmen

wàishāng 外傷 an external injury; a bruise

wàishěng 外省 other provinces

wàishěngrén 外省人 persons from another province

wàisheng 外甥 a nephew

wàishengnǚ 外甥女 a niece

wàisù 外宿 to stay outside (one's own home or dormitory) overnight

wàisūn 外孫 a son of one's daughter; grandson

wàisūnnǚ 外孫女 a daughter of one's daughter; granddaughter

wàitàikōng 外太空 outer space

wàitào 外套 1. an overcoat 2. overalls in the Qing Dynasty

wàitou 外頭 outside

wàiwéi 外圍 the perimeter

wàiwéi shèbèi 外圍設備 (computer) peripheral device

wàiwén 外文 a foreign language

wàiwù 外務 1. foreign affairs 2. affairs or work which do not really concern one or which one is not obliged to handle

wàixiàng 外向 extrovert; extroversion

wàixiāo 外銷 to export; export

wàixīngrén 外星人 an E.T. (extraterrestrial)

wàixíng 外形 an appearance; a contour

wàiyě 外野 (baseball) outfield

wàiyěshǒu 外野手 an outfielder

wàiyī 外衣 a coat; a jacket; outer clothing

wàiyòng 外用 external use; external application

wàiyǔ 外語 a foreign language

wàiyù 外遇 to have extramarital affairs

wàiyuán 外援 outside help; foreign aid

wàiyuán 外緣 1. the outer rim (of an object) 2. desires that come from outside temptations

wàizài 外在 external; extrinsic

wàizhài 外債 international loans

wàizhuàn 外傳 a narrative of events not recorded in history

wàizī 外資 foreign capital

wàizǐ 外子 a reference to one's own husband

wàizǔfù 外祖父 one's maternal grandfather

wàizǔmǔ 外祖母 one's maternal grandmother

wān 剜

to scoop out; to gouge out; to carve out

wānkōng xīnsi 剜空心思 to exhaust one's wits

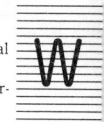

wān 蜿
to creep; to wriggle; to wind up

wānyán 蜿蜒 creeping; snaky

wān 豌
peas; garden peas

wāndòu 豌豆 peas; garden peas

wān 彎
to bend; to curve

wānlù 彎路 1. a tortuous path 2. a detour

wānqū 彎曲 bent; curved

wānwān qūqū 彎彎曲曲 having many bends or curves

wān 灣
1. a bay; a gulf; a cove 2. the bend of a stream 3. to anchor; to moor

wán 丸
1. a pellet; a small ball; a pill 2. an egg 3. used in Japanese indicating completion or completeness

wánzi 丸子 1. a meat ball 2. a medical pill

wán 完
1. to finish; to complete; to bring to a conclusion 2. to run out; to use up 3. whole; complete; perfect; intact

wánbèi 完備 complete with everything

wánbì 完畢 finished; completed

wánbì guī Zhào 完璧歸趙 to return something intact to its owner

wánchéng 完成 to accomplish; to complete

wándàn 完蛋 (colloquial) ruined; busted

wángōng 完工 finished or completed

wánhǎo 完好 flawless; faultless; perfect

wánhǎo wúquē 完好無缺 intact; undamaged

wánhūn 完婚 to get married

wánjié 完結 to come to an end; to end

wánjùn 完竣 finished or completed

wánle 完了 hopeless

wánliǎo 完了 finished; over

wánmǎn 完滿 (said of meetings, negotiations, etc.) satisfactory; successful

wánměi 完美 perfect

wánměi zhǔyì 完美主義 perfectionism

wánquán 完全 complete; entire

wánshàn 完善 immaculate perfect

wánzhěng 完整 complete; whole

wán 玩
1. to play (with); to toy with 2. to find pleasure in; to amuse oneself with 3. (also **wàn**) to joke; to take things lightly 4. (also **wàn**) something to amuse oneself with—as antiques, etc. 5. (also **wàn**) to learn

wánbǎxì 玩把戲 to play little tricks; to juggle

wánhuāyàng 玩花樣 to play tricks; to cheat

wánhuǒ zìfén 玩火自焚 Whoever plays with fire will get burnt.

wánjù 玩具 a toy

wánnòng 玩弄 1. to toy with 2. to juggle with 3. to fool; to play jokes on

wán'ǒu 玩偶 a doll

wánpiào 玩票 to do a payless job

wánrmìng 玩兒命 to play with one's life at stake; to do daredevil tricks

wànshì bùgōng 玩世不恭 to be a cynic, beatnik or hippie; to take everything lightly

wánshuǎ 玩耍 to play

wánwèi 玩味 to ponder

wánwù 玩物 a plaything; a toy

wánxiào 玩笑 1. a joke; a jest 2. to take something less seriously than it deserves

wányìr 玩意兒 1. a toy 2. activities for entertainment or relaxation 3. a thing 4. (slang) a louse

wán 紈

processed fine and light silk

wánkù zǐdì 紈袴子弟 a good-for-nothing young man from a wealthy family

wán 頑

1. stupid; dull; ignorant 2. obstinate; stubborn 3. recalcitrant; unruly; defiant 4. to play 5. naughty or impish

wángù 頑固 1. stubborn; obstinate; headstrong 2. ultraconservative

wánkàng 頑抗 to resist stubbornly; stubborn resistance

wánliè 頑劣 good-for-nothing; stubborn and stupid

wánpí 頑皮 naughty or impish (children)

wánqiáng 頑強 stubborn; obstinacy; tenacious

wánshí diàntóu 頑石點頭 (said of statements or teachings) so persuasive and moving that even the rocks nod in agreement

wántóng 頑童 naughty or unruly children; an urchin

wǎn 宛

1. as if; as though 2. crooked; roundabout 3. a Chinese family name

wǎnrú 宛如 as if; as though; like

wǎnyán 宛延 long and winding

wǎnzhuǎn 宛轉 (to persuade, explain, etc.) mildly and indirectly; tactfully

wǎn 浣

refer to **huàn** 浣

wǎn 挽

1. to draw (a bow, etc.); to pull 2. to restore 3. to seize 4. to roll up (sleeves, etc.)

wǎnhuí 挽回 to try with effort to turn back an adverse tide; to retrieve

wǎnjiù 挽救 to save (a situation, a failing concern, etc.)

wǎnliú 挽留 to request to stay; to urge to stay

wǎnshǒu 挽手 to hold hands; arm in arm

wǎn 婉

complaisant

wǎn 惋 also **wàn**

1. to regret 2. to be alarmed

wǎnxī 惋惜 to feel sorry for (a loss, etc.); to regret

wǎnxí 惋惜 refer to **wǎnxī** 惋惜

wǎn 婉

1. amiable; genial; agreeable; pleasant 2. good-looking; beautiful

wǎnxiè 婉謝 to decline (an invitation, a present, etc.) with great gentleness and courtesy

wǎnyán xiāngquàn 婉言相勸 to persuade gently

wǎnyuē 婉約 1. (said of speech) gentle, smooth and courteous 2. (style of poetry) restrained; soft; plaintive

wǎnzhuǎn 婉轉 (to persuade or state something) mildly; gently; suavely—without hurting another's feelings

wǎn 晚

1. sunset; evening; night 2. late 3. drawing toward the end 4. younger; junior

wǎn'ān 晚安 Good evening! Good night!

wǎnbān 晚班 the night shift

wǎnbào 晚報 an evening (or an afternoon) paper

wǎnbèi 晚輩 the younger generation; one's juniors

wǎncān 晚餐 dinner; supper

wǎnchǎng 晚場 an evening show

wǎndiǎn 晚點 (said of a train, ship, etc.) late behind schedule

wǎnfàn 晚飯 dinner; supper

wǎnhuì 晚會 an evening gathering or meeting

wǎnhūn 晚婚 late marriage

wǎnjiān 晚間 evening; night

wǎnjìn 晚近 lately; recently; modern

wǎnjǐng 晚景 1. scenes at sunset 2. circumstances in one's old age

wǎnlǐfú 晚禮服 formal evening

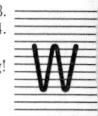

dress

wǎnnián 晚年 old age; one's later (or remaining) years

wǎnniáng 晚娘 a stepmother

wǎnniáng miànkǒng 晚娘面孔 an unsmiling face

wǎnqī 晚期 the later period

wǎnqī 晚期 refer to **wǎnqī** 晚期

wǎnqǐ 晚起 to rise or get up late

wǎnshang 晚上 in the evening or night

wǎnxiá 晚霞 sunset clouds

wǎnyàn 晚宴 a dinner party

wǎn 莞

smiling

wǎn'ěr 莞爾 smiling

wǎn 琬

1. a kind of jade tablet slightly tapering at the top 2. the virtue of a gentleman

wǎnyǎn zhīzhāng 琬琰之章 an esteemed letter

Wǎn 皖

1. name of an ancient state in what is today's Anhui Province 2. an alternative name of Anhui Province

wǎn 碗

a bowl (especially a small one)

wǎndié 碗碟 bowls and dishes

wǎnguì 碗櫃 a cupboard

wǎnkuài 碗筷 bowls and chopsticks

wǎn 輓

1. to draw or pull (a cart) 2. to mourn 3. (晚) late

wǎn'gē 輓歌 a funeral hymn; a dirge; an elegy

wǎnlián 輓聯 funeral scrolls

wàn 玩

refer to **wán** 玩 3, 4, 5

wàn 惋

refer to **wǎn** 惋

wàn 曼

refer to **màn** 曼

wàn 腕

the wrist

wànzi 腕子 the wrist

wàn 萬

1. ten thousand 2. all; omni- 3. a very great number; myriad 4. very; extremely; absolutely 5. name of an ancient dance 6. a Chinese family name

wànbù déyǐ 萬不得已 1. if the worst comes to happen 2. to have no alternative; to have to do it; very reluctantly

wànfēn 萬分 very; extremely

wàngǔ liúfāng 萬古流芳 a good name that will last forever

wànguàn jiāsī 萬貫家私 very wealthy; very rich

Wànguó Yīnbiāo 萬國音標 International Phonetic Alphabet (IPA)

wànhuātǒng 萬花筒 a kaleidoscope

wànlài jùjí 萬籟俱寂 refer to **wànlài jùjì** 萬籟俱寂

wànlài jùjì 萬籟俱寂 All sounds are hushed (in the dead of the night).

Wànlǐ Chángchéng 萬里長城 the Great Wall (of China)

wànlíngyào 萬靈藥 a panacea; a cure-all

wànmín 萬民 all the people

wànnéng 萬能 omnipotent; almighty

wànniánqīng 萬年青 a Chinese evergreen

wànniàn jùhuī 萬念俱灰 completely discouraged; extremely pessimistic

wànqiān 萬千 numerous; myriads

wànquán zhījì 萬全之計 an absolutely safe measure, plan, device, etc.

wànrén kōngxiàng 萬人空巷 Everyone (in a city) turns out (to watch a spectacle, to welcome a hero, etc.)

Wànshèngjié 萬聖節 All Saints' Day; Halloween

wànshì shībiǎo 萬世師表 (literally) a paragon for all generations—Confucius

wànshòu wújiāng 萬壽無疆 May you attain boundless longevity!

wànsuì 萬歲 (a slogan) Long live the...

wànwú yīshī 萬無一失 not the least mishap or mistake; absolutely safe or sure; certain to succeed

wànwù 萬物 all things under the sun; all God's creation

wànxiàng gēngxīn 萬象更新 a new year—as all things change from old to new

wànxìng 萬幸 extremely lucky; very fortunate indeed

wànyī 萬一 1. one ten thousandth—a very tiny fraction 2. just in case that; if by any chance 3. something not anticipated or happening accidentally

wànzhàng shēnyuān 萬丈深淵 an abyss of 100,000 feet—a bottomless abyss

wànzhòng yīxīn 萬眾一心 all for one and one for all; with one aspiration in their hearts; solidarity

wànzǐ qiānhóng 萬紫千紅 (said of flowers) a vast display of dazzling colors

wàn 翫
1. careless or casual due to familiarity 2. to play

wànwèi 翫味 appreciation

wāng 汪
1. (said of water) deep and extensive 2. a puddle 3. (said of liquid) to soak; to collect; to accumulate

wāngwāng 汪汪 1. (said of water) deep and extensive 2. the barking of dogs; a bowwow 3. brimming with tears

wāngyáng dàhǎi 汪洋大海 the vast expanse of the sea

wáng 亡
1. to perish 2. to flee 3. lost; dead 4. the late

wánggù 亡故 dead; died

wángguó 亡國 1. a subjugated nation 2. fall of a nation

wángguónú 亡國奴 conquered (or subjugated) people

wánghún 亡魂 the spirit of the dead

wángmìng 亡命 to go into exile; to escape (from justice) to a place far away from home

wángmìng zhītú 亡命之徒 criminals

wángyáng bǔláo 亡羊補牢 to take precaution after suffering a loss

wáng 王
1. a king; a ruler 2. a prince, the highest rank of nobility 3. great; of a tremendous size 4. the strongest or most powerful 5. a salutation of respect 6. an audience with the ruler or emperor 7. a Chinese family name

wángba 王八 1. a turtle; a tortoise 2. a cuckold 3. a man who works in a brothel 4. an s.o.b.

wángbadàn 王八蛋 a term of revilement similar to s.o.b.

wángcháo 王朝 a dynasty

wángchú 王儲 refer to **wángchǔ** 王儲

wángchǔ 王儲 a crown prince

wánfǎ 王法 the law

wángfēi 王妃 a prince's concubine

wánggōng 王宮 a royal palace

wángguān 王冠 a crown

wángguó 王國 a kingdom

wánghòu 王后 the queen

wángpái 王牌 a trump card

wángshì 王室 1. the royal family 2. the imperial or royal court

wángsūn gōngzǐ 王孫公子 blue-blooded young men; aristocrats

wángwèi 王位 the throne; the crown

wángye 王爺 1. a nobleman 2. Your Imperial Highness

wángzǐ 王子 a prince

wáng 忘

wángba 忘八 1. a tortoise 2. a cuckold

wǎng 罔
1. to libel; to slander; to deceive
2. not

wǎng 往
1. to go toward; to depart; to be bound for 2. formerly; past; bygone

wǎngcháng 往常 usually; heretofore; in the past

wǎngfǎn 往返 to come and go; to and fro

wǎnghòu 往後 1. backward 2. hereafter

wǎnghuán 往還 1. coming and going 2. contact between two people or parties

wǎnglái 往來 1. to go and return 2. personal contact between two parties, etc.

wǎngnián 往年 in the years past

wǎngrì 往日 in the past

wǎngshì 往事 things that have come to pass

wǎngwǎng 往往 usually; often; frequently

wǎngwǎng rúcǐ 往往如此 It happens frequently that....

wǎngxī 往昔 in the past; in ancient times

wǎngxí 往昔 refer to **wǎngxī** 往昔

wǎng 枉
1. crooked 2. to waste; useless; in vain 3. to wrong; to do or suffer wrong; aggrieved; oppression 4. (in polite language) to request another to deign or condescend to

wǎngfǎ 枉法 to abuse law

wǎngfèi 枉費 to waste; to be of no avail

wǎngfèi gōngfu 枉費工夫 to spend time and work in vain

wǎngfèi xīnjī 枉費心機 to scheme, plan or cudgel one's brains to no purpose or in vain

wǎngjià 枉駕 I'm honored by your visit.

wǎngqū 枉曲 bent; crooked; warped

wǎngrán 枉然 useless; to no purpose; in vain

wǎngsǐ 枉死 to die through injustice

wǎng 惘
dejected; frustrated; discouraged

wǎngrán 惘然 in a daze; stupefied; at a loss

wǎng 網
1. a net; a network; a web 2. (figuratively) the dragnet; the arms of law 3. to bring together; to collect

wǎngkāi yīmiàn 網開一面 to leave one side of the net open —to give a wrongdoer a way out

wǎnglù 網路 a network; the internet

wǎngluó 網羅 to bring together; to collect

wǎngluò 網絡 the internet

wǎngmó 網膜 a retina

wǎngqiú 網球 tennis

wǎngqiúchǎng 網球場 a tennis court

wǎngqiúpāi 網球拍 a racket (for playing tennis)

wǎngzi 網子 a net

wǎng 魍
a kind of monster

wǎngliǎng 魍魎 a kind of monster

wàng 王
to rule; to govern

wàng 妄
1. absurd; untrue; false 2. ignorant; stupid 3. reckless; rash 4. wild

wàngxiǎng 妄想 a daydream; to desire wildly

wàngzì fěibó 妄自菲薄 to underestimate oneself

wàngzì zūndà 妄自尊大 self-importance; conceited

wàng 忘
1. to forget 2. to omit; to miss (a line, etc.) 3. to neglect; to overlook

wàngběn 忘本 ungrateful

wàngbuliǎo 忘不了 will not or cannot forget

wàngdiào 忘掉 to forget

wàng'ēn fùyì 忘恩負義 ungrateful

wànghuái 忘懷 unmindful; to forget; forgetful

wàngjì 忘記 1. to fail to remember; to forget 2. to neglect

wàngle 忘了 to forget; to have forgotten

wàngqí suǒyǐ 忘其所以 to be beside oneself with enthusiasm, etc.

wàngqíng 忘情 to be unmindful of all emotions and the ups and downs of life; to be unmoved

wàngquè 忘卻 to forget

wàngwǒ 忘我 oblivious of self-existence

wàngxíng 忘形 to get carried away

wàngyōucǎo 忘憂草 day lily

wàng 旺
1. prosperous; to prosper; to flourish 2. vigorous; prolific; productive 3. (said of light, fires, etc.) brilliant; bright or brightly

wàngjì 旺季 (said of business) a boom season; a busy season

wàngshèng 旺盛 1. prosperous; vigorous 2. high (morale)

wàngxiāo 旺銷 to be in great demand; to sell well; to have a ready market

wàng 往
an adverb indicating time or direction

wàng hǎochu xiǎng 往好處想 to think of the better possibilities of a situation, etc.

wàngqiánkàn 往前看 to look forward

wàngxiàshuō 往下說 to talk on; Go ahead.

wàngyòuzhuǎn 往右轉 to turn right

wàng 望
1. to view; to watch; to gaze into the distance 2. to hope; to expect

3. the 15th day of each month of the lunar calendar 4. reputation; prestige 5. to call on; to visit

wàngchén mòjí 望塵莫及 to be left far behind

wàngchuān qiūshuǐ 望穿秋水 to aspire earnestly

wàngfēng pīmí 望風披靡 to flee helter-skelter at the mere sight of the oncoming force

wàngméi zhǐkě 望梅止渴 to console oneself with false hopes

wàngyǎn yùchuān 望眼欲穿 to aspire earnestly

wàngyuǎnjìng 望遠鏡 a telescope

wàngzǐ chénglóng 望子成龍 to hope one's children will have a bright future

wàngzú 望族 a family of renown

wēi 危 also **wéi**
1. danger; dangerous; precarious; perilous 2. restless 3. to fear; to be upset or afraid 4. lofty; high 5. just; honest; straightforward

wēihài 危害 to endanger; to harm; to injure

wēijī chóngchóng 危機重重 crisis-ridden

wēijí 危急 urgent; (in) a state of emergency

wēinàn 危難 (in) danger, peril, trouble, or distress

wēirú lěiluǎn 危如累卵 extremely dangerous

wēixiǎn 危險 danger; dangerous; unsafe

wēixiǎn fènzǐ 危險份子 dangerous elements

wēiyán sǒngtīng 危言聳聽 to stir up others with sensational statements

wēizài dànxī 危在旦夕 1. (said of a city under enemy attack) may fall at any moment 2. may die soon; dying

wēizǎi dànxì 危在旦夕 refer to **wēizài dànxī** 危在旦夕

wēi 委

wēiyí 委蛇 in a carefree manner

wēi 威

1. dignity; majesty 2. authority; power; might 3. awe-inspiring; awe

wēibī lìyòu 威逼利誘 to threaten and to bribe

wēifēng 威風 1. power and prestige 2. imposing; awe-inspiring

wēifēng lǐnlǐn 威風凜凜 awe-inspiring; imposing

wēilì 威力 1. the force that inspires awe 2. military force 3. the destructive force (of a typhoon, earthquake, nuclear device, etc.)

wēimíng 威名 prestige

Wēinísī 威尼斯 Venice, a city in Italy

wēishìjì 威士忌 whisky

wēiwàng 威望 prestige

wēiwǔ 威武 an awe-inspiring display of military force, etc.

wēixié 威脅 to threaten; intimidation; a threat; intimidation

wēiyán 威嚴 1. sternness; severity 2. an awe-inspiring air

wēi 倭

wēichí 倭遲 winding; circuitous; meandering

wēi 偎

1. to cuddle; to embrace 2. intimate; very dear to 3. to lean on

wēiyī 偎依 to cuddle or curl up

wēi 葳

refer to **wěi** 萎

wēi 微 also **wéi**

1. small; minute; little; slight 2. low; mean; humble 3. a polite expression for I, my, me 4. weak; sickly; feeble 5. subtle 6. obscure 7. hidden; concealed 8. to spy 9. if not; but for

wēibōlú 微波爐 a microwave oven

wēibó 微薄 low; mean; trifling; thin; little

wēibù zúdào 微不足道 insignificant

wēicí 微詞 a hint or circumlocution (to point out another's mistake, etc.)

wēidiànnǎo 微電腦 a microcomputer

wēifēng 微風 a breeze

wēifú chūyóu 微服出遊 to make a tour in disguise

wēiguān 微觀 microscopic

wēihū qíwēi 微乎其微 extremely trifling or minute; an iota

wēijīfēn 微積分 calculus

wēiliàng 微量 trace; micro

wēimiào 微妙 subtle (positions); delicate (relations); obscure and mysterious (meanings, etc.)

wēiruò 微弱 weak or feeble

wēishēngwù 微生物 microbes; microorganisms

wēiwēi 微微 small; minute; diminutive

wēixiǎo 微小 1. very small; minute 2. very low (voices, sounds, etc.)

wēixiào 微笑 to smile; a smile

wēixiěguǎn 微血管 refer to **wēixuěguǎn** 微血管

wēixuěguǎn 微血管 (anatomy) capillaries

wēixūn 微醺 slightly drunk

wēiyàng 微恙 a slight indisposition

wēiyǔ 微雨 a light rain; a drizzle

wēi 逶

winding; curved; tortuous (road, way)

wēiyí 逶迤 1. to wind; winding (river, road, etc.) 2. long; distant

wēi 薇 also **wéi**

a kind of fern; thorn-ferns

wēi 巍 also **wéi**

towering; lofty; majestic

wēirán sǒnglì 巍然聳立 to stand out majestically

wēiwēi 巍巍 towering; lofty; imposing

wéi 危

refer to **wěi** 危

wéi 韋

1. tanned leather 2. a Chinese

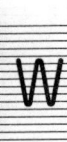

family name

wéi 桅

the mast of a ship

wéigān 桅竿 the mast of a boat

wéiqiáng 桅檣 a mast

wéi 惟

1. to think; to meditate 2. only; alone 3. but; however

wéidú 惟獨 only; alone

wéikǒng 惟恐 for fear that; lest; afraid of nothing but

wéilì shìtú 惟利是圖 interested only in material gain

wéimiào wéixiào 惟妙惟肖 so skillfully imitated as to be indistinguishable from the original

wéimìng shìcóng 惟命是從 always do as one is told; to be slavishly obedient

wéiwǒ dúzūn 惟我獨尊 egoistic; arrogant

wéiyī 惟一 the only one

wéi 唯

only

wéidú 唯獨 only or alone; an exception

wéidú jìyìtǐ 唯讀記憶體 (computer) read-only memory; ROM

wéikǒng 唯恐 for fear that; for fear of

wéilì shìtú 唯利是圖 to be bent solely on profit

wéiměi zhǔyì 唯美主義 aestheticism

wéimìng shìcóng 唯命是從 obsequious; to do whatever is told

wéiyī 唯一 the only one, the only kind, etc.

wéiyǒu 唯有 only

wéi 帷

a curtain; a screen; a tent

wéimàn 帷幔 screens; cloth partitions

wéimù 帷幕 1. a tent 2. a military tent

wéiwò 帷幄 a military tent

wéi 爲

1. to do; to act 2. to manage; to

handle; to exercise; to administer; to govern 3. to serve as 4. to become 5. to be

wéifēi zuòdǎi 爲非作歹 to do evil

wéifù bùrén 爲富不仁 wealthy but unkind

wéihài 爲害 to bring trouble

wéihuàn 爲患 to bring trouble

wéinán 爲難 1. troubled; in difficulties or a dilemma 2. to make things difficult (for another)

wéipíng 爲憑 to use as proof; to use as evidence

wéiqī bùyuǎn 爲期不遠 in the near future; soon

wéiqí bùyuǎn 爲期不遠 refer to **wéiqī bùyuǎn** 爲期不遠

wéirén 爲人 one's personality, character or temperament

wéirén shībiǎo 爲人師表 to be a model of virtue for others

wéishēng 爲生 to make a living

wéishí guòzǎo 爲時過早 premature; too early

wéishǒu 爲首 1. to be the head or leader 2. headed by; led by

wéisuǒ yùwéi 爲所欲爲 to do as one pleases

wéiwǔ 爲伍 to associate or mix (with)

wéixué 爲學 to engage in studies

wéiyè 爲業 as a means of livelihood

wéizhèng 爲證 to serve as proof; to serve as evidence

wéizhǐ 爲止 1. until; till; up to 2. no further

wéizhǔ 爲主 mainly; to be the most important

wéi 圍

1. to surround; to enclose; to encircle; to hem in 2. surroundings; environment 3. the circumference of a circle formed by a person's arms

wéibór 圍脖兒 a scarf; a muffler

wéibǔ 圍捕 to arrest (a criminal) by closing in on him from all sides

wéigōng 圍攻 to besiege; to beleaguer

W

wéijiǎo 圍剿 to attack (bandits or rebels) from all sides

wéijīn 圍巾 a scarf; a muffler

wéikùn 圍困 to besiege; to beleaguer

wéilú 圍爐 to sit and chat around the fireplace

wéiqí 圍棋 the encirclement chess

wéiqiáng 圍牆 an enclosing wall; a fence

wéiqún 圍裙 an apron

wéirào 圍繞 to surround; to encircle

wéirào 圍繞 refer to **wéirào** 圍繞

wéi 微
refer to **wēi** 微

wéi 違
1. to go against; to defy; to disobey; to disregard 2. to be separated 3. to avoid 4. evil; fault

wéibèi 違背 to defy; to disobey; to disregard; to be contrary to

wéifǎ 違法 to be against the law; to be unlawful; to violate the law; to be illegal

wéifǎn 違反 to contradict; to disregard (the rules, etc.)

wéiguī 違規 to be against regulations

wéijìn 違禁 to defy a prohibition

wéijǐng 違警 to break a police regulation

wéikàng 違抗 to defy and oppose; to disobey

wéixiàn 違憲 unconstitutional; violation of the constitution

wéixīn zhīlùn 違心之論 insincere utterances, comments, etc.

wéiyuē 違約 a breach of contract; to break a contract or agreement

wéiyuējīn 違約金 a forfeit or penalty

wéizhāng jiànzhú 違章建築 refer to **wéizhāng jiànzhú** 違章建築

wéizhāng jiànzhú 違章建築 buildings erected without a license or against the provisions of the building code; illegal con-

struction

wéi 維
1. to tie; to hold fast; to secure 2. to maintain; to safeguard 3. to unite; to hold together 4. long and slender—as fibers 5. an initial particle—only, but, etc. 6. a pattern or rule

wéichí 維持 to maintain; to keep; to guard and support; to sustain; to preserve

wéichí zhì'ān 維持治安 to maintain public order

wéichí zhìxù 維持秩序 to keep order

wéihù 維護 to safeguard; to preserve; to uphold

wéimiào wéixiào 維妙維肖 so skillfully imitated as to be indistinguishable from the original; remarkably true to life

Wéinàsī 維納斯 Venus

wéishēngsù 維生素 vitamins

wéitāmìng 維他命 vitamins

wéixì 維繫 to maintain; to keep

wéixiū 維修 to keep in (good) repair; to service; to maintain

Wéiyěnà 維也納 Vienna

wéi 薇
refer to **wēi** 薇

wéi 闈
1. the side doors of a palace 2. the living quarters of the queen and the imperial concubines 3. ladies' living quarters; private quarters 4. (formerly) a hall where the civil service examination took place

wéi 巍
refer to **wēi** 巍

wěi 尾
1. the tail; the rear; the stern (of a ship); rear; back 2. last; final 3. remaining 4. a Chinese family name

wěiba 尾巴 a tail

wěidà bùdiào 尾大不掉 to have subordinates too powerful to control

wěishēng 尾聲 1. a coda 2. an epilog 3. an end

wěishù 尾數 1. an odd sum; odd change 2. the balance of an account

wěisuí 尾隨 to follow close behind; to tail

wěizhuī 尾追 to chase after

wěi 委

1. to depute; to deputize 2. to send; to put in charge of; to commission 3. to give up; to abandon 4. to be frustrated, weakened or tired 5. really; truly; indeed 6. a grievance; a wrong 7. to stoop or lower oneself (in order to avoid an open conflict, etc.)

wěimǐ bùzhèn 委靡不振 dispirited and lethargic; in low spirits

Wěinèiruìlā 委內瑞拉 Venezuela

wěipài 委派 to appoint; to commission

wěiqū qiúquán 委曲求全 to make great concessions for the purpose of accommodating to a situation

wěiqu 委屈 1. a grievance; complaints 2. to be frustrated or wronged 3. to take an office, etc. far below one's ability 4. to put someone to inconvenience

wěirèn 委任 to appoint; to commission

wěishēn 委身 1. to become the wife of... 2. to consign oneself to someone or something

wěishí 委實 really; indeed

wěisuǒ 委瑣 1. petty; trifling 2. of a wretched appearance 3. being a stickler for forms

wěituō 委託 to commission; to entrust

wěiwǎn 委婉 tactful; unobtrusively

wěiyǐ zhòngrèn 委以重任 to entrust someone with an important task

wěiyuán 委員 a member of a committee

wěiyuánhuì 委員會 a committee; a council

wěizuì 委罪 to impute

wěi 娓

1. complying; subservient 2. attractive; beautiful

wěiwěi 娓娓 (to talk) tirelessly

wěiwěi dòngtīng 娓娓動聽 persuasive (accounts, narration, etc.)

wěi 萎 also **wèi**

1. to wither 2. ill; sick 3. to fall; to decline; to weaken

wěimǐ bùzhèn 萎靡不振 unable to pick oneself up; despondent; lethargic

wěisuō 萎縮 1. to dry up and shrink; to shrink back 2. to atrophy

wěixiè 萎謝 (said of flowers) to wither; to fade

wěi 偉

extraordinary; great; big

wěidà 偉大 great; extraordinary

wěirén 偉人 a great man

wěiyè 偉業 monumental accomplishments

wěi 唯

yes or no; the words one answers

wěiwěi nuònuò 唯唯諾諾 to say yes to a superior's suggestion; to be a yes man

wěi 猥

1. vulgar; wanton; low; lewd and licentious 2. varied; numerous; many; multitudinous 3. the bark of a dog

wěixiè 猥褻 obscene; obscenity; lewd

wěi 瑋

1. a kind of jade 2. rare; precious; splendorous

wěi 偽 also **wèi**

1. false; counterfeit 2. simulated; artificial 3. illegal; not legally constituted

wěibì 偽幣 1. counterfeit money 2. money issued by a puppet government

wěichāo 偽鈔 a counterfeit bank note

wěijūnzǐ 偽君子 a hypocrite

wěishàn 偽善 hypocrisy; hypo-

W

critical

wěizào 偽造 to forge; to falsify

wěizào wénshū 偽造文書 a forgery; counterfeit documents

wěizhèng 偽證 perjury

wěizhuāng 偽裝 disguise; camouflage

wěi 緯

1. the woof 2. parallels showing latitude on a map

wěidù 緯度 degrees of latitude (in geography)

wěi 鮪

a tuna

wěidiāo 鮪釣 a tuna liner

wèi 未

1. not yet 2. not 3. the eighth of the Twelve Terrestrial Branches 4. 1:00–3:00 p.m.

wèibì 未必 not always; not necessarily

wèibì jìnrán 未必盡然 not always so

wèibǔ xiānzhī 未卜先知 to foresee accurately

wèicéng 未曾 never before

wèicháng 未嘗 1. not necessarily 2. never

wèicháng bùkě 未嘗不可 It is not necessarily impermissible or impossible.

wèichéngnián 未成年 not yet come of age; minor

wèidìng 未定 uncertain; unfixed; undefined

wèigǎn gǒutóng 未敢苟同 (literary language) can not agree

wèihūn 未婚 unmarried; single

wèihūnfū 未婚夫 one's fiancé

wèihūnqī 未婚妻 one's fiancée

wèijí 未及 not enough time left to do it

wèijīng 未經 to have not yet (gone through)

wèijìng zhīzhì 未竟之志 an unfulfilled ambition

wèijué 未決 undecided; uncertain; unsettled

wèikāifā 未開發 (said of land, resources, etc.) undeveloped

wèilái 未來 future; in the future

wèilǎo xiānshuāi 未老先衰 to become senile before one's time

wèiliǎo 未了 unsettled; unfixed; unfinished

wèimiǎn 未免 1. It must be admitted that.... 2. necessarily; unavoidably

wèinéng 未能 to fail to; cannot

wèinéng miǎnsú 未能免俗 incapable of being exempted from usual custom

wèisuì 未遂 attempted without success

wèiwán 未完 unfinished; not completed

wèiwángrén 未亡人 a widow

wèiyǔ chóumóu 未雨綢繆 to take precautions before it is too late

wèizhīshù 未知數 1. (mathematics) an unknown number 2. unknown; uncertain

wèi 位

1. position; rank 2. location

wèijū jīnyào 位居津要 to occupy a key position

wèiyú 位於 situated at; located at

wèiyuán 位元 (computers) a bit

wèiyuánzǔ 位元組 (computer) a byte

wèizhi 位置 1. position (in space); location 2. position (in an organization)

wèizi 位子 a seat

wèi 味

1. a taste; a flavor 2. a smell; an odor 3. a delicacy; a dainty

wèidao 味道 1. a taste; a flavor 2. a smell 3. a feeling

wèijīng 味精 monosodium glutamate

wèijué 味覺 the sense of taste; gustation

wèi 畏

1. to stand in awe of; to fear; to dread; to be afraid of 2. to revere; to respect

wèibì 畏避 to evade because of

fear

wèijù 畏懼 to dread; to be scared of; to fear

wèiqiè 畏怯 to fear; to be scared of

wèishǒu wèiwěi 畏首畏尾 to harbor fear fore and aft

wèisuō 畏縮 to shrink; to recoil; to cringe; to flinch

wèitú 畏途 a dangerous path

wèizuì 畏罪 to be afraid of punishment

wèizuì zìshā 畏罪自殺 to kill oneself from fear of punishment

wèi 胃

the stomach; the gizzard (of birds and fowls)

wèi'ái 胃癌 a gastric carcinoma

wèibìng 胃病 a stomach ailment

wèicháng 胃腸 the stomach and intestines

wèijìng 胃鏡 a gastroscope

wèikǒu 胃口 appetite

wèikuìyáng 胃潰瘍 a gastric ulcer

wèitòng 胃痛 a stomach pain or ache

wèiyán 胃炎 gastritis

wèiyè 胃液 gastric juice

wèi 尉

1. a company-grade military officer 2. (in former times) a grade of military official

wèiguān 尉官 a junior officer

wèi 為

for; for the good of; for the sake of

wèicǐ 為此 because of this; for this reason

wèiguó juānqū 為國捐軀 to sacrifice one's life for the fatherland

wèiguó zhēngguāng 為國爭光 to struggle for the glory of one's country

wèihé 為何 why; for what reason

wèihǔ zuòchāng 為虎作倀 to help an evil person do evil

wèimín chúhài 為民除害 to remove the evils from the people

wèi...qǐjiàn 為……起見 in order to...; for the purpose of...

wèirén shuōxiàng 為人說項 to say a good word for someone

wèirén zuòjià 為人作嫁 to work for others without profiting oneself

wèishénme 為什麼 What for? Why?

wèi 喂

hallo; hello; please; if you please; I say

wèi 偽

refer to **wěi** 偽

wèi 衛

1. to guard; to protect; to defend 2. a keeper; a bodyguard; a guard

wèibīng 衛兵 (military) a guard; a sentry

wèimiǎn 衛冕 to defend a title

wèishēng 衛生 sanitation; sanitary; public health

wèishēngjiān 衛生間 a toilet

wèishēngmián 衛生棉 a sanitary napkin

wèishēng shèbèi 衛生設備 sanitary facilities

wèishēngsuǒ 衛生所 a public health clinic

wèishēngyī 衛生衣 a kind of tight cotton underwear

wèishēngzhǐ 衛生紙 tissue paper; toilet paper

wèixīng 衛星 satellites

wèi 蔚

(said of vegetation) luxuriant; ornamental and colorful

wèilán 蔚藍 sky-blue

wèiwéi qíguān 蔚為奇觀 to present a magnificent sight; to offer a thrilling view

wèi 慰

to console; to comfort; to soothe; to assuage; to relieve

wèijiè 慰藉 to console

wèiláo 慰勞 to entertain and cheer (sometimes by means of material gifts)

wèilào 慰勞 refer to **wèiláo** 慰勞

wèiliú 慰留 to try to retain (a person intending to resign) in office

wèiwèn 慰問 to show sympathy by making inquiries

wèiwènjīn 慰問金 money sent to express one's gratitude or sympathy

wèi 謂
1. to tell; to say 2. to name; to call; to designate 3. to think; to be of the opinion; to assume 4. meaning; sense

wèi 遺
1. to send or present as a gift 2. to be left to; to be laid upon

wèi 餵
to feed; to raise

wèinǎi 餵奶 to feed a baby with milk; to breast-feed

wèiyǎng 餵養 to raise; to rear; to keep

wèi 魏
1. lofty; stately; magnificent 2. a Chinese family name

wēn 溫
1. warm; lukewarm; to warm 2. to review; to revise 3. temperature 4. a Chinese family name

wēnbǎo 溫飽 adequately fed and clothed

wēnchā 溫差 difference in temperature

wēnchuáng 溫床 a hotbed

wēncún 溫存 tender; loving; caressing

wēndài 溫帶 the Temperate Zone

wēndài qìhòu 溫帶氣候 temperate climate

wēndù 溫度 temperature

wēndùjì 溫度計 a thermometer

wēngù zhīxīn 溫故知新 to learn new things by reviewing old things

wēnhé 溫和 gentle; mild; temperate

wēnhuo 溫和 warm

wēnjiǔ 溫酒 to heat wine; lukewarm wine

wēnkāishuǐ 溫開水 lukewarm boiled water

wēnnuǎn 溫暖 warm; warmth

wēnqíng 溫情 kindness; warmheartedness

wēnquán 溫泉 a hot spring; a spa

wēnróu 溫柔 warm and tender; sweet-natured

wēnróuxiāng 溫柔鄉 (literally) land of the tender—1. a brothel 2. the enthralling experience of enjoying female charms in an intimate manner

wēnrùn 溫潤 1. mild and smooth 2. beautiful and tender

wēnshì 溫室 a greenhouse

wēnshùn 溫順 gentle; good-natured; docile; obedient

wēnwén ěryǎ 溫文爾雅 gentle and graceful

wēnxí 溫習 to review (what has been learned)

wēnxīn 溫馨 warm and fragrant

wēnxǔ 溫煦 refer to **wēnxù** 溫煦

wēnxù 溫煦 gentle; mild; temperate; warm

wēnxún 溫馴 meek; docile; tame

wēn 瘟
an epidemic; a plague; a pestilence

wēnyì 瘟疫 an epidemic; a plague; a pestilence

wén 文
1. a composition; an article 2. language 3. literature; education; culture 4. elegant; civil; polite; polished; mild; suave; cultured; urbane 5. civilian or civil (as opposed to military) 6. a former monetary unit 7. (also **wèn**) to cover up; to conceal; to gloss over

wénbǐ 文筆 the pen; literary talent

wénbù duìtí 文不對題 The content of the writing is inconsistent with the title.

wéncǎi 文采 1. elegant appearances 2. beautiful or gorgeous color

wéncí 文辭 diction; phraseology;

W

language

wéndàn 文旦 a shaddock; a pomelo

wéndìng 文定 to become betrothed

wénfǎ 文法 grammar

wénfēng 文風 1. literary style 2. popular interest in learning

wénfēng búdòng 文風不動 1. no change from origin 2. calm; quiet

wéngǎo 文稿 a manuscript

wéngào 文告 a public notice; a manifesto

wénguān 文官 a civil servant

wénguò shìfēi 文過飾非 to cover up one's fault by clever use of words in writing

wénháo 文豪 a literary lion; a great writer

wénhuà 文化 culture; civilization

wénhuà jiāoliú 文化交流 cultural exchange

wénhuà shìyè 文化事業 cultural enterprises

wénhuà shuǐzhǔn 文化水準 the cultural standing or level

wénjiàn 文件 documents; legal papers

wénjù 文具 writing tools; stationery

wénkē 文科 the liberal arts

wénmáng 文盲 an illiterate

wénmíng 文明 civilized; civilization

wénpíng 文憑 a diploma

wénqíng bìngmào 文情並茂 Both the language and the content are excellent.

wénrén 文人 1. a man of letters 2. a man with a civilian background

wénruò shūshēng 文弱書生 an effeminate scholar

wénshū 文書 1. documents; records 2. an archivist

wénshū chǔlǐ 文書處理 (computer) text processing

wéntán 文壇 the literary circles, world, or arena

wéntǐ 文體 literary style

wénwǔ bǎiguān 文武百官 all the civil and military officials

wénwǔ quáncái 文武全才 a master of both the pen and the sword

wénwù 文物 cultural artifacts

wénxiàn 文獻 records; documents

wénxuǎn 文選 a selection of literary works; an anthology

wénxué 文學 literature

wénxuéjiā 文學家 a literary man; a litterateur

wénxuéjiè 文學界 the literary world, circles, or arena

wénxuéyuàn 文學院 a college of liberal arts

wénxué zuòpǐn 文學作品 literary works

wényǎ 文雅 graceful; refined; polished

wényì 文義 the meaning of a written article

wényì 文藝 literature (as one of the fine arts); belles-lettres

Wényì Fùxīng 文藝復興 the Renaissance

wényìjiè 文藝界 the literary circles

wénzhāi 文摘 an abstract; a digest

wénzhāng 文章 an article; a composition

wénzhí 文職 a civil post

wénzhí bīnbīn 文質彬彬 refer to **wénzhì bīnbīn** 文質彬彬

wénzhì bīnbīn 文質彬彬 elegant and refined in manner

wénzhōuzhōu 文縐縐 pedantic

wénzì 文字 1. a letter; a character; written language 2. writing

wénzì chǔlǐ 文字處理 (computer) text processing

wén 紋

1. stripes; lines; streaks; veins 2. ripples (of water) 3. (finger) prints 4. wrinkles (on the face) 5. to tattoo

wénlǐ 紋理 lines; stripes; veins; grain

wénshēn 紋身 tattoo; to tattoo the body

wén 蚊
a mosquito; a gnat

wénxiāng 蚊香 a mosquito coil; mosquito incense

wénzhàng 蚊帳 a mosquito net

wén 雯
the coloring on the clouds

wén 聞
1. to hear; to have heard 2. to learn; learning; to understand 3. to convey, forward or transmit (a message, etc.) 4. to smell 5. to make known 6. a Chinese family name 7. (also **wèn**) reputation

wéndá 聞達 eminent; famous and influential

wénfēng érqǐ 聞風而起 to rise up on hearing the news

wénfēng sàngdǎn 聞風喪膽 to become terror-stricken at the news

wénfēng xiǎngyìng 聞風響應 to hear the news and rise up in response

wénmíng 聞名 1. famous; distinguished 2. to hear of someone's name

wénmíng tiānxià 聞名天下 world-famous; known far and wide

wénxùn 聞訊 to hear of the message

wěn 刎
to cut the throat

wěnjǐng zhījiāo 刎頸之交 profound mutual devotion between friends

wěn 吻
1. the lip 2. the tone of one's speech 3. to kiss; a kiss

wěnbié 吻別 to kiss someone good-bye

wěnhé 吻合 (said of two things) to agree, correspond, match, or tally with

wěn 紊 also **wèn**
confused; tangled; involved; disorderly

wěnluàn 紊亂 confused; tangled; chaotic

wěn 穩
1. stable; stability; steady; firm 2. sure; certain 3. secure; security

wěndang 穩當 proper and secure

wěndìng 穩定 1. to stabilize 2. stable; steady

wěngù 穩固 stable and firm; secure

wěnjiàn 穩健 firm and steady

wěnzhā wěndǎ 穩紮穩打 to proceed steadily and step by step

wěnzhòng 穩重 steady, calm, and dignified

wèn 文
refer to **wén** 文 7

wèn 紊
refer to **wěn** 紊

wèn 問
1. to ask; to inquire 2. to interrogate; to examine 3. to ask after; to inquire after 4. to hold responsible

wèn'ān 問安 (usually to elders) to wish somebody good health

wèn'àn 問案 to try (or hear) a case

wèndá 問答 questions and answers; a dialogue

wèngòng 問供 to interrogate a criminal suspect

wènguà 問卦 to consult oracles

wènhǎo 問好 to ask about a person's health or welfare

wènhào 問號 an interrogation mark

wènhòu 問候 to ask about a person's health or welfare

wènhuà 問話 to ask questions

wènjuàn 問卷 a questionnaire

wènshì 問世 (said of a new book) to come out

wèntí 問題 a problem; a question; an issue

wèntí értóng 問題兒童 a problem child

wèntí shàonián 問題少年 a juvenile delinquent

wènxīn wúkuì 問心無愧 to examine oneself and find nothing to be ashamed of

wènxùn 問訊 1. to inquire after a person 2. to ask; to inquire

wènzhǎn 問斬 to execute a prisoner by beheading him

wènzuì 問罪 to reprimand; to rebuke; to condemn

wèn 聞

refer to **wén** 聞 7

wēng 翁

1. the father 2. the father-in-law 3. an old man 4. a title of respect 5. a Chinese family name

wēnggū 翁姑 woman's parents-in-law

wēng ‖翁

the hum or buzz of insects

wěng 蓊

(said of vegetation) luxuriant; flourishing; lush

wěngyù 蓊鬱 the lush or luxuriant growth of vegetation

wèng 甕

a jar; a jug; a pot

wèngzhōng zhībiē 甕中之鱉 something that can be caught easily

Wō 倭

name of a human race; an old name for Japan

Wōkòu 倭寇 (ancient usage) the dwarf pirates; the Japs

wō 喔 also wò

the crowing of a cock; the cackling of fowls

wō 渦

a whirlpool; an eddy

wōlúnjī 渦輪機 a turbine

wō 窩

1. a cave; a den; a nest 2. an apartment; living quarters; a house 3. to hide; to harbor (a criminal, etc.) 4. to bend; to crease 5. a hollow part of the human body; a pit

wōcáng 窩藏 to harbor (outlaws); to keep (stolen goods)

wōnang 窩囊 1. stupid, cowardly and timid; good-for-nothing 2. to feel vexed

wōrlǐfǎn 窩兒裏反 an intramural fight

wō 蝸 also guā

a snail

wōniú 蝸牛 a snail

wǒ 我 also ě

1. I; me; my 2. we; our; us 3. self

wǒfāng 我方 our side; we

wǒguó 我國 our country

wǒjiā 我家 my home; my house

wǒmen 我們 we; us

wǒxíng wǒsù 我行我素 to act according to one's will regardless of others' opinions

wò 沃

1. to irrigate 2. (said of land) fertile

wòrǎng 沃壤 fertile soil

wòtǔ 沃土 fertile land

wòyě qiānlǐ 沃野千里 an endless expanse of fertile land

wò 臥

1. to lie down; to rest; to sleep 2. to lay or place across; to lie across

wòbìng 臥病 bedridden on account of illness

wòdǎo 臥倒 to lie down (on the ground to escape enemy fire or detection)

wòdǐ 臥底 (said of thieves, etc.) to act as a stool pigeon

wòfáng 臥房 a bedroom

wòpù 臥鋪 a sleeping berth on a train or ship

wò 握

1. to hold fast; to grasp 2. a handful

wòbié 握別 to part; to shake hands at parting

wòjǐn 握緊 to hold fast; to grasp firmly

wòlì 握力 a grip

wòquán 握拳 to clench one's fist

wòshǒu 握手 to shake hands

wòshǒu yánhuān 握手言歡 to hold hands and converse cheerfully

wò 渥
1. to dye 2. great (kindness)

wòzé 渥澤 profound benefaction

wò 喔
refer to **wō** 喔

wò 斡
to revolve; to turn; to rotate

wòxuán 斡旋 to mediate; mediation

wò 齷
wòchuò 齷齪 1. narrow; small 2. dirty

wū 污
1. dirty; filthy 2. to stain; to mar 3. corrupt

wūdiǎn 污點 a blot; a stain; a smear; a defect; a flaw

wūgòu 污垢 dirt; filth

wūhuì 污穢 dirty; filthy

wūhuì bùkān 污穢不堪 intolerably dirty or filthy

wūlì 污吏 a corrupt official

wūmiè 污衊 to libel; to slander

wūní 污泥 mud

wūrǎn 污染 to contaminate; to pollute

wūrǔ 污辱 1. to humiliate 2. to rape

wūshuǐ 污水 sewage; filthy water

wūsǔn 污損 to stain and damage

wūzhuó 污濁 muddy; dirty; foul; filthy

wū 巫 also **wú**
1. a witch; a wizard 2. a Chinese family name

wūpó 巫婆 a witch

Wūshān yúnyǔ 巫山雲雨 a rendezvous between two lovers —coitus

wūshī 巫師 a sorcerer; a wizard

wūshù 巫術 black magic; witchery; sorcery

wūyī 巫醫 a witch doctor

wū 屋
a house; a room; a shelter

wūdǐng 屋頂 a roof

wūjǐ 屋脊 the ridge of a roof

wūyán 屋簷 the eaves

wūzhǔ 屋主 the owner of a house

wū 烏
1. a crow, raven or rook 2. dark color 3. how; what; when 4. Alas! 5. (now rarely) the sun 6. a Chinese family name

wūgǔjī 烏骨雞 dark-skinned and dark-boned chicken

wūguī 烏龜 1. a turtle; a tortoise 2. a cuckold

wūhé zhīzhòng 烏合之眾 a mob; a rabble

wūhēi 烏黑 pitch-dark (night); raven black (hair)

wūliūliū 烏溜溜 (said of eyes) dark and liquid

wūlóngchá 烏龍茶 oolong tea

wūméi 烏梅 dried plums

wūmù 烏木 ebony

wūtuōbāng 烏托邦 1. utopia —an ideal place or state 2. Utopia

wūyā 烏鴉 a crow; a raven

wūyān zhàngqì 烏煙瘴氣 (said of air) heavily polluted; now also used figuratively to indicate corruption, confusion, etc.

wūyǒu 烏有 nothingness

wūyú 烏魚 black mullet

wūyúzǐ 烏魚子 mullet's roe

wūyún 烏雲 1. dark clouds 2. (figuratively) a woman's black hair

wūyún mìbù 烏雲密佈 as dark clouds mass up—A heavy downpour is in the making or the situation is getting dangerous or imminent.

wūzéi 烏賊 the cuttlefish; the inkfish

wū 嗚
1. to weep; to sob 2. to toot; to hoot; to zoom 3. Alas!

wūhū āizāi 嗚呼哀哉 (usually

used in lamenting someone's death) What a tragedy!

wūyè 嗚咽 sobs; to sob; to weep

wū 鎢 also **wù**

wolfram; tungsten

wūsī 鎢絲 a tungsten filament

wū 誣 also **wú**

to accuse falsely

wūgào 誣告 to bring a false charge against

wūlài 誣賴 to incriminate falsely

wú 毋

(imperative) do not; no

wúníng 毋寧 refer to **wúnìng** 毋寧

wúnìng 毋寧 rather... (than); (not so much...) as

wúxū 毋需 do not need

wúyòng 毋庸 need not

wúyòng huìyán 毋庸諱言 There's no need for reticence.

wú 无

the ancient form of **wú** 無—not; no; negative; without

wúwàng zhīzāi 无妄之災 an unexpected trouble or bad break

Wú 吳

1. name of a state in the Epoch of the Three Kingdoms 2. name of a state in the Warring States period 3. a Chinese family name

wúguōyú 吳郭魚 a mouth-breeder

wú 巫

refer to **wū** 巫

wú 吾

1. I, me, we, or us (in literary usage) 2. my; our

wú'ài 吾愛 my love; my darling

wúbèi 吾輩 we; us

wúchái 吾儕 we; us

wúrén 吾人 we

wú 梧

1. a firmiana 2. a support; a prop 3. to support; to prop up

wúshǔ jìqióng 梧鼠技窮 at one's wits' end

wútóng 梧桐 a firmiana

wú 無

1. negative; not; no; none 2. without; destitute of; wanting: to lack; to have not 3. no matter what (or how); not yet

wú'ài 無礙 1. no harm; all right 2. (Buddhism) apratihata

wúbǐ 無比 incomparable; peerless

wúbìng shēnyín 無病呻吟 1. to groan for no reason 2. (said of writing) affected sentimentality

wúbù 無不 all without exception

wúchǎn jiējí 無產階級 the proletariat

wúchǐ 無恥 shameless; brazen; impudent

wúchū qíyòu 無出其右 Nobody can better him.; second to none

wúdí 無敵 matchless; invincible

wúdì fàngshǐ 無的放矢 (literally) to shoot without a target —indiscriminate; to attack without a cause

wúdì zìróng 無地自容 extremely embarrassed or ashamed

wúdòng yúzhōng 無動於衷 1. unmoved; flinty-hearted 2. to remain firm

wúdú yǒu'ǒu 無獨有偶 It happens that there is a similar case.

wúduān 無端 without cause or reason

wú'è bùzuò 無惡不作 to stop at nothing in doing evil

wúfǎ 無法 unable; incapable

wúfǎ wútiān 無法無天 lawless and godless

wúfáng 無妨 1. doesn't matter 2. there's no harm

wúfáng 無妨 refer to **wúfāng** 無妨

wúfēi 無非 no other than; nothing but

wúfēn xuānzhì 無分軒輊 well-matched; a draw

wúfēng bù qǐlàng 無風不起浪 There must be a cause or reason for this.

wúgū 無辜 innocent; guiltless

wúgù 無故 uncalled-for; without cause or reason

wúguān 無關 irrelevant; to have nothing to do with

wúguān jǐnyào 無關緊要 not important; of no consequence or significance

wúhòu 無後 heirless; without posterity

wúhuà bùtán 無話不談 to keep no secrets from each other

wújí zhītán 無稽之談 groundless utterances; wild talks; rumors

wújí érzhōng 無疾而終 to die without any apparent ailment or disease

wújì 無際 (said of space) boundless

wújì kěshī 無計可施 helpless; at one's wit's end

wújì yúshì 無濟於事 won't help the matter; to no avail

wújiā kěguī 無家可歸 homeless

wújià zhībǎo 無價之寶 a priceless treasure

wújiān bùcuī 無堅不摧 to overrun all fortifications

wújīng dǎcǎi 無精打采 listless; dejected; despondent; low-spirited

wújū wúshù 無拘無束 freely; unconstrained; carefree

wúkě hòufēi 無可厚非 shouldn't be blamed too much for that—no serious mistakes committed

wúkě jiùyào 無可救藥 incorrigible; incurable

wúkě nàihé 無可奈何 having no alternative; to have to

wúkǒng bùrù 無孔不入 to let no opportunity slip by (in the pursuit of one's selfish ends)

wúlài 無賴 a villain; a rascal

wúlǐ 無理 unreasonable

wúlǐ qǔnào 無理取鬧 to make trouble without a cause

wúlì 無力 1. feeble; weak 2. cannot afford

wúlì kětú 無利可圖 profitless

wú lìzhuī zhīdì 無立錐之地 very poor; stark poverty

wúliáo 無聊 1. ennui; boredom 2. nonsensical; silly

wúlù kězǒu 無路可走 at the end of one's rope; no way out

wúlùn 無論 1. no matter; whatever 2. let alone; to say nothing of

wúlùn rúhé 無論如何 anyway; in any case

wúmínghuǒ 無名火 fury; wrath; anger

wúmíng xiǎozú 無名小卒 a nobody; an unimportant person

wúmíngzhǐ 無名指 the ring finger

wúnài 無奈 can't help it

wúnéng 無能 incompetent; incapable

wúnéng wéilì 無能為力 unable to help; can't do anything about it; powerless

wúqī túxíng 無期徒刑 life imprisonment

wúqí bùyǒu 無奇不有 Nothing is too strange (in the world, this school, etc.).

wúqí túxíng 無期徒刑 refer to **wúqī túxíng**

wúqiān wúguà 無牽無掛 to have no cares

wúqíng 無情 callous; heartless; ruthless

wúqióng 無窮 endless; boundless; limitless

wúshāng dàyǎ 無傷大雅 It doesn't matter.

wúshàng guāngróng 無上光榮 the highest honor

wúshēng 無聲 noiseless; silent

wúshēng diànhuà 無繩電話 a radiophone

wúshī zìtōng 無師自通 to acquire a skill without being taught

wúshì 無視 to pay no attention to

wúshù 無數 1. countless; numerous 2. an uncertain number of

wúshuāng 無雙 peerless; matchless; unique; unrivaled

wúsī 無私 selfless; unselfish

wúsuǒ bùnéng 無所不能 omnipotent

wúsuǒ bùwéi 無所不為 ready to do anything, however bad it may be

wúsuǒ bùzài 無所不在 omnipresent; ubiquitous

wúsuǒ bùzhī 無所不知 to know everything; omniscient

wúsuǒ shìcóng 無所適從 don't know where to turn to; indecisive

wúsuǒ shìshì 無所事事 to do nothing; to idle away one's time

wúsuǒwèi 無所謂 do not care

wúwǎng bùlì 無往不利 successful in whatever one does

wúwàng 無望 1. hopeless; to despair of 2. do not expect that...

wúwàng zhīzāi 無妄之災 unexpected misfortunes

wúwēi bùzhì 無微不至 very thoughtful; to considerate in every way

wúwéi bùzhì 無微不至 refer to **wúwēi bùzhì** 無微不至

wúwèi 無味 1. tasteless; dull (offers, etc.) 2. unpalatable

wúwù 無誤 correct; right

wúxì kěchéng 無隙可乘 to have no loophole to exploit

wúxiá 無瑕 without blemish, defect or fault—perfect

wúxiàn 無限 limitless; boundless; infinite

wúxiàndiàn 無線電 radio; wireless

wúxiàn diànhuà 無線電話 a radiophone

wúxiào 無效 1. ineffective; useless; to no avail 2. invalid; null and void

wúxiè kějī 無懈可擊 flawless; invulnerable

wúxiè kějī 無懈可擊 refer to **wúxiè kějī** 無懈可擊

wúxīn 無心 1. unintentional 2. in no mood

wúxíng 無形 invisible

wúxíngzhōng 無形中 insidiously; unknowingly

wúxū 無須 unnecessary; no need to

wúyàng 無恙 to feel well; all right

wúyè yóumín 無業遊民 a vagrant

wúyī bùjīng 無一不精 to be an expert in everything

wúyī wúkào 無依無靠 with no one to turn to or rely on

wúyì 無益 useless; without benefit

wúyì 無異 not different from; tantamount to

wúyì 無意 to have no interest in; to have no intention (of doing something)

wúyìshí 無意識 1. (psychology) unconsciousness 2. unintentional

wúyìshí 無意識 refer to **wúyìshí** 無意識

wúyìzhōng 無意中 unexpectedly; accidentally

wúyín 無垠 (said of space) boundless; limitless

wúyǐng wúzōng 無影無蹤 (to vanish or disappear) without a trace

wúyōng zhìyí 無庸置疑 unquestionable

wúyòng 無用 useless; of no use

wúyōu wúlǜ 無憂無慮 carefree

wúyú kuìfá 無虞匱乏 no fear of deficiency

wúyǔ lúnbǐ 無與倫比 beyond comparison; peerless; unique; unparalleled

wúyuán 無緣 1. no opportunity or chance 2. unable to 3. an inexplicable animosity toward somebody

wúyuán wúgù 無緣無故 without cause or reason

wúzhī 無知 ignorant; (said of a child) innocent

wúzhōng shēngyǒu 無中生有 (literally) to make something out of nothing—to fabricate; to invent; to frame up

wúzú qīngzhòng 無足輕重 of little significance

wúzuì 無罪 innocent; guiltless; not guilty

wú 蜈
a centipede

wúgong 蜈蚣 a centipede

wú 誣
refer to **wū** 誣

wú 蕪
1. a luxuriant growth of weeds 2. decayed or rotten vegetation 3. confused; mixed-up; in disorder 4. waste; neglected, as land

wújīng 蕪菁 the turnip

wúzá 蕪雜 disorderly and confusing

wú 鼯
a flying squirrel

wúshǔ 鼯鼠 a flying squirrel

wúshǔ jìqióng 鼯鼠技窮 at one's wit's end

wǔ 五
five; fifth

wǔcǎi 五彩 blue, yellow, red, white and black

wǔdàzhōu 五大洲 the five continents—Asia, Africa, Europe, the Americas, and Oceania

wǔfēnzhōng rèdù 五分鐘熱度 short-lived enthusiasm

wǔgēng 五更 the fifth watch of the night which is about 4 a.m.

wǔgǔ 五穀 grains of all sorts

wǔguān 五官 1. the five organs—the ear, the eye, the mouth, the nose and the heart 2. the five senses—visual, auditory, olfactory, gustatory and tactile senses

wǔhuā bāmén 五花八門 rich in variety

wǔhuāròu 五花肉 streaky pork

wǔjīn 五金 1. the five metals—gold, silver, copper, iron, and tin 2. metals in general 3. hardware

Wǔjīng 五經 The Five Classics—the Confucian canon comprising The Book of Changes (**Yìjīng** 易經), The Book of Odes (**Shījīng** 詩經), The Book of History (**Shūjīng** 書經), The Book of Rites (**Lǐjì** 禮記), and The Spring and Autumn Annals

(**Chūnqiū** 春秋)

Wǔquán Xiànfǎ 五權憲法 the five-power constitution of the Republic of China outlined by Dr. Sun Yat-sen

wǔrì jīngzhào 五日京兆 office held for a short time only

wǔshíbù xiào bǎibù 五十步笑百步 The pot calls the kettle black.

wǔtǐ tóudì 五體投地 1. to prostrate oneself 2. to admire someone with the utmost sincerity

wǔwèi 五味 the five flavors—sweet, sour, bitter, pungent, salty

wǔxiànpǔ 五線譜 (music) a staff

wǔxíng 五行 the five primary elements—metal, wood, water, fire and earth

wǔyán liùsè 五顏六色 of variegated colors

Wǔ Yī Láodòngjié 五一勞動節 May (or Labor) Day

wǔyuè 五月 1. May 2. the fifth moon of the lunar calendar 3. five months

wǔzàng 五臟 the five viscera—the heart, the lungs, the liver, the kidneys, and the spleen

wǔzhǐ 五指 the five fingers—the thumb, the index finger, the middle finger, the ring finger, the little finger

wǔ 午
1. noon; high noon 2. (in old Chinese time measurement) 11 a.m. to 1 p.m. 3. the seventh of the Twelve Terrestrial Branches (**Dìzhī** 地支)

wǔfàn 午飯 lunch; a midday meal

wǔhòu 午後 afternoon

wǔqián 午前 before noon; the forenoon

wǔshuì 午睡 an afternoon nap; a siesta

wǔxiū 午休 a noon break; a noontime rest

wǔyè 午夜 midnight

wǔyèchǎng 午夜場 movie marathon

wǔ 伍
1. a military unit of five soldiers (in the Zhou Dynasty) 2. to associate 4. five

wǔ 忤
1. recalcitrant; disobedient 2. a blunder; a mistake; wrong

wǔnì 忤逆 1. recalcitrant; stubborn defiance 2. disobedient to one's parents

wǔ 武
1. force; military 2. warlike; martial 3. footprints; steps 4. the length of half a pace 5. the string of an ancient hat 6. to inherit

wǔdǎpiàn 武打片 Kungfu movies

wǔduàn 武斷 to decide arbitrarily

wǔgōng 武功 1. military achievements 2. fighting skills

wǔháng 武行 (in Chinese opera) actors and actresses who play acrobatic roles or the role of warriors

wǔlì 武力 military might; (by) force

wǔqì 武器 weapons; arms

wǔshēng 武生 a male actor in Peking opera who plays the role of a young warrior or acrobat

wǔshì 武士 1. a warrior 2. a samurai 3. a knight or cavalier

wǔshù 武術 martial arts

wǔxiápiàn 武俠片 motion pictures depicting the chivalry and prowess of ancient swordsmen

wǔxiá xiǎoshuō 武俠小說 a novel of swordsmen

wǔzhuāng 武裝 1. armed; to arm; armament 2. military uniform

wǔzhuāng bùduì 武裝部隊 armed forces

wǔ 迕 also wù
1. to meet 2. to oppose; to disobey

wǔnì 迕逆 1. to go against one's superiors 2. delinquent in filial piety

wǔ 侮
1. to bully 2. to disgrace; to insult; to humiliate 3. an insult; a bully

wǔmàn 侮慢 1. to insult 2. haughty and rude

wǔmiè 侮蔑 to disgrace; to slight

wǔrǔ 侮辱 1. to insult; to humiliate 2. an insult

wǔ 摀
1. to cover; to conceal; to hide 2. to put into an airtight container (in cooking)

wǔgài 摀蓋 to cover up; to hide

wǔzhe ěrduo 摀著耳朵 to cover one's ears

wǔ 嫵
attractive; lovely

wǔmèi 嫵媚 lovely; charming

wǔ 舞
1. to dance; to prance 2. to brandish; to wave 3. to stir up

wǔbì 舞弊 misconduct, malpractice or irregularities (of an official); to bribe

wǔchí 舞池 a dance floor

wǔdǎo 舞蹈 a dance

wǔdòng 舞動 1. to dance 2. to brandish

wǔhuì 舞會 a dancing party; a dance; a ball

wǔlóng 舞龍 a dragon dance

wǔnǚ 舞女 a taxi dancer; a dancing girl

wǔqǔ 舞曲 dance music; a dance tune

wǔshī 舞獅 a lion dance

wǔtái 舞臺 a stage (in a theater)

wǔtīng 舞廳 a dance hall

wǔwén nòngmò 舞文弄墨 1. to amuse oneself with writing 2. to tamper with documents (for fraudulent purposes)

wù 兀
1. to cut off the feet 2. high and flat on the top 3. this 4. ignorant looking

wùzì 兀自 still

wù 勿

    do not; not; never; a negative word used in formal speech

wù 戊

    the fifth of the Ten Celestial Stems

wù 物

    1. a thing; matter; a being 2. content; substance 3. the physical world; nature 4. other people

wùguī yuánzhǔ 物歸原主 Things return to their proper owners.

wùhuàn xīngyí 物換星移 vicissitudes of human affairs with the elapse of time

wùjí bìfǎn 物極必反 As soon as a thing reaches its extremity, it reverses its course.

wùjià 物價 commodity prices

wùjià zhǐshù 物價指數 a price index

wùlǐxué 物理學 physics

wùměi jiàlián 物美價廉 (said of merchandise) excellent quality and reasonable price

wùpǐn 物品 things; articles

wùsè 物色 to seek (talent); to scout for (talent)

wùtǐ 物體 (physics) a body; an object

wùyǐ lèijù 物以類聚 Birds of a feather flock together.

wùyǐ xīwéi guì 物以稀為貴 A thing is valued if it is rare.

wùzhèng 物證 material evidence

wùzhǐ 物質 refer to **wùzhì** 物質

wùzhì 物質 (physics) matter

wùzhǔ 物主 the owner (of a thing)

wùzī 物資 materials; supplies; goods

wù 迕

    refer to **wǔ** 迕

wù 悟

    to become aware of; to realize; to awake to; to comprehend

wùdào 悟道 (Buddhism) to awake to Truth

wùxìng 悟性 understanding; the capacity for understanding

wù 晤

    1. to meet; to see face to face 2. enlightened; wise

wùshāng 晤商 a face-to-face negotiation; to discuss in an interview

wùtán 晤談 to meet and talk; to converse

wù 務

    1. to attend to; to strive after; to be engaged in 2. duty; business; affairs 3. must; necessary

wùbì 務必 must; by all means

wùnóng 務農 to be engaged in farming

wùshí 務實 to strive for thoroughness

wùshǐ 務使 to make sure; to ensure

wùxū 務須 must; by all means

wù 惡

    to hate; to detest; to dislike; to abhor; to loathe

wù 塢

    1. a low wall around a village for defense; an entrenchment; a fortified building; a castle 2. a structure which slants to a lower center on all sides

wù 誤

    1. an error; a mistake 2. to harm; to suffer 3. to delay 4. to miss 5. by accident

wùchā 誤差 (mathematics) an error

wùchuán 誤傳 to transmit (facts) incorrectly

wùdǎo 誤導 to mislead

wùdiǎn 誤點 (said of trains, etc.) to be behind time

wùhuì 誤會 to misunderstand; to misinterpret; to misconstrue; a misunderstanding

wùjiě 誤解 to misunderstand; to misinterpret; to misconstrue; a misunderstanding

wùmiù 誤謬 a mistake; an error

wùrén zǐdì 誤人子弟 to mislead the children of others

wùrèn 誤認 to identify incorrectly

wùrù qítú 誤入歧途 to go astray (morally)

wùshā 誤殺 1. unintentional homicide; manslaughter 2. to kill or murder a person mistaken for the intended victim

wùshí 誤食 to eat (something poisonous or inedible) by mistake

wùshì 誤事 to ruin a plan through mismanagement, etc.; to bungle matters

wùxìn 誤信 to believe what is unreliable

wù 鎢
refer to **wū** 鎢

wù 鶩
1. to rush; to speed 2. unrestrained; uninhibited

wùyuǎn 鶩遠 impractically ambitious; overambitious

wù 霧
fog; mist; vapor

wùlǐ kànhuā 霧裏看花 (literally) to look at flowers in a fog —failing eyesight of the aged

wùqì 霧氣 fog or mist

xī 夕 also **xì**
1. dusk; sunset; evening 2. night 3. slant; oblique 4. to meet in the evening

xīyáng 夕陽 the setting sun

xīyáng chǎnyè 夕陽產業 failing business

xī 兮
a particle of pause used in ancient poetry and still used in eulogies

xī 汐 also **xì**
the flow of the tide at night

xī 西
1. west; the west; western 2. Western; the West; European; American; Occidental; foreign

Xībānyá 西班牙 Spain

Xībànqiú 西半球 the Western Hemisphere

xīběi 西北 northwest

Xībólìyà 西伯利亞 Siberia

xībù 西部 the western part (of a territory); the West

Xīcān 西餐 Western food; European or American meals

Xīdiǎn 西點 1. Western-style dessert 2. West Point

xīfāng 西方 1. west; the West or Western 2. a Buddhist paradise

xīfēng 西風 a west wind; a westerly; a wester

Xīfēng dōngjiān 西風東漸 the spread of Western influences to the East

xīguā 西瓜 watermelons

xīhóngshì 西紅柿 a tomato

Xīlì 西曆 the Gregorian calendar

xī'nán 西南 southwest

Xīshì 西式 Western-style; Occidental style; European or American style

xīxíng 西行 to go west; to travel westward

Xīxué 西學 Western learning

Xīyàn 西諺 a Western proverb; European or American aphorisms

Xīyángrén 西洋人 Westerners

Xīyángshǐ 西洋史 history of Europe and America

Xīyào 西藥 Western medicines or pharmaceuticals

Xīyuán 西元 the Gregorian calendar, which begins with the year in which Christ was supposedly born; A.D.

Xīzàng 西藏 1. Tibet 2. Tibetan

Xīzhuāng 西裝 Western-style clothes; a Western suit

xī 吸
to absorb; to imbibe; to suck in; to attract; to draw; to inhale

xīchénqì 吸塵器 a vacuum cleaner

xīdú 吸毒 to smoke opium

xīguǎn 吸管 1. a pipette 2. a straw

xīlì 吸力 1. (physics) gravitation 2. attraction

xīqì 吸氣 to inhale

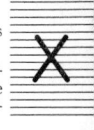

xīqǔ 吸取 1. to absorb (knowledge) 2. to suck (liquid)

xīshí 吸食 to suck; to take in

xīshōu 吸收 1. to absorb; to take in 2. to recruit or enlist

xīshǔn 吸吮 to suck; to absorb

xīxiěguǐ 吸血鬼 refer to **xīxuèguǐ** 吸血鬼

xīxuèguǐ 吸血鬼 a vampire

xīyān 吸煙 to smoke; smoking

xīyānqū 吸煙區 a smoking area

xīyǐn 吸引 to attract; to draw

xīyǐnlì 吸引力 1(physics) gravitation 2. attraction

xī 希
1. rare; strange 2. to hope; to wish; to desire 3. to come to a stop gradually 4. to become silent 5. very; much

xīhan 希罕 1. rare; uncommon 2. to care; to value

xījì 希冀 to desire; to wish for

Xīlà 希臘 Greece; Greek

Xīlàrén 希臘人 a Greek

xīmù 希慕 to long for; to be desirous of

xīqí 希奇 strange; rare; uncommon

xīqì 希企 to hope for

xīqiú 希求 to hope for

xīshì zhīzhēn 希世之珍 a very rare treasure

xītú 希圖 to hope and scheme for

xīwàng 希望 a hope; a wish; expectations; to hope; to wish; to desire

xīwēi 希微 extremely little (amount); very little

xīwéi 希微 refer to **xīwēi** 希微

xīyǒu 希有 very rare

xī 矽 also **xì**
silicium

Xīgǔ 矽谷 Silicium Valley

xī 析
1. to split; to divide; to separate 2. to interpret; to explain; to analyze

xīyí 析疑 to explain a doubt; to clarify a doubt

xīyì 析義 interpretation and elaboration of the meaning of something

xī 昔 also **xí**
1. bygone; of old; formerly; ancient 2. a night; an evening 3. the end

xīrén 昔人 the ancient people

xīrì 昔日 in former days (or times)

xī 奚
1. why; how; what; which 2. a servant

xīluò 奚落 to laugh at; to make a fool of

xī 息 also **xí**
1. a breath 2. news; tidings 3. to stop; to end 4. interest (on money) 5. a son 6. to rest

xījì 息跡 to live in retirement

xīkuǎn 息款 interest (on money)

xīnù 息怒 to let one's anger cool off

xīshì níngrén 息事寧人 to settle disputes and bring about peace

xīxī xiāngguān 息息相關 related as closely as each breath is to the next

xī 唏
to weep or sob with sorrow; to grieve

xīxū 唏噓 to sob

xī 畦
refer to **qí** 畦

xī 悉
1. to know 2. all; whole; total; entire

xīshù 悉數 to enumerate in full detail

xīshù 悉數 all; the entire sum (of money)

xīxīn 悉心 with one's whole heart

xī 淅
1. water for washing rice; to wash rice 2. name of a river in Henan Province

xīlì 淅瀝 1. the sound of rain-

drops 2. the sound of falling leaves in the wind

xīmǐ 淅米 to wash rice

xī 歔

to sob

xīxū 歔欷 to sob

xī 惜 also **xí**

1. to pity; to sympathize; to regret; to feel sorry for somebody 2. to value highly; to have a high opinion of (something); to show love or fondness for 3. to spare; to grudge

xībié 惜别 to say good-bye

xīfú 惜福 to refrain from leading an excessively comfortable life

xī 棲(栖)

refer to **qī** 棲(栖)

xī 稀

1. thin (liquids, etc.); watery; diluted 2. rare; scarce; uncommon 3. scattered; sparse

xībó 稀薄 (said of air) thin or rare

xīfàn 稀飯 congee; gruel; porridge

xīhan 稀罕 1. rare; rarity; scarce 2. to care

xīkè 稀客 a guest who seldom comes to visit

xīqí 稀奇 1. strange; rare 2. to care

xīshǎo 稀少 few; little; scarce; rare; sparse

xīshì 稀釋 to dilute (liquids)

xīshū 稀疏 scattered or dispersed; sparse

xī 晰

clear; clearly; distinct

xī 晳

1. (said of one's skin) fair; white 2. to discriminate; to distinguish

xī 犀

1. (said of armor, weapons, etc.) sharp-edged and hard 2. a rhinoceros

xījiǎo 犀角 1. a rhinoceros horn 2. bone of the forehead

xīlì 犀利 1. hard and sharp 2.

trenchant; sharp

xīniú 犀牛 the rhinoceros

xī 溪 also **qī**

a mountain stream

xīgǔ 溪谷 a valley; a canyon; a gorge

xījiàn 溪澗 a mountain stream

xīliú 溪流 a brook

xīshuǐ 溪水 a mountain stream

xī 熙

1. bright and brilliant; glorious 2. expansive; spacious 3. flourishing; prosperous; booming 4. peaceful and happy

xīlái rǎngwǎng 熙來攘往 the hustle and bustle of large crowds

xīxī rǎngrǎng 熙熙攘攘 crowded and noisy; hustle and bustle

xī 蜥

a lizard

xīyì 蜥蜴 a lizard

xī 熄 also **xí**

1. to extinguish (a fire); to put out (a light) 2. to quash; to destroy; to obliterate

xīdēng 熄燈 to turn or switch off the light

xīhuǒ 熄火 1. to stop the fire (in the boiler)—to stop operation 2. to turn off the lamp or light

xīmiè 熄滅 to extinguish (a fire); to put out (a light); to die out

xī 膝

the knee

xīgài 膝蓋 the knee

xīxià chénghuān 膝下承歡 to please one's parents by living with them

xī 嬉

to have fun; to sport; to play; to frolic

xī'nào 嬉鬧 to romp

xīpí 嬉皮 hippies

xīpí xiàoliǎn 嬉皮笑臉 grinning cheekily; smiling and grimacing

xīxì 嬉戲 to frolic; to play; to

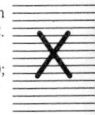

sport

xīxiào 嬉笑 to be laughing and playing

xī 嘻
1. an interjection of grief or surprise 2. laughing happily

xīpí xiàoliǎn 嘻皮笑臉 laughing in a frolicsome manner

xīxī hāhā 嘻嘻哈哈 laughing and talking happily

xīxiào 嘻笑 to giggle; to titter

xī 錫 also **xí**
1. tin 2. to bestow...on; to confer...on

xībó 錫箔 tinfoil; tinfoil (or silver) paper

xīkuàng 錫礦 1. tin ore 2. tin mine

xīzhǐ 錫紙 tinfoil; tinfoil (or silver) paper

xī 熹
1. faint sunlight; dawn 2. giving out faint light

xīwēi 熹微 1. faint light at dawn 2. (said of morning sunlight) dim; pale

xīwéi 熹微 refer to **xīwēi** 熹微

Xī 羲
Fu Xi (**Fúxī** 伏羲), a legendary ruler who introduced houses

xī 禧
refer to **xǐ** 禧

xī 谿
1. a valley; a gorge 2. (溪) a stream; a creek; a brook

xīgǔ 谿谷 a valley

xīhuò 谿壑 a ravine

xī 蹊
1. a path; a footpath 2. to trample; to tread

xīqiāo 蹊蹺 extraordinary; strange; queer

xī 蟋
a cricket (insect)

xīshuài 蟋蟀 a cricket

xī 犧
1. sacrifice (as homage to a

deity); a beast of a uniform color for sacrifice 2. to give up (for the sake of something of greater value); to sacrifice

xīshēng 犧牲 1. sacrifice (offered to a deity) 2. to sacrifice

xīshēngpǐn 犧牲品 1. a loss leader—a popular article sold for a fraction of its normal price 2. a sacrificial lamb

xī 曦
sunshine; sunlight

xī 攜
refer to **xié** 攜

xí 昔
refer to **xī** 昔

xí 席
1. a mat 2. a feast 3. a seat 4. to take a seat 5. to rely on

xíbù xiánuǎn 席不暇暖 very busy

xícì 席次 the order of seats

xídì érzuò 席地而坐 to sit on the ground

xíjuǎn 席捲 1. to take away everything 2. to sweep across

xíwèi 席位 a seat (at a conference, etc.)

xí 息
refer to **xī** 息

xí 惜
refer to **xī** 惜

xí 習
1. to learn; to familiarize oneself with; to receive training in 2. habit; custom; practice 3. to follow; to repeat

xífēi chéngshì 習非成是 Through usage the wrong becomes the right.

xíguàn 習慣 habit; to be accustomed to

xísú 習俗 custom; practice

xítí 習題 problems to be worked out in the course of study; exercises

xíxìng 習性 temperament; dispositions

xíyǐ wéicháng 習以為常 hav-

ing been accustomed to it

xízuò 習作 to learn to do

xí 媳
a daughter-in-law

xífù 媳婦 a daughter-in-law

xí 蓆
a mat, especially a straw mat

xí 熄
refer to **xī** 熄

xí 錫
refer to **xī** 錫

xí 檄
a summons to arms in ancient times

xíwén 檄文 a written summons to arms for a cause

xí 隰
1. low, marshy land 2. newly opened farmland

xí 襲
1. to put on; to clothe in; to wear 2. a suit (of clothes); a set (of dress) 3. repeated; double 4. hereditary; to inherit 5. to raid; to assail 6. to plagiarize; to appropriate

xíjí 襲擊 1. a surprise attack 2. to raid

xíjí 襲擊 refer to **xíjí** 襲擊

xǐ 洗
1. to wash; to rinse; to cleanse; to clean; to clear 2. to baptize

xǐcháng 洗腸 to purge the bowels

xǐchén 洗塵 to give a welcome dinner (for someone arriving after a long trip)

xǐdí 洗滌 to wash; to cleanse; to rinse

xǐdíjì 洗滌劑 washing fluid; a detergent

xǐ'ěr gōngtīng 洗耳恭聽 to listen respectfully

xǐfàjīng 洗髮精 refer to **xǐfàjīng** 洗髮精

xǐfàjīng 洗髮精 shampoo

xǐjié 洗劫 to sack everything

xǐjìng 洗淨 to wash something

until it's clean

xǐlǐ 洗禮 1. to baptize 2. a severe test

xǐliǎn 洗臉 to wash one's face

xǐliǎnpén 洗臉盆 a washbasin

xǐliàn 洗練 (said of literary writings) refined; polished; elegant

xǐnǎo 洗腦 to brainwash; to indoctrinate

xǐpái 洗牌 to shuffle playing cards or mah-jong pieces; a shuffle

xǐshèn 洗腎 dialysis or hemodialysis

xǐshǒu 洗手 1. to wash one's hands 2. to wash one's hands of evil ways

xǐshǒu bùgàn 洗手不幹 to wash one's hands of an evil practice

xǐshǒujiān 洗手間 a toilet; a water closet; a lavatory

xǐshuā 洗刷 1. to scrub; to clean 2. to vindicate oneself

xǐtóu 洗頭 to shampoo; to wash one's hair

xǐwǎnjī 洗碗機 a dishwasher

xǐwèi 洗胃 (medicine) gastric lavage

xǐxīn gémiàn 洗心革面 to reform oneself

xǐxuě 洗雪 1. to cleanse (both literally and figuratively) 2. to revenge; to vindicate

xǐyī 洗衣 to wash clothes

xǐyīdiàn 洗衣店 a laundry shop

xǐyījī 洗衣機 a washing machine

xǐzǎo 洗澡 to take a bath

xǐzǎojiān 洗澡間 a bathroom

xǐzǎopén 洗澡盆 a bathtub

xǐzhuó 洗濯 to wash; to rinse

xǐ 徙
1. to move one's abode; to migrate 2. to be exiled

xǐjū 徙居 to move; to migrate

xǐshàn 徙善 to change for the better

xǐ 喜
1. a joyful thing; a happy event 2. joy 3. to like; to love; to be fond of 4. joyful; happy; delight-

ful; pleasant; auspicious

xǐ'ài 喜愛 to like; to love; to be fond of

xǐbù zìshèng 喜不自勝 to be delighted beyond measure

xǐchū wàngwài 喜出望外 joy over unexpected good luck; unexpected joy

xǐhào 喜好 to be fond of; to delight in

xǐhuan 喜歡 to like; to be fond of; to love

xǐjiǔ 喜酒 a wedding feast

xǐjù 喜劇 a comedy

Xǐmǎlāyǎshān 喜馬拉雅山 the Himalayas

xǐnù āilè 喜怒哀樂 the feelings of joy, anger, sorrow and delight

xǐqì yángyáng 喜氣洋洋 1. a joyful atmosphere 2. a cheerful look or expression

xǐqìng 喜慶 auspicious or happy occasions

xǐque 喜鵲 the magpie

xǐshì 喜事 an occasion for joy (especially a wedding)

xǐtiě 喜帖 a wedding invitation

xǐxīn yànjiù 喜新厭舊 to like the new and dislike the old

xǐxùn 喜訊 happy news; good news

xǐyángyáng 喜洋洋 beaming with joy; radiant

xǐyángyáng 喜洋洋 refer to **xǐyángyáng** 喜洋洋

xǐyuè 喜悅 joy; delight; gratification

xǐ 禧 also **xī** happiness; blessings; auspiciousness

xǐ 璽 1. the seal of an emperor or a king 2. the formal seal of a state; the national emblem

xì 夕 refer to **xī** 夕

xì 汐 refer to **xī** 汐

xì 系

1. a system; a line; a connecting link; a connection 2. lineage; a genealogy 3. (politics) a clique; a theoretic or party line 4. (in a college or a university) a department or school 5. to relate to; to bear on 6. to be

xìliè 系列 1. a line or lineage 2. a row; a series

xìtǒng 系統 a system; systematic

xìzhǔrèn 系主任 the head or chairman of a department (in a college)

xì 矽 refer to **xī** 矽

xì 係

1. to bind; to belong to; to attach to; to connect with 2. to be

xìshù 係數 (mathematics) coefficient

xì 細

1. tiny; small; little 2. thin; slender; tall but lean; slim 3. fine 4. petty; trifling; detailed 5. precise; exquisite; delicate (workmanship, etc.)

xìbāo 細胞 a cell

xìbù 細部 details (of a drawing); minute parts

xìmì 細密 1. (said of materials) fine and delicate 2. careful; cautious

xìmù 細目 detailed items

xìwēi 細微 tiny; minute

xìwēi 細微 refer to **xìwēi** 細微

xìyǔ 細雨 a misty rain; drizzle

xìyǔ 細語 low and tender talk; pillow talk

xì 隙(隟)

1. a crack; a fissure; a crevice 2. a grudge; a dislike; a dispute; a quarrel; a complaint 3. spare time; leisure 4. an opportunity; a loophole 5. an important passageway or corridor

xìxià 隙縫 a crack, crevice, or fissure

xì 戲

1. to play; to toy; to sport 2. to jest; to have fun; to make fun 3. a drama; a play; a show 4. a

game
xìbān 戲班 a dramatic troupe
xìcí 戲詞 an actor's lines
xìfǎ 戲法 jugglery; a trick; magic
xìjù 戲劇 a drama; the theater
xìjùhuà 戲劇化 to dramatize; dramatic
xìjùjiā 戲劇家 a playwright; a dramatist
xìmǎ 戲碼 a repertoire
xìmí 戲迷 a drama fan
xìnòng 戲弄 to play a trick on; to tease
xìnüè 戲謔 refer to **xìxuè** 戲謔
xìpiào 戲票 an admission ticket for a play
xìqǔ 戲曲 a drama; a play
xìshuǐ 戲水 to play in water
xìtái 戲臺 a stage (for plays)
xìxuè 戲謔 a joke; a witticism; a jest; fun
xìyán 戲言 a joke; a witticism
xìyuánzi 戲園子 a playhouse; a theater
xìyuàn 戲院 a theater; a movie house
xìzhuāng 戲裝 theatrical (or stage) costume
xìzi 戲子 a dramatic player

xì 鬩
to quarrel; to conflict
xìqiáng 鬩牆 to quarrel within the family; an intramural fight

xì 繫
to connect; to link; to join
xìniàn 繫念 to feel concerned about

xiā 蝦
a shrimp
xiāmi 蝦米 dried shrimps

xiā 瞎
1. blind; blindly 2. rash; reckless; heedless; (to do things, etc.) without purpose or reason; at random; groundlessly 3. (dialect) to become tangled (said of thread, etc.)
xiābāi 瞎掰 to make a futile effort

xiāchě 瞎扯 to talk recklessly; to tell lies
xiāgǎo 瞎搞 to do a thing without any plan or method
xiāle yǎnjing 瞎了眼睛 Blind fool!
xiāmáng 瞎忙 to be busy for nothing
xiā'nào 瞎鬧 to make nonsense; to fool around
xiāshuō 瞎說 to talk nonsense; wild talks
xiāzi 瞎子 a blind man

xiá 匣
1. a case; a small box 2. a cage

xiá 狎
to show familiarity, intimacy, or disrespect
xiáwǔ 狎侮 to be impolite to; to treat with disrespect

xiá 洽
refer to **qià** 洽

xiá 俠
1. a person adept in martial arts and dedicated to helping the poor and weak 2. chivalry
xiáyì 俠義 chivalry; honor and gallantry

xiá 挾
refer to **xié** 挾

xiá 狹
narrow; narrow-minded
xiá'ài 狹隘 narrow-minded; parochial; narrow
xiácháng 狹長 long and narrow
xiálù xiāngféng 狹路相逢 enemies or rivals coming face to face
xiáxiǎo 狹小 (said of rooms, etc.) narrow and small
xiáyì 狹義 the narrow sense
xiázhǎi 狹窄 narrow; cramped

xiá 峽
1. a gorge 2. an isthmus 3. straits
xiágǔ 峽谷 (geography) a dale; a gorge
xiáwān 峽灣 (geography) a fiord

xiá 瑕

1. a flaw, spot, or blemish in a piece of jade 2. a fault, error, blemish or flaw

xiábù yǎnyú 瑕不掩瑜 The defects do not out weigh the merits.

xiácī 瑕疵 defects; flaws; blemishes

xiáyú hùjiàn 瑕瑜互見 (said of a single person) to have both good and bad qualities

xiá 遐

1. distant; far 2. a long time 3. advanced in years 4. to die down; to vanish 5. to abandon; to cast off 6. Why not? How? What?

xiáxiǎng 遐想 wild and fanciful thoughts

xiá 暇 also **xià**

leisure; free time; spare time

xiá 轄

1. a linchpin 2. to govern; to administer; administration; to manage 3. the noise of wheels

xiáqū 轄區 an area under the jurisdiction (of a magistrate, etc.); magistracy

xiá 霞

colored, low-hanging clouds; rosy clouds

xiáguāng 霞光 rays of morning or evening sunlight

xiá 黠

1. smart; clever; shrewd 2. crafty; cunning; artful; wily

xiáhuì 黠慧 clever; smart; shrewd

xià 下

1. to put down 2. to lay 3. to fall 4. to descend 5. to begin 6. below; under 7. inferior; lower 8. next

xiàba 下巴 the chin

xiàbǎi 下擺 the lower part of a Chinese gown

xiàbài 下拜 to bow

xiàbān 下班 to knock off

xiàbàn bèizi 下半輩子 the

latter half of one's life

xiàbànchǎng 下半場 the second half (of a game)

xiàbànqí 下半旗 to fly a flag at half-mast

xiàbàntiān 下半天 the last half day; afternoon

xiàbànyè 下半夜 the wee hours

xiàbèizi 下輩子 the next life; the next incarnation

xiàbǐ 下筆 to start writing

xiàbǐ chéngzhāng 下筆成章 to write quickly and skillfully

xiàbian 下邊 as follows; following; below; under

xiàbù 下部 1. the lower part 2. the private parts

xiàbù wéilì 下不爲例 This does not constitute a precedent. Don't do it again!

xiàbuliǎotái 下不了臺 1. cannot bring to a conclusion 2. to be put on the spot

xiàcè 下策 a bad strategy, measure or policy

xiàcéng 下層 1. a lower stratum, layer or deck 2. low-ranking

xiàchǎng 下場 1. to get to the playground to compete, play ball, etc. 2. an exịt on the stage

xiàchang 下場 the conclusion; the end

xiàchē 下車 to get off (trains or vehicles, etc.)

xiàchén 下沈 to sink; to subside

xiàchú 下廚 to go to the kitchen; to prepare food

xiàchuán 下船 to go ashore

xiàchuáng 下床 to get up

xiàchuí 下垂 1. to hang down; to droop 2. (medicine) prolapse

xiàdàn 下蛋 to lay eggs

xiàděng 下等 1. lowgrade 2. mean; depraved

xiàdì 下地 1. to go to the fields 2. to leave a sickbed

xiàdìyù 下地獄 to go to hell

xiàdìngyì 下定義 to define; to give a definition

xiàdú 下毒 to poison

xiàdúshǒu 下毒手 to lay violent hands on someone

xià'è 下顎 the lower jaw; the mandible

xiàfàn 下飯 (said of dishes) to go along with rice

xiàfāng 下方 1. south and west 2. below; under 3. the earth

xiàfáng 下房 the servant's quarters

xiàfēng 下風 1. in an inferior position 2. leeward

xiàgǎng 下崗 refer to **xiàgǎng** 下崗

xiàgǎng 下崗 to come or go off sentry duty

xiàgōng 下工 to stop working

xiàgōngfu 下工夫 to devote much time and energy to a task

xiàguì 下跪 to kneel down

xiàhǎi 下海 1. to turn professional (usually referring to show personalities) 2. to go to sea 3. People who have no commercial background start to do business.

xiàhuí 下回 next time

xiàjí 下級 1. lower levels 2. subordinates

xiàjià 下嫁 to marry someone beneath her station

xiàjiàn 下賤 low; cheap; degrading

xiàjiàng 下降 to descend; to drop

xiàjiè 下屆 next (term, election, etc.)

xiàjiǔ 下酒 (said of food) to go with wine

xiàjiǔcài 下酒菜 a dish that goes with wine

xiàjuéxīn 下決心 to make a resolution

xiàkè 下課 to get out of class; to finish class

xiàlai 下來 to come down

xiàliè 下列 1. as follows 2. what are listed below

xiàliú 下流 1. downstream 2. to flow down 3. low; nasty; mean; scurrilous

xiàliúhuà 下流話 foul language; obscenities

xiàlóu 下樓 to descend the stairs; to go downstairs

xiàluò 下落 whereabouts

xiàmǎ 下馬 to dismount from a horse

xiàmǎwēi 下馬威 to warn against insubordination, etc. by enforcing strict disciplinary action when one first takes office

xiàmiàn 下麵 to cook noodles

xiàmian 下面 1. underneath 2. following 3. lower levels; subordinates

xiàmìnglìng 下命令 to give orders

xiànǚ 下女 a maid

xiàpiàn 下片 to stop showing a movie

xiàpiān 下片 refer to **xiàpiān** 下片

xiàpǐn 下品 lowgrade; inferior

xiàpìn 下聘 to present betrothal gifts

xiàpōlù 下坡路 a descending road

xiàpù 下鋪 the lower berth

xiàqí 下棋 to play chess

xiàqu 下去 1. to go down 2. to go on

xiàrén 下人 a servant

xiàshān 下山 to go down a mountain

xiàshēn 下身 1. the lower part of the body 2. the privates

xiàshì 下士 (military rank) corporal

xiàshǒu 下手 1. to start doing something 2. to commit a crime 3. a helper

xiàshǔ 下屬 a subordinate

xiàshuǐ 下水 to launch a boat

xiàshuǐdào 下水道 sewers; the sewerage system

xiàshuǐlǐ 下水禮 the ceremony of launching a ship

xiàshui 下水 internal organs of animals

xiàtà 下榻 to take up abode; to stay

xiàtái 下臺 1. to get off stage 2. to be relieved from office

xiàtǐ 下體 the privates; the genitals

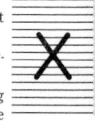

xiàtián 下田 to work on farmland

xiàtiě 下帖 to send an invitation

xiàwén 下文 1. the statement that follows 2. further development or information

xiàwǔ 下午 an afternoon

xiàxián 下弦 the last quarter of the moon

xiàxiàn 下限 lower limit

xiàxiāng 下鄉 to go to the country; to rusticate

xiàxíngchē 下行車 the down train

xiàxué 下學 to leave for home after school

xiàxuéqī 下學期 next semester

xiàxuéqī 下學期 refer to **xiàxuéqī** 下學期

xiàxuě 下雪 to snow

xiàxún 下旬 the last ten days of a month

xiàyàn 下嚥 to swallow

xiàyě 下野 to quit or resign from official posts

xiàyìshì 下意識 subconscious

xiàyìshì 下意識 refer to **xiàyìshì** 下意識

Xiàyìyuàn 下議院 the Lower House

xiàyóu 下游 downstream

xiàyǔ 下雨 to rain

xiàyù 下獄 to put behind bars

xiàyuè 下月 next month

xiàzàng 下葬 to bury

xiàzhǒng 下種 to sow seed

xià zhúkèlìng 下逐客令 to ask an unwelcome guest or visitor to leave

xiàzhù 下注 to put stake; to wager

xiàzhù 下箸 to start eating

xiàzhuì 下墜 to fall

xià 夏
1. summer 2. big; spacious 3. a big house; a mansion 4. Cathay, the ancient name of China 5. a dynasty in Chinese history (2205-1782 B.C.)

xiàjì 夏季 the summer season

xiàlìng 夏令 summer; summer time

xiàlìngyíng 夏令營 summer camps

xiàtiān 夏天 summer; summer days

Xiàwá 夏娃 (the Bible) Eve

Xiàwēiyí 夏威夷 Hawaii

xiàzhì 夏至 the summer solstice which falls on June 21 or 22 on the Northern Hemisphere

xiàzhuāng 夏裝 a summer dress

xià 廈
refer to **shà** 廈

xià 暇
refer to **xiá** 暇

xià 嚇
to frighten; to startle; to scare

xiàhu 嚇唬 to scare; to frighten

xiàrén 嚇人 1. to frighten people 2. horrible; terrible

xiān 仙
1. a god; an immortal; a fairy 2. a divine

xiāndān 仙丹 a panacea; a cure-all; an elixir

xiānfēng dàogǔ 仙風道骨 divine poise or bearing

xiānjìng 仙境 1. a fairyland 2. a place of exquisite natural beauty

xiānnǚ 仙女 a fairy

xiānréntiào 仙人跳 a badger game

xiānrénzhǎng 仙人掌 a cactus

xiānshì 仙逝 to die; to pass away

xiāntáo 仙桃 a divine peach

xiānzǐ 仙子 a fairy; an immortal

xiān 先
1. first; foremost 2. before; earlier; in advance 3. the late...; the deceased... 4. one's forebears 5. the abbreviation for Mister or Sir

xiāndǎo 先導 1. to lead the way 2. a model; a teacher 3. a guide

xiāndǔ wéikuài 先睹為快 to eagerly await a look at (something) ahead of others

xiānfā zhìrén 先發制人 to take the initiative

xiānfēng 先鋒 a vanguard; a forerunner; the trailblazer

xiānfū 先夫 my late husband

xiānfù 先父 my late father

xiānhé 先河 a harbinger; a forerunner

xiānhòu 先後 1. the order (of things narrated, placed, etc.) 2. the ins and outs of an incident

xiānjiàn zhīmíng 先見之明 the ability to discern what is coming

xiānjìn 先進 predecessors; seniors

xiānjué 先覺 a prophet

xiānlái hòudào 先來後到 First come, first served.

xiānlǐ hòubīng 先禮後兵 diplomacy (or courtesy) before the use of force

xiānliè 先烈 the national martyrs

xiānmín 先民 ancients

xiānmǔ 先母 my late mother

xiānqián 先前 before; previously

xiānqū 先驅 a vanguard; a forerunner; a pioneer

xiānrén 先人 1. previous generations 2. forebears

xiānrù wéizhǔ 先入為主 One usually favors the very first idea entering his mind.

xiānsheng 先生 1. an honorable title for a teacher 2. a name for the elderly and learned 3. Mister; Sir 4. a husband

xiāntiān 先天 1. natural physical endowments 2. congenital; innate; inherent

xiāntiān bùzú 先天不足 inborn deficiency

xiānwáng 先王 1. the late king 2. ancient sage sovereigns

xiān xiàshǒu wéiqiáng 先下手為強 It's always advantageous to make the first move (or take the initiative).

xiānxián 先賢 ancient saints and sages

xiānyán 先嚴 my deceased father

xiānzhǎn hòuzòu 先斬後奏 (in a modern sense) to take action before reporting to one's superior

xiānzhào 先兆 an omen; a portent; a sign

xiānzhé 先哲 ancient saints and sages

xiānzhī 先知 1. a prophet 2. a person of foresight or forethought

xiānzhī xiānjué 先知先覺 1. a person of foresight or forethought 2. having foresight

xiān 掀

1. to lift with the hands; to raise 2. to stir; to stir up; to cause to rise

xiāndòng 掀動 to raise; to stir up; to instigate

xiānkāi 掀開 to open; to uncover or unveil (a secret, etc.)

xiānqǐ 掀起 to stir up (a movement, etc.)

xiān 鮮

1. fresh; new 2. delicious; tasty 3. bright; attractive

xiānhóng 鮮紅 bright red

xiānhuā 鮮花 fresh flowers

xiānměi 鮮美 fresh and delicious

xiānmíng 鮮明 1. sharp; distinct 2. bright-colored

xiānnèn 鮮嫩 fresh and tender

xiānxiě 鮮血 refer to **xiānxuè** 鮮血

xiānxiě línlí 鮮血淋漓 refer to **xiānxuè línlí** 鮮血淋漓

xiānxuè 鮮血 fresh blood; blood

xiānxuè línlí 鮮血淋漓 drenched with blood

xiānyàn 鮮豔 bright-colored; resplendent; attractively

xiānyàn duómù 鮮豔奪目 bright-colored; resplendent; attractively

xiān 孅

slender; thin; small; fine; delicate

xiānruò 孅弱 frail; weak; deli-

cate

xiān 纖
tiny; minute; fine; delicate; slender

xiānruò 纖弱 fragile; delicate

xiānshòu 纖瘦 delicate and slender

xiānwéi 纖維 fiber

xiānxì 纖細 fine; tiny; minute

xiānyāo 纖腰 a slender waist (of a woman)

xián 弦
1. strings (of bows, etc.) 2. the chord of an arc 3. the first or last quarter of a lunar month

xiánwài zhīyīn 弦外之音 overtones; connotations

xiányuè 弦月 a crescent moon

xiányuèduì 弦樂隊 a string orchestra (or band)

xiányuèqì 弦樂器 a stringed instrument

xián 咸
all; completely; fully; wholly

xián 涎
saliva

xiánmò 涎沫 saliva

xiánpí làiliǎn 涎皮賴臉 shameless; brazen

xián 絃
1. the string of a musical instrument; a cord 2. first and last quarters of the moon

xiánwài zhīyīn 絃外之音 overtones; connotations; suggestion

xiányuè 絃樂 string music

xiányuèduì 絃樂隊 a string band

xián 啣
1. a bridle 2. to hold in the mouth 3. to harbor

xián 閑
1. a fence; a bar; a barrier 2. to defend 3. big 4. familiar with; accustomed to 5. (閒) leisure 6. laws or regulations 7. a stable

xiánjìng 閑靜 peaceful and calm in mind—without desires

xiánkěyá 閑磕牙 leisure talks or conversation about nothing in particular

xiánshū 閑書 books for killing time, as novels, etc.

xiánxí 閑習 to be well versed in or familiar with

xiánxiá 閑暇 leisure; spare time

xián 閒
1. quiet; tranquil; calm; placid 2. leisure; spare time

xiándàng 閒蕩 to saunter; to stroll; to loaf

xiángōngfu 閒工夫 leisure; spare time

xiánguàng 閒逛 to saunter; to stroll

xiánhuà 閒話 1. random or idle talk; gossip; complaint 2. to talk casually about; to chat about

xiánjū 閒居 to lead an idle, leisure, or quiet life

xiánliáo 閒聊 1. to chat; to gossip 2. a gossip; a chat

xiánqíng yìzhì 閒情逸致 a peaceful and comfortable mood

xiánrén 閒人 1. idlers; persons with nothing to do 2. persons not concerned

xiánshì 閒事 matters not of one's concern; others' business; matters one has nothing to do with

xiánshì 閒適 quiet and comfortable

xiántán 閒談 idle talk; to chat

xiányán xiányǔ 閒言閒語 sarcastic remarks or complaints; gossip

xiánzá 閒雜 without fixed duties

xiánzhì 閒置 to leave unused; to let something lie idle; to set aside

xián 嫌
1. to detest; to dislike 2. ill will; a grudge 3. to suspect; suspicion 4. to complain; to reject; to object

xiánqì 嫌棄 to reject; to give up in disgust

xiánxì 嫌隙 the suspicion born out of dislike; an old grudge

xiányí 嫌疑 suspicion; to suspect

xiányífàn 嫌疑犯 a suspect (of a crime, etc.)

xián 銜

1. a bit (in a horse's mouth) 2. the title (of an official) 3. to hold in the mouth 4. to harbor; to cherish 5. to follow (orders)

xiánjiē 銜接 to adjoin; to lie next to; to connect; to dovetail

xián 賢

1. capable; able; versatile; talented 2. good; worthy; virtuous 3. to admire; to praise; to esteem 4. a term of respectful address to another

xiánhuì 賢慧 (usually said of women) virtuous and intelligent

xiánliáng 賢良 virtuous; the virtuous

xiánmíng 賢明 capable and virtuous

xiánnèizhù 賢內助 a good wife

xiánqī liángmǔ 賢妻良母 a dutiful wife and loving mother

xiánrén 賢人 a person of virtue and talents

xiánshū 賢淑 (usually said of women) virtuous and understanding

xiánshú 賢淑 refer to **xiánshū** 賢淑

xián 嫻（嫺）

1. refined; gracious 2. skillful; skilled

xiánjìng 嫻靜 quiet and refined (women)

xiánshú 嫻熟 expert; adept in; skilled in

xiányǎ 嫻雅 polished; cultured; refined

xián 鹹

saltish; salty; briny; salted

xiáncài 鹹菜 pickled vegetables; pickles

xiándàn 鹹蛋 salted eggs

Xiánhǎi 鹹海 Lake Aral

xiánròu 鹹肉 salted meat

xiánshuǐ 鹹水 saline water; salt water

xiánshuǐhú 鹹水湖 salt lakes

xiánwèi 鹹味 a salty taste; saltiness

xiányú 鹹魚 salted fish

Xiǎn 洗

a Chinese family name

xiǎn 洒

1. respectful 2. deep 3. alarmed; surprised

xiǎn 險

1. dangerous; danger 2. obstructed; difficult 3. a strategic pass 4. mean and crafty; cunning; sinister 5. nearly; almost

xiǎn'è 險惡 1. dangerous; perilous; ominous; precarious 2. devious; diabolic

xiǎnjìng 險境 a dangerous situation

xiǎnjùn 險峻 (said of terrain) of highly strategic significance; (said of hills, etc.) precipitous

xiǎnshèng 險勝 to win by a narrow margin

xiǎntān 險灘 a dangerous shoal; rapids

xiǎnxiàng huánshēng 險象環生 dangers lurking on all sides; to be beset with danger

xiǎnyào 險要 (said of a place) strategic and capable of being easily defended

xiǎnzāo bùcè 險遭不測 to escape death by a hair's breadth

xiǎnzāo dúshǒu 險遭毒手 to have a narrow escape from assassination, murder, etc.

xiǎnzhà 險詐 treacherous; treachery

xiǎnzǔ 險阻 hazardous; precarious (situations, etc.); difficult (terrain)

xiǎn 鮮

rare; few; seldom

xiǎnyǒu 鮮有 seldom to have; rare

xiǎn 蘚

(botany) moss; lichen

xiǎntái 蘚苔 (botany) moss; lichen

xiǎn 癬

refer to **xuǎn** 癬

xiǎn 顯

1. evident; manifest; clear 2. high-positioned; eminent; prominent 3. well-known; renowned; famed; reputed 4. to expose; to make known; to display; to show; to manifest 5. a prefix referring to one's forebears

xiǎndá 顯達 to attain high office; to achieve prominence in officialdom

xiǎnde 顯得 to look; to seem; to appear

xiǎn'ér yìjiàn 顯而易見 evidently; apparently

xiǎnguì 顯貴 bigwigs; eminent personages

xiǎnhè 顯赫 outstanding; illustrious; renowned; powerful; mighty; prominent

xiǎnhuā zhíwù 顯花植物 a flowering plant

xiǎnhuàn 顯宦 a ranking or high official

xiǎnlíng 顯靈 omens, etc. given by the soul of a dead person; a divine manifestation

xiǎnlù 顯露 to appear; to show; to unveil; to manifest

xiǎnlù tóujiǎo 顯露頭角 to show one's promise

xiǎnmíng 顯明 evident; clear; remarkable

xiǎnran 顯然 evident; clearly visible; obvious

xiǎnshēnshǒu 顯身手 to show one's talent or skill

xiǎnshì 顯示 to indicate; to show; to reveal

xiǎnwēijìng 顯微鏡 a microscope

xiǎnwéijìng 顯微鏡 refer to **xiǎnwēijìng** 顯微鏡

xiǎnxiàn 顯現 to appear; to reveal

xiǎnxìng jīyīn 顯性基因 a dominant gene

xiǎnyǎn 顯眼 conspicuous; striking; eye-catching

xiǎnyáng 顯揚 to cite; to commend; to praise

xiǎnyào 顯要 bigwigs; notables; VIPs (very important persons)

xiǎnzhù 顯著 evident; clear; notable; eye-catching; marked; remarkable

xiàn 限

1. a boundary; a line 2. a doorsill or threshold 3. limits; restriction; to limit or restrict 4. to specify; to fix

xiàndìng 限定 to limit

xiàndù 限度 limits; limitation; degree

xiàn'é 限額 a quota

xiànjià 限價 price control; a price fixed under a government specified ceiling

xiànliàng 限量 limits; limitation

xiànqī 限期 1. a time limit; a deadline 2. within a definite time

xiànqí 限期 refer to **xiànqī** 限期

xiànshí 限時 to fix or set the time; to set a time limit or deadline

xiànshí zhuānsòng 限時專送 prompt delivery

xiànzhì 限制 limitations; to restrict

xiàn 現

1. to emerge; to appear 2. current; now 3. in time of need; extempore 4. cash 5. ready; available 6. actual

xiànchǎng 現場 the scene (of an incident); a site

xiànchéng 現成 ready; ready-made

xiàndài 現代 modern; the present world

xiàndàihuà 現代化 to modernize; modernization

xiànfáng 現房 houses available for rent or purchase

xiànhuò 現貨 stock goods; goods on hand

xiànjiēduàn 現階段 the present stage

xiànjīn 現今 nowadays; at present; now

xiànjīn 現金 cash; ready money

xiànjīn jiāoyì 現金交易 business transactions in cash; cash transactions

xiànkuǎn 現款 cash; ready money

xiànrèn 現任 present (job, or employment)

xiànshēn shuōfǎ 現身說法 to act as an example to others

xiànshí 現實 1. reality 2. pragmatic; real

xiànshì 現世 1. the world nowadays; present 2. to bring shame on oneself

xiànxiàng 現象 phenomena; appearances

xiànxíng 現行 existing; presently valid

xiànxíng 現形 to reveal one's true form

xiànxíngfàn 現行犯 (law) flagrante delicto

xiànyì jūnrén 現役軍人 military personnel on active service

xiànyǒu 現有 to have on hand; existing

xiànzài 現在 now; at present

xiànzhuàng 現狀 things as they are; the status quo

xiàn 陷
1. to sink; to fall; to submerge; to stick; to bog 2. to frame (up); to harm another with trumped-up charges 3. to entrap; to beguile 4. to crush (the enemy position); to fall; to capture (a city, etc.) 5. a defect; a deficiency

xiànhài 陷害 to frame; to snare; to harm another with a trumped-up charge, slander, etc.

xiànjǐng 陷阱 a trap; a snare; a booby trap

xiànluò 陷落 1. to sink; to submerge 2. (said of a city, position, etc.) to be lost to the enemy

xiànnì 陷溺 to sink; to submerge; to be drowned

xiànrù juéjìng 陷入絕境 to get into extreme difficulty

xiàn 羨
to envy; to covet

xiànmù 羨慕 to envy; to covet

xiàn 腺
a gland

xiàntǐ 腺體 a gland

xiàn 線(綫)
1. a line 2. threads 3. wires

xiànlù 線路 1. (electricity) a circuit 2. a narrow path

xiànmín 線民 a stool pigeon; an informer

xiànquān 線圈 a coil

xiànsuǒ 線索 a clue; a lead

xiàntiáo 線條 lines; streaks

xiànzhuāngběn 線裝本 a book bound in the traditional Chinese style

xiànzhuāngshū 線裝書 a book bound in the traditional Chinese style

xiàn 縣
a county; a prefecture

xiànyìhuì 縣議會 a county council

xiànyìyuán 縣議員 members of a district council

xiànzhǎng 縣長 the chief hsien (or county) executive

xiànzhèngfǔ 縣政府 a county government

xiàn 憲
1. law; a code; a statute; an ordinance; a constitution 2. intelligent 3. a reference to superiors

xiànbīng 憲兵 military police; gendarmes

xiànfǎ 憲法 constitution (of a national government)

xiànlìng 憲令 laws and ordinances

xiànzhāng 憲章 a charter

xiànzhèng 憲政 constitutional government (or rule)

xiàn 餡
anything serving as stuffing for dumplings, etc.

xiànr 餡兒 stuffing

xiàn 獻
1. to present; to forward; to offer; to dedicate; to donate 2. to

display; to show; to stage 3. to curry (favor, etc.); to flatter or cater to

xiànbǎo 獻寶 1. to present a treasure 2. to offer a scheme or one's valuable experience 3. to show off what one treasures

xiànchǒu 獻醜 to show my poor skill or talent (a polite expression)

xiàncí 獻詞 a dedication; a dedication speech

xiànhuā 獻花 to present flowers or bouquets; to lay a wreath

xiànjì 獻技 to display one's feat

xiànjì 獻計 to present or offer advice or a scheme for adoption

xiànlǐ 獻禮 1. the ceremony of offering presents 2. to present a gift

xiànmèi 獻媚 to curry favor; to toady

xiànshēn 獻身 to offer or dedicate oneself (to a cause, one's nation, etc.)

xiànyīnqín 獻殷勤 to flatter; to ingratiate

xiāng 香

1. sweet-smelling; fragrant; aromatic; balmy 2. tasty; delicious 3. fair; beautiful 4. spicy; balm; incense

xiāngbīn 香檳 champagne

xiāngcǎo 香草 1. vanilla 2. a fragrant herb

xiāngcháng 香腸 sausage

Xiānggǎng 香港 Hong Kong (Hongkong)

Xiānggǎngjiǎo 香港腳 athlete's foot

xiānggū 香菇 a kind of edible mushroom grown on wooden logs

xiāngguā 香瓜 a muskmelon; a cantaloupe

xiāngguī 香閨 a lady's chamber

xiānghuā 香花 fragrant flowers

xiānghuī 香灰 ashes of incense

xiānghuǒ 香火 1. incense burned and candles lighted in honor of a deity, an ancestor, etc. 2. an oath; a vow

xiāngjiāo 香蕉 a banana

xiāngjiāoshuǐ 香蕉水 banana oil

xiāngjiāoyóu 香蕉油 banana oil

xiāngjīng 香精 essence

xiāngkè 香客 visitors to temples; pilgrims

xiāngliào 香料 spice; balm

xiānglú 香爐 a thurible; a censer

xiāngnáng 香囊 a sachet

xiāngpēnpēn 香噴噴 smelling very good; sweet-smelling

xiāngpiàn 香片 jasmine tea

xiāngqì 香氣 a sweet smell; a pleasant odor; fragrance

xiāngròu 香肉 (euphemism) dog meat

xiāngshuǐ 香水 perfume; scent

xiāngtián 香甜 1. sweet; delicious 2. (to sleep) soundly

xiāngwèi 香味 spicy taste; aromatic flavor

xiāngxiāo yùyǔn 香消玉殞 (literally) The fragrance is gone and the jade is fallen.—The beauty is dead.

xiāngyān 香煙 1. cigarettes 2. continuity of the family line 3. smoke of burning incense

xiāngyóu 香油 1. perfumed oil; aromatic oil 2. sesame oil

xiāngzào 香皂 perfumed soap; toilet soap

xiāngzhú 香燭 incense and candles—materials for the altar

xiāng 相

1. each other; one another; mutually; reciprocal 2. substance

xiāng'ài 相愛 to love each other

xiāng'ān wúshì 相安無事 at peace with each other

xiāngbàn 相伴 to accompany somebody

xiāngbǐ 相比 to compare with each other

xiāngchà 相差 to differ

xiāngchèn 相稱 to fit each other; to match each other; to be symmetrical

xiāngchí bùxià 相持不下 persistently opposing each other with neither giving way

xiāngchǔ 相處 to spend time together; to live together

xiāngchuán 相傳 1. (said of a report) to be transmitted from person to person 2. to be passed or handed down from generation to generation

xiāngdāng 相當 1. equivalent; to correspond to 2. considerable 3. appropriate; fit

xiāngdé yìzhāng 相得益彰 Each gains in appearance from the presence of the other.

xiāngděng 相等 equal; equivalent

xiāngduì 相對 1. corresponding 2. relative 3. opposite; face to face

xiāngfǎn 相反 contrary; opposed to each other

xiāngféng 相逢 to come across

xiāngfú 相符 to tally; to correspond

xiāngfǔ xiāngchéng 相輔相成 to complement each other; to reciprocate and complement

xiānggān 相干 related; connected; to have to do with

xiānggào 相告 to tell; to pass information

xiānggé 相隔 to be separated by; to be apart

xiānggù shīsè 相顧失色 to look at each other in dismay

xiāngguān 相關 related; connected; to have to do with

xiānghù 相互 one another; mutually; reciprocally

xiānghuì 相會 to meet together

xiāngjì 相繼 in succession

xiāngjiàn hènwǎn 相見恨晚 to regret having not met earlier

xiāngjìn 相近 close (in amount, quality, degree, etc.); approximate

xiāngjiù 相救 to rescue; to help out of difficulty

xiāngjù 相距 away from

xiāngjù 相聚 to meet together; to assemble

xiāngkè 相剋 mutually destructive

xiānglián 相連 connected; joined; linked

xiāngpèi 相配 to match well

xiāngqīn xiāng'ài 相親相愛 to be kind to each other and love each other

xiāngqiú 相求 to ask for a favor; to beg; to entreat

xiāngqù wújǐ 相去無幾 The difference is insignificant.

xiāngquàn 相勸 to persuade; to offer advice

xiāngróng 相容 (computer) compatible

xiāngshí 相識 1. to know each other 2. an acquaintance

xiāngshì 相識 refer to **xiāngshí** 相識

xiāngsī 相思 to miss each other

xiāngsībìng 相思病 lovesickness

xiāngsì 相似 alike; similar

xiāngtí bìnglùn 相提並論 to mention (two things or persons of different worth) in the same breath

xiāngtóng 相同 1. the same 2. similar

xiāngxiàng 相像 to resemble; to be similar

xiāngxìn 相信 to believe; to have faith in

xiāngxíng jiànchù 相形見絀 to be outshone

xiāngxíng zhīxià 相形之下 in comparison with

xiāngyī wéimìng 相依為命 to rely upon each other for life

xiāngyìng bùlǐ 相應不理 to disregard another's request

xiāngyìng chéngqù 相映成趣 to form an interesting or delightful contrast

xiāngyù 相遇 to meet each other

xiāngyuē 相約 to make an appointment

xiāngzèng 相贈 to present a gift; to give a present

xiāngzhī 相知 1. bosom friends;

great friends 2. to know each other well

xiāngzhù 相助 to help; to help each other

xiāngzhuàng 相撞 to collide with each other

xiāngzuǒ 相左 to disagree; to differ; to conflict with each other

Xiāng 湘

1. name of a river flowing through Hunan 2. an alternative name of Hunan

Xiāngjiāng 湘江 the Xiang River, flowing through Hunan

Xiāngxiù 湘繡 Hunan-style embroideries

xiāng 廂

1. a side room 2. a box in the theater 3. the vicinity or outskirts of a city

xiāngfáng 廂房 a side room

xiāng 鄉

1. a village; the country, as contrasted with a city or town 2. rural 3. a small administrative unit comprising several villages 4. one's native place or birthplace; one's village

xiāngbalǎo 鄉巴佬 a country bumpkin; a hillbilly; an unsophisticated villager

xiāngchóu 鄉愁 homesickness; nostalgia

xiāngcūn 鄉村 a village; a country; a rural area

xiāngcūn yīnyuè 鄉村音樂 country music

xiānggōngsuǒ 鄉公所 a public office in charge of the administration of a group of villages

xiāngjiān 鄉間 in the countryside; in the rural area

xiānglǐ 鄉里 1. the village where one resides or grew up 2. people from the same hometown

xiāngmín 鄉民 villagers; countryfolk

xiāngqīn 鄉親 1. people hailing from the same area 2. local people; villagers

xiāngtǔ 鄉土 1. one's hometown

or native place 2. local geography and history

xiāngxia 鄉下 countryside; a rural area

xiāngxiarén 鄉下人 villagers; rustics; countryfolk; the country people

xiāngyě 鄉野 rural; pastoral

xiāngyīn 鄉音 one's native accent; a local accent

xiāngyuàn 鄉愿 a hypocrite or an impostor in the countryside

xiāngzhèn 鄉鎮 a small town which is essentially a rural village

xiāng 箱

1. a box; a chest; a trunk 2. the box or body of a carriage

xiānglóng 箱籠 refer to **xiānglóng** 箱籠

xiānglóng 箱籠 boxes; chests; trunks

xiāng 襄

1. to help; to assist 2. to achieve; to accomplish; to complete 3. to rise; to raise 4. high 5. to remove

xiānglǐ 襄理 an assistant manager (of a bank)

xiāngzhù 襄助 to help; to assist

xiāng 鑲

1. to fill in (a tooth, etc.); to mount; to inlay; to set (jewels, etc.) 2. to edge; to border; to hem

xiāngbiān 鑲邊 to edge or hem

xiāngyá 鑲牙 to fill in an artificial tooth; to crown a tooth

xiáng 降

1. to surrender; to submit to 2. to conquer

xiángfú 降服 1. to surrender and give allegiance to the new master 2. to bring to terms; to subdue

xiánglóng fúhǔ 降龍伏虎 to overcome powerful adversaries

xiángqí 降旗 the white flag signifying surrender

xiáng 祥

auspicious; propitious; favorable

X

xiángruì 祥瑞 a good (or an auspicious) omen

xiáng 翔
1. to soar 2. (詳) detailed

xiáng 詳
1. complete; detailed; details 2. to know the details 3. please see... for details 4. to explain; to interpret

xiángjiě 詳解 to explain in detail

xiángjìn 詳盡 detailed and complete

xiánglüè 詳略 detailed or brief

xiángmì 詳密 detailed and comprehensive

xiángqíng 詳情 details of an event, etc.

xiángshù 詳述 to narrate in complete detail

xiángtán 詳談 to speak in detail

xiángxì 詳細 in every detail and particular

xiǎng 享
1. to enjoy; to receive 2. to offer 3. to entertain

xiǎngfú 享福 to enjoy happiness and prosperity

xiǎnglè 享樂 to seek pleasure; to make merry

xiǎngnián 享年 the number of years lived (by one who dies old)

xiǎngshòu 享受 to enjoy; to indulge oneself in

xiǎngyòng 享用 to enjoy the use of

xiǎngyǒu 享有 to possess; to have in possession

xiǎng 想
1. to think; to consider; to suppose 2. to hope; to expect 3. to plan 4. to remember with longing; to miss 5. to want; would like to

xiǎngbì 想必 presumably; probably

xiǎngbudào 想不到 to one's surprise; unexpectedly

xiǎngbukāi 想不開 to take some misfortune too seriously

xiǎngbutōng 想不通 can't figure it out

xiǎngdào 想到 to think of; to remember

xiǎngfázi 想法子 to devise means; to think of a scheme

xiǎngfa 想法 an idea; an opinion; a view

xiǎngjiā 想家 homesick; nostalgic

xiǎngjiàn 想見 to infer; to gather

xiǎngniàn 想念 to miss (something or someone)

xiǎngrù fēifēi 想入非非 to indulge in wishful thinking

xiǎngtōng 想通 to straighten out one's thinking

xiǎngxiàng 想像 to imagine; to fancy

xiǎngxiànglì 想像力 imagination

xiǎng 餉
1. pay, provisions, rations, etc. for the military or the police 2. to entertain with food; to feast; to present food as a gift

xiǎng 饗
1. to dine and wine guests; to give a big party or a banquet 2. a sacrificial ceremony

xiǎngyàn 饗宴 a feast

xiǎng 響
1. a report; a sound; an echo 2. (said of sound) loud or high 3. to make a sound; to ring

xiǎngliàng 響亮 1. sonorous; loud and clear; stentorian 2. straightforward

xiǎngwěishé 響尾蛇 the sidewinder; the rattlesnake

xiǎngyìng 響應 to echo in support; to respond favorably; to rise in support

xiàng 向
1. to turn; to face 2. a direction; a trend 3. until now 4. a Chinese family name

xiàngbì xūzào 向壁虛造 to fabricate

xiàngguāngxìng 向光性 (biol-

ogy) phototropism

xiànghòu 向後 1. in the future 2. to turn around

xiànglái 向來 hitherto; heretofore; until now

xiàngliàng 向量 vector

xiàngrìkuí 向日葵 the sunflower

xiàngshàng 向上 1. to turn upward 2. to strive upward

xiàngwài 向外 1. to turn outside 2. upwards of, or more (used after a number)

xiàngxīnlì 向心力 centripetal force

xiàngxué 向學 to determine or to be inclined to study

xiàng 相

1. to examine; to study; to read 2. a countenance; facial features 3. the prime minister (in feudal times) 4. to assist; to help

xiàngcè 相冊 a photo album

xiàngjī 相機 a camera

xiàngjī xíngshì 相機行事 to act as circumstances dictate

xiàngmào 相貌 a countenance; a physiognomy; a face; facial features

xiàngmào tángtáng 相貌堂堂 to have a dignified appearance

xiàngpiàn 相片 a photograph; a photo

xiàngqīn 相親 an interview prior to marriage

xiàngsheng 相聲 a Chinese comic dialogue; a cross talk

xiàngshì 相士 1. a fortuneteller 2. to appraise a person's latent ability

xiàngzhǐ 相紙 (photography) printing paper; photographic paper

xiàng 巷

a lane; an alley

xiàngdào 巷道 a lane; an alley

xiàngkǒu 巷口 an entrance to a lane

xiàngyì 巷議 local rumors or gossips

xiàngzi 巷子 a lane; an alley

xiàng 象

1. an elephant 2. a portrait; an image snapshot 3. a phenomenon; the outward appearance or expression of anything—especially weather, heavenly bodies, etc.; shape; an image 4. ivory

xiàngqí 象棋 Chinese chess

xiàngyá 象牙 ivory; elephant tusks

xiàngyámù 象牙木 ivorywood

xiàngyátǎ 象牙塔 the ivory tower

xiàngzhēng 象徵 1. to symbolize 2. a symbol

xiàng 項

1. the back of the neck; the nape 2. the back of a cap or crown 3. an item; an article; a matter; a kind; a class 4. funds; a sum of money 5. (mathematics) a term

xiàngliàn 項鍊 a necklace

xiàngmù 項目 an item; an article (in an agreement, etc.)

xiàng 像

1. an image; a portrait 2. to resemble; resemblance 3. like; as

xiàngshì 像是 to look like; to seem

xiàngyàng 像樣 presentable; decent

xiàng 橡

an acorn

xiàngjiāo 橡膠 rubber

xiàngjiāoshù 橡膠樹 a rubber tree

xiàngpí 橡皮 1. an eraser 2. rubber

xiàngpíjīn 橡皮筋 a rubber band

xiàngshù 橡樹 an oak

xiàng 嚮

1. to guide; to direct; to lead 2. to lean toward; to be inclined toward

xiàngbì xūzào 嚮壁虛造 to fabricate out of nothing

xiàngdǎo 嚮導 a guide

xiàngwǎng 嚮往 to aspire; to

X

long

xiāo 枵

empty

xiāofù cōnggōng 枵腹從公 to do one's duty even with an empty stomach

xiāo 消

1. to vanish; to disappear; to die out 2. to disperse; to eliminate; to remove; to alleviate; to allay; to extinguish; to quench 3. to need; to take

xiāochén 消沈 depressed; dejected; low-spirited

xiāochóu jiěmèn 消愁解悶 to quench sorrow and dissipate worry

xiāochú 消除 to eliminate; to get rid of

xiāodú 消毒 to disinfect; to sterilize

xiāodúshuǐ 消毒水 antiseptic solution

xiāofáng 消防 fire fighting

xiāofángchē 消防車 a fire engine

xiāofángduì 消防隊 a fire brigade

xiāofáng duìyuán 消防隊員 a fire fighter; a fireman

xiāofángshuān 消防栓 a fireplug; a hydrant

xiāofèi 消費 consumption; to consume

xiāofèi hézuòshè 消費合作社 a consumers' cooperative

xiāofèipǐn 消費品 consumer goods

xiāofèizhě 消費者 a consumer

xiāohào 消耗 to consume (or expend)

xiāohàozhàn 消耗戰 a war of attrition

xiāohuà 消化 1. to digest (food); digestion 2. to absorb mentally

xiāohuà bùliáng 消化不良 indigestion; dyspepsia

xiāohuà qìguān 消化器官 the digestive organs

xiāohuà xìtǒng 消化系統 the digestive apparatus

xiāohún 消魂 to be held spellbound (by a beautiful woman)

xiāojí 消極 negative; pessimistic; passive

xiāojiǎn 消減 to decrease; to lessen; to diminish

xiāomǐ 消弭 to put an end to; to terminate; to bring to an end

xiāomiè 消滅 1. to annihilate 2. to die out

xiāomó 消磨 to while away (time)

xiāoqì 消氣 to allay one's anger

xiāoqiǎn 消遣 pastimes; diversions; recreation

xiāoróng 消融 to melt

xiāosàn 消散 to scatter and disappear

xiāoshī 消失 to vanish; to disappear

xiāoshì 消逝 to die away; to vanish

xiāoshòu 消受 1. to endure 2. to enjoy

xiāoshòu 消瘦 skinny; emaciated; wasted

xiāoshǔ 消暑 to relieve summer heat

xiāoshǔ zhǐkě 消暑止渴 (said of a drink) to relieve summer heat and quench thirst

xiāoxi 消息 news; tidings; information

xiāoxi língtōng 消息靈通 well-informed

xiāoyán 消炎 to eliminate inflammation

xiāoyánpiàn 消炎片 sulfaguanidine tablets

xiāoyè 消夜 a midnight snack

xiāoyīnqì 消音器 a silencer; a muffler

xiāozāi 消災 to prevent calamities

xiāozhǎng 消長 rise and fall; vicissitudes

xiāozhǒng 消腫 to remove or reduce a swelling

xiāo 宵

night; dark; evening

xiāojìn 宵禁 a curfew

xiāoxiǎo 宵小 thieves; evildoers

xiāoyè 宵夜 a snack before going to bed

xiāoyī gànshí 宵衣旰食 diligent in discharging official duties

xiāo 哮
1. to wheeze; to gasp; to breathe with difficulty 2. (also **xiào**) a roar; a howl

xiāochuǎn 哮喘 1. asthma 2. to wheeze

xiāo 梟
1. an owl; a legendary bird said to eat its own mother 2. a smuggler of contraband, narcotics, etc. 3. brave and unscrupulous

xiāoxióng 梟雄 an unscrupulous, brave and capable person

xiāo 逍
1. to wander in a leisurely manner; to saunter; to loiter 2. free and unfettered; to be leisurely and carefree

xiāoyáo 逍遙 to loiter about; to saunter about

xiāoyáo fǎwài 逍遙法外 to remain out of the law's reach; to get off scot-free

xiāo 霄
1. the sky 2. night 3. to exhaust; to dissolve 4. clouds or mist

xiāorǎng 霄壤 heaven and earth

xiāo 銷
1. to melt 2. to be marketed; to be circulated; to sell 3. (消) to vanish; to dispel; to cancel 4. pig iron; crude iron

xiāohuǐ 銷毀 to destroy

xiāohún 銷魂 enraptured; transported; carried away

xiāojià 銷假 to begin work anew after a leave of absence or vacation

xiāojià 銷價 the (retail) price of a commodity)

xiāolù 銷路 a sale; a market

xiāoshēng nìjī 銷聲匿跡 to vanish without leaving any trace behind; to go into hiding

xiāoshòuliàng 銷售量 sales volume

xiāo 蕭
1. a common variety of artemisia; oxtail-southernwood 2. reverent; respectful 3. quiet; lonely; desolate 4. a Chinese family name

xiāorán 蕭然 1. desolate; deserted 2. in commotion; disorderly

xiāosǎ 蕭灑 elegant; stately and easy (in one's appearance and manner)

xiāosà 蕭颯 cool and soothing winds of autumn

xiāosè 蕭瑟 1. chilly, desolate, deserted, lonely, etc. 2. to rustle; to sough

xiāotiáo 蕭條 1. (said of a place or situation) deserted; desolate 2. (said of business) sluggish; depressed; slack

xiāo 簫
a vertical flute of bamboo

xiāo 瀟
1. the sound of beating rain and whistling wind; the roar of a strong wind 2. name of a stream in Hunan

xiāosǎ 瀟灑 (usually said of a man's manner) dashing and refined

xiāoxiāo 瀟瀟 a whistling wind and rushing rain

xiāo 囂
1. noise; clamor; hubbub 2. to be haughty or proud

xiāozhāng 囂張 haughty; rampant; arrogant; aggressive

xiāo 驍
1. having courage and agility; brave; valiant 2. a fine horse

xiāoxióng 驍雄 capable and ambitious

xiáo 淆 also **yáo**
confuse; mix

xiáoluàn shìtīng 淆亂視聽 to confuse and muddle the truth

xiáozá 淆雜 mixed; miscellaneous

xiáo 殽 also **yáo**
confusion; disorder; mess

xiáoluàn 殽亂 messy; disorderly; confused

xiáo 學
refer to **xué** 學

xiǎo 小
1. small; little; tiny 2. minor 3. young; junior 4. humble; mean 5. slight; unimportant; trivial

xiǎobáiliǎn 小白臉 a handsome young man with effeminate features

xiǎobān 小班 1. the lowest of the three grades of kindergarten children 2. a first-rate brothel (in Beijing)

xiǎoběn jīngyíng 小本經營 (business) to run or operate with a small capital

xiǎobiàn 小便 1. to urinate; to make water 2. urine; urination

xiǎobiāotí 小標題 a subheading; a subhead

xiǎobiēsān 小瘪三 (dialect) a bum; a trash

xiǎobùfèn 小部份 a small part; the minority

xiǎobudiǎnr 小不點兒 a very small or tiny thing or person

xiǎocài 小菜 a plain dish (as distinct from expensive courses)

xiǎocèzi 小冊子 a pamphlet or brochure

xiǎochǎn 小產 a miscarriage

xiǎocháng 小腸 the small intestine

xiǎochī 小吃 a snack

xiǎochīguǎn 小吃館 a small restaurant; an eatery

xiǎochǒu 小丑 a clown

xiǎochǒu tiàoliáng 小醜跳梁 petty thieves going on the rampage

xiǎocōngming 小聰明 clever or smart in a small way

xiǎodàn 小旦 (Chinese opera) a female role

xiǎodāo 小刀 1. a small sword 2. a pocket knife

xiǎodǎo 小島 an islet

xiǎodào xiāoxi 小道消息 hearsay; the grapevine

xiǎodì 小弟 1. a little brother 2. a little boy 3. a young male servant

xiǎodiàn 小店 1. an inn; a lodging house 2. a small store 3. my or our store (a self-depreciatory term)

xiǎodiànyǐng 小電影 (slang) a porno film

xiǎodiào 小調 a folk song; a ballad

xiǎodòngzuò 小動作 petty action; little tricks

xiǎo'érkē 小兒科 1. pediatrics 2. (slang) parsimonious

xiǎo'ér mábì zhèng 小兒麻痺症 poliomyelitis; polio

xiǎo'érduo 小耳朵 1. (slang) DBS, Direct Broadcasting Satellite 2. a spy

xiǎo'èr 小二 (formerly) a waiter at a tavern

xiǎofàn 小販 a stall holder; a peddler

xiǎofèi 小費 a tip (given to a waiter, porter, etc.)

xiǎofù 小腹 the lower abdomen

xiǎogèzi 小個子 a little chap; a small fellow

xiǎogǒu 小狗 a young dog; a puppy

xiǎogū 小姑 one's husband's younger sister

xiǎogū dúchǔ 小姑獨處 to remain a spinster

xiǎogūniang 小姑娘 a missy; a young girl

xiǎoguǐ 小鬼 1. the spirits serving the ruler of the lower world 2. an imp; a mischievous child

xiǎoguò 小過 1. a minor mistake 2. a minor demerit

xiǎoháir 小孩兒 a child

xiǎohào 小號 1. small size (as distinct from medium and large sizes) 2. to urinate

xiǎohé 小河 a rivulet

xiǎohù rénjiā 小戶人家 a poor, humble family

xiǎohuāyàng 小花樣 a little

stunt

xiǎohuǒzi 小夥子 a young fellow

xiǎojī 小雞 a chick

xiǎojiā bìyù 小家碧玉 a daughter of a humble family

xiǎojiātíng 小家庭 a small family

xiǎojiě 小解 1. to urinate; to make water 2. urine; urination

xiǎojie 小姐 a young (unmarried) lady

xiǎojiùzi 小舅子 a brother-in-law (one's wife's younger brother)

xiǎokāi 小開 a businessman's son

xiǎokàn 小看 to think little of; to slight

xiǎokāng 小康 1. (said of a family) well-to-do 2. (said of a nation) fairly prosperous and secure

xiǎokǎo 小考 a quiz or test conducted for students by the teacher

xiǎolǎba 小喇叭 a trumpet

xiǎolǎopo 小老婆 a concubine

xiǎolǎotóuér 小老頭兒 a man who ages prematurely

xiǎoliǎngkǒu 小兩口 a young couple

xiǎolóuluo 小嘍囉 a lackey; a underling

xiǎolù 小路 a path; a trail

xiǎomǎimai 小買賣 small business

xiǎomài 小麥 wheat

xiǎomāo 小貓 a kitten

xiǎomèi 小妹 1. a little sister 2. a little girl 3. a young female servant

xiǎomǐ 小米 millet

Xiǎoniányè 小年夜 the night before Lunar New Year's Eve

xiǎoniǎo yīrén 小鳥依人 (said of a child or young girl) lovely and pliant like a little bird

xiǎoniūér 小妞兒 a small girl; a young girl

xiǎonǚ 小女 (a self-depreciatory term) my daughter

xiǎopiányi 小便宜 a small advantage

xiǎopǐnwén 小品文 an essay

xiǎopùzi 小舖子 a small store

xiǎoqì 小器 1. narrow-minded 2. niggardly

xiǎoqìguǐ 小氣鬼 a niggard

xiǎoqiǎo línglóng 小巧玲瓏 1. (said of a woman) petite 2. (said of a decorative item) small and exquisite

xiǎoqǔ 小曲兒 a ditty

xiǎoquǎn 小犬 1. (a self-depreciatory term) my son 2. a puppy

xiǎorén 小人 a mean person

xiǎoshěn 小嬸 a sister-in-law

xiǎoshēng 小生 the young man's role (especially in Chinese opera)

xiǎoshēng 小聲 to lower one's voice; to speak low

xiǎoshí 小時 an hour

xiǎoshíhou 小時候 as a child; in childhood

xiǎoshí liǎoliǎo 小時了了 very intelligent when young

xiǎoshì 小事 a trifle; a trivial matter

xiǎoshìmín 小市民 the urban petty bourgeois

xiǎoshū 小叔 a brother-in-law

xiǎoshù 小數 a decimal fraction; a decimal

xiǎoshù 小樹 a sapling

xiǎoshùdiǎn 小數點 the decimal point

xiǎoshuō 小說 a novel; fiction

xiǎoshuōjiā 小說家 a novelist

xiǎosī 小廝 a servant (especially a mean one); a subaltern; an underling

xiǎotí dàzuò 小題大做 to make much of a trifle; a storm in a teacup

xiǎotíqín 小提琴 a violin

xiǎotǐng 小艇 a small boat; a skiff

xiǎotōu 小偷 a thief; a burglar

xiǎotuǐ 小腿 the calf (of the leg)

xiǎowáwa 小娃娃 a small child

xiǎowányìr 小玩藝兒 a small

toy or plaything

xiǎowǒ 小我 the individual; the ego; the self

xiǎoxiě 小寫 lowercase (of the Roman alphabet)

xiǎoxīn 小心 careful; cautious

xiǎoxīnyǎnr 小心眼兒 narrow-minded

xiǎoxīn yìyì 小心翼翼 very timidly; very gingerly

xiǎoxíng 小型 small-sized; miniature

xiǎoxué 小學 a primary school; an elementary school

xiǎoxuéshēng 小學生 a (primary school) pupil

xiǎoyā 小鴨 a duckling

xiǎoyātou 小丫頭 a little girl (expressing contempt or endearment)

xiǎoyáng 小羊 a lamb

xiǎoyèqǔ 小夜曲 (music) a serenade

xiǎoyízi 小姨子 a sister-in-law (one's wife's younger sister)

xiǎoyìsi 小意思 1. a trifle; a triviality 2. a small token of regard (such as a gift)

xiǎozhǐ 小指 the little finger

xiǎozhù 小住 to sojourn

xiǎozhuàn 小篆 small seal characters

xiǎozhuó 小酌 a little drink or a few drinks (of some alcoholic beverage)

xiǎozi 小子 a young fellow (usually with slight contempt)

xiǎozǔ 小組 a group formed for a specific purpose

xiǎozǔ tǎolùn 小組討論 a group discussion

xiǎo 曉

1. daybreak; dawn 2. to explain 3. to know; to understand

xiǎode 曉得 to know; to be aware of

xiǎofēng cányuè 曉風殘月 (literally) the morning breeze and the lingering moon—nature at daybreak

xiǎoyǐ dàyì 曉以大義 (to persuade someone to follow the

right path) by telling him what is right

xiǎoyù 曉諭 to explain; to tell; to give explicit instructions

xiào 孝

filial piety; of or having to do with filial piety

xiàodào 孝道 the principle of filial piety

xiàofú 孝服 mourning dress

xiàojìng 孝敬 to show filial piety and respect for one's parents

xiàoshùn 孝順 to show filial obedience or devotion for (one's parents)

xiàosī 孝思 the heart of filial piety

xiàotì 孝悌 to be a dutiful son and to be respectful to one's elder brothers

xiàoxīn 孝心 filial piety

xiàoxíng 孝行 filial conduct

xiàozǐ 孝子 1. a devoted child 2. a bereaved son

xiào 肖

to resemble; to be like; alike; similar

xiàoxiàng 肖像 a portrait

xiào 笑

1. to laugh; to smile; to grin; to giggle; to titter; to chuckle; to snicker 2. to ridicule; to deride; to jeer

xiàobǐng 笑柄 a laughingstock; a joke

xiàohua 笑話 1. a joke 2. a ridiculous error 3. Nonsense! 4. to ridicule

xiàohua bǎichū 笑話百出 to make many ridiculous mistakes

xiàokǒu chángkāi 笑口常開 grinning all the time

xiàolǐ cángdāo 笑裏藏刀 (literally) to conceal a dagger behind a smile—very treacherous

xiàoliǎn 笑臉 a smiling face

xiàoróng 笑容 a smile

xiàoróng kějū 笑容可掬 to be radiant with smiles

xiàoróng kějú 笑容可掬 refer to **xiàoróng kějú** 笑容可掬

xiàoshēng 笑聲 sound of laughter

xiàotán 笑談 1. a laughingstock 2. laughing conversation 3. to laugh over

xiàowō 笑渦 dimples appearing with a smile

xiàoyè 笑靨 dimples appearing with a smile

xiàozhú yánkāi 笑逐顏開 to beam with smiles

xiào 校

1. a school 2. field-grade (officers)

xiàochē 校車 a school bus

xiàoduì 校隊 the school team

xiàofú 校服 school uniform

xiàogē 校歌 a school song; a college song

xiàoguī 校規 school regulations

xiàohuā 校花 a campus queen; a school belle

xiàohuī 校徽 a school emblem; a badge

xiàojǐng 校警 the police guards of a school

xiàokān 校刊 a school magazine

xiàomén 校門 a gate of a school or college

xiàoqí 校旗 a school flag

xiàoqìng 校慶 anniversary celebrations of a school

xiàoshè 校舍 school premises

xiàowù 校務 school administration

xiàoxùn 校訓 a school motto

xiàoyī 校醫 a school doctor or physician

xiàoyǒu 校友 an alumnus or alumna

xiàoyù 校譽 the reputation or prestige of a school or college

xiàoyuán 校園 the school ground; the campus

xiàozhǎng 校長 a principal; a schoolmaster

xiào 哮

refer to **xiào** 哮 2

xiào 效

1. to imitate; to mimic; to follow 2. effect; effectiveness; efficacy 3. to devote 4. to offer

xiàofǎ 效法 to take as a model; to imitate

xiàoguǒ 效果 effect; result

xiàoláo 效勞 to render service; to work for

xiàolì 效力 1. effect; efficacy 2. to render service

xiàolǜ 效率 efficiency

xiàomìng 效命 1. to obey orders 2. to pursue an end at the cost of one's life

xiàonéng 效能 effect

xiàoyì 效益 beneficial result; benefit

xiàoyòng 效用 usefulness; use; utility

xiàozhōng 效忠 to be loyal to; allegiance

xiào 傚

to model after; to imitate; to copy; to emulate

xiàofǎng 傚仿 emulation

xiàoyóu 傚尤 emulation

xiào 酵

refer to **jiào** 酵

xiào 嘯

1. to whistle 2. to howl; to cry or shout in a sustained voice; to roar

xiē 些

a small quantity or number; a little; a few; some

xiēwēi 些微 1. very little 2. slightly

xiēwéi 些微 refer to **xiēwēi** 些微

xiē 楔 also **xiè**

1. to wedge 2. a gatepost 3. a wedge

xiēxíng wénzì 楔形文字 cuneiform; sphenogram

xiēzi 楔子 1. a wedge 2. a preface; a foreword; a prologue

xiē 歇

1. to rest 2. to sleep 3. to come

to an end; to stop 4. to lodge

xiēdiàn 歇店 to stay or lodge at an inn

xiēhòuyǔ 歇後語 a common expression whose last part is omitted

xiējiǎo 歇腳 to rest the feet after walking

xiēshǒu 歇手 to stop doing something

xiēsīdǐlǐ 歇斯底里 hysteria

xiēsù 歇宿 to spend the night; to stay for the night

xiētuǐ 歇腿 1. to rest one's feet after a long walk 2. to rest at a place; to stay at an inn

xiēxi 歇息 to take a rest

xiēyè 歇業 to close shop

xiē 蠍

a scorpion

xiēzi 蠍子 a scorpion

xié 邪

1. evil; depraved; wicked; mean; vicious 2. pertaining to sorcery or demonism; abnormal

xiébù shèngzhèng 邪不勝正 The evil will not triumph over the virtuous.

xié'è 邪惡 evil and wicked; debauchery

xiéjiào 邪教 paganism; heathendom

xiémén wāidào 邪門歪道 crooked ways; dishonest practices

xiéshuō 邪說 heresy; perverted views

xié 協

1. to agree; an agreement 2. to be united; to bring into harmony; to coordinate 3. to assist; to aid; to help

xiédìng 協定 an agreement

xiéhé 協和 harmony; to harmonize

xiéhuì 協會 an association; a society

xiélì 協力 to exert together

xiéshāng 協商 to negotiate; to discuss

xiétiáo 協調 to coordinate; harmony

xiétóng 協同 to work with (others); to join others in (accomplishing an undertaking, etc.)

xiéyì 協議 1. an agreement 2. to discuss

xiézhù 協助 to assist; to help mutually

xiézòuqǔ 協奏曲 (music) a concerto

xié 挾　also **xiá**

1. to clasp or hold under the arm 2. to embrace; to bosom 3. to presume upon (one's influence, advantage, etc.) 4. to extort

xiéchí 挾持 1. to grasp someone on both sides by the arms 2. to hold someone under duress

xiédài 挾帶 to carry under arms

xiéguì zìzhòng 挾貴自重 to be proud of one's high position

xié 脅

1. the sides of the trunk from armpits to ribs; the flank 2. to threaten with force; to force 3. to shrug (shoulders); to shrink

xiéchí 脅持 1. to take somebody on both sides by the arms 2. to hold somebody by violence

xiécóng 脅從 to be forced to join (rebellion, banditry, etc.)

xiépò 脅迫 to threaten with force; to coerce; coercion

xié 斜

inclined; sloping; slanting; leaning; oblique; diagonal

xiéduìmiàn 斜對面 diagonally opposite

xiémiàn 斜面 1. (mathematics) an inclined plane 2. (machinery) a bevel (face); the oblique plane

xiépō 斜坡 a slope

xiéshì 斜視 1. to look askance 2. squint

xiétǐzì 斜體字 italics

xiéxiàn 斜線 an oblique line

xiéyáng 斜陽 the setting sun

xié 偕　also **jiē**

1. to accompany 2. together

xiétóng 偕同 in company with; along with

xié 鞋

shoes; footwear

xiébázi 鞋拔子 a shoehorn; a shoe lifter

xiédài 鞋帶 a shoestring; a shoelace

xiédǐ 鞋底 the sole of a shoe

xiédiàn 鞋店 a shoe shop

xiédiàn 鞋墊 a shoepad; an insole

xiégēn 鞋跟 the heel of a shoe

xiéjiang 鞋匠 a shoemaker; a cobbler

xiémiàn 鞋面 the vamp

xiétóng 鞋童 a shoeshine boy

xiéyóu 鞋油 shoe polish

xié 諧

1. harmonious; congruous 2. to come to an agreement; to settle 3. to joke; to jest

xiéhé 諧和 harmony; harmonious; accord; agreement; concordant

xiéxīng 諧星 a comedian

xiéyīn 諧音 1. (said of characters) representing sound 2. (physics) resonance

xié 擷 also **jié**

to pick; to collect; to gather

xiéqǔ jīnghuá 擷取精華 to pick the best

xié 攜 also **xī**

1. to take; to carry 2. to help; to lead

xiédài 攜帶 to carry with oneself; to take along

xiéshǒu 攜手 1. to hold each other's hand 2. to cooperate

xié 血

refer to **xuè** 血

xié 寫

to write; to sketch; to draw; to represent

xiégǎo 寫稿 to write for (or contribute to) a magazine, etc.

xiéshēng 寫生 to draw, or paint, from nature; to sketch

xiéshí 寫實 realistic (as distinct from romantic)

xiéyì 寫意 (said of painting) to make an impressionistic portrayal

xiězhào 寫照 an image; portrayal; a description

xiézhēn 寫真 to draw or paint a portrait

xiézì 寫字 to write

xiézìlóu 寫字樓 an office

xiézuò 寫作 writing

xiè 卸

1. to get rid of; to remove 2. to unload (cargoes, etc.) 3. to resign; to retire from office

xièhuò 卸貨 to unload (or discharge) cargoes

xièrèn 卸任 to quit a public office

xièzhuāng 卸妝 to remove make-up and ornaments

xiè 泄

1. to leak out; to reveal 2. to vent 3. to scatter; to disperse

xiè 洩 (泄)

to drain; to vent; to let out; to dissipate; to leak out

xièdǐ 洩底 to disclose a secret

xièfèn 洩憤 to give vent to one's anger

xièhèn 洩恨 to vent one's grudge

xièhóng 洩洪 to let water flow out from the reservoir

xièlòu 洩漏 to disclose; to divulge; to reveal; to leak out

xièmì 洩密 to divulge a secret; to betray confidential matters

xièqì 洩氣 1. to lose strength, momentum, etc. 2. discouraging; disappointed 3. to give vent to one's pent-up resentment, frustration, etc.

xiè 屑

1. chips; crumbs; bits; odds and ends; trifles 2. to care; to mind

xiè 械 also **jiè**

1. weapons 2. implements; machinery; machines 3. shackles; fetters 4. to arrest and put in prison

xiè 楔

refer to **xiē** 楔

xiè 榭

a pavilion; an arbor; a kiosk

xiè 懈

negligent; remiss; relaxed; inattentive

xièdài 懈怠 to neglect; slack; negligent

xièmàn 懈慢 neglectful; negligent

xiè 謝

1. to thank 2. to decline 3. to fade; to wither

xiècí 謝詞 a thank-you speech

xiè'ēn 謝恩 to express thanks for great favors

xièhán 謝函 a letter of thanks; a thank-you note; a thank-you letter

xièjué 謝絕 to decline (an offer, etc.)

xièjué cānguān 謝絕參觀 No visitors allowed.

xièlǐ 謝禮 1. a gift sent as a token of gratitude 2. an honorarium

xièmù 謝幕 a curtain call; to bow to the audience on stage at the end of the show

xièshīyàn 謝師宴 a dinner party given by graduating students in honor of their teachers

xiètiān xièdì 謝天謝地 Thank Heaven! (or God!)

xiètiě 謝帖 a letter of thanks; a thank-you note; a thank-you letter

xièxie 謝謝 Thank you. Thanks.

xièzuì 謝罪 to apologize

xiè 邂

to meet without a prior engagement; to meet by chance

xiègòu 邂逅 refer to **xièhòu** 邂逅

xièhòu 邂逅 to meet by chance; to meet accidentally; to meet (a relative, friend, etc.) unexpectedly

xiè 褻

1. underwear; clothes worn in one's bedroom or house 2. dirty;

filthy 3. intimate (sometimes denoting a degree of indecency) 4. to slight; to look down upon

xièdú 褻瀆 1. to slight; to abuse; to insult; to blaspheme; to desecrate 2. (a polite expression) to bother others with trifles, etc.

xiè 瀉

1. to drain; water flowing down 2. diarrhea; to have loose bowels

xièchū 瀉出 to leak out; to spurt out

xièdùzi 瀉肚子 diarrhea

xièyào 瀉藥 laxatives; purgatives

xiè 蟹

a crab

xīn 心

1. the heart 2. the mind 3. conscience; moral nature 4. intention; idea; ambition 5. the core; the inside 6. one of the constellations

xīn'ài 心愛 (things or persons) dear to one's heart

xīn'ān lǐdé 心安理得 to feel at ease and justified

xīnbìng 心病 1. mental disorder 2. worries which one cannot share with another

xīnbù zàiyān 心不在焉 absent-minded

xīncháng 心腸 1. heart 2. affections; sympathies 3. conscience 4. a natural bent of the mind

xīndǎn jùliè 心膽俱裂 to be terror-stricken

xīndàng shénchí 心蕩神馳 to be infatuated (with a stunning beauty, etc.); rapt

xīndé 心得 what one gains from intense study, meditation or long practice

xīndì 心地 conscience; intentions

xīndì guāngmíng 心地光明 clear conscience; upright

xīndì shànliáng 心地善良 good-natured; kind-hearted

xīndiàn gǎnyìng 心電感應 telepathy

xīndiàntú 心電圖 an electrocardiogram

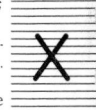

xīndòng 心動 1. palpitation or fluttering of the heart 2. to become interested in something

xīndú shǒulà 心毒手辣 callous and cruel; cold-blooded

xīnfán 心煩 piqued; annoyed; fretful

xīnfán yìluàn 心煩意亂 fretful and confused

xīnfáng 心房 1. (anatomy) auricles 2. soul; mind

xīnfēi 心扉 (figuratively) the door of one's heart

xīnfú kǒufú 心服口服 to admit somebody's superiority, etc. with sincerity

xīnfú qìzào 心浮氣躁 to be unsettled and short-tempered

xīnfù 心腹 1. loyalty 2. a region of great strategic importance 3. a confidant

xīnfù zhīhuàn 心腹之患 the threat from within

xīn'gān 心肝 1. a darling; a honey; a sweetheart 2. conscience

xīn'gān qíngyuàn 心甘情願 to be totally willing; willingly

xīn'gāo qì'ào 心高氣傲 proud and arrogant

xīnguǎng tǐpán 心廣體胖 A clear conscience contributes to physical well-being.

xīnhěn 心狠 hardhearted; flinty; heartless

xīnhuā nùfàng 心花怒放 to be brimming with joy

xīnhuái 心懷 to cherish; to harbor

xīnhuāng 心慌 to be greatly shaken and perturbed; panicky

xīnhuāng yìluàn 心慌意亂 to lose one's wits totally

xīnhuī yìlěng 心灰意冷 to feel discouraged and hopeless

xīnjì 心跡 real intentions

xīnjī 心機 schemes; designs; craftiness

xīnjí 心急 impatient

xīnjì 心悸 palpitation of the heart

xīnjiāo 心焦 anxious; worried; vexed

xīnjīng dǎnzhàn 心驚膽戰 shuddering and terrified; to tremble with fear

xīnjīng ròutiào 心驚肉跳 trembling with fear trepidation

xīnjìng 心境 a mood; a humor

xīnjìng 心靜 calm

xīnkǎn 心坎 1. the heart's chord 2. bosom 3. the center of the heart

xīnkǒu 心口 1. the bosom 2. one's utterance and what he really thinks

xīnkǒu rúyī 心口如一 to speak one's mind frankly

xīnkuàng shényí 心曠神怡 to feel way above par; to feel on top of the world

xīnlǐ 心理 1. mentality; psychology 2. thought and ideas 3. mental

xīnlǐ cèyàn 心理測驗 a mental test

xīnlǐ fǔdǎo 心理輔導 psychological counseling

xīnlǐ jiànshè 心理建設 mental readjustment

xīnlǐxué 心理學 psychology

xīnlǐ zuòyòng 心理作用 mental reaction

xīnlì jiāocuì 心力交瘁 to feel exhausted both mentally and physically

xīnlǐ yǒushù 心裡有數 aware of something without speaking out

xīnliánxīn 心連心 heart linked to heart

xīnlíng 心靈 mind; spirit; spiritual

xīnlǐng 心領 1. to understand without verbal exchange 2. to appreciate

xīnlǐng shénhuì 心領神會 to know or understand without being told

xīnluàn rúmá 心亂如麻 extremely confused and disturbed

xīnmǎn yìzú 心滿意足 to be fully contented; complacent

xīnmùzhōng 心目中 1. in one's heart or mind 2. in one's mem-

ory

xīnpíng qìhé 心平氣和 1. calmly 2. to be very fair, without involving one's personal feelings

xīnqíng 心情 a mood; a humor

xīnrú dāogē 心如刀割 heartbroken

xīnrú zhǐshuǐ 心如止水 a mind without worries, cares, ambitions or worldly desires

xīnruǎn 心軟 soft-hearted; tender-hearted

xīnshangrén 心上人 a sweetheart; a lover

xīnshén bùdìng 心神不定 a confused state of mind

xīnshēng 心聲 1. spoken language 2. the heart's desire; intentions

xīnshì 心室 ventricles

xīnshì 心事 something weighing on one's mind; a load on one's mind; worry

xīnshù 心術 designs; schemes; intentions

xīnsi 心思 1. ideas 2. intentions 3. a mood

xīnsuān 心酸 heartsore; grief-stricken; to sadden

xīnsuàn 心算 mental arithmetic

xīnsuì 心碎 heartbreak; heartbroken

xīntài 心態 mentality

xīnténg 心疼 1. (literally) heartache 2. to love dearly

xīntián 心田 1. one's heart 2. one's disposition

xīntiào 心跳 1. heartbeat 2. palpitation of the heart caused by fear

xīntòng 心痛 to feel the pangs of heart

xīntóu 心頭 1. the heart; the mind 2. the heart of an animal

xīnwōr 心窩兒 1. in one's heart 2. the region between the ribs

xīnwú pángwù 心無旁鶩 single-minded

xīnxì 心細 cautious; careful(ness)

xīnxián 心弦 the heart's chord

xīnxiě 心血 refer to **xīnxuè** 心血

xīnxiě láicháo 心血來潮 refer to **xīnxuè láicháo** 心血來潮

xīnxīn xiāngyìn 心心相印 a complete meeting of minds

xīnxìng 心性 temperament; tempers

xīnxiōng 心胸 1. will; ambition 2. capacity for tolerance

xīnxū 心虛 a guilty conscience

xīnxù 心緒 a mood; the state of mind

xīnxuán liǎngdì 心懸兩地 divided attention; to have worries at two places at the same time

xīnxuè 心血 energy; painstaking care

xīnxuè láicháo 心血來潮 to hit upon a sudden idea

xīnyǎnr 心眼兒 1. one's intention; conscience 2. mind 3. cleverness or wits

xīnyí 心儀 to look upon someone as a model due to admiration

xīnyì 心意 1. ideas; intentions; opinions 2. regard

xīn yǒuyú ér lì bùzú 心有餘而力不足 resources or ability at one's command inadequate to achieve what is desired, or to do what one wishes

xīnyǒu yújì 心有餘悸 one's heart still fluttering with fear

xīnyuán yìmǎ 心猿意馬 cannot make up one's mind; indecision

xīnyuàn 心願 1. a wish aspiration 2. a promise to a god

xīnyuè chéngfú 心悅誠服 to concede or submit willingly

xīnzàng 心臟 the heart (as an organ)

xīnzàngbìng 心臟病 heart disease

xīnzhào bùxuān 心照不宣 a tacit understanding or agreement

xīnzhí kǒukuài 心直口快 honest and outspoken

xīnzhì 心智 mentality

xīnzhōng 心中 in one's heart or mind

xīnzhōng yǒushù 心中有數

to know fairly well

xīnzuì 心醉 1. to admire without reserve 2. to be captivated or held spellbound

xīn 辛

1. the eighth of the Ten Celestial Stems 2. bitter; acrid 3. hard; toilsome; laborious

Xīnhài Gémìng 辛亥革命 the Revolution of 1911 (the year of **xīnhài** 辛亥), which led to the overthrow of the Qing Dynasty

xīnkǔ 辛苦 1. laborious; toilsome 2. to work hard; to go through hardships

xīnlà 辛辣 pungent; hot; bitter; acrid and peppery

xīnláo 辛勞 pains; toil

xīnqín 辛勤 hardworking; industrious; diligent

xīnsuān 辛酸 sad; bitter; miserable

xīn 芯

pith of rushes

xīnpiàn 芯片 (computer) chip

xīn 欣

glad; gladly; joyful; joyfully; delighted; happy

xīnféng 欣逢 happy to be present (on a joyful occasion)

xīnrán 欣然 gladly; with pleasure

xīnshǎng 欣賞 to appreciate, enjoy or admire

xīnwèi 欣慰 comforted; contented; satisfaction

xīnxī 欣悉 delighted to learn; to have happily learned that

xīnxǐ 欣喜 joyful; happy; delight

xīnxǐ ruòkuáng 欣喜若狂 to be beside oneself with joy

xīnxiàn 欣羨 to admire or envy

xīnxīn xiàngróng 欣欣向榮 1. (said of flowers in spring) blossoming 2. (said of business, financial situations, etc.) flourishing; thriving; prospering

xīn 莘

refer to **shēn** 莘

xīn 歆

1. (said of gods, etc.) to accept offerings, etc. 2. to admire; to submit to willingly; to envy 3. to move; to touch 4. to inhale; to smell 5. sacrificial food

xīnxiàn 歆羨 to admire; to envy (another's beauty or luck)

xīn 新

1. new; fresh; novel 2. modern; recent 3. beginning; starting 4. the prefix "neo"

xīnbǎn 新版 the new edition (of a book)

xīnbiān 新編 1. a new version 2. newly organized

xīnbīng 新兵 recruits

xīnchén dàixiè 新陳代謝 1. (biology) metabolism 2. the new superseding the old

xīnchuàng 新創 newly devised; newly started; newly founded

xīnchūn 新春 1. the early spring 2. the Lunar New Year

xīnfáng 新房 1. a bridal chamber 2. a new house

xīnhūn 新婚 newly married

xīnhūn fūfù 新婚夫婦 newlyweds

xīnjìyuán 新紀元 a new era

Xīnjiāpō 新加坡 Singapore

xīnjìn 新近 recently; newly; lately

xīnjìn rényuán 新進人員 1. new employees of an organization 2. a novice

xīnjiù jiāotì 新舊交替 the transition from the old to the new

xīnjū 新居 a new residence

xīnláng 新郎 a bridegroom

xīnlì 新曆 the solar calendar; the Gregorian calendar

xīnmíngcí 新名詞 new terms; new terminology

xīnnián 新年 New Year

xīnniáng 新娘 a bride

xīnqí 新奇 novel; new

xīnqìxiàng 新氣象 a prevailing new atmosphere

xīnrén 新人 1. new employees 2. a bride 3. a new love 4. a man with modern thoughts

xīnrèn 新任 newly appointed

xīnshēng 新生 1. newborn 2. a new student 3. a new life; rebirth

xīnshēngdì 新生地 reclaimed land; tidal land

xīnshì 新式 of a new style; modern

xīnshǒu 新手 a new hand (at a job); a greenhorn; a novice

Xīntáibì 新臺幣 New Taiwan Dollar (NT$)

xīnwén 新聞 news

xīnwén guǎngbō 新聞廣播 a news broadcast; a newscast

xīnwén jìzhě 新聞記者 a journalist; a reporter; a correspondent

xīnwénjiè 新聞界 the circle of journalists; the press circle

xīnwén méitǐ 新聞媒體 news media

xīnwén rénwù 新聞人物 people in the news

xīnwén zìyóu 新聞自由 freedom of the press

xīnxiān 新鮮 1. fresh 2. new; original; novel

xīnxīng 新興 newly risen; burgeoning

xīnxiù 新秀 a person who has begun to distinguish himself in a given field

Xīn Yīnggélán 新英格蘭 New England

xīnyíng 新穎 novel; new; original

Xīnyuē Quánshū 新約全書 the New Testament

xīnyuè 新月 1. (astronomy) a new moon 2. a crescent

Xīnzhú 新竹 a city in Taiwan

xīnzhuāng 新裝 1. a new dress 2. newly installed

xīn 鋅 zinc

xīnbǎn 鋅版 zincotype; zincograph

xīn 薪 1. firewood; fuel; fagots 2. salary; pay

xīnfèng 薪俸 salary; pay

xīnshuǐ 薪水 salary; pay; wages

xīn 馨 also **xīng** fragrance or aroma (especially that which comes from afar)

xīn 鑫 a word of no definite meaning, used only in names, with a connotation of prosperity or good profit

xín 尋 to beg; to entreat

xínqián 尋錢 to beg for money

xìn 芯 the central part of an object

xìn 信 1. honesty; truthfulness; faith; confidence; trust 2. believing; true 3. to believe or trust 4. an envoy; an emissary; a messenger 5. news; a message; information; word 6. a letter

xìnbǐ 信筆 to write freely or aimlessly

xìnbù 信步 to wander; to stroll aimlessly

xìnchā 信插 a mail rack

xìnchāi 信差 a mailman; a postman

xìnfēng 信封 an envelope

xìnfēng 信風 trade wind; seasonal wind

xìnfèng 信奉 to believe in (a religion, etc.)

xìnfú 信服 to believe in; to trust

xìn'gē 信鴿 a carrier pigeon

xìnhào 信號 a signal (with flags, lamps, etc.)

xìnhàodēng 信號燈 a semaphore; a signal lamp

xìnhuì 信匯 mail transfer (M/T)

xìnjiān 信箋 letter papers

xìnjiàn 信件 mail or letters (collectively)

xìnjiào 信教 to believe in a religion

xìnkǒu cíhuáng 信口雌黃 to criticize wildly

xìnkǒu húshuō 信口胡說 to talk nonsense

xìnkǒu kāihé 信口開河 to talk at random; to brag

xìnlài 信賴 1. trust 2. to trust

xìnniàn 信念 a belief; a conviction

xìnrèn 信任 1. to trust; to have faith in 2. trust

xìnrèn tóupiào 信任投票 a vote of confidence

xìnshǎng bìfá 信賞必罰 to give rewards or punishments strictly and impartially

xìnshǒu 信守 to abide by; to keep (a promise)

xìnshǒu niānlái 信手拈來 to take without forethought

xìnshǒu niánlái 信手拈來 refer to **xìnshǒu niānlái** 信手拈來

xìntiáo 信條 a creed or code; a dogma

xìntú 信徒 a believer (of a religion, etc.)

xìntuō 信託 1. trust 2. to trust

xìntuō gōngsī 信託公司 a trust company

xìnxī 信息 news; information; a message

xìnxī gāosù gōnglù 信息高速公路 information highway

xìnxí 信息 refer to **xìnxī** 信息

xìnxiāng 信箱 a postbox; a letter box

xìnxīn 信心 faith; confidence

xìnyǎng 信仰 belief; to believe in

xìnyì 信義 good faith; faith

xìnyòng 信用 credit

xìnyòng hézuòshè 信用合作社 a credit cooperative

xìnyòngkǎ 信用卡 a credit card

xìnyòngzhuàng 信用狀 a letter of credit

xìnyù 信譽 credit and reputation

xìnzhǐ 信紙 letter paper

xìn 釁
1. to anoint (drums, bells, etc.) with blood in worship 2. to anoint (the body) 3. a rift (between people)

xìnduān 釁端 the cause of a fight

xīng 星
1. any heavenly body that shines; stars, planets, satellites, etc. 2. a spark or sparks 3. droplets; small particles of anything; very tiny 4. name of one of the constellations 5. a movie star 6. by night; nocturnal

xīngchén 星辰 stars; heavenly bodies

xīngdǒu 星斗 stars; heavenly bodies

xīngguāng 星光 starlight

xīngguāng cànlàn 星光燦爛 a star-studded gathering

xīnghào 星號 an asterisk (☆)

Xīnghé 星河 (astronomy) the Milky Way

xīngjì 星際 interplanetary; interstellar

xīngluó qíbù 星羅棋布 numerous and arrayed like stars in heaven or pieces on a chessboard (usually said of archipelagos, etc.)

xīngqī 星期 week

xīngqí 星期 refer to **xīngqī** 星期

xīngqiú 星球 planets; stars

xīngsàn 星散 to scatter and spread like stars

xīngsù 星宿 a person who is considered an incarnation of a star

xīngtuán 星團 (astronomy) a constellation

xīngxì 星系 (astronomy) a galaxy

xīngxiàngxué 星象學 astrometry

xīngxīng 星星 tiny spots

xīngxīng zhīhuǒ, kěyǐ liáoyuán 星星之火，可以燎原 Small things may cause big trouble.

xīngxīng zhīhuǒ, kěyǐ liáoyuán 星星之火，可以燎原 refer to **xīngxīng zhīhuǒ, kěyǐ liáoyuán** 星星之火，可以燎原

xīngxíng 星形 a star-polygon

xīngxing 星星 stars, planets and

satellites

xīngxiù 星宿 planets or stars in heaven

xīngyè 星夜 1. night; a starlit night 2. (to travel, escape, etc.) by night

xīngyuè jiāohuī 星月交輝 any gathering or congregation of famous or august personalities

xīngyún 星雲 (astronomy) a nebula

xīngzuò 星座 (astronomy) a constellation

xīng 猩

1. scarlet; red 2. a yellow-haired ape

xīnghóng 猩紅 scarlet; bloodred

xīnghóngrè 猩紅熱 scarlet fever

xīngxing 猩猩 a chimpanzee; an orangutan

xīng 惺

1. clever; intelligent; wise 2. wavering; indecisive 3. (also **xíng**) to become aware of; to awake from ignorance

xīngsōng 惺忪 1. indecisive 2. (said of eyes) not yet fully open on waking up

xīngxing zuòtài 惺惺作態 to be affected; to simulate (friendship, innocence, etc.)

xīng 腥

1. raw, undressed meat 2. an offensive smell, especially of fish or blood

xīngfēng xiěyǔ 腥風血雨 refer to **xīngfēng xuèyǔ** 腥風血雨

xīngfēng xuèyǔ 腥風血雨 (literally) winds carrying an offensive smell of flesh and rain of blood—the carnage of war

xīngwèir 腥味兒 an offensive smell of fish, etc.

xīng 興

1. to rise; to thrive; to prosper; to flourish 2. to happen; to take place; to occur 3. to start; to begin; to launch; to initiate; to establish; to found; to open

xīngbàn 興辦 to set up; to initiate

xīngfèn 興奮 excited; stimulated; excitement

xīngfènjì 興奮劑 a stimulant

xīngfēng zuòlàng 興風作浪 to cause unrest

xīngjiàn 興建 to establish; to build; to construct

xīnglóng 興隆 prosperous; thriving; vigorous

xīngqǐ 興起 to gain power; to rise

xīngshèng 興盛 prosperous; thriving; vigorous

xīngshī wènzuì 興師問罪 to mobilize troops to chastise rebels

xīngshuāi 興衰 rise and fall; vicissitudes

xīngwáng 興亡 rise and fall; prosperity and adversity

xīngwàng 興旺 prosperous; thriving

xīng 馨

refer to **xīn** 馨

xíng 刑

penalty; punishment

xíngchǎng 刑場 an execution ground

xíngfǎ 刑法 criminal law; the criminal code

xíngjù 刑具 an instrument of torture

xíngqī 刑期 a term of imprisonment

xíngqī 刑期 refer to **xíngqī** 刑期

xíngqiú 刑求 to exact confession by means of torture

xíngshì 刑事 criminal; penal

xíngshìfàn 刑事犯 a criminal

xíngshì sùsòngfǎ 刑事訴訟法 the code of criminal procedure

xíng 行

1. to walk; to go on foot 2. to move; to go; to travel 3. to act; to do; to work 4. to publish 5. to be current; to prevail 6. able; capable 7. all right; O.K.; enough 8. baggage for travel 9. a road; a path 10. (also **xìng**) one's behavior or conduct

xíngchē 行車 1. the movement

xíngchéng 行程 1. a traveler's route or itinerary 2. to embark on a journey 3. a march; a journey

xíngcì 行刺 to assassinate

xíngdòng 行動 to act; to move; to make a move

xíngdòng diànhuà 行動電話 the cellular telephone

xíngdòng zìrú 行動自如 to move freely or without impairment

xínghuì 行賄 to bribe; to offer a bribe

xíngjiāng jiùmù 行將就木 dying; nearing death

xíngjìn 行進 (military) to move forward; to march

xíngjìng 行徑 1. one's conduct or behavior; actions 2. a path; a trail

xíngjūn 行軍 1. the movement of an army; a march 2. the deployment of military forces

xínglǐ 行禮 1. to salute; to bow curtsey or kowtow to show respect 2. to undergo a ceremony

xíngli 行李 baggage; luggage

xíngnáng 行囊 one's baggage and money for travel

xíngpiàn 行騙 to cheat; to deceive; to swindle

xíngqǐ 行乞 to beg; to be a beggar

xíngqiè 行竊 to steal

xíngrén 行人 pedestrians; passers-by

xíngréndào 行人道 sidewalks of a street

xíngrén túbùqū 行人徒步區 pedestrian precinct

xíngsè cōngcōng 行色匆匆 in a hurry to leave

xíngshàn 行善 to do good deeds; to do charitable work

xíngshī zǒuròu 行尸走肉 a walking corpse—an absolutely useless person

xíngshǐ 行駛 to drive (cars); to sail or steer (boats)

xíngshìlì 行事曆 a calendar

xíngshū 行書 running-style characters

xíngwéi 行為 1. behavior; conduct 2. (law) acts

xíngxiāo 行銷 to sell; to effect sales; to be on sale

xíngxīng 行星 the planets

xíngxíng 行刑 1. to execute (criminals); execution 2. to torture (prisoners)

xíngxiōng 行兇 to commit killing or murder

xíngyī 行醫 to practice medicine

xíngyǒu yúlì 行有餘力 to have extra resources

xíngyún liúshuǐ 行雲流水 (literally) moving clouds and flowing water—a natural and flowing style of writing, etc.

xíngzhèng 行政 1. government; administration of public affairs 2. the executive branch of a government

xíngzhèng jīguān 行政機關 administrative organizations

Xíngzhèngyuàn 行政院 Executive Yuan

xíngzōng 行蹤 tracks or whereabouts of a person

xíngzǒu 行走 to walk

xíng 形

1. a form; a shape 2. a complexion 3. a terrain; a contour 4. expression; to describe 5. in comparison 6. to show

xíngchéng 形成 to form; to take shape

xíngdān yǐngzhī 形單影隻 to be all alone

xínghái 形骸 one's body or skeleton

xíngjī 形跡 1. one's behavior or conduct 2. one's appearance and manner

xíngmào 形貌 a countenance

xíngróng 形容 1. to describe 2. shape; form

xíngróngcí 形容詞 an adjective

xíngróng kūgǎo 形容枯槁 a thin, bony, or emaciated appearance

xíngsè cānghuáng 形色倉皇

to look anxious and tense

xíngshì 形式 1. form 2. formality 3. style

xíngshì 形勢 1. a situation 2. a terrain or contour

xíngshìshang 形式上 nominally

xíngsì 形似 to resemble; to look like

xíngtài 形態 an appearance; a form; a state

xíngtǐ 形體 the human body which has a form or shape

xíngtóng xūshè 形同虛設 to exist in name only

xíngxiàng 形象 1. a form; an image 2. (fine arts) form as contrasted to substance

xíngxíng sèsè 形形色色 of all shapes and colors; a great variety and diversity

xíngyǐng bùlí 形影不離 (usually said of lovers and devoted couples) inseparable, like a person and his shadow

xíngyǐng xiāngdiào 形影相弔 solitary; lonely

xíngyǐng xiāngsuí 形影相隨 inseparable; very intimate

xíngzhuàng 形狀 the appearance, or shape of a thing

xíngzōng 形蹤 1. the whereabouts of a person 2. the behavior or conduct of a person

xíngzōng bùdìng 形蹤不定 to wander here and there unpredictably

xíng 型

1. an earthen mold for casting 2. a model; a pattern; a standard 3. a statute; a law 4. a style; a fashion; a type

xínghào 型號 a model; a type

xǐng 省

1. to examine (oneself, etc.); to reflect; to introspect 2. to understand; to know 3. to visit (one's seniors, etc.) 4. to test; an examination 5. memory

xǐngchá 省察 1. to examine 2. to introspect

xǐngshì 省視 to survey; to inspect

xǐngwù 省悟 to realize; awakening; realization; to awaken to (truth, etc)

xīng 惺

refer to **xīng** 惺 3

xǐng 醒

1. to recover from (drunkenness, a stupor, etc.) 2. to awake; to wake up; to be roused 3. to be clear or cool in mind

xǐngjiǔ 醒酒 to sober up from drunkenness

xǐngmù 醒目 1. to catch the eye; to attract attention; eye-catching; refreshing 2. awake; not asleep

xǐngwù 醒悟 to awake (from errors, illusions, etc.)

xǐng 擤

to blow (the nose)

xǐngbítì 擤鼻涕 to blow the nose

xíng 行

refer to **xíng** 行 10

xìng 杏

1. an apricot 2. almonds—apricot kernels 3. apricot flowers

xìnghuā 杏花 apricot blossoms

xìngliǎn shēngchūn 杏臉生春 to have a cheerful look

xìnglín 杏林 a term used in praising a good and kind physician or referring to the medical profession in general

xìngrén 杏仁 almonds; apricot kernels

xìngtán 杏壇 (in a broad sense) the teaching profession

xìngyǎn 杏眼 apricot-like eyes —a woman's large eyes

xìngyǎn táosāi 杏眼桃腮 large eyes and rosy cheeks (of a beauty)

xìng 性

1. nature; natural property; temper 2. a quality or property 3. sex

xìngbiàntài 性變態 sexual perversion

xìngbié 性別 the sex of a person —male or female

xìngbìng 性病 venereal diseases —VD

xìnggǎn 性感 sex appeal; sexy

xìnggé 性格 disposition; personality; character

xìngjí 性急 impetuous; impulsive; impatient

xìngjiāo 性交 sexual intercourse

xìngjiāoyù 性教育 sex education

xìngmìng 性命 a person's life

xìngnéng 性能 1. natural ability 2. qualities and capabilities of machinery

xìngqìguān 性器官 sexual organs; genitals

xìngqíng 性情 disposition

xìngsāorǎo 性騷擾 sexual harassment

xìngxiàng 性向 disposition

xìngxiàng cèyàn 性向測驗 aptitude test

xìngxíngwéi 性行爲 sexual behavior

xìngyù 性欲 sexual desire or urge

xìngzhí 性質 refer to **xìngzhì** 性質

xìngzhì 性質 property; characteristics; nature

xìngzi 性子 1. a temper; a disposition 2. strength; potency

xìng 姓

1. surname; one's family name 2. a clan; a family; people

xìngmíng 姓名 the full name of a person

xìngshì 姓氏 the surname; the family name

xìng 幸

1. well-being and happiness 2. fortunately; luckily; thanks to 3. to feel happy about; to favor 4. an imperial tour

xìng'ér 幸而 luckily; fortunately; thanks to

xìngfú 幸福 happiness and well-being; bliss

xìnghǎo 幸好 luckily; fortunately

xìngkuī 幸虧 luckily; fortunately

xìngmiǎn yú'nàn 幸免於難 to have luckily survived an accident or incident

xìngyùn 幸運 1. good luck 2. lucky

xìngyùn zhīshén 幸運之神 the goddess of fortune

xìngzāi lèhuò 幸災樂禍 to take pleasure in others' misfortune

xìng 倖

1. good luck; lucky; by luck or chance; fortunate 2. to dote on; to spoil

xìngcún 倖存 to survive by good luck

xìngmiǎn 倖免 to escape (punishment) by luck

xìng 悻

angry; indignant; enraged

xìngxìngrán 悻悻然 angry; huff; enraged

xìng 興

1. cheerful; happy; gay; merry 2. interest; enthusiasm

xìngchōngchōng 興沖沖 cheerful; sprightly; gay

xìnggāo cǎiliè 興高采烈 cheerful; elated; in high spirits; jubilant

xìngqù 興趣 interest

xìngzhì 興致 interest; eagerness; enthusiasm

xiōng 凶

1. evil; bad 2. famine 3. unlucky; unfortunate 4. fear; fearsome 5. very; excessive; excess

xiōngbào 凶暴 fierce and brutal

xiōngcán 凶殘 bloodthirsty; merciless

xiōngduō jíshǎo 凶多吉少 to bode ill rather than well

xiōng'è 凶惡 brutish; fearful; ferocious

xiōnghàn 凶悍 fierce and tough

xiōnghěn 凶狠 fierce and malicious

xiōngměng 凶猛 violent; ferocious

xiōngnián 凶年 a year of famine

xiōngqì 凶器 a lethal weapon

xiōngshā 凶殺 homicide; murder

xiōngshén èshà 凶神惡煞 devils; fiends

xiōngshǒu 凶手 a murderer; an assassin

xiōngxiǎn 凶險 danger; dangerous

xiōngzhái 凶宅 a haunted house

xiōngzhào 凶兆 a bad omen

xiōng 兄
1. one's elder brother 2. a term used in addressing a senior of the same generation to show respect

xiōngdì 兄弟 brothers

xiōngdì xìqiáng 兄弟鬩牆 an intramural fight

xiōngdi 兄弟 1. one's younger brother 2. a designation for juniors of the same generation among one's relatives 3. I (a modest term)

xiōngyǒu dìgōng 兄友弟恭 to show love and respect as good brothers should

xiōngzhǎng 兄長 an elder brother

xiōng 兇
1. fierce; violent; cruel; ferocious 2. truculent; inhuman

xiōngbào 兇暴 cruel and violent

xiōng'è 兇惡 evil; wicked; malignant

xiōngfàn 兇犯 a criminal; a murderer

xiōnghàn 兇悍 ferocious, truculent, savage, fierce, etc.

xiōnghěn 兇狠 ferocious, truculent, savage, fierce, etc.

xiōngměng 兇猛 fierce; ferocious

xiōngqì 兇器 the murderous weapon

xiōngshā 兇殺 murder; homicide

xiōngshǒu 兇手 the murderer; the killer

xiōngxiǎn 兇險 cruel and mean

xiōng 匈
1. the breast; the bosom; the thorax 2. to clamor

Xiōngnú 匈奴 the Huns, an ancient nationality in China

Xiōngyálì 匈牙利 Hungary

xiōng 洶
1. unquiet; restless; turbulent; tumultuous 2. noisy; uproarious; clamorous

xiōngxiōng 洶洶 tumultuous; turbulent; agitated

xiōngyǒng 洶湧 (said of water) turbulent; tumultuous

xiōng 胸
1. the chest; the breast; the bosom; the bust; the thorax 2. one's ambition or aspiration 3. the mind (as narrow-minded, etc.); one's capacity

xiōngbù 胸部 the chest

xiōnghuā 胸花 a corsage

xiōnghuái 胸懷 ambition or aspiration; mind

xiōngjīn kāikuò 胸襟開闊 broad-minded; large-minded

xiōngkǒu 胸口 the middle of the chest

xiōngtáng 胸膛 the breast or bosom; the thorax

xiōngyī 胸衣 corsets

xiōngyǒu chéngzhú 胸有成竹 to have had ready or well-thought-out plans or designs in one's mind (in coping with a matter, situation, etc.)

xiōngzhēn 胸針 a brooch

xióng 雄
1. male; masculine; virile 2. a person or state having great power and influence 3. heroic; brave; strong; ambitious 4. to win; to triumph; victory 5. to scold others with insulting words

xióngbà yìfāng 雄霸一方 to hold a part of the country and to exercise undisputed authority

xióngbiàn 雄辯 a forceful pre-

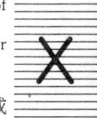

sentation of one's points in a debate; eloquence

xióngcái dàlüè 雄才大略 (said of a ruler) extremely capable

xióngfēng 雄風 an awe-inspiring air; a gallant and stately manner

xiónghòu 雄厚 ample; plentiful; rich; abundant

xiónghún 雄渾 powerful; grand; grandiose

xióngjiàn 雄健 powerful; vigorous; strapping

xióngjiūjiū 雄赳赳 imposing; looking brave and resolute; valiantly

xióngshī 雄師 crack troops; a powerful army

xióngwěi 雄偉 grandeur; majestic; stately

xióngxīn 雄心 ambition; great expectations

xióngzhuàng 雄壯 virile; powerful; strong; majestic

xióngzī 雄姿 a dashing look; a manly form

xióng 熊

1. a bear 2. shining bright 3. a Chinese family name

xióngxīn bāodǎn 熊心豹膽 tremendous bravery or courage

xióngxióng 熊熊 flaming and glorious; shining

xióngxióng dàhuǒ 熊熊大火 a blazing fire

xiū 休

1. rest; to rest 2. to stop; to cease 3. happiness; joy; weal

xiūbīng 休兵 1. to stop fighting 2. a truce; an armistice

xiūhuì 休會 to adjourn a meeting

xiūhuǒshān 休火山 a dormant volcano

xiūjià 休假 a holiday; to have a holiday

xiūkè 休克 shock

xiūqī xiāngguān 休戚相關 to share joys and sorrows with each other

xiūxi 休息 to take a rest; rest

xiūxián 休閒 leisure; relaxation; ease

xiūxiánfú 休閒服 casual wear; sports wear

xiūxiǎng 休想 to stop thinking

xiūxué 休學 a leave of absence (for a considerable period of time) from school

xiūyǎng 休養 to rest; to recuperate

xiūyǎng shēngxī 休養生息 to recuperate and multiply

xiūyǎng shēngxī 休養生息 refer to **xiūyǎng shēngxī** 休養生息

xiūyè 休業 to suspend business; to close the store (for a holiday)

xiūyèshì 休業式 a semester closing ceremony

xiūzhàn 休戰 1. to stop fighting 2. a truce; an armistice

xiūzhǐ 休止 to stop; to cease

xiūzhǐfú 休止符 a sign of rests in staff notation

xiū 修

1. to repair; to mend 2. to adorn; to decorate 3. to construct; to build 4. long; slender 5. to prune; to cut; to sharpen; to trim 6. to study; to cultivate 7. to write; to compile; to edit

xiūbǔ 修補 to repair; to mend

xiūcháng 修長 tall and thin; slender

xiūcí 修辭 rhetoric; diction

xiūcíxué 修辭學 rhetoric (as a subject of study)

xiūdào 修道 to cultivate oneself according to a religious doctrine

xiūdàoyuàn 修道院 1. a monastery 2. a nunnery; a convent

xiūdìng 修訂 to revise

xiūdìngbǎn 修訂版 a revision; the revised edition

xiūdìngběn 修訂本 a revision; the revised edition

xiūfù 修復 to complete a repair job

xiūgǎi 修改 to correct; to alter

xiūjiǎn 修剪 to trim, cut, clip, or prune

xiūjiàn 修建 to repair and build

xiūlǐ 修理 1. to repair 2. to torture

xiūmiàn 修面 to shave one's face

xiūnǚ 修女 a Catholic nun; a sister

xiūpèi 修配 to repair and supply replacements

xiūqì 修葺 to repair; to mend

xiūróng 修容 to make up one's features

xiūshēn 修身 to cultivate oneself

xiūshēn qíjiā 修身齊家 to cultivate oneself and put family in order

xiūshì 修士 a monk

xiūshì 修飾 to doll up

xiūxíng 修行 to practice Buddhist or Taoist rules

xiūyǎng 修養 1. to seek perfection in scholastic or ethical pursuits 2. man's moral culture as the result of training

xiūyè 修業 to pursue academic studies

xiūzhěng 修整 1. to repair and maintain 2. to prune; to trim

xiūzhèng 修正 to correct; to alter

xiūzhǐjia 修指甲 to manicure (or trim) fingernails

xiūzhǐjia 修指甲 refer to **xiūzhǐjia** 修指甲

xiūzhú 修築 refer to **xiūzhù** 修築

xiūzhù 修築 to build; to construct

xiū 羞
1. ashamed; abashed 2. shy; bashful 3. to disgrace; to insult; to shame

xiūchǐ 羞恥 a sense of shame

xiūdādā 羞答答 shy; bashful

xiūfèn 羞憤 ashamed and resentful

xiūkuì 羞愧 mortified; disgraced

xiūqiè 羞怯 shy and nervous

xiūquè 羞怯 refer to **xiūqiè** 羞怯

xiūrǔ 羞辱 to shame; to insult; to disgrace

xiūsè 羞澀 1. to act awkwardly

because of shame 2. to be short of

xiūyú qǐchǐ 羞於啓齒 too shy to speak out one's mind

xiǔ 朽
1. to rot; to decay 2. old and useless

xiǔbài 朽敗 decayed and rotten

xiǔhuài 朽壞 to decay; to rot; decayed

xiǔmù 朽木 1. rotten wood; decayed trees 2. a good-for-nothing

xiǔmù bùkě diāo 朽木不可雕 A congenital defeatist cannot be taught to succeed.

xiǔmù fèntǔ 朽木糞土 decayed wood and filthy soil—a hopeless person

xiǔ 宿
night

xiù 秀
1. brilliant; excellent; competent; outstanding 2. beautiful; elegant; graceful; delicate; fine 3. (said of grain crops) to put forth new flowers or ears

xiùlì 秀麗 beautiful; elegant; graceful; fine

xiùqì 秀氣 beautiful; elegant; graceful; fine

xiùsè kěcān 秀色可餐 (said of a woman) very attractive

xiùwài huìzhōng 秀外慧中 beautiful and intelligent

xiù 袖
1. the sleeve 2. to hide or put things in sleeves

xiùkǒu 袖口 the cuff (of a sleeve); the far ends of sleeves; a wristband

xiùkòu 袖扣 cuff links

xiùshǒu pángguān 袖手旁觀 to look on without even lifting a finger (to help, etc.)

xiùzhēn 袖珍 pocket-size; pocket

xiùzhēnběn 袖珍本 a pocket book; a pocket edition

xiù 臭
1. scent; smells; odors 2. to smell

xiù 宿
an ancient term for a constellation; an asterism

xiù 嗅
to smell; to scent; to sniff

xiùjué 嗅覺 the sense of smell

xiù 銹(鏽)
rust

xiùbān 銹斑 rust stains

xiù 繡(綉)
1. to embroider 2. embroidery

xiùhuā 繡花 1. embroidery 2. to embroider

xiùhuāxié 繡花鞋 embroidered shoes

xiùqiú 繡球 a ball of rolled silk

xū 戌
the eleventh of the Twelve Terrestrial Branches

xūshí 戌時 7—9 p.m.

xū 吁
a sigh

xū 須
1. to have to; must; to need 2. necessary; proper 3. probably 4. a beard 5. a moment; a while 6. to wait for 7. to stop at 8. a Chinese family name

xūyú 須臾 in an instant; a short while

xūzhī 須知 1. to have to know; should know 2. that which is essential to know—common knowledge; to note

xū 虛
1. empty; hollow; void; unoccupied 2. unreal; false; deceptive; unfounded; groundless 3. weak; feeble 4. abstract; shapeless

xūdù 虛度 to fritter away; to dream away

xūgòu 虛構 made-up; to trump up; to frame

xūhuái ruògǔ 虛懷若谷 to be open-minded

xūhuàn 虛幻 illusory; visionary; unreal

xūjiǎ 虛假 false; unreal; dishon-

est

xūjīng 虛驚 a false alarm

xūmíng 虛名 an empty reputation

xūqíng jiǎyì 虛情假意 hypocrisy; insincerity

xūróng 虛榮 vanity; empty glory; vainglorious

xūróngxīn 虛榮心 vainglory; vanity

xūruò 虛弱 debility; weak; feeble

xūshí 虛實 1. true or false 2. the actual situation

xūsuì 虛歲 age according to Chinese calculation

xūtuō 虛脫 (medicine) collapse; prostration

xūwěi 虛偽 spurious; insincere; hypocrisy

xūwú 虛無 nothingness; emptiness; nil; void

xūxiàn 虛線 1. a dotted line 2. an imaginary line

xūxīn 虛心 open-minded

xūyǒu qíbiǎo 虛有其表 to appear better than it is

xūzhāng shēngshì 虛張聲勢 to bluff

xū 需
1. to need; to require; to demand 2. expenses; provisions; needs; necessaries 3. hesitation; delay

xūqiú 需求 to need; to require; needs; demands

xūyào 需要 to need or require; needs or requirements

xū 噓
1. to warm with exhaled air 2. to speak well of (another) 3. a deep sigh 4. to hiss; to boo

xūhán wēnnuǎn 噓寒問暖 to show a kind concern for another's comfort

xū 墟
1. a high mound 2. an ancient town; a ghost town 3. wild, waste land 4. a periodical marketplace where goods are bartered 5. to ruin; to destroy

xū 鬚
1. beard; whiskers 2. whiskers

(of a cat, etc.) 3. an awn

xūméi 鬚眉 1. beard and eye-brows 2. men

xú 徐

slow; calm; composed; gently

xúbù 徐步 to walk slowly

xúhuǎn 徐緩 slowly; unhurriedly

Xúniáng bànlǎo 徐娘半老 a flirtatious middle-aged woman who still retains traces of her erstwhile beauty

xúxú 徐徐 1. steady; relaxed and dignified 2. slow

xúxú érlái 徐徐而來 to come with relaxed and dignified steps

xǔ 栩

1. a species of oak 2. glad; pleased

xǔxǔ rúshēng 栩栩如生 (said of a portrait, etc.) true to life; lifelike; to the life

xǔ 許

1. to promise; to approve; to per-mit 2. to praise; to commend 3. (said of a young girl) to be betrothed 4. to expect 5. per-haps; maybe 6. about

xǔduō 許多 many; numerous; much

xǔhūn 許婚 (said of a girl) to betroth

xǔjiǔ 許久 for a long time

xǔkě 許可 to approve; to permit or allow

xǔkězhèng 許可證 a permit; a license

xǔnuò 許諾 to promise; a prom-ise

xǔpèi 許配 to betroth; to affi-ance

xǔyuàn 許願 1. to make a vow (to a god) 2. to promise some-body a reward

xǔ 煦

refer to **xù** 煦

xù 旭

1. brightness or radiance of day-break 2. the rising sun 3. smug, proud or complacent

xùrì 旭日 the rising sun

xù 序

1. a preface; a foreword 2. order

xùlùn 序論 an introduction (in a piece of writing)

xùmù 序幕 the prologue; the prelude

xùqǔ 序曲 a prelude

xùshù 序數 an ordinal number

xùwén 序文 a preface; a fore-word

xùyán 序言 a preface; a fore-word

xù 恤(卹)

1. to relieve; to help 2. to sympa-thize; to be considerate

xùgū 恤孤 to relieve orphans

xùpín 恤貧 to give relief to the poor

xù 畜

to rear or raise (livestock or children)

xùmù 畜牧 animal husbandry

xùyǎng 畜養 to raise

xù 敍

1. to tell; to narrate; to describe; to express 2. to talk about; to chat 3. to arrange in order 4. to rate or evaluate (as a basis for reward, appointment, etc.); to assess

xùbié 敍別 to get together for talk before a separation

xùjiù 敍舊 to talk about the old days

xùshù 敍述 to tell; to narrate

xùshuō 敍說 to tell; to narrate

xùwén 敍文 a preface; a fore-word

xùyán 敍言 a preface; a fore-word

xù 酗

to lose one's temper when drunk

xùjiǔ 酗酒 to indulge in exces-sive drinking

xù 絮

1. raw, coarse, old, waste cotton or silk 2. wooly; fluffy 3. catkins and similar blossoms 4. padding; cushioning 5. (said of chatter,

writing, etc.) windy 6. to wad with cotton

xùdao 絮叨 tiresomely talkative; to nag

xùxù bùxiū 絮絮不休 to din; to chatter

xù 婿

1. one's son-in-law 2. one's husband

xù 煦 also xǔ

1. warm and cozy 2. kindness; favors; good graces; kind and gracious

xùxù 煦煦 1. kind; gracious; benevolent 2. (said of weather) warm and fine

xù 蓄

1. to collect; to store; to save up; to reserve 2. to cultivate (long hair or a beard); to grow 3. to raise; to rear; to breed 4. to wait; to expect

xùfà 蓄髮 refer to **xùfà** 蓄髮

xùfà 蓄髮 to grow or cultivate long hair

xùhóng 蓄洪 to store floodwater

xùjī 蓄積 to store or save up; storage or savings

xùshuǐchí 蓄水池 a reservoir

xùyì 蓄意 to harbor certain intentions or ideas; premeditated (murder, etc.)

xù 緒

1. the end of a thread or string 2. a clue 3. a beginning 4. a task; an enterprise 5. mood 6, remnants; remains; leftovers

xùlùn 緒論 a preface; a foreword; an introduction

xù 續

1. to continue; to extend; to renew 2. to add; to supply more

xùdìng 續訂 to renew one's subscription

xùjí 續集 the sequel (of a movie, etc.)

xùjiè 續借 to renew (a library book)

xùpìn 續聘 to continue to employ (a person)

xùxián 續絃 (said of a man) to remarry

xùyuē 續約 to renew a contract

xuān 宣

1. to announce; to declare 2. to propagate; to circulate 3. a Chinese family name

xuānbù 宣布 to announce

xuānchēng 宣稱 to claim; to assert

xuānchuán 宣傳 to publicize; (sales) propaganda

xuānchuánchē 宣傳車 a propaganda car

xuānchuánpǐn 宣傳品 propaganda material

xuāndǎo 宣導 to guide (the people) by creating a better understanding

xuāndú 宣讀 to read out (a declaration, an announcement, etc.) in public

xuān'gào 宣告 to announce; to declare

xuānláo 宣勞 to contribute one's labor, time and energy, to a public cause

xuānlào 宣勞 to comfort (people in distress) by an official message

xuānpàn 宣判 to announce the verdict

xuānshì 宣示 to make publicly known

xuānshì 宣誓 to take an oath

xuānshì jiùzhí 宣誓就職 (said of government officials) to be sworn in

xuānxiè 宣泄 1. to reveal, disclose, or divulge (a secret) 2. to drain (liquid)

xuānyán 宣言 a declaration; a manifesto

xuānyáng 宣揚 to publicize and exalt

xuānzhàn 宣戰 to declare war

xuān 軒

1. a carriage formerly used by high officials 2. the high front of a chariot or carriage 3. a balcony; a porch 4. a window 5. open; wide 6. high; lofty 7. smiling; laughing; delighted 8. a stu-

dio; a room

xuānrán dàbō 軒然大波 (literally) towering waves—great repercussions

xuānzhì 軒輊 difference in height, rank, excellence, etc.

xuān 喧

1. to talk noisily; to clamor 2. noise; hubbub; uproar; noisy

xuānbīn duózhǔ 喧賓奪主 to act like a boss where one does not belong

xuānhuá 喧嘩 uproar; turmoil

xuānnào 喧鬧 hubbub; noisy

xuānrǎng 喧嚷 clamor; hubbub; din; racket

xuānténg 喧騰 noise and excitement; hubbub

xuānxiāo 喧囂 noise; din; uproar

xuān 萱

a daylily (Hemerocallis fulva)

xuāntáng 萱堂 one's mother

xuān 暄

1. comfortable and genial (climates); warm 2. (dialect) fluffy

xuānnuǎn 暄暖 warm and comfortable

xuān 瑄

an ornamental piece of jade about 6.5 inches in diameter

xuān 諠

to bawl; to shout

xuānhuá 諠譁 turmoil; a hubbub; tumult; an uproar

xuán 玄

1. far and obscure; occult or mystic 2. dark or black 3. deep and profound; abstruse and subtle 4. silent and meditative 5. pretending 6. a Chinese family name

xuán'ào 玄奧 1. abstruse and subtle 2. mysteries; profundities

xuánguān 玄關 1. the entrance to Buddhism 2. The door of a house 3. a vestibule

xuánjī 玄機 (Taoism) the profound and mysterious truth

xuánmiào 玄妙 profound,

abstruse and subtle

xuánsūn 玄孫 great-great-grandson

xuán 旋

1. to return; to turn back 2. to revolve; to circle; to spin; to move in an orbit 3. a very short while 4. to urinate

xuánjí 旋即 forthwith; immediately afterwards

xuánlǜ 旋律 melody

xuánqián zhuǎnkūn 旋乾轉坤 immense power to reverse a situation

xuánzhǒng 旋踵 a very short time

xuánzhuǎn 旋轉 to turn round and round

xuánzhuǎnmén 旋轉門 a revolving door

xuán 漩 also **xuàn**

a whirlpool

xuánwō 漩渦 1. a whirlpool 2. a dispute; a quarrel

xuán 璇

1. fine jade 2. name of a constellation

xuángōng 璇宮 an exquisite room ornamented with fine gems; a swanky palace

xuán 縣

to hang

xuán 懸

1. to hang or be hanged or hung; to suspend or be suspended 2. to be in suspension; to be in suspense; unsettled; unsolved 3. unfounded; without a basis; unsupported 4. far apart 5. to be concerned for

xuán'àn 懸案 an unsettled case

xuán'ér wèijué 懸而未決 suspense; in suspense

xuánguà 懸掛 to hang (decorations)

xuánhú jìshì 懸壺濟世 to practice medicine or pharmacy

xuánkōng 懸空 to be suspended (or hung) in the air

xuánliáng zìjìn 懸梁自盡 to

X

hang oneself

xuánniàn 懸念 worry and concern for a friend or close family member far away

xuánqí 懸旗 to hoist a flag; to hang a flag

xuánshǎng 懸賞 to offer a prize, or reward (for the capture of a criminal, etc.)

xuánshū 懸殊 very different

xuányá 懸崖 a precipice

xuányá lèmǎ 懸崖勒馬 to stop just before committing a serious blunder

xuányá qiàobì 懸崖峭壁 overhanging precipices and steep cliffs

xuányí 懸疑 suspense

xuǎn 選

1. to select; to choose; choice 2. to elect; elections

xuǎnbá 選拔 to select

xuǎnchū 選出 to pick out; to select; to elect

xuǎndìng 選定 to decide on a selection

xuǎndú 選讀 1. to take an elective course in a college 2. selected readings

xuǎngòu 選購 to select and make purchase

xuǎnjǔ 選舉 to elect; to vote; elections

xuǎnjǔquán 選舉權 the right to vote

xuǎnjǔrén 選舉人 a voter

xuǎnkè 選課 to take courses in a college

xuǎnměi 選美 a beauty contest

xuǎnmín 選民 the eligible voters among the citizenry; constituency

xuǎnshǒu 選手 a member of a sports team or delegation representing a school, an area or a country; a contestant

xuǎnxián yǔ'néng 選賢與能 to pick the good and select the capable for public posts

xuǎnyòng 選用 to select and appoint to a post

xuǎnzé 選擇 a choice; to choose

xuǎnzétí 選擇題 a multiple-choice question

xuǎn 癬 also xiǎn

ringworm; tetter

xuàn 炫

1. to show off; to display; to flaunt 2. dazzling; bright; shining

xuànhuò 炫惑 to dazzle and confuse

xuànyào 炫耀 1. to flaunt; to show off 2. bright and brilliant

xuàn 眩

1. to confuse; to dazzle 2. dizzy; giddy; confused vision

xuànhuò 眩惑 to confuse and cheat (the people); to mislead

xuànyào 眩耀 to dazzle; dazzling

xuànyùn 眩暈 dizziness

xuàn 旋

1. to whirl; a whirl 2. at the time; at the last moment; as soon as 3. to heat wine

xuànfēng 旋風 a whirlwind

xuàn 衒

1. to brag; to boast; to show off 2. to recommend oneself

xuàn 絢

bright and brilliant; adorned and stylish

xuànlàn 絢爛 bright and brilliant

xuànlì 絢麗 gorgeous; magnificent

xuàn 渲

to color with paint

xuànrǎn 渲染 1. to color with paint 2. to make exaggerated additions in a story or report; to play up

xuàn 漩

refer to **xuán** 漩

xuē 削 also xiāo, xuè

1. to cut; to pare; to shave; to whittle 2. to deprive

xuēchú 削除 to take out; to omit

xuēfà 削髮 refer to **xuēfā** 削髮

xuēfà 削髮 to shave the head

xuējià 削價 to cut price to the cost level

xuējiǎn 削減 to curtail; to cut down

xuēpíng 削平 1. to pare; to smooth 2. to put down; to conquer

xuēqiānbǐ 削鉛筆 to sharpen a pencil

xuēruò 削弱 to enfeeble; to weaken; to devitalize

xuēzúshìlǚ 削足適履 an impractical solution of a problem

xuē 靴
boots

xuēdǐ 靴底 soles of boots

xuē 噱
refer to **xué** 噱

xuē 薛
1. a kind of marsh grass 2. name of an ancient state in today's Shandong Province 3. a Chinese family name

xué 穴 also **xuè**
1. a cave; a den; a hole 2. points in the human body where acupuncture can be applied 3. (Chinese boxing) points in the human body where nerve centers are supposed to be located, a strike at which may cause paralysis or even death

xuédào 穴道 1. points in the human body where acupuncture can be applied 2. (Chinese boxing) points in the human body where nerve centers are supposed to be located, a strike at which may cause paralysis or even death 3. an underground channel

xué 噱 also **jué**, **xuē**
laugh

xuétóu 噱頭 words or act meant to amuse or to excite laughter

xué 學 also **xiáo**
1. to learn; to study; to imitate 2. of or having to do with learning; academic

xuébù 學步 (said of a child) to learn to walk

xuécháo 學潮 a student strike

xuéfèi 學費 tuition

xuéfēn 學分 units, credits, or semester hours

xuéfēng 學風 school traditions

xuéfǔ 學府 an institute of higher learning

xuéhuì 學會 1. a learned society; an institute 2. to succeed in learning (a skill)

xuéjí 學籍 one's status as a student of a particular school

xuéjiū 學究 a pedagogue; a pedant

xuékē 學科 a subject; a course

xuélì 學歷 educational background

xuélíng 學齡 school age

xuénián 學年 an academic (or a school) year

xuépài 學派 a school (of thought)

xuéqī 學期 a (school) term; a semester

xuéqí 學期 refer to **xuéqī** 學期

xuérén 學人 a scholar

xuéshè 學舍 a school building

xuésheng 學生 a student; a pupil

xuésheng shídài 學生時代 school days

xuéshēngzhèng 學生證 a student's identity card

xuéshí 學識 erudition; learning; scholarship

xuéshì 學士 a holder of the bachelor's degree

xuéshì 學識 refer to **xuéshí** 學識

xuéshù 學術 learning; science

xuéshùjiè 學術界 academic circles

xuéshuō 學說 a theory

xuétáng 學堂 a school

xuétóng 學童 a school child

xuétú 學徒 1. an apprentice 2. a student

xuéwèi 學位 an academic degree

xuéwen 學問 learning; scholarship; erudition

xuéwú zhìjìng 學無止境 There is no limit to knowledge.

xuéxí 學習 to learn; to study

xuéxiào 學校 a school

xuéyè 學業 schoolwork

xuéyè chéngjī 學業成績 scholastic attainments (or achievements)

xuéyǐ zhìyòng 學以致用 to make use of what one has learned

xuéyì 學藝 1. sciences and arts 2. to learn a trade

xuéyǒu zhuāncháng 學有專長 to have acquired a specialty from study

xuéyuàn 學院 1. a college (in a university) 2. an academy

xuézhǎng 學長 one's senior at school

xuézhě 學者 a scholar; a learned person

xuézhì 學制 an educational system

xuézǐ 學子 a student; a pupil

xué 雪 1. snow 2. to clean; to wash or wipe away 3. (also xuè) pure white; bright

xuěbái 雪白 snow-white

xuěbēng 雪崩 snowslide

xuěchǐ 雪恥 to wipe out a shame; to avenge an insult or humiliation

xuěduī 雪堆 a snowbank; a snowdrift

xuěhèn 雪恨 to avenge one's grudge; to avenge wrongs done to one

xuěhuā 雪花 a snowflake

xuějiā 雪茄 a cigar

xuějǐng 雪景 a landscape of snow; a snow scene

xuěliàng 雪亮 bright as snow; shiny

xuění hóngzhuǎ 雪泥鴻爪 (literally) talon marks on the snow —traces of past events

xuěpiàn 雪片 1. a snowflake 2. to come in like an avalanche

xuěqiāo 雪橇 a sled; a toboggan; a sledge

xuěqiú 雪球 a snowball

xuěrén 雪人 snowman

xuěshàng jiāshuāng 雪上加霜 disasters coming one after another in succession

xuězhōng sòngtàn 雪中送炭 to give timely assistance; to send things which are in urgent need, as food for hungry refugees

xuě 鱈 a cod

xuè 穴 refer to xué 穴

xuè 血 also xiě 1. blood 2. blood relationship

xuèběn wúguī 血本無歸 no return of hard-earned capital

xuèguǎn 血管 a blood vessel

xuèhǎi shēnchóu 血海深仇 blood feud; intense and deep-seated hatred

xuèhàn 血汗 blood and sweat —hard toil

xuèhànqián 血汗錢 money earned by very hard work or toil; hard-earned money

xuèhóng 血紅 as red as blood; scarlet

xuèjì 血跡 bloodstained; a bloodstain

xuèkǒu pēnrén 血口噴人 to curse and slander; to make false accusations against others

xuèkù 血庫 a blood bank

xuèlèi 血淚 tears and blood —extreme sorrow

xuèlínlín 血淋淋 blood-dripping; bloody; sanguinary

xuènóng yúshuǐ 血濃於水 Blood is thicker than water.

xuèqì fānggāng 血氣方剛 (said of youths) hot-tempered; easily excited; full of vigor

xuèqīn 血親 a blood relative

xuèqiú 血球 a blood corpuscle; a blood cell

xuèròu móhú 血肉模糊 (said of human bodies) badly mutilated; mutilated beyond recognition

xuètáng 血糖 blood sugar; blood glucose

xuètǒng 血統 blood relationship; a strain; lineage; consanguinity; pedigree

xuèxīng 血腥 reeking of blood; bloody; sanguinary

xuèxíng 血型 a blood type; a blood group

xuèyā 血壓 blood pressure

xuèyè 血液 the blood

xuèyuán 血緣 blood; blood relationship; a strain

xuè 削
refer to **xuē** 削

xuè 雪
refer to **xuě** 雪 3

xūn 熏 (燻)
1. smoke; to smoke; to burn; smoked (meat, fish, etc.) 2. (said of smell) to assail nostrils 3. warm; mild 4. to move or touch 5. (薰) to cauterize 6. (薰) to scent; to fumigate; to perfume; to embalm

xūnhēi 熏黑 to blacken by smoke

xūnrǎn 熏染 to influence

xūnròu 熏肉 to smoke meat; smoked meat; bacon

xūnsǐ 熏死 suffocated to death (by fumes, stench, etc.)

xūntáo 熏陶 to influence; to educate; to train

xūntiān 熏天 overwhelming

xūnxīn 熏心 to becloud the mind

xūnyú 熏魚 1. to smoke fish 2. smoked fish

xūnzhì 熏炙 to cauterize

xūn 勳
merits; honors; meritorious services; achievements

xūnzhāng 勳章 a medal of honor; a decoration

xūn 薰
1. to cauterize 2. to perfume; to embalm 3. to smoke; to fumigate 4. warm

xūntáo 薰陶 to edify

xūnxīn 薰心 to becloud the mind

xūn 醺
drunk; intoxicated; tipsy

xún 旬
1. a period of ten days 2. a period of ten years (usually used to indicate a person's age) 3. widespread; throughout 4. to tour; to inspect

xúnnián 旬年 1. a full year 2. ten years

xúnrì 旬日 ten days

xúnyuè 旬月 1. a whole month 2. ten months

xún 巡
1. to patrol; to inspect; to cruise 2. a round (of drinks) 3. a policeman; a cop

xúnbǔ 巡捕 (formerly) a policeman

xúnchá 巡查 to patrol and investigate

xúnfáng 巡防 1. a patrolman 2. to patrol

xúnháng 巡航 to cruise; a cruise

xúnhuí 巡迴 to go the rounds; to tour

xúnjī 巡緝 to patrol to arrest thieves and smugglers

xúnjǐng 巡警 1. a policeman 2. to inspect

xúnlǐ 巡禮 1. a pilgrimage to a holy land 2. an inspection or sightseeing tour

xúnluó 巡邏 to patrol

xúnluóchē 巡邏車 a squad car

xúnluóduì 巡邏隊 a military patrol

xúnqì 巡緝 refer to **xúnjī** 巡緝

xúnshì 巡視 (said of ranking officials) to inspect

xúnxíng 巡行 to make the rounds of inspection

xúnyángjiàn 巡洋艦 a cruiser

xúnyì fēidàn 巡弋飛彈 a cruise missile

xún 徇
refer to **xùn** 徇 6, 7

xún 荀
1. name of an ancient state 2. a kind of herb 3. a Chinese family

name

xún 循

1. to follow; to comply with 2. to postpone 3. in orderly fashion 4. (obsolete) to touch 5. to inspect

xúnguī dǎojǔ 循規蹈矩 law-abiding; to obey the rules and regulations

xúnhuán 循環 circulation

xúnhuánsài 循環賽 a round robin

xúnhuán xìtǒng 循環系統 the circulatory system

xúnhuán xiǎoshù 循環小數 recurring decimals

xúnlì 循例 according to rules

xúnxù jiànjìn 循序漸進 to follow in proper sequence and make gradual progress

xúnxún shànyòu 循循善誘 to lead students gradually and patiently on the right path

xún 尋

1. a measure of length in former times (roughly equivalent to eight feet) 2. to seek; to search

xúnbǎo 尋寶 to hunt for treasure

xúncháng 尋常 usual; ordinary; common

xúnduǎnjiàn 尋短見 to end one's own life; to commit suicide

xúnfǎng 尋訪 to look for (somebody whose whereabouts is unknown)

xúngēn jiūdǐ 尋根究底 to probe deeply

xúnhuā wènliǔ 尋花問柳 1. to enjoy natural beauty in springtime 2. to seek carnal pleasure

xúnhuān zuòlè 尋歡作樂 to seek amusement

xúnkāixīn 尋開心 (dialect) to make fun of; to joke

xúnmì 尋覓 to search for; to look for

xúnrén qǐshì 尋人啓事 a notice in a missing person column

xúnyōu tànshèng 尋幽探勝 to visit scenic spots

xúnzhǎo 尋找 to look for; to

xún 馴 also **xùn**

1. tame 2. mild; well-bred; obedient; docile 3. gradual 4. to tame; to put under control; to break (an animal)

xúnfú 馴服 to tame; to subdue; to break in; subdued; obedient

xúnhé 馴和 gentle; mild; good-natured

xúnliáng 馴良 docile; obedient; tractable; gentle

xúnlù 馴鹿 a reindeer

xúnyǎng 馴養 to raise (animals); to domesticate (animals); to tame

xún 詢

1. to inquire 2. to deliberate and plan 3. truely

xúnchá 詢察 to investigate and inquire

xúnwèn 詢問 to inquire; to ask

xúnwènchù 詢問處 an information desk

xùn 汛

1. to sprinkle 2. abundant water; a flood 3. menses; menstruation

xùnqī 汛期 (irrigation) the flood season

xùnqí 汛期 refer to **xùnqī** 汛期

xùn 迅

swift; rapid; sudden

xùnléi bùjí yǎn'ěr 迅雷不及掩耳 as swift as a sudden clap of thunder which leaves no time for covering the ears; out of the blue

xùnsù 迅速 by leaps and bounds; quick; swift; rapid

xùn 徇

1. to show 2. to issue orders in the army 3. to follow; to comply with 4. quick 5. to die for a cause 6. (also **xún**) pervading 7. (also **xún**) to profit

xùnnàn 徇難 to die for a just cause

xùnsī 徇私 to profit oneself; favoritism; nepotism

xùn 殉

1. to die for a cause 2. (originally) to be buried with the dead (usually said of slaves, loyal servants, concubines, etc.)

xùndào 殉道 to die for the right cause; to die a martyr's death

xùndàozhě 殉道者 a martyr

xùnguó 殉國 to die for one's country

xùnqíng 殉情 to die for love

xùnzhí 殉職 to die while performing one's work

xùn 訓

1. to lecture; to teach; to exhort 2. (to serve as) a lesson 3. an old proverb, etc.

xùnchì 訓斥 to reprimand; to rebuke

xùndǎo 訓導 to teach and guide

xùnhuà 訓話 to lecture; to exhort

xùnjiè 訓誡 to admonish

xùnliàn 訓練 to drill; to train; training

xùnliànbān 訓練班 a training class

xùnmiǎn 訓勉 to exhort and encourage

xùnshì 訓示 instructions; to admonish

xùn 訊

1. to ask; to inquire; to question 2. information; news 3. to put on trial; to question in court; to interrogate

xùnxī 訊息 news; information; tidings

xùnxí 訊息 refer to **xùnxī** 訊息

xùn 馴

refer to **xún** 馴

xùn 遜 also **sùn**

1. respectful and compliant; obedient 2. to resign; resigning; to surrender; to abdicate; yielding 3. humble; modest 4. not as good as; inferior to

xùnràng 遜讓 to surrender (a position) to another; to yield

xùnsè 遜色 inferior to; not as good as

xùnwèi 遜位 to abdicate; abdica-

tion

yā 丫

something that branches or forks upward

yātou 丫頭 1. (in ancient China) a slave girl; a maid 2. (in modern usage) a small girl, especially one's own daughter

yā 呀

a creaking sound

yā 押

1. to mortgage; to pawn; to pledge 2. to detain or imprison (temporarily) 3. to escort 4. a signature

yādàng 押當 1. to pawn 2. a pawnshop

yāhuì 押匯 documentary draft negotiation

yājiè 押解 to transfer or deport (suspects, prisoners, goods, etc.) from one place to another under escort or guard

yājīn 押金 a cash pledge; a deposit

yāsòng 押送 to send (goods or criminals) to another place under escort or guard

yāyùn 押韻 to rhyme

yā 椏

the forking branch of a tree

yā 鴉

a crow; a raven

yāpiàn 鴉片 opium

yāquè wúshēng 鴉雀無聲 so quiet that not a single voice can be heard

yā 鴨

a duck

yādàn 鴨蛋 1. a duck's egg 2. (slang) scoreless; zero

yādànliánr 鴨蛋臉兒 an oval face (regarded as an ideal shape for a woman's face)

yāshémào 鴨舌帽 a cap with a visor

yāzi 鴨子 a duck

yā 壓

1. to press 2. to control; to quell

Y

yā 壓

3. to crush 4. (said of enemy troops, etc.) to close in; to press near 5. to hold (a document, etc.) without taking action; to pigeonhole 6. a way of making a stroke in Chinese calligraphy 7. to excel; to surpass others 8. refer to **yà** 壓

yādǎo 壓倒 to surpass; to overwhelm

yādǎoxìng shènglì 壓倒性勝利 an overwhelming victory

yājǐ 壓擠 to extrude; extrusion

yājìng 壓境 (usually said of enemy troops) to mass on, or approach the border

yākèlì 壓克力 (chemistry) acrylic resin

yālì 壓力 pressure

yāpò 壓迫 1. to oppress; to pressure; to force 2. oppression; pressure

yāsuì 壓碎 to crush to pieces

yāsuìqián 壓歲錢 money given to children by elders on the Lunar New Year's Eve

yāsuō 壓縮 to compress; to condense

yāyì 壓抑 to curb; to repress

yāzhà 壓榨 1. to oppress 2. to extract (liquids) by applying high pressure

yāzhì 壓制 1. to suppress (one's anger, etc.); to restrain (usually by force) 2. (military) to neutralize (enemy fire by massive bombardment)

yāzhóu hǎoxì 壓軸好戲 refer to **yāzhòu hǎoxì** 壓軸好戲

yāzhòu hǎoxì 壓軸好戲 the last but best one of a series of performances

yāzhù 壓住 to suppress; to put down by force

yá 牙

1. teeth 2. to bite 3. ivory articles 4. a broker

yáfèngr 牙縫兒 space between the teeth

yágāo 牙膏 toothpaste

yágòu 牙垢 tartar on the teeth

yákē 牙科 dentistry

yáqiān 牙籤 a toothpick

yáshuā 牙刷 a toothbrush

yáténg 牙疼 toothache

yáxiàn 牙線 dental floss

yáyá xuéyǔ 牙牙學語 (said of an infant) to begin to babble, prattle, or lisp

yáyī 牙醫 a dentist

yáyín 牙齦 gums

yázhōubìng 牙周病 periodontosis

yá 芽

a sprout; a shoot; a bud

yá 涯

1. the water's edge; a bank 2. a limit 3. faraway places

yájì 涯際 the edge; the limit

yá 崖 also **yái**

1. a cliff; a precipice 2. the brink; the verge 3. precipitous; high and steep; forbidding

yábì 崖壁 a precipice

yá 衙

1. a government office 2. to meet; to gather; to congregate 3. (Tang Dynasty) a front hall of the palace

yámen 衙門 a government office in feudal China

yǎ 亞

refer to **yà** 亞

yǎ 啞

1. dumb; mute 2. hoarse; husky 3. a phrase-final particle

yǎba 啞巴 (a) deaf-mute (person)

yǎkǒu wúyán 啞口無言 to be speechless

yǎlíng 啞鈴 a dumbbell

yǎmí 啞謎 a riddle; an enigma

yǎ 雅

1. refined; polished; sophisticated; not common or vulgar 2. elegant; graceful 3. usually; often; frequently; much 4. name of an ancient musical instrument 5. friendship; acquaintance 6. (now rarely) a wine vessel

yǎguān 雅觀 graceful and ele-

gant in appearance

yǎliàng 雅量 1. broad-mindedness; generous; magnanimity 2. a great capacity for drinking

Yǎměizú 雅美族 the Yamis, an aborigine tribe on Orchid Island

Yǎpǐ 雅痞 Yuppie or Yuppy (a young, ambitious, and well-educated city-dweller who has a professional career and an affluent lifestyle)

yǎshì 雅事 refined activities of the intelligentsia

yǎsú 雅俗 the refined and the vulgar; the sophisticated and the simple-minded

yǎsú gòngshǎng 雅俗共賞 to appeal to both the sophisticated and the simple-minded

yǎxìng 雅興 enthusiasm in refined pursuits

yǎyán 雅言 1. things one often talks about 2. well-intentioned criticism; honest advice

yǎzéi 雅賊 a thief who steals only books and works of art

yǎzhì 雅致 1. refined tastes; refinement 2. fine; delicate; elegant; tasteful

yǎzuò 雅座 a nicely fixed chamber or room in a restaurant for customers who desire privacy

yà 亞 also yǎ
1. second (in excellence) 2. Asia

Yàdāng 亞當 Adam

yàjūn 亞軍 the runner-up

yàmá 亞麻 flax

Yàmǎxùnhé 亞馬遜河 the Amazon River in South America

yàrèdài 亞熱帶 the subtropical zone

Yàzhōu 亞洲 Asia

yà 軋
to crush; to grind

yà 訝
surprised or to express surprise; to wonder

yà 揠
to pull up or out

yàmiáo zhùzhǎng 揠苗助長

to spoil things by excessive enthusiasm

yà 壓 also yā

yàgēnr 壓根兒 totally; entirely; completely

ya 呀
1. a particle used after a phrase for expressing surprise, etc. 2. to gape (as in surprise)

yái 崖
refer to **yá** 崖

yān 奄
refer to **yǎn** 奄 3, 4, 5

yān 咽
the throat; the larynx; the pharynx

yānhóu 咽喉 1. the larynx; the throat 2. a narrow, throat-like passage of strategic importance

yān 胭
1. cosmetics, especially referring to rouge and face powder 2. (咽) the throat

yānzhi 胭脂 rouge

yān 殷
dark red

yānhóng 殷紅 dark red

yān 焉
1. an interrogative—how, why, when, etc. 2. a pronoun—it 3. an adverb—there; here 4. a conjunctive—and so; so that 5. a final particle indicating numerous senses

yāngǎn 焉敢 How dare...?

yānnéng 焉能 How can (one do it, succeed, etc.)?

yānzhī fēifú 焉知非福 How could you know it is not a blessing?

yān 淹
1. to submerge; to drown; to soak; to steep in; to flood 2. to delay; to procrastinate 3. to stay; to be stranded

yānmò 淹沒 1. drowned 2. to waste a talent as if by submerging it

yānsǐ 淹死 drowned

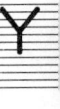

yāntōng gǔjīn 淹通古今 to be thoroughly acquainted with the old and modern

yān 菸

a tobacco leaf

yāncǎo 菸草 tobacco

yānjiǔ 菸酒 tobacco and alcoholic drinks

yān 腌

to salt; to pickle

yān 湮 also **yīn**

1. to bury 2. to block 3. long (in time)

yānmiè 湮滅 to bury; to destroy (evidence)

yānmò 湮沒 to bury or be buried

yān 煙(烟)

1. smoke; fumes 2. tobacco; a smoke; a cigarette 3. mist; vapor 4. opium

yāncǎo 煙草 tobacco

yāncōng 煙囪 a chimney; a stovepipe

yāndì 煙蒂 a cigarette butt

yāndǒu 煙斗 a pipe (for smoking)

yāndú 煙毒 the poisoning effect of opium-smoking

yānguǐ 煙鬼 an opium smoker or addict; a heavy smoker

yānhuā liǔxiàng 煙花柳巷 a red-light district

yānhuī 煙灰 cigarette ashes; cigar ashes

yānhuīgāng 煙灰缸 an ashtray

yānhuǒ 煙火 1. kitchen smoke which suggests presence of humans 2. cooked food (as distinct from herbs and fruits which are supposed to be the food of immortals) 3. a signal fire or beacon 4. smoke and fire

yānhuǒ 煙火 fireworks

yānjìn 煙禁 prohibition of opium smoking

yānmù 煙幕 a smoke screen

yānsī 煙絲 cut-tobacco for pipe smoking

yānwù 煙霧 smoke; mist; vapor; smog

yānxiāo yúnsàn 煙消雲散 to vanish completely; to disappear

yānyǐn 煙癮 1. opium or tobacco addiction 2. a craving for tobacco

yānzuǐr 煙嘴兒 a cigarette holder

yān 嫣

captivating; charming; lovely; fascinating

yānhóng 嫣紅 bright red; rich crimson

yān 醃

to pickle; to salt

yāncài 醃菜 pickled vegetables

yānròu 醃肉 salted pork; salted meat

Yān 燕

a state in what is Hebei today during the Epoch of Warring States

yān 閹

1. to castrate 2. a eunuch

yān'gē 閹割 to castrate

yānrén 閹人 a castrated person; a eunuch

yán 言

1. speech; words 2. to say; to talk; to speak; to mean; to express 3. a language; a dialect

yán bì xìn, xíng bì guǒ 言必信, 行必果 Promises must be kept and action must be resolute.

yánbù jíyì 言不及義 to make idle talks; to talk frivolously

yánbù yóuzhōng 言不由衷 not speaking one's mind; not to talk from the bottom of one's heart

yánchū rúshān 言出如山 A promise is a promise.

yáncí 言辭 words or expressions; statements; wording; diction

yán'ér yǒuxìn 言而有信 to be as good as one's word

yánguī yúhǎo 言歸於好 to resume friendship; to be on good terms again; to reconcile

yánguī zhèngzhuàn 言歸正

傳 Let's go back to the main topic.

yánguò qíshí 言過其實 to exaggerate; to boast or brag; to overstate

yánhé 言和 to make peace; to reconcile

yánjiǎn yìgāi 言簡意賅 Few words were spoken, but none of the major points was missing.

yánjiào 言敎 to give verbal directions

yánlùn 言論 speech

yánlùn zìyóu 言論自由 freedom of speech

yánmíng 言明 to state clearly; to make a statement; to declare

yántán 言談 words and speech; conversation

yántīng jìcóng 言聽計從 to have full confidence in someone

yánwài zhīyì 言外之意 overtones

yánxíng 言行 words and deeds

yánxíng yīzhì 言行一致 to practice what one preaches

yányóu zài'ěr 言猶在耳 The words are still ringing in the ear.

yányǔ 言語 spoken language; speech; words

yánzhī chénglǐ 言之成理 to present in a reasonable way; to talk sense

yánzhī guòzǎo 言之過早 still too early to say; premature to say

yánzhī yǒuwù 言之有物 (said of a speech or writing) having substance; convincing

yán 延
1. to lengthen; to spread; to extend 2. to delay; to defer 3. to prolong 4. to invite 5. to procrastinate

yáncháng 延長 to lengthen; to extend; to prolong

yánchángxiàn 延長線 an extension

yánchí 延遲 to delay; to be delayed

yándàng 延宕 to procrastinate

yánhuǎn 延緩 to postpone; to put off; to defer

yánjǐng qǐzú 延頸企足 to expect or look forward anxiously

yánjǐng qìzú 延頸企足 refer to **yánjǐng qǐzú** 延頸企足

yánlǎn 延攬 to recruit the service of (talented men)

yánnián yìshòu 延年益壽 to lengthen one's life

yánpìn 延聘 to invite the service of

yánqī 延期 to be postponed; to be put off

yánqí 延期 refer to **yánqī** 延期

yánqǐng 延請 to invite (talented people to provide assistance)

yánshāo 延燒 (said of fire) to spread

yánshēn 延伸 to extend; to stretch

yánshòu 延壽 to prolong one's life

yánsuǐ 延髓 medulla oblongata; the afterbrain

yánwù 延誤 to fail because of procrastination

yánxù 延續 to continue; to be continued

yánzhǎnxìng 延展性 (physics) ductility

yán 岩
1. a large rock 2. a mountain

yán'àn 岩岸 (geography) a rocky coast

yánbì 岩壁 1. (geology) a dyke 2. a cliff

yáncéng 岩層 a rock stratum; a rock formation

yándòng 岩洞 a cavern; a grotto

yánjiāng 岩漿 (geology) magma; lava

yánshí 岩石 a rock; a crag

yánxué 岩穴 a cavern; a grotto

yánxuè 岩穴 refer to **yánxué** 岩穴

yányán 岩鹽 rock salt

yán 沿
1. to follow; to go along; along

2. to hand down; to continue 3. successive; continuous 4. (also **yàn**) the edge; the brim

yán'àn 沿岸 along the coast of...; littoral

yánbiānr 沿邊兒 along the edge

yán'gé 沿革 vicissitudes or history (of a system, institution, etc.)

yánhǎi 沿海 1. along the coast 2. offshore

yánhé 沿河 along the river

yánlù 沿路 along the road; along the way

yántú 沿途 along the way

yánxí 沿襲 to follow the old or traditional (practices, customs, precedents, etc.)

yánxiàn 沿線 along a railway or highway

yányòng 沿用 to continue following the old practices, customs, etc.

yánzhe 沿著 to follow or go along...

yán 炎 1. burning; hot; sultry 2. to blaze; to flame; to flare up 3. inflammation

yánliáng 炎涼 1. (said of weather) hot and cold 2. snobbishness

yánrè 炎熱 (said of weather) very hot

yánxià 炎夏 hot summer

yányán 炎炎 1. awe-inspiring 2. very hot

yán 妍 1. beautiful; pretty; good-looking; cute; attractive; charming 2. seductive; coquettish

yánlì 妍麗 attractive; charming; beauty

yán 研 1. to go to the very source; to study; to investigate; to research; to examine 2. to grind; to powder

yánjiū 研究 to study and research

yánjiūshēng 研究生 a graduate student

yánjiūshì 研究室 a research laboratory

yánjiūsuǒ 研究所 a research laboratory; a research institute; a graduate school

yánjiūyuán 研究員 a researcher

yánjiūyuàn 研究院 a research institute

yánmó 研磨 1. to grind; to pestle 2. to abrade; to polish

yántǎo 研討 to study and discuss; to investigate and research

yántǎohuì 研討會 a seminar; a symposium

yánxí 研習 to research and study

yánxíhuì 研習會 a study meeting or conference

yánzhì 研製 1. to manufacture; to develop 2. (Chinese medicine) to prepare medicinal powder by grinding

yán 焰(燄)
refer to **yàn** 焰(燄)

yán 筵
1. a bamboo mat 2. a feast; a banquet

yánxí 筵席 1. a mat for sitting on 2. a feast; a banquet

yán 閻
1. a village gate; the gate of a lane 2. a Chinese family name

yánluówang 閻羅王 1. the Ruler of Hades; the King of Hell 2. a tyrant; one who is feared by all others

yán 檐
1. eaves of a house 2. the brim

yán 癌
refer to **ái** 癌

yán 顏
1. face (physically); countenance; features 2. reputation 3. dyes; colors 4. a Chinese family name

yánliào 顏料 dyestuffs; pigments

yánmiàn 顏面 1. honor 2. countenance; face

yánsè 顏色 1. color; hue; pigment 2. countenance; facial expression 3. a lesson

yánsè zìruò 顏色自若 to be composed with the face unchanged

yán 簷

1. the eaves of a house 2. the edge or brim of anything sloping downward—as that of a hat, umbrella, etc.

yán 嚴

1. stern; strict; severe; grim; inclement; inexorable; relentless; rigorous; rigid; grave; solemn 2. reverence 3. tight 4. father 5. a Chinese family name

yánbàn 嚴辦 to deal with severely

yánchéng 嚴懲 to punish severely

yáncí 嚴慈 father and mother

yáncí qiǎnzé 嚴詞譴責 to condemn sternly

yándōng 嚴冬 severe winter; very cold winter

yánfáng 嚴防 to guard carefully

yán'gé 嚴格 strict; stringent; rigid; rigorous

yánhán 嚴寒 severe cold

yánjǐn 嚴謹 careful; cautious; well-knit

yánjìn 嚴禁 to prohibit or forbid strictly

yánkē 嚴苛 harsh

yánkù 嚴酷 inclement; caustic

yánlì 嚴厲 strict; stringent; rigid; rigorous

yánmì 嚴密 rigid; rigorous; strict; exact

yánshī 嚴師 a stern or strict teacher

yánsù 嚴肅 serious-looking; serious

yánxíng jùnfǎ 嚴刑峻法 severe punishments under strict laws

yánxíng kǎodǎ 嚴刑拷打 to torture cruelly

yánzhěng 嚴整 well-disciplined; in neat formation

yánzhòng 嚴重 serious; severe; grave

yán 巖

1. a rock; a crag 2. a cave

yándòng 巖洞 a mountain cave

yánxué 巖穴 a cave or cavern

yánxué 巖穴 refer to **yánxué** 巖穴

yán 鹽

common salt; salt

yánbā 鹽巴 (dialect) salt; common salt

yánjǐng 鹽井 a salt well

yánkuàng 鹽礦 a salt mine

yánshuǐ 鹽水 salt solution; salt water; brine

yánsuān 鹽酸 hydrochloric acid

yántián 鹽田 a salt garden; a salt pond

yánwèi 鹽味 a salty taste; saltiness

yǎn 奄

1. to cover; to surround 2. suddenly 3. (also **yān**) to soak; to bathe; to drown 4. (also **yān**) to remain 5. (also **yān**) to castrate; a castrated man

yǎnyǎn yīxī 奄奄一息 dying

yǎnyǎn yīxī 奄奄一息 refer to **yǎnyǎn yīxī** 奄奄一息

yǎn 衍

1. to overflow; to spread out 2. ample; plenty and abundant 3. (said of fields or plains) level; plane and even 4. a lake; a marsh 5. a slope 6. superfluous

yǎnshēng 衍生 to derive from

yǎn 眼

1. the eye 2. a look; a glance 3. a tiny hole; an opening; an orifice; an aperture 4. a key point

yǎnbābā 眼巴巴 1. expectantly; eagerly; anxiously 2. helplessly (watching something unpleasant happen)

yǎngāo shǒudī 眼高手低 to have great aims but poor abilities

yǎnguāng 眼光 sight; insight; vision; eye—discerning ability; power of judgment

yǎnhóng 眼紅 1. red-eyed 2. covetous; envious 3. angry

yǎnhuā 眼花 eyesight blurred;

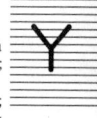

Y

dim of sight

yǎnhuā liáoluàn 眼花撩亂 (scenes so varied and confusing as) to dazzle the eyes

yǎnjiǎn 眼瞼 eyelids

yǎnjiémáo 眼睫毛 eyelashes

yǎnjiè 眼界 one's field of vision; an outlook

yǎnjìng 眼鏡 glasses; spectacles

yǎnjìngshé 眼鏡蛇 a cobra

yǎnjing 眼睛 the eyes

yǎnkuàng 眼眶 an orbit; an eye socket

yǎnlèi 眼淚 tears

yǎnlì 眼力 1. eyesight; vision 2. discerning ability

yǎnmíng shǒukuài 眼明手快 to see things clearly and act speedily

yǎnpí 眼皮 eyelids

yǎnqián 眼前 1. right before one's eyes 2. at this moment; now; at present

yǎnqiú 眼球 an eyeball

yǎnshén 眼神 expression of the eyes

yǎnshú 眼熟 seemingly familiar by sight

yǎnwō 眼窩 an orbit; an eye socket

yǎnxiàn 眼線 (said of crime investigation) a contact, a stool pigeon, or an informer

yǎnyàoshuǐ 眼藥水 eyewash; eyewater; eyedrops

yǎnzhào 眼罩 1. an eyeshade 2. blinkers (for a horse)

yǎnzhēngzhēng 眼睜睜 1. right before one's eyes; publicly 2. attentively; to watch helplessly

yǎnzhōngdīng 眼中釘 an eyesore

yǎnzhū 眼珠 an eyeball

yǎn 偃

1. to cease; to be at rest; to stop; to suppress; to lay off 2. to lie on one's back 3. an embankment

yǎnqí xīgǔ 偃旗息鼓 1. to stop the fanfare 2. to stop fighting

yǎnqí xígǔ 偃旗息鼓 refer to

yǎnqí xīgǔ 偃旗息鼓

yǎn 掩

1. to cover; to hide; to conceal; to cover up 2. to shut; to close 3. to mount a surprise attack; to take or catch by surprise

yǎnbì 掩蔽 to cover; to conceal; to shelter

yǎncáng 掩藏 to hide; to conceal

yǎn'ěr dàolíng 掩耳盜鈴 to deceive oneself

yǎn'gài 掩蓋 to cover up; to conceal

yǎnhù 掩護 1. to cover (friendly troops on a special assignment) 2. camouflage

yǎnkǒu érxiào 掩口而笑 to laugh in secret

yǎnmái 掩埋 to bury

yǎnmiàn érqì 掩面而泣 to cover one's face and weep

yǎnrén ěrmù 掩人耳目 to hoodwink people

yǎnshì 掩飾 to cover; to conceal

yǎnyìng 掩映 1. the mingling, or contrast, of light and shadow (usually said of enchanting scenery) 2. to set off (one another)

yǎn 演

1. to perform for entertainment; to act; to play 2. to expound 3. to exercise; to practice 4. to evolve; to develop

yǎnbiàn 演變 to develop and change; to evolve

yǎnchàng 演唱 to sing on stage

yǎnchū 演出 (said of entertainers) to perform; to present (a play)

yǎnjì 演技 acting

yǎnjiǎng 演講 to deliver a speech; to orate

yǎnjiǎng bǐsài 演講比賽 an oratorical contest

yǎnjìn 演進 to evolve; to develop

yǎnliàn 演練 drill

yǎnshuō 演說 to deliver a speech

yǎnshuōjiā 演說家 an orator

yǎnsuàn 演算 to do mathemati-

Y

cal problems

yǎnxí 演習 military exercises; maneuvers

yǎnxì 演戲 1. to act in a play 2. to playact

yǎnyuán 演員 an actor or actress

yǎnzòu 演奏 (said of musicians) to perform

yǎnzòuhuì 演奏會 a concert; a recital

yǎn 儼
1. majestic; respectable 2. (to act, talk, appear, etc.) as if; like

yǎnrán 儼然 dignified-looking

yàn 沿
1. bank; water's edge 2. refer to **yán** 沿 4

yàn 咽
to swallow; to gulp

yàn 彥
a man of ability and virtue; an erudite scholar

yàn 唁
for to condole with or express sympathy

yàndiàn 唁電 a condolatory telegram

yànhán 唁函 a letter (or message) of condolence

yàn 宴
1. to entertain; to feast 2. leisurely; comfort; ease

yàn'ěr xīnhūn 宴爾新婚 the bliss of the newlyweds

yànhuì 宴會 a banquet; a feast

yànkè 宴客 to entertain guests at a banquet

yànqǐng 宴請 to entertain (to dinner)

yànxí 宴席 a banquet; a feast

yànxiǎng 宴饗 (said of the emperor) to give a great dinner

yànyǐn 宴飲 to feast; to dine and wine

yàn 晏
1. clear (sky, sea, water, etc.) 2. late 3. peaceful; quiet 4. a Chinese family name

yànqǐ 晏起 to get up late

yànqǐn 晏寢 to sit up late

yànrán 晏然 peaceful and easy; quiet and comfortable

yànrú 晏如 peaceful and easy

yàn 雁
the wild goose

yànháng 雁行 1. to walk like flying wild geese, one after another 2. brothers

yànzú chuánshū 雁足傳書 to bring a message

yàn 硯
an inkstone

yàntái 硯臺 an ink-slab; an ink-stone

yàn 焰(燄) also **yán**
1. flames; blazes 2. glowing; brilliant

yàn 厭
1. to dislike; to detest; to hate 2. to get tired of 3. satiated; surfeited

yànfán 厭煩 bored; wearied

yànjuàn 厭倦 to be tired of; to be weary of

yànqì 厭棄 to reject; to get rid of

yànshí 厭食 lack of appetite

yànshì 厭世 1. to be disgusted with the world 2. to die 3. misanthropy

yànwù 厭惡 to loathe; to dislike

yàn 燕
1. a swallow 2. comfort; ease 3. to feast; to enjoy

yàn'ān 燕安 comfort; ease; peace

yàn'ěr xīnhūn 燕爾新婚 marital happiness

yànhǎo 燕好 (said of husband and wife) very fond of each other

yànmài 燕麥 oats

yànmàipiàn 燕麥片 oatmeal

yànshòu huánféi 燕瘦環肥 beautiful women, each of whom is attractive in her own way

yànwěifú 燕尾服 a swallowtail; a tailcoat

Y

yànyǔ ní'nán 燕語呢喃 the soft chirping of swallows

yànzi 燕子 a swallow

yàn 諺

a proverb; a saying; a saw; an adage

yànyǔ 諺語 a proverb; a saying; a saw; an adage

yàn 嚥

to swallow

yànqì 嚥氣 to breathe one's last; to die

yàn 贋

a counterfeit; a sham; a fake; bogus; spurious; forged

yànpǐn 贋品 a counterfeit; an imitation; a phony; a sham; a fake; a forgery

yàn 驗

1. to test; to examine; to analyze 2. to produce an effect 3. to verify; to prove

yànguāng 驗光 optometry

yànmíng 驗明 to ascertain by a test or examination

yànmíng zhèngshēn 驗明正身 to make a positive identification of a criminal before execution

yànniǎo 驗尿 a urine test; a urinalysis

yànshāng 驗傷 to examine an injury by competent authorities of law

yànshī 驗屍 a postmortem examination; an autopsy

yànshōu 驗收 to accept (goods, buildings, etc.) after ascertaining that the quality or quantity meets requirements

yànsuàn 驗算 to check computations

yànxiě 驗血 a blood test

yànzhèng 驗證 to test and verify

yàn 饜

1. full-stomached; sufficient; surfeited; satiated 2. to partake plentifully of

yànzú 饜足 surfeited; satiated

yàn 豔(艷)

1. plump; voluptuous 2. beautiful and captivating (literary writings, etc.) 3. gorgeous; colorful; gaudy 4. anything pertaining to love, as a love story, love song, etc.; amorous 5. a beauty 6. radiant 7. to admire or envy

yànlì 豔麗 radiantly beautiful; magnificent; charming

yànyángtiān 豔陽天 bright sunny skies

yànyù 豔遇 an encounter with a beautiful woman

yāng 央

1. the center; central; middle 2. the finish or conclusion; to finish 3. to request; to entreat

yāngqiú 央求 to beg; to entreat; to implore; to plead

yāng 泱

1. great; profound 2. (said of clouds) turbulent

yāngyāng dàguó 泱泱大國 a great country

yāng 殃

1. disaster; misfortune; calamities 2. the return of the spirit of the deceased

yāngjí chíyú 殃及池魚 to cause trouble or bring disaster to innocent people

yāngjí wúgū 殃及無辜 Trouble involves the innocent people.

yāng 秧

1. a rice seedling 2. a tree sapling; a very young plant for transplanting 3. fry 4. (now rarely) to cultivate; to grow

yāngmiáo 秧苗 a rice seedling

yāng 鴦

the female mandarin duck

yáng 羊

a sheep; a goat

yángcháng xiǎojìng 羊腸小徑 a narrow, winding path

yángmáo 羊毛 wool

yángqún 羊群 a flock of sheep

or goats

yángròu 羊肉 mutton

yángrù hǔkǒu 羊入虎口 (literally) a sheep in a tiger's mouth —a hopelessly perilous situation

yángshuǐ 羊水 amniotic fluid

yáng 佯

1. to pretend; to feign; to sham 2. false; deceitful; feigning

yángbìng 佯病 to pretend to be ill

yángkuáng 佯狂 to feign madness

yángsǐ 佯死 to feign death; to pretend to be dead

yángzuò bùzhī 佯作不知 to feign ignorance; to pretend not to know

yáng 洋

1. an ocean 2. foreign; Western; Occidental 3. imported

yángcài 洋菜 agar

yángcōng 洋葱 an onion

yángfáng 洋房 a Western-style house

yángfú 洋服 Western clothes; Occidental dress

yángháng 洋行 a foreign business firm

yánghuà 洋化 to be westernized

yánghuò 洋貨 foreign goods

yángjiǔ 洋酒 imported wine and spirits

yángliú 洋流 the marine current

yángrén 洋人 a Westerner; a foreigner

yángsǎn 洋傘 a Western-style umbrella

yángtiě 洋鐵 tin plate; galvanized iron

yángwáwa 洋娃娃 a doll

yángwén 洋文 a foreign language

yángxiàng 洋相 to make an exhibition of oneself

yángyáng dàguān 洋洋大觀 grand; magnificent

yángyáng déyì 洋洋得意 proud and happy; elated

yángyáng sǎsǎ 洋洋灑灑 (said of expository writing, etc.) copious and fluent

yángyì 洋溢 to be filled with; to brim with

yángyù 洋芋 a potato

yángzhuāng 洋裝 1. Western dress 2. Western binding (for books)

yáng 揚

1. to raise 2. (said of flames) blazing 3. to wave; to flutter 4. to praise; to acclaim 5. to display; to expose; to make evident; to make known 6. high or raised (voice, cry, etc.) 7. to scatter; to spread 8. to stir; to get excited 9. a Chinese family name

yángcháng érqù 揚長而去 to stride away without looking back; to stalk off

yángfān 揚帆 to set sail

yángfān 揚帆 refer to **yángfān** 揚帆

yángméi tǔqì 揚眉吐氣 to feel proud and elated after one suddenly comes to fame, wealth or good luck

yángmíng tiānxià 揚名天下 to have one's name spread far and wide; to become world-famous

yángqì 揚棄 to discard; to renounce

yángwēi 揚威 to show one's great authority, superiority, power, etc. to attain eminence (in a certain field, etc.)

yángyán 揚言 to exaggerate; to declare in public

yángyáng déyì 揚揚得意 to be smug and complacent

yángyáng zìdé 揚揚自得 to be complacent

yáng 陽

1. positive (electricity, etc.) 2. male; masculine 3. the sun; solar; sunlight 4. the north of a stream 5. the south of a hill 6. bright; brilliant 7. the male genitals 8. pertaining to this world, as opposed to Hades

yángchūn 陽春 springtime

yángchūnmiàn 陽春麵 cooked noodles without any dressing

Y

yángfèng yīnwéi 陽奉陰違 to observe rules or obey orders ostensibly; to pretend to obey

yánggāng 陽剛 tough, strong, positive, stern, etc. in character

yángguāng 陽光 sunshine; sunlight; sunbeams

yángjiān 陽間 the world of the living

yánglì 陽曆 the solar calendar; the Gregorian calendar

Yángmíngshān 陽明山 Mt. Yang-ming in Taiwan

yángpíng 陽平 (Chinese phonetics) the second tone

yángsǎn 陽傘 a parasol; an umbrella

yángshòu 陽壽 one's predestined life span

yángtái 陽臺 1. a veranda or balcony 2. a trysting place; a tryst

yángxìng 陽性 1. positive (electricity, etc.) 2. the male sex; masculinity

yángzhái 陽宅 a human habitation; a house; the residence of the living

yáng 楊

1. a poplar 2. a willow 3. a Chinese family name

yánghuā 楊花 poplar blossoms; poplar filaments

yángliǔ 楊柳 a willow

yángtáo 楊桃 a carambola or star fruit

yáng 瘍

skin diseases or infections; sores; an ulcer

yǎng 仰

1. to look up 2. to adore, admire or revere 3. to lean or rely upon 4. to swallow

yǎngjiǎo 仰角 an angle of elevation

yǎnglài 仰賴 to look to (somebody for help); to rely upon

yǎngmù 仰慕 to adore; to admire and respect

yǎngrén bíxí 仰人鼻息 to rely on others and have to watch

their every expression

yǎngrén bíxí 仰人鼻息 refer to **yǎngrén bíxí** 仰人鼻息

yǎngtiān chángxiào 仰天長嘯 to make a long cry into the air

yǎngwàng 仰望 1. to look up at 2. to respectfully seek guidance or help from; to look up to

yǎngwò 仰臥 to lie on the back

yǎngwò qǐzuò 仰臥起坐 (sports) sit-up

yǎngyǒng 仰泳 (sports) backstroke

yǎngzhàng 仰仗 to rely on

yǎng 氧

oxygen

yǎnghuà 氧化 to oxidize or be oxidized; oxidation

yǎnghuàwù 氧化物 the oxide

yǎng 養

1. to grow; to raise; to breed; to rear; to bring up 2. to support or keep (a family, etc.) 3. to give birth to 4. to nourish; to cultivate (one's mind, etc.) 5. to educate 6. to nurse (a wound or illness) 7. (also **yàng**) to support one's parents

yǎngbīng 養兵 to maintain and train soldiers (in preparation for war)

yǎngbīng qiānrì, yòngzài yīzhāo 養兵千日, 用在一朝 (literally) to maintain an army for a thousand days to use it for a moment

yǎngbìng 養病 1. to convalesce; to recuperate 2. convalescence; recuperation

yǎngchéng 養成 to discipline and train; to cultivate (good habits, etc.)

yǎng'ér fánglǎo 養兒防老 to raise sons as insurance against the insecurity of old age

yǎngfèn 養分 the amount of nutritious substance in a given food item; nutrition

yǎngfù 養父 a foster father

yǎnghǔ yíhuàn 養虎遺患 To keep a tiger is to invite calamity.—Appeasement brings disas-

ter.

yǎnghuo 養活 1. to support or keep (a family or somebody) 2. to rear; to bring up

yǎngjiā huókǒu 養家活口 to support one's family

yǎngjīng xùruì 養精蓄銳 to nourish and discipline one's stamina; to nurse one's strength (in preparation for a challenging task ahead)

yǎnglǎo 養老 1. (said of persons) to retire and enjoy the fruit of one's work in the past 2. to provide for the aged

yǎnglǎojīn 養老金 an old age pension

yǎnglǎoyuàn 養老院 a home for destitute old people

yǎngliào 養料 nutrition; nutritious value

yǎngmǔ 養母 a foster mother

yǎngnǚ 養女 an adopted daughter; a foster daughter

yǎngshāng 養傷 to nurse one's injuries or wounds

yǎngshén 養神 to have mental relaxation; to give one's mental faculty a rest

yǎngshēng 養生 to preserve one's health; to keep in good condition

yǎngshēng sòngsǐ 養生送死 to support one's parents when they are alive and to look after their funeral arrangement upon their death (which is the duty of a son)

yǎngshēng zhīdào 養生之道 a regimen; the formula of healthy living

yǎngyù 養育 to rear; to raise and educate

yǎngzhí 養殖 to breed (aquatics)

yǎngzǐ 養子 1. a foster or an adopted son 2. to bring up children

yǎngzūn chǔyōu 養尊處優 to live in luxury (or clover)

yǎng 癢
to itch; to tickle

yàng 怏
discontented; disheartened;

dispirited

yàng 恙
1. disease 2. worry

yàng 養
refer to **yǎng** 養 7

yàng 樣
1. appearances; looks 2. a style; a pattern; a mode; a form 3. a sort; a kind; a variety 4. a sample

yàngbǎn 樣板 1. a sample plate 2. a templet 3. a model; a prototype; an example

yàngběn 樣本 a sample

yàngpǐn 樣品 a specimen; a sample (of a commodity)

yàngshì 樣式 style; modes; patterns

yàngyàng 樣樣 each and every; all; every kind

yàngzhāng 樣張 a specimen sheet

yàngzi 樣子 1. appearance; shape 2. manner 3. sample; model 4. tendency; likelihood

yāo 幺(么)
1. tiny; small; insignificant 2. the youngest son or daughter of a family 3. one on dice; one 4. lone; alone

yāo'ér 幺兒 the youngest son

yāo 夭
1. young; fresh-looking; tender 2. (also **yǎo**) to die young; to suppress; to repress

yāoshòu 夭壽 to die young

yāozhé 夭折 1. to die young 2. to come to a premature end

yāo 吆
to shout; to cry

yāohe 吆喝 1. to shout; to cry 2. to hawk

yāo 妖
1. weird; unaccountable; monstrous; supernatural 2. an evil; a monster; a goblin; a phantom; a ghost 3. (usually said of a woman) bewitching

yāoguài 妖怪 1. a monster or demon 2. a Circe; a siren 3. a

spirit transformed from a very old animal, tree

yāojing 妖精 1. a monster or demon 2. a Circe; a siren 3. a spirit transformed from a very old animal, tree

yāoli yāoqì 妖裏妖氣 seductive and bewitching

yāomèi 妖媚 bewitching

yāomó guǐguài 妖魔鬼怪 a general term for evil spirits

yāoniè 妖孽 1. unlucky omens 2. the monsters who cause great calamities 3. a person like a devil

yāonǚ 妖女 a fairy enchantress

yāoshù 妖術 sorcery; witchcraft

yāoyán huòzhòng 妖言惑衆 to cheat people with sensational speeches

yāoyàn 妖艶 seductive; bewitchingly pretty

yāo 殀 also **yǎo**

1. to die young or untimely 2. to be wronged or aggrieved

yāo 要

1. to invite 2. to engage; to make an agreement 3. to ask for; to demand 4. to coerce; to threaten

yāoqiú 要求 1. to demand; to request 2. a demand; a request

yāoxié 要脅 to blackmail; to put pressure on; to coerce; to threaten

yāo 腰

1. the midriff; the waist 2. the kidneys 3. the middle of something; the waist portion of a region

yāobāo 腰包 1. a purse; a billfold; a wallet 2. one's money

yāobù 腰部 the waist

yāochán wànguàn 腰纏萬貫 very rich; loaded

yāodài 腰帶 1. a girdle; a waistband 2. (anatomy) a pelvic girdle

yāoguǒ 腰果 a cashew nut

yāosuān bèiténg 腰酸背疼 a sore waist and an aching back

yāowéi 腰圍 1. the waist; the waistline 2. a girdle

yāo 邀

1. to invite; to ask; to request 2. to intercept 3. (now rarely) to weigh or measure

yāogōng 邀功 to take credit for the deeds achieved by someone else

yāoqǐng 邀請 to invite; invitation

yāoyàn 邀宴 1. to invite to a feast 2. an invitation to a luncheon or dinner party

yāoyuē 邀約 1. an engagement; an invitation 2. to invite; to make an appointment

yáo 肴

cooked food, especially meat and fish; dishes

yáozhuàn 肴饌 rich food; sumptuous dishes

yáo 姚

1. handsome; good-looking; elegant 2. a Chinese family name

yáo 淆

refer to **xiáo** 淆

yáo 堯

1. Yao, a legendary sage king in ancient China whose reign is said to have extended from 2357 to 2255 B.C. 2. high; eminent; lofty

yáo 殽

1. refer to **xiáo** 殽 2. dishes

yáo 搖

1. to wag; to shake; to wave; to rock 2. (said of one's confidence, determination, etc.) to sway, wobble, shake 3. to scull; to row (a boat, etc.) 4. to agitate; to incite; to annoy

yáobǎi 搖擺 to swing to and fro; to oscillate; to vacillate

yáodàng 搖盪 to sway; unstable (situations, etc.)

yáodòng 搖動 to shake; to rock; to sway

yáogǔnyuè 搖滾樂 rock'n'roll; rock music

yáohuàng 搖晃 to shake (a bottle, etc.)

yáolán 搖籃 a cradle

yáolánqǔ 搖籃曲 a cradle song; a lullaby

yáoqí nàhǎn 搖旗吶喊 to cheer or encourage

yáoshēn yībiàn 搖身一變 1. (often said of an upstart, turncoat, etc.) to transform into another person all of a sudden 2. (in fairy tales) to change to another form in the twinkle of the eye

yáotóu bǎiwěi 搖頭擺尾 to act obsequiously

yáowěi qǐlián 搖尾乞憐 to fawn and be obsequious

yáoyáo huǎnghuàng 搖搖晃晃 shaky; tottering; faltering

yáoyáo yùzhuì 搖搖欲墜 shaky; on the verge collapse of

yáoyè 搖曳 1. wavering gently 2. (said of light) flickering 3. (said of a girl's hips) to sway enticingly

yáoyǐ 搖椅 a rocking chair

yáoyì 搖曳 refer to **yáoyè** 搖曳

yáo 徭

compulsory labor service; conscript labor

yáoyì 徭役 compulsory labor service; corvee

yáo 瑤

1. a precious jade or stone 2. clean, pure and white 3. treasurable; valuable; precious

yáochí 瑤池 a fairyland

yáohán 瑤函 (a polite expression) your letter

yáo 遙

distant; far; remote

yáokòng 遙控 remote control; teleneontrol

yáowàng 遙望 to take a distant look

yáoyáo lǐngxiān 遙遙領先 to be far ahead

yáoyáo wúqī 遙遙無期 in the indefinite future

yáoyáo wúqí 遙遙無期 refer to **yáoyáo wúqī** 遙遙無期

yáoyuǎn 遙遠 far and remote

yáo 窯

1. a kiln; a brick furnace 2. pottery 3. a pit in a coal mine; a coal shaft 4. a cave—for human dwelling 5. a brothel

yáozi 窯子 a brothel; a prostitute

yáo 餚

dishes and foods

yáo 謠

1. rumor 2. a ballad; a folk song; a song

yáochuán 謠傳 1. unfounded report; hearsay 2. according to rumor; it is rumored

yáoyán 謠言 unfounded report; rumor

yǎo 夭

refer to **yāo** 夭 2

yǎo 妖

refer to **yāo** 妖

yǎo 杳

1. deep and expansive 2. quiet; silent

yǎorán 杳然 quiet and silent; lonely

yǎowú yīnxìn 杳無音信 without any news of someone for a long time

yǎowú wúzōng 杳杳無蹤 gone without leaving a trace

yǎo 咬

to bite; gnaw

yǎojǐn yáguān 咬緊牙關 to endure pain or hardships with determination; to persevere

yǎopò 咬破 to bite through

yǎowén jiáozì 咬文嚼字 to be overcareful or pedantic about the use of each word

yǎoyá qièchǐ 咬牙切齒 to gnash the teeth (in anger or hatred)

yǎozhù 咬住 to bite into

yǎo 窈

1. deep; obscure; secluded 2. tranquil

yǎotiǎo 窈窕 1. (said of young women) attractive and charming 2. far and deep

Y

yǎo 舀 also **kuǎi**

to ladle out (water)

yāo 拗

refer to **ào** 拗

yào 要

1. necessary; important; essential; necessity 2. must; should; ought to 3. to want; to demand; to need; to require; to desire; to take 4. to summarize; a summary; a generalization; a synopsis 5. will; shall—to indicate the future tense 6. brief 7. if; in case

yàobude 要不得 extremely bad; inappropriate; condemnable

yàoburán 要不然 otherwise; or

yàobushì 要不是 If it were not for.... But for....

yàochōng 要衝 a strategic position; a key place; a communication hub

yàodào 要道 1. an important road or passage 2. the essential points of what is good and appropriate

yàodé 要得 1. good; well done; bravo 2. acceptable; okay

yàodiǎn 要點 the important or main points; the gist; the essential points

yàofàn 要犯 an important or dangerous criminal; a most-wanted criminal

yàofànde 要飯的 a beggar

yàohài 要害 1. fatal points; a vital part; a crucial point 2. strategic locations or points

yàohǎo 要好 1. to desire to excel 2. to be friend 3. to be in love with

yàojǐn 要緊 important and urgent

yàojué 要訣 the secret of doing something; the key to doing something successfully

yàolǐng 要領 essential points; essentials

yàomiànzi 要面子 to be keen on face-saving

yàomìng 要命 1. very; extremely; awfully 2. too much to endure

yàorén 要人 a VIP; a prominent figure

yàosài 要塞 a fortress; a strategic point

yàoshì 要事 an important matter; an urgent business

yàoshi 要是 if; in case

yàosù 要素 essentials; chief ingredients or elements or factors

yàozhí 要職 an important post

yàozhǐ 要旨 key points; themes; epitomes

yào 葯 also **yuè**

angelica

yào 樂

to love; to be fond of; to delight in

yàoqún 樂群 fond of company and learning from one's friends

yào 藥 also **yuè**

1. medicine; remedy; a drug; pharmaceuticals 2. to kill with poison; to poison

yàocái 藥材 medicinal substance

yàocǎo 藥草 medicinal herbs

yàodān 藥單 a (medicinal) prescription

yàofāng 藥方 a (medicinal) prescription

yàofáng 藥房 a druggist's store; a dispensary; a pharmacy

yàofěn 藥粉 medicinal powder

yàogāo 藥膏 ointment; salve

yàoguànzi 藥罐子 1. a drug boiler 2. one who is perennially ill

yàojìshī 藥劑師 a pharmacist; a druggist

yàojú 藥局 a druggist's store; a dispensary; a pharmacy

yàolì 藥力 the potency or effect of a drug

yàoliàng 藥量 dosage

yàopiàn 藥片 a tablet of medicine

yàopǐn 藥品 pharmaceutical products; drugs

yàoshuǐ 藥水 liquid medicine

yàowán 藥丸 a pill medicine; a

pill

yàoxiāng 藥箱 a medicine chest; a medical kit

yào 耀 also **yuè**
1. to shine; to dazzle 2. to show off

yàowǔ yángwēi 耀武揚威 1. bluff and bluster; to show off one's strength or power 2. to parade military prowess

yàoyǎn 耀眼 dazzling; to dazzle

yào 鷂
a hawk; a sparrow hawk

yàozi 鷂子 1. a sparrow hawk 2. a kite (a toy)

yàozi fānshēn 鷂子翻身 a hawk's turn (a fast bodily motion in Chinese pugilism)

yào 躍
refer to **yuè** 躍

yào 鑰 also **yuè**
1. a key 2. a lock

yàoshi 鑰匙 a key

yē 耶
transliteration of English names

Yēdànjié 耶誕節 Christmas

Yēdàn kǎpiàn 耶誕卡片 a Christmas card

Yēdànshù 耶誕樹 a Christmas tree

Yēsū Jīdū 耶穌基督 Jesus Christ

yē 掖
1. to conceal; to tuck away; to hide 2. to fold; to roll up (part of one's clothing)

yē 椰 also **yé**
a coconut; a coconut palm; a coconut tree

yēzi 椰子 a coconut

yē 噎
1. to be choked with food 2. to choke off

yé 耶
a phrase-final particle for a question

yé 揶

to jeer at; to ridicule; to play a joke on

yéyú 揶揄 to ridicule; to jeer at

yé 椰
refer to **yē** 椰

yé 爺
1. father 2. master; sir 3. god

yérliǎng 爺兒倆 father and son; father and daughter

yérmen 爺兒們 men and boys

yéye 爺爺 1. grandfather; grandpa 2. sir

yě 也
1. and; also; besides; either; too 2. still 3. even 4. an expletive in Chinese writing

yěhǎo 也好 That's fine.

yěkěyǐ 也可以 1. may also 2. It makes no difference. It's okay.

yěshì 也是 also the same

yěxíng 也行 All right! That will do too.

yěxǔ 也許 perhaps; probably

yě 冶
1. to smelt; to fus metals 2. seductive; fascinating

yějīn 冶金 metallurgy

yěyóu 冶遊 to frequent brothels

yě 野
1. the countryside; fields; the wilderness 2. the people (as opposed to the government) 3. wild; uncultured; undomesticated; coarse; barbarous; rude

yěcān 野餐 a picnic; a barbecue

yěcǎo 野草 a weed

yědì 野地 1. the countryside 2. the wilderness

yěháizi 野孩子 an urchin; a street urchin

yěhé 野合 illicit copulation or connection

yěhuā 野花 1. a wild flower 2. a harlot

yěhuǒ 野火 1. will-o'-the-wisp 2. prairie fire; bushfire; wildfire 3. farm fire (for clearing the field)

yějī 野雞 1. a pheasant 2. a streetwalker 3. unlicensed taxi-

cabs

yěmǎ 野馬 a wild horse; a mustang

yěmán 野蠻 1. barbarous; savage; uncivilized 2. unreasonable; rude; brutal

yěrén 野人 1. a rustic 2. a barbarian; a savage

yěrén xiànpù 野人獻曝 (literally) a rustic offering sunshine —a trivial contribution

yěshēng 野生 wild; undomesticated

yěshēng dòngwù 野生動物 undomesticated animals

yěshǐ 野史 unofficial history

yěshòu 野獸 a wild beast; a brute

yěwài 野外 the outdoors; the open

yěxīn 野心 1. ambition; careerism 2. greediness

yěxīn bóbó 野心勃勃 full of ambition

yěxìng 野性 jungle instincts; ungovernableness; untamedness; unruliness

yěyíng 野營 outdoor camping

yězhàn 野戰 (military) field operations

yè 曳 also **yì**

to haul; to tug; to drag; to trail

yèyǐnjī 曳引機 a tractor

yè 夜

1. night; dark(ness) 2. a night trip; night traveling

yèbān 夜班 night shifts; night work

yèbù bìhù 夜不閉戶 There's no need to close doors at night.

yècān 夜餐 supper

yècháng mèngduō 夜長夢多 There'll be twists and obstacles if a problem or an issue is not settled promptly.

yèchē 夜車 1. a night train 2. (figuratively) to study late at night

yèdàxué 夜大學 an evening university

yègōng 夜工 night work; a night

job

yèhú 夜壺 a chamber pot

yèjiān 夜間 at night; in the night

yèjiānbù 夜間部 the night department (of a school, college or university)

yèjǐng 夜景 night scenes (of a locality)

yèláixiāng 夜來香 (botany) the tuberose

yèlán rénjìng 夜闌人靜 deep in the night; at the dead of night

Yèláng zìdà 夜郎自大 ignorant and boastful

yèliáng rúshuǐ 夜涼如水 chilling (autumn) night

yèmángzhèng 夜盲症 night blindness; nyctalopia

yèmāozi 夜貓子 1. the owl 2. a person who enjoys night life

yèmù 夜幕 gathering darkness

yèsè 夜色 the dim light of night —moonlight

yèsè cāngmáng 夜色蒼茫 twilight at dusk

yèshēnghuó 夜生活 night life

yèshì 夜市 business activities in night hours; markets devoted to nighttime business

yèwǎn 夜晚 at night; in the night

yèxí 夜襲 to launch an attack under the cover of night

yèxiào 夜校 a night school

yèyè 夜夜 night after night

yèyǐ jìrì 夜以繼日 around the clock; night and day

yèyīng 夜鶯 the nightingale

yèzǒnghuì 夜總會 a nightclub

yè 頁

a page (in books, etc.); a sheet (of paper, etc.)

yècì 頁次 the page number

yèmǎ 頁碼 the page number

yè 咽

to be choked; to weep or speak in a choked voice; to sob

yè 射

refer to **shè** 射 5

yè 液 also **yì**

liquid; juices; secretions; sap

yèhuà 液化 to liquefy or be liquefied; liquefaction

yèhuà tiānránqì 液化天然氣 liquefied natural gas

yètǐ 液體 liquid

yèzhī 液汁 liquid; fluid; juices; sap

yè 掖 also yì

1. to support another; to extend a helping hand; to promote 2. armpits; side; by the side

yè 腋 also yì

the armpits; the part under the forelegs of animals

yèmáo 腋毛 armpit hair

yèwō 腋窩 the armpits

yè 葉

1. a leaf; a petal (of a flower) 2. a leaf or two pages (of a book) 3. a period; an era or epoch 4. something light and tiny—as a small boat in a lake 5. a Chinese family name

yèlǜsù 葉綠素 (biochemistry) chlorophyll

yèluò guīgēn 葉落歸根 When a person gets old, he thinks of going back home.

yèluò zhīqiū 葉落知秋 Revealing signs foretell things to come.

yèzi 葉子 a leaf

yè 業

1. work; occupations; professions; vocations; callings; trades 2. estate; property 3. already

yèjī 業績 the track record

yèjīng 業經 to have already been

yèwù 業務 business activities

yèyǐ 業已 to have already been

yèyú 業餘 1. amateur 2. spare time

yèzhǔ 業主 the proprietor; the owner

yè 謁

to have an audience with; to see a superior

yèjiàn 謁見 to have an audience with; to see a superior

yèlíng 謁陵 to pay homage to a great leader by visiting his tomb or mausoleum

yè 靨

dimples in the face

yī 一

1. union; uniformity; uniform 2. one; unit 3. single; alone 4. whole; all; throughout 5. a; an; the 6. to unify; to unite 7. once; as soon as 8. each; per; every time (Note: When **yī** precedes a 4th-tone sound, it is pronounced as **yí**. When the sound followed **yī** is a 1st-, 2nd-, or 3rd-tone sound, **yī** is pronounced as **yì**.)

yībāzhang 一巴掌 (to give someone) a slap

yībǎ 一把 a handful; a bundle

yībǎi 一百 one hundred

yībǎi zhōunián jìniàn 一百 週年紀念 a centenary; a centennial

yībài túdì 一敗塗地 a complete failure

yībān 一般 common; general; commonly; generally

yībān jiànshi 一般見識 to hold the same kind of view

yībānxìng 一般性 generality

yībàn 一半 a half; half; in part

yībāng 一幫 a gang; a clique

yībèi 一輩 a generation

yībèizi 一輩子 as long as one lives; a lifetime

yīběn 一本 a copy; a volume

yīběn wànlì 一本萬利 to gain enormous profit out of small capital investment

yīběn zhèngjīng 一本正經 in a serious manner

yībíkǒng chūqì 一鼻孔出氣 to sing the same tune

yībízi huī 一鼻子灰 to meet rejection, humiliation or frustration

yībǐ 一筆 1. one stroke 2. a sum of money (debt, account, etc.)

yībǐ gōuxiāo 一筆勾消 1. all cancelled 2. to settle an account once (and) for all

yībǐ mǒshā 一筆抹殺 totally

Y

negate

yībì zhīlì 一臂之力 help; assistance

yībiān 一邊 1. on one side; by the side 2. at the same time

yībiǎo réncái 一表人材 handsome; dashing

yībìng 一併 all; wholly; together with

yībìng bùqǐ 一病不起 to die of illness

yībō sānzhé 一波三折 hitting one snag after another

yībō wèipíng, yībō yòuqǐ 一波未平，一波又起 One trouble follows another.

yībù 一部 a (book, motion picture, etc.)

yībù dēngtiān 一步登天 fast advancement in one's career, etc.

yībùfen 一部分 a part; a portion; partially

yīcéng 一層 1. one story or floor 2. a stratum

yīchà'nà 一刹那 in a moment

yīchángkōng 一場空 all in vain; futile

yīchǎng 一場 1. a performance 2. a (long period of association) 3. a (dream) 4. a (period of happiness, grief, etc.)

yīchàng yīhè 一唱一和 One echoes the other.

yīchén bùrǎn 一塵不染 immaculate; spotless

yīchéng 一成 10 percent

yīchéng bùbiàn 一成不變 fixed; unchangeable; invariable; inflexible

yīchóu mòzhǎn 一籌莫展 knowing not what to do; helpless

yīchù jífā 一觸即發 (literally) One slight touch and off it goes —imminent

yīcì 一次 once

yīcù érjī 一蹴而幾 to succeed in doing something at the first try

yīdàn 一旦 1. once; whenever 2. a day

yīdǎng zhuānzhèng 一黨專政 one-party dictatorship

yīdāo liǎngduàn 一刀兩斷 to sever relations by one stroke; to be through with

yīdào 一道 1. together 2. a (problem, etc.) 3. on the same path

yīděng 一等 first-class; first-rate

yīdiǎn 一點 1. a point 2. a little bit

yīdiǎnr 一點兒 1. a little bit 2. somewhat

yīdiǎn yīdī 一點一滴 every drop; every bit

yīdìng 一定 certainly; surely; necessarily

yīdòng bùrú yījìng 一動不如一靜 Unless one is absolutely sure that he can succeed in doing something, he should not try it.

yīdù 一度 once; on one occasion; for a time

yīduān 一端 1. one end 2. one aspect

yī'èr 一二 a little; a few

yīfà qiānjūn 一髮千鈞 refer to yīfā qiānjūn 一髮千鈞

yīfà qiānjūn 一髮千鈞 a critical situation

yīfān fēngshùn 一帆風順 to proceed smoothly without a hitch

yīfān hǎoyì 一番好意 well-intentioned; good will

yīfán fēngshùn 一帆風順 refer to yīfān fēngshùn 一帆風順

yīfǎn chángtài 一反常態 to act out of one's normal behavior

yīfāng 一方 1. an area or region 2. a party

yīfāngmiàn 一方面 1. one side 2. on the one hand..., on the other hand....

yīfēn gēngyún, yīfēn shōuhuò 一分耕耘，一分收穫 One reaps no more than what he has sown.

yīfēn qián, yīfēn huò 一分錢，一分貨 The higher the price, the better the quality of the merchandise.

yīfèn 一份 a part, portion or share

yīfū dāngguān 一夫當關 to hold a key position single-handedly

yīfū yīqī 一夫一妻 monogamy

yīgài 一概 all; without exception; totally

yīgài érlùn 一概而論 discussed or regarded in the same frame of mind or in an indiscriminating manner

yīge 一個 one; a; an

yīgege 一個個 1. one by one 2. each and every one

yīgejìnr 一個勁兒 full of zest or enthusiasm

yīgòng 一共 altogether; in all; all told

yīgǔ zuòqì 一鼓作氣 to brace oneself (for a challenge)

yīguàn zuòfēng 一貫作風 the consistent way of doing things

yīguàn zuòyè 一貫作業 integrated operation

yīhōng érsàn 一哄而散 refer to **yīhòng érsàn** 一哄而散

yīhòng érsàn 一哄而散 (said of crowds) to disperse in a hubbub

yīhuī érjiù 一揮而就 to finish writing an article or drawing a painting very quickly

yīhuí 一回 1. an occasion; a round (in boxing) 2. once

yīhuí shēng, èrhuí shú 一回生，二回熟 awkward at first but skillful later on

yīhuíshì 一回事 1. one and the same (thing) 2. one thing

yīhuǐr 一會兒 refer to **yīhuìr** 一會兒

yīhuìr 一會兒 1. in a moment 2. now... now...

yījǐ zhīsī 一己之私 one's own selfish interests

yījì zhīcháng 一技之長 proficiency in a particular line (or field); professional skill

yījiǎzǐ 一甲子 a cycle of sixty years

yījiàn rúgù 一見如故 to become intimate at the first meeting

yījiàn shuāngdiāo 一箭雙鵰 1. to win the affection of two beauties at the same time 2. to kill two birds with one stone

yījiàn zhōngqíng 一見鍾情 to fall in love at first sight

yījiǎo 一腳 1. a kick 2. to take part in something (often unsolicited)

yījīn 一斤 one catty

yī...jiù 一 …… 就 …… no sooner...than...

yījǔ 一舉 with one action; at a blow; at one fell swoop

yījǔ liǎngdé 一舉兩得 to gain two advantages by a single move; to kill two birds with one stone

yījǔ yīdòng 一舉一動 every movement and every action

yījué 一絕 a special skill; a unique talent

yījué bùzhèn 一蹶不振 unable to recover from a failure

yījué cíxióng 一決雌雄 to fight it out

yīkè 一刻 fifteen minutes; a quarter

yīkè qiānjīn 一刻千金 Time is precious.

yīkǒu 一口 1. a mouthful; a bite 2. (to promise or grant a favor) without hesitation 3. to insist (often falsely that somebody has done something bad)

yīkǒu dāyìng 一口答應 to promise without hesitation

yīkǒuqì 一口氣 1. in one breath; without stop 2. breath

yīkǒu yǎodìng 一口咬定 to insist on saying something

yīkuài 一塊 a piece; a block

yīkuàir 一塊兒 together; altogether

yīlái 一來 1. on the one hand 2. as soon as (someone) arrives

yīlǎnbiǎo 一覽表 a table list, or chart

yīlǎn wúyú 一覽無餘 (literally) A single glance takes in all—a panoramic view

yīláo yǒngyì 一勞永逸 to make a great effort to accomplish something once (and) for

all

yīlèng 一愣 taken aback

yīlián 一連 1. successively 2. a company

yīliánchuàn 一連串 a series of

yīliǎo bǎiliǎo 一了百了 To solve the key issue will expedite the solution of the whole problem.

yīliú 一流 1. first-rate 2. of the same class

yīliùyān 一溜煙 (to get away) quickly

yīlù 一路 all the way

yīlǜ 一律 without exception (or discrimination)

yīluò qiānzhàng 一落千丈 to nose-dive or decline drastically

yīmài xiāngchuán 一脈相傳 derived from the same origin

yīmáo bùbá 一毛不拔 very stingy; parsimonious

yīméi 一枚 a (coin, medal, etc.)

yīmiàn 一面 one side; an aspect

yīmiàndǎo 一面倒 excessively dependent upon

yīmiàn zhīcí 一面之詞 one-sided statements

yīmiàn zhījiāo 一面之交 a nodding acquaintance

yīmíng jīngrén 一鳴驚人 to become famous overnight; to achieve enormous success at the very first try

yīmìng guīyīn 一命歸陰 to die

yīmìng wūhū 一命嗚呼 to die

yīmù liǎorán 一目了然 to understand fully at a glance

yīmù shíháng 一目十行 (said of the ability to read very fast) to read ten lines at one glance

yīnián bànzǎi 一年半載 a relatively short time

yīnián dàotóu 一年到頭 all (the) year round

yīnián sìjì 一年四季 all the year round

yīnián yīdù 一年一度 once a year; annual(ly)

yīnián zhījì zàiyú chūn 一年之計在於春 Spring is the best time to do the year's work.

yīniàn zhīchā 一念之差 a false step (which brings untold woes)

yīnuò qiānjīn 一諾千金 a solemn promise

yīpāi jíhé 一拍即合 to become good friends after brief contact

yīpài 一派 a school; a faction

yīpài húyán 一派胡言 complete nonsense

yīpán sǎnshā 一盤散沙 utterly lacking cohesion; disunited

yīpáng 一旁 one side; on the sideline

yīpào érhóng 一砲而紅 to become famous all at once

yīpén 一盆 a plate or tray (of food); a pot (of flower); a basin (of water)

yīpī 一批 a batch; a shipment (of goods)

yīpǐ 一匹 a (horse, etc.)

yīpǐ 一疋 a roll

yīpiān 一篇 a literary article; a chapter

yīpiàn 一片 a denominative adjective for any object which is flat and thin

yīpiē 一瞥 a glimpse; a glance

yīpín rúxǐ 一貧如洗 penniless; in utter destitution

yīpù shíhán 一暴十寒 to do something by fits and starts

yīqí 一齊 at the same time

yīqǐ 一起 1. in the same place 2. together

yīqiào bùtōng 一竅不通 completely ignorant

yīqiè 一切 all; everything

yīqīn fāngzé 一親芳澤 to caress, kiss, or sleep with a woman

yīqiū zhīhé 一丘之貉 people of the same ilk

yīqǔ 一曲 a song

yīqù bùhuí 一去不回 to leave for good

yīquān 一圈 1. a circle 2. one round (in a mah-jong game)

yīqún 一群 a group; a crowd; a herd; a pack; a flock

yīrèn 一任 a tour, term, or tenure (of duty)

yīrì 一日 one day; such a day

yīrì qiānlǐ 一日千里 to make progress or improvement at a tremendous pace

yīrì sānqiū 一日三秋 longing for loved ones or close friends far away

yīrì wéishī, zhōngshēn wéifù 一日爲師，終身爲父 One should respect his teacher as if the teacher were his own father, even if the teacher-student relationship has existed for only a single day.

yīrì zhījì zàiyú chén 一日之計在於晨 Morning hours are the best time of the day to work.

yīrú jìwǎng 一如既往 as before; as always

yīsǎo érkōng 一掃而空 completely removed

yīshàn 一扇 a (door, window, etc.)

yīshēn shìdǎn 一身是膽 to have plenty of guts; very brave

yīshēn shìzhài 一身是債 (said of individuals) to be deep in debt

yīshēng 一生 a lifetime

yīshēng bùxiǎng 一聲不響 do not say a word

yīshīzú chéng qiāngǔ hèn 一失足成千古恨 One pitfall leads to endless misery and regret.

yīshí 一時 1. for a moment 2. a period of time 3. accidentally

yīshí bànkè 一時半刻 a short time; a little while

yīshì 一世 1. an epoch; an age 2. a lifetime 3. I (used after the name of an emperor such as Napoleon I)

yīshì tóngrén 一視同仁 without discrimination

yīshì wúchéng 一事無成 to accomplish nothing

yīshì zhīxióng 一世之雄 a great hero of his time

yīshǒu 一手 single-handedly

yīshǒu bāobàn 一手包辦 1. dictatorial; arbitrary 2. to do something all by oneself

yīshǒu jiāoqián, yīshǒu jiāohuò 一手交錢，一手交貨 cash on delivery

yīshǒu zhētiān 一手遮天 to hide the truth from the masses

yīshuāng 一雙 a couple

yīshùn 一瞬 the twinkling of an eye; in an instant

yīsī bùgǒu 一絲不苟 No detail is overlooked.

yīsī bùguà 一絲不掛 stark-naked

yīsī yīháo 一絲一毫 a tiny bit; an iota; a trace

yīsī liǎozhī 一死了之 to end one's troubles or worries by death

yīsuǒ 一所 a (school, charity institute, etc.)

yītā hútú 一塌糊塗 in a great mess; topsy-turvy

yītàng 一趟 a trip; a ride

yītào 一套 a suit; a set 2. phony promise; trick; flattery

yītiān 一天 1. a whole day 2. one day

yītiān dàowǎn 一天到晚 from morning till night; all day long

yītiáo 一條 1. a (rope, whip, snake, etc.) 2. an article (of a law) 3. a carton (of cigarettes)

yītiáoxīn 一條心 to be of one mind

yītōng 一通 a (telegram, etc.)

yītóng 一同 together with; in the company of

yītóu 一頭 1. a head (covered with gray hair, dust, skin ailments, etc.) 2. (said of cattle, hogs, mules, etc.) a head 3. a jerky motion of the head

yītóu wùshuǐ 一頭霧水 (slang) in bewilderment or confusion; not knowing what's the matter

yītuán héqì 一團和氣 full of goodwill toward one another

yītuánzāo 一團糟 in a hopeless mess

yīwǎng dǎjìn 一網打盡 to round up all (the criminals or other undesirable elements)

yīwǎng qíngshēn 一往情深

Y

to fall deeply in love

yīwàng wújì 一望無際 to spread out far beyond the horizon

yīwèi 一味 habitually; invariably

yīwén bùzhí 一文不值 not worth a penny

yīwèn sānbùzhī 一問三不知 to say I don't know to every question

yīwōfēng 一窩蜂 (said of a crowd of people) to swarm

yīwú shìchù 一無是處 without a single redeeming feature

yīwú suǒcháng 一無所長 do not have a single skill

yīwú suǒhuò 一無所獲 to achieve or gain nothing (after all the efforts made)

yīwú suǒyǒu 一無所有 to own nothing at all

yīwú suǒzhī 一無所知 to know nothing at all

yīwǔ yīshí 一五一十 to narrate in detail

yīxī shàngcún 一息尚存 so long as one is alive (often followed by a vow to do something)

yīxì shàngcún 一息尚存 refer to **yīxī shàngcún** 一息尚存

yīxìliè 一系列 a series of

yīxiàzi 一下子 1. at once 2. at one stroke

yīxiàn 一線 a thread; a ray

yīxiàn xīwàng 一線希望 a gleam of hope

yīxiāng qíngyuàn 一廂情願 unilateral willingness

yīxiàng 一向 1. hitherto 2. consistently

yīxiào qiānjīn 一笑千金 an enchanting smile

yīxiào zhìzhī 一笑置之 to dismiss with a laugh

yīxiē 一些 1. some; a few 2. somewhat

yīxīn 一心 1. wholeheartedly 2. at one

yīxīn yīyì 一心一意 of one heart and mind

yīxiǔ 一宿 one night; an over-

night stay

yīyán bùfā 一言不發 to keep one's mouth shut

yīyán bùhé 一言不合 A single jarring note in conversation (between two persons is immediately followed by a quarrel, fist fight, etc.).

yīyán jiǔdǐng 一言九鼎 a solemn promise or pledge

yīyán nánjìn 一言難盡 It is a long story.

yīyán wéidìng 一言爲定 to reach a binding agreement verbally

yīyán xīngbāng 一言興邦 A timely warning may avert a national crisis.

yīyǎn kànqù 一眼看去 1. to take a sweeping look 2. at first glance

yīyǎnghuàtàn 一氧化碳 carbon monoxide (CO)

yīyàng 一樣 1. alike; in the same manner 2. an (object, item or article)

yīyè 一頁 one page

yīyè zhīqiū 一葉知秋 any sign foretelling things to come

yīyī 一一 one by one; each separately

yīyì gūxíng 一意孤行 to do something against the advice of others

yīyǐn érjìn 一飲而盡 to empty the glass at one gulp

yīyīng jùquán 一應俱全 complete with everything

yīyìng jùquán 一應俱全 refer to **yīyīng jùquán** 一應俱全

yīyōng érshàng 一擁而上 to rush up in a crowd

yīyǔ dàopò 一語道破 to hit the nail on the head

yīyuánhuà 一元化 centralized; unified

yīyuè 一月 1. January 2. one month

yīzài 一再 repeatedly; again and again

yīzǎo 一早 in the early morning

yīzé 一則 1. one item 2. on the one hand

yīzhǎyǎn 一眨眼 the twinkling of an eye; in an instant

yīzhǎn 一盞 a (lamp); a (cup)

yīzhāng 一張 a sheet (of paper); a (table, desk, painting or calligraphic work)

yīzhāng 一章 a chapter (of a book)

yīzhāo 一朝 1. in one day 2. once

yīzhāo qiāngǔ 一朝千古 to die suddenly

yīzhāo yīxī 一朝一夕 a short period of time

yīzhāo yīxì 一朝一夕 refer to yīzhāo yīxī 一朝一夕

yīzhé 一折 1. a 90 percent discount 2. one fold

yīzhēn jiànxiě 一針見血 exactly right; to the point

yīzhèn 一陣 a sudden gust (of wind, laughter, etc.)

yīzhènzi 一陣子 for a while

yīzhī 一枝 1. a (flower, pen, cigarette, etc.); a piece of (chalk) 2. a branch

yīzhī bànjiě 一知半解 incomplete comprehension

yīzhī dúxiù 一枝獨秀 to outshine others

yīzhí 一直 always; constantly

yīzhí qiānjīn 一擲千金 refer to yīzhì qiānjīn 一擲千金

yīzhì 一致 unanimously; one and all; consistent

yīzhì qiānjīn 一擲千金 to spend money recklessly

yīzhǒng 一種 1. one kind or type 2. a species

yīzhōu 一周 1. a week 2. a revolution, or circle

yīzhū 一株 a (tree, weed, flower, etc.)

yīzhuāng 一樁 an (affair); a (matter)

yīzǒu liǎozhī 一走了之 to evade the solution of a problem by walking away from where it exists

yīzǔ 一組 a set; a group

yīzūn 一尊 1. a (Buddha statue) 2. a jug (of wine)

yīzuò 一座 a (bridge, mountain, etc.)

yī 伊

1. he; she 2. a Chinese family name

Yīdiànyuán 伊甸園 the Garden of Eden

Yīlākè 伊拉克 Iraq

Yīlǎng 伊朗 Iran

Yīsuǒ Yùyán 伊索寓言 Aesop's Fables

yī 衣

1. clothing; dress; apparel; garments; attire 2. a coating; a covering 3. skin or peel of fruits 4. (also **yì**) to clothe; to wear; to dress

yībō 衣缽 teaching, skill, etc. handed down from a master to his pupil

yīchú 衣櫥 a wardrobe; a clothespress

yīfu 衣服 clothes; clothing; dress

yīguān bùzhěng 衣冠不整 sloppily dressed

yīguān chǔchǔ 衣冠楚楚 in immaculate attire; dressed like a gentleman

yīguān qínshòu 衣冠禽獸 a gentleman in appearance but a beast in conduct

yīguì 衣櫃 a wardrobe; a chest of drawers for clothing

yījià 衣架 a rack for clothes; a clotheshorse; a coat hanger

yījīn 衣襟 lapels of a garment

yījǐn huánxiāng 衣錦還鄉 to return home in glory

yīliào 衣料 clothing material

yīlǐng 衣領 a collar

yīmàojiān 衣帽間 a cloakroom (in restaurants, etc.); a checkroom

yīshān lánlǚ 衣衫襤褸 ragged clothing

yīshang 衣裳 clothes; garments; clothing

Yīsuǒbǐyà 衣索比亞 Ethiopia

yīwù 衣物 clothing and other articles of daily use

yīxiāng 衣箱 a box or chest for

Y

storing clothes

yīzhuó 衣著 clothing; attire; apparel; dress

yī 依
1. to depend on; to lean to 2. to follow; to comply with; to consent; to yield to 3. to be tolerant to; to forgive 4. according to

yīcǐ lèituī 依此類推 The rest may be deduced by analogy.

yīcì 依次 in order (in proper sequence or position); one by one

yīcóng 依從 to comply with; to follow

yīcún 依存 interdependent

yīfǎ 依法 according to law

yīfù 依附 1. to depend on 2. to submit to

yījiù 依舊 as usual; as before

yījù 依據 according to; in accordance with

yīkào 依靠 to rely on; to depend on

yīlài 依賴 to depend on

yīliàn 依戀 to be reluctant to leave

yīpíng 依憑 to rely on; to depend on

yīrán 依然 as before; as usual; still

yīshùn 依順 to be obedient

yīsuí 依隨 to follow (a person, a wish)

yīwéi liǎngkě 依違兩可 shilly-shally

yīxī 依稀 unclear; uncertain; not distinct

yīyàng huà húlu 依樣畫葫蘆 to imitate others

yīyī bùshě 依依不捨 unwilling to part

yīyuē 依約 in accordance with the promise

yīzhàng 依仗 1. someone or something to fall back upon 2. to rely on or count on

yīzhào 依照 according to; in accordance with

yī 咿
a form used to represent a sound

yīyā xuéyǔ 咿啞學語 (said of a baby) to begin to babble, prattle, or lisp

yī 揖
1. to bow with hands folding in front 2. to yield politely; to defer to

yīràng 揖讓 1. courtesy between the host and his guests to 2. abdicate

yī 壹
an elaborate form of **yī** 一 used mostly in accounting and especially in checks to prevent forgery or alterations

yī 漪
ripples

yī 翳
refer to **yì** 翳

yī 醫
1. to cure or treat (diseases) 2. a doctor; a physician; a surgeon 3. medical science; medical service

yīdé 醫德 medical ethics

yījiè 醫界 the medical circles; the medical world

yīkē 醫科 the department of medicine (at a university)

yīshēng 醫生 a doctor; a physician; a surgeon

yīshī 醫師 a doctor; a physician; a surgeon

yīshù 醫術 medical skill; the art of healing

yīxué 醫學 medical science

yīxuéyuàn 醫學院 a college of medicine

yīyàofèi 醫藥費 a hospital bill; a doctor's fee; medical expenses

yīyuàn 醫院 a hospital

yīzhì 醫治 to cure (a disease); medical treatment; to doctor

yí 夷
1. (in ancient China) barbarians in the east 2. foreign tribes or foreigners 3. at ease; peaceful 4. to level; to make level, even or smooth 5. safe 6. to eliminate; to exterminate; to kill; to execute 7. injuries; wounds 8. grades; classes 9. common; usual; ordinary 10. great; big

yíwéi píngdì 夷為平地 to level (a town, etc.) with the ground

yí 宜
1. right; fitting; proper; good 2. should; ought to; had better 3. a matter 4. to fit; to suit; to put in order 5. a Chinese family name

yírén 宜人 pleasant; agreeable; delightful

yíshì yíjiā 宜室宜家 to make a harmonious and orderly home (used as a congratulatory message on wedding)

yí 怡
1. harmony; on good terms 2. pleasure; joy; jubilation

yíqíng yǎngxìng 怡情養性 (said of things or environs) to contribute to one's peace of mind or inner tranquility

yírán zìdé 怡然自得 happy and contented

yíshén 怡神 to inspire peace and harmony in one's mind

yíyǎng 怡養 to enjoy good health and live a happy life

yí 姨
1. the sisters of one's wife 2. the sisters of one's mother 3. a concubine

yífu 姨父 an uncle

yímā 姨媽 the married sisters of one's mother

yímǔ 姨母 the married sisters of one's mother

yíniáng 姨娘 a concubine of one's father

yípó 姨婆 a grandaunt

yítàitai 姨太太 a concubine

yízhàng 姨丈 an uncle

yí 胰
the pancreas

yízàng 胰臟 the pancreas

yí 移
1. to change; to alter; to influence; to affect 2. to shift; to move 3. to forward; to transmit; to transplant; to convey 4. to give; to endow

yídòng 移動 to move; to shift; to change

yíhuā jiēmù 移花接木 1. to cheat by sleight of hand 2. to graft

yíjiāo 移交 to turn over

yíjū 移居 to move to another town, country, etc. for settlement

yíkāi 移開 to move away

yímín 移民 1. to immigrate; immigration 2. to emigrate; to settle people (in a new region, etc.); to colonize 3. an immigrant 4. an emigrant

yíqíng biéliàn 移情別戀 to shift one's love to another person

yízhí 移植 1. to transplant 2. grafting; transplanting

yízhuǎn 移轉 to transfer (certain rights, holdings, etc.)

yí 貽
1. to give to; to present to 2. to hand down; to transmit; to pass on to; to bequeath; to leave behind

yíwù 貽誤 to cause hindrance or delay; to bungle

yíxiào dàfāng 貽笑大方 to become a laughingstock

yí 疑
1. doubtful; dubious; skeptical; doubt; to doubt; to question 2. suspicious; to suspect 3. strange; incomprehensible; mysterious; questionable; sham; dummy; false

yí'àn 疑案 an unsettled case; an uncertain case

yídiǎn 疑點 1. a doubtful or questionable point 2. a suspicious point

yífàn 疑犯 a criminal suspect

yíhuò 疑惑 to doubt; to suspect

yílǜ 疑慮 anxiety; misgivings

yínàn 疑難 a question; a problem; a puzzle

yíshén yíguǐ 疑神疑鬼 to have unnecessary suspicions

yísì 疑似 could be; suspected to be

yíwèn 疑問 a question; doubt;

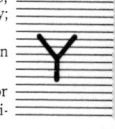

uncertainty

yíwènjù 疑問句 an interrogative sentence

yíxīn 疑心 1. to doubt 2. suspicion

yíxīnbìng 疑心病 1. hypochondria 2. skepticism

yíxìn cānbàn 疑信參半 do not believe entirely

yíyì 疑義 dubious interpretation

yíyún 疑雲 clouds of suspicion or misgivings (darkening one's mind)

yí 誼

refer to **yì** 誼

yí 儀

1. appearance; deportment; manners; looks; demeanor 2. ceremonies; rites 3. a rule, regulation, form or standard 4. customs 5. an instrument; an apparatus

yíbiǎo 儀表 1. appearance and deportment 2. a rule; a model

yíduì 儀隊 an honor guard

yíqì 儀器 (laboratory, medical, etc.) an instrument; an apparatus

yíróng 儀容 looks; appearance and deportment

yíshì 儀式 ceremonies; rites

yítài 儀態 bearing; deportment; demeanor

yítài wànfāng 儀態萬方 (usually said of girls) charming poises and exquisite bearing

yí 遺

1. to lose; lost 2. things lost 3. to miss; an omission due to negligence 4. to forget 5. to leave over 6. remnants; leftovers 7. to abandon; to desert 8. anything left behind by the deceased; to bequeath; to hand down; a legacy 9. to urinate 10. short for nocturnal emission

yíchǎn 遺產 1. property left behind by a deceased person 2. a legacy

yíchòu wànnián 遺臭萬年 a bad reputation that will be long remembered

yíchuán 遺傳 to inherit; hereditary; heredity

yígū 遺孤 orphans

yíhái 遺骸 one's remains; one's corpse

yíhàn 遺憾 to regret; regret; to feel sorry; regrettable

yíhèn 遺恨 to regret; regret; to feel sorry; regrettable

yíjī 遺跡 relics; vestiges; traces

yíjiào 遺教 1. exhortation of a dying person 2. teachings of a dead person

yílǎo 遺老 1. ministers of the preceding emperor (father of the current emperor) 2. ministers of the preceding dynasty 3. old, experienced men in the country

yíliú 遺留 to leave behind either intentionally or unintentionally

yílòu 遺漏 to omit or miss; an omission; an oversight

yíluò 遺落 1. to lose; lost 2. carefree; indifferent to what's happening around

yímìng 遺命 the injunctions of a dead person

yíqì 遺棄 1. (law) to desert, or to fail to support one's legal dependents 2. to cast away; to abandon

yíróng 遺容 1. the portrait of a dead person 2. remains (of the deceased)

yíshī 遺失 to lose; lost

yíshū 遺書 1. letters written by a suicide 2. ancient books scattered or lost 3. manuscripts published posthumously

yíshuāng 遺孀 a widow

yítǐ 遺體 1. the remains (of a deceased person); the corpse 2. one's body (handed down by one's parents)

yíwàng 遺忘 to forget; to neglect

yíwù 遺物 things left behind by a dead person

yíxiàng 遺像 the portrait of a dead person

yíyán 遺言 instructions, words, etc. of a dying person; a will

yízhǐ 遺址 the old site of some building or a city which no long-

er exists

yízhì 遺志 the ideal or wish not carried out before one's death

yízhǔ 遺囑 1. the will of a dead person 2. instructions of a dying person

yízhù 遺著 a posthumous book

yízú 遺族 survivors of a deceased person's family

yí 頤
1. the cheeks 2. to nourish; to rear; to take care of oneself

yíyǎng 頤養 to nourish; to keep fit; to take care of oneself; to recuperate

yízhǐ qìshǐ 頤指氣使 to order about; to be extremely bossy

yǐ 乙
1. the second of the Ten Celestial Stems 2. one 3. someone

yǐchún 乙醇 ethanol; alcohol

yǐ 已
1. to cease 2. to come to an end; to finish 3. already 4. used to indicate the past 5. excessive; very; much 6. a final particle to add emphasis

yǐgù 已故 the deceased; the late...

yǐjīng 已經 already

yǐ kāifā guójiā 已開發國家 a developed country

yǐrán 已然 to be already so

yǐsǐ 已死 already dead

yǐwǎng 已往 before; in the past

yǐ 以
by means of; because of

yǐbào yìbào 以暴易暴 to displace violence with violence

yǐbèi wànyī 以備萬一 to provide against any accidental happenings

yǐbiàn 以便 so as to; in order to

yǐcí hàiyì 以詞害意 to sacrifice clarity in the use of wrong words for expression

yǐcǐ lèituī 以此類推 The rest can be done in the same manner.

yǐcǐ wéijiè 以此爲戒 to take this as a lesson

yǐdà qīxiǎo 以大欺小 to bully

the weak

yǐdé bàoyuàn 以德報怨 to repay injury with kindness; to return good for evil

yǐdú gōngdú 以毒攻毒 to fight evil with evil

yǐdù hòuhuàn 以杜後患 to forestall future trouble

yǐ'é chuán'é 以訛傳訛 to convey incorrectly what is already incorrect

yǐgōng wéishǒu 以攻爲守 to take the offensive in a basically defensive operation

yǐguǎ dízhòng 以寡敵衆 to fight a numerically superior enemy

yǐguǎng zhāolái 以廣招徠 in order to promote patronage or sales

yǐhòu 以後 after; afterward

yǐjí 以及 and; including; as well as

yǐjiǎ luànzhēn 以假亂眞 to mix the spurious with the genuine

yǐjǐng xiàoyóu 以儆效尤 to warn others against making the same mistake

yǐlái 以來 since

yǐlǐ xiāngdài 以禮相待 to treat somebody with due respect

yǐlín wéihè 以鄰爲壑 to profit oneself at the expense of others

yǐlín wéihuò 以鄰爲壑 refer to **yǐlín wéihè** 以鄰爲壑

yǐluǎn tóushí 以卵投石 to fight a hopeless battle

yǐmào qǔrén 以貌取人 to judge a person by his appearance or looks

yǐmiǎn 以免 in order to avoid; so as not to

yǐnèi 以內 within

yǐnóng lìguó 以農立國 a nation based on agricultural economy

yǐqián 以前 before

yǐróu kègāng 以柔克剛 Soft and fair goes far.

Yǐsèliè 以色列 Israel

yǐshàng 以上 above

yǐshēn shìfǎ 以身試法 to defy the law; to dare to violate the law

yǐshēn xiāngxǔ 以身相許 (said of girls) to pledge to marry somebody

yǐshēn xùnzhí 以身殉職 to die at one's post

yǐshēn zuòzé 以身作則 to set examples by one's own action

yǐtuì wéijìn 以退為進 to make concessions in order to gain advantages

yǐwài 以外 1. other than; besides 2. outside; beyond

yǐwǎng 以往 in the past; formerly

yǐwéi 以為 to regard...as; to think; to consider

yǐwén huìyǒu 以文會友 to gather friends together for literary activities

yǐxià 以下 below

yǐyá huányá 以牙還牙 an eye for an eye, a tooth for a tooth

yǐyī dāngshí 以一當十 to tip one against ten

yǐyì dàiláo 以逸待勞 to wait in comfort for an exhausted enemy

yǐyuàn bàodé 以怨報德 to bite the hand that feeds one

yǐzhì 以至 1. up to; until 2. so... that

yǐzhì 以致 so that; with the result that

yǐ 矣
1. a final particle denoting the perfect tense 2. an auxiliary denoting determination 3. (in usage) both particles or auxiliaries indicating exclamations or questions

yǐ 倚
1. to rely on; to depend on 2. to lean toward; to rest on 3. biased; partial

yǐbàng 倚傍 to pattern after; to emulate

yǐkào 倚靠 1. to lean against 2. to rely on; to depend on 3. support

yǐlài 倚賴 to depend on; to rely

on (others)

yǐlǎo màilǎo 倚老賣老 to presume on age to despise the youth

yǐshì língrén 倚勢凌人 to take advantage of one's position to bully people

yǐzhàng 倚仗 to presume on (one's position, authority, etc.)

yǐzhòng 倚重 to entrust a person with heavy responsibility

yǐ 椅
a chair; a bench

yǐbèi 椅背 the back of a chair

yǐdiàn 椅墊 a chair cushion

yǐtào 椅套 chair covers

yǐzi 椅子 a chair; a bench

yǐ 旖
1. romantic; tender 2. charming; lovely; attractive; graceful 3. the fluttering of flags

yǐní 旖旎 1. (said of flags) fluttering 2. (said of scenery) enchanting

yǐní fēngguāng 旖旎風光 a romantic or charming sight

yǐ 蟻
an ant

yǐfù 蟻附 to swarm over (as ants swarm over their prey)

yì 弋
1. to catch; to take 2. to shoot with arrow and bow

yìhuò 弋獲 to catch (game in hunting, a thief, etc.)

yì 刈
to mow; to reap

yìcǎojī 刈草機 a mower

yì 衣
refer to **yī** 衣 4

yì 曳
refer to **yè** 曳

yì 屹
to rise high; to stand erect

yìlì 屹立 to stand erect; to stand magnificent (like a mountain)

yìrán 屹然 firm and erect (like a mountain)

Y

yì 亦

also; too

yìbù yìqū 亦步亦趨 to follow the example of another person at each move

yìjí 亦即 that is; i.e.; namely; viz.

yìrán 亦然 also; too; similarly

yì 邑

1. a town 2. a political district in ancient China 3. a county 4. a state 5. a capital city 6. (悒) sad or melancholy

yì 役

1. military service 2. to guard the frontier 3. to dispatch 4. to employ as a servant 5. to serve 6. to do

yìshǐ 役使 to make (someone) work

yì 抑

1. to press down; to repress 2. to restrain; to force to (do, perform, etc.) 3. to bend or lower (one's head) 4. or; or if; still; else; either; then 5. but; an opening particle of an expression 6. an exclamatory, roughly equivalent to "oh", or "alas" 7. to stop

yìhuò 抑或 besides; moreover; or

yìyáng dùncuò 抑揚頓挫 melodious; cadence

yìyù 抑鬱 sad and melancholy

yìzhǐ 抑止 to restrain; to suppress; to repress

yìzhì 抑制 to restrain; to suppress; to repress

yì 泄

1. mild and easy 2. many; crowded

yìtà 泄沓 1. garrulous and disorderly 2. easygoing; lax in moral attitude

yì 易

1. to exchange; to barter 2. easy 3. to change (places, jobs, owners, etc.) 4. amiable; lenient 5. the Book of Changes 6. a Chinese family name

yìdì érchù 易地而處 to look at a matter from the other fellow's viewpoint

yìkāiguàn 易開罐 a ring-pull can

yìlāguàn 易拉罐 a ring-pull can

yìránwù 易燃物 combustibles; inflammables

yìrú fǎnzhǎng 易如反掌 as easy as turning over the palm of one's hand

yìshǒu 易手 to change hands

yìwèi 易位 1. to change places or positions; to transpose 2. to dethrone

yìzhǔ 易主 to change owners or masters

yì 疫

an epidemic; a plague; a pestilence

yìmiáo 疫苗 vaccine

yì 奕

1. great; grand; abundant 2. gorgeous; elegant; good-looking 3. worried; unsettled; anxious 4. in good order; in sequence

yì 弈

the "go" game

yìqí 弈棋 the "go" game

yì 射

refer to **shè** 射 4

yì 益

1. to increase; to add to; to augment 2. in a higher degree; to a greater extent; more 3. benefit; profit; advantage

yìchu 益處 advantages; benefit; profit

yìfā 益發 increasingly; more and more; all the more

yìzhì 益智 1. to grow in intelligence or wisdom 2. the longan

yì 異

1. different; difference 2. peculiar; extraordinary; uncommon; strange; unusual 3. foreign; unfamiliar; unknown 4. to marvel; to wonder 5. to separate

yìbāng 異邦 a foreign country

yìcháng 異常 extraordinary; different; unusual; strange

yìduān xiéshuō 異端邪說 heretical beliefs; heresy

Y

yìguó qíngdiào 異國情調 an exotic touch or mood on a foreign land

yìjǐ 異己 a dissident

yìjiàotú 異教徒 a heathen; a pagan

yìkǒu tóngshēng 異口同聲 People are unanimous in their opinion.

yìlèi 異類 those of a different class or kind

yìqǔ tónggōng 異曲同工 The writings are different, but the excellence is the same.

yìqù 異趣 different tastes or interests

yìrì 異日 1. another day 2. bygone days

yìwèi 異味 uncommon smell

yìwén 異聞 unusual news; a strange story

yìxiāng 異鄉 a strange land; a foreign land

yìxiǎng tiānkāi 異想天開 to have fantastic notions

yìyàng 異樣 unusual; extraordinary

yìyì 異議 dissent; objections

yì 液

refer to **yè** 液

yì 掖

refer to **yè** 掖

yì 翌

tomorrow

yìrì 翌日 tomorrow

yì 腋

refer to **yè** 腋

yì 逸

1. to flee; to escape; to run away 2. to go beyond; to exceed 3. to rusticate; to live in retirement 4. ease; leisure 5. to let loose; to let go 6. a fault; an error; a mistake 7. quick; rapid 8. lost 9. superior; outstanding

yìlè 逸樂 enjoyment of an easy life

yìqù héngshēng 逸趣橫生 replete with humor or refined interest

yìshì 逸事 an anecdote; an episode

yì 軼

1. to excel; to surpass 2. to be scattered; to go loose

yìshì 軼事 an anecdote (not included in history)

yìwén 軼聞 an anecdote

yì 詣

1. to go (to a place); to arrive 2. to visit; to call on 3. achievements

yì 意

1. a thought; an idea; sentiments 2. intention; inclination 3. expectations 4. meaning 5. a hint; a suggestion

Yìdàlì 意大利 Italy

yìhuì 意會 to sense; to perceive spontaneously (not through explanations)

yìjiàn 意見 an opinion; a suggestion; a view

yìjiànxiāng 意見箱 a suggestion box

yìjìng 意境 a frame of mind; conception

yìliào 意料 expectations

yìniàn 意念 an idea

yìqì 意氣 spirits; heart; emotion

yìqì fēngfā 意氣風發 highspirited and vigorous

yìqì xiāngtóu 意氣相投 congenial; to share the same aspirations and have the same temperament

yìqì yòngshì 意氣用事 to act on impulse

yìshí 意識 consciousness

yìshí 意識 refer to **yìshí** 意識

yìsi 意思 1. meaning 2. intention; desire 3. interest

yìsi yìsi 意思意思 to serve as a token

yìtú 意圖 to intend to do something; intention

yìwài 意外 1. unexpected; accidental 2. a surprise; an accident

yìwài tíngjī 意外停機 (computer) unexpected failure or shut down

yìwèi 意味 1. an impression 2. to portend

yìwèi 意謂 It seems to say....

yìwèi shēncháng 意味深長 meaningful; profound in meaning

yìxià rúhé 意下如何 How about it? What do you think?

yìxiǎng bùdào 意想不到 never thought of; unexpectedly

yìxiàng 意向 intentions; inclinations

yìxìng lánshān 意興闌珊 to feel dispirited

yìyì 意義 meaning; significance

yìyì 意譯 free translation

yìyóu wèijìn 意猶未盡 to wish to continue doing something one has done for a long time

yìyù 意欲 volition; desire; to want to do something

yìyuàn 意願 inclination; wish; volition

yìzhǐ 意旨 intention; meaning; will

yìzhì 意志 volition; will; will power

yìzhì xiāochén 意志消沈 dejected; low-spirited

yìzhōngrén 意中人 the person with whom one is in love

yì 義

1. justice; righteousness 2. generosity; charity; philanthropy; chivalry 3. meaning; connotations 4. artificial; unreal; false 5. a Chinese family name

yìbù róngcí 義不容辭 Moral obligation prohibits declination of the call.

yìfù 義父 a foster father

yìgōng 義工 a volunteer worker

yìjǔ 義舉 an act of charity; a chivalrous deed

yìmài 義賣 a charity sale; a bazaar

yìmǔ 義母 a foster mother

yìnǚ 義女 a foster daughter

yìqì 義氣 1. spirit of justice or righteousness 2. loyalty to friends

yìshì 義士 a patriot; a freedom-seeker

yìwú fǎngù 義無反顧 to pursue justice without ever turning back

yìwù 義務 duty; obligation

yìwù jiàoyù 義務教育 compulsory education

yìyǎn 義演 a charity performance (by entertainers); a charity show

yìzhèng cíyán 義正詞嚴 to speak sternly out of a sense of justice

yìzhī 義肢 artificial limbs

yìzǐ 義子 a foster son

yì 溢

1. to flow over; to brim over 2. excessive

yìchū 溢出 to brim over; to flow over

yìyú yánbiǎo 溢於言表 (said of emotions or inner feelings) to show clearly in one's utterances and manners

yì 肄

1. to study; to learn; to practice 2. to toil; to work hard 3. remnants; leftovers 4. fresh twigs

yìyè 肄業 to learn; to study (at a certain school)

yì 裔

1. descendants; posterity 2. the hem of a garment, robe, etc. 3. remote or border regions

yì 億

1. a hundred million 2. tranquility; repose 3. (according to) estimates

yìwàn fùwēng 億萬富翁 a billionaire

yì 誼 also **yí**

1. friendship 2. (義) justice; righteousness

yì 毅

firm; resolute; endurance; fortitude

yìlì 毅力 perseverance; indomitability

yìrán 毅然 firmly; courageously

yì 縊

to strangle; to hang

yìsǐ 縊死 to hang oneself

yì 憶

to remember; to bear in mind; to recall; to recollect

yìqǐ 憶起 to call to mind; to recall

yì 翳 also yī

1. to screen; to conceal 2. the haziness of objects due to weakened vision 3. the chariot cover made of feathers 4. the film over a diseased eye

yì 翼

1. wings 2. fins 3. to assist; to help 4. to protect; to patronize

yì 臆

1. one's breast, heart, thoughts, etc. 2. one's personal views or feelings

yìcè 臆測 to guess or conjecture; speculation

yìduàn 臆斷 an arbitrary judgment

yìduó 臆度 to guess or conjecture; speculation

yìduò 臆度 refer to **yìduó** 臆度

yì 藝

art; skill; talent; craft; dexterity

yìjì 藝妓 a geisha girl; a geisha

yìmíng 藝名 a stage name, or a screen name (of an entertainer)

yìrén 藝人 an entertainer

yìshù 藝術 art

yìshùjiā 藝術家 an artist

yìshùpǐn 藝術品 a work of art; an object of art

yì 議

1. to discuss; to argue; to debate; to negotiate; to talk over 2. an opinion; a view 3. to criticize; to comment; criticism; comment 4. argumentative writing; argumentation; an essay; a treatise

yì'àn 議案 a bill; a proposal

yìchéng 議程 an agenda

yìdìng 議定 to arrive at a decision after discussion or negotiation

yìdìngshū 議定書 a protocol

yìhé 議和 to negotiate peace

yìhuì 議會 a parliament; an assembly; a council

yìjià 議價 1. to negotiate over the price 2. the negotiated price

yìlùn 議論 1. argument; debate 2. to discuss; to talk 3. comments

yìlùnwén 議論文 argumentative writing

yìtí 議題 a topic for discussion; a subject of debate

yìyuán 議員 a councilor; a parliamentarian

yìyuàn 議院 a parliament; a legislature

yìzhǎng 議長 the speaker, president, or chairman of an assembly, parliament, etc.

yì 譯

to translate; translation

yìběn 譯本 a translation

yìmǎqì 譯碼器 a decoder; a decipher

yìmíng 譯名 a translated name

yìwén 譯文 translated texts

yìyīn 譯音 transliteration

yìzhě 譯者 a translator

yì 懿

1. virtuous; fine; good; exemplary 2. having to do with womanly virtue; modest; chaste

yìdé 懿德 fine virtue

yìxíng 懿行 a virtuous deed

yìyán 懿言 fine words

yì 囈

to talk in sleep; somniloquy

yìyǔ 囈語 to talk while asleep; somniloquy

yì 驛

a station where couriers rested in former times; a courier station

yìmǎchē 驛馬車 a stagecoach

yìzhàn 驛站 a courier station

yīn 因

1. cause; reason 2. for; because of 3. in accordance with; according to; on the basis of; in the

light of 4. to follow (a practice, convention, etc.); to carry on

yīncái shījiào 因材施教 to teach according to the student's ability or aptitude

yīncǐ 因此 therefore; hence; thus

yīndì zhìyí 因地制宜 to take actions that suit local circumstances

yīn'ér 因而 therefore; and so; thereupon

yīnguǒ 因果 1. cause and effect 2. karma; preordained fate

yīnguǒ bàoyìng 因果報應 retribution for sin

yīnhuò défú 因禍得福 to profit from a misfortune

yīnlòu jiùjiǎn 因陋就簡 1. to do things in the easy, simple way 2. to make do with whatever is available

yīnshí zhìyí 因時制宜 to do what is appropriate according to the circumstances

yīnsù 因素 factors; elements

yīnwèi 因為 inasmuch as; since; because; as

yīnxí 因襲 to follow conventions and traditions

yīnxiǎo shīdà 因小失大 to try to save a little only to lose a lot

yīnxún 因循 1. to follow (old customs) 2. to procrastinate

yīnxún gǒuqiě 因循苟且 to follow routines without thinking about improvement

yīnyè fèishí 因噎廢食 to refuse making renovations for fear of a little trouble

yīnzi 因子 (mathematics) a factor

yīn 姻

1. one's husband's family 2. marriage 3. relations or connections through marriage

yīnqī 姻戚 relatives by marriage

yīnqīn 姻親 relatives by marriage

yīnyuán 姻緣 the invisible bond that makes a man and a woman husband and wife

yīn 音

1. sound; voice 2. tone; accent; timbre 3. a musical note 4. (usually used in correspondence) news; information

yīnbiāo 音標 phonetic signs

yīnchā 音叉 a tuning fork

yīndiào 音調 1. the pitch of a sound; tone 2. musical pitch according to the standard of ancient pitch pipes

yīnfú 音符 (music) notes

yīnjié 音節 a syllable

yīnliàng 音量 the volume (of sound)

yīnróng wǎnzài 音容宛在 His or her voice and appearance seem to be still with us.

yīnsè 音色 timbre; tone color

yīnsù 音速 the speed of sound

yīnxiǎng 音響 1. audio 2. sound; acoustics

yīnxìn 音信 news; messages; tidings; letters; information

yīnxùn 音訊 news; messages; tidings; letters; information

yīnyì 音譯 transliteration by sound rather than meaning

yīnyù 音域 (music) the range; the compass; the register

yīnyuè 音樂 music

yīnyuèhuì 音樂會 a concert; a musical recital

yīnyuèjiā 音樂家 a musician

yīnyùn 音韻 a rhyme

yīnzhí 音質 refer to **yīnzhì** 音質

yīnzhì 音質 tonality; tone quality

yīn 茵

mattress

yīn 殷

1. flourishing; prosperous 2. polite; courteous 3. sad; sorrowful 4. eager; eagerly 5. an alternative name for the latter half of the Shang Dynasty

yīnfù 殷富 wealthy; prosperous; well off

yīnqiè 殷切 ardent; eager

yīnqín 殷勤 courteous; polite; civil

yīnshèng 殷盛 thriving; flourish-

ing; prosperous; abundant

yīn 氤

the spirit of harmony (between heaven and earth)

yīnyūn 氤氳 1. the spirit of harmony (between heaven and earth) 2. misty; dense 3. the spirit of vigor or prosperity

yīn 陰

1. negative (as opposite to positive, as electricity) 2. feminine; female 3. cloudy; dark 4. shady 5. secret 6. the back side 7. the north side of a mountain 8. the south side of a stream 9. reproductive organs of both sexes 10. Hades; hell 11. cunning and crafty 12. time 13. a Chinese family name

yīn'àn 陰暗 dim; dark; gloomy; overcast

yīncáo dìfǔ 陰曹地府 Hades; the nether world

yīnchén 陰沈 1. gloomy (sky) 2. quiet and designing (persons)

yīncuò yángchā 陰錯陽差 due to all sorts of accidental mishaps

yīndé 陰德 one's unpublicized good deeds

yīn'gān 陰乾 to be placed in the shade to dry; to dry in the shade

yīn'gōu 陰溝 1. a covered drain; a sewer 2. the vagina

yīnhún bùsàn 陰魂不散 The soul (or spirit) refuses to leave.

yīnjí 陰極 the cathode; the negative pole

yīnjiān 陰間 Hades; the shades; the underworld

yīnlěng 陰冷 1. (said of weather) gloomy and cold; raw 2. (said of a person's look) somber; glum

yīnlì 陰曆 the lunar calendar

yīnliáng 陰涼 shady and cool

yīnmái 陰霾 haze; thin mist

yīnmóu 陰謀 a plot; a secret scheme; a conspiracy

yīnmóu guǐjì 陰謀詭計 schemes and intrigues; dark schemes and tricks

yīnpíng 陰平 (Chinese phonetics) the first tone

yīnsēnsēn 陰森森 gloomy; weird; ominous

yīntiān 陰天 a cloudy day

yīnxiǎn 陰險 cunning; crafty; deceitful; sinister

yīnxìng 陰性 1. negative 2. female

yīnyáng 陰陽 yin (shade) and yang (light)

yīnyáng guàiqì 陰陽怪氣 1. to act or speak in an odd or queer manner 2. eccentric; queer

yīnyīn chénchén 陰陰沈沈 gloomy; dusky; dreary

yīnyǐng 陰影 shades; shadows

yīnyǔ 陰雨 cloudy and rainy; overcast and rainy

yīn 湮

refer to **yān** 湮

yīn 慇

1. mournful; sorrowful 2. regardful; respectful

yīnqín 慇懃 polite; courteous; civil

yīnyīn 慇慇 mournful; sad; melancholy

yīn 蔭 also **yìn**

1. the shade of trees; shade 2. to shelter

yín 吟

1. to chant; to intone; to sing; to recite 2. to moan

yínsòng 吟誦 to recite (a verse)

yínxiào 吟嘯 1. to whistle or shout in freedom 2. to lament

yínyóu shīrén 吟遊詩人 a troubadour; a minstrel

yín 垠

1. the bank (of a stream) 2. a boundary; a limit

yín 淫

1. licentious; lewd; lascivious; libidinous; dissolute 2. obscene; pornographic 3. to seduce; to debauch; to tempt; temptation 4. things related to sexual desire and behavior

yíncí 淫辭 obscene expressions; wanton language

yíndàng 淫蕩 (said of women) wanton and lascivious

yínhuì 淫穢 dirty (books, etc.); obscene

yínluàn 淫亂 debauchery

yínshū 淫書 obscene books

yínwēi 淫威 1. despotic power 2. excessive use of powers and punishments

yínyì 淫逸 debauchery; wantonness

yínyù 淫慾 wanton desires; sexual desire

yín 寅
1. the third of the Twelve Terrestrial Branches 2. a fellow officer; a colleague 3. a horary sign (for the period from 3 to 5 a.m.)

yínchī mǎoliáng 寅吃卯糧 unable to make both ends meet

yínshí 寅時 the period of the day from 3 a.m. to 5 a.m.

yín 夤
1. to hang on (power, glory, etc.) 2. to respect 3. a remote place

yínyè 夤夜 deep in the night

yín 銀
1. silver 2. money; wealth 3. silvery

yínbì 銀幣 a silver coin; silver

yínháng 銀行 a bank

Yínhé 銀河 the Milky Way; the Galaxy

yínhūn 銀婚 a silver wedding; the 25th wedding anniversary

yínhuò liǎngqīng 銀貨兩清 completion of a business transaction with goods delivered and payment made

yínkuàng 銀礦 1. silver ore 2. silver mine

yínlóu 銀樓 a jeweler's shop

yínmù 銀幕 (motion-picture) screen

yínpái 銀牌 a silver medal

yínqì 銀器 silverware

yínsè 銀色 silvery

yínsè shìchǎng 銀色市場 market (marketed) for the senior

yínyuán 銀圓 silver dollar

yín 齦
gums (of the teeth)

yǐn 引
1. to pull 2. to guide 3. to introduce 4. to quote 5. to retire 6. a unit of length (=33⅓ meters) 7. to cause

yǐnbào 引爆 to ignite; to detonate

yǐnbì 引避 to avoid

yǐnchū 引出 to draw forth; to lead

yǐndǎo 引導 to guide; to lead

yǐndù 引渡 to extradite; extradition

yǐnfā 引發 (chemistry) initiation

yǐnháng gāogē 引吭高歌 to sing aloud

yǐnhào 引號 a quotation mark; a quote

yǐnhuǒ 引火 to ignite; to light; to kindle a fire

yǐnjiàn 引見 to present a person to the emperor, etc.

yǐnjiàn 引薦 to recommend

yǐnjìn 引進 1. to recommend 2. to introduce from elsewhere

yǐnjīng jùdiǎn 引經據典 1. to quote from classics 2. pedantic

yǐnjiù 引咎 to take the blame on oneself

yǐnjiù cízhí 引咎辭職 to resign from office as a gesture to show self-reproach

yǐnláng rùshì 引狼入室 to bring in a troublemaker

yǐnlì 引力 gravitation

yǐnlǐng érwàng 引領而望 to long for; to expect eagerly

yǐnlù 引路 to lead the way

yǐnqǐ 引起 to cause; to give rise to

yǐnqíng 引擎 an engine

yǐnrén rùshèng 引人入勝 1. to lead one into wonderland 2. (said of books) absorbing

yǐnrén zhùmù 引人注目 noticeable; conspicuous

yǐnrù 引入 to lead into; to draw into

yǐnrù qítú 引入歧途 to lead

Y

(somebody) astray

yǐnshēn 引伸 to expound

yǐntuì 引退 to retire; to resign

yǐnwén 引文 a quoted passage; a quotation

yǐnxiàn 引線 1. a sewing needle 2. a go-between 3. a fuse

yǐnyǐ wéijiè 引以為戒 to learn a lesson (from a previous error)

yǐnyòng 引用 to quote

yǐnyòu 引誘 to induce; to lure; to entice; to tempt

yǐnzhèng 引證 to cite supporting evidence

yǐn 飲

1. to drink 2. drinks 3. to swallow (insult, anger, etc.) 4. to be hit (by a bullet, an arrow, etc.)

yǐnchá 飲茶 1. (in Guangdong) to drink tea along with refreshments 2. to drink tea

yǐnhèn 飲恨 1. to swallow grievances 2. to be defeated in a competition

yǐnjiǔ 飲酒 to drink wine or liquor

yǐnliào 飲料 beverages; drinks

yǐnqì 飲泣 to weep in deep sorrow

yǐnshí 飲食 1. to drink and eat 2. drink and food

yǐnshuǐ 飲水 1. drinking water 2. to drink water

yǐnshuǐjī 飲水機 a drinking fountain; a water fountain

yǐnshuǐ sīyuán 飲水思源 grateful for favors received; not to forget one's origin

yǐn 隱

1. hidden; concealed; secret; mysterious 2. dark; obscure; not evident or obvious 3. to retire; to reject public life; to live like a hermit 4. painful; grievous 5. a riddle 6. destitute; poor 7. to examine and study 8. a low wall

yǐncáng 隱藏 to hide; to conceal

yǐndùn 隱遁 to retire from public life; to live in reclusion

yǐn'è yángshàn 隱惡揚善 to cover up another's bad deeds

and praise his virtues

yǐnhuì 隱諱 1. taboo (on the parent's or emperor's personal name) 2. to avoid mentioning; to cover up

yǐnjí 隱疾 1. ailments beneath one's garment 2. ailments one wants to keep to oneself, as syphilis, impotence, etc.

yǐnjū 隱居 to retire from public life; to live in reclusion

yǐnmán 隱瞞 to hide the truth; to cover up

yǐnmì 隱祕 1. to conceal; to hide 2. a secret

yǐnnì 隱匿 to hide; to go into hiding; to lie low

yǐnqíng 隱情 secrets; things which cannot be revealed to others

yǐnrěn 隱忍 to bear patiently; to forbear

yǐnshì 隱士 a retired scholar; a recluse

yǐnsī 隱私 one's secrets; private matters one wants to hide

yǐnsīquán 隱私權 privacy

yǐntuì 隱退 to retire; retirement

yǐnxíng yǎnjìng 隱形眼鏡 contact lenses

yǐnxìng 隱性 (genetics) recessive

yǐnxìng máimíng 隱姓埋名 to live incognito

yǐnyì 隱逸 a recluse; a retired person

yǐnyǐn zuòtòng 隱隱作痛 to feel dull pain

yǐnyōu 隱憂 hidden or latent worries

yǐnyù 隱喻 a metaphor

yǐnyuē 隱約 indistinct; obscure; ambiguous; abstruse

yǐn 癮

1. addiction; a habitual craving 2. strong interest (in a sport or pastime)

yǐnjūnzǐ 癮君子 an opium eater; a heavy smoker

yǐntóu 癮頭 addiction

yìn 印

1. a seal; a stamp; a chop 2. to

print; to stamp; to imprint 3. an imprint

yìnbiǎojī 印表機 a printer

Yìndù 印度 India

Yìndù bàndǎo 印度半島 the subcontinent of India

Yìndùyáng 印度洋 the Indian Ocean

yìnfā 印發 to print and distribute

yìnhuā 印花 a revenue stamp

yìnhuāshuì 印花税 stamp tax

yìnjiàn 印鑑 an imprint or impression of one's chop filed with agencies concerned for checking purposes

Yìnní 印尼 Indonesia

yìnní 印泥 ink for imprinting of seals

yìnshuā 印刷 to print

yìnshuāpǐn 印刷品 printed matter

yìntái 印台 an ink pad; a stamp pad

yìnxiàng 印象 an impression; a mental image

yìnxíng 印行 to publish

yìnzhāng 印章 a general name for stamps, seals and chops

yìnzhèng 印證 to confirm; to corroborate

yìn 胤

long successions of descendants; posterity

yìn 飲

to make animals drink

yìnmǎ 飲馬 to water a horse

yìn 廕

to shelter; to harbor; to protect

yìn 蔭

1. (with) the support or blessing of 2. refer to **yīn** 蔭

yīng 英

1. a flower; a leaf; a petal 2. surpassing; outstanding; prominent; distinguished 3. fine; handsome 4. English; British 5. a hero; an outstanding person 6. a Chinese family name

yīngbàng 英鎊 the pound sterling

yīngcái 英才 a person of outstanding ability or talent

yīngchǐ 英尺 foot

yīngcùn 英寸 (linear measure) inch

Yīnggélán 英格蘭 England

Yīngguó 英國 Great Britain; Britain; the United Kingdom; England

Yīng Hàn cídiǎn 英漢辭典 an English-Chinese dictionary

yīngjùn 英俊 (said of a man) handsome

yīnglǐ 英里 (linear measure) mile

Yīng Měi 英美 Britain and America

yīngmíng 英名 fame; glory; renown

yīngmíng 英明 (said of leaders) intelligent; sagacious; perspicacious

yīngmǔ 英畝 (square measure) acre

yīngtǐng 英挺 outstanding; prominent

Yīngwén 英文 the (written) English language; English

yīngxióng 英雄 a hero; a great man

yīngyǒng 英勇 brave; courageous

Yīngyǔ 英語 the (spoken) English language; English

yīngzī 英姿 a dashing appearance

yīng 瑛

1. the glitter or sheen of jade 2. a transparent piece of jade; a crystal

yīng 膺

1. the breast of a person 2. (now rarely) a belt across the breast of a horse 3. to receive; to be given (a responsibility, etc.); to undertake; to shoulder; to bear; to sustain 4. (now rarely) to punish (the enemy, etc.) by war

yīngrèn 膺任 to be appointed to or given (an office, etc.)

yīngxuǎn 膺選 to be elected

yīng 嬰

an infant; a baby; a suckling

yīng'ér 嬰兒 a baby; an infant

yīnghái 嬰孩 a baby; an infant

yīng 應

1. should; ought to; need 2. (also **yìng**) to assent to

yīngdāng 應當 duty-bound; should; ought to

yīngdé 應得 that one deserves to receive; deserved

yīngfǒu 應否 should or should not

yīnggāi 應該 should; ought to; need

yīngjiè bìyèshēng 應屆畢業生 graduating students or pupils

yīngyǒu 應有 due; proper; deserved

yīngyǒu jìnyǒu 應有盡有 to have every thing that one expects to find

yīngyǔn 應允 to assent; to consent

yīng 罌

a jar with a small mouth

yīngsù 罌粟 an opium poppy

yīng 鶯

a greenfinch; a Chinese oriole

yīngtí yànyǔ 鶯啼燕語 Orioles sing and swallows chatter. (a phrase descriptive of a fine spring day)

yīngyīng yànyàn 鶯鶯燕燕 a crowd of women chattering together pleasantly

yīng 櫻

the cherry; the cherry blossoms

yīngchún 櫻唇 the small, beautiful mouth of a woman

yīnghuā 櫻花 the oriental cherry

yīngtáo 櫻桃 cherries

yīng 鷹

a hawk; an eagle; a falcon

yīnggōu bízi 鷹鉤鼻子 an aquiline nose

yīngjià 鷹架 a scaffold

yīngquǎn 鷹犬 1. falcons and dogs used in hunting 2. hired ruffians; rapacious underlings

yīng 鸚

a parrot

yīngwǔ 鸚鵡 a parrot

yīngwǔ xuéshé 鸚鵡學舌 to parrot another's statement, theory, etc.

yíng 迎

to receive; to greet; to meet; to welcome

yíngfēng 迎風 1. facing the wind; against the wind 2. down the wind; with the wind

yíngfēng zhāozhǎn 迎風招展 to flutter in the wind

yínghé 迎合 1. to cater to 2. to make an appointment to meet each other in the future

yíngjiē 迎接 to receive; to greet; to welcome

yíngmiàn 迎面 right against one's face in the opposite direction

yíngqīn 迎親 to go to meet one's bride at her home before escorting her back to one's own home for the wedding

yíngrèn érjiě 迎刃而解 (said of a difficult problem) to be solved neatly

yíngtóu 迎頭 head-on; directly

yíngtóu gǎnshàng 迎頭趕上 to try hard to catch up

yíngtóu tòngjī 迎頭痛擊 to make a frontal attack

yíngtóu tòngjí 迎頭痛擊 refer to **yíngtóu tòngjī 迎頭痛擊**

yíngxīn 迎新 1. to see the New Year in 2. to welcome new arrivals

yíngxīn sòngjiù 迎新送舊 to usher in the new and send off the old

yíng 盈

to fill; to become full

yíngkuī 盈虧 1. (said of the moon) waxing and waning 2. profits and losses

yínglì 盈利 profit; gains; surpluses

yíngyíng 盈盈 1. (said of water) clear and abundant 2. (said of a woman's bearing) easy and graceful

yíngyú 盈餘 profit; gains; surpluses

yíng 楹

a pillar; a column

yínglián 楹聯 the scrolls hung on a pillar

yíng 熒

1. bright; shining; luminous 2. dazzling; glittering; sparkling; glimmering 3. to doubt; to suspect

yíng 瑩

1. the luster of jade 2. a jade like pebble 3. smooth and glossy; clean and shining 4. transparent; pure 5. (said of a person) bright and clever

yíngrùn 瑩潤 clear and lustrous

yíng 縈

1. to coil; to entwine; to wind around and around; to twine; to round 2. to entangle; to preoccupy; to bog

yínghuái 縈懷 to linger; to be constantly on one's mind

yíngrǎo 縈繞 to linger; to encircle; to wind around

yíngrào 縈繞 refer to **yíngrǎo** 縈繞

yíng 螢

a luminous insect; a firefly; a glowworm

yínghuǒchóng 螢火蟲 a firefly; a glowworm

yíngmù 螢幕 a screen

yíng 營

1. military barracks; a camp; a battalion 2. to manage; to administer; to handle; to operate; to run

yíngdì 營地 campsite; camping ground

yíngfáng 營房 barracks

yínghuǒ 營火 a campfire

yíngjiàn 營建 to manage or handle the construction of; to construct

yíngjiù 營救 to rescue or deliver

yínglì 營利 to engage in making profit

yíngshēng 營生 to make a living

yíngsī wǔbì 營私舞弊 to seek personal gain illicitly while holding a public post; to practice graft

yíngyǎng 營養 nutrition; nourishment

yíngyè 營業 to engage in business; business operation

yíngzào 營造 to construct; to build

yíngzhǎng 營長 a battalion commander

yíng 蠅

a fly

yíngtóu wēilì 蠅頭微利 petty profits

yíngtóu wéilì 蠅頭微利 refer to **yíngtóu wēilì** 蠅頭微利

yíng 贏(贏)

1. to win; to beat 2. gains; profits

yíngdé 贏得 to win (honor, a privilege, etc.)

yíngjiā 贏家 the winner

yǐng 影(景)

1. a shadow; an image 2. a trace; a vague impression 3. to copy and imitate 4. to hide 5. a sundial

yǐngběn 影本 a facsimile edition; a rubbing

yǐngdiépiàn 影碟片 a videodisk

yǐngjí 影集 a miniseries (or a mini series)

yǐngjùjiè 影劇界 movie and drama circles

yǐngmí 影迷 a movie fan

yǐngpiàn 影片 a motion picture; movies

yǐngpíng 影評 brief comments on motion pictures

yǐngpíngrén 影評人 a movie critic

yǐngshè 影射 1. to counterfeit

(trademarks, etc.); to delude; to humbug 2. to hint by suggestive remarks

yǐngtán 影壇 the movie circles; moviedom

yǐngxiǎng 影響 to affect; to influence

yǐngxiàng 影像 an image; a portrait

yǐngxīng 影星 a movie star

yǐngyìn 影印 1. photogravure 2. xerography

yǐngzhǎn 影展 a photographic exhibition; a film festival

yǐngzi 影子 1. a shadow 2. (figuratively) a trace

yǐng 穎

outstanding; remarkable; talented; distinguished

yǐnghuì 穎慧 clever; bright; intelligent

yǐngxiù 穎秀 outstandingly talented

yìng 映

1. to mirror; to reflect; a reflection 2. to project (slides, pictures, etc.) 3. to shine; shining; to blind; blinding (glare, light, etc.)

yìngshè 映射 to shine upon; to cast light upon

yìngxiàng 映象 image

yìngzhào 映照 to shine and reflect

yìng 硬

1. hard; stiff; solid; firm 2. rigid; inflexible; obstinate; very insistent; unyielding 3. to solidify; to harden; to stiffen 4. by force; to manage to do something in a forced manner 5. (said of quality) good 6. able (person)

yìngbāngbāng 硬幫幫 1. hard and firm 2. stiff

yìngbī 硬逼 to compel or force

yìngbì 硬幣 hard money (as opposed to paper money); coins; specie

yìngchēng 硬撐 to hold on firmly despite extreme adversity, pain, etc.

yìngdié 硬碟 (computer) hard disc

yìngdù 硬度 hardness

yìnggàn 硬幹 to do something in disregard of obstacles

yìnghàn 硬漢 a man of fortitude

yìnghuà 硬化 1. to stiffen; to solidify 2. sclerosis

yìngjiàn 硬件 (computer) hardware

yìnglang 硬朗 (said of the aged) sturdy and strong

yìngpán 硬盤 (computer) hard disc

yìngpīn 硬拼 to fight recklessly

yìngshuō 硬說 to insist on saying; to assert

yìngtǐ 硬體 (computers) hardware

yìngxìng guīdìng 硬性規定 rigid and inflexible ruling

yìngyào 硬要 to want or demand insistently

yìngzhe tóupí 硬著頭皮 to do something against one's will

yìngzhǐbǎn 硬紙板 cardboard

yìng 應

1. to respond to; to answer; to echo; to react to 2. to comply with; to grant 3. to deal with; to cope with 4. refer to **yīng** 應 2

yìngbiàn 應變 1. to prepare oneself for change 2. to adapt oneself to changes

yìngbiàn cuòshī 應變措施 an emergency measure

yìngchéng 應承 to agree; to promise; to consent

yìngchou 應酬 1. social appointments 2. to treat with courtesy

yìngdá 應答 to reply; to answer

yìngduì 應對 1. to answer questions 2. repartee

yìngduì rúliú 應對如流 to answer questions fluently

yìngfu 應付 to deal with; to cope with; to handle

yìngjí 應急 to meet an emergency

yìngjiē bùxiá 應接不暇 too busy to make proper response to

yìngjǐng 應景 to do something appropriate on the occasion

Y

yìngkǎo 應考 to participate in an examination

yìngmén 應門 1. to keep the gate 2. to answer the door

yìngpìn 應聘 to accept an offer of employment

yìngshēngchóng 應聲蟲 a servile sycophant

yìngshí 應時 1. seasonable 2. to adapt oneself to the times

yìngshì 應試 to take examinations

yìngyàn 應驗 to come true; to be fulfilled

yìngyāo 應邀 at somebody's invitation

yìngyòng 應用 1. to utilize; to make use of 2. for practical application

yìngyòngwén 應用文 practical writing

yìngyùn érshēng 應運而生 to come with the tide of fashion

yìngzhàn 應戰 to accept a challenge; to meet the enemy on the battle field

yìngzhào nǚláng 應召女郎 a call girl

yìngzhào rùwǔ 應召入伍 to be drafted (for military service)

yìngzhěn 應診 (said of a doctor) to see patients

yìngzhēng 應徵 1. to respond to a want ad 2. to be recruited

yōng 庸 also **yǒng**

1. mediocre; common 2. stupid 3. a hired laborer 4. to require 5. to reward 6. an interrogative (as how, etc.)

yōngcái 庸才 a man of mediocre ability

yōngdìng 庸訂 a commonplace; a platitude

yōngfū yúfù 庸夫愚婦 simple, ignorant people

yōngmín 庸民 the common people; the masses

yōngrén 庸人 a mediocre person

yōngrén zìrǎo 庸人自擾 (literally) Stupid people create trouble for themselves.

yōngsú 庸俗 vulgar; unrefined

yōngyī 庸醫 a quack doctor; a quack

yōngyōng lùlù 庸庸碌碌 mediocre; common

yōng 雍

1. harmonious; harmony; peaceful; union 2. to block up; to obstruct

yōngróng 雍容 a majestic, stately or imposing appearance

yōngróng huáguì 雍容華貴 (said of a woman) graceful and poised; regal

yōngróng zìdé 雍容自得 in the peace of mind

yōng 傭 also **yǒng**

1. to hire 2. a servant; a domestic help

yōngbīng 傭兵 mercenaries

yōnggōng 傭工 1. to hire laborers 2. hired laborers or servants

yōng 慵 also **yǒng**

indolent; lazy; idle

yōngduò 慵惰 lazy; indolent; idle

yōnglǎn 慵懶 lazy; indolent; idle

yōng 擁 also **yǒng**

1. to hug; to embrace; to hold 2. to have; to possess 3. to crowd; to throng; to swarm 4. to follow; to support

yōngbào 擁抱 to embrace; to hug; to hold in one's arms

yōngdài 擁戴 to support a leader or ruler; (to) support

yōnghù 擁護 to advocate; to support; to back

yōngjǐ 擁擠 crowded; packed

yōngsè 擁塞 to block up; a jam

yōngyǒu 擁有 to have; to possess; to own

yōng 壅 also **yǒng**

1. to stop; to block up 2. to bank up the roots of plants

yōngsè 壅塞 to block up; to obstruct; to impede

yōng 臃 also **yǒng**

1. to swell; a swelling 2. fat and

Y

clumsy

yǒngzhǒng 臃腫 fat and clumsy

yōng 饔
1. cooked food 2. breakfast 3. slaughtered animals

yōngsūn bùjì 饔飧不繼 discontinuation of supper after breakfast—poverty-stricken

yóng 庸
refer to **yōng** 庸

yóng 傭
refer to **yōng** 傭

yóng 慵
refer to **yōng** 慵

yǒng 永
long in time; everlasting; eternal; permanent

yǒngbié 永別 to part for good; to die

yǒngbù 永不 will never

yǒngchuí bùxiǔ 永垂不朽 immortal (accomplishment, fame, etc.)

yǒngcún 永存 to remain forever; to live for ever and ever

yǒnghéng 永恆 eternity; eternal; everlasting; perpetual

yǒngjiǔ 永久 permanent; perpetual; eternal; lasting

yǒngjué 永訣 to be gone forever —to die

yǒngshēng 永生 1. for ever 2. eternal life

yǒngshì 永世 forever; eternity

yǒngwú níngrì 永無寧日 Never will there be days of peace.

yǒngyuǎn 永遠 forever; eternally; perpetually

yǒngzhì bùwàng 永誌不忘 to remember forever

yǒng 甬
1. a measure of capacity 2. alternative name of Ningbo, Zhejiang

yǒngdào 甬道 the central path in a hall

yǒng 泳
1. to swim 2. types or methods of swimming

yǒng 俑
wooden or earthen figures of men and women buried with the dead; a tomb figure; a figurine

yǒng 勇
1. brave; courageous; bold; valiant; intrepid; fearless 2. a soldier; a conscript 3. bravery; courage

yǒnggǎn 勇敢 brave; courageous

yǒngměng 勇猛 brave and fierce

yǒngqì 勇氣 courage; bravery; valor

yǒngshì 勇士 a brave fighter; a warrior

yǒngwǎng zhíqián 勇往直前 to march fearlessly onward

yǒngyú 勇於 to be brave in; to have the courage to

yǒng 湧（涌）
1. to gush; to pour 2. to rise

yǒngchū 湧出 to well out; to spring out

yǒngjìn 湧進 to swarm (or sweep) into

yǒngquán 湧泉 a fountain; a spring

yǒngxiàn 湧現 to crop up (in one's mind)

yǒng 詠
1. to sing; to hum 2. the chirping of birds

yǒngtàn 詠歎 to sigh (usually in admiration)

yǒng 蛹
a chrysalis; a pupa

yǒng 踴（踊）
to leap up

yǒngyuè 踴躍 1. to leap 2. enthusiastically

yǒng 擁
refer to **yōng** 擁

yǒng 壅
refer to **yōng** 壅

yǒng 臃
refer to **yōng** 臃

yòng 用
1. to use; to employ 2. to exert 3. use 4. effect 5. finance 6. to need; need 7. to eat; to drink

yòngbīng 用兵 to manipulate troops

yòngbuguàn 用不慣 unaccustomed to the use of

yòngbuzháo 用不著 there is no need to

yòngchu 用處 a purpose

yòngdezháo 用得著 1. to need 2. it is necessary to

yòngdì 用地 land for a specific use

yòngfǎ 用法 directions for using or operating something

yònggōng 用功 to study diligently; to study hard

yòngguāng 用光 to use up; to run out of; to exhaust

yònghù 用戶 a customer (of a utility); a user; a consumer

yòngjù 用具 a tool; an appliance; an implement

yònglì 用力 to exert oneself; to make an effort; to put forth one's strength

yòngpǐn 用品 articles for use

yòngqián 用錢 1. to spend money 2. commission

yòngqíng bùzhuān 用情不專 to be frivolous in affairs of the heart

yòngrén 用人 to employ people

yòngren 用人 a servant

yòngshuǐ 用水 1. to use water 2. water for a specific use

yòngtú 用途 a purpose

yòngxīn 用心 to take care; to pay attention

yòngxīn liángkǔ 用心良苦 well-intentioned but little understood

yòngxíng 用刑 to torture

yòngyì 用意 an intention; a purpose; an idea

yòngyǔ 用語 terminology; phraseology

yòngzhī bùjié 用之不竭 It cannot be used up.

yòng 佣
a commission

yòngjīn 佣金 a bribe; a commission

yōu 幽
1. dark; gloomy 2. lonely; solitary 3. quiet; tranquil 4. deep; profound 5. hidden; secret 6. to imprison; to confine

yōu'àn 幽暗 dim; gloomy

yōufèn 幽憤 resentment; to sulk

Yōufú 幽浮 UFO (unidentified flying object)

yōugǔ 幽谷 a deep valley

yōuhuì 幽會 a tryst, or secret meeting (between a couple in love)

yōuhún 幽魂 the spirit of a dead person; a ghost

yōujìn 幽禁 to confine; to imprison

yōujìng 幽靜 tranquil; placid; serene

yōulíng 幽靈 the disembodied spirit of a dead person; a ghost

yōuměi 幽美 pathetically beautiful

yōumíng 幽冥 1. dark; obscure 2. (Buddhism) hell

yōumíng yìlù 幽明異路 The dead and the living do not mix.

yōumò 幽默 humorous; humor

yōuxián 幽閑 1. (said of a woman) gentle and graceful 2. leisurely and carefree

yōuyǎ 幽雅 chaste and elegant

yōuyōu 幽幽 1. deep; profound; unfathomable 2. dim

yōuyuàn 幽怨 hidden bitterness (of a lady frustrated in love)

yōu 悠
1. far; long; vast; extensive 2. sad; pensive; meditative 3. gentle; slow; soft 4. to swing

yōucháng 悠長 long in time

yōujiǔ 悠久 long in time

yōurán 悠然 unhurriedly; in a leisurely manner; naturally

yōuxián 悠閑 leisurely; unrestrained; unhurried

yōuyáng 悠揚 1. flowing gently sometimes high, sometimes low (as sound) 2. extending far (as scenery)

yōuyuǎn 悠遠 distant; far (in time or space)

yōuzāi 悠哉 1. anxiously 2. free from restraint; carefree

yōu 憂

1. pensive; mournful; grieved; sad 2. anxiety; to worry about; concerned about; anxious; apprehensive

yōuchóu 憂愁 melancholy; grief; sad

yōufèn 憂憤 grieved and indignant

yōuhuàn 憂患 suffering; hardship; misery

yōujù 憂懼 anxious and fearful

yōuláo chéngjí 憂勞成疾 to lose one's health because of care

yōulǜ 憂慮 worried; anxious

yōuqī 憂慼 sad and worried

yōushāng 憂傷 worried and grieved

yōuxīn chōngchōng 憂心忡忡 care-ridden; to have a heart loaded with worry

yōuyù 憂鬱 melancholy; depressed; dejected

yōu 優

1. good; excellent 2. abundant; plenty 3. players (as in an opera) 4. victory; winning 5. soft

yōudài 優待 favorable treatment

yōudàiquàn 優待券 1. a discount ticket 2. a free ticket (for a show, etc.)

yōuděng 優等 an excellent grade; first-rate

yōudiǎn 優點 merits; good qualities; advantages

yōuhòu 優厚 munificent; liberal; favorable

yōuhuì 優惠 preferential; favorable

yōuliáng 優良 fine; good

yōuliè 優劣 1. good and bad 2. bright and dull 3. fit and unfit

yōuluòrǔ 優酪乳 yoghurt; sour milk

yōuměi 優美 1. wonderful; graceful; fine 2. anything that inspires a sense of joy

yōuróu guǎduàn 優柔寡斷 to be peaceable and easygoing but lacking the strength of making quick decisions

yōushēngxué 優生學 eugenics

yōushèng 優勝 winning; superior

yōushèng lièbài 優勝劣敗 survival of the fittest

yōushèngzhě 優勝者 a winner; a champion

yōushì 優勢 supremacy; superiority

yōuwò 優渥 munificent

yōuxiān 優先 priority; to take precedence

yōuxiānquán 優先權 priority

yōuxiù 優秀 outstanding; remarkable

yōuyì 優異 excellent; remarkable; brilliant

yōuyóu 優游 1. carefree 2. indecisive 3. to leave one's life to fate

yōuyuè 優越 superior; outstanding

yōuyuègǎn 優越感 a sense of superiority

yōuzāi yóuzāi 優哉游哉 leisurely and carefree

yóu 尤

1. to feel bitter against; to reproach; to blame 2. a mistake; an error 3. especially or particularly 4. special or outstanding 5. a Chinese family name

yóuqí 尤其 above all; in particular; particularly; especially

yóushèn 尤甚 1. more than; worse than 2. especially so; particularly so

yóuwù 尤物 1. an uncommon person 2. a woman of extraordinary beauty

yóu 由

1. reason; cause; a source; derivation 2. from 3. up to (someone to make a decision) 4. by;

through

yóubude 由不得 involuntarily; unable to do as one pleases

yóucǐ 由此 hence; from this; therefore

yóucǐ kějiàn 由此可見 thus it can be seen; this shows; that proves

yóulái 由來 1. derivation; a source 2. so far; up to now

yóulái yǐjiǔ 由來已久 It has been so for quite some time.

yóuyú 由於 because of; owing to; due to; as a result of

yóuzhōng 由衷 from the depth of one's heart; heartfelt

yóuzhōng zhīyán 由衷之言 words uttered in sincerity

yóu 油

1. a general name for oil, fat, grease, either animal or vegetable 2. anything in liquid form which is inflammable, as gasoline, etc. 3. to oil 4. to varnish; to paint 5. greasy 6. sly; polished and over-experienced 7. luxuriant; prospering; flourishing

yóubù 油布 oilcloth (used as a waterproof covering)

yóucài 油菜 rape

yóucéng 油層 an oil reservoir; an oil layer

yóuchǎng 油廠 1. an oil refinery 2. an oil extracting mill

yóuchuán 油船 a tanker

yóudēng 油燈 an oil lamp

yóudòufu 油豆腐 fried bean curd

yóugāo 油膏 ointment

yóuguǎn 油管 an oil pipe; an oil pipeline

yóuhuà 油畫 an oil painting

yóujǐng 油井 an oil well

yóukuàng 油礦 an oil field; oil deposit

yóuliàng 油亮 glossy; shiny

yóuliào 油料 petroleum, oil and lubricant (POL)

yóulún 油輪 an oil tanker; a tanker; an oiler

yóumén 油門 1. a throttle 2. an accelerator

yóumò 油墨 printing ink

yóunì 油膩 (said of food) greasy; oily

yóuqī 油漆 1. paint; varnish 2. to paint

yóuqiāng huádiào 油腔滑調 suave and sly; glib

yóurán 油然 1. copious; luxuriant; flourishing 2. (rarely) halting

yóurán érshēng 油然而生 (said of love, etc.) to well up

yóushāng 油商 an oil dealer; an oilman

yóushuǐ 油水 1. the cream or essence of something 2. side profit or outside gains in a deal —as kickbacks, etc.

yóutián 油田 an oil field

yóutiáo 油條 1. fritters of twisted dough—a Chinese specialty usually for breakfast 2. a suave, well-oiled person, long on experience but short on sincerity

yóutǒng 油桶 an oil drum

yóutóu fěnmiàn 油頭粉面 pomaded hair and powdered face—descriptive of a frivolous youngster

yóuwū 油污 greasy dirt

yóuxiāng 油箱 a fuel tank

yóuyān 油煙 soot; lampblack

yóuyìn 油印 to mimeograph

yóuyìnjī 油印機 a mimeograph

yóuzhī 油脂 1. (chemistry) olein 2. oil and grease; fats

yóuzhǐ 油紙 oilpaper

yóuzuǐ huáshé 油嘴滑舌 sweet and smooth words which are not backed by sincerity

yóu 柚 also yòu

a teak; a teaktree

yóumù 柚木 1. a teak (tree) 2. teak; teakwood

yóu 郵

1. a post office 2. postal 3. to deliver mails, letters, etc. 4. a wayside station where couriers on government service change horses 5. a hut; a lodge in the field

yóubāo 郵包 a postal parcel

yóuchāi 郵差 a mailman; a postman

yóuchuō 郵戳 a postmark; a postal dater

yóudì 郵遞 to send by mail; to deliver through postal service; mail service

yóudì qūhào 郵遞區號 a zip code

yóudìyuán 郵遞員 a postman

yóufèi 郵費 postal charges

yóugòu 郵購 1. mail order 2. to buy by mail order

yóují 郵寄 to send by mail; to mail

yóujiǎn 郵簡 an air letter

yóujiàn 郵件 mail matter; postal items; the post; mail

yóujú 郵局 a post office

yóupiào 郵票 a postal stamp

yóutǒng 郵筒 a postbox; a mailbox; a letter box

yóuxiāng 郵箱 a postbox; a mailbox; a letter box

yóuzhèng 郵政 postal administration; postal service; postal affairs

yóuzhèng chǔjīn 郵政儲金 savings deposits in a department of the post office

yóuzhèng xìnxiāng 郵政信箱 a post-office box (P.O.B.)

yóuzī 郵資 postal charges

yóu 猶

1. like; similar to; tantamount to; as if 2. still; yet; even; especially; while 3. a kind of monkey 4. a Chinese family name 5. strategy; scheme; plot

yóurú 猶如 just like

Yóutàijiào 猶太教 Judaism

Yóutàirén 猶太人 the Jewish people; Jews

yóuyi 猶疑 undecided; to hesitate

yóuyù 猶豫 undecided; to hesitate

yóu 游

1. to swim; to float; to waft; to drift 2. (遊) to wander about 3. part of a river 4. a Chinese family name

yóubiāo 游標 (computer) cursor

yóudàng 游蕩 loitering about and doing nothing; loafing

yóudòng 游動 to move about

yóují 游擊 a hit-and-run attack

yóujíduì 游擊隊 a guerrilla band; guerrillas

yóujíshǒu 游擊手 (baseball) a shortstop

yóují 游擊 refer to **yóují** 游擊

yóujíduì 游擊隊 refer to **yóujíduì** 游擊隊

yóujíshǒu 游擊手 refer to **yóujíshǒu** 游擊手

yóuláng 游廊 a covered corridor; a veranda

yóulí 游離 (said of a radical, valence, nucleus, etc., in chemistry) free; ionization; liberation

yóumù mínzú 游牧民族 nomadic people; nomads

yóushǒu hàoxián 游手好閒 loitering about and doing nothing; loafing

yóushuì 游說 to lobby; to canvass (for a cause, project, etc.)

yóusī 游絲 gossamer

yóuyí bùdìng 游移不定 undecided; hesitating

yóuyǒng 游泳 swimming

yóuyǒngchí 游泳池 a swimming pool

yóuyǒngyī 游泳衣 a swimming suit

yóuzī 游資 idle capital; idle money

yóu 鈾

uranium

yóu 遊

1. to travel; to go to a distance 2. to roam; to saunter 3. to befriend; to make friends 4. freely wield (a sword), move (one's eyes), stretch (one's sight), etc.

yóubàn 遊伴 a travel companion

yóudàng 遊蕩 to fool around; to act like a bum or vagrant

yóují 遊記 a travelogue (in writing); a writing about one's travels

yóukè 遊客 a traveler; a tourist

yóulǎn 遊覽 1. to visit; to tour; sightseeing 2. to read extensively

yóulǎnchē 遊覽車 a bus or train for tourists or sightseers

yóulè 遊樂 to make merry; entertainment

yóulèchǎng 遊樂場 an amusement park

yóurèn yǒuyú 遊刃有餘 to handle a difficult task with great ease

yóushān wánshuǐ 遊山玩水 to travel high and low and enjoy the sights of mountains and rivers

yóushǒu hàoxián 遊手好閒 to be a lazy good-for-nothing; to lead a parasitic life

yóushuì 遊說 to travel around and try to talk people into accepting one's views; to lobby; to canvass

yóutǐng 遊艇 a yacht

yóuwán 遊玩 to play; to recreate

yóuxì 遊戲 to play; play

yóuxíng 遊行 1. to parade; a parade 2. to demonstrate (in protest)

yóuxué 遊學 to study abroad; to pursue advanced study far away from home

yóuzǐ 遊子 a traveler; a wanderer

yóu 魷
a cuttlefish

yǒu 友
1. a friend; friendly; friendship 2. fraternity; fraternal love 3. to befriend

yǒu'ài 友愛 friendship; fraternal love

yǒubāng 友邦 friendly nations; allies

yǒuhǎo 友好 friendly; amity (treaty, etc.)

yǒujūn 友軍 friendly forces

yǒuqíng 友情 friendship

yǒurén 友人 friends

yǒushàn 友善 friendly

yǒuyí 友誼 refer to **yǒuyì** 友誼

yǒuyì 友誼 friendship

yǒu 有
to have; to be present; to exist; there is

yǒu'ài 有礙 detrimental; harmful

yǒu'ài guānzhān 有礙觀瞻 to be an eyesore

yǒu'àn kěchá 有案可查 to be on record

yǒubǎn yǒuyǎn 有板有眼 1. (said of singing performances) rhythmical 2. (said of speech) articulate 3. (said of conduct) systematic

yǒubànfǎ 有辦法 1. to have a way to solve some problem 2. to be resourceful

yǒubèijǐng 有背景 to have powerful connections

yǒubèi wúhuàn 有備無患 There is no danger when there is preparedness.

yǒudài 有待 1. to wait until 2. to require or need (improvement, investigation, etc.)

yǒudiǎnr 有點兒 some; a little; somewhat

yǒufū zhīfù 有夫之婦 a married woman

yǒufú tóngxiǎng, yǒuhuò tóngdāng 有福同享，有禍同當 to share bliss and misfortune together

yǒugǎn érfā 有感而發 to make a comment out of personal feeling

yǒugōng 有功 to make contributions to

yǒuguān 有關 to concern

yǒuguǐ 有鬼 There's something fishy.

yǒuhài 有害 detrimental; harmful

yǒuhài wúyì 有害無益 not helpful but harmful

yǒuhé bùkě 有何不可 Why not?

yǒuhéng 有恆 persistent; persevering

yǒujī kěchéng 有機可乘 to have loopholes to exploit

yǒujiàn yúcǐ 有鑒於此 in view

of this

yǒujiāo wúlèi 有教無類 to provide education for all people without discrimination

yǒukòng 有空 to have time (for doing something)

yǒukǒu jiēbēi 有口皆碑 praised by all

yǒukǒu nányán 有口難言 unable to speak for self-defense or self-justification under certain circumstances

yǒukuī zhíshǒu 有虧職守 to have neglected one's responsibility or duty

yǒulái yǒuwǎng 有來有往 (said of exchanging gifts or rendering help to others) reciprocal

yǒulài 有賴 to depend on; to rest on

yǒuláo 有勞 to have troubled (you); Please do me a favor by....

yǒule 有了 1. to have obtained what was wanted 2. to have found the answer or solution 3. to become pregnant

yǒulǐ 有理 reasonable justified

yǒulǐ 有禮 polite; courteous; civil

yǒulì 有利 profitable; advantageous; favorable; beneficial; helpful; conducive

yǒulì kětú 有利可圖 · (said of material profit) profitable

yǒumáobing 有毛病 1. sick; ill 2. something wrong; out of order

yǒumíng wúshí 名無實 to exist only in name

yǒumù gòngdǔ 有目共睹 to be obvious to all

yǒupíng yǒujù 有憑有據 well-founded

yǒu qífù bìyǒu qízǐ 有其父必有其子 Like father, like son.

yǒuqián 有錢 rich; wealthy; well-to-do

yǒuqián néngshǐ guǐ tuīmò 有錢能使鬼推磨 Money can work miracles.

yǒuqíngrén zhōngchéng juànshǔ 有情人終成眷屬 The lovers finally got married.

yǒuqǐng 有請 So-and-so requests the pleasure of seeing you.

yǒuqiú bìyìng 有求必應 to respond to every plea

yǒuqù 有趣 interesting; amusing; fascinating

yǒurǎn 有染 to have an affair with

yǒurén 有人 some people; anyone; somebody

yǒurú 有如 just like; as if; as though

yǒushēng yǐlái 有生以來 since one's birth

yǒushēng yǒusè 有聲有色 (said of a description or performance) vivid; impressive

yǒushēng zhīnián 有生之年 for the rest of one's life

yǒushī shēnfen 有失身份 to be beneath one's dignity

yǒushí 有時 sometimes; now and then; occasionally

yǒushí zhīshì 有識之士 knowledgeable people; farsighted people; thinking people

yǒushǐ yǐlái 有史以來 since the dawn of history

yǒushǐ yǒuzhōng 有始有終 to carry out an undertaking from start to finish—not to give up halfway

yǒushì 有事 1. to be busy 2. to meet with an accident

yǒushì wúkǒng 有恃無恐 There is no fear when one has something to fall back upon.

yǒushì zhīshì 有識之士 refer to **yǒushí zhīshì** 有識之士

yǒushuō yǒuxiào 有說有笑 to talk and laugh

yǒusuǒ bùzhī 有所不知 to be unaware of something

yǒutiáo bùwèn 有條不紊 systematic; orderly

yǒutiáo bùwèn 有條不紊 refer to **yǒutiáo bùwèn** 有條不紊

yǒutiáo yǒulǐ 有條有理 logical; systematic

yǒutóu yǒuliǎn 有頭有臉 honored; respected presentable

yǒutóu yǒuwěi 有頭有尾 complete; finished; to do a job from beginning to end

yǒuwàng 有望 hopeful; promis-

ing

yǒuwéi 有爲 capable of great achievements

yǒuwèn bìdá 有問必答 to answer all questions asked

yǒuxǐ 有喜 pregnant

yǒuxì kěchéng 有隙可乘 There is a flaw or chance for attack.

yǒuxiàn 有限 limited; restricted; finite

yǒuxiào 有效 effective; effectual; valid

yǒuxiē 有些 1. some; a few 2. somewhat

yǒuxīn 有心 to have a mind to

yǒuxīnrén 有心人 a person who has a mind to do something useful

yǒuyán zàixiān 有言在先 to have agreed before

yǒuyǎn bùshì Tàishān 有眼不識泰山 to fail to recognize a great person

yǒuyǎn bùshì Tàishān 有眼不識泰山 refer to **yǒuyǎn bùshì Tàishān** 有眼不識泰山

yǒuyǎn wúzhū 有眼無珠 to lack discerning power

yǒuyīcì 有一次 on one occasion; once

yǒuyì 有益 advantageous; useful; profitable; beneficial

yǒuyì 有意 1. to intend; purposeful 2. to be interested

yǒuyìshí 有意識 conscious

yǒuyìshí 有意識 refer to **yǒuyìshí** 有意識

yǒuyìsi 有意思 interesting; exciting; enjoyable; amusing

yǒuyǒng wúmóu 有勇無謀 to be foolhardy

yǒuyòng 有用 useful; practical; beneficial

yǒuyuán 有緣 linked by ties of fate

yǒuzēng wújiǎn 有增無減 1. to increase steadily 2. to get steadily worse or serious

yǒuzhāo yīrì 有朝一日 some day in the future

yǒuzhì jìngchéng 有志竟成

Where there is a will, there is a way.

yǒuzhì yītóng 有志一同 to be of the same mind

yǒuzhǒng 有種 to have guts

yǒuzhùyú 有助於 to be conducive to

yǒu 酉

1. the tenth of the Twelve Terrestrial Branches 2. 5:00-7:00 p.m.

yǒu 莠 also **yòu**

1. foxtail (a kind of weed) 2. bad; ugly; undesirable

yǒu 黝

bluish black

yǒuhēi 黝黑 (said of a complexion) dark; swarthy

yòu 又

1. also; again; in addition to; and 2. moreover; furthermore 3. and (used in a mixed fraction such as one and three fourths)

yòujī yòukě 又飢又渴 both hungry and thirsty

yòujīng yòuxǐ 又驚又喜 alarmed and happy at the same time

yòukuài yòuhǎo 又快又好 (to do something) very fast with excellent results; efficient

yòu 幼

1. young; delicate 2. to take care of the young

yòuchóng 幼蟲 a larva

yòu'ér 幼兒 an infant; a baby

yòumiáo 幼苗 a tender seedling

yòunèn 幼嫩 young and tender; delicate

yòunián 幼年 childhood

yòu nǚtóngjūn 幼女童軍 a brownie

yòutóng 幼童 a young child

yòutóngjūn 幼童軍 a cub scout

yòuxiǎo 幼小 young and small

yòuyá 幼芽 a young bud; a plumule

yòuzhì 幼稚 immature; naive

yòuzhìyuán 幼稚園 a kinder-

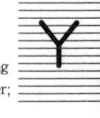

Y

garten

yòuzǐ 幼子 a young son

yòu 右

1. right (as opposed to left). 2. west 3. to assist; to aid 4. to emphasize

yòubian 右邊 the right-hand side

yòupài 右派 1. the right wing 2. the rightists; the conservatives

yòushǒu 右手 1. the right hand 2. the right-hand side

yòushǒu 右首 the right-hand side

yòuxián 右舷 the starboard

yòuxīnshì 右心室 the right ventricle

yòuyì fēnzǐ 右翼份子 a right-winger

yòu 佑(祐)

to help; to protect; to aid; to bless

yòuzhù 佑助 (said of a diety) to help (a mortal)

yòu 囿

1. an enclosure for keeping animals; a menagerie; a garden 2. to confine; to enclose

yòuyú chéngjiàn 囿於成見 bound by prejudice; biased

yòuyú yīyú 囿於一隅 confined to a corner

yòu 柚

1. a pumelo or pomelo; a shaddock 2. refer to **yóu** 柚

yòuzi 柚子 a pomelo; a shaddock

yòu 莠

refer to **yǒu** 莠

yòu 釉

glaze

yòuyào 釉藥 substance used to produce glaze for pottery; glaze

yòu 誘

1. to guide; to lead 2. to decoy; to tempt; to allure; to lure; to captivate

yòudǎo 誘導 to guide; to induce; induction

yòudí 誘敵 to induce the enemy

(to make a wrong move)

yòu'ěr 誘餌 1. a bait 2. a shill

yòuguǎi 誘拐 to seduce; to entice; to abduct; to kidnap

yòuhuò 誘惑 1. to entice; to lure; to allure; to tempt; to beguile 2. to attract; attractive

yòupiàn 誘騙 to induce by deceit; to beguile

yòuyīn 誘因 an inducement

yòu 鼬

a weasel

yòushǔ 鼬鼠 a weasel

yū 迂

1. impractical; unrealistic; stale; old-fashioned; trite 2. roundabout; indirect; circuitous; winding 3. to make a detour 4. absurd; preposterous

yūfǔ 迂腐 stale; hackneyed; pedantic

yūhuí 迂迴 1. twisty; circuitous (road) 2. (military) detouring tactics; flanking tactics

yū 紆

1. to wind; to spiral; to bend; to twist; to distort; to meander 2. a knot in one's heart; melancholy

yūhuǎn 紆緩 slow; dilatory

yūhuí 紆迴 circuitous; winding (roads)

yū 淤

1. muddy sediment; mud; sediment 2. stalemated; blocked; to silt up

yūjī 淤積 to silt up; to clog up

yūní 淤泥 sediment at the bottom of a river, ditch, etc.; silt

yūsè 淤塞 to silt up; to block

yūxiě 淤血 refer to **yūxuè** 淤血

yūxuè 淤血 blood clot

yū 瘀

a hematoma

yūnóng 瘀膿 pus

yūshāng 瘀傷 a contusion; a bruise

yūxiě 瘀血 refer to **yūxuè** 瘀血

yūxuè 瘀血 a hematoma

yú 于

1. (a particle in literary use) in; at; by; to 2. (a verb in literary use) to go or proceed; to take

yúguī 于歸 (said of a girl) to enter into matrimony

yúshì 于是 hence; consequently; thereupon

yú 予
I; me

yú 余
1. (in formal speech) I; me 2. a Chinese family name

yú 盂
1. a basin; a broad-mouthed receptacle for holding liquid; a jar 2. a party for hunting

yú 於
1. in; on; at; by; from 2. than; then; to; with reference to 3. compared with 4. a Chinese family name

yúshì 於是 then; so; thus; thereafter

yúshì wúbǔ 於事無補 It doesn't help the situation.

yú 娛
to amuse; to give pleasure to; to entertain; amusement; entertainment; pleasure

yúlè 娛樂 amusement; entertainment; to amuse; to entertain

yúlè chǎngsuǒ 娛樂場所 entertainment establishments

yú 魚
fish

yúchā 魚叉 a harpoon; a gaff; a fish spear

yúchí 魚池 a fishpond

yúchì 魚翅 shark's fins

yúdùbái 魚肚白 silver-gray (like the belly of a fish)—gray dawn

yú'ěr 魚餌 fish bait

yúfàn 魚販 a fishmonger

yúgān 魚竿 a fishing rod; a fish pole

yúgānyóu 魚肝油 cod-liver oil

yúgāng 魚缸 a fish globe

yúgōu 魚鉤 a fishhook

yúguàn 魚貫 in a column; in procession

yúléi 魚雷 a torpedo

yúlèi 魚類 fishes; Pisces

yúlín 魚鱗 scales (of fish)

yúluǎn 魚卵 roe; spawn

yúmǐ zhīxiāng 魚米之鄉 land of agriculture and fishery; land of plenty

yúmiáo 魚苗 fry (of fish)

yúmù hùnzhū 魚目混珠 (literally) to pass fish eyes as pearls —1. to masquerade 2. to offer something bogus

yúròu 魚肉 1. fish and meat 2. victims of oppression 3. to oppress; to bully

yúròu xiāngmín 魚肉鄉民 to oppress the people

yúshì 魚市 a fish market

yúsōng 魚鬆 dried fish floss

yúwán 魚丸 a fish ball

yúwǎng 魚網 a fishnet; a fishing net

yúwěiwén 魚尾紋 crow's-feet

yúwēn 魚塭 a fish farm

yúxiā 魚蝦 fish and shrimps

yúxīngwèi 魚腥味 a fishy smell

yúyán zhīlì 魚鹽之利 gain from marine resources

yúyāng 魚秧 fry (of fish)

yúyǔ xióngzhǎng 魚與熊掌 unable to make up one's mind as to which of two desirable things to choose

yúzǐjiàng 子魚醬 caviar

yú 愉
happy; contented; pleased

yúkuài 愉快 cheerful; happy; pleased; delighted

yúyuè 愉悅 joyful; glad; happy

yú 渝
1. to change one's mind 2. another name of Chongqing 3. another name of the Jialing River in Sichuan

yú 隅
1. a corner; a nook 2. an angle 3. an out-of-the-way place; a recess

yú 楡

an elm

yú 逾
1. to exceed; to pass over; more than 2. (踰) to transgress 3. added

yújǔ 逾矩 to transgress what is right

yúqī 逾期 to exceed a time limit

yúqí 逾期 refer to **yúqī** 逾期

yúyuè 逾越 1. to pass over; to scale (a wall, etc.) 2. to do what one is not supposed to do

yú 與(歟)
one of the interrogative particles

yú 腴
1. fat 2. plump and soft 3. fertile 4. intestines of dogs and hogs 5. rich

yú 瑜
1. a fine and flawless piece of jade; a perfect gem 2. the brilliancy of jade; the luster of gems 3. excellences; virtues

yújiā 瑜珈 yoga, a mystic and ascetic practice in Hindu philosophy

yú 愚
1. stupid; foolish; silly; unwise; unintelligent 2. to fool; to cheat; to deceive 3. (courteous self-reference) I; me

yúbèn 愚笨 stupid; foolish

yúchǔn 愚蠢 stupid; dull

yúdùn 愚鈍 dull-witted; stupid

yújiàn 愚見 my humble opinion

yúmèi 愚昧 benighted; stupid; ignorant

yúnòng 愚弄 to make a fool of somebody

yúrén 愚人 a fool; a simpleton

Yúrénjié 愚人節 All Fools' Day

yú 漁
1. to fish 2. to seek; to pursue 3. to seize 4. to acquire forcibly

yúchuán 漁船 a fishing boat

yúcūn 漁村 a fishing village

yúfū 漁夫 a fisherman

yúgǎng 漁港 a fishing harbor

yúhuì 漁會 a fishermen's associ-ation

yúhuòliàng 漁獲量 a catch

yúlì 漁利 to seek profits or gains by unethical means

yúliè 漁獵 1. fishing and hunting 2. to seek (illegal gains)

yúmín 漁民 fishermen

yúwǎng 漁網 a fishing net

yúwēng 漁翁 an old fisherman

yúwēng délì 漁翁得利 The fisherman catches both (while the snipe and the clam are locked in a fight).

yúyè 漁業 fishery

yúzhōu 漁舟 a fishing boat

yú 餘
1. remaining; the remnant or remainder; the rest 2. a surplus; an overplus; an excess 3. a balance 4. a complement of a number or figure; odd 5. after

yúbō dàngyàng 餘波蕩漾 The effect (of a major event) is still being felt.

yúdǎng 餘黨 remnants of an outlawed faction or disbanded gang

yúdì 餘地 a spare space; an alternative; elbowroom; leeway

yú'é 餘額 1. a surplus amount; a balance 2. vacancies to be filled

yúhuī 餘暉 twilight at sunset

yújì 餘悸 a lingering shock or fear

yúkuǎn 餘款 remaining funds; a favorable balance; surplus funds

yúlì 餘力 strength or energy to spare

yúliáng 餘糧 surplus grain

yúnián 餘年 the remaining years of one's life

yúniè 餘孽 remnants of rebel groups, secret societies, etc.

yúshēng 餘生 1. the remaining years of one's life; old age 2. a survival (after a disaster)

yúshù 餘數 1. the balance 2. (mathematics) the complement of a number 3. the residue; the remainder

yúwēi 餘威 the influence or power of someone that remains

Y

after his death

yúwèi 餘味 pleasant memories; an aftertaste

yúxiá 餘暇 spare time; leisure

yúxìng 餘興 1. an entertainment program arranged for a gathering 2. a lingering interest

yúyīn ràoliáng 餘音繞梁 The thrilling voice keeps reverberating in the air after the vocalist has stopped singing.

yúzhèn 餘震 aftershocks in the wake of a strong earthquake

yú 諛

to flatter; to toady

yúcí 諛辭 flattery

yú 踰

1. (逾) to pass over; to cross; to go beyond; to transgress; to exceed 2. excessive; overly

yújǔ 踰矩 to transgress the bounds of correctness

yúyuè 踰越 to go beyond; to transgress

yú 輿

1. a carriage; a vehicle 2. a sedan chair 3. the land; the earth 4. all; general 5. to carry; to transport

yúlùn 輿論 public opinion

yúlùnjiè 輿論界 the media; press circles

yúqíng 輿情 public sentiment; public feeling

yú 歟

a final particle indicating doubt, surprise, exclamation, etc.

yǔ 予

to give

yǔ 宇

1. a house; a roof 2. look; appearance; countenance 3. space

yǔhángyuán 宇航員 an astronaut; a cosmonaut

yǔzhòu 宇宙 the universe

yǔzhòufú 宇宙服 a space suit

yǔzhòu tōngxìn 宇宙通信 space communication

yǔzhòuzhàn 宇宙站 space station

yǔ 羽

1. a feather; a plume 2. a wing of a bird 3. one of the five notes in the Chinese musical scale

yǔmáo 羽毛 a feather; a plume; down

yǔmáoqiú 羽毛球 badminton

yǔyì 羽翼 an assistant; a helper

yǔ 雨

rain; rainy

yǔdī 雨滴 a raindrop

yǔdiǎn 雨點 a raindrop

yǔguò tiānqīng 雨過天青 (literally) When the rain is over, the sky clears up.— When the incident (or confusion) is over, everything goes back to normal.

yǔhòu chūnsǔn 雨後春筍 mushroom like bamboo shoots after rain

yǔjì 雨季 the rainy season; the monsoon

yǔjù 雨具 things for wet weather

yǔliàng 雨量 (meteorology) the amount of rainfall or precipitation; rainfall

yǔlù 雨露 favors and kindness; benevolence

yǔmào 雨帽 a rain hat; a rain cap

yǔpéng 雨棚 a rainshed

yǔsǎn 雨傘 an umbrella

yǔshuǐ 雨水 1. rain water 2. one of 24 climatic periods in the solar calendar, which falls on February 19 or 20

yǔtiān 雨天 a rainy day

yǔxié 雨鞋 rainshoes; galoshes

yǔyī 雨衣 a raincoat

yǔ 禹

1. Yu, the legendary founder of the Xia Dynasty (21st-16th century B.C.) 2. a Chinese family name

yǔ 與

1. and; with; together with 2. to give; to impart

yǔhǔ móupí 與虎謀皮 to try

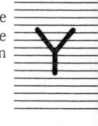

to persuade someone to do what is against his interest

yǔqí...bùrú 與其……不如 It's better to ... than (rather than) ...; ...rather than...

yǔrì jùzēng 與日俱增 to be on the increase

yǔshì chángcí 與世長辭 to pass away

yǔshì wúzhēng 與世無爭 to stand aloof from worldly success

yǔzhòng bùtóng 與眾不同 extraordinary; uncommon

yǔ 語
1. language; speech 2. a word; a sentence 3. a saying; a proverb 4. a sign; a signal 5. to speak; to say; to talk

yǔbìng 語病 illogical use of words

yǔcí 語詞 words; phrases

yǔdiào 語調 the tone of one's speech; intonation

yǔfǎ 語法 wording; grammar; syntax

yǔhuì 語彙 vocabulary

yǔjīng sìzuò 語驚四座 The statement was received with raised eyebrows.

yǔjù 語句 a sentence; a phrase

yǔlù 語錄 quotations

yǔqì 語氣 1. (grammar) mood 2. the tone (of one's speech); the manner of speaking

yǔtài 語態 (grammar) voice

yǔwén 語文 language and literature

yǔwú lúncì 語無倫次 to talk incoherently

yǔyān bùxiáng 語焉不詳 The statement is too brief to be clear.

yǔyán 語言 a language; speech

yǔyì 語意 the meaning (of a word, etc.)

yǔyīn 語音 1. a phone 2. pronunciation

yǔzhòng xīncháng 語重心長 One's words are serious and (one's) heart is thoughtful.

yǔzhùcí 語助詞 a grammatical particle; an auxiliary

yǔ 嶼
an islet; an island

yǔ 齬
1. uneven teeth 2. to disagree; to have discord

yù 玉
1. a precious stone—especially jade; a gem 2. a polite expression for your 3. a designation of things belonging to a girl or young woman 4. (said of a person, especially a woman) pure; fair; beautiful 5. a Chinese family name

yùchéng qíshì 玉成其事 to assist another in accomplishing a task or attaining a goal

Yùhuáng Dàdì 玉皇大帝 the Jade Emperor, the supreme deity in Taoism

yùlánhuā 玉蘭花 magnolia blossoms

yùmǐ 玉米 maize; Indian corn

yùnǚ 玉女 1. a young and beautiful girl 2. your daughter 3. an angel in the fairyland

yùpèi 玉佩 a jade pendant on a girdle

yùqì 玉器 a jade article

yùshí jùfén 玉石俱焚 to destroy indiscriminately, be it jade or rock

yùshǒu 玉手 fair hands; hands of a pretty lady

yùshǔshǔ 玉蜀黍 maize; Indian corn

yùxǐ 玉璽 the imperial seal

yùxiāo 玉簫 a jade flute

yùyè qióngjiāng 玉液瓊漿 top-quality wine

yùyǔn xiāngxiāo 玉殞香消 the death of a woman

yùzhào 玉照 your photograph or picture

yùzhuó 玉鐲 a jade bracelet

yù 芋
a taro

yù 育
1. to produce; to give birth to; to breed 2. to raise; to bring up; to

nourish; to nurse 3. to educate

yùyòuyuàn 育幼院 a nursery school; an orphanage

yùzhǒng 育種 breeding

yù 抑

to restrain; to repress; to curb; to suppress

yù 郁

1. adorned; colorfully ornamented; beautiful; refined 2. a Chinese family name

yùliè 郁烈 permeated with strong aroma

yù 浴

1. to bathe; to wash 2. a bath

yùjīn 浴巾 a bath towel

yùpén 浴盆 a bath; a bathtub

yùshì 浴室 a bathroom

yùxiě kǔzhàn 浴血苦戰 refer to **yùxuè kǔzhàn** 浴血苦戰

yùxuè kǔzhàn 浴血苦戰 to fight a bloody battle

yùyī 浴衣 a bathrobe; a bathing gown

yù 御

1. to drive a chariot or carriage 2. a driver; an attendant 3. to resist; to keep out 4. to control; to manage; to superintend; to tame (a shrew); to harness 5. imperial 6. to wait on; to set before, as food; to present to

yùcì 御賜 bestowed by the emperor

yùhuāyuán 御花園 an imperial garden

yùjià 御駕 1. the imperial carriage 2. the emperor

yùjià qīnzhēng 御駕親征 The emperor personally led his soldiers in a military operation.

yùlínjūn 御林軍 imperial guards

yùqián 御前 in the presence of the emperor

yùshàn 御膳 the imperial cuisine

yùshànfáng 御膳房 the imperial kitchen

yùyī 御醫 the emperor's physician

yùyòng 御用 (said of articles, etc.) used by the emperor

yùzhǐ 御旨 an imperial decree

yù 域

1. a frontier; a boundary 2. a region; a country; an area 3. to live; to stay

yù 欲

1. to desire; to intend; to long for; to want; wish; desire; expectation; longing 2. about to; on the point of

yùbà bùnéng 欲罷不能 unable to stop even if one wants to

yùgài mízhāng 欲蓋彌彰 The more one tries to cover up (a secret, etc.), the better-known it will become.

yùqín gùzòng 欲擒故縱 to try to get something by feigning uninterestedness or making concessions

yùsù bùdá 欲速不達 Haste makes waste.

yùwàng 欲望 desires; to long for; longings

yùyán yòuzhǐ 欲言又止 to wish to speak but keep silent on second thought

yù 寓

1. to live temporarily; to sojourn; to dwell 2. to consign

yùsuǒ 寓所 one's residence or dwelling

yùyán 寓言 a fable; an allegory

yùyì 寓意 a moral (of a fable)

yùyì shēnkè 寓意深刻 to be pregnant with meaning

yù 喻

1. to use a figure of speech; an illustration; a parable 2. to know; to be acquainted with 3. to explain; to make clear; to tell the meaning of; to instruct 4. a Chinese family name

yù 馭

1. to drive 2. to govern; to rule; to control 3. a driver

yù 裕

1. abundance; affluent; plenty; to be abundant 2. tolerant (adminis-

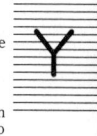

tration, etc.); lenient (punishment, etc.) 3. generous; magnanimous 4. slowly; to take time

yù 與

to take part in; to participate in

yùhuì 與會 to participate in a conference

yù 遇

1. to meet; to run into; to come across; to encounter 2. to treat; treatment 3. opportunity; luck 4. meeting of minds; to win confidence (of a superior, king, etc.) 5. to rival; to match with

yùcì 遇刺 to be attacked by an assassin

yùdào 遇到 to run into; to meet with; to encounter

yùhài 遇害 to be murdered or assassinated

yùjiàn 遇見 to meet with; to run into; to come across; to bump into

yù'nàn 遇難 1. to get killed in an accident 2. to be murdered by enemy troops, rebels, etc.

yùrén bùshū 遇人不淑 to have married a bad husband

yùrén bùshú 遇人不淑 refer to yùrén bùshū 遇人不淑

yù 愈

1. (癒) to recover (from illness); to heal 2. to a greater degree; even more

yùjiā 愈加 increasingly; more and more

yùshèn 愈甚 intenser; to become intense

yùyì 愈益 increasingly; more and more

yù 預

1. beforehand; previously; in advance 2. to prepare; to make ready; reserve (funds, troops, etc.) 3. to take part in

yùbào 預報 a forecast; an advance notice

yùbèi 預備 to prepare; to get ready beforehand; preparatory

yùcè 預測 to predict; to make a forecast

yùdìng 預定 1. to reserve (seats,

rooms, etc.) 2. to set (a date, etc.); to be scheduled

yùfáng 預防 to prevent beforehand; to nip in the bud; to prepare against

yùgǎn 預感 1. a premonition; a presentiment 2. to have a premonition

yùgào 預告 to inform or notify beforehand; advance notice; to herald

yùjì 預計 to estimate; to surmise; estimates; to calculate in advance

yùliào 預料 to predict; to surmise; to anticipate; to expect

yùliú 預留 to put aside for later use; to keep something in reserve

yùmóu 預謀 to scheme or plan beforehand

yùqī 預期 to expect; to estimate; to anticipate

yùqí 預期 refer to yùqī 預期

yùsài 預賽 a preliminary competition

yùshòuwū 預售屋 soon to be available housing

yùsuàn 預算 an estimate; a budget; to calculate in advance

yùxí 預習 1. (said of students) to prepare lessons before class 2. to rehearse or drill; a rehearsal or drill

yùxiān 預先 beforehand; in advance

yùyán 預言 1. prophecy; a prediction; a forecast 2. to predict; to foretell

yùyánjiā 預言家 a prophet; a fortuneteller

yùyǎn 預演 a preview; a rehearsal

yùyuē 預約 a preliminary agreement; to make an appointment

yùzhào 預兆 an omen; premonition; a presage; a sign; a harbinger

yùzhī 預支 to draw (salary) in advance

yùzhī 預知 to know beforehand or in advance; a foreknowledge

yùzhù 預祝 to congratulate (vic-

tory or success) beforehand

yù 語
to tell; to inform; to admonish

yù 獄
1. jail; prison 2. a lawsuit
yùlì 獄吏 a jailer; a warden
yùzú 獄卒 a jailer; a gaoler

yù 熨
to settle (matters)

yù 慾
desire; appetite; passion; lust; greed
yùhuǒ fénshēn 慾火焚身 The fire of lust is so hot that it consumes the body.
yùlìng zhǐhūn 慾令智昏 Greed can benumb reason.
yùniàn 慾念 desire; a longing; a craving
yùwàng 慾望 desire; a longing; an aspiration

yù 禦
to guard against; to take precautions against
yùdí 禦敵 to guard against the enemy
yùhán 禦寒 to protect oneself from cold

yù 諭
1. to notify by a directive, etc.; to instruct; to tell 2. a decree; an edict
yùshì 諭示 to notify or announce by an edict

yù 豫
1. comfort; to be at ease 2. (預) to get ready; beforehand 3. to travel; to make a trip 4. to cheat; to lie 5. to hesitate 6. short for Henan 7. happy; delighted; pleased

yù 燠
warm

yù 癒
healed; cured

yù 譽
1. fame; honor; glory 2. to eulogize; to praise

yùmǎn quánqiú 譽滿全球 world-famous

yù 鬻
1. to sell 2. to bring up 3. young; childish
yùwén 鬻文 to write for pay

yù 鷸
a snipe
yùbàng xiāngzhēng 鷸蚌相爭 a quarrel which benefits only a third party

yù 籲(籲)
to call for; to make an appeal for
yùtiān cìfú 籲天賜福 to implore Heaven for a blessing

yù 鬱
1. a tulip 2. a plum (*Prunus japonica*) 3. held in check; pent-up; stagnant 4. luxuriant; lush
yùjī 鬱積 pent-up (feelings); to smolder
yùjīnxiāng 鬱金香 a tulip
yùmèn 鬱悶 to have pent-up emotions or thoughts
yùyù guǎhuān 鬱鬱寡歡 to mope; to feel low; one's spirits droop

yuān 冤
1. oppression; injustice; a grievance; a wrong 2. feud; animosity; enmity 3. to cheat; to lie 4. to spend money recklessly 5. to make false accusations
yuānchóu 冤仇 feud; enmity; animus
yuāndàtóu 冤大頭 a fathead
yuānjiā 冤家 an enemy (but also used for lovers)
yuānjiā lùzhǎi 冤家路窄 Enemies often cross each other's path.
yuānqíng 冤情 the details of a grievance or wrong
yuānqū 冤屈 a grievance; a wrong
yuānwang 冤枉 to wrong; to accuse a person with a false charge
yuānyù 冤獄 miscarriage of jus-

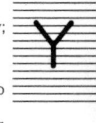

Y

tice

yuān 淵
1. deep waters; a gulf; an abyss
2. profound; depth; erudition;
extensive

yuānbó 淵博 (said of learning)
erudite

yuānsǒu 淵藪 the place where
things or persons flock together
—a hotbed

yuānyuán 淵源 1. the source 2.
relationship

yuān 鳶
1. a kite; a hawk 2. a kite (a
toy)

yuānfēi yúyuè 鳶飛魚躍 kites
flying and fishes jumping—natural freedom of things in the universe

yuān 鴛
the male mandarin duck

yuānyang 鴛鴦 mandarin
ducks, which always live in
pairs—a symbol of lovers

yuānyang húdié pài 鴛鴦蝴
蝶派 literature characterized by
shallow love stories

yuán 元
1. the beginning; the first; original 2. the head 3. a dollar 4. the
eldest; chief; big 5. (Chinese
astrology) 60 years 6. the Yuan
Dynasty

yuánbǎo 元寶 a silver or gold
ingot

Yuándàn 元旦 New Year's Day

yuánjiàn 元件 (computer) an
element

yuánlǎo 元老 an elder person
who has held high positions for
long period of time and is highly
respected by the nation

yuánnián 元年 the first year of
a reign, dynasty, etc.

yuánpèi 元配 a man's first wife

yuánqì 元氣 vitality and constitution

yuánqìjiàn 元器件 (computer)
an element

yuánshǒu 元首 1. the chief of
state; the king; the president,

etc. 2. the beginning

yuánshuài 元帥 the commander
in chief

yuánsù 元素 (chemistry) the elements

yuánxiāo 元宵 1. the Lantern
Festival 2. small rice-flour dumplings eaten on the Lantern Festival

yuánxiōng 元兇 the chief cul-
prit; a ringleader (of a crime)

yuánxūn 元勳 1. great achievements 2. a founding father

yuányuè 元月 1. the first month
of the lunar calendar 2. January

yuán 員
1. a member (of an organization,
etc.) 2. a person engaged in some
field of activity 3. outer limits
(of land, space, etc.)

yuángōng 員工 employees (collectively)

yuán 袁
1. the graceful look of a flowing
robe 2. a Chinese family name

yuán 原
1. the source; the origin; the
beginning 2. original; primary 3.
a steppe; a vast plain; level 4.
a graveyard 5. to excuse; to pardon

yuánbǎn 原版 the original print
or edition

yuándònglì 原動力 1. power 2.
action

yuánfēng bùdòng 原封不動
(kept or left) intact or unopened

yuángǎo 原稿 a manuscript

yuángào 原告 the plaintiff; the
prosecutor

yuánjí 原籍 hailing from; a
native of

yuánlái 原來 originally or formerly

yuánlái rúcǐ 原來如此 1. I see.
2. It was as it is now.

yuánlǐ 原理 a principle

yuánliàng 原諒 forgiveness; to
forgive; to pardon

yuánliào 原料 raw materials

yuánmù 原木 a log

Y

yuánrèn 原任 1. the predecessor 2. formerly held the post of...

yuánshǐ 原始 1. primitive; backward 2. a source

yuánshǐ fēnshù 原始分數 a raw score

yuánshǐrén 原始人 a primitive

yuánwěi 原委 the reason why a thing happened; the ins and outs (of a case, story, etc.)

yuánwén 原文 the original text

yuánxiān 原先 in the beginning; originally

yuánxíng bìlù 原形畢露 to reveal the true nature or colors (of a person) completely

yuányì 原意 1. original intentions 2. original meaning

yuányīn 原因 a reason; a cause

yuányóu 原油 crude oil; crude petroleum

yuányuán běnběn 原原本本 in detail; the whole (story or thing)

yuánzé 原則 a principle

yuánzhǐ 原址 the former address

yuánzhùmín 原住民 an aborigine

yuánzhuàng 原狀 1. the original condition 2. the status quo

yuánzǐ 原子 an atom

yuánzǐbǐ 原子筆 a ball-point pen

yuánzǐdàn 原子彈 an atomic bomb

yuánzǐnéng 原子能 atomic energy

yuánzuò 原作 the original work

yuán 援 1. to lead 2. to take hold of; to pull by hand 3. to aid; to help; to reinforce 4. to rescue 4. to invoke (a law, precedent, etc.)

yuánjiù 援救 to rescue

yuánjūn 援軍 reinforcements

yuánlì 援例 to follow a precedent

yuánshǒu 援手 1. to extend a helping hand 2. a helper

yuányǐn 援引 to cite (a prece-

dent) as proof, etc.

yuányòng 援用 to invoke or quote (a precedent, provisions of laws, etc.)

yuánzhù 援助 to aid; aid; to help

yuán 源 a source; a head (of a stream)

yuánliú 源流 full particulars; all the details; the whole story

yuántóu 源頭 a head or a source (of a stream)

yuánwěi 源委 full particulars; all the details; the whole story

yuányuán bùjué 源源不絕 to continue without end

yuányuǎn liúcháng 源遠流長 to have a long history

yuán 圓 1. round; circular; spherical 2. complete; to complete; to make plausible; to justify 3. satisfactory; tactful 4. a monetary unit 5. a circle

yuánchǎng 圓場 to mediate

yuánguī 圓規 a pair of compasses

yuánhú 圓弧 an arc

yuánhuá 圓滑 tactful; slick and sly

yuánjí 圓寂 refer to **yuánjì** 圓寂

yuánjì 圓寂 (said of Buddhist monks or nuns) to die; to pass away

yuánmǎn 圓滿 1. satisfactory 2. rounded out 3. complete

yuánpán 圓盤 a disc

yuánquān 圓圈 a circle; a ring

yuántǒng 圓筒 a cylinder

yuánwǔqǔ 圓舞曲 waltz

yuánxīn 圓心 the center of a circle

yuánxíng 圓形 round; spherical; circular

yuánzhōu 圓周 the circumference of a circle

yuánzhūbǐ 圓珠筆 a ball-point pen

yuánzhù 圓柱 a cylinder

yuán 園

1. a piece of ground used for growing flowers, fruit or vegetables; a garden; a plantation 2. a public garden, park or recreation ground

yuándì 園地 1. a garden 2. (in a periodical) a space reserved for publishing articles or letters from readers

yuándīng 園丁 a gardener

yuányì 園藝 gardening; horticulture

yuányóuhuì 園遊會 a garden party

yuánzhǔ 園主 the owner of a park or a garden

yuán 猿

an ape; a gibbon

yuánhóu 猿猴 apes and monkeys

yuánlèi 猿類 anthropoid

yuán 緣

1. a cause; a reason 2. to go along; to follow 3. a hem; a margin; an edge; a fringe 4. relationship by fate; predestined relationship

yuánfèn 緣分 predestined relationship

yuángù 緣故 a cause; a reason

yuánqǐ 緣起 1. origins 2. a preface

yuányóu 緣由 a cause; a reason

yuǎn 遠

1. far; distant; remote 2. deep; profound 3. to keep at a distance

yuǎnchù 遠處 distant; located far away; distant places

yuǎndà 遠大 very promising (person, etc.); (to look) far ahead

yuǎndào 遠道 faraway; distant; afar

yuǎnfāng 遠方 a distant place; a remote place

yuǎnfáng 遠房 related through remote ancestry; distantly related

yuǎnjiàn 遠見 foresight; a farsighted view; prescience

yuǎnjiāo jìngōng 遠交近攻 to make friends with distant countries and attack the neighboring ones

yuǎnjìn 遠近 1. far and near 2. remote or close (relatives, etc.) 3. distance

yuǎnjǐng 遠景 1. a vista; a distant view; a long-range perspective 2. (movies) a long shot

yuǎnjù jiāoxué 遠距教學 distant learning

yuǎnjùlí jiāoyù 遠距離教育 distant learning

yuǎnlí 遠離 1. to depart for a distant place 2. to keep away at a great distance

yuǎnlí chénxiāo 遠離塵囂 far from the madding crowd

yuǎnqīn bùrú jìnlín 遠親不如近鄰 Distant relatives are not as helpful as close neighbors.

yuǎnshè chóngyáng 遠涉重洋 to cross many seas—to go abroad

yuǎnshì 遠視 1. farsightedness (as a physical defect); hypermetropia 2. to look from a distance

yuǎnshuǐ jiùbùliǎo jìnhuǒ 遠水救不了近火 Water from afar cannot quench a nearby fire.

yuǎnxíng 遠行 to travel to a distant place; a journey to a distant place

yuǎnyáng 遠洋 1. an ocean 2. of the open sea beyond the littoral zone; oceanic

yuǎnzhēng 遠征 to do battle in a distant land; an expedition

yuǎnzǒu gāofēi 遠走高飛 to go (or flee) far away

yuǎnzú 遠足 an excursion; an outing

yuàn 怨

1. ill will; hatred; enmity; animus; resentment 2. to resent; to complain; to blame (others); to impute

yuànduì 怨懟 ill will; hatred; a grudge

yuànfèn 怨忿 animus; bitterness; a grudge

yuànhèn 怨恨 ill will; enmity; animus

yuàn'ǒu 怨偶 an unharmonious couple

yuànqì 怨氣 spite; complaints; resentment

yuànshēng zàidào 怨聲載道 (said of bad administration, etc.) Complaints can be heard everywhere.

yuàntàn 怨歎 to sigh with bitterness

yuàntiān yóurén 怨天尤人 (figuratively) to impute all faults and wrongs to others; to be neurotically dissatisfied

yuànyán 怨言 complaints; grumbles

yuànyóu 怨尤 complaining; a grudge; a grumble

yuàn 苑
1. a garden; a park 2. a gathering place

yuàn 院
1. a courtyard; a yard 2. a designation for certain government offices and public places 3. short for the Executive Yuan, Legislative Yuan, Examination Yuan, Judicial Yuan, or Control Yuan

yuànxiáshì 院轄市 a special municipality

yuànzhǎng 院長 the dean of a college or court of law; the director of a hospital, museum, etc.

yuànzi 院子 a yard; a courtyard

yuàn 遠
to keep at a distance; to keep away from; to avoid; to shun

yuànxiǎorén 遠小人 to keep away from mean persons

yuàn 願
1. to be willing; to be desirous of; to hope; to wish 2. anything one wishes or desires; an ambition or aspiration 3. a vow 4. to think

yuàn tiānxià yǒuqíngrén jiēchéng juànshǔ 願天下有情人皆成眷屬 May all lovers unite in marriage!

yuànwàng 願望 one's wish or aspiration; what one's heart desires

yuànyì 願意 1. to be willing 2. to like; to want 3. to approve of

yuē 曰
1. (an archaic usage) to say 2. to call; to name

yuē 約
1. an agreement; a covenant; a contract; a treaty 2. brief(ly); simply 3. about; around; approximately; estimated 4. a date; an appointment or engagement; a rendezvous; to make an appointment; to date 5. poor; poverty; hardship; straitened 6. (mathematics) to reduce 7. to bind; to restrain 8. vague(ly)

yuēdìng 約定 to agree upon; to agree to

yuēhuì 約會 an appointment or engagement; a date

yuēlüè 約略 1. brief(ly); sketchy 2. approximate

yuēmo 約莫 or so; about; approximately

yuēqī 約期 an appointment or engagement; to make an appointment

yuēqí 約期 refer to **yuēqī** 約期

yuēqǐng 約請 to invite

yuēshù 約束 to bind or restrain; restraint; restriction

yuè 月
1. the moon 2. the month

yuèbàn 月半 the 15th day of a month

yuèbào 月報 1. a monthly report 2. a monthly journal

yuèbǐng 月餅 a moon cake

yuèchū 月初 the beginning of a month

yuèdǐ 月底 the end of a month

yuèguāng 月光 moonlight

yuèguì 月桂 a laurel

yuèjīng 月經 menses; periods; monthlies

yuèkān 月刊 a monthly (publication)

yuèlì 月利 monthly interest

Y

yuèlì 月曆 a calendar, each page of which is a table of the days of a month

yuèliang 月亮 the moon

yuèpiào 月票 a monthly ticket

yuèqiú 月球 the moon

yuèsè 月色 moonlight

yuèshí 月食 (astronomy) a lunar eclipse

yuèshí 月蝕 (astronomy) a lunar eclipse

yuètái 月臺 a platform (at a railway station)

yuètáipiào 月臺票 a platform ticket

yuètóur 月頭兒 the beginning of a month

yuèxī 月息 monthly interest

yuèxí 月息 refer to **yuèxī** 月息

yuèxià lǎorén 月下老人 a matchmaker

yuèxīn 月薪 a monthly salary

yuèyè 月夜 a moonlight night; a moonlit night

yuè 岳
1. a great mountain; a high mountain 2. the parents of one's wife

yuèfù 岳父 one's father-in-law

yuèmǔ 岳母 one's mother-in-law

yuèzhàng 岳丈 one's father-in-law

yuè 悅
to delight; to gratify; to please; contented; pleased; gratified

yuè'ěr 悅耳 pleasant to the ear; musical

yuèmù 悅目 pleasant to the eye

yuè 越
1. to go beyond; to transgress 2. to skip; to climb over; to cross over; to go across 3. even more; the more 4. name of an ancient state 5. a Chinese family name

yuèguǐ 越軌 to go beyond what is proper

yuèguò 越過 1. to exceed; to overstep 2. to go across; to cross

yuèjiè 越界 to go beyond the boundary

yuèláiyuè... 越來越…… more and more; increasingly more

yuè léichí yībù 越雷池一步 to transgress the bounds

Yuènán 越南 Vietnam

yuèquán 越權 to act without authorization

yuèyě sàipǎo 越野賽跑 a cross-country race

yuèyù 越獄 to break jail; a jail-break

Yuè 粵
1. Guangdong Province 2. Guangdong and Guangxi Provinces

Yuèjù 粵劇 Guangdong opera

yuè 葯
refer to **yào** 葯

yuè 閱
1. to read; to go over (examination papers) 2. to review; to inspect; to examine; to observe 3. to experience 4. to pass

yuèbào 閱報 to read newspapers

yuèbīng 閱兵 to inspect or review troops

yuèdú 閱讀 to read

yuèjuàn 閱卷 to grade examination papers

yuèlǎn 閱覽 to read

yuèlǎnshì 閱覽室 a reading room

yuèlì 閱歷 1. to see, hear, or do for oneself 2. experience; background

yuè 樂
1. music 2. a Chinese family name

yuèduì 樂隊 a band; an orchestra

yuèpǔ 樂譜 a score (of music); musical notes

yuèqì 樂器 a musical instrument

yuèqǔ 樂曲 a piece of music; a musical composition

yuèshī 樂師 a musician

yuètuán 樂團 1. a philharmonic society 2. a philharmonic orchestra

yuèzhāng 樂章 a movement (of a symphony, sonata, etc.)

Y

yuè 龠
1. a kind of flute 2. a kind of measuring vessel

yuè 嶽
a high mountain

yuè 藥
refer to **yào** 藥

yuè 耀
refer to **yào** 耀

yuè 躍 also **yào**
to jump; to leap; to bound; to spring

yuèrán zhǐshàng 躍然紙上
(said of things portrayed in literature or paintings) full of life; vivid

yuèyuè yùshì 躍躍欲試 impatient to have a try; eager to do something

yuè 鑰
refer to **yào** 鑰

yūn 暈
1. to faint; to swoon 2. giddy and dizzy 3. (usually used sarcastically) to do things without a purpose

yūndǎo 暈倒 to faint and fall; to swoon

yūnguoqu 暈過去 to pass out; to faint

yūnjué 暈厥 (medicine) syncope; to faint

yūntóu zhuànxiàng 暈頭轉向 1. to feel dizzy and giddy 2. so confused that one doesn't know what to do, say, etc.

yún 匀
uniform; even

yúnchèn 匀稱 symmetrical; even

yún 云
to say; to speak

yún 芸
1. a strong-scented herb; rue 2. (耘)to weed

yúnyún zhòngshēng 芸芸眾生 1. people of the world 2. all living things

yún 耘
to weed

yún 雲
1. clouds 2. a cloud of; a large number of 3. short for Yunnan Province

yúnbìn 雲鬢 the hairdo of a beautiful woman—like floating clouds

yúncai 雲彩 clouds illuminated by the rising or setting sun

yúncéng 雲層 layers of clouds

yúnhǎi 雲海 a sea of clouds

yúnjí 雲集 to congregate; to gather; to flock together

yúnkāi jiànrì 雲開見日 (literally) When the clouds part, one sees the sun.—a turn of fortune for the better

yúnliàng 雲量 cloud cover; cloud amount; cloudiness

Yúnnán 雲南 Yunnan Province

yúnqì 雲氣 thin, floating clouds

yúnquè 雲雀 a skylark; a meadowlark

yúntī 雲梯 a scaling ladder

yúntūn 雲吞 Chinese ravioli

yúnwù 雲霧 clouds and fog —obscure places

yúnxiá 雲霞 1. clouds 2. one who is unmoved by monetary gains or high positions; a person of high virtue

yúnxiāo 雲霄 the sky—very high

yúnxiāo fēichē 雲霄飛車 a roller coaster

yúnxiāo wùsàn 雲消霧散 (literally) clouds dissipating and fog melting away—The troubles are over.

yúnyān 雲煙 clouds and smog

yúnyóu 雲遊 to travel without a destination; to wander about

yúnyǔ 雲雨 1. grace and favor 2. sexual intercourse; making love

yǔn 允
1. to allow; to consent; to grant 2. appropriate; proper 3. sincere; loyal; faithful; truly

yǔncóng 允從 to follow (one's

advice, etc.)

yǔnnuò 允諾 to assent; to consent; to grant; to permit

yǔnwén yǔnwǔ 允文允武 to be good at wielding both pen and weapon

yǔnxǔ 允許 to assent; to consent; to grant; to permit

yǔn 隕

1. to fall 2. to die

yǔnluò 隕落 1. to fall from the sky or outer space 2. to pass away; to die

yǔnshí 隕石 a meteorite

yǔn 殞

1. to die; to perish 2. (隕) to fall

yǔnluò 殞落 to fall

yǔnmìng 殞命 to perish; to die

yǔnshí 殞石 a meteorite

yǔn 磒

to fall down

yǔnshí 磒石 a meteor; a meteorite

yùn 孕

to be pregnant; to conceive

yùnfù 孕婦 a pregnant woman

yùnyù 孕育 to nourish; to foster

yùn 暈

1. (meteorology) a halo; vapors; a mist 2. dazzled; to feel faint or dizzy

yùnchē 暈車 to be bussick, train-sick or carsick

yùnchuán 暈船 to be seasick

yùnjī 暈機 airsick

yùn 運

1. to move; to revolve 2. to transport; to ship 3. to utilize; to make use of 4. one's luck or fortune

yùndòng 運動 1. sports; physical exercises 2. motion; movement 3. a social movement; a campaign; a drive 4. lobby

yùndòngchǎng 運動場 a playground; a stadium; a gymnasium; a sports arena

yùndònghuì 運動會 an athletic meet; a sports meeting; games

yùndòngyuán 運動員 1. an athlete; a sportsman 2. a lobbyist

yùnfèi 運費 a freight charge; freight

yùnhé 運河 1. a canal 2. the Grand Canal in China

yùnhuò 運貨 to transport goods

yùnqì 運氣 (Chinese pugilism) dynamic tension of muscles

yùnqi 運氣 luck or fortune

yùnshū 運輸 transportation; to transport

yùnsòng 運送 to convey; to transport; to deliver; to ship

yùnsuàn 運算 (mathematics) an operation

yùnxiāo 運銷 to ship (goods) for sales; shipping and marketing

yùnxíng 運行 to move in an orbit, as a planet or satellite

yùnyòng 運用 to employ; to make use of; to exercise

yùnzhuǎn 運轉 1. to revolve; revolution 2. to work; to operate; to run

yùn 慍

angry; indignant; displeased; irritated; vexed

yùnduì 慍懟 to resent

yùnnù 慍怒 angry; irritated; displeased

yùnsè 慍色 a displeased look

yùn 熨

to iron (clothes or cloth)

yùndǒu 熨斗 an iron (for pressing clothes)

yùnyīfú 熨衣服 to iron clothes

yùn 醞

1. to brew; to ferment 2. to deliberate on; deliberation 3. wine

yùnniàng 醞釀 1. to brew (wine or liquor) 2. (said of a storm, disturbance, etc.) to begin to form; to brew

yùn 韻

1. rhymes 2. harmony of sound 3. refined; sophisticated; polished; elegant 4. vowels

yùnjiǎo 韻腳 rhyme at the end

of a line of poetry

yùnlǜ 韻律 rhythm; rhyme; scheme; meter

yùnlǜwǔ 韻律舞 an aerobic dance

yùnmǔ 韻母 a vowel

yùnshì 韻事 a romantic incident of an intellectual which smacks of refined taste and elegant style

yùnwèi 韻味 refined and sophisticated taste; lingering charm

yùnwén 韻文 a rhymed composition

yùn 蘊

1. to collect; to gather 2. to store; to have in store 3. deep; profound 4. sweltering; sultry

yùncáng 蘊藏 to have in store; to be rich in

yùnjiè 蘊藉 refined and cultivated

yùnniàng 蘊釀 (said of a storm, trouble, etc.) to brew; to foment

zā 匝

to make a revolution round; to encompass; to circle

zā 咂

to take in food with the tongue; to suck

zā 紮(紥) also **zhá**

to bind; to tie; to fasten

zājǐn 紮緊 to tighten; to fasten securely

zá 砸

1. to crash and break; to squash; to smash; to knock; to pound 2. to ruin; to fail; to be bungled 3. to mash; to beat to a pulp

zálàn 砸爛 to crush to a mash

záshāng 砸傷 to be injured by a crashing object

zásuì 砸碎 to break to pieces; to smash

zá 雜

1. to mix; to blend; mixed; blended 2. miscellaneous 3. motley; medley 4. petty and numerous

zácǎo 雜草 weeds

záfèi 雜費 miscellaneous expenses; sundry charges

záhuì 雜燴 a dish of mixed food items

záhuò 雜貨 groceries; sundry goods

záhuòdiàn 雜貨店 a sundry store; a grocery

zájì 雜記 a miscellany; miscellaneous notes; random notes; jottings

zájiāo 雜交 1. (biology) to hybridize; to cross 2. hybridization; crossbreed; a cross; interbreeding 3. promiscuity

záliáng 雜糧 miscellaneous grain crops, as oat, millet, etc. (as opposed to rice and wheat which are staple foods)

záluàn 雜亂 confused and disorderly; to be jumbled

záluàn wúzhāng 雜亂無章 motley; disorderly

zániàn 雜念 distracting thoughts

zápái 雜牌 a less known and inferior brand

záqī zábā 雜七雜八 a motley; a jumble of various things; odds and ends

zásè 雜色 motley; parti-colored; variegated

záshuǎ 雜耍 juggler's feats; a vaudeville or variety show

záwén 雜文 an essay

záwù 雜物 miscellaneous articles or objects; odds and ends

záwù 雜務 chores; miscellaneous duties

záyīn 雜音 noises; (recording) humming or other unwanted sounds

zázhí 雜質 refer to **zázhì** 雜質

zázhì 雜誌 a magazine; a periodical; a journal

zázhì 雜質 impurities

zázhǒng 雜種 1. a mixed breed; a hybrid 2. (in ancient China) a foreign race or tribe 3. a bastard; son of a bitch

zāi 災

a disaster; a calamity; a catastrophe

zāihài 災害 disasters; calamities

zāihuàn 災患 disasters; calam-

ities

zāihuāng 災荒 famine caused by floods or droughts

zāimín 災民 refugees created by disasters

zāinàn 災難 disasters; calamities

zāiqíng 災情 the extent of a disaster or calamity

zāiqíng cǎnzhòng 災情慘重 1. The situation in the afflicted area is serious. 2. (now often used comically) heavy losses

zāiqū 災區 the afflicted area; the disaster area

zāi 哉

a phrase-final particle expressing surprise, admiration, doubt, etc.

zāi 栽

1. to plant 2. to care; to assist 3. to fall; to fail 4. young trees, saplings, cuttings for planting

zāigēntou 栽跟頭 1. to stumble (both literally and figuratively) 2. to be greatly embarrassed

zāipéi 栽培 1. to plant and cultivate 2. to educate people 3. to give special favor

zāizāng 栽贓 to place stolen goods in somebody's place with the intention of incriminating him

zāizhí 栽植 to plant; to raise; to grow

zāizhòng 栽種 to plant; to raise; to grow

zǎi 仔

1. refer to **zǐ** 仔 2 2. one who tends cattle

zǎi 宰

1. to preside; to govern 2. to slaughter 3. a Chinese family name

zǎigē 宰割 1. to cut up (meat) 2. to partition or dismember (a country) 3. to kill; to destroy

zǎishā 宰殺 to slaughter; to butcher; to kill

zǎixiàng 宰相 a prime minister (in former times)

zǎi 載

1. a year 2. (also **zài**) to record; to publish

zài 再

1. again; repeated 2. still; further; then

zàibǎn 再版 the second printing or edition (of a book)

zàicì 再次 once more; once again

zàidù 再度 once more; once again

zàifàn 再犯 1. to repeat an offense 2. a second-time offender

zàihuì 再會 good-bye; see you again

zàihūn 再婚 to remarry after the annulment of a former marriage; digamy

zàijiàn 再見 good-bye; see you again

zàijiàoyù 再教育 reeducation

zàijiē zàilì 再接再勵 to forge ahead in disregard of obstructions

zàiqǐ 再起 1. to rise again 2. to assume public office again

zàisān 再三 time and again; repeatedly

zàishěn 再審 a retrial

zàishēng fùmǔ 再生父母 second parents—an expression of deep gratitude to benefactors for great help rendered

zàishēng jìyìtǐ 再生記憶體 (computer) regenerative

zàishuō 再說 furthermore; besides

zàixiàn 再現 reappearance

zài 在

1. at; in; on; up to 2. to rest with; to consist in; to depend on 3. to be alive; living; to be present; to exist 4. used to indicate a progressive tense

zàichǎng 在場 to be present

zàidìrén 在地人 the local people

zàiháng 在行 to be an expert at something

zàihu 在乎 1. to care; to mind 2. to consist in; to depend on (whether...)

zàijiā 在家 to be at home; to be in

zàijié nántáo 在劫難逃 If one is doomed, one is doomed.

zàinèi 在內 1. including; inclusive 2. inside

zàishì 在世 alive; in this world

zàisuǒ bùcí 在所不辭 will not hesitate to

zàisuǒ bùxī 在所不惜 regardless of the cost or sacrifice

zàisuǒ bùxí 在所不惜 refer to **zàisuǒ bùxī** 在所不惜

zài suǒ nánmiǎn 在所難免 unavoidable; inevitable

zàitáo 在逃 (said of a criminal) on the loose or still at large

zàiwài 在外 1. excluding 2. outside

zàiwàng 在望 1. to be visible 2. to be in sight

zàiwèi 在位 in the position; on the throne

zàixià 在下 my humble self; I

zàixiān 在先 1. before; formerly; beforehand 2. in front; ahead

zàixué 在學 to be at school

zàiyā 在押 being imprisoned

zàiyì 在意 to mind; to care about

zàizhí 在職 to be at one's post

zàizhí xùnliàn 在職訓練 in-service training

zàizuò 在座 to be present (at a gathering)

zài 載

1. (said of vehicles, vessels, etc.) to carry (loads); to load 2. refer to **zài** 載 3. to fill

zàigē zàiwǔ 載歌載舞 to sing and dance at the same time

zàiyùn 載運 to transport; to carry

zàizhòng 載重 1. to carry heavy loads; heavily loaded 2. carrying capacity

zān 簪 also **zēn**

1. a clasp for clipping the cap and hair together 2. a hairpin for women 3. to stick (in the hair, etc.); to wear

zānzi 簪子 a hair clasp

zán 咱

I, me (in North China dialect)

zánmen 咱們 (inclusive) we; you and I

zàn 暫 also **zhàn**

1. temporarily; for a short time; not lasting 2. suddenly; abruptly

zànbié 暫別 to part for a short time

zàndìng 暫定 1. (said of time) tentatively set on, at, etc. 2. (said of a number, price, place, etc.) tentatively fix at

zànhuǎn 暫緩 to postpone or delay for a while; to put off; to defer

zànjì ránméi 暫濟燃眉 to temporarily relieve an urgent need

zànjiè 暫借 to borrow for a short time

zànqiě 暫且 for the time being

zànshí 暫時 for the time being; temporarily

zàntíng 暫停 1. to stop, halt or suspend temporarily 2. a time-out

zànxíng 暫行 temporary; provisional

zàn 贊

1. to assist; to aid; to help; to support; to back 2. to praise; to commend; to exalt; to glorify; to extol; to eulogize

zànbù juékǒu 贊不絕口 to praise profusely; to heap praises on...

zànchéng 贊成 to agree to; to be in favor of

zànměi 贊美 to praise; to extol; to exalt

zànshǎng 贊賞 to commend; to praise; to extol; to admire

zàntàn 贊歎 to exclaim in praise

zàntóng 贊同 to consent to; to approve of; to agree

zànxǔ 贊許 to approve of

zànyáng 贊揚 to exalt; to glorify; to extol; to praise

zànzhù 贊助 to sponsor; to patronize; support

zànzhùrén 贊助人 a patron; a sponsor

zàn 讚

to commend; to eulogize; to praise; to applaud; to laud

zànměi 讚美 to praise; to eulogize; eulogy; laud; praise

zànpèi 讚佩 to esteem; to admire

zànshǎng 讚賞 to praise; to appreciate

zàntàn 讚歎 to sing the praises of

zànxǔ 讚許 to speak favorably of

zànyáng 讚揚 to glorify; to exalt; to uphold; commendation; glorification

zāng 臟

1. bribes; to bribe 2. loot; booty; stolen goods; plunder; spoils

zāngkuǎn 臟款 money acquired illicitly

zāngwù 臟物 plunder; booty; loot; spoils

zāng 髒

dirty; filthy

zānghuà 髒話 on obscene word; a swearword; a profane word

zāngxīxī 髒兮兮 very much soiled; very dirty

zàng 葬

to bury, inter or consign to a grave

zànglǐ 葬禮 a funeral or burial service

zàngshēn 葬身 to be buried

zàngshēn zhīdì 葬身之地 a burial ground

zàngsòng 葬送 to bury or waste (one's talent, future, hopes, etc.)

zàngyí 葬儀 burial or funeral rites

zàng 藏

1. Tibet; Tibetans 2. a storage; a warehouse; a depository 3. a collective name for the Buddhist and Taoist scriptures

zàngqīng 藏青 indigo blue

Zàngwén 藏文 the Tibetan language

zàng 臟

a general name of all the internal organs in the chest and abdomen; the viscera

zàngfǔ 臟腑 1. viscera; entrails 2. one's integrity, aspirations, etc.

zāo 遭

1. to meet with; to incur; to be victimized; to suffer 2. times of binding or turning around, as with a rope 3. a time; a turn

zāoféng 遭逢 1. to meet with 2. vicissitudes in one's life

zāonàn 遭難 to meet with difficulty, misfortune, or death

zāoshòu 遭受 to incur (losses, etc.); to be subjected to

zāoyāng 遭殃 to meet with misfortune or disaster

zāoyù 遭遇 1. to meet with; to encounter 2. vicissitudes in one's life

zāo 糟

1. sediment or dregs of wine 2. to soak food items (as fish, meat, etc.) in wine or wine sediment 3. (said of a plan, arrangement, etc.) to become a mess, or in bad shape 4. decayed; rotten; spoiled 5. not sturdy or strong 6. lousy; a louse

zāogāo 糟糕 What a mess! Too bad!

zāota 糟蹋 1. to waste (talent, great ability, etc. on trifles); to degrade or debase 2. to insult

zāo 蹧

to spoil; to ruin

zāota 蹧蹋 to spoil; to ruin

záo 鑿 also zuò

1. to chisel or dig; to bore or pierce through 2. a chisel 3. real; true; actual; indisputable; authentic; conclusive 4. to make a forced interpretation of text

záobì tōuguāng 鑿壁偷光 very studious

záodòng 鑿洞 to bore or drill a hole

zǎo 早

1. early; earlier; soon; beforehand; previous; premature; in

advance 2. morning 3. ago; before 4. Good morning!

zǎo'ān 早安 Good morning!

zǎobān 早班 the morning shift

zǎocān 早餐 breakfast

zǎocāo 早操 morning calisthenics

zǎochǎn 早產 premature birth

zǎochǎng 早場 a morning show (at a cinema, theater, etc.)

zǎochén 早晨 daybreak; (early) morning; dawn

zǎochū wǎnguī 早出晚歸 to go out early and return late

zǎochūn 早春 1. early spring 2. early spring tea

zǎodào 早到 to arrive early

zǎodiǎn 早點 breakfast

zǎodiǎnr 早點兒 earlier; sooner

zǎohūn 早婚 to marry young; early marriage

zǎonián 早年 years ago; in bygone years

zǎoqí 早期 the early stage

zǎoqī 早期 refer to **zǎoqí** 早期

zǎoqǐ 早起 to get up early; to rise early

zǎorì 早日 at an earlier date; soon

zǎoshang 早上 early in the morning

zǎoshì 早市 a morning market

zǎoshú 早熟 1. (said of plants, etc.) to ripen early 2. (said of a person) to reach puberty early 3. precocious

zǎowǎn 早晚 1. morning and evening 2. sooner or later

zǎoxiān 早先 some time ago; before

zǎoyǐ 早已 to have already...

zǎozhī rúcǐ 早知如此 If it had been known that things would turn out this way....

zǎo 蚤

a flea

zǎo 棗

jujube, commonly called date

zǎohóng 棗紅 purplish red

zǎoní 棗泥 jujube paste, used as stuffing for pastry or dumplings

zǎoshù 棗樹 a jujube tree

zǎo 澡

to wash; to bathe

zǎopén 澡盆 a bathtub

zǎotáng 澡堂 a public bath; a bathhouse

zǎo 藻

1. algae; pondweeds 2. diction; wording; language

zǎoshì 藻飾 1. embellishment in writing 2. to polish writings

zào 皂(皁)

1. black 2. menial labor 3. a menial; a lictor 4. soap

zàobái bùfēn 皂白不分 to fail to distinguish between right and wrong

zào 灶

1. a place for cooking; a kitchen 2. a cooking stove or furnace

Zàoshén 灶神 the God of Kitchen

zào 造

1. to create; to make 2. to manufacture; to produce 3. to make up; to invent 4. to build 5. to arrive at; to reach 6. (law) a party concerned in the suit 7. an era; a period 8. to institute

zàochéng 造成 1. to complete; to build up; to compose 2. to result in

zàochuán 造船 to build a ship

zàochuánchǎng 造船廠 a shipbuilding yard; a dockyard

zàofǎn 造反 to rebel; to rise up against; revolt; uprising

zàofú rénqún 造福人群 to do good deeds to benefit mankind

Zàohuà 造化 Heaven; Mother Nature; the Creator

zàohua 造化 one's luck or fortune

zàohua nòngrén 造化弄人 to be a sport of fate

zàojiù 造就 1. to educate; to bring up 2. one's achievement or accomplishment

zàojù 造句 to make a sentence

zàoniè 造孽 to do evil things

Z

Zàowùzhǔ 造物主 the Creator

zàoxíng 造型 1. modeling; mold-making 2. a model; a mold 3. (machinery) molding

zàoyáo 造謠 to start a rumor

zàoyáo shēngshì 造謠生事 to spread rumors to cause trouble

zàoyì 造詣 1. one's scholastic attainment, depth or profundity 2. to call on; to visit

zàozì 造字 to coin words

zàozuò 造作 to make

zàozuo 造作 affectations

zào 噪

1. to be noisy 2. (said of birds, insects, etc.) to chirp

zàoyīn 噪音 unpleasant noise; a din

zào 燥

1. arid; dry; parched 2. impatient; restless

zàorè 燥熱 dry and hot

zào 躁

1. irritable; hot-tempered 2. uneasy 3. rashness

zàojí 躁急 impatient; uneasy

zé 咋

refer to **zhā** 咋 2

zé 則

1. a law; a rule; a regulation; a standard; a norm; a criterion 2. a particle indicating consequence (usually used after a supposition) or a reason 3. a numerary particle used before news reports, advertisements, etc. 4. but; however 5. to imitate; to follow

zé 窄

refer to **zhǎi** 窄

zé 責

1. one's duty, responsibility, obligation, etc. 2. to demand; to be strict with 3. to punish; punishment 4. to upbraid; to censure; to reprimand; to blame

zébèi 責備 to upbraid; to reprimand; to reproach

zéfá 責罰 to punish; a penalty

zéguài 責怪 to blame

zémà 責罵 to upbraid; to blame; to scold

zé'nàn 責難 to urge someone to a difficult task; to hold high expectations for another person

zé'nàn 責難 to upbraid; to censure

zérèn 責任 1. duty; responsibility; an obligation 2. responsibility for a fault; blame

zéwèn 責問 to blame and demand an explanation

zéwú pángdài 責無旁貸 There's no shirking the responsibility.

zé 賊

refer to **zéi** 賊

zé 嘖

1. an interjection of approval or admiration 2. to argue; to dispute

zé 擇 also **zhái**

to select; to choose; to pick out

zé'ǒu 擇偶 to select a spouse or a mate

zéqī 擇期 to select a good time or day (for an undertaking, a wedding, etc.)

zéqí 擇期 refer to **zéqī** 擇期

zéshàn gùzhí 擇善固執 to choose what is good and stick to it

zéyǒu 擇友 to choose friends

zé 澤

1. the place where water gathers; a marsh 2. grace; favors; kindness 3. brilliance; radiance; luster; bright; glossy; smooth 4. to benefit; to enrich

zébèi tiānxià 澤被天下 Benefits spread to all people.

zě 怎

refer to **zěn** 怎

zě 仄

1. oblique 2. said of the three tones other than the even tone (in ancient Chinese phonology) 3. narrow 4. uneasy

zéi 賊 also **zé**

1. a thief; a burglar; a robber; a

bandit 2. a rebel; a traitor 3. to harm 4. to kill 5. pests on the farm 6. a term of reviling 7. clever; cunning; crafty

zéichuán 賊船 a pirate ship; a ship owned by bandits or rebels

zéihài 賊害 to cause harm or injury to another

zéikòu 賊寇 rebels; bandits

zéitóu zéinǎo 賊頭賊腦 acting stealthily; thief-like

zéixìng nán'gǎi 賊性難改 The habitual criminal is incorrigible.

zéiyíng 賊營 the camp of rebels, bandits, etc.

zēn 簪
refer to **zān** 簪

zěn 怎 also **zě**
why; how; what

zěn'gǎn 怎敢 how can one dare; don't dare

zěnme 怎麼 why; how; what

zěnme déliǎo 怎麼得了 There is no telling the serious consequences.

zěnnài 怎奈 but alas; except that

zěnnéng 怎能 how can (he do this to me?); how could (you...?)

zěnyàng 怎樣 how; in what way

zēng 曾
1. older or younger by three generations 2. a Chinese family name

zēngsūn 曾孫 one's great-grandchildren

zēngsūnnǚ 曾孫女 one's great-granddaughter

zēngzǔfù 曾祖父 one's great-grandfather

zēngzǔmǔ 曾祖母 one's great-grandmother

zēng 增
to add to; to increase; to grow; to enlarge

zēngbǔ 增補 to add to; to supplement

zēngchǎn 增產 to increase production

zēngdìngběn 增訂本 a revised and enlarged edition

zēngguāng 增光 to do credit to

zēngguǎng 增廣 to widen (one's knowledge, etc.)

zēngjiā 增加 to add to; to increase

zēngjiǎn 增減 increases and decreases

zēngjìn 增進 to promote (friendship, etc.); to increase (knowledge, etc.)

zēngkān 增刊 a supplement—as of newspaper, etc.

zēngqiáng 增強 to strengthen; to enhance

zēngyuán 增援 to send reinforcements

zēngzhǎng 增長 a rise; to grow

zēngzhí 增值 appreciation; increment

zēngzhíshuì 增值稅 VAT (value-added tax)

zēng 憎
to hate; to loathe; to abhor; to abominate; to detest

zēnghèn 憎恨 to hate

zēngwù 憎惡 to abominate; to detest; to abhor

zèng 贈
to send (gifts); to confer or bestow (titles); to give

zèngpǐn 贈品 a gift; a present

zèngsòng 贈送 to present; to give; to donate

zèngyán 贈言 words of advice

zèngyuè 贈閱 (said of publications) given free of charge

zhā 扎
to pierce; to prick

zhāgēn 扎根 to take root

zhāshi 扎實 solid; firm

zhāshǒu 扎手 1. to prick the hand 2. difficult to handle

zhāyǎn 扎眼 dazzling; garish

zhā 咋
to shout blusteringly

Zhā 查
a Chinese family name

zhā 渣

dregs; lees; grounds; sediment

zhāzǐ 渣滓 grounds; sediment; dregs; lees

zhá 扎
to struggle; to strive

zháyíng 扎營 to pitch a tent; to encamp

zhá 札
1. (in ancient China) a thin wooden tablet for writing 2. correspondence; a letter 3. (in ancient China) documents or instructions to a subordinate 4. (now rarely) to die before one comes of age

zhájì 札記 a notebook in which one records his comments on the book he is reading

zhá 炸
to fry in oil or fat; to deep-fry

zhájī 炸雞 1. to fry chicken 2. fried chicken

zhájiàngmiàn 炸醬麵 a kind of noodles served with fried bean sauce and mincemeat

zhá 紮(紮)
1. refer to **zā** 紮 (紮) 2. to stop; to post

zháyíng 紮營 to bivouac; to station troops; to encamp

zhá 閘
1. a floodgate; a lock; a sluice 2. a brake 3. a switch or similar devices

zhámén 閘門 a floodgate

zhá 箚
1. correspondence; letters 2. (in former times) written directives or instructions to a lower government agency

zhájì 箚記 1.a notebook 2. to put down by items

zhá 鍘
1. a long knife hinged at one end for cutting hay; a fodder chopper 2. to cut up with a hay cutter

zhǎ 眨
to wink; to blink

zhà 乍
1. at first; for the first time 2. suddenly; unexpectedly

zhàjiàn 乍見 1. to meet for the first time 2. to see suddenly

zhà 咋
1. all of a sudden; suddenly 2. (also **zé**) to bite; to gnaw

zhàshé 咋舌 to show one's surprise or regret

zhà 柵
a fence of bamboos or wood; a palisade; a railing of posts

zhàlan 柵欄 a fence; a palisade; a railing

zhà 炸
1. to explode; to burst; to bomb 2. to get mad 3. to disperse boisterously; to flee in terror

zhàdàn 炸彈 a bomb

zhàhuǐ 炸燬 to blow up; to blast

zhàshāng 炸傷 to be injured in bombing or explosion

zhàsǐ 炸死 to kill by bombing

zhàyào 炸藥 dynamite; explosives

zhà 蚱
a locust; a grasshopper

zhàměng 蚱蜢 a locust; a grasshopper

zhà 詐
1. deceitful; false; fake; crafty 2. to deceive; to cheat; to lie; to swindle; to pretend; to feign 3. to trick into; to bluff somebody into giving information

zhàcái 詐財 to cheat for money

zhàpiàn 詐騙 to swindle

zhàqī 詐欺 fraud; imposture; cheating

zhàshù 詐術 fraud; cheating; guile; chicanery

zhàsǐ 詐死 to fake death; to play dead

zhà 搾(榨)
to press (for juice or oil); to extract; to squeeze; to wring

zhàcài 搾菜 a kind of salted vegetable root

zhàqǔ 搾取 1. to extract 2. to extort; to exploit; to rob

zhàyóu 搾油 to extract oil

zhàzhījī 搾汁機 a juicer

zhāi 摘 also **zhé**
1. to take off (one's hat, etc.); to pluck; to pick 2. to choose; to select 3. to jot down (notes) 4. to expose; to unveil (a conspiracy, etc.)

zhāichú 摘除 to excise

zhāijì 摘記 notes or observations (by an author)

zhāilù 摘錄 an excerpt

zhāiqǔ 摘取 to select; to pick; to take

zhāixia 摘下 to pick off (flowers, etc.); to take off

zhāiyào 摘要 1. to summarize 2. an abstract

zhāi 齋
1. pious; respectful; chaste; pure 2. to abstain from meat; to fast 3. to purify oneself 4. to provide Buddhist monks with meals 5. a room for study; a study; a school 6. a vegetarian meal

zhāifàn 齋飯 a vegetarian meal for a Buddhist monk

zhāijiè 齋戒 to abstain from meat, wine, etc. (when offering sacrifices to gods); to fast

zhāijiè mùyù 齋戒沐浴 to purify oneself by observing abstinent rules and bathing

zhāisēng 齋僧 to provide Buddhist monks with meals

zhāishè 齋舍 1. a room for fasting 2. a study; a school

zhāitáng 齋堂 a dining room in a Buddhist temple

zhái 宅 also **zhè**
a dwelling; a residence; a house

zháidì 宅第 a mansion

zháixīn rénhòu 宅心仁厚 a benevolent and generous nature

zháiyuàn 宅院 a house with a courtyard

zháizi 宅子 a residence; a house

zhái 擇
refer to **zé** 擇

zhǎi 窄 also **zé**
1. narrow; contracted; tight 2. mean; narrow-minded

zhǎixiǎo 窄小 1. (said of a dress) tight and small 2. (said of a room, etc.) narrow and small

zhài 債
a debt; an obligation

zhàihù 債戶 a debtor

zhàikuǎn 債款 a loan

zhàiquánrén 債權人 a creditor

zhàiquàn 債券 bonds issued by a government or debentures issued by a company

zhàitái gāozhú 債臺高築 refer to **zhàitái gāozhú** 債臺高築

zhàitái gāozhú 債臺高築 to be deep in debt

zhàiwù 債務 debt or obligation

zhàiwùrén 債務人 a debtor

zhàizhǔ 債主 a creditor

zhài 寨
a stockade

zhàizi 寨子 a stockaded village

zhān 占
to divine

zhānbǔ 占卜 1. to divine 2. to observe

zhānxīngshù 占星術 astrology

zhān 沾
1. to moisten; to wet 2. to tinge; to stain; to contaminate 3. to be imbued with; to be infected with 4. to benefit from 5. to touch

zhānbiān 沾邊 1. to touch on (or upon) only lightly 2. to be relevant

zhānguāng 沾光 to benefit from the support or influence of someone

zhānjīn 沾襟 to moisten sleeves with tears

zhānqīn dàigù 沾親帶故 1. having personal connections, close or remote 2. to rub off some glory on friends and relatives

zhānrǎn 沾染 to become addicted to (bad habits, practices, etc.)

Z

zhānshī 沾濕 1. to moisten; damp or wet 2. steeped in; imbued with

zhānzhān zìxǐ 沾沾自喜 smug and complacent

zhānzì 沾漬 imbued with; to soak in

zhān 詹

1. to talk too much; verbosity 2. to reach 3. a Chinese family name

zhān 霑

1. soaked; to become wet or damp; to moisten 2. to receive (benefits, etc.)

zhānrǎn 霑染 1. to get affected by a communicable disease 2. to gain a small advantage

zhān 氈

1. felt 2. a blanket

zhānmào 氈帽 a felt cap or hat

zhān 瞻

1. to look; to look up 2. to regard respectfully; to reverence

zhānqián gùhòu 瞻前顧後 (literally) to look forward and backward—very cautious

zhānwàng 瞻望 to look forward to a faraway place

zhānyǎng 瞻仰 1. to pay respects to 2. to look up to

zhǎn 展

1. to open 2. to stretch; to extend 3. to unfold; to unroll 4. to expand; to dilate 5. to prolong 6. to visit

zhǎnchì 展翅 to spread the wings; to fly

zhǎnkāi 展開 1. to spread out; to unfold 2. to start (an activity, task, etc.)

zhǎnlǎn 展覽 to exhibit; to display

zhǎnlǎnhuì 展覽會 an exhibition or exposition

zhǎnshì 展示 to show; to display; to exhibit

zhǎnshìhuì 展示會 an exhibition; a trade show

zhǎnwàng 展望 the prospects of an undertaking

zhǎnxiàn 展現 to present before one's eyes; to develop

zhǎnzhuǎn 展轉 1. to turn round and round 2. indirectly

zhǎn 斬

1. to cut 2. to kill; to behead

zhǎncǎo chúgēn 斬草除根 to eliminate the cause of trouble completely

zhǎndīng jiétiě 斬釘截鐵 to speak, or act, with determination and courage

zhǎnshǒu 斬首 to guillotine; to behead

zhǎnshǒu shìzhòng 斬首示眾 to behead a criminal and exhibit the severed head to the public as a warning to would-be offenders

zhǎnxīn 斬新 brand-new

zhǎn 盞

1. a small shallow container; a small cup 2. a numerical adjunct denoting lamps

zhǎn 嶄

1. (said of a mountain) high and steep 2. towering (above) 3. novel; new

zhǎnxīn 嶄新 brand-new

zhǎn 輾

to turn over; to roll over

zhǎnzhuǎn 輾轉 1. to roll about; to toss 2. to take a roundabout course; to pass through many places

zhǎnzhuǎn fǎncè 輾轉反側 to toss about in bed

zhàn 占（佔）

to occupy

zhànjù 占據 to occupy illegally or by force

zhànlǐng 占領 to occupy

zhànyǒu 占有 to take possession of

zhàn 佔

to seize; to usurp; to occupy; to take by force

zhànjù 佔據 to occupy; to take possession of

zhànlǐng 佔領 to occupy; to capture

zhànpiányi 佔便宜 to take advantage

zhànshàngfēng 佔上風 to have the upper hand

zhànxiàn 佔線 The line's busy (or engaged).

zhànyǒu 佔有 1. to own; to have 2. to occupy

zhàn 站

1. to stand 2. a station; a stop; a center for rendering certain services

zhàn'gǎng 站崗 to stand guard; to stand sentry

zhànlì 站立 to stand

zhànpiào 站票 a ticket for standing room; an SRO (standing room only) ticket

zhànwěn 站穩 to stand firm

zhànzhǎng 站長 the head of a station; a stationmaster

zhànzhù 站住 (word of command) halt; to stop; to stand

zhàn 湛

1. dewy 2. deep; profound 3. a Chinese family name

zhànlán 湛藍 dark blue; azure

zhànrán 湛然 1. (said of water) transparent 2. quiet; calm

zhànxīn 湛新 brand-new

zhàn 棧

1. a storehouse; a warehouse 2. a tavern; an inn 3. a road made along a cliff

zhàndào 棧道 a log-formed road along a steep cliff

zhànfáng 棧房 1. a storehouse; a warehouse 2. a tavern; an inn

zhàn 暫

refer to **zàn** 暫

zhàn 戰

1. war; warfare; fighting; battle 2. to contest; to fight; to contend 3. to shudder 4. a Chinese family name

zhànbài 戰敗 to suffer (a) defeat; to be defeated

zhànbèi 戰備 war preparations

zhànchǎng 戰場 a battlefield

zhànchē 戰車 1. a tank (an armored vehicle) 2. a chariot

zhàndì 戰地 a battlefield

zhàndòu 戰鬥 1. to fight; to combat; to engage in a battle 2. (military) action

zhàndòujī 戰鬥機 a fighter plane; a fighter

zhàndòuyuán 戰鬥員 a combatant

zhànfàn 戰犯 a war criminal

zhànfú 戰俘 prisoners of war

zhàngǔ 戰鼓 a battle drum

Zhànguó Shídài 戰國時代 the Epoch of Warring States (403-221B.C.)

zhànguǒ 戰果 military achievements; war results

zhànháo 戰壕 a trench

zhànhuǒ 戰火 flames of war

zhànjī 戰機 1. an opportunity for combat 2. a fighter

zhànjī 戰績 military successes (or exploits)

zhànjī huīhuáng 戰績輝煌 brilliant combat performances

zhànjiàn 戰艦 a warship; a battleship

zhànjú 戰局 the war situation

zhànkuàng 戰況 the war situation

zhànlì 戰慄 to tremble; to shudder; to shiver

zhànlìpǐn 戰利品 a trophy; booty; a prize; loot

zhànluàn 戰亂 chaos and social upheavals brought about by war

zhànlüè 戰略 strategy

zhànmǎ 戰馬 a war-horse; a battle steed

zhànqū 戰區 a war zone or area

zhànshèng 戰勝 to conquer; to win a victory

zhànshí 戰時 wartime

zhànshì 戰士 a warrior; a fighting man

zhànshì 戰事 war; hostilities

zhànshū 戰書 a written declaration of war

zhànshù 戰術 tactics; the art of war

zhànyì 戰役 a (military) cam-

Z

paign; a battle

zhànyǒu 戰友 a comrade in arms

zhànzhàn jīngjīng 戰戰兢兢 trembling with fear; very cautious

zhànzhēng 戰爭 war

zhàn 顫

refer to **chàn** 顫

zhàn 蘸

to dip

zhànbǐ 蘸筆 to dip a writing brush in ink

zhāng 章

1. a piece of writing; a chapter 2. a system; a statute; an organized body 3. an emblem; a seal; a stamp 4. to make clear; to make known 5. a pattern; an example 6. a Chinese family name

zhāngchéng 章程 a set of regulation; constitution

zhānghuí xiǎoshuō 章回小說 a serial novel

zhāngjié 章節 chapters and sections (of a piece of writing)

zhāngyú 章魚 an octopus

zhāng 張

1. to open; to stretch; to extend 2. to display 3. a sheet (of paper); a leaf (of a book)

zhāngdēng jiécǎi 張燈結彩 decorated with lanterns and colored hangings (for a joyous occasion)

Zhāngguān Lǐdài 張冠李戴 wrong attribution; misappropriation

zhānghuáng shīcuò 張皇失措 to lose composure; panicky

zhāngkāi 張開 to stretch open; to open

zhāngkǒu jiéshé 張口結舌 agape and tongue-tied

zhāngkuáng 張狂 to dissipate without inhibition

zhānglì 張力 tensile strength; tension

zhāngluó 張羅 to set a snare for birds

zhāngluó 張羅 1. to raise funds 2. to serve guests 3. to take care of; to get busy about

Zhāng Sān Lǐ Sì 張三李四 anybody; every Tom, Dick, and Harry

zhāngtiē 張貼 to paste up

zhāngwàng 張望 to look around; to look about

zhāngyá wǔzhǎo 張牙舞爪 (said of wild beasts) to frighten people by showing the fangs and flourishing the paws

zhāngyáng 張揚 to publicize; to make widely known

zhāngzuǐ 張嘴 1. to open the mouth 2. to ask for a loan or a favor

zhāng 獐(麞)

the roe deer; the hornless river deer

zhāngtóu shǔmù 獐頭鼠目 facial features suggesting cunning and meanness

zhāng 彰

1. ornamental 2. evident; obvious; clear 3. to manifest; to make known

zhāngmíng 彰明 to manifest; to clarify

zhāngmíng jiàozhù 彰明較著 extremely obvious and ostensible

zhāngxiǎn 彰顯 to manifest

zhāng 璋

an ancient jade ornament used in state ceremonies; a jade tablet

zhāng 樟

a camphor tree

zhāngmù 樟木 1. a camphor tree 2. the wood of a camphor tree

zhāngnǎo 樟腦 camphor

zhāngnǎowán 樟腦丸 a camphor ball; a mothball

zhāngnǎoyóu 樟腦油 camphor oil

zhāng 蟑

a cockroach; a roach

zhāngláng 蟑螂 a cockroach; a roach

zhǎng 長

1. senior; old 2. the eldest 3. a head; a chief; a leader; a commander; a chairman 4. to grow 5. to increase; to advance 6. to look; to appear; to become

zhǎngbèi 長輩 the senior generation; the older member of a family; an elder

zhǎngdà 長大 to grow up; to attain manhood; to mature

zhǎngguān 長官 one's superior in office, etc.; (a polite expression) officers or officials; a commanding officer

zhǎngjìn 長進 to make progress

zhǎnglǎo 長老 1. a senior or an oldster. an presbyter 3. reverent address for a monk

Zhǎnglǎohuì 長老會 the Presbyterian Church

zhǎngshàng 長上 elders and superiors

zhǎngsūn 長孫 1. the eldest of one's grandsons 2. a Chinese compound surname

zhǎngxiàng 長相 one's looks or appearances

zhǎngyòu 長幼 young and old; seniority among family members

zhǎngzhě 長者 a senior; an elder; a person of virtue

zhǎngzǐ 長子 the eldest son

zhǎng 掌

1. the palm of the hand; the sole of the foot; paws of an animal 2. to slap with one's hand; to smack 3. to have charge of; to supervise; to control

zhǎngduò 掌舵 1. to steer a ship 2. the steersman 3. the man in charge

zhǎngguǎn 掌管 to take charge of; to supervise

zhǎngguì 掌櫃 a shopkeeper

zhǎngquán 掌權 to be in power or authority

zhǎngshàng míngzhū 掌上明珠 a beloved daughter; the apple of one's eye

zhǎngshàngxíng diànzǐ yóulèqì 掌上型電子遊樂器 a

hand-held electronic vedio game

zhǎngshēng 掌聲 clapping; applause

zhǎngshēng rúléi 掌聲如雷 thunderous applause

zhǎngwò 掌握 in one's grasp; within one's power

zhǎngxīn 掌心 the center of the palm

zhǎngzhèng 掌政 to head a government

zhǎng 漲

to go up or rise (as prices, water, etc.)

zhǎngcháo 漲潮 (said of the tide) to flow

zhǎngdié 漲跌 price fluctuation

zhǎngfú 漲幅 (said of commodity prices, stocks, etc.) the rate of increase or rise

zhǎngjià 漲價 to raise prices; appreciation

zhàng 丈

1. a unit in Chinese lineal measurement slightly longer than 10 feet 2. an elder; a senior 3. to measure; to survey

zhàngfu 丈夫 a man.

zhàngfū qìgài 丈夫氣概 manly; manliness

zhàngfu 丈夫 a husband

zhàngliáng 丈量 to measure; to survey

zhàngmuniáng 丈母娘 a mother-in-law

zhàngren 丈人 a father-in-law

zhàng 仗

1. weapony 2. to lean upon; to rely upon; to depend on 3. battle; war

zhàngshì qīrén 仗勢欺人 to bully the weaker on one's strength or power, or connection with powerful people

zhàngyì shūcái 仗義疏財 to think little of one's fortune in one's enthusiasm for charity, etc.

zhàngyì zhíyán 仗義執言 to speak in accordance with justice

zhàng 杖

1. a stick; a staff; a cane 2. (an

old punishment) to beat with a cane; flogging with a stick 3. (now rarely) a mourning staff 4. to presume on (one's connections, influence, etc.)

zhàngjī 杖擊 to hit or beat with a cane

zhàngjí 杖擊 refer to **zhàngjī** 杖擊

zhàng 長

a surplus; a remainder

zhàngwù 長物 property; belongings

zhàng 帳

1. a canopy above the bed 2. a tent 3. a curtain; a mosquito net 4. a scroll (sent as a gift for a wedding, funeral, etc.) 5. (賬) accounts

zhàngbù 帳簿 an account book

zhàngdān 帳單 a bill; a check

zhàngfáng 帳房 1. a cashier 2. a cashier's office

zhànghù 帳戶 a bank account

zhàngkuǎn 帳款 funds on account; credit

zhàngmù 帳目 accounts; itemized bills

zhàngpeng 帳篷 a tent; a mat-shed

zhàngzi 帳子 a mosquito net

zhàng 脹

1. full-stomached; glutted 2. swelling of the skin, etc. 3. to expand; expansion

zhàngqì 脹氣 1. inflated with air 2. (medicine) flatulence

zhàng 幛

a scroll of silk or cloth embroidered with appropriate wording sent as a gift for a wedding, funeral, etc.

zhàng 嶂

a precipitous mountain

zhàng 障

1. to separate; to screen; a barrier; a screen 2. a dike; an embankment 3. to defend; to guard; to shield 4. to guarantee 5. to hinder; to obstruct

zhàng'ài 障礙 1. obstacles; barriers; obstructions 2. a malfunction; a handicap

zhàngbì 障蔽 to screen; to obstruct

zhàngyǎnfǎ 障眼法 1. legerdemain 2. a cover-up; camouflage

zhàng 漲

to swell; to expand

zhàng 賬

1. accounts 2. debts 3. credits; loans; bills

zhàngbù 賬簿 an account; an account book

zhàngdān 賬單 a bill; an invoice

zhàngfáng 賬房 1. a cashier's office 2. a cashier; a teller

zhàngmù 賬目 accounts

zhàng 瘴

miasma; swamp vapor

zhànglì 瘴癘 disease or epidemic attributed to miasma; poisonous vapor

zhàngqì 瘴氣 miasma; swamp vapor

zhāo 招

1. to beckon with one's hand; to summon 2. to raise (an army, capital, etc.); to recruit 3. to confess; to admit 4. a poster; a notice; a signboard 5. to cause; to effect; to incite; to incur; to invite 6. to entice; to induce 7. to welcome; to receive 8. to infect; to be infectious 9. (now rarely) a target; a bull's eye 10. a move; a trick; a device

zhāo'ān 招安 to grant amnesty and enlistment to bandits, etc.

zhāobiāo 招標 invitation to bid at a tender

zhāobīng mǎimǎ 招兵買馬 to raise an army (usually in preparation for an insurrection)

zhāocái jìnbǎo 招財進寶 to bring in wealth and riches

zhāodài 招待 1. to serve; to entertain 2. a reception 3. a receptionist

zhāodàihuì 招待會 a reception

zhāodàiquàn 招待券 a free ticket

zhāodàisuǒ 招待所 a guest house; a hostel

zhāofēng yǐndié 招蜂引蝶 (said of a woman) to act like a habitual flirt

zhāofǔ 招撫 to call to surrender; to pacify

zhāogòng 招供 1. to confess (to a crime, etc.) 2. a confession (by a criminal)

zhāohu 招呼 1. to beckon; to call 2. to take care of 3. to engage in a fight 4. to watch out; to mind

zhāohuzhàn 招呼站 a designated bus or taxi stop

zhāojià 招架 to resist; to defend; to ward off blows

zhāojià bùzhù 招架不住 to be unable to hold on (or off)

zhāokǎo 招考 to advertise for employees or students through competitive examinations

zhāolái 招徠 to solicit customers

zhāolǎn 招攬 1. to collect; to gather together 2. to canvass; to solicit customers

zhāolǐng 招領 to advertise for the claimant or legal owner of a lost article

zhāomù 招募 1. to enlist troops (usually mercenaries) 2. to solicit (investment, capital, etc.)

zhāopai 招牌 1. the signboard of a store or any other business concern 2. the reputation of a large business firm or a quality product

zhāopaicài 招牌菜 brand dish

zhāopìn 招聘 to advertise for office vacancies

zhāoqīn 招親 to take a husband

zhāore 招惹 to incur; to bring upon oneself

zhāorèn 招認 1. confession 2. to confess (to a certain crime, etc.)

zhāoshēng 招生 to enroll students

zhāoshì 招式 a stance or posture in Chinese martial art

zhāoshōu 招收 to advertise for students, apprentices, etc.

zhāoshǒu 招手 to wave a hand

zhāoshù 招數 1. a scheme; a trick; a device 2. one move in Chinese martial art

zhāoxiáng 招降 to call for surrender (of the enemy, etc.)

zhāoyáo 招搖 to act ostentatiously

zhāoyuàn 招怨 to inspire hatred; to incur animosity or grudges

zhāozhì 招致 to bring about; to incur

zhāozū 招租 (said of a house) for rent

zhāo 昭

1. bright; luminous 2. prominent; eminent; evident; obvious 3. to make open; to display

zhāogào 昭告 to declare or announce to the public

zhāorán ruòjiē 昭然若揭 very obvious

zhāoshì 昭示 to decree, declare, etc. officially

zhāoxuě 昭雪 to redress (a miscarriage of justice)

zhāozhāng 昭彰 prominent; eminent; obvious; evident

zhāozhù 昭著 famous; eminent

zhāo 朝

1. morning 2. a day

zhāobù bǎoxī 朝不保夕 precarious

zhāobù bǎoxì 朝不保夕 refer to **zhāobù bǎoxī** 朝不保夕

zhāohuì 朝會 a morning rally (in schools)

zhāolìng xīgǎi 朝令夕改 to change rules very frequently

zhāolìng xìgǎi 朝令夕改 refer to **zhāolìng xīgǎi** 朝令夕改

zhāolù 朝露 morning dew—a symbol of transience

zhāoqì 朝氣 fresh spirit

zhāoqì péngbó 朝氣蓬勃 full of vigor and vitality

zhāo Qín mù Chǔ 朝秦暮楚 to be fickle or capricious

zhāosān mùsì 朝三暮四 to be

Z

inconsistent

zhāosī mùxiǎng 朝思暮想 to yearn day and night

zhāoxī 朝夕 1. day and night 2. a very brief period of time

zhāoxì 朝夕 refer to **zhāoxī** 朝夕

zhāoyáng 朝陽 the morning sun

zhāoyáng chǎnyè 朝陽產業 thriving business

zhāozhāo mùmù 朝朝暮暮 every day; always; day and night

zhāo 著(着)

1. to bear; to take 2. a plan; a method 3. (also **zhuó**) a move (on the chessboard, in action, plans, etc.)

zháo 著(着)

1. to make a move or take action; to use 2. to catch (fire, cold, etc.) 3. refer to **zhuó** 著 4

zháohuāng 著慌 anxious or worried

zháojí 著急 anxious or worried

zháoliáng 著涼 to catch a cold

zháomí 著迷 to be fascinated

zháomó 著魔 to be bewitched; to be possessed

zhǎo 爪

1. a nail 2. a claw; a talon

zhǎoyá 爪牙 lackeys; cat's paws

zhǎoyìn 爪印 a trace; a print; a nail mark

zhǎo 找

1. to seek; to look for; to search for; to find 2. to return (change)

zhǎobiàn 找遍 to have searched or looked everywhere

zhǎochár 找碴兒 to pick (up) quarrels

zhǎoduìxiàng 找對象 to look for a partner in marriage

zhǎomáfan 找麻煩 1. to ask for trouble 2. to pick on somebody; to find fault

zhǎoménlu 找門路 to look for employment by seeking help from the right connections

zhǎoqí 找齊 1. to make equal; to even up 2. to make up a deficiency

zhǎoqián 找錢 to give change

zhǎoshì 找事 1. to look for jobs 2. to look for trouble

zhǎosǐ 找死 to invite death; to seek death

zhǎoxún 找尋 to search for; to look for

zhǎo 沼

a lake; a pond; a pool; a marsh

zhǎoqì 沼氣 marsh gas; methane

zhǎozé 沼澤 a marsh; a swamp

zhào 召

1. to summon; to call up 2. to cause; to invite

zhàohuàn 召喚 to call; to summon

zhàohuí 召回 to recall (a diplomat from abroad)

zhàojí 召集 1. to convene (a meeting, etc.) 2. to call to arms

zhàojiàn 召見 to summon a subordinate; to be summoned by a superior

zhàokāi 召開 to convene; to convoke

zhàomù 召募 to enlist or recruit (soldiers)

zhào 兆

1. a sign (in fortune-telling) 2. to portend; to foretell 3. an omen 4. a trillion (1,000,000,000,000); a billion 5. to begin; beginning

zhàotou 兆頭 a sign; an omen; a portent

zhào 詔

1. to proclaim; to announce 2. to instruct; to teach and direct; to coach 3. an imperial decree or mandate

zhàolìng 詔令 an imperial decree or edict

zhào 照

1. to shine upon; to light or illumine 2. a certificate or license 3. according to; in accordance with; to pattern on or after 4. to compare, collate, survey, etc. 5. to photograph; to take a picture; to shoot 6. to look after; to take care of 7. to notify or proclaim 8. sunshine 9. a picture

zhàobàn 照辦 to act upon; to comply with; to manage, or handle something according to instructions, orders, etc.

zhàoběn xuānkē 照本宣科 to repeat what the book says

zhàocháng 照常 as usual

zhàochāo 照抄 to copy exactly as what is written

zhàofā 照發 to issue as before

zhàogu 照顧 1. to look after; to take care of 2. to patronize 3. to consider

zhàojiù 照舊 as usual; as before

zhàolì 照例 to follow precedents or usual practices; as a rule

zhàoliào 照料 to take care of; to look after

zhàomiànr 照面兒 to meet; to come face to face

zhàomíng shèbèi 照明設備 illuminating equipment

zhàopiàn 照片 a photograph; a snapshot

zhàoshè 照射 to shine or light upon; to radiate

zhàoshuō 照說 as a rule

zhàosuàn 照算 1. to calaulate or charge (the listed items) accordingly 2. to charge without deduction, discount, etc.

zhàoxiàng 照相 to take a picture or photograph

zhàoxiàngguǎn 照相館 a photostudio

zhàoxiàngjī 照相機 a camera

zhàoyàng 照樣 1. to pattern after; to copy 2. as usual; in the old manner

zhàoyào 照耀 to radiate; to light up; to shine

zhàoyìng 照應 1. to take care of; to look after 2. to correlate

zhàozhǔn 照准 to approve (a request); to grant

zhào 罩
1. a bamboo basket for catching fish 2. to coop; to cover; to wrap 3. a cover; a shade 4. a mantle; a cloak

zhàobùzhù 罩不住 (informal) unable to control a situation

zhàopáo 罩袍 a dust-robe; a dust-gown; an overall

zhàoshān 罩衫 an overall; a dustcoat

zhào 肇
1. to begin; to start; to commence 2. to found; to devise 3. to incur (misfortune, etc.) 4. to adjust; to make right

zhàoduān 肇端 the beginning; the start; to originate or initiate

zhàohuò 肇禍 to incur or court misfortune

zhàoshǐ 肇始 to begin

zhàoshì 肇事 to stir up trouble or disturbances

Zhào 趙
1. name of an ancient feudal state 2. a Chinese family name

zhē 折
1. to turn upside down; to fall head over heels 2. to pour all out

zhēgēntou 折跟頭 to somersault; to fall head over heels

zhēteng 折騰 1. to turn upside down 2. to waste 3. to toss about

zhē 遮
1. to hide; to cover; to screen; to shade; to shield; to conceal; to shut out 2. to intercept; to block

zhēbì 遮蔽 to cover; to screen

zhēchǒu 遮醜 to hide one's shame

zhēdǎng 遮擋 to fend

zhēgài 遮蓋 to cover; to cover up

zhēxiū 遮羞 to hush up a scandal

zhēyǎn 遮掩 1. to hide; to cover up; to conceal 2. to cover; to envelop

zhēyáng 遮陽 to protect from the sunlight

zhēyìn 遮蔭 to shade

zhēzhù 遮住 to obstruct; to block; to cover

zhē 蜇 also **shì**
1. a poisonous insect; a scorpion 2. to sting

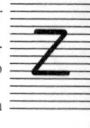

zhé 折
1. to break; to snap 2. to bend; to humble; to bow 3. to judge; to decide a course 4. to sell, barter or exchange 5. a discount in the price 6. to fold 7. to tear into halves; to destroy 8. to submit to; to be willing

zhébàn 折半 to reduce by half

zhéduàn 折斷 to snap; to break

zhéfú 折服 1. to acknowledge the superiority of others 2. to submit

zhéhé 折合 (said of two currencies, etc.) equivalent to

zhéhuí 折回 to turn back (half way)

zhéjià 折價 (said of an article used in repaying a debt, etc.) equivalent to

zhéjiù 折舊 depreciation (especially said of machinery in use)

zhékou 折扣 abatement; a discount in the price

zhémo 折磨 to submit to an ordeal; trials and afflictions

zhéshā 折煞 to break one's luck

zhéshā 折煞 refer to **zhéshā** 折煞

zhéshàn 折扇 a folding fan

zhéshè 折射 refraction; to refract

zhéshòu 折壽 (said of excessive happiness, blessings, etc.) that will cut one's natural allotment of life expectancy

zhésuàn 折算 calculated at; equivalent to

zhésǔn 折損 to damage

zhéxiàn 折現 to convert into cash

zhézhōng 折衷 to compromise; a compromise

zhé 哲
1. a sage; a thinker; a philosopher 2. wise; wisdom; sagacious

zhélǐ 哲理 a philosophical principle

zhéxué 哲學 philosophy

zhéxuéjiā 哲學家 a philosopher; a thinker

zhé 摘
refer to **zhāi** 摘

zhé 摺
1. to fold (paper, etc.); to plait 2. a folder; a folded brochure 3. curved and winding 4. to pull and break

zhéchǐ 摺尺 a folding ruler

zhéchuáng 摺床 a folding bed

zhédié 摺疊 to fold up (clothing, etc.)

zhéhén 摺痕 a crease; a fold

zhéjiǎo 摺角 to make a dog-ear; to dog-ear

zhéshàn 摺扇 a folding fan

zhé 褶
refer to **zhě** 褶

zhé 蟄 also **zhí**
to hibernate; hibernation

zhéfú 蟄伏 to hibernate; hibernation

zhé 謫
1. to censure; to reproach 2. to punish; to penalize 3. one's fault 4. to exile; to banish (an official) to a distant place

zhéjū 謫居 to live in exile

zhéxiān 謫仙 an immortal living among mortals—a genius; a prodigy

zhé 慴
refer to **shè** 慴

zhě 者
1. those who; he who 2. a particle combining with some words to form adverbials

zhě 褶 also **zhé**
to fold; pleated

zhěqún 褶裙 a pleated skirt

zhè 宅
refer to **zhái** 宅

Zhè 浙
1. Zhejiang 2. name of a river

zhè 這 also **zhèi**
1. this (a pronoun) 2. this (a demonstrative adjective); such

zhèbiān 這邊 1. this side; here 2. this side; our side

zhèbù tiándì 這步田地 (to) such a pass; (to) such a deplorable situation

zhècì 這次 this time; present; current

zhèhuǐr 這會兒 refer to **zhèhuìr** 這會兒

zhèhuìr 這會兒 now; at the moment

zhèlǐ 這裡 here; this place; where we are

zhème 這麼 so; thus; (in) this way; like this

zhèshān wàngzhe nàshān gāo 這山望著那山高 (figuratively) One is never satisfied with one's own present circumstance, position, etc.

zhè 蔗

sugarcane

zhètáng 蔗糖 sugar from sugarcane; cane sugar

zhe 著(着)

an adverbial particle

zhèi 這

refer to **zhè** 這

zhēn 貞 also **zhēng**

1. chastity of a woman 2. pure; virtuous 3. to be incorruptible; to be correctly firm 4. devotion; dedication 5. to divine; to inquire by divination

zhēncāo 貞操 1. purity and chastity in one's conduct 2. a woman's chastity or virginity

zhēnjié 貞節 1. tenacity to hold on to one's virtuous way or integrity 2. (said of a woman) chastity; purity; virtue

zhēnjié 貞潔 chaste and pure; virtuous

zhēn 珍

1. precious; rare; very valuable 2. valuables; treasures 3. delicacies

zhēn'ài 珍愛 to value; to love dearly

zhēncáng 珍藏 to treasure

zhēnguì 珍貴 valuable; treasurable; precious

zhēnpǐn 珍品 delicacies; treasures

zhēnqí 珍奇 rare and precious

zhēnqín yìshòu 珍禽異獸 rare birds and animals

zhēnshì 珍視 to value highly

zhēnwán 珍玩 curios of great value

zhēnwàn 珍玩 refer to **zhēnwán** 珍玩

zhēnxī 珍惜 to treasure

zhēnxí 珍惜 refer to **zhēnxī** 珍惜

zhēnxiū 珍饈 dainties; rare delicacies

zhēnzhòng 珍重 1. to value highly 2. to take good care of (yourself)

zhēnzhū 珍珠 a pearl

zhēn 針

1. a needle; a pin; a probe 2. a stitch

zhēnbiān 針砭 1. acupuncture 2. remonstrance

zhēnduì 針對 1. to aim directly at; to focus on 2. in accordance with

zhēnfēng xiāngduì 針鋒相對 to oppose each other with equal harshness

zhēnjiǔ 針灸 acupuncture and moxibustion; acupuncture and cauterization

zhēnxiàn 針線 1. a needle and thread 2. needlework

zhēnzhīpǐn 針織品 knit goods; knitwear; knitting

zhēn 砧

1. a rock with a flat top on which the laundry is beaten and washed; an anvil 2. an ancient instrument for torture

zhēnbǎn 砧板 a chopping block

zhēn 振

benevolent and generous

zhēnzhēn 振振 benevolent and generous; noble

zhēn 眞

1. true; real; factual; substantial; actual; truly 2. the highest sincerity one is capable of

zhēn'ài 眞愛 true love

Z

zhēncái shíliào 眞材實料 genuine material and solid substance

zhēncái shíxué 眞才實學 1. solid learning; genuine talent 2. truly learned; highly competent

zhēnchéng 眞誠 sincere; genuine; true

zhēndì 眞諦 the real meaning; the essence

zhēngōngfu 眞工夫 a true skill or accomplishment

zhēnhuà 眞話 the truth

zhēnjiǎ 眞假 true and false; real and fake

zhēnjīn bùpà huǒliàn 眞金不怕火煉 Truth is ultimately louder than lies or slanders.

zhēnkōng 眞空 vacuum

zhēnlǐ 眞理 1. truth 2. righteousness

zhēnmiànmù 眞面目 (literally) the real face—true colors; true character; the actual thing behind a false front

zhēnpí 眞皮 1. dermis 2. genuine leather

zhēnpíng shíjù 眞憑實據 indisputable proof

zhēnqiāng shídàn 眞槍實彈 real guns and bullets

zhēnqiè 眞切 1. true and concise; vivid 2. (to see or hear) clearly

zhēnqíng 眞情 1. actual happenings (of an incident, etc.) 2. real affections

zhēnquè 眞確 authentic; true; accurate

zhēnshí 眞實 actual; true; real; factual

zhēnshíxìng 眞實性 reliability; truthfulness

zhēnxiàng 眞相 the truth (about a happening, etc.)

zhēnxiàng dàbái 眞相大白 The truth is out.

zhēnxīn 眞心 from the bottom of one's heart; sincere; wholehearted

zhēnxīnhuà 眞心話 words from the bottom of one's heart

zhēnzhèng 眞正 1. actually; real 2. genuine

zhēnzhì 眞摯 sincere; sincerity; faithful; true

zhēnzhū 眞珠 a natural pearl

zhēn 偵

1. to detect; to spy; to scout 2. a scout; a spy; a detective

zhēnchá 偵查 to investigate

zhēnchá 偵察 reconnaissance; to reconnoiter

zhēnchájī 偵察機 a reconnaissance plane

zhēnjī 偵緝 to track down and arrest

zhēnpò 偵破 to crack a criminal case

zhēnqì 偵緝 refer to **zhēnjī** 偵緝

zhēntàn 偵探 1. a detective 2. to investigate

zhēntàn xiǎoshuō 偵探小說 detective stories

zhēnxún 偵詢 to examine a suspect or someone concerned to gather information

zhěn 診

refer to **zhěn** 診

zhēn 椹

a block

zhēnbǎn 椹板 a chopping board

zhēn 斟

1. to fill a cup with (tea or wine) 2. to consider

zhēnjiǔ 斟酒 to pour wine or liquor into a cup or glass

zhēnzhuó 斟酌 1. to fill a cup, or glass, with wine or liquor 2. to consider

zhēn 甄

1. a potter's wheel 2. to make pottery ware 3. to examine; to discern 4. to grade (competence, etc.) by examinations 5. to make clear

zhēnxuǎn 甄選 to select (talented people, etc.)

zhēnyòng 甄用 to employ by an examination

zhēn 榛

a hazel

zhēnmǎng 榛莽 thickets; bushes

zhēn 箴

1. a probe; a needle 2. to warn; to admonish

zhēnyán 箴言 a maxim; warning words; an admonition

zhēn 鍼(針)

a needle; a pin; a probe

zhěn 枕

1. a pillow 2. (also **zhèn**) to use something as a pillow; to pillow

zhěnbiānrén 枕邊人 wife (who shares the same pillow with her husband)

zhěn'gē dàidàn 枕戈待旦 to be on the alert

zhěnjiè 枕藉 to lie in complete disarray or to lie about on each other

zhěnjīn 枕巾 a pillow cover

zhěnjīng jièshǐ 枕經藉史 to be excessively fond of ancient books

zhěnmù 枕木 a railway sleeper; a railroad tie

zhěnpàn 枕畔 beside the pillow

zhěntào 枕套 a pillowcase; a pillowslip

zhěntou 枕頭 a pillow

zhěnxí nán'ān 枕席難安 cannot sleep—very worried and anxious

zhěn 疹

a rash

zhěnzi 疹子 measles; carbuncles

zhěn 診 also **zhēn**

1. to examine (diseases, ailments, etc.); to diagnose 2. to tell; to report

zhěnduàn 診斷 to diagnose (a disease); a diagnosis

zhěnduànshū 診斷書 a written diagnosis

zhěnliáo 診療 to diagnose and treat

zhěnmài 診脈 to feel the pulse

zhěnsuǒ 診所 a clinic; a dispensary

zhěnzhì 診治 to diagnose and treat

zhěn 軫

the wooden bumper at the rear of a cart

zhěnniàn 軫念 to remember with deep emotion

zhěn 縝

fine; close; minute

zhěnmì 縝密 minute; fine

zhěn 枕

refer to **zhěn** 枕 2

zhèn 振

1. to arouse to action; to raise; to rise 2. to pull up; to save; to relieve 3. to shake; to flap as wings 4. to restore order

zhènbǐ zhíshū 振筆直書 to write rapidly; to wield the pen furiously

zhènbì yīhū 振臂一呼 to arouse to action

zhèndàng 振盪 1. (physics) vibration 2. (electricity) oscillation

zhèndòng 振動 (physics) vibration; to vibrate

zhènfèn 振奮 1. to arouse; to stimulate 2. encouraging; exciting

zhènxīng 振興 to promote or develop (industrial endeavor, etc.); to prosper

zhènzhèn yǒucí 振振有詞 to talk fluently and loudly (as if one has all the reasons on his side)

zhènzuò 振作 to arouse (oneself)

zhèn 陣

1. a column or row of troops; the army; the rank and file 2. to battle; to go to war 3. anything that occurs in a certain duration or spell of time

zhèndì 陣地 a (military) position

zhènjiǎo 陣腳 1. a front line 2. position; situation; circumstances

zhènróng 陣容 1. the appearance of 2 military deployment; the layout of troops 2. the lineup of a cabinet 3. the cast of a movie

zhènshì 陣勢 order of battle;

Z

battle array

zhèntòng 陣痛 labor pangs

zhènwáng 陣亡 to be killed in action

zhènxiàn 陣線 line of battle

zhènyíng 陣營 a camp; an encampment

zhènyǔ 陣雨 occasional drizzle; showers

zhèn 朕

1. the royal we (used exclusively by the emperor or king to mean I) 2. an omen; an augury; a portent; a sign

zhènzhào 朕兆 an omen; a portent; an augury; a sign

zhèn 陳(陣)

tactical deployment of troops

zhèn 賑

1. to relieve or give aid to the distressed; to support 2. rich; wealthy; prosperous

zhènjì 賑濟 to relieve or give aid to the distressed; to provide relief for

zhènzāi 賑災 to relieve the afflicted area; to relieve victims of a natural disaster

zhèn 震

1. to shake; to tremble, as an earthquake 2. to excite; to shock 3. terrified; scared 4. (now rarely) thunder; a thunderclap 5. the 4th of the Eight Diagrams

zhèndòng 震動 1. to vibrate; to shake; to move 2. to be shocked or shaken

zhèn'ěr yùlóng 震耳欲聾 deafening; earsplitting

zhèngǔ shuòjīn 震古鑠今 unprecedented; peerless

zhènhàn 震撼 to shake; shaken

zhènjīng 震驚 greatly surprised

zhènnù 震怒 greatly infuriated; wrath; rage

zhènshè 震懾 to awe; to frighten

zhènzhé 震慴 refer to **zhènshè** 震懾

zhèn 鴆

1. a kind of venomous bird 2.

poisoned wine

zhèndú 鴆毒 1. poison; venom 2. to slander; to harm by devious means

zhèn 鎮

1. to subdue; to suppress; to quell; to put down 2. to cool with water or ice 3. weight 4. whole 5. a town; a township 6. a garrison post

zhènbào 鎮暴 riot control

zhèndìng 鎮定 self-composed; calm; cool

zhèngōngsuǒ 鎮公所 a town hall; a town house

zhènjìng 鎮靜 self-composed; calm; cool

zhènjìngjì 鎮靜劑 a sedative; a tranquilizer

zhènyā 鎮壓 to suppress; to put down; suppression

zhēng 丁

sound

zhēng 正

the first in the lunar calendar

zhēngyuè 正月 the first month of the lunar year

zhēng 征

1. to journey far away 2. to attack; to conquer; to tame 3. to levy taxes; to collect taxes 4. to take; to snatch

zhēngfá 征伐 to battle; to be on the warpath

zhēngfú 征服 to conquer; conquest

zhēngshōu 征收 to levy and collect (taxes); to impose

zhēngtǎo 征討 to quell; to subjugate

zhēngyī 征衣 1. traveling clothes 2. warrior's costume

zhēngzhàn 征戰 to fight in battle

zhēng 怔

terrified; stunned; scared

zhēngchōng 怔忡 severe palpitation

zhēngzhōng 怔忪 scared and nervous; fearful

zhēng 爭

1. to contend; to struggle; to strive 2. to fight; to dispute; to argue; to quarrel 3. short of; to lack; to be deficient in

zhēngbà 爭霸 to contend (or struggle) for hegemony

zhēngbàzhàn 爭霸戰 a fight for hegemony; a power struggle

zhēngbiàn 爭辯 to argue; to debate; to dispute

zhēngchǎo 爭吵 to quarrel; to wrangle

zhēngdòu 爭鬥 to struggle; to conflict

zhēngduān 爭端 the cause of dispute, or quarrel

zhēngduó 爭奪 to struggle for; to contend for

zhēngfēng chīcù 爭風吃醋 to fight for the affection of a man or woman

zhēnggōng 爭功 to contend for credit

zhēngguāng 爭光 to win glory

zhēnglùn 爭論 to dispute; to argue

zhēngmiànzi 爭面子 to try to win or excel for the sake of face

zhēngqì 爭氣 don't let down; to try to win credit for

zhēngqiáng dòushèng 爭強鬥勝 to desire to excel over others

zhēngqǔ 爭取 to win over; to compete for

zhēngquán duólì 爭權奪利 to fight for selfish gains

zhēngxiān kǒnghòu 爭先恐後 anxious to be ahead of others

zhēngxióng 爭雄 to struggle or contend for supremacy

zhēngyán dòuyàn 爭妍鬥艷 to contend in beauty and fascination

zhēngyì 爭議 to dispute; to argue

zhēngzhí 爭執 to argue or dispute obstinately

zhēng 貞

refer to **zhēn** 貞

zhēng 烝

1. to rise—as steam 2. many; numerous 3. lewdness, incest, etc. among the older generation 4. (蒸) to steam

zhēngmín 烝民 the people; the masses

zhēng 猙

fierce-looking; hideous; repulsive

zhēngníng 猙獰 fierce-looking; hideous; repulsive

zhēng 掙

1. to make efforts; to strive 2. to get free from

zhēngkāi 掙開 to get free with effort

zhēngtuō 掙脫 to break away with force; to shake off

zhēngzhá 掙扎 to struggle; a struggle; to strive

zhēng 峥

1. lofty 2. outstanding 3. steep 4. harsh

zhēngróng 峥嶸 1. lofty and steep 2. (said of a person) distinguished; outstanding

zhēng 睜

to open the eyes

zhēng yǎnjing shuō xiāhuà 睜開眼睛說瞎話 to tell a barefaced lie

zhēng yìzhīyǎn, bì yìzhīyǎn 睜一隻眼，閉一隻眼 to pretend not to see—to overlook purposely

zhēng 箏

a kite

zhēng 蒸

1. steam; to steam; to cook by steaming 2. to evaporate 3. twigs or slender branches as fuel 4. crowded; crowds; the masses

zhēngfā 蒸發 evaporation; to evaporate

zhēngjiǎo 蒸餃 a steamed dumpling

zhēngliú 蒸餾 distillation; to distill

zhēngliúshuǐ 蒸餾水 distilled

water

zhēnglóng 蒸籠 a tight basket and sieve of bamboo for steaming food

zhēngqì 蒸汽 steam; vapor

zhēngqìjī 蒸汽機 a steam engine

zhēngzhēng rìshàng 蒸蒸日上 (usually said of business, etc.) getting more and more prosperous

zhēng 諍

refer to **zhèng** 諍

zhēng 徵

1. to summon 2. to levy or raise (taxes) 3. to call to arms 4. to ask; to inquire 5. to request; to seek for 6. to prove; to evidence 7. a sign

zhēngbīng 徵兵 to draft able-bodied male citizens for military service

zhēngbīngzhì 徵兵制 the conscription system

zhēngdiào 徵調 to issue orders to conscript men and make military deployment

zhēnggòu 徵購 requisition by purchase

zhēnghòu 徵候 a symptom, or an indication

zhēnghòuqún 徵候群 a symptom group

zhēngjí 徵集 to collect or requisition; to levy

zhēngpìn 徵聘 to solicit a competent person for a vacancy

zhēngqiú 徵求 to seek; to solicit (answers, etc.); to want (an office clerk, etc.)

zhēngshōu 徵收 to collect (taxes, duty, etc.)

zhēngshuì 徵稅 to levy and collect taxes

zhēngwén 徵文 to solicit writings publicly

zhēngxìnsuǒ 徵信所 a credit information office

zhēngxún 徵詢 to solicit opinions, consent, etc.

zhēngyòng 徵用 to requisition; to conscript

zhēngzhào 徵召 to draft the capable and virtuous for public service

zhēngzhào 徵兆 a symptom; an omen

zhēng 錚

1. a clang of metal 2. a gong

zhēngzhēng 錚錚 1. a clang of metal 2. righteous; incorruptible; upright

zhēng 癥

obstruction of the bowels

zhēngjié 癥結 1. obstruction of the bowels 2. a difficult point (of a problem); a bottleneck; a crux

zhěng 拯

1. to save; to deliver 2. to raise; to lift up

zhěngjiù 拯救 1. deliverance 2. to save; to rescue; to deliver

zhěngxù 拯恤 to save and help (the refugees, the poor, etc.)

zhěng 整

1. orderly; systematic; neat; tidy 2. sharp 3. whole; complete; entire; intact 4. to tidy; to set in order; to adjust; to arrange; to repair; to make ready

zhěngbiān 整編 to reorganize troops

zhěngchì 整飭 1. orderly; systematic 2. to set to order

zhěngchú 整除 to divide exactly

zhěngduì 整隊 1. (said of troops, etc.) to form neat lines; to file 2. the whole unit, band, column, etc.

zhěngdùn 整頓 to put in order, or to put to right a poorly managed organization, firm, etc.

zhěnghé 整合 (geology) conformity

zhěngjié 整潔 neat and clean

zhěnglǐ 整理 to arrange; to put in order; to adjust

zhěngliúqì 整流器 (physics) 1. a rectifier 2. a commutator

zhěngpī 整批 a batch

zhěngqí 整齊 1. neat; tidy 2. even

zhěngqí huàyī 整齊劃一 neat

and uniform

zhěngrén 整人 (slang) to give someone a hard time; to fix somebody

zhěngróng 整容 1. to improve one's looks by plastic surgery 2. to tidy one's appearance (by shaving, a haircut, etc.); face-lifting

zhěngshù 整數 a whole number; an integer; a round sum

zhěngsù 整肅 1. strict; rigid; stern 2. to purge (a government or political leader) 3. to rectify

zhěngtào 整套 the whole set

zhěngtǐ 整體 the whole

zhěngtiān 整天 the whole day; all day long

zhěngxíng 整形 orthopedics

zhěngxíng shǒushù 整形手術 plastic operation

zhěngxiū 整修 to rebuild; to renovate

zhěngzhì 整治 1. to set in order; to adjust and repair 2. to dredge (a river)

zhěngzhuāng 整裝 to dress up

zhěngzhuāng dàifā 整裝待發 (usually said of troops on an expedition) to pack up and be ready to go

zhèng 正

1. the obverse side; the right side 2. appropriate; proper 3. formal 4. to rectify; to correct 5. pure; not contaminated 6. straightforward and unbending; honest and virtuous 7. the person in charge; the person in command; the principal (as against the secondary) 8. to mete out punishment for a criminal 9. original (texts, etc.) 10. exactly; just; right 11. positively 12. main; principal 13. sharp; punctually 14. just; unbiased

zhèngběn 正本 the original copy

zhèngběn qīngyuán 正本清源 to overhaul thoroughly

zhèngbǐ 正比 direct proportion

zhèngbù 正步 the goose step; the parade step

zhèngcháng 正常 normal; common; usually

zhèngdà guāngmíng 正大光明 fair and frank

zhèngdāng 正當 right at that time; just when

zhèngdàng 正當 proper; justifiable; legitimate

zhèngdào 正道 the right course

zhèngdiàn 正殿 the main hall

zhèngduì 正對 face to face; directly opposite

zhèngfǎ 正法 1. the proper law or rule 2. to execute (a death convict); execution

zhèngfāngxíng 正方形 (geometry) a square

zhèngfù 正負 positive and negative

zhèngguī 正規 regular; standard

zhèngguǐ 正軌 the proper way or course

zhènghǎo 正好 exactly (at the right moment); exactly right; it just happened that...

zhèngjīn wēizuò 正襟危坐 to sit upright and look straight ahead

zhèngjīn wēizuò 正襟危坐 refer to **zhèngjīn wēizuò** 正襟危坐

zhèngjīng bābǎi 正經八百 serious; earnest

zhèngjing 正經 (said of manners, conducts, etc.) very proper; respectable; serious

zhèngkǎi 正楷 the standard script (in Chinese calligraphy)

zhèngmén 正門 the front door; the main entrance

zhèngmiàn 正面 the right side; the obverse side; the head (of a coin)

zhèngpài 正派 honest, proper and straightforward; virtuous

zhèngqì 正氣 righteousness

zhèngquè 正確 accurate; correct; right; proper

zhèngquèxìng 正確性 accuracy; correctness

zhèngrén jūnzǐ 正人君子 a gentleman

zhèngshì 正式 formally; official

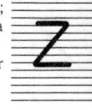

zhèngshì 正事 1. one's job; one's duty or obligation 2. serious business

zhèngshì 正視 to look straight in the eye; to look at something without bias or distortion

zhèngtí 正題 1. the subject (or topic) of a talk or an essay 2. (philosophy) a thesis

zhèngtīng 正廳 1. the main hall 2. stalls (in a theater)

zhèngtǒng 正統 orthodox; authorized

zhèngtú 正途 the right course

zhèngwén 正文 text

zhèngwǔ 正午 high noon; noon

zhèngyán lìsè 正顏厲色 a stern and severe look; a serious manner

zhèngyè 正業 1. a respectable job 2. one's main job as contrasted to his side jobs

zhèngyì 正義 righteousness; justice

zhèngyìgǎn 正義感 the sense of justice or righteousness

zhèngzài 正在 1. (said of a position) exactly at 2. a term used before a verb to form a progressive tense

zhèngzhí 正直 upright and honest; candid and fair

zhèngzhí 正值 just at that time; exactly during; it happened just when...

zhèngzhōng 正中 right in the center

zhèngzhōng xiàhuái 正中下懷 exactly as one wishes or hopes for

zhèngzōng 正宗 orthodox

zhèng 政

1. government 2. politics; political affairs 3. administration; management

zhèngbiàn 政變 a coup d'état; a coup

zhèngcè 政策 a policy

zhèngdǎng 政黨 a political party

zhèngfǔ 政府 a government

zhèngfǔ jīguān 政府機關 a government agency

zhènggāng 政綱 the platform (of a political party)

zhèngjiàn 政見 political views; politics

zhèngjiè 政界 political circles; officialdom

zhèngjú 政局 the political situation or scene

zhèngkè 政客 a politician who places personal gain above public interests

zhènglìng 政令 a government order (or decree)

zhènglùn 政論 articles, statements or comments about politics

zhènglüè 政略 a government policy

zhèngquán 政權 regime; political power

zhèngshì 政事 affairs of the government

zhèngtǐ 政體 a political system; a polity

zhèngwù 政務 affairs of the government

zhèngyào 政要 government VIPs

zhèngzhì 政治 1. politics 2. government administration

zhèngzhì bìhù 政治庇護 political asylum

zhèngzhìfàn 政治犯 a political prisoner

zhèngzhìjiā 政治家 a statesman

zhèng 症

1. disease; an ailment 2. symptoms or manifestations of a disease

zhènghou 症候 symptoms or manifestations of a disease

zhèngzhuàng 症狀 symptoms or manifestations of a disease

zhèng 掙

1. to struggle (for one's life, etc.) 2. to earn (money, etc.)

zhèngqián 掙錢 to earn money

zhèng 幀

1. a numerary adjunct (for paint-

ings, pictures, photos, etc.) 2. one
of a pair—as of scrolls

zhèng 諍 also **zhēng**

1. to expostulate; to remonstrate;
to admonish 2. to dispute; to
compete

zhèngyán 諍言 a remonstrance;
an expostulation; forthright
admonition

zhèng 鄭

1. solemn; formal; serious 2. a
Chinese family name 3. name of
an ancient state in what is
today's Henan

zhèngzhòng 鄭重 1. cautious;
careful 2. solemn; serious

zhèngzhòng qíshì 鄭重其事 1.
to treat it with seriousness 2.
very careful or cautious

zhèng 證(証)

1. to give evidence; to bear testimony; to bear witness; to prove;
to testify 2. evidence; proof; testimony 3. a certificate; a card 4.
a symptom

zhèngcí 證詞 testimony given at
a court of law

zhènghūnrén 證婚人 a witness
at a wedding

zhèngjiàn 證件 papers supporting a claim; documentary proof;
credentials

zhèngjù 證據 testimony; evidence; witness; proof

zhèngmíng 證明 to prove; to
testify

zhèngmíngshū 證明書 a certificate; a voucher

zhèngquàn 證券 securities
(bills, bonds, etc.); stocks and
bonds

zhèngren 證人 a witness

zhèngshí 證實 to prove; to testify

zhèngshū 證書 a certificate; a
diploma; credentials

zhèngwù 證物 physical evidence; an exhibit

Zhī 氏

name of an ancient barbarian
tribe

zhī 支

1. to pay; to disburse; to defray
2. to support; to sustain 3. to
prop up; to put up 4. to prick up;
to raise 5. to send away; to put
somebody off 6. a branch; a subdivision 7. a term for indicating
amount or number 8. (textile)
count 9. the Terrestrial
Branches used in calculation
with the Celestial Stems

zhīcheng 支撐 to prop up; to
support

zhīchí 支持 to support; to sustain

zhīchū 支出 expense; expenditure

zhīfù 支付 to pay (what is owed);
to defray

zhījiě 支解 to dismember

zhīlí 支離 1. to disintegrate 2. incoherent; fragmented; broken

zhīlí pòsuì 支離破碎 completely disintegrated

zhīlǐng 支領 to draw money

zhīliú 支流 a tributary (of a
river) nonessentials

zhīpài 支派 a subdivision; a
branch (of a school of thought)

zhīpai 支派 to appoint

zhīpèi 支配 to dominate to manage

zhīpiào 支票 a cheque or check

zhīpiàobù 支票簿 a checkbook

zhīqìguǎn 支氣管 a bronchus

zhīqǔ 支取 to draw money

zhīshǐ 支使 1. to order about 2.
to send away

zhīwú qící 支吾其詞 to speak
haltingly or ambiguously

zhīxiàn 支線 a branch line

zhīyìng 支應 1. to take charge
of cash receipts and payments 2.
to look after; to take care of

zhīyòng 支用 to disburse

zhīyuán 支援 to aid; to support;
to assist

zhīzhù 支柱 a prop; a support; a
stay

zhī 之

1. to go to; to leave for; to
arrive at 2. zigzag; winding 3. an

expletive 4. third person objective case (it; her; him; them) 5. this; that; these; those 6. (possessive particle) of

zhīhòu 之後 after this; afterward

zhīqián 之前 before this; before; prior to

zhīzìlù 之字路 an S-shaped road

zhī 汁
juice; the natural fluid; sap

zhī 枝
1. the branches of a tree; a branch 2. limbs 3. to branch off

zhīgàn 枝幹 the trunk and the branches

zhījié 枝節 1. branches and knots —minor matters 2. an obstacle; a complication

zhītiáo 枝條 a twig

zhītou 枝頭 on the branch

zhīyā 枝椏 a branch; a twig

zhīyè 枝葉 1. branches and leaves 2. complications and diversities 3. children; offspring

zhīyè fúshū 枝葉扶疏 (said of trees) luxuriant

zhīzi 枝子 a branch; a bough

zhī 肢
1. the four limbs of a person 2. the legs of an animal 3. the wings or feet of a bird

zhījiě 肢解 to dismember; dismemberment

zhītǐ 肢體 the body

zhī 知
1. knowledge 2. to know; to understand; to recognize; to be aware of 3. to acquaint; to be familiar with; to befriend 4. to control; to operate; to direct 5. to wait on

zhīdao 知道 to know; to realize; to understand

zhījǐ 知己 1. a close or intimate friend 2. intimate 3. to know oneself

zhījué 知覺 1. consciousness 2. perception

zhīliǎo 知了 the cicada, or broad locust

zhīmíng 知名 well-known

zhīmíngdù 知名度 name recognition; name familiarity

zhīnán értuì 知難而退 to withdraw or quit after learning of the difficulties, hardships, etc. involved

zhīqù 知趣 knowing what to do in a delicate situation

zhīshi 知識 knowledge; learning; information

zhīshi fènzǐ 知識分子 intellectuals; the intelligentsia

zhīxī 知悉 to know; to be aware of

zhīxiǎo 知曉 to know; to be aware of

zhīxīnhuà 知心話 secrets from the bottom of one's heart

zhīyīn 知音 a close or intimate friend

zhīzú 知足 to be content with what one has had

zhīzú chánglè 知足常樂 Contentment brings happiness.

zhī 芝
1. a kind of purplish fungus symbolizing nobility 2. a kind of fragrant herb 3. a Chinese family name

zhīma 芝麻 a sesame

zhī 祇
refer to **zhǐ** 祇

zhī 指 also **zhǐ**
zhījia 指甲 a fingernail

zhī 脂
1. the fat of animals; grease; lard; tallow 2. the gum or sap of trees; resin 3. to anoint; to grease; to lubricate 4. cosmetics

zhīfáng 脂肪 the fat of animals or plants

zhīfěn 脂粉 rouge and face powder—cosmetics

zhīfěnqì 脂粉氣 feminine; sissy

zhī 隻
1. a numerary adjunct for a hen, pigeon, bird, ox, hand, foot, etc. 2. single; alone; one of a pair 3. odd (number)

zhīshēn 隻身 alone; all by one-

self

zhīyán piànyǔ 隻言片語 a few words

zhī 梔
a gardenia

zhīzihuā 梔子花 a gardenia

zhī 蜘
a spider

zhīzhū 蜘蛛 a spider

zhī 織
to weave; to knit

zhībǔ 織補 to darn; to mend

zhībù 織布 to weave cloth

zhībùjī 織布機 a loom

zhī 擲
refer to **zhì** 擲

zhí 直
1. straight; to straighten 2. upright and honest; fair; unbiased 3. vertical; longitudinal; from top to bottom 4. outspoken; frank; straightforward 5. directly; firsthand 6. continuous; uninterrupted 7. stiff; numb 8. just; simply; only; merely 9. a vertical stroke (in Chinese characters)

zhícháng 直腸 the rectum

zhíchén 直陳 to describe truthfully; to state frankly

zhíchǐ 直尺 a straightedge

zhídá 直達 to go nonstop to; through

zhídáchē 直達車 a through train, bus, etc.

zhídào 直到 1. till; until 2. up to

zhíjiē 直接 direct; firsthand; directly

zhíjié liǎodāng 直截了當 straightforward; flatly

zhíjìng 直徑 1. a straight path 2. a diameter

zhíjué 直覺 intuition

zhílì 直立 to stand erect

zhíshàng qīngyún 直上青雲 to hit the highest literary honors

zhíshēngjī 直昇機 a helicopter

zhíshǔ 直屬 to be under the direct control or jurisdiction of

zhíshuài 直率 straight-forward;

candid; frank

zhíshuǎng 直爽 straight-forward; candid; frank

zhíxiáshì 直轄市 a special municipality

zhíxiàn 直線 1. a straight line 2. steep; sharp

zhíxiāo 直銷 to sell directly or direct sale by a manufacturer instead of through an agent

zhíxìngzi 直性子 frank; straightforward

zhíyán 直言 1. to speak out 2. outspoken remarks

zhíyán bùhuì 直言不諱 to speak plainly and frankly

zhíyì 直譯 word-for-word translation

zhí 指 also **zhǐ**
a finger

zhítou 指頭 a finger

zhí 姪
1. the children of one's brother —nephews or nieces 2. I; me (when speaking to a family friend of one's father's generation)

zhí'ér 姪兒 a nephew

zhízi 姪子 a nephew

zhínǚ 姪女 a niece

zhí 值
1. prices of commodities; value; cost; to cost; to be worth 2. at the time of... 3. to meet; to happen

zhíbān 值班 to be on duty

zhíde 值得 to be worthy of; to deserve

zhíqián 值錢 valuable; expensive

zhíqín 值勤 to be on duty

zhírì 值日 to be one's turn to be on duty

zhírìshēng 值日生 the student on duty

zhíxīng 值星 (said of army officers) to be on duty for the week

zhí 執
1. to hold; to grasp; to seize 2. to detain; to arrest 3. to maintain or uphold (a principle, etc.); to

Z

hold on stubbornly to

zhí'ào 執拗 refer to **zhíniù** 執拗

zhíbǐ 執筆 to write

zhífǎ 執法 to enforce (or execute) the law

zhífú 執紼 to attend a funeral

zhímí bùwù 執迷不悟 to adhere stubbornly to errors

zhíniù 執拗 presistent

zhíxíng 執行 to execute (an order); to carry out

zhíyè 執業 1. to engage in a profession or trade 2. a vocation or trade

zhíyì 執意 to stick to one's own view; to insist on

zhízhǎng 執掌 to manage; to superintend

zhízhào 執照 a license; a permit

zhízhèng 執政 to be in power; to hold the reins of the government

zhízhuó 執著 inflexible; to persist in

zhí 植

1. to plant; to set up; to erect 2. (now rarely) to lean on 3. plants; vegetation

zhídǎng yíngsī 植黨營私 to form a faction for selfish ends

zhíshù 植樹 to plant trees

zhíwù 植物 vegetable; plants; floras

zhíwùjiè 植物界 the vegetable kingdom

zhíwùrén 植物人 a vegetable

zhíwùxué 植物學 botany

zhíwùxuéjiā 植物學家 a botanist

zhíwùyóu 植物油 vegetable oil

zhíwùyuán 植物園 a botanical garden; an arboretum

zhí 殖

1. to grow in abundance; to prosper 2. to plant 3. to become wealthy 4. to colonize; colonization

zhímín 殖民 to colonize

zhímíndì 殖民地 a colony

zhí 質

refer to **zhì** 質 3, 4, 5, 6, 7

zhí 蟄

refer to **zhé** 蟄

zhí 職

1. a profession or a vocation; a career 2. a post; a position 3. an office; official duties 4. to govern; to direct; to manage 5. used in place of I in documents to a superior 6. only; particularly

zhíděng 職等 official rank; grade of position

zhíshǒu 職守 one's official duties, charge, etc.

zhíwèi 職位 one's office; one's position in an office

zhíwù 職務 one's official duties or obligations

zhíyè 職業 a profession; a vocation; an occupation

zhíyè fùnǚ 職業婦女 career women

zhíyè jièshàosuǒ 職業介紹所 an employment agency

zhíyè xuéxiào 職業學校 a vocational school

zhíyè xùnliàn 職業訓練 vocational training

zhíyuán 職員 staff members or employees of a company, office, etc.

zhízé 職責 one's position and responsibility; charge

zhí 擲

refer to **zhǐ** 擲

zhí 躑

to falter; to hesitate

zhízhú 躑躅 1. to falter; to hesitate; to loiter around 2. (botany) an azalea

zhǐ 止

1. to stop; to desist; to still 2. to rest in; to stay 3. deportment 4. to detain 5. to prohibit 6. to come to; to arrive at 7. still; calm; stagnant 8. only

zhǐbù 止步 to stop; to go no further

zhǐfù 止付 to stop payment

zhǐjìng 止境 limits; the terminal point; the end

zhǐké 止咳 to stop coughing

zhǐkě 止渴 to quench thirst

zhǐtòng 止痛 to stop pain; to kill pain

zhǐtòngyào 止痛藥 the painkiller; the anodyne

zhǐxī 止息 to cease; to stop

zhǐxí 止息 refer to **zhǐxī** 止息

zhǐxiě 止血 refer to **zhǐxuè** 止血

zhǐxiè 止瀉 to stop diarrhea

zhǐxuè 止血 to stop bleeding or hemorrhage

zhǐyǎng 止癢 to stop or alleviate itching

zhǐ 只
1. only; merely 2. but; yet

zhǐbùguò 只不過 only; just; merely

zhǐdé 只得 to have to

zhǐdú cúnchǔqì 只讀存儲器 (computer) read-only memory; ROM

zhǐguǎn 只管 (do anything) as you wish; please don't hesitate to...

zhǐhǎo 只好 the only alternative is to...; to have to

zhǐpà 只怕 afraid of no one (or nothing) except...

zhǐshì 只是 1. but; yet 2. merely; only; just

zhǐyào 只要 1. to want only... 2. all one has to do is to...

zhǐyīn 只因 only because; for the simple reason that...

zhǐyǒu 只有 1. to have...only; only; alone 2. to have to (do or be)

zhǐ 旨
1. a purpose; will; intention; an objective 2. an imperial decree 3. good; excellent; beautiful 4. tasty; pleasant to the palate; delicious

zhǐqù 旨趣 purposes and intentions

zhǐyì 旨意 1. will; intention 2. an imperial decree; God's will

zhǐ 沚
a sandy islet in a stream; a small sandbank

zhǐ 址
1. land on which to build a house; a location; a site 2. a foundation

zhǐ 祇(只) also **zhī**
only; merely

zhǐhǎo 祇好 to have to

zhǐyào 祇要 only if

zhǐ 指
1. refer to **zhī**, **zhí** 2. to point; to direct 3. to indicate; to refer to; to mean 4. the number of people 5. intentions 6. the main theme 7. to hope 8. to depend on

zhǐbiāo 指標 1. (mathematics) characteristic 2. an index sign

zhǐdǎo 指導 1. direction or guidance 2. to instruct; to direct; to guide

zhǐdiǎn 指點 to teach; to advise

zhǐdìng 指定 1. to appoint 2. to indicate clearly and with certainty 3. to allot

zhǐfù wéihūn 指腹為婚 a prenatal betrothal

zhǐhuī 指揮 to conduct or direct (an orchestra, etc.); to command (an army, etc.)

zhǐhuīguān 指揮官 the commander

zhǐhuī ruòdìng 指揮若定 to retain full composure even in command of a big operation

zhǐjiāo 指教 1. direction and guidance 2. (a polite expression) your advice or counsel

zhǐkòng 指控 to accuse; to charge

zhǐlìng 指令 a directive

zhǐlù wéimǎ 指鹿為馬 to confound right and wrong

zhǐmíng 指名 to mention by name

zhǐmíng 指明 to indicate clearly; to point out

zhǐmíng dàoxìng 指名道姓 to mention someone's name

zhǐnán 指南 a directory; a guidebook; a primer

zhǐnánzhēn 指南針 a compass

zhǐpài 指派 to appoint; to assign

Z

zhǐrèn 指認 to identify (a suspect, a lost item, etc.) from a group

zhǐrì kědài 指日可待 can be expected very shortly or soon

zhǐsāng màhuái 指桑罵槐 to scold somebody indirectly

zhǐshǐ 指使 to hire or entice another to a task for oneself

zhǐshì 指示 1. instruction; indication 2. to direct; to instruct

zhǐshù 指數 an index; an exponent

zhǐwàng 指望 to hope for; to expect

zhǐwén 指紋 a fingerprint

zhǐxiàng 指向 to point to; to direct to

zhǐyǐn 指引 to direct; to guide; guidance

zhǐyìn 指印 a fingerprint

zhǐzé 指責 to accuse; to censure

zhǐzhēn 指針 1. a guide; a manual 2. an index

zhǐzhèng 指正 1. to correct 2. (a polite expression) to present herewith for your correction

zhǐzhèng 指證 to produce evidence (in court, etc.); to prove

zhǐzhǐ diǎndiǎn 指指點點 1. gesticulating 2. to point; to indicate

zhǐ 咫

1. the foot measure of the Zhou Dynasty (divided into eight inches) 2. near

zhǐchǐ tiānyá 咫尺天涯 so near and yet so far

zhǐ 砥

refer to **dǐ** 砥

zhǐ 紙

paper

zhǐbǎn 紙板 cardboard

zhǐbì 紙幣 paper money; bank notes

zhǐhé 紙盒 a carton; a paper box

zhǐjiāng 紙漿 paper pulp

zhǐpái 紙牌 playing cards

zhǐqián 紙錢 paper money burnt as offerings to the dead

zhǐshàng tánbīng 紙上談兵 impractical schemes; empty talks

zhǐtiáo 紙條 a slip of paper

zhǐzhāng 紙張 paper; sheets of paper

zhǐzuì jīnmí 紙醉金迷 to indulge in a wanton life

zhǐ 趾

1. a toe 2. a foot 3. a footprint; a track

zhǐgāo qìyáng 趾高氣揚 (literally) to walk in a vain, swaggering manner—elated and proud

zhǐjiǎ 趾甲 a toenail

zhǐ 黹

embroidery; needlework

zhǐ 徵

one of the five musical notes in Chinese scale

zhì 至

1. to arrive at; to reach (a destination) 2. very; extremely; to indicate the superlative degree —the most

zhìchéng 至誠 sincere; the greatest sincerity

zhìcǐ 至此 1. to come here 2. to have developed to this point

zhìduō 至多 at (the) most

zhìgāo wúshàng 至高無上 the highest; the most exalted; the supreme

zhìjiāo 至交 one's closest friend

zhìjīn 至今 until now; so far; up to the present time

zhìlǐ míngyán 至理名言 a proverb of lasting value

zhìqīn hǎoyǒu 至親好友 close relatives and dear friends

zhìshǎo 至少 at least; the least

zhìsǐ bùyú 至死不渝 to remain faithful until death

zhìyǒu 至友 the closest friend; a close friend

zhìyú 至於 1. as to; with regard to 2. to the extent of

zhì 志

1. to make up one's mind to pursue some object; to be bent on

doing something 2. will; purpose 3. an ideal; ambition; wish 4. annals; records

zhìbù zàicǐ 志不在此 to have an ambition for things beyond what is presently available or obtainable

zhìdé yìmǎn 志得意滿 fully satisfied or contented; complacent

zhìqi 志氣 ambition; will

zhìqù 志趣 purpose and interest; inclination; a bent

zhìqù xiāngtóu 志趣相投 of similar purpose and interest

zhìshì 志士 1. a man of purpose and virtue 2. a man of high ambitions

zhìshì rénrén 志士仁人 people of purpose and virtues

zhìtóng dàohé 志同道合 to share the same ambition and purpose; of one mind

zhìxiàng 志向 purpose; ambition

zhìyuàn 志願 1. voluntary 2. aspiration; ambition

zhìzài bìdé 志在必得 to get it at any cost

zhìzài qiānlǐ 志在千里 cherishing a great ambition

zhì 炙

to burn; to cauterize; to roast; to broil; to heat

zhìshǒu kěrè 炙手可熱 very influential and powerful

zhì 知（智）

the learned; the wise; brains

zhì 制

1. to establish; to institute; to set up 2. to prevail; to overpower; to control 3. a system 4. used before the signature in letter writing to indicate the writer is in mourning

zhìcái 制裁 to chastise; to sanction

zhìdí jīxiān 制敵機先 to gain an advantage over the enemy by taking steps to forestall him

zhìdìng 制定 to institute; to establish

zhìdù 制度 a system; an institu-

tion

zhìfú 制伏 to subdue; to subjugate; to overcome

zhìfú 制服 a uniform

zhìhéng 制衡 to check and balance

zhìkōngquán 制空權 air supremacy

zhìxiàn 制憲 to draw up a national constitution

zhìyuē 制約 to restrict; to condition

zhìzhǐ 制止 to stop; to prevent

zhì 治

1. (also chí) to administer; to control; to govern; to manage; to rule 2. to regulate; to harness (a river) 3. the seat of the local government 4. to treat (a disease); to cure 5. (also chí) to study 6. (also chí) to punish 7. peaceful and orderly

zhì'ān 治安 public security

zhìběn 治本 to deal with (or cure) a trouble, etc. at the source

zhìbiāo 治標 to cope with the symptoms only

zhìbìng 治病 to treat a disease or ailment

zhìchǎn 治產 to manage property

zhìguó 治國 to govern a nation

zhìjī 治績 the merits or achievements of an administration

zhìjiā 治家 to manage a household

zhìlǐ 治理 1. to administer; to manage; to govern 2. to harness; to regulate

zhìliáo 治療 to treat or cure (a disease); therapy

zhìluàn 治亂 order and disorder; peace and upheaval

zhìluàn xīngwáng 治亂興亡 the rise and fall of a nation

zhìsāng 治喪 to manage a funeral

zhìshì 治世 a time of peace and order as a result of enlightened government

zhìshì 治事 to transact business

zhìxué 治學 to devote oneself to learning

zhìyù 治愈 to succeed in curing a disease; to heal

zhìzhuāng 治裝 to pack or arrange one's baggage before taking a trip

zhìzuì 治罪 to punish a criminal according to law

zhì 致

1. to send; to present; to convey; to transmit; to extend (thanks, etc.) 2. to cause to come; to cause (injury, death, etc.) 3. to achieve; to attain; to amass (fortune) 4. one's principle, interest, hobby, etc. 5. to bring about; to occasion or result in 6. to retire; to resign

zhì'ái wùzhì 致癌物質 (medicine) carcinogen

zhìcí 致辭 to address; to deliver a speech

zhìdiàn 致電 to send a telegram or cable

zhìfù 致富 to become rich

zhìhè 致賀 to extend or offer congratulations

zhìjìng 致敬 to salute

zhìlì 致力 to devote or dedicate oneself to

zhìmìng 致命 1. to sacrifice one's life 2. fatal; fatality

zhìmìngshāng 致命傷 1. a mortal wound 2. vulnerability; the weak point

zhìshì 致仕 to resign from office

zhìsǐ 致死 to cause death; to result in death

zhìxiè 致謝 to offer thanks; to thank

zhìyán wùzhì 致癌物質 refer to **zhì'ái wùzhì** 致癌物質

zhìyì 致意 to convey one's best wishes or regards

zhì 陟

1. to mount; to ascend 2. to advance; to elevate; to promote

zhì 桎

1. fetters; shackles 2. to fetter 3. to suffocate

zhìgù 桎梏 fetters; shackles

zhì 秩

1. order; orderly 2. official ranks 3. official salaries 4. a decade

zhìxù 秩序 1. order 2. arrangement

zhìxù jǐngrán 秩序井然 in perfect order

zhì 痔

piles; hemorrhoids

zhìchuāng 痔瘡 piles; hemorrhoids

zhì 窒

to block; to stop up; to obstruct; to stuff up

zhìxī 窒息 to suffocate; to smother

zhìxí 窒息 refer to **zhìxī** 窒息

zhì 智

1. talented; capable; intelligent; clever; wisdom; wit 2. prudence 3. a Chinese family name

zhìhuì 智慧 wisdom; intelligence

zhìhuì cáichǎn quán 智慧財產權 intellectual property rights

zhìlì 智力 intelligence

Zhìlì 智利 Chile, or Chili

zhìlì cèyàn 智力測驗 an intelligence test; an IQ test

zhìlì shāngshù 智力商數 intelligence quotient (I.Q.)

zhìmóu 智謀 tactics; strategy

zhìnáng 智囊 a wise person; a wise advisor

zhìnángtuán 智囊團 a brain trust; a think tank

zhìnéng 智能 intelligence and capability

zhìnéng bùzú 智能不足 mental retardation

zhìyǒng shuāngquán 智勇雙全 both intelligent and brave

zhì 痣

a mole; nevus

zhì 稚

young and tender; small; delicate; immature; childish

zhìnèn 稚嫩 1. tender and deli-

cate 2. young and tender

zhìqì 稚氣 innocence of a child; childishness

zhìzi 稚子 young children

zhì 置

1. to put; to place 2. to establish; to set 3. to procure; to purchase

zhìchǎn 置產 to buy an estate

zhìshēn shìwài 置身事外 to stay away from an affair

zhìxìn 置信 to believe

zhìyí 置疑 to doubt

zhìzhī bùlǐ 置之不理 to disregard it totally; to ignore

zhìzhī dùwài 置之度外 to give no thought to

zhì 雉

1. a pheasant 2. a unit of volume measure in ancient China (about 30′ square by 10′)

zhì 製

1. to produce; to manufacture; to make; to create 2. to compose (writings, literature, etc.); literary works 3. to cut out garments and make them 4. a form; a model; a pattern

zhìbǎn 製版 to make a printing plate

zhìpǐn 製品 products; manufactures

zhìtú 製圖 to make (or draw) maps, charts, etc.

zhìzào 製造 to produce; to manufacture; to make; to create

zhìzuò 製作 to make; to produce; to manufacture

zhìzuòrén 製作人 a producer

zhì 誌

1. to write down; to put down; to record 2. a record

zhì'āi 誌哀 to condole

zhìqìng 誌慶 to offer congratulations

zhìxǐ 誌喜 to offer congratulations

zhì 滯

at a standstill; stagnant; impeded; blocked; stationary

zhì'ài 滯礙 to obstruct; to impede

zhìliú 滯留 1. to remain at a standstill 2. to loiter; to detain

zhìmèn 滯悶 to have pent-up feeling

zhìxiāo 滯銷 sales slump

zhì 幟

1. a flag; a pennant; a pennon 2. a mark; a sign

zhì 質

1. to pawn 2. a pledge; a hostage 3. (also **zhí**) matters; substances; elements 4. (also **zhí**) one's disposition or temperament; qualities 5. (also **zhí**) simple; plain 6. (also **zhí**) to question 7. (also **zhí**) to confront

zhìdì 質地 1. quality of something 2. one's disposition or endowments 3. material of piece goods

zhìliàng 質量 1. (physics) mass 2. quality

zhìliàng guǎnlǐ 質量管理 quality control

zhìliào 質料 quality; raw materials

zhìpú 質樸 refer to **zhìpǔ** 質樸

zhìpǔ 質樸 simple and unadorned

zhìwèn 質問 1. to interrogate 2. to raise questions in order to resolve one's doubt

zhìxún 質詢 to interpellate; interpellation

zhìyā 質押 to mortgage

zhìyí 質疑 to question; to query

zhì 緻

fine; close; dense; delicate

zhì 摯

1. sincere; cordial 2. a Chinese family name

zhìyǒu 摯友 a bosom friend

zhì 櫛 also **jié**

1. a comb; a comb of many fine teeth 2. to comb the hair 3. to weed out; to eliminate; to delete

zhìbǐ 櫛比 (said of houses) joined closely together

zhìfēng mùyǔ 櫛風沐雨 hardworking; industrious

zhì 擲 also **zhī, zhí**

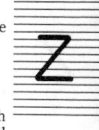

to throw; to cast

zhìbiāoqiāng 擲標槍 (sports) 1. javelin throw 2. to throw the javelin

zhìqiānqiú 擲鉛球 (sports) shot put

zhìtiěbǐng 擲鐵餅 (sports) discus throw

zhōng 中

1. the middle; among; within; between 2. China or Chinese; Sino-

zhōngbù 中部 the central part; the middle part

Zhōngcài 中菜 Chinese dishes

zhōngcān 中餐 1. a midday meal 2. Chinese meal

zhōngchǎn jiējí 中產階級 the middle class; bourgeois

zhōngchuò 中輟 to give up halfway

zhōngděng 中等 middle-class; medium

zhōngděng jiàoyù 中等教育 secondary education

Zhōngdōng 中東 the Middle East (Asia)

zhōngduàn 中斷 suspension; interruption

zhōngduì 中隊 1. a squadron 2. a unit composed of several groups

zhōngfàn 中飯 lunch; luncheon

zhōngfēng 中鋒 the center (in basketball, soccer, military operations, etc.)

zhōnggǔ 中古 the Middle Ages; medieval

Zhōngguó 中國 1. China; Cathay 2. the Middle Kingdom

Zhōngguóchéng 中國城 Chinatown

Zhōngguóhuà 中國話 Chinese; the Chinese language

zhōnghé 中和 1. justice and peace 2. (chemistry) to neutralize

zhōnghé zuòyòng 中和作用 neutralization

Zhōnghuá 中華 (originally, the region along the Yellow River where the Chinese people thrived) the Chinese nation; the

Chinese people

zhōngjí 中級 middle rank; intermediate

zhōngjìzhàn 中繼站 a relay station

zhōngjiān 中堅 1. the main force (of an army); crack troops 2. a cadre; underpinning

zhōngjiān 中間 in the middle; in the center

zhōngjiānpài 中間派 the middle-of-the-roaders

zhōngjiānrén 中間人 a middleman; a mediator; an agent

zhōngjiàng 中將 (army, marine and air force) lieutenant general; (navy) viceadmiral

zhōnglì 中立 neutral; neutrality

zhōnglìguó 中立國 a neutral nation

zhōngliàngjí 中量級 (sports) middle weight

zhōngluò 中落 a sudden fall of one's family fortune; to decline

Zhōng Měizhōu 中美洲 Central America

Zhōngnán Bàndǎo 中南半島 Indochina

zhōngnián 中年 middle age

Zhōng Ōu 中歐 the central part of Europe

zhōngpiān xiǎoshuō 中篇小說 a novelette

Zhōngqiūjié 中秋節 the Mid-Autumn Festival or the Moon Festival

Zhōng Rì Zhànzhēng 中日戰爭 the Sino-Japanese War

Zhōngshā Qúndǎo 中沙群島 the Zhongsha Islands

Zhōngshānlíng 中山陵 Dr. Sun Yat-sen Mausoleum

zhōngshì 中士 a sergeant

Zhōngshì 中式 the Chinese style or fashion

zhōngshū 中樞 the central administration

zhōngtíqín 中提琴 a viola

zhōngtú 中途 midway; halfway; on the way

Zhōngwài 中外 Chinese and foreign

zhōngwàiyěshǒu 中外野手 (baseball) a center fielder

zhōngwèi 中尉 (army and air force) first lieutenant; (navy) lieutenant

Zhōngwén 中文 the Chinese language

zhōngwǔ 中午 noon; high noon; midday

Zhōng Xī hébì 中西合璧 a (good) combination or blending of Chinese and Western (fashion, style, etc.)

zhōngxiàn 中線 (sports) the center line; halfway line

zhōngxiào 中校 (army and air force) lieutenant colonel; (navy) commander

zhōngxīn 中心 1. center 2. central point

zhōngxīn rénwù 中心人物 the central (or key) figure

zhōngxīn sīxiǎng 中心思想 the gist; a central idea or thought

zhōngxīng 中興 revival (of a nation or family); rejuvenation; resurgence

zhōngxíng 中型 medium-sized; middle-sized

zhōngxìng 中性 1. (chemistry) neutral(ity) 2. (grammar) the neuter gender

zhōngxué 中學 middle school; secondary school; high school

zhōngxún 中旬 the middle part of a month

Zhōng Yà 中亞 Central Asia

zhōngyāng 中央 the center; the middle

zhōngyāng jíquán 中央集權 a centralized government

Zhōngyāng Qíngbàojú 中央情報局 Central Intelligence Agency (CIA)

zhōngyāng yùsuàn 中央預算 the central budget

Zhōngyāng Zhèngfǔ 中央政府 Central Government

Zhōngyào 中藥 Chinese medicine (mostly herbs)

Zhōngyī 中醫 a Chinese herb doctor

zhōngyōng 中庸 mediocre

zhōngyuán 中原 1. the Central Plains—the downstream regions of the Yellow River 2. the midst of a plain

Zhōngyuánjié 中元節 the Ghost Festival on the 15th day of the seventh lunar month

zhōngzhǐ 中止 to suspend; to interrupt

zhōngzhǐ 中指 the middle finger

zhōngzǐ 中子 neutron

zhōng 忪
1. agitated 2. frightened

zhōng 忠
1. faithful; loyal; sincere; patriotic 2. devoted; honest

zhōngchéng 忠誠 loyal; faithful; staunch

zhōnggān yìdǎn 忠肝義膽 having good faith, virtue and patriotism

zhōnggào 忠告 honest or sincere advice; sincere counsel

zhōnghòu 忠厚 honest and tolerant; kind and big-hearted

zhōngliáng 忠良 1. faithful and honest 2. virtuous persons

zhōngliè 忠烈 to be loyal till death; martyrdom

zhōngliècí 忠烈祠 a martyrs' shrine

zhōngshí 忠實 1. loyal and faithful 2. reliable or truthful (reports, etc.)

zhōngxiào liǎngquán 忠孝兩全 both loyal to one's country and filial to one's parents

zhōngxīn 忠心 loyalty; faithfulness; sincerity

zhōngxīn gěnggěng 忠心耿耿 loyal, faithful and true

zhōngxìn 忠信 faithful and honest

zhōngyán nì'ěr 忠言逆耳 Truth seldom sounds pleasant.

zhōngyì 忠義 1. faithful and virtuous 2. people of loyalty and virtue

zhōngyǒng 忠勇 loyal and courageous

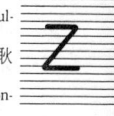

zhōngzhēn 忠貞 loyal (subjects, etc.); patriotic

zhōngzhēn bù'èr 忠貞不貳 the loyalty that can stand all tests and trials

zhōng 盅

a small cup

zhōng 衷

1. the bottom of one's heart; honest; sincere 2. good and virtuous; goodness 3. proper; appropriate; befitting; propriety 4. undergarments

zhōngcháng 衷腸 innermost feelings; sincere words

zhōngqū 衷曲 the voice of one's heart; inner feelings; words from the bottom of one's heart

zhōngqǔ 衷曲 refer to **zhōngqū** 衷曲

zhōngxīn 衷心 cordial; heartfelt; wholehearted

zhōngxīn gǎnxiè 衷心感謝 to thank sincerely

zhōng 終

1. the end; to come to the end; the conclusion 2. death; to die 3. finally; at last; in the end; after all 4. whole; all

zhōngdiǎn 終點 1. the terminus; the final point; the end; a destination 2. (sports) finish

zhōngduānjī 終端機 a terminal

zhōngguī 終歸 1. the conclusion; to end or conclude 2. finally; after all; at last

zhōngjí 終極 the finality or end

zhōngjié 終結 the end, conclusion, termination, etc.

zhōnglǎo 終老 throughout one's life; until death

zhōngliǎo 終了 to end; to complete; to conclude; to terminate

zhōngnián 終年 1. the whole year; throughout the year 2. the age at which one dies

zhōngqí yīshēng 終其一生 throughout one's life

zhōngrì 終日 throughout the day

zhōngshēn bànlǚ 終身伴侶 a life company—wife or husband

zhōngshēn shìyè 終身事業 a lifelong career

zhōngshēng 終生 the whole life

zhōngxū 終須 to have to...in the end

zhōngyú 終於 in the end; finally; at last

zhōngzhàn 終站 the terminal stop or station

zhōngzhǐ 終止 to stop; to end

zhōng 鍾

1. a kind of wine container 2. to concentrate; to accumulate 3. a Chinese family name

zhōng'ài 鍾愛 to cherish; to dote on; to love deeply (especially children)

zhōngqíng 鍾情 to fall in love

zhōng 鐘

1. a bell (which tolls as distinct from that which jingles) 2. a clock 3. a Chinese family name

zhōngbǎi 鐘擺 a pendulum

zhōngbiǎo 鐘錶 a timepiece; a clock and a watch

zhōngbiǎodiàn 鐘錶店 a watchmaker's shop

zhōngdiǎnfèi 鐘點費 remuneration paid by the hour

zhōnglóu 鐘樓 a bell tower; a belfry

zhōngrǔshí 鐘乳石 a stalactite

zhōngshēng 鐘聲 the toll of a bell

zhōngtóu 鐘頭 an hour

zhǒng 冢

1. a high grave 2. a peak; a summit 3. the eldest 4. great; supreme; prime

zhǒng 腫

to swell; a swelling; a boil

zhǒngliú 腫瘤 (medicine) a tumor

zhǒngzhàng 腫脹 to swell; swelling

zhǒng 塚

a high tomb; a mound; a grave

zhǒng 種

1. seeds of grain 2. races (of

human beings) 3. descendants; posterity 4. a species; a genus; a kind or sort

zhǒnglèi 種類 a sort, kind, variety or class

zhǒngzhǒng 種種 1. various kinds 2. shortcropped hair 3. simple and sincere (as rural people)

zhǒngzǐ 種子 a seed

zhǒngzú 種族 (said of people) a race or tribe

zhǒngzú qíshì 種族歧視 racial discrimination

zhǒng 踵

1. the heel 2. to follow 3. to call personally at; to go personally to; to call in person

zhǒngzhì 踵至 to arrive just behind

zhòng 中

1. to hit (the target); to attain (a goal) 2. to be hit by; to be affected by

zhòngdàn 中彈 to get shot

zhòngdì 中的 to hit the bull's-eye

zhòngdú 中毒 to be poisoned; toxicosis

zhòngfēng 中風 to suffer from a stroke of paralysis or apoplexy

zhòngjì 中計 to walk (or fall) into a trap

zhòngjiǎng 中獎 to win a (lottery) prize

zhòngkàn 中看 good to look at

zhòngkěn 中肯 to the point; fair; relevant

zhòngqiān 中籤 to be chosen by lot

zhòngshāng 中傷 to hurt somebody insidiously

zhòngshǔ 中暑 to have a sunstroke

zhòngtīng 中聽 pleasant to the ear

zhòngxuǎn 中選 to be chosen; to be selected

zhòngyì 中意 to suit one's fancy; agreeable

zhòngyòng 中用 useful; serviceable

zhòng 仲

1. in the middle; between two entities 2. the second in order of birth

zhòngcái 仲裁 to arbitrate; arbitration

zhòngchūn 仲春 midspring

zhòngdōng 仲冬 midwinter

zhòngqiū 仲秋 midautumn

zhòngxià 仲夏 midsummer

zhòng 重

1. heavy; weighty; much 2. to weigh; weight 3. difficult 4. serious; grave 5. severe 6. important; significant 7. to value; to emphasize

zhòngbìng 重病 a serious illness

zhòngchóu 重酬 a substantial reward; a handsome reward

zhòngchuāng 重創 1. a serious wound 2. to inflict a severe blow on (the enemy)

zhòngchuāng 重創 refer to zhòngchuāng 重創 2

zhòngdà 重大 1. important; of great consequence; significant 2. serious; grave

zhòngdàn 重擔 a heavy burden (or responsibility)

zhòngdiǎn 重點 the point or center of emphasis

zhòngdú 重讀 to stress

zhòngfàn 重犯 an important criminal; a criminal who is guilty of a serious crime

zhònggōngyè 重工業 heavy industry

zhòngjīn lǐpìn 重金禮聘 to employ with good pay

zhòngjīnshǔ 重金屬 heavy metals

zhònglì 重力 gravity

zhòngliàng 重量 weight

zhòngrèn 重任 an important mission; an important office or post

zhòngshāng 重傷 a serious injury

zhòngshǎng 重賞 to reward

generously

zhòngshǎng zhīxià, bìyǒu yǒngfū 重賞之下，必有勇夫 Generous rewards rouse one to heroism.

zhòngshì 重視 to pay much attention to; to consider important

zhòngtīng 重聽 weak in hearing; hard of hearing

zhòngtóuxì 重頭戲 1. a play involving much singing and action 2. a role involving much singing and action

zhòngxīn 重心 the center of gravity

zhòngxíng 重刑 severe punishment

zhòngyào 重要 important; significant; vital

zhòngyìqi 重義氣 particular about loyalty to friends

zhòngyīn 重音 (phonetics) accent; stress

zhòngyòng 重用 to give (someone) an important assignment

zhòngyú Tàishān 重於泰山 (literally) heavier than Mount Tai—very weighty; very important

zhòngzhèn 重鎮 1. key positions (in military operations); an important city 2. a key figure

zhòng 眾

1. many; numerous 2. a crowd; a multitude; all; the masses 3. public or popular (opinion, views, etc.)

zhòngduō 眾多 numerous

zhòngkǒu shuòjīn 眾口鑠金 public clamour can confound right and wrong

zhòngmù kuíkuí 眾目睽睽 the glare of the public; the public gaze

zhòngpàn qīnlí 眾叛親離 (said of a dictator at his downfall) opposed by the masses and deserted by followers—to be utterly isolated

zhòngrén 眾人 all people; the multitude

zhòngshēng 眾生 1. all living creatures 2. beasts or animals

zhòngshǐ zhīdì 眾矢之的 the target of public censure (or attacks)

zhòngshuō fēnyún 眾說紛紜 Opinions vary.

zhòngsuǒ zhōuzhī 眾所週知 universally known; as everyone knows

zhòngwàng suǒguī 眾望所歸 to command public respect and support

zhòngyì fēnyún 眾議紛紜 Public opinions or views are divergent.

zhòng 種

1. to plant; to sow; to cultivate 2. to vaccinate

zhòngdòu 種痘 vaccination (against smallpox); to vaccinate

zhòngguā déguā, zhòngdòu dédòu 種瓜得瓜，種豆得豆 One reaps what he sows.

zhòngtián 種田 to farm; to till the land

zhòngzhí 種植 to plant

zhōu 舟

a boat; a ship; a vessel

zhōují 舟楫 1. a ship; a vessel 2. a capable assistant

zhōu 州

1. an administrative district in ancient China 2. (Zhou Dynasty) a region with 2,500 families 3. (in old China) a county 4. a state (in the USA) 5. a place surrounded by water; an islet; a sand bar

zhōuxiàn 州縣 a county within an administrative district

zhōuzhǎng 州長 a governor

zhōu 周

1. the Zhou Dynasty 2. a circumference; a circuit 3. complete 4. all around; everywhere 5. to aid; to provide for 6. a Chinese family name

zhōubào 周報 a weekly

zhōubiān shèbèi 周邊設備 (computer) peripheral device

zhōudao 周到 thorough; considerate

zhōujì 周濟 to help the poor with money

zhōukān 周刊 a weekly

zhōumì 周密 careful and thorough

zhōumò 周末 the weekend

zhōunián 周年 an anniversary

zhōuqī 周期 a period; a cycle

zhōuqī 周期 refer to **zhōuqī** 週期

zhōuquán 周全 1. to aid; to help 2. complete with all that is desired

zhōusuì 周歲 one full year of life

zhōuwéi 周圍 1. surroundings; environment 2. the circumference

zhōuxiáng 周詳 complete and detailed

zhōuxuán 周旋 1. to attend to guests or friends 2. to deal with; to fight

zhōuxuán dàodǐ 周旋到底 (said of litigation, quarrels, etc.) to fight to the end

zhōuzāo 周遭 around

zhōuzhé 周折 a complicated or troublesome course of development

zhōuzhuǎn bùlíng 周轉不靈 (said of business firms) to be in financial straits

zhōu 洲
1. an island in a river 2. a continent

zhōujì dàndào fēidàn 洲際彈道飛彈 the intercontinental ballistic missile; the ICBM

zhōuzhǔ 洲渚 an island in a river

zhōu 週
1. a week; a period 2. a cycle; a revolution; to revolve

zhōudao 週到 (often said of service, etc.) thoughtful; considerate

zhōu'ér fùshǐ 週而復始 to repeat the cycle all over again

zhōuhuì 週會 a weekly meeting

zhōukān 週刊 a weekly periodical; a weekly

zhōumì 週密 careful; thorough

zhōumò 週末 a weekend

zhōunián 週年 a full year; an anniversary

zhōunián jìniàn 週年紀念 commemoration of an anniversary

zhōuqī 週期 a period; a cycle

zhōuqī 週期 refer to **zhōuqī** 週期

zhōuquán 週全 1. complete and perfect 2. to help; assistance

zhōusuì 週歲 a full year (especially said of a child's age)

zhōuzhuǎn 週轉 1. circulating or revolving (funds) 2. to have enough to meet the need

zhōu 粥 also **zhù**
congee; rice gruel

zhōushǎo sēngduō 粥少僧多 (literally) The congee is not enough for the many monks —not enough for circulation or distribution

zhōu 賙
to give; to aid; to relieve

zhōujì 賙濟 to relieve the needy

zhóu 妯
sisters-in-law

zhóuli 妯娌 sisters-in-law (a reference among the wives of one's husband's brothers)

zhóu 軸 also **zhòu**, **zhú**
1. an axis; a pivot; an axle 2. (said of mounted paintings or calligraphic works) a scroll

zhóuxīn 軸心 an axis

zhǒu 肘
1. the elbow 2. to catch one by the elbow

zhǒuzi 肘子 1. the upper part of a leg of pork 2. the elbow

zhǒu 帚
a broom; a besom

zhòu 咒
1. to curse; to swear 2. words used as charms by Buddhist monks or Taoist priests to exorcize ghosts

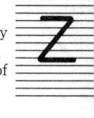

zhòumà 咒罵 to swear at; to curse

zhòuyǔ 咒語 1. curses; imprecations 2. exorcism; incantation 3. hocus-pocus

zhòu 宙

infinite time; time without beginning or end; eternity

zhòu 紂

1. the last emperor of the Yin Dynasty, whose name stands for tyranny 2. the crupper of a saddle

zhòu 胄

1. descendants; posterity; offspring 2. the eldest (son, etc.) 3. a helmet

zhòujiǎ 胄甲 a helmet and armor

zhòu 晝

day; daytime; daylight

zhòuqǐn 晝寢 to take a nap; a siesta

zhòuyè 晝夜 day and night

zhòu 軸

refer to **zhóu** 軸

zhòu 皺

1. wrinkles; creases; folds; rumples 2. to wrinkle; to fold; to contract; to crease; to crumple

zhòuméitóu 皺眉頭 to frown; to knit the brows

zhòuwén 皺紋 wrinkles; creases; folds; rumples

zhòuwénzhǐ 皺紋紙 crepe paper

zhòu 縐

1. crepe; crape 2. wrinkled; crinkled; creased

zhòushā 縐紗 crepe silk

zhòu 驟 also zòu

1. to gallop 2. swift; sudden 3. frequent

zhòujiàng 驟降 a rapid fall (of snow)

zhòurán 驟然 suddenly

zhòuzhì 驟至 to arrive suddenly

zhū 朱

1. red; vermilion 2. a Chinese family name

zhūhóng 朱紅 bright red; vermilion

zhūmén 朱門 rich and influential families

zhūpī 朱批 writing comments or remarks in red with a brush

zhūshā 朱砂 cinnabar

zhū 侏

1. short 2. a pigmy or dwarf

zhūrú 侏儒 1. a dwarf 2. a court jester

zhū 珠

1. a pearl 2. a bead; a drop 3. the pupil of the eye

zhūbǎo 珠寶 jewelry; pearls and valuables

zhūguāng bǎoqì 珠光寶氣 to be richly bejeweled

zhūjī 珠璣 exquisite or excellent wording of a piece of writing

zhūlián bìhé 珠聯璧合 an excellent match

zhūsuàn 珠算 calculation with an abacus

zhūtāi ànjié 珠胎暗結 to be pregnant (as a result of a love affair)

zhūyuán yùrùn 珠圓玉潤 1. smooth and sweet (voice) 2. smooth and easy (style in writing)

zhū 株

1. a tree; a numeral auxiliary for counting trees or similar things 2. roots that grow above the ground

zhūlián 株連 to involve others in a crime one committed

zhū 硃

1. vermilion 2. imperial (the signature and instructions of an emperor were written in red)

zhūpī 硃批 an imperial rescript

zhūshā 硃砂 cinnabar

zhūshāzhì 硃砂痣 a red mole

zhū 蛛

a spider

zhūsī mǎjī 蛛絲馬跡 clues;

leads

zhūwǎng 蛛網 a spider's web; a cobweb

zhū 誅
1. to kill; to execute; execution 2. to punish 3. to weed out; to exterminate

zhūmiè 誅滅 to eliminate; to eradicate

zhū 銖
1. an ancient unit of weight; the ancient coinage of Han 2. blunt; dull

zhū 豬
1. a pig; a hog 2. a pigheaded person

zhūgān 豬肝 pig's liver

zhūjuàn 豬圈 a pigsty; a pigpen; a hogpen

zhūpái 豬排 a pork chop

zhūròu 豬肉 pork

zhūyóu 豬油 lard

zhūzōng 豬鬃 hog's bristles

zhū 諸
1. all; various 2. in, to, from, etc.

zhūduō 諸多 many; numerous

zhūhóu 諸侯 the feudal princes; dukes or princes under an emperor

zhūrú 諸如 such as

zhūrú cǐlèi 諸如此類 various things like this

zhūwèi 諸位 Ladies and Gentlemen!

zhūzǐ bǎijiā 諸子百家 the numerous schools of thinkers, or their works in the late Zhou Dynasty

zhú 竹
1. bamboo 2. slips of bamboo for writing

zhúfá 竹筏 a bamboo raft

zhúgān 竹竿 a bamboo pole or cane

zhúlán 竹籃 a bamboo basket

zhúlín 竹林 a bamboo grove

zhúsǔn 竹筍 a bamboo shoot

zhútǒng 竹筒 a bamboo tube

zhúyǐ 竹椅 a bamboo chair

zhú 逐
1. to chase; to pursue; to follow 2. to drive off; to banish; to exile; to expel 3. little by little; gradually

zhúbù 逐步 step by step; to proceed orderly

zhújiàn 逐漸 little by little; gradually; by degrees

zhúkèlìng 逐客令 an announcement to a visitor that he is unwelcome

zhúlì 逐利 to pursue material gains

zhúnián 逐年 year by year; year after year

zhúzì 逐字 word by word; word for word

zhú 軸
refer to **zhóu** 軸

zhú 筑
1. an alternative name of Guiyang 2. refer to **zhù** 築

zhú 燭
1. a candle 2. to illuminate; to shine upon

zhúguāng 燭光 1. (physics) candle power 2. candlelight

zhútái 燭臺 a candlestick; a candlestand

zhúxīn 燭心 candlewick

zhúxìn 燭芯 candlewick

zhǔ 主
1. a master; a leader; a chief; a host 2. Jesus Christ; God; Lord 3. to officiate at; to preside over; to take charge of 4. main; chief; primary; principal

zhǔbàn 主辦 to sponsor; to take charge of

zhǔbǐ 主筆 an editorial writer of a newspaper

zhǔbiān 主編 an editor in chief

zhǔchí 主持 to officiate at; to preside over

zhǔchí zhèngyì 主持正義 to uphold justice

zhǔcí 主詞 the subject

zhǔcóng 主從 1. the master and his servant 2. the principal and

the secondary (criminals)

zhǔcún 主存 (computer) main memory

zhǔdǎo 主導 leading; dominant; guiding

zhǔdòng 主動 to take the initiative

zhǔdòngmài 主動脈 (anatomy) the aorta

zhǔfàn 主犯 the principal criminal

zhǔfù 主婦 a housewife; a hostess

zhǔgàn 主幹 1. the trunk 2. the main force

zhǔgù 主顧 a customer; a client

zhǔguān 主觀 the subjective point of view

zhǔguǎn 主管 1. the boss; the chief 2. to take charge of

zhǔhūn 主婚 to preside over a wedding ceremony

zhǔhūnrén 主婚人 the guardians of the marrying couple at a wedding ceremony

zhǔjì 主祭 1. to officiate at a religious rite or service 2. a person officiating at such a service

zhǔjìshì 主計室 the auditing department

zhǔjìyìtǐ 主記憶體 (computer) main memory

zhǔjiàn 主見 the ideas or thoughts of one's view

zhǔjiǎng 主講 1. to lecture; to speak on a special subject 2. the main speaker

zhǔjiàng 主將 1. the commanding general 2. the most important athlete in a sports team

zhǔjiào 主教 a bishop

zhǔjué 主角 the leading player; the leading character in a novel; a hero or heroine; a protagonist

zhǔkè 主客 the guest of honor

zhǔlì 主力 the main force

zhǔlìjiàn 主力艦 a battleship; a capital ship

zhǔlìjūn 主力軍 the main force

zhǔliáng 主糧 the staple food grain

zhǔliú 主流 1. the mainstream 2.

the essential or main aspect

zhǔmóu 主謀 the mastermind

zhǔnǎo 主腦 the mastermind; the chief; the leader

zhǔpú 主僕 master and servant

zhǔquán 主權 1. sovereignty 2. the right of autonomy

zhǔrén 主人 1. an owner 2. a host 3. a master

zhǔréngōng 主人公 the leading character in a novel; a hero or heroine; a protagonist

zhǔrénwēng 主人翁 1. a respectful term for a host 2. a master

zhǔrèn 主任 the head of an office

zhǔshí 主食 staple food

zhǔshǐ 主使 a mastermind; a ringleader

zhǔshuài 主帥 an address to the commander in chief

zhǔsuí kèbiàn 主隨客便 A host respects his guest's wishes.

zhǔtí 主題 the main theme (of an essay); the gist

zhǔtǐ 主體 1. the subjective (as against the objective) 2. the main body or the most important part of something

zhǔxí 主席 a chairman; a president

zhǔxiū 主修 to specialize in (a subject); to major

zhǔyǎn 主演 to star; to play the leading role in a play or a motion picture

zhǔyào 主要 essential; important; major

zhǔyì 主意 an idea; a suggestion

zhǔyì 主義 a principle; a doctrine

zhǔyīn 主因 the major (or principal) cause

zhǔzǎi 主宰 1. the man in charge 2. a god

zhǔzhànpài 主戰派 the hawks

zhǔzhāng 主張 1. an opinion 2. to advocate

zhǔzhèng 主政 1. to head the administration 2. the person in charge

Z

zhǔzhǐ 主旨 the gist, substance, or purport

zhǔzhì yīshī 主治醫師 a physician in charge of a case

zhǔzi 主子 1. the emperor 2. one's master

zhǔ 貯

refer to **zhù** 貯

zhǔ 渚

a sand bar in a river

zhǔ 煮

to cook; to boil; to stew; to decoct

zhǔcài 煮菜 to prepare food or dishes

zhǔdòu ránqí 煮豆燃其 fraternal persecution

zhǔfàn 煮飯 to cook rice; to cook meals

zhǔfèi 煮沸 to boil

zhǔhè fénqín 煮鶴焚琴 to destroy something fine by behaving rudely

zhǔlàn 煮爛 to stew something until it's tender

zhǔshú 煮熟 to cook thoroughly

zhǔ 麈

1. a kind of deer 2. to whisk; to dust

zhǔwěi 麈尾 a duster

zhǔ 屬

1. to compose (a piece of writing) 2. to instruct

zhǔmù 屬目 to gaze; to look at eagerly

zhǔtuō 屬託 to ask or instruct somebody to do something

zhǔyì 屬意 to have a preference for

zhǔ 囑

to ask another to do something; to instruct; to enjoin; to direct; to entrust; to charge

zhǔfu 囑咐 to instruct or bid (a person to do something)

zhǔtuō 囑託 to entrust (a person with a task); to request (a person to do something)

zhǔ 矚

to watch; to observe or gaze at carefully; to pay attention to

zhǔmù 矚目 to be the focus of attention

zhù 住

1. to dwell; to inhabit; to live 2. to stop 3. used after verb to complement its meaning

zhùchù 住處 a residence; a dwelling; lodging; a domicile

zhùhù 住戶 a resident family

zhùjiā 住家 a residence; a home

zhùkǒu 住口 1. to stop talking 2. Shut up!

zhùshǒu 住手 1. Stop! 2. to halt; to hold

zhùsù 住宿 to stay overnight; to lodge

zhùyuàn 住院 to be hospitalized

zhùyuàn yīshī 住院醫師 a resident (in a hospital)

zhùzhái 住宅 a residence; a dwelling; a house

zhùzháiqū 住宅區 a residential area, district or quarter

zhùzhǐ 住址 address

zhù 助

to help; to aid; to assist; help; assistance

zhùchǎnshì 助產士 a midwife

zhùdòngcí 助動詞 an auxiliary verb

zhùjiào 助教 a teaching assistant; a TA

zhùlǐ 助理 1. an assistant 2. to assist

zhùpǎo 助跑 a run-up; an approach

zhùshǒu 助手 an assistant; a helper; an aide

zhùtīngqì 助聽器 an audiophone

zhùxìng 助興 to liven things up; to add to the amusement

zhùxuéjīn 助學金 a stipend; a scholarship

zhùzhǎng 助長 to encourage (a tendency); to promote the development of

zhùzhèn 助陣 to cheer or root for

zhù Zhòu wéinüè 助紂爲虐

to help the wicked perpetrate wicked deeds; to help a tyrant to do evil

zhù 佇(竚)

1. to stand (for a long time) 2. to hope; to expect

zhùlì 佇立 to stand still; to stand motionless

zhù 注

1. to pour (liquid) 2. to concentrate; to engross; preoccupation 3. (註) to annotate 4. stakes (in gambling)

zhùdìng 注定 to be doomed; to be destined

zhùjiě 注解 1. to annotate 2. a footnote; an annotation

zhùmù 注目 to gaze at; to stare at

zhùmùlǐ 注目禮 (military) a parade salute

zhùrù 注入 to pour into; to empty into

zhùshè 注射 to inject; to get a shot

zhùshì 注視 to look attentively

zhùshì 注釋 1. to annotate 2. a footnote; an annotation

zhùshū 注疏 notes and commentaries

zhùxiāo 注銷 to nullify; to cancel; to annul

zhùyì 注意 to pay attention to; to watch

zhùyìlì 注意力 attention

zhùyīn 注音 to make phonetic transcriptions

Zhùyīn Fúhào 注音符號 the National Phonetic Symbols (for Mandarin)

zhùzhòng 注重 to lay stress on; to emphasize

zhù 柱

1. a pillar; a post 2. a cylinder 3. to support 4. to stab; to pierce

zhùláng 柱廊 a colonnade

zhùzi 柱子 a pillar; a post

zhù 祝

1. to wish someone happiness; to pray for happiness 2. to congratulate; to felicitate 3. to celebrate

4. a Chinese family name

zhùfú 祝福 1. to bless 2. to wish happiness to

zhùhè 祝賀 to congratulate; to felicitate; congratulations

zhùróng 祝融 the god of fire

zhùshòu 祝壽 to celebrate someone's birthday

zhù 蛀

1. worms that eat into wood or books 2. (said of worms) to eat into; to bore

zhùchǐ 蛀齒 decayed teeth; dental caries

zhùchóng 蛀蟲 a moth

zhùyá 蛀牙 decayed teeth; dental caries

zhù 粥

refer to **zhōu** 粥

zhù 註

1. (注) an explanatory note; a footnote; a commentary or remark 2. to register; to record or list

zhùcè 註冊 to register; registration

zhùcè shāngbiāo 註冊商標 a registered trademark

zhùdìng 註定 destined; predestined doomed

zhùjiǎo 註脚 an explanatory note; a footnote

zhùjiě 註解 an explanatory note; to explain

zhùmíng 註明 to explain or state clearly in writing

zhùshì 註釋 an explanatory note

zhùxiāo 註銷 to cancel; to nullify; to annul

zhù 貯 also **zhǔ**

to store zp; to hoard; to save up; to deposit

zhùcáng 貯藏 1. to store up; to hoard 2. (mineral) deposits

zhùcángshì 貯藏室 a storage room

zhùcún 貯存 to store up; to stockpile; to deposit

zhùshuǐchí 貯水池 a pond for storing water; a reservoir

zhùxù 貯蓄 to store up; to hoard

zhù 著
1. apparent; obvious; famous 2. to write; to author 3. writings; a literary work; books 4. to set forth; to manifest; to make known

zhùchēng 著稱 famous; renowned; celebrated

zhùmíng 著名 famous; renowned; celebrated

zhùshù 著述 1. to write 2. a literary work

zhùzuò 著作 1. to write 2. a literary work

zhùzuòquán 著作權 copyright

zhù 箸
chopsticks

zhù 駐
1. to halt 2. to remain temporarily; to station (troops, diplomatic representatives, etc.)

zhùbīng 駐兵 to station troops

zhùfáng 駐防 to garrison (a place)

zhùjūn 駐軍 1. to station troops 2. an occupation force 3. a garrison; garrison troops

zhùshǒu 駐守 to station troops at a place for defense purpose

zhùtún 駐屯 (said of troops) to be stationed at

zhùyán 駐顏 to preserve a youthful complexion

zhùyán yǒushù 駐顏有術 to possess the secret of preserving a youthful complexion

zhùzhá 駐紮 (said of troops) to be stationed at

zhù 築 also **zhú**
to build (out of earth, rock, etc.)

zhùcháo 築巢 to build a nest

zhùdī 築堤 to build a dike or embankment

zhùlù 築路 to build roads

zhùtí 築堤 refer to **zhùdī** 築堤

zhù 鑄
1. to melt or cast metal; to coin; to mint 2. to make or commit (blunders, etc.) 3. to educate and

influence (a person) 4. a Chinese family name

zhùchéng dàcuò 鑄成大錯 to commit a serious mistake; to make a gross error

zhùxiàng 鑄像 to erect a metal statue

zhuā 抓
1. to scratch 2. to grasp; to seize; to take; to snatch; to make a snatch at; to catch 3. to arrest

zhuābiànzi 抓辮子 to seize on someone's mistake

zhuā'ěr náosāi 抓耳撓腮 1. to tweak one's ears and scratch one's cheeks 2. impatient 3. agitated 4. depressed

zhuājǐn 抓緊 to grasp firmly

zhuākōngzi 抓空子 to find time

zhuāpò 抓破 to injure skin by scratching

zhuāpòliǎn 抓破臉 1. to hurt the face by scratching 2. to break off friendly relations

zhuāqǔ 抓取 to take by grasping

zhuārén 抓人 to arrest

zhuāyǎng 抓癢 to scratch an itchy part

zhuāyào 抓藥 to buy (Chinese herbal) medicine according to a doctor's prescription

zhuāzéi 抓賊 to catch a thief

zhuāzhù 抓住 1. to grasp; to grip; to clutch 2. to keep from going away; to hold 3. to grip somebody's attention

zhuǎ 爪
a claw; a paw; a talon

zhuǎzi 爪子 a claw; a paw; a talon

zhuān 專
1. to concentrate; to focus 2. to monopolize 3. to specialize 4. exclusive; special

zhuān'àn 專案 a special case (to be dealt with separately)

zhuāncái 專才 a specialist

zhuāncháng 專長 a special skill; a specialty

zhuānchē 專車 a train or bus

run for a particular purpose

zhuānchéng 專程 a special trip

zhuānchéng 專誠 with the exclusive purpose of

zhuānduàn 專斷 arbitrary

zhuānfǎng 專訪 a report produced by a journalist after having paid a special visit to the person or persons concerned

zhuāngōng 專攻 to specialize in

zhuānhán 專函 a letter written for a specific purpose

zhuānhèng 專橫 dictatorial; arbitrary; despotic; tyrannical

zhuānjī 專機 a plane designated for a special use

zhuānjiā 專家 a specialist; an expert

zhuānkē xuéxiào 專科學校 a junior college

zhuānkuǎn 專款 the fund designated for a specific use

zhuānlán 專欄 a special column (in a newspaper or magazine)

zhuānlán zuòjiā 專欄作家 a columnist

zhuānlì 專利 a monopoly; a patent

zhuānlìpǐn 專利品 a patent; a patent article

zhuānmài 專賣 a monopoly

zhuānměi 專美 to attain distinction alone

zhuānmén 專門 1. a specialty; a special field 3. exclusively

zhuānmén réncái 專門人才 the people with professional skill

zhuānquán 專權 to be dictatorial

zhuānrén 專人 a person specially assigned for a task

zhuānshǐ 專使 a special envoy

zhuāntí 專題 a special subject

zhuāntí bàodǎo 專題報導 a report on a special topic

zhuāntí yǎnjiǎng 專題演講 a lecture on a special topic

zhuānxiàn 專線 1. a special railway line 2. a special telephone line

zhuānyè 專業 1. a special field of study; a specialty 2. a special-

ized trade

zhuānyèhuà 專業化 specialization

zhuānyè rényuán 專業人員 the personnel in a specific field

zhuānyè xùnliàn 專業訓練 training in a specialty

zhuānyè zhīshì 專業知識 professional knowledge

zhuānyī 專一 to concentrate one's attention on; single-minded

zhuānyòng 專用 to use exclusively

zhuānyǒu míngcí 專有名詞 proper noun

zhuānyuán 專員 a specialist in the government

zhuānzhèng 專政 dictatorship

zhuānzhí 專職 1. sole duty; specific duty 2. full-time

zhuānzhì 專制 tyrannical; despotic; autocratic

zhuānzhù 專注 to concentrate one's attention on

zhuān 甎(磚、塼) brick

zhuānchǎng 甎廠 a brickfield; a brickyard

zhuānwǎ 甎瓦 bricks and tiles

zhuānyáo 甎窯 a brick kiln

zhuǎn 轉

1. to turn 2. to take a turn; to shift; to change 3. to transport; to convey; to transfer 4. indirect; roundabout 5. to roll 6. to migrate; to move

zhuǎnbài wéishèng 轉敗爲勝 to turn a defeat into a victory; to turn the tables (on someone)

zhuǎnbiàn 轉變 1. to undergo changes; to change 2. a change or shift (of attitude, thinking, etc.)

zhuǎnbō 轉播 to relay a broadcast or telecast

zhuǎnbōzhàn 轉播站 a relay station

zhuǎnchē 轉車 to change trains or buses; to transfer to another train or bus

zhuǎndá 轉達 to transmit through another person or office;

Z

to convey

zhuǎndòng 轉動 1. to turn; to revolve; to rotate 2. to budge; to move

zhuǎn'gào 轉告 to pass on (words); to communicate; to transmit

zhuǎnhuà 轉化 1. to change; to transform 2. to react chemically

zhuǎnhuàn 轉換 transition; to change; to switch

zhuǎnjī 轉機 a turning point (usually from bad to good); a favorable turn

zhuǎnjià 轉嫁 1. (said of a woman) to remarry 2. to transfer (a tax burden upon consumers, etc.)

zhuǎnjiāo 轉交 to send or deliver through or in care of another person

zhuǎnkǒu 轉口 transit

zhuǎnlièdiǎn 轉捩點 a turning point

zhuǎnmài 轉賣 to resell

zhuǎnniàn 轉念 to change one's mind; to have second thoughts

zhuǎnràng 轉讓 to transfer (ownership, title, etc.)

zhuǎnshēn 轉身 to turn the body; to turn round

zhuǎnshì 轉世 (said of the soul) to transmigrate into another body

zhuǎnshǒu 轉手 1. to fall into another's hands; to change hands 2. a very brief period of time

zhuǎnshǒu wéigōng 轉守爲攻 to change from the defensive to the offensive

zhuǎnsòng 轉送 to pass on; to transmit on

zhuǎnwān 轉彎 to take a turn; to turn in another direction

zhuǎnwān mòjiǎo 轉彎抹角 1. to go along a zigzag course 2. to talk in a roundabout way; to beat around the bush; to mince

zhuǎnwān wéi'ān 轉危爲安 1. to become safe; to avert a danger; to turn the corner 2. (said of a gravely ill patient) out of danger

zhuǎnwēi wéi'ān 轉危爲安
refer to **zhuǎnwēi wéi'ān**

zhuǎnxiàng 轉向 (said of wind) to change directions

zhuǎnxué 轉學 to transfer to another school

zhuǎnyǎn 轉眼 a very brief period of time; in the twinkling of an eye; an instant

zhuǎnyè 轉業 to change one's trade; to change one's career

zhuǎnyí 轉移 to change in position or direction; to divert; to shift; to turn; to transfer

zhuǎnyùn 轉運 1. to transport; to convey; to forward 2. to be in a constant cyclic motion 3. to have a turn of luck (for the better)

zhuǎnzhàng 轉賬 to transfer accounts (in banking)

zhuàn 囀
refer to **zhuàn** 囀

zhuàn 傳
a biography

zhuànjì 傳記 a biography

zhuàn 撰
to write; to compose

zhuàn'gǎo 撰稿 to prepare manuscripts; to write

zhuànshù 撰述 to write an account of (facts, happenings, etc.); to narrate

zhuànwén 撰文 to compose; to write

zhuànxiě 撰寫 to write or compose (usually light works)

zhuàn 篆
1. the seal type, an ancient calligraphic style 2. a seal

zhuànkè 篆刻 to cut a seal in the seal type

zhuànshū 篆書 the seal type, an ancient calligraphic style

zhuàn 賺
1. to earn; to make money; to gain 2. to cheat; to deceive

zhuànqián 賺錢 to earn money; to make a profit

zhuàn 轉

to turn round and round; to rotate; to revolve; to gyrate

zhuànxiàng 轉向 1. to lose one's bearings; to lose one's way 2. a change in one's philosophy, beliefs, etc.

zhuànyǐ 轉椅 a swivel chair

zhuàn 饌

1. to prepare food 2. food and drink; dainties 3. to eat and drink

zhuànjù 饌具 a food vessel

zhuàn 囀 also zhuǎn

1. to warble; to twitter; to chirp 2. pleasing to the ear

zhuāng 妝 (粧)

1. to doll up; to adorn oneself; to apply makeup 2. jewels, etc. for adornment 3. to disguise; to pretend

zhuāngbàn 妝扮 to doll up

zhuānglián 妝奩 a bride's trousseau; a dowry

zhuāngshì 妝飾 to adorn; to dress up

zhuāng 莊 (庄)

1. solemn; dignified; stately; august; sober; gravity 2. a large farmhouse; a manor house 3. a village; a hamlet 4. a market; a shop; a store; a bank 5. a Chinese family name

zhuāngjia 莊家 1. a farmhouse 2. the banker (in gambling games)

zhuāngjia 莊稼 1. farming 2. crops; harvests

zhuāngjiādì 莊稼地 a farm; a field

zhuāngjiāhàn 莊稼漢 a farmer

zhuāngyán 莊嚴 1. dignified; solemn; stately; august 2. to make solemn

zhuāngyuán 莊園 a manor

zhuāngzhòng 莊重 dignified; solemn

zhuāng 裝

1. to fill in or up; to pack; to load 2. to pretend; to feign 3. to adorn; to dress or make up; ornamental dressing; to decorate

(a room, etc.) 4. to disguise 5. to store; to keep 6. to install (machines, equipment, etc.) 7. clothes and personal effects

zhuāngbàn 裝扮 1. adornment; make-up; to dress or doll up; attire 2. to disguise

zhuāngbèi 裝備 equipment or an outfit

zhuāngbìng 裝病 to pretend illness; to malinger

zhuāngdìng 裝訂 to bind pages into a volume or book; binding

zhuāngfēng màishǎ 裝瘋賣傻 to pretend to be crazy and stupid; to play the fool

zhuānghútu 裝糊塗 to pretend not to know; to feign ignorance

zhuānghuáng 裝潢 to decorate (a room, shop, etc.); decoration

zhuānghuò 裝貨 to load or pack goods

zhuāngjiǎ bùduì 裝甲部隊 armored troops or units

zhuāngjiǎchē 裝甲車 an armored vehicle; a tank

zhuānglóng zuòyǎ 裝聾作啞 to pretend to hear and know nothing

zhuāngmǎn 裝滿 to fill up

zhuāngmú zuòyàng 裝模作樣 to act affectedly; to be pretentious; to strike a pose

zhuāngpèi 裝配 to assemble (a machine)

zhuāngqiāng zuòshì 裝腔作勢 affected; pretentious; to strike an attitude

zhuāngshè 裝設 to install; to equip

zhuāngshì 裝飾 1. to doll up; to deck; to make up 2. to adorn; to embellish

zhuāngsuàn 裝蒜 to be pretenious or affected

zhuāngxiāng 裝箱 to pack in a box or chest; to box

zhuāngyùn 裝運 to pack and transport; to load and ship

zhuāngzài 裝載 loaded with; to pack; to stow

zhuāng 椿

1. a stake; a post; a pile 2. a numerary auxiliary for affairs or matters

zhuàng 壯

1. big; great 2. strong; robust; vigorous; sturdy 3. portly; stout 4. to strengthen 5. the prime of one's life

zhuàngdà 壯大 1. big and strong; vigorous 2. to expand

zhuàngdǎn 壯膽 to embolden

zhuàngdīng 壯丁 1. an able-bodied man 2. an adult fit for military service

zhuàngguān 壯觀 a grand sight; a great sight

zhuàngjǔ 壯舉 a great achievement

zhuàngkuò 壯闊 magnificent; grandiose

zhuànglì 壯麗 splendorous

zhuàngliè 壯烈 courageous

zhuàngliè xīshēng 壯烈犧牲 to die as a martyr

zhuàngnián 壯年 the prime of one's life

zhuàngshì 壯士 a brave man; a hero

zhuàngzhì língyún 壯志凌雲 a soaring ambition

zhuàngzhì wèichóu 壯志未酬 to die before the fulfillment of his ambition or aspiration

zhuàng 狀

1. appearance; look; shape; form 2. a condition; a state; a situation 3. written appeal 4. a certificate 5. to describe; to narrate; description

zhuàngkuàng 狀況 a situation; circumstances; conditions

zhuàngtài 狀態 a situation; a state; a condition

zhuàngyuán 狀元 1. the top successful candidate in the imperial examination 2. the very best

zhuàngzi 狀子 a plaint

zhuàng 僮

Zhuàngzú 僮族 the name of a small tribe in southwestern China

zhuàng 撞

1. to bump; to run into; to collide; to dash 2. to meet by chance

zhuàngdǎo 撞倒 to knock down by bumping

zhuàngguǐ 撞鬼 to encounter a ghost

zhuàngjí 撞擊 to ram; to dash

zhuàngjí 撞擊 refer to **zhuàngjí** 撞擊

zhuàngjiàn 撞見 to meet unexpectedly; to run into

zhuàngkāi 撞開 to burst open

zhuàngpiàn 撞騙 to swindle

zhuàngqiú 撞球 1. billiards 2. billiard balls

zhuàngqiúchǎng 撞球場 a billiard room; a billiard saloon

zhuàngshāng 撞傷 to injure by bumping (as in car accidents)

zhuī 隹

a general name of short-tailed birds, such as pigeons

zhuī 追

1. to chase; to pursue; to follow; to trace 2. to drive; to expel 3. to demand insistently; to dun for 4. to try to recover (stolen goods, etc.)

zhuībén sùyuán 追本溯源 to trace to the very source of something

zhuībǔ 追捕 to pursue and apprehend; to chase

zhuīchá 追查 to investigate; to trace (by observing marks, tracks, bits of evidence, etc.)

zhuīdào 追悼 to commemorate (the dead)

zhuīgǎn 追趕 to pursue; to chase; to try to catch up with

zhuīgēn jiūdǐ 追根究底 to raise one question after another (in order to reach the bottom of a matter)

zhuīgēn jiūdǐ 追根究底 refer to **zhuīgēn jiūdǐ** 追根究底

zhuīhuí 追回 1. to recover (what has been taken away illicitly) 2. to catch up with someone on the way and make him come back

zhuījí 追擊 to chase and attack; to give chase

zhuījí 追擊 refer to **zhuījí** 追擊

zhuījiā 追加 to make an addition (to a document, etc.)

zhuījiū 追究 1. to try insistently to find out (the ultimate cause, etc.) 2. to investigate (a fault, offense, etc.) and punish (the guilty)

zhuījiù 追究 refer to **zhuījiū** 追究

zhuīniàn 追念 to remember with nostalgia or gratitude

zhuīqiú 追求 1. to seek; to pursue; to go after 2. to court (a woman); courtship

zhuīsù 追溯 to trace the origin of; to trace back

zhuīsuí 追隨 to follow

zhuīwèn 追問 to question insistently

zhuīxún 追尋 to seek; to pursue

zhuīyì 追憶 to call to memory; to remember; to look back

zhuīzhú 追逐 to pursue

zhuīzōng 追蹤 1. to follow the examples of the predecessors 2. to trace; to trail

zhuī 椎 also **chuí**

1. a hammer; a mallet; a bludgeon; a mace 2. to beat; to hammer; to hit; to strike 3. a vertebra

zhuīgǔ 椎骨 a vertebra

zhuījí 椎擊 to strike with a hammer

zhuījí 椎擊 refer to **zhuījí** 椎擊

zhuīxīn qìxiě 椎心泣血 refer to **zhuīxīn qìxuè** 椎心泣血

zhuīxīn qìxuè 椎心泣血 deep sorrow; extreme grief

zhuī 錐

1. an awl 2. to pierce; to bore; to drill; to make a hole 3. conical

zhuīchǔ nángzhōng 錐處囊中 Real talent will be discovered.

zhuīxíng 錐形 a taper; a cone

zhuì 綴

1. to put together; to combine; to

compose 2. to mend clothes; to patch up; to sew; to stitch 3. to decorate; to stud

zhuìbǔ 綴補 to patch up (clothes)

zhuì 墜

to fall down; to sink; the fall (of a person, a state, etc.)

zhuìdì 墜地 1. to fall 2. failure 3. to come to this world

zhuìlóu 墜樓 to fall from a building

zhuìluò 墜落 to fall; to drop

zhuìmǎ 墜馬 to fall off a horse

zhuì 贅

1. useless; superfluous; redundant 2. repetition; to repeat; repetitious 3. to follow around, as children 4. to be burdensome 5. to pawn things for money 6. to meet; to congregate 7. a son-in-law who takes the place of a son in his wife's parental family which is lacking for an heir

zhuìliú 贅瘤 a wen; an excrescence

zhuìshù 贅述 a repetitious or superfluous statement

zhuìyán 贅言 verbosity

zhūn 諄

patient or earnest (in explaining, teaching, etc.)

zhūnzhūn jiàohuì 諄諄教誨 to teach and admonish with patience

zhǔn 准

1. to approve; to permit; to grant 2. in accordance with 3. equivalent; equal

zhǔnjiàng 准將 a brigadier general

zhǔnxǔ 准許 to approve; to permit; to allow

zhǔn 準

1. level; even 2. a rule; a criterion; a standard; accurate; accuracy 3. to aim; to sight 4. would-be (son-in-law, bride, etc.); to-be 5. (law) quasi 6. certainly

zhǔnbèi 準備 1. to prepare; to get ready 2. to plan

zhǔnquè 準確 correct; accurate; precise

zhǔnshéng 準繩 1. a criterion; a standard 2. (carpenter's) a marking line

zhǔnshí 準時 punctual; punctuality

zhǔntou 準頭 accuracy; a standard

zhǔnxīnláng 準新郎 a would-be bridegroom

zhǔnxīnniáng 準新娘 a would-be bride

zhǔnzé 準則 a rule; a standard; a criterion

zhuó 拙 also **zhuó**

1. stupid; crude; poor (works, etc.); slow and clumsy 2. a conventional term referring to oneself

zhuōjiàn 拙見 (used in polite conversation) my humble idea or view

zhuōjīng 拙荊 (used in polite conversation) my stupid wife

zhuōliè 拙劣 clumsy and inferior

zhuōzhù 拙著 (used in polite conversation) my (poor) writing

zhuó 卓 also **zhuó**

1. lofty; high 2. profound; brilliant; eminent 3. (to stand) erect; upright

zhuōjiàn 卓見 a brilliant idea or view

zhuōjué 卓絕 eminent; prominent; outstanding

zhuōyǒu chéngxiào 卓有成效 fruitful; highly effective

zhuōyuè 卓越 excellent; remarkable

zhuó 捉

1. to seize; to grasp; to catch; to hold 2. to apprehend; to arrest

zhuōdāo 捉刀 to ghostwrite

zhuōjiān 捉奸 to catch a person in the act of adultery (usually by the wronged husband or wife)

zhuōjǐn jiànzhǒu 捉襟見肘 hard-pressed for money; in financial straits

zhuōmícáng 捉迷藏 1. to play hide-and-seek; hide-and-seek 2. to beat about the bush

zhuōmō bùdìng 捉摸不定 unpredictable

zhuōná 捉拿 to apprehend; to arrest

zhuōnòng 捉弄 to play a joke (or trick) on (somebody); to make fun of

zhuōyāo 捉妖 (Taoism) to exorcise

zhuōzéi 捉賊 to catch thieves

zhuōzhù 捉住 to catch; to seize

zhuó 桌 also **zhuó**

1. a table; a desk 2. dishes for guests around the table—usually consisting of 20 courses 3. a tableful of guests (10 to 12 persons at a round table)

zhuōbù 桌布 a tablecloth

zhuōdēng 桌燈 a desk lamp

zhuōmiàn 桌面 the top of a table

zhuōqiú 桌球 table tennis; ping-pong

zhuōshàngxíng diànnǎo 桌上型電腦 a desktop computer

zhuó 灼

1. to burn; to cauterize 2. bright; clear; luminous; brilliant 3. flowers in full bloom

zhuórè 灼熱 intense heat; red-hot

zhuóshāng 灼傷 a burn

zhuó 卓

refer to **zhuó** 卓

zhuó 拙

refer to **zhuó** 拙

zhuó 茁

1. sprouting; growing 2. strong; sturdy; vigorous

zhuózhuàng 茁壯 vigorous; strong

zhuó 酌

1. to drink 2. to pour (wine) 3. to weigh and consider

zhuójiǔ 酌酒 to pour wine

zhuóliàng 酌量 to weigh and consider

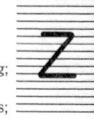

zhuó 啄

(said of a bird) to peck

zhuómùniǎo 啄木鳥 a woodpecker

zhuóshí 啄食 to eat by pecking

zhuó 琢

1. to cut, chisel or polish jade, gems 2. to improve; to polish; to refine 3. refer to **zuó** 琢

zhuómó 琢磨 1. to cut and polish 2. to study and improve

zhuó 著(着)

1. to wear (garments, etc.) 2. refer to **zhāo** 著 3. to apply (color, etc.); to start 4. (also **zhāo**) to hit the bull's eye; right to the point; very worthwhile

zhuóbǐ 著筆 to begin to write or paint

zhuólì 著力 to apply force; to exert

zhuólù 著陸 (said of an airplane) to land; to alight; to descend to the ground

zhuóluò 著落 whereabouts; results

zhuósè 著色 to apply coloring; to color

zhuóshǒu 著手 to start doing something

zhuóxiǎng 著想 for the sake of

zhuóyǎn 著眼 to watch; to eye with attention

zhuózhòng 著重 to emphasize; emphasis

zhuó 濁

1. (said of water) turbid or muddy 2. (said of the world) evil, corrupt, tumultuous 3. (said of a person) stupid and idiotic 4. name of a constellation

zhuóliú 濁流 a turbid stream

zhuóshuǐ 濁水 turbid or muddy water

zhuóyīn 濁音 a voiced sound

zhuó 擢

1. to take out; to pull out; to extract; to pick out; to select 2. to promote; to raise (in rank)

zhuóshēng 擢升 to advance; to promote (to a higher position or rank)

zhuóyòng 擢用 to pick and promote (promising employees or subordinates)

zhuó 濯

1. to wash 2. to eliminate vices 3. grand; magnificent 4. a Chinese family name

zhuózhuó 濯濯 1. bright and brilliant 2. (said of mountains) bare; bald 3. to be fat and sleek

zhuó 鐲

1. a kind of bell used in the army in ancient times 2. a bracelet; an armlet

zī 孜

never weary; unwearied and diligent

zīzī bùjuàn 孜孜不倦 to work with diligence and without fatigue

zī 吱

squeaky cries of an animal

zīzhā 吱喳 chatter (made by birds or animals)

zī 咨

1. to inquire; to consult 2. a very formal official communication between offices of equal rank

zīxún 咨詢 to inquire; to consult

zīzhèng 咨政 a political advisor (to the Chinese presidency)

zī 姿

1. the manner; an air; carriage; bearing 2. looks

zīsè 姿色 (female) beauty

zīshì 姿勢 1. carriage; deportment; bearing 2. (in photography) a pose

zītài 姿態 1. carriage; deportment; bearing 2. a gesture

zī 茲

1. this 2. now; here; at present 3. year

zīshì tǐdà 茲事體大 This is a big problem. This is a serious matter.

zī 孳

1. to bear or beget in large numbers 2. to work with sustained diligence

zīshēng 孳生 to grow and multiply

zīxī 孳息 1. to grow 2. interest (from money)

zīxí 孳息 refer to **zīxī** 孳息

zī 滋

1. to grow 2. to increase; to multiply 3. to nourish 4. to give rise to 5. to spurt out 6. juice; sap

zībǔ 滋補 to nourish; nutritious; tonic

zīrǎo 滋擾 to disturb peace and order; to harass

zīrùn 滋潤 1. to freshen; to enrich 2. to moisten; moist

zīshēng 滋生 to reproduce in large numbers

zīshì 滋事 to create trouble

zīwèi 滋味 taste; flavor

zīyǎngpǐn 滋養品 nutrient; nutritive food; nourishment

zīzhǎng 滋長 to grow; to thrive

zī 資

1. money; wealth; property; means; capital 2. expenses; fees; charges 3. natural endowments or gifts; one's disposition 4. to avail of 5. to aid or help; to assist; to subsidize; to support 6. to supply; to provide 7. one's qualifications, position, or record of service 8. to trust to

zīběn 資本 funds; capital

zīběnjiā 資本家 a capitalist

zīchǎn 資產 1. property; real estate 2. (accounting) assets

zīfāng 資方 the management (of a shop, factory, etc.); capital

zīge 資格 qualifications, requirements, or seniority of a person

zījīn 資金 funds; capital

zīlì 資歷 qualifications and experiences (of an applicant, etc.); professional background

zīliào 資料 data

zīqiǎn 資遣 to dismiss (employees) with severance pay

zīshēn 資深 senior; seniority

zīxùn 資訊 information

zīxùn gāosù gōnglù 資訊高速公路 information highway

zīyōushēng 資優生 a student with a high IQ

zīyuán 資源 resources; natural resources

zīzhí 資質 refer to **zīzhì** 資質

zīzhì 資質 one's natural gifts or endowments

zīzhù 資助 to help another with money

zī 輜

1. a curtained carriage 2. a wagon for supplies

zīzhòng 輜重 1. luggage 2. military supplies

zī 錙

an ancient unit of weight (said to equal 8 taels)

zīzhū bìjiào 錙銖必較 to be particular even about a trifling amount

zī 髭

moustaches

zīxū 髭鬚 moustaches and beards

zī 諮

1. to inquire; to confer; to consult 2. an official communication between offices of the same level

zīshāng 諮商 (psychology) counseling

zīxún 諮詢 to inquire and consult; to seek advice

zī 齜

1. to open the mouth and show the teeth 2. uneven teeth

zīyá 齜牙 to open the mouth and show the teeth

zǐ 子

1. a child; a son; an offspring 2. a seed; an egg 3. the first of the twelve Terrestrial Branches 4. a rank of the nobility equivalent to a viscount 5. a designation used in speaking of or to a man in former times (somewhat similar to "mister")

zǐdàn 子彈 a bullet

zǐdì 子弟 young dependents; children

zǐgōng 子宮 the womb; the uterus

zǐgōng'ái 子宮癌 uterine cancer

zǐjù 子句 (grammar) a clause

zǐjué 子爵 a viscount

zǐmín 子民 the people

zǐnǚ 子女 sons and daughters; children

zǐshí 子時 the period of the day from 11 p.m. to 1 a.m.

zǐsì 子嗣 a son; a male offspring

zǐsūn 子孫 descendants; posterity

zǐwǔxiàn 子午線 a meridian

zǐxū wūyǒu 子虛烏有 pure imagination

zǐyīn 子音 a consonant

zǐzǐ sūnsūn 子子孫孫 generation after generation of descendants

zǐ 仔

1. careful 2. (also **zǎi**) (said of animals or fowls) young

zǐxì 仔細 careful; punctilious; attentive

zǐ 姊 also **jiě**

one's elder sister or sisters

zǐmèi 姊妹 sisters

zǐmèihuā 姊妹花 beautiful sisters

zǐmèishì 姊妹市 sister cities

zǐ 梓

1. a tall, stately tree with palm-shaped leaves and yellow flowers in summer 2. one's native place or hometown 3. to carve words on a woodboard; printing blocks

zǐ 紫

purple; violet

zǐcài 紫菜 (botany) laver

zǐdīngxiāng 紫丁香 a lilac

zǐluólán 紫羅蘭 (botany) the violet

zǐsè 紫色 purple; violet

zǐwàixiàn 紫外線 ultraviolet rays

zǐyàoshuǐ 紫藥水 gentian violet solution

zǐ 滓

dregs; lees; sediment

zì 自

1. self; personal; private; in person; personally 2. from 3. natural; naturally 4. a Chinese family name

zì'ài 自愛 self-respect

zìbái 自白 confession

zìbáishū 自白書 an affidavit

zìbào zìqì 自暴自棄 to abandon oneself to a dissipated life

zìbēi 自卑 to underestimate oneself

zìbēigǎn 自卑感 a sense of inferiority

zìbèi 自備 self-provided

zìbìzhèng 自閉症 (psychiatry) autism

zìbù liànglì 自不量力 to do something beyond one's ability

zìcán xínghuì 自慚形穢 to feel inferior to others

zìchēng 自稱 to call oneself; to claim

zìchuī zìléi 自吹自擂 refer to **zìchuī zìlèi** 自吹自擂

zìchuī zìlèi 自吹自擂 to brag; to boast

zìcóng 自從 since then; ever since

zìdà 自大 conceited; egomaniacal; egotistic

zìdé qílè 自得其樂 to find joy in one's own way (no matter what others may think)

zìdòng 自動 1. voluntary; of one's own free will 2. automatic

zìdòng fànmàijī 自動販賣機 a vending machine

zìdònghuà 自動化 automation; to automate

zìdòng tíkuǎnjī 自動提款機 a cashomat

zìfèi 自費 to pay one's own expenses

zìfén 自焚 to burn oneself to death—self-immolation

zìfù 自負 conceited

zìgān duòluò 自甘墮落 to

abandon oneself to wanton ways

zìgào fènyǒng 自告奮勇 to volunteer

zìgēngnóng 自耕農 an owner-farmer

zìgǔ yǐlái 自古以來 since ancient times

zìgù bùxiá 自顧不暇 to have trouble even in taking care of oneself

zìháo 自豪 to feel proud of; to take pride in

zìhuàxiàng 自畫像 a self-portrait

zìjǐ 自己 self; oneself; one's person

zìjǐrén 自己人 persons closely related with each other

zìjǐ zìzú 自給自足 self-sufficient

zìjìn 自盡 to commit suicide; to kill oneself

zìjū 自居 to consider oneself to be (a genius, VIP, famous figure, etc.)

zìjué 自覺 1. to feel something concerning oneself; aware 2. self-consciousness

zìkuā 自誇 to brag; to boast

zìláishuǐ 自來水 running water; tap water

zìlì 自立 independent; self-supporting

zìlì gēngshēng 自力更生 to achieve self-renewal with one's own effort; self-reliance

zìlì ménhù 自立門戶 to establish one's own school of thought or clique

zìliàn 自戀 narcissism

zìmǎn 自滿 complacency; to be satisfied with oneself

zìmíng déyì 自鳴得意 smug

zìmìng bùfán 自命不凡 conceited

zìqī qīrén 自欺欺人 to deceive oneself and others as well

zìqǔ mièwáng 自取滅亡 to take the road to one's doom

zìqǔ qírǔ 自取其辱 to ask for an insult

zìrán 自然 1. nature 2. certainly; surely; of course 3. (in primary

school) a subject or course of study concerning natural sciences

zìrán érrán 自然而然 a matter of course

zìrán 自然 at ease; natural

zìrèn 自認 1. to believe 2. to accept adversity with resignation

zìshā 自殺 to commit suicide; suicide

zìshēn 自身 oneself

zìshēn nánbǎo 自身難保 unable even to protect oneself

zìshēng zìmiè 自生自滅 to grow and die without outside interference

zìshí qíguǒ 自食其果 to reap the fruit of what one has sown

zìshí qílì 自食其力 to live by one's own exertion

zìshǐ zhìzhōng 自始至終 from beginning to end

zìshì 自視 to consider, to think or to imagine oneself

zìshǒu 自首 to give oneself up to the law

zìshù 自述 to narrate one's own story or experience

zìsī 自私 selfish; selfishness

zìtàn bùrú 自歎不如 to admit with regret that one is not as good

zìtǎo kǔchī 自討苦吃 to ask for trouble

zìtǎo méiqù 自討沒趣 You ask for it!—to get an insult unnecessarily

zìtóu luówǎng 自投羅網 to walk right into a trap

zìwèi 自衛 self-defense; to defend oneself

zìwèi 自慰 1. self-consolation 2. onanism

zìwèiduì 自衛隊 militia corps

zìwèn 自問 to ask oneself

zìwǒ 自我 self; ego

zìwǒ táozuì 自我陶醉 to indulge in daydreaming

zìxí 自習 to learn and practice by oneself

zìxiāng cánshā 自相殘殺 to

engage in an intramural fight

zìxiāng máodùn 自相矛盾 inconsistent

zìxīn 自新 to make a new person out of oneself; self-renewal

zìxìn 自信 self-confidence

zìxíngchē 自行車 a bicycle; a bike

zìxǐng 自省 self-examination; introspection

zìxiū 自修 to learn and practice by oneself

zìxǔ 自許 to regard oneself as; conceited

zìxǔ 自詡 to brag; to boast

zìxún fánnǎo 自尋煩惱 to look for trouble

zìyán zìyǔ 自言自語 to talk to oneself

zìyǐ wéishì 自以為是 self-approbation

zìyì 自縊 to hang oneself

zìyóu 自由 1. freedom; liberty 2. at ease 3. of one's own free will

zìyóu liàn'ài 自由戀愛 free love

zìyóushì 自由式 (swimming) freestyle

zìyóu xíngdòng 自由行動 free action

zìyóu zìzài 自由自在 carefree

zìyòu 自幼 since childhood

zìyú 自娛 to amuse oneself

zìyuán qíshuō 自圓其說 to explain oneself away

zìyuàn 自願 voluntary

zìyuàn zìyì 自怨自艾 to blame and censure oneself

zìzài 自在 freely

zìzai 自在 at ease (with oneself and the world)

zìzé 自責 to blame oneself; self-reproach

zìzhǎo máfan 自找麻煩 to look for trouble

zìzhì 自治 1. self-discipline 2. autonomy

zìzhì 自制 self-restraint; self-discipline

zìzhòng 自重 self-respect; self-discipline; self-esteem

zìzhǔ 自主 independent; autonomy

zìzhǔquán 自主權 sovereignty (of a state)

zìzhùcān 自助餐 a buffet lunch or supper

zìzhù cāntīng 自助餐廳 a cafeteria

zìzhù xǐyīdiàn 自助洗衣店 a launderette

zìzhuǎn 自轉 refer to **zìzhuàn** 自轉

zìzhuàn 自傳 an autobiography

zìzhuàn 自轉 (astronomy) rotation

zìzūn 自尊 1. self-respect; self-esteem 2. egotistic

zìzūnxīn 自尊心 a sense of self-respect; self-esteem

zìzuò zìshòu 自作自受 to reap the fruit of what one has sown

zìzuò cōngmíng 自作聰明 presumptuous; pretentious

zìzuò duōqíng 自作多情 to imagine oneself as the favorite of one of the opposite sex

zìzuò zhǔzhāng 自作主張 to take liberties; to decide for oneself

zìzuò zìshòu 自作自受 refer to zìzuò zìshòu 自作自受

zì 字

1. a word; a character; a letter; a logograph 2. to betroth a girl 3. (formerly) a name or style taken at the age of 20, by which one was sometimes called

zìdiǎn 字典 a dictionary; a lexicon; a thesaurus

zìduàn 字段 (computer) field

zìfú 字符 (computer) character

zìhao 字號 1. a mark made with letters or characters 2. the name of a shop

zìhuà 字畫 1. the strokes in a character 2. calligraphy and painting

zìhuì 字彙 1. vocabulary 2. a glossary

zìjī 字跡 one's handwriting

zìjié 字節 (computer) byte

zìjù 字據 a receipt; a certificate

zìlǐ hángjiān 字裡行間 between the lines; the overtone (of a piece of writing)

zìmǔ 字母 an alphabet; a letter (of an alphabet)

zìmù 字幕 subtitle

zìshǒu 字首 a prefix

zìtǐ 字體 (printing) a style of letter or character; a type

zìtiáor 字條兒 a brief note

zìtiè 字帖 a copybook

zìwěi 字尾 a suffix

zìyǎn 字眼 a word; a character

zìyì 字義 the definition, connotation, or meaning of a word

zìyuán 字元 (computer) character

zìzhǐlǒu 字紙簍 a wastebasket

zì 恣 to throw off restraint; to dissipate; to debauch

zìsì 恣肆 licentious; willful

zìyì 恣意 unscrupulous; willful; unbridled

zìyì wàngwéi 恣意妄為 to act willfully

zì 漬 1. to soak 2. to dye 3. to be caked with

zìhén 漬痕 a stain; a spot; a smear

zōng 宗 1. an ancestor; a clan 2. a sect; a religion 3. to believe in 4. a Chinese family name

zōngjiào 宗教 religion

zōngjiào xìnyǎng 宗教信仰 religious belief

zōngjiào yíshì 宗教儀式 religious rites; ritual

zōngmiào 宗廟 the imperial ancestral temple

zōngqīn 宗親 members of the same clan

zōngshī 宗師 one whose virtue and learning command the respect of others

zōngshì 宗室 1. the imperial family 2. the ancestral shrine of a large clan

zōngzhǐ 宗旨 a purpose; an objective

zōngzú 宗族 a clan; a paternal clan

zōng 從(縱) from north to south

zōng 棕 the palm tree

zōnglǘshù 棕櫚樹 the palm tree

zōngsè 棕色 brown, the color of palm fibers

zōngsuō 棕簑 a coir rain cape; a coir raincoat

zōng 綜 also **zòng** 1. to sum up 2. in view of; to take account of 3. to arrange 4. synthesis 5. to examine into

zōnghé 綜合 synthesis; synthesize

zōnghé bàodǎo 綜合報導 a comprehensive dispatch

zōnghé suǒdéshuì 綜合所得稅 consolidated income tax

zōngkuò 綜括 to sum up; to encompass all

zōnglǎn 綜覽 to view generally

zōnglǐ 綜理 to be in overall charge

zōngyì jiémù 綜藝節目 a variety show

zōng 縱 refer to **zòng** 縱 4

zōng 蹤(踪) 1. a footprint; a track; traces; a vestige 2. to follow the tracks of; to keep track of; to trail

zōngjì 蹤跡 1. a track; traces; a vestige 2. to keep track of; to follow up clues

zōngyǐng 蹤影 traces; a vestige

zǒng 總 1. to gather; to collect; to assemble; to unite 2. always 3. all; general; overall; complete; total 4. chief; principal; central 5. at any rate; in any event

zǒngbiānjí 總編輯 an editor-in-chief

zǒngbù 總部 headquarters

zǒngcái 總裁 a director general, president or governor (of a bank, political party, etc.)

zǒngchēng 總稱 a generic name; a general term

zǒngdàilǐ 總代理 (business) a general agent

zǒngděi 總得 to have to; somehow

zǒngdòngyuán 總動員 general mobilization

zǒngdū 總督 a viceroy; a governor-general

zǒng'é 總額 the total amount; the sum total

zǒng'ér yánzhī 總而言之 in short; in brief; in a word; in conclusion; to sum up

zǒnggāng 總綱 general principles

zǒnggòng 總共 altogether; in all; all told

zǒngguǎn 總管 1. a superintendent; a supervisor 2. to supervise

zǒngguī 總歸 anyhow; eventually; after all

zǒngháng 總行 a head office (of a business firm)

zǒnghé 總和 the sum total; the total

zǒngjī 總機 a telephone switchboard

zǒngjiān 總監 an inspector general; a chief inspector

zǒngjiàoliàn 總教練 a chief coach (of a sport delegation)

zǒngjīnglǐ 總經理 a general manager

zǒngkuò 總括 to sum up; to summarize

zǒnglǎn dàquán 總攬大權 to be in full power

zǒnglǐ 總理 1. a prime minister; a premier 2. a president (of a political party, etc.)

zǒngliàng 總量 the total amount

zǒnglùn 總論 a summary; an introduction

zǒngpíng 總評 general comment; overall appraisal

zǒngpíngjūn 總平均 an overall average

zǒngshì 總是 always; without exception

zǒngshù 總數 the total amount; the sum total

zǒngsīlìng 總司令 a commander in chief

zǒngsuàn 總算 1. on the whole; in general 2. finally

zǒngtǒng 總統 the president (of a state)

zǒngtǒngfǔ 總統府 the presidential office

zǒngwù 總務 general affairs

zǒngyùsuàn 總預算 a general budget

zǒngzé 總則 general principles

zǒngzhàng 總帳 (bookkeeping) a ledger

zǒngzhī 總之 in short; in brief; in a word; in conclusion; to sum up

zǒngzhí 總值 total value; a total price

zǒngzhòngliàng 總重量 gross weight

zòng 從
refer to **cóng** 從 4

zòng 綜
refer to **zōng** 綜

zòng 粽
glutinous rice tamale—made by wrapping the rice in broad leaves of reeds and boiled for a few hours—usually with other ingredients, such as dates, meat, oysters, beans, etc.

zòngzi 粽子 a glutinous rice dumpling; rice tamale

zòng 縱
1. to allow to move or work freely; to let go; to let fly 2. to indulge; indulgence 3. even if; although 4. (also **zōng**) vertical; longitudinal

zòngduì 縱隊 a column of troops

zòngguān 縱觀 to take a free, wide look; to take a sweeping look

zòngguàn tiělù 縱貫鐵路 the main north-south railway of Tai-

Z

wan

zònghéng jiāocuò 縱橫交錯 arranged in a crisscross pattern

zònghǔ guīshān 縱虎歸山 to allow an evildoer to escape

zònghuǒ 縱火 to commit arson

zònglǎn 縱覽 to look freely and extensively

zòngrán 縱然 even though; even if

zòngróng 縱容 to connive at

zòngshǐ 縱使 even though; even if

zòngyǒu 縱有 even if there is...

Zōu 鄒
1. name of a state in the Epoch of Warring States 2. a Chinese family name

zǒu 走
1. to walk; to go on foot 2. to run; to go swiftly 3. to go; to travel 4. to leave; to go away; to depart 5. to let out or lose (unintentionally); to leak out 6. to visit

zǒubì 走避 to run away from; to shun; to evade

zǒubiàn 走遍 to travel all over (an area)

zǒudào 走道 1. a pavement; a sidewalk 2. a path; a footpath 3. an aisle

zǒudòng 走動 1. to take a walk; to go for a stroll 2. to have intercourse; to visit

zǒudúshēng 走讀生 a nonresident student

zǒufǎng 走訪 1. to interview; to have an interview with 2. to visit

zǒugǒu 走狗 a lackey; a tool

zǒuhuǒ 走火 1. (said of firearms) to go off accidentally 2. (electricity) a short circuit

zǒukāi 走開 Beat it! Get out of the way!

zǒuláng 走廊 a corridor; a hall; a veranda

zǒulòu 走漏 (said of secrets, plots, etc.) to leak

zǒulù 走路 to walk; to go on foot

zǒumǎ kànhuā 走馬看花 to examine a thing hurriedly

zǒusàn 走散 1. to walk away in different directions 2. to get separated from other travelers

zǒushī 走失 (said of persons, animals, etc.) to get lost; to be missing

zǒusī 走私 to smuggle

zǒutóu wúlù 走投無路 to have no one to turn to

zǒuwèi 走味 to turn stale; to lose flavor

zǒuxiàng 走向 1. the run; the trend 2. (geology) strike 3. to move toward; to head for; to be on the way to

zǒuyàng 走樣 1. to get out of shape; to lose shape; to deviate from the original 2. to be different from what is expected or intended

zǒuyùn 走運 to be in luck; to have good luck

zǒuzheqiáo 走著瞧 to wait and see

zòu 奏
1. to report to the throne 2. to play (music or musical instruments) 3. to move; to advance

zòujié 奏捷 to win; to be victorious

zòumíngqǔ 奏鳴曲 (music) a sonata

zòuxiào 奏效 effective; efficacious

zòuyuè 奏樂 to play music (in solemn ceremonies)

zòu 揍
1. to beat; to slug (somebody); to hit hard 2. to smash

zòurén 揍人 to slug a person

zòu 驟
refer to **zhòu** 驟

zū 租
1. to rent; to lease; to let; to hire; to charter 2. rent; rental 3. a tax; to tax

zūfèi 租費 a royalty

zūhù 租戶 a tenant

zūjiè 租界 a foreign settlement

or concession

zūjiè 租借 lend-lease; to rent

zūjīn 租金 rent or rental

zūlìn 租賃 to rent (a house, etc.); to lease

zūshòu 租售 for rent or sale

zūyòng 租用 to rent for use; to be tenanted

zūyuē 租約 a lease

zú 足

1. the foot; the leg 2. the base (of an object) 3. sufficient; full; enough; adequate

zúbù chūhù 足不出戶 to refrain from stepping outside the house

zúgòu 足夠 enough; sufficient; full; ample

zújī 足跡 1. whereabouts 2. a footprint; a footmark; a track

zújiàn 足見 it serves to show

zújīn 足金 pure gold

zúqiú 足球 football; soccer

zúqiúduì 足球隊 a football team

zúqiúsài 足球賽 a football game; a soccer game

zúsuì 足歲 to have actually reached a certain age

zúyǐ 足以 sufficient to; enough to

zúzhì duōmóu 足智多謀 wise and resourceful

zúzú 足足 full; no less than; as much as

zú 卒

1. a servant; an underling; a lackey 2. a soldier 3. a unit of one hundred soldiers 4. at last; after all; at long last 5. to complete; to finish 6. dead; to die 7. a community of 300 families 8. a pawn in Chinese chess

zú 族

1. a tribe; a family 2. a race (of people) 3. a class or group of things with common features

zúpǔ 族譜 the pedigree of a clan

zúrén 族人 fellow clansmen

zǔ 阻

1. to prevent; to stop; to prohibit

2. to separate; separated 3. to hinder; to obstruct; to impede; to blockade 4. difficulty; to suffer 5. to rely on 6. a strategic pass

zǔ'ài 阻礙 an obstacle or hindrance; to obstruct; obstruction; to impede

zǔdǎng 阻擋 to stop; to be in the way

zǔgé 阻隔 1. to be separated; to be isolated 2. to cut off

zǔlì 阻力 the force of resistance

zǔsè 阻塞 1. to block up; to clog; to obstruct 2. a jam; a block

zǔzhǐ 阻止 to stop or prevent; to prohibit or proscribe; to block

zǔ 祖

1. one's grandfather or grandmother 2. ancestors; forebears 3. a founder; an originator 4. to follow the example of; to imitate 5. a Chinese family name

zǔchǎn 祖產 ancestral estate

zǔchuán 祖傳 inherited from one's ancestors; hereditary

zǔfén 祖墳 an ancestral grave

zǔfù 祖父 one's grandfather

zǔguó 祖國 one's homeland; one's fatherland

zǔjí 祖籍 one's ancestral home

zǔmǔ 祖母 one's grandmother

zǔsūn 祖孫 ancestors and descendants

zǔxiān 祖先 forefathers; ancestors; forebears

zǔzōng 祖宗 forefathers; ancestors; forebears

zǔ 組

1. a group; a team; a section; a department; an organization; a union 2. to organize; to arrange; to unite; to form 3. tassels; a fringe; a girdle; a tape

zǔchéng 組成 to form; to constitute

zǔgé 組閣 (government) to form a cabinet

zǔhé 組合 1. (mathematics) combinations 2. to unite; to make up 3. a company; a union

zǔqǔ 組曲 (music) a suite

zǔzhǎng 組長 the chief of a

Z

department or section in a government agency

zǔzhī 組織 1. to organize; to constitute 2. an organization; a formation 3. (biology) tissue; texture

zǔ 詛

1. to curse; to imprecate 2. to vow; to pledge

zǔzhòu 詛咒 to curse; to imprecate

zuān 鑽

1. to pierce; to drill; to bore; to dig through; to penetrate 2. to go through; to make one's way into 3. to gain (profit, a position, etc.) through special favor, contact, relations, etc. 4. to study intensively; to dig into; to bury oneself in 5. (also **zuǎn**) to bore or pierce a hole

zuānkǒng 鑽孔 to make a hole; to perforate

zuān niújiǎojiān 鑽牛角尖 to get oneself into a dead-end alley through sheer stubbornness

zuānyán 鑽研 to study or scrutinize thoroughly

zuānyíng 鑽營 to seek advantage for oneself by all means

zuǎn 纂

1. a kind of red cloth 2. to compile; to collect

zuǎnxiū 纂修 to compile; to edit

zuǎn 鑽

refer to **zuān** 鑽 5

zuàn 鑽

1. a gimlet; an awl or auger; a borer; a drill 2. a diamond; a jewel

zuànjiè 鑽戒 a diamond ring

zuànshí 鑽石 a diamond

zuǐ 嘴

1. the mouth; the bill or beak (of a bird); the snout (of a pig, etc.) 2. a nozzle

zuǐba 嘴巴 the mouth

zuǐchán 嘴饞 gluttonous

zuǐchún 嘴唇 the lips

zuǐjǐn 嘴緊 tight-lipped; close-mouthed

zuǐtián 嘴甜 honeymouthed

zuǐyìng 嘴硬 1. to talk toughly 2. to refuse to admit a mistake

zuì 最

extreme; superlative

zuì'ǎi 最矮 (said of stature) the shortest; (said of houses) the lowest

zuìchū 最初 1. the first; the earliest 2. at first; in the beginning

zuìdà 最大 the biggest; the largest; the greatest; the maximum

zuìdī 最低 the lowest; the minimum; the least

zuìdī lùqǔ biāozhǔn 最低錄取標準 the minimum scores; requirement for admission

zuìdī xiàndù 最低限度 1. the lowest limit 2. at least

zuìduō 最多 the most; at most

zuìgāo 最高 the highest; the superlative; the supreme

zuìgāo dāngjú 最高當局 the highest authorities

Zuìgāo Fǎyuàn 最高法院 the Supreme Court

zuìgāofēng 最高峰 the summit; the climax

zuìgāojí 最高級 1. the highest; the summit 2. (linguistics) the superlative degree

zuìhǎo 最好 1. the best 2. had better

zuìhòu 最後 the last; the ultimate; the final

zuìhòu tōngdié 最後通牒 an ultimatum

zuìhuài 最壞 the worst; the meanest

zuìhuìguó 最惠國 the most favored nation

zuìjiā 最佳 the best

zuìjìn 最近 1. the nearest; the closest 2. recently; lately

zuìshǎo 最少 the least; the minimum

zuìxiān 最先 1. the first; the earliest; the foremost 2. at first; in the beginning

zuìxiǎo 最小 the least; the smallest; the minimum

zuìxīn 最新 the newest; the latest

zuìzhōng 最終 the final; the last; the ultimate

zuì 罪
1. sin; crime; fault; vice; evil; guilt 2. suffering; pain

zuìdà èjí 罪大惡極 a heinous crime; a capital offense

zuì'è 罪惡 sin; crime; vice; evil; guilt

zuìfàn 罪犯 a criminal; an offender

zuìgāi wànsǐ 罪該萬死 The crime deserves death for ten thousand times.

zuìkuí huòshǒu 罪魁禍首 a ringleader; a chief offender

zuìniè 罪孽 sin

zuìrén 罪人 1. a criminal; a sinner 2. to blame others

zuìxíng 罪行 criminal acts; atrocities; offenses

zuìyǒu yīngdé 罪有應得 The punishment is well deserved.

zuìzhèng 罪證 proof of a crime; evidence of one's guilt

zuì 醉
1. drunk; intoxicated 2. infatuated; charmed

zuìguǐ 醉鬼 a drunkard; a drunken person

zuìshēng mèngsǐ 醉生夢死 to live a befuddled life

zuìwēng zhīyì bùzài jiǔ 醉翁之意不在酒 to be secretly interested in something while pretending to show interest in another

zuìxīn 醉心 infatuated with (a pursuit)

zuìxūnxūn 醉醺醺 inebriated; sottish; drunk

zuì 蕞
very small; tiny

zuì'ěr xiǎoguó 蕞爾小國 a very small state

zūn 尊
1. to honor; to respect; to venerate; to revere; to esteem 2. honored; honorable; noble;

esteemed; respectable

zūnbēi 尊卑 1. seniors and juniors 2. superiors and inferiors

zūnchēng 尊稱 an honorific term; a title of respect

zūnfūrén 尊夫人 (courteously) your wife

zūnguì 尊貴 noble; honorable; respectable

zūnjià 尊駕 (courteously) you; your esteemed self

zūnjìng 尊敬 to respect; to revere; respect; reverence

zūnqīn 尊親 (courteously) your parents

zūnshī zhòngdào 尊師重道 to respect the teacher and his teachings

zūnxìng dàmíng 尊姓大名 (courteously) your name

zūnyán 尊嚴 dignity; honor; respectability

zūnyánsǐ 尊嚴死 euthanasia

zūnzhǎng 尊長 an elder; a senior

zūn 樽
1. a wine vessel; a goblet; a bottle; a wine jar 2. (said of vegetation) luxuriant

zūn 遵
1. to follow 2. to observe (rules, regulations, etc.); to abide by (laws, etc.)

zūncóng 遵從 to follow; to comply with; to obey (orders, etc.)

zūnfèng 遵奉 to observe; to obey

zūnmìng 遵命 to obey orders; to observe instructions

zūnshǒu 遵守 to observe; to abide by; to keep (a promise)

zūnxún 遵循 1. to accord with; to obey; to go by 2. to hesitate

zūnzhào 遵照 to follow; to observe; to accord with; to obey

zūnzhǐ 遵旨 to follow imperial orders or decrees

zuò 作

zuòfang 作坊 a small workshop

zuònòng 作弄 to tease; to make

a fool of

zuó 作

zuójian 作踐 to abuse; to waste; to treat harshly

zuóxīng 作興 1. allowable 2. to be in good spirits 3. in vogue 4. to hold in high regard 5. perhaps; likely

zuó 昨

yesterday; lately; past

zuórì 昨日 yesterday

zuósǐ jīnshēng 昨死今生 to be reborn; to lead a new life from now on

zuótiān 昨天 yesterday

zuówǎn 昨晚 last night

zuó 琢 also **zhuó**

to ponder over; to consider

zuómo 琢磨 to ponder over; to consider

zuǒ 左

1. the left side 2. the east side 3. improper 4. supporting (documents, etc.); to assist 5. to be demoted; to descend 6. inconvenience 7. erroneous; mistaken 8. unduly stubborn 9. to disregard

zuǒbian 左邊 the left side; the left-hand side

zuǒcè 左側 on the left side

zuǒfāng 左方 on the left; to the left

zuǒgù yòupàn 左顧右盼 inattentive

zuǒlín yòushè 左鄰右舍 neighbors

zuǒlúnqiāng 左輪鎗 a revolver; a six-shooter

zuǒpài 左派 1. a radical; a leftist 2. a leftist faction

zuǒpiězi 左撇子 a left-handed person; a southpaw; a portsider

zuǒqīng 左傾 left-leaning

zuǒshǒu 左手 the left hand

zuǒsī yòuxiǎng 左思右想 to think over and over; to ponder

zuǒyì 左翼 1. (politics) the left wing or leftist 2. (ball games) the left wing 3. (military operations) the left flank

zuǒyòu 左右 1. left and right —nearby; at hand 2. servants; aides 3. to sway

zuǒyòu féngyuán 左右逢源 to get help from all sides

zuǒyòu kāigōng 左右開弓 to slap someone's face with both hands

zuǒyòushǒu 左右手 1. left and right hands 2. top aides

zuǒyòu wéinán 左右爲難 to be in a dilemma

zuǒzhī yòuchù 左支右絀 not have enough money to cover the expenses

zuǒzhuǎn 左轉 to turn left

zuǒ 佐

to assist; to aid; to second

zuǒcān 佐餐 to be eaten together with rice

zuǒlǐ 佐理 to assist

zuǒzhèng 佐證 the evidence

zuò 坐

1. to sit; a seat 2. to ride (on a bus, train, etc.) 3. to kneel 4. to reach; to arrive at 5. (said of a building) to have its back towards 6. to get (profit, etc.) without work 7. to keep on; to persist in 8. (said of a building) to fall back from pressure; to sink 9. (said of guns, etc.) to recoil; to kick

zuòbiāo 坐標 (mathematics) coordinates

zuòchī shānkōng 坐吃山空 One cannot live in security without a dependable source of income.

zuòcì 坐次 the order of seats in a meeting or feast

zuòdiàn 坐墊 a seat cushion

zuòguān chéngbài 坐觀成敗 to look on coldly

zuòhuái bùluàn 坐懷不亂 to be immune from the temptation of feminine charms

zuòjì 坐騎 refer to **zuòqí** 坐騎

zuòjǐng guāntiān 坐井觀天 a very limited view, usually implying shortsightedness, ignorance, shallowness, etc.

zuòkùn 坐困 to be confined or walled in

zuòláo 坐牢 to be jailed or imprisoned

zuò lěngbǎndèng 坐冷板凳 to hold a position with little or no power

zuòlì bù'ān 坐立不安 fidgety; restless

zuòluò 坐落 (said of a house, building, etc.) to be located or situated at

zuòqí 坐騎 one's horse for riding

zuòshī liángjī 坐失良機 to let a golden chance slip by

zuòshì 坐視 to keep hands off

zuòxí 坐席 1. to take one's seat at a banquet table 2. a seat

zuòxia 坐下 to sit down

zuòxiǎng qíchéng 坐享其成 to enjoy the fruit without toil

zuòyǐ dàibì 坐以待斃 to do nothing to avert a crisis, peril, etc.

zuòzhèn 坐鎮 personally take charge of (an operation or mission)

zuò 作

1. to do; to make 2. the works (of a writer, etc.) 3. to rise up 4. to pretend; to affect 5. to regard...as; to take...for 6. to write; to compose

zuò'àn 作案 to commit a crime

zuòbà 作罷 to drop; to give up

zuòbàn 作伴 to keep (someone) company; to serve as a companion

zuòbǎo 作保 to guarantee; to vouch for

zuòbì 作弊 to cheat (especially in examinations); to indulge in corrupt practices

zuòdōng 作東 to stand treat

zuòduì 作對 to oppose; to act against

zuò'è duōduān 作惡多端 to indulge in all sorts of evildoing

zuòfǎ 作法 a way of doing or handling things

zuòfǎ zìbì 作法自斃 to get into trouble through one's own scheme

zuòfèi 作廢 to nullify; to cancel

zuòfēng 作風 one's way of doing things

zuògěng 作梗 to oppose secretly

zuògōng 作工 to labor; to work

zuògǔ 作古 to die; to pass away

zuòguài 作怪 mischievous; to act mischievously

zuòguān 作官 to be a government official

zuòhuó 作活 to work (for a living)

zuòjiā 作家 a writer; an author

zuòjiǎ 作假 to pretend; to make an imitation copy

zuòjià 作嫁 to earn a living by working for others

zuòjiān fànkē 作姦犯科 to do evil; to break the law

zuòjiǎn zìfú 作繭自縛 refer to **zuòjiǎn zìfù** 作繭自縛

zuòjiǎn zìfù 作繭自縛 to get into trouble by one's own schemes

zuòkè 作客 1. to be a guest 2. to stay outside of one's hometown

zuòlè 作樂 to make merry; to have fun

zuòluàn 作亂 to rebel; to start an uprising

zuòméi 作媒 to act as a go-between in marriage

zuòmèng 作夢 1. to dream 2. to imagine as in a dream; to have daydreams

zuòniè 作孽 to do evil

zuònòng 作弄 refer to **zuōnòng** 作弄

zuò'ǒu 作嘔 to nauseate

zuòpéi 作陪 to accompany

zuòpǐn 作品 the works

zuòqǔ 作曲 to compose

zuòqǔjiā 作曲家 a composer

zuòshēng 作聲 to speak; to break silence

zuòshī 作詩 to write poems; to versify

zuòshì 作勢 to put on airs; to pretend

zuòshòu 作壽 to celebrate a

birthday

zuò shūsǐzhàn 作殊死戰 to fight to the bitter end

zuòsuì 作祟 1. (said of spirits) to haunt 2. (said of people) to make mischief

zuòtài 作態 to strike an attitude

zuòwēi zuòfú 作威作福 to overexert one's power and position by acting impudently

zuòwéi 作為 1. conduct; behavior 2. to accomplish 3. to serve as; to look upon as

zuòwěi 作偽 to pretend; to make an imitation copy

zuòwén 作文 1. to write a composition 2. a composition

zuòwù 作物 crops

zuòxiù 作秀 (informal) 1. to appear in a stage show 2. to grandstand

zuòyè 作業 students' homework

zuòyè xìtǒng 作業系統 (computers) the operating system

zuòyòng 作用 1. functions 2. effect

zuòzhàn 作戰 to go to battle; to fight against

zuòzhě 作者 a writer; an author

zuòzhèng 作證 to act as a witness in court

zuòzhǔ 作主 to take up responsibility for making a decision

zuò 座

a seat; a stand

zuòbiāo 座標 (mathematics) coordinates

zuòcì 座次 seating order

zuòluò 座落 to be situated or located at

zuòshàngkè 座上客 a guest of honor

zuòtánhuì 座談會 a discussion meeting; a symposium

zuòwèi 座位 a seat

zuòwú xūxí 座無虛席 There is standing room only.

zuòyòumíng 座右銘 a motto

zuò 做

1. to work; to make; to do 2. to act as 3. to pretend to be

zuò'ài 做愛 to make love

zuòbàn 做伴 to keep somebody company

zuòdào 做到 to accomplish; to achieve

zuòdōng 做東 to play the host; to host

zuòfǎ 做法 way of doing a thing; practice

zuòfàn 做飯 to prepare food

zuògōng 做工 to work

zuòguān 做官 to become an official

zuòjiǎ 做假 to cheat

zuòkè 做客 to be a guest

zuòlǐbài 做禮拜 to go to church; to be at church

zuòméi 做媒 to be a matchmaker

zuòmèng 做夢 1. to dream 2. to daydream

zuònòng 做弄 to make fun of; to play jokes upon

zuòrén 做人 to conduct oneself; to behave

zuòrénqíng 做人情 to do something as a favor

zuòshēng 做聲 to make a sound

zuòshēngyi 做生意 to do business transactions

zuòshì 做事 1. to handle affairs; to do a deed; to act 2. to work; to have a job

zuòshòu 做壽 to celebrate one's birthday

zuòtóufa 做頭髮 to have one's hair done at a beauty parlor

zuòwénzhāng 做文章 1. to write an essay 2. to make an issue of

zuòxiǎo 做小 to be someone's concubine

zuòyàngzi 做樣子 to go through the motion of doing something; to pretend to do something

zuòyīfu 做衣服 to tailor; to have a dress made

zuòzéi xīnxū 做賊心虛 One who has done something bad secretly cannot look others in the eye.

zuòzhǔ 做主 to take charge of; to be responsible for; to decide

zuòzhuāng 做莊 (gambling) to be the banker

zuòzuo 做作 1. affectation; pretentious 2. to behave unnaturally

zuò 鑿

refer to **záo** 鑿

Radical List

Radicals are arranged according to the stroke numbers used in writing them. The page number to the right of each radical indicates where the radical is located in the Radical Index.

Radical	Page Number	Radical	Page Number	Radical	Page Number	Radical	Page Number	Radical	Page Number
一	788	厂	790	辶	794	毋(母)	799	白	803
丨	788	厶	790	廾	794	比	799	皮	803
丶	788	又	790	弋	794	毛	799	皿	803
丿	788	口	790	弓	794	氏	799	目(罒)	803
乙	788	囗	792	彐(彑⇒)	795	气	799	矛	803
亅	788	土	792	彡	795	水(氵氺)	799	矢	803
二	788	士	792	彳	795	火(灬)	801	石	803
亠	788	夂	792	心(忄小)	795	爪(爫)	801	示(礻)	804
人(亻)	788	夕	792	戈	796	父	801	禸	804
儿	789	大	792	戶	796	爻	801	禾	804
入	789	女	792	手(扌)	796	爿	801	穴	804
八	789	子	793	支	797	片	801	立	804
冂	789	宀	793	支(攵)	797	牙	801	竹	804
冖	789	寸	793	文	797	牛(牜)	801	米	805
冫	789	小	793	斗	797	犬(犭)	802	糸	805
几	789	尢(尢)	793	斤	797	玄	802	缶	805
凵	789	尸	793	方	797	玉(王)	802	网(罓	805
刀(刂)	789	屮	794	无	797	瓜	802	罔罓)	
力	790	山	794	日	797	瓦	802	羊(羋)	806
勹	790	巛	794	曰	798	甘	802	羽	806
匕	790	工	794	月	798	生	802	老	806
匚	790	己	794	木	798	用	802	而	806
匸	790	巾	794	欠	799	田	802	耒	806
十	790	干	794	止	799	疋(疋)	802	耳	806
卜	790	幺	794	歹(歺)	799	疒	802	聿	806
卩(㔾)	790	广	794	殳	799	癶	803	肉(月)	806

Radical	Page Number	Radical	Page Number	Radical	Page Number	Radical	Page Number
臣	806	足	810	飛	813	鼻	814
自	806	身	810	食(飠)	813	齊	814
至	807	車	810	首	813	齒	814
臼(臼)	807	辛	810	香	813	龍	814
舌	807	辰	810	馬	813	龜	814
舛	807	辵(辶)	810	骨	813	龠	814
舟	807	邑(阝)	811	高	813		
艮	807	酉	811	髟	813		
色	807	釆	811	鬥	814		
艸(艹)	807	里	811	鬯	814		
虍	808	金	811	鬲	814		
虫	808	長(镸)	812	鬼	814		
血	808	門	812	魚	814		
行	808	阜(阝)	812	鳥	814		
衣(衤)	808	隶	812	鹵	814		
襾(覀)	808	隹	812	鹿	814		
見	808	雨	812	麥	814		
角	809	青	812	麻	814		
言	809	非	812	黃	814		
谷	809	面	813	黍	814		
豆	809	革	813	黑	814		
豕	809	韋	813	黹	814		
豸	809	韭	813	黽	814		
貝	809	音	813	鼎	814		
赤	810	頁	813	鼓	814		
走	810	風	813	鼠	814		

Radical Index

In this index the characters are listed under their respective radicals. Characters with the same radical are arranged in the ascending order according to the number of strokes used in writing them. The figure to the right of each character is the page number under which the character can be found in the body of the dictionary.

The first step in looking for a character is to find out the radical under which it is listed. The next step is to look for the character in the index according to the number of strokes (i.e. the total number of strokes used in writing the whole character minus the number of strokes used in writing the radial). With the page number as a guide, one can locate in the dictionary the character and the entries beneath it.

候	224	傍	14	僧	320	**6**		**7**		凶	638
借	280		15	儗	405	兒	141	冠	196	**3**	
俱	296	備	22	僻	418	**9**			198	凹	5
	298	傖	52	儀	678	兜	129	**8**		出	77
倨	298	傅	168	億	683	**12**		冥	385	凸	568
倦	300	傢	201	**14**		兢	287	冤	709		569
倔	301	傢	258	儐	33	**入**	472	冢	754	**6**	
	302	傑	277		34	**2**		**14**		函	210
倆	340	傀	322	價	57	內	397	冪	378	**刀(刂)**	
	344	傘	477	儒	76	**4**		**冫**		刀	110
倫	361	傚	626	儘	283	全	458	**3**		刁	122
們	375	**11**		儒	472	**6**		冬	127	**1**	
倩	442	傲	6	**15**		兩	343	**4**		刃	467
倏	519	傳	83	償	61	**八**		冰	34	**2**	
	522	催	92	儡	333	**2**		**5**		分	157
倘	548	僅	283	優	696	公	184	冷	334	切	446
偶	554	傾	314	**16**		六	354	冶	667	刈	680
倭	584		451	儲	80	兮	601	**8**		**3**	
	593		453		81	**4**		凋	123	刊	307
倖	638	傻	481	**19**		共	188	凍	128	划	229
修	640	傷	485	儺	340	兵	35	凌	349	列	346
倚	680	傭	693	**20**		**6**		准	768	刎	592
值	745		694	儻	659	典	119	**9**		刑	635
9		債	725	**儿**		具	298	湊	91	**5**	
側	53	傳	765	**1**		其	431	**13**		別	33
假	258	**12**		兀	599	**8**		凜	348	初	79
	259	僖	266	**2**		兼	260	**14**		利	338
健	265	僥	273	元	710	**14**		凝	403	判	411
偕	276	僚	345	允	715	冀	255	**几**		刨	412
偶	408	僕	427	**3**		**冂**		几	245	刪	483
偏	419	僑	444	充	73	**3**			252	**6**	
偌	475	僧	479	兄	639	冊	53	**1**		刺	89
停	561	僮	565	**4**		冉	462	凡	146	到	111
偷	566		767	光	199	**4**		**9**		剁	
偎	584	僞	589	先	610	再	718	凰	235	刮	194
偉	587	像	620	兒	639	**5**		**10**		劫	276
偽	587	**13**		兆	732	冒	370	凱	307	刻	311
偕	627	價	260	**5**		冑	758	**12**			313
優	658	儉	263	兌	135	冕	379	凳	115	券	460
偵	736		266	克	313	**冖**		**凵**		刷	523
做	783	僵	268	免	379			**2**			524
10		徹	289	兔	570					制	749

7		力	337	**勹**		**2**			584	**6**	
剋	313	**3**		**1**		匹	416	印	688	取	457
剌	325	功	186	勺	489		418	**5**		受	516
前	439	加	256	**2**		**9**		即	250	叔	518
剃	554	**4**		勾	189	區	29	卵	360		520
削	646	劣	346		190	匿	399	卻	461	**7**	
	649	**5**		勿	600	區	456	**6**		叛	411
則	722	努	406	匀	715	**十**		卷	300	**16**	
8		劬	457	**3**		十	503	卸	628	叢	91
剝	16	劭	490	包	15	**1**		**10**		**口**	
	37	助	761	匆	90	千	437	卿	451	口	316
剛	174	**6**		**4**		**2**		**厂**		**2**	
剖	426	劾	218	匈	639	升	497	**2**		叭	7
剔	552	**7**		**7**		午	598	厄	139	斥	73
剜	577	勃	38	匍	427	半	13	**7**		叨	110
9		勁	284	**9**		卉	239	厚	223		549
副	167		290	匐	164	**6**		**8**		叼	122
剪	262	勉	379	**匕**		卑	20	厤	94	叮	125
10		勇	694	**2**		卒	92	原	710	古	191
創	84	**9**		匕	25	協	627	**10**		叫	273
	85	動	128	化	229	卓	769	厥	301	句	298
割	179	勘	308	**3**		卒	778	厭	659	可	312
剩	500		309	北	21	**7**		**13**			313
11		勒	331		39	南	394	厲	339	叩	317
劇	58		332	**9**		**10**		**厶**		另	351
剮	272	務	600	匙	72	博	38	**3**		叵	425
劂	420	**10**			513	**卜**		去	458	史	507
	421	勞	329	**匚**		卜	39	**9**		司	530
12			331	**3**		**3**		參	50	台	543
劃	229	勝	499	匝	717	卡	305		54	右	702
	231		500	**4**			436		477	召	732
13		勠	358	匠	269	占	725		459	只	747
劊	203	**11**		匡	321		726	**又**		**3**	
	320	募	392	**5**		**6**		又	701	吃	71
劍	266	勤	448	匣	607	卦	195	**1**			249
劇	299	勢	512	**8**		**冂**		叉	54	吋	94
劉	354	**14**		匪	154	**(巳)**			56	各	180
劈	417	勳	649	**11**		**3**		**2**		合	216
	418	**15**		匯	240	卯	370	反	147	后	223
14		勵	339	**12**		**4**		及	249	吉	249
劓	255	**18**		匵	322	危	583	友	699	吏	338
力		勸	460	**匸**						名	383

居	295
屈	456
屋	554
6	
屍	502
屎	508
屋	594
7	
屑	628
展	726
8	
屏	35
屏	424
9	
屍	57
屠	569
11	
屢	359
12	
層	54
履	359
18	
屬	522
	761
屮	
1	
屯	573
山	
山	482
3	
屹	680
4	
岔	56
岌	249
5	
岸	4
岡	174
	175
岬	258
岩	655
岳	714
7	

島	110
峰	160
峻	304
峭	445
峽	607
8	
崩	24
崇	75
崔	92
崗	175
	175
崛	301
崎	431
崖	652
	653
崢	739
9	
嵐	326
嵌	438
	442
10	
嵩	535
11	
嶇	456
嶄	726
嶂	730
12	
嶙	348
嶔	447
14	
嶺	351
嶼	706
嶽	715
18	
巍	584
	586
20	
巖	657
巛	
川	82
3	
巡	649

州	756
8	
巢	62
工	
工	183
2	
巨	297
巧	445
左	781
4	
巫	595
7	
差	54
	56
	57
	88
己	
己	252
巳	533
巳	679
1	
巴	7
6	
巷	620
巾	
巾	281
2	
布	46
市	509
3	
帆	146
4	
希	602
5	
帛	38
帘	340
帕	408
帖	559
	560
帚	757
6	
帝	118

帥	524
	530
7	
幫	14
師	502
席	604
8	
常	60
帶	104
帷	585
帳	730
9	
幃	164
帽	370
幀	742
10	
幌	236
11	
幕	392
幛	730
12	
幣	27
幟	751
干	
干	171
2	
平	422
3	
年	400
5	
并	36
幸	638
10	
幹	174
幺	
1	
幻	233
2	
幼	701
6	
幽	695
9	

幾	246
	252
7	
广	
4	
庇	26
床	84
序	643
5	
底	116
店	120
府	165
6	
庚	182
庖	412
度	133
	138
7	
庫	318
庭	561
8	
座	783
庵	4
康	309
庶	522
庸	693
	694
9	
廁	54
廂	618
10	
廊	328
廉	341
廈	481
	610
11	
廄	295
廓	323
廖	346
廳	689
12	
廠	61
廚	80

廢	154
廣	200
廟	381
廝	532
16	
廬	357
龐	412
22	
廳	561
夂	
4	
廷	561
延	655
6	
建	265
廾	
2	
弁	30
4	
弄	355
	405
6	
弈	681
12	
弊	27
弋	
弋	680
3	
式	509
10	
弒	511
弓	
弓	184
1	
弔	123
引	687
2	
弗	163
弘	221
3	
弛	72
	507

永	694	**5**		洞	128	浙	734	渡	133		354
2		波	37	洪	221	**8**		港	175	滅	382
氾	148		425	洇	238	淳	87	渦	204	溟	386
求	455	泊	38	活	242	淙	90	湖	226	溺	399
汀	560		425	津	282	淬	93	渙	234	滂	411
汁	744	治	72	流	352	淡	107	渾	241	溥	428
3			749	洛	363	涵	211	湔	261	溶	469
池	72	法	144	派	410	涸	215	減	263	溿	473
汞	188		145	洽	436		218	渴	312	濕	503
汗	210	泛	148	洒	475	淮	231	湄	372	溲	536
	211	沸	154	洗	605	混	241	湎	379	潮	538
汞	223	沾	191		613		242	渺	381	滔	549
江	267	河	217	洽	607	淨	290	湃	410	溪	430
汝	472	泓	221	洒	613	淚	333	渠	457	溢	683
汕	484	沮	295	洩	628	涼	343	湯	485	源	711
污	594		297	洵	639	淋	347		547	準	768
汐	601		298	洋	661	渝	361	湍	570	滋	771
	606	況	321	洲	757	淼	381	溫	590	滓	772
汛	650	泠	349	**7**		淖	396	渦	593	**11**	
4		泌	26	浮	38	淒	429	渥	594	漕	53
沖	74		378	涍	54	淺	441	**10**		滴	115
沌	136	泯	383	浮	162	清	449	滄	52	嫡	116
汩	192	沫	388		164	深	494	潦	116	溉	171
沆	213	泥	398	海	208	淑	519	滇	119	漢	212
汲	249		399	浩	215		520		557	滸	227
決	301	泡	412	浣	233	涮	525	溝	189	漸	262
沒	371		413		579	潤	548	滑	192		266
汨	378	泣	434	浸	284	渺	550		229	漿	268
沒	388	泅	455	涇	286	添	556	滾	203	連	341
沐	392	泉	459	涓	300	淅	602	潤	242	漏	356
沛	414	泰	545	浚	304	淯	622	溢	314	滷	357
沏	429	泄	628	浪	328		664	溜	352	滿	367
汽	434		681	浬	336	涯	652			漫	367
沏	448	沿	655	浼	373	淹	653			漠	389
泐	456		659	涅	402	液	668			漂	420
沙	479	浃	660	浦	427		682				421
沈	496	泳	694	涉	491	淫	686			漆	430
沓	543	油	697	涕	554	淤	702				458
汰	545	沾	725	涎	612	淵	710			滲	497
汪	581	沼	732	消	621	**9**				漱	522
沃	593	注	762	湧	694	渤	38				
沚	747	**6**		浴	707	測	54				

	536	濟	252	**3**		煩	146	熿	6	爾	142		
澌	645		255	灸	293	煥	234		709	**爿**			
	646	濬	304		749	煎	261	爍	52	**4**		戕	442
演	658	濫	327	災	717	煉	342	燷	239				443
瀁	676	濛	375	灶	721	煤	372	繪	240	**片**			
漁	704	濘	398	灼	769	煞	481	燮	541	片	419		
漲	729		403	**4**		煦	643	營	691		420		
	730	濡	472	炒	63		644	燥	722	**4**		版	13
滯	751	濤	549	炊	85	煙	654	燭	759	**8**			
潰	775		550	炕	310	煮	761	**14**		牌	409		
12		濯	770	炎	656	**10**		燼	286	**牙**			
潯	57	**15**		**5**		熔	469	**15**		牙	652		
潮	63	瀑	20	炳	35	煽	483	爆	20	**牛(牜)**			
澈	64		428	炯	292	熙	603	爍	530	牛	403		
澄	70	瀆	132	炬	298	熄	603	**16**		**2**			
潢	236	瀠	267	炮	16		605	爐	357	牟	389		
潤	266	瀏	354		412	熊	640	**17**		牝	422		
澆	271	濾	360		413	熏	649	爛	327	**3**			
潔	279	潘	496	炭	547	熒	691	**爪(爫)**		牢	328		
潰	321	瀉	629	炫	646	**11**		爪	732	牡	390		
潦	331	**16**		炸	724	熬	5		763	牠	543		
	345	瀨	34	**6**		熱	463	**4**			550		
	346	瀚	212	烘	221	熟	514	爬	408		573		
潘	410	瀝	340	烤	310		520	爭	739	**4**			
澎	415	瀟	622	烙	331	熨	709	**8**		牧	392		
潑	425	**17**			363		716	為	585	物	600		
潛	440	瀾	326	烈	347	**12**			589	**5**			
潤	474		327	烏	594	熾	73	**14**		牴	117		
澀	479	瀰	377	烝	739	燈	114	爵	302	牲	499		
潸	483	**18**		**7**		燉	137	**父**		**6**			
潭	546	灌	199	烽	160	燎	345	父	165	特	550		
13		**19**		烹	415		346		166	**7**			
澳	6	灘	475	焉	653	燗	374	**4**		犁	334		
澱	122	灢	545	**8**			375	爸	8	牽	437		
激	247	**21**		焙	22	燃	462	爹	124	**8**			
濃	405	灨	8	焚	157	燒	489	**9**		犄	246		
澡	721	**22**		焦	271	燙	548	爺	667	犀	603		
澤	722	灣	578	然	462	熹	604	**爻**		**9**			
濁	770	**火(灬)**		無	595	燕	654	**7**		犍	261		
14		火	243	焰	656		659	爽	525	**10**			
濱	33	**2**			659	**13**		**10**		**10**			
濠	213	灰	236	**9**									

疾	250	瘴	730	**5**		盡	285	睫	278	**3**						
痂	257	**12**		皋	177	**10**		睛	286	知	744					
疱	413	癌	1	**6**		盤	410	睦	392		749					
疲	417		656	皎	272	**11**		睡	528	**5**						
疼	551	癆	329	**7**		盬	199	睜	739	矩	297					
疹	737	療	345	皓	215	盧	357	**9**		**7**						
症	742	**13**		皖	580	目(罒)		睹	132	短	133					
6		癖	418	**10**		目	391	睽	322	**8**						
痕	220	**14**		皚	1	**3**		瞄	381	矮	2					
痊	459	癘	33	**皮**		盲	369	睿	474	**12**						
癢	663	**15**		皮	417	直	745	**10**		矯	273					
痔	750	癩	740	**5**		**4**		瞌	311	**石**						
7		**16**		皰	413	盹	136	瞑	380	石	504					
痘	130	癩	326	**10**		盾	136		386	**3**						
痙	290	**17**		皺	758		528	瞎	607	矽	602					
痢	339	癬	614	**皿**		看	307	**11**			606					
痞	418		646	皿	383		308	瞠	67	**4**						
痠	538	癰	688		386	眉	372	瞞	367	砍	308					
痛	565	**19**		**3**		眇	381	**12**		砒	417					
痣	750	癲	119	盂	703	盼	411	瞪	115	砌	434					
8		癱	545	**4**		省	499	瞭	346	砂	480					
凝	71	**ㄗㄜ**		盃	20	相	616	瞥	421	研	656					
瘁	93	**4**		盆	415		620	瞧	445	**5**						
瘟	194	癸	202	盈	690	省	637	瞬	529	砥	117					
麻	364	**7**		盅	754	**5**		瞳	565	砝	145					
痰	546	登	114	**5**		眛	374	**13**		礆	413					
瘃	702	發	142	盎	5	眼	378	瞻	726	砰	415					
9		**白**		盍	218	眩	646	**14**		破	425					
瘋	160	白	9	**6**		眨	724	矇	375	砸	717					
瘓	234	**1**		盛	70	眞	735		376	砧	735					
瘌	325	百	10	盒	218	**6**		**19**		砥	748					
瘡	407		38	盜	321	眷	300	矗	82	**6**						
瘍	662	**2**		盛	500	眸	389	**21**		硅	201					
癒	709	皂	721	**7**		眺	559	矚	761	硫	353					
10		**3**		盜	112	眼	657	**矛**		硃	758					
瘡	84	的	114	**8**		眾	756	矛	370							
瘠	251		116	盟	375	**7**		**4**		硯	659					
瘤	354		118	盞	726	睏	323	矜	282	硬	692					
瘦	518	**4**		**9**		**8**		**矢**		**8**						
瘟	590	皈	201	監	261	睬	50	矢	507	碑	21					
11		皇	234		266	督	130	**2**		碘	119					
瘸	461	皆	275			睪	177	矣	680	碉	123					

碟	358	社	491	**8**			756	**7**		竿	172
硼	415	祀	534	禽	448	**10**		窗	84	**4**	
礁	416			**禾**		稻	112	窖	274	笆	7
碎	540	**4**		禾	215	稿	178	窨	292	筍	541
碗	580	歧	430	**2**		穀	193	**8**		笑	625
9		祈	431	私	530	稽	246	窠	311	**5**	
碧	27	祇	431	禿	568		434	窟	318	笨	24
碟	124		744	秀	641	稷	255	**9**		笛	116
碩	507		747	**3**		稼	259	窪	575	第	118
	530	**5**		秉	35	**11**		窩	593	符	164
碳	547	祕	26	**4**		積	247	**10**		笠	339
10			378	科	311	穆	393	窮	454	笙	499
磅	15	祠	88	秒	381	穌	537	窯	665	**6**	
	412	祛	456	秋	454	穎	692	**11**		筆	25
磁	88	神	495	**5**		**12**		窺	322	策	54
磋	94	祟	540	秤	71	穗	540	**12**		答	95
磕	311	祝	762		424	**13**		窿	355	等	114
磊	333	祖	778	秦	448	機	240	**13**		筏	144
碼	365	**6**		秧	660	檅	405	竄	92	筋	283
礦	401	祭	254	秩	750	**14**		竅	446	筐	321
磬	410	票	421	租	777	穫	245	**17**		筒	564
磅	411	祥	618	**6**		穩	592	竊	446		565
確	461	**8**		移	677	**穴**		**立**		**7**	
磧	716	禁	283	**7**		穴	648	立	337	筷	320
11			285	程	70	**2**		**5**		筵	656
磨	387	祿	358	稈	173	究	292	站	727	**8**	
	389	**9**		稍	489		294	竚	762	箔	39
磧	436	福	165	稅	528	**3**		**6**		管	198
礦	236	禍	245	稀	603	空	314	竟	290	箕	246
礁	271	**11**		**8**			316	章	728	箋	262
磷	348	禦	709	稗	12	穿	454	**7**		箱	440
13		**12**		稟	36	**4**		竣	304	算	539
礎	81	禪	57	稠	76	穿	82	竦	535	箏	724
14			485	稜	333	突	568	童	565	箏	739
礙	2	禧	604	稔	467		569	**9**		**9**	
15			606	稚	750	**5**		端	133	範	149
礦	321	**13**		**9**		窈	665	竭	278	箭	266
礪	340	禮	337	稱	66	窄	722	**15**		節	278
礫	340	**14**			67		725	競	291	篇	419
示(礻)		禱	111		71	**6**		**竹**		箱	618
示	509	**內**		糯	407	窈	559	竹	759	箴	737
3		**4**		種	754	窒	750	**3**		箸	763
		禹	705								

篆 765	**6**	約 713	絮 643	線 615	繼 255
10	粟 538	紂 758	絢 646	緒 644	繩 441
篝 92	粵 714	**4**	紫 772	緣 712	纂 779
篤 132	粥 757	純 87	**7**	**10**	**15**
篙 177	762	紡 151	綁 15	縛 165	纏 57
篩 482	**7**	紛 156	繁 147	169	纍 333
築 759	粲 52	級 250	經 286	縣 615	續 644
763	糧 343	納 393	絹 300	645	**17**
11	梁 343	紐 404	綏 539	緦 683	纖 612
簇 92	**8**	紕 417	繡 642	縈 691	**21**
簍 356	粹 93	紗 480	**8**	縝 737	纜 327
篷 415	精 287	紓 518	綃 24	緞 758	**缶**
12	粽 776	素 537	綹 50	**11**	**3**
簧 236	**9**	索 541	綱 76	縫 161	缸 174
簡 264	糊 226	542	綽 87	162	**4**
簫 622	糅 404	紋 591	緋 153	績 248	缺 460
簪 719	470	紊 592	綱 175	縷 360	**5**
723	**10**	紮 717	緊 283	縹 420	缽 37
13	糕 177	724	綾 350	421	**11**
簿 47	糜 456	紙 748	綠 358	縮 538	罄 454
簾 342	糖 548	**5**	360	541	**12**
簽 438	**11**	絆 14	綿 379	總 775	罈 546
簷 657	糙 53	累 332	綺 434	775	**14**
14	糞 157	333	綣 460	776	罌 690
籌 77	糧 269	紹 490	網 582	**12**	**18**
籍 252	糠 309	紳 493	綰 768	繚 345	罐 199
籃 326	糜 377	細 606	綜 775	繞 463	**网**
15	糟 720	絃 612	776	繕 485	(罒冗冈罓)
籤 439	**糸**	終 754	**9**	織 745	**3**
16	**1**	組 778	編 28	**13**	罕 211
籠 355	系 606	**6**	締 119	繪 241	罔 582
19	**2**	給 181	緞 134	繭 264	**6**
籬 335	糾 292	252	緩 233	繮 175	罣 195
籮 363	293	絞 272	緝 246	268	**8**
米	**3**	結 276	430	繳 273	罩 733
米 377	紅 187	277	436	繩 499	置 751
4	222	絕 301	緘 262	繫 255	罪 780
粉 157	紀 252	絡 331	練 342	607	**9**
5	253	363	緬 379	**14**	罰 144
粗 91	紉 467	絨 469	緯 588	辮 30	署 521
粒 339	紈 579	絲 531		繽 34	522
粘 400	紆 702	統 565			**10**

罷	8		9		4		3		脅	627		11	
	418	羈	263	耽	105	肚	132	胸	639	臚	162	
罵	365	翩	419	耿	182		133	胭	653	膠	271	
11		甋	581	5		肝	172	胰	677	膜	387	
罹	335	10		聊	345	肛	174	脂	744		389	
14		翰	6	聆	349	肖	625	7		膣	548	
羅	363	翰	212	6		肘	757	脖	38	膝	603	
19		11		聒	194	脯	165		12		
羈	249	翳	676		204	4			427	膩	399	
羊(芏)			684	7		肪	150	脫	574	膨	415	
羊	660	翼	684	聘	422		151	8		膳	485	
3		12		聖	501	肥	153	腕	1	13		
美	373	翻	146	8		股	192		5	臂	22	
4		藩	146	聚	298	肩	260		654		28	
羔	177	翹	445	聞	592	肯	314	腑	165	膽	106	
5			446		593	肴	664	腐	166	臟	193	
羚	349	14		11		育	706	脾	418	膾	320	
羞	641	耀	667	聰	90	肢	744	腔	442	臉	342	
7			715	聯	341	5		腎	496	膿	405	
群	461	老		聲	499	胞	16	腕	580	臊	478	
羨	615	老	329	聳	535	背	20	腋	669		479	
義	683	4		12			21		682	臀	573	
10		耆	431	職	746	肺	154	腴	730	臆	684	
羲	604	5		16		胡	226	9		膺	689	
12		者	734	聾	355	脈	388	腸	60	臃	693	
羵	483	而		聽	560	胖	410	腹	169		694	
13		而	141		562		412	腳	272	14		
羹	182	3		聿		胚	413		302	臍	432	
羸	332	耐	394	7		胎	543	腫	379	15		
羽		耍	523	肆	534	胃	589	腦	396	臘	325	
羽	705	耒		肅	538	胤	689	肥	475	18		
4		4		肄	683	6		腺	615	臟	720	
翅	73	耙	8	8		脆	93	腥	635	臣		
翁	593		408	肇	733	胴	128	腰	664	臣	64	
5		耕	182	肉(月)		胳	170	腴	704	2		
翌	604		286	肉	470		178	腫	754	臥	593	
翌	682	耗	215		473	脫	200	10		11		
6		耘	715	2		脊	250	膀	15	臨	348	
翔	619	耳		肌	245		252		412	自		
8		耳	141	肓	314	腈	319	膊	39	自	772	
翠	93	3		肋	331	脈	366	膏	177	4		
翡	154	耶	667		333	能	398	腿	572	臭	77	

	641
至	
至	748
3	
致	750
8	
臺	543
臼(⺽)	
臼	294
4	
舀	319
	666
5	
舂	74
7	
舅	295
與	704
	705
	708
9	
興	635
	638
10	
舉	297
12	
舊	295
舌	
舌	490
2	
舍	490
	491
4	
舐	511
6	
舒	520
8	
舔	558
舛	
舛	84
6	
舜	529
8	
舞	599
舟	
舟	756
3	
舢	483
4	
般	12
	37
航	213
5	
舶	38
船	83
舵	138
7	
艇	562
10	
艙	52
艘	478
	536
14	
艦	267
艮	
艮	182
1	
良	343
11	
艱	262
色	
色	479
	482
艸(艹)	
艸	53
2	
艾	2
3	
芒	369
芍	489
	530
芋	706
4	
芭	7
芻	80
芳	150
芬	156
芙	164
花	228
芥	280
芹	448
芯	632
	633
芽	652
芸	715
芝	744
5	
苞	16
范	148
苟	189
苛	311
苦	318
茅	370
茂	370
	390
苗	381
茉	388
茄	446
苒	462
若	463
	474
苔	543
英	689
苑	713
茁	769
6	
草	53
茶	55
荒	234
荊	286
落	331
	363
荔	338
茫	369
茗	386
荏	466
茹	471
	473
荀	649
茵	685
茲	770
7	
荻	116
荳	130
荷	218
莢	258
莖	286
莒	297
莉	339
莽	369
莓	372
莫	389
莎	481
莘	493
	632
荼	569
莞	580
莠	701
	702
莊	766
8	
菠	37
菜	50
菖	59
萃	93
萏	107
菲	153
	154
菇	191
菡	212
華	229
	230
菅	261
菁	286
菊	296
菌	304
萊	326
菱	349
萌	375
萍	424
菩	427
萋	430
萄	550
萎	584
	587
菸	654
9	
葱	90
蒂	119
董	128
葛	180
葫	226
葷	241
葵	322
落	363
葡	427
葺	436
葉	492
	669
萬	580
萱	645
葯	666
	714
葬	720
著	732
	735
	763
	770
10	
蓓	22
蒼	52
蓋	171
蒞	339
蒙	375
	376
蒲	427
蓉	469
蒐	536
蒜	539
蓑	541
蓊	593
蓆	605
蓄	644
蒸	739
11	
蔔	39
蔡	50
蔣	268
蔻	317
蓮	341
蔓	368
蔑	382
蓬	415
蔬	520
蔚	589
蔭	686
	689
蔗	735
12	
蔽	27
蕩	109
蕃	147
蕙	240
蕉	271
蕨	302
蕊	474
蕪	598
蕭	622
蕞	780
13	
薄	16
	39
薈	240
薦	267
薑	268
蕾	333
薔	443
薇	584
	586
薪	633
薛	647
14	
藏	52

親	447	**5**		誣	595	諛	705	讀	130	**9**	
	453	詞	88		598	論	709		132	貓	369
10		詆	117	誤	600	諸	759	**16**		**貝**	
覎	255	詎	298	誘	702	**10**		變	31	貝	21
13		評	424	語	706	謗	15	讎	58	**2**	
覺	275	訴	538		709	謊	236	**19**		負	167
	302	詠	694	誌	751	講	268	讚	720	貞	735
14		詐	724	**8**		謎	374	**谷**			739
覽	327	詔	732	諂	58		377	谷	192	**3**	
18		診	736	調	124		378	**10**		財	49
觀	197		737		558		378	谿	242	貢	188
角		註	762	誹	154	謙	438		245	**4**	
角	272	詛	779	諒	345	謄	551		604	販	148
	301	**6**		論	362	謝	629	**豆**		貫	198
6		詫	56	請	453	謠	665	豆	130	貨	244
解	279	誠	70	誰	492	**11**		**3**		貧	421
11		該	170		526	謹	284	豈	433	貪	545
觸	486	詰	190	談	546	謾	368	**8**		責	722
13		詭	203	誼	678	謬	386	豎	523	**5**	
觸	82	話	230		683		404	豌	578	貶	29
言		誃	237	諍	740	謳	407	**11**		貸	105
言	654	詰	278		743	謫	734	豐	160	貳	142
2		誇	319	諄	768	**12**		**21**		費	154
訂	126	詮	459	**9**		譁	229	豔	660	貴	203
訃	167	詩	503	諳	4	議	249	**象**		賀	219
計	253	試	511	謀	124	謫	302	**5**		買	366
3		詳	619	諷	160	譜	428	象	620	貿	370
記	254	詢	650		161	識	507	**7**		貼	559
訖	435	詣	682		162		513	豪	213	貽	677
訕	484	詹	726	諺	240	譚	546	**9**		貯	761
討	550	誅	759	諢	242	證	743	豫	709		762
託	574	**7**		諫	266	**13**		豬	759	**6**	
訊	651	誕	107	謀	390	警	289	**豸**		賈	192
訓	651	誥	178	謔	407	譬	418	**3**			259
4		誨	239	諾	407	議	684	豹	18	賄	238
訛	139		240	諡	513	譯	684	豺	57		239
訪	151	誠	281	謂	590	**14**		**5**		賃	349
訣	301	認	467	諧	628	護	228	貂	123	賂	358
設	492	誓	512	諡	645	讁	441	**7**		賊	722
訟	536	說	528	諺	660	譽	709	貌	371	資	771
許	643		529	調	669	**15**				**7**	
訝	653	誦	536							賓	33

透	568	**11**		邱	454	酪	331		344	鋒	160
途	569	遨	6	邵	490		363	**11**		銀	328
逍	622	遯	137	**6**		酩	386	**金**		鋁	359
造	721	適	512	郊	270	**7**		金	281	鋪	426
這	734	遭	720	郎	327	酷	318	**2**			428
	735	遮	733	郁	707	酸	275	釘	125	銳	474
逐	759	**12**		**7**			626		127	鋌	562
8		遲	72	郝	214	**8**		釜	165	銷	622
逮	103	遼	345		218	醇	87	針	735	鋅	633
	105	遴	348	郡	304	醋	92	**3**		鏽	642
進	284	遷	438	**8**		醃	654	釣	123	**8**	
透	584	**13**		部	47	醉	780	釦	212	錶	33
逸	682	透	463	郭	204		538	釧	317	錘	86
週	757	遺	590	郵	697	**9**		**4**		錯	94
9			678	**9**		醒	637	鈔	62	錠	127
逼	24	選	646	都	129	**10**			63	鋼	175
遍	30	**13**			130	醜	77	鈍	136	鋼	194
達	95	避	28	**10**		醞	716	鈣	171	錦	283
道	112	還	208	鄉	618	**11**		鈎	189	鋸	299
遁	136	邂	299	鄒	777	醫	269	鈞	304	錄	358
遇	140	邁	366	**11**		醫	676	鈕	404	錳	376
過	206	邀	629	鄙	26	**14**		**5**		錢	441
遑	236	邀	664		27	醺	649	鈷	191	錫	604
遍	420	**14**		**12**		**17**		鉀	259		605
遒	456	邀	381	鄧	115	釀	401	鉅	298	錚	740
遂	539	**15**		鄰	347	**18**		鈴	349	錐	768
	540	邊	29	**15**		釁	634	鉛	438	錙	771
違	586	邏	324	鄺	743	**釆**		鉗	440	**9**	
遐	608	**19**		**酉**		采	49	鈾	698	鍍	133
遊	698	邐	363	酉	701	**5**		**6**		鍛	134
逾	704	**邑(⻏)**		**2**		釉	702	鉸	273	鍋	204
遏	708	邑	681	酋	455	**13**		銬	310	鍰	233
運	716	**4**		**3**		釋	513	銘	386	鍵	267
10		邦	14	酒	293	**里**		銓	459	鍊	342
遘	119	那	393	配	414	里	335	銅	565	錨	370
遛	354		397	酌	769	**2**		銜	613	鎂	373
遣	441		398	**4**		重	74	銀	687	鍥	446
遜	541	哪	397	酗	643		755	銖	759	鍘	724
	651	邪	627	酥	536	**4**		**7**		鍼	737
遙	665	**5**		**6**		野	667	鋤	80	鍾	754
遠	712	邸	116	酬	76	**5**		鉎	94	**10**	
	713					量	343				

鏹 15	鑲 402	闇 5	陝 483	**隹**	**5**
鎧 307	**19**	闊 13	院 713	隹 767	電 121
鎳 402	鑾 360	闋 323	陣 737	**2**	雷 332
鎗 442	鑼 363	闌 326	陟 750	隻 744	零 349
鎔 470	鑽 779	闈 458	**8**	**3**	**6**
鎖 542	**20**	闔 586	陳 65	461	需 642
鎢 595	784	**10**	738	**4**	**7**
601	**長(镸)**	闖 84	陵 349	雁 194	霉 372
鏹 738	長 59	闐 218	陸 354	集 251	霄 622
11	729	闕 461	357	雄 639	震 738
钁 6	730	461	陪 413	雅 652	**8**
鏢 32	**門**	**11**	陶 550	雁 659	霏 153
鍾 58	門 374	關 197	陷 615	**5**	霍 245
鏡 291	**1**	**12**	陰 686	雋 300	霖 348
鏗 314	閂 524	闡 58	飲 689	304	霓 399
鏈 342	**2**	**13**	**9**	雍 693	霑 726
鏪 356	閃 483	闢 418	隊 135	雊 751	**9**
鐯 443	**3**	**阜(阝)**	階 276	**6**	霜 525
鐵 481	閉 27	阜 166	隆 354	雌 88	霞 608
12	**4**	**3**	隋 539	雎 248	**11**
鐐 345	間 261	阡 437	隅 703	**8**	霧 601
346	265	**4**	**10**	雕 123	**12**
鐃 396	開 305	阤 139	隘 2	**9**	露 356
鐘 754	閏 474	防 150	隔 180	雖 539	358
13	閑 612	阱 289	隙 606	540	**13**
鐺 109	閑 612	阮 473	隕 716	**10**	霸 8
鐸 138	**5**	**5**	**11**	雛 80	霹 417
鑊 300	閘 724	阿 1	際 255	**11**	**14**
鐮 342	**6**	139	障 730	雞 248	霽 255
鐵 560	閥 144	附 166	**13**	雙 525	**16**
鐲 770	閣 180	陀 574	隨 539	雜 717	靄 2
14	閨 201	阻 778	隧 540	**11**	靈 350
鑑 267	閩 218	**6**	險 613	離 335	**青**
鑒 267	閫 383	降 269	**14**	難 395	青 449
鑄 763	**7**	618	隰 605	396	**5**
16	閬 359	陋 356	隱 688	**雨**	靖 291
鑫 633	閱 714	陌 388	**16**	雨 705	**7**
17	**8**	限 614	隴 355	**3**	靚 291
鑭 618	閹 654	**7**	**隶**	雪 648	**8**
鑰 667	閻 656	陛 26	**8**	649	靜 291
715	**9**	除 80	隸 340	**4**	**非**
18		陡 130		雯 592	非 152
				雲 715	

Stroke Numbers Index

In this index the characters are arranged according to the total number of strokes used in writing the character. Characters with the same number of strokes are arranged according to the order of their appearance in this dictionary. The figure to the right of each character is the page number under which the character can be found in the body of the dictionary. Using the page number as a guide, he can locate in the dictionary the character and the entries beneath it.

1		口	316	反	147	少	489		763	弗	163
一	669	女	406	方	149		490	支	743	仆	166
乙	679	乞	432	分	155	升	497	之	743	甘	171
2		千	437	丰	158	什	504	止	746	功	186
几	6	刃	467	夫	162	氏	508	中	752	古	191
七	25	三	475		163		163		755	瓜	194
卜	110	山	482	父	165	手	514	**5**		禾	215
刀	110	上	486		166	水	526	凹	5	弘	221
刁	122	勺	489	丐	171	太	544	叭	7	乎	225
丁	125	尸	501	戈	178	天	554	扒	7	加	256
	738	士	508	公	184	屯	573		408	甲	258
二	142	巳	533	勾	189	王	581	白	9	叫	273
几	245	土	570		190		582	半	13	巨	297
	252	丸	578	戶	227	文	590	包	15	句	298
九	292	亡	581	互	227		592	北	21	卡	305
了	332	兀	599	化	229	毋	595		39		436
	345	夕	601	幻	233	无	595	本	23	刊	307
力	337		606	火	243	午	598	必	30	可	312
匕	382	下	608	及	249	五	598	弁	35	叩	313
乃	393	小	623	介	280	勿	600	丙	37	尻	337
匕	428	丫	651	今	281	心	629	冊	46	立	337
人	464	幺	663	斤	281	凶	638	叱	53	令	349
入	472	也	667	井	289	牙	652	斥	73		350
十	503	已	679	亢	309	夭	663	出	77		351
又	701	弋	680	孔	315	刈	680	勿	90	另	351
3		于	702	六	354	引	687	打	95	卯	370
才	48	丈	729	毛	369	尤	696		96	矛	382
叉	54	子	771	木	391	友	699	代	103	民	382
	56	**4**		內	397	予	703	石	106	皿	383
川	82	巴	7	牛	403		705		504		386
寸	94	比	25	匹	416	元	710	且	107	末	388
大	98		26		418	月	713	叩	110	母	390
	103	不	40	片	419	日	713		549	目	391
凡	146	尺	72		420	云	715	氏	115	奶	398
千	171	仇	76	仆	426	匀	715		116	尼	405
工	183	丑	77	欠	441	允	715	叼	122	奴	416
弓	184	歹	103	切	446	仄	722	叮	125	丕	417
己	252	丹	105	犬	460	扎	723	多	127	皮	417
子	276	弔	123	仁	466		724	乏	144	疋	418
巾	281	斗	129	壬	466	犯	732	犯	148	平	422
久	292	厄	139	仍	468			氾	148	叵	425
叉	300	歹	139	日	468	爪				扑	426

字	頁	字	頁	字	頁	字	頁	字	頁	字	頁
仟	437	用	695	地	117	江	267	汕	484	伊	675
巧	445	由	696	町	125	交	269	舌	490	衣	675
且	446	幼	701	丟	127	匠	269	式	509		680
丘	454	右	702	多	137	臼	294	收	513	夷	676
囚	455	玉	706		138	扛	309	守	515	屹	680
去	458	孕	716	朵	138	优	309	戍	522	亦	681
冉	462	叵	717	耳	141	考	310	死	532	因	684
扔	467	仔	718	而	141	扣	317	寺	534	印	688
冗	470		772	伐	142	夸	319	夙	537	有	699
仁	475	乍	724	帆	146	匡	321	她	543	字	705
申	492	札	724	妃	152	老	329	同	563	羽	705
生	497	占	725	分	157	肋	331	吐	570	再	718
失	501		726	伏	163		333	托	573	在	718
史	507	仗	729	各	180	吏	338	妄	582	早	720
矢	507	召	738	互	182	劣	346	危	583	宅	725
世	508	正	741		183	列	346		584	兆	732
示	509	汁	744	艮	182	忙	368	刎	592	宅	734
市	509	只	747	丞	188	米	377	污	594	旨	747
仕	509	主	759	共	188	名	383	伍	599	至	748
甩	524	左	781	光	199	年	389	西	601	仲	755
司	530	**6**		圭	201	兵	400	汐	601	舟	756
四	533	艾	2	亥	209		411		606	州	756
他	542	安	3	汗	210	仳	418	先	610	朱	758
它	542	百	10	行	635	乒	422	向	619	竹	759
	573		38		637	牝	422	血	628	自	772
台	543	艸	53	好	214	朴	425		648	字	774
田	557	臣	64	合	216	企	433	刑	635	**7**	
汀	560	丞	67	后	223		434	匈	639	呆	1
凸	568	成	67	划	229	阡	455	兇	639		103
瓦	575	吃	71	灰	236	求	456	休	640	吧	7
	576		249	回	237	曲	457	朽	641		8
外	576	池	72	卉	239	全	458	吁	642	把	7
未	588	弛	72	伙	244	任	466	戌	642		8
戊	600	充	73	乩	245		467	旭	643	伯	11
仙	610	舛	84	肌	245	戎	470	旬	647		38
兄	639	次	89	吉	249	肉	470	汛	649	扳	12
玄	645	此	89	伎	252	如	471	羊	660	邦	14
穴	648	存	93	奸	260	汝	472	仰	662	份	14
央	660	吋	94	尖	260	色	479	吃	663	伴	14
以	679	忖	94	件	264		482	曳	668	貝	21
永	694								680	姚	25
										妣	26

枸	189	架	259	苦	318		412	神	495	哇	575
苟	189	姦	260	垮	319	叛	411	省	499		576
垢	190	柬	262	表	32	盼	411	牲	499	歪	576
故	193	建	265	括	323	炮	412	施	502	紈	579
括	194	姜	267	剌	325		413	屍	502	委	583
冠	196	降	269	姥	331	胚	413	虺	502	韋	584
	198	郊	270	俚	336	盆	415	食	504	為	585
枴	196	妓	271	俐	338	砒	417	拾	505		589
皈	201	狡	272	亮	344	毗	417	屎	508	畏	588
癸	202	皆	275	咧	346	品	422	是	510	胃	589
軌	202	拮	277	玲	349	迫	425	柿	511	屋	594
哈	207	界	280	流	352	珀	425	室	511	侮	599
孩	208	疥	280	柳	354	匍	427	拭	511	洗	605
咳	208	津	282	陋	356	柒	429	恃	511		613
	209	矜	282	侶	359	契	434	首	516	係	606
曷	218	勁	284	律	360	砌	434	狩	517	洽	607
狠	220		290	洛	363	恰	436	述	522	俠	607
很	220	炯	292	冒	370	洽	436	耍	523	咸	612
恨	220	迴	292	茂	370	前	439	帥	524	洒	613
恆	220	赳	292	茅	370	俏	445		530	限	614
虹	221		293	眉	372	茄	446	拴	524	香	616
哄	221	韭	293	昧	373	契	446	閂	524	相	616
	223	柩	294	美	373	侵	447	盾	528		620
洪	221	倔	296	咪	376	秋	454	思	531	降	618
侯	223	炬	298	弭	377	酋	455	俗	537	巷	620
厚	223	軍	303	祕	378	祛	456	胎	543	枵	621
後	223	俊	304	勉	379	泉	459	苔	545	洩	628
胡	226	咳	305	面	380	卻	461	泰	547	信	633
徊	231		307	眇	381	芮	462	炭	547	星	634
宦	233		311	秒	381	染	462	剃	554	省	637
皇	234	看	307	苗	381	若	463	殄	557	型	637
恢	236		308	陌	388		474	恬	557	洶	639
恍	236	砍	308	茉	388	紉	467	畋	557	恤	643
洄	238	拷	310	茂	390	柔	470	迢	558	宣	644
徊	238	柯	311	某	390	洒	475	挑	558	炫	646
活	242	苛	311	面	394	砂	480		559	削	646
即	250	科	311	耐	394	舢	483	亭	561		649
亟	250	恪	313	怒	406	珊	483	恫	562	徇	649
急	250		461	虐	407	甚	490	突	568		650
紀	253	剋	313	趴	408				495		569	咽	653
計	253	客	313	派	410		496	娃	575		659
柵	257	枯	317	胖	410	拾	491	挖	575		668

	340	挪	407	桑	477	剔	552	屑	628	宰	718
狸	334	旁	411	紗	480	偶	554	倖	638	蚤	721
浬	336	畔	411	扇	483	俤	554	胸	639	窄	722
栗	338	袍	412		484	涕	554	修	640		725
荔	338	疱	413	陝	483	庭	561	袖	641	眨	724
屚	339	皰	413	閃	483	挺	561	徐	643	展	726
倆	340	訕	413	訕	484	徒	569	栩	644	站	727
	344	珮	414	啕	486	退	572	軒	644	浙	734
料	346	配	414	捎	489	託	574	眩	646	哲	734
烈	347	砰	415	哨	490	剜	577	荀	649	眞	735
凌	349	疲	417	涉	491	挽	579	殉	650	振	735
留	353	紕	417	射	491	訊	584		651		737
旅	359	娉	417		681	訓	584	胭	653	砧	735
倫	361	破	422	師	502	朏	585	股	653	針	737
埋	365	剖	425	時	505	股	587		685	陣	737
	366	浦	427	舐	511		591	晏	659	疹	737
馬	365	圃	428	紓	518	晏	591	宴	659	朕	738
脈	366	埔	428	書	518	宴	592	唁	659	烝	739
茫	369	期	430	殊	519	唁	593	秩	660	症	742
洸	373	耆	431	恕	522	秧	593	氧	662	隻	744
眛	374	豈	433	候	522	氧	594	羔	663	脂	744
們	375	起	433	衰	524	羔	600	窈	665	值	745
迷	376	氣	435	栓	525	窈	602	舀	666	紙	748
眠	378	訖	435	朔	530	舀	602	射	668	砥	748
娓	379	虔	440	送	535	射	604	胰	677	秩	750
	579	倩	442	悚	535	胰	604	倚	680	桎	750
哞	382	峭	445	素	537	倚	607	益	681	陟	750
冥	385	俏	445	崇	540	益	607	茵	685	冢	754
茗	386	挐	446	孫	541	茵	607	蚓	686	衷	754
歃	391	衾	447	婆	541	蚓	612	娛	694	珠	758
娜	393		448	索	541	娛	621	浴	703	株	758
	407	秦	448		542	浴	621	袁	707	貯	762
納	393	拳	459	唆	541	袁	621	員	710	追	767
哪	393	缺	460	祖	547	員	622	原	710	準	769
拿	393	茌	466	倘	548	原	626	院	710	酌	769
能	398	容	469	唐	548	院	626	悅	713	捉	769
逆	399	茹	471	逃	549	悅	626	耘	714	桌	769
娘	401		473	桃	549	耘	627	砸	715	茲	770
捏	402	辱	472	套	550	砸	627	栽	717	恣	775
涅	402	弱	474	特	550	栽	627		718	租	777
紐	404			討	550					座	783
哦	407			疼	551						

廝	532		638	鳩	738	操	52	霏	153	冀	255
嘶	532	嘘	642	震	738	艙	52	墳	157	臀	255
飆	534	銹	642	靜	740	禪	57	奮	157	劑	255
慫	535	墟	642	徵	740	儕	57	憤	157	暨	255
踏	543	緒	644	靜	743	橙	66	諷	160	頰	258
諂	546	璇	645	鄭	743		70		161	撿	263
潭	546	鴉	651	質	746	瞳	67		162	餞	266
彈	546	醃	654		751	癡	71	縛	165	諫	266
歎	547	養	662	徵	748	達	72		169	蕉	271
趟	548		663	緻	751	熾	73	輻	165	徼	273
膛	548	樣	663	幟	751	儔	76	橄	174	醛	275
躺	548	窯	665	摯	751	瘡	84	擗	174	盡	283
踢	552	拗	666	鬧	757	錘	86	鋼	175	錦	283
鋌	562	嘻	668	歠	758	褰	93	糕	177	喋	286
褪	572	儀	678	箸	763	橇	93	篙	177	頸	289
	573	誼	678	駐	763	錯	94	骼	180	靜	291
駝	574		683	甄	764	擔	106	錮	194	橘	296
魄	575	毅	683	篆	765		108	館	198	舉	297
豌	578	億	683	撰	765	殫	106	盥	199	鋸	299
盨	581	蔭	686	撞	766	噹	108	龜	201	據	299
緯	588	影	691	墜	767	蕩	109		304	蕨	302
慰	589	瑩	691	諄	768	擋	109	骸	208	嗉	302
蔚	589	憂	696	輻	771		110	憨	210	墾	314
瘟	590	魷	699	粽	776	導	111	駁	210	窺	322
嫵	599	餘	704	醉	780		112	憾	212	賴	326
嬉	603	慾	709	**16**		燈	114	頷	212	播	332
膝	603	緣	712	曖	2	澱	122	撼	212		333
嘻	604	閱	714	嬡	2	雕	123		212	罹	335
蝦	607	碩	716	譖	4	諜	124	翰	212	歷	339
瞎	607	熨	716	澳	6	錠	127	衡	220	曆	339
賢	613	暫	719	懊	6	懂	128	橫	220	燦	345
嫻	613	遭	720	辦	14	獨	131		221		346
線	615	憎	723	鮑	20	篤	132	樺	231	遼	345
箱	618	增	723	憊	22	賭	132	寰	232	霖	348
銷	622	暫	727	蔽	27	顢	136	諱	240	遴	354
霄	622	璋	728	壁	28		137	蕙	240	盧	357
學	623	樟	728	辨	30	燉	137	諢	242	錄	358
噓	626	賬	730	憨	33	蹉	138	錕	242	褸	360
鞋	628	遮	733	儐	33		139	霍	245	駱	364
寫	628	蔗	735	錶	33	氌	140	機	246	螞	365
鋅	633	箴	737	餐	50	翻	146	積	247	瞞	367
興	635					番	147	激	247		
								輯	252		

翹	445	雜	717	夒	182	麓	358	蟹	629	籃	326
	446	簪	719	關	197	羅	363	簷	657	攔	326
鞘	446		723	瀚	212	饅	367	價	660	鶿	335
竅	446	蹧	720	毇	218	矇	375	嚥	660	礪	340
鞦	454	贍	726	鬍	227		376	藥	666	礫	345
軀	457	謫	734	譁	229	懵	376		715	鐐	346
鬈	460	鎮	738	壞	231	廮	377	蟻	680	齡	350
闋	461	織	745	懷	231	難	395	藝	684	露	356
繞	463	擲	745	繪	241		396	蠅	691		358
擾	463		746	穫	245	藕	408	願	713	蘆	357
鎔	470		751	譏	249	攀	410	韻	716	爐	357
薩	475	職	746	繭	264	龐	412	贊	719	彌	377
鬆	481	轉	764	疆	268	鵬	415	贈	723	鐃	396
繚	485		765	繮	268	騙	420	證	743	孽	402
觴	486	贅	768	繳	273	曝	428	**20**		囁	402
嬌	496	蹤	775	轎	275	譜	428	講	2	糯	407
瀋	496	**19**		覺	275	麒	432	寶	18	譬	420
薯	522	癒	2		302	簽	438	辮	30	飄	420
曙	523	鑒	6	櫛	279	鏘	443	繽	34	蘋	425
雙	525	瓣	14		751	蹺	444	攙	57	繼	441
鬆	535	爆	20	饉	284	鵲	445	懺	58	點	453
餿	536	邊	29	鯨	288		461	闡	58	勸	460
鎖	542	鏢	32	鏡	291	瓊	454	籌	77	壞	462
檳	544	癟	33	譊	302	鏡	481	韵	80	攘	462
縛	546	瞽	33	鏗	314	癱	483	觸	82	嚷	462
題	553	瀨	34	曠	321	繩	499	黨	109	饒	463
魍	582	簿	47	邊	324	識	507	環	202	蠐	472
魏	590	蟾	57	臘	325		513	蠔	213	鰓	475
甕	593	鎽	58	艦	326	獸	518	饑	249	騷	478
鎢	595	懲	70	懶	327	爍	530	籍	252	贍	485
	601	寵	75	贏	332	瀨	543	卿	255	釋	513
闖	607	疇	77	類	333	譚	546	鐢	255	媚	525
點	608	櫓	81	離	335	艚	549	繼	255	蘇	537
簫	622	鵓	87	歷	340	藤	551	艦	267	騰	551
瀉	629	辭	89	麗	340	穩	592	徹	275	韶	559
繡	642	蹲	94	簾	342	鶩	601	警	289	襪	576
薰	649		136	鏈	342	霧	601	競	291	顧	598
顏	656	顚	119	隴	355	璽	606	齟	297	蠐	604
醫	676	鶣	123	壟	355	繫	607	瓖	321	曦	604
䰾	702	犢	132	鏌	356	嚮	620	饋	322	孅	611
歟	705	藩	147	櫓	357	瀟	622	瀾	326	鹹	613
癒	709	繮	175	廬	357	蠍	627		327		

Table 1   837   Appendices

Table 1   Countries and Capitals

Country Guójiā	Capital Shǒudū
Afghanistan	Kabul
Āfùhàn	Kèbù'ěr
Albania	Tirana
Ā'ěrbāníyà (Ā'ěrbāníyǎ)	Dìlā'nà
Algeria	Algiers
Ā'ěrjílìyà (Ā'ěrjílìyǎ)	Ā'ěrjí'ěr
Angola	Luanda
Āngēlā	Luó'āndá
Antigua and Barbuda	St. John's
Āntíguādǎo (Āndìkǎ)	Shèngyuēhàn
Argentina	Buenos Aires
Āgēntíng	Bùyínuòsī'àilìsī
Armenia	Yerevan
Yàměiníyà (Yàměiníyǎ)	Yělìwēn
Australia	Canberra
Àodàlìyà (Àozhōu)	Kānpéilā (Kānpéilā)
Austria	Vienna
Àodìlì	Wéiyěnà
Azerbaijan	Baku
Yàsèbàirán (Yǎsèbàirán)	Bākù
Bahamas	Nassau
Bāhāmǎ	Násāo (Násuǒ)
Bahrain	Manama
Bālín	Màinàmài (Màinàmǎ)
Bangladesh	Dacca
Mèngjiālā	Dákǎ
Barbados	Bridgetown
Bābāduōsī (Bābèiduō)	Bùlǐqídùn (Qiáozhèn)

Table 1 838 Appendices

Belgium	Brussels
Bǐlìshí	Bùlǔsài'ěr
Belize	Belmopan
Bólìzī(Bèilǐsī)	Bèi'ěrmòpān(Bèi'ěrmòbāng)
Benin	Porto Novo
Bèiníng(Bèinán)	Bōduōnuòfú(Xīn'gǎng)
Bhutan	Thimphu
Bùdān	Tíngbù(Xīnbù)
Bolivia	La Paz
Bōlìwéiyà(Bōlìwéiyǎ)	Lābāsī
Bosnia and Herzegovina	Sarajevo
Bōsīníyà(Bōsīníyǎ)	Sèlāyēfó
Botswana	Gaborone
Bócíwǎ'nà(Bōzhá'nà)	Hābóluónèi(Jiābólónglǐ)
Brazil	Brasilia
Bāxī	Bāxīlìyà(Bāxīlìyǎ)
Brunei	Bandar Seri Begawan
Wénlái(Wènlái)	Sīlǐbājiāwānshì
Bulgaria	Sofia
Bǎojiālìyà(Bǎojiālìyǎ)	Suǒfēiyà(Suǒfēiyǎ)
Burkina Faso	Ouagadougou
Bùjī'nàfǎsuǒ	Wǎjiādùgǔ
Burundi	Bujumbura
Bùlóngdí(Púlóngdì)	Bùqióngbùlā(Bùsōngbùlā)
Belarus	Minsk
Bái'éluósī	Míngsīkè
Cambodia	Phnom Penh
Jiǎnpǔzhài	Jīnbiān
Cameroon	Yaounde
Kēmàilóng	Yǎwēndé(Yǎ'ēndé)

Table 1   839   Appendices

Canada	Ottawa
Jiā'nádà	Wòtàihuá
Cape Verde	Praia
Fódéjiǎo (Wéidéjiǎo)	Pǔlàyǎ (Péiyǎ)
Central African Republic	Bangui
Zhōngfēi Gònghéguó	Bānjí (Bānjī)
Chad	Ndjamena
Zhādé (Chádé)	Ēnjiǎméinà (Ēnjiāngnà)
Chile	Santiago
Zhìlì	Shèngdìyàgē (Shèngdìyágē)
China	Beijing
Zhōngguó	Běijīng
Colombia	Bogota
Gēlúnbǐyà (Gēlúnbǐyǎ)	Bōgēdà
Comoros	Moroni
Kēmóluó (Gēmó)	Mòluóní (Mòluòní)
Congo	Brazzaville
Gāngguǒ	Bùlācháiwéi'ěr (Bùlāzhá)
Costa Rica	San Jose
Gēsīdálíjiā (Gēsīdàlíjiā)	Shèngyuēsè (Shènghéxī)
Croatia	
Kèluó'āixīyà (Kèluó'āixīyǎ)	
Cuba	Havana
Gǔbā	Hāwǎ'nà
Cyprus	Nicosia
Sàipǔlùsī (Sàipǔlèsī)	Níkēxīyà (Nígǔxīyǎ)
Czech Republic	Prague
Jiékè	Bùlāgé
Denmark	Copenhagen
Dānmài	Gēběnhāgēn

Djibouti	Djibouti
Jíbùtí (Jíbùdì)	Jíbùtí (Jíbùdì)
Dominica	Roseau
Duōmínjiādǎo (Duōmíníkè)	Luósuǒ (Luósuō)
Dominican Republic	Santo Domingo
Duōmínjiā (Duōmíngníjiā)	Shèngduōmínggè (Shèngduō-mínggē)
Ecuador	Quito
Èguāduō'ěr (Èguāduō)	Jíduō
Egypt	Cairo
Āijí	Kāiluó
El Salvador	San Salvador
Sà'ěrwǎduō	Shèngsà'ěrwǎduō
Equatorial Guinea	Malabo
Chìdàojǐ'nèiyà (Chìdàojǐ'nèi-yǎ)	Mǎlābó
Estonia	Tallinn
Āishāníyà (Àishāníyǎ)	Tǎlín
Ethiopia	Addis Ababa
Āisè'èbǐyà (Yīsuǒbǐyà)	Yàdīsīyàbèibā (Ādísī'àbèibā)
Fiji	Suva
Fěijī	Sūwǎ
Finland	Helsinki
Fēnlán	Hè'ěrxīnjī
France	Paris
Fǎguó	Bālí
Gabon	Libreville
Jiāpéng	Lìbówéi'ěr (Zìyóushì)
Gambia	Banjul
Gāngbǐyà (Gānbǐyà)	Bānzhū'ěr

Georgia	Tbilisi
Qiáozhìyà (Qiáozhǐyǎ)	Dìbǐlìsī
Germany	Berlin
Déguó	Bólín
Ghana	Accra
Jiā'nà	Ākèlā
Greece	Athens
Xīlà	Yǎdiǎn
Grenada	St. George's
Gélínnàdá (Géruìnàdá)	Shèngqiáozhì (Shèngqiáozhìshì)
Guatemala	Guatemala City
Wēidìmǎlā (Guādìmǎlā)	Wēidìmǎlā (Guādìmǎlāshì)
Guinea	Conakry
Jǐ'nèiyà (Jǐ'nèiyǎ)	Kē'nàkèlǐ
Guinea-Bissau	Bissau
Jǐ'nèiyàbǐshào (Jǐ'nèiyàbǐsuǒ)	Bǐshào (Bǐsuǒ)
Guyana	Georgetown
Guīyànà (Gàiyǎnà)	Qiáozhìdūn (Qiáozhìchéng)
Haiti	Port-au-Prince
Hǎidì	Tàizǐgǎng
Holy See	Vatican
Jiàotíng	Fàndìgāng
Honduras	Tegucigalpa
Hóngdūlāsī	Tègǔxíjiā'ěrbā (Dégǔxíjiābā)
Hungary	Budapest
Xiōngyálì	Bùdápèisī
Iceland	Reykjavik
Bīngdǎo	Léikèyǎwèikè

Table 1 842 Appendices

India	New Delhi
Yìndù	Xīndélǐ
Indonesia	Jakarta
Yìnní (Yìndùníxīyà)	Yǎjiādá
Iran	Teheran
Yīlǎng	Déhēilán
Iraq	Baghdad
Yīlākè	Bāgédá
Ireland	Dublin
Ài'ěrlán	Dūbólín
Israel	Jerusalem
Yǐsèliè	Yēlùsālěng
Italy	Rome
Yìdàlì	Luómǎ
Ivory Coast	Abidjan
Xiàngyáhǎi'àn	Ābǐrǎng (Ābǐshàng)
Jamaica	Kingston
Yámǎijiā	Jīnsīdūn (Jīngsīdūn)
Japan	Tokyo
Rìběn	Dōngjīng
Jordan	Amman
Yuēdàn	Ānmàn
Kazakhstan	Alma Ata
Hāsàkè	Ālāmǔtú
Kenya	Nairobi
Kěnníyà (Kěnyǎ)	Nèiluóbǐ (Nèiluòbǐ)
Kirghizia	Bishkek
Jí'ěrjísī	Bǐsīkǎikè
Kuwait	Kuwait City
Kēwēitè	Kēwēitè (Kēwēitèshì)

Table 1 843 Appendices

Laos	Vientiane
Lǎoguō (Liáoguó)	Wànxiàng (Yǒngzhēn)
Latvia	Riga
Lātuōwéiyà (Lātuōwéiyà)	Lǐjiā
Lebeanon	Beirut
Líbā'nèn	Bèilǔtè
Lesotho	Maseru
Láisuǒtuō (Làisuótuō)	Mǎsèlǔ (Mǎsàilǔ)
Liberia	Monrovia
Lìbǐlìyà (Làibǐruìyà)	Méngluówéiyà (Méngluówéiyà)
Libya	Tripoli
Lìbǐyà (Lìbǐyǎ)	Dìlǐbōlǐ
Liechtenstein	Vaduz
Lièzhīdūnshìdēng	Wǎdūzī (Wǎdūzī)
Lithuania	Vilnius
Lìtáowǎn	Wéi'ěrniǔsī
Luxembourg	Luxembourg
Lúsēnbǎo	Lúsēnbǎo
Madagascar	Tananarive
Mǎdájiāsījiā	Tǎ'nà'nàlǐfó (Ǎntǎ'nà'nàlǐfó)
Malawi	Lilongwe
Mǎlāwéi (Mǎlāwēi)	Lǐlóngguī (Lǐlǎngwēi)
Malaysia	Kuala Lumpur
Mǎláixīyà (Mǎláixīyǎ)	Jílóngpō
Maldives	Male
Mǎ'ěrdàifū (Mǎ'ěrdìfū)	Mǎlěi (Mǎlù)
Mali	Bamako
Mǎlǐ (Mǎlǐ)	Bāmǎkē
Malta	Valletta
Mǎ'ěrtǎ	Wǎláitǎ (Wǎlètǎ)

Table 1 844 Appendices

Marshall Islands	Majuro
Mǎshào'ěrqúndǎo	
Mauritania	Nouakchott
Máolǐtǎníyà (Máolǐtǎníyà)	Nǔwǎkèxiàotè (Nuòkèshā)
Mauritius	Port Louis
Máolǐqiúsī (Mólǐxīsī)	Lùyǐgǎng (Lùyìshìgǎng)
Mexico	Mexico City
Mòxīgē	Mòxīgēshì
Micronesia	
Mǐkèluóníxīyà (Mǐkèluóníxīyǎ)	
Monaco	Monaco-Ville
Mónàgē	Mónàgē (Mónàgēshì)
Mongolia	Ulan Bator
Ménggǔ	Wūlánbātuō
Morocco	Rabat
Móluògē	Lābātè
Mozambique	Maputo
Mòsāngbǐkè (Mòsānbǐkè)	Mǎpútuō (Mǎbùduō)
Myanmar	Rangoon
Miǎndiàn	Yǎngguāng
Namibia	Windhoek
Nàmǐbǐyà (Nàmǐbǐyà)	Wēndéhékè (Wēntúkè)
Nepal	Kathmandu
Níbó'ěr	Jiādémǎndū
Netherlands	Amsterdam
Hélán	Āmǔsītèdān
New Zealand	Wellington
Xīnxīlán (Niǔxīlán)	Huìlíngdùn (Wēilíngdùn)
Nicaragua	Managua
Níjiālāguā	Mǎ'nàguā

Table 1   845   Appendices

Niger	Niamey
Nírì'ěr (Nírì)	Níyàměi (Nǐ'ǎměi)
Nigeria	Lagos
Nírìlìyà (Nàijílìyà)	Lāgèsī
North Korea	Ryongyang
Běicháoxiān (Běihán)	Píngrǎng
Norway	Oslo
Nuówēi	Àosīlù
Oman	Muscat
Āmàn	Mǎsīkètè
Pakistan	Islamabad
Bājīsītǎn	Yīsīlánbǎo (Yīsīlánmǎbādé)
Panama	Panama City
Bā'námǎ	Bā'námǎchéng (Bā'námǎshì)
Papua New Guinea	Port Moresby
Bābùyàxīnjǐnèiyà (Bābùyǎniǔjǐ'nèiyǎ)	Mò'ěrzībǐgǎng (Mó'ěrsībèigǎng)
Paraguay	Asuncion
Bālāguī	Yàsōngsēn (Yǎsōngsēn)
Peru	Lima
Mìlǔ	Lìmǎ
Philippines	Manila
Fēilǜbīn	Mǎnílā
Poland	Warsaw
Bōlán	Huáshā
Portugal	Lisbon
Pútáoyá	Lǐsīběn
Qadar	Doha
Kǎtǎ'ěr (Kǎdá)	Duōhā (Dùhā)

Table 1 846 Appendices

Rumania	Bucharest
Luómǎníyà (Luómǎníyǎ)	Bùjiālèsītè
Russian Federation	Moscow
Èluósī	Mòsīkē
Rwanda	Kigali
Lúwàngdá (Lú'āndá)	Jíjiālì (Jíjiālì)
St. Kitts-Nevis	Basseterre
Shèngjīcǐ-Níwéisī (Shèngqísī-Nàwéisī)	Bāsītè'ěr (Bāshìdì)
St. Lucia	Castries
Shènglúxīyàdǎo (Shènglùxīyǎ)	Kǎsītèlǐ (Kǎsīcuī)
St. Vincent and the Grenadines	Kingstown
Shèngwénsēntèdǎo (Shèngwénsēn)	Jīnsīdūn (Jīngshìzhèn)
San Marino	San Marino
Shèngmǎlìnuò	Shèngmǎlìnuò
Sao Tome and Principe	Sao Tome
Shèngduōměi hé Pǔlínxībǐ (Shèngduōměi jí Pǔlínxībǐ)	Shèngduōměi
Saudi Arabia	Riyadh
Shātè'ālābó (Shāwūdì'ālābó)	Lǐyǎdé
Senegal	Dakar
Sè'nèijiā'ěr	Dákè'ěr (Dákǎ)
Seychelles	Victoria
Sèshé'ěr (Sàixī'ěr)	Wéiduōlìyà (Wéiduōlìyǎ)
Sierra Leone	Freetown
Sèlālì'áng (Shīzishān)	Fúlìdūn (Zìyóuchéng)

Table 1   847   Appendices

Singapore	Singapore
Xīnjiāpō	Xīnjiāpō
Slovakia	Bratislava
Sīluòfákè	Bùlātísīlāfán
Solomon Islands	Honiara
Suǒluóménqúndǎo	Huòníyàlā (Hénī'ālā)
Somalia	Mogadishu
Suǒmǎlǐ (Suǒmǎlìyǎ)	Mójiādíshā (Mójiādíxiū)
South Africa	Pretoria
Nánfēi	Bǐlètuólìyà (Pǔlètuōlìyǎ)
South Korea	Seoul
Náncháoxiān (Nánhán)	Hànchéng
Spain	Madrid
Xībānyá	Mǎdélǐ
Sri Lanka	Colombo
Sīlǐlánkǎ	Kēlúnpō
Sudan	Khartoum
Sūdān	Kātúmù (Kātǔmù)
Suriname	Paramaribo
Sūlǐ'nán (Sūlì'nán)	Pālāmǎlǐbó (Bālāmǎlìbō)
Swaziland	Mbabane
Sīwēishìlán (Shǐwǎjìlán)	Mǔbābā'nà (Mòbābèn)
Sweden	Stockholm
Ruìdiǎn	Sīdégē'ěrmó
Switzerland	Berne
Ruìshì	Bó'ěrní (Bó'ēn)
Syria	Damascus
Xùlìyà (Xùlìyǎ)	Dàmǎshìgé
Tadzhikistan	Dushanbe
Tǎjíkè	Dùsāngbèi

Table 1 848 Appendices

Tanzania	Dar es Salaam
Tǎnsāngníyà (Tǎnshàngníyǎ)	Dálèisīsàlāmǔ
Thailand	Bangkok
Tàiguó	Mǎngǔ
Togo	Lome
Duōgē	Luòmǎi (Luòméi)
Trinidad and Tobago	Port of Spain
Tèlìnídá hé Duōbāgē (Qiānlǐdá jí Tuōbèigē)	Xībānyágǎng
Tunisia	Tunis
Túnísī (Túníxīyǎ)	Túnísī
Turkey	Ankara
Tǔěrqí	Ānkǎlā
Turkmenistan	Ashkhabad
Tǔkùmàn	Āshíhābādé
Uganda	Kampala
Wūgāndá	Kǎnpàlā
Ukraine	Kiev
Wūkèlán	Jīfū
United Arab Emirates	Abu Dhabi
Ālābó liánhé Qiúzhǎngguó (Ālābó liánhé Dàgōngguó)	Ābùzhábǐ (Ābùdábǐ)
United Kingdom	London
Yīngguó (Liánhéwángguó)	Lúndūn
United States	Washington
Měiguó	Huáshèngdùn
Uruguay	Montevideo
Wūlāguī	Méngdéwéidìyà (Méngtè-wéiduō)
Uzbekistan	Tashkent
Wūzībiékè	Tǎshígān

Vanuatu	Port Vila
Wànnàdù	Wéilāgǎng
Venezuela	Caracas
Wěinèiruìlā	Jiālājiāsī (Jiālākǎsī)
Vietnam	Hanoi
Yuènán	Hénèi
Western Samoa	Apia
Xīsàmóyà (Xīsàmóyǎ)	Āpíyà (Ābìyǎ)
Yemen	San'a
Yěmén (Yèmén)	Sà'nà (Shā'nà)
Yugoslavia	Belgrade
Nánsīlāfū	Bèi'ěrgélè
Zaire	Kinshasa
Zhāyī'ěr (Sàyī)	Jīnshāsà (Jīnxiàshā)
Zambia	Lusaka
Zànbǐyà (Shàngbǐyǎ)	Lúsàkǎ (Lùshākǎ)
Zimbabwe	Harare
Jīnbābùwéi (Xīnbāwēi)	Hālāléi

Table 2 A Comparative Table of Hanyu Pinyin (HP) and Mandarin Phonetic Symbols (MPS)

Initials			
MPS	HP	MPS	HP
ㄅ	b	ㄐ	j
ㄆ	p	ㄑ	q
ㄇ	m	ㄒ	x
ㄈ	f	ㄓ	zh
ㄉ	d	ㄔ	ch
ㄊ	t	ㄕ	sh
ㄋ	n	ㄖ	r
ㄌ	l	ㄗ	z
ㄍ	g	ㄘ	c
ㄎ	k	ㄙ	s
ㄏ	h		

Finals			
MPS	HP	MPS	HP
ㄚ	a	ㄧㄢ	ian
ㄛ	o	ㄧㄣ	in
ㄜ	e	ㄧㄤ	iang
ㄝ	ê	ㄧㄥ	ing
ㄞ	ai	ㄨ	u
ㄟ	ei	ㄨㄚ	ua
ㄠ	ao	ㄨㄛ	uo
ㄡ	ou	ㄨㄞ	uai
ㄢ	an	ㄨㄟ	ui
ㄣ	en	ㄨㄢ	uan
ㄤ	ang	ㄨㄣ	un
ㄥ	eng	ㄨㄤ	uang
ㄦ	er	ㄨㄥ	-ong
ㄧ	i	ㄩ	ü
ㄧㄚ	ia	ㄩㄝ	üe
ㄧㄝ	ie	ㄩㄢ	üan
ㄧㄞ	iai	ㄩㄣ	ün
ㄧㄠ	iao	ㄩㄥ	iong
ㄧㄡ	iu		

Tones		
	MPS	HP
1st tone		‒
2nd tone	′	′
3rd tone	ˇ	ˇ
4th tone	`	`
neutral tone	•	

Table 3   Hanyu Pinyin Table

Initials / Finals		b	p	m	f	d	t	n	l	g	k	h	j	q	x	zh	ch	sh	r	z	c	s
a	a	ba	pa	ma	fa	da	ta	na	la	ga	ka	ha				zha	cha	sha		za	ca	sa
o	o	bo	po	mo	fo															za	ca	sa
e	e					de	te	ne	le	ge	ke	he				zhe	che	she	re	ze	ce	se
ê	ê																					
ai	ai	bai	pai	mai		dai	tai	nai	lai	gai	kai	hai				zhai	chai	shai		zai	cai	sai
ei	ei	bei	pei	mei	fei	dei		nei	lei	gei	kei	hei				zhei		shei		zei		
ao	ao	bao	pao	mao		dao	tao	nao	lao	gao	kao	hao				zhao	chao	shao	rao	zao	cao	sao
ou	ou		pou	mou	fou	dou	tou	nou	lou	gou	kou	hou				zhou	chou	shou	rou	zou	cou	sou
an	an	ban	pan	man	fan	dan	tan	nan	lan	gan	kan	han				zhan	chan	shan	ran	zan	can	san
en	en	ben	pen	men	fen			nen		gen	ken	hen				zhen	chen	shen	ren	zen	cen	sen
ang	ang	bang	pang	mang	fang	dang	tang	nang	lang	gang	kang	hang				zhang	chang	shang	rang	zang	cang	sang
eng	eng	beng	peng	meng	feng	deng	teng	neng	leng	geng	keng	heng				zheng	cheng	sheng	reng	zeng	ceng	seng
er	er																					
-i																zhi	chi	shi	ri	zi	ci	si
i	yi	bi	pi	mi		di	ti	ni	li				ji	qi	xi							
ia	ya								lia				jia	qia	xia							
io	yo																					
ie	ye	bie	pie	mie		die	tie	nie	lie				jie	qie	xie							
iai	yai																					
iao	yao	biao	piao	miao		diao	tiao	niao	liao				jiao	qiao	xiao							
iu	you			miu		diu		niu	liu				jiu	qiu	xiu							
ian	yan	bian	pian	mian		dian	tian	nian	lian				jian	qian	xian							
in	yin	bin	pin	min				nin	lin				jin	qin	xin							
iang	yang							niang	liang				jiang	qiang	xiang							
ing	ying	bing	ping	ming		ding	ting	ning	ling				jing	qing	xing							
u	wu	bu	pu	mu	fu	du	tu	nu	lu	gu	ku	hu				zhu	chu	shu	ru	zu	cu	su
ua	wa									gua	kua	hua				zhua	chua	shua				
uo	wo					duo	tuo	nuo	luo	guo	kuo	huo				zhuo	chuo	shuo	ruo	zuo	cuo	suo
uai	wai									guai	kuai	huai				zhuai	chuai	shuai				
ui	wei					dui	tui			gui	kui	hui				zhui	chui	shui	rui	zui	cui	sui
uan	wan					duan	tuan	nuan	luan	guan	kuan	huan				zhuan	chuan	shuan	ruan	zuan	cuan	suan
un	wen					dun	tun		lun	gun	kun	hun				zhun	chun	shun	run	zun	cun	sun
uang	wang									guang	kuang	huang				zhuang	chuang	shuang				
ong	weng					dong	tong	nong	long	gong	kong	hong				zhong	chong		rong	zong	cong	song
ü	yu							nü	lü				jü	qü	xü							
üe	yue							nüe	lüe				jüe	qüe	xüe							
üan	yuan								lüan				jüan	qüan	xüan							
ün	yun												jün	qün	xün							
iong	yong												jiong	qiong	xiong							

國家圖書館出版品預行編目資料

遠東拼音漢英辭典 = Far East Pinyin Chinese-
　English Dictionary / 葉德明主編.
　--初版. --臺北市：遠東, 2000 [民89]
　　面；　公分
　　含索引
　　ISBN 957-612-462-X(48K平裝)
　　ISBN 957-612-463-8(60K平裝)
　1.中國語言－字典，辭典－英國語言
805.133　　　　　　　　　　　　89001812

Far East Pinyin
Chinese-English Dictionary
遠東拼音漢英辭典
2005年版

60K 道林紙本 定價新台幣450元 （外埠酌加運匯費）

主　　　　編 / 葉	德	明
編 輯 者 / 遠東圖書公司編審委員會		
發 行 人 / 浦	永	強
印 刷 者 / 遠　東　圖　書　公　司		
發 行 所 / 遠　東　圖　書　公　司		

地　　　址 / 台北市重慶南路一段66號
電 話 總 機 / (02)23118740　傳 真/(02)23114184
郵 政 劃 撥 / 00056691
美 國 發 行 所 / U.S. 國際出版公司
　　　　　　　　U.S. International Publishing Inc.
　　　　　　　　39 West 38th Street,
　　　　　　　　New York, N.Y. 10018, U.S.A.
登 記 證 / 局版台業字第0820號
　　　　　　　www.fareast.com.tw

Far East Pinyin

Chinese-English Dictionary

遠東拼音漢英辭典

2005年版

發行所　U.S. International Publishing Inc.
39 West 38th Street,
New York, N.Y. 10018, U.S.A.
www.fareast.com.tw

國家圖書館出版品預行編目資料

遠東拼音漢英辭典 = Far East Pinyin Chinese-
English Dictionary / 葉德明主編.
  --初版. --臺北市 : 遠東, 2000 [民89]
    面； 公分
    含索引
  ISBN 957-612-462-X(48K平裝)
  ISBN 957-612-463-8(60K平裝)
  1.中國語言－字典，辭典－英國語言
805.133   89001812

Far East Pinyin
Chinese-English Dictionary
遠東拼音漢英辭典

2005年版

60K 道林紙本 定價新台幣450元 （外埠酌加運匯費）

主   編 / 葉   德   明
編 輯 者 / 遠東圖書公司編審委員會
發 行 人 / 浦   永   強
印 刷 者 / 遠 東 圖 書 公 司
發 行 所 / 遠 東 圖 書 公 司
地   址 / 台北市重慶南路一段66號
電話總機 / (02)23118740 傳 真/(02)23114184
郵政劃撥 / 00056691
美國發行所 / U.S. 國際出版公司
            U.S. International Publishing Inc.
            39 West 38th Street,
            New York, N.Y. 10018, U.S.A.
登 記 證 / 局版台業字第0820號
            www.fareast.com.tw

Far East Pinyin
Chinese-English Dictionary
遠東拼音漢英辭典

2005 年版

U.S. International Publishing Inc.
50 West 34th Street,
New York, N.Y. 10018, U.S.A.

www.fareast.com.tw